Readings in
SOCIOLOGY

EDGAR A. SCHULER
MICHIGAN STATE UNIVERSITY

THOMAS F. HOULT
ARIZONA STATE UNIVERSITY

DUANE L. GIBSON
MICHIGAN STATE UNIVERSITY

WILBUR B. BROOKOVER
MICHIGAN STATE UNIVERSITY

Readings in
SOCIOLOGY

THIRD EDITION

Thomas Y. Crowell ♣ NEW YORK ♣ ESTABLISHED 1834

To the memory of
MAUDE L. FIERO

Preface

TO THE THIRD EDITION

Since the publication of our second edition in 1960, both the nature of the world to which man must address himself and the character of the tools available to the behavioral sciences for coping with that world have changed so drastically as to require a substantial re-examination of the contents of our book. In our revision we have attempted to incorporate new material that reflects these dramatic changes while retaining those selections whose enduring quality renders them continuously useful.

We view sociology as an integral part of the great tradition of liberal studies. It is our hope that the study of sociology as a liberal discipline will help students bring their minds to the highest functioning level, at home with the heritage of the past, engaged in a continuing quest for enlightenment regarding the present, and actively involved in a search for a better future. Concerning the specific social-science objectives of our book, we can do no better than to quote our statement in the second edition, a position to which we remain committed:

"The editors have sought constantly to produce a book that would make a contribution to genuinely *liberal* education; to expand the reader's horizon and human concerns beyond his own immediate place and time; to inculcate a truly scientific humility in the face of diverse peoples, customs and beliefs; and to affirm their own belief in the values of a maturing social science for our own democratic society and for an increasingly rich and humane life for all peoples everywhere."

We have been pleased to learn that our first two editions, in addition to finding wide acceptance among teachers and students, have also been read for both pleasure and edification by an increasing number of persons in the general adult population. Our selections, though chosen solely because they impressed us as contributing to sociological understanding through apt illustration and readability for use in introductory courses in colleges and universities, have added up to a volume that has proven useful and interesting to those whose formal education lies behind them. This unanticipated development has been very gratifying to us, for we are now perhaps more sharply aware than ever before of the increasing importance of continuing adult education, informal as well as formal.

A manual has been prepared for the convenience of teachers who use this book. It contains a correlations table, developed by the editors, of suggested linkages between the chapters of current texts in the field and each of our 100 selections. It also contains objective questions, prepared by Carleton W. Smith, based on each of the readings.

We wish to thank all authors and publishers who made their work available for incorporation in this volume. Individual acknowledgment is given in a footnote at the beginning of each selection. As in the earlier editions, biographical data are presented about each author.

The cooperation and assistance of numerous librarians and library staff members at Michigan State University, Arizona State University, Wayne State University, and the East Lansing, Michigan, Public Library are gratefully acknowledged.

Mrs. Anne Berkey assembled most of the data on which the new and the updated biographical notes are based and, in addition, efficiently and conscientiously prepared the manuscript for submission to the publisher. Mr. Terry Tomaselli gave extensive help in preparing the correlations table. To both of them, and to our able and dependable secretarial colleagues—at Michigan State, Mrs. Josephine Wharton, Mrs. Almeda Ritter, and Mrs. Sharon Anthes; and at Arizona State, Miss Norma Fisher, who helped particularly on the permissions correspondence—we are glad to express our appreciation.

We feel indebted beyond measure to our students and professional colleagues who by their candid reactions to the contents of the earlier editions added to our own enlightenment, and by their continued use of its predecessors encouraged us to undertake the preparation of this third edition.

As is conventional but nonetheless sincere, we wish to express to the members of our respective families our heartfelt appreciation for much and prized assistance, and for patient forbearance during the long period required to complete our third cooperative editorial project.

With sorrow we record the passing of our cherished friend and colleague, Maude L. Fiero, whose broad-ranging mind and fearless spirit made her an invaluable partner in this venture. In spite of serious illness she undertook with habitual vigor her share of this third edition, but her untimely death prevented her completing the job.

E.A.S.   D.L.G.
T.F.H.   W.B.B.

Contents

III. PERSON AND GROUP

IV. SOCIAL ORGANIZATION: TYPES OF GROUP RELATIONSHIPS

VIII. SOCIAL ORGANIZATION: ECOLOGICAL

IX. SOCIAL PROCESSES

X. SOCIAL AND CULTURAL CHANGE: DISORGANIZATION, PLANNING, AND VALUES

APPENDICES. SOCIOLOGISTS AT WORK

Social Science in Liberal Education

PERSPECTIVES OF STUART CHASE, PETER BERGER, ROBERT REDFIELD, AND ROBERT BIERSTEDT

Now that the practical usefulness of the social sciences in general, and sociology in particular, has become more widely accepted, many will study sociology because it will help them to earn a living. But acquaintance with sociology can have far more than economic value. Properly approached, the study of sociology can help us to improve the quality of our lives and realize our capabilities as human beings—in other words, it will help us to become liberally educated. In this prologue, the editors have assembled the ideas of four well-known writers and scholars, which they believe provide justification of sociology as a humanistic study. It is hoped that many of the subsequent selections, chosen with great care, will exemplify the position of Bierstedt, which is that "Sociology has an honorable place in the realm of humane letters and it belongs with the liberal arts as well as with the sciences."

Mr. Chase

✧　✧　✧　✧　✧

To cope with the tough problems ahead of us we should be able to see all the way around them. Experts and specialists are invaluable, but, as specialists, they see only the trees, sometimes only the twigs under the trees. We need power to see the woods. We need generalists who do not get lost in the trees. This does not mean two kinds of people, for everyone is a specialist in some degree, perhaps as a typist, perhaps as a nuclear physicist. It means more room in our minds for the over-all view, especially for relationships and balancing of alternatives.

　. . . The competence of the specialist today has overawed the intelligent layman until he says: "It's way over my head; I'll leave it to the experts." How often do we all say or think something like that? Yet it is a dangerous

SOURCE: Stuart Chase, *Some Things Worth Knowing.* Copyright © 1958 by Stuart Chase. Reprinted by permission of Harper & Row, Publishers. ✧ Stuart Chase is the author of many interpretive works in social science, especially in economics and communications. He has been an investigator for the Federal Trade Commission and has acted as a consultant for many organizations among which are the United States Treasury, SEC, and UNESCO. His books include *The Proper Study of Mankind, The Tyranny of Words,* and *The Economy of Abundance.*

attitude in this day and age. It tends to create an oligarchy of knowledge, which can become a monopoly of power, a series of tight little principalities with no minds left to survey the whole country.

I know a generalist who is also a learned specialist. He has written me that he would like to tell his specialist confreres: "Wake up! Live at the level of your time! Crawl out of that talent-trap which you refer to as your 'field' and look around. You may learn something about the only era you will ever live in, and about the only species you will ever be a member of. You will certainly learn something about yourself!"

To leave learning exclusively to specialists is not only dangerous but weak. It deprives civilized people of an essential part of their life on earth, something that many primitive peoples have naturally exercised—the full expression of curiosity, honestly confronting the mystery of existence, trying to understand their world and themselves. It is pitiful to retreat from this facing of life, especially at a time when so much new knowledge is coming in. Even if the astrophysicists have shown the universe to be far grander and more complex than we used to think, shall we say: "It's all beyond me," and turn our backs and go indoors? Or shall we look up with new wonder and delight, trying to imagine the vast recesses of the whirling sky? Similarly for the marvels unfolding before the electronic microscope, and for new aspects of human behavior now being revealed.

❖   ❖   ❖   ❖   ❖

A mature mind combines reliable information with good judgment, and one definition of good judgment is appreciation of relationships between fields of information. . . .

The intelligent layman . . . also wants to know what knowledge is available to promote negotiation and accommodation between the great powers. This is a question in the area of the behavioral sciences.

He wants to understand too what can be done to lessen tension between the races, and between worker and employer, and how to improve community relations. He would especially like to understand himself better, and why he often has so much trouble doing what he thinks he ought to do, and how he can get on more happily with his family, and in his personal relations generally.

Aside from these rather practical motives a good generalist possesses a healthy curiosity. . . . How and where [Homo sapiens] originally developed, how he survived as a hunter for many thousands of years, as a farmer and city dweller for a few more thousands; the purpose of his excess brain capacity even beyond what he needs for the intricate skills of language— these are some of the mysteries. The study of various cultures (where indeed the behavioral sciences begin) answers some questions but raises others: for example, which traits are common to man of every age and place, which are unique in a given society or even individual; why can the same complex customs arise independently in widely separate cultures?

❖   ❖   ❖   ❖   ❖

. . . Specialists have distorted the environment of the world today and pulled human behavior out of scale. Generalists are needed in great numbers to offset what the specialists are doing to us. To put it in another way, we need more specialists equipped with wide perspective, to exert critical judgment on what they are doing as specialists. This, I take it, was Robert Oppenheimer's motive when he demurred about working on the hydrogen bomb: his general philosophy came in conflict with his expert knowledge. Almost everyone, as I said earlier, is both specialist and generalist; but the latter function has grown more and more neglected as specialties become more complex and demanding.

In *Fables for Our Time*, James Thurber imagines a conference of ostriches concerned with the loss of their ability to fly. One of them named Oliver complains that men can fly sitting down, while ostriches cannot fly at all. "The old ostrich glared at Oliver severely, first with one eye and then with the other. 'Man is flying too fast for a world that is round,' he said. 'Soon he will catch up with himself, in a great rear-end collision, and man will never know that what hit Man from behind was Man.' "

Mr. Berger

Any intellectual activity derives excitement from the moment it becomes a trail of discovery. In some fields of learning this is the discovery of worlds previously unthought and unthinkable. This is the excitement of the astronomer or of the nuclear physicist on the antipodal boundaries of the realities that man is capable of conceiving. But it can also be the excitement of bacteriology or geology. In a different way it can be the excitement of the linguist discovering new realms of human expression or of the anthropologist exploring human customs in faraway countries. In such discovery, when undertaken with passion, a widening of awareness, sometimes a veritable transformation of consciousness, occurs. The universe turns out to be much more wonder-full than one had ever dreamed. The excitement of sociology is usually of a different sort. Sometimes, it is true, the sociologist penetrates into worlds that had previously been quite unknown to him—for instance, the world of crime, or the world of some bizarre religious sect, or the world fashioned by the exclusive concerns of some group such as medical specialists or military leaders or advertising executives. However, much of the time the sociologist moves in sectors of

SOURCE: Peter L. Berger, *Invitation to Sociology*, pp. 20–24, 175. Copyright © 1963 by Peter L. Berger. Reprinted by permission of Doubleday & Company, Inc. ❖ Peter L. Berger is associate professor of sociology at Hartford Seminary Foundation. His special interests include the sociology of religion, the sociology of knowledge, the sociology of politics, and sociological theory. In addition to *Invitation to Sociology*, he has written *Noise of Solemn Assemblies* and *Precarious Vision*.

experience that are familiar to him and to most people in his society. He investigates communities, institutions and activities that one can read about every day in the newspapers. Yet there is another excitement of discovery beckoning in his investigations. It is not the excitement of coming upon the totally unfamiliar, but rather the excitement of finding the familiar becoming transformed in its meaning. The fascination of sociology lies in the fact that its perspective makes us see in a new light the very world in which we have lived all our lives. This also constitutes a transformation of consciousness. Moreover, this transformation is more relevant existentially than that of many other intellectual disciplines, because it is more difficult to segregate in some special compartment of the mind. The astronomer does not live in the remote galaxies, and the nuclear physicist can, outside his laboratory, eat and laugh and marry and vote without thinking about the insides of the atom. The geologist looks at rocks only at appropriate times, and the linguist speaks English with his wife. The sociologist lives in society, on the job and off it. His own life, inevitably, is part of his subject matter. Men being what they are, sociologists too manage to segregate their professional insights from their everyday affairs. But it is a rather difficult feat to perform in good faith.

The sociologist moves in the common world of men, close to what most of them would call real. The categories he employs in his analyses are only refinements of the categories by which other men live—power, class, status, race, ethnicity. As a result, there is a deceptive simplicity and obviousness about some sociological investigations. One reads them, nods at the familiar scene, remarks that one has heard all this before and don't people have better things to do than to waste their time on truisms—until one is suddenly brought up against an insight that radically questions everything one had previously assumed about this familiar scene. This is the point at which one begins to sense the excitement of sociology.

Let us take a specific example. Imagine a sociology class in a Southern college where almost all the students are white Southerners. Imagine a lecture on the subject of the racial system of the South. The lecturer is talking here of matters that have been familiar to his students from the time of their infancy. Indeed, it may be that they are much more familiar with the minutiae of this system than he is. They are quite bored as a result. It seems to them that he is only using more pretentious words to describe what they already know. Thus he may use the term "caste," one commonly used now by American sociologists to describe the Southern racial system. But in explaining the term he shifts to traditional Hindu society, to make it clearer. He then goes on to analyze the magical beliefs inherent in caste tabus, the social dynamics of commensalism and connubium, the economic interests concealed within the system, the way in which religious beliefs relate to the tabus, the effects of the caste system upon the industrial development of the society and vice versa—all in India. But suddenly India is not very far away at all. The lecture then goes back to its Southern theme. The familiar now seems not quite so familiar any more. Questions are raised that are new, perhaps raised angrily, but raised all the same. And at least some of the students have begun to understand that there are functions involved in this business of race that they have not read about in the newspapers (at least not those in their hometowns) and that their parents have not told them—partly, at least, because neither the newspapers nor the parents knew about them.

It can be said that the first wisdom of sociology is this—things are not what they seem. This too is a deceptively simple statement. It ceases to be simple after a while. Social reality turns out to have many layers of meaning. The discovery of each new layer changes the perception of the whole.

Anthropologists use the term "culture shock" to describe the impact of a totally new culture upon a newcomer. . . .

. . . The first encounters with polygamy or with puberty rites or even with the way some nations drive their automobiles can be quite a shock to an American visitor. With the shock may go not only disapproval or disgust but a sense of excitement that things can *really* be that different from what they are at home. To some extent, at least, this is the excitement of any first travel abroad. The experience of sociological discovery could be described as "culture shock" minus geographical displacement. In other words, the sociologist travels at home—with shocking results.

. . . The discovery, for instance, that his own church has considerable money invested in the missile industry or that a few blocks from his home there are people who engage in cultic orgies may not be drastically different in emotional impact. Yet we would not want to imply that sociological discoveries are always or even usually outrageous to moral sentiment. Not at all. What they have in common with exploration in distant lands, however, is the sudden illumination of new and unsuspected facets of human existence in society. This is the excitement and the humanistic justification of sociology.

People who like to avoid shocking discoveries, who prefer to believe that society is just what they were taught in Sunday School, who like the safety of the rules and the maxims of what Alfred Schuetz has called the "world-taken-for-granted," should stay away from sociology. People who feel no temptation before closed doors, who have no curiosity about human beings, who are content to admire scenery without wondering about the people who live in those houses on the other side of that river, should probably also stay away from sociology. They will find it unpleasant or, at any rate, unrewarding. People who are interested in human beings only if they can change, convert or reform them should also be warned, for they will find sociology much less useful than they hoped. And people whose interest is mainly in their own conceptual constructions will do just as well to turn to the study of little white mice. Sociology will be satisfying, in the long run, only to those who can think of nothing more entrancing than to watch men and to understand things human.

❖   ❖   ❖   ❖   ❖

We maintain that the teaching of sociology is justified insofar as a liberal education is assumed to have a more than etymological connection with intellectual liberation. Where this assumption does not exist, where education is understood in purely technical or professional terms, let sociology be eliminated from the curriculum. It will only interfere with the smooth operation of the latter, provided, of course, that sociology has not also been emasculated in accordance with the educational ethos prevailing in such situations. Where, however, the assumption still holds, sociology is justified by the belief that it is better to be conscious than unconscious and that consciousness is a condition of freedom. To attain a greater measure of awareness, and with it of freedom, entails a certain amount of suffering and even risk. An educational process that would avoid this becomes simple technical training and ceases to have any relationship to the civilizing of the mind. We contend that it is part of a civilized mind in our age to have come in touch with the peculiarly modern, peculiarly timely form of critical thought that we call sociology.

Mr. Redfield

It is part of a general education to understand, in the first place, that there is a social science, as distinct from common-sense knowledge about society and as distinct from social reform. Every educated person should know that to a great extent society can be studied objectively and systematically, as can starfish or the action of glaciers. One can get impersonal, organized, verifiable knowledge about housing, crime, and race relations, as one can get such knowledge about any other phenomena of nature. An educated person will know how to distinguish the scientific way of attacking a social problem from those ways of attacking it which are more generally practiced around him. He will understand that in a great many instances people do something about a social problem because they feel badly about it rather than because they understand it and that what they do corresponds with their feelings rather than with the facts underlying the problem. He will understand that this is true, whether the action taken be to write a letter to the newspapers, to pass a law, or to demand changes in the school curriculum. It is a part of general education to understand that scientific knowledge is different from feeling strongly about something and from

s o u r c e s :   Robert Redfield, "Research in the Social Science: Its Significance for General Education," *Social Education* (December, 1941). Reprinted by permission. Robert Redfield, "The Art of Social Science," *American Journal of Sociology*, LIX, 3 (November, 1948), 189–90. Copyright 1948 by The University of Chicago. Reprinted by permission of The University of Chicago Press. ❖ For biographical data on Robert Redfield see selection 5.

common-sense knowledge and that it is a more secure basis for social action than either.

The successful teacher of the social studies will make clear that there is a difference between the analysis of processes, which are matters of efficiency, and other objective judgments. The citizen must know what are his values, and he should understand how to act so as to protect or realize them. The uneducated person confuses values and processes, ends and means; a good education in social science will help to keep them distinct.

As a part of this understanding, the educated man or woman will have been taught that a social problem is not a simple thing. Social problems are closely intermeshed with one another. If one makes a beginning with the problem of housing, one finds that it is only one aspect of the larger problem of national insecurity. It is also related to the problem of the national income and to that of the national health. The solutions given in the form of new housing projects or in zoning laws encounter the problems of racial intolerance. It follows from this that a social problem does not mean the same thing to everybody.

. . . The problem of housing looks very differently to laymen, landowners, builders, tax officials, and city planners, and . . . full understanding of the problem depends upon special scientific knowledge of economists, sociologists, and students of government. The contribution of social-science research to a general education is not made use of when a social problem is presented to young people as if it existed with simple reference to some social ideal. It is not made use of if the problem is presented as if all one had to do was to take note of the social injustice attending the present state of things. That is not functional education; it does not prepare the young person for life.

A further contribution which social-science research can make to general education is the understanding that although social science is like physical or biological science in that it is objective, systematic description of the world around us, it differs from physical and biological science in that all the facts and all the problems are controversial. The social scientist is studying, chiefly, to put it strongly, himself, and one cannot help feeling and caring about one's self. We, as human beings, care about the institutions and social problems which the social scientist studies. Therefore it is harder for the social scientist to maintain objectivity than it is for the physicist, and it is harder for Society, with a capital "S," to keep from interfering with the social scientist than with the physicist. This is one of the elements of understanding of social-science research which belongs in a general education. If social problems are presented . . . so as to communicate this general knowledge of the nature of social science it will be made clear to the learner that the mere facts of social science lie within a realm of controversy and prejudice. As Professor Wirth has pointed out even the number of people living in a given city of the United States is a controversial matter in the sense that if the city has been losing population the

Chamber of Commerce will not want the fact to get abroad. The number of people unemployed in this country is a controversial fact, first, in the sense that various interest groups care as to what criterion is selected for determining who is unemployed, and, second, because even if it is decided who are unemployed, various groups will interpret the fact according to their interests. For some employers there will be just enough unemployed to assure a labor reserve, while for other of our citizens these same unemployed constitute a problem of providing relief.

At the same time the educated man or woman will understand that this special difficulty under which the social scientist labors has its compensation in a special advantage enjoyed by the social scientist and understanding of the nature of social-science research is not complete until another general characteristic of it is recognized. It is a peculiarity of the scientific method as applied to man in society that the investigator can get a more intimate knowledge of his subject matter than can the physicist of his, just because he is part of it. The physical scientist learns of his subject matter only as caliper and scales can tell him about it. The social scientist can ask questions of his subject matter and get answers, and he can project his own humanity imaginatively into the subject matter and so increase his understanding of it. The contribution of social-science research to a general education is provided in part by an understanding of the advantages and the dangers of this essential characteristic of social-science research. The social scientist does not abolish his own prejudices any more than he abolishes his own human nature. But he controls prejudice by making it explicit. So, too, he develops controlled use of his human insights. It is more important to a general education that the individual knows that there is a problem of using and controlling the human faculty of insight as a scientific instrument than that he know the latest facts with regard to any problem studied by that method.

✣   ✣   ✣

The humanistic aspect of social science is the aspect of it that is today not well appreciated. Social science is essentially scientific in that its propositions describe, in general terms, natural phenomena; in that it returns again and again to special experience to verify and to modify these propositions. It tells what is, not what ought to be. It investigates nature. It strives for objectivity, accuracy, competency. It employs hypotheses and formal evidence; it values negative cases; and, when it finds a hypothesis to be unsupported by the facts, it drops it for some other which is. But these are all aspects of social science so well known that it is tedious to list them again. What is less familiar, but equally true, is that to create the hypothesis, to reach the conclusion, to get, often, the very first real datum as to what are A's motives or what is the meaning of this odd custom or that too-familiar institution, requires on the part of one who studies persons and societies, and not rocks or proteins, a truly humanistic and freely imaginative insight into people, their conventions and interests and motives, and that this requirement in the social scientist calls for gifts and for a kind of education different from that required of any physicist and very similar to what is called for in a creative artist.

If this be seen, it may also be seen that the function of social science in our society is a double function. Social science is customarily explained and justified by reason of what social science contributes to the solution of particular problems that arise in the management of our society, as a help in getting particular things done. As social scientists we take satisfaction in the fact that today, as compared with thirty years ago, social scientists are employed because their employers think that their social science is applicable to some practical necessity. Some knowledge of techniques developed in social science may be used: to select taxicab drivers that are not likely to have accidents; to give vocational guidance; to discover why one business enterprise has labor troubles while a similar enterprise does not; to make more effective some governmental program carried into farming communities. . . .

All these contributions to efficiency and adjustment may be claimed with justice by social scientists. What is also to be claimed, and is less commonly stressed, is that social science contributes to that general understanding of the world around us which, as we say, "liberalizes," or "enriches." The relation of social science to humanistic learning is reciprocal. Social scientists need humanistic learning the better to be social scientists. And the understanding of society, personality, and human nature which is achieved by scientific methods returns to enrich that humanistic understanding without which none can become human and with which some few may become wise. Because its subject matter is humanity, the contribution of social science to general, liberal education is greater than is the contribution of those sciences with subject matter that is physical. In this respect also, creative artist and social scientist find themselves side by side. The artist may reveal something of universal human or social nature. So too may the social scientist. No one has ever applied, as a key to a lock, Sumner's *Folkways* or Tawney's *Religion and the Rise of Capitalism* or James's *The Varieties of Religious Experience*. These are not the works of social science that can be directly consulted and applied when a government office or a business concern has an immediate problem. But they are the books of lasting influence. Besides what influence they have upon those social scientists who come to work in the government office, or the business concern, in so far as they are read and understood and thought about by men and women who are not social scientists, or even as they are communicated indirectly by those who have read them to others, they are part of humanistic education, in the broad sense. Releasing us from our imprisonment in the particular, we are freed by seeing how we are exemplifications of the general. For how many young people has not Sumner's book, or

Veblen's book, or some work by Freud, come as a swift widening of the doors of vision, truly a liberation, a seeing of one's self, perhaps for the first time, as sharing the experiences, the nature, of many other men and women? So I say that social science, as practiced, is something of an art and that, as its best works are communicated, it has something of the personal and social values of all the arts.

Mr. Bierstedt

Sociology has an honorable place in the realm of humane letters and it belongs with the liberal arts as well as with the sciences. We have seldom been able to escape the public belief that it is the principal business of sociology to solve social problems; and the identification of our discipline with such problems is too well known to require comment. That sociology might also have something to do with culture in the narrower and non-sociological sense of intellectual cultivation seems seldom to have occurred to anyone, including sociologists.

I invite your attention, therefore, to the fact that sociology, like the other arts, is one of the ornaments of the human mind, that its literature extending from Plato to our contemporaries is in a great and humane tradition, that sociology—like all of the liberal arts—liberates us from the provincialisms of time and place and circumstance, that the social order is a study worthy of a free man, and that society itself, like every other thing that has ever agitated the restless and inquisitive mind of man, is a fit and dignified subject of inquiry.

SOURCE :   Robert Bierstedt, "Sociology and Humane Learning," *American Sociological Review*, Vol. 25 (February, 1960), 8–9. Reprinted by permission of The American Sociological Association. ✧ Robert Bierstedt is professor of sociology and anthropology at New York University. He is an advisory editor of Dodd, Mead & Company, Inc., and has served in an editorial capacity on the *American Sociological Review* and the *American Journal of Sociology*. In 1960–61 he was executive officer of the American Sociological Association. He is chiefly interested in sociological theory and is the author of *The Social Order* and *The Making of Society*.

CHAPTER I

Introduction

❖ 1 ❖

THE TRANSITION TO SCIENCE
IN HUMAN RELATIONS

George A. Lundberg

Sociology consists of the scientific study of human groups. To consider sociology a science means that we stand ready to observe human behavior as scientists would observe any natural phenomenon and to look for systematic regularities in this human behavior. In this selection Lundberg, long an exponent of the rigorous application of the natural science approach to the study of human behavior, describes some of the practical results of this approach and presents the future steps which he feels must be taken if the social sciences are to help achieve a more rational "management of social relations."

I. Consensus on Methods

I have expressed the view that the best hope for man in his present social predicament lies in a type of social science strictly comparable to the other natural sciences. We have reviewed some of the objections that have been urged both by physical and social scientists to this proposal. I am not under the illusion that my argument can be established conclusively in so brief a compass. Actually, of course, only time and future scientific devel-

SOURCE: George A. Lundberg, *Can Science Save Us?* (New York: David McKay Company, Inc., 1961), 42–51. Reprinted by permission. ❖ The author (1895–1966) was professor emeritus of sociology, University of Washington. He was the editor of *Sociometry*, 1941–1945, and served as consultant to the National Resources Planning Board for many years. Among his publications are *Foundations of Sociology*; *Social Research*; and *Sociology*, of which he was the coauthor. He was a past president of the American Sociological Association.

opment can finally demonstrate the validity of the position which I have outlined.

In the meantime, we are confronted with the necessity of proceeding on *some* hypothesis as to the way out of our difficulties. It is generally agreed, even by those who differ most radically as to the proper approach, that our first need is a unified, coherent theory on which to proceed. A society cannot achieve its adjustments by mutually incompatible or contradictory behavior, any more than can an individual organism. However we may differ on details and on ends, we must agree on certain broad means, certain principles of action toward whatever ends we do agree upon.

In short, we all apparently agree with Comte's appraisal of the situation as he saw it a hundred years ago. Speaking of the theological, the metaphysical, and the positive scientific approaches, he said: "Any one of these might alone secure some sort of social order: but, while the three co-exist, it is impossible for us to understand one another upon any essential point whatever."

Of course there are some who find in our present predicament merely further evidence of the futility of the scientific approach in human affairs. They overlook the fact that, actually, science has as yet not been tried on social problems. Consequently, they advocate a return to theology, or "the" classics, either in their historic forms or in new versions in which the advocates of these approaches personally can play the role of major prophets. If I could see any chance of bringing about a return to theology or "the" classics, I might give it serious consideration, because any one unified approach might be better than two or more contradictory ones. But I see no such possibility in the long run. The commitments we have already made to science, chiefly in our technological culture, are of such character that we can neither go back nor stand still.

Our technological developments and our methods of communication have resulted in a fundamental interdependence which dominates our lives. This state of affairs requires, as we shall see, that we bring our social arrangements into line with this basic technological pattern, rather than vice versa. This basic technological pattern unquestionably rests upon natural science. On this ground, rather than on any assumption of absolute or intrinsic superiority of science as a philosophy of life, I think the following conclusion is inescapable: *In our time and for some centuries to come, for better or for worse, the sciences, physical and social, will be to an increasing degree the accepted point of reference with respect to which the validity (Truth) of all knowledge is gauged.*

II. What Can Be Done—Some Examples

What are some examples of types of work by social scientists that are of vast importance in managing human relations?

When we speak of *types* of work by social scientists, we are obviously announcing an undertaking so large as to prevent even a summary within the confines of this book. There are at least five well-recognized social sciences, and if we use the larger category of "behavioral science," the number rises to twelve or more. The social sciences are well-recognized in the sense that they are firmly established as departments in nearly all leading universities and colleges as well as in professional, industrial, and governmental circles. Over a hundred journals publish every year hundreds of research reports of studies large and small, designed to yield new knowledge or to test and refine previous conclusions and to predict behavior under stipulated conditions. We shall confine ourselves to a few illustrations selected chiefly because they are individually of interest to more than one of the social sciences. Readers interested in more comprehensive accounts, including methodological details, will find a large literature readily available.

For our present purpose we shall not here become involved in the question of the degree of scientific refinement attained in the different sciences. My argument has been based in large part on what appears to me to be warranted anticipations regarding *future developments* of the social sciences. Here I shall rather take the view that, *even with their present shortcomings*, the social sciences must be taken seriously. The recent (1960) elevation of the Office of Social Sciences to full divisional status in the National Science Foundation is an indication of this growing recognition.

The work of such agencies at the Census Bureau is known to all and is more or less taken for granted. Without the data and the analyses which it provides, the administration of public affairs would certainly dissolve in chaos and perhaps in civil war. It is equally certain that no international organization can function without an elaborate organization of this kind to provide the essential facts regarding people and their characteristics and activities. Perhaps the most permanently valuable contribution of the ill-fated League of Nations was its establishment of an international statistical bureau which managed to survive until taken over by the larger information agencies of the United Nations. The Office of Population Research at Princeton University has engaged in detailed studies of local and international population trends in various parts of the world and has predicted the future areas of population pressure. This knowledge is of the utmost practical importance in the administration of national and international organization of any kind. The Scripps Foundation, the Milbank Memorial Fund, and many others are engaged in similar or related work of a character that measures up very well to the standards of the physical sciences.

Social scientists have also been prominent in pointing out one of the most serious of the world's *problems*, namely, the problem of overpopulation. As a result of the drastic decline in the death rate resulting from the application of medical science, world population is increasing at an unprecedented rate. For example, although it took thousands of years for the human species to reach the number of one billion of living people (about 1830) it required only one century to add the second billion. It is now taking less than thirty-five years for the world population to add a third billion—probably before 1965. The United Nations' population experts estimate that it will take only fifteen years to add a fourth billion, and another ten years to add the fifth billion if present rates should continue. The idea that any expansion of the food supply could do more than temporarily alleviate the starvation of people under such rates of population increase is merely a confusion of wishful thinking with stern realities.

However, just as the application of science to health and sanitation has produced this situation, science has provided the means for its control. Further improvements in the latter are highly likely and imminent. The distinctively social problem of securing the widespread adoption of known methods of control involve a number of problems of a type not yet fully solved, but under extensive inquiry by social scientists. In the meantime we have an example of successful population control in the case of postwar Japan. We are not here concerned with these problems in themselves, but with the role of scientifically gathered and analyzed human social data in the prediction of future population, and the solution of a problem which some regard as more dangerous than nuclear war. Also in other ways, statistics of individual countries, and the data collected by the United Nations organization, are of fundamental importance to the work of many scientists engaged in a wide variety of particular projects. Human ecology, which cuts across the conventional boundaries of demography, geography, sociology, economics, political science (and perhaps others), has produced very impressive work both of applied and theoretical significance.

Reliable and objective knowledge of other peoples and cultures constitutes another field in which social scientists have made distinguished contributions. This knowledge has thrown a flood of light on our own civilization and permits the formulation and test of hypotheses regarding human behavior patterns in general. The Human Relations Area Files contain, systematically filed and indexed, virtually all present reliable knowledge regarding some two hundred cultures. To make a long story short, if a researcher happens to be interested in some subject as, for example, divorce, crime, education, law (and about a thousand other topics), in other cultures, he can go to one of the twenty or more libraries which subscribe to the File, and find all the known information on any or all of these subjects for each of about two hundred cultures. The information is neatly filed away in a separate drawer for each subject. Information which it might take years to locate as scattered in hundreds of books in a library can be secured in a few hours from the File. The importance of this kind of knowledge and its ready availability in facilitating our contacts with people of other lands and cultures became very evident during and after World War II.

We [have recognized] the importance of instruments and methods of observation and measurement in the social as well as in the physical sciences. Social scientists have produced revolutionary developments in this field in the last thirty years. Thousands of such instruments have been invented by means of which vocational aptitudes, success in college and other undertakings, and social behavior of great variety can be accurately measured and predicted. Instruments and scales for the measurement of attitudes have opened vast new fields for investigation.

Perhaps the best known, but by no means the only one, of these devices is the public opinion poll. We have in this technique an illustration of how a development in the social sciences may be as significant for the future of social organization as many physical inventions have been in our industrial development. The mechanisms by which the "public will" can make itself reliably felt in government and community action has always been in the foreground of political discussion. With the expansion of the areas in which public opinion must operate, many students of the problem have despaired of the capacity of the town meeting technique adequately to make operative the "public will." In the face of this situation, the scientific public opinion poll constitutes an instrument which cheaply and accurately permits us to learn the beliefs, the attitudes, and the wishes of the rank and file of the population. Public opinion polls are at present frequently thought of as interesting devices mainly for predicting the outcome of elections. They do permit such prediction, but this is a very minor aspect of their full possible importance. Polls were extensively used in the armed forces in World War II as a guide to the administration of the invaded areas, the return of the armed forces after the war, and in many other ways.

Public opinion polling may be a device through which can be resolved one of the principal impasses of our time, namely, the apparent irreconcilability of authoritarian control on the one hand and the "public will" on the other. It may be that through properly administered public opinion polls professionalized public officials can give us all the efficiency now claimed for authoritarian centralized administration and yet have that administration at all times subject to the dictates of a more delicate barometer of the peoples' wills than is provided by all the technologically obsolete paraphernalia of traditional democratic processes. In short, it is not impossible that as the advancing technology in the physical adjustments of our lives leads to a threatened breakdown of democracy, so an improved social research instrument may restore and even increase the dominance of the people's voice in the control of human society.

The time may come when the reliable polling of public opinion will be a science comparable to meteorology. Charts of all kinds of social weather, its movements and trends, whether it be anti-Semitism, anti-Negro sentiment, or mob-mindedness will be at the disposal of the administrators of the people's will in every land. A barometer of international tension has been designed to detect reliably and early the tensions that lead to war. It is true that mere knowledge of these tensions does not necessarily operate to alleviate them. But it is also true that a reliable diagnosis of the tension and an understanding of the feelings and sentiments that underlie tensions is essential for an effective approach to the problem.

"Statesmen" will doubtless continue for some time to value their intuitions more highly than scientific prediction. Pious platitudes doubtless will continue to be heard about the "unpredictability" of human behavior. It remains a fact that social scientists predicted within a fraction of 1 per cent the actual voting behavior of sixty-eight million voters in the U.S.A. in the presidential election of 1960. The pollsters have been doing so regularly since 1936 with a maximum error of 6 per cent. Nor are such results limited to voting behaviors. The late Professor Stouffer of Harvard predicted, also within a fraction of 1 per cent, the number of discharged soldiers after World War II who would take advantage of the educational privileges of the G.I. Bill of Rights. Hundreds of other cases could be reported from a great variety of fields of human social behavior, including the vast areas of market research.

To those who constantly have their minds on quick and dramatic solutions to the world's troubles this type of research is likely to seem offensively trivial—a kind of fiddling while Rome burns. "Writers" are fond of referring contemptuously to basic scientific work as an "ivory tower" and as "lecturing on navigation while the ship sinks." Navigation today is what it is because some people were willing to study the *principles* of their subject while their individual ships went down, instead of rushing about with half-baked advice as to how to save ships that could not be saved, or were not worth saving anyway. As A. J. Carlson has recently said: "The failure of bacteria to survive in close proximity to certain moulds looked trivial at first, but few informed people would label the discovery of that initial fact *trivial* today."

So much, then, for a few illustrations, rather than a summary, of the type of work that is being done and that needs to be done in the social sciences. Is there enough of it being done? Clearly not, or we would not need to flounder as we are in national and international affairs, pursuing diametrically opposite courses within the same decade. Can the social sciences ever hope to catch up with the other sciences, the increasingly rapid advance of which constantly creates new social problems? Certainly we can, if we devote ourselves to the business with something like the seriousness, the money, and the equipment that we have devoted to physical research. Consider how the physical scientists are today given vast resources to concentrate on the invention of a new submarine detector or a new bomb, not to mention the peacetime occupations of these scientists with penicillin and sulpha drugs. Obviously, I am not criticizing this action. On the contrary, it is the way to proceed if you want results. Is there anything like that going on regarding the world organization and its numerous subsidiary problems, all of them important to peace and prosperity?

Comparatively speaking, there is almost nothing that could be called fundamental research into the basic nature of human relations. To be sure, there are endless petty projects, surveys, conferences, oratory, and arguments by representatives of pressure groups, as if argument ever settled any scientific questions. Of basic social research there is very little. Why isn't there more? It is not yet realized that scientific knowledge is relevant to successful world organization. We still think that common sense, good will, eloquent leaders, and pious hopes are sufficient when it comes to management of social relations.

* 2 *

A STUDY IN FERTILITY CONTROL

Bernard Berelson and Ronald Freedman

Students often ask, "What good is sociological knowledge? What is its practical value?" Answers to such questions are suggested by Berelson and Freedman, authors of this selection, as they describe an apparently successful attempt to teach family planning in Taiwan. The authors term the attempt "one of the most extensive and elaborate social science experiments ever carried out in a natural setting." One may infer, on the basis of the experiment as described, that even though favorable social changes may occur without planning, sociological knowledge can be used to influence social change in a desired direction.

It is widely recognized that in many parts of the world there is a "population problem": the high rate of increase in population makes social and economic development difficult if not impossible. Can anything be done about the problem? Practical means of fertility control are available to individual couples, but can the control of fertility actually be implemented on a large scale in the developing areas? This article will describe an experiment designed to find out what can be done in one of the world's most

SOURCE: *Scientific American*, Vol. 210, No. 5 (May, 1964). Reprinted with permission. Copyright © 1964 by Scientific American, Inc. All rights reserved. Available separately @ 20¢ as offprint No. 621 from W. H. Freeman and Company, 660 Market Street, San Francisco, California. ✧ Bernard Berelson is on the staff of the Communication Research Programs, Population Council, and was formerly Dean of the Graduate School, University of Chicago. He is the author of *The Library Public* and *Content Analysis*, and the coauthor of *Voting* and *Human Behavior: An Inventory of Scientific Findings*. ✧ Ronald Freedman is professor of sociology and the Director of the Population Studies Center at the University of Michigan. His special interests include population trends and urban community organization, and he is the coauthor of *Principles of Sociology*.

densely populated places: the island of Taiwan off the coast of mainland China.

Large-scale efforts to control fertility are, to be sure, not unknown. A number of governments have assumed the responsibility of providing their people with information and services on family planning, and some countries have organized major national programs. Lowering a birthrate is a novel objective for a government, however, and no country has yet managed to achieve widespread family limitation through a planned social effort. Current programs are therefore handicapped by a lack of information on attitudes toward fertility control and by a lack of experience with programs to implement family planning.

Since any change in birthrate depends on individual decisions by large numbers of husbands and wives, it is essential to know first of all how the people concerned feel about family size and limitation. Do they need to be motivated toward family planning? If they are so motivated, how can they best be helped to accomplish their aim? To investigate these questions the Taiwan study was inaugurated a year and a half ago [1962] under the sponsorship of the provincial health department of Taiwan with the support of the Population Council, a U.S. foundation that advances scientific training and study in population matters. The most significant preliminary finding is that the people do not need to be motivated. They want to plan their families, but they need to know how. Teaching them how—implementing a family-planning program—has proved to be feasible.

Taiwan has a population of about 12 million in an area of 14,000 square miles, and its population is increasing rapidly. In recent years mortality has fallen almost to Western levels: life expectancy is more than 60 years and the death rate is less than eight per 1,000 of population per year. The birthrate is about 37 per 1,000, so the rate of increase is almost 3 per cent per year, or enough to double the population in 25 years. Nevertheless, compared with other parts of Asia, Taiwan provides a favorable situation for the diffusion of family planning. The island is relatively urbanized and industrialized, the farmers are oriented toward a market economy, literacy and popular education are fairly widespread, there is a good transportation and communication system and a solid network of medical facilities. The standard of living is high for a population of this size in Asia outside of Japan. The society is highly organized. Women are not sharply subordinated and there are few religious or ideological objections to contraception.

❖   ❖   ❖   ❖   ❖

Although the situation in Taiwan was quite favorable for family planning and the birthrate trend had been downward, this was not to say that it would be a simple matter to accelerate the decline in fertility. As a first step in that effort the Population Studies centers in Taiwan and at the

University of Michigan undertook a survey that would serve as a base line and also as a guide for a program of action. Between October, 1962, and January, 1963, public health nurses interviewed nearly 2,500 married women of the city of Taichung in the prime reproductive age group (ages 20 to 39) as to their attitudes toward family planning, their information about it and what they did about it. The survey made it clear that these women as a group wanted to have a moderate number of children, were having more children than they wanted, approved of the idea of family limitation and were trying—ineffectively—to limit the size of their families.

The number of children most of the women wanted was four, and women who had already borne more than that number acknowledged that they would have preferred fewer children (see illustration, page 22). More than 90 per cent of Taichung's wives (and their husbands too, according to the wives) were favorably inclined toward limiting family size. They had few objections in principle, they saw, the value of such limitation for the economic welfare of their families and they did not believe that the number of children should be left to "fate" or "providence." In this regard (and the same has been found to be true in other countries) their attitudes are more advanced than some officials believe them to be.

The women were in general poorly informed about family-planning methods and indeed about the physiology of reproduction. About a fourth of them had employed some means of contraception, but in most cases only after four or five pregnancies and in many cases without success. The women expressed strong interest in learning and adopting better methods. And in their own minds family planning did not conflict with their traditional feelings about the Chinese family or its central role in their lives.

Experience with contraception or other methods of limiting family size was naturally most common in the "modernized" sectors of the population: the best-educated women, the most literate and those with an urban background. The women's actual and desired fertility were also related to these characteristics, but we found that on every educational level the average woman between 35 and 39, when childbearing is not yet over, had borne more children than she wanted. This was true even of groups in which substantial numbers of women had tried to limit the size of their families: contraception had arrived on the scene too late and was too ineffective to enable such women to attain their goals.

The survey data made it clear that the women had become aware of the decline of infant mortality in their community. This is an important perception, and one that does not follow automatically on the event. (Other surveys have shown that women sometimes perceive a decrease in infant mortality as an increase in births.) Because they recognized that more children were surviving, the women appreciated that, unlike their parents, they did not need to have five or seven children in order to see three or four survive to adulthood.

The salient message of the survey was that in Taichung people have more children than they want. There are indications that the same thing is true in many similar societies. It seems clear that if throughout the world unwanted children were not conceived, a large part of the "population problem" would disappear.

The next task was to facilitate the matching of behavior to attitude— to implement family planning. Several things were required beyond the mere wish to limit the number of children: information and knowledge, supplies and services, public acceptance and social support. To study how best to enable the people of Taiwan to do what they themselves said they wanted to do, the provincial health authorities undertook to develop a program of action to make the practice of family planning more readily available in the city of Taichung. This effort, we think, is one of the most extensive and elaborate social science experiments ever carried out in a natural setting.

Taichung has a population of about 300,000, including about 36,000 married women from 20 to 39 years old, of whom 60 per cent have had three or more children. Most of the people live in a central region of shops, offices and residences, but there are also rural areas within the city's administrative limits. A number of government health stations and hospital clinics provide focal points for the action program.

The city as a whole was exposed to only two aspects of the program: a general distribution of posters pointing out the advantages of family planning and a series of meetings with community leaders to inform them about the program, get their advice and enlist their support. That was the extent of the community-wide effort; the remainder of the program was designed as a differentiated experiment involving various kinds and degrees of effort. The objective was to learn how much family planning could be achieved at how much cost in money, personnel and time. To this end the local health authorities and a cooperating team from the U.S. devised four different "treatments," and applied one of them to each of the 2,389 *lin's,* or neighborhoods of 20 to 30 families, into which Taichung is divided. In order of increasing effort,, the treatments were designated "Nothing," "Mail," "Everything (wives only)" and "Everything (wives and husbands)."

In the "Nothing" *lin's* there was no activity beyond the distribution of posters and the meetings with leaders. In the "Mail" *lin's* there was a direct-mail campaign addressed to two groups: newlywed couples and parents with two or more children. It was in the "Everything" neighborhoods that the major effort was made to increase family planning. The primary procedure was a personal visit to the home of every married woman from 20 to 39 years old by a specially trained staff of nurse-midwives. The fieldworkers made appointments for people at the health stations, provided contraceptive supplies, answered questions and did whatever else was necessary to satisfy a couple's desire for family-planning guidance. In half of the "Everything" *lin's* the visits were made to wives only; in the other half the visits were extended to both husbands and wives, who were seen either separately or together.

Rather than apply each of these treatments to a different part of the city, the investigators decided to arrange matters so as to test a central economic issue: How much "circulation effect" can one expect in a program of this kind? To what extent can one depend on the population itself to spread the desired innovation, and how large an initial effort is required to prime the process? There has been substantial testimony that word-of-mouth diffusion played a large role in spreading ideas about family planning in the West and Japan; any such effect would clearly be of major importance to national efforts in the underdeveloped countries, which must influence large numbers of people and do so with limited resources.

In order to investigate this question of "spread" it seemed advisable to apply the four treatments in different concentrations in different parts of the city. Taichung was divided into three sectors roughly equivalent in urban-rural distribution, socioeconomic status and fertility, and designated as areas of heavy, medium and light "density." In the heavy-density sector the two "Everything" treatments were administered to half of the *lin's*, in the medium sector to a third of them and in the light sector to a fifth. In each sector the remaining *lin's* were assigned to the "Nothing" and the "Mail" treatment groups. The *lin's* were assigned at random, although always in the proper proportion, and those designated for a particular treatment received exactly the same program regardless of their location in the city. They differed only in their environment; in the heavy-density sector, for example, "Nothing" *lin's* were much more closely surrounded by "Everything" *lin's* than were the "Nothing" neighborhoods in the two lighter-density sectors.

The program got under way in mid-February of 1963: the posters went up, meetings were held, 18 fieldworkers fanned out through the "Everything" *lin's* and the health stations prepared to receive inquiries. A set of educational materials was prepared for group and individual discussion, primarily visual aids dealing with the elementary facts about the physiology of reproduction, the reasons for practicing family planning and the major methods of contraception. The fieldworkers offered a wide choice of methods, encouraging couples to select whichever seemed most suitable: jelly, foam tablet, diaphragm, condom, rhythm, withdrawal, the oral pill and the new intra-uterine device. (The last is a recent development that holds great promise for mass programs to reduce fertility because it does not require continued supply, sustained motivation or repeated actions on the part of the user. A plastic ring or coil is inserted in the uterus by a physician and remains there; it is extremely effective as a contraceptive, although its mode of action is still unclear.) Contraceptive supplies were

provided at or below cost, or free if necessary; the pills sold for the equivalent of 75 cents for a cycle of 20. The same charge was made for the insertion of an intra-uterine device.

By the end of June fieldworkers had visited each of the nearly 12,000
designated homes at least once and more than 500 neighborhood meetings
had been held. Between then and the middle of October follow-up visits
were made to women or couples who had indicated interest and to women
who had been pregnant or had been nursing infants earlier in the year. A
final phase began in late October and is still continuing; direct action has
been terminated, but services and supplies are still available at the health
stations, and the momentum of the program is continuing to have effect
as of this writing.

There are three ways in which the effectiveness of the whole program
will be measured. One is through case records kept for all couples who
were visited in their homes or came to clinics as a result of the action
program. The second is a before-and-after survey of a random sample of
2,432 women of childbearing age. The final story will be told in fertility
statistics to be compiled eventually from the official register.

So far one result has emerged from the before-and-after survey, and
it is a key measure of the outcome: at the end of 1962, 14.2 per cent of the
women in the sample were pregnant, and at the end of 1963, 11.4 per cent
were pregnant, a decline of about a fifth.

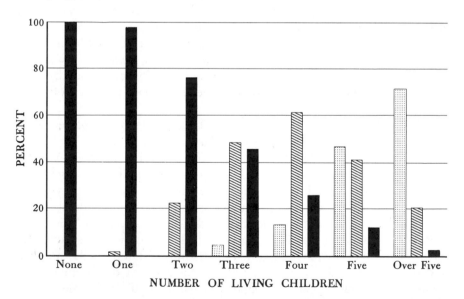

FAMILY-SIZE PREFERENCES are charted for Taichung wives according to the number of children they have. The chart shows the per cent of wives
in each group who said they would have preferred fewer children (dotted bars)
or more children (black bars) than they had or were satisfied with the number
of children they had (striped bars).

Aside from this one statistic, only the case records are available. Even for the people directly involved it is too early to measure the effect of the program on fertility; an immediate effect would take at least nine months to begin to show up! A presumptive effect, however, can be gauged from the record of "acceptances," defined as the insertion of an intra-uterine device or the receipt of instructions and the purchase of supplies for other methods, together with expressed intent to practice contraception. In the 13 months ending in mid-March of this year the action program was responsible for a total of 5,297 acceptances of family planning, 4,007 of which were from women living within Taichung proper. (The remainder came from outside the city even though no direct action was carried on there.)

How good is that record? There are different ways to appraise the figures of 4,000-odd acceptances within the city. First, the accepters constitute 11 per cent of the married women from 20 to 39. Not all the women in that age group, however, were "eligible" to accept family planning as a result of this program. About 16 per cent were already practicing contraception to their own satisfaction. Another 16 per cent had been sterilized or were believed to be sterile. Nine per cent were pregnant, 3 per cent lactating and 1 per cent experiencing menstrual irregularities of one kind or another. If these women are eliminated, only about 55 per cent of the 36,000 in the age group were "eligible." Of these 20,000 or so women, the program secured about 20 per cent as family planners. Included in that definition of eligibility, however, are women who actively want another child—young wives who have not completed their families or those who want a son. If they are considered not really eligible for contraception at this time, the "currently eligible" category is reduced to some 10,000 women, and those who have taken up contraception in the first 13 months come to about 40 per cent of this truly eligible population.

This arithmetic helps to define a "success" in the spread of family planning in the underdeveloped countries. At any given time somewhere between half and three-fourths of the target population is simply out of bounds for the purpose. If a program can get as many as half—or even a third or a fourth—of the remaining group to begin practicing contraception within a few years, it has probably achieved a good deal. In this kind of work, then, having an impact on 10 per cent of the target population in a year or so is not a disappointing failure but a substantial success; one should report "Fully 10 per cent," not "Only 10 per cent"! Another way to appraise the Taichung results to date is to recognize that whereas in February, 1963, about 16 per cent of the married women from 20 to 39 were practicing contraception, by March of this year about 27 per cent were doing so, an increase of nearly 70 per cent.

The impact of such a program is not felt immediately or at one time or evenly. At the outset the acceptance rate was remarkably constant, but after some seven weeks, when 40 per cent of the home visits had been made and word-of-mouth reports of the program were well established, the curve began to climb steadily. It hit a plateau in about four weeks and stayed there for about a month before declining. This was the height of the program, when two-thirds of the home visits had been completed and interest was strong. By the beginning of June, when nearly all the visits had been made, the cream had been skimmed: the women who were strongly motivated toward family planning had heard of the program and had decided what they would do about it. By the end of the summer follow-up visits were reaching less motivated women and the curve returned to its starting point. In the fall, when home visits ended but supplies and services were still available, the acceptances settled to a lower but steady rate.

A program of this kind, then, apparently starts off reasonably well, builds up quite rapidly and achieves roughly half of its first year's return within the first four months. The important thing is to develop a "critical mass" that can generate enough personal motivation and social support to carry on without further home visits. A poor country simply cannot afford visits to the entire population, so any realistic plan must rely heavily on personal and informal contacts from trusted sources; it may be that the job will have to be done by relatives, neighbors and friends or not at all. The task of a planned program will thus be to develop enough knowledgeable and convinced users of contraceptives to start a movement that reaches out to the ill-informed and unconvinced.

The indirect effects were extremely important in Taichung. The most dramatic indication is the fact that by the end of 1963 some 20 per cent of the acceptances had come from women who did not even live in the city. (That figure has since risen to almost 25 per cent.) Within the city about 60 per cent of the acceptances were from "Everything" *lin's*; the other 40 per cent were divided about equally between the "Nothing" and the "Mail" *lin's*. Even in the "Everything" neighborhoods about a sixth of those who accepted contraceptives actually came forward before their scheduled home visits had been made. Direct home visits, in other words, accounted for only some 40 per cent of the acceptances by the end of December.

The nature of the contraceptive method has more of an effect on the success of a program than may have been generally recognized. A "one-time" method requires far less field effort over a long term than a method dependent on resupply and sustained motivation. In Taichung the choice turned out to be overwhelmingly for the intra-uterine devices, which were preferred by 78 per cent of those who accepted contraceptives; 20 per cent selected one of the more traditional methods (mainly foam tablets or condoms) and 2 per cent chose the oral pill (which was, to be sure, the most expensive method). The women themselves, in other words, elected the "one-time" method. This was particularly significant in view of the method's high effectiveness and what might be called its "accountability" through scheduled medical follow-ups. The six-month checkup shows that only some 20 per cent of the devices have been removed or involuntarily expelled, whereas about 30 per cent of the women who chose the traditional methods are no longer practicing contraception regularly.

✧   ✧   ✧   ✧   ✧

Family planning does not, of course, diffuse evenly among the different kinds of people in a community. Acceptance varies with education and age and—in Taichung at least—above all with number of children and number of sons. When couples in Taiwan have four children, they have all they want and they are ready to do something about it—if there is something available that is reasonably effective, inexpensive and easy to use. The evidence here is that whereas the slow long-term "natural" spread of contraception through a population reaches the better-educated people first, a deliberate and accelerated effort like the Taichung program can quickly have a major impact on the families that already have large numbers of children.

Taiwan is one of many low-income countries where rapid increases in population thwart economic development and threaten to slow further improvements in the standard of living. In the long run, to be sure, it seems likely that economic and social pressures combined with personal aspirations will lead individuals to limit their families. The underdeveloped countries, however, cannot wait for a long-term solution to their present crisis. The program in Taichung suggests that fertility control can be spread by a planned effort—not so easily or so fast as death control, but nevertheless substantially, in a short period of time and economically. (The cost of each acceptance was between $4 and $8, far below the eventual economic value of each prevented birth, which has been estimated as being between one and two times the annual per capita income.)

A good deal of the story in Taiwan remains to be told, of course, including the results of the sample survey and the critical check of official birth statistics over the next months and years. Health agencies in Taiwan are now extending the program to a larger segment of the population, testing the Taichung results and trying out new approaches in the slum areas of cities and in poor fishing and mining villages. At this point one can at least say that fertility in Taiwan is changing and can be changed—changing over the long run as the result of unplanned social processes but, most significantly, changeable in the short run as the result of a planned effort to help people have the number of children they really want.

WHAT DO ATTITUDE SURVEYS
TELL US?

Paul F. Lazarsfeld

Sociologists are not infrequently accused by laymen of "elaborating the obvious"—of investing much time, energy, and dollars in surveys which, in the end, only reveal "what everybody already knows." But there are dangers inherent in too-heavy dependence on common-sense generalizations about attitudes and behavior, as Paul Lazarsfeld demonstrates dramatically here. He makes his point as a part of a review of two publications which set forth the findings of extensive attitude surveys conducted by the Army during World War II—the results of which were used in a new and wholly unprecedented fashion to improve the selection, training, assignment, and morale of American soldiers.

It will be helpful to consider the special role played by attitude surveys in contemporary social science. Although surveys are only one of the many techniques available, at the moment they undoubtedly constitute the most important and promising step forward that has been made in recent years.

The limitations of survey methods are obvious. They do not use experimental techniques; they rely primarily on what people say, and rarely include objective observations; they deal with aggregates of individuals rather than with integrated communities; they are restricted to contemporary problems—history can be studied only by the use of documents remaining from earlier periods.

In spite of these limitations survey methods provide one of the foundations upon which social science is being built. The finding of regularities is the beginning of any science, and surveys can make an important contribution in this respect. For it is necessary that we know what people usually do under many and different circumstances if we are to develop theories explaining their behavior. Furthermore, before we can devise an

SOURCE: Paul F. Lazarsfeld, "The American Soldier—An Expository Review," *The Public Opinion Quarterly*, Vol. 13, No. 3 (Fall, 1949), 378–80. Reprinted by permission. ❖ The author is the Quételet Professor of Social Science at Columbia University and was formerly director of the Bureau of Applied Social Research. He has acted as a consultant for agencies concerned with problems of communication by radio, newspaper, or magazine. He is a former president of the American Sociological Association and the coauthor of *The People's Choice, Continuities in Social Research*, and *Language of Social Research*.

experiment we must know what problems are worthwhile; which should be investigated in greater detail. Here again surveys can be of service.

Finding regularities and determining criteria of significance are concerns the social sciences have in common with the natural sciences. But there are crucial differences between the two fields of inquiry. The world of social events is much less "visible" than the realm of nature. That bodies fall to the ground, that things are hot or cold, that iron becomes rusty, are all immediately obvious. It is much more difficult to realize that ideas of right and wrong vary in different cultures; that customs may serve a different function from the one which the people practising them believe they are serving; that the same person may show marked contrasts in his behavior as a member of a family and as a member of an occupational group. The mere description of human behavior, of its variation from group to group and of its changes in different situations, is a vast and difficult undertaking. It is this task of describing, sifting and ferreting out interrelationships which surveys perform for us. And yet this very function often leads to serious misunderstandings. For it is hard to find a form of human behavior that has not already been observed somewhere. Consequently, if a study reports a prevailing regularity, many readers respond to it by thinking "of course that is the way things are." Thus, from time to time, the argument is advanced that surveys only put into complicated form observations which are already obvious to everyone.

Understanding the origin of this point of view is of importance far beyond the limits of the present discussion. The reader may be helped in recognizing this attitude if he looks over a few statements which are typical of many survey findings and carefully observes his own reaction. A short list of these, with brief interpretive comments, will be given here in order to bring into sharper focus probable reactions of many readers.

1. Better educated men showed more psycho-neurotic symptoms than those with less education. (The mental instability of the intellectual as compared to the more impassive psychology of the-man-in-the-street has often been commented on.)
2. Men from rural backgrounds were usually in better spirits during their Army life than soldiers from city backgrounds. (After all, they are more accustomed to hardships.)
3. Southern soldiers were better able to stand the climate in the hot South Sea Islands than Northern soldiers. (Of course, Southerners are more accustomed to hot weather.)
4. White privates were more eager to become non-coms than Negroes. (The lack of ambition among Negroes is almost proverbial.)
5. Southern Negroes preferred Southern to Northern white officers. (Isn't it well known that Southern whites have a more fatherly attitude toward their "darkies"?)
6. As long as the fighting continued, men were more eager to be returned to the States than they were after the German surrender. (You cannot blame people for not wanting to be killed.)

We have in these examples a sample list of the simplest type of inter-relationships which provide the "bricks" from which our empirical social science is being built. But why, since they are so obvious, is so much money and energy given to establish such findings? Would it not be wiser to take them for granted and proceed directly to a more sophisticated type of analysis? This might be so except for one interesting point about the list. *Every one of these statements is the direct opposite of what actually was found.* Poorly educated soldiers were more neurotic than those with high education; Southerners showed no greater ability than Northerners to adjust to a tropical climate; Negroes were more eager for promotion than whites; and so on.

If we had mentioned the actual results of the investigation first, the reader would have labelled these "obvious" also. Obviously something is wrong with the entire argument of "obviousness." It should really be turned on its head. Since every kind of human reaction is conceivable, it is of great importance to know which reactions actually occur most frequently and under what conditions; only then will a more advanced social science develop.

✦ 4 ✦

MANIFEST AND LATENT FUNCTIONS

Robert K. Merton

Most social scientists are "functionalists." That is, they are more concerned with the functions of various phenomena than with trying to ascertain the "real nature" of the phenomena. Stated in another way, modern social science is more concerned with what things do than with what things allegedly are. As one investigator has expressed it, the usefulness of electricity was limited as long as physicists concerned themselves with the vain attempt to find out what electricity is; progress came only when men turned to the task of finding what electricity could do and contented themselves with defining electricity as "that which does such and such." In this article Robert K. Merton applies the same approach to political

SOURCE: Reprinted from *Social Theory and Social Structure*, pp. 71–81, by permission of The Free Press, Glencoe, Illinois. Copyright 1949. ✦ The author is the Giddings Professor of Sociology, Columbia University, and associate director of the Bureau of Applied Social Research. He is a past president of the American Sociological Association. His main interests include the sociology of professions, the sociology of science, sociological theory, and mass communications. He is the author of *Social Theory and Social Structure* and the coeditor of *Sociology Today* and *Reader in Bureaucracy*.

machines. He is not here concerned with what political machines may be in any ultimate sense; he concentrates on what they do, that is, how they function. In using this approach, Merton illustrates the basic point that a function may be manifest (obvious or intended) or latent (hidden or unintended). The author demonstrates that the scientist, as scientist, aims to describe, not judge; he analyzes political machines but he does not blame or praise them.

Some Functions of the Political Machine

Without presuming to enter into the variations of detail marking different political machines—a Tweed, Vare, Crump, Flynn, Hague are by no means identical types of bosses—we can briefly examine the functions more or less common to the political machine, as a generic type of social orgnization. We neither attempt to itemize all the diverse functions of the political machine nor imply that all these functions are similarly fulfilled by each and every machine.

The key structural function of the Boss is to organize, centralize and maintain in good working condition "the scattered fragments of power" which are at present dispersed through our political organization. By this centralized organization of political power, the boss and his apparatus can satisfy the needs of diverse subgroups in the larger community which are not adequately satisfied by legally devised and culturally approved social structures.

To understand the role of bossism and the machine, therefore, we must look at two types of sociological variables: (1) the *structural context* which makes it difficult, if not impossible, for morally approved structures to fulfill essential social functions, thus leaving the door open for political machines (or their structural equivalents) to fulfill these functions and (2) the subgroups whose distinctive needs are left unsatisfied, except for the latent functions which the machine in fact fulfills.

Structural Context

The constitutional framework of American political organization specifically precludes the legal possibility of highly centralized power and, it has been noted, thus "discourages the growth of effective and responsible leadership. The framers of the Constitution, as Woodrow Wilson observed, set up the check and balance system 'to keep government at a sort of mechanical equipoise by means of a standing amicable contest among its several organic parts.' They distrusted power as dangerous to liberty: and therefore they spread it thin and erected barriers against its concentration." This dispersion of power is found not only at the national level but in local areas as well. "As a consequence," Sait goes on to observe, "when *the people* or *particular groups* among them demanded positive action, no one had adequate authority to act. The machine provided an antidote."

The constitutional dispersion of power not only makes for difficulty of effective decision and action but when action does occur it is defined and hemmed in by legalistic considerations. In consequence, there develops "a much *more human system* of partisan government, whose chief object soon became the circumvention of government by law. . . . The lawlessness of the extra-official democracy was merely the counterpoise of the legalism of the official democracy. The lawyer having been permitted to subordinate democracy to the Law, the Boss had to be called in to extricate the victim, which he did after a fashion and for a consideration."

Officially, political power is dispersed. Various well-known expedients were devised for this manifest objective. Not only was there the familiar separation of powers among the several branches of the government but, in some measure, tenure in each office was limited, rotation in office approved. And the scope of power inherent in each office was severely circumscribed. Yet, observes Sait in rigorously functional terms, "Leadership is necessary; and *since* it does not develop readily within the constitutional framework, the Boss provides it in a crude and irresponsible form from the outside."

Put in more generalized terms, *the functional deficiencies of the official structure generate an alternative (unofficial) structure to fulfill existing needs somewhat more effectively.* Whatever its specific historical origins, the political machine persists as an apparatus for satisfying otherwise unfulfilled needs of diverse groups in the population. By turning to a few of these subgroups and their characteristic needs, we shall be led at once to a range of latent functions of the political machine.

Functions of the Political Machine for Diverse Subgroups

It is well known that one source of strength of the political machine derives from its roots in the local community and the neighborhood. The political machine does not regard the electorate as a vague, undifferentiated mass of voters. With a keen sociological intuition, the machine recognizes that the voter is primarily a man living in the specific neighborhood, with specific personal problems and personal wants. Public issues are abstract and remote; private problems are extremely concrete and immediate. It is not through the generalized appeal to large public concerns that the machine operates, but through the direct, quasi-feudal relationships between local representatives of the machine and voters in their neighborhood. Elections are won in the precinct.

The machine welds its link with ordinary men and women by elaborate networks of personal relations. Politics is transformed into personal ties.

The precinct captain "must be a friend to every man, assuming, if he does not feel, sympathy with the unfortunate, and utilizing in his good works the resources which the boss puts at his disposal." The precinct captain is forever a friend in need. In our prevailingly impersonal society, the machine, through its local agents, fulfills the important social *function of humanizing and personalizing all manner of assistance* to those in need. Food-baskets and jobs, legal and extra-legal advice, setting to rights minor scrapes with the law, helping the bright poor boy to a political scholarship in a local college, looking after the bereaved—the whole range of crises when a feller needs a friend, and, above all, a friend who knows the score and who can do something about it—all these find the ever-helpful precinct captain available in the pinch.

To assess this function of the political machine adequately, it is important to note not only the fact that aid *is* provided but *the manner in which it is provided*. After all, other agencies do exist for dispensing such assistance. Welfare agencies, settlement houses, legal aid clinics, medical aid in free hospitals, public relief departments, immigration authorities— these and a multitude of other organizations are available to provide the most varied types of assistance. But in contrast to the professional techniques of the welfare worker which may typically represent in the mind of the recipient the cold, bureaucratic dispensation of limited aid following upon detailed investigation of *legal* claims to aid of the "client," are the unprofessional techniques of the precinct captain who asks no questions, exacts no compliance with legal rules of eligibility and does not "snoop" into private affairs.

For many, the loss of "self-respect" is too high a price for legalized assistance. In contrast to the gulf between the settlement house workers who so often come from a different social class, educational background and ethnic group, the precinct worker is "just one of us," who understands what it's all about. The condescending lady bountiful can hardly compete with the understanding friend in need. In *this struggle between alternative structures for fulfilling the nominally same function* of providing aid and support to those who need it, it is clearly the machine politician who is better integrated with the groups which he serves than the impersonal, professionalized, socially distant and legally constrained welfare worker. And since the politician can at times influence and manipulate the official organizations for the dispensation of assistance, whereas the welfare worker has practically no influence on the political machine, this only adds to his greater effectiveness. More colloquially and also, perhaps, more incisively, it was the Boston ward-leader, Martin Lomasny, who described this essential function to the curious Lincoln Steffens: "I think," said Lomasny, "that there's got to be in every ward somebody that any bloke can come to—no matter what he's done—and get help. *Help, you understand; none of your law and justice, but help*."

The "deprived classes," then, constitute one subgroup for whom the political machine clearly satisfies wants not adequately satisfied in the same fashion by the legitimate social structure.

For a second subgroup, that of business (primarily "big" business but also "small"), the political boss serves the function of providing those political privileges which entail immediate economic gains. Business corporations, among which the public utilities (railroads, local transportation companies, communications corporations, electric light) are simply the most conspicuous in this regard, seek special political dispensations which will enable them to stabilize their situation and to near their objective of maximizing profits. Interestingly enough, corporations often want to avoid a chaos of uncontrolled competition. They want the greater security of an economic czar who controls, regulates and organizes competition, providing this czar is not a public official with his decisions subject to public scrutiny and public control. (The latter would be "government control," and hence taboo.) The political boss fulfills these requirements admirably.

Examined for a moment apart from any "moral" considerations, the political apparatus of the Boss is effectively designed to perform these functions with a minimum of inefficiency. Holding the strings of diverse governmental divisions, bureaus and agencies in his competent hands, the Boss rationalizes the relations between public and private business. He serves as the business community's ambassador in the otherwise alien (and sometimes unfriendly) realm of government. And, in strict business-like terms, he is well-paid for his economic services to his respectable business clients. In an article entitled, "An Apology to Graft," Steffens suggested that "Our economic system, which held up riches, power and acclaim as prizes to men bold enough and able enough to buy corruptly timber, mines, oil fields and franchises and 'get away with it,' was at fault." And, in a conference with a hundred or so of Los Angeles business leaders, he described a fact well known to all of them: the Boss and his machine were an *integral part* of the organization of the economy. "You cannot build or operate a railroad, or a street railway, gas, water, or power company, develop and operate a mine, or get forests and cut timber on a large scale, or run any privileged business, without corrupting or joining in the corruption of the government. You tell me privately that you must, and here I am telling you semi-publicly that you must. And that is so all over the country. And that means that we have an organization of society in which, *for some reason*, you and your kind, the ablest, most intelligent, most imaginative, daring, and resourceful leaders of society, are and must be against society and its laws and its all-around growth."

Since the demand for the services of special privileges are built into the structure of the society, the Boss fulfills diverse functions for this second subgroup of business-seeking-privilege. These "needs" of business, as presently constituted, are not adequately provided for by "conventional" and "culturally approved" social structures; consequently, the extra-legal but more-or-less efficient organization of the political machine comes to provide these services. To adopt an *exclusively* moral attitude toward the "corrupt political machine" is to lose sight of the very structural conditions which generate the "evil" that is so bitterly attacked. To adopt a functional outlook on the political machine is not to provide an apologia, but a more solid base for modifying or eliminating the machine, *providing* specific structural arrangements are introduced either for eliminating these effective demands of the business community or, if that is the objective, of satisfying these demands through alternative means.

A third set of distinctive functions fulfilled by the political machine for a special subgroup is that of providing alternative channels of social mobility for those otherwise excluded from the more conventional avenues for personal "advancement." Both the sources of this special "need" (for social mobility) and the respect in which the political machine comes to help satisfy this need can be understood by examining the structure of the larger culture and society. As is well known, the American culture lays enormous emphasis on money and power as a "success" goal legitimate for all members of the society. By no means alone in our inventory of cultural goals, it still remains among the most heavily endowed with positive affect and value. However, certain subgroups and certain ecological areas are notable for the relative absence of opportunity for achieving these (monetary and power) types of success. They constitute, in short, sub-populations where "the cultural emphasis upon pecuniary success has been absorbed, but where there is *little access to conventional and legitimate* means for attaining such success. The conventional occupational opportunities of persons in (such areas) are almost completely limited to manual labor. Given our cultural stigmatization of manual labor, and its correlate, the prestige of white-collar work," it is clear that the result is a tendency to achieve these culturally approved objectives *through whatever means are possible.* These people are on the one hand, "asked to orient their conduct toward the prospect of accumulating wealth [and power] and, on the other, they are largely denied effective opportunities to do so institutionally."

It is within this context of social structure that the political machine fulfills the basic function of providing avenues of social mobility for the otherwise disadvantaged. Within this context, even the corrupt political machine and the racket "represent the triumph of amoral intelligence over morally prescribed 'failure' when the channels of vertical mobility are closed or narrowed *in a society which places a high premium on economic affluence, [power] and social ascent for all its members.*" As one sociologist has noted on the basis of several years of close observation in a "slum area":

The sociologist who dismisses racket and political organizations as deviations from desirable standards thereby neglects some of the major elements of slum life. . . . *He does not discover the functions they perform for the members* [of the groupings in the slum]. The Irish and later immigrant peoples have had the greatest difficulty in finding places for themselves in our urban social and economic structure. Does anyone believe that the immigrants and their children could have achieved their present degree of social mobility without gaining control of the political organization of some of our largest cities? The same is true of the racket organization. *Politics and the rackets have furnished an important means of social mobility for individuals, who, because of ethnic background and low class position,* are blocked from advancement in the "respectable" channels.

This, then, represents a third type of function performed for a distinctive subgroup. This function, it may be noted in passing, is fulfilled by the *sheer* existence and operation of the political machine, for it is in the machine itself that these individuals and subgroups find their culturally induced needs more or less satisfied. It refers to the services which the political apparatus provides for its own personnel. But seen in the wider social context we have set forth, it no longer appears as *merely* a means of self-aggrandizement for profit-hungry and power-hungry *individuals,* but as an organized provision for *subgroups* otherwise excluded or restricted from the race for "getting ahead."

Just as the political machine performs services for "legitimate" business, so it operates to perform not dissimilar services for "illegitimate" business: vice, crime and rackets. Once again, the basic sociological role of the machine in this respect can be more fully appreciated only if one temporarily abandons attitudes of moral indignation, to examine with all moral innocence the actual workings of the organization. In this light, it at once appears that the subgroup of the professional criminal, racketeer, gambler, has basic similarities of organization, demands and operation to the subgroup of the industrialist, man of business, speculator. If there is a Lumber King or an Oil King, there is also a Vice King or a Racket King. If expansive legitimate business organizes administrative and financial syndicates to "rationalize" and to "integrate" diverse areas of production and business enterprise, so expansive rackets and crime organize syndicates to bring order to the otherwise chaotic areas of production of illicit goods and services. If legitimate business regards the proliferation of small business enterprises as wasteful and inefficient, substituting, for example the giant chain stores for the hundreds of corner groceries, so illegitimate business adopts the same businesslike attitude, and syndicates crime and vice.

Finally, and in many respects, most important, is the basic similarity, if not near-identity, of the economic role of "legitimate" business and "illegitimate" business. *Both are in some degree concerned with the provision of goods and services for which there is an economic demand.* Morals aside, they are both business, industrial and professional enterprises, dispensing goods and services which some people want, for which there is a market in which goods and services are transformed into commodities. And, in a prevalently market society, we should expect appropriate enterprises to arise whenever there is a market demand for given goods or services.

As is well known, vice, crime and the rackets *are* "big business." Consider only that there have been estimated to be about 500,000 professional prostitutes in the United States, and compare this with the approximately 200,000 physicians and 200,000 nurses. It is difficult to estimate which have the larger clientele: the professional men and women of medicine or the professional men and women of vice. It is, of course, difficult to estimate the economic assets, income, profits and dividends of illicit gambling in this country and to compare it with the economic assets, income, profits and dividends of, say, the shoe industry, but it is altogether possible that the two industries are about on a par. No precise figures exist on the annual expenditures on illicit narcotics, and it is probable that these are less than the expenditures on candy, but it is also probable that they are larger than the expenditure on books.

It takes but a moment's thought to recognize that, *in strictly economic terms*, there is no relevant difference between the provision of licit and illicit goods and services. The liquor traffic illustrates this perfectly. It would be peculiar to argue that prior to 1920 (when the 18th amendment became effective), the provision of liquor constituted an economic service, that from 1920 to 1933, its production and sale no longer constituted an economic service dispensed in a market, and that from 1934 to the present, it once again took on a serviceable aspect. Or, it would be *economically* (not morally) absurd to suggest that the sale of bootlegged liquor in the dry state of Kansas is less a response to a market demand than the sale of publicly manufactured liquor in the neighboring wet state of Missouri. Examples of this sort can of course be multiplied many times over. Can it be held that in European countries, with registered and legalized prostitution, the prostitute contributes an economic service, whereas in this country, lacking legal sanction, the prostitute provides no such service? Or that the professional abortionist is in the economic market where he has approved legal status and that he is out of the economic market where he is legally taboo? Or that gambling satisfies a specific demand for entertainment in Nevada, where it is one of the largest business enterprises of the largest city in the state, but that it differs essentially in this respect from movie houses in the neighboring state of California?

The failure to recognize that these businesses are only *morally* and not *economically* distinguishable from "legitimate" businesses has led to badly scrambled analysis. Once the economic identity of the two is recognized, we may anticipate that if the political machine performs functions for "legitimate big business" it will be all the more likely to perform not dissimilar functions for "illegitimate big business." And, of course, such is often the case.

The distinctive function of the political machine for their criminal, vice and racket clientele is to enable them to operate in satisfying the economic demands of a large market without due interference from the government. Just as big business may contribute funds to the political party war-chest to ensure a minimum of governmental interference, so with big rackets and big crime. In both instances, the political machine can, in varying degrees, provide "protection." In both instances, many features of the structural context are identical: (1) market demands for goods and services; (2) the operators' concern with maximizing gains from their enterprises; (3) the need for partial control of government which might otherwise interfere with these activities of businessmen; (4) the need for an efficient, powerful and centralized agency to provide an effective liaison of "business" with government.

Without assuming that the foregoing pages exhaust either the range of functions or the range of subgroups served by the political machine, we can at least see that *it presently fulfills some functions for these diverse subgroups which are not adequately fulfilled by culturally approved or more conventional structures.*

Several additional implications of the functional analysis of the political machine can be mentioned here only in passing, although they obviously require to be developed at length. First, the foregoing analysis has direct implications for *social engineering.* It helps explain why the periodic efforts at "political reform," "turning the rascals out" and "cleaning political house" are typically short-lived and ineffectual. It exemplifies a basic theorem: *any attempt to eliminate an existing social structure without providing adequate alternative structures for fulfilling the functions previously fulfilled by the abolished organization is doomed to failure.* (Needless to say, this theorem has much wider bearing than the one instance of the political machine.) When "political reform" confines itself to the manifest task of "turning the rascals out," it is engaging in little more than sociological magic. The reform may for a time bring new figures into the political limelight; it may serve the casual social function of reassuring the electorate that the moral virtues remain intact and will ultimately triumph; it may actually effect a turnover in the personnel of the political machine; it may even, for a time, so curb the activities of the machine as to leave unsatisfied the many needs it has previously fulfilled. But, inevitably, unless the reform also involves a "re-forming" of the social and political structure such that the existing needs are satisfied by alternative structures or unless it involves a change which eliminates these needs altogether, the political machine will return to its integral place in the social scheme of things. *To seek social change, without due recognition of the manifest and latent functions performed by the social organization undergoing change, is to indulge in social ritual rather than social engineering.* The concepts of manifest and latent functions (or their equivalents) are indispensable elements in the theoretic repertoire of the social engineer. In this crucial sense, these concepts are not "merely" theoretical (in the abusive sense of the term), but are eminently practical. In the deliberate enactment of social change, they can be ignored only at the price of considerably heightening the risk of failure.

A second implication of our analysis of the political machine also has a bearing upon areas wider than the one we have considered. The "paradox" has often been noted that the supporters of the political machine include both the "respectable" business class elements who are, of course, opposed to the criminal or racketeer and the distinctly "unrespectable" elements of the underworld. And, at first appearance, this is cited as an instance of very strange bedfellows. The learned judge is not infrequently called upon to sentence the very racketeer beside whom he sat the night before at an informal dinner of the political bigwigs. The district attorney jostles the exonerated convict on his way to the back room where the Boss has called a meeting. The big business man may complain almost as bitterly as the big racketeer about the "extortionate" contributions to the party fund demanded by the Boss. Social opposites meet—in the smoke-filled room of the successful politician.

In the light of a functional analysis all this of course no longer seems paradoxical. Since the machine serves both the businessman and the criminal man, the two seemingly antipodal groups intersect. This points to a more general theorem: *the social functions of an organization help determine the structure (including the recruitment of personnel involved in the structure), just as the structure helps determine the effectiveness with which the functions are fulfilled.* In terms of social status, the business group and the criminal group are indeed poles apart. But status does not fully determine behavior and the inter-relations between groups. Functions modify these relations. Given their distinctive needs, the several sub-groups in the large society are "integrated," whatever their personal desires or intentions, by the centralizing structure which serves these several needs. In a phrase with many implications which require further study, *structure affects function and function affects structure.*

A CRITIQUE OF
CULTURAL RELATIVISM

Robert Redfield

In this discussion of the basic theoretical viewpoint known as "cultural relativity," Robert Redfield does not argue against the obvious fact that truths may be regarded as relative to time, place, and a particular culture. But he does assert that acceptance of relativity does not necessitate rejection of all value commitments. Redfield's assertion has immense practical significance because he points to the dangers, as well as to the logical fallacies, of those who would say, for example, "since everything is right in terms of its own logic, I cannot condemn the excesses of totalitarianism." As Redfield shows, science itself would cease to exist if such an attitude were carried to its logical extreme.

I will consider some of the questions that arise when we look at the primitive or the precivilized cultures with a view to the goodness or the badness of them. . . . My own behavior, as an anthropologist, is relevant to the subject now to be discussed, for I am interested here in the way anthropologists do or do not place values on the things they see in prehistoric or in contemporary nonliterate or illiterate societies, and what comes of it if they do. I shall venture to anthropologize the anthropologists, and shall not leave myself out of their number.

. . . Writing of Petalesharoo, the Pawnee Indian who in the face of the customs of his tribe rescued a woman prisoner about to be put to death ceremonially and strove to end human sacrifice among his people, I called him "a hint of human goodness." Plainly I placed a value on his conduct. Looking back twenty-five years, I recall when as a student I first heard the story of Petalesharoo from Professor Fay-Cooper Cole, anthropologist. He told the story with great human warmth, and I know that then I responded sympathetically. Now I begin to wonder if he or I *could* tell the tale barely, neutrally, without implying admiration of the deed.

In my writings, I have not infrequently indicated my admiration for some act, my approval of some turn in human events. The long story of

SOURCE: Robert Redfield, *The Primitive World and Its Transformations* (Ithaca, N.Y.: Cornell University Press, 1953), 139–64, passim. ❖ Robert Redfield (1897–1958) was chairman of the Department of Anthropology and Distinguished Service Professor at the University of Chicago. His chief interests lay in ethnological studies. From 1930 to 1947 he directed ethnological field work in Yucatan and Guatemala. Among his books are *The Folk Culture of Yucatan, The Primitive World and Its Transformations, The Little Community,* and *The Social Uses of Science.*

human affairs which I have been sketchily recounting is a story in which
I have not pretended to be disinterested. It is the human biography; it is
your story and mine; how can we help but care? I have not tried to conceal
a certain sense of satisfaction that in the childhood of our race, before
there were cities, precivilized men, like the preliterates of today, recognized moral obligations, even if the moral rules were not my rules. I
think this better than the unrestrained selfishness which Hobbes imagined
wrongly to characterize the behavior of men before political society developed. So when in the course of these discussions I have encountered
in some uncivilized society a custom which I liked or disliked, I think I
have in many cases shown how I felt about it. I regret that the Siriono in
the Bolivian forest abandon their dying kinsmen without a word, while I
come to understand the rigors of their life that make such conduct excus-
able. I am pleased that the Yagua in their big communal houses respect
even a child's desire to be alone, and refrain from speaking to him when he
turns his face to the wall. . . .

This is, perhaps, a shocking admission. What right have I, who
admit to caring about the human career, to speak as an anthropologist?
For are not anthropologists enjoined to adopt in their work a rigid objectivity? Professor Kroeber has written that "there is no room in anthropology for a shred of ethnocentricity, of homino-centricity." My ethnocentricity appears in the positive valuations I have placed on the increase and
widening of humane standards, for are not such standards a special pride
of Euro-American civilization? And my homini-centricity is patent: I have
placed myself squarely on the side of mankind, and have not shamed to
wish mankind well.

My predicament stimulates an examination of some of the problems
of objectivity and value judgment that arise in anthropology. There are a
good many of these problems, and I shall try to sort them out and to reach
at least the first points of understanding as to what is involved in some of
them.

❖   ❖   ❖   ❖   ❖

Since Westermarck wrote two books to show that it is not possible to
establish one way of thought or action as better than another, if not
before that time, anthropologists have taken this position. It has come
to have a name: cultural relativism. Most anthropologists would, I
think, accept the term as naming their position, or would take the position
without perhaps accepting the name. Cultural relativism means that the
values expressed in any culture are to be both understood and themselves
valued only according to the way the people who carry that culture see
things. In looking at a polygamous society and a monogamous society, we
have no valid way to assert that the one is better than the other. Both
systems provide for human needs; each has values discoverable only when
we look at marriage from the point of view of the man who lives under
the one system or the other. This is, necessarily then, also to be said in

comparing cultures which practice torture, infanticide, in-group sorcery, and homosexuality with those that do not. The gist of cultural relativism as stated by Professor Herskovits, who has discussed the concept at length, is that "judgments are based on experience, and experience is interpreted by each individual in terms of his own enculturation."

With this proposition I do not disagree. I fail to see that having accepted it one finds it necessary to accept everything else that Professor Herskovits says about cultural relativism. . . .

. . . I am persuaded that cultural relativism is in for some difficult times. Anthropologists are likely to find the doctrine a hard one to maintain. The criticisms of philosophers will be directed more sharply against it. Moreover, the experiences of anthropologists are changing, and these changed experiences will work changes in their judgments as to the relativity of values. (It occurs to me that this proposition is itself an application of the principle!) It was easy to look with equal benevolence upon all sorts of value systems so long as the values were those of unimportant little people remote from our own concerns. But the equal benevolence is harder to maintain when one is asked to anthropologize the Nazis, or to help a Point Four administrator decide what to do for those people he is committed to help. The Point Four man is committed to do something to change that people, for he cannot help them without changing them, and what is the anthropologist to say when the Point Four man asks him just what he ought to do? Perhaps the anthropologist can keep on saying: "Do A, and X will result, but Y will result from doing B—*you* choose which to do." But I doubt that if the anthropologist says only this, he and the administrator will get on very well together. And perhaps the anthropologist, if he continues this neutrality, and yet sees a smash coming, will be just a little restless at night.

At any rate, I should like to point out that the doctrine of cultural relativism does enjoin the benevolence. It is a doctrine of ethical neutralism, but it is not a doctrine of ethical indifference. Ruth Benedict's *Patterns of Culture* is an exemplification of cultural relativism. She wrote in large part to tell us that all cultures are "equally valid." But this meant, for her, not that we are to value none of them, but that we are to value all of them. The book is a call to positive sympathetic valuation of other ways of life than our own. Malinowski has gone so far as to write of "the respect due even to savages." And Herskovits states the positive element in the doctrine very clearly. He is not confused into supposing that cultural relativism is a mere scientific method, a procedure instrumental in reaching statements as to fact. No, he says, "cultural relativism is a *philosophy* which, in recognizing the values set up by every society to guide its own life, lays stress on the dignity inherent in every body of custom, and on the need for tolerance of conventions though they may differ from one's own." And again: "Emphasis on the worth of many ways of life, not one, is an affirmation of the values of each culture."

However, the two parts of this doctrine are not logically or necessarily interdependent. The first part says that people are brought up to see the value in things that their local experience has suggested. The second part says that we should respect all cultures. But there is no true "therefore" between these two parts. It cannot be proved, from the proposition that values are relative, that we ought to respect all systems of values. We might just as well hate them all. . . . It is Professor Herskovits who has intruded upon the objectivity of science a moral judgment, which I personally admire, but for which he can show no demonstration of proof.

The anthropologist is, then, ethically neutral, but unlike him of whom the partisan demanded, "Just who are you neutral *for?*," the anthropologist is neutral for everybody. This, at least, is the way anthropologists represent their position. It seems to me that their success in living up to their doctrine may be questioned.

The difficulties of doing so were remarked by not a few of the anthropologists themselves when in 1947 the Executive Board of their American professional association submitted a statement to the Commission on Human Rights of the United Nations. The statement urged the Commission to recognize that, not only should the personality of the individual be accorded respect, but that "respect for the cultures of differing human groups is equally important." It declared the principle of cultural relativity and told the UN Commission that therefore any attempt it might make to write something about human rights ("formulate postulates") "that grow out of the beliefs or moral codes of one culture must to that extent detract from the applicability of any declaration of Human Rights to mankind as a whole." So the Commission was advised to incorporate in the Declaration of Human Rights a statement of the right of men to live in terms of their own traditions.

I understand that the UN Commission did not follow this advice. I imagine that some anthropologists are rather relieved that they did not. Such a declaration might seem to authorize the head-hunting peoples to continue head hunting, for would they not, by continuing head hunting, be living in terms of their own traditions? Of course the anthropologists who drafted this statement were not thinking of the head hunters. They knew, as well as you or I, that the head hunters and the cannibals will not be permitted to live in terms of these particular traditions if it is our heads and bodies they go for. They were thinking of the great and influential world civilizations—Indonesian, Indian, Chinese, African, Euro-American. But even here it is not clear just what the writers of the declaration expected to guarantee to these traditional ways of life—the right of a Mississippi human group to maintain its traditional white supremacy, of Russia to maintain a dehumanizing, fear-ridden way of life? At the time the anthropologists wrote their statement it was perhaps nazism that presented to their minds most plainly the difficulties with their statement, for they wrote in the following sentence: "Even where political systems exist that deny citizens the right of participation in their government, or seek to conquer weaker peoples, underlying cultural values may be called on to bring the peoples of such states to a realization of the consequences of the acts of their governments." If we call upon underlying values to save us, it is we, on the outside of the culture, who are making them effective. And what if the underlying approved values are not there? The sentence is, to put it bluntly, a weasel; by including it, the declaration was made self-contradictory. You either respect all values or you do not. If the Nazis had come to have values approving the subjugation of everybody else, we, or the United Nations, would have either to respect this traditional way of life or not respect it. . . .

✧   ✧   ✧   ✧   ✧

As soon as the anthropologist puts his attention on the particular human individuals in a primitive society, it becomes difficult to avoid the suggestion if not the fact that he is valuing one culture, or cultural situation, as better than another. It is not uncommon for an anthropologist, now studying a primitive culture disorganized by its contact with civilization, to see that the people he is studying are less comfortable than they were. Some of them, indeed, as those Oceanic natives whom Rivers described, appear now on their way to extinction just because they do not find life worth living any more. The anthropologist can hardly convince us—or himself—that so far as he is concerned a disorganized culture that fails to provide a desire to live is as valid as any other. Equal validity can be safely attributed only to cultures that arrange it so people do what they want to do and are convinced that it is the right thing to do.

But even among such cultures, the well-integrated and the motive-providing, it is not always possible for the anthropologist to avoid at least the suggestion that he is preferring one of them to another. Ruth Benedict was a cultural relativist who told us that cultures are equally valid. Nevertheless, in reading some of her pages, one doubts that she found them equally good. In the seventh chapter of *Patterns of Culture* she introduces the concept of "social waste." Here she leads the reader to see a resemblance between the values of Kwakiutl society and those of his own (Middletown); both emphasize rivalry. But rivalry, wrote Benedict, is "notoriously wasteful. It ranks low in the scale of human values." One asks, Whose scale? Is there a universal scale of values which ranks rivalry low? She goes on to point out not only that "Kwakiutl rivalry produces a waste of material goods," but also that "the social waste is obvious." In Middletown, also, rivalry is "obsessive." Thus she is led to the conclusion that "it is possible to scrutinize different institutions and cast up their cost in terms of social capital, in terms of the less desirable behavior traits they stimulate, and in terms of human suffering and frustration." . . .

✧   ✧   ✧   ✧   ✧

It is that disturbing fellow, the living human individual, who makes trouble for the scientist's stern principle of perfect objectivity. Whenever the anthropologist looks at him, something human inside the anthropologist stirs and responds. It is easy enough to be objective toward objects; but the human individual refuses to be only an object. When he is there before you, he insists on being judged as human beings are judged in life, if not in science. While the anthropologist is looking at the bones of the dead, at flint implements, or at institutions formally conceived and named—the Omaha kinship system or the tribal ideology—he is not much distracted by these claims upon his own human nature. But when the anthropologist meets and talks with some particular Indian or Oceanic islander, then he is apt to feel for that native while he is trying to describe him objectively. If the society is one that is running along the traditional ways of life, the field ethnologist is apt to respond with sympathy and indeed with favor toward the culture that keeps men's lives going in directions that they find good. If the ethnologist is himself gifted in communicating the human warmth of an exotic scene, as was Malinowski, an account results which communicates not only the humanity of the life described, but something of the enjoyment and satisfactions which the ethnologist himself experienced in coming to know that life. If the culture is one which puts the people who live by it into constant and fearful anxieties, the anthropologist is apt to show the disfavor he feels toward such a life. Reo Fortune's Dobuans are familiar; so I mention here instead the Tzeltal Indians of Chiapas, where Alfonso Villa Rojas found a people often sick, always believing that each sickness was the result of some moral transgression committed by the sufferer or, more terribly, by some one of his near kinsmen, and who are continually ridden by anxiety and compulsions to confess sins. Villa has described this people objectively, in the sense that his report is well documented and obviously trustworthy. But it would be untrue to assert that he has not shown, strongly in conversation and of course much more reservedly in his written description, his own unfavorable view of such a life. Furthermore, if one reads such an account of people whose traditional ways of life have been disrupted, as, for example, McGregor's account of a reservation community of Sioux Indians, one finds oneself making value judgments that seem to reflect those of the writer, as to the somewhat unhappy predicament in which these people find themselves.

I think that the objectivity claimed by the anthropologist must admit of difficulties and qualifications. Professor Herskovits declares that "a basic necessity of ethnographic research . . . calls for a rigid exclusion of value judgments." This seems a little too strongly put. Rather, I should say, ethnographic research calls for as much objectivity as can be combined with the necessity to come to know the values of the people one is studying. The exception to allow the ethnographer to respect—i.e., value positively—all cultures has already been noted. Professor R. H. Tawney is then expressing an opinion with which we may suppose that Professor Herskovits would agree when he writes that the student of a society must bring to his study "respect and affection." The necessity to understand the values of the people one is studying requires, I should say, the projection into unfamiliar words and actions of human qualities—sympathy, pride, wish to be appreciated, and so on. Otherwise the ethnologist will not find out what the people he is studying are proud about or what, for them, deserves appreciation. My own opinion is that it is not possible to make use of these human qualities in field work, as I think one must, without also valuing what one sees. In the very necessity to describe the native, one must feel for him—or perhaps against him. The feelings are mixed with valuations. In Indian communities in which I have worked, I have found myself constantly liking and disliking some people as compared with others, some customs as compared with others, and some aspects of the total culture as compared with others. I remember, after having spent a good deal of time in Chan Kom, Yucatan, how I had come to admire a certain quality of decency and dignity about the people, and how bored I had become with their—to me—overemphasis on the prudent and the practical. If they would only once admire a sunset or report a mystic experience, I used to hear myself thinking. I would not know how to find out about a culture without this sort of valuing. Objectivity requires that I hold in suspense each formulation I make about the native life. It requires me to become aware of the values I have that may lead me in one direction rather than another. It demands that I subject my descriptions to the tests of documentation, internal consistency, and if possible the evidence and judgments of other observers. But I do not think that it asks of me that I divest myself of the human qualities, including valuing. I could not do my work without them.

. . . Perhaps we should ask of the field ethnologist, not that he divest himself of values, for that it impossible, nor that he emphasize in every case values predominating in his own times with regard to applied science, increased production, and adjusted personalities, but that he make plain what he does find that is good or bad about the people he reports. And then, also, perhaps he can help to bring it about that he is followed in the same community to be studied by an ethnologist with a contrasting value emphasis! It was the *New Yorker* that suggested that we do not want balanced textbooks; we want balanced libraries. We do not want ethnologists so balanced that they have no humanity. We want a balanced profession, a varied lot of anthropologists.

My praise of Petalesharoo here receives explanation, if not justification. Petalesharoo acted against the customary practice of his people. It is a little easier to do that after civilization than before; in precivilized societies it was harder. So Petalesharoo gets my praise on that count. And when he acted, he acted in conformity with the trend of the human career of which he was ignorant, but which I know about, being some thousands of years older in civilization than was he. So it is not remarkable that I praise him. Perhaps also you, my reader, do too.

If you do, and you are not an anthropologist, no one will scold. But I am an anthropologist, and have taken the oath of objectivity. Somehow the broken pledge—if it is broken—sits lightly on my conscience. In me, man and anthropologist do not separate themselves sharply. I used to think I could bring about that separation in scientific work about humanity. Now I have come to confess that I have not effected it, and indeed to think that it is not possible to do so. All the rules of objectivity I should maintain: the marshaling of evidence that may be confirmed by others, the persistent doubting and testing of all important descriptive formulations that I make, the humility before the facts, and the willingness to confess oneself wrong and begin over. I hope I may always strive to obey these rules. But I think now that what I see men do, and understand as something that human beings do, is seen often with a valuing of it. I like or dislike as I go. This is how I reach understanding of it. The double standard of ethical judgment toward primitive peoples is a part of my version of cultural relativity. It is because I am a product of civilization that I value as I do. It is because I am a product of civilization that I have both a range of experience within which to do my understanding-valuing and the scientific disciplines that help me to describe what I value so that others will accept it, or recognizing it as not near enough the truth, to correct it. And if, in this too I am wrong, those others will correct me here also.

❖ 6 ❖

THE JUKE MYTH

Samuel Hopkins Adams

In this amusing account, Samuel Hopkins Adams illustrates the importance, to science in general and to social science in particular, of carefully gathered data. Fortunately for the valid development

SOURCE: "The Juke Myth," by Samuel Hopkins Adams. First published in the *Saturday Review*, Vol. 38, No. 14 (April 2, 1955), 13, 48–49. Copyright, 1955, by Saturday Review, Inc. ❖ The author (1871–1958) was a distinguished essayist and a former staff member of *McClure's Magazine*. Among his works are *The Santa Fe Trail*, *Erie Canal*, and *Grandfather Stories*.

of sociology, our standards of data collection and interpretation today have changed radically from those which prevailed during the
time when the Juke study was considered sound research. Another
important change that occurred has been in our basic theory of
human behavior. Early in this century, as the popularity of the
Juke study illustrates, most people were convinced that the behavior of humans is largely inborn. Now, as the following selection
and as some of the selections in Chapter II suggest, the great majority of professional students of human behavior are agreed that
the most important factors in human action are learned.

No other family in American annals is so well and unfavorably known
as the Jukes. The name is a synonym for depravity. What the Rothschilds
embody in finance the Jukes represent in misdemeanor. If there were an
International Hall of Ill Fame they would get top billing.

And they never existed otherwhere than in the brain of an amateur
criminologist. Richard L. Dugdale did not precisely invent them; rather,
he compiled them from an assortment of human derelicts whom he collected after a method peculiarly his own, for the purpose of bolstering his
theory of criminal heredity. He passed on his findings to posterity in his
*magnum opus, The Jukes: A Study in Crime, Pauperism, Disease, and
Insanity.*

This classic has permeated the sociology of nations. Geneticists like
Giddings, East, and Walter have swallowed it whole. The New York State
Prison Association sponsored it. Putnam's brought out three large editions,
which were accepted as sociological gospel. Dugdale became the recognized
authority on crime. His qualifications as an expert are peculiar. When the
Dugdale family came to this country from England in 1851 Richard was
ten years old. It was intended that he should go to college. After three
years of schooling in New York something went awry in his education. He
left school and became assistant to a sculptor. In the evenings he attended
classes at Cooper Union, where he won something of a reputation as a
debater on social topics.

His career, if such it were, was interrupted by the departure of the
family to try farming in the Middle-west. The venture was unsuccessful.
The Dugdales returned to New York and Richard turned his hands to
manufacturing. He was then twenty-three. The business failed. Richard
had a nervous breakdown and withdrew from active endeavor. "For four
years I could neither earn nor learn," he records. Such was his technical
equipment as a sociologist.

The Jukes came into his life quite by chance. He happened to be in
a Kingston, N.Y., police court in 1873, where a youth was on trial for
receiving stolen goods. Five relatives were present as witnesses. They came
of a breed, to quote the incipient investigator, "so despised that their
family name had come to be used generically as a term of reproach." They
were alleged to live like haggards of the rock, in the caves of a nearby lake

region. "Crime-cradles," our author calls the locality. He was a neat hand at a phrase.

He invented the name Juke for the clan.

The fact that the Juke at the bar of justice was acquitted in no wise discouraged young Dugdale. He made inquiries about the others present. An uncle of the accused is set down as a burglar. No proof is adduced. Two male cousins had been charged with pushing a boy over a cliff, one of whom was convicted. The remaining witnesses, two girls, he lists as harlots. By the Dugdale method "under the heading of harlots are included all women who have made lapses, however seldom." This is fairly indicative of his standards of investigation and attribution.

With this auspicious start he canvassed the neighborhood for further specimens.

With comparatively little inquiry [he writes], it was found that out of twenty-nine male adults, the immediate blood relations of the six, seventeen were criminals and fifteen others convicted of some degree of offense.

Impressed by this suggestive ratio—as who would not be by thirty-two out of a possible twenty-nine?—Dugdale went sleuthing back through the generations until he came upon an old Dutch reprobate who kept a turnpike hostelry in Orange County about the middle of the eighteenth century. Old Max appears to have been a sporting character. Several illegitimate children were imputed to him. He enjoyed a local reputation for drinking, gaming, and wenching, divertissements fairly general in those lusty pioneer days. He became Exhibit A in the Dugdale rogues' gallery, though nothing criminal appears in his record.

Max had two legitimate sons who married into a family of six sisters. With the discovery of the sisterhood Dugdale really hits his stride. The family line of the six is obscure; it "has not been absolutely ascertained," he admits. "One, if not all, of them were illegitimate," he surmises, on what grounds he does not explain. Delia, is recorded as a "harlot before marriage," and Bell as a "harlot after marriage." Clara, he notes (presumptively with reluctance), was "reputed chaste." She did, however, marry a man who shot a neighbor. Effie's reputation was unknown to author Dugdale, which was certainly a break for Effie.

Another sister *circa* 1760 is Dugdale's prize specimen. "Margaret, Mother of Criminals," he calls her, although her name was Ada. Apt alliteration's artful aid again! To her goes the credit for "the distinctly criminal line of the family." But, what family? For all that he reveals Margaret-Ada, of unascertained parentage, may have been a Van Rensselaer, a Livingston, a Saltonstall, a Biddle, or the granddaughter of the original Joe Doakes. To be sure, he later characterizes the whole lot as "belonging to the Juke blood." Pure assumption. As their derivation was unknown and they were suspectedly illegitimate anyway, how could Dugdale or anybody else know anything of their ancestry?

As a "Mother of Criminals" Margaret (or Ada) hardly lives up to her name. Her daughter is designated as a harlot, but, by way of palliation perhaps, our author adds, "not industrious." One son was a laborer, "somewhat industrious." The other, a farmer, is stigmatized as having been "indolent" and "licentious in youth." The same might be said of some eminent non-Jukes, including Robert Burns and the Apostle Paul.

Margaret-Ada was married to one of old Max's sons. She had a son of her own, whom Dugdale holds to be co-responsible for the evil Juke inheritance. But this son was a Juke only in name. He was illegitimate. Dugdale says so.

Thus, the notorious criminal-Juke strain derives on one side from a progenitor who was not criminal (Old Max) and on the other from a line which was not Juke except by Dugdale fiat. (Margaret-Ada through her illegitimate son.)

It sufficed Dugdale. He had his theory; now he set out after supporting facts. He made a year's tour of prisons, almshouses, and asylums, collecting Jukes. The result he published in 1875. It is still regarded by those who have not read it, and even some who have, as an authoritative document. It established the Jukes as the type-family of degeneration.

Dugdale invented a terminology to go with his Jukes. His thesis is based, so he states, upon "Positive Statistics and Conjectural Statistics . . . Conjectural Statistics consists in Political Arithmetic and the Theory of Probabilities." This recondite process "reduces the method of study to one of historico-biographical synthesis united to statistical analysis," which sounds as if it might have come out of Lewis Carroll.

Applying this yardstick, Dugdale lists 709 alleged Jukes of whom 507 were social detrimentals. Such conventional crimes as murder, arson, rape, and robbery, quite lacking in proof for the most part, are cited. But there were not enough of them to support satisfactorily the Dugdale political arithmetic and theory of probabilities. So he fattens up the record with entries like the following:

> Reputed sheep-stealer, but never caught.
> Thief, but never caught.
> Petty thief, though never convicted.
> Guilty of murder, but escapes punishment.
> Unpunished and cautious thief.
> Bastardy prosecution.
> Supposed to have attempted rape.
> Cruelty to animals.
> Habitual criminal.
> Impossible to get any reliable information, but it is evident that at nineteen he was a leader in crime.

And such scattered attributions as "pauper," "harlot," "brothel-keeper," "vagrant," "lazy," "intemperate," "drunkard," "immoral," "lecherous," etc., etc., etc. There was also a "contriver of crime," and a hardened character who, in addition to frequenting a saloon, was accused of breaking a deaf man's ear-trumpet. Like the Juke who started it all, he was acquitted. It did not matter to our investigator; the non-breaker of the ear trumpet comes down the ages, embalmed in criminal history.

All this might seem rather attenuated evidence on which to indict an entire family. It sufficed Dugdale. He followed the long and proliferating branches of the clan through the generations and worked out a diagram as framework for the composite portrait. This he calls "Leading Facts."

```
                    Consanguinity
                         F
   C    Prostitution     O    Illegitimacy    P
                         R                    A
   R                     N                    U
                         I                    P
   I    Exhaustion       C    Intemperance    E
                         A                    R
   M                     T                    I
                         I                    S
   E    Disease          O    Extinction      M
                         N
                 Not Consanguineous
```

In other words, *fornication* [the italics are his], either consanguineous or not, is the backbone of their habits, flanked on the one side by *pauperism*, on the other by *crime*. The secondary features are *prostitution*, with its complement of *bastardy*, and its resultant of miseducated childhood: *exhaustion*, with its complement, *intemperance*, and its resultant, unbalanced minds; and *disease*, with its complement, *extinction*.

Dugdale's investigations into hygiene and morality are on a par with his criminological efforts. Insanity, epilepsy, deformity, impotency, and tuberculosis appear to have been as typical Juke phenomena as thievery, bastardy, and general lawlessness. Some of the evidence cited is calculated to astonish students of heredity. For example, it is recorded that the original Max went blind and transmitted the affliction to his posterity. As he lost his sight late in life, after his children were born, it is difficult to see how he can be held responsible for their blindness unless he poked them in the eye with a burnt stick.

Our author's figures on tuberculosis are confident, but where he found them is left a mystery. Nobody bothered to keep statistics in those days. Still more difficult would it have been to gather reliable data on venereal disease. Yet our conjectural statistician specifies, in one branch of the Jukes, forty harlots who contaminated 440 men, presumably eleven per harlot. In another genealogical line he states that 23½ per cent of the females were immoral. That ½ per cent is fairly awe-inspiring.

Not until long after the author's death did anyone rise to challenge his thesis. The late Thomas Mott Osborne, of prison-reform fame and at one time president of that same prison association which certified the Dugdale revelations, studied the Juke records with growing skepticism. Himself a practised investigator, he raised questions about the Dugdale methods which that author might have found awkward to answer.

Whence, Mr. Osborne wished to know, did Dugdale derive those cocksure figures on disease, insanity, and death? Vital statistics at the time of his inquiry were practically non-existent. How did he acquire his data on criminality when court records for the period were notoriously unreliable, if, indeed, they were available at all? What genealogical method did he use in tracing back the Juke line through the mazes of its prevalent bastardy, for a century and a quarter? Legitimate family lines, Mr. Osborne pointed out, were difficult enough to trace; illegitimate were flatly impossible, beyond a generation or two. Further, the objector indicated, a specially trained sociological investigator would have required at least three years to do the work which Dugdale completed in one.

Analyzing the indicated method of investigation, Mr. Osborne suggested that Dugdale based it on a formula of retroactive hypothesis as follows:

That every criminal was a putative Juke.

That every Juke was a presumptive criminal.

By the system which Dugdale employed in tracing down his Jukes, Mr. Osborne concluded, it would be possible to asperse the morality, sanity, and legitimacy of any family in America. As for the Jukes, they were "pure folklore."

Another dissident raised objections in *The Clinical Review* for April 1902. Was it credible, Edmund Andrews asked, that Old Max possessed "such a miraculous energy of vicious propagation that, by his sole vital force, he begat and transmitted the degeneracy of all the Jukes for five generations?" Each descendant in the fifth generation, the critic pointed out, had fifteen other progenitors. Why assign his or her lawless, shiftless, or bawdy habits to Max any more than to any other of the uncharted Jukes or Jakes or Jeeks or Jenkins? A sturdy breeder like Max might well be the ancestor of a couple of thousand great-great-grandchildren, 1,500 of whom, for all that Dugdale knew to the contrary, might have been missionaries.

"It is sheer nonsense," Mr. Andrews contends "to suppose that he (a fifth-generation Juke degenerate) got them all (his vicious proclivities) from that one lazy, but jovial old Rip Van Winkle, the original Juke."

These were but voices crying in a wilderness. To scotch a good, sturdy historical fake, once it has got its growth, is impossible. Nine-tenths of America devoutly believes that Robert Fulton invented the steamboat and that Abner Doubleday was the founder of baseball. So the Jukes will doubtless continue to furnish texts to trusting sociologists, and no great harm done.

But they are in the wrong category. The proper place of a Juke is not in criminology. It is in mythology.

A WITNESS AT THE SCOPES TRIAL

Fay-Cooper Cole

Facts never speak for themselves. For the scientist they speak in terms of theoretical assumptions. For the layman they are inter-preted to fit his basic beliefs. If, for example, one assumed the earth were flat, then data that suggested that the world has a spheri-cal shape could be discounted as optical illusions. Action would likewise be affected; sailors who believed the world was flat would hesitate to sail far from land. Similarly, if one believed that man was created just as he exists today—a conception that was widely accepted for centuries—then one would hardly be motivated to search for data throwing light on the development of man through the ages. This is the significance of the Scopes trial discussed by Fay-Cooper Cole. It represented the most famous dramatic public test of the traditional belief about the nature of man. By 1925, almost all respected scientists and other learned people had ac-cepted the theory that man and his works were products of evolu-tionary forces that extended back countless thousands of years. This theory has had a profound effect upon teaching and research in social science and religion. It should be noted, however, that the theory does not and cannot say anything about man's ultimate beginnings.

"This is Clarence Darrow," said the voice at the other end of the wire, "I suppose you have been reading the papers, so you know Bryan and his outfit are prosecuting that young fellow Scopes. Well, Malone, Colby and I have put ourselves in a mess by offering to defend. We don't know much about evolution. We don't know whom to call as witnesses. But we do know we are fighting your battle for academic freedom. We need the help of you fellows at the University, so I am asking three of you to come to my office to help lay plans."

That afternoon in Darrow's office three of us from the University of Chi-cago—Horatio Hackett Newman, professor of biology; Shailer Mathews, dean of the Divinity School; and I—met to outline the strategy for what turned out to be one of the most publicized trials of the century. The Scopes trial proved also to be a historic occasion in the cause of popular understanding of science. A century ago the educated world was shaken

SOURCE: *Scientific American,* Vol. 200, No. 1 (January, 1959), 121–30. Reprinted by permission. ✧ The author (1881–1961) was professor emeritus of anthropology at the University of Chicago. He had done archeological work in the United States and abroad. His books include *Peoples of Malaysia, Kincaid—A Prehistoric Illinois Metropolis,* and *The Bukidnon of Mindanao.*

by the discoveries of Charles Darwin and Alfred Russel Wallace, and the evidence they presented for the evolution of life on this planet. In 1959, as we celebrate the centenary of the *Origin of Species*, few informed persons, if any, question the theory of evolution. However, the century has witnessed several attempts to stifle investigation and outlaw the teaching of the theory. The best known of these was the Scopes trial, held in Dayton, Tenn., in 1925. The trial resulted in an immense revival of public interest in Darwin and in evolution; there has been no comparable effort since then to suppress this advance in man's understanding of himself and the world he lives in.

To understand the trial and what lay back of it, one must recall the climate of the 1920s. It was a time of uncertainty, unrest and repression. We had just emerged from a world war. Old standards were badly shaken; the young were labeled "the lost generation"; intolerance was rampant. The Ku Klux Klan was on the march, not only in the South but in the North as well. In many towns in Illinois, Indiana and other parts of the Midwest, staid business men—even members of the clergy—put on "white nighties" and burned fiery crosses to put the Negro, the Jew, the Catholic and the immigrant "in their places." The Fundamentalists, under the leadership of William Jennings Bryan, had organized in some 20 states and were putting pressure on all institutions of learning to curb the teaching of science, particularly evolution, which they considered in contradiction to the Bible. Prohibitive bills had been passed in Tennessee and Mississippi and were pending in six other states.

Then came the great opportunity. In the little town of Dayton the high-school science teacher and football coach, 24-year-old John Thomas Scopes, found himself engaged in a discussion of the new law with George W. Rappelyea, a young mining engineer and superintendent of the local coal mines. Scopes expressed bewilderment that the state should supply him with a textbook that presented the theory of evolution, yet make him a lawbreaker if he taught the theory. Rappelyea agreed that it was a crazy law and clearly unconstitutional. Then suddenly he asked: "Why don't I have you arrested for teaching evolution from that text and bring the whole thing to an end?" Scopes replied: "Fair enough."

Scopes was duly arrested. But neither of the principals had any idea of what they were starting. Within a few hours the Chattanooga papers carried the story. Soon it was spread across the nation. The Fundamentalists were quick to realize the opportunity to dramatize their battle against evolution. Bryan and his associates offered their services to the Prosecution. They were accepted. Here was big news.

At this point, it happened, three lawyers met in New York City for a conference on some business matters. They were Clarence Darrow, controversialist and defender of unpopular causes; Bainbridge Colby, an eminent corporation lawyer and, like Bryan, a former Secretary of State; and Dudley Field Malone, a leading Catholic layman and a fashionable barrister. Their conversation turned to the Tennessee situation. One said: "It is a shame. That poor teacher, who probably doesn't know what it is all about, is to be sacrificed by the Fundamentalists." Another said: "Someone ought to do something about it." The third replied: "Why don't we?" Through the American Civil Liberties Union they offered to defend young Scopes. Their offer was accepted.

This was real news! Bryan, three times candidate for the presidency of the U.S., the great Fundamentalist leader and orator, on one side. On the other, three of the nation's most famous lawyers, including Darrow, master jury-pleader. The papers were full of the story.

This was the background of Darrow's call to me and of our meeting at his office in Chicago early in the summer of 1925. By telephone, wire and letter we proceeded to assemble a panel of expert witnesses: scientists to testify on the theory of evolution and theologians to give evidence on the history and interpretation of the Bible. In addition to Newman, Mathews and myself, our panel finally included Kirtley Mather, professor of geology at Harvard; Jacob G. Lipman, director of the New Jersey Agricultural Experiment Station at Rutgers University; W. C. Curtis, professor of zoology at the University of Missouri; Wilbur Nelson, state geologist of Tennessee; Maynard Metcalf, professor of zoology at Johns Hopkins University; Charles Judd, head of the University of Chicago School of Education; and Rabbi Herman Rosenwasser of San Francisco, a noted Hebrew scholar. All of us, along with our counsel, undertook to go to Dayton at our own expense and to serve without fee.

The trial was scheduled for Friday, July 10. But long before that date the town was crowded with newspapermen, Fundamentalist supporters and others who were just curious. No one was willing to house "the heretics," that is, the scientific witnesses and defense attorneys. So an old "haunted house" on a hill overlooking the town was fitted out as a dormitory.

When I reached town, I took care not to associate myself at once with the Defense group, and was able to wander about for a time listening to the talk of the local people. For the most part they were extremely partisan to the Fundamentalist cause. But they were apprehensive of the famous Darrow, and they were not yet aware of his plan to present expert testimony on evolution and the scriptures.

That evening I joined the group at the "haunted house" and there met young Scopes for the first time. He was a fine, clean-cut young man, a little shy and apparently overwhelmed by the controversy he had stirred up. He expressed amazement that famous lawyers like Darrow, Colby, Malone and Arthur Garfield Hays (counsel to the American Civil Liberties Union) should come to his defense, and that a group of well-known scientists should join them.

Little happened on the first day of the trial beyond the selection of the jury. A panel was offered, and Darrow accepted it without change after a casual examination. But he did bring out the fact that 11 jurors were Fundamentalist church members. All admitted that they knew little about science or evolution. One said that the only Darwin he had ever heard about ran a local notion store. One could not read or write.

The events of Sunday provided us with an interesting insight into the local climate of opinion. Charles Francis Potter, a liberal Unitarian minister and writer who had been invited to conduct services at the Methodist-Episcopal church, was barred from the pulpit by the parishioners. Meanwhile Bryan addressed an overflow house at the Southern Methodist church. That afternoon, in an open courtyard in the center of town, Bryan talked to an immense audience. He said he welcomed the opportunity to bring "this slimy thing, evolution, out of the darkness. . . . Now the facts of religion and evolution would meet at last in a duel to the death." It was a fine example of Bryan's oratory, and it swept the crowd.

The court opened on Monday with a prayer in which a local clergyman urged God to preserve his sacred word against attack. It was a scarcely veiled plea to the jury.

The Defense filed a motion to quash the indictment on the ground that the act violated the Constitution of the State of Tennessee and Section 1 of the Fourteenth Amendment of the Constitution of the United States, which extends the Bill of Rights to limit action by the governments of the states. The Defense argued further that the indictment was contrary to a U.S. Supreme Court decision which says: "The law knows no heresy, and is committed to the support of no dogma, nor to the establishment of any sect." In support of this attack on the indictment, the Defense declared that it wished to offer the testimony of scientists and biblical scholars. These expert witnesses, the Defense contended, would show that there was no necessary conflict between evolution and Christianity.

Though the Defense asked that judgment on its motion to dismiss should be reserved until its witnesses had been heard, Judge John T. Raulston ordered the argument to proceed. On motion of the Prosecution, he sent the jury from the courtroom. Apparently the introduction of scientific witnesses had taken Bryan and his associates by surprise. Their ultimate response to our efforts to argue the underlying issues of the case was to lose them the trial in the minds of the American people.

That afternoon Darrow pressed for dismissal with an eloquent attack on ignorance and bigotry. Coatless in the sweltering courtroom, tugging at his suspenders, he paced up and down, firing shot after shot at the Prosecution. He stressed the danger to freedom of press, church and school if men like Bryan could impose their opinions and interpretations on the law of the land. "The fires of bigotry and hate are being lighted," he said. "This is as bold an attempt to destroy learning as was ever made in the Middle Ages. . . . The statute says you cannot teach anything in conflict with the Bible." He argued that in the U.S. there are over 500 churches and sects which differ over certain passages in the Bible. If the law were to prevail, Scopes would have to be familiar with the whole Bible and all its interpretations; among all the warring sects, he would have to know which one was right in order not to commit a crime.

Darrow said: "Your Honor, my client is here because ignorance and bigotry are rampant, and that is a mighty strong combination. . . . If today you can make teaching of evolution in the public schools a crime, tomorrow you can make it a crime to teach it in the private schools. At the next session of the Legislature you can ban books and newspapers. You can set Catholic against Protestant, and Protestant against Protestant, when you try to foist your own religion upon the minds of men. If you can do the one, you can do the other. After a while, Your Honor, we will find ourselves marching backward to the glorious days of the 16th century when bigots lighted the fagots to burn men who dared to bring any intelligence and enlightenment to the human mind."

The speech made a profound impression. Townspeople agreed that anything might happen with that man Darrow around. Judge Raulston adjourned court until Wednesday in order that he might consider the motion to quash.

That night, as we gathered in our haunted house for a conference, a terrific storm swept the town. When a brilliant flash of lightning struck nearby, Darrow said: "Boys, if lightning strikes this house tonight . . . !"

Tuesday was a quiet day. At Rappelyea's office, where he had been invited to take advantage of the secretarial facilities, Potter found that the stenographer would not take dictation from any Unitarian minister. Rappelyea himself was arrested three times for speeding in the course of his service to us as guide and chauffeur. We were besieged by Holy Rollers, who came in from the hills to convert us. We also had to protect ourselves from a supporter. H. L. Mencken had come to town. His vitriolic articles so antagonized the people we wanted most to reach that we had to persuade him to leave the scene.

After the jury was sworn in on Wednesday, the Court ruled against the Defense motion to quash the indictment. The law, said Judge Raulston, did not deprive anyone of speech, thought or opinion, for no one need accept employment in Tennessee. He ruled the law constitutional, saying that the public has the right to say, by legislative act or referendum, whether Latin, chemistry or astronomy might be taught in its schools.

The Prosecution then called the county superintendent of schools, the heads of the school board and seven students. All testified to what Scopes had taught. Darrow limited his cross-examination to establishing simply that the State had furnished the textbook. After offering the King James version of the Bible as an exhibit, the Prosecution rested.

The first witness for the Defense was Maynard Metcalf. A recognized scientist, he was also an eminent Congregational layman and teacher of one of the largest Bible classes in the country. Darrow established his competence as a witness, then asked a question on evolution. The Prosecution at once challenged the testimony as irrelevant; according to them the only question was: Did Scopes violate the law?

The judge agreed to hear arguments on this point the next day. Meanwhile he excused the jury, with instructions not to enter the courtroom or to remain within hearing of the loudspeakers. A lot of angry jurors filed out. They had not only lost their reserved seats, but also were barred from the proceedings entirely.

The trial reached its high point on Thursday. After an impassioned plea by the State's Attorney against the admission of expert testimony, Bryan took over for the Prosecution. Instead of making good on his challenge of "a duel to the death," he argued against the presentation of scientific evidence. He said that the jury did not need the help of scientists or Bible experts to decide the facts and to interpret the law: "The law is what the people decided." He then presented an enlargement of the picture of the evolutionary tree from the textbook Scopes had used; it showed man in a circle with other mammals. Bryan shouted: "Talk about putting Daniel in the lions' den. How dare these scientists put man in a little ring with lions and tigers and everything that smells of the jungle. . . . One does not need to be an expert to know what the Bible says. . . . Expert testimony is not needed!"

With that speech Bryan lost the argument with the press and with the radio audience. When Malone had finished his reply, Bryan had also lost the argument, for a time, with most of his Dayton followers.

Malone was a Patrick Henry that day. He asked whether our children are to know nothing of science beyond that permitted by certain sects. "I have never seen greater need for learning," he declared, "than is exhibited by the Prosecution, which refuses information offered by expert witnesses. . . . Why this fear of meeting the issue? Mr. Bryan has said this is to be a duel to the death. I know little about dueling, Your Honor, but does it mean that our only weapon, the witnesses, is to be taken away while the Prosecution alone carries the sword? This is not my idea of a duel. . . . We do not fear all the truth they can present as facts. We are ready. We stand with progress. We stand with science. We stand with intelligence. We feel that we stand with the fundamental freedoms in America. We are not afraid. Where is the fear? We defy it." Then, turning toward Bryan and pointing his finger, he cried: "There is the fear!"

The crowd went out of control—cheering, stamping, pounding on desks—until it was necessary to adjourn court for 15 minutes to restore order.

I was sitting next to the aisle. Beside me was a Chattanooga policeman, one of the squad brought in to protect us from the Ku Klux Klan. As Malone finished, my guard beat the desk in front of me so hard with his club that a corner of the desk broke off. His chief came up and asked:

"Why didn't you cheer when Malone made that speech?" My guard replied: "Hell. What did you think I was doing? Rapping for order?"

We had won for the day. Even the hostile crowd was with us.

That night Darrow said: "Today we have won, but by tomorrow the judge will have recovered and will rule against us. I want each one of you to go to the stenographer's room the first thing in the morning and prepare a statement for the press, saying what you would have said if allowed to testify in court."

As we were preparing our statements next morning, Judge Raulston looked in. I was nearest to the door. He asked what we were doing. When I told him, he asked the others in turn. Then he went to Darrow and told him he must not release the testimony: "It might reach the jury." Darrow replied: "Your Honor, you can do what you please with that jury. You can lock it up, but you cannot lock up the American people. The testimony will be released."

When court resumed, the judge ruled against us on all points. Rising and pushing his long hair from his forehead, Darrow spoke slowly and clearly. "The outcome is plain. We expect to protect our rights in some other court. Is that plain?" The judge replied: "I hope, Colonel Darrow, you don't attempt to reflect upon the Court." To which Darrow drawled: "Your Honor has the right to hope." The insult was deliberate. For an instant there was complete silence, then the judge mumbled that he had the right to do something else. A moment later he adjourned court until Monday.

Public reaction to the ruling was emphatic, and Bryan's prestige was shaken. Townspeople admitted to me, one of the "heretics," that they could not understand why Bryan had backed down. They asked: "What can you do now, if you can't talk?"

On Monday Darrow apologized to the Court, momentarily relieving the tension. Then, in order to secure the foundation for appeal, Hays read into the record the prepared statements of the scientific and other scholarly witnesses, and concluded by placing in evidence three versions of the Bible that differed from one another and from the King James version submitted by the Prosecution. Suddenly Hays electrified the crowd with the announcement that the Defense wished to call Bryan to the stand "as a biblical witness."

Darrow submitted Bryan to grueling examination. In reply to Darrow's questions Bryan stated that he accepted the Bible literally as God's revealed word. What he didn't understand he accepted on simple faith. He believed that Eve was the first woman, created from Adam's rib; that God had sent childbirth pains to all women because of her transgression; that the snake must crawl on its belly because it tempted Eve; that everything outside the Ark, except fish, perished in the flood; that all existing animals had descended from the pairs saved by Noah; that all men spoke one language until the Tower of Babel; and that present languages had developed since then. Only once did he falter, when he admitted that the seven days of creation might mean seven epochs. He conceded that he was not familiar with the work of archaeologists, who had uncovered civilizations more than 5,000 years old, but he declared that he had never had much interest in those scientists who disputed the Bible. Repeatedly the State's Attorney tried to stop the questioning, but always Bryan replied: "No. Let it go on. I am not afraid to defend my religion."

Finally Malone intervened, saying he would have asked the same questions, but only to challenge Bryan's literal interpretation of the King James version. As a churchman and a Christian, however, he objected to any effort by counsel for the State to pin Darrow's views of religion on the defense. "I don't want this case to be changed by Mr. Darrow's agnosticism or Mr. Bryan's brand of religion." Malone further observed that this was supposed to be a trial by jury, yet the jury had not been permitted in the court for more than 15 minutes since being sworn in.

On Tuesday Judge Raulston struck the examination of Bryan from the record. The only question remaining, he said, was: What did Scopes teach? To this ruling Darrow replied: "Your Honor, we are wasting time. You should call the jury and instruct it to bring in a verdict of guilty." The Court did so, and Scopes was fined $100.

Scopes had come on to graduate study in geology at the University of Chicago when the Tennessee Supreme Court heard Darrow's appeal and at last handed down its decision in January, 1927. The court narrowly affirmed the anti-evolution statute, but threw out the $100 fine on a technicality. It brought an end to the formal proceedings by advising the State to desist from further prosecution: "We see nothing to be gained by prolonging the life of this bizarre case."

The Defense was also content to accept the Court's advice. No attempt at repression has ever backfired so impressively. Where one person had been interested in evolution before the trial, scores were reading and inquiring at its close. Within a year the prohibitive bills which had been pending in other states were dropped or killed. Tennessee had been made to appear so ridiculous in the eyes of the nation that other states did not care to follow its lead.

At the University of Chicago I had been teaching modest-sized classes. When the University resumed in the autumn my lecture hall was filled. Students were standing along the walls and sitting in the windows. I thought I was in the wrong room. When I asked a boy at the door what class was meeting, he replied: "Anthropology. The prof who teaches it defended that fellow Scopes." From that time on Introductory Anthropology had to be limited to lecture-hall capacity. My mail, mostly hostile, increased until the University gave up trying to put it in my box, but tied it in bundles and sent it to my office.

Some time after the trial I was summoned to the office of Frederick Woodward, acting president of the University. He handed me a long document, a series of resolutions from a Southern Baptist conference. They took the University to task for the part members of its faculty had taken in the trial, taking note of the University's strong Baptist origins. They voiced objections to Professors Judd, Newman and Mathews, but reserved the real condemnation for me—the witness on human evolution. I was "a snake in the grass corrupting the youth of a nation," and so on, concluding with "and we have been investigating Professor Cole still further, and we find that he is not even a Baptist."

I began to laugh, but the president said: "This is no laughing matter. You are a rather new man here, but already we have more demands for your removal than any other man who has been on our faculty. These resolutions are typical and were considered of such importance that they were read yesterday at the meeting of the Board of Trustees." "Yes," I replied. "And what did they do?" He reached across his desk and handed me a piece of paper. They had raised my salary.

Environmental Factors

❖ 8 ❖

HOW DIFFERENCES IN ENVIRONMENT AFFECTED SEPARATED ONE-EGG TWINS

Horatio H. Newman

A long-standing controversy in American social science concerns the relative importance of heredity and environment in the development of human personality: To what extent is human behavior the result of biological inheritance? How do culture, social experience, or learning influence behavior? One way to answer questions of this type is to study the adult personalities of identical twins who were separated early in life. Since such one-egg twins have the same genetic origin, differences that are found in later life presumably result from differences in education, family relationships, and other social experiences. Although the Newman study, summarized here, is based on the relatively few available cases and thus constitutes inadequate grounds for firm generalization, still it suggests that even when genetic equipment is the same, personalities differ as environments differ.

In each of the twenty cases of separated one-egg twins every effort was made to reconstruct the life experiences of the twins and to discover any differences in environment or experience that might have tended to

SOURCE: Horatio H. Newman, *Multiple Human Births* (Garden City N.Y.: Doubleday & Company, Inc., 1940), chap. XV. Copyright 1940 by H. H. Newman, reprinted by permission of the author and Doubleday & Company, Inc. ❖ The author (1875–1957) was professor emeritus of zoology at the University of Chicago. He had done extensive research in genetics, embryology, and marine life. Among his books are *The Physiology of Twinning, Evolution Yesterday and Today*, and *The Phylum Chordata*.

produce differences in ability, personality or physical condition. We roughly subdivided environment into three categories: educational, social and physical-health.

It was found that whenever the educational experiences of a pair of twins differed to a marked extent the twin with the greater amount of education had a distinctly higher score on all ability and scholastic achievement tests, while in those cases where there was no difference in education, or only a small difference, the scores of the twins of a pair tended to be about as similar as the average of one-egg twins reared together. A few examples of this close correlation between differences in education and those in mental ability will make this important point clear.

The Effects of Differences in Education

In the case of twins *Gladys* and *Helen*, Gladys stopped school after the third grade, while Helen went on through college and became a teacher. There was a difference of about thirteen years of formal schooling in favor of Helen. In the Stanford-Binet Test Helen's I.Q. was one hundred and sixteen (high normal) and Gladys' was ninety-two (low normal), a large difference of twenty-four points. On the Otis S.A.[1] Test Helen had an I.Q. of one hundred and six, Gladys ninety-four, a difference of twelve points. On the International Test Helen scored one hundred and eighty-eight points, Gladys one hundred and forty-three, a difference of forty-five points. On the Stanford Achievement Test Helen had a mental age of eighteen years, ten months, Gladys a mental age of thirteen years and one month, a difference of sixty-nine months. It seems certain that in the case of Gladys the great deficiency in education had inhibited the development of the rather high grade of mental ability with which she was endowed by heredity and which was well developed in her twin sister.

In the second case, that of twins *James* and *Reece*, the differences in both education and ability were less striking but quite noteworthy. James completed grade and high school in a town of about two thousand inhabitants, while Reece attended a rural grade school in the mountains which was open only during five months in the year. He attended only when he felt like it and stopped at the eighth grade. On the Stanford-Binet Test James's I.Q. was ninety-six (almost up to average), while Reece's I.Q. was only seventy-seven (commonly regarded as bordering on the "dull and backward" classification), a difference of nineteen points. On the Otis S.A. Test James's I.Q. was one hundred and four (above average) and Reece's was eighty-four, a difference of twenty points. On the International Test James scored one hundred and twenty-four points, Reece eighty-nine, a difference of thirty-five points. On the Stanford Achievement Test James had a mental age of sixteen years, Reece thirteen years, one month, a difference of thirty-five months.

[1] Scholastic Achievement

In the third case, that of twins *Eleanore* and *Georgiana*, Eleanore stopped school at the end of the fifth grade, while Georgiana finished grade school and high school and then had three years at normal school, a difference in favor of Georgiana of ten years of schooling. In this case, though both girls were quite efficient as office assistants, their mental rating was considerably below the average. Nevertheless, Georgiana was consistently superior to Eleanore. Georgiana's I.Q. on the Stanford-Binet was seventy-eight, Eleanore's was only sixty-six, a difference of twelve points, but in a part of the scale where a few points are rather significant. On the Otis S.A. Test Georgiana's I.Q. was eighty-four and Eleanore's sixty-nine, a difference of fifteen points. On the International Test Georgiana scored ninety-eight points, Eleanore sixty-nine, a difference of twenty-nine points. On the Stanford Achievement Test Georgiana's mental age was fourteen years, one month, Eleanore's ten years, eleven months, a difference of thirty-eight months. This case shows that with a good education a poorly endowed person can improve his ability to a moderate degree but cannot reach the level of a potentially able but poorly educated person such as the twin Gladys of our first case. Some comment might be made here as to the minimal endowment necessary for successfully completing a course in some normal schools and qualifying as a teacher.

The fourth and last case where there was a considerable difference in education is that of twins *Mabel* and *Mary*. Mary was educated through grade school and three years of high school in a medium-sized city and finished her last year in the high school of a large city. Mabel finished the eighth grade in a small country school near her farm home. As is usually the case in country schools, the terms were short. The difference in years of education was actually about five. On the Stanford-Binet Test Mary had an I.Q. of one hundred and six, Mabel of eighty-nine, a difference of seventeen points. On the Otis S.A. Test Mary's I.Q. was one hundred and eleven and Mabel's ninety-seven, a difference of fourteen points. On the International Test Mary scored one hundred and four points, Mabel ninety-six, a difference of only eight points, but in the same direction as the other differences. On the Stanford Achievement Test Mary had a mental age of seventeen years, three months, Mabel fourteen years, five months, a difference of thirty-four months.

Out of the twenty cases studied, these four cases were the only ones in which the differences in schooling between twins of a pair differed more than a year or two. It will be noted that in each of these four cases the better educated twin had a distinctly higher rating on *all* the tests. The consistency of the results on the various tests increases our confidence in the validity of the tests themselves and in the reality of the differences in mental ability of the twins examined. One can hardly question the conclusion that mental ability within certain limits can be improved by education or suffer for the lack of it. In each of these cases we must assume that the twin with the lower I.Q. had an inherited capacity to reach at least the rating of the twin partner with the higher I.Q. If the differences in education had been greater, presumably the differences in I.Q. would have been greater. One's I.Q., then, is not fixed by heredity alone but may be raised or lowered many points according to the type and amount of education the individual experiences.

Remarkably enough, however, the remaining sixteen cases of separated twins, in which differences in education had amounted to no more than a year or two, showed an average difference in I.Q. even slightly less than that of one-egg twins reared together. From this we may draw the conclusion that small differences in education do not appreciably affect ability, but that large differences in education may induce important differences in ability.

Effects of Differences in Social Environment

Differences in social environment are difficult to estimate in terms comparable to those in education. The method of estimating these differences was that of rating them by five independent judges and averaging their estimates. When these rated differences in social environment were compared with differences in scores on personality tests there was no reliable correlation of the group as a whole between differences in social environment and differences in personality traits. What is the explanation of this unexpected result? There seem to be two possible answers to this question. Either differences in social environment have no effect on personality traits or else the tests of personality do not bear any direct relation to our rather rough-and-ready estimates of differences in the total social environment. We regard the second answer as more probable than the first.

We find in some cases of separated twins that the chief difference in social environment is one between city life and country life. In other cases the difference is one between relative wealth and relative poverty. In still other cases the difference is mainly one of contacts with cultured as over against relatively uncultured family groups and associates. In one pair of twins one twin had led a respectable life and the other had had a more or less lawless career. In another pair the life of one twin had been full of stimulating social contacts, while the other had led a decidedly sheltered and isolated existence without stimulating contacts of any sort. In another case one twin had a large family of children to whom she had devoted all her energy and affection, while the twin sister, though married, was childless and had followed a professional career. In still another case one twin girl had spent most of her life in London, England, while the other had, since eighteen months of age, lived in a small town in Ontario. These varied types of social environmental difference are so unrelated to each other that one would not expect any summation of such differences to be correlated with differences in scores made on any particular kind of personality test.

If, then, we are to discover any relation between differences in social environment and 'differences in personality we shall have to find them through the study of individual cases. When this was done we found clear evidence that differences in social experience actually do produce differences in personality.

Perhaps the most striking personality difference of all was that found between twins *Mildred* and *Ruth*. Mildred was the foster child of a banker who was also the mayor of a medium-sized city. He was a well-educated man whose home was a gathering place of interesting and cultured people. Mildred entered into all of these activities. Ruth, on the other hand, was the foster child of a man of little education who was a foreman of laborers. The foster mother disapproved of Ruth's normal associates and kept her at home after school hours, with dolls as her only companions. On all the personality tests Ruth showed an inhibited character, shy, diffident, silent, with lisping speech and an unhappy expression, while Mildred was much more confident, unembarrassed, talkative, happy in facial expression and spoke without a trace of lisping. Although both girls were high school seniors in two different cities and had had equal educational opportunities, Mildred's I.Q. on both the Stanford-Binet and the Otis S.A. tests was fifteen points higher than that of Ruth. From this it might be inferred that the cultured and stimulating home life of Mildred, as contrasted with the barren home life of Ruth, had made a difference in mental ability equal to that of several years of formal schooling in some of the other cases.

Another interesting case was that of *Mary* and *Mabel*. These twins, in addition to the educational differences already described, had lived very different lives. Mary had lived all her life in a town and had devoted herself to her studies and to music and music teaching. Mabel had lived on a large and prosperous farm, participating actively in all the work commonly done by an able-bodied farm woman. On all of the personality tests the scores of these twenty-nine-year-old women were among the most different of the whole twenty pairs. Mabel, the farm woman, was slow and phlegmatic; Mary was far more excitable and responsive, almost neurotic. On the other hand, Mabel was more aggressive and was evidently the leader and manager. She had fewer fears and was less readily shocked by unpleasant words and ideas. She walked about with a firm, almost masculine stride, in contrast with Mary's ladylike step and manner. The two women seemed totally unlike in overt behavior and gave the impression of having very different personalities.

The case of *Gladys* and *Helen*, who had the greatest difference in schooling, also illustrates the effects of social differences on personality. These social differences are inherent in the fact that Helen had gone through college and was a teacher, while Gladys had been an industrial worker most of her life. In some of the personality tests the scores were very similar; on others very different. It appears that these twins are alike in fundamental personality traits but differ greatly in their reactions to different social situations. The largest contrast was in overt behavior. Helen, the teacher, was much more suave and polished, was much more interested in her personal appearance and made more of an effort to produce a favorable personal impression. Gladys was all business, without social charm or concern about how she impressed others.

In contrast to these cases in which the differences in social environment seemed definitely to have produced appropriate differences in personality was the case of twins *James* and *Reece*. James had always lived in town with his maternal grandparents. He had had a good high-school education and was engineer for a sand-and-gravel company. He was a steady, respected citizen. Reece, on the contrary, had lived the life of a mountaineer, had never worked steadily, had engaged in illegal pursuits characteristic of his environment and had been caught and punished several times. In spite of this great difference in social experience, these twins, who had never spent a night together since babyhood, were almost indistinguishable as to their behavior when with us. They made highly similar scores on all the personality tests. It appears that the differences in environment and experience have not modified their fundamental personality traits but have merely served to direct the primitive impulses, common to both, into modes of behavior in one case characteristic of a primitive environment and in the other case into those more in accord with the ideals of a higher level of civilized life. Neither of these men is criminalistic in character, but both are rather individualistic, rather stubborn and both tend to resist opposition vigorously. One expressed his strong character by primitive modes of action; the other restrained his primitive impulses in favor of actions which are more socially acceptable in a modern urban community.

Effects of Differences in Physical Environment

Under the head of physical environment we include differences in climate, housing, food, physical exercise, hygiene and disease. In no two pairs of separated twins did we find the same combination of these physical environmental differences. In some pairs one of these types of environmental difference was well marked; in others another type. Here again, as in the study of differences in social environment, the case-study method is more likely to reveal the effects of specific differences in the physical environment than is the statistical method.

There were two pairs of twins in which there was a great difference in health. The first of these is the case of twins *Thelma* and *Zelma*, twenty-nine-year-old married women. Thelma was a victim of advanced tuberculosis and was exceedingly frail, weighing only seventy-two pounds; while Zelma was quite healthy and weighed ninety-eight pounds, normal for such a small, delicately formed woman. Apart from this great difference in weight, Thelma was a sort of shrunken replica of Zelma. The second case where the health condition constituted the only marked environmental effect was the case of fifty-eight-year-old twins *Ada* and *Ida*. Ada was a robust and normally healthy woman, while Ida had an enormous goiter and showed very pronounced symptoms of goiter disease (thyroxin deficiency). Ada was vigorous and active, Ida easily fatigued and somewhat sluggish. Ada weighed two hundred and eight pounds, Ida two hundred and twenty-seven, the extra weight due to excess water in the tissues, a condition characteristic of goiter disease.

There were two cases of twins with pronounced difference in muscular development. The first is the case of *Mabel* and *Mary*, twice previously referred to in this chapter. Mabel was a muscular farm worker and Mary a sedentary, ladylike music teacher and store clerk. Mabel weighed one hundred and thirty-eight pounds and was hard muscled; Mary weighed only one hundred and ten pounds and her muscles were soft and poorly developed. It is obvious that the great difference in the occupations of these two women was responsible for most of their difference in muscularity and weight. The second of these cases was that of the twins *Paul O.* and *Paul C.* Paul C. had been addicted to gymnastics and Paul O. had led a sedentary life. Paul C. was very well developed, muscularly, while Paul O. was much less so. The difference in weight was over ten pounds in favor of Paul C. and was due entirely to excess muscle.

There was one case of marked differences in the condition of the teeth. The twins *Edith* and *Fay* showed a striking contrast in this respect. Fay, at the age of thirty-eight years, had one of the most perfect sets of teeth I have examined, while Edith's teeth were in extremely bad condition, the incisors discolored and much worn and cheek teeth much decayed. It appears that Edith had had several children in rapid succession while she and her husband were trying to establish claim on a North Dakota farm. During this period food was scarce, especially those foods rich in tooth-building ingredients. It was during this period that Edith's potentially fine teeth deteriorated. Fay, who lived in a city and always had everything a prosperous husband could supply, took care of her teeth and was rewarded by having them in perfect condition.

Statistical Comparisons

Comparisons were made between the fifty pairs of one-egg twins reared together and twenty pairs of one-egg twins reared apart. In these two sets of twins the only difference is in the environment. Let us see which characters are least affected and which are most affected by differences in environment.

The twins reared apart were, on the average, no more different than those reared together in measurable physical characters except for one character, body weight, which in twins is largely a measure of differences in food, health and physical exercise. The average difference in weight for twins reared apart was twice as great as that for twins reared together. In all other physical measurements, except those directly dependent on differences in weight, the average differences in the two sets of twins was almost exactly the same.

The situation is quite different when we come to deal with mental differences. The average difference in I.Q. of twins reared together was 5.3 points and for twins reared apart 8.2 points, an excess of nearly three points. This difference was almost entirely accounted for by the four cases in which there was a great difference in education.

The average difference in scholastic achievement for the twins reared apart was more than twice as great as for twins reared together, indicating that achievement tests register more accurately differences in schooling than do ability tests.

Since only one personality test was given to the twins reared together, it was not easy to compare the two sets of twins with respect to differences in personality, but there are many evidences that environmental differences have caused greater differences in personality than in any other traits.

In conclusion, we may fairly say that our researches have done at least two things: 1, they have shown conclusively that the human heredity-environment problem is extremely complex, that it is not one problem but many, that the problem differs with respect to every character studied and that there is therefore no general solution for the problem as a whole; 2, that solutions can be given only for well-defined heredity-environment setups, such as that for children in the same family reared together, and for a limited number of one-egg twins reared under a variety of different environmental conditions.

We realize that while we have helped to solve with some degree of success a few parts of the heredity-environment problem, there remains much to be done. We have at least untangled some of the threads in that very intricate mesh that constitutes the organism we call man.

A STUDY OF VALUES

Evon Z. Vogt and John M. Roberts

If it can be shown that the inborn characteristics of people in com-munities do not differ significantly, and at the same time one ob-serves that such groups solve similar problem quite differently, then the differences must be ascribed to the learned factors which sociologists and anthropologists call "culture." This point is illus-trated by Evon Z. Vogt and John M. Roberts as they demonstrate that persons basically similar biologically, but having different cul-tures, may settle in the same general geographical area and yet de-velop markedly different modes of life.

"No tenet of intellectual folklore has been so damaging to our life and times as the cliché that 'science has nothing to do with values.' If the consideration of values is to be the exclusive property of religion and the humanities, a scientific understanding of human experience is im-possible."

In these words the anthropologist Clyde Kluckhohn recently defined a major challenge and frontier of social research. The forming and choosing of values is a central concern of all men and societies. Conceptions of the desirable, the fitting and the good vary widely among the world's 3,000 or so cultures. They strongly influence the selection of the modes, the means and the ends of human behavior. The social scientist cannot view "man in culture" as conditioned only by economic forces and biological impulses. People see the world through cultural lenses compounded of particular combinations of values; they respond in different ways in accord-ance with their differing values. We must recognize that people are not just "driven" by situational pressures: they are also "pulled" by the ideals and goals of their cultures.

As we advance the frontiers of the social sciences it becomes increas-ingly clear that values must be studied as a part of our actual subject

SOURCE: *Scientific American*, Vol. 195, No. 1 (July, 1956), 25–30. Reprinted by permission. ❖ Evon Z. Vogt is professor of anthropology at Harvard University. His interests include social anthropology, cultural change, primitive religion, and American ethnology. Among his books are *Modern Homesteaders, The Life of a Twentieth-Century Frontier Family, Navaho Veterans,* and *Walter Witching, U.S.A.* ❖ John M. Roberts is professor of sociology and anthropology at Cornell University. His fields of study are southwestern ethnology, small group cultures, codes and models, values, high-way studies, and primitive law and government. He has written *Three Navaho Households, Zuni Law,* and *Zuni Daily Life* as well as coauthored *Language of Experience.*

matter and not left entirely to the humanists and philosophers. Values are, in fact, the subject of an increasing number of investigations today. But how can values be brought under the same kind of objective study as linguistic systems and the techniques of salmon fishing?

The apparent difficulty is reduced if we recall that the object of such study is not to make an ethical judgment of goodness or badness. We want to know, rather, how values function in organizing behavior. Since it is virtually impossible to experiment with human cultures, the social scientist must find his laboratory situation ready-made. Preferably he should be able to observe and compare the role of values in one or two cultures other than his own. Ideally he will find a situation where he can observe variations in values against a background in which other variables are relatively constant.

This article is concerned with . . . the region south of Gallup, N.M., where communities of five different cultural traditions—Zuñi and Navaho Indians, Mormons, Catholic Spanish-Americans and Protestant-American homesteaders from Texas—all contend with the same high-altitude semiarid environment. Since our research has not yet reached the phase of synthesis and final theory construction, it is still too early to summarize the project's over-all results. At this stage, however, we are able to report that the Gallup region has given us a practically ideal laboratory for investigation of the manifold questions presented by the role of values in human life.

The value study . . . has engaged the collaboration of 30 investigators from the disciplines of anthropology, sociology, psychology, philosophy, history, government and law. They have approached their common concern with values through a wide variety of topical interests, such as religion, cultural change, politics, land use, child rearing, adult personality, mythology, music and graphic arts. The full battery of research techniques —direct observation, participant observation, personal interviews, group discussions, interaction analysis, psychological tests and questionnaires— is represented in the immense documentation now assembled. Since the populations of the five communities are small (3,000 Zuñis, 650 Navahos, 700 Spanish-Americans, 250 Mormons, 250 Texans) it has been possible to emphasize intensive methods and reduce the problems of sampling and statistical analysis which attend so much social research. The extensive existing literatures on some of the cultures have helped to give the study historical depth.

In all its undertakings the values study has been faced with the delicate problem of rapport and public relations in the five communities. No research could be conducted that might endanger future investigations. Among the Zuñi, for example, it has so far not been politic to study prayers, ceremonials and other religious matters at close range. Because we have had to be careful to protect individuals and groups in every way, this is the first over-all account of the project to be published outside a few specialized professional journals and monographs.

The geography of the Gallup region establishes some much-needed constants for a study that is otherwise bedeviled by a multiplicity of un-controlled variables. Each of the peoples of the five cultures see the same plateau and mesa country, sparsely covered with gramagrass, sagebrush, pinyon and juniper and with stands of ponderosa pines at the higher elevations. All of the people must contend with the same fluctuation in rainfall, averaging only 12 to 15 inches per year, and with the short, changeable growing season typical of the American Southwest at this 7,000-foot altitude. There are permanent springs in the region, but the small Zuñi River, a tributary of the Little Colorado, is the only year-round stream. Soils, however, are fertile and productive when watered.

To meet the problems of making a living in this landscape, each of the five communities has essentially the same technology available to it. In face-to-face contact with one another for a generation or more, all have been subjected to markedly similar historical pressures. These pressures have mounted during the last 10 years, as hard-surface roads, telephone lines and public power have spread through their country. The five communities remain distinct, however, and present significant contrasts.

Each of the cultures, for example, has worked out its own solution for the problem of physical survival. The Zuñis, oldest of the peoples in the region, conduct a long-established irrigation agriculture supplemented by stock-raising and by crafts, notably the making of silver jewelry. The Navahos were originally roving hunters and gatherers and came into the region only a century ago; they have become dry farmers and sheepherders with wage work providing an increasing percentage of their income as contact with our American culture becomes more extensive. Livestock ranching and wage work provide the principal income for the three Spanish-American villages, which were settled about 75 years ago. The Mormons, also established in this region since the 1880's, have been conspicuously successful at irrigation farming; they also engage in livestock ranching and wage work. The Texans staked out the last Homestead Act lands in the region during the 1930's, as refugees from the dust bowl to the east; they raise cattle and carry on a commercial and largely mechanized dry-land farming, with pinto beans as their principal crop.

The five cultures present corresponding contrasts in their community organization and family life. The sedentary Zuñis spend their winters in the stone houses of their large central pueblo, moving in the agricultural season to three farming villages. Their social structure is based on the matrilocal household (with the husband living with his wife's kinfolk), matrilineal clans, and various priesthoods and other religious groupings. The Navahos also have matrilocal extended families and matrilineal clans. They are less tightly organized, however, and families dwell in widely scattered hogans: hexagonal log houses with dirt roofs. As compared to the other two non-Indian cultures, the Mormons resemble the Zuñis in having a strong sense of identity with their community. Their life centers around the single village of Ramah, where the values study maintains its field headquarters. For the Spanish-Americans the family and the Catholic church are paramount institutions. The Texan homesteads are scattered over several townships; their identity is loosely maintained by competing Protestant churches and cliques.

The values study seeks answers to a number of questions that are suggested by the differences among these five cultures. It has set out to define, first of all, the value system of each of them and to establish the role that values play in making these cultures different from one another. The changes in values that are occurring in each culture represent another important line of inquiry. Of equal challenge is the question of why their different value systems persist, despite their contact with each other and their exposure to the same environmental pressures.

One of the most promising areas of investigation is the connection between the values and the social structures of the various communities. For example, the Spanish-Americans lay strong emphasis upon "lineality" —the view that social relations are desirable when they are consistent with the hierarchy of their society. In their communities younger relatives are subordinate to older kinsmen, females to males, and the *peón* to his *patrón*. The secular structure gears into the hierarchically arranged Catholic church with its offices extending from the parish priest through the bishops, archbishops, cardinals and on up to the Pope. Much the same type of hierarchy is found in the sacred world of the Spanish-Americans, from the local images of the saints up to the Deity.

The Texan homesteaders, in marked contrast, place a strong American-frontier stress upon individualistic social relations in which each man is expected to be self-reliant and to be "his own boss." The social order of the community is composed of relatively isolated families, each living on its own farm and competing with other families for position and prestige. Instead of the single, hierarchically arranged church, the homesteaders subscribe to no less than 10 competing Christian denominations, each distinguished by a slightly different doctrine and type of service.

The Texan homesteaders fail to understand why "anybody wants to live all bunched up in a little village and take orders from the big landholders and the priests." The Spanish-Americans say of the Texans that "everybody tries to be his own *patrón*."

The Mormons present still another picture. The formal structure of the Mormon church has hierarchical aspects with lines of authority running upward from the local ward bishops through the state presidents to the 12 apostles and church president in Salt Lake City, Utah. But within this framework the local community enjoys much autonomy to work out its own affairs, and great value is placed upon collateral, cooperative economic and social relationships. Around the village and the large cohesive family system there is a proliferation of cooperatives in economic affairs. The little village of Ramah boasts a mutual irrigation company, a cooperative land and cattle company and a cooperative dairy. The spirit of individualistic competition which pervades the Texan community is consciously suppressed in favor of the values of cooperation in the Mormon village.

These values have deep roots in Mormon history. Joseph Smith, the founder of the church, proposed the "law of consecration" which required that all who had surplus wealth must impart it through the church to the poor. Although this "law" was abandoned as early as 1838, the values it expressed lent a strong cooperative bias to much of later Mormon activity. The compact village settlement was a social invention of the Mormons, motivated by a sense of urgent need to prepare a dwelling place for the "Savior" at "His second coming." Through the years cooperation became a strong defense against "persecution" by the "gentiles," first in the Middle West and later in the Far West, when the political and legal movements to stamp out Mormon polygamy came to a head. The cooperative spirit was also strongly reinforced in the arid West by the requirements of irrigation agriculture—the construction of storage reservoirs, the building and maintaining of networks of ditches, and the necessity of organized arrangements for the distribution of scarce water supplies among the various farms within a village.

The Spanish-Americans, Texans and Mormons, different as they are, belong to a single major historical tradition which contrasts with that of the Zuñis and Navahos. In former times Zuñi was ruled by a theocracy. Today personal relationships among the Zuñis are organized in a complicated series of interlocking religious, kinship and secular units, in which the individual strikes a delicate balance with external authority. No true Zuñi wishes to live away from Zuñi, particularly in the wintertime. The Zuñis have been characterized as having a kind of "middle of the road," "avoidance of excess" approach to life, in the manner of the ancient Greeks. Although this characterization must be qualified, it still symbolizes the Zuñi ideal.

While both Mormons and Zuñis can be characterized as "cooperative" and both societies manifest important linkages between their cooperative value systems and the requirements of irrigation agriculture, there are some interesting differences between them. In the Mormon community the values of cooperation are propounded by a single organized church which embraces the entire community. The Zuñi spirit of cooperation is expressed and institutionalized in the activities of a whole series of priesthoods, dancing groups and curing societies, in which the individual Zuñi may hold two or more memberships. Cooperation is stressed also as a matter of Zuñi kinship obligation. Kinship is important to the Mormons, but sustained kinship-based activity seldom goes beyond the closest relatives. In Zuñi there are large groups of near and distant relatives to whom one owes duties and from whom one derives benefits and position.

The Navahos, with their scattered hogans are more like the Texans in their settlement pattern. Except near agencies and railroad towns, they have no villages. From the core of the extended matrilineal family the Navaho views his relationships as reaching outward to include an ever-widening circle of kinsmen, some of whom he may rarely, if ever, see during the course of a year or more. Until recent times the Navahos have had no organized political leadership, the "tribe" consisting merely of a series of local bands which shared the same language and customs.

Although the Texans and Navahos can be characterized as being less communally inclined and more "individualistic" than the Mormons and Zuñis, there are, again, interesting differences in pattern and emphasis. The Texan focus is upon the individual farmer and his immediate family engaged in a competitive struggle with others for economic wealth and social prestige within the community. The Navaho sense of kinship involves no idea of striving and competing. Navahos cooperate easily with kinsmen and neighbors when the occasion arises, such as the work of putting on the larger ceremonials. But there are no organized and regular cooperative activities on a community-wide basis, unless these are actively promoted by Indian Service officials or other whites.

Differences in culture can thus be related to differences in values. The relationship comes into sharper focus when we consider the varying cultures in the context of their adjustment to their relatively unvarying natural environment, the constant in our laboratory situation. First we shall describe the general orientations of the five groups toward nature and time. Then we shall see how the values thus expressed relate to the way each of the groups reacts to the environmental problem of drought.

The Spanish-Americans have what might be called a "normal curve" view of the workings of nature. Out of so many children born, so many die before maturity; from every row of seeds, only so many plants come up; and out of every 10 or so summers, two or three are bound to be without rain. One can do little but accept what comes. Corresponding to this view of nature is an orientation in time that lays stress upon the present, as opposed to the past, which slowly recedes into obscurity, or to the even more elusive future. Life flows secure in the traditional familial mold; the important thing is the present, with its immediate drama, color and spontaneity. It is foolish to work too hard, and to worry about the future is even more ridiculous. About the mysteries of the world neither curiosity nor knowledge extend much beyond a shrug of the shoulders and a *"Quién sabe?"* These Spanish-American values find concrete expression in the traditional fiesta, a combined religious and recreational affair which is conducted each year in honor of the patron saint of the village. Catholic Masses and processions, combined with drinking, dancing, singing and visiting, express at once the solemn traditionalism and the love of present excitement and drama in the life of the small Spanish-American village.

By contrast the Texan frontier homesteaders manifest a drive for mastery over the workings of nature. Nature is defined as something to be controlled and exploited by man for his own ends and material comfort. The homesteader therefore equips himself with the most modern type of tractor, practices modern farming methods and attempts to extend even further his control over nature in the face of great odds in this semi-arid environment. The past can be forgotten, even rejected, and the present is merely a step along the road to the future. If the crops fail, there is always the hope that "next year we'll make it." There is strong perennial optimism that "progress" will continue and that their crossroads will eventually grow into a modern city. While the homesteaders feel that their Spanish-American neighbors are lazy and "not getting any place," the latter feel just as strongly that the homesteaders are senselessly working themselves to death in a life in which one should live fully in the present.

The Mormon villagers share with the Texan homesteaders the view that mastery over nature is desirable. Indeed, in some respects they carry this idea much further, for they hold the theological view that the Mormon people have "put on the uniform of the flesh" and live out this earthly life in order to learn about and attain mastery over gross matter. "The Latter-Day Saints," as the Mormons call themselves, have developed a work-health-education-recreation value complex to guide their activities: work to gain mastery over the world; health to keep man effective in the struggle for continuing progress; education to accelerate his progress; and recreation to strengthen both man's body and the community he lives in. Like the Texans, they emphasize the future, but not so much for the purpose of economic development as for participation in the eternal progress of the universe in which man himself progresses toward godhood.

To the Zuñi the universe looks very different. He neither feels that he is a master of nature nor that he is its victim. In his colorful and beautiful religion he has developed techniques of cooperating with nature. This attitude is of course sustained by a body of realistic information on ways to make a living in a difficult environment. The Zuñi equivalent of the Spanish-American fiesta has an important place in his life, but he is less taken with its recreational aspects. He lives in the present, but in many things, much more than any of his neighbors, he looks back to the past. It is a glorious past, an ancient mythological time when Zuñis came up from the "wombs" of the earth, wandered around, and finally settled at "the middle place," where their descendants to this day still maintain a shrine to mark the center of the universe.

The Navahos resemble the Spanish-Americans and the Zuñis in their orientation to nature and time. Like the Zuñis, the Navahos view man as having an integral part to play in a general cosmic scheme. But they see the universe as more powerful than man and profoundly threatening. In dealing with nature circumspection is the best guide to action, and fear is the dominant emotional theme. Yet the Navaho is not completely fatalistic. There are small things one can do to maintain and restore harmony in the scheme. Thus individual curing ceremonials, performed with care, can keep matters from becoming worse. The present is the important time-dimension, but the Navahos also recall a "holy people" who came up from the underworld, created four sacred mountains and the "earth surface people" and then departed for their permanent homes in the six directions: east, south, west, north, zenith and nadir.

For all five cultures the annual drought is a serious common concern. Each group responds differently to this problem in terms of its distinctive value-orientation. The Zuñis increase the intensity and tempo of their ceremonial activity; they give more attention to the planting of prayer feathers and to the fasting and prayers of the rain priests. This is in line with their view of the ultimate harmony of nature; man need only do his part and the gods will do the rest. With centuries of summer rains to testify to the soundness of this view, Zuñi is deeply opposed to rainmaking with airplanes and silver iodide.

The Navahos also tend to respond to drought by increasing ceremonial activity. But they are not so certain of the efficacy of their rainmaking ceremonies. They direct less ritual to that purpose and are more humble in the face of a more threatening universe.

The Spanish-Americans, on the other hand, seem to do little or nothing about drought beyond collecting in small groups on the plaza to talk about it. In their view, to attempt to alter the course of natural events by ceremonial is as useless as trying to alter it by rainmaking.

Against the ceremonial response of the Zuñis and Navahos and the fatalistic response of the Spanish-Americans, the behavior of the Mormons and Texans draws a dramatic contrast. They actively support the artificial rainmaking projects; they reduce their livestock herds and crop acreages, and they organize to enlist government aid in meeting the drought conditions. The Navahos and Zuñis, in contrast, have to be forced by the government to practice acreage restriction in bad years.

Ceremonial and ritual responses are not entirely lacking, however, in the Mormon and Texan communities. Mormons occasionally say prayers in church for rain. The Texans have held special prayer meetings during droughts; indeed, the governor of Texas set aside a special day for such meetings during the recent severe southwestern drought. A minority within each community also feels that seeding the clouds is "interfering with the work of the Lord." But the majority responds in the vein expressed by one of the more articulate farmers in the Texan community, who declared: "The Lord will look down and say, 'Look at those poor ignorant people. I gave them the clouds, the airplanes and the silver iodide, and they didn't have the sense to put them together.'"

Thus systems of values may promote and justify radically different modes of behavior among people confronted with the same objective problem. Why do such different values persist in the same tiny region among peoples living so close to one another? There appear to be at least two basic aspects to this question. First, we know that the values are intricately related to the total structure of each culture. Accordingly, unless the structure breaks down completely, values will tend to persist as functional parts of the whole. Second, we have also discovered that face-to-face contacts between the five cultural groups have not always encouraged the easy communication and interaction which might eventually level the differences between them. In fact, some of the intercultural contacts appear to have reinforced, rather than changed, the original value systems. There is, for example, good evidence that Navahos and Zuñis cling tenaciously to certain of their aboriginal values precisely because missionaries and other agents of white culture bring strong pressure upon them to change.

❖ 10 ❖

THE CONCEPT OF CULTURE

Clyde Kluckhohn

Among the environmental factors that have the most significant effect on man's behavior are those that man himself has created. The term that social scientists use to describe this social heritage is "culture," but this word has a variety of popular meanings with which it may be confused. A close reading of the following statement by Clyde Kluckhohn should help you to understand the unique definition given to "culture" by social scientists. You will further comprehend this concept by examining some patterns of culture from different societies.

Why do the Chinese dislike milk and milk products? Why would the Japanese die willingly in a Banzai charge that seemed senseless to Americans? Why do some nations trace descent through the father, others through the mother, still others through both parents? Not because different peoples have different instincts, not because they were destined by God or Fate to different habits, not because the weather is different in China and Japan and the United States. Sometimes shrewd common

SOURCE: Clyde Kluckhohn, *Mirror for Man* (New York: McGraw-Hill Book Company, Inc., 1949), 17–36. Reprinted by permission. ❖ Clyde Kluckhohn (1905–1960) was professor of anthropology and director of the Russian Research Center at Harvard University. He was the author of *To the Foot of the Rainbow*, the coauthor of *Navaho Means People* and *How the Soviet System Works*, and the coeditor of *Personality in Nature, Society and Culture*.

sense has an answer that is close to that of the anthropologist: "because they were brought up that way." By "culture" anthropology means the total life way of a people, the social legacy the individual acquires from his group. Or culture can be regarded as that part of the environment that is the creation of man.

This technical term has a wider meaning than the "culture" of history and literature. A humble cooking pot is as much a cultural product as is a Beethoven sonata. In ordinary speech a man of culture is a man who can speak languages other than his own, who is familiar with history, literature, philosophy, or the fine arts. In some cliques that definition is still narrower. The cultured person is one who can talk about James Joyce, Scarlatti, and Picasso. To the anthropologist, however, to be human is to be cultured. There is culture in general, and then there are the specific cultures such as Russian, American, British, Hottentot, Inca. The general abstract notion serves to remind us that we cannot explain acts solely in terms of the biological properties of the people concerned, their individual past experience, and the immediate situation. The past experience of other men in the form of culture enters into almost every event. Each specific culture constitutes a kind of blueprint for all of life's activities.

One of the interesting things about human beings is that they try to understand themselves and their own behavior. While this has been particularly true of Europeans in recent times, there is no group which has not developed a scheme or schemes to explain man's actions. To the insistent human query "why?" the most exciting illumination anthropology has to offer is that of the concept of culture. Its explanatory importance is comparable to categories such as evolution in biology, gravity in physics, disease in medicine. A good deal of human behavior can be understood, and indeed predicted, if we know a people's design for living. Many acts are neither accidental nor due to personal peculiarities nor caused by supernatural forces nor simply mysterious. Even those of us who pride ourselves on our individualism follow most of the time a pattern not of our own making. We brush our teeth on arising. We put on pants—not a loincloth or a grass skirt. We eat three meals a day—not four or five or two. We sleep in a bed—not in a hammock or on a sheep pelt. I do not have to know the individual and his life history to be able to predict these and countless other regularities, including many in the thinking process, of all Americans who are not incarcerated in jails or hospitals for the insane.

To the American woman a system of plural wives seems "instinctively" abhorrent. She cannot understand how any woman can fail to be jealous and uncomfortable if she must share her husband with other women. She feels it "unnatural" to accept such a situation. On the other hand, a Koryak woman of Siberia, for example, would find it hard to understand how a woman could be so selfish and so undesirous of feminine companionship in the home as to wish to restrict her husband to one mate.

Some years ago I met in New York City a young man who did not speak a word of English and was obviously bewildered by American ways. By "blood" he was as American as you or I, for his parents had gone from Indiana to China as missionaries. Orphaned in infancy, he was reared by a Chinese family in a remote village. All who met him found him more Chinese than American. The facts of his blue eyes and light hair were less impressive than a Chinese style of gait, Chinese arm and hand movements, Chinese facial expression, and Chinese modes of thought. The biological heritage was American, but the cultural training had been Chinese. He returned to China. Another example of another kind: I once knew a trader's wife in Arizona who took a somewhat devilish interest in producing a cultural reaction. Guests who came her way were often served delicious sandwiches filled with a meat that seemed to be neither chicken nor tuna fish yet was reminiscent of both. To queries she gave no reply until each had eaten his fill. She then explained that what they had eaten was not chicken, not tuna fish, but the rich, white flesh of freshly killed rattlesnakes. The response was instantaneous—vomiting, often violent vomiting. A biological process is caught in a cultural web.

A highly intelligent teacher with long and successful experience in the public schools of Chicago was finishing her first year in an Indian school. When asked how her Navaho pupils compared in intelligence with Chicago youngsters, she replied, "Well, I just don't know. Sometimes the Indians seem just as bright. At other times they just act like dumb animals. The other night we had a dance in the high school. I saw a boy who is one of the best students in my English class standing off by himself. So I took him over to a pretty girl and told them to dance. But they just stood there with their heads down. They wouldn't even say anything." I inquired if she knew whether or not they were members of the same clan. "What difference would that make?"

"How would you feel about getting into bed with your brother?" The teacher walked off in a huff, but, actually, the two cases were quite comparable in principle. To the Indian the type of bodily contact involved in our social dancing has a directly sexual connotation. The incest taboos between members of the same clan are as severe as between true brothers and sisters. The shame of the Indians at the suggestion that a clan brother and sister should dance and the indignation of the white teacher at the idea that she should share a bed with an adult brother represent equally nonrational responses, culturally standardized unreason.

All this does not mean that there is no such thing as raw human nature. The very fact that certain of the same institutions are found in all known societies indicates that at bottom all human beings are very much alike. The files of the Cross-Cultural Survey at Yale University are organized according to categories such as "marriage ceremonies," "life crisis rites," "incest taboos." At least seventy-five of these categories are represented in every single one of the hundreds of cultures analyzed. This is hardly surprising. The members of all human groups have about the same biological equipment. All men undergo the same poignant life experiences such as birth, helplessness, illness, old age, and death. The biological potentialities of the species are the blocks with which cultures are built. Some patterns of every culture crystallize around focuses provided by the inevitables of biology: the difference between the sexes, the presence of persons of different ages, the varying physical strength and skill of individuals. The facts of nature also limit culture forms. No culture provides patterns for jumping over trees or for eating iron ore.

There is thus no "either-or" between nature and that special form of nurture called culture. Culture determinism is as one-sided as biological determinism. The two factors are interdependent. Culture arises out of human nature, and its forms are restricted both by man's biology and by natural laws. It is equally true that culture channels biological processes—vomiting, weeping, fainting, sneezing, the daily habits of food intake and waste elimination. When a man eats, he is reacting to an internal "drive," namely, hunger contractions consequent upon the lowering of blood sugar, but his precise reaction to these internal stimuli cannot be predicted by physiological knowledge alone. Whether a healthy adult feels hungry twice, three times, or four times a day and the hours at which this feeling recurs is a question of culture. *What* he eats is of course limited by availability, but is also partly regulated by culture. It is a biological fact that some types of berries are poisonous; it is a cultural fact that, a few generations ago, most Americans considered tomatoes to be poisonous and refused to eat them. Such selective, discriminative use of the environment is characteristically cultural. In a still more general sense, too, the process of eating is channeled by culture. Whether a man eats to live, lives to eat, or merely eats and lives is only in part an individual matter, for there are also cultural trends. Emotions are physiological events. Certain situations will evoke fear in people from any culture. But sensations of pleasure, anger, and lust may be stimulated by cultural cues that would leave unmoved someone who has been reared in a different social tradition.

Except in the case of newborn babies and of individuals born with clear-cut structural or functional abnormalities we can observe innate endowments only as modified by cultural training. In a hospital in New Mexico where Zuñi Indian, Navaho Indian, and white American babies are born, it is possible to classify the newly arrived infants as unusually active, average, and quiet. Some babies from each "racial" group will fall into each category, though a higher proportion of the white babies will fall into the unusually active class. But if a Navaho baby, a Zuñi baby, and a white baby—all classified as unusually active at birth—are again observed at the age of two years, the Zuñi baby will no longer seem given to quick and restless activity—*as compared with the white child*—though he may seem so as compared with the other Zuñis of the same age. The Navaho child is likely to fall in between as contrasted with the Zuñi and the white, though he will probably still seem more active than the average Navaho youngster.

It was remarked by many observers in the Japanese relocation centers that Japanese who were born and brought up in this country, especially those who were reared apart from any large colony of Japanese, resemble in behavior their white neighbors much more closely than they do their own parents who were educated in Japan.

I have said "culture channels biological processes." It is more accurate to say "the biological functioning of individuals is modified if they have been trained in certain ways and not in others." Culture is not a disembodied force. It is created and transmitted by people. However, culture, like well-known concepts of the physical sciences, is a convenient abstraction. One never sees gravity. One sees bodies falling in regular ways. One never sees an electromagnetic field. Yet certain happenings that can be seen may be given a neat abstract formulation by assuming that the electromagnetic field exists. Similarly, one never sees culture as such. What is seen are regularities in the behavior or artifacts of a group that has adhered to a common tradition. The regularities in style and technique of ancient Inca tapestries or stone axes from Melanesian islands are due to the existence of mental blueprints for the group.

Culture is a way of thinking, feeling, believing. It is the group's knowledge stored up (in memories of men; in books and objects) for future use. We study the products of this "mental" activity: the overt behavior, the speech and gestures and activities of people, and the tangible results of these things such as tools, houses, cornfields, and what not. It has been customary in lists of "culture traits" to include such things as watches or lawbooks. This is a convenient way of thinking about them, but in the solution of any important problem we must remember that they, in themselves, are nothing but metals, paper, and ink. What is important is that some men know how to make them, others set a value on them, are unhappy without them, direct their activities in relation to them, or disregard them.

It is only a helpful shorthand when we say "The cultural patterns of the Zulu were resistant to Christianization." In the directly observable world of course, it was individual Zulus who resisted. Nevertheless, if we do not forget that we are speaking at a high level of abstraction, it is justifiable to speak of culture as a cause. One may compare the practice of saying "syphilis caused the extinction of the native population of the island." Was it "syphilis" or "syphilis germs" or "human beings who were carriers of syphilis"?

"Culture," then, is "a theory." But if a theory is not contradicted by any relevant fact and if it helps us to understand a mass of otherwise chaotic facts, it is useful. Darwin's contribution was much less the accumulation of new knowledge than the creation of a theory which put in order data already known. An accumulation of facts, however large, is no more a science than a pile of bricks is a house. Anthropology's demonstration that the most weird set of customs has a consistency and an order is comparable to modern psychiatry's showing that there is meaning and purpose in the apparently incoherent talk of the insane. In fact, the inability of the older psychologies and philosophies to account for the strange behavior of madmen and heathens was the principal factor that forced psychiatry and anthropology to develop theories of the unconscious and of culture.

Since culture is an abstraction, it is important not to confuse culture with society. A "society" refers to a group of people who interact more with each other than they do with other individuals—who cooperate with each other for the attainment of certain ends. You can see and indeed count the individuals who make up a society. A "culture" refers to the distinctive ways of life of such a group of people. Not all social events are culturally patterned. New types of circumstances arise for which no cultural solutions have as yet been devised.

A culture constitutes a storehouse of the pooled learning of the group. A rabbit starts life with some innate responses. He can learn from his own experience and perhaps from observing other rabbits. A human infant is born with fewer instincts and greater plasticity. His main task is to learn the answers that persons he will never see, persons long dead, have worked out. Once he has learned the formulas supplied by the culture of his group, most of his behavior becomes almost as automatic and unthinking as if it were instinctive. There is a tremendous amount of intelligence behind the making of a radio, but not much is required to learn to turn it on.

The members of all human societies face some of the same unavoidable dilemmas posed by biology and other facts of the human situation. This is why the basic categories of all cultures are so similar. Human culture without language is unthinkable. No culture fails to provide for aesthetic expression and aesthetic delight. Every culture supplies standardized orientations toward the deeper problems, such as death. Every culture is designed to perpetuate the group and its solidarity, to meet the demands of individuals for an orderly way of life and for satisfaction of biological needs.

However, the variations on these basic themes are numberless. Some languages are built up out of twenty basic sounds, others out of forty. Nose plugs were considered beautiful by the predynastic Egyptians but are not by the modern French. Puberty is a biological fact. But one culture ignores it, another prescribes informal instructions about sex but no ceremony, a third has impressive rites for girls only, a fourth for boys and girls. In this culture, the first menstruation is welcomed as a happy, natural event; in that culture the atmosphere is full of dread and supernatural threat. Each culture dissects nature according to its own system of categories. The Navaho Indians apply the same word to the color of a robin's egg and to that of grass. A psychologist once assumed that this meant a difference in the sense organs, that Navahos didn't have the physiological equipment to distinguish "green" from "blue." However, when he showed them objects of the two colors and asked them if they were exactly the same colors, they looked at him with astonishment. His dream of discovering a new type of color blindness was shattered.

Every culture must deal with the sexual instinct. Some, however, seek to deny all sexual expression before marriage, whereas a Polynesian adolescent who was not promiscuous would be distinctly abnormal. Some cultures enforce lifelong monogamy, others, like our own, tolerate serial monogamy; in still other cultures, two or more women may be joined to one man or several men to a single woman. Homosexuality has been a permitted pattern in the Greco-Roman world, in parts of Islam, and in various primitive tribes. Large portions of the population of Tibet, and of Christendom at some places and periods, have practiced complete celibacy. To us marriage is first and foremost an arrangement between two individuals. In many more societies marriage is merely one facet of a complicated set of reciprocities, economic and otherwise, between two families or two clans.

The essence of the cultural process is selectivity. The selection is only exceptionally conscious and rational. Cultures are like Topsy. They just grew. Once, however, a way of handling a situation becomes institutionalized, there is ordinarily great resistance to change or deviation. When we speak of "our sacred beliefs," we mean of course that they are beyond criticism and that the person who suggests modification or abandonment must be punished. No person is emotionally indifferent to his culture. Certain cultural premises may become totally out of accord with a new factual situation. Leaders may recognize this and reject the old ways in theory. Yet their emotional loyalty continues in the face of reason because of the intimate conditionings of early childhood.

A culture is learned by individuals as the result of belonging to some particular group, and it constitutes that part of learned behavior which is shared with others. It is our social legacy, as contrasted with our organic heredity. It is one of the important factors which permits us to live together in an organized society, giving us ready-made solutions to our problems, helping us to predict the behavior of others, and permitting others to know what to expect of us.

Culture regulates our lives at every turn. From the moment we are born until we die there is, whether we are conscious of it or not, constant pressure upon us to follow certain types of behavior that other men have created for us. Some paths we follow willingly, others we follow because we know no other way, still others we deviate from or go back to most unwillingly. Mothers of small children know how unnaturally most of this comes to us—how little regard we have, until we are "culturalized," for the "proper" place, time, and manner for certain acts such as eating, excreting, sleeping, getting dirty, and making loud noises. But by more or less adhering to a system of related designs for carrying out all the acts of living, a group of men and women feel themselves linked together by a powerful chain of sentiments. Ruth Benedict gave an almost complete definition of the concept when she said, "Culture is that which binds men together."

It is true any culture is a set of techniques for adjusting both to the external environment and to other men. However, cultures create problems as well as solve them. If the lore of a people states that frogs are dangerous creatures, or that it is not safe to go about at night because of witches or ghosts, threats are posed which do not arise out of the inexorable facts of the external world. Cultures produce needs as well as provide a means of fulfilling them. There exist for every group culturally defined, acquired drives that may be more powerful in ordinary daily life than the biologically inborn drives. Many Americans, for example, will work harder for "success" than they will for sexual satisfaction.

Most groups elaborate certain aspects of their culture far beyond maximum utility or survival value. In other words, not all culture promotes physical survival. At times, indeed, it does exactly the opposite. Aspects of culture which once were adaptive may persist long after they have ceased to be useful. An analysis of any culture will disclose many features which cannot possibly be construed as adaptations to the total environment in which the group now finds itself. However, it is altogether likely that these apparently useless features represent survivals, with modifications through time, of cultural forms which were adaptive in one or another previous situation.

Any cultural practice must be functional or it will disappear before long. That is, it must somehow contribute to the survival of the society or to the adjustment of the individual. However, many cultural functions are not manifest but latent. A cowboy will walk three miles to catch a horse which he then rides one mile to the store. From the point of view of manifest function this is positively irrational. But the act has the latent function of maintaining the cowboy's prestige in the terms of his own subculture. One can instance the buttons on the sleeve of a man's coat, our absurd English spelling, the use of capital letters, and a host of other apparently nonfunctional customs. They serve mainly the latent function of assisting individuals to maintain their security by preserving continuity with the past and by making certain sectors of life familiar and predictable.

Every culture is a precipitate of history. In more than one sense history is a sieve. Each culture embraces those aspects of the past, which, usually in altered form and with altered meanings, live on in the present. Discoveries and inventions, both material and ideological, are constantly being made available to a group through its historical contacts with other peoples or being created by its own members. However, only those that fit the total immediate situation in meeting the group's needs for survival or in promoting the psychological adjustment of individuals will become part of the culture. The process of culture building may be regarded as an addition to man's innate biological capacities, an addition providing instruments which enlarge, or may even substitute for, biological functions, and to a degree compensating for biological limitations—as in ensuring that death does not always result in the loss to humanity of what the deceased has learned.

Culture is like a map. Just as a map isn't the territory but an abstract representation of a particular area, so also a culture is an abstract description of trends toward uniformity in the words, deeds, and artifacts of a human group. If a map is accurate and you can read it, you won't get lost; if you know a culture, you will know your way around in the life of a society.

Many educated people have the notion that culture applies only to exotic ways of life or to societies where relative simplicity and relative homogeneity prevail. Some sophisticated missionaries, for example, will use the anthropological conception in discussing the special modes of living of South Sea Islanders, but seem amazed at the idea that it could be applied equally to inhabitants of New York City. And social workers in Boston will talk about the culture of a colorful and well-knit immigrant group but boggle at applying it to the behavior of staff members in the social-service agency itself.

In the primitive society the correspondence between the habits of individuals and the customs of the community is ordinarily greater. There is probably some truth in what an old Indian once said, "In the old days there was no law; everybody did what was right." The primitive tends to find happiness in the fulfillment of intricately involuted cultural patterns; the modern more often tends to feel the pattern as repressive to his individuality. It is also true that in a complex stratified society there are numerous exceptions to generalizations made about the culture as a whole. It is necessary to study regional, class, and occupational subcultures. Primitive cultures have greater stability than modern cultures; they change—but less rapidly.

However, modern men also are creators and carriers of culture. Only in some respects are they influenced differently from primitives by culture. Moreover, there are such wide variations in primitive cultures that any black-and-white contrast between the primitive and the civilized is altogether fictitious. The distinction which is most generally true lies in the field of conscious philosophy.

The publication of Paul Radin's *Primitive Man as a Philosopher* did much toward destroying the myth that an abstract analysis of experience was a peculiarity of literate societies. Speculation and reflection upon the nature of the universe and of man's place in the total scheme of things have been carried out in every known culture. Every people has its characteristic set of "primitive postulates." It remains true that critical examination of basic premises and fully explicit systematization of philosophical concepts are seldom found at the nonliterate level. The written word is an almost essential condition for free and extended discussion of fundamental philosophic issues. Where dependence on memory exists, there seems to be an inevitable tendency to emphasize the correct perpetuation of the precious oral tradition. Similarly, while it is all too easy to underestimate the extent to which ideas spread without books, it is in general true that tribal or folk societies do not possess competing philosophical systems. The major exception to this statement is, of course, the case where part of the tribe becomes converted to one of the great proselytizing religions such as Christianity or Mohammedanism. Before contact with rich and powerful civilizations, primitive peoples seem to have absorbed new ideas piecemeal, slowly integrating them with the previously existing ideology. The abstract thought of nonliterate societies is ordinarily less self-critical, less systematic, nor so intricately elaborated in purely logical dimensions. Primitive thinking is more concrete, more implicit—perhaps more completely coherent than the philosophy of most individuals in larger societies which have been influenced over long periods by disparate intellectual currents.

No participant in any culture knows all the details of the cultural map. The statement frequently heard that St. Thomas Aquinas was the last man to master all the knowledge of his society is intrinsically absurd. St. Thomas would have been hard put to make a pane of cathedral glass or to act as a midwife. In every culture there are what Ralph Linton has called "universals, alternatives, and specialties." Every Christian in the thirteenth century knew that it was necessary to attend mass, to go to confession, to ask the Mother of God to intercede with her Son. There were many other universals in the Christian culture of Western Europe. However, there were also alternative cultural patterns even in the realm of religion. Each individual had his own patron saint, and different towns developed the cults of different saints. The thirteenth-century anthropologist could have discovered the rudiments of Christian practice by questioning and observing whomever he happened to meet in Germany, France, Italy, or England. But to find out the details of the ceremonials honoring St. Hubert or St. Bridget he would have had to seek out certain individuals or special localities where these alternative patterns were practiced. Similarly, he could not learn about weaving from a professional soldier or about canon law from a farmer. Such cultural knowledge belongs in the realm of the specialties, voluntarily chosen by the individual or ascribed to him by birth. Thus, part of a culture must be learned by everyone, part may be selected from alternative patterns, part applies only to those who perform the roles in the society for which these patterns are designed.

Many aspects of a culture are explicit. The explicit culture consists in those regularities in word and deed that may be generalized straight from the evidence of the ear and the eye. The recognition of these is like the recognition of style in the art of a particular place and epoch. If we have examined twenty specimens of the wooden saints' images made in the Taos valley of New Mexico in the late eighteenth century, we can predict

that any new images from the same locality and period will in most respects exhibit the same techniques of carving, about the same use of colors
and choice of woods, a similar quality of artistic conception. Similarly, if,
in a society of 2,000 members, we record 100 marriages at random and find
that in 30 cases a man has married the sister of his brother's wife, we can
anticipate that an additional sample of 100 marriages will show roughly the
same number of cases of this pattern.

The above is an instance of what anthropologists call a behavioral
pattern, the practices as opposed to the rules of the culture. There are also,
however, regularities in what people say they do or should do. They do
tend in fact to prefer to marry into a family already connected with their
own by marriage but this is not necessarily part of the official code of conduct. No disapproval whatsoever is attached to those who make another
sort of marriage. On the other hand, it is explicitly forbidden to marry a
member of one's own clan even though no biological relationship is traceable. This is a regulatory pattern—a Thou Shalt or a Thou Shalt Not. Such
patterns may be violated often, but their existence is nevertheless important.
A people's standards for conduct and belief define the socially approved
aims and the acceptable means of attaining them. When the discrepancy
between the theory and the practice of a culture is exceptionally great,
this indicates that the culture is undergoing rapid change. It does not
prove that ideals are unimportant, for ideals are but one of a number of
factors determining action.

Cultures do not manifest themselves solely in observable customs and
artifacts. No amount of questioning of any save the most articulate in the
most self-conscious cultures will bring out some of the basic attitudes common to the members of the group. This is because these basic assumptions
are taken so for granted that they normally do not enter into consciousness.
This part of the cultural map must be inferred by the observer on the
basis of consistencies in thought and action. Missionaries in various societies are often disturbed or puzzled because the natives do not regard
"morals" and "sex code" as almost synonymous. The natives seem to feel
that morals are concerned with sex just about as much as with eating—no
less and no more. No society fails to have some restrictions on sexual behavior, but sex activity outside of marriage need not necessarily be furtive
or attended with guilt. The Christian tradition has tended to assume that
sex is inherently nasty as well as dangerous. Other cultures assume that sex
in itself is not only natural but one of the good things of life, even though
sex acts with certain persons under certain circumstances are forbidden.
This is implicit culture, for the natives do not announce their premises.
The missionaries would get further if they said, in effect, "Look, our
morality starts from different assumptions. Let's talk about those assumptions," rather than ranting about "immorality."

A factor implicit in a variety of diverse phenomena may be generalized
as an underlying cultural principle. For example, the Navaho Indians

always leave part of the design in a pot, a basket, or a blanket unfinished. When a medicine man instructs an apprentice he always leaves a little bit of the story untold. This "fear of closure" is a recurrent theme in Navaho culture. Its influence may be detected in many contexts that have no explicit connection.

If the observed cultural behavior is to be correctly understood, the categories and presuppositions constituting the implicit culture must be worked out. The "strain toward consistency" which Sumner noted in the folkways and mores of all groups cannot be accounted for unless one grants a set of systematically interrelated implicit themes. For example, in American culture the themes of "effort and optimism," "the common man," "technology," and "virtuous materialism" have a functional inter-dependence, the origin of which is historically known. The relationship between themes may be that of conflict. One may instance the competition between Jefferson's theory of democracy and Hamilton's "government by the rich, the wellborn, and the able." In other cases most themes may be integrated under a single dominant theme. In Negro cultures of West Africa the mainspring of social life is religion; in East Africa almost all cultural behavior seems to be oriented toward certain premises and categories centered on the cattle economy. If there be one master principle in the implicit culture, this is often called the "ethos" or *Zeitgeist*.

Every culture has organization as well as content. There is nothing mystical about this statement. One may compare ordinary experience. If I know that Smith, working alone, can shovel 10 cubic yards of dirt a day, Jones 12, and Brown 14, I would be foolish to predict that the three working together would move 36. The total might well be considerably more; it might be less. A whole is different from the sum of its parts. The same principle is familiar in athletic teams. A brilliant pitcher added to a nine may mean a pennant or may mean the cellar; it depends on how he fits in.

And so it is with cultures. A mere list of the behavioral and regulatory patterns and of the implicit themes and categories would be like a map on which all mountains, lakes, and rivers were included—but not in their actual relationship to one another. Two cultures could have almost identical inventories and still be extremely different. The full significance of any single element in a culture design will be seen only when that element is viewed in the total matrix of its relationship to other elements. Naturally, this includes accent or emphasis, as well as position. Accent is manifested sometimes through frequency, sometimes through intensity. The indispensable importance of these questions of arrangement and emphasis may be driven home by an analogy. Consider a musical sequence made up of three notes. If we are told that the three notes in question are A, B, and G, we receive information which is fundamental. But it will not enable us to predict the type of sensation which the playing of this sequence is likely to evoke. We need many different sorts of relationship data. Are the notes to be played in that or some other order? What duration will each receive?

How will the emphasis, if any, be distributed? We also need, of course, to know whether the instrument used is to be a piano or an accordion.

Cultures vary greatly in their degree of integration. Synthesis is achieved partly through the overt statement of the dominant conceptions, assumptions, and aspirations of the group in its religious lore, secular thought, and ethical code; partly through habitual but unconscious ways of looking at the stream of events, ways of begging certain questions. To the naïve participant in the culture these modes of categorizing, of dissecting experience along these planes and not others, are as much "given" as the regular sequence of daylight and darkness or the necessity of air, water, and food for life. Had Americans not thought in terms of money and the market system during the depression they would have distributed unsalable goods rather than destroyed them.

Every group's way of life, then, is a structure—not a haphazard collection of all the different physically possible and functionally effective patterns of belief and action. A culture is an interdependent system based upon linked premises and categories whose influence is greater, rather than less, because they are seldom put in words. Some degree of internal coherence which is felt rather than rationally constructed seems to be demanded by most of the participants in any culture. As Whitehead has remarked, "Human life is driven forward by its dim apprehension of notions too general for its existing language."

In sum, the distinctive way of life that is handed down as the social heritage of a people does more than supply a set of skills for making a living and a set of blueprints for human relations. Each different way of life makes its own assumptions about the ends and purposes of human existence, about what human beings have a right to expect from each other and the gods, about what constitutes fulfillment or frustration. Some of these assumptions are made explicit in the lore of the folks; others are tacit premises which the observer must infer by finding consistent trends in word and deed.

THE AMISH: A CULTURAL ISLAND

John Hostetler

One of the most effective ways of learning the meaning of the culture is to compare the codes of proper behavior in different societies. A case study of a "foreign" culture is frequently used to provide this comparison. We have chosen in this book to achieve the same purpose through a description of a cultural island within American society. Hostetler's examination of strongly traditional Amish codes of behavior and the symbols associated with these codes helps us to understand not only the concept of culture, but also the means by which groups such as the Amish resist assimilation into the larger society.

The Amish Charter

We turn now to the moral principles of the contemporary Amish community. By moral we mean that which is considered right and wrong, and the principles for which life is worth living. The fundamentals of right and wrong are made relevant in the life of the society. Behavior in the Amish community is oriented to absolute values, involving a conscious belief in religious and ethical ends, entirely for their own sake, and quite independent of any external rewards. This orientation to *Wert-rational*, or absolute values, requires of the individual certain unconditional demands. Regardless of any possible cost to themselves, the members are required to put into practice what is required by duty, honor, personal loyalty, and religious calling. The fundamental values and common ends of the group, recognized by the people and accepted by them, have been designated as the charter. A charter need not be reduced to writing to be effective in the little community; it may be thought of as the common purpose of the community, corresponding to a desire or a set of motives embodied in tradition. Although Amish life is oriented to absolute values, there is an almost automatic reaction to habitual stimuli that guides behavior in a

SOURCE: John A. Hostetler, *Amish Society* (Baltimore: The Johns Hopkins Press, 1963). Reprinted by permission. ❖ John A. Hostetler is associate professor of sociology and anthropology at Temple University. He was born in Mifflin County, Pennsylvania, and was reared as an Amishman, but he left his Plain Folk community for an education. His special interests include social change, problems of the marginal man, and cultural anthropology. His research and numerous publications have focused on the Amish, Mennonites, and Hutterites. He is the author of *Annotated Bibliography on the Amish*, which was awarded the International Folklore Prize, University of Chicago; *The Sociology of Mennonite Evangelism*; and *Education and Marginality in the Communal Society of the Hutterites*.

course which has been repeatedly followed. Behavior is traditionally oriented by belief and the habit of long experience.

The Amish view of reality is conditioned by a dualistic world view. They believe, as have many other ascetic brotherhoods, that light and truth coexist with the powers of darkness and falsehood. Purity and goodness are in conflict with impurity and evil. The rejection of the world is based upon this dualistic conception of reality and is manifest in specific life situations. While the Amish share this fundamental doctrine of the two worlds with other believers, it becomes a reality to the Amish, while to many Christian people it is greatly modified.

Separation from the World

To the Amish there is a divine spiritual reality, the Kingdom of God, and a Satanic Kingdom that dominates the present world. It is the duty of a Christian to keep himself "unspotted from the world" and separate from the desires, intent, and goals of the worldly person. Amish preaching and teaching draws upon passages from the Bible which emphasize the necessity of separation from the world. Two passages, perhaps the most often quoted, epitomize for the Amishman the message of the Bible. The first is: "Be not conformed to this world, but be ye transformed by the renewing of your mind that ye may prove what is that good and acceptable and perfect will of God." This to the Amishman means among other things that one should not dress and behave like the world. The second is: "Be ye not unequally yoked together with unbelievers; for what fellowship hath righteousness with unrighteousness? and what communion hath light with darkness?" This doctrine forbids the Amishman from marrying a non-Amish person or from being in business partnership with an outsider. It is applied generally to all social contacts that would involve intimate connections with persons outside the ceremonial community. This emphasis upon literalness and separateness is compatible with the Amish view of themselves as a "chosen people" or "peculiar people."

The principle of separation conditions and controls the Amishman's contact with the outside world; it colors his entire view of reality and being. Bible teaching is conditioned by the totality of the traditional way of life. Compatible with the doctrine of separation is the doctrine of nonresistance. By the precepts of Christ, the Amish are forbidden to take part in violence and war. In time of war they are conscientious objectors, basing their stand on biblical texts, such as "My kingdom is not of this world: if my kingdom were of this world, then would my servant fight." The Amish have no rationale for self-defense or for defending their possessions. Like many early Anabaptists they are "defenseless Christians." Problems of hostility are met without retaliation. The Amish farmer, in difficulty with the hostile world around him, is admonished by his bishop to follow the example of Isaac: after the warring Philistines had stopped up all the wells of his father Abraham, Isaac moved to new lands and dug new wells. This advice is taken literally, so that in the face of hostility, the Amish move to new locations without defending their rights.

The Amish share with the Mennonites the principles of Anabaptism as evidenced by their common endorsement of the Dortrecht Confession. Both practice adult rather than infant baptism, non-resistance and refusal to bear arms, and refusal to swear an oath, and both refrain from holding public offices. Religion tends to be pervasive and associated with a total way of life, not a specialized activity. The Amish today differ from the Mennonites mainly in the extent to which external changes have effected the groups. The Amish are more literal in the observance of certain practices such as fasting and shunning, in practical informal mutual aid, and in keeping the young on the farm. The Mennonites have been readier to accept changes and to incorporate them into their religious values. Mennonites are technologically modern, and they generally accept higher education. Furthermore, during the nineteenth century they founded institutions of higher education to train missionaries. Mennonites developed along the lines of modern Protestantism, while the Amish have retained literalism, limited education, and agrarianism.

The Amish are "otherworldly" minded, in contrast to the many Christian churches that are concerned with making the world a better place in which to live. The Amish show little interest in improving the world or their environment. They profess to be "strangers and pilgrims" in the present world.

❖   ❖   ❖   ❖   ❖

Amish preaching and moral instruction emphasize self-denial and obedience to the teaching of the Word of God, which is equated with the rules of the church. All ministers constantly warn their members to beware of worldliness. Long passages from the Old Testament are retold, giving prominence to crucial events in the lives of Abraham, Isaac, Jacob, Joseph, and Moses. The escape of the Israelites from Egyptian bondage and Moses's giving of the law are sermon themes; punishments meted out to the lawbreakers are emphasized. The themes: "Offenders were executed for breaking the law," and "we are not better than they," are emphatically stressed. The choice put before the congregation is to obey or die. To disobey the church is to die. To obey the church and strive for "full fellowship," that is, complete harmony with the order of the church, is to have *lebendige Hoffnung*, a living hope of salvation. An Amish person simply puts faith in God, obeys the order of the church, and patiently hopes for the best.

Separation from the world is a basic tenet of the Amish charter; yet the Amish are not highly ethnocentric in their relationships with the outside world. They accept as a matter of course other people as they are, without attempting to convert them to the Amish way of life. But for those who are born into the Amish society, the sanctions for belonging are deeply rooted in the belief in separatism.

The people of the little community have an "inside view" as well as a contrasting "outside view" of things. The doctrine of separation shapes the "outside view," and in discussing further aspects of the Amish charter we turn now to the "inside view."

The Vow of Obedience

The ceremony of baptism may be viewed as a rite of passage from youth to adulthood, but it also reveals the "inside view" of things. The meaning of baptism to the individual and the community reflects ethos. Taking the baptismal vow admits one to full fellowship in the church. When young people reach late adolescence, they are urged to become members of the church. In their sermons, ministers challenge young people to join the church. The parents are concerned that young people take this step. In most cases no overt urging by the parents is necessary, since it is normal for young people to follow the role expectation and be baptized. No young person could be married in the Amish church without first being baptized in the faith.

After the spring communion, a class of instruction is held for all those who wish to join the church. This is known as *die Gemee nooch geh,* or literally, "to follow the church." The applicants meet with the ministers on Sunday morning at worship service in the *Kämmerli,* the consultation room where the ordained customarily meet. The ministers very simply acquaint the applicants for baptism with the incidents in the Bible that suggest the right relationship with God. At the same time the *Regel und Ordnung* (rules and order) of the Amish church are explained. After six or eight periods of instruction, roughly from about May to August, a day is set for the baptismal service. The consent of the members is obtained to receive the applicants into fellowship. Baptism occurs prior to the fall *Ordnungsgemee* (preparatory service), which is followed by *Grossgemee* (communion). Great emphasis is placed upon the difficulty of walking the "straight and narrow way." The applicants are told that it is better not to make a vow than to vow and later break it; on a Saturday prior to baptism they are asked to meet with the ministers where they are given opportunity to "turn back" if they so desire. The young men are asked to promise that they will accept the duties of a minister should the lot ever fall on them.

❖   ❖   ❖   ❖   ❖

The Rules for Living

Once the individual has been baptized, he is committed to keep the *Ordnung* or the rules of the church. For a single person this means keeping one's behavior more in line with the rules than before. With marriage the individual assumes responsibility for keeping the rules as well as for "building the church," which means taking an active part in promoting the rules.

The little Amish community is distinctive from other church groups in that the rules governing life are traditional ways not specified in writing. These rules can be known only by being a participant. The rules for living tend to form a body of sentiments that are essentially a list of taboos within the environment of the small Amish community.

All Amish members know the *Ordnung* of their church district and these generally remain oral and unwritten. Perhaps most rules are taken for granted and it is usually those questionable or borderline issues which are specified in the *Ordnung*. These rules are repeated at the *Ordnungsgemee* just preceding communion Sunday. They must have been unanimously endorsed by the ordained body. At the members' meeting following the regular service they are presented orally, after which members are asked to give assent. If there is any change from previous practice, allowing a new innovation or adaptation, this change is not announced. The former taboo is simply not mentioned. A unanimous expression of unity and "peace" with the *Ordnung* makes possible the communion. But without unity there can be no communion.

The following *Ordnung* of a contemporary group, published in English, appears to be representative of the Old Order Amish, except for those portions indicated by brackets. That it appears in print at all is evidence of change from the traditional practice of keeping it oral. This *Ordnung* allows a few practices not typically sanctioned by the Old Order: the giving of tithes, distribution of tracts, belief in assurance of salvation, and limited missionary activity.

ORDNUNG OF A CHRISTIAN CHURCH

Since it is the duty of the church, especially in this day and age, to decide what is fitting and proper and also what is not fitting and proper for a Christian to do, (in points that are not clearly stated in the Bible), we have considered it needful to publish this booklet listing some rules and ordinances of a Christian Church.

We hereby confess to be of one faith with the 18 articles of Faith adopted at Dortrecht, 1632, also with nearly all if not all articles in booklet entitled "Article und Ordnung der Christlichen Gemeinde."

No ornamental bright, showy form-fitting, immodest or silk-like clothing of any kind. Colors such as bright red, orange, yellow and pink not allowed. Amish form of clothing to be followed as a general rule. Costly Sunday clothing to be discouraged. Dresses not shorter than half-way between knees and floor, nor over eight inches from floor. Longer advisable. Clothing in every way modest, serviceable and as simple as scripturally possible. Only outside pockets allowed are on work eberhem or vomas and pockets on large overcoats. Dress shoes, if any, to be plain and black only. No high heels and pomp slippers, dress socks, if any, to be black except white for foot hygiene for both sexes. A plain, unshowy suspender without buckles.

Hat to be black with no less than 3-inch rim and not extremely high in crown. No stylish impression in any hat. No pressed trousers. No sweaters.

Prayer covering to be simple, and made to fit head. Should cover all the hair as nearly as possible and is to be worn wherever possible. [Pleating of caps to be discouraged.] No silk ribbons. Young children to dress according to the Word as well as parents. No pink or fancy baby blankets or caps.

Women to wear shawls, bonnets, and capes in public. Aprons to be worn at all times. No adorning of hair among either sex such as parting of hair among men and curling or waving among women.

A full beard should be worn among men and boys after baptism if possible. No shingled hair. Length at least half-way below tops of ears.

No decorations of any kind in buildings inside or out. No fancy yard fences. Linoleum, oilcloth, shelf and wall paper to be plain and unshowy. Over-stuffed furniture or any luxury items forbidden. No doilies or napkins. No large mirrors, (fancy glassware), statues or wall pictures for decorations.

[No embroidery work of any kind.] Curtains either dark green rollers or black cloth. No boughten dolls.

No bottle gas or high line electrical appliances.

Stoves should be black if bought new.

Weddings should be simple and without decorations. [Names not attached to gifts.]

No ornaments on buggies or harness.

Tractors to be used only for such things that can hardly be done with horses. Only either stationary engines or tractors with steel tires allowed. No airfilled rubber tires.

Farming and related occupations to be encouraged. Working in cities or factories not permissible. Boys and girls working out away from home for worldly people forbidden except in emergencies.

Worldly amusements as radios, card playing [party games], movies, fairs, etc., forbidden. [Reading, singing, tract distribution, Bible games, relief work, giving of tithes, etc., are encouraged.]

Musical instruments or different voice singing not permissible. No dirty, silly talking or sex teasing of children.

Usury forbidden in most instances. No government benefit payments or partnership in harmful associations. No insurance. No photographs.

No buying or selling of anything on Sunday. It should be kept according to the principles of the Sabbath. [Worship of some kind every Sunday.]

[Women should spend time doing good or reading God's Word instead of taking care of canaries, goldfish or house flowers.]

Church confession is to be made if practical where transgression was made. If not, a written request of forgiveness should be made to said church. All manifest sins to be openly confessed before church before being allowed to commune. I Tim. 5, 20. A period of time required before taking new members into full fellowship.

Because of great falling away from sound doctrine, we do not care to fellowship, that is hold communion, with any churches that allow or uphold any unfruitful works of darkness such as worldliness, fashionable attire, [bed-courtship, habitual smoking or drinking, old wives fables, non-assurance of salvation, anti-missionary zeal] or anything contrary to sound doctrine.

The rules of the Amish church cover the whole range of human experience. In a society where the goal is directed toward keeping the world out, there are many taboos, and customs become symbolic. There are variations in what is allowed from one community to another in the United States and Canada. Custom is regional and therefore not strictly uniform. The most universal of all Amish norms across the United States and Canada are the following: no electricity, telephones, central-heating systems, automobiles, or tractors with pneumatic tires; required are beards but not moustaches for all married men, long hair (which must be parted in the center, if allowed at all), hooks-and-eyes on dresscoats, and the use of horses for farming and travel. No formal education beyond the elementary grades is a rule of life.

The *Ordnung* is an essential part of the Amish charter. It is the way in which the moral postulates of society are expressed and carried out in life. The charter is constantly subjected to forces of change, a source of conflict to be discussed later.

The Punishment of the Disobedient

A moral principle in the little Amish community is the practice of *Bann und Meidung.* These words rendered in English mean excommunication and shunning. *Meidung* was the crucial question in the controversy that gave rise to the Amish as a sect movement in their secession from the Swiss Brethren. This doctrine was intrinsic in the Anabaptist movement from its very beginning and appeared in the earliest confession of faith. The Anabaptist concept of the church was that it should be a pure church of believers only; persons who fall into sin must be first excommunicated, then shunned. Menno Simons taught that the ban applies to "all—great and small, rich and poor, without any respect of persons, who once passed under the Word but have now fallen back, those living or teaching offensively in the house of the Lord—until they repent." The method of dealing with a backslider is that given by Christ in Matthew 18:15–17, and "If he neglect to hear the church, let him be unto thee as a heathen man and a publican." In other words, a person who has broken his vow and will not mend his ways must be expelled just as the human body casts off an ulcer or infectious growth. Through the years the *Meidung* has been applied in different ways. The doctrine among the Mennonites of Holland and Switzerland was of a mild character, in which the offender was excluded from communion. But a stricter conception of the ban was advanced by Jakob Ammann. The strict interpretation requires shunning of all (1) members who leave the Amish church to join another and (2) members who marry outside the brotherhood. *Meidung* requires that members receive no favors from the excommunicated person, that they do not buy from or sell to an excommunicated person, that no member shall eat at the same table with an excommunicated person, and if the case involves husband or wife, they are to suspend their usual marital relations.

The Amish make no effort to evangelize or proselyte the outsider, nor are they concerned with the redemption of the outside society to the extent that they wish to draw members from the outer society into the brotherhood. It is their primary concern to keep their own baptized members from slipping into the outer world, or into other religious groups. With greater mobility and ease of travel and communication, isolation is breaking down, and Amish solidarity is threatened by more and more of their members wanting to become like outsiders. The Amish leaders meet this threat with the ban. Members who wish to have automobiles, radios, or the usual comforts of modern living, face the threat of being excommunicated and shunned. Thus the ban is used as an instrument of discipline, not only for the drunkard or the adulterer, but for the person who transgresses the order of the church. It is a powerful instrument for keeping the church intact and for preventing members from involvement in the wider society.

The meaning of *Bann und Meidung* is made clearer if we understand how it works in life situations. Let us take the case of a young man whom we shall fictitiously name Joseph. Joseph grew up in a very strict Amish home, under the guidance of parents who were known for their orthodoxy. He was baptized at the age of twenty. Three years after his baptism Joseph was excommunicated and shunned. Charges laid against him included the following: he had attended a revival meeting, began to chum with excommunicated persons, bought an automobile, and began to attend a Mennonite church.

Joseph was excommunicated with the counsel of the assembly and was informed in their presence. After being asked to leave the service he thought to himself: "It is strange to think that I am now to be 'mited.' I don't feel very comfortable." At home, the young man was shunned: he could no longer eat at the family table. He ate at a separate table, with the younger children, or after the baptized persons finished eating. Joseph was urged to mend his ways, to make good his broken promise. His normal work relations and conversational pattern were strained. Several times he attended preaching services with his family. Since members may not accept services, goods, or favors from excommunicated members, he could not take his sisters to church, even if he used a buggy instead of his offensive automobile, but they could drive a buggy and take him along. It was not long until Joseph accepted employment with a non-Amish person and began using his automobile for transportation to and from home. When shunned friends came to his home for conversation, Joseph's parents met them at the gate and turned them away. It was not long until father and mother asked him to leave home. He explained: "I had to move away from home or my parents could not take communion. My parents were afraid that younger persons in the family would be led astray. They didn't exactly chase me off the place, but I was no longer welcome at home."

One of the purposes of excommunication is to restore the erring member by showing him his lost condition so that he will turn to repentance. The excommunication service itself is a painful and sober procedure. John Umble's description is fitting: "The excommunication of members was an awful and solemn procedure. The members to be expelled had been notified in advance and were present. An air of tenseness filled the house. Sad-faced women wept quietly; stern men sat with faces drawn. The bishop arose; with trembling voice and with tears on his cheek he announced that the guilty parties had confessed their sin, that they were cast off from the fellowship of the church and committed to the devil and all his angels (*dem Teufel und allen seinen Engeln übergeben*). He cautioned all the members to exercise 'shunning rigorously.'"

Once an individual is in a state of *Bann* (or *Bond* as the Amish call it), members are to receive no favors from him. In a very real sense he is "an outcast, rejected of God and man. His only hope is not to die before he should be reinstated, lest he should be an outcast also in the world to come."

Among the Amish communities today there are numerous divisions as a result of differing opinions on shunning. The moderate interpretation of the ban, taken by most of the midwestern groups, holds that moral transgressors should be excommunicated and shunned, but if the offender is restored to another Christian church of the non-resistant faith, then shunning should no longer be applied. But this, according to the adherents of the strict ban, is a departure from Jakob Ammann. In speaking of a former Amish member who joined the Mennonites a bishop told the writer: "The only way for us to lift the ban is for him to make peace with the Old Order church, going back to one of them and living his promise he made in his baptismal vow on his knees before God and the church. It does not need to be here but in any of the churches that are in peace with us." According to this view, an excommunicated person must be shunned for life unless he restores his previous relationship with the group. The ban becomes an effective means of dispensing with the offender. By shunning him in all social relations, he is given a status that minimizes the threat to other members of the community. This perpetuation of the controversy undoubtedly aids the Old Order group to remain distinct and socially isolated.

Closeness to Nature

The little Amish community has a strong affinity for the soil and for nature. Unlike science, which is occupied with the theoretical reconstruction of the order of the world, the Amish view comes from direct contact with nature by the reality of work. The physical world is good, and in itself not corrupting or evil. The beautiful is apprehended in the universe, by the orderliness of the seasons, the heavens, the world of growing plants as well as the many species of animals, and by the forces of living and dying. While it is wrong to attend a show in a theater, it is not uncommon for an Amish family to visit the zoo or the circus to see the animals God has made.

The Amishman feels contact with the world through the working of his muscles and the aching of his limbs. In the little Amish community toil is proper and good, religion provides meaning, and the bonds of family and church provide human satisfaction and love.

The charter of Amish life requires members to limit their occupation to farming or closely associated activity such as operating a saw mill, carpentry, or mason work. In Europe the Amish lived in rural areas, always having a close association with the soil, so that the community was entirely agrarian in character. It is only in America that the Amish have found it necessary to make occupational regulations for protection from the influence of urbanism.

The preference for rural living is reflected in attitudes and in the informal relations of group life, rather than in an explicit dogma. For the Amish, God is manifest more in closeness to nature, in the soil and in the weather, and among plants and animals, than he is in the man-made city. Hard work, thrift, and mutual aid find sanction in the Bible. The city by contrast is held to be the center of leisure, of non-productive spending, and often of wickedness. The Christian life, they contend, is best maintained away from the cities. God created Adam and Eve to "replenish the earth, and subdue it; and have dominion over the fish of the sea, and over the fowl of the air, and over every living thing that moveth upon the earth." In the same way, man's highest place in the universe today is to care for the things of creation. One Amishman said, "The Lord told Adam to replenish the earth and to rule over the animals and the land—you can't do that in cities." Another said, "While the Lord's blessings were given to the people who remained in the country, sickness and ruination befell Sodom. Shows, dances, parties, and other temptations ruin even the good people who now live in cities. Families are small in cities; in the city you never know where your wife is, and city women can't cook. People go hungry in the cities but you will never starve if you work hard in the country."

The Amish have generally prospered on the land more often than their neighbors. Lancaster County, Pennsylvania, which is the center of Amish life, has long been distinguished as the garden spot of the nation, representing an intensive kind of farming on relatively small holdings. Their success is based upon long experience with agricultural practices in the Old World and upon a philosophy of work and thrift.

❖   ❖   ❖   ❖   ❖

. . . The Amish attribute their material success in farming to divine blessing.

The main objective of their farming, as Walter Kollmorgen has pointed out, "is to accumulate sufficient means to buy enough land to keep all the children on farms. To this end the Amish work hard, produce abundantly, and save extensively."

❖ ❖ ❖ ❖ ❖

There are other moral directives in the little community but these form the essential core of what is viewed as right and wrong. The view of life and of man's place in the total scheme of things are determined by the sacred guides to life. These guide are: a biblical view of separation from the world, the vow of obedience, observance of the *Ordnung*, upholding the true doctrine of shunning, and living close to the God-created environment. In all of these tradition plays an important part. The people of the little Amish community tend to regard the ways of their ancestors as sacred and to believe that these time-hallowed practices should be carefully guarded.

The Symbolic Community

The Amish community is a multibonded community. The members are held together not by a single interest but by many symbolic ties which they have in common. The ecologic and ceremonial functions are bounded by the limits of horse-and-buggy travel. But there exists also a symbolic community made up of many social rules for living and a culture that has set definite boundaries. A member of the Amish faith is bound to the norms and practices of his social group. He is a member of the in-group or *unser Satt Leit* (our sort of people) and is marked by certain symbols. The out-group is *anner Satt Leit* (other sorts of people), who are distinguished by their symbols. This sharp line of distinction gives rise to a general principle by which in-groups tend to stereotype out-groups, and any threat from an out-group tends to intensify the cohesion of the in-group.

Before observing in detail the intimately shared activities which make the Amish community a multibonded one, it is well to note the over-all complexity of these ties. Language provides a guide to a social reality that is different from that of other people. All new members with rare exceptions are offspring and they are assimilated gradually by a majority of the old members. Physical property, including farms that were the abodes of the forefathers, and preference for certain soils and topography come to have sentimental attachment. Common traditions and ideals which have been revered by the whole community from generation to generation embody the expectations of all. All relatives are Amish or of Amish descent. There are formal church rules that guide the members in their conduct with each other and with outsiders. The specialists, the lifetime ordained persons, carry on the functions of the church and enable it to act as a unit in maintaining separation from the world. The size of each church district is kept to a minimum, enabling it to function as a small, intimate, and informally controlled group, whereas largeness would make consensus more difficult. There are special means to resist shock such as mutual aid in times of fire, death, and sickness. The life of the community is prolonged because the basic needs of the individual are met from the cradle to the grave. The Amish baby grows up strongly attached to those of his kind and remains indifferent to contacts outside his culture. The tendency to symbolize all of life provides a basis for action in meeting the future. It assures internal unity and community longevity.

Symbols, Convention, and Tradition

Symbols form an important maintenance function in everyday life. The symbols are different from the non-Amish or "English" symbols. In the world around them, the Amish see the symbols of worldly civilization. They are such objects as the cathedral, the skyscraper, the modernistically designed automobile and house, the television set, the missile, and modern ways of clothing the body. To the Amishman these symbols represent the world. They are a reminder of danger to him and are to be avoided.

The Amish have their own symbolism which provides a basis for common consciousness and a common course of action. We may hypothesize that in a simple society like the Amish the people themselves become symbolic, and not their achievements as in world civilization. The horse and buggy, the beard of the married man, and the styles of dress—all take on symbolic meaning. All Amish know that this is the accepted way of doing things, and symbolism becomes an effective means of social control as the nonconformist can quickly be detected from the conformist. Symbols which are universal in all Amish communities include the following: hooks-and-eyes on the Sunday coat and vest of all men, trouser styles that have no fly-closing but a flap that buttons along the waist, wide-brimmed black-felt hats for men, white organdy caps for women, plain rather than patterned or striped dresses for women, uncut hair for women, and long hair cut in bangs for men. All these symbols together constitute a world of social reality, a way of life that teaches how people should live and what they should imitate.

An illustration of convention which is symbolic is the way courtesy is expressed among the Amish. Acts rather than words perform this function. In a small society where convention is understood few words are needed between actor and alter to make meanings precise. Words of courtesy, as expressed by the English-speaking world, are conspicuously absent among members of the Amish family and community. The dialect contains few if any words of endearment between husband and wife, but young people of courting age frequently employ English words of endearment. Amish parents who hear "English" couples exchange words like "honey" and "sweetheart" have remarked that such a relationship is probably anything but "sweet." There are no words in the Amish spoken language that correspond to "pardon me" or "excuse me." Children might use such English terms in their play but persistence in using them in family relationships would not be approved. They would be accused of trying to be "society" persons. "Oops" is sometimes used to indicate that a certain act was not intentional. "Please" and "thank you" are not a part of table manners nor a part of everyday conversation, but children are taught to say *Denki* (thank you) and *Willkomm* (you are welcome) when giving or receiving gifts on special occasions.

Acts of politeness are much more characteristic than words. The wife may brush the husband's hat on Sunday morning before he gets around to it. The act requires no "thank you." If the husband is thoughtful he will carry the toddler, help his wife into the carriage, and tuck the blankets around her. Belching is a normal occurrence around the dinner table and conceived as a sign of good appetite with no thought of discourtesy. A boy who was chewing his food vigorously at the breakfast table was greeted by his older brother with the words: "Fer was machst so wiescht?" (Why do you make so ugly?) The boy did not reply but modified his behavior. However, in the presence of English people the Amish will adopt the polite language of the outsider. An Amish woman walking along a village sidewalk who approached a woman washing her sidewalk said "pardon me" as she stepped over the washed part of the sidewalk.

Symbolism in Amish life performs the functions of communication. When much of life is governed by symbols, fewer words are needed for communication. The conspicuous absence of words of courtesy in the Amish dialect would appear to be a function of the importance of symbols, making such words unnecessary. Like dress patterns, the speech habits have also been preserved in the New World. Polite language in Medieval Europe was characteristic of the nobility and not of the peasant groups. Actions among the Amish speak louder than words of courtesy. Acts and intentions are understood, while words of courtesy which might be adopted from the English language would not be understood. The large number of symbols which function within the Amish society aid the growing Amish child to find his place within the family, the community, and within the world of the Amish people.

The Language of Dress

Anything that can be perceived through the senses can be symbolized, and in Amish society styles of dressing become very important as symbols of group identity. The garb not only admits the individual to full fellowship but also clarifies his role and status within his society.

The hat, for example, distinguishes the Amishman from the outsider and also symbolizes his role within his social structure. When the two-year-old boy discards a dress and begins wearing trousers for the first time, he also receives a stiff jet-black hat with three or more inches of brim. Hat manufacturers produce at least twenty-eight different sizes and a dozen different styles of Amish hats. The bridegroom in Pennsylvania gets a telescopic hat that is worn during the early married years. The hat is distinguished by a permanent crease around the top of the crown. Grandfather's hat has a four-inch crown and a four-inch brim. The bishop's hat has a four- and one-half-inch crown, slightly rounded, and a wide seam around the brim. A hat which has a flatter crown is worn by the rank and file of Amish fathers. The outsider may never notice these differences, or if he does he may regard them as accidental. But to the Amish these symbols indicate whether people are fulfilling the expectations of the group. A young man who wears a hat with a brim that is too narrow is liable for sanction. The very strict Amish congregations can be distinguished from the more progressive ones by the width of the brim and the band around the crown. Thus when the writer's family moved from Pennsylvania to Iowa, one of the first adaptations to make was to take out the scissors and cut off some of the brim. This made my brothers and myself more acceptable to the new community of Amish. At the same time the act symbolized other adaptations that had to be made to adjust to a more "westernized" group of Old Order Amish.

❖   ❖   ❖   ❖   ❖

One of the most highly symbolic of all garments among the women is the *Kapp* or head cap worn by every woman and even by infants. Girls from about age twelve to marriage wear a black cap for Sunday dress and a white cap at home. After marriage a white cap is always worn. The size, style, and color of caps varies slightly with regions and with degrees of orthodoxy in a single community. The fine pleats ironed into some of these caps requires hours of tedious work. The specific way in which they are made, including the width of the *fedderdeel* (front part) and the *hinnerdeel* (back part), and the width of the pleats and seams are sacred symbols of the community. Though this headpiece has undergone some changes in detail, the present Amish cap is essentially the same as that worn by the Palatine women of earlier centuries. Among most American Mennonites of Swiss-German origin the cap has become a "prayer cap" or "veiling" required of women "when praying or prophesying." (I Corinthians 11:5)

These few illustrations of Amish dress could be supported with still many others. But this is sufficient to indicate how dress styles serve as symbols for a group. The symbols function very effectively in maintaining separatism and continuity. The language of dress forms a common understanding and mutual appreciation among those who share the same traditions and expectations. Dress keeps the insider separate from the world and also keeps the outsider out. These shared conventions are given sacred sanction and biblical justification: *unser Satt Leit* (our sort of people) are distinguishable from *englische Leit* (English people) or *anner Satt Leit* (other people). The attempts by theatricals to reproduce the dress of the

Amish never quite measure up to the authentic. They appear ludicrous if not hilarious to the Amish.

The Language of Speech

The Amish community is also a speech community. Language provides familiarity in which individuals find common grounds for understanding. Although the Amish came from Switzerland, from Alsace and Lorraine in France, and from the Rhineland of Germany, yet their conversational speech is remarkably uniform. The reason for this is that they came from the same (Allemanic) dialect-speaking area. Some of the Alsatian Amish could speak French when they arrived in America and a few French words have been incorporated into their dialect which is Pennsylvania Dutch (or German). Dutch in this instance is a usage from "Deutsch" meaning German, and not the language of the Netherlands. The four districts of Amish in Adams County, Indiana, around Berne, speak a Swiss dialect, but it poses no real barrier for interaction with other Amish. An Amish person traveling from Pennsylvania through the midwestern states on a kinship visit can speak his own familiar dialect and be understood.

Linguists have observed that the Amish are trilingual, that is, they can speak three somewhat distinctive yet intermixed tongues. These are: Pennsylvania Dutch, High German, and English. The usage of three distinctive tongues, rather than one or two languages, lends itself to social isolation in that there are speech groupings within the community. Roles and functions tend to organize around each language; thus when speaking English the Amishman tends to think and behave like the English-speaking person.

Pennsylvania Dutch is the familiar tongue of children at home and in informal conversation. It is the mother tongue of children born to Amish parents. Professor Albert Buffington has made it clear that this speech is not a "garbled English" or "corrupted German in the mouths of ignorant people who speak with a heavy accent," but a distinct dialect of the German language. The dialect resembles the Palatine German folk speech. It is, of course, spoken by many Pennsylvania Dutch people who are not Amish.

The second language of the growing Amish child is English. A child is introduced to English when he attends school; as he learns it he also learns that his non-Amish playmates are "English" or *Englischer* in the dialect. They are *anner Satt Leit* (the other sort of people). Amish children learn to speak the two languages without difficulty and without noticeable accent. Upon entering school the child frequently has no English vocabulary, but he readily learns his second language.

English is used when speaking with non-Amish persons in town, at school, or when talking to an "English" visitor or salesman. Thus Amishmen employ the English language on "forced" occasions. An Amish person may shift his conversation from the dialect to English, or from English to the dialect, whichever he finds most convenient for the situation. An outsider as a guest at an Amish table may find that dialect chatter prevails at one end of the table, while one or two members of the family keep the general conversation in English for the benefit of the guest. Frey has described the Amish use of English as "American English built on a framework of Pennsylvania Dutch language patterns and interjected continually with whole or part loan-translations from the dialect." The Amish generally experience little difficulty in speaking correct English.

High German, or more precisely "Amish High German," is used exclusively for the preaching service and at formal ceremonial occasions.

❖　❖　❖　❖　❖

The Amish nomenclature denoting an outsider as an *Englischer* has symbolic meaning. Such a general term means that he may be Methodist, Baptist, Lutheran, or anything but Amish. The Mennonites are not classed as English. Since the Mennonites are only a step removed from the Amish they are *Mennischte* and not really as "English" as other people. On the other hand a person of Catholic affiliation is called a *Gedolischer* (from the German word *Katholischer*). Outsiders who are neighbors of the Amish people often refer to the Amish as "The Dutch."

Conversation in the dialect becomes an especially important function of community life as the Amish are very sociable and hospitable people. The Amish devote more space to the subject of visiting in their weekly newspaper than to any other topic. Visits to the homes, preaching services, particularly before and after the service, funerals, weddings, sales, quiltings, barn-raisings, frolics of various kinds, sewings, singings, and Sunday visiting are all occasions for conversing at length.

Controlled and Limited Education

Limiting education to the elementary grades prevents exposure to many areas of scientific knowledge and vocational training. It functions also as a form of boundary maintenance. New inventions and knowledge find their way into the little Amish community by many diffuse and delayed means. As soon as the law will allow, Amish children are taken out of school for work at home. The Amish viewpoint is that "Our people are engaged in some form of agriculture and we feel positive that as farmers we are better off with only a common school education. Education does not build muscle like tilling the soil in the open field and sunshine with lots of hard work. If a boy does little hard work before he is twenty-one, he probably never gets to like it afterward. In other words, he will not amount to much as a farmer."

Conflict over the school question arose in Pennsylvania, a few years later in Ohio, and continues in some areas. Pennsylvania law requires that children attend school until their seventeenth birthday but that children engaged in farm work may be excused through permits when they reach the age of fifteen. The conflict arose when it became clear that some Amish children completed grade eight more than once because their parents were opposed to sending them to high schools. When the parents were summoned to court and refused to pay their fines on grounds that this would admit to being guilty, they were sent to jail. Friends and businessmen paid the fines to release the parents. Some were arrested as many as ten times. The Amish took the position that compulsory attendance beyond the elementary grades interferes with the exercise of their religious liberty. Meanwhile a compromise plan has been worked out in Pennsylvania where pupils who have completed grade eight report to special "Saturday" schools conducted by the Amish themselves. Some of the more progressive Amish groups have allowed their children to enter the high school believing that it is not wrong to comply with the law. The Old Order Amish state that their children are needed for agricultural labor at home and that farming does not require higher education. The Amish leaders believe that exposure to the consolidated high school would constitute a real danger to their future community life. An Amishman who was called to court for challenging the school attendance law said: "We teach our children not to smoke or use profane language and do such things as that. I know most of the high school pupils smoke cigarettes and many girls I guess too. . . . It is better to have them at home. . . ."

The Amish strategy is merely one of withdrawal from the world. In some areas school boards have been able to keep the one-room school open in deference to the Amish, and in other areas where consolidation has occurred the Amish have built their own schools. The establishment of their own schools in recent times is an attempt to avoid participation in the centralized school and to bypass its whole socializing influence, rather than for the purpose of religious indoctrination. However, there seems to be a tendency after several years of experience for some schools to take over from the home the function of teaching religion.

The Old Order Amish are firm in their stand against formal education in the American high school. It is an effective means of maintenance, especially when linked to the doctrine of shunning. With set limits to the amount of knowledge a young person can acquire on one hand, and with the dread of censure (and of excommunication) on the other, one can scarcely find a more effective way of bounding the little community. A person who receives knowledge outside of the Amish bounds equips himself for capable living outside of the Amish community but makes himself liable to the severe sanctions of the ban and shunning. Limited knowledge preserves the existing order of things; it reinforces traditional values by keeping alternate courses of action to a minimum. Traditional values and stereotypes are thus maintained by unfamiliarity with alternate courses of action. Furthermore, questions about in-group practices are kept to a minimum.

SEXUAL CODES IN
TEEN-AGE CULTURE

Ira L. Reiss

Some contemporary sociologists maintain that the adolescent age group develops a subculture somewhat divergent from the main stream of adult culture. Others suggest that the adolescent differences we observe are only imperfect reflections of the dominant group behavior. Regardless of the position one takes, it is important to recognize that adolescents spend much of their time in association with their own age group. Thus the teen-age codes will greatly affect behavior within this age group, although adult, particularly parental, norms will remain important. This selection analyzes the modern code in an important realm of adolescent behavior.

Teen-age sexual codes reflect quite clearly the bold outlines of adult sexual codes. The high degree of conformity in teen-age culture increases the observability of teen-age beliefs and adds to our understanding of adult beliefs. The teen-ager exists in a world somewhere between youthful idealism and adult realism, and his sexual codes reflect this state of being. In a very real sense, he is a marginal man with one foot in the world of the child and the other foot in the world of the adult.

The teen-ager is at the stage at which it is vitally important for him to learn how to exist in society independent of his parents. For this reason, he transfers his dependence to his peers and strives to learn from them the secrets of entrance into the adult world. One would think that this vaguely defined status of "almost adult" would lead to confusion and weak statements of belief. To a large extent, this is the case, but, nevertheless, it is equally true that it leads to dogmatic statements of belief and a search for conviction through conformity. Teen-agers translate and adapt the sexual codes of adults to fit their particular circumstance and state of mind.

Going Steady

When unchaperoned dating gained prevalence in the early part of this century, it involved a much more rapid change of dating partners than

SOURCE: *The Annals of the American Academy of Political & Social Science,* Vol. 338 (November, 1961), 53–62. Reprinted by permission. ✧ The author is associate professor of sociology and anthropology at the State University of Iowa. His chief interests include the sociology of the family, theory, and methodology. He is the author of *Premarital Sexual Standards in America.*

occurs today. Nevertheless, by the time of World War II, going steady had taken root, and, today, it seems that slightly more than half of the high school students have some going-steady experience. Even among the early teen-agers, possibly one quarter go steady.

Class differences are important in examining the going-steady complex. It seems that those high school people who go steady and plan to go to college are not likely to marry their high school steadies, and those who are from lower economic classes and who do not plan to go to college are much more likely to marry their high school steadies. Thus, in looking at the custom of going steady, one must realize that there are different subtypes and that the consequences differ for each type.

Although a psychologist may point to the security of going steady as its chief reason for being, as a sociologist, I would point out how Western society has, for centuries, been developing an association of sexual behavior with mutual affection. This association is hard to achieve in casual dating; but, in steady dating, sex and affection can quite easily be combined, and, in this way, a potential strain in the social system is reduced. Another area of strain which is reduced by going steady is the conflict a girl may feel between her desire for sexual experience and her desire to maintain her reputation. For many, sexual behavior is made respectable by going steady. In these ways, one may say that no other dating custom is quite as central to the understanding of teen-age sexual codes as going steady.

Girls' Sexual Codes

One of the most popular sexual codes among teen-age girls is petting-with-affection. This code is a modern day subtype of our formal abstinence standard. This subtype of abstinence seems extremely popular among high school couples who are going steady. Such couples feel it is proper to engage in heavy petting if they are going steady, the justification being that they are in love or at least extremely fond of each other. The petting-with-affection sex code probably grew along with the going-steady custom; they both illustrate adaptations of our dating institution to the newer unchaperoned dating circumstances.

What evidence do we have for such petting behavior among teen-agers? Though surely not perfect, the most extensive study of sexual behavior is that done by the Institute for Sex Research, formerly headed by Alfred C. Kinsey and now run by Paul H. Gebhard. It should be noted that the Kinsey studies are most valid for urban, white, northeastern, college-educated people, and, thus, great care must be taken when applying the results to other groups. The reader should keep in mind the tenuousness of any such generalizations made in this paper.

Kinsey's data show that, of the females who were twenty years old or older when interviewed, about one fifth to one fourth admitted they had petted to orgasm while still in their teens. Most of this behavior occurred between the ages of sixteen and twenty. About three-quarters of all the girls twenty years old or more admitted being aroused by some form of petting or kissing in their teens, and approximately 90 per cent stated they had a least been kissed during their teens.

Those girls who marry in their teens start their petting and kissing behavior earlier than those who marry later. In general, the few years previous to marriage are by far the most sexually active for girls. Lower class females marry earlier, and, thus, they are more active in their teens and more likely to marry their teen-age steadies.

The above rates are averages for Kinsey's entire sample of several thousand females; were we to take only the females born in more recent decades, the rates would be considerably higher. For example, of those females born before 1900, only 10 per cent ever petted to orgasm in their teens, whereas, of those girls born in the 1920's, almost 30 per cent, or three times the proportion, petted to orgasm in their teens.

It seems clear that we have developed not only new dating forms such as going steady but also, as we have seen, new sexual codes to go with them. These new codes allow females much more freedom in heavy petting, provided affection is involved. Of course, other girls, particularly in the early teens, adhere to standards which only permit kissing, and a few others adhere to standards which allow full sexual relations, but, by and large, petting-with-affection seems the increasingly popular sex code for high school girls.

The most recent evidence of the nature of teen-age sex codes also supports these contentions. This evidence comes from research which the author is engaged in at present. Some preliminary reports on this study were made in the author's book *Premarital Sexual Standards in America*. The study involves 1,000 high school and college students, most of whom are teen-agers. Although final analysis of the study has not been completed, it is clear that petting-with-affection is an extremely popular code with teen-age girls, particularly with the teen-agers who are high school juniors and seniors.

Finally, one should note that, in my own study and in the Kinsey study, religion was another key factor affecting girls' sexual beliefs and behaviors. Those girls who were devout in their religion were much more conservative in their sexual behavior and belief. Religion was not as strong a factor for boys and did not control their behavior as much. As we shall see, amount of education was the key determinant for male sexual behavior.

Boys' Sexual Codes

Among the teen-age boys, we find a quite different code dominant. Abstinence is given some form of lip service, particularly among the more highly educated classes, but, by and large, it is not an operational code; it is not adhered to in the behavior of the majority of the teen-age boys. Even among the males destined for college, about half have coitus in their teens;

among those who stop their education in high school, about three-quarters have coitus in their teens, and, among those whose education stops before high school, about eight-tenths have coitus in their teens. Thus, it is clear that the majority of all males, in this sample of Kinsey's at least, experienced full sexual relations before reaching twenty years of age.

For teen-age girls, the rate of nonvirginity appears to be considerably lower. Kinsey reports approximately 20 per cent nonvirginity for females by age twenty. Of course, the greater liberality of the boys does not involve a single standard; that is, they are predominantly adherents of the double standard which allows boys to have coitus but condemns girls for the same thing. This is an ancient standard reaching back many thousands of years in Western culture. It is by no means a universal standard, however, for we do find many cultures where the sexes are treated equally.

Although in recent generations, due to our greater equalitarianism and the evolving nature of the dating institution, the double standard seems to have been weakened sharply, it is still quite dominant among teen-age boys. The greater freedom allowed the male child in almost all areas of life constantly buttresses this standard and makes it seem obvious to teen-agers. Teen-agers are not sufficiently objective or sophisticated to be bothered by the contradictions in this or any other sexual code. For example, if all women abided fully by the double standard, then no men could, for the men would have no partners! Thus, this code operates only to the extent that someone violates it.

Some of these double standard teen-age boys will condemn a girl who accepts petting-with-affection, for they believe heavy petting is improper for girls. However, my own data indicate that most of these teen-age males will accept heavy petting in a going-steady relationship. They, of course, allow themselves to go further and may try to have coitus with a steady in order to see if she is a "good" girl. It is not unusual to find a relationship either broken up or its affectionate nature altered if a girl gives in to her double standard steady. Such condemnatory behavior on the part of double standard males keeps many girls from going as far sexually as they might want to. Thus, the double standard male eliminates many potential sex partners because of the attitude he takes toward such sex partners.

Teen-age double standard males are often stricter than their older brothers who accept coitus for a girl when she is in love and/or engaged. These teen-age males are supported in this rigidity by the conformity of their peer group. Double standard males typically view the act of coitus as a conquest, as a source of peer group prestige. Thus, they are quite prone to tell their friends all of the details of any affair. This characteristic tends further to discourage females from yielding to double standard males. Instead, the girl is encouraged to be, in part at least, a tease, that is, to show just enough sexual activity to keep the male interested but not enough to arouse his condemnation. Sexual behavior in this sense involves a great deal of the aspect of a game. Sex comes to be used as a power leverage to control the relationship. Under such circumstances, sexual desire is developed so sharply in the male and so differently in the female that the male wants the female to be both sexually active and sexually pure. Under such conditions, sexual behavior can only with great difficulty relate directly to feelings of affection. This is particularly true for the act of coitus. In fact, one finds very often an inverse relation, in that boys prefer to have coitus with girls they do not care for, because they regard the girls they do care for as "too good" for such behavior. Girls, too, may control their sexual reactions, particularly with someone they care for, until they are sure they will not be condemned for their sexual response.

Thus, in the area of coitus among teen-agers, the double standard does seem to block the association of sex and affection. However, one should quickly add that, on the level of petting, sex and affection can more easily be combined, for this behavior is much more likely to be accepted for both sexes by both males and females.

Minor Standards

There are minor teen-age standards which are more permissive than petting-with-affection or the double standard. For the older teen-ager, the most popular minor standard is what I shall call permissiveness-with-affection. This standard accepts full sexual intercourse for both boys and girls, provided they are involved in a stable, affectionate relationship. The degree of stability and affection required varies among adherents from feeling strong affection to being in love and engaged. Some teen-age couples who are going steady have coitus in accord with this standard. The situation here is quite different from that of the double standard boy and his girl friend, for, in permissiveness-with-affection, both the boy and girl accept for each other what they are doing. They combine sex with affection and use affection as one of the key justifications of the sexual act.

There is a class difference in sexual standards among boys. My evidence indicates that the lower classes are more likely to be strong supporters of the double standard, while the upper classes, though still mostly double standard, contain a large proportion of boys who are not so dogmatic in their beliefs and a minority who accept permissiveness-with-affection. In general, the upper classes seem to stress equality of the sexes and the importance of affection more than the lower classes. A permissiveness-without-affection code seems more widespread at the lower levels.

Age is a crucial factor among teen-agers. Teen-agers under sixteen are much more likely to accept only kissing than are older teen-agers, who may accept petting or coitus. As noted earlier, religion does not restrict sexual behavior as much among boys as it does among girls. Education is a more important factor, with the more highly educated groups being the most conservative.

Promiscuity

The newspapers from time to time pick up stories of high school "sex clubs" and other forms of promiscuous teen-age sexual behavior. The available evidence indicates that promiscuous coitus is common predominantly for double standard males and a few females. Promiscuous coitus is not common on an equalitarian basis, that is, where both male and female accept the behavior as right for each other. Our culture has stressed the association of sex-with-affection to such an extent that it is difficult, at least for many females, to violate this association in coitus. In the case of petting, one finds more likelihood of violation of this norm by both men and women, but, in the case of coitus, it is much more often violated by males. Ehrmann's study of 1,000 college students supports this difference between male and female sexual activity and attitudes. Females, in addition to associating love with sexual behavior more than males, also have more non-sexual motives for sexual behavior, such as the desire to please the boy or to cement a relationship.

During the teens, the sexual outlets of boys and girls differ considerably. The chief outlet for girls seems to be masturbation and petting, whereas for boys the chief outlets include coitus at the fore. In Kinsey's sample, about one third of the girls masturbated to orgasm in their teens, while over 90 per cent of the boys have so masturbated in their teens. Despite their high rate of masturbation, males also have a high rate of coitus. The lower class boys rely less on masturbation and petting and more on coitus for their sexual outlets than do those boys who go to college.

The teen-age girl today is still typically the much more conservative partner and the guardian of sexual limits. However, she appears increasingly to be a half-willing guardian who more and more seeks her self-satisfaction and strives to achieve sexual equality.

There is a general trend in American society toward more equalitarian and more permissive sexual codes in all areas. This is true for teen-age sexual codes, too. The growth within abstinence of petting-with-affection is one sign of this increasing equalitarian and permissive force. Also, within the double standard, one finds increased willingness by males to accept some coitus on the part of females, especially if it occurs when the girl is in love and/or engaged. Finally, in the minor standard of permissiveness-with-affection, one sees this trend in the increased strength of this standard among teen-agers, particularly among older, college teen-agers. And these trends toward equalitarianism and permissiveness seem even stronger among older dating couples in their twenties. The teen-agers are relatively new at sexual behavior, and they, at first, grab the basic outlines of the older couples' codes. With the passage of time, they come to behave in a somewhat more equalitarian and permissive manner.

In my current research, there is evidence that the real change-over in a teen-ager's sexual code is more one of integrating attitudes and changing overt behavior than of changing basic attitudes. In short, it seems that a person holds his basic sexual attitudes in rudimentary form in his teens, but he is not fully ready to act upon them and has not fully learned how to combine these values into a coherent code of living. As he learns to do this, his behavior changes and so does his awareness of his beliefs and their unity, but his basic beliefs may well remain the same. This entire area of how our sexual beliefs are formed and how they change is in need of more careful study. My own research is aimed at probing some aspects of this problem.

Parents are prone to be most aware of what they consider excessive sexual behavior, for they are concerned about the consequences of such behavior as they may affect their children. Thus, parents complain about sexual acts of which they become aware, and they often believe teen-agers are sexually promiscuous. Actually, according to our best estimates, the real increases in teen-age sexual behavior over the last generation are not in the area of sexual intercourse but rather in the area of petting and in the public nature of some petting behavior. Thus, these parents of today have probably had similar rates of coitus but perhaps lower rates of petting. In addition, one should note that the petting behavior today very often is not promiscuous but occurs in a stable affectionate relationship.

Youth Culture: Tame or Wild?

About twenty years ago, Kingsley Davis and Talcott Parsons wrote of a youth culture and of a parent-youth conflict and, in doing so, implied in part that youth culture was largely irresponsible, impulsive, and antiadult. Many people have come to share this view and to expect rather extreme sexual behavior from teen-agers. I myself formerly accepted this view of the teen-ager as valid. However, after examining the evidence in the key areas of teen-age sexual behavior, I must admit that I can no longer accept such a conception of youth culture without serious modification and quali-fication. I would submit that the vast majority of our approximately twenty million teen-agers are not only not extreme but are quite conservative and restrained in the area of premarital sexual codes and behavior when we compare them to their older brothers and sisters.

There is evidence to show that teen-agers are unsure of how far to go sexually, that they feel ill at ease on dates, and that they are concerned with such "tame" issues as whether one should kiss good night on a first date. A recent study showed that teen-agers rate themselves lower in com-parison to adults than adults rate them. Teen-agers in this study rated adults considerably higher than themselves on most all "good" qualities. These are hardly the attitudes of an arrogant or antiadult youth. They seem more those of a group desirous of becoming like adults and striving toward that goal.

Further, when we look at the rates of female petting to orgasm in the Kinsey studies, we find considerably more of this behavior among girls in their twenties than among girls in their teens. The coitus rate for females doubles between the ages of twenty and twenty-five. Masturbation rates also increase considerably after the teens. In all these ways, the teen-agers seem more conservative than those individuals who are in their twenties.

August Hollingshead's excellent study of a midwest community also gives evidence on the conservatism of youth. He found a very close correspondence between social class of parents and social class of teen-agers' dating partners. In this study, too, we are given a picture of youth culture that is very much like adult culture in its status consciousness. Hollingshead and others have also noted the fact that a large proportion of the teen-age population is virtually not involved in any dating. A good estimate for the high school age group would be that about one third of the boys and one fifth of the girls are not involved in dating.

Venereal Disease and Pregnancy

Let us now examine two key indices, venereal disease and pregnancy, which should give us additional insights into the behavior of teen-agers. Teen-agers do have significant rates of venereal disease and illegitimacy. However, the press has largely exaggerated such rates. The teen-age rate of venereal disease for ages fifteen to nineteen is only about a third of the rate for the twenty to twenty-four age group and is also lower than that of the twenty-five to twenty-nine age group.

There has been a slight rise in the number of teen-age venereal disease cases in recent years, and this has received much publicity. It is quite likely that the actual rates for teen-agers are not higher and that this slight increase is due to the greater number of teen-agers today. More than 80 per cent of the venereal disease reported is from older groups of people. Finally, the rate of venereal disease among teen-agers is not evenly distributed in the teen-age group. As far as we can tell from reported cases, it is highly concentrated in the lower social classes.

When one examines the national figures for unwed mothers, one finds that 40 per cent are teen-agers. Here, too, several qualifications are needed. First, most of these reported cases are Negro, and class status in general is low. The upper classes, according to Paul Gebhard's recent study, are much more willing to resort to abortion. The upper classes, also, have a greater ability to stay out of public statistics and may, thus, show lower rates. According to Clark Vincent's study, when upper class females become pregnant before marriage, it is more likely to be the result of a love affair, whereas, when lower class females become pregnant, it is more likely to be a result of a casual affair. Thus, there are important class differences here, too.

When we compare teen-age unwed motherhood with that for girls in their twenties, we find that the older girls have about the same proportion of the illegitimate children. We also find that the teen-age rates are not increasing as much as the rates for older groups. For example, in 1940 teen-age mothers were 40 per cent of the total; in 1957 they were 40 per cent.

Thus, from the evidence of national figures, it seems reasonable to conclude that it is a small and specific segment of the teen-age population that becomes involved with venereal disease or premarital pregnancy. Furthermore, the people in their twenties seem somewhat more likely to be involved in such circumstances. Also, these older couples are much more involved in adult culture in terms of their occupations and their nearness to marriage, and yet their sexual behavior is less conservative.

A warning must be added at this point concerning the venereal disease rates and unwed motherhood rates. They are far from perfect indices and, as mentioned, many higher class people manage to be excluded from them because they can afford more private means of coping with their problems. However, to the extent that we use these rates, we fail to find support for the charges made about teen-agers. It is no doubt true that teen-agers are irresponsible in the sense that they seek "to have a good time," but I would suggest that, in the area of sexual codes and behavior, the evidence shows more conservatism and responsibility than one might otherwise suspect. It may be well to avoid the over-all impressions given by a general use of the term "youth culture" as described by Parsons. Here, as elsewhere, qualification and specific research is a step toward better theoretical formulation and better understanding.

A Final Overview

What has occurred in teen-age sexual codes in recent generations is a working out of sexual practices acceptable to teen-agers. Many of these practices are at the level of petting. In short, as unchaperoned dating came into vogue and as adolescence became more prolonged due to our specialized industrial culture, young people worked out additional sexual codes to supplement and modify the older codes of abstinence and the double standard. There always were people who engaged in coitus; today there are more, but, for girls in their teens, it is still a minor activity. When we look at petting, we note something different, for here we see a much more continuous and current change among teen-agers—it is here in this middle ground that teen-agers have come to accept a petting-with-affection standard. The equalitarian and permissive aspects of this standard in many cases lead at later ages to acceptance of the more radical permissiveness-with-affection standard. However, during the teens, petting-with-affection is probably the major standard involved in stable affectionate relationships at middle and upper class levels.

At the present time, it is impossible to predict precise changes in sexual codes. This is especially true because, as we have seen, there are differences according to social class, religion, educational level, and so forth. But one can say that all the signs indicate a continued trend toward equalitarian and permissive codes. The trend seems to be toward that which now obtains in the Scandinavian countries, with the inclusion of sex education in the schools and with permissive attitudes on the formal as well as covert levels. This does not forebode the end of the double standard, for the double standard is still deeply rooted in our male dominant culture, but it does mean a continued weakening of the double standard and more qualifications of its mandates.

Teen-agers are a paradoxical group. They are not as wild as their parents or they themselves sometimes think. Teen-agers do want independence. But, judging by their sexual codes, they want independence from their parents, not from the total adult culture.

* 13 *

FUNDAMENTAL NOTIONS OF THE FOLKWAYS AND OF THE MORES

William Graham Sumner

The manners, usages, folkways, mores, and institutions of every society tend to be regarded by the members of that society as the only right and proper ones. Perhaps Sumner's famous book, Folkways, published in 1906, did more than any other to demonstrate the great variety of human behavior patterns thus regarded. As a result, it has induced many people to pause before they say—or even to refrain from thinking—"My ways—our ways—are the only civilized ways of behaving." The terms "folkways" and "mores," first given currency as sociological terms in Sumner's book, are now a part of our everyday language.

Definition and Mode of Origin of the Folkways

If we put together all that we have learned from anthropology and ethnography about primitive men and primitive society, we perceive that the first task of life is to live. Men begin with acts, not with thoughts.

SOURCE: William Graham Sumner, *Folkways* (Ginn and Company, 1940, Centennial Edition), sect. 1–3, 28–29, 31–32, 34–35, 66–68. Reprinted by permission. ✧ The author (1840–1910) was one of the pioneer American sociologists with Ward, Giddings, Small and Ross. He was also an economist and a rector. In 1872 he became professor of political and social science at Yale University. He was the second president of the American Sociological Association. He wrote *A History of American Currency* and *What Social Classes Owe to Each Other* and was the coauthor of *The Science of Society*.

Every moment brings necessities which must be satisfied at once. Need was the first experience, and it was followed at once by a blundering effort to satisfy it. It is generally taken for granted that men inherited some guiding instincts from their beast ancestry, and it may be true, although it has never been proved. If there were such inheritances, they controlled and aided the first efforts to satisfy needs. Analogy makes it easy to assume that the ways of beasts had produced channels of habit and predisposition along which dexterities and other psychophysical activities would run easily. Experiments with newborn animals show that in the absence of any experience of the relation of means to ends, efforts to satisfy needs are clumsy and blundering. The method is that of trial and failure, which produces repeated pain, loss, and disappointments. Nevertheless, it is a method of rude experiment and selection. The earliest efforts of men were of this kind. Need was the impelling force. Pleasure and pain, on the one side and the other, were the rude constraints which defined the line on which efforts must proceed. The ability to distinguish between pleasure and pain is the only psychical power which is to be assumed. Thus ways of doing things were selected, which were expedient. They answered the purpose better than other ways, or with less toil and pain. Along the course on which efforts were compelled to go, habit, routine, and skill were developed. The struggle to maintain existence was carried on, not individually, but in groups. Each profited by the other's experience; hence there was concurrence towards that which proved to be most expedient. All at last adopted the same way for the same purpose; hence the ways turned into customs and became mass phenomena. Instincts were developed in connection with them. In this way folkways arise. The young learn them by tradition, imitation, and authority. The folkways, at a time, provide for all the needs of life then and there. They are uniform, universal in the group, imperative, and invariable. As time goes on, the folkways become more and more arbitrary, positive, and imperative. If asked why they act in a certain way in certain cases, primitive people always answer that it is because they and their ancestors always have done so. A sanction also arises from ghost fear. The ghosts of ancestors would be angry if the living should change the ancient folkways.

The Folkways Are a Societal Force

The operation by which folkways are produced consists in the frequent repetition of petty acts, often by great numbers acting in concert or, at least, acting in the same way when face to face with the same need. The immediate motive is interest. It produces habit in the individual and custom in the group. It is, therefore, in the highest degree original and primitive. By habit and custom it exerts a strain on every individual within its range; therefore it rises to a societal force to which great classes of societal phenomena are due. Its earliest stages, its course, and laws may be studied; also its influence on individuals and their reaction on it. It is our present purpose so to study it. We have to recognize it as one of the chief forces by which a society is made to be what it is. Out of the unconscious experiment which every repetition of the ways includes, there issues pleasure or pain, and then, so far as the men are capable of reflection, convictions that the ways are conducive to societal welfare. These two experiences are not the same. The most uncivilized men, both in the food quest and in war, do things which are painful, but which have been found to be expedient. Perhaps these cases teach the sense of social welfare better than those which are pleasurable and favorable to welfare. The former cases call for some intelligent reflection on experience. When this conviction as to the relation to welfare is added to the folkways they are converted into mores, and, by virtue of the philosophical and ethical element added to them, they win utility and importance and become the source of the science and the art of living.

Folkways Are Made Unconsciously

It is of the first importance to notice that, from the first acts by which men try to satisfy needs, each act stands by itself, and looks no further than the immediate satisfaction. From recurrent needs arise habits for the individual and customs for the group, but these results are consequences which were never conscious, and never foreseen or intended. They are not noticed until they have long existed, and it is still longer before they are appreciated. Another long time must pass, and a higher stage of mental development must be reached, before they can be used as a basis from which to deduce rules for meeting, in the future, problems whose pressure can be foreseen. The folkways, therefore, are not creations of human purpose and wit. They are like products of natural forces which men unconsciously set in operation, or they are like the instinctive ways of animals, which are developed out of experience, which reach a final form of maximum adaptation to an interest, which are handed down by tradition and admit of no exception or variation, yet change to meet new conditions, still within the same limited methods, and without rational reflection or purpose. From this it results that all the life of human beings, in all ages and stages of culture, is primarily controlled by a vast mass of folkways handed down from the earliest existence of the race, having the nature of the ways of other animals, only the topmost layers of which are subject to change and control, and have been somewhat modified by human philosophy, ethics, and religion, or by other acts of intelligent reflection. We are told of savages that "It is difficult to exhaust the customs and small ceremonial usages of a savage people. Custom regulates the whole of a man's actions,—his bathing, washing, cutting his hair, eating, drinking, and fasting. From his cradle to his grave he is the slave of ancient usage. In his life there is nothing free, nothing original, nothing spontaneous, no progress towards a higher and better life, and no attempt to improve his condition, mentally, morally, or spiritually." All men act in this way with only a little wider margin of voluntary variation.

❖   ❖   ❖   ❖   ❖

Folkways Due to False Inference

Folkways have been formed by accident, that is, by irrational and incongruous action, based on pseudo-knowledge. In Molembo a pestilence broke out soon after a Portuguese had died there. After that the natives took all possible measures not to allow any white man to die in their country. On the Nicobar islands some natives who had just begun to make pottery died. The art was given up and never again attempted. White men gave to one Bushman in a kraal a stick ornamented with buttons as a symbol of authority. The recipient died leaving the stick to his son. The son soon died. Then the Bushmen brought back the stick lest all should die. Until recently no building of incombustible materials could be built in any big town of the central province of Madagascar, on account of some ancient prejudice. A party of Eskimos met with no game. One of them returned to their sledges and got the ham of a dog to eat. As he returned with the ham bone in his hand he met and killed a seal. Ever afterwards he carried a ham bone in his hand when hunting. The Belenda women (peninsula of Malacca) stay as near to the house as possible during the period. Many keep the door closed. They know no reason for this custom. "It must be due to some now forgotten superstition." Soon after the Yakuts saw a camel for the first time smallpox broke out amongst them. They thought the camel to be the agent of the disease. A woman amongst the same people contracted an endogamous marriage. She soon afterwards became blind. This was thought to be on account of the violation of ancient customs. A very great number of such cases could be collected. In fact they represent the current mode of reasoning of nature people. It is their custom to reason that, if one thing follows another, it is due to it. A great number of customs are traceable to the notion of the evil eye, many more to ritual notions of uncleanness. No scientific investigation could discover the origin of the folkways mentioned, if the origin had not chanced to become known to civilized men. We must believe that the known cases illustrate the irrational and incongruous origin of many folkways. In civilized history also we know that customs have owed their origin to "historical accident,"—the vanity of a princess, the deformity of a king, the whim of a democracy, the love intrigue of a statesman or prelate. By the institutions of another age it may be provided that no one of these things can affect decisions, acts, or interests, but then the power to decide the ways may have passed to clubs, trades unions, trusts, commercial rivals, wire-pullers, politicians, and political fanatics. In these cases also the causes and origins may escape investigation.

Harmful Folkways

There are folkways which are positively harmful. Very often these are just the ones for which a definite reason can be given. The destruction of a man's goods at his death is a direct deduction from other-worldliness; the dead man is supposed to want in the other world just what he wanted here. The destruction of a man's goods at his death was a great waste of capital, and it must have had a disastrous effect on the interests of the living, and must have very seriously hindered the development of civilization. With this custom we must class all the expenditure of labor and capital on graves, temples, pyramids, rites, sacrifices, and support of priests, so far as these were supposed to benefit the dead. The faith in goblinism produced other-worldly interests which overruled ordinary worldly interests. Foods have often been forbidden which were plentiful, the prohibition of which injuriously lessened the food supply. There is a tribe of Bushmen who will eat no goat's flesh, although goats are the most numerous domestic animals in the district. Where totemism exists it is regularly accompanied by a taboo on eating the totem animal. Whatever may be the real principle in totemism, it overrules the interest in an abundant food supply. "The origin of the sacred regard paid to the cow must be sought in the primitive nomadic life of the Indo-European race," because it is common to Iranians and Indians of Hindostan. The Libyans ate oxen but not cows. The same was true of the Phœnicians and Egyptians. In some cases the sense of a food taboo is not to be learned. It may have been entirely capricious. Mohammed would not eat lizards, because he thought them the offspring of a metamorphosed clan of Israelites. On the other hand, the protective taboo which forbade killing crocodiles, pythons, cobras, and other animal enemies of man was harmful to his interests, whatever the motive. "It seems to be a fixed article of belief throughout southern India, that all who have willfully or accidentally killed a snake, especially a cobra, will certainly be punished, either in this life or the next, in one of three ways: either by childlessness, or by leprosy, or by ophthalmia." Where this faith exists man has a greater interest to spare a cobra than to kill it. India furnishes a great number of cases of harmful mores. "In India every tendency of humanity seems intensified and exaggerated. No country in the world is so conservative in its traditions, yet no country has undergone so many religious changes and vicissitudes." "Every year thousands perish of disease that might recover if they would take proper nourishment, and drink the medicine that science prescribes, but which they imagine that their religion forbids them to touch." "Men who can scarcely count beyond twenty, and know not the letters of the alphabet, would rather die than eat food which had been prepared by men of lower caste, unless it had been sanctified by being offered to an idol; and would kill their daughters rather than endure the disgrace of having unmarried girls at home beyond twelve or thirteen years of age." In the last case the rule of obligation and duty is set by the mores. The interest comes under vanity. The sanction of the caste rules is in a boycott by all members of the caste. The rules are often very harmful. "The authority of caste rests partly on written laws, partly on legendary fables or narratives, partly on the injunctions of instructors and priests, partly on custom and usage, and partly on the caprice and convenience of its votaries." The harm of caste rules is so great that of late they have been broken in some cases, especially in regard to travel over sea, which is a great advantage to Hindoos. The Hindoo folkways in regard to widows and child marriages must also be recognized as socially harmful.

❖   ❖   ❖   ❖   ❖

The Folkways Are "Right"

The folkways are the "right" ways to satisfy all interests, because they are traditional, and exist in fact. They extend over the whole of life. There is a right way to catch game, to win a wife, to make one's self appear, to cure disease, to honor ghosts, to treat comrades or strangers, to behave when a child is born, on the warpath, in council, and soon in all cases which can arise. The ways are defined on the negative side, that is, by taboos. The "right" way is the way which the ancestors used and which has been handed down. The tradition is its own warrant. It is not held subject to verification by experience. The notion of right is in the folkways. It is not outside of them, of independent origin, and brought to them to test them. In the folkways, whatever is, is right. This is because they are traditional, and therefore contain in themselves the authority of the ancestral ghosts. When we come to the folkways we are at the end of our analysis. The notion of right and ought is the same in regard to all the folkways, but the degree of it varies with the importance of the interest at stake. The obligation of conformable and coöperative action is far greater under ghost fear and war than in other matters, and the social sanctions are severer, because group interests are supposed to be at stake. Some usages contain only a slight element of right and ought. It may well be believed that notions of right and duty, and of social welfare, were first developed in connection with ghost fear and other-worldliness, and therefore that, in that field also, folkways were first raised to mores. "Rights" are the rules of mutual give and take in the competition of life which are imposed on comrades in the in-group, in order that the peace may prevail there which is essential to the group strength. Therefore rights can never be "natural" or "God-given," or absolute in any sense. The morality of a group at a time is the sum of the taboos and prescriptions in the folkways by which right conduct is defined. Therefore morals can never be intuitive. They are historical, institutional, and empirical.

World philosophy, life policy, right, rights, and morality are all products of the folkways. They are reflections on, and generalizations from, the experience of pleasure and pain which is won in efforts to carry on the struggle for existence under actual life conditions. The generalizations are very crude and vague in their germinal forms. They are all embodied in folklore, and all our philosophy and science have been developed out of them.

The Folkways Are "True"

The folkways are necessarily "true" with respect to some world philosophy. Pain forced men to think. The ills of life imposed reflection and taught forethought. Mental processes were irksome and were not undertaken until painful experience made them unavoidable. With great unanimity all over the globe primitive men followed the same line of thought. The dead were believed to live on as ghosts in another world just like this one. The ghosts had just the same needs, tastes, passions, etc., as the living men had had. These transcendental notions were the beginning of the mental outfit of mankind. They are articles of faith, not rational convictions. The living had duties to the ghosts, and the ghosts had rights; they also had power to enforce their rights. It behooved the living therefore to learn how to deal with ghosts. Here we have a complete world philosophy and a life policy deduced from it. When pain, loss, and ill were experienced and the question was provoked, Who did this to us? the world philosophy furnished the answer. When the painful experience forced the question, Why are the ghosts angry and what must we do to appease them? the "right" answer was the one which fitted into the philosophy of ghost fear. All acts were therefore constrained and trained into the forms of the world philosophy by ghost fear, ancestral authority, taboos, and habit. The habits and customs created a practical philosophy of welfare, and they confirmed and developed the religious theories of goblinism.

❖   ❖   ❖   ❖   ❖

Definition of the Mores

When the elements of truth and right are developed into doctrines of welfare, the folkways are raised to another plane. They then become capable of producing inferences, developing into new forms, and extending their constructive influence over men and society. Then we call them the mores. The more are the folkways, including the philosophical and ethical generalizations as to societal welfare which are suggested by them, and inherent in them, as they grow.

Taboos

The mores necessarily consist, in a large part, of taboos, which indicate the things which must not be done. In part these are dictated by mystic dread of ghosts who might be offended by certain acts, but they also include such acts as have been found by experience to produce unwelcome results, especially in the food quest, in war, in health, or in increase or decrease of population. These taboos always contain a greater element of philosophy than the positive rules, because the taboos contain reference to a reason, as, for instance, that the act would displease the ghosts. The primitive taboos correspond to the fact that the life of man is environed by perils. His food quest must be limited by shunning poisonous plants. His appetite must be restrained from excess. His physical strength and health must be guarded from dangers. The taboos carry on the accumulated wisdom of generations, which has almost always been purchased by pain, loss, disease, and death. Other taboos contain inhibitions of what will be injurious to the group. The laws about the sexes, about property, about war, and about ghosts, have this character. They always include some social philosophy. They are both mystic and utilitarian, or compounded of the two.

Taboos may be divided into two classes, (1) protective and (2) destructive. Some of them aim to protect and secure, while others aim to repress or exterminate. Women are subject to some taboos which are directed against them as sources of possible harm or danger to men, and they are subject to other taboos which put them outside of the duties or risks of men. On account of this difference in taboos, taboos act selectively, and thus affect the course of civilization. They contain judgments as to societal welfare.

❖   ❖   ❖   ❖   ❖

More Exact Definition of the Mores

We may now formulate a more complete definition of the mores. They are the ways of doing things which are current in a society to satisfy human needs and desires, together with the faiths, notions, codes, and standards of well living which inhere in those ways, having a genetic connection with them. By virtue of the latter element the mores are traits in the specific character (ethos) of a society or a period. They pervade and control the ways of thinking in all the exigencies of life, returning from the world of abstractions to the world of action, to give guidance and to win revivification. "The mores [*Sitten*] are, before any beginning of reflection, the regulators of the political, social, and religious behavior of the individual. Conscious reflection is the worst enemy of the mores, because mores begin unconsciously and pursue unconscious purposes, which are recognized by reflection often only after long and circuitous processes, and because their expediency often depends on the assumption that they will have general acceptance and currency, uninterfered with by reflection." "The mores are usage in any group, in so far as it, on the one hand, is not the expression or fulfillment of an absolute natural necessity [e.g. eating or sleeping], and, on the other hand, is independent of the arbitrary will of the individual, and is generally accepted as good and proper, appropriate and worthy."

Ritual

The process by which mores are developed and established is ritual. Ritual is so foreign to our mores that we do not recognize its power. In primitive society it is the prevailing method of activity, and primitive religion is entirely a matter of ritual. Ritual is the perfect form of drill and of the regulated habit which comes from drill. Acts which are ordained by authority and are repeated mechanically without intelligence run into ritual. If infants and children are subjected to ritual they never escape from its effects through life. Galton says that he was, in early youth, in contact with the Mohammedan ritual idea that the left hand is less worthy than the right, and that he never overcame it. We see the effect of ritual in breeding, courtesy, politeness, and all forms of prescribed behavior. Etiquette is social ritual. Ritual is not easy compliance with usage; it is strict compliance with detailed and punctilious rule. It admits of no exception or deviation. The stricter the discipline, the greater the power of ritual over action and character. In the training of animals and the education of children it is the perfection, inevitableness, invariableness, and relentlessness of routine which tells. They should never experience any exception or irregularity. Ritual is connected with words, gestures, symbols, and signs. Associations result, and, upon a repetition of the signal, the act is repeated, whether the will assents or not. Association and habit account for the phenomena. Ritual gains further strength when it is rhythmical, and is connected with music, verse, or other rhythmical acts. Acts are ritually repeated at the recurrence of the rhythmical points. The alternation of night and day produces rhythms of waking and sleeping, of labor and rest, for great numbers at the same time, in their struggle for existence. The seasons also produce rhythms in work. Ritual may embody an idea of utility, expediency, or welfare, but it always tends to become perfunctory, and the idea is only subconscious. There is ritual in primitive therapeutics, and it was not eliminated until very recent times. The patient was directed, not only to apply remedies, but also to perform rites. The rites introduced mystic elements. This illustrates the connection of ritual with notions of magical effects produced by rites. All ritual is ceremonious and solemn. It tends to become sacred, or to make sacred the subject-matter with which it is connected. Therefore, in primitive society, it is by ritual that sentiments of awe, deference to authority, submission to tradition, and disciplinary coöperation are inculcated. Ritual operates a constant suggestion, and the suggestion is at once put in operation in acts. Ritual, therefore, suggests sentiments, but it never inculcates doctrines. Ritual is strongest when it is most perfunctory and excites no thought. By familiarity with ritual any doctrinal reference which it once had is lost by familiarity, but the habits persist. Primitive religion is ritualistic, not because religion makes ritual, but because ritual makes religion. Ritual is something to be done, not something to be thought or felt. Men can always perform the prescribed act, although they cannot always think or feel prescribed thoughts or emotions. The acts may bring up again, by association, states of the mind and sentiments which have been connected with them, especially in childhood, when the fantasy was easily affected by rites, music, singing, dramas, etc. No creed, no moral code, and no scientific demonstration can ever win the same hold upon men and women as habits of action, with associated sentiments and states of mind, drilled in from childhood. Mohammedanism shows the power of ritual. Any occupation is interrupted for the prayers and prescribed genuflections. The Brahmins also observe an elaborate daily ritual. They devote to it two hours in the morning, two in the evening, and one at midday. Monks and nuns have won the extreme satisfaction of religious sentiment from the unbroken habit of repeated ritual, with undisturbed opportunity to develop emotional effects of it.

The Ritual of the Mores

The mores are social ritual in which we all participate unconsciously. The current habits as to hours of labor, meal hours, family life, the social intercourse of the sexes, propriety, amusements, travel, holidays, education, the use of periodicals and libraries, and innumerable other details of life fall under this ritual. Each does as everybody does. For the great mass of mankind as to all things, and for all of us for a great many things, the rule to do as all do suffices. We are led by suggestion and association to believe that there must be wisdom and utility in what all do. The great mass of the folkways give us discipline and the support of routine and habit. If we had to form judgments as to all these cases before we could act in them, and were forced always to act rationally, the burden would be unendurable. Beneficent use and wont save us this trouble.

POPULATION

Kingsley Davis

For a number of years, competent students of population trends and natural resources have contended that present high rates of population growth in the nonindustrial areas of the world are the most serious social problem of our time. They point out, for example, that if present trends continue unchecked, within a hundred years there will be six times as many people on this earth as there are today. Thus, Edward A. Ross's discussion of "standing room only" half a century ago was more realistic than generally thought. Certainly, massive population growth can nullify most of the gains brought about by economic and technological development, especially in the face of limited arable land and other environmental resources. However, Kingsley Davis suggests that recent demographic history indicates that motivations to improve standards of living combined with the pressure of painful scarcities will accelerate reproductive restraint.

Just as the nation-state is a modern phenomenon, so is the explosive increase of the human population. For hundreds of millenniums *Homo sapiens* was a sparsely distributed animal.

❖   ❖   ❖   ❖   ❖

. . . Indeed, the rate of growth of the world population remained low right up to the 16th and 17th centuries.

Then came a spectacular quickening of the earth's human increase. Between 1650 and 1850 the annual rate of increase doubled, and by the 1920's it had doubled again. After World War II, in the decade from 1950 to 1960, it took another big jump. The human population is now growing at a rate that is impossible to sustain for more than a moment of geologic time.

Since 1940 the world population has grown from about 2.5 billion to

SOURCE: *Scientific American*, Vol. 209 (September, 1963), 62–71. Reprinted with permission. Copyright © 1963 by Scientific American, Inc. All rights reserved. ❖ The author is professor of sociology and Director of International Population and Urban Research at the University of California, Berkeley, and chairman of the National Research Council's newly created Behavioral Science Division. He has served as U.S. representative to the Population Commission of the United Nations and was a former president of the American Sociological Association. His main interests are population, urbanization, and family. Among his books are *Youth in Depression, Human Society*, and *The Pattern of World Urbanization*.

3.2 billion. This increase, within 23 years, is more than the *total* estimated population of the earth in 1800. If the human population were to continue to grow at the rate of the past decade, within 100 years it would be multiplied sixfold.

Projections indicate that in the next four decades the growth will be even more rapid. The United Nations' "medium" projections give a rate during the closing decades of this century high enough, if continued, to multiply the world population sevenfold in 100 years. These projections are based on the assumption that the changes in mortality and fertility in regions in various stages of development will be roughly like those of the recent past. They do not, of course, forecast the actual population, which may turn out to be a billion or two greater than that projected for the year 2000 or to be virtually nil. So far the UN projections, like most others in recent decades, are proving conservative. In 1960 the world population was 75 million greater than the figure given by the UN's "high" projection (published in 1958 and based on data up to 1955).

In order to understand why the revolutionary rise of world population has occurred, we cannot confine ourselves to the global trend, because this trend is a summation of what is happening in regions that are at any one time quite different with respect to their stage of development. For instance, the first step in the demographic evolution of modern nations—a decline in the death rate—began in northwestern Europe long before it started elsewhere. As a result, although population growth is now slower in this area than in the rest of the world, it was here that the unprecedented upsurge in human numbers began. Being most advanced in demographic development, northwestern Europe is a good place to start in our analysis of modern population dynamics.

In the late medieval period the average life expectancy in England, according to life tables compiled by the historian J. C. Russell, was about 27 years. At the end of the 17th century and during most of the 18th it was about 31 in England, France and Sweden, and in the first half of the 19th century it advanced to 41.

The old but reliable vital statistics from Denmark, Norway and Sweden show that the death rate declined erratically up to 1790, then steadily and more rapidly. Meanwhile the birth rate remained remarkably stable (until the latter part of the 19th century). The result was a marked increase in the excess of births over deaths, or what demographers call "natural increase." In the century from about 1815 until World War I the average annual increase in the three Scandinavian countries was 11.8 per 1,000—nearly five times what it had been in the middle of the 18th century, and sufficient to triple the population in 100 years.

For a long time the population of northwestern Europe showed little reaction to this rapid natural increase. But when it came, the reaction was emphatic; a wide variety of responses occurred, all of which tended to reduce the growth of the population. For example, in the latter part of the

19th century people began to emigrate from Europe by the millions, mainly to America, Australia and South Africa. Between 1846 and 1932 an estimated 27 million people emigrated overseas from Europe's 10 most advanced countries. The three Scandinavian countries alone sent out 2.4 million, so that in 1915 their combined population was 11.1 million instead of the 14.2 million it would otherwise have been.

In addition to this unprecedented exodus there were other responses, all of which tended to reduce the birth rate. In spite of opposition from church and state, agitation for birth control began and induced abortions became common. The age at marriage rose. Childlessness became frequent. The result was a decline in the birth rate that eventually overtook the continuing decline in the death rate. By the 1930's most of the industrial European countries had age-specific fertility rates so low that, if the rates had continued at that level, the population would eventually have ceased to replace itself.

In explaining this vigorous reaction one gets little help from two popular clichés. One of these—that population growth is good for business—would hardly explain why Europeans were so bent on stopping population growth. The other—that numerical limitation comes from the threat of poverty because "population always presses on the means of subsistence"—is factually untrue. In every one of the industrializing countries of Europe economic growth outpaced population growth.

❖   ❖   ❖   ❖   ❖

. . . Clearly the strenuous efforts to lessen population growth were due to some stimulus other than poverty.

The stimulus, in my view, arose from the clash between new opportunities on the one hand and larger families on the other. The modernizing society of northwestern Europe necessarily offered new opportunities to people of all classes: new ways of gaining wealth, new means of rising socially, new symbols of status. In order to take advantage of those opportunities, however, the individual and his children required education, special skills, capital and mobility—none of which was facilitated by an improvident marriage or a large family. Yet because mortality was being reduced (and reduced more successfully in the childhood than in the adult ages) the size of families had become potentially larger than before. In Sweden, for instance, the mortality of the period 1755–1775 allowed only 6.1 out of every 10 children born to reach the age of 10, whereas the mortality of 1901–1910 allowed 8.5 to survive to that age. In order to avoid the threat of a large family to his own and his children's socioeconomic position, the individual tended to postpone or avoid marriage and to limit reproduction within marriage by every means available. Urban residents had to contend particularly with the cost and inconvenience of young children in the city. Rural families had to adjust to the lack of enough land to provide for new marriages when the children reached marriageable age. Land had become less available not only because of the plethora of families with numerous youths but also because, with modernization, more capital was needed per farm and because the old folks, living longer, held on to the property. As a result farm youths postponed marriages, flocked to the cities or went overseas.

In such terms we can account for the paradox that, as the progressive European nations became richer, their population growth slowed down. The process of economic development itself provided the motives for curtailment of reproduction, as the British sociologist J. A. Banks has made clear in his book *Prosperity and Parenthood*. We can see now that in all modern nations the long-run trend is one of low mortality, a relatively modest rate of reproduction and slow population growth. This is an efficient demographic system that allows such countries, in spite of their "maturity," to continue to advance economically at an impressive speed.

Naturally the countries of northwestern Europe did not all follow an identical pattern. Their stages differed somewhat in timing and in the pattern of preference among the various means of population control. France, for example, never attained as high a natural increase as Britain or Scandinavia did. This was not due solely to an earlier decline in the birth rate, as is often assumed, but also to a slower decline in the death rate. . . .

❖   ❖   ❖   ❖   ❖

. . . Throughout northwestern Europe the population upsurge resulting from the fall in death rates brought about a multiphasic reaction that eventually reduced the population growth to a modest pace. The main force behind this response was not poverty or hunger but the desire of the people involved to preserve or improve their social standing by grasping the opportunities offered by the newly emerging industrial society.

Is this an interpretation applicable to the history of any industrialized country, regardless of traditional culture? According to the evidence the answer is yes. We might expect it to be true, as it currently is, of the countries of southern and eastern Europe that are finally industrializing. The crucial test is offered by the only nation outside the European tradition to become industrialized: Japan. How closely does Japan's demographic evolution parallel that of northwestern Europe?

If we superpose Japan's vital-rate curves on those of Scandinavia half a century earlier, we see basically similar, although more rapid, development. The reported statistics, questionable up to 1920 but good after that, show a rapidly declining death rate as industrialization took hold after World War I. The rate of natural increase during the period from 1900 to 1940 was almost exactly the same as Scandinavia's between 1850 and 1920, averaging 12.1 per 1,000 population per year compared with Scandinavia's 12.3. And Japan's birth rate, like Europe's, began to dip until it was falling faster than the death rate, as it did in Europe. After the usual baby boom following World War II the decline in births was precipitous, amounting to 50 per cent from 1948 to 1960—perhaps the swiftest drop in reproduction that has ever occurred in an entire nation. The rates of childbearing for women in various ages are so low that, if they continued indefinitely, they would not enable the Japanese population to replace itself.

In thus slowing their population growth have the Japanese used the same means as the peoples of northwestern Europe did? Again, yes. Tabooridden Westerners have given disproportionate attention to two features of the change—the active role played by the Japanese government and the widespread resort to abortion—but neither of these disproves the similarity. It is true that since the war the Japanese government has pursued a birth-control policy more energetically than any government ever has before. It is also clear, however, that the Japanese people would have reduced their childbearing of their own accord. A marked decline in the reproduction rate had already set in by 1920, long before there was a government policy favoring this trend.

As for abortion, the Japanese are unusual only in admitting its extent. Less superstitious than Europeans about this subject, they keep reasonably good records of abortions, whereas most of the other countries have no accurate data. According to the Japanese records, registered abortions rose from 11.8 per 1,000 women of childbearing age in 1949 to a peak of 50.2 per 1,000 in 1955. We have no reliable historical information from Western countries, but we do know from many indirect indications that induced abortion played a tremendous role in the reduction of the birth rate in western Europe from 1900 to 1940, and that it still plays a considerable role. Furthermore, Christopher Tietze of the National Committee for Maternal Health has assembled records that show that in five eastern European countries where abortion has been legal for some time the rate has shot up recently in a manner strikingly similar to Japan's experience. In 1960–1961 there were 139 abortions for every 100 births in Hungary, 58 per 100 births in Bulgaria, 54 in Czechoslovakia and 34 in Poland. The countries of eastern Europe are in a developmental stage comparable to that of northwestern Europe earlier in the century.

Abortion is by no means the sole factor in the decline of Japan's birth rate. Surveys made since 1950 show the use of contraception before that date, and increasing use thereafter. There is also a rising frequency of sterilization. Furthermore, as in Europe earlier, the Japanese are postponing marriage. The proportion of girls under 20 who have ever married fell from 17.7 per cent in 1920 to 1.8 per cent in 1955. In 1959 only about 5 per cent of the Japanese girls marrying for the first time were under 20, whereas in the U.S. almost half the new brides (48.5 per cent in the registration area) were that young.

Finally, Japan went through the same experience as western Europe in another respect—massive emigration. Up to World War II Japan sent millions of emigrants to various regions of Asia, Oceania and the Americas.

In short, in response to a high rate of natural increase brought by declining mortality, Japan reacted in the same ways as the countries of northwestern Europe did at a similar stage. Like the Europeans, the Japanese limited their population growth in their own private interest and that of their children in a developing society, rather than from any fear of absolute privation or any concern with overpopulation in their homeland. The nation's average 5.4 per cent annual growth in industrial output from 1913 to 1958 exceeded the performance of European countries at a similar stage.

As our final class of industrialized countries we must now consider the frontier group—the U.S., Canada, Australia, New Zealand, South Africa and Russia. These countries are distinguished from those of northwestern Europe and Japan by their vast wealth of natural resources in relation to their populations; they are the genuinely affluent nations. They might be expected to show a demographic history somewhat different from that of Europe. In certain particulars they do, yet the general pattern is still much the same.

One of the differences is that the riches offered by their untapped resources invited immigration. All the frontier industrial countries except Russia received massive waves of emigrants from Europe. They therefore had a more rapid population growth than their industrializing predecessors had experienced. As frontier countries with great room for expansion, however, they were also characterized by considerable internal migration and continuing new opportunities. As a result their birth rates remained comparatively high. In the decade from 1950 to 1960, with continued immigration, these countries grew in population at an average rate of 2.13 per cent a year, compared with 1.76 per cent for the rest of the world. It was the four countries with the sparsest settlement (Canada, Australia, New Zealand and South Africa), however, that accounted for this high rate; in the U.S. and the U.S.S.R. the growth rate was lower—1.67 per cent per year.

Apparently, then, in pioneer industrial countries with an abundance of resources population growth holds up at a higher level than in Japan or northwestern Europe because the average individual feels it is easier for himself and his children to achieve a respectable place in the social scale. The immigrants attracted by the various opportunities normally begin at a low level and thus make the status of natives relatively better. People marry earlier and have slightly larger families. But this departure from the general pattern for industrial countries appears to be only temporary.

In the advanced frontier nations, as in northwestern Europe, the birth rate began to fall sharply after 1880, and during the depression of the 1930's it was only about 10 per cent higher than in Europe. Although the postwar baby boom has lasted longer than in other advanced countries, it is evidently starting to subside now, and the rate of immigration has diminished. There are factors at work in these affluent nations that will likely limit their population growth. They are among the most urbanized countries in the world, in spite of their low average population density. Their birth rates are extremely sensitive to business fluctuations and social changes. Furthermore, having in general the world's highest living standards, their demand for resources, already staggering, will become fantastic if both population and per capita consumption continue to rise rapidly, and their privileged position in the world may become less tolerated.

Let us shift now to the other side of the population picture: the nonindustrial, or underdeveloped, countries.

As a class the nonindustrial nations since 1930 have been growing in population about twice as fast as the industrial ones. This fact is so familiar and so taken for granted that its irony tends to escape us. When we think of it, it is astonishing that the world's most impoverished nations, many of them already overcrowded by any standard, should be generating additions to the population at the highest rate.

The underdeveloped countries have about 69 per cent of the earth's adults—and some 80 per cent of the world's children. Hence the demographic situation itself tends to make the world constantly more underdeveloped, or impoverished, a fact that makes economic growth doubly difficult.

How can we account for the paradox that the world's poorest regions are producing the most people? One is tempted to believe that the underdeveloped countries are simply repeating history: that they are in the same phase of rapid growth the West experienced when it began to industrialize and its death rates fell. If that is so, then sooner or later the developing areas will limit their population growth as the West did.

It is possible that this may prove to be true in the long run. But before we accept the comforting thought we should take a close look at the facts as they are.

In actuality the demography of the nonindustrial countries today differs in essential respects from the early history of the present industrial nations. Most striking is the fact that their rate of human multiplication is far higher than the West's ever was. The peak of the industrial nations' natural increase rarely rose above 15 per 1,000 population per year; the highest rate in Scandinavia was 13, in England and Wales 14, and even in Japan it was slightly less than 15. True, the U.S. may have hit a figure of 30 per 1,000 in the early 19th century, but if so it was with the help of heavy immigration of young people (who swelled the births but not the deaths) and with the encouragement of an empty continent waiting for exploitation.

In contrast, in the present underdeveloped but often crowded countries the natural increase per 1,000 population is everywhere extreme. In the decade from 1950 to 1960 it averaged 31.4 per year in Taiwan, 26.8 in Ceylon, 32.1 in Malaya, 26.7 in Mauritius, 27.7 in Albania, 31.8 in Mexico, 33.9 in El Salvador and 37.3 in Costa Rica. These are not birth rates; they are the *excess* of births over deaths! At an annual natural increase of 30 per 1,000 a population will double itself in 23 years.

The population upsurge in the backward nations is apparently taking place at an earlier stage of development—or perhaps we should say *unde*velopment—than it did in the now industrialized nations. In Britain, for instance, the peak of human multiplication came when the country was already highly industrialized and urbanized, with only a fifth of its working males in agriculture. Comparing four industrial countries at the peak of their natural increase in the 19th century (14.1 per 1,000 per year) with five nonindustrial countries during their rapid growth in the 1950's (32.2 per 1,000 per year), I find that the industrial countries were 38.5 per cent urbanized and had 27.9 per cent of their labor force in manufacturing, whereas now the nonindustrial countries are 29.4 per cent urbanized and have only 15.1 per cent of their people in manufacturing. In short, today's nonindustrial populations are growing faster and at an earlier stage than was the case in the demographic cycle that accompanied industrialization in the 19th century.

As in the industrial nations, the main generator of the population upsurge in the underdeveloped countries has been a fall in the death rate. But their resulting excess of births over deaths has proceeded faster and farther. . . .

In most of the underdeveloped nations the death rate has dropped with record speed. For example, the sugar-growing island of Mauritius in the Indian Ocean within an eight-year period after the war raised its average life expectancy from 33 to 51—a gain that took Sweden 130 years to achieve. Taiwan within two decades has increased its life expectancy from 43 to 63; it took the U.S. some 80 years to make this improvement for its white population. According to the records in 18 underdeveloped countries, the crude death rate has dropped substantially in each decade since 1930; it fell some 6 per cent in the 1930's and nearly 20 per cent in the 1950's, and according to the most recent available figures the decline in deaths is still accelerating.

The reasons for this sharp drop in mortality are in much dispute. There are two opposing theories. Many give the credit to modern medicine and public health measures. On the other hand, the public health spokesmen, rejecting the accusation of complicity in the world's population crisis, belittle their own role and maintain that the chief factor in the improvement of the death rate has been economic progress.

Those in the latter camp point out that the decline in the death rate in northwestern Europe followed a steadily rising standard of living. Improvements in diet, clothing, housing and working conditions raised the population's resistance to disease. As a result many dangerous ailments disappeared or subsided without specific medical attack. The same process, say the public health people, is now at work in the developing countries.

On the other side, most demographers and economists believe that economic conditions are no longer as important as they once were in strengthening a community's health. The development of medical science has provided lifesaving techniques and medicines that can be transported overnight to the most backward areas. A Stone Age people can be endowed with a low 20th-century death rate within a few years, without waiting for the slow process of economic development or social change. International agencies and the governments of the affluent nations have been delighted to act as good Samaritans and send out public health missionaries to push disease-fighting programs for the less developed countries.

The debate between the two views is hard to settle. Such evidence as we have indicates that there is truth on both sides. Certainly the newly evolving countries have made economic progress. Their economic advance, however, is not nearly rapid enough to account for the very swift decline in their death rates, nor do they show any clear correlation between economic growth and improvement in life expectancy. For example, in Mauritius during the five-year period from 1953 to 1958 the per capita income fell by 13 per cent, yet notwithstanding this there was a 36 per cent drop in the death rate. On the other hand, in the period between 1945 and 1960 Costa Rica had a 64 per cent increase in the per capita gross national product and a 55 per cent decline in the death rate. There seems to be no consistency—no significant correlation between the two trends when we look at the figures country by country. In 15 underdeveloped countries for which such figures are available we find that the decline in death rate in the 1950's was strikingly uniform (about 4 per cent per year), although the nations varied greatly in economic progress—from no improvement to a 6 per cent annual growth in per capita income.

Our tentative conclusion must be, therefore, that the public health people are more efficient than they admit. The billions of dollars spent in public health work for underdeveloped areas has brought down death rates, irrespective of local economic conditions in these areas. The programs instituted by outsiders to control cholera, malaria, plague and other diseases in these countries have succeeded. This does not mean that death control in underdeveloped countries has become wholly or permanently independent of economic development but that it has become temporarily so to an amazing degree.

Accordingly the unprecedented population growth in these countries bears little relation to their economic condition. The British economist Colin G. Clark has contended that rapid population growth stimulates economic progress. This idea acquires plausibility from the association between human increase and industrialization in the past and from the fact that in advanced countries today the birth rate (but not the death rate) tends to fluctuate with business conditions. In today's underdeveloped countries, however, there seems to be little or no visible connection between economics and demography.

In these countries neither births nor deaths have been particularly responsive to economic change. Some of the highest rates of population growth ever known are occurring in areas that show no commensurate economic advance. In 34 such countries for which we have data, the correlation between population growth and economic gain during the 1950's was negligible, and the slight edge was on the negative side: − .2. In 20 Latin American countries during the period from 1954 to 1959, while the annual gain in per capita gross domestic product fell from an average of 2 per cent to 1.3 per cent, the population growth rate *rose* from 2.5 to 2.7 per cent per year.

All the evidence indicates that the population upsurge in the underdeveloped countries is not helping them to advance economically. On the contrary, it may well be interfering with their economic growth. A surplus of labor on the farms holds back the mechanization of agriculture. A rapid rise in the number of people to be maintained uses up income that might otherwise be utilized for long-term investment in education, equipment and other capital needs. To put it in concrete terms, it is difficult to give a child the basic education he needs to become an engineer when he is one of eight children of an illiterate farmer who must support the family with the produce of two acres of ground.

By definition economic advance means an increase in the amount of product per unit of human labor. This calls for investment in technology, in improvement of the skills of the labor force and in administrative organization and planning. An economy that must spend a disproportionate share of its income in supporting the consumption needs of a growing population—and at a low level of consumption at that—finds growth difficult because it lacks capital for improvements.

A further complication lies in the process of urbanization. The shifts from villages and farmsteads to cities is seemingly an unavoidable and at best a painful part of economic development. It is most painful when the total population is skyrocketing; then the cities are bursting both from their own multiplication and from the stream of migrants from the villages. The latter do not move to cities because of the opportunities there. The opportunities are few and unemployment is prevalent. The migrants come, rather, because they are impelled by the lack of opportunity in the crowded rural areas. In the cities they hope to get something—a menial job, government relief, charities of the rich. I have recently estimated that if the population of India increases at the rate projected for it by the UN, the net number of migrants to cities between 1960 and 2000 will be of the order of 99 to 201 million, and in 2000 the largest city will contain between 36 and 66 million inhabitants. One of the greatest problems now facing the governments of underdeveloped countries is what to do with these millions of penniless refugees from the excessively populated countryside.

Economic growth is not easy to achieve. So far, in spite of all the talk and the earnest efforts of underdeveloped nations, only one country outside the northwestern European tradition has done so: Japan. The others are struggling with the handicap of a population growth greater than any industrializing country had to contend with in the past. A number of them now realize that this a primary problem, and their governments are pursuing or contemplating large-scale programs of birth-limitation. They are receiving little help in this matter, however, from the industrial nations, which have so willingly helped them to lower their death rates.

The Christian nations withhold this help because of their official taboos against some of the means of birth-limitation (although their own people privately use all these means). The Communist nations withhold it because limitation of population growth conflicts with official Marxist dogma (but Soviet citizens control births just as capitalist citizens do, and China is officially pursuing policies calculated to reduce the birth rate).

The West's preoccupation with the technology of contraception seems unjustified in view of its own history. The peoples of northwestern Europe utilized all the available means of birth limitation once they had strong motives for such limitations. The main question, then, is whether or not the peoples of the present underdeveloped countries are likely to acquire such motivation in the near future. There are signs that they will. Surveys in India, Jamaica and certain other areas give evidence of a growing desire among the people to reduce the size of their families. Furthermore, circumstances in the underdeveloped nations today are working more strongly in this direction than they did in northwestern Europe in the 19th century.

As in that earlier day, poverty and deprivation alone are not likely to generate a slowdown of the birth rate. But personal aspirations are. The agrarian peoples of the backward countries now look to the industrialized, affluent fourth of the world. They nourish aspirations that come directly from New York, Paris and Moscow. No more inclined to be satisfied with a bare subsistence than their wealthier fellows would be, they are demanding more goods, education, opportunity and influence. And they are beginning to see that many of their desires are incompatible with the enlarged families that low mortality and customary reproduction are giving them.

They live amid a population density far greater than existed in 19th-century Europe. They have no place to which to emigrate, no beckoning continents to colonize. They have rich utopias to look at and industrial models to emulate, whereas the Europeans of the early 1800's did not know where they were going. The peoples of the underdeveloped, overpopulated countries therefore seem likely to start soon a multiphasic limitation of births such as began to sweep through Europe a century ago. Their governments appear ready to help them. Government policy in these countries is not quibbling over means or confining itself to birth-control technology; its primary task is to strengthen and accelerate the peoples' motivation for reproductive restraint.

Meanwhile the industrial countries also seem destined to apply brakes to their population growth. The steadily rising level of living, multiplied by the still growing numbers of people, is engendering a dizzying rate of consumption. It is beginning to produce painful scarcities of space, of clean water, of clean air and of quietness. All of this may prompt more demographic moderation than these countries have already exercised.

❖ 15 ❖

THE WIND THAT MEANS
LIFE TO INDIA

Santha Rama Rau

This selection describes the struggles of an entire society with the persistent question of how to relate to a dominant feature of its geographical environment, the great rain-bearing wind called the "monsoon." Note that man's behavior is not simply determined by geographical phenomena, but rather, society systematically seeks ways to cope with them, or harness them to serve man's ends. As W. D. Wallis has said, "Geographical environment is the cradle in which man's genius awaits the promptings of motives which give him mastery over his fate."

Sometime at the end of every April winds spring up off the west coast of South America and these, so the meteorologists tentatively suggest, travel westward across more than half the world to produce one of the world's most spectacular climatic phenomena. In the early part of their annual journey they are not particularly dramatic winds. They move easily at about fifteen or twenty miles an hour as part of the trade winds of the southern hemisphere, blow across the Marquesas Islands, include Tahiti in their scope and carry with them, for the most part, clear days and warm nights.

By the middle of May the winds have reached the Samoan Islands and continue along the course determined for them by the turning earth. They

SOURCE: *The New York Times Magazine* (June 8, 1952), 12, 24, 26–27. Copyright © 1952 by Santha Rama Rau. ✧ The author was educated at Wellesley College and now lives in India. A free-lance writer since 1945, she has many articles, short stories, and books to her credit. Among her books are *Home to India, This Is India, My Russian Journey*, and *Gifts of Passage*.

move across the Ellice Islands, the Solomons and New Guinea, and the long island chain of Indonesia.

In June the winds reach the Indian Ocean, and it is only then that their whole character changes. They sweep entirely out of their course, slacken their speed, acquire a special name and such enormous importance that without them the 500 million people who live in India, Pakistan, Ceylon, Burma, Indo-China and Siam would not be able to survive in their homelands. By the time the first rain clouds burst over the Malabar coast those winds have become the great southwest monsoon, India's most valued—and most capricious—blessing.

From the time of the spring equinox onward, as the sun's rays strike the earth more and more directly, the huge land mass of continental Asia begins to heat up. With growing intensity through the weeks that follow, the heat continues unrelieved. In late May and early June temperatures recorded in North India have reached as high as 126 degrees F. The capital city, Delhi, has an average daytime temperature for May of 104 degrees. Then the Government offices and the foreign embassies switch to summer hours—the working day begins at 7:30 A.M. and finishes at 1:30 P.M. A large part of every day becomes devoted simply to avoiding the heat. Chiks (the slatted, bamboo screens) are lowered all day over windows and verandas to keep the interiors of homes and offices cool and shaded from the sun and glare. Only after sunset are windows and houses opened up to the slightly cooler air of evening. Only in the late short twilight do people sit in their gardens or walk in the parks.

The sea's moderating influence does not spread very far inland and only the cities immediately on the coast benefit by reasonably temperate weather. But in the plains of the north and east of the great plateaus of the center of India the heat is a strong and a curiously personal enemy. The earth bakes into a hard cracked surface, rivers dry up entirely or shrink to thin opaque trickles, and all farming comes to a standstill. This is also the season of the Loo, a dreaded, searingly hot wind that blows in from the Rajasthan desert, raises the temperature by 15 or 20 degrees and sweeps the surface soil into dust storms. All kinds of illnesses and nervous ailments are attributed to it, heat-stroke, hysteria and uncertain tempers, and, at the first hint of the rising Loo, doors and windows are shut and bolted against its dust, heat and evil influence.

At the end of May the prolonged and acute heat has formed an enormous low pressure area in the atmosphere over India, and something like a huge whirlwind begins to circulate around its edges. As the heat increases, the speed of the air circulation grows until at last it has acquired suction strong enough to reach below the equator and pull the southeastern trade winds into India. Here, as the monsoon, for three months they move east and north across the country pouring out the water accumulated over 10,000 miles of ocean. Eventually they are checked by the great mountain barriers of the Himalayas which serve to contain the monsoon and conserve the major force of the rains for India. This mountain wall makes it possible for parts of Assam to have a rainfall of 450 inches in one summer while beyond the Himalayas Tibet gets between five and ten inches a year.

As the sun enters its autumnal phase, the earth, already cooled by the rains, is further cooled by the sun's declining intensity, and gradually the monsoon retreats from India to rejoin its old route south of the equator. If anything were to interfere with the process—if, for instance, a string of large volcanic islands were to spring up between the African Coast and Cape Gormorin, the southern tip of India, to deflect the monsoon, or if the heat in Central Asia should, by the cooling of the earth, be reduced and the force to pull in the monsoon should vanish—then India would become a desert. Only a thin coastal strip and the banks of the Ganges might remain green and habitable.

It is not surprising, then, that the chief of the Vedic gods, the oldest of all India's deities and the father of the whole pantheon of gods is Indra, the god of rain. A child born under his auspices is certain to be fortunate and prosperous, and the monsoon, his season, is traditionally connected with fertility, production and richness.

For weeks before the rains begin priests in the temples of the west coast compute from ancient scriptures and old astronomical charts the exact date the monsoon will arrive. With equal seriousness (and, according to the priests, hardly more reliable results) scientists and Government meteorologists collect data from their many coastal stations, study advance reports of weather conditions from island outposts in the Indian Ocean and attempt to predict when the rains will come. For days beforehand, prayers and chanting in the temples urge Indra not to withhold his gift. In some parts of India raindances and drumbeats are performed to call the rain. In Delhi, Government officials more prosaically get on with the job of seeing that plans for water storage, more and deeper wells and bigger irrigation schemes are completed in case this year, again, the monsoon should fail.

Some years ago, one of India's former Ministers of Finance, in presenting his budget to the Indian Parliament, opened his speech with the remark, "The Indian budget is a gamble in rain." Just as Indian agriculture depends entirely on the monsoon to provide its water to fill the country's rivers and reservoirs, and to make irrigation possible, so Indian industry relies to a great extent on the same sources for its power. The electric light and power supply in all the major cities depends on the water reserves which, in turn, are replenished only by the monsoon. Without question, the greatest single factor in maintaining the functioning economy of India is the rain of high summer.

Although the monsoon has never entirely failed to appear, there has never been a recorded year in which the rains have been satisfactory in every part of the country. The day the rains break there is an extraordinary relaxing of tension everywhere. Strangers in city streets smile at each other in relief that the heat has broken. Children rush out yelling in excitement to stand in the first downpour and adults touch the damp ground in gratitude. Every newspaper carries the news on the front page, and compares the arrival of this year's rain with previous monsoons. But after a night of singing and exhilaration and thanksgiving, the anxiety begins again.

So many things can go wrong. There can be too much rain all at once and this will cause floods. Lives will be lost, property damaged, and yet more of India's thin, infinitely precious top soil will get washed away. There may be too little rain and that will result in droughts and famine. There may be long breaks in the monsoon which can mean that the seeds which are sown immediately the rains begin don't germinate, or that later, seedlings wither.

The rains may begin too early or too late, and continue too long or end too abruptly. Then crops will rot in the fields before they are ripe for harvesting, or they may dry up before they are fully grown. In fact, one of the most important of the monsoon festivals, Bombay's Coconut Day, comes at the end of the heavy rains. At that time the gods of the ocean are appeased and offerings of food and flowers and fruit are taken down to all the beaches so that the monsoon seas will abate and allow the fishing craft to leave the harbors again. In all the aspects of the arrival, distribution, timing and departure of the monsoon the Indian farmer most of all, the industrialist and the Indian Government must gamble on the rains.

Just how uncertain a gamble it is and how disastrous the results of losing it, the last five years have shown more clearly than any other period since 1876. The monsoon, which has been known to give some places thirty inches of rain in one day, can equally give other parts of India only five inches for the whole year. Normally, over two or three seasons things even themselves out, but recently the monsoon shortcomings have been so widespread and so consistent as to produce in some areas what is described by the meteorologists as "a chronic condition of the failure of the rains."

❖   ❖   ❖   ❖   ❖

In the countryside around Delhi . . . things are getting serious. Wells are drying up and the new program for sinking tube wells in many of the drought areas cannot move fast enough to alleviate the immediate crisis— there is too much survey work and experimentation to be done first. In a desperate attempt to find short cuts to the findings of the geological surveys, the Government of India has even hired a waterdiviner. . . .

The Point Four technicians who are arriving now in India . . . deal first with the water problem. Tube well experts have arrived to work with Indian geologists, and the plans go ahead. But however such schemes may insure the prosperity of the future, and to whatever extent they may remove the country's reliance on the uncertainties of the monsoon rains, at the moment nothing can keep the country from widespread drought and famine except a good, or better still, a series of good and well-distributed monsoons. Meanwhile, Indians have three months in which to watch with anxious speculation the fluctuations of the monsoon, and finally a winter of either rejoicing or of tragedy. In September, they will know which.

❖ 16 ❖

THE SOCIAL LIFE OF BABOONS

S. L. Washburn and Irven DeVore

Over the years studies conducted on different kinds of animals have demonstrated that a form of social life exists among some nonhumans. Interesting comparisons have been made between the societies of nonhumans and humans. For instance, the pecking order among chickens, first observed some years ago, seems to have its counterpart among humans in various organizations; and the term is now frequently used to refer to the status differences of men in these organizations. A more relevant comparison with human society is provided in the following study of baboon social life. The study may give us some valuable insight into the kind of social behavior that characterized the ancestors of man a million years ago, though we know too little about man's origins to be sure. But the study does illustrate the importance of the group as the arena within which individual (human or nonhuman) behavior is learned.

The behavior of monkeys and apes has always held great fascination for men. In recent years plain curiosity about their behavior has been reinforced by the desire to understand human behavior. Anthropologists have come to understand that the evolution of man's behavior, particularly his social behavior, has played an integral role in his biological evolution. In

SOURCE: *Scientific American*, Vol. 204 (June, 1961), 62–71. Reprinted with permission. Copyright © 1961 by Scientific American, Inc. All rights reserved. Available separately @ 20¢ as offprint No. 601 from W. H. Freeman and Company, 660 Market Street, San Francisco, California. ❖ S. L. Washburn is professor of anthropology at the University of California, Berkeley, and a research associate at the Wenner-Gren Foundation of Anthropological Research. He was the Managing Editor of the *American Journal of Physical Anthropology* from 1955 to 1957. ❖ Irven DeVore is associate professor of anthropology at Harvard University. He has done field work in Africa and is the author of *Field Studies of Monkeys and Apes*, the coauthor of *The Primates*, and the editor of *Primate Behavior*.

the attempt to reconstruct the life of man as it was shaped through the ages, many studies of primate behavior are now under way in the laboratory and in the field. As the contrasts and similarities between the behavior of primates and man — especially preagricultural, primitive man—become clearer, they should give useful insights into the kind of social behavior that characterized the ancestors of man a million years ago.

With these objectives in mind we decided to undertake a study of the baboon. We chose this animal because it is a ground-living primate and as such is confronted with the same kind of problem that faced our ancestors when they left the trees. Our observations of some 30 troops of baboons, ranging in average membership from 40 to 80 individuals, in their natural setting in Africa show that the social behavior of the baboon is one of the species' principal adaptations for survival. Most of a baboon's life is spent within a few feet of other baboons. The troop affords protection from predators and an intimate group knowledge of the territory it occupies. Viewed from the inside, the troop is composed not of neutral creatures but of strongly emotional, highly motivated members. Our data offer little support for the theory that sexuality provides the primary bond of the primate troop. It is the intensely social nature of the baboon, expressed in a diversity of interindividual relationships, that keeps the troop together. This conclusion calls for further observation and experimental investigation of the different social bonds. It is clear, however, that these bonds are essential to compact group living and that for a baboon life in the troop is the only way of life that is feasible.

Many game reserves in Africa support baboon populations but not all were suited to our purpose. We had to be able to locate and recognize particular troops and their individual members and to follow them in their peregrinations day after day. In some reserves the brush is so thick that such systematic observation is impossible. A small park near Nairobi, in Kenya, offered most of the conditions we needed. Here 12 troops of baboons, consisting of more than 450 members, ranged the open savanna. The animals were quite tame; they clambered onto our car and even allowed us to walk beside them. In only 10 months of study, one of us (DeVore) was able to recognize most of the members of four troops and to become moderately familiar with many more. The Nairobi park, however, is small and so close to the city that the pattern of baboon life is somewhat altered. To carry on our work in an area less disturbed by humans and large enough to contain elephants, rhinoceroses, buffaloes and other ungulates as well as larger and less tame troops of baboons, we went to the Amboseli game reserve and spent two months camped at the foot of Mount Kilimanjaro. In the small part of Amboseli that we studied intensively there were 15 troops with a total of 1,200 members, the troops ranging in size from 13 to 185 members. The fact that the average size of the troops in Amboseli (80) is twice that of the troops in Nairobi shows the need to study the animals in several localities before generalizing.

A baboon troop may range an area of three to six square miles but it utilizes only parts of its range intensively. When water and food are widely distributed, troops rarely come within sight of each other. The ranges of neighboring troops overlap nonetheless, often extensively. This could be seen best in Amboseli at the end of the dry season. Water was concentrated in certain areas, and several troops often came to the same water hole, both to drink and to eat the lush vegetation near the water. We spent many days near these water holes, watching the baboons and the numerous other animals that came there.

On one occasion we counted more than 400 baboons around a single water hole at one time. To the casual observer they would have appeared to be one troop, but actually three large troops were feeding side by side. The troops came and went without mixing, even though members of different troops sat or foraged within a few feet of each other. Once we saw a juvenile baboon cross over to the next troop, play briefly and return to his own troop. But such behavior is rare, even in troops that come together at the same water hole day after day. At the water hole we saw no fighting between troops, but small troops slowly gave way before large ones. Troops that did not see each other frequently showed great interest in each other.

When one first sees a troop of baboons, it appears to have little order, but this is a superficial impression. The basic structure of the troop is most apparent when a large troop moves away from the safety of trees and out onto open plains. As the troop moves the less dominant adult males and perhaps a large juvenile or two occupy the van. Females and more of the older juveniles follow, and in the center of the troop are the females with infants, the young juveniles and the most dominant males. The back of the troop is a mirror image of its front, with less dominant males at the rear. Thus without any fixed or formal order, the arrangement of the troop is such that the females and young are protected at the center. No matter from what direction a predator approaches the troop, it must first encounter the adult males.

When a predator is sighted, the adult males play an even more active role in defense of the troop. One day we saw two dogs run barking at a troop. The females and juveniles hurried, but the males continued to walk slowly. In a moment an irregular group of some 20 adult males was interposed between the dogs and the rest of the troop. When a male turned on the dogs, they ran off. We saw baboons close to hyenas, cheetahs and jackals, and usually the baboons seemed unconcerned—the other animals kept their distance. Lions were the only animals we saw putting a troop of baboons to flight. Twice we saw lions near baboons, whereupon the baboons climbed trees. From the safety of the trees the baboons barked and threatened the lions, but they offered no resistance to them on the ground.

With nonpredators the baboons' relations are largely neutral. It is common to see baboons walking among topi, eland, sable and roan antelopes, gazelles, zebras, hartebeests, gnus, giraffes and buffaloes, depending on which ungulates are common locally. When elephants or rhinoceroses walk through an area where the baboons are feeding, the baboons move out of the way at the last moment. We have seen wart hogs chasing each other, and a running rhinoceros go right through a troop, with the baboons merely stepping out of the way. We have seen male impalas fighting while baboons fed beside them. Once we saw a baboon chase a giraffe, but it seemed to be more in play than aggression.

Only rarely did we see baboons engage in hostilities against other species. On one occasion, however, we saw a baboon kill a small vervet monkey and eat it. The vervets frequented the same water holes as the baboons and usually they moved near them or even among them without incident. But one troop of baboons we observed at Victoria Falls pursued vervets on sight and attempted, without success, to keep them out of certain fruit trees. The vervets easily escaped in the small branches of the trees.

The baboons' food is almost entirely vegetable, although they do eat meat on rare occasions. We saw dominant males kill and eat two newborn Thomson's gazelles. Baboons are said to be fond of fledglings and birds' eggs and have even been reported digging up crocodile eggs. They also eat insects. But their diet consists primarily of grass, fruits, buds and plant shoots of many kinds; in the Nairobi area alone they consume more than 50 species of plant.

For baboons, as for many herbivores, association with other species on the range often provides mutual protection. In open country their closest relations are with impalas, while in forest areas the bushbucks play a similar role. The ungulates have a keen sense of smell, and baboons have keen eyesight. Baboons are visually alert, constantly looking in all directions as they feed. If they see predators, they utter warning barks that alert not only the other baboons but also any other animals that may be in the vicinity. Similarly, a warning bark by a bushbuck or an impala will put a baboon troop to flight. A mixed herd of impalas and baboons is almost impossible to take by surprise.

Impalas are a favorite prey of cheetahs. Yet once we saw impalas, grazing in the company of baboons, make no effort to escape from a trio of approaching cheetahs. The impalas just watched as an adult male baboon stepped toward the cheetahs, uttered a cry of defiance and sent them trotting away.

The interdependence of the different species is plainly evident at a water hole, particularly where the bush is thick and visibility poor. If giraffes are drinking, zebras will run to the water. But the first animals to arrive at the water hole approach with extreme caution. In the Wankie reserve, where we also observed baboons, there are large water holes surrounded by wide areas of open sand between the water and the bushes.

The baboons approached the water with great care, often resting and playing for some time in the bushes before making a hurried trip for a drink. Clearly, many animals know each other's behavior and alarm signals.

A baboon troop finds its ultimate safety, however, in the trees. It is no exaggeration to say that trees limit the distribution of baboons as much as the availability of food and water. We observed an area by a marsh in Amboseli where there was water and plenty of food. But there were lions and no trees and so there were no baboons. Only a quarter of a mile away, where lions were seen even more frequently, there were trees. Here baboons were numerous; three large troops frequented the area.

At night, when the carnivores and snakes are most active, baboons sleep high up in big trees. This is one of the baboon's primary behavioral adaptations. Diurnal living, together with an arboreal refuge at night, is an extremely effective way for them to avoid danger. The callused areas on a baboon's haunches allow it to sleep sitting up, even on small branches; a large troop can thus find sleeping places in a few trees. It is known that Colobus monkeys have a cycle of sleeping and waking throughout the night; baboons probably have a similar pattern. In any case, baboons are terrified of the dark. They arrive at the trees before night falls and stay in the branches until it is fully light. Fear of the dark, fear of falling and fear of snakes seem to be basic parts of the primate heritage.

Whether by day or night, individual baboons do not wander away from the troop, even for a few hours. The importance of the troop in ensuring the survival of its members is dramatized by the fate of those that are badly injured or too sick to keep up with their fellows. Each day the troop travels on a circuit of two to four miles; it moves from the sleeping trees to a feeding area, feeds, rests and moves again. The pace is not rapid, but the troop does not wait for sick or injured members. A baby baboon rides its mother, but all other members of the troop must keep up on their own. Once an animal is separated from the troop the chances of death are high. Sickness and injuries severe enough to be easily seen are frequent. For example, we saw a baboon with a broken forearm. The hand swung uselessly, and blood showed that the injury was recent. This baboon was gone the next morning and was not seen again. A sickness was widespread in the Amboseli troops, and we saw individuals dragging themselves along, making tremendous efforts to stay with the troop but falling behind. Some of these may have rejoined their troops; we are sure that at least five did not. One sick little juvenile lagged for four days and then apparently recovered. In the somewhat less natural setting of Nairobi park we saw some baboons that had lost a leg. So even severe injury does not mean inevitable death. Nonetheless, it must greatly decrease the chance of survival.

Thus, viewed from the outside, the troop is seen to be an effective way of life and one that is essential to the survival of its individual members. What do the internal events of troop life reveal about the drives and motivations that cause individual baboons to "seek safety in numbers"? One of the best ways to approach an understanding of the behavior patterns within the troop is to watch the baboons when they are resting and feeding quietly.

Most of the troop will be gathered in small groups, grooming each other's fur or simply sitting. A typical group will contain two females with their young offspring, or an adult male with one or more females and juveniles grooming him. Many of these groups tend to persist, with the same animals that have been grooming each other walking together when the troop moves. The nucleus of such a "grooming cluster" is most often a dominant male or a mother with a very young infant. The most powerful males are highly attractive to the other troop members and are actively sought by them. In marked contrast, the males in many ungulate species, such as impalas, must constantly herd the members of their group together. But baboon males have no need to force the other troop members to stay with them. On the contrary, their presence alone ensures that the troop will stay with them at all times.

Young infants are equally important in the formation of grooming clusters. The newborn infant is the center of social attraction. The most dominant adult males sit by the mother and walk close beside her. When the troop is resting, adult females and juveniles come to the mother, groom her and attempt to groom the infant. Other members of the troop are drawn toward the center thus formed, both by the presence of the protective adult males and by their intense interest in the young infants.

In addition, many baboons, especially adult females, form preference pairs, and juvenile baboons come together in play groups that persist for several years. The general desire to stay in the troop is strengthened by these "friendships," which express themselves in the daily pattern of troop activity.

Our field observations, which so strongly suggest a high social motivation, are backed up by controlled experiment in the laboratory. In the troop this social drive is expressed in strong individual preferences, by "friendship," by interest in the infant members of the troop and by the attraction of the dominant males. Field studies show the adaptive value of these social ties. Solitary animals are far more likely to be killed, and over the generations natural selection must have favored all those factors which make learning to be sociable easy.

The learning that brings the individual baboon into full identity and participation in the baboon social system begins with the mother-child relationship. The newborn baboon rides by clinging to the hair on its mother's chest. The mother may scoop the infant on with her hand, but the infant must cling to its mother, even when she runs, from the day it is born. Experimental studies demonstrate this clinging reflex; field observations show why it is so important.

In the beginning the baboon mother and infant are in contact 24 hours a day. The attractiveness of the young infant, moreover, assures that he and his mother will always be surrounded by attentive troop members. Experiments show that an isolated infant brought up in a laboratory does not develop normal social patterns. Beyond the first reflexive clinging, the development of social behavior requires learning. Behavior characteristic of the species depends therefore both on the baboon's biology and on the social situations that are present in the troop.

As the infant matures it learns to ride on its mother's back, first clinging and then sitting upright. It begins to eat solid foods and to leave the mother for longer and longer periods to play with other infants. Eventually it plays with the other juveniles many hours a day, and its orientation shifts from the mother to this play group. It is in these play groups that the skills and behavior patterns of adult life are learned and practiced. Adult gestures, such as mounting, are frequent, but most play is a mixture of chasing, tail-pulling and mock fighting. If a juvenile is hurt and cries out, adults come running and stop the play. The presence of an adult male prevents small juveniles from being hurt. In the protected atmosphere of the play group the social bonds of the infant are widely extended.

Grooming, a significant biological function in itself, helps greatly to establish social bonds. The mother begins grooming her infant the day it is born, and the infant will be occupied with grooming for several hours a day for the rest of its life. All the older baboons do a certain amount of grooming, but it is the adult females who do most. They groom the infants, juveniles, adult males and other females. The baboons go to each other and "present" themselves for grooming. The grooming animal picks through the hair, parting it with its hands, removing dirt and parasites, usually by nibbling. Grooming is most often reciprocal, with one animal doing it for a while and then presenting itself for grooming. The animal being groomed relaxes, closes its eyes and gives every indication of complete pleasure. In addition to being pleasurable, grooming serves the important function of keeping the fur clean. Ticks are common in this area and can be seen on many animals such as dogs and lions; a baboon's skin, however, is free of them. Seen in this light, the enormous amount of time baboons spend in grooming each other is understandable. Grooming is pleasurable to the individual, it is the most important expression of close social bonds and it is biologically adaptive.

The adults in a troop are arranged in a dominance hierarchy, explicitly revealed in their relations with other members of the troop. The most dominant males will be more frequently groomed and they occupy feeding and resting positions of their choice. When a dominant animal approaches a subordinate one, the lesser animal moves out of the way. The observer can determine the order of dominance simply by watching the reactions of the baboons as they move past each other. In the tamer troops these observations can be tested by feeding. If food is tossed between two baboons, the more dominant one will take it, whereas the other may not even look at it directly .

The status of a baboon male in the dominance hierarchy depends not only on his physical condition and fighting ability but also on his relationships with other males. Some adult males in every large troop stay together much of the time, and if one of them is threatened, the others are likely to back him up. A group of such males outranks any individual, even though another male outside the group might be able to defeat any member of it separately. The hierarchy has considerable stability and this is due in large part to its dependence on clusters of males rather than the fighting ability of individuals. In troops where the rank order is clearly defined, fighting is rare. We observed frequent bickering or severe fighting in only about 15 per cent of the troops. The usual effect of the hierarchy, once relations among the males are settled, is to decrease disruptions in the troop. The dominant animals, the males in particular, will not let others fight. When bickering breaks out, they usually run to the scene and stop it. Dominant males thus protect the weaker animals against harm from inside as well as outside. Females and juveniles come to the males to groom them or just to sit beside them. So although dominance depends ultimately on force, it leads to peace, order and popularity.

Much has been written about the importance of sex in uniting the troop. It has been said, for example, that "the powerful social magnet of sex was the major impetus to subhuman primate sociability." Our observations lead us to assign to sexuality a much lesser, and even at times a contrary, role. The sexual behavior of baboons depends on the biological cycle of the female. She is receptive for approximately one week out of every month, when she is in estrus. When first receptive, she leaves her infant and her friendship group and goes to the males, mating first with the subordinate males and older juveniles. Later in the period of receptivity she goes to the dominant males and "presents." If a male is not interested, the female is likely to groom him and then present again. Near the end of estrus the dominant males become very interested, and the female and a male form a consort pair. They may stay together for as little as an hour or for as long as several days. Estrus disrupts all other social relationships, and consort pairs usually move to the edge of the troop. It is at this time that fighting may take place, if the dominance order is not clearly established among the males. Normally there is no fighting over females, and a male, no matter how dominant, does not monopolize a female for long. No male is ever associated with more than one estrus female; there is nothing resembling a family or a harem among baboons.

Much the same seems to be true of other species of monkey. Sexual behavior appears to contribute little to the cohesion of the troop. Some monkeys have breeding seasons, with all mating taking place within less than half the year. But even in these species the troop continues its normal existence during the months when there is no mating. It must be remembered that among baboons a female is not sexually receptive for most of her life. She is juvenile, pregnant or lactating; estrus is a rare event in her life. Yet she does not leave the troop even for a few minutes. In baboon troops, particularly small ones, many months may pass when no female member comes into estrus; yet no animals leave the troop, and the highly structured relationships within it continue without disorganization.

The sociableness of baboons is expressed in a wide variety of behavior patterns that reinforce each other and give the troop cohesion. As the infant matures the nature of the social bonds changes continually, but the bonds are always strong. The ties between mother and infant, between a juvenile and its peers in a play group, and between a mother and an adult male are quite different from one another. Similarly, the bond between

	ECOLOGY			ECONOMIC SYSTEM	
	GROUP SIZE, DENSITY AND RANGE	HOME BASE	POPULATION STRUCTURE	FOOD HABITS	ECONOMIC DEPENDENCE
MEN	Groups of 50–60 common but vary widely. One individual per 5–10 square miles. Territorial rights; defend boundaries against strangers.	Occupy improved sites for variable times where sick are cared for and stores kept.	Tribal organization of local, exogamous groups.	Omnivorous. Food-sharing. Men specialize in hunting, women and children in gathering.	Infants are dependent on adults for many years. Maturity of male delayed biologically and culturally. Hunting, storage and sharing of food.
APES	10–200 in group. 10 individuals per square mile. Range 3–6 square miles; no territorial defense.	None: sick and injured must keep up with troop.	Small, inbreeding groups.	Almost entirely vegetarian. No food sharing, no division of labor.	Infant economically independent after weaning. Full maturity biologically delayed. No hunting, storage or sharing of food.

APES AND MEN are contrasted in this chart, which indicates that although apes often seem remarkably "human," there are fundamental differences in behavior. Baboon characteristics, which may be taken as representative of ape and monkey behavior in general, are based on laboratory and field studies;

two females in a friendship group, between the male and female in a consort pair or among the members of a cluster of males in the dominance hierarchy is based on diverse biological and behavioral factors, which offer a rich field for experimental investigation.

In addition, the troop shares a considerable social tradition. Each troop has its own range and a secure familiarity with the food and water sources, escape routes, safe refuges and sleeping places inside it. The counterpart of the intensely social life within the troop is the coordination of the activities of all the troop's members throughout their lives. Seen against the background of evolution, it is clear that in the long run only the social baboons have survived.

When comparing the social behavior of baboons with that of man,

SOCIAL SYSTEM					COMMU-NICATION
ORGANIZATION	SOCIAL CONTROL	SEXUAL BEHAVIOR	MOTHER-CHILD RELATIONSHIP	PLAY	
Bands are dependent on and affiliated with one another in a semi-open system. Subgroups based on kinship.	Based on custom.	Female continuously receptive. Family based on prolonged male-female relationship and incest taboos.	Prolonged; infant helpless and entirely dependent on adults.	Interpersonal but also considerable use of inanimate objects.	Linguistic community. Language crucial in the evolution of religion, art, technology and the co-operation of many individuals.
Troop self-sufficient, closed to outsiders. Temporary subgroups are formed based on age and individual preferences.	Based on physical dominance.	Female estrus. Multiple mates. No prolonged male-female relationship.	Intense but brief; infant well developed and in partial control.	Mainly interpersonal and exploratory.	Species-specific, largely gestural and concerned with immediate situations.

human characteristics are what is known of preagricultural Homo sapiens. The chart suggests that there was a considerable gap between primate behavior and the behavior of the most primitive men known.

there is little to be gained from laboring the obvious differences between modern civilization and the society of baboons. The comparison must be drawn against the fundamental social behavior patterns that lie behind the vast variety of human ways of life. For this purpose we have charted the salient features of baboon life in a native habitat alongside those of human life in preagricultural society [*see chart*]. Cursory inspection shows that the differences are more numerous and significant than are the similarities.

The size of the local group is the only category in which there is not a major contrast. The degree to which these contrasts are helpful in understanding the evolution of human behavior depends, of course, on the degree to which baboon behavior is characteristic of monkeys and apes in general and therefore probably characteristic of the apes that evolved into men. Different kinds of monkeys do behave differently, and many more field studies will have to be made before the precise degree of difference can be understood.

For example, many arboreal monkeys have a much smaller geographical range than baboons do. In fact, there are important differences between the size and type of range for many monkey species. But there is no suggestion that a troop of any species of monkey or ape occupies the hundreds of square miles ordinarily occupied by preagricultural human societies. Some kinds of monkey may resent intruders in their range more than baboons do, but there is no evidence that any species fights for complete control of a territory. Baboons are certainly less vocal than some other monkeys, but no nonhuman primate has even the most rudimentary language. We believe that the fundamental contrasts in our chart would hold for the vast majority of monkeys and apes as compared with the ancestors of man. Further study of primate behavior will sharpen these contrasts and define more clearly the gap that had to be traversed from ape to human behavior. But already we can see that man is as unique in his sharing, cooperation and play patterns as he is in his locomotion, brain and language.

The basis for most of these differences may lie in hunting. Certainly the hunting of large animals must have involved co-operation among the hunters and sharing of the food within the tribe. Similarly, hunting requires an enormous extension of range and the protection of a hunting territory. If this speculation proves to be correct, much of the evolution of human behavior can be reconstructed, because the men of 500,000 years ago were skilled hunters. In locations such as Choukoutien in China and Olduvai Gorge in Africa there is evidence of both the hunters and their campsites. We are confident that the study of the living primates, together with the archaeological record, will eventually make possible a much richer understanding of the evolution of human behavior.

Person and Group

* 17 *

FINAL NOTE ON A CASE OF
EXTREME ISOLATION

Kingsley Davis

For centuries there have been reports of children who were raised by animals or in some other way managed to live in complete iso- lation from human beings. If such feral men could be found, they would have great significance for social science, since they would provide a· crucial means of determining the nature and extent of sociocultural influence on human behavior. Investigation of all re- ported cases has, however, shown them to have little validity and to be heavily laden with myth and rumor. It is highly doubtful if any child ever lived without at least some human association. In recent years, however, a few verified instances have been found in which extremely limited association with humans has occurred. Kingsley Davis gives here his final report on such a case and makes some comparisons between the child, Anna, and another child, Isabelle, who lived under similar circumstances. One cannot be sure to what extent Anna's failure to achieve the level of socializa- tion of a normal ten-year-old was due to organic deficiency. Clearly, however, a tremendous change took place in her behavior after the isolation was ended. It seems certain that many typically human behavior patterns were not achieved until Anna was able to associate with other humans from whom she could learn such behavior.

Early in 1940 there appeared . . . an account of a girl called Anna.[1] She had been deprived of normal contact and had received a minimum of human care for almost the whole of her first six years of life. At that time

S O U R C E : *The American Journal of Sociology*, Vol. 52, No. 5 (March, 1947), 432–37. Reprinted by permission of the University of Chicago Press and the author. ✧ For biographical data on the author, see selection 14.

[1] Kingsley Davis, "Extreme Social Isolation of a Child," *American Journal of Sociology*, XLV (January, 1940), 554–65.

observations were not complete and the report had a tentative character. Now, however, the girl is dead, and, with more information available, it is possible to give a fuller and more definitive description of the case from a sociological point of view.

Anna's death, caused by hemorrhagic jaundice, occurred on August 6, 1942. Having been born on March 1 or 6, 1932, she was approximately ten and a half years of age when she died. The previous report covered her development up to the age of almost eight years; the present one recapitulates the earlier period on the basis of new evidence and then covers the last two and a half years of her life.

Early History

The first few days and weeks of Anna's life were complicated by frequent changes of domicile. It will be recalled that she was an illegitimate child, the second such child born to her mother, and that her grandfather, a widowed farmer in whose house her mother lived, strongly disapproved of this new evidence of the mother's indiscretion. This fact led to the baby's being shifted about.

Two weeks after being born in a nurse's private home, Anna was brought to the family farm, but the grandfather's antagonism was so great that she was shortly taken to the house of one of her mother's friends. At this time a local minister became interested in her and took her to his house with an idea of possible adoption. He decided against adoption, however, when he discovered that she had vaginitis. The infant was then taken to a children's home in the nearest large city. This agency found that at the age of only three weeks she was already in a miserable condition, being "terribly galled and otherwise in very bad shape." It did not regard her as a likely subject for adoption but took her in for a while anyway, hoping to benefit her. After Anna had spent nearly eight weeks in this place, the agency notified her mother to come to get her. The mother responded by sending a man and his wife to the children's home with a view to their adopting Anna, but they made such a poor impression on the agency that permission was refused. Later the mother came herself and took the child out of the home and then gave her to this couple. It was in the home of this pair that a social worker found the girl a short time thereafter. The social worker went to the mother's home and pleaded with Anna's grandfather to allow the mother to bring the child home. In spite of threats, he refused. The child, by then more than four months old, was next taken to another childen's home in a near-by town. A medical examination at this time revealed that she had impetigo, vaginitis, umbilical hernia, and a skin rash.

Anna remained in this second children's home for nearly three weeks, at the end of which time she was transferred to a private foster-home. Since, however, the grandfather would not, and the mother could not, pay

for the child's care, she was finally taken back as a last resort to the grandfather's house (at the age of five and a half months). There she remained,
kept on the second floor in an attic-like room because her mother hesitated
to incur the grandfather's wrath by bringing her downstairs.

The mother, a sturdy woman weighing about 180 pounds, did a
man's work on the farm. She engaged in heavy work such as milking cows
and tending hogs and had little time for her children. Sometimes she went
out at night, in which case Anna was left entirely without attention.
Ordinarily, it seems, Anna received only enough care to keep her barely
alive. She appears to have been seldom moved from one position to another. Her clothing and bedding were filthy. She apparently had no instruction, no friendly attention.

It is little wonder that, when finally found and removed from the room
in the grandfather's house at the age of nearly six years, the child could
not talk, walk, or do anything that showed intelligence. She was in an
extremely emaciated and undernourished condition, with skeleton-like
legs and a bloated abdomen. She had been fed on virtually nothing except
cow's milk during the years under her mother's care.

Anna's condition when found, and her subsequent improvement, have
been described in the previous report. It now remains to say what happened to her after that.

Later History

In 1939, nearly two years after being discovered, Anna had progressed,
as previously reported, to the point where she could walk, understand
simple commands, feed herself, achieve some neatness, remember people,
etc. But she still did not speak, and, though she was much more like a
normal infant of something over one year of age in mentality, she was far
from normal for her age.

On August 30, 1939, she was taken to a private home for retarded
children, leaving the county home where she had been for more than a
year and a half. In her new setting she made some further progress, but
not a great deal. In a report of an examination made November 6 of the
same year, the head of the institution pictured the child as follows:

Anna walks about aimlessly, makes periodic rhythmic motions of her
hands, and, at intervals, makes guttural and sucking noises. She regards her
hands as if she had seen them for the first time. It was impossible to hold her
attention for more than a few seconds at a time—not because of distraction
due to external stimuli but because of her inability to concentrate. She ignored
the task in hand to gaze vacantly about the room. Speech is entirely lacking.
Numerous unsuccessful attempts have been made with her in the hope of
developing initial sounds. I do not believe that this failure is due to negativism
or deafness but that she is not sufficiently developed to accept speech at this
time. . . . The prognosis is not favorable. . . .

More than five months later, on April 25, 1940, a clinical psychologist, the late Professor Francis N. Maxfield, examined Anna and reported the following: large for her age; hearing "entirely normal"; vision apparently normal; able to climb stairs; speech in the "babbling stage" and "promise for developing intelligible speech later seems to be good." He said further that "on the Merrill-Palmer scale she made a mental score of 19 months. On the Vineland social maturity scale she made a score of 23 months."

Professor Maxfield very sensibly pointed out that prognosis is difficult in such case of isolation. "It is very difficult to take scores on tests standardized under average conditions of environment and experience," he wrote, "and interpret them in a case where environment and experience have been so unusual." With this warning he gave it as his opinion at that time that Anna would eventually "attain an adult mental level of six or seven years."

The school for retarded children, on July 1, 1941, reported that Anna had reached 46 inches in height and weighed 60 pounds. She could bounce and catch a ball and was said to conform to group socialization, though as a follower rather than a leader. Toilet habits were firmly established. Food habits were normal, except that she still used a spoon as her sole implement. She could dress herself except for fastening her clothes. Most remarkable of all, she had finally begun to develop speech. She was characterized as being at about the two-year level in this regard. She could call attendants by name and bring in one when she was asked to. She had a few complete sentences to express her wants. The report concluded that there was nothing peculiar about her, except that she was feeble-minded —"probably congenital in type."

A final report from the school, made on June 22, 1942, and evidently the last report before the girl's death, pictured only a slight advance over that given above. It said that Anna could follow directions, string beads, identify a few colors, build with blocks, and differentiate between attractive and unattractive pictures. She had a good sense of rhythm and loved a doll. She talked mainly in phrases but would repeat words and try to carry on a conversation. She was clean about clothing. She habitually washed her hands and brushed her teeth. She would try to help other children. She walked well and could run fairly well, though clumsily. Although easily excited, she had a pleasant disposition.

Interpretation

Such was Anna's condition just before her death. It may seem as if she had not made much progress, but one must remember the condition in which she had been found. One must recall that she had no glimmering of speech, absolutely no ability to walk, no sense of gesture, not the least capacity to feed herself even when the food was put in front of her, and no comprehension of cleanliness. She was so apathetic that it was hard to tell whether or not she could hear. And all this at the age of nearly six years. Compared with this condition, her capacities at the time of her death seem striking indeed, though they do not amount to much more than a two-and-a-half-year mental level. One conclusion therefore seems safe, namely, that her isolation prevented a considerable amount of mental development that was undoubtedly part of her capacity. Just what her original capacity was, of course, is hard to say; but her development after her period of confinement (including the ability to walk and run, to play, dress, fit into a social situation, and, above all, to speak) shows that she had at least this much capacity—capacity that never could have been realized in her original condition of isolation.

A further question is this: What would she have been like if she had received a normal upbringing from the moment of birth? A definitive answer would have been impossible in any case, but even an approximate answer is made difficult by her early death. If one assumes, as was tentatively surmised in the previous report, that it is "almost impossible for any child to learn to speak, think, and act like a normal person after a long period of early isolation," it seems likely that Anna might have had a normal or near-normal capacity, genetically speaking. On the other hand, it was pointed out that Anna represented "a marginal case, [because] she was discovered before she had reached six years of age," an age "young enough to allow for some plasticity." While admitting, then, that Anna's isolation *may* have been the major cause (and was certainly a minor cause) of her lack of rapid mental progress during the four and a half years following her rescue from neglect, it is necessary to entertain the hypothesis that she was congenitally deficient.

In connection with this hypothesis, one suggestive though by no means conclusive circumstance needs consideration, namely, the mentality of Anna's forebears. Information on this subject is easier to obtain, as one might guess, on the mother's than on the father's side. Anna's maternal grandmother, for example, is said to have been college educated and wished to have her children receive a good education, but her husband, Anna's stern grandfather, apparently a shrewd, hard-driving, calculating farmowner, was so penurious that her ambitions in this direction were thwarted. Under the circumstances her daughter (Anna's mother) managed, despite having to do hard work on the farm, to complete the eighth grade in a country school. Even so, however, the daughter was evidently not very smart. "A schoolmate of [Anna's mother] stated that she was retarded in school work; was very gullible at this age; and that her morals even at this time were discussed by other students." Two tests administered to her on March 4, 1938, when she was thirty-two years of age, showed that she was mentally deficient. On the Stanford Revision of the Binet-Simon Scale her performance was equivalent to that of a child of eight years, giving her an I.Q. of 50 and indicating mental deficiency of "middle-grade moron type."

As to the identity of Anna's father, the most persistent theory holds that he was an old man about seventy-four years of age at the time of the girl's birth. If he was the one, there is no indication of mental or other biological deficiency, whatever one may think of his morals. However, someone else may actually have been the father.

To sum up: Anna's heredity is the kind that *might* have given rise to innate mental deficiency, though not necessarily.

Comparison with Another Case

Perhaps more to the point than speculations about Anna's ancestry would be a case for comparison. If a child could be discovered who had been isolated about the same length of time as Anna but had achieved a much quicker recovery and a greater mental development, it would be a stronger indication that Anna was deficient to start with.

Such a case does exist. It is the case of a girl found at about the same time as Anna and under strikingly similar circumstances. A full description of the details of this case has not been published, but, in addition to newspaper reports, an excellent preliminary account by a speech specialist, Dr. Marie K. Mason, who played an important role in the handling of the child, has appeared. Also the late Dr. Francis N. Maxfield, clinical psychologist at Ohio State University, as was Dr. Mason, has written an as yet unpublished but penetrating analysis of the case. Some of his observations have been included in Professor Zingg's book on feral man. The following discussion is drawn mainly from these enlightening materials. The writer, through the kindness of Professors Mason and Maxfield, did have a chance to observe the girl in April, 1940, and to discuss the features of her case with them.

Born apparently one month later than Anna, the girl in question, who has been given the pseudonym Isabelle, was discovered in November, 1938, nine months after the discovery of Anna. At the time she was found she was approximately six and a half years of age. Like Anna, she was an illegitimate child and had been kept in seclusion for that reason. Her mother was a deaf-mute, having become so at the age of two, and it appears that she and Isabelle had spent most of their time together in a dark room shut off from the rest of the mother's family. As a result Isabelle had no chance to develop speech; when she communicated with her mother, it was by means of gestures. Lack of sunshine and inadequacy of diet had caused Isabelle to become rachitic. Her legs in particular were affected; they "were so bowed that as she stood erect the soles of her shoes came nearly flat together, and she got about with a skittering gait." Her behavior toward strangers, especially men, was almost that of a wild animal, manifesting much fear and hostility. In lieu of speech she made only a strange croaking sound. In many ways she acted like an infant. "She was apparently utterly unaware of relationships of any kind. When presented with a ball for the first time, she held it in the palm of her hand, then reached out and stroked my face with it. Such behavior is comparable to that of a child of six months." At first it was even hard to tell whether or not she could hear, so unused were her senses. Many of her actions resembled those of deaf children.

It is small wonder that, once it was established that she could hear, specialists working with her believed her to be feeble-minded. Even on nonverbal tests her performance was so low as to promise little for the future. Her first score on the Stanford-Binet was 19 months, practically at the zero point of the scale. On the Vineland social maturity scale her first score was 39, representing an age level of two and a half years. "The general impression was that she was wholly uneducable and that any attempt to teach her to speak, after so long a period of silence, would meet with failure."

In spite of this interpretation, the individuals in charge of Isabelle launched a systematic and skillful program of training. It seemed hopeless at first. The approach had to be through pantomime and dramatization, suitable to an infant. It required one week of intensive effort before she even made her first attempt at vocalization. Gradually she began to respond, however, and, after the first hurdles had at last been overcome, a curious thing happened. She went through the usual stages of learning characteristic of the years from one to six not only in proper succession but far more rapidly than normal. In a little over two months after her first vocalization she was putting sentences together. Nine months after that she could identify words and sentences on the printed page, could write well, could add to ten, and could retell a story after hearing it. Seven months beyond this point she had a vocabulary of 1,500–2,000 words and was asking complicated questions. Starting from an educational level of between one and three years (depending on what aspect one considers), she had reached a normal level by the time she was eight and a half years old. In short, she covered in two years the stages of learning that ordinarily require six. Or, to put it another way, her I.Q. trebled in a year and a half. The speed with which she reached the normal level of mental development seems analogous to the recovery of body weight in a growing child after an illness, the recovery being achieved by an extra fast rate of growth for a period after the illness until normal weight for the given age is again attained.

When the writer saw Isabelle a year and a half after her discovery, she gave him the impression of being a very bright, cheerful, energetic little girl. She spoke well, walked and ran without trouble, and sang with gusto and accuracy. Today she is over fourteen years old and has passed the sixth grade in a public school. Her teachers say that she participates in all school activities as normally as other children. Though older than her classmates, she has fortunately not physically matured too far beyond their level.

Clearly the history of Isabelle's development is different from that of Anna's. In both cases there was an exceedingly low, or rather blank, intellectual level to begin with. In both cases it seemed that the girl might be congenitally feeble-minded. In both a considerably higher level was reached later on. But the Ohio girl achieved a normal mentality within two years, whereas Anna was still markedly inadequate at the end of four and a half years. This difference in achievement may suggest that Anna had less initial capacity. But an alternative hypothesis is possible.

One should remember that Anna never received the prolonged and expert attention that Isabelle received. The result of such attention, in the case of the Ohio girl, was to give her speech at an early stage, and her subsequent rapid development seems to have been a consequence of that. "Until Isabelle's speech and language development, she had all the characteristics of a feeble-minded child." Had Anna, who, from the standpoint of psychometric tests and early history, closely resembled this girl at the start, been given a mastery of speech at an earlier point by intensive training, her subsequent development might have been much more rapid.

The hypothesis that Anna began with a sharply inferior mental capacity is therefore not established. Even if she were deficient to start with, we have no way of knowing how much so. Under ordinary conditions she might have been a dull normal or, like her mother, a moron. Even after the blight of her isolation, if she had lived to maturity, she might have finally reached virtually the full level of her capacity, whatever it may have been. That her isolation did have a profound effect upon her mentality, there can be no doubt. This is proved by the substantial degree of change during the four and a half years following her rescue.

Consideration of Isabelle's case serves to show, as Anna's case does not clearly show, that isolation up to the age of six, with failure to acquire any form of speech and hence failure to grasp nearly the whole world of cultural meaning, does not preclude the subsequent acquisition of these. Indeed, there seems to be a process of accelerated recovery in which the child goes through the mental stages at a more rapid rate than would be the case in normal development. Just what would be the maximum age at which a person could remain isolated and still retain the capacity for full cultural acquisition is hard to say. Almost certainly it would not be as high as age fifteen; it might possibly be as low as age ten. Undoubtedly various individuals would differ considerably as to the exact age.

Anna's is not an ideal case for showing the effects of extreme isolation, partly because she was possibly deficient to begin with, partly because she did not receive the best training available, and partly because she did not live long enough. Nevertheless, her case is instructive when placed in the record with numerous other cases of extreme isolation. This and the previous article about her are meant to place her in the record. It is to be hoped that other cases will be described in the scientific literature as they are discovered (as unfortunately they will be), for only in these rare cases of extreme isolation is it possible "to observe *concretely separated* two factors in the development of human personality which are always otherwise only analytically separated, the biogenic and the sociogenic factors."

KILLERS OF THE DREAM:
WHEN I WAS A CHILD

Lillian Smith

The previous selection illustrates the importance of association with other human beings in the development of human personality. Since the transmission to children of human habits, attitudes, and beliefs begins very early, and goes on constantly in every family, school, and other groups, we are often not keenly aware of this pervasive social process. In this selection Lillian Smith reveals, with sensitivity and candor, how she was taught a particular pattern of behavior and attitudes considered appropriate for white southern Christian girls of her generation.

Even its children knew that the South was in trouble. No one had to tell them; no words said aloud. To them, it was a vague thing weaving in and out of their play, like a ghost haunting an old graveyard or whispers after the household sleeps—fleeting mystery, vague menace to which each responded in his own way. Some learned to screen out all except the soft and the soothing; others denied even as they saw plainly, and heard. But all knew that under quiet words and warmth and laughter, under the slow ease and tender concern about small matters, there was a heavy burden on all of us and as heavy a refusal to confess it. The children knew this "trouble" was bigger than they, bigger than their family, bigger than their church, so big that people turned away from its size. They had seen it flash out and shatter a town's peace, had felt it tear up all they believed in. They had measured its giant strength and felt weak when they remembered.

This haunted childhood belongs to every southerner of my age. We ran away from it but we came back like a hurt animal to its wound, or a murderer to the scene of his sin. The human heart dares not stay away too long from that which hurt it most. There is a return journey to anguish that few of us are released from making.

SOURCE: Reprinted from *Killers of the Dream* (revised and enlarged), 15–28 passim, by Lillian Smith. By permission of W. W. Norton & Company, Inc. Copyright © 1949, 1961 by Lillian Smith. ✦ The author (1897–1966), a novelist, held honorary doctorate degrees from Oberlin College and Howard University. During her early career, she was principal of a two-teacher mountain school and later spent three years in China teaching music at a private school. For ten years she was editor and publisher of *South Today*. In 1950 she was granted the Southern Author's Award and also a Special Citation for Distinguished Contribution to American Letters by the National Book Award Committee. Her books include *Strange Fruit, One Hour, The Journey,* and *Now Is the Time*.

❖   ❖   ❖   ❖   ❖

The mother who taught me what I know of tenderness and love and compassion taught me also the bleak rituals of keeping Negroes in their "place." The father who rebuked me for an air of superiority toward schoolmates from the mill and rounded out his rebuke by gravely reminding me that "all men are brothers," trained me in the steel-rigid decorums I must demand of every colored male. They who so gravely taught me to split my body from my mind and both from my "soul," taught me also to split my conscience from my acts and Christianity from southern tradition.

Neither the Negro nor sex was often discussed at length in our home. We were given no formal instruction in these difficult matters but we learned our lessons well. We learned the intricate system of taboos, of renunciations and compensations, of manners, voice modulations, words, feelings, along with our prayers, our toilet habits, and our games. I do not remember how or when, but by the time I had learned that God is love, that Jesus is His Son and came to give us more abundant life, that all men are brothers with a common Father, I also knew that I was better than a Negro, that all black folks have their place and must be kept in it, that sex has its place and must be kept in it, that a terrifying disaster would befall the South if ever I treated a Negro as my social equal and as terrifying a disaster would befall my family if ever I were to have a baby outside of marriage. I had learned that God so loved the world that He gave His only begotten Son so that we might have segregated churches in which it was my duty to worship each Sunday and on Wednesday at evening prayers. I had learned that white southerners are a hospitable, courteous, tactful people who treat those of their own group with consideration and who as carefully segregate from all the richness of life "for their own good and welfare" thirteen million people whose skin is colored a little differently from my own.

I knew by the time I was twelve that a member of my family would always shake hands with old Negro friends, would speak graciously to members of the Negro race unless they forgot their place, in which event icy peremptory tones would draw lines beyond which only the desperate would dare take one step. I knew that to use the word "nigger" was unpardonable and no well-bred southerner was quite so crude as to do so; nor would a well-bred southerner call a Negro "mister" or invite him into the living room or eat with him or sit by him in public places.

I knew that my old nurse who had cared for me through long months of illness, who had given me refuge when a little sister took my place as the baby of the family, who soothed, fed me, delighted me with her stories and games, let me fall asleep on her deep warm breast, was not worthy of the passionate love I felt for her but must be given instead a half-smiled-at affection similar to that which one feels for one's dog. I knew but I never believed it, that the deep respect I felt for her, the tenderness, the love, was a childish thing which every normal child outgrows, that such love begins with one's toys and is discarded with them, and that somehow—though it seemed impossible to my agonized heart—I too, must outgrow these feelings. I learned to use a soft voice to oil my words of superiority. I learned to cheapen with tears and sentimental talk of "my old mammy" one of the profound relationships of my life. I learned the bitterest thing a child can learn: that the human relations I valued most were held cheap by the world I lived in.

From the day I was born, I began to learn my lessons. I was put in a rigid frame too intricate, too twisting to describe here so briefly, but I learned to conform to its slide-rule measurements. I learned it is possible to be a Christian and a white southerner simultaneously; to be a gentlewoman and an arrogant callous creature in the same moment; to pray at night and ride a Jim Crow car the next morning and to feel comfortable in doing both. I learned to believe in freedom, to glow when the word *democracy* was used, and to practice slavery from morning to night. I learned it the way all of my southern people learn it: by closing door after door until one's mind and heart and conscience are blocked off from each other and from reality.

I closed the doors. Or perhaps they were closed for me. One day they began to open again. Why I had the desire or the strength to open them, or what strange accident or circumstance opened them for me would require in the answering an account too long, too particular, too stark to make here. And perhaps I should not have the wisdom that such an analysis would demand of me, nor the will to make it. I know only that the doors opened, a little; that somewhere along that iron corridor we travel from babyhood to maturity, doors swinging inward began to swing outward, showing glimpses of the world beyond, of that bright thing we call "reality."

I believe there is one experience which pushed these doors open, a little. And I am going to tell it here, although I know well that to excerpt from a life and family background one incident and name it as a "cause" of a change in one's life direction is a distortion and often an irrelevance. The hungers of a child and how they are filled have too much to do with the way in which experiences are assimilated to tear an incident out of life and look at it in isolation. Yet, with these reservations, I shall tell it, not because it was in itself a severe trauma, but because it became a symbol of buried experiences that I did not have access to. It is an incident that has rarely happened to other southern children. In a sense, unique. But it was an acting-out, a private production of a little script that is written on the lives of most southern children before they know words. Though they may not have seen it staged this way, each southerner has had his own private showing.

I should like to preface the account by giving a brief glimpse of my family, hoping the reader, entering my home with me, will be able to blend the edges of this isolated experience into a more full life picture and in doing so will see that it is, in a sense, everybody's story.

I was born and reared in a small Deep South town whose population was about equally Negro and white. There were nine of us who grew up freely in a rambling house of many rooms, surrounded by big lawn, back yard, gardens, fields, and barn. It was the kind of home that gathers memories like dust, a place filled with laughter and play and pain and hurt and ghosts and games. We were given such advantages of schooling, music, and art as were available in the South, and our world was not limited to the South, for travel to far places seemed a natural thing to us, and usually one of the family was in a remote part of the earth.

We knew we were a respected and important family of this small town but beyond this we gave little thought to status. Our father made money in lumber and naval stores for the excitement of making and losing it— not for what money can buy nor the security which it sometimes gives. I do not remember at any time wanting "to be rich" nor do I remember that thrift and saving were ideals which our parents considered important enough to urge upon us. In the family there was acceptance of risk, a mild delight in burning bridges, an expectant "What next?" We were not irresponsible; living according to the pleasure principle was by no means our way of life. On the contrary we were trained to think that each of us should do something of genuine usefulness, and the family thought it right to make sacrifices if necessary, to give each child preparation for such work. We were also trained to think learning important, and books; but "bad" books our mother burned. We valued music and art and craftsmanship but it was people and their welfare and religion that were the foci around which our lives seemed naturally to move. Above all else, the important thing was what we "planned to do." That each of us must do something was as inevitable as breathing for we owed a "debt to society which must be paid." This was a family commandment.

While many neighbors spent their energies in counting limbs on the family tree and grafting some on now and then to give symmetry to it, or in licking scars to cure their vague malaise, or in fighting each battle and turn of battle of the Civil War which has haunted the southern conscience so long, my father was pushing his nine children straight into the future. "You have your heritage," he used to say, "some of it good, some not so good; and as far as I know you had the usual number of grandmothers and grandfathers. Yes, there were slaves, too many of them in the family, but that was your grandfather's mistake, not yours. The past has been lived. It is gone. The future is yours. What are you going to do with it? He asked this question often and sometimes one knew it was but an echo of a question he had spent his life trying to answer for himself. For the future held my father's dreams; always there, not in the past, did he expect to find what he had spent his life searching for.

We lived the same segregated life as did other southerners but our parents talked in excessively Christian and democratic terms. We were told ten thousand times that status and money are unimportant (though we were well supplied with both); we were told that "all men are brothers," that we are a part of a democracy and must act like democrats. We were told that the teachings of Jesus are important and could be practiced if we tried. We were told that to be "radical" is bad, silly too; and that one must always conform to the "best behavior" of one's community and make it better if one can. We were taught that we were superior to hate and resentment, and that no member of the Smith family could stoop so low as to have an enemy. No matter what injury was done us, we must not injure ourselves further by retaliating. That was a family commandment.

We had family prayers once each day. All of us as children read the Bible in its entirety each year. We memorized hundreds of Bible verses and repeated them at breakfast, and said "sentence prayers" around the family table. God was not someone we met on Sunday but a permanent member of our household. It never occurred to me until I was fourteen or fifteen years old that He did not chalk up the daily score on eternity's tablets.

Despite the strain of living so intimately with God, the nine of us were strong, healthy, energetic youngsters who filled days with play and sports and music and books and managed to live most of the time on the careless level at which young lives should be lived. We had our times of anxiety of course, for there were hard lessons to be learned about the soul and "bad things" to be learned about sex. Sometimes I have wondered how we learned them with a mother so shy with words.

She was a wistful creature who loved beautiful things like lace and sunsets and flowers in a vague inarticulate way, and took good care of her children. We always knew this was not her world but one she accepted under duress. Her private world we rarely entered, though the shadow of it lay heavily on our hearts.

Our father owned large business interests, employed hundreds of colored and white laborers, paid them the prevailing low wages, worked them the prevailing long hours, built for them mill towns (Negro and white), built for each group a church, saw to it that religion was supplied free, saw to it that a commissary supplied commodities at a high price, and in general managed his affairs much as ten thousand other southern businessmen managed theirs.

✧　✧　✧　✧　✧

Against this backdrop the drama of the South was played out one day in my life:

A little white girl was found in the colored section of our town, living with a Negro family in a broken-down shack. This family had moved in a few weeks before and little was known of them. One of the ladies in my mother's club, while driving over to her washerwoman's, saw the child swinging on a gate. The shack, as she said, was hardly more than a pigsty and this white child was living with dirty and sick-looking colored folks. "They must have kidnapped her," she told her friends. Genuinely shocked, the clubwomen busied themselves in an attempt to do something, for the child was very white indeed. The strange Negroes were subjected to a grueling questioning and finally grew evasive and refused to talk at all. This only increased the suspicion of the white group. The next day the clubwomen, escorted by the town marshal, took the child from her adopted family despite their tears.

She was brought to our home. I do not know why my mother consented to this plan. Perhaps because she loved children and always showed concern for them. It was easy for one more to fit into our ample household and Janie was soon at home there. She roomed with me, sat next to me at the table; I found Bible verses for her to say at breakfast; she wore my clothes, played with my dolls and followed me around from morning to night. She was dazed by her new comforts and by the interesting activities of this big lively family; and I was as happily dazed, for her adoration was a new thing to me; and as time passed a quick, childish, and deeply felt bond grew up between us.

But a day came when a telephone message was received from a colored orphanage. There was a meeting at our home. Many whispers. All afternoon the ladies went in and out of our house talking to Mother in tones too low for children to hear. As they passed us at play, they looked at Janie and quickly looked away again, though a few stopped and stared at her as if they could not tear their eyes from her face. When my father came home Mother closed her door against our young ears and talked a long time with him. I heard him laugh, heard Mother say, "But Papa, this is no laughing matter!" And then they were back in the living room with us and my mother was pale and my father was saying, "Well, work it out, Mame, as best you can. After all, now that you know, it is pretty simple."

In a little while my mother called my sister and me into her bedroom and told us that in the morning Janie would return to Colored Town. She said Janie was to have the dresses the ladies had given her and a few of my own, and the toys we had shared with her. She asked me if I would like to give Janie one of my dolls. She seemed hurried, though Janie was not to leave until next day. She said, "Why not select it now?" And in dreamlike stiffness I brought in my dolls and chose one for Janie. And then I found it possible to say, "Why is she leaving? She likes us, she hardly knows them. She told me she had been with them only a month."

"Because," Mother said gently, "Janie is a little colored girl."

"But she's white!"

"We were mistaken. She is colored."

"But she looks—"

"She is colored. Please don't argue!"

"What does it mean?" I whispered.

"It means," Mother said slowly, "that she has to live in Colored Town with colored people."

"But why? She lived here three weeks and she doesn't belong to them, she told me so."

"She is a little colored girl."

"But you said yourself she has nice manners. You said that," I persisted.

"Yes, she is a nice child. But a colored child cannot live in our home."

"Why?"

"You know, dear! You have always known that white and colored people do not live together."

"Can she come to play?"

"No."

"I don't understand."

"I don't either," my young sister quavered.

"You're too young to understand. And don't ask me again, ever again, about this!" Mother's voice was sharp but her face was sad and there was no certainty left there. She hurried out and busied herself in the kitchen and I wandered through that room where I had been born, touching the old familiar things in it, looking at them, trying to find the answer to a question that moaned like a hurt thing. . . .

And then I went out to Janie, who was waiting, knowing things were happening that concerned her but waiting until they were spoken aloud.

I do not know quite how the words were said but I told her she was to return in the morning to the little place where she had lived because she was colored and colored children could not live with white children.

"Are you white?" she said.

"I'm white," I replied, "and my sister is white. And you're colored. And white and colored can't live together because my mother says so."

"Why?" Janie whispered.

"Because they can't," I said. But I knew, though I said it firmly, that something was wrong. I knew my mother and father whom I passionately admired had betrayed something which they held dear. And they could not help doing it. And I was shamed by their failure and frightened, for I felt they were no longer as powerful as I had thought. There was something Out There that was stronger than they and I could not bear to believe it. I could not confess that my father, who always solved the family dilemmas easily and with laughter, could not solve this. I knew that my mother who was so good to children did not believe in her heart that she was being good to this child. There was not a word in my mind that said it but my body knew and my glands, and I was filled with anxiety.

But I felt compelled to believe they were right. It was the only way my world could be held together. And, slowly, it began to seep through me: *I was white. She was colored. We must not be together. It was bad to be together. Though you ate with your nurse when you were little, it was bad to eat with any colored person after that. It was bad just as other things were bad that your mother had told you. It was bad that she was to sleep in the room with me that night. It was bad. . . .*

I was overcome with guilt. For three weeks I had done things that white children were not supposed to do. And now I knew these things had been wrong.

I went to the piano and began to play, as I had always done when I was in trouble. I tried to play my next lesson and as I stumbled through it, the little girl came over and sat on the bench with me. Feeling lost in the deep currents sweeping through our house that night, she crept closer and put her arms around me and I shrank away as if my body had been uncovered. I had not said a word, I did not say one, but she knew, and tears slowly rolled down her little white face. . . .

And then I forgot it. For more than thirty years the experience was wiped out of my memory. But that night, and the weeks it was tied to, worked its way like a splinter, bit by bit, down to the hurt places in my memory and festered there. And as I grew older, as more experiences collected around that faithless time, as memories of earlier, more profound hurts crept closer, drawn to that night as if to a magnet, I began to know that people who talked of love and children did not mean it. That is a hard thing for a child to learn. I still admired my parents, there was so much that was strong and vital and sane and good about them and I never forgot this; I stubbornly believed in their sincerity, as I do to this day, and I loved them. Yet in my heart they were under suspicion. Something was wrong.

Something was wrong with a world that tells you that love is good and people are important and then forces you to deny love and to humiliate people. I knew, though I would not for years confess it aloud, that in trying to shut the Negro race away from us, we have shut ourselves away from so many good, creative, honest, deeply human things in life. I began to understand slowly at first but more clearly as the years passed, that the warped, distorted frame we have put around every Negro child from birth is around every white child also. Each is on a different side of the frame but each is pinioned there. And I knew that what cruelly shapes and cripples the personality of one is as cruelly shaping and crippling the personality of the other. I began to see that though we may, as we acquire new knowledge, live through new experiences, examine old memories, gain the strength to tear the frame from us, yet we are stunted and warped and in our lifetime cannot grow straight again any more than can a tree, put in a steel-like twisting frame when young, grow tall and straight when the frame is torn away at maturity.

As I sit here writing, I can almost touch that little town, so close is the memory of it. There it lies, its main street lined with great oaks, heavy with matted moss that swings softly even now as I remember. A little white town rimmed with Negroes, making a deep shadow on the whiteness. There it lies, broken in two by one strange idea. Minds broken. Hearts broken. Conscience torn from acts. A culture split in a thousand pieces. That is segregation. I am remembering: a woman in a mental hospital walking four steps out, four steps in, unable to go further because she has drawn an invisible line around her small world and is terrified to take one step beyond it. . . . A man in a Disturbed Ward assigning "places" to the other patients and violently insisting that each stay in his place. . . . A Negro woman saying to me so quietly, "We cannot ride together on the bus, you know. It is not legal to be human down here."

Memory, walking the streets of one's childhood . . . of the town where one was born.

❖ 19 ❖

STATUS AND ROLE

Ralph Linton

Through their behavior in various groups people come to perform certain roles and acquire statuses. Ralph Linton's discussion of these two concepts has become a classic. He examines the theory of status and role with illustrations from both nonliterate and complex societies.

The term *status*, like the term *culture*, has come to be used with a double significance. A *status*, in the abstract, is a position in a particular pattern. It is thus quite correct to speak of each individual as having many statuses, since each individual participates in the expression of a number of patterns. However, unless the term is qualified in some way, *the status* of any individual means the sum total of all the statuses which he occupies. It represents his position with relation to the total society. Thus the status of Mr. Jones as a member of his community derives from a combination of all the statuses which he holds as a citizen, as an attorney, as a Mason, as a Methodist, as Mrs. Jones's husband, and so on.

SOURCE: *The Study of Man* by Ralph Linton, 113–21. Copyright 1936, by D. Appleton-Century Company, Inc. Reprinted by permission of Appleton-Century-Crofts. ❖ The author (1893–1953) was Sterling Professor of Anthropology at Yale University. He was Assistant Curator of North American Ethnology, Field Museum of Natural History. He has been described as one of the greatest anthropologists of the present era. Among his works are *Acculturation in Seven American Indian Tribes; The Cultural Background of Personality; Most of the World: The Peoples of Africa, Latin America, and the East Today;* and *The Tree of Culture.*

A status, as distinct from the individual who may occupy it, is simply a collection of rights and duties. Since these rights and duties can find expression only through the medium of individuals, it is extremely hard for us to maintain a distinction in our thinking between statuses and the people who hold them and exercise the rights and duties which constitute them. The relation between any individual and any status he holds is somewhat like that between the driver of an automobile and the driver's place in the machine. The driver's seat with its steering wheel, accelerator, and other controls is a constant with ever-present potentialities for action and control, while the driver may be any member of the family and may exercise these potentialities very well or very badly.

A *rôle* represents the dynamic aspect of a status. The individual is socially assigned to a status and occupies it with relation to other statuses. When he puts the rights and duties which constitute the status into effect, he is performing a rôle. Rôle and status are quite inseparable, and the distinction between them is of only academic interest. There are no rôles without statuses or statuses without rôles. Just as in the case of *status*, the term *rôle* is used with a double significance. Every individual has a series of rôles deriving from the various patterns in which he participates and at the same time a *rôle*, general, which represents the sum total of these rôles and determines what he does for his society and what he can expect from it.

Although all statuses and rôles derive from social patterns and are integral parts of patterns, they have an independent function with relation to the individuals who occupy particular statuses and exercise their rôles. To such individuals the combined status and rôle represent the minimum of attitudes and behavior which he must assume if he is to participate in the overt expression of the pattern. Status and rôle serve to reduce the ideal patterns for social life to individual terms. They become models for organizing the attitudes and behavior of the individual so that these will be congruous with those of the other individuals participating in the expression of the pattern. Thus if we are studying football teams in the abstract, the position of quarterback is meaningless except in relation to the other positions. From the point of view of the quarterback himself it is a distinct and important entity. It determines where he shall take his place in the line-up and what he shall do in various plays. His assignment to this position at once limits and defines his activities and establishes a minimum of things which he must learn. Similarly, in a social pattern such as that for the employer-employee relationship the statuses of employer and employee define what each has to know and do to put the pattern into operation. The employer does not need to know the techniques involved in the employee's labor, and the employee does not need to know the techniques for marketing or accounting.

It is obvious that, as long as there is no interference from external sources, the more perfectly the members of any society are adjusted to their statuses and rôles the more smoothly the society will function. In its attempts to bring about such adjustments every society finds itself caught on the horns of a dilemma. The individual's formation of habits and attitudes begins at birth, and, other things being equal, the earlier his training for a status can begin the more successful it is likely to be. At the same time, no two individuals are alike, and a status which will be congenial to one may be quite uncongenial to another. Also, there are in all social systems certain rôles which require more than training for their successful performance. Perfect technique does not make a great violinist, nor a thorough book knowledge of tactics an efficient general. The utilization of the special gifts of individuals may be highly important to society, as in the case of the general, yet these gifts usually show themselves rather late, and to wait upon their manifestation for the assignment of statuses would be to forfeit the advantages to be derived from commencing training early.

Fortunately, human beings are so mutable that almost any normal individual can be trained to the adequate performance of almost any rôle. Most of the business of living can be conducted on a basis of habit, with little need for intelligence and none for special gifts. Societies have met the dilemma by developing two types of statuses, the *ascribed* and the *achieved*. Ascribed statuses are those which are assigned to individuals without reference to their innate differences or abilities. They can be predicted and trained for from the moment of birth. The *achieved* statuses are, as a minimum, those requiring special qualities, although they are not necessarily limited to these. They are not assigned to individuals from birth but are left open to be filled through competition and individual effort. The majority of the statuses in all social systems are of the ascribed type and those which take care of the ordinary day-to-day business of living are practically always of this type.

In all societies certain things are selected as reference points for the ascription of status. The things chosen for this purpose are always of such a nature that they are ascertainable at birth, making it possible to begin the training of the individual for his potential statuses and rôles at once. The simplest and most universally used of these reference points is sex. Age is used with nearly equal frequency, since all individuals pass through the same cycle of growth, maturity, and decline, and the statuses whose occupation will be determined by age can be forecast and trained for with accuracy. Family relationships, the simplest and most obvious being that of the child to its mother, are also used in all societies as reference points for the establishment of a whole series of statuses. Lastly, there is the matter of birth into a particular socially established group, such as a class or caste. The use of this type of reference is common but not universal. In all societies the actual ascription of statuses to the individual is controlled by a series of these reference points which together serve to delimit the field of his future participation in the life of the group.

The division and ascription of statuses with relation to sex seems to be basic in all social systems. All societies prescribe different attitudes and activities to men and to women. Most of them try to rationalize these prescriptions in terms of the physiological differences between the sexes or their different rôles in reproduction. However, a comparative study of the statuses ascribed to women and men in different cultures seems to show that while such factors may have served as a starting point for the development of a division the actual ascriptions are almost entirely determined by culture. Even the psychological characteristics ascribed to men and women in different societies vary so much that they can have little physiological basis. Our own idea of women as ministering angels contrasts sharply with the ingenuity of women as torturers among the Iroquois and the sadistic delight they took in the process. Even the last two generations have seen a sharp change in the psychological patterns for women in our own society. The delicate, fainting lady of the middle eighteen-hundreds is as extinct as the dodo.

When it comes to the ascription of occupations, which is after all an integral part of status, we find the differences in various societies even more marked. Arapesh women regularly carry heavier loads than men "because their heads are so much harder and stronger." In some societies women do most of the manual labor; in others, as in the Marquesas, even cooking, housekeeping, and baby-tending are proper male occupations, and women spend most of their time primping. Even the general rule that women's handicap through pregnancy and nursing indicates the more active occupations as male and the less active ones as female has many exceptions. Thus among the Tasmanians seal-hunting was women's work. They swam out to the seal rocks, stalked the animals, and clubbed them. Tasmanian women also hunted opossums, which required the climbing of large trees.

Although the actual ascription of occupations along sex lines is highly variable, the pattern of sex division is constant. There are very few societies in which every important activity has not been definitely assigned to men or to women. Even when the two sexes coöperate in a particular occupation, the field of each is usually clearly delimited. Thus in Madagascar rice culture the men make the seed beds and terraces and prepare the fields for transplanting. The women do the work of transplanting, which is hard and back-breaking. The women weed the crop, but the men harvest it. The women then carry it to the threshing floors, where the men thresh it while the women winnow it. Lastly, the women pound the grain in mortars and cook it.

When a society takes over a new industry, there is often a period of uncertainty during which the work may be done by either sex, but it soon falls into the province of one or the other. In Madagascar, pottery is made by men in some tribes and by women in others. The only tribe in which it is made by both men and women is one into which the art has been introduced within the last sixty years. I was told that during the fifteen years preceding my visit there had been a marked decrease in the number of male potters, many men who had once practised the art having given it up. The factor of lowered wages, usually advanced as the reason for men leaving one of our own occupations when women enter it in force, certainly was not operative here. The field was not overcrowded, and the prices for men's and women's products were the same. Most of the men who had given up the trade were vague as to their reasons, but a few said frankly that they did not like to compete with women. Apparently the entry of women into the occupation had robbed it of a certain amount of prestige. It was no longer quite the thing for a man to be a potter, even though he was a very good one.

The use of age as a reference point for establishing status is as universal as the use of sex. All societies recognize three age groupings as a minimum: child, adult, and old. Certain societies have emphasized age as a basis for assigning status and have greatly amplified the divisions. Thus in certain African tribes the whole male population is divided into units composed of those born in the same years or within two- or three-year intervals. However, such extreme attention to age is unusual, and we need not discuss it here.

The physical differences between child and adult are easily recognizable, and the passage from childhood to maturity is marked by physiological events which make it possible to date it exactly for girls and within a few weeks or months for boys. However, the physical passage from childhood to maturity does not necessarily coincide with the social transfer of the individual from one category to the other. Thus in our own society both men and women remain legally children until long after they are physically adult. In most societies this difference between the physical and social transfer is more clearly marked than in our own. The child becomes a man not when he is physically mature but when he is formally recognized as a man by his society. This recognition is almost always given ceremonial expression in what are technically known as puberty rites. The most important element in these rites is not the determination of physical maturity but that of social maturity. Whether a boy is able to breed is less vital to his society than whether he is able to do a man's work and has a man's knowledge. Actually, most puberty ceremonies include tests of the boy's learning and fortitude, and if the aspirants are unable to pass these they are left in the child status until they can. For those who pass the tests, the ceremonies usually culminate in the transfer to them of certain secrets which the men guard from women and children.

The passage of individuals from adult to aged is harder to perceive. There is no clear physiological line for men, while even women may retain their full physical vigor and their ability to carry on all the activities of the adult status for several years after the menopause. The social transfer of men from the adult to the aged group is given ceremonial recognition in a few cultures, as when a father normally surrenders his official position and titles to his son, but such recognition is rare. As for women, there appears to be no society in which the menopause is given ceremonial recognition, although there are a few societies in which it does alter the individual's status. Thus Comanche women, after the menopause, were released from their disabilities with regard to the supernatural. They could handle sacred objects, obtain power through dreams and practise as shamans, all things forbidden to women of bearing age.

The general tendency for societies to emphasize the individual's first change in age status and largely ignore the second is no doubt due in part to the difficulty of determining the onset of old age. However, there are also psychological factors involved. The boy or girl is usually anxious to grow up, and this eagerness is heightened by the exclusion of children from certain activities and knowledge. Also, society welcomes new additions to the most active division of the group, that which contributes most to its perpetuation and well-being. Conversely, the individual who enjoys the thought of growing old is atypical in all societies. Even when age brings respect and a new measure of influence, it means the relinquishment of much that is pleasant. We can see among ourselves that the aging usually refuse to recognize the change until long after it has happened.

In the case of age, as in that of sex, the biological factors involved appear to be secondary to the cultural ones in determining the content of status. There are certain activities which cannot be ascribed to children because children either lack the necessary strength or have not had time to acquire the necessary technical skills. However, the attitudes between parent and child and the importance given to the child in the family structure vary enormously from one culture to another. The status of the child among our Puritan ancestors, where he was seen and not heard and ate at the second table, represents one extreme. At the other might be placed the status of the eldest son of a Polynesian chief. All the *mana* (supernatural power) of the royal line converged upon such a child. He was socially superior to his own father and mother, and any attempt to discipline him would have been little short of sacrilege. I once visited the hereditary chief of a Marquesan tribe and found the whole family camping uncomfortably in their own front yard, although they had a good house built on European lines. Their eldest son, aged nine, had had a dispute with his father a few days before and had tabooed the house by naming it after his head. The family had thus been compelled to move out and could not use it again until he relented and lifted the taboo. As he could use the house himself and eat anywhere in the village, he was getting along quite well and seemed to enjoy the situation thoroughly.

The statuses ascribed to the old in various societies vary even more than those ascribed to children. In some cases they are relieved of all heavy labor and can settle back comfortably to live off their children. In others they perform most of the hard and monotonous tasks which do not require great physical strength, such as the gathering of firewood. In many societies the old women, in particular, take over most of the care of the younger children, leaving the younger women free to enjoy themselves. In some places the old are treated with consideration and respect; in others they are considered a useless incumbrance and removed as soon as they are incapable of heavy labor. In most societies their advice is sought even when little attention is paid to their wishes. This custom has a sound practical basis, for the individual who contrives to live to old age in an uncivilized group has usually been a person of ability and his memory constitutes a sort of reference library to which one can turn for help under all sorts of circumstances.

In certain societies the change from the adult to the old status is made more difficult for the individual by the fact that the patterns for these statuses ascribe different types of personality to each. This was the case among the Comanche, as it seems to have been among most of the Plains tribes. The adult male was a warrior, vigorous, self-reliant, and pushing. Most of his social relationships were phrased in terms of competition. He took what he could get and held what he had without regard to any abstract rights of those weaker than himself. Any willingness to arbitrate differences or to ignore slights was a sign of weakness resulting in loss of prestige. The old man, on the other hand, was expected to be wise and gentle, willing to overlook slights and, if need be, to endure abuse. It was his task to work for the welfare of the tribe, giving sound advice, settling feuds between the warriors, and even preventing his tribe from making new enemies. Young men strove for war and honor, old men strove for peace and tranquillity. There is abundant evidence that among the Comanche the transition was often a difficult one for the individual. Warriors did not prepare for old age, thinking it a better fate to be killed in action. When waning physical powers forced them to assume the new rôle, many of them did so grudgingly, and those who had strong magic would go on trying to enforce the rights which belonged to the younger status. Such bad old men were a peril to young ones beginning their careers, for they were jealous of them simply because they were young and strong and admired by the women. The medicine power of these young men was still weak, and the old men could and did kill them by malevolent magic. It is significant that although benevolent medicine men might be of any age in Comanche folklore, malevolent ones were always old.

CULTURAL CONTRADICTIONS
AND SEX ROLES

Mirra Komarovsky

As is implied by the preceding article, difficulties arise for those who have conflicting statuses. In our own society, such contradictory statuses may be particularly serious for college women. Many college coeds who read this article will recognize some of the problems reported by Mirra Komarovsky. They are dilemmas that confront the individual in our changing contemporary society when the norms associated with her various statuses and roles are incompatible.

Profound changes in the roles of women during the past century have been accompanied by innumerable contradictions and inconsistencies. With our rapidly changing and highly differentiated culture, with migrations and multiplied social contacts, the stage is set for myriads of combinations of incongruous elements. Cultural norms are often functionally unsuited to the social situations to which they apply. Thus they may deter an individual from a course of action which would serve his own, and society's, interests best. Or, if behavior contrary to the norm is engaged in, the individual may suffer from guilt over violating mores which no longer serve any socially useful end. Sometimes culturally defined roles are adhered to in the face of new conditions without a conscious realization of the discrepancies involved. The reciprocal actions dictated by the roles may be at variance with those demanded by the actual situation. This may result in an imbalance of privileges and obligations or in some frustration of basic interests.

Again, problems arise because changes in the mode of life have created new situations which have not as yet been defined by culture. Individuals left thus without social guidance tend to act in terms of egotistic or "short-run hedonistic" motives which at times defeat their own long-term interests or create conflict with others. The precise obligation of a gainfully employed wife toward the support of the family is one such undefined situation.

SOURCE: *American Journal of Sociology*, Vol. 52, No. 3 (November, 1946), 184–89. Reprinted by permission of the University of Chicago Press and the author. ❖ The author is professor of sociology at Barnard College. She is the author of *The Unemployed Man and His Family* and *Women in the Modern World: Their Education and Their Dilemmas*, and the coauthor of *Leisure, A Suburban Study*.

Finally, a third mode of discrepancy arises in the existence of incompatible cultural definitions of the same social situation, such as the clash of "old-fashioned" and "radical" mores, of religion and law, of norms of economic and familial institutions.

The problems raised by these discrepancies are social problems in the sense that they engender mental conflict or social conflict or otherwise frustrate some basic interest of large segments of the population.

This article sets forth in detail the nature of certain incompatible sex roles imposed by our society upon the college woman. It is based on data collected in 1942 and 1943. Members of an undergraduate course on the family were asked for two successive years to submit autobiographical documents focused on the topic; 73 were collected. In addition, 80 interviews, lasting about an hour each, were conducted with every member of a course in social psychology of the same institution—making a total of 153 documents ranging from a minimum of five to a maximum of thirty typewritten pages.

The generalization emerging from these documents is the existence of serious contradictions between two roles present in the social environment of the college woman. The goals set by each role are mutually exclusive, and the fundamental personality traits each evokes are at points diametrically opposed, so that what are assets for one become liabilities for the other, and the full realization of one role threatens defeat in the other.

One of these roles may be termed the "feminine" role. While there are a number of permissive variants of the feminine role for women of college age (the "good sport," the "glamour girl," the "young lady," the domestic "home girl," etc.), they have a common core of attributes defining the proper attitudes to men, family, work, love, etc., and a set of personality traits often described with reference to the male sex role as "not as dominant, or aggressive as men" or "more emotional, sympathetic."

The other and more recent role is, in a sense, no sex role at all, because it partly obliterates the differentiation in sex. It demands of the women much the same virtues, patterns of behavior, and attitude that it does of the men of a corresponding age. We shall refer to this as the "modern" role.

Both roles are present in the social environment of these women throughout their lives, though, as the precise content of each sex role varies with age, so does the nature of their clashes change from one stage to another. In the period under discussion the conflict between the two roles apparently centers about academic work, social life, vocational plans, excellence in specific fields of endeavor, and a number of personality traits.

One manifestation of the problem is in the inconsistency of the goals set for the girl by her family.

Forty, or 26 per cent, of the respondents expressed some grievance against their families for failure to confront them with clearcut and consistent goals. The majority, 74 per cent, denied having had such experiences. One student writes:

How am I to pursue any course single-mindedly when some way along the line a person I respect is sure to say, "You are on the wrong track and are wasting your time." Uncle John telephones every Sunday morning. His first question is: "Did you go out last night?" He would think me a "grind" if I were to stay home Saturday night to finish a term paper. My father expects me to get an "A" in every subject and is disappointed by a "B." He says I have plenty of time for social life. Mother says, "That 'A' in Philosophy is very nice dear. But please don't become so deep that no man will be good enough for you." And finally, Aunt Mary's line is careers for women. "Prepare yourself for some profession. This is the only way to insure yourself independence and an interesting life. You have plenty of time to marry."

A senior writes:

I get a letter from my mother at least three times a week. One week her letters will say, "Remember that this is your last year at college. Subordinate everything to your studies. You must have a good record to secure a job." The next week her letters are full of wedding news. This friend of mine got married; that one is engaged; my young cousin's wedding is only a week off. When, my mother wonders, will I make up my mind? Surely, I wouldn't want to be the only unmarried one in my group. It is high time, she feels, that I give some thought to it.

A student reminisces:

All through high school my family urged me to work hard because they wished me to enter a first-rate college. At the same time they were always raving about a girl schoolmate who lived next door to us. How pretty and sweet she was, how popular, and what taste in clothes! Couldn't I also pay more attention to my appearance and to social life? They were overlooking the fact that this carefree friend of mine had little time left for school work and had failed several subjects. It seemed that my family had expected me to become Eve Curie and Hedy Lamarr wrapped up in one.

Another comments:

My mother thinks that it is very nice to be smart in college but only if it doesn't take too much effort. She always tells me not to be too intellectual on dates, to be clever in a light sort of way. My father, on the other hand, wants me to study law. He thinks that if I applied myself I could make an excellent lawyer and keeps telling me that I am better fitted for this profession than my brother.

Another writes:

One of my two brothers writes: "Cover up that high forehead and act a little dumb once in a while"; while the other always urges upon me the importance of rigorous scholarship.

The students testified to a certain bewilderment and confusion caused by the failure on the part of the family to smooth the passage from one role to another, especially when the roles involved were contradictory. It seemed to some of them that they had awakened one morning to find their world upside down: what had hitherto evoked praise and rewards from relatives, now suddenly aroused censure. A student recollects:

I could match my older brother in skating, sledding, riflery, ball, and many of the other games we played. He enjoyed teaching me and took great pride in my accomplishments. Then one day it all changed. He must have suddenly become conscious of the fact that girls ought to be feminine. I was walking with him, proud to be able to make long strides and keep up with his long-legged steps when he turned to me in annoyance, "Can't you walk like a lady?" I still remember feeling hurt and bewildered by his scorn, when I had been led to expect approval.

Once during her freshman year in college, after a delightful date, a student wrote her brother with great elation:

"What a wonderful evening.at———fraternity house! You should be proud of me, Johnny! I won all ping-pong games but one!"
"For heaven's sake," came the reply, "when will you grow up? Don't you know that a boy likes to think he is better than a girl? Give him a little competition, sure, but miss a few serves in the end. Should you join the Debate Club? By all means, but don't practice too much on the boys." Believe me I was stunned by this letter but then I saw that he was right. To be a success in the dorms one must date, to date one must not win too many ping-pong games. At first I resented this bitterly. But now I am more or less used to it and live in hope of one day meeting a man who is my superior so that I may be my natural self.

It is the parents and not the older sibling who reversed their expectations in the following excerpt:

All through grammar school and high school my parents led me to feel that to do well in school was my chief responsibility. A good report card, an election to student office, these were the news Mother bragged about in telephone conversations with her friends. But recently they suddenly got worried about me: I don't pay enough attention to social life, a woman needs *some* education but not that much. They are disturbed by my determination to go to the School of Social Work. Why my ambitions should surprise them after they have exposed me for four years to some of the most inspired and stimulating social scientists in the country, I can't imagine. They have some mighty strong arguments on their side. What is the use, they say, of investing years in training for a profession, only to drop it in a few years? Chances of meeting men are slim in this profession. Besides, I may become so preoccupied with it as to sacrifice social life. The next few years are, after all, the proper time to find a mate. But the urge to apply what I have learned, and the challenge of this profession is so strong that I shall go on despite the family opposition.

The final excerpt illustrates both the sudden transition of roles and the ambiguity of standards:

I major in English composition. This is not a completely "approved" field for girls so I usually just say "English." An English Literature major is quite liked and approved by boys. Somehow it is lumped with all the other arts and even has a little glamour. But a composition major is a girl to beware of because she supposedly will notice all your grammar mistakes, look at your letters too critically, and consider your ordinary speech and conversation as too crude.

I also work for a big metropolitan daily as a correspondent in the city room. I am well liked there and may possibly stay as a reporter after graduation in February. I have had several spreads [stories running to more than eight or ten inches of space], and this is considered pretty good for a college correspondent. Naturally, I was elated and pleased at such breaks, and as far as the city room is concerned I'm off to a very good start on a career that is hard for a man to achieve and even harder for a woman. General reporting is still a man's work in the opinion of most people. I have a lot of acclaim but also criticism, and I find it confusing and difficult to be praised for being clever and working hard and then, when my efforts promise to be successful, to be condemned and criticized for being unfeminine and ambitious.

Here are a few of these reactions:

My father: "I don't like this newspaper set-up at all. The people you meet are making you less interested in marriage than ever. You're getting too educated and intellectual to be attractive to men."

My mother: "I don't like your attitude toward people. The paper is making you too analytical and calculating. Above all, you shouldn't sacrifice your education and career for marriage."

A lieutenant with two years of college: "It pleased me greatly to hear about your news assignment—good girl."

A Navy pilot with one year of college: "Undoubtedly, I'm old-fashioned, but I could never expect or feel right about a girl giving up a very promising or interesting future to hang around waiting for me to finish college. Nevertheless, congratulations on your job on the paper. Where in the world do you get that wonderful energy? Anyway I know you were thrilled at getting it and feel very glad for you. I've an idea that it means the same to you as that letter saying 'report for active duty' meant to me."

A graduate metallurgist now a private in the Army: "It was good to hear that you got that break with the paper. I am sure that talent will prove itself and that you will go far. But not too far, as I don't think you should become a career woman. You'll get repressed and not be interested enough in having fun if you keep after that career."

A lieutenant with a year and a half of college: "All this career business is nonsense. A woman belongs in the home and absolutely no place else. My wife will have to stay home. That should keep her happy. Men are just superior in everything, and women have no right to expect to compete with them. They should do just what will keep their husbands happy."

A graduate engineer—my fiancé: "Go right ahead and get as far as you can in your field. I am glad you are ambitious and clever, and I'm as anxious to see you happily successful as I am myself. It is a shame to let all those brains go to waste over just dusting and washing dishes. I think the usual home life and children are small sacrifices to make if a career will keep you happy. But I'd rather see you in radio because I am a bit wary of the effect upon our marriage of the way of life you will have around the newspapers.

Sixty-one, or 40 per cent, of the students indicated that they have occasionally "played dumb" on dates, that is, concealed some academic honor, pretended ignorance of some subject, or allowed the man the last word in an intellectual discussion. Among these were women who "threw games" and in general played down certain skills in obedience to the unwritten law that men must possess these skills to a superior degree. At the same time, in other areas of life, social pressures were being exerted upon these women to "play to win," to compete to the utmost of their abilities for intellectual distinction and academic honors. One student writes:

I was glad to transfer to a woman's college. The two years at the co-ed university produced a constant strain. I am a good student; my family expects me to get good marks. At the same time I am normal enough to want to be invited to the Saturday night dance. Well, everyone knew that on that campus a reputation of a "brain" killed a girl socially. I was always fearful lest I say too much in class or answer a question which the boys I dated couldn't answer.

Here are some significant remarks made from the interviews:

When a girl asks me what marks I got last semester I answer, "Not so good—only one 'A.' " When a boy asks the same question, I say very brightly with a note of surprise, "Imagine, I got an 'A!' "

I am engaged to a southern boy who doesn't think too much of the woman's intellect. In spite of myself, I play up to his theories because the less one knows and does, the more he does for you and thinks you "cute" into the bargain. . . . I allow him to explain things to me in great detail and to treat me as a child in financial matters.

One of the nicest techniques is to spell long words incorrectly once in a while. My boy-friend seems to get a great kick out of it and writes back, "Honey, you certainly don't know how to spell."

When my date said that he considers Ravel's *Bolero* the greatest piece of music ever written, I changed the subject because I knew I would talk down to him.

A boy advised me not to tell of my proficiency in math and not to talk of my plans to study medicine unless I knew my date well.

My fiancé didn't go to college. I intend to finish college and work hard at it, but in talking to him I make college appear a kind of a game.

Once I went sailing with a man who so obviously enjoyed the role of a protector that I told him I didn't know how to sail. As it turned out he didn't either. We got into a tough spot, and I was torn between a desire to get a hold of the boat and a fear to reveal that I had lied to him.

It embarrassed me that my "steady" in high school got worse marks than I. A boy should naturally do better in school. I would never tell him my marks and would often ask him to help me with my homework.

I am better in math than my fiancé. But while I let him explain politics to me, we never talk about math even though, being a math major, I could tell him some interesting things.

Mother used to tell me to lay off the brains on dates because glasses make me look too intellectual anyhow.

I was once at a work camp. The girls did the same work as the boys. If some girls worked better, the boys resented it fiercely. The director told one capable girl to slow down to keep peace in the group.

How to do the job and remain popular was a tough task. If you worked your best, the boys resented the competition; if you acted feminine, they complained that you were clumsy.

On dates I always go through the "I-don't-care-anything-you-want-to-do" routine. It gets monotonous but boys fear girls who make decisions. They think such girls would make nagging wives.

I am a natural leader and, when in the company of girls, usually take the lead. That is why I am so active in college activities. But I know that men fear bossy women, and I always have to watch myself on dates not to assume the "executive" role. Once a boy walking to the theater with me took the wrong street. I knew a short cut but kept quiet.

I let my fiancé make most of the decisions when we are out. It annoys me, but he prefers it.

I sometimes "play dumb" on dates, but it leaves a bad taste. The emotions are complicated. Part of me enjoys "putting something over" on the unsuspecting male. But this sense of superiority over him is mixed with feeling of guilt for my hypocrisy. Toward the "date" I feel some contempt because he is "taken in" by my technique, or if I like the boy, a kind of a maternal condescension. At times I resent him! Why isn't he my superior in all ways in which a man should excel so that I could be my natural self? What am I doing here with him, anyhow? Slumming?

And the funny part of it is that the man, I think, is not always so unsuspecting. He may sense the truth and become uneasy in the relation. "Where do I stand? Is she laughing up her sleeve or did she mean this praise? Was she really impressed with that little speech of mine or did she only pretend to know nothing about politics?" And once or twice I felt that the joke was on me: the boy saw through my wiles and felt contempt for me for stooping to such tricks.

Another aspect of the problem is the conflict between the psychogenic personality of the girl and the cultural role foisted upon her by the milieu. At times it is the girl with "masculine" interests and personality traits who chafes under the pressure to conform to the "feminine" pattern. At other times it is the family and the college who thrust upon the reluctant girl the "modern" role.

While, historically, the "modern" role is the most recent one, onto-genetically it is the one emphasized earlier in the education of the college girl, if these 153 documents are representative. Society confronts the girl with powerful challenges and strong pressure to excel in certain competitive lines of endeavor and to develop certain techniques of adaptation very similar to those expected of her brothers. But, then, quite suddenly as it appears to these girls, the very success in meeting these challenges begins to cause anxiety. It is precisely those most successful in the earlier role who are now penalized.

It is not only the passage from age to age but the moving to another region or type of campus which may create for the girl similar problems. The precise content of sex roles, or, to put it in another way, the degree of their differentiation, varies with regional class, nativity, and other sub-cultures.

Whenever individuals show differences in response to some social situation, as have our 153 respondents, the question naturally arises as to the causes. It will be remembered that 40 per cent admitted some difficulties in personal relations with men due to conflicting sex roles but that 60 per cent said that they had no such problems. Inconsistency of parental expec tations troubled 26 per cent of the students.

To account for individual differences would require another study, involving a classification of personalities in relation to the peculiar social environments of each. Generally speaking, it would seem that it is the girl with a "middle-of-the-road personality" who is most happily adjusted to the present historical moment. She is not a perfect incarnation of either role but is flexible enough to play both. She is a girl who is intelligent enough to do well in school but not so brilliant as to "get all A's"; informed and alert but not consumed by an intellectual passion; capable but not talented in areas relatively new to women; able to stand on her own feet and to earn a living but not so good a living as to compete with men; capable of doing some job well (in case she does not marry or, otherwise, has to work) but not so identified with a profession as to need it for her happiness.

A search for less immediate causes of individual reactions would lead us further back to the study of genesis of the personality differences found relevant to the problem. One of the clues will certainly be provided by the relation of the child to the parent of the same and of the opposite sex. This relation affects the conception of self and the inclination for a particular sex role.

The problems set forth in this article will persist, in the opinion of the writer, until the adult sex roles of women are redefined in greater harmony with the socioeconomic and ideological character of modern society. Until then neither the formal education nor the unverbalized sex roles of the adolescent woman can be cleared of intrinsic contradictions.

CONTINUITIES AND DISCONTINUITIES IN CULTURAL CONDITIONING

Ruth Benedict

This article has been widely reprinted because it so effectively demonstrates how a particular aspect of culture, "continuities and discontinuities," affects personality development. As used by Ruth Benedict, the term "continuity" refers primarily to types of child-rearing which gradually prepare a child for his adult roles and thus help to prevent maladjustment. An example of cultural discontinuity is the fact that in our society unmarried young adults are expected to have no sexual experience, yet are supposed to become, "overnight" so-to-speak, adequate husbands and wives.

All cultures must deal in one way or another with the cycle of growth from infancy to adulthood. Nature has posed the situation dramatically: on the one hand, the newborn baby, physiologically vulnerable, unable to fend for itself, or to participate of its own initiative in the life of the group, and, on the other, the adult man or woman. Every man who rounds out his human potentialities must have been a son first and a father later, and the two roles are physiologically in great contrast; he must first have been dependent upon others for his very existence, and later he must provide such security for others. This discontinuity in the life cycle is a fact of nature and is inescapable. Facts of nature, however, in any discussion of human problems, are ordinarily read off not at their bare minimal but surrounded by all the local accretions of behavior to which the student of human affairs has become accustomed in his own culture. For that reason, it is illuminating to examine comparative material from other societies in order to get a wider perspective on our own special accretions. The anthropologist's role is not to question the facts of nature, but to insist upon the interposition of a middle term between "nature" and

SOURCE: Copyright Patrick Mullahy. Published by Thomas Nelson & Sons, New York. Originally published in *Psychiatry*, Vol. 1 (1938), 161–67. ✧ The author (1887–1948) was an anthropologist, educator, and poet (under the name Ann Singleton). She was a member of the staff of the Department of Anthropology at Columbia University. Her researches helped to guide Allied propaganda in World War II. She studied Mission, Blackfoot, Apache, Pueblo, and Pima Indians on location and made special studies of mythology, folklore, and primitive religions. Among her books are *Patterns of Culture, Race, Science and Politics*, and *The Chrysanthemum and the Sword*.

"human behavior"; his role is to analyze that term, to document local man-made doctorings of nature, and to insist that these doctorings should not be read off in any one culture as nature itself. Although it is a fact of nature that the child becomes a man, the way in which this transition is effected varies from one society to another, and no one of these particular cultural bridges should be regarded as the "natural" path to maturity.

From a comparative point of view, our culture goes to great extremes in emphasizing contrasts between the child and the adult. The child is sexless, the adult estimates his virility by his sexual activities; the child must be protected from the ugly facts of life, the adult must meet them without psychic catastrophe; the child must obey, the adult must command this obedience. These are all dogmas of our culture, dogmas which, in spite of the facts of nature, other cultures commonly do not share. In spite of the physiological contrasts between child and adult, these are cultural accretions.

It will make the point clearer if we consider one habit in our own culture in regard to which there is not this discontinuity of conditioning. With the greatest clarity of purpose and economy of training, we achieve our goal of conditioning everyone to eat three meals a day. The baby's training in regular food periods begins at birth, and no crying of the child and no inconvenience to the mother is allowed to interfere. We gauge the child's physiological make-up and at first allow it food oftener than adults, but, because our goal is firmly set and our training consistent, before the child is two years old it has achieved the adult schedule. From the point of view of other cultures, this is as startling as the fact of three-year-old babies perfectly at home in deep water is to us. Modesty is another sphere in which our child training is consistent and economical; we waste no time in clothing the baby, and, in contrast to many societies where the child runs naked till it is ceremonially given its skirt or its public sheath at adolescence, the child's training fits it precisely for adult conventions.

In neither of these aspects of behavior is there need for an individual in our culture to embark before puberty, at puberty, or at some later date upon a course of action which all his previous training has tabooed. He is spared the unsureness inevitable in such a transition.

The illustration I have chosen may appear trivial, but, in larger and more important aspects of behavior, our methods are obviously different. Because of the great variety of child training in different families in our society, I might illustrate continuity of conditioning from individual life histories in our culture, but even these, from a comparative point of view, stop far short of consistency; and I shall, therefore, confine myself to describing arrangements in other cultures in which training, which with us is idiosyncratic is accepted and traditional and does not, therefore, involve the same possibility of conflict. I shall choose childhood rather than infant and nursing situations, not because the latter do not vary strikingly in different cultures but because they are nevertheless more circumscribed by the baby's physiological needs than is its later training. Childhood situations provide an excellent field in which to illustrate the range of cultural adjustments which are possible within a universally given, but not so drastic, set of physiological facts.

The major discontinuity in the life cycle is of course that the child who is at one point a son must later be a father. These roles in our society are strongly differentiated; a good son is tractable, and does not assume adult responsibilities; a good father provides for his children and should not allow his authority to be flouted. In addition the child must be sexless so far as his family is concerned, whereas the father's sexual role is primary in the family. The individual in one role must revise his behavior from almost all points of view when he assumes the second role.

I shall select for discussion three such contrasts that occur in our culture between the individual's role as child and as father: (1) responsible-nonresponsible status role; (2) dominance-submission; (3) contrasted sexual role. It is largely upon our cultural commitments to these three contrasts that the discontinuity in the life cycle of an individual in our culture depends.

1. *Responsible-Nonresponsible Status Role*

The techniques adopted by societies which achieve continuity during the life cycle in this sphere in no way differ from those we employ in our uniform conditioning to three meals a day. They are merely applied to other areas of life. We think of the child as wanting to play and the adult as having to work, but in many societies the mother takes the baby daily in her shawl or carrying net to the garden or to gather roots, and adult labor is seen even in infancy from the pleasant security of its position in close contact with its mother. When the child can run about, it accompanies its parents still, doing tasks which are essential and yet suited to its powers, and its dichotomy between work and play is not different from that [which] its parents recognize, namely, the distinction between the busy day and the free evening. The tasks it is asked to perform are graded to its powers, and its elders wait quietly by, not offering to do the task in the child's place. Everyone who is familiar with such societies has been struck by the contrast with our child training. Dr. Ruth Underhill tells me of sitting with a group of Papago elders in Arizona when the man of the house turned to his little three-year-old granddaughter and asked her to close the door. The door was heavy and hard to shut. The child tried, but it did not move. Several times the grandfather repeated: "Yes, close the door." No one jumped to the child's assistance. No one took the responsibility away from her. On the other hand there was no impatience, for after all the child was small. They sat gravely waiting till the child succeeded and her grandfather gravely thanked her. It was assumed that the task would not be asked of her unless she could perform it, and, having been asked, the responsibility was hers alone just as if she were a grown woman.

The essential point of such child training is that the child is from infancy continuously conditioned to responsible social participation, while at the same time the tasks that are expected of it are adapted to its capacity. The contrast with our society is very great. A child does not make any labor contribution to our industrial society except as it competes with an adult; its work is not measured against its own strength and skill but against high-geared industrial requirements. Even when we praise a child's achievement in the home, we are outraged if such praise is interpreted as being of the same order as praise of adults. The child is praised because the parent feels well disposed, regardless of whether the task is well done by adult standards, and the child acquires no sensible standard by which to measure its achievement. The gravity of a Cheyenne Indian family ceremoniously making a feast out of the little boy's first snowbird is at the furthest remove from our behavior. At birth the little boy was presented with a toy bow, and from the time he could run about serviceable bows suited to his stature were specially made for him by the man of the family. Animals and birds were taught him in a graded series beginning with those most easily taken, and as he brought in his first of each species his family duly made a feast of it, accepting his contribution as gravely as the buffalo his father brought. When he finally killed a buffalo, it was only the final step of his childhood conditioning, not a new adult role with which his childhood experience had been at variance.

The Canadian Ojibwa show clearly what results can be achieved. This tribe gains its livelihood by winter trapping, and the small family of father, mother, and children live during the long winter alone on their great frozen hunting grounds. The boy accompanies his father and brings in his catch to his sister as his father does to his mother; the girl prepares the meat and skins for him just as his mother does for her husband. By the time the boy is 12, he may have set his own line of traps on a hunting territory of his own and return to his parents' house only once in several months—still bringing the meat and skins to his sister. The young child is taught consistently that it has only itself to rely upon in life, and this is as true in the dealings it will have with the supernatural as in the business of getting a livelihood. This attitude he will accept as a successful adult just as he accepted it as a child.

2. Dominance-Submission

Dominance-submission is the most striking of those categories of behavior where like does not respond to like, but where one type of behavior stimulates the opposite response. It is one of the most prominent ways in which behavior is patterned in our culture. When it obtains between classes, it may be nourished by continuous experience; the difficulty in its use between children and adults lies in the fact that an individual conditioned to one set of behavior in childhood must adopt the opposite as an adult. Its opposite is a pattern of approximately identical reciprocal behavior; the societies which rely upon continuous conditioning characteristically invoke this pattern. In some primitive cultures the very terminology of address between father and son, and, more commonly, between grandfather and grandson or uncle and nephew, reflects this attitude. In such kinship terminologies, one reciprocal expresses each of these relationships so that son and father, for instance, exchange the same term with one another, just as we exchange the same term with a cousin. The child later will exchange it with his son. "Father-son," therefore, is a continuous relationship he enjoys throughout life. The same continuity, backed up by verbal reciprocity, occurs far oftener in the grandfather-grandson relationship or that of mother's brother-sister's son. When these are "joking" relationships, as they often are, travellers report wonderingly upon the liberties and pretensions of tiny toddlers in their dealing with these family elders. In place of our dogma of respect to elders, such societies employ in these cases a reciprocity as nearly identical as may be. The teasing and practical joking the grandfather visits upon his grandchild, the grandchild returns in like coin; he would be led to believe that he failed in propriety if he did not give like for like. If the sister's son has right of access without leave to his mother's brother's possessions, the mother's brother has such rights also to the child's possessions. They share reciprocal privileges and obligations which in our society can develop only between age mates.

From the point of view of our present discussion, such kinship conventions allow the child to put in practice from infancy the same forms of behavior which it will rely upon as an adult; behavior is not polarized into a general requirement of submission for the child and dominance for the adult.

It is clear from the techniques described above, by which the child is conditioned to a responsible status role, that these depend chiefly upon arousing in the child the desire to share responsibility in adult life. To achieve this, little stress is laid upon obedience but much stress upon approval and praise. Punishment is very commonly regarded as quite outside the realm of possibility, and natives in many parts of the world have drawn the conclusion from our usual disciplinary methods that white parents do not love their children. If the child is not required to be submissive, however, many occasions for punishment melt away; a variety of situations which call for it do not occur. Many American Indian tribes are especially explicit in rejecting the ideal of a child's submissive or obedient behavior. Prince Maximilian von Wied, who visited the Crow Indians over a hundred years ago, describes a father's boasting about his young son's intractability even when it was the father himself who was flouted; "He will be a man," his father said. He would have been baffled at the idea that his child should show behavior which would obviously make him appear a poor creature in the eyes of his fellows if he used it as an adult. Dr. George Devereux tells me of a special case of such an attitude among the Mohave at the present time. The child's mother was white and protested to its father that he must take action when the child disobeyed and struck him. "But why?" the father said, "he is little. He cannot possibly injure me." He did not know of any dichotomy according to which an adult expects obedience and a child must accord it. If his child had been docile he would simply have judged that it would become a docile adult— an eventuality of which he would not have approved.

Child training which brings about the same result is common also in other areas of life than that of reciprocal kinship obligations between child and adult. There is a tendency in our culture to regard every situation as having in it the seeds of a dominance-submission relationship. Even where dominance-submission is patently irrelevant we read in the dichotomy, assuming that in every situation there must be one person dominating another. On the other hand some cultures, even when the situation calls for leadership do not see it in terms of dominance-submission. To do justice to this attitude, it would be necessary to describe their political and especially their economic arrangements, for such an attitude to persist must certainly be supported by economic mechanisms that are congruent with it. But it must also be supported by—or what comes to the same thing, express itself in—child training and familial situations.

3. Contrasted Sexual Role

Continuity of conditioning in training the child to assume responsibility and to behave no more submissively than adults is quite possible in terms of the child's physiological endowment if his participation is suited to his strength. Because of the late development of the child's reproductive organs, continuity of conditioning in sex experience presents a difficult problem. So far as their belief that the child is anything but a sexless being is concerned, they are probably more nearly right than we are with an opposite dogma. But the great break is presented by the universally sterile unions before puberty and the presumably fertile ones after maturation. This physiological fact no amount of cultural manipulation can minimize or alter, and societies, therefore, which stress continuous conditioning most strongly sometimes do not expect children to be interested in sex experience until they have matured physically. This is striking among American Indian tribes like the Dakota; adults observe great privacy in sex acts and in no way stimulate children's sexual activity. There need be no discontinuity, in the sense in which I have used the term, in such a program if the child is taught nothing it does not have to unlearn later. In such cultures, adults view children's experimentation as in no way wicked or dangerous, but merely as innocuous play which can have no serious consequences. In some societies such play is minimal and the children manifest little interest in it. But the same attitude may be taken by adults in societies where such play is encouraged and forms a major activity among small children. This is true among most of the Melanesian cultures of Southeast New Guinea;

adults go as far as to laugh off sexual affairs within the prohibited class, if the children are not mature, saying that since they cannot marry there can be no harm done.

It is this physiological fact of the difference between children's sterile unions and adults' presumably fertile sex relations which must be kept in mind in order to understand the different mores which almost always govern sex expression in children and in adults in the same culture. A great many cultures with preadolescent sexual license require marital fidelity, and a great many which value premarital virginity in either male or female arrange their marital life with great license. Continuity in sex experience is complicated by factors which it was unnecessary to consider in the problems previously discussed. The essential problem is not whether or not the child's sexuality is consistently exploited—for even where such exploitation is favored, in the majority of cases the child must seriously modify his behavior at puberty or at marriage. Continuity in sex expression means rather that the child is taught nothing it must unlearn later. If the cultural emphasis is upon sexual pleasure, the child who is continuously conditioned will be encouraged to experiment freely and pleasurably, as among the Marquesans; if emphasis is upon reproduction, as among the Zuni of New Mexico, childish sex proclivities will not be exploited, for the only important use which sex is thought to serve in his culture is not yet possible to him. The important contrast with our child training is that, although a Zuni child is impressed with the wickedness of premature sex experimentation, he does not run the risk as in our culture of associating this wickedness with sex itself rather than with sex at his age. The adult in our culture has often failed to unlearn the wickedness or the dangerousness of sex, a lesson which was impressed upon him strongly in his most formative years.

4. *Discontinuity in Conditioning*

Even from this very summary statement of continuous conditioning, the economy of such mores is evident. In spite of the obvious advantages, however, there are difficulties in its way. Many primitive societies expect as different behavior from an individual as child and as adult as we do, and such discontinuity involves a presumption of strain.

Many societies of this type, however, minimize strain by the techniques they employ; and some techniques are more successful than others in ensuring the individual's functioning without conflict. It is from this point of view that age-grade societies reveal their fundamental significance. Age-graded cultures characteristically demand different behavior of the individual at different times of his life and persons of a like age-grade are grouped into a society whose activities are all oriented toward the behavior desired at that age. Individuals "graduate" publicly and with honor from one of these groups to another. Where age society members are enjoined to loyalty and mutual support, and are drawn not only from the local group but from the whole tribe, as among the Arapaho, or even from other tribes as among the Wagawaga of Southeast New Guinea, such an institution has many advantages in eliminating conflicts among local groups and fostering intratribal peace. This seems to be also a factor in the tribal military solidarity of the similarly organized Masai of East Africa. The point that is of chief interest for our present discussion, however, is that by this means an individual who at any time takes on a new set of duties and virtues is supported not only by a solid phalanx of age mates but by the traditional prestige of the organized "secret" society into which he has now graduated. Fortified in this way, individuals in such cultures often swing between remarkable extremes of opposite behavior without apparent psychic threat. For example, the great majority exhibit prideful and non-conflicted behavior at each stage in the life cycle, even when a prime of life devoted to passionate and aggressive head hunting must be followed by a later life dedicated to ritual and to mild and peaceable civic virtues.

Our chief interest here, however, is in discontinuity which primarily affects the child. In many primitive societies, such discontinuity has been fostered not because of economic or political necessity or because such discontinuity provides for a socially valuable division of labor, but because of some conceptual dogma. The most striking of these are the Australian and Papuan cultures where the ceremony of the "Making of Man" flourishes. In such societies it is believed that men and women have opposite and conflicting powers, and male children, who are of undefined status, must be initiated into the male role. In Central Australia the boy child is of the woman's side, and women are taboo in the final adult stages of tribal ritual. The elaborate and protracted initiation ceremonies of the Arunta, therefore, snatch the boy from the mother, dramatize his gradual repudiation of her. In a final ceremony he is reborn as a man out of the men's ceremonial "baby pouch." The men's ceremonies are ritual statements of a masculine solidarity, carried out by fondling one another's *churingas*, the material symbol of each man's life, and by letting out over one another blood drawn from their veins. After this warm bond among men has been established through the ceremonies, the boy joins the men in the men's house and participates in tribal rites. The enjoined discontinuity has been tribally bridged.

West of the Fly River in southern New Guinea, there is a striking development of this Making of Men cult which involves a childhood period of passive homosexuality. Among the Keraki it is thought that no boy can grow to full stature without playing the role for some years. Men slightly older take the active role, and the older man is a jealous partner. The life cycle of the Keraki Indians includes, therefore, in succession, passive homosexuality, active homosexuality, and heterosexuality. The Keraki believe that pregnancy will result from post-pubertal passive homosexuality and see evidences of such practices in any fat man, whom, even as an old man, they may kill or drive out of the tribe because of their fear. The ceremony that is of interest in connection with the present discussion takes place at the end of the period of passive homosexuality. This ceremony consists in burning out the possibility of pregnancy from the boy by pouring lye down his throat, after which he has no further protection if he gives way to the practice. There is no technique for ending active homosexuality, but this is not explicitly taboo for older men; heterosexuality and children, however, are highly valued. Unlike the neighboring Marindanim, who share their homosexual practices, Keraki husband and wife share the same house and work together in the gardens.

I have chosen illustrations of discontinuous conditioning where it is not too much to say that the cultural institutions furnish adequate support to the individual as he progresses from role to role or interdicts the previous behavior in a summary fashion. The contrast with arrangements in our culture is very striking, and against this background of social arrangements in other cultures the adolescent period of *Sturm und Drang* with which we are so familiar becomes intelligible in terms of our discontinuous cultural institutions and dogmas rather than in terms of physiological necessity. It is even more pertinent to consider these comparative facts in relation to maladjusted persons in our culture who are said to be fixated at one or another pre-adult level. It is clear that if we were to look at our social arrangements as an outsider, we should infer directly from our family institutions and habits of child training that many individuals would not "put off childish things"; we should have to say that our adult activity demands traits that are interdicted in children, and that, far from redoubling efforts to help children bridge this gap, adults in our culture put all the blame on the child when he fails to manifest spontaneously the new behavior or, overstepping the mark, manifests it with untoward belligerence. It is not surprising that in such a society many individuals fear to use behavior which has up to that time been under a ban and trust instead, though at great psychic cost, to attitudes that have been exercised with approval during their formative years. Insofar as we invoke a physiological scheme to account for these neurotic adjustments we are led to overlook the possibility of developing social institutions which would lessen the social cost we now pay; instead, we elaborate a set of dogmas which prove inapplicable under other social conditions.

G. H. MEAD'S THEORY OF
INDIVIDUAL AND SOCIETY

Charles W. Morris

G. H. Mead's great contribution to sociology was his theoretical analysis of the basic relationship between the person and the group. His "social behaviorism" emphasized the crucial function of language and social interaction in the development of human behavior and stressed that the human mind is a social phenomenon. This selection, taken from Charles Morris' introduction to a compilation of Mead's lectures entitled Mind, Self, and Society, presents some of the concepts central to his theory. Mead's formulation has come to be known as the "symbolic interaction" theory of behavior.

The transformation of the biologic individual to the minded organism or self takes place, on Mead's account, through the agency of language, while language in turn presupposes the existence of a certain kind of society and certain physiological capacities in the individual organisms.

The minimal society must be composed of biologic individuals participating in a social act and using the early stages of each other's actions as gestures, that is, as guides to the completion of the act. In the "conversation of gestures" of the dog fight each dog determines his behavior in terms of what the other dog is beginning to do; and the same holds for the boxer, the fencer, and the chick which runs to the hen at the hen's cluck. Such action is a type of communication; in one sense the gestures are symbols, since they indicate, stand for, and cause action appropriate to the later stages of the act of which they are early fragments, and secondarily to the objects implicated in such acts. In the same sense, the gestures may be said to have meaning, namely, they mean the later stages of the oncoming act and, secondarily, the objects implicated: the clenched fist means the blow, the outstretched hand means the object being reached for. Such meanings are not subjective, not private, not mental, but are objectively there in the social situation.

SOURCE: George Herbert Mead, *Mind, Self, and Society, from the Standpoint of a Social Behaviorist* (Chicago: The University of Chicago Press, 1934), pp. xx–xxvi. Edited, with introduction by Charles W. Morris. Reprinted by permission of the publisher. ❖ Charles W. Morris is Research Professor of Philosophy at the University of Florida. During the year 1956–57 he was a Fellow at the Center for Advanced Study in the Behavioral Sciences, Palo Alto, Calif. He is the editor of *Works of George H. Mead* and the author of *Six Theories of Mind; Logical Positivism, Pragmatism and Scientific Empiricism*; and *Signs, Language and Behavior*.

Nevertheless, this type of communication is not language proper; the meanings are not yet "in mind"; the biologic individuals are not yet consciously communicating selves. For these results to transpire the symbols or gestures must become significant symbols or gestures. The individual must know what he is about; he himself, and not merely those who respond to him, must be able to interpret the meaning of his own gesture. Behavioristically, this is to say that the biologic individual must be able to call out in himself the response his gesture calls out in the other, and then utilize this response of the other for the control of his own further conduct. Such gestures are significant symbols. Through their use the individual is "taking the rôle of the other" in the regulation of his own conduct. Man is essentially the rôle-taking animal. The calling out of the same response in both the self and the other gives the common content necessary for community of meaning.

As an example of the significant symbol Mead uses the tendency to call out "Fire!" when smoke is seen in a crowded theater. The immediate utterance of the sound would simply be part of the initiated act, and would be at the best a non-significant symbol. But when the tendency to call out "Fire!" affects the individual as it affects others, and is itself controlled in terms of these effects, the vocal gesture has become a significant symbol; the individual is conscious of what he is about; he has reached the stage of genuine language instead of unconscious communications; he may now be said to use symbols and not merely respond to signs; he has now acquired a mind.

In looking for gestures capable of becoming significant symbols, and so of transforming the biologic individual into a minded organism, Mead comes upon the vocal gesture. No other gesture affects the individual himself so similarly as it affects others. We hear ourselves talk as others do, but we do not see our facial expressions, nor normally watch our own actions. For Mead, the vocal gesture is the actual fountainhead of language proper and all derivative forms of symbolism; and so of mind.

Mind is the presence in behavior of significant symbols. It is the internalization within the individual of the social process of communication in which meaning emerges. It is the ability to indicate to one's self the response (and implicated objects) that one's gesture indicates to others, and to control the response itself in these terms. The significant gesture, itself a part of a social process, internalizes and makes available to the component biologic individuals the meanings which have themselves emerged in the earlier, non-significant stages of gestural communication. Instead of beginning with individual minds and working out to society, Mead starts with an objective social process and works inward through the importation of the social process of communication into the individual by the medium of the vocal gesture. The individual has then taken the social act into himself. Mind remains social; even in the inner forum so developed thought goes on by one's assuming the rôles of others and controlling one's behavior in terms of such rôle-taking. Since the isolation of the physical thing is for Mead dependent upon the ability to take the rôle of the other, and since thought about such objects involves taking their rôles, even the scientist's reflection about physical nature is a social process, though the objects thought about are no longer social.

It is the same agency of language which on this theory makes possible the appearance of the self. Indeed, the self, mind, "consciousness of," and the significant symbol are in a sense precipitated together. Mead finds the distinguishing trait of selfhood to reside in the capacity of the minded organism to be an object to itself. The mechanism by which this is possible on a behavioristic approach is found in the rôle-taking which is involved in the language symbol. In so far as one can take the rôle of the other, he can, as it were, look back at himself from (respond to himself from) that perspective, and so become an object to himself. Thus again, it is only in a social process that selves, as distinct from biological organisms, can arise—selves as beings that have become conscious of themselves.

Nor is it merely the process of being aware of one's self that is social: the self that one becomes conscious of in this manner is itself social in form, though not always in content. Mead stresses two stages in the development of the self: the stages of play and the game. In play the child simply assumes one rôle after another of persons and animals that have in some way or other entered into its life. One here sees, writ large as it were, the assumption of the attitudes of others through the self-stimulation of the vocal gesture, whereas later in life such attitudes are more abbreviated and harder to detect. In the game, however, one has become, as it were, all of the others implicated in the common activity—must have within one's self the whole organized activity in order to successfully play one's own part. The person here has not merely assumed the rôle of a specific other, but of any other participating in the common activity; he has generalized the attitude of rôle-taking. In one of Mead's happiest terms and most fertile concepts he has taken the attitude or rôle of the "generalized other."

Through a social process, then, the biologic individual of proper organic stuff gets a mind and a self. Through society the impulsive animal becomes a rational animal, a man. In virtue of the internalization or importation of the social process of communication, the individual gains the mechanism of reflective thought (the ability to direct his action in terms of the foreseen consequences of alternative courses of action); acquires the ability to make himself an object to himself and to live in a common moral and scientific world; becomes a moral individual with impulsive ends transformed into the conscious pursuit of ends-in-view.

Because of the emergence of such an individual, society is in turn transformed. It receives through the reflective social self the organization distinctive of human society; instead of playing his social part through physiological differentiation (as in the case of the insect) or through the bare influence of gestures upon others, the human individual regulates his part in the social act through having within himself the rôles of the others implicated in the common activity. In attaining a new principle of social organization, society has gained a new technique of control, since it has now implanted itself within its component parts, and so regulates, to the degree that this is successfully done, the behavior of the individual in terms of the effect on others of his contemplated action.

✤ 23 ✤

RIESMAN ON SOCIETY
AND CHARACTER

David Riesman, with Nathan Glazer and Reuel Denney

The book titled The Lonely Crowd *by David Riesman and his co-workers created a sensation outside as well as inside the "sociological fraternity." The reason for this is the contention of the authors regarding the basic nature of modern Western society. Our society, they assert, has gradually become one in which people are decreasingly "inner-directed" and increasingly "other-directed." To Riesman et al., the inner-directed person is one who makes decisions with little regard to their current social acceptability; the other-directed individual is one who tends to commit himself to values or programs only after he has assessed their general social acceptability. These definitions are developed more fully in the following extracts from* The Lonely Crowd. *It should be noted parenthetically (in the selection by Bell, for example) that the trend from inner- to other-direction (if there is such a trend) means that ours is becoming a "mass" society.*

SOURCE: *The Lonely Crowd* (1953) by David Riesman, pp. 25–40 passim, permission granted by Yale University Press. ❖ David Riesman is the Henry Ford II Professor of Social Sciences at Harvard University. He was trained as a lawyer and served as a law clerk to Justice Brandeis. In addition to *The Lonely Crowd*, his books include *Faces in the Crowd, Thorstein Veblen, Individualism Reconsidered and Other Essays*, and *Constraint and Variety in American Education.* ❖ Nathan Glazer is a professor of sociology and of social science at the University of California, Berkeley. His chief interests are race relations in the United States and problems of large cities. He is the author of *American Judaism* and *Social Basis of American Communism*, and the coauthor of *Beyond the Melting Pot.* ❖ Reuel Denney is professor of social science at the University of Chicago. He is the author of *Connecticut River* and *Astonished Muse.*

A Definition of Inner-Direction

In western history the society that emerged with the Renaissance and Reformation and that is only now vanishing serves to illustrate the type of society in which inner-direction is the principal mode of securing conformity. Such a society is characterized by increased personal mobility, by a rapid accumulation of capital (teamed with devastating technological shifts), and by an almost constant *expansion:* intensive expansion in the production of goods and people, and extensive expansion in exploration, colonization, and imperialism. The greater choices this society gives—and the greater initiatives it demands in order to cope with its novel problems —are handled by character types who can manage to live socially without strict and self-evident tradition-direction. These are the inner-directed types.

The concept of inner-direction is intended to cover a very wide range of types. Thus, while it is essential for the study of certain problems to differentiate between Protestant and Catholic countries and their character types, between the effects of the Reformation and the effects of the Renaissance, between the puritan ethic of the European north and west, and the somewhat more hedonistic ethic of the European east and south, while all these are valid and, for certain purposes, important distinctions, the concentration of this study on the development of modes of conformity permits their neglect. It allows the grouping together of these otherwise distinct developments because they have one thing in common: *the source of direction for the individual is "inner" in the sense that it is implanted early in life by the elders and directed toward generalized but nonetheless inescapably destined goals.*

We can see what this means when we realize that, in societies in which tradition-direction is the dominant mode of insuring conformity, attention is focused on securing external *behavioral* conformity. While behavior is minutely prescribed, individuality of character need not be highly developed to meet prescriptions that are objectified in ritual and etiquette—though to be sure, a social character *capable* of such behavioral attention and obedience is requisite. By contrast, societies in which inner-direction becomes important, though they also are concerned with behavioral conformity, cannot be satisfied with behavioral conformity alone. Too many novel situations are presented, situations which a code cannot encompass in advance. Consequently the problem of personal choice, solved in . . . [a tradition-directed period] by channeling choice through rigid social organization, in the period of . . . [inner-direction] is solved by channeling choice through a rigid though highly individualized character.

This rigidity is a complex matter. While any society dependent on inner-direction seems to present people with a wide choice of aims—such as money, possessions, power, knowledge, fame, goodness—these aims are ideologically interrelated, and the selection made by any one individual remains relatively unalterable throughout his life. Moreover, the means to those ends, though not fitted into as tight a social frame of reference as in the society dependent on tradition-direction, are nevertheless limited by the new voluntary associations—for instance, the Quakers, the Masons, the Mechanics' Associations—to which people tie themselves. Indeed, the term "tradition-direction" could be misleading if the reader were to conclude that the force of tradition has no weight for the inner-directed character. On the contrary, he is very considerably bound by traditions: they limit his ends and inhibit his choice of means. The point is rather that a splintering of tradition takes place, connected in part with the increasing division of labor and stratification of society. Even if the individual's choice of tradition is largely determined for him by his family, as it is in most cases, he cannot help becoming aware of the existence of competing traditions—hence of tradition as such. As a result he possesses a somewhat greater degree of flexibility in adapting himself to ever changing requirements and in return requires more from his environment.

❖   ❖   ❖   ❖   ❖

A Definition of Other-Direction

The type of character I shall describe as other-directed seems to be emerging in very recent years in the upper middle class of our larger cities: more prominently in New York than in Boston, in Los Angeles than in Spokane, in Cincinnati than in Chillicothe. Yet in some respects this type is strikingly similar to *the* American, whom Tocqueville and other curious and astonished visitors from Europe, even before the Revolution, thought to be a new kind of man. Indeed, travelers' reports on America impress us with their unanimity. The American is said to be shallower, freer with his money, friendlier, more uncertain of himself and his values, more demanding of approval than the European. It all adds up to a pattern which, without stretching matters too far, resembles the kind of character that a number of social scientists have seen as developing in contemporary, highly industrialized, and bureaucratic America: Fromm's "marketer," Mills's "fixer," Arnold Green's "middle class male child."

It is my impression that the middle-class American of today is decisively different from those Americans of Tocqueville's writings who nevertheless strike us as so contemporary, and much of this book will be devoted to discussing these differences. It is also my impression that the conditions I believe to be responsible for other-direction are affecting increasing numbers of people in the metropolitan centers of the advanced industrial countries. My analysis of the other-directed character is thus at once an analysis of the American and of contemporary man. Much of the time I find it hard or impossible to say where one ends and the other begins. Tentatively, I am inclined to think that the other-directed type does find itself most at home in America, due to certain unique elements in American society, such as its recruitment from Europe and its lack of any feudal past. As against this, I am also inclined to put more weight on capitalism, industrialism, and urbanization—these being international tendencies—than on any character-forming peculiarities of the American scene.

Bearing these qualifications in mind, it seems appropriate to treat contemporary metropolitan America as our illustration of a society—so far, perhaps, the only illustration—in which other-direction is the dominant mode of insuring conformity. It would be premature, however, to say that it is already the dominant mode in America as a whole. But since the other-directed types are to be found among the young, in the larger cities, and among the upper income groups, we may assume that, unless present trends are reversed, the hegemony of other-direction lies not far off.

If we wanted to cast our social character types into social class molds, we could say that inner-direction is the typical character of the "old" middle class—the banker, the tradesman, the small entrepreneur, the technically oriented engineer, etc.—while other-direction is becoming the typical character of the "new" middle class—the bureaucrat, the salaried employee in business, etc. Many of the economic factors associated with the recent growth of the "new" middle class are well known. They have been discussed by James Burnham, Colin Clark, Peter Drucker, and others. There is a decline in the numbers and in the proportion of the working population engaged in production and extraction—agriculture, heavy industry, heavy transport—and an increase in the numbers and the proportion engaged in white-collar work and the service trades. People who are literate, educated, and provided with the necessities of life by an ever more efficient machine industry and agriculture, turn increasingly to the "tertiary" economic realm. The service industries prosper among the people as a whole and no longer only in court circles.

These developments lead, for large numbers of people, to changes in paths to success and to requirement of more "socialized" behavior both for success and for marital and personal adaptation. Connected with such changes are changes in the family and in child-rearing practices. In the smaller families of urban life, and with the spread of "permissive" child care to ever wider strata of the population, there is a relaxation of older patterns of discipline. Under these newer patterns the peer-group (the group of one's associates of the same age and class) becomes much more important to the child, while the parents make him feel guilty not so much about violation of inner standards as about failure to be popular or otherwise to manage his relations with these other children. Moreover, the pressures of the school and the peer-group are reinforced and continued—in a manner whose inner paradoxes I shall discuss later—by the mass media: movies, radio, comics, and popular culture media generally. Under these conditions types of character emerge that we shall here term other-directed.
. . . *What is common to all the other-directed people is that their contemporaries are the source of direction for the individual—either those*

known to him or those with whom he is indirectly acquainted, through friends and through the mass media. This source is of course "internalized" in the sense that dependence on it for guidance in life is implanted early. The goals toward which the other-directed person strives shift with that guidance: it is only the process of striving itself and the process of paying close attention to the signals from others that remain unaltered throughout life. This mode of keeping in touch with others permits a close behavioral conformity, not through drill in behavior itself, as in the tradition-directed character, but rather through an exceptional sensitivity to the actions and wishes of others.

Of course, it matters very much who these "others" are: whether they are the individual's immediate circle or a "higher" circle or the anonymous voices of the mass media; whether the individual fears the hostility of chance acquaintances or only of those who "count." But his need for approval and direction from others—and contemporary others rather than ancestors—goes beyond the reasons that lead most people in any era to care very much what others think of them. While all people want and need to be liked by some of the people some of the time, it is only the modern other-directed types who make this their chief source of direction and chief area of sensitivity.

❖   ❖   ❖   ❖   ❖

. . . We must differentiate the nineteenth-century American—gregarious and subservient to public opinion though he was found to be by Tocqueville, Bryce, and others—from the other-directed American as he emerges today, an American who in his character is more capable of and more interested in maintaining responsive contact with others both at work and at play. This point needs to be emphasized, since the distinction is easily misunderstood. The inner-directed person, though he often sought and sometimes achieved a relative independence of public opinion and of what the neighbors thought of him, was in most cases very much concerned with his good repute and, at least in America, with "keeping up with the Joneses." These conformities, however, were primarily external, typified in such details as clothes, curtains, and bank credit. For, indeed, the conformities were to a standard, evidence of which was provided by the "best people" in one's milieu. In contrast with this pattern, the other-directed person, though he has his eye very much on the Joneses, aims to keep up with them not so much in external details as in the quality of his inner experience. That is, his great sensitivity keeps him in touch with others on many more levels than the externals of appearance and propriety. Nor does any ideal of independence or of reliance on God alone modify his desire to look to the others—and the "good guys" as well as the best people—for guidance in what experiences to seek and in how to interpret them.

THE ORGANIZATION MAN

William H. Whyte, Jr.

Like the previous selection, this one is taken from a recent book that has attracted much attention. Whyte's popular treatment has helped to define and clarify the concept of "The Organization Man" and thereby to add a distinctive new term to our evolving language. This excerpt from the book bearing the same title briefly analyzes several typical aspects of human behavior in American bureaucratic organizations. It shows how the changing structure of American society, particularly in business, has produced dramatic changes in human behavior and ideology.

This . . . is about the organization man. If the term is vague, it is because I can think of no other way to describe the people I am talking about. They are not the workers, nor are they the white-collar people in the usual, clerk sense of the word. These people only work for The Organization. The ones I am talking about *belong* to it as well. They are the ones of our middle class who have left home, spiritually as well as physically, to take the vows of organization life, and it is they who are the mind and soul of our great self-perpetuating institutions. Only a few are top managers or ever will be. In a system that makes such hazy terminology as "junior executive" psychologically necessary, they are of the staff as much as the line, and most are destined to live poised in a middle area that still awaits a satisfactory euphemism. But they are the dominant members of our society nonetheless. They have not joined together into a recognizable elite—our country does not stand still long enough for that—but it is from their ranks that are coming most of the first and second echelons of our leadership, and it is their values which will set the American temper.

The corporation man is the most conspicuous example, but he is only one, for the collectivization so visible in the corporation has affected almost every field of work. Blood brother to the business trainee off to join Du Pont is the seminary student who will end up in the church hierarchy, the doctor headed for the corporate clinic, the physics Ph.D. in a government laboratory, the intellectual on the foundation-sponsored team project, the engi-

SOURCE: William H. Whyte, Jr., *The Organization Man*, pp. 3–15. Copyright © 1956 by William H. Whyte, Jr. Reprinted by permission of Simon and Schuster, Inc. ✧ The author was Assistant Managing Editor of *Fortune*. In 1953, he received the Benjamin Franklin Magazine writing award and the Liberty and Justice book award. In addition to *The Organization Man*, his works include *Is Anybody Listening?* and numerous articles.

neering graduate in the huge drafting room at Lockheed, the young apprentice in a Wall Street law factory.

They are all, as they so often put it, in the same boat. Listen to them talk to each other over the front lawns of their suburbia and you cannot help but be struck by how well they grasp the common denominators which bind them. Whatever the differences in their organization ties, it is the common problems of collective work that dominate their attentions, and when the Du Pont man talks to the research chemist or the chemist to the army man, it is these problems that are uppermost. The word *collective* most of them can't bring themselves to use—except to describe foreign countries or organizations they don't work for—but they are keenly aware of how much more deeply beholden they are to organization than were their elders. They are wry about it, to be sure; they talk of the "treadmill," the "rat race," of the inability to control one's direction. But they have no great sense of plight; between themselves and organization they believe they see an ultimate harmony and, more than most elders recognize, they are building an ideology that will vouchsafe this trust.

. . . America has paid much attention to the economic and political consequences of big organization—the concentration of power in large corporations, for example, the political power of the civil-service bureaucracies, the possible emergence of a managerial hierarchy that might dominate the rest of us. These are proper concerns, but no less important is the personal impact that organization life has had on the individuals within it. A collision has been taking place—indeed, hundreds of thousands of them, and in the aggregate they have been producing what I believe is a major shift in American ideology.

Officially, we are a people who hold to the Protestant Ethic. Because of the denominational implications of the term many would deny its relevance to them, but let them eulogize the American Dream, however, and they virtually define the Protestant Ethic. Whatever the embroidery, there is almost always the thought that pursuit of individual salvation through hard work, thrift, and competitive struggle is the heart of the American achievement.

But the harsh facts of organization life simply do not jibe with these precepts. This conflict is certainly not a peculiarly American development. In their own countries such Europeans as Max Weber and Durkheim many years ago foretold the change, and though Europeans now like to see their troubles as an American export, the problems they speak of stem from a bureaucratization of society that has affected every Western country.

It is in America, however, that the contrast between the old ethic and current reality has been most apparent—and most poignant. Of all peoples it is we who have led in the public worship of individualism. One hundred years ago De Tocqueville was noting that though our special genius—and failing—lay in co-operative action, we talked more than others of personal independence and freedom. We kept on, and as late as the twenties, when big organization was long since a fact, affirmed the old faith as if nothing had really changed at all.

Today many still try, and it is the members of the kind of organization most responsible for the change, the corporation, who try the hardest. It is the corporation man whose institutional ads protest so much that Americans speak up in town meeting, that Americans are the best inventors because Americans don't care that other people scoff, that Americans are the best soldiers because they have so much initiative and native ingenuity, that the boy selling papers on the street corner is the prototype of our business society. Collectivism? He abhors it, and when he makes his ritualistic attack on Welfare Statism, it is in terms of a Protestant Ethic undefiled by change—the sacredness of property, the enervating effect of security, the virtues of thrift, of hard work and independence. Thanks be, he says, that there are some people left—e.g., businessmen—to defend the American Dream.

He is not being hypocritical, only compulsive. He honestly wants to believe he follows the tenets he extols, and if he extols them so frequently it is, perhaps, to shut out a nagging suspicion that he, too, the last defender of the faith, is no longer pure. Only by using the language of individualism to describe the collective can he stave off the thought that he himself is in a collective as pervading as any ever dreamed of by the reformers, the intellectuals, and the utopian visionaries he so regularly warns against.

The older generation may still convince themselves; the younger generation does not. When a young man says that to make a living these days you must do what somebody else wants you to do, he states it not only as a fact of life that must be accepted but as an inherently good proposition. If the American Dream deprecates this for him, it is the American Dream that is going to have to give, whatever its more elderly guardians may think. People grow restive with a mythology that is too distant from the way things actually are, and as more and more lives have been encompassed by the organization way of life, the pressures for an accompanying ideological shift have been mounting. The pressures of the group, the frustrations of individual creativity, the anonymity of achievement: are these defects to struggle against—or are they virtues in disguise? The organization man seeks a redefinition of his place on earth—a faith that will satisfy him that what he must endure has a deeper meaning than appears on the surface. He needs, in short, something that will do for him what the Protestant Ethic did once. And slowly, almost imperceptibly, a body of thought has been coalescing that does that.

I am going to call it a Social Ethic. With reason it could be called an organization ethic, or a bureaucratic ethic; more than anything else it rationalizes the organization's demands for fealty and gives those who offer it wholeheartedly a sense of dedication in doing so—*in extremis*, you might say, it converts what would seem in other times a bill of no rights into a restatement of individualism.

But there is a real moral imperative behind it, and whether one inclines to its beliefs or not he must acknowledge that this moral basis, not mere expediency, is the source of its power. Nor is it simply an opiate for those who must work in big organizations. The search for a secular faith that it represents can be found throughout our society—and among those who swear they would never set foot in a corporation or a government bureau. Though it has its greatest applicability to the organization man, its ideological underpinnings have been provided not by the organization man but by intellectuals he knows little of and toward whom, indeed, he tends to be rather suspicious.

Any groove of abstraction, Whitehead once remarked, is bound to be an inadequate way of describing reality, and so with the concept of the Social Ethic. It is an attempt to illustrate an underlying consistency in what in actuality is by no means an orderly system of thought. No one says, "I believe in the social ethic," and though many would subscribe whole-heartedly to the separate ideas that make it up, these ideas have yet to be put together in the final, harmonious synthesis. But the unity is there.

In looking at what might seem dissimilar aspects of organization society, it is this unity I wish to underscore. The "professionalization" of the manager, for example, and the drive for a more practical education are parts of the same phenomenon; just as the student now feels technique more vital than content, so the trainee believes managing an end in itself, an *expertise* relatively independent of the content of what is being managed. And the reasons are the same. So too in other sectors of our society; for all the differences in particulars, dominant is a growing accommodation to the needs of society—and a growing urge to justify it.

Let me now define my terms. By social ethic I mean that contemporary body of thought which makes morally legitimate the pressures of society against the individual. Its major propositions are three: a belief in the group as the source of creativity; a belief in "belongingness" as the ultimate need of the individual; and a belief in the application of science to achieve the belongingness.

. . . The gist can be paraphrased thus: Man exists as a unit of society. Of himself, he is isolated, meaningless; only as he collaborates with others does he become worthwhile, for by sublimating himself in the group, he helps produce a whole that is greater than the sum of its parts. There should be, then, no conflict between man and society. What we think are conflicts are misunderstandings, breakdowns in communication. By applying the methods of science to human relations we can eliminate these obstacles to consensus and create an equilibrium in which society's needs and the needs of the individual are one and the same.

Essentially, it is a utopian faith. Superficially, it seems dedicated to the practical problems of organization life, and its proponents often use the word *hard* (versus *soft*) to describe their approach. But it is the long-range promise that animates its followers, for it relates techniques to the vision of a finite, achievable harmony. . . .

Like the utopian communities, it interprets society in a fairly narrow, immediate sense. One can believe man has a social obligation and that the individual must ultimately contribute to the community without believing that group harmony is the test of it. In the Social Ethic I am describing, however, man's obligation is in the here and now; his duty is not so much to the community in a broad sense but to the actual, physical one about him, and the idea that in isolation from it—or active rebellion against it— he might eventually discharge the greater service is little considered. In practice, those who most eagerly subscribe to the Social Ethic worry very little over the long-range problems of society. It is not that they don't care but rather that they tend to assume that the ends of organization and morality coincide, and on such matters as social welfare they give their proxy to the organization.

It is possible that I am attaching too much weight to what, after all, is something of a mythology. Those more sanguine than I have argued that this faith is betrayed by reality in some key respects and that because it cannot long hide from organization man that life is still essentially competitive the faith must fall of its own weight. They also maintain that the Social Ethic is only one trend in a society which is a prolific breeder of counter-trends. The farther the pendulum swings, they believe, the more it must eventually swing back.

I am not persuaded. We are indeed a flexible people, but society is not a clock and to stake so much on counter-trends is to put a rather heavy burden on providence. . . .

. . . No one can say whether these trends will continue to outpace the counter-trends, but neither can we trust that an equilibrium-minded providence will see to it that excesses will cancel each other out. Counter-trends there are. There always have been, and in the sweep of ideas ineffectual many have proved to be.

It is also true that the Social Ethic is something of a mythology, and there is a great difference between mythology and practice. An individualism as stringent, as selfish as that often preached in the name of the Protestant Ethic would never have been tolerated, and in reality our predecessors co-operated with one another far more skillfully than nineteenth-century oratory would suggest. Something of the obverse is true of the Social Ethic; so complete a denial of individual will won't work either, and even the most willing believers in the group harbor some secret misgivings, some latent antagonism toward the pressures they seek to deify.

But the Social Ethic is no less powerful for that, and though it can never produce the peace of mind it seems to offer, it will help shape the nature of the quest in the years to come. The old dogma of individualism betrayed reality too, yet few would argue, I dare say, that it was not an immensely powerful influence in the time of its dominance. So I argue of the Social Ethic; call it mythology, if you will, but it is becoming the dominant one.

This . . . is not a plea for nonconformity. Such pleas have an occasional therapeutic value, but as an abstraction, nonconformity is an empty goal, and rebellion against prevailing opinion merely because it is prevailing should no more be praised than acquiescence to it. Indeed, it is often a mask for cowardice, and few are more pathetic than those who flaunt outer differences to expiate their inner surrender.

I am not, accordingly, addressing myself to the surface uniformities of U.S. life. There will be no strictures . . . against "Mass Man"—a person the author has never met—nor will there be any strictures against ranch wagons, or television sets, or gray flannel suits. They are irrelevant to the main problem, and, furthermore, there's no harm in them. I would not wish to go to the other extreme and suggest that these uniformities per se are good, but the spectacle of people following current custom for lack of will or imagination to do anything else is hardly a new failing, and I am not convinced that there has been any significant change in this respect except in the nature of the things we conform to. Unless one believes poverty ennobling, it is difficult to see the three-button suit as more of a strait jacket than overalls, or the ranch-type house than old law tenements.

And how important, really, are these uniformities to the central issue of individualism? We must not let the outward forms deceive us. If individualism involves following one's destiny as one's own conscience directs, it must for most of us be a realizable destiny, and a sensible awareness of the rules of the game can be a condition of individualism as well as a constraint upon it. The man who drives a Buick Special and lives in a ranch-type house just like hundreds of other ranch-type houses can assert himself as effectively and courageously against his particular society as the bohemian against his particular society. He usually does not, it is true, but if he does, the surface uniformities can serve quite well as protective coloration. The organization people who are best able to control their environment rather than be controlled by it are well aware that they are not too easily distinguishable from the others in the outward obeisances paid to the good opinions of others. And that is one of the reasons they do control. They disarm society.

I do not equate the Social Ethic with conformity, nor do I believe those who urge it wish it to be, for most of them believe deeply that their work will help, rather than harm, the individual. I think their ideas are out of joint with the needs of the times they invoke, but it is their ideas, and not their good will, I wish to question. As for the lackeys of organization and the charlatans, they are not worth talking about.

Neither do I intend . . . a censure of the fact of organization society. We have quite enough problems today without muddying the issue with misplaced nostalgia, and in contrasting the old ideology with the new I mean no contrast of paradise with paradise lost, an idyllic eighteenth century with a dehumanized twentieth. Whether or not our own era is worse than former ones in the climate of freedom is a matter that can be left to later historians, but . . . I write with the optimistic promise that individualism is as possible in our times as in others.

I speak of individualism *within* organization life. This is not the only kind, and someday it may be that the mystics and philosophers more distant from it may prove the crucial figures. But they are affected too by the center of society, and they can be of no help unless they grasp the nature of the main stream. Intellectual scoldings based on an impossibly lofty ideal may be of some service in upbraiding organization man with his failures, but they can give him no guidance. The organization man may agree that industrialism has destroyed the moral fabric of society and that we need to return to the agrarian virtues, or that business needs to be broken up into a series of smaller organizations, or that it's government that needs to be broken up, and so on. But he will go his way with his own dilemmas left untouched.

I . . . argue that he should fight the organization. But not self-destructively. He may tell the boss to go to hell, but he is going to have another boss, and, unlike the heroes of popular fiction, he cannot find surcease by leaving the arena to be a husbandman. If he chafes at the pressures of his particular organization, either he must succumb, resist them, try to change them, or move to yet another organization.

Every decision he faces on the problem of the individual versus authority is something of a dilemma. It is not a case of whether he should fight against black tyranny or blaze a new trail against patent stupidity. That would be easy—intellectually, at least. The real issue is far more subtle. For it is not the evils of organization life that puzzle him, *but its very beneficence.* He is imprisoned in brotherhood. Because his area of maneuver seems so small and because the trapping so mundane, his fight lacks the heroic cast, but it is for all this as tough a fight as ever his predecessors had to fight.

Thus to my thesis, I believe the emphasis of the Social Ethic is wrong for him. People do have to work with others, yes; the well-functioning team is a whole greater than the sum of its parts, yes—all this is indeed true. But is it the truth that now needs belaboring? Precisely because it *is* an age of organization, it is the other side of the coin that needs emphasis. We do need to know how to co-operate with The Organization but, more than ever, so do we need to know how to resist it. Out of context this would be an irresponsible statement. Time and place are critical, and history has taught us that a philosophical individualism can venerate conflict too much and co-operation too little. But what is the context today? The tide has swung far enough the other way, I submit, that we need not worry that a counteremphasis will stimulate people to an excess of individualism.

The energies Americans have devoted to the co-operative, to the social, are not to be demeaned; we would not, after all, have such a problem to discuss unless we had learned to adapt ourselves to an increasingly collective society as well as we have. An ideal of individualism which denies the obligations of man to others is manifestly impossible in a society such as ours, and it is a credit to our wisdom that while we preached it, we never fully practiced it.

But in searching for that elusive middle of the road, we have gone very far afield, and in our attention to making organization work we have come close to deifying it. We are describing its defects as virtues and denying that there is—or should be—a conflict between the individual and organization. This denial is bad for the organization. It is worse for the individual. What it does, in soothing him, is to rob him of the intellectual armor he so badly needs. For the more power organization has over him, the more he needs to recognize the area where he must assert himself against it. And this, almost because we have made organization life so equable, has become excruciatingly difficult.

To say that we must recognize the dilemmas of organization society is not to be inconsistent with the hopeful premise that organization society can be as compatible for the individual as any previous society. We are not hapless beings caught in the grip of forces we can do little about, and wholesale damnations of our society only lend a further mystique to organization. Organization has been made by man; it can be changed by man. It has not been the immutable course of history that has produced such constrictions on the individual as personality tests. It is organization man who has brought them to pass and it is he who can stop them.

The fault is not in organization, in short; it is in our worship of it. It is in our vain quest for a utopian equilibrium, which would be horrible if it ever did come to pass; it is in the soft-minded denial that there is a conflict between the individual and society. There must always be, and it is the price of being an individual that he must face these conflicts. He cannot evade them, and in seeking an ethic that offers a spurious peace of mind, thus does he tyrannize himself.

There are only a few times in organization life when he can wrench his destiny into his own hands—and if he does not fight then, he will make a surrender that will later mock him. But when is that time? Will he know the time when he sees it? By what standards is he to judge? He does feel an obligation to the group; he does sense moral constraints on his free will. If he goes against the group, is he being courageous—or just stubborn? Helpful—or selfish? Is he, as he so often wonders, right after all? It is in the resolution of a multitude of such dilemmas, I submit, that the real issue of individualism lies today.

THE THEORY OF MASS SOCIETY

Daniel Bell

This selection provides another perspective on the ideas contained in the two preceding articles. It is Bell's contention that there is no really substantial evidence to show that our Western world is becoming increasingly a "mass society"—stifling and preventing the expression of individual interest. He feels that "the theory of the mass society no longer serves as a description of Western society, but as an ideology of romantic protest against contemporary society." In developing this thesis, Bell examines and refutes some basic assumptions widely held by many popular writers and social scientists.

The sense of a radical dehumanization of life which has accompanied events of the past several decades has given rise to the theory of "mass society." One can say that, Marxism apart, it is probably the most influential social therapy in the Western world today. While no single individual has stamped his name on it—to the extent that Marx is associated with the transformation of personal relations under capitalism into commodity values, or Freud with the role of the irrational and unconscious in behavior—the theory is central to the thinking of the principal aristocratic, Catholic, or Existentialist critics of bourgeois society today. These critics—Ortega y Gasset, Karl Mannheim, Karl Jaspers, Paul Tillich, Gabriel Marcel, Emil Lederer, and others—have been concerned, less with the general conditions of freedom, than with the freedom of the *person*, and with the possibility for some *few* persons of achieving a sense of individual self in our mechanized society.

The conception of "mass society" can be summarized as follows: The revolutions in transport and communications have brought men into closer contact with each other and bound them in new ways; the division of labor has made them more interdependent; tremors in one part of society affect all others. Despite this greater interdependence, however, individuals have grown more estranged from one another. The old primary group ties of family and local community have been shattered; ancient parochial faiths

SOURCE: Reprinted from *Commentary*, Vol. 22, No. 1 (July, 1956), 75–83. Copyright by the American Jewish Committee. The essay also appears, in revised form, in Daniel Bell, *The End of Ideology* (Glencoe, Ill.: The Free Press, 1950). ✧ The author is labor editor of *Fortune* and associate professor of sociology at Columbia University. His chief interests are in industrial relations and industrial sociology. He has edited *The New American Right* and is the author of *American Marxist Parties*, *Work in the Life of an American*, and *Work and Its Discontents*.

are questioned; few unifying values have taken their place. Most important, the critical standards of an educated elite no longer shape opinion or taste. As a result, mores and morals are in constant flux, relations between individuals are tangential or compartmentalized rather than organic. At the same time greater mobility, spatial and social, intensifies concern over status. Instead of a fixed or known status symbolized by dress or title, each person assumes a multiplicity of roles and constantly has to prove himself in a succession of new situations. Because of all this, the individual loses a coherent sense of self. His anxieties increase. There ensues a search for new faiths. The stage is thus set for the charismatic leader, the secular messiah, who, by bestowing upon each person the semblance of necessary grace, and of fullness of personality, supplies a substitute for the older unifying belief that the mass society has destroyed.

In a world of lonely crowds seeking individual distinction, where values are constantly translated into economic calculabilities, where in extreme situations shame and conscience can no longer restrain the most dreadful excesses of terror, the theory of the mass society seems a forceful, realistic description of contemporary society, an accurate reflection of the *quality* and *feeling* of modern life. But when one seeks to apply the theory of mass society analytically, it becomes very slippery. Ideal types, like the shadows in Plato's cave, generally never give us more than a silhouette. So, too, with the theory of "mass society." Each of the statements making up the theory, as set forth in the second paragraph above, might be true, but they do not follow necessarily from one another. Nor can we say that all conditions described are present at any one time or place. More than that, there is no organizing principle—other than the general concept of a "breakdown of values"—which puts the individual elements of theory together in a logical, meaningful—let alone historical—manner. And when we examine the way the "theory" is used by those who employ it, we find ourselves even more at a loss.

As commonly used in the term "mass media," "mass" implies that standardized material is transmitted to "all groups of the population uniformly." As understood generally by sociologists, a *mass* is a heterogeneous and undifferentiated audience as opposed to a *class*, or any parochial and relatively homogeneous segment. Some sociologists have been tempted to go further and make "mass" a rather pejorative term. Because the mass media subject a diverse audience to a common set of cultural materials, it is argued that these experiences must necessarily lie outside the personal —and therefore meaningful—experiences to which the individual responds directly. A movie audience, for example, is a "mass" because the individuals looking at the screen are, in the words of the American sociologist Herbert Blumer, "separate, detached, and anonymous." The "mass" divorces—or "alienates"—the individual from himself.

❖   ❖   ❖   ❖   ❖

Presumably a large number of individuals, because they have been subjected to similar experiences, now share some common psychological reality in which the differences between individual and individual become blurred; and accordingly we get the sociological assumption that each person is now of "equal weight," and therefore a sampling of what such disparate individuals say they think constitutes "*mass* opinion." But is this so? Individuals are not *tabulae rasae*. They bring varying social conceptions to the same experience, and go away with dissimilar responses. They may be silent, separate, detached, and anonymous while watching the movie, but afterward they talk about it with friends and exchange opinions and judgments. They are once again members of particular social groups. Would one say that several hundred or a thousand individuals home alone at night, but all reading the same book, constitutes a "mass"?

One could argue, of course, that reading a book is a qualitatively different experience from going to a movie. But this leads precisely to the first damaging ambiguity in the theory of the mass society. Two things are mixed up in that theory: a judgment as to the *quality* of modern experience—with much of which any sensitive individual would agree—and a presumed scientific statement concerning the disorganization of society created by industrialization and by the demand of the masses for equality. It is the second of these statements with which this essay quarrels, not the first.

Behind the theory of social disorganization lies a romantic notion of the past that sees society as having once been made up of small "organic," close-knit communities (called *Gemeinschaften* in the terminology of the sociologists) that were shattered by industrialism and modern life, and replaced by a large impersonal "atomistic" society (called *Gesellschaft*) which is unable to provide the basic gratifications and call forth the loyalties that the older communities knew.

✧   ✧   ✧   ✧   ✧

It is asserted that the United States is an "atomized" society composed of lonely, isolated individuals. One forgets the truism, expressed sometimes as a jeer, that Americans are a nation of joiners. There are in the United States today at least 200,000 voluntary organizations, associations, clubs, societies, lodges, and fraternities with an aggregate (but obviously overlapping) membership of close to eighty million men and women. In no other country in the world, probably, is there such a high degree of voluntary communal activity, expressed sometimes in absurd rituals, yet often providing real satisfactions for real needs.

"It is natural for the ordinary American," wrote Gunnar Myrdal, "when he sees something that is wrong to feel not only that there should be a law against it, but also that an organization should be formed to combat it." Some of these voluntary organizations are pressure groups—business, farm, labor, veterans, trade associations, the aged, etc., etc.—

but thousands more are like the National Association for the Advancement of Colored People, the American Civil Liberties Union, the League of Women Voters, the American Jewish Committee, the Parent-Teachers Associations, local community-improvement groups, and so on, each of which affords hundreds of individuals concrete, emotionally shared activities.

Equally astonishing are the number of ethnic group organizations in this country carrying on varied cultural, social, and political activities. The number of Irish, Italian, Jewish, Polish, Czech, Finnish, Bulgarian, Bessarabian, and other national groups, their hundreds of fraternal, communal, and political groups, each playing a role in the life of America, is staggering. In December 1954, for example, when the issue of Cyprus was first placed before the United Nations, the Justice for Cyprus Committee, "an organization of American citizens," according to its statement, took a full-page advertisement in the New York *Times* to plead the right of that small island to self-determination. Among the groups listed in the Justice for Cyprus Committee were: the Order of Ahepa, the Daughters of Penelope, the Pan-Laconian Federation, the Cretan Federation, the Pan-Messian Federation, the Pan-Icarian Federation, the Pan-Epirotic Federation of America, the Pan-Thracian Association, the Pan-Elian Federation of America, the Dodecanesian League of America, the Pan-Macedonian Association of America, the Pan-Samian Association, the Federation of Sterea Ellas, the Cyprus Federation of America, the Pan-Arcadian Federation, the GAPA, and the Federation of Hellenic Organizations.

We can be sure that if, in a free world, the question of the territorial affiliation of Ruthenia were to come up before the United Nations, dozens of Hungarian, Rumanian, Ukrainian, Slovakian, and Czech "organizations of American citizens" would rush eagerly into print to plead the justice of the claims of their respective homelands to Ruthenia.

Even in urban neighborhoods, where anonymity is presumed to flourish, the extent of local ties is astounding. Within the city limits of Chicago, for example, there are eighty-two community newspapers with a total weekly circulation of almost 1,000,000; within Chicago's larger metropolitan area, there are 181. According to standard sociological theory, these local papers providing news and gossip about neighbors should slowly decline under the pressure of the national media. Yet the reverse is true. In Chicago, the number of such newspapers has increased 165 per cent since 1910; in those forty years circulation has jumped 770 per cent. As sociologist Morris Janowitz, who studied these community newspapers, observed: "If society were as impersonal, as self-centered and barren as described by some who are preoccupied with the one-way trend from 'Gemeinschaft' to 'Gesellschaft' seem to believe, the levels of criminality, social disorganization and psychopathology which social science seeks to account for would have to be viewed as very low rather than (as viewed now) alarmingly high."

It may be argued that the existence of such a large network of voluntary associations says little about the cultural level of the country concerned. It may well be, as Ortega maintains, that cultural standards throughout the world have declined (in everything—architecture, dress, design?), but nonetheless a greater proportion of the population today participates in worth-while cultural activities. This has been almost an inevitable concomitant of the doubling—*literally*—of the American standard of living over the last fifty years. The rising levels of education have meant rising appreciation of culture. In the United States more dollars are spent on concerts of classical music than on baseball. Sales of books have doubled in a decade. There are over a thousand symphony orchestras, and several hundred museums, institutes, and colleges purchasing art in the United States today. Various other indices can be cited to show the growth of a vast middlebrow society. And in coming years, with steadily increasing productivity and leisure, the United States will become even more actively a "consumer" of culture. . . .

It has been argued that the American mass society imposes an excessive conformity upon its members. But it is hard to discern who is conforming to what. The *New Republic* cries that "hucksters are sugar-coating the culture." The *National Review*, organ of the "radical right," raises the banner of iconoclasm against the liberal domination of opinion-formation in our society. *Fortune* decries the growth of "organization man." Each of these tendencies exists, yet in historical perspective, there is probably less conformity to an over-all mode of conduct today than at any time within the last half-century in America. True, there is less bohemianism than in the twenties (though increased sexual tolerance), and less political radicalism than in the thirties (though the New Deal enacted sweeping reforms). But does the arrival at a political dead-center mean the establishment, too, of a dead norm? I do not think so. One would be hard put to it to find today the "conformity" *Main Street* exacted of Carol Kennicott thirty years ago. With rising educational levels, more individuals are able to indulge a wider variety of interests. ("Twenty years ago you couldn't sell Beethoven out of New York," reports a record salesman. "Today we sell Palestrina, Monteverdi, Gabrielli, and Renaissance and Baroque music in large quantities.")

One hears, too, the complaint that divorce, crime, and violence demonstrate a widespread social disorganization in the country. But the rising number of divorces . . . indicates not the disruption of the family, but a freer, more individualistic basis of choice, and the emergence of the "companionship" marriage. And as regards crime . . . , there is actually much *less* crime and violence (though more vicarious violence through movies and TV, and more "windows" onto crime, through the press) than was the case twenty-five and fifty years ago. Certainly, Chicago, San Francisco, and New York were much rougher and tougher cities in those years. But violent crime, which is usually a lower-class phenomenon, was then contained within the ecological boundaries of the slum; hence one can recall quiet, tree-lined, crime-free areas and feel that the tenor of life was more even in the past. But a cursory look at the accounts of those days—the descriptions of the gang wars, bordellos, and street-fighting in San Francisco's Barbary Coast, New York's Five Points, or Chicago's First Ward—would show how much more violent in the past the actual life of those cities was.

At this point it becomes quite apparent that such large-scale abstractions as "the mass society," with the implicit diagnoses of social disorganization and decay that derive from them, are rather meaningless without standards of comparison. Social and cultural change is probably greater and more rapid today in the United States than in any other country, but the assumption that social disorder and *anomie* inevitably attend such change is not borne out in this case.

This may be owing to the singular fact that the United States is probably the first large society in history to have change and innovation "built into" its culture. Almost all human societies, traditionalist and habit-ridden as they have been and still are, tend to resist change. The great efforts to industrialize underdeveloped countries, increase worker mobility in Europe, and broaden markets—so necessary to the raising of productivity and standards of living—are again and again frustrated by ingrained resistance to change. Thus in the Soviet Union change has been introduced only by dint of wholesale coercion. In the United States—a culture with no feudal tradition; with a pragmatic ethos, as expressed by Jefferson, that regards God as a "workman"; with a boundless optimism and a restless eagerness for the new that has been bred out of the original conditions of a huge, richly endowed land—change, and the readiness to change, have become the norm. This indeed may be why those consequences of change predicted by theorists basing themselves on European precedent find small confirmation.

The mass society is the product of change—and is itself change. But the *theory* of the mass society affords us no view of the relations of the parts of the society to each other that would enable us to locate the sources of change. We may not have enough data on which to sketch an alternative theory, but I would argue that certain key factors, in this country at least, deserve to be much more closely examined than they have been.

The change from a society once geared to frugal saving and now impelled to spend dizzily; the break-up of family capitalism, with the consequent impact on corporate structure and political power; the centralization of decision-making, politically, in the state and, economically, in a group of large corporate bodies; the rise of status and symbol groups replacing specific interest groups—indicate that new social forms are in the making, and with them still greater changes in the complexion of life under mass society. With these may well come new status anxieties—

aggravated by the threats of war—changed character structures, and new moral tempers.

The moralist may have his reservations or give approval—as some see in the break-up of the family the loss of a source of essential values, while others see in the new, freer marriages a healthier form of companionship—but the singular fact is that these changes emerge in a society that is now providing one answer to the great challenge posed to Western—and now world—society over the last two hundred years: how, within the framework of freedom, to increase the living standards of the majority of people, and at the same time maintain or raise cultural levels. American society, for all its shortcomings, its speed, its commercialism, its corruption, still, I believe, shows us the most humane way.

The theory of the mass society no longer serves as a description of Western society, but as an ideology of romantic protest against contemporary society. This is a time when other areas of the globe are beginning to follow in the paths of the West, which may be all to the good as far as material things are concerned; but many of the economically underdeveloped countries, especially in Asia, have caught up the shopworn self-critical Western ideologies of the 19th century and are using them against the West, to whose "materialism" they oppose their "spirituality." What these Asian and our own intellectuals fail to realize, perhaps, is that one may be a thoroughgoing critic of one's own society without being an enemy of its promises.

Social Organization:

TYPES OF GROUP RELATIONSHIPS

❖ 26 ❖

PRIMARY GROUPS

Charles Horton Cooley

Professor Cooley, the author of this selection, is recognized as a pioneer in the field of social psychology. One of his very fruitful contributions to sociology is the concept of primary groups as the "nursery of human nature." Here he explains the universality of primary groups and contrasts their characteristics with what we now designate as secondary groups. He carefully defines "human nature," which he declares to be fundamentally the same the world over. Although more recent discoveries have revealed certain limitations in his data, such as his statement in this selection about differences in racial capacities, in most essentials his thinking is sound and illuminating. Since 1909, when the book in which this selection appears was published, much progress has been made in developing the scientific research methods of both psychology and sociology; but many of Cooley's ideas, of which the primary-group concept is one, have a timeless quality.

By primary groups I mean those characterized by intimate face-to-face association and coöperation. They are primary in several senses, but chiefly in that they are fundamental in forming the social nature and ideals of the individual. The result of intimate association, psychologically, is a certain fusion of individualities in a common whole, so that one's very

SOURCE: Reprinted with the permission of Charles Scribner's Sons from *Social Organization* by Charles Horton Cooley. Copyright 1909 Charles Scribner's Sons; renewal copyright 1937 Elsie Jones. ❖ The author (1864–1929), an American social philosopher, was professor of sociology at the University of Michigan and a president of the American Sociological Association. He made contributions of great range and depth to the field of sociology. Among his important works are *Personal Competition, Human Nature and the Social Order, Social Organization,* and *Social Process.*

self, for many purposes at least, is the common life and purpose of the group. Perhaps the simplest way of describing this wholeness is by saying that it is a "we"; it involves the sort of sympathy and mutual identification for which "we" is the natural expression. One lives in the feeling of the whole and finds the chief aims of his will in that feeling.

It is not to be supposed that the unity of the primary group is one of mere harmony and love. It is always a differentiated and usually a competitive unity, admitting of self-assertion and various appropriative passions; but these passions are socialized by sympathy, and come, or tend to come, under the discipline of a common spirit. The individual will be ambitious, but the chief object of his ambition will be some desired place in the thought of the others, and he will feel allegiance to common standards of service and fair play. So the boy will dispute with his fellows a place on the team, but above such disputes will place the common glory of his class and school.

The most important spheres of this intimate association and coöperation—though by no means the only ones—are the family, the play-group of children, and the neighborhood or community group of elders. These are practically universal, belonging to all times and all stages of development; and are accordingly a chief basis of what is universal in human nature and human ideals. The best comparative studies of the family, such as those of Westermarck or Howard, show it to us as not only a universal institution, but as more alike the world over than the exaggeration of exceptional customs by an earlier school had led us to suppose. Nor can any one doubt the general prevalence of play-groups among children or of informal assemblies of various kinds of among their elders. Such association is clearly the nursery of human nature in the world about us, and there is no apparent reason to suppose that the case has anywhere or at any time been essentially different.

As regards play, I might, were it not a matter of common observation, multiply illustrations of the universality and spontaneity of the group discussion and coöperation to which it gives rise. The general fact is that children, especially boys after about their twelfth year, live in fellowships in which their sympathy, ambition and honor are engaged even more often, than they are in the family. Most of us can recall examples of the endurance by boys of injustice and even cruelty, rather than appeal from their fellows to parents or teachers—as, for instance, in the hazing so prevalent at schools, and so difficult, for this very reason, to repress. And how elaborate the discussion, how cogent the public opinion, how hot the ambitions in these fellowships.

Nor is this facility of juvenile association, as is sometimes supposed, a trait peculiar to English and American boys; since experience among our immigrant population seems to show that the offspring of the more restrictive civilizations of the continent of Europe form self-governing play-groups with almost equal readiness. Thus Miss Jane Addams, after pointing out that the "gang" is almost universal, speaks of the interminable discussion which every detail of the gang's activity receives, remarking th .t "in these social folk-motes, so to speak, the young citizen learns to act upon his own determination."

Of the neighborhood group it may be said, in general, that from the time men formed permanent settlements upon the land, down, at least, to the rise of modern industrial cities, it has played a main part in the primary, heart-to-heart life of the people. Among our Teutonic forefathers the village community was apparently the chief sphere of sympathy and mutual aid for the commons all through the "dark" and middle ages, and for many purposes it remains so in rural districts at the present day. In some countries we still find it with all its ancient vitality, notably in Russia, where the mir, or self-governing village group, is the main theatre of life, along with the family, for perhaps fifty millions of peasants.

In our own life the intimacy of the neighborhood has been broken up by the growth of an intricate mesh of wider contacts which leaves us strangers to people who live in the same house. And even in the country the same principle is at work, though less obviously, diminishing our economic and spiritual community with our neighbors. How far this change is a healthy development, and how far a disease, is perhaps still uncertain.

Besides these almost universal kinds of primary association, there are many others whose form depends upon the particular state of civilization; the only essential thing, as I have said, being a certain intimacy and fusion of personalities. In our own society, being little bound by place, people easily form clubs, fraternal societies and the like, based on congeniality, which may give rise to real intimacy. Many such relations are formed at school and college, and among men and women brought together in the first instance by their occupations—as workmen in the same trade, or the like. Where there is a little common interest and activity, kindness grows like weeds by the roadside.

But the fact that the family and neighborhood groups are ascendant in the open and plastic time of childhood makes them even now incomparably more influential than all the rest.

Primary groups are primary in the sense that they give the individual his earliest and completest experience of social unity, and also in the sense that they do not change in the same degree as more elaborate relations, but form a comparatively permanent source out of which the latter are ever springing. Of course they are not independent of the larger society, but to some extent reflect its spirit; as the German family and the German school bear somewhat distinctly the print of German militarism. But this, after all, is like the tide setting back into creeks, and does not commonly go very far. Among the German, and still more among the Russian, peasantry are found habits of free coöperation and discussion almost uninfluenced by the character of the state; and it is a familiar and well-supported view that the village commune, self-governing as regards local affairs and habituated to discussion, is a very widespread institution in settled communities, and the continuator of a similar autonomy previously existing in the clan. "It is man who makes monarchies and establishes republics, but the commune seems to come directly from the hand of God."

In our own cities the crowded tenements and the general economic and social confusion have sorely wounded the family and the neighborhood, but it is remarkable, in view of these conditions, what vitality they show; and there is nothing upon which the conscience of the time is more determined than upon restoring them to health.

These groups, then, are springs of life, not only for the individual but for social institutions. They are only in part moulded by special traditions, and, in larger degree, express a universal nature. The religion or government of other civilizations may seem alien to us, but the children or the family group wear the common life, and with them we can always make ourselves at home.

By human nature, I suppose, we may understand those sentiments and impulses that are human in being superior to those of lower animals, and also in the sense that they belong to mankind at large, and not to any particular race or time. It means, particularly, sympathy and the innumerable sentiments into which sympathy enters, such as love, resentment, ambition, vanity, hero-worship, and the feeling of social right and wrong.

Human nature in this sense is justly regarded as a comparatively permanent element in society. Always and everywhere men seek honor and dread ridicule, defer to public opinion, cherish their goods and their children, and admire courage, generosity, and success. It is always safe to assume that people are and have been human.

It is true, no doubt, that there are differences of race capacity, so great that a large part of mankind are possibly incapable of any high kind of social organization. But these differences, like those among individuals of the same race, are subtle, depending upon some obscure intellectual deficiency, some want of vigor, or slackness of moral fibre, and do not involve unlikeness in the generic impulses of human nature. In these all races are very much alike. The more insight one gets into the life of savages, even those that are reckoned the lowest, the more human, the more like ourselves, they appear. Take for instance the natives of Central Australia, as described by Spencer and Gillen, tribes having no definite government or worship and scarcely able to count to five. They are generous to one another, emulous of virtue as they understand it, kind to their children and to the aged, and by no means harsh to women. Their faces . . . are wholly human and many of them attractive.

And when we come to a comparison between different stages in the development of the same race, between ourselves, for instance, and the Teutonic tribes of the time of Cæsar, the difference is neither in human nature nor in capacity, but in organization, in the range and complexity of relations, in the diverse expression of powers and passions essentially much the same.

There is no better proof of this generic likeness of human nature than in the ease and joy with which the modern man makes himself at home in literature depicting the most remote and varied phases of life—in Homer, in the Nibelung tales, in the Hebrew Scriptures, in the legends of the American Indians, in stories of frontier life, of soldiers and sailors, of criminals and tramps, and so on. The more penetratingly any phase of human life is studied the more an essential likeness to ourselves is revealed.

To return to primary groups: the view here maintained is that human nature is not something existing separately in the individual, but a *group-nature or primary phase of society*, a relatively simple and general condition of the social mind. It is something more, on the one hand, than the mere instinct that is born in us—though that enters into it—and something less, on the other, than the more elaborate development of ideas and sentiments that makes up institutions. It is the nature which is developed and expressed in those simple, face-to-face groups that are somewhat alike in all societies; groups of the family, the playground, and the neighborhood. In the essential similarity of these is to be found the basis, in experience, for similar ideas and sentiments in the human mind. In these, everywhere, human nature comes into existence. Man does not have it at birth; he cannot acquire it except through fellowship, and it decays in isolation.

If this view does not recommend itself to common-sense I do not know that elaboration will be of much avail. It simply means the application at this point of the idea that society and individuals are inseparable phases of a common whole, so that wherever we find an individual fact we may look for a social fact to go with it. If there is a universal nature in persons there must be something universal in association to correspond to it.

What else can human nature be than a trait of primary groups? Surely not an attribute of the separate individual—supposing there were any such thing—since its typical characteristics, such as affection, ambition, vanity, and resentment, are inconceivable apart from society. If it belongs, then, to man in association, what kind or degree of association is required to develop it? Evidently nothing elaborate, because elaborate phases of society are transient and diverse, while human nature is comparatively stable and universal. In short the family and neighborhood life is essential to its genesis and nothing more is.

Here as everywhere in the study of society we must learn to see mankind in psychical wholes, rather than in artificial separation. We must see and feel the communal life of family and local groups as immediate facts, not as combinations of something else. And perhaps we shall do this best by recalling our own experience and extending it through sympathetic observation. What, in our life, is the family and the fellowship; what do we know of the we-feeling? Thought of this kind may help us to get a concrete perception of that primary group-nature of which everything social is the outgrowth.

CONTRASTING TYPES OF
GROUP RELATIONSHIPS

John B. Holland

Sociologists have introduced a number of terms to characterize types of social relationships. The primary group concept described in the previous selection, the contrasting secondary group concept, and the Gemeinschaft and Gesellschaft concepts developed by Ferdinand Tönnies are probably most widely used to indentify differing patterns of social interaction. In this selection John Holland defines Gemeinschaft and Gesellschaft and illustrates their usefulness in social analysis. In the selection following this, you will find an illustration of the combination of Gemeinschaft, or primary relations, and Gesellschaft, or secondary relations, in a bureaucratic setting.

The individual lives in a world made up of many groups of people. While we think of ourselves as individuals, separate and distinct from all other individuals, we do not, nor can we live without others. We are not only individuals, we are at the same time group members. We participate in many kinds of social groups. More than that we find ourselves at times, both as individuals and as group members, in conflict with other groups. And in a complex modern world we find ourselves affected by still other groups about whom we may be unaware.

The nature of these many associations that we as individuals have with other people is complex, varied, and often difficult to determine. Some progress may be made toward clarifying these relations, however, if we will distinguish between two quite different kinds of human relations. We shall use the classification of Tönnies, a German sociologist, and explore the meaning of the terms Gemeinschaft and Gesellschaft.

Before doing so it is necessary to be critical of any attempt to classify all human relations into only two general categories. Further, rather than thinking of Gemeinschaft and Gesellschaft as two separate and distinct kinds of human relations, it would seem more nearly correct to think of them as occupying the extreme ends of a straight line.

The extreme ends of such a scale represent pure types or polar extremes. Our own concrete and real experiences with other people usually fall

SOURCE: Leo A. Haak, ed., *Source Book for Effective Living* (East Lansing: Michigan State University, 1950), 196–99, reprinted by permission. ❖ Professor Holland (1910–1953) was a member of the Department of Sociology and Anthropology and of the Social Science Department at Michigan State University. He was the coauthor of *Community Involvement*.

somewhere along this scale rather than at one end or the other. Our relations with others are generally in terms of more or less rather than all or none, for usually these relations involve both Gemeinschaft and Gesellschaft. Nevertheless, by clearly defining the polar extremes we may classify many of our relations as an individual in the group, for generally one or the other kind of relationship is predominant. The scale furnishes us with a convenient device to measure many of the kinds of associations we have as group members, though we need not assume that all human relations can be made to fit into one or the other of these categories.

This way of classifying our relations with others is not new. The ideas we are to explore here have been most explicitly developed by Tönnies, but they are really a refinement of the thinking of many others who have gone before. Confucius and Plato, Aristotle and Cicero, St. Augustine and Thomas Aquinas, to mention only a few, have attempted to understand and account for the different kinds of human relationships which they observed. Their classifications are similar to that of Tönnies. This way of looking at people, therefore, is not new, it has been useful to many of the great thinkers of the ages, and it is useful to us because it gives us a new pair of glasses with which we may look at facts which are familiar to all of us.

Gesellschaft Relations

First, let us define Gesellschaft, not because it comes first, but because it is the easiest to explain. A brief definition may be given as "Rational relations based on calculation of individual self-interest." Like all brief statements there are many points covered in that definition. What are some of them?

❖   ❖   ❖   ❖   ❖

First of all, our Gesellschaft relations with others are based upon reason and not feeling. Second, we are concerned with our individual self-interest. Third, our obligations are limited to whatever specific contract is stated or implied. Fourth, our relationship with others covers only a specific and clearly-defined area of interest. Fifth, it is not necessary, in fact it is entirely irrelevant whether or not we have any interests in common other than these specific, individual interests which we hope to further by our relationship.

In terms of concrete, flesh and blood people what does this mean? What kind of relations do we have with other people which serve our immediate interests and are largely Gesellschaft in character?

Take an inventory of your daily activities. Whom do you see and what do you do when you are with other people? When you buy a loaf of bread is it primarily an intimate and friendly exchange, or is it a contract between buyer and seller? If you get a check from Veterans Administration do you have a warm personal feeling for the man who signed the check, or do you look to see if it is made out correctly and delivered on time? If you have a part-time job, do you usually prop your feet upon the boss's desk for an hour of friendly conversation, or do you have specific, well-defined duties which you are expected to perform? When you registered at this college, although the cashier may have been very friendly, was this principally Gesellschaft or otherwise? The illustrations could be multiplied indefinitely in terms of your own experiences, but these serve to point out the fact that you and I, living as we do in a complex society, spend a great deal of time busily engaged with the pursuit of our own self-interests. And we have many contacts with other human beings who are likewise concerned with their own interests. In this pursuit of self-interest, people have little reality for us as human beings, as personalities who think, feel, and act, and have personal problems even as we. Because so many of our relations with others are largely Gesellschaft in character it is not surprising that we sometimes fail to recognize the reality of groups and the effect on us and our personalities of our many associations with others.

Gemeinschaft Relations

Just as Gesellschaft is a polar type which characterizes one kind of human relations, so Gemeinschaft is the other. Broadly stated Gemeinschaft is everything that Gesellschaft is not. Gemeinschaft comes logically first in human relations.

Gemeinschaft is easier to define but harder to explain. A brief definition is: "Intimate relations based on sentiment." That is, Gemeinschaft relations are based on the way we feel about people. They are intimate relations. In such contacts with others people are real. Our concern is not with rational calculations and limited obligations but with flesh and blood people and our felt obligations to them.

We may make further contrasts. Whereas in Gesellschaft we enter into a relationship because of rational consideration of individual self-interest, in Gemeinschaft our motives are general and indefinite in character. This is so because they are not carefully calculated but are a part of our feelings. Gemeinschaft relations cover a multitude of interests not well defined at all. For example, if you are married why did you marry? There are many answers, not one or two single, specific reasons. You married for love, to have a home, to raise children, to obtain what we may call psychic security—that is, emotional security and approval. If I ask you why you entered the college bookstore you can tell me exactly. But if I ask you why you married this particular person, why you like certain friends, why you have a friendly feeling for the old home town, it is difficult to explain. This is natural since sentiments and feelings, being nonrational, are hard to explain by rational means. Frequently, however, we feel called upon to justify our feelings and in so doing we depend upon rationalizations which we offer as "good reasons" to explain our behavior.

A second contrast with Gesellschaft relations is that in Gemeinschaft obligations are unspecified and unlimited. There is no specific contract. The burden of proof is on him who would evade an obligation arising out of a Gemeinschaft relation. Let us examine the obligations in marriage. In a general sense a marriage between two people involves a ceremony in which certain obligations are stated. But these are blanket obligations which in the final analysis mean an obligation on each of the marriage partners to help in whatever contingencies arise in their common life together. A married veteran is going to school. There is nothing in the marriage contract which says that his wife will take a full or part-time job to help him in that process. And yet many veterans' wives are doing just that. If a friend of yours is down and out and needs ten dollars there is no written obligation on your part to meet his need. But if you've got the money and if he is a real friend of yours, one for whom you have an intimate and deep-seated liking, you loan him the money, even though you do not expect to get it back.

A third point that may be made about Gemeinschaft relations is that not only are obligations unlimited but they can be ignored only because of the prior obligations of another Gemeinschaft relationship. To illustrate, if you are a doctor you would not, as a husband, ordinarily leave your wife's bridge party. But if it were necessary for you to make an emergency call you would do so. Or again if you were about to meet with a friend who was in a tough spot and needed you to help him regain his bearings, you would cancel the engagement if your child were to be injured or suddenly taken ill. But it should be noted that you are relieved of one Gemeinschaft obligation only because another and higher Gemeinschaft obligation supersedes. You do not customarily ignore Gemeinschaft obligations for Gesellschaft obligations, or if you do we may safely say that there was no deep Gemeinschaft feeling on your part in the first place.

Finally, Gemeinschaft obligations are both moral and ethical in character. I mean by that that individuals in a Gemeinschaft relationship have individual interests but these interests are integrated and a part of the ultimate values of the group. It is safe to say that as a member of a family, insofar as you have intimate feelings for that family, you share in common certain beliefs and ideals. There are certain moral responsibilities that you feel and these moral responsibilities are a part of your individual codes of ethics, your standards, your values. Gemeinschaft relations are shared relations. They extend beyond individual self-interest. In Gemeinschaft relations your individual purposes and ends are integrated and a part of the purposes and ends of the group.

These are the principal characteristics of Gemeinschaft. Relations are intimate and based on feelings or sentiment, not upon reason or calculation. In Gemeinschaft there is what we might call a bond or feeling of belonging. Thus we speak of the bond that unites man and wife or friends or a group of neighbors who are intimately acquainted with each other.

We can illustrate Gemeinschaft concretely for ourselves again in terms of the groups of people with whom we associate in a day. Whom did you see today? How intimately are you concerned with their welfare? Not abstract persons, but real people about whose welfare you are genuinely and personally concerned? What bonds do you have with others and what would it take to break them?

In summary, then, Gemeinschaft relations are intimate relations based on sentiment; Gesellschaft relations are rational relations based on calculation of individual interest. These two types of relations are polar extremes and our actual relations with others vary from extreme, intimate, personal relations with others to extreme, rational calculation of people as means to serve our own immediate ends. It is useful to make this classification because it enables us to analyze more clearly our relations with others and to see in proper perspective our actions as they affect and are affected by others. But even beyond that we need to appraise what is involved in gaining and losing Gemeinschaft relations because we live in a world which is based increasingly upon Gesellschaft. How well each of us personally can survive by rational concern with limited and specific interests alone is a problem which confronts us both as individuals and as group members.

* 28 *

THE SOCIAL "WORLD" OF THE TRANSIENTS' CAMP

John Steinbeck

The talented novelist often describes aspects of social reality more clearly and vividly than the restrained accounts of social scientists. This skill is well illustrated in The Grapes of Wrath, *the classic story of the migrant farm family "tractored out" of Oklahoma but hopeful of finding a better life in California. The following selection from the novel shows how quickly human relationships can develop regularities, become "organized," even in so transitory a situation as the overnight camp of the westward-moving migrant farm families.*

SOURCE: *The Grapes of Wrath* by John Steinbeck, Copyright © 1939 by John Steinbeck. Reprinted by permission of the Viking Press, Inc. ✧ The author, a renowned American novelist, received the Pulitzer Prize in 1940 and was awarded the Nobel prize for literature in 1962. Among his many books are *Tortilla Flat, Of Mice and Men, The Moon Is Down,* and *Winter of Our Discontent.*

The cars of the migrant people crawled out of the side roads onto the great cross-country highway, and they took the migrant way to the West. In the daylight they scuttled like bugs to the westward; and as the dark caught them, they clustered like bugs near to shelter and to water. And because they were lonely and perplexed, because they had all come from a place of sadness and worry and defeat, and because they were all going to a new mysterious place, they huddled together; they talked together; they shared their lives, their food, and the things they hoped for in the new country. Thus it might be that one family camped near a spring, and another camped for the spring and for company, and a third because two families had pioneered the place and found it good. And when the sun went down, perhaps twenty families and twenty cars were there.

In the evening a strange thing happened: the twenty families became one family, the children were the children of all. The loss of home became one loss, and the golden time in the West was one dream. And it might be that a sick child threw despair into the hearts of twenty families, of a hundred people; that a birth there in a tent kept a hundred people quiet and awestruck through the night and filled a hundred people with the birth-joy in the morning. A family which the night before had been lost and fearful might search its goods to find a present for a new baby. In the evening, sitting about the fires, the twenty were one. They grew to be units of the camps, units of the evenings and the nights. A guitar unwrapped from a blanket and tuned—and the songs, which were all of the people, were sung in the nights. Men sang the words, and women hummed the tunes.

Every night a world created, complete with furniture—friends made and enemies established; a world complete with braggarts and with cowards, with quiet men, with humble men, with kindly men. Every night relationships that make a world, established; and every morning the world torn down like a circus.

At first the families were timid in the building and tumbling worlds, but gradually the technique of building worlds became their technique. Then leaders emerged, then laws were made, then codes came into being. And as the worlds moved westward they were more complete and better furnished, for their builders were more experienced in building them.

The families learned what rights must be observed—the right of privacy in the tent; the right to keep the past black hidden in the heart; the right to talk and to listen; the right to refuse help or to accept, to offer help or to decline it; the right of son to court and daughter to be courted; the right of the hungry to be fed; the rights of the pregnant and the sick to transcend all other rights.

And the families learned, although no one told them, what rights are monstrous and must be destroyed: the right to intrude upon privacy, the right to be noisy while the camp slept, the right of seduction or rape, the right of adultery and theft and murder. These rights were crushed, because the little worlds could not exist for even a night with such rights alive.

And as the worlds moved westward, rules became laws, although no one told the families. It is unlawful to foul near the camp; it is unlawful in any way to foul the drinking water; it is unlawful to eat good rich food near one who is hungry, unless he is asked to share.

And with the laws, the punishments—and there were only two—a quick and murderous fight or ostracism; and ostracism was the worst. For if one broke the laws his name and face went with him, and he had no place in any world, no matter where created.

In the worlds, social conduct became fixed and rigid, so that a man must say "Good morning" when asked for it, so that a man might have a willing girl if he stayed with her, if he fathered her children and protected them. But a man might not have one girl one night and another the next, for this would endanger the worlds.

The families moved westward, and the technique of building the worlds improved so that the people could be safe in their worlds; and the form was so fixed that a family acting in the rules knew it was safe in the rules.

There grew up government in the worlds, with leaders, with elders. A man who was wise found that his wisdom was needed in every camp; a man who was a fool could not change his folly with his world. And a kind of insurance developed in these nights. A man with food fed a hungry man, and thus insured himself against hunger. And when a baby died a pile of silver coins grew at the door flap, for a baby must be well buried, since it has had nothing else of life. An old man may be left in a potter's field, but not a baby.

A certain physical pattern is needed for the building of a world—water, a river bank, a stream, a spring, or even a faucet unguarded. And there is needed enough flat land to pitch the tents, a little brush or wood to build the fires. If there is a garbage dump not too far off, all the better; for there can be found equipment—stove tops, a curved fender to shelter the fire, and cans to cook in and to eat from.

And the worlds were built in the evening. The people, moving in from the highways, made them with their tents and their hearts and their brains.

In the morning the tents came down, the canvas was folded, the tent poles tied along the running board, the beds put in place on the cars, the pots in their places. And as the families moved westward, the technique of building up a home in the evening and tearing it down with the morning light became fixed; so that the folded tent was packed in one place, the cooking pots counted in their box. And as the cars moved westward, each member of the family grew into his proper place, grew into his duties; so that each member, old and young, had his place in the car; so that in the weary, hot evenings, when the cars pulled into the camping places, each member had his duty and went to it without instruction: children to gather wood, to carry water; men to pitch the tents and bring down the beds; women to cook the supper and to watch while the family fed. And this was done without command. The families, which had been units of which the boundaries were a house at night, a farm by day, changed their boundaries. In the long hot light, they were silent in the cars moving slowly westward; but at night they integrated with any group they found.

Thus they changed their social life—changed as in the whole universe only man can change. They were not farm men any more, but migrant men. And the thought, the planning, the long staring silence that had gone out to the fields, went now to the roads, to the distance, to the West. That man whose mind had been bound with acres lived with narrow concrete miles. And his thought and his worry were not any more with rainfall, with wind and dust, with the thrust of the crops. Eyes watched the tires, ears listened to the clattering motors, and minds struggled with oil, with gasoline, with the thinning rubber between air and road. Then a broken gear was tragedy. Then water in the evening was the yearning, and food over the fire. Then health to go on was the need and strength to go on, and spirit to go on. The wills thrust westward ahead of them, and fears that had once apprehended drought or flood now lingered with anything that might stop the westward crawling.

The camps became fixed—each a short day's journey from the last.

And on the road the panic overcame some of the families, so that they drove night and day, stopped to sleep in the cars, and drove on to the West, flying from the road, flying from movement. And these lusted so greatly to be settled that they set their faces into the West and drove toward it, forcing the clashing engines over the roads.

But most of the families changed and grew quickly into the new life. And when the sun went down——

Time to look out for a place to stop.

And—there's some tents ahead.

The car pulled off the road and stopped, and because others were there first, certain courtesies were necessary. And the man, the leader of the family, leaned from the car.

Can we pull up here an' sleep?

Why, sure, be proud to have you. What State you from?

Come all the way from Arkansas.

They's Arkansas people down that fourth tent.

That *so?*

And the great question, How's the water?

Well, she don't taste so good, but they's plenty.

Well, thank ya.

No thanks to me.

But the courtesies had to be. The car lumbered over the ground to the end tent, and stopped. Then down from the car the weary people climbed, and stretched stiff bodies. Then the new tent sprang up; the children went for water and the older boys cut brush or wood. The fires started and supper was put on to boil or to fry. Early comers moved over, and States were exchanged, and friends and sometimes relatives discovered.

Oklahoma, huh? What county?

Cherokee.

Why, I got folks there. Know the Allens? They's Allens all over Cherokee. Know the Willises?

Why, sure.

And a new unit was formed. The dusk came, but before the dark was down the new family was of the camp. A word had been passed with every family. They were known people—good people.

* 29 *

SOCIAL RELATIONS IN A BUREAUCRACY

George C. Homans

To the uninitiated, a bureaucracy, with its many rules of operation and its highly organized and formalized structure, has little room for any informal interaction, either in relation to the job or in a purely social sense. Actually, however, the work of large and complex organizations is mediated through a network of many small, interrelated groups. This selection, written by George Homans but based upon case material from Peter Blau's The Dynamics of Bureaucracy, examines the interpersonal processes which develop in the work situation and explores the reasons for the behavior which takes place. After reading this article, the student will find it instructive to observe, utilizing Homans' approach, some small group with which he is acquainted.

A Federal Agency: Consultation Among Colleagues

The group consisted of a supervisor, sixteen agents, and one clerk, who formed in 1949 a department in a local branch of a Federal agency that had its headquarters in Washington, D.C. In order to protect the

SOURCE: Abridged from *Social Behavior: Its Elementary Forms* by George C. Homans, © 1961, by Harcourt, Brace & World, Inc., and reprinted with their permission. ✧ The author is professor of sociology at Harvard University. His major interests include industrial relations and sociological theory. In addition to *Social Behavior: Its Elementary Forms*, his writings include *The Human Group* and *English Villagers of the Thirteenth Century*. He is a former president of the American Sociological Association.

anonymity of the group, the investigator does not tell us what the precise job of the agency was. Broadly it was concerned with the enforcement of a certain set of Federal laws. Since we are not interested in formal organization, and since he was hardly a member of the group, we shall not have much to say about the supervisor; nor was the clerk a member. Our business is with the sixteen agents.

The members of the department were fairly experienced in their work: only one had been with the agency for less than five years. Two held the civil-service grade 9, which was the highest represented among the agents; two were in grade 7; and the rest, the great majority, were in the middle with grade 8. But regardless of their different grades, all did much the same kind of work. Only three were women, and only one was a Negro. On the average an agent spent about 40 per cent of his time in the home office, where he had a desk of his own along with the other agents. But because their duties took them often into the field, not all the agents were together in the office at any one time.

An agent's main duty was investigation. On assignment by the supervisor, he went to the office of a business firm, obtained from it a wide variety of information, then came back to the agency where, from the information he had collected, he wrote a report stating whether or not and in what way the firm had violated Federal law. In order to determine whether a violation had occurred, an agent had to know how a large and complex body of legal rulings applied to the circumstances of a particular case. And since his report might become the basis of legal action against the firm, an agent had to be sure of his facts, his argument, and the clarity of his presentation.

The quality of the reports an agent turned in to the supervisor determined more than anything else the kind of efficiency rating the latter gave him, and this in turn affected his chances for promotion to a higher grade in the civil service. Thus an agent had to do a job difficult in itself, and his success in doing it made a difference to his future. Moreover, unlike the members of many industrial groups, the agents believed strongly in the value of the work the agency was doing, and so were doubly motivated to do it right.

Yet in spite of his long experience, an agent was often in doubt which legal rules might be applicable to the case under consideration and what decision he ought to reach about it. An agent was left free to make his own decision, the only formal rule being that if he had any doubt or question, he was to bring it to the supervisor without consulting any of his colleagues. But like many formal rules, this one was disregarded. Not unnaturally the agents believed that to take a question to the supervisor was to confess one's incompetence and so to prejudice one's efficiency rating; accordingly they did go to their colleagues for help and advice, and the supervisor seems to have winked at the practice.

Although the agents all had much experience, they still recognized that some of their number were better than others at solving the problems that came up over writing reports. Blau's first job was to ask every agent to put all the others in order of their competence as he saw it. The individual rankings were highly in agreement with one another, and they agreed also with the supervisor's ranking of the competence of the different agents.

The investigator next tried to relate the perceived competence of the different agents to the number of times other agents went to them for help and advice. In the course of his observations of behavior in the department, the investigator kept a record of every contact between agents, however brief it might have been, such as a word spoken in passing. He discovered that an agent, while he was in the office, had an average of five contacts per hour with colleagues. Some of these were casual and social conversations, but many were discussions of technical problems. The investigator decided that the latter were probably the longer, and so in studying the distribution of technical consultations he included only contacts that lasted more than three minutes. The investigator also asked every agent to name the other agents whom he consulted when he ran into difficulties with his work.

The results showed a rather marked pattern. As we should expect, the more competent an agent, the more contacts he was apt to receive, and the higher was the esteem in which he was held. But the correlation was not perfect. Two of the agents who their colleagues believed were competent seem to have discouraged people that came to them for help and so to have choked off further advances. As Blau says, "The two experts who were considered uncooperative by their colleagues were generally disliked and received only few contacts. To become accepted, an expert had to share the advantages of his superior skill with his co-workers."

But most agents were ready to help. A few of them, and these among the most competent of all, were consulted by a large number of others, but did not themselves go regularly for advice to any one agent. Thus four agents had no regular partners, but all four were highly competent. Three of them were also very popular as consultants. "These three were by no means isolated from the exchange of advice. On the contrary, they participated so widely in it that they did not spend much time with any single co-worker." The fourth agent had only recently been assigned to the department and had not yet been brought into much use as a consultant. The rest of the agents, on the other hand, were apt to take regular partners. Each one of them, though occasionally consulting the few highly competent men, was apt to be especially closely linked with one or two others whose competence was more nearly equal to his own. On any occasion when he needed help, he felt free to consult his partner, as long as he was ready to allow the latter the same kind of privilege in return.

Rewards and Costs of Consultation

Now let us see what the investigator has to say about the social economics of consultation:

A consultation can be considered an exchange of values; both participants gain something, and both have to pay a price. The questioning agent is enabled to perform better than he could otherwise have done, without exposing his difficulties to the supervisor. By asking for advice, he implicitly pays his respect to the superior proficiency of his colleague. This acknowledgment of inferiority is the cost of receiving assistance. The consultant gains prestige, in return for which he is willing to devote some time to the consultation and permit it to disrupt his own work. The following remark of an agent illustrates this: "I like giving advice. It's flattering, I suppose, if you feel that the others come to you for advice."

The expert who was willing to give advice got various advantages incidental to his rise in esteem. From the consultation he drew renewed confidence in his own capacity to solve technical problems. He might, indeed, pick up ideas useful to him in doing his own work without paying the price of an admission of inferiority. Each of the three most popular consultants, whom many others asked for help, could, moreover, when he needed help in return, scatter his requests among these many and did not need to concentrate them on any single agent, which would have made more conspicuous the fact that it was help he was asking for. As the investigator puts it: "Besides, to refrain from asking any particular individual too many questions helped to maintain his reputation as an expert. Consequently, three of the most popular consultants had no regular partners."

The cost that an expert incurred in getting his prestige is obvious: he had to take time from his own work. "All agents liked being consulted, but the value of any one of very many consultations became deflated for experts, and the price they paid in frequent interruptions became inflated. . . . Being approached for help was too valuable an experience to be refused, but popular consultants were not inclined to encourage further questions."

The investigator is quite explicit that asking a colleague for help incurred an agent costs: "Asking a colleague for guidance was less threatening than asking the supervisor, but the repeated admission of his inability to solve his own problems also undermined the self-confidence of an agent and his standing in the group. The cost of advice became prohibitive, if the consultant, after the questioner had subordinated himself by asking for help, was in the least discouraging—by postponing a discussion or by revealing his impatience during one."

The cost in inferiority of asking a colleague for help was rendered greater in this group than it would have been in some others by the fact that, formally, the agents were not greatly unequal: all held the same job-title, all did the same kind of work, and most of them held the same civil-service grade. A man who is already another's inferior has much less to lose in asking a service of him than one who began as his equal.

That asking for help did indeed incur a man costs is shown by the practice some agents adopted of asking for help while elaborately pretending that they were doing nothing of the sort. Such an agent would bring his problem to a colleague as if it were a case presenting special points of interest well worthy of dispassionate analysis between two discriminating judges. As one of the agents said, "Casey asks me sometimes, too, but he does it with a lot of finesse. He will just seem to ask what my opinion is, not as if he were worried about the question." And the investigator makes the comment: "Such manipulative attempts to obtain advice without reciprocating by acknowledging the need for the other's help were resented. . . . If his advice was needed, the agent demanded that the respect due him be paid by *asking* for his assistance. An official whose deliberate disguise of a consultation was discovered created resentment without averting loss of esteem." In short, this maneuver broke the rules of fair exchange: it attempted to get help without conceding superiority in return. . . .

As we have seen, three of the most competent agents did not enter into partnerships, did not regularly exchange help and advice with particular other agents. Two highly competent agents did take regular partners, but upon the whole partnerships were confined to people of middle and low competence. The investigator implies that it was precisely the costs a man incurred in asking the most competent agents for advice that led the rest to seek out partners among people more nearly of their own rank, with whom they could exchange help without losing status; for the essence of partnership was that if one man asked his partner for help on one occasion, the partner might ask the same favor back on the next. Speaking of the fact that an agent who tried to consult one of his more competent colleagues might meet with a refusal, Blau says:

To avoid such rejections, agents usually consulted a colleague with whom they were friendly, even if he was not an expert. . . . The establishment of partnerships of mutual consultation virtually eliminated the danger of rejections as well as the status threat implicit in asking for help, since the roles of questioner and consultant were intermittently reversed. These partnerships also enabled agents to reserve their consultations with an expert whom they did not know too well for their most complicated problems.

That is, the advice a man got from his partner might not be of the highest value, but it was purchased at low cost since a partner was apt to be his social equal. And thus he was enabled to save his really difficult problems for the most competent agents, whose advice, since it did come high in confessed inferiority, he did not want to ask often. . . .

. . . Social behavior is an exchange of more or less valuable rewards. The expert agents provided for the others a service that these others found valuable and rare. In return, the experts received much interaction and were able to command from the rest a high degree of esteem, thus establishing a social ranking in the group. But in getting these rewards both parties to the exchange incurred costs—the experts in time taken away from their own work, the others in implicit admissions of inferiority. The costs, moreover, increased and the rewards declined with the number of exchanges, thus tending to cut off further exchange. The experts began to rebuff new requests, and the rest began to hesitate before approaching the experts. Indeed the rest began to look for sources of help they could exploit at lower cost. In the nature of the case, these sources could only be agents more nearly of their own rank than the experts. With such people they could both give and take advice without net loss in esteem.

Finally, most agents met the conditions of distributive justice. For instance, the experts who were ready to give help got much esteem but incurred heavy costs in time taken away from their own work: their costs were proportional to their rewards. Therefore the other agents not only respected but liked them. To win esteem it was not enough to *be* expert: a man had to devote his expert knowledge to the service of others. Thus a couple of agents, known to be competent, who repelled others approaching them with requests for help, were much disliked and left much alone. In failing to enter into exchange at all they had deprived the others of services that the others had come to expect of people with so much to give.

"Social" Interaction

The investigator next turned to the relations between the agents' competence and their more purely "social" behavior. Of the latter he made two different kinds of observations. In his period of watching the group he had kept a record of all the contacts (interactions) an agent received from others, but in mapping out the pattern of consultations he had included only the relatively long contacts—three minutes or more—on the ground that long contacts were more likely than short ones to have to do with the official business of the agency. Now, in mapping out "social" behavior—passing the time of day, gossiping, telling jokes—he included all the contacts an agent received, long or short, and called this a measure of *contacts received*. The investigator also asked each agent to keep a record every day of the colleagues he lunched with. "If a luncheon engagement is defined as eating with one colleague once, the total number of engagements reported (which often included several colleagues on the same day, and the same colleague on repeated days), divided by the number of days on which the respondent went out to lunch from the office, defines the value of this index,"—which the investigator called a measure of an agent's *informal relations*.

He then proceeded to study the interrelations of these three variables: competence, contacts received, and informal relations. For this purpose, he divided the rank-order of the agents on each variable into two parts, but the division did not necessarily come at the mid-point of the distribution. Thus seven agents were rated as high in competence and eight low, but six were rated as high in contacts received and nine low. (One agent transferred out of the department in the course of the study, reducing the total number of the agents considered for the present purpose to fifteen.)

Agents high in competence were statistically likely to be high also in contacts received. Not all were: the two highly competent agents who were unwilling to give the others the benefit of their competence and who were accordingly disliked received few social contacts; but the tendency was in this direction. By the same token, the less competent agents tended statistically to get few contacts.

Perhaps this finding tells us little more than we know already. An expert who was willing to share his knowledge with others was much sought after by the others for consultation, and we know that many of the contacts an expert received were of this sort. But not all were: some were more purely "social." Once a man has won esteem by providing others with rare and valuable services, another reason for their seeking him out comes into play: he is now able to offer a new kind of service. . . .

. . . Some members of a group, those not unduly troubled about their self-respect, seek out social interaction with a member of high status for reasons other than getting the service that first won him the status. But how will a member of high status receive their advances? If he is in any doubt about his status, social contacts with his inferiors will tend to bring him down to their level, and he is apt to rebuff them; but if his status is so firmly established that he need not worry about it, his willingness to allow them social access to him provides them with a new and valuable service and enhances the esteem in which they hold him.

"Contacts received" was measured by the number of interactions a man received in the office, and this might include "business" contacts as well as "social" ones. The best index of purely "social" contacts was "informal relations," which was measured by luncheons. The investigator found that, statistically speaking, agents of high competence were apt to have few informal relations and agents of low competence to have many. Some of the competent agents did not use their competence to help others; therefore they did not enjoy high status, and the others were not much interested in getting their company for lunch. Some enjoyed a status both high and secure, and could afford to wait until others approached them. And some may not have been quite sure of their high status, which may have led them to rebuff the advances of their inferiors. All of these effects tended to reduce the informal relations of the more competent people. But the less competent people, who on the average were less secure in their status than the more competent ones, tended actively to seek others out for luncheon dates. They sought out the agents of high status if they could get them, but if they could not, they found lunching with somebody better than lunching alone. No doubt man is a gregarious animal and enjoys lunching with his fellows regardless of what it does to his status. Our only point is that differences in status provide additional reasons for (or against) social contacts. By lunching with any one of his fellows an agent of low status could at least make good the fact that he was the other's equal, that he was at least an accepted member of the group. At any rate, the less competent agents "lunched in larger groups than experts and made greater efforts to arrange their work so that they would have to eat alone as rarely as possible." By eating in large groups they necessarily rolled up a high score in informal relations, since each person present at the table added to the score.

Though the competent agents tended to have fewer informal relations than the less competent, lunching more often alone or with fewer companions, the relationship was statistical and did not hold good of all of them. One agent of whom it did not hold good was the one who, in the office, was most encouraging to people who came and asked him for help. He was better liked than any other agent, and became, as we shall soon see, the informal leader of the group. In short, his status was both high and secure. "His great willingness to assist others," the investigator comments, "was his price for maintaining this position." But this was not the only service he did for them: he was also willing to provide them with the secondary reward of lunching with him. "He was particularly hospitable to colleagues who consulted him, and he deliberately fostered informal relations with them. 'If anyone asks me for lunch,' he told the observer, 'I never say, "I have a date with another fellow; I can't." I always say, "Of course, come along." ' In contrast to most experts, this agent had very extensive informal relations."

The investigator finally turned to the third of the possible relations between the three variables, the relation between informal relations and contacts received, and he found that agents who had many informal relations (luncheons) were statistically likely to receive many contacts.

✧   ✧   ✧   ✧   ✧

It is interesting to reconstruct from the investigator's data what the actual pattern of social engagements among the agents must have been. We shall not give here the tedious reasoning that leads to the reconstruction but only its conclusions. The less competent agents must have lunched with one another a great deal, and in large groups, without the more competent agents' being present—indeed the investigator implies as much. The competent agents must also have lunched with one another a good deal without the less competent agents' being present—but in small groups. This suggests that they may have rebuffed some of the social advances made to them by the less competent agents. And, finally, some of the less competent managed to get some of the more competent to lunch with them fairly often, in large groups. In fact the investigator tells us that the informal leader was one of the competent men who thus allowed himself to be lunched with by his social inferiors. Equals, then, tended in general to lunch with equals, but some inferiors made successful advances to their superiors in status.

We have here further evidence of the complex interplay of two tendencies we have encountered again and again: a tendency for a man to interact with his superiors in status, and a tendency for him to interact with his equals. A man establishes superior status by providing superior services for others. By the same token, accepting the superior services becomes a cost to a man, since he thereby recognizes his inferiority. Sooner or later he will turn to others who can provide him with services that no doubt reward him less but that also cost him less in inferiority. In the nature of the case, these others can only be his equals. As the partnerships in the Federal agency show, he will turn to his equals for services at work that he can return in kind; but he is particularly apt to turn to them in the "social" field of activity, just because it is *not* the field in which his superiors win their high esteem—and he his low. A secondary development then builds on this primary one. The rest of mankind can "see" the equations of elementary social behavior just as clearly in their way as we social scientists can, and once the relation between social interaction and equality of status is established, it provides new rewards for interaction. By interacting with his fellows a man can then provide evidence for himself and for them that he is at least their equal. Still better, if he can get his superior to interact with him he may do something to raise his apparent status.

Esteem and Authority

As we have just seen, people of high status tend to receive much interaction. Indeed to maneuver a man into coming to you is to establish the presumption that you are his superior. But people of high status also give much interaction, especially in the sense of originating activity. They tell a relatively large number of others what they ought to do, and the others often do it. The higher the esteem, the higher the authority, is a proposition for which the Federal agency provided much evidence.

Let us consider particularly the agent who the investigator believes was the top informal leader in the department. (The supervisor was of course the formal leader.) He was highly competent at his job, and recognized as being so both by the supervisor and by the other agents. Of the more competent agents, he was also the one most receptive and least discouraging to requests for help from others. That is, he was the most willing to incur the cost of taking time off from his own work. And he was highly popular. . . .

. . . He received high rewards in esteem from the group, but in so doing he incurred, as they saw it, high costs too.

He rewarded the others not only in the business side of their life but in the social one too. He was always ready to accept an invitation to lunch with his social inferiors, and in this he was unlike most of the other competent agents. But the very liberality with which he distributed his favors prevented his becoming identified with any one of the cliques whose members met regularly for lunch. He was in touch with everybody and not exclusively in touch with any single person or subgroup. . . .

. . . The more competent agents tended to take the lead in any undertaking in which several members of the group were engaged. They made most suggestions, and their suggestions were most often followed, whether the question was where to go for lunch or what to do about a project on which a number of agents were working together. And of all the competent agents, the one held in highest esteem was the one who also held highest authority. When a committee was appointed to draft a change in one of the regulations, he dominated the discussion, and his opinion was the one finally adopted. Above all he stood up for the other agents against the supervisor. In this connection the investigator says of him:

This agent became the informal leader of the group, whose suggestions the others often followed and who acted as their spokesman. For example, in a departmental meeting the supervisor criticized certain deficiencies in the performance of most agents, clearly exempting experts from his criticism. Nevertheless, this official spoke up on behalf of the group and explained that agents could not be blamed for these deficiencies, since a legal regulation that restricted their operations was responsible for them. Generally, the high regard in which this agent was held made his advice and opinion influential among colleagues, and even among superiors.

A man to whom many others come singly for valuable services, in this case advice on how to do their work, and who in rendering the services incurs costs visibly proportional to the esteem they have given him, earns the right to tell them jointly what to do in new conditions that may affect the welfare of many of them, himself among the rest. By serving he becomes a leader. We must always remember that the services he provides need not be ones that you or I should find rewarding or even approve of. Leaders get to be where they are by doing some of the strangest things, and the rest of us are always asking ourselves, "What's he got that I haven't got?" The answer is that what he has got does actually reward some other men, whether or not it ought to do so, and what he has got is rare in the actual circumstances, whether or not it would be rare in others.

Nor should we lay too much stress on the difference between the followers' coming to him singly and his telling them jointly what to do. In both cases, whether he gives them advice they take or orders they obey, the important point is that he controls their behavior; and the fact that a new occasion may call for his advising them jointly is a nonessential detail. His past behavior has won him the capability of doing so, should the occasion present itself, but it may not. The advice he has given them singly they have in the past rewarded with approval, and so he is more likely to give advice again on a new occasion. He has, as we say, acquired confidence in his ability to give them advice. Nor is it just that he has more confidence but that the others have less: persons whose status is less than his own are persons whose advice has less often won approval in the past, and who are therefore less apt to have the gall to speak up now: what wise ideas they have do them no good if they lack the confidence to come out with them.

The relation between past behavior and present that holds good for the leader holds good also for the followers. Having taken his advice singly and found it rewarding, they are more ready to take it jointly—to obey him when he tells them what to do for their welfare and his own. In doing so, he puts his social capital at hazard, since if they obey and fail to find the outcome rewarding, he has done injury to his esteem and their future willingness to obey. But he has much capital to risk, and if they do find the outcome to their satisfaction, he has replaced his capital and more. Finally, though the leader may lay himself open to the social advances of his followers, he cannot allow himself to get too close to any one of them or any single clique; for frequent social interaction implies equality, and equality between people tends to be incongruent with the fact that one of their number gives orders to the rest. But the best guarantee that he shall not be too close to anyone lies in the very profusion with which he scatters his favors abroad.

Nonconformity and Isolation

A member of a group acquires high esteem by providing rare and valuable services for the other members. But these are obviously not the only services a member can perform: he can also perform services that, without being rare, nevertheless have their value. Prominent among them is conformity to the norms of the group—a norm being a statement of what behavior ought to be, to which at least some members of the group find it valuable that their own actual behavior and that of other members should conform. Since a norm envisages that a relatively large number of members will behave similarly in some respect, conformity to a norm cannot be a rare service: any fool can conform if he will only take the trouble; and therefore if all a man did was conform, he would never get much esteem, though he would always get some. But it does not follow that if conformity will not win a man much esteem, nonconformity will not lose him much—if he has any to lose. For his failure to conform, when the other members see no just reason why he should not, deprives them unfairly of a valuable service, and so earns him their positive hostility.

Among themselves the agents had, over time, worked out several unofficial norms. They felt that no agent, as a maximum, should complete more than the eight cases a month that the supervisor expected of every agent as a minimum. And they felt that no agent should take a report home from the office in order to work on it in the evening. Agents who showed any sign of doing these things were kidded until they stopped. Violation of these norms was an injury to the members of the group, and conformity a value to them, because an agent who finished more than eight cases a month or worked on cases at home might have gotten an advantage over the others in the race for promotion; and if everyone had started to violate the norms, they would all have found themselves, through competition, working harder than they ever had before—not that the supervisor was at all discouraged with the quantity and quality of their present work: the agents were devoted civil servants. In practice, these output norms conspired to perpetuate existing differences in competence, since they prevented slower agents from catching up with their superiors by working harder.

The agents laid an even more severe taboo against reporting to the supervisor that firms had offered them bribes, though by the official rules of the agency they were bound to report such offers. It was not that the agents accepted bribes and wanted to prevent a colleague who was puritanical about such matters from spoiling their game. Far from it: when they suspected that an officer of a firm was working up to offering a bribe, they did their best to cut him off before he could commit himself openly. In the agents' view, it was inevitable that businessmen, given the pressures they worked under, should think of bribery; therefore it ought not to be held against them, and an agent reporting them and so making them subject to legal action was a "squealer." The agents also had a more practical interest in the norm against reporting bribes. If possible an agent was expected to induce the firm he was investigating to obey the law voluntarily and not under the compulsion of legal action expensive to both parties. An offer of a bribe, however tactfully it was made, put into an agent's hand a lever by which he might without legal action get the firm to comply with the law. But it was a lever that became worse than useless once the proffered bribe was officially reported. Indeed the report might make the company all the more ready to fight it out with the government in the courts. Accordingly, agents discouraged all tendencies in their colleagues to "get tough with" and "crack down on" companies, except as a last resort. Should the agency get the reputation of behaving this way, their work would become much more difficult: all companies would meet every agent with automatic hostility, and the chances of persuading them instead of compelling them to compliance would be gone forever. For these reasons most agents felt they had a direct personal interest in seeing that all their colleagues conformed to this norm.

With these norms in mind, let us look at one of the isolates in the department. When we call him an isolate, we mean that he received few social contacts and often lunched alone. Although he appears to have been considered fairly competent, he not only was not ready to use his competence for the benefit of others but spent his time instead turning out more work than the others considered right. Already held in low esteem for behavior of this sort, he proceeded to take a "get tough" attitude toward the firms he investigated; indeed this was generally more apt to be true of the less popular agents than of the more popular ones. And he was the only agent who violated the strongest taboo of all and reported to the supervisor that a bribe had been offered him. The investigator tells us little or nothing about the social background of any of the agents, including this one, and so we cannot tell what features of his past history may have predisposed him to behave as he did. He himself admitted he had made a mistake: though he had violated the norm, he was ready to say it was a good one.

For his action the group had for a time deliberately ostracized him. Cutting off interaction with a member and thus depriving him of any social reward whatever is the most severe punishment a group can inflict on him; in fact he ceases to be a member. But once a man has stood that, he can, so to speak, stand anything; and the group has lost control of him, for it has left him with nothing more to lose. Certainly the department had pretty well lost control of this agent. Though he reported no more bribes, he did much as he pleased in other ways. For instance, the agents felt that he wasted their time by talking a great deal too much in department meetings, where the agents of higher esteem usually took the largest part in the discussion. But in spite of the laughter his remarks provoked, he kept at it and could not be cowed. In a better cause he might have been a hero. The investigator believes that this agent provided only the most conspicuous example of a general tendency: that agents of established low status conformed least closely to the norms of the group, while those of middle status—particularly those, like newcomers, whose esteem was least well established—were the greatest conformers of all.

Social behavior, in a group as elsewhere, is a continuous process of members influencing other members, and the success of influence in the past changes the probability of its success in the future. One result of the process of influence is that the members of a group become differentiated in a more or less stable way—stable so long as external circumstances do not change much. As some members, for instance, succeed in providing, under the influence of requests from others, more valuable services for these others than they can provide for themselves, the members become differentiated in esteem. This fairly stable differentiation in some pattern other than a random one is what we mean by the structure or organization of the group. But the structure is never so stable that it does not itself sow the seeds of further change, and we have been studying a particular example of this. The process of influence that has landed a man at the bottom of the ladder of esteem may render any future influence, so far as it comes from other members, still less likely to succeed with him. Suppose he would ordinarily lose esteem by doing something other than what they want, but he happens as a result of his past behavior to be left without any esteem to lose. If there is any other way in which he finds the action rewarding—and it may be rewarding just because it vexes *them*—the fact that its costs have been reduced to zero raises the odds in favor of his taking it.

A group controls its members by creating rewards for them which it can then threaten to withdraw. If the group has to make good the threat too often, it may wind up with nothing left to withdraw. Its control is always precarious as long as the members have any alternative to accepting the control, such as the alternative offered by another group they can make their escape to. We have been speaking of the low-status member who is going lower. But very high status may have something of the same effect as very low. A man who has so much status to lose that he will not mind if he loses a little of it can afford to try something new and take the risk that it may not turn out to be acceptable to the membership. He too, in his way, is exempt from the control of the group. There are deviates and deviates, some from the point of view of the group are bad deviates, some are good ones. But both are innovators; and if one looked only at the innovations they propose, it would often be hard to tell which is which.

We try to describe what happens in human behavior without taking any moral stand about it—unless laughter is a moral stand. Or rather we take only one stand out of the many open to us. We have nothing to say in favor of conformity or against it. All we have done is point out that a man who does not conform takes certain risks. But a man is born to take risks. Morally we cannot object to him unless he wants his nonconformity made easy, unless he wants to kick the group in the teeth and have it like him too. For then he is being unfair to the rest of us by asking that an exception to the human condition be made in his favor.

CHAPTER V

Social Organization:

COLLECTIVE BEHAVIOR

✦ 30 ✦

THE MEN FROM MARS

John Houseman

Collective behavior depends upon some form of communication
functioning within the framework of a shared culture. Under these
conditions any enlargement in the available means of communica-
tion, such as radio, television and the communication satellites,
increases the potential size of the audience whose attention may
be attracted and whose behavior may be influenced for either de-
sirable or undesirable ends through control of the content trans-
mitted. In the selection which follows, John Houseman gives a
graphic account of a startling and rather disquieting episode pre-
cipitated by a radio program designed only for entertainment.
Realism was necessary to ensure the full dramatic effect in its pres-
entation. So skillful was the technique used, however, that thou-
sands believed an actual invasion from Mars was taking place. The
panic, the irrational behavior of many people who chanced to tune
in, is an interesting example of the propaganda potential of radio
and television. Houseman rejects the idea that the incident can be
dismissed as an example of the "incredible stupidity and gullibility
of the American public." Instead, he indicates many other impor-
tant factors that must be considered in any explanation of the
effects stimulated by the broadcast.

RADIO WAR TERRORIZES U.S.—N.Y. *Daily News, October 31, 1938*

Everybody was excited I felt as if I was going crazy and kept on saying what
can we do what difference does it make whether we die sooner or later? We

SOURCE: *Harper's Magazine,* Vol. 197, No. 1183 (December, 1948),
74–82. Reprinted by permission of the author and the publisher. ✧ The
author was cofounder of Mercury Theater, New York, in the 1930's. He supervised Voice of America programs during World War II for the Radio
Program Bureau, Office of War Information.

were holding each other. Everything seemed unimportant in the face of death.
I was afraid to die, just kept on listening.—*A listener*

Nothing about the broadcast was in the least credible.—*Dorothy Thompson*

The show came off. There is no doubt about that. It set out to
dramatize, in terms of popular apprehension, an attempted invasion of
our world by hostile forces from the planet Mars. It succeeded. Of the
several million American citizens who, on the evening of October 30, 1938,
milled about the streets, clung sobbing to one another or drove wildly in
all directions to avoid asphyxiation and flaming death, approximately
one-half were in terror of Martians—not of Germans, Japanese, or unknown
enemies—but, specifically, of Martians. Later, when the excitement was
over and the shadow of the gallows had lifted, some of us were inclined to
take credit for more deliberate and premeditated villainy than we deserved.
The truth is that at the time, nobody was more surprised than we were.
In fact, one of the most remarkable things about the broadcast was the
quite haphazard nature of its birth.

In October 1938, the Mercury Theater, of which Orson Welles and I
were the founding partners, had been in existence for less than a year. Our
first Broadway season had been shatteringly successful—"Julius Caesar,"
"The Cradle Will Rock," "Shoemaker's Holiday," and "Heartbreak House"
in the order of their appearance. In April, Orson, in a straggly white beard,
made the cover of *Time* Magazine. In June, the Columbia Broadcasting
System offered him a radio show—"The Mercury Theater on the Air," a
series of classic dramatizations in the first person singular with Orson as
master of ceremonies, star, narrator, writer, director, and producer. He
accepted. So, now, in addition to an empty theater, a movie in progress,
two plays in rehearsal, and all seven of the chronicle plays of William
Shakespeare in preparation, we had a radio show.

We opened on July 11. Among our first thirteen shows were "Treasure
Island," "39 Steps," "Abraham Lincoln," "Three Short Stories" (by
Saki, Sherwood Anderson, and Carl Ewald), "Jane Eyre," "Julius Caesar"
(with running commentary by Kaltenborn out of Plutarch), and "The
Man Who Was Thursday." Our second series, in the fall, began with
Booth Tarkington's "Seventeen," "Around the World in Eighty Days,"
and "Oliver Twist." Our fifth show was to be "Life with Father." Our
fourth was "The War of the Worlds."

No one, as I remember, was very enthusiastic about it. But it seemed
good programming, between the terrors of Dickens' London slums, and
the charm of Clarence Day's New York in the nineties, to throw in something of a contrasting and pseudo-scientific nature. We thought of Shiel's
Purple Cloud, Conan Doyle's *Lost World*, and several others before we
settled on H. G. Wells' twenty-year-old novel, which neither of us, as it
turned out later, remembered at all clearly. It is just possible that neither
of us had ever read it.

II

Those were our golden days of unsponsored radio. We had no advertising agency to harass us, no client to cut our withers. Partly because we were perpetually overworked and partly because that was the way we did things at the Mercury, we never seemed to get more than a single jump ahead of ourselves. Shows were created week after week under conditions of soul- and health-destroying pressure. On the whole they were good shows. And we *did* develop a system—of sorts.

It worked as follows: I was editor of the series. With Welles, I chose the shows and then laid them out. The writing, most of it, was done by Howard Koch—earnest, spindly, six-foot-two—a Westchester lawyer turned playwright. To write the first draft of an hour's radio script took him about five days, working about fifteen hours a day. Our associate producer was Paul Stewart, a Broadway actor turned director. His function was to put the broadcast through its first paces and preliminary rehearsals. Every Thursday, musicless and with rudimentary sound effects, a wax record of the show was cut. From this record, played back later that night, Orson would give us his reactions and revisions. In the next thirty-six hours the script would be reshaped and rewritten, sometimes drastically. Saturday afternoon there was another rehearsal, with sound—with or without Welles. It was not until the last day that Orson really took over.

Sundays, at eight, we went on the air. Beginning in the early afternoon—when Bernard Herrmann arrived with his orchestra of twenty-seven high-grade symphony players—two simultaneous dramas were regularly unfolded in the stale, tense air of Studio Number One: the minor drama of the current show and the major drama of Orson's gargantuan struggle to get it on. Sweating, howling, disheveled, and single-handed he wrestled with Chaos and Time—always conveying an effect of being alone, traduced by his collaborators, surrounded by treachery, ignorance, sloth, indifference, incompetence and—more often than not—downright sabotage! Every Sunday it was touch and go. As the hands of the clock moved relentlessly toward air time the crisis grew more extreme, the peril more desperate. Often violence broke out. Scripts flew through the air, doors were slammed, batons smashed. Scheduled for six—but usually nearer seven—there was a dress rehearsal, a thing of wild improvisations and irrevocable disaster. (One show was found to be twenty-one minutes overlength, another fourteen and one-half minutes short.)

After that, with only a few minutes to go, there was a final frenzy of correction and reparation, of utter confusion and absolute horror, aggravated by the gobbling of sandwiches and the bolting of oversized milkshakes. By now it was less than a minute to air time. . . .

At that instant, quite regularly week after week—with not one second to spare . . . the titanic buffoonery stopped. Suddenly out of chaos, the show emerged—delicately poised, meticulously executed, precise as clock-work, and smooth as satin. And above us all, like a rainbow over storm clouds, stood Orson on his podium, sonorous and heroic, a leader of men surrounded by his band of loyal followers; a giant in action, serene and radiant with the joy of a hard battle bravely fought—a great victory snatched from the jaws of disaster.

In later years, when the Men from Mars had passed into history, there was some bickering among members of the Mercury as to who, exactly, had contributed precisely what, to that particular evening's entertainment. The truth is that a number of us made a number of essential and incalculable contributions to the broadcast. (Who can accurately assess, for instance, the part played by Johnny Dietz's perfect engineering, in keeping unbroken the shifting illusion of imperfect reality? How much did the original old H. G. Wells, who noisily repudiated us, have to do with it? Or the second assistant sound man? Or individual actors? Or Dr. Goebbels? Or Charlie McCarthy?) Orson Wells had virtually nothing to do with the writing of the script and less than usual to do with its preliminary rehearsals. Yet first and last it was his creation. If there had been a lynching that night, it is Welles the outraged populace would have strung up—and rightly so. Orson was the Mercury. "The War of the Worlds," like everything we did, was his show.

Actually, it was a narrow squeak. Those Men from Mars barely escaped being stillborn. Tuesday afternoon—five days before the show—Howard Koch telephoned. He was in deep distress. After three days of slaving on H. G. Wells' scientific fantasy he was ready to give up. Under no circumstances, he declared, could it be made interesting or in any way credible to modern American ears. Koch was not given to habitual alarmism. To confirm his fears, Annie, our secretary, came to the phone. She was an acid and emphatic girl from Smith College with fine blond hair, who smelled of fading spring flowers. "You can't do it!" she whined. "Those old Martians are just a lot of nonsense. It's all too silly! We're going to make fools of ourselves! Absolute fools!"

For some reason which I do not clearly remember our only possible alternative for that week was a dreary one—"Lorna Doone." I tried to reach Welles. He was at the theater and wouldn't come to the phone.

The reason he wouldn't come to the phone was that he was in his thirty-sixth successive hour of dress-rehearsing "Danton's Death," a beautiful, fragmentary play by Georg Buechner out of which Max Reinhardt, in an augmented form, had made a successful mass-spectacle in the twenties. Not to be outdone, Orson had glued seventeen hundred masks on to the back wall of the Mercury Theater, and ripped out the entire stage. Day after day actors fell headlong into the rat-ridden basement, leaped on and off erratically moving elevators, and chanted the "Carmagnole" in chorus under the supervision of Marc Blitzstein.

Unable to reach Welles, I called Koch back. I was severe. I taxed him with defeatism. I gave him false comfort. I promised to come up and help. When I finally got there—around two the next morning—things were better. He was beginning to have fun laying waste the State of New Jersey. Annie had stopped grinding her teeth. We worked all night and through the next day. Wednesday at sunset the script was finished.

Thursday, as usual, Paul Stewart rehearsed the show, then made a record. We listened to it rather gloomily, long after midnight in Orson's room at the St. Regis, sitting on the floor because all the chairs were covered with coils of unrolled and unedited film. We agreed it was a dull show. We all felt its only chance of coming off lay in emphasizing its newscast style—its simultaneous, eyewitness quality.

All night we sat up, spicing the script with circumstantial allusions and authentic detail. Friday afternoon it went over to CBS to be passed by the network censor. Certain name alterations were requested. Under protest and with a deep sense of grievance we changed the Hotel Biltmore to a non-existent Park Plaza, Trans-America to Intercontinent, the Columbia Broadcasting Building to Broadcasting Building. Then the script went over to mimeograph and we went to bed. We had done our best and, after all, a show is just a show. . . .

Saturday afternoon Paul Stewart rehearsed with sound effects but without Welles. He worked for a long time on the crowd scenes, the roar of cannon echoing in the Watchung Hills and the sound of New York Harbor as the ships with the last remaining survivors put out to sea.

Around six we left the studio. Orson, phoning from the theater a few minutes later to find out how things were going, was told by one of the CBS sound men, who had stayed behind to pack up his equipment, that it was not one of our better shows. Confidentially, the man opined, it just didn't come off. Twenty-seven hours later, quite a few of his employers would have found themselves a good deal happier if he had turned out to be right.

III

On Sunday, October 30, at 8:00 P.M., E.S.T., in a studio littered with coffee cartons and sandwich paper, Orson swallowed a second container of pineapple juice, put on his earphones, raised his long white fingers and threw the cue for the Mercury theme—the Tchaikovsky Piano Concerto in B Flat Minor ♯ 1. After the music dipped, there were routine introductions—then the announcement that a dramatization of H. G. Wells' famous novel, *The War of the Worlds*, was about to be performed. Around 8:01 Orson began to speak, as follows:

WELLES

We know now that in the early years of the twentieth century this world was being watched closely by intelligences greater than man's and yet as mortal as his own. We know now that as human beings busied themselves about their various concerns they were scrutinized and studied, perhaps almost as narrowly as a man with a microscope might scrutinize the transient creatures that swarm and multiply in a drop of water. With infinite complacence people went to and fro over the earth about their little affairs, serene in the assurance of their dominion over this small spinning fragment of solar driftwood which by chance or design man has inherited out of the dark mystery of Time and Space. Yet across an immense ethereal gulf minds that are to our minds as ours are to the beasts in the jungle, intellects vast, cool, and unsympathetic regarded this earth with envious eyes and slowly and surely drew their plans against us. In the thirty-ninth year of the twentieth century came the great disillusion-ment.

It was near the end of October. Business was better. The war scare was over. More men were back at work. Sales were picking up. On this particular evening, October 30, the Crossley service estimated that thirty-two million people were listening in on their radios. . . .

Neatly, without perceptible transition, he was followed on the air by an anonymous announcer caught in a routine bulletin:

ANNOUNCER

. . . for the next twenty-four hours not much change in temperature. A slight atmospheric disturbance of undetermined origin is reported over Nova Scotia, causing a low pressure area to move down rather rapidly over the northeastern states, bringing a forecast of rain, accompanied by winds of light gale force. Maximum temperature 66; minimum 48. This weather report comes to you from the Government Weather Bureau. . . . We now take you to Meridian Room in the Hotel Park Plaza in downtown New York, where you will be entertained by the music of Ramon Raquello and his orchestra.

At which cue, Bernard Herrmann led the massed men of the CBS house orchestra in a thunderous rendition of "La Cumparsita." The entire hoax might well have exploded there and then—but for the fact that hardly anyone was listening. They were being entertained by Charlie McCarthy —then at the height of his success.

The Crossley census, taken about a week before the broadcast, had given us 3.6 per cent of the listening audience to Edgar Bergen's 34.7 per cent. What the Crossley Institute (that hireling of the advertising agencies) deliberately ignored was the healthy American habit of dial-twisting. On that particular evening, Edgar Bergen in the person of Charlie McCarthy temporarily left the air about 8:12 P.M. E.S.T., yielding place to a new and not very popular singer. At that point, and during the follow-ing minutes, a large number of listeners started twisting their dials in search of other entertainment. Many of them turned to us—and when they did, they stayed put! For by this time the mysterious meteorite had fallen at Grovers Mill in New Jersey, the Martians had begun to show their foul leathery heads above the ground, and the New Jersey State Police were racing to the spot. Within a few minutes people all over the United States were praying, crying, fleeing frantically to escape death from the Martians. Some remembered to rescue loved ones, others telephoned farewells or warnings, hurried to inform neighbors, sought information from newspapers or radio stations, summoned ambulances and police cars.

The reaction was strongest at points nearest the tragedy—in Newark, New Jersey, in a single block, more than twenty families rushed out of their houses with wet handkerchiefs and towels over their faces. Some began moving household furniture. Police switchboards were flooded with calls inquiring, "Shall I close my windows?" "Have the police any extra gas masks?" Police found one family waiting in the yard with wet cloths on faces contorted with hysteria. As one woman reported later:

I was terribly frightened. I wanted to pack and take my child in my arms, gather up my friend and get in the car and just go north as far as we could. But what I did was just sit by one window, praying, listening, and scared stiff, and my husband by the other sniffling and looking out to see if people were running. . . .

In New York hundreds of people on Riverside Drive left their homes ready for flight. Bus terminals were crowded. A woman calling up the Dixie Bus Terminal for information said impatiently, "Hurry please, the world is coming to an end and I have a lot to do."

In the parlor churches of Harlem evening service became "end of the world" prayer meetings. Many turned to God in that moment:

I held a crucifix in my hand and prayed while looking out of my open window for falling meteors. . . . When the monsters were wading across the Hudson River and coming into New York, I wanted to run up on my roof to see what they looked like, but I couldn't leave my radio while it was telling me of their whereabouts.

Aunt Grace began to pray with Uncle Henry. Lily got sick to her stomach. I don't know what I did exactly but I know I prayed harder and more earnestly than ever before. Just as soon as we were convinced that this thing was real, how petty all things on this earth seemed; how soon we put our trust in God!

The panic moved upstate. One man called up the Mt. Vernon Police Headquarters to find out "where the forty policemen were killed." Another took time out to philosophize:

I thought the whole human race was going to be wiped out—that seemed more important than the fact that we were going to die. It seemed awful that everything that had been worked on for years was going to be lost forever.

In Rhode Island weeping and hysterical women swamped the switchboard of the Providence *Journal* for details of the massacre, and officials of the electric light company received a score of calls urging them to turn off all lights so that the city would be safe from the enemy. The Boston *Globe* received a call from one woman "who could see the fire." A man in Pittsburgh hurried home in the midst of the broadcast and found his wife in the bathroom, a bottle of poison in her hand, screaming, "I'd rather die this way than that." In Minneapolis a woman ran into church screaming, "New York destroyed this is the end of the world. You might as well go home to die I just heard it on the radio."

The Kansas City Bureau of the AP received inquiries about the "meteors" from Los Angeles; Salt Lake City; Beaumont, Texas; and St. Joseph, Missouri. In San Francisco the general impression of listeners seemed to be that an overwhelming force had invaded the United States from the air—was in process of destroying New York and threatening to move westward. "My God," roared an inquirer into a telephone, "where can I volunteer my services, we've got to stop this awful thing!"

As far south as Birmingham, Alabama, people gathered in churches and prayed. On the campus of a Southeastern college——

The girls in the sorority houses and dormitories huddled around their radios trembling and weeping in each other's arms. They separated themselves from their friends only to take their turn at the telephones to make long distance calls to their parents, saying goodbye for what they thought might be the last time. . . .

There are hundreds of such bits of testimony, gathered from coast to coast.

IV

At least one book[1] and quite a pile of sociological literature has appeared on the subject of "The Invasion from Mars." Many theories have been put forward to explain the "tidal wave" of panic that swept the nation. I know of two factors that largely contributed to the broadcast's extraordinarily violent effect. First, its historical timing. It came within thirty-five days of the Munich crisis. For weeks, the American people had been hanging on their radios, getting most of their news no longer from the press, but over the air. A new technique of "on-the-spot" reporting had been developed and eagerly accepted by an anxious and news-hungry world. The Mercury Theater on the Air by faithfully copying every detail of the new technique—including its imperfections—found an already enervated audience ready to accept its wildest fantasies. The second factor was the show's sheer technical brilliance. To this day it is impossible to sit in a room and hear the scratched, worn, off-the-air recording of the broadcast, without feeling in the back of your neck some slight draft left over from that great wind of terror that swept the nation. Even with the element of credibility totally removed it remains a surprisingly frightening show.

Radio drama was taken seriously in the thirties—before the Quiz and the Giveaway became the lords of the air. In the work of such directors as

[1] *The Invasion from Mars* by Hadley Cantril, Princeton University Press, from which many of the above quotations were taken.

Reis, Corwin, Fickett, Welles, Robson, Spier, and Oboler there was an eager, excited drive to get the most out of this new, all too rapidly freezing medium. But what happened that Sunday, up on the twentieth floor of the CBS building was something quite special. Beginning around two, when the show started to take shape under Orson's hands, a strange fever seemed to invade the studio—part childish mischief, part professional zeal.

First to feel it were the actors. I remember Frank Readick (who played the part of Carl Phillips, the network's special reporter) going down to the record library and digging up the Morrison recording of the explosion of the Hindenburg at Lakehurst. This is a classic reportage—one of those wonderful, unpredictable accidents of eyewitness description. The broadcaster is casually describing a routine landing of the giant gasbag. Suddenly he sees something. A flash of flame! An instant later the whole thing explodes. It takes him time—a full second—to react at all. Then seconds more of sputtering ejaculations before he can make the adjustment between brain and tongue. He starts to describe the terrible things he sees —the writhing human figures twisting and squirming as they fall from the white burning wreckage. He stops, fumbles, vomits, then quickly continues. Readick played the record to himself, over and over. Then, recreating the emotion in his own terms, he described the Martian meteorite as he saw it lying inert and harmless in a field at Grovers Mill, lit up by the headlights of a hundred cars—the coppery cylinder suddenly opening, revealing the leathery tentacles and the terrible pale-eyed faces of the Martians within. As they begin to emerge he freezes, unable to translate his vision into words; he fumbles, retches—and then after a second continues.

A few moments later Carl Phillips lay dead, tumbling over the microphone in his fall—one of the first victims of the Martian Ray. There followed a moment of absolute silence—an eternity of waiting. Then, without warning, the network's emergency fill-in was heard—somewhere in a quiet studio, a piano, close on mike, playing "Clair de Lune," soft and sweet as honey, for many seconds, while the fate of the universe hung in the balance. Finally it was interrupted by the manly reassuring voice of Brigadier General Montgomery Smith, Commander of the New Jersey State Militia, speaking from Trenton, and placing "the counties of Mercer and Middlesex as far west as Princeton and east to Jamesburg" under Martial Law! Tension—release—then renewed tension. For soon after that came an eyewitness account of the fatal battle of the Watchung Hills; and then, once again, that lone piano was heard—now a symbol of terror, shattering the dead air with its ominous tinkle. As it played, on and on, its effect became increasingly sinister—a thin band of suspense stretched almost beyond endurance.

That piano was the neatest trick of the show—a fine specimen of the theatrical "retard," boldly conceived and exploited to the full. It was one of the many devices with which Welles succeeded in compelling, not merely the attention, but also the belief of his invisible audience. "The War of the Worlds" was a magic act, one of the world's greatest, and Orson was just the man to bring it off.

For Welles is at heart a magician whose particular talent lies not so much in his creative imagination (which is considerable) as in his proven ability to stretch the familiar elements of theatrical effect far beyond their normal point of tension. For this reason his productions require more elaborate preparation and more perfect execution than most. At that—like all complicated magic tricks—they remain, till the last moment, in a state of precarious balance. When they come off, they give —by virtue of their unusually high intensity—an impression of great brilliance and power; when they fail—when something in their balance goes wrong or the original structure proves to have been unsound—they provoke, among their audience, a particularly violent reaction of unease and revulsion. Welles' flops are louder than other men's. The Mars broadcast was one of his unqualified successes.

Among the columnists and public figures who discussed the affair during the next few days (some praising us for the public service we had rendered, some condemning us as sinister scoundrels) the most general reaction was one of amazement at the "incredible stupidity" and "gullibility" of the American public, who had accepted as real, in this single broadcast, incidents which in actual fact would have taken days or even weeks to occur. "Nothing about the broadcast," wrote Dorothy Thompson with her usual aplomb, "was in the least credible." She was wrong. The first few minutes of our broadcast were, in point of fact, strictly realistic in time and perfectly credible, though somewhat boring, in content. Herein lay the great tensile strength of the show; it was the structural device that made the whole illusion possible. And it could have been carried off in no other medium than radio.

Our actual broadcasting time, from the first mention of the meteorites to the fall of New York City, was less than forty minutes. During that time men traveled long distances, large bodies of troops were mobilized, cabinet meetings were held, savage battles fought on land and in the air. And millions of people accepted it—emotionally if not logically.

There is nothing so very strange about that. Most of us do the same thing, to some degree, most days of our lives—every time we look at a movie or listen to a broadcast. Not even the realistic theater observes the literal unities; motion pictures and, particularly, radio (where neither place nor time exists save in the imagination of the listener) have no difficulty in getting their audiences to accept the telescoped reality of dramatic time. Our special hazard lay in the fact that we purported to be, not a play, but reality. In order to take advantage of the accepted convention, we had to slide swiftly and imperceptibly out of the "real" time of a news report into the "dramatic" time of a fictional broadcast. Once that was achieved—without losing the audience's attention or arousing their skepticism, if they could be sufficiently absorbed and bewitched not to notice the transition—then, we felt, there was no extreme of fantasy through which they would not follow us. We were keenly aware of our problem; we found what we believed was the key to its solution. And if, that night, the American public proved "gullible," it was because enormous pains and a great deal of thought had been spent to make it so.

In the script, "The War of the Worlds" started extremely slowly— dull meteorological and astronomical bulletins alternating with musical interludes. These were followed by a colorless scientific interview and still another stretch of dance music. These first few minutes of routine broadcasting "within the existing standards of judgment of the listener" were intended to lull (or maybe bore) the audience into a false security and to furnish a solid base of realistic time from which to accelerate later. Orson, in making over the show, extended this slow movement far beyond our original conception. "La Cumparsita," rendered by "Ramon Raquello, from the Meridian Room of the Hotel Park Plaza in downtown New York," had been thought of as running only a few seconds; "Bobby Millette playing 'Stardust' from the Hotel Martinet in Brooklyn," even less. At rehearsal Orson stretched both these numbers to what seemed to us, in the control room, an almost unbearable length. We objected. The interview in the Princeton Observatory—the clock-work ticking monotonously overhead, the woolly-minded professor mumbling vague replies to the reporters' uninformed questions—this, too, he dragged out to a point of tedium. Over our protests, lines were restored that had been cut at earlier rehearsals. We cried there would not be a listener left. Welles stretched them out even longer.

He was right. His sense of tempo, that night, was infallible. When the flashed news of the cylinder's landing finally came—almost fifteen minutes after the beginning of a fairly dull show—he was able suddenly to spiral his action to a speed as wild and reckless as its base was solid. The appearance of the Martians; their first treacherous act; the death of Carl Phillips; the arrival of the militia; the battle of the Watchung Hills; the destruction of New Jersey—all these were telescoped into a space of twelve minutes without overstretching the listeners' emotional credulity. The broadcast, by then, had its own reality, the reality of emotionally felt time and space.

V

At the height of the crisis, around 8:31, the Secretary of the Interior came on the air with an exhortation to the American people. His words, as you read them now, ten years later, have a Voltairean ring. (They were admirably spoken—in a voice just faintly reminiscent of the President's—by a young man named Kenneth Delmar, who has since grown rich and famous as Senator Claghorn.)

THE SECRETARY
     Citizens of the nation: I shall not try to conceal the gravity of the situation that confronts the country, nor the concern of your Government in protecting the lives and property of its people. However, I wish to impress upon you—private citizens and public officials, all of you—the urgent need of calm and resourceful action. Fortunately, this formidable enemy is still confined to a comparatively small area, and we may place our faith in the military forces to keep them there. In the meantime placing our trust in God, we must continue the performance of our duties, each and every one of us, so that we may confront this destructive adversary with a nation united, courageous, and consecrated to the preservation of human supremacy on this earth. I thank you.

     Toward the end of this speech (*circa* 8:22 E.S.T.), Davidson Taylor, supervisor of the broadcast for the Columbia Broadcasting System, received a phone call in the control room, creased his lips, and hurriedly left the studio. By the time he returned, a few moments later—pale as death—clouds of heavy smoke were rising from Newark, New Jersey, and the Martians, tall as skyscrapers, were astride the Pulaski Highway preparatory to wading the Hudson River. To us in the studio the show seemed to be progressing splendidly—how splendidly Davidson Taylor had just learned outside. For several minutes now, a kind of madness had seemed to be sweeping the continent—somehow connected with our show. The CBS switchboards had been swamped into uselessness, but from outside sources vague rumors were coming in of deaths and suicides and panic injuries.
     Taylor had requests to interrupt the show immediately with an explanatory station-announcement. By now the Martians were across the Hudson and gas was blanketing the city. The end was near. We were less than a minute from the Station Break. The organ was allowed to swirl out under the slackening fingers of its failing organist and Ray Collins, superb as the "last announcer," choked heroically to death on the roof of Broadcasting Building. The boats were all whistling for a while as the last of the refugees perished in New York Harbor. Finally, as they died away, an amateur shortwave operator was heard from heaven knows where, weakly reaching out for human companionship across the empty world:

> 2X2L Calling CQ
> 2X2L Calling CQ
> 2X2L Calling CQ
> Isn't there anyone on the air?
> Isn't there anyone?

     Five seconds of absolute silence. Then, shattering the reality of World's End—the Announcer's voice was heard, suave and bright:

ANNOUNCER
     You are listening to the CBS presentation of Orson Welles and the Mercury Theater on the Air in an original dramatization of *The War of the Worlds*, by H. G. Wells. The performance will continue after a brief intermission.

The second part of the show was extremely well written and most sensitively played—but nobody heard it. It recounted the adventures of a lone survivor, with interesting observations on the nature of human society; it described the eventual death of the Martian Invaders, slain—"after all man's defenses had failed by the humblest thing that God in his wisdom had put upon this earth"—by bacteriological action; it told of the rebuilding of a brave new world. After a stirring musical finale, Welles, in his own person, delivered a charming informal little speech about Halloween, which it happened to be.

I remember, during the playing of the final theme, the phone starting to ring in the control room and a shrill voice through the receiver announcing itself as belonging to the mayor of some Midwestern city, one of the big ones. He is screaming for Welles. Choking with fury, he reports mobs in the streets of his city, women and children huddled in the churches, violence and looting. If, as he now learns, the whole thing is nothing but a crummy joke—then he, personally, is coming up to New York to punch the author of it on the nose! Orson hangs up quickly. For we are off the air now and the studio door bursts open. The following hours are a nightmare. The building is suddenly full of people and dark blue uniforms. We are hurried out of the studio, downstairs, into a back office. Here we sit incommunicado while network employees are busily collecting, destroying, or locking up all scripts and records of the broadcast. Then the press is let loose upon us, ravening for horror. How many deaths have we heard of? (Implying they know of thousands.) What do we know of the fatal stampede in a Jersey hall? (Implying it is one of many.) What traffic deaths? (The ditches must be choked with corpses.) The suicides? (Haven't you heard about the one on Riverside Drive?) It is all quite vague in my memory and quite terrible.

Hours later, instead of arresting us, they let us out a back way. We scurry down to the theater like hunted animals to their hole. It is surprising to see life going on as usual in the midnight streets, cars stopping for traffic, people walking. At the Mercury the company is still stoically rehearsing—falling downstairs and singing the "Carmagnole." Welles goes up on stage, where photographers, lying in wait, catch him with his eyes raised up to heaven, his arms outstretched in an attitude of crucifixion. Thus he appeared in a tabloid that morning over the caption, "I Didn't Know What I Was Doing!" The New York Times quoted him as saying, "I don't think we will choose anything like this again."

We were on the front page for two days. Having had to bow to radio as a news source during the Munich crisis, the press was now only too eager to expose the perilous irresponsibilities of the new medium. Orson was their whipping boy. They quizzed and badgered him. Condemnatory editorials were delivered by our press-clipping bureau in bushel baskets. There was talk, for a while, of criminal action.

Then gradually, after about two weeks, the excitement subsided. By then it had been discovered that the casualties were not as numerous or as serious as had at first been supposed. One young woman had fallen and broken her arm running downstairs. Later the Federal Communications Commission held some hearings and passed some regulations. The Columbia Broadcasting System made a public apology. With that the official aspects of the incident were closed.

As to the Mercury—our new play, "Danton's Death," finally opened after five postponements. Not even our fantastic publicity was able to offset its generally unfavorable notices. On the other hand, that same week the Mercury Theater on the Air was signed up by Campbell Soups at a most lavish figure.

Of the suits that were brought against us—amounting to over three quarters of a million dollars for damages, injuries, miscarriages, and distresses of various kinds—none was substantiated or legally proved. We did settle one claim however, against the advice of our lawyers. It was the particularly affecting case of a man in Massachusetts, who wrote:

"I thought the best thing to do was to go away. So I took three dollars twenty-five cents out of my savings and bought a ticket. After I had gone sixty miles I knew it was a play. Now I don't have money left for the shoes that I was saving up for. Will you please have someone send me a pair of black shoes size 9B!"

We did.

❖ 31 ❖

WHERE VIOLENCE BEGINS

Norman Cousins

The development of distrust and hostility between people who have long lived together in harmony is sometimes hard to understand. This selection by Norman Cousins, however, demonstrates how close friends may be caught up in mass suspicion and resort to violence against each other. The function of fear and rumor in breaking down the mutual confidence developed through long association is clearly evident.

In addition to illustrating the role of suspicion and rumor in the development of violence between people, this article calls

SOURCE: *Saturday Review*, Vol. 37, No. 3 (January 16, 1954), 22–24, 33. ❖ The author is editor of the *Saturday Review*. He has received several honorary doctorates as well as awards for journalism and public service, one of these being the Thomas Jefferson award for Advancement of Democracy in Journalism. Some of his books include *The Good Inheritance, Who Speaks for Man?* and *Modern Man Is Obsolete*.

attention to the role of the United States as a great power in international affairs. Cousins points out that America is not isolated from the problems of relations between India and Pakistan, and that our knowledge and understanding are not yet commensurate with our power in the world.

This is about Kamilal Deridas of India, who killed his friend. The killing occurred about seven years ago. All his life Deridas had followed the non-violence teachings of Mahatma Gandhi. He kept his thoughts free of fear and hate. And then one day, suddenly, he reached for a knife and slew his friend. Up until now that killing has had no direct connection with the American people; but it now becomes important for us to think about it as hard and carefully as we have thought about anything in our lives.

I met Deridas at a refugee camp on the outskirts of Delhi in February 1951. When I returned to India recently I tried to find him and learned that he had made himself a new home somewhere to the north of Delhi; no one knew exactly where. But, though I was unable to locate him, I shall never forget the things he told me about his experiences during India's ordeal in the summer of 1947, when the country was partitioned into three units—India proper, Pakistan West, and Pakistan East. The two sections of the new Pakistan were united politically, but they were separated by the geographical expanse of India at its widest. If you can imagine that Mexico, instead of being situated south of the United States, were to be split in half, with one part in Southern California and the other in New England, then you may have a fair idea of the geographic relationship of Pakistan to India, as well as the difficulties surmounted so heroically by the Pakistani leaders in operating a unified and free government.

The background of partition is long and involved. It was the culmination of more than a century of dual struggle—the struggle for national independence against England, and the struggle for power inside India between Hindu and Moslem. Centuries ago the Moslems ruled the northern part of India. When the British quit India in 1947 there were perhaps 100,000,000 Moslems in all of India, as against more than 325,000,000 Hindus. With partition some sixty-five million Moslems formed the population of the new Pakistan, the balance remaining in India. Today the population of Pakistan is more than seventy-five million, with close to forty million Moslems still in India proper.

Partition and national independence were part of the same historical event. Neither was then possible without the other. But the sudden rupture of a great nation caused it to bleed hideously. The struggle for national independence had been waged for centuries but it came virtually overnight and no one was prepared for it. The new Free India had only a bare governmental skeleton with which to administer the affairs of the second most populous nation in the world. Pakistan started absolutely from scratch, having to use empty crates for government desks.

And in those early days of uncertainty and confusion people became panicky. Whatever the animosity had been between Hindu and Moslem before Independence, the people had managed to live side by side. There had been recurrent violent flare-ups, to be sure, but they were not too serious. With partition, however, millions of people suddenly became jittery and insecure. A Hindu who lived in a city near the border like Lahore wondered what was to happen to him now that Lahore was to become part of Pakistan. A Moslem who lived on the outskirts of Calcutta wondered what was to happen now that there would be a separate Moslem Government in Pakistan that did not include him. The insecurity and confusion became multiplied as millions of people decided to move in order to be governed by their own group.

Then came violence. At first there were only sporadic incidents. A Moslem in Dacca, for example, would smash the shopwindows of a clothing store owned by a Hindu, claiming he had heard that Hindus were looting Moslem shops in Calcutta or Delhi. A Hindu in Calcutta would set fire to a Moslem home, in open view of a crowd, yelling that he had heard that Moslems were burning homes of Hindus who remained behind in Dacca or Karachi. Some Hindus or Moslems would try to take advantage of the national turmoil by seizing business properties or homes.

Each incident, of course, fed on rumors and begat even greater rumors. Outrages were carried out in the name of retaliation. Soon a civil war without battle-lines or armies raged throughout the subcontinent. People rushed through the streets with sticks or torches or whatever could be used to kill a man.

Kamilal Deridas was one of those who used a knife. When he spoke to me about it, four years later, he found it difficult to believe that it was his own arm that swung the knife over the shoulder and into the chest of a man who had been his friend.

Like millions of others who lived through the dark days of 1947, Deridas doesn't like to talk about what happened or his own part in it. It was only after we had spent many hours together, discussing the event in a general way, that he began to speak in terms of his individual experiences. I had told him that I found it difficult to understand how people who achieved so much through their belief in non-violence could suddenly abandon that belief at the very moment of its fulfillment. It was inexplicable that a non-violent victory should produce such volcanic violence within the nation itself. And what about the people, I asked. How could they allow themselves to become something they had never been? The Hindus and Moslems I knew were gentle people, peaceable people. I couldn't imagine them as killers. And Deridas's reply to my question was simple and vivid.

"I can answer you because I know how it was. I was part of it. From the very beginning I was part of it all. I was twenty-six at the time. My wife, my two little boys, and I lived with my parents in a nice house on the edge of Lahore. My father operated an arts-and-crafts shop. Lahore was something of a world convention city. The weather is clear and good almost the entire year and there were generally meetings that brought many people to the city.

"I had gone to college, studying law, but had deferred setting up an office of my own because my father was ailing and it was necessary for me to look after the business, which had prospered over the years. I had many friends in Lahore—among both Hindus and Moslems. Those of us who had gone to college thought all the old antagonisms were foolish, and we were bored by the traditional hostilities of the older people. Two of my closest friends were Moslems and they were as indifferent to the old religious and cultural rivalries as I was. The name of one was Faiz; the other Ahmed.

"After plans for the partition were made in 1947 Faiz came to me and said that he was worried about talk he had heard in town. He had heard that certain Hindu homes would be requisitioned after Pakistan came into being in order to make room for the many Moslems who could be coming to the city. And our home was on one of the lists.

"My father dismissed this talk as nonsense. He said that the new Pakistan would not tolerate such outrages because there were more Moslems in India than Hindus in what was to be the new Pakistan. He said the new Government would know only too well how much worse it would fare than India in any contest of seizure of private property. He told me to forget about it.

"But as the time for partition neared, and as reports reached Lahore of local riots in sections where there were mixed populations, I became very alarmed. One night Faiz came to my home through the back door and begged me to get my belongings together as quickly as I could, take my family, and flee Lahore.

"He said that there had been a secret meeting a few hours earlier in town and that reports were read which told of Hindu looting of Moslem shops in Delhi and Bombay and also that in several places Moslem women had been violated by Hindus and put on public exhibition. He said there were also reports that many, many thousands of Moslem homes had been seized by Hindu crowds throughout India. The men at the meeting were hysterical with rage and called for immediate retaliatory action.

"There were some at the meeting who cautioned against anything that might start a riot. They pointed out that they had lived side by side with their Hindu neighbors for many years and that these people were not responsible for the outrages that happened to Moslems many hundreds of miles away. But most of the others turned on these cautious few and shouted them down, saying they were traitors, and then the cautious few spoke no more. My friend said he knew terrible things were going to happen, and that the police would be powerless to do anything.

"I made up my mind that we would have to leave within a week at most and began to plan a way out and also to plan some way of getting the most valuable items in our store to a place of safety. I sought the help of Ahmed, who agreed to keep the most valuable items in the cellar of his home. That night and the next night, between one A.M. and four A.M., we transported the valuables in Ahmed's car from our store to his home. It was a courageous thing for him to do. It would have meant his death if he had been discovered.

"Then Ahmed and Faiz and I met in order to make plans for us to get out of Lahore until some measure of stability returned to the city. My father was difficult to persuade about this but something terrible that happened to us two days after Faiz came to warn me changed his mind. Our store was located in the resort section, which is the far side of the city. Early in the morning, shortly after I had opened the shop, I heard the sounds of a great commotion coming from afar. I locked the store, then rushed towards the center of the town. As I approached I saw the looting and the burning had already begun. There was smashed glass all over the streets. Not far away I could see smoke rising from the heart of the city.

"I ran back to the store. My father and my brother-in-law were waiting when I got there. They were very agitated. My twenty-one-year-old sister had been missing since eight A.M. It was now ten A.M. We barricaded the store to the best of our ability, then rushed home. We never saw my sister again. That night my brother-in-law learned that she had been abducted, along with sixty or seventy young Hindu wives. We could only pray for her life and her integrity of physical self, but I feared the worst.

"That night, in accordance with our plan, we left the house one by one, dressed in Moslem style, and were picked up by Faiz and Ahmed in their cars and brought to Ahmed's house, where we were to stay secretly until we completed arrangements for getting out of Lahore. It was lucky we had left our house when we did. Part of it was wrecked the very next day and the part that remained was occupied.

"Our plan for leaving Lahore was a simple one. We would travel in three pony carts. My wife, my two sons, and I would be in one cart. My father and mother would be in another. My brother-in-law and his little boy in the third. After a day's travel from Lahore we would slip over the border at night and then get a train to Delhi, 250 or 300 miles distance. At Delhi, we would try to find a place to live.

"But much was to happen to us before we left Lahore. In no time at all the riots had swept all through the city. We heard incredible stories of what was happening not only in Lahore but throughout India and Pakistan. Thousands of women and young girls on both sides were being abducted and violated. Mobs were rushing through streets, seizing people and tearing them apart. It was unbelievable—but it was happening.

"Then one night—it was after mid-night—Ahmed came to the small room in his house where we were all hiding. I could see that there was something wrong. He was almost hysterical. He had just been told that his parents had been burned to death the night before in their beds. They lived in Batala, just over the border. My father tried to calm him by saying it could not be so, that Hindus would not do such a thing; and Ahmed said that there was no doubt about it. He said he knew that there were outrages on both sides; he had wanted to stay free of them, and had risked his life and the lives of his immediate family to help Hindus, and that this was now his reward—a mother and father burned in their beds by Hindus.

"My father again insisted that it was not so, and that someone had lied to Ahmed, and before I knew what was happening my father and Ahmed were quarreling and shouting at each other. I begged them to be quiet, for they were certain to rouse the entire neighborhood. But those were no days of calm tempers; we had all been without sleep and were on edge and had been infected by the ugly passions that were sweeping over the two countries. My father and Ahmed continued to shout at each other, accusing each other; then my father in a moment of rage said that he was certain that all Ahmed was after was our valuables which we had stored with him. And Ahmed, insane with grief over the killing of his parents, went into a blind fury, reached for a knife, and started after my father.

"Right then something happened to me. I don't remember it clearly; in fact, I don't remember it at all, but my wife told me about it later. The sight of the knife after everything that had happened in the past few days— the burning and the lootings and the killings and the attacks on women and having to be huddled together secretly wondering what would happen to us—all this made me lose my senses when I saw Ahmed going at my father with a knife. I took a knife that Ahmed had given me earlier for my own safety. I killed him. I reached over his shoulder with my knife and I killed him.

"Right after that we left the house, taking Ahmed's car, even though it had been decided earlier, that we would not use an automobile because cars on the road going to the border attracted too much suspicion. We knew the pony carts were small enough for the back roads. But now we had no choice. How we finally made the border is almost too incredible to tell. But we made it. Anyway, that is not what you wanted to know about. You wanted to know how peaceable men could forget all their convictions, forget everything, and kill. I have tried to tell you.

"There are many, many thousands of people like me. No one knows how many people became killers, during those dark days. What we know is that maybe 300,000 were killed; maybe half a million; maybe a million. No one stopped to count. But we do know that twelve million people lost their homes and fled in terror. Seven or eight million Hindus. Four or five million Moslems. Maybe more.

"I have talked about my part in the dark days to a very few people. But one man to whom I spoke had known Gandhiji, and you know that Gandhi himself was killed in that terrible period during partition. And this man, who would know what Gandhiji would say if he knew what I had done, told me that what had happened was not my sin alone but the sin of all the people of India and Pakistan. Gandhiji made no distinction in his life between Hindu and Moslem; he loved us all. And his friend told me that Gandhi would have said that I had temporarily lost my sanity with all the others but that I should work for friendship between Hindu and Moslem as the only way of paying for my crime.

"What he said helps. It also helps to remember that when men are soldiers they kill because they are caught up in something larger than themselves. I hope I have answered your question."

I said that he had; but I could see there was something more he had to say.

"Perhaps you are wondering," he resumed after a minute or two, "whether these terrible things happened here in India and Pakistan only because—well, because there is something perhaps primitive or uncivilized about these people; and that this could never happen to people like yourselves who are educated and refined. One thing I surely learned during that time was that everything is swept aside in panic. I was a college man; Ahmed was a college man. College men were in the crowds that set fire to the shops and the homes. And in the Western world a high literacy rate didn't keep the German people from going in for mass murder. And there were many outrages in your own Civil War. I'm afraid I would have to say that what happened to us could happen to anyone when suddenly the structure of law and order is removed and the people are governed only by their fears. It is then that the worst elements in the society can set the pattern for society itself.

"At a time like that is when the very great men in a society show themselves. And it was then that the world really knew that Jawaharlal Nehru was fit to wear the mantle of Gandhiji. For it was Nehru who risked his life to save Moslems during the Delhi riots. It was Nehru who rushed out into Connaught Circle late at night and thrust himself between a Hindu looter and his intended victim. And it was Nehru who while on the spot ordered Hindu police to shoot at Hindu looters. And the rioting and the killing receded faster in Delhi than anywhere else—because of Nehru.

"And it is Nehru's presence in the Government that has caused many millions of Moslems to stay behind in India. By working for Moslem-Hindu friendship in India he is fulfilling the debt we must all pay to our consciences for what happened during those awful days. Both Hindus and Moslems have sinned deeply. Only in friendship can they clear those miserable stains. And Nehru is trusted by the Moslems in India. They shudder —and I shudder with them—when we think of what would happen in India if anything happened to him.

"For there is still great uneasiness in the two countries. And I tremble with my entire being lest something might happen that would throw things out of balance and bring on again even more bloodier and darker days.

"There are many issues which are unsettled between Hindus and Moslems as the result of partition. And the people are pressing for settlement. I have had to live with my family in tents or shacks, without proper sanitary facilities, since 1947. What about our property in, Lahore? Shouldn't there be some payment for our store and our home? And what about the abducted women? Pakistani have many of the same claims against India. Then, to top everything, of course, is the Kashmir dispute.

"The situation between the two countries is far from ideal. Zealots on both sides are trying to inflame the people. Moslem religious fanatics think Pakistan ought to wage a holy war against India and unite the entire country on the basis of Moslem rule. And we have our own Hindu fanatics who want to sweep into Pakistan and bring about reunification through force and then set up a theocratic Hindu state.

"That is why I pray that these two countries may have peace."

I began this account by saying that Deridas's story about the dark days of 1947 in India has a special meaning today for the American people. America is in a position today to exercise a profound influence on the affairs of India and Pakistan. If we are wise we can contribute to the peace and well-being of both countries. If we are foolish or insensitive we can upset a precarious equilibrium and help to touch off a subcontinental civil war.

Of all the issues outstanding between India and Pakistan today none is more difficult or more combustible than the Kashmir dispute. There is no clear-cut question of right and wrong here between India and Pakistan. Anyone who has attempted to study the problem on the spot knows the difficulty of striking a balance between the claims of both parties. Similarly, anyone who has made a sensitive appraisal of the situation knows that the present Prime Ministers of both countries are far more moderate in their approaches, far more convinced of the necessity for and possibility of a peaceful settlement, than large segments of public opinion in their respective countries. Both Mohammed Ali and Jawaharlal Nehru have demonstrated a sense of total responsibility in opposing the growing extremist factions.

In the midst of this touch-and-go situation comes the report that America is preparing to send arms to Pakistan. The effect has been exactly what was to be expected. In India it has already strengthened the hands of the extremists who want to press for a forcible seizure of the Kashmir. It gives the Communists the most powerful weapon they have had since India became independent. It puts them in a position where they could claim leadership against what they denounced as the vacillating policies of Nehru. It enables them to exploit the passions of the militant Hindus, playing upon their fears that the religious fanatics in Pakistan would seize the upper hand and use American arms against India. It makes the entire nation fearful that Pakistan would be in a stronger position in the event of a showdown over the Kashmir.

There are forty million Moslems in India. If Nehru's policies of mod-

eration are to be swept aside by an alliance of Communists and militant
Hindus then the last barrier will have been removed to a resumption of the
dark days of 1947.

America says it is against Communism. Nothing that organized Communism has done in Asia—whether in China or India—can compare with
the impetus we will give Communism in Asia as the result of the chaos
resulting from a Hindu-Moslem explosion. Russia does not want peace in
Asia. Russia has no way of coping with peace in Asia. Russia wants chaos
in Asia. We are proposing to make her that gift.

It is one of history's most stupendous paradoxes that step by step, day
by day, in the name of anti-Communism we seem to be doing the very
things that will give Communism control over the majority of the world's
peoples.

Our business in the world is the business of peace. If we are to do
anything for Asia let us do the things that are in keeping with the American
character. If we want to help Pakistan build real defenses against Communism let us put up giant dams and power installations. Let us help her
develop her farms and her industries. If we are concerned about Communism in India let us fight the threat where it exists today—in the farms
and villages and factories—by helping to prove to the Indian people that
Communism is the false answer to famine, poverty, illiteracy. We can
prove that democracy is the right answer by putting democracy to work.
But if we can do none of these things let us not set the stage for mass
murder.

We have yet to develop our knowledge of the world to match our
power in the world. For we will survive not through power alone but
through a deep sensitivity to the wants and the hurts of others, and through
the appeal of great ideas. This is the test of the American moral fiber if
there ever was one.

❖ 32 ❖

A CUP OF COFFEE

Lillian Smith

*One form of nonviolent collective action common in the early six-
ties in the Negro's struggle to gain equality in America was the
"sit-in." The following piece of fiction provides us with an intimate
picture of this form of protest. It helps us to understand what
would motivate an upper middle class southern Negro boy, so-*

SOURCE: Reprinted from *Our Faces, Our Words* by Lillian Smith. By
permission of W. W. Norton & Company, Inc. Copyright © 1964 by Lillian
Smith. ❖ For biographical data on the author, see selection 18.

cialized to an acceptance of the norms for his race, to take the lead-
ership in organizing a sit-in.

To go back four years: that day, I'd been reading. *Franny and Zooey.*
Everybody was reading it in our dorm. There were other books on Bill's
shelf and mine, the usual things: Camus' *Sisyphus*, Dylan Thomas, Mailer,
Sartre; I had just read *Borstal Boy.* We were English majors. I was trying
out for an Ionesco play in French. All this is to suggest, I guess, that I
didn't go in for the racial stuff, "sociological problems," our English prof
called it. I hadn't even read Dick Wright. I just didn't like race talk.

My uncle kept his life raw with it. He was that kind, couldn't pass up
a slight. Had to bleed. Active in NAACP. Always fighting the white man.
Before I was born he was going after the Negro's rights. Once, I was about
six or so, he said to me, "Tell me, do you know who you are?" I saw Mama
look up, put her hand out to stop him, then as suddenly, she went back
to stringing the beans for supper.

"I'm Jim," I said.

"Jim who?"

I told him.

"That's not important."

"Yes, it is," Mama said. "Jim is a person, he has a name, and he's
going to make us proud of it, some day."

Uncle laughed. I thought it a mean laugh; maybe it was just an unhappy one. "Your mama don't want you to learn the facts of life," he said.
"The most important fact for you, Jim, is that you are a Negro." He looked
at Mama (she's his sister) as if to say, You can lie to him but not to me.
"You're not a nigger—and don't you ever let anybody call you one. But
you are a Negro. And the sooner you learn it the better. You're as good as
anybody technically, but you are not, actually, until you get your rights
as an American. White folks are not going to give them to you even though
they belong to you. Remember: they stole 'em from you. Remember: folks
don't like to return what they steal. You'll have to take 'em back. And to
do it you'll have to work to get them; you can never let up, never for one
minute let up."

Mama said, "Jim and I—we look at it another way. Jim's a human
being, you're one, too (though you're not acting like one now)." She
smiled. Uncle snorted. "Jim knows he's human—much like the other two
and a half billion humans across the earth. He knows he's an individual
and different from others; he knows it is good to be different and every
human being has a right to be different. But color is a false difference; it is
not important to Jim nor to me. It shouldn't be to anybody."

Uncle looked at me. Things were being said I couldn't hear, I felt
them whizzing between the two. Uncle's voice snagged on his words, "You
believe all this, what your mother is saying?"

"Yes sir."

"Well, young man, what you going to do with all these fine notions?"

"He's going to grow up to be a real man, intelligent, decent, hard-working, who will leave a good mark on the world, I hope," said Mama.

"Ha!" said Uncle. "Just like that! Easy, too, huh?" My pup began chasing a chicken, I ran to help him. I didn't like Uncle's voice and I shied away from him after that day.

Mom works in the branch library, called the James Weldon Johnson Branch. (It is integrated, today, but it wasn't four years ago.) I used to go down most every afternoon to read and look around. We had a lot of good juveniles at home, too; of course they were about white children, no little Negroes, but I accepted that. I guess I vaguely thought it strange not to put little Negroes in books, too—but it wasn't a hurting thought. Mom took me to the plays and concerts at the Negro college; I'd go sound to sleep but I liked going. I accepted my world; I didn't know any other; most children accept the world they're born into, even when it is a place where earthquakes play around.

After high school, I went to the college here at home. I lived in the dorm—and that day I am telling about, I was reading *Franny and Zooey*, and I was with it. I wasn't thinking, "I'm a Negro and all this is alien to me. It wasn't, it was real and human. A guy named Dan was talking to my roommate. I heard him say, "My mom was just getting over flu, see? And she'd been shopping all morning. She'd bought about fifty-five dollars' worth of stuff; she was matching a spool of thread when suddenly everything began to black out. She knew if she could sit down a few minutes and have a cup of coffee she'd be OK. But where in that store or anywhere else downtown could she get it! She fainted. They had a time: somebody got her ammonia, somebody found a cot for her, and somebody else brought her a cup of coffee."

Bill laughed. "One way to get it. It's not funny, Dan. But there's a terrible irony—"

Dan nodded. "When it's your own mother you don't think about irony."

I closed the book. To hell with *Franny and Zooey* . . .

If Mom was tired and needed a cup of coffee where could she get it downtown? Dammit to hell, where could she get it? Jesus Christ! She could buy out the store and still couldn't buy one cup of coffee and sit down quietly and drink it. You never thought about it before—how about going to the john—did they let her go to a restroom—

I saw Mom, suddenly. Right there, standing in front of my whole life. Gray-eyed, gentle, poised. Always so quietly poised. My God, where did her serenity come from! She'd never said a bitter word in her life against the whites, not to me; and she wasn't a handkerchief-head, either; talk about white folks giving you back your "dignity"—Mom's dignity couldn't have been taken from her, it went down to the center of her soul. I saw all this. I saw all she'd tried to keep me from looking at, cesspools and stinking ways, dirty alleys in streets and minds—Mom all the time turning me toward books, music, poetry, drama, ideas, science, hoping, I guess, that I'd never catch on to what it was really about. She couldn't stand hate —I guess she didn't want me poisoned by it.

"Dan," I said, "let's make em open up those places."

"OK by me," said Dan.

That's the way the revolution started for us. We were suddenly *there.* In it. We'd never been a black boy, like Dick Wright down in Mississippi. We'd never felt invisible, way Ralph Ellison felt. We never felt we were Nothing; I was always sure I was Something. Well, I admit it: we'd been mighty sheltered; our race had never had it so good, I guess, as the middle-class Negro in some of the upper-South cities had it when I was growing up. I'd never seen a Klansman in my life; had never seen a race murder, never heard a mob on the loose. I knew such things happened, read about them but I guess I pushed them off. *They didn't get on my mind.* I knew there were places I couldn't go but having the college we were able to enjoy many advantages even the whites in our city didn't have. Somehow my pride never got tangled up in it; oh, I knew I couldn't enter certain places but I honestly believe I didn't worry about this much more than the average middle-class white southern kid worries who knows he can't join a million-aire's club; I knew about Negro slums, Harlem, South Side but thought about it in the same way most white boys think about slums and bad housing for whites. I was *sound asleep,* let me settle for that. My mother was a lady to her fingertips; I guess I pretended she was exactly like any white lady with access to the same civilities and courtesies.

Well—we were waking up. We dressed in our Sunday clothes to look like the gentlemen we made like we were, took our Bibles and school books and started our sit-in. But before we sat in, we did read up on what the others had done in Greensboro and Tallahassee. We knew we'd better get with this nonviolence thing. We didn't have time to read Martin Buber or Gandhi or Thoreau but we did take time out to read Martin Luther King —all about redemption through suffering, "absorbing" the cruelties of others . . . conciliation . . . compassion. I read it. Dan read it.

"My God," Dan said, "what the hell is redemption?"

I stared at him. There was nothing in *Franny and Zooey* about redemption. Somebody said—Bill, I think—"maybe we'd better read Camus' *The Fall.*" We decided we didn't have time. We wouldn't say it but I think we felt we'd better get going before we lost our nerve. "We'll get redeemed, later," Bill said solemnly, "we'd better go sit now." Dan was staring hard at me, it made me tremble, I felt things turning upsidedown. "Let's get going," I said. Voice sort of loud.

Well, we got going and sat in at Walgreen's. Don't know why we picked that one but we did. Maybe because we knew it was a chain store and might be more sensitive to pressures—but I don't know, we actually weren't doing much thinking. We walked to the counter, sat down, opened

our books. Bill opened the Bible—and read it, too. I had my physics textbook; read one paragraph sixteen times without knowing what was in it.
The white girl behind the counter, awfully young, turned pink then deathly
white. She didn't say a word. Bill looked up, smiled, said quietly, "We'd
like some coffee, please, and some doughnuts." She swallowed, swallowed
again, shook her head. "I can't," she said. She wasn't mean. I felt sorry
for her. "Please go away," she whispered, "they won't let me serve you."
We sat there.

Pretty soon, two or three white kids came in, stared at us, one sat
down next to me, hummed something, got up, walked out. We kept on
reading. Some more came in; we didn't turn round to see but they were
making a lot of noise. Then it happened: that cigarette; the goon stuck
the burning thing into my back. Sit tight, don't move, take it; this is nonviolence, I told myself, you have to take it. A white guy came in, knocked
the cigarette out of the other guy's hand; there was scuffling back of me;
I didn't turn. A cop came in. Walgreen's closed the counter. We left.

That's how we started. Three weeks later, the lunch counter opened
to everybody. By then, we were sitting in at Kress's. There were about
twenty-five or more students helping us now, and more high-school kids
than we needed; the high-school kids just poured into the movement, completely unafraid, having a ball, but serious, too, deepdown.

We felt we had to hold meetings now to decide what to do, what not
to do; we had to learn you can't lose your temper, you can't talk back, you
can't hit back; you keep everything under control. Two of the college men
couldn't make it; we told them to stay out of things until they could control their feelings; the high school kids were cool, and they listened. "You
got to feel compassionate toward the whites," a worker from CORE told
us; at our request he had come to train us. So we talked about compassion, forgiveness, talked about absorbing evil through our own suffering.
"You'll find it works," the CORE adviser told us; "if a white has any good
in him, he'll respond to compassion and friendly talk; you got to remember
that you can hate evil without hating the man who does the evil; it's like
a doctor treating the evil of smallpox without hating the man who has it."

"Yeah," said one kid, "but you'd better fear that smallpox." Everybody
laughed.

"Sure," said the teacher of nonviolence, "you've got to have sense; be
wary, be shrewd, nobody was more shrewd than Gandhi, don't be reckless;
but remember: negative nonviolence is not enough; it's got to be positive;
you feel all the time that the other man, the one fighting you, can be
redeemed; he's got to feel something good in you."

This was tough on most of us; we didn't want to be cowards; we felt
it would do us a world of good to punch a white bully in the nose; we
wondered if these goons possessed souls; maybe terror had to be met with
terror; maybe those cops actually couldn't respond to love. We talked
about this; but we knew, somewhere in us, that strategically a minority

can't change things by violence, it would be suicide to try; and we began to see that while one goon may fail to respond to conciliation and friendly reason and this thing we called "love," hundreds of thousands of the public, white and Negro looking on, would begin to respond, begin to understand; and we dimly saw that when this happens change comes, real change. For this is the beginning of dialogue, of response of one human to another.

Well, back to the Kress business. Six girls were sitting in with us, very brave and gay. There was a lot of laughter and singing; maybe no movement in the world's history has ever been such a singing movement as this one. But things were getting tougher. A mean editorial appeared in the morning paper; the editor couldn't grasp the basic idea of truth and compassion in human relations; he honestly didn't believe we as Americans should protest the lack of our civil rights; he seemed to think we should just keep on as our grandfathers had done; but the editor was caught fast in the first decade of the century.

A week later, Kress's opened up. We moved on from Kress's to picketing the biggest department store in town. Somehow, I got in jail. That hurt Mom. *Her* son. They sent us there because we had "trespassed." I wanted to say, "Mom, I'm in jail so you can have a cup of coffee when you want one." I didn't say it. That cup of coffee had metamorphosed into everything Negroes lacked that was rightfully theirs as human beings. It looked like we'd have to open up the whole city, the whole region; then we'd have to go North and help them open up things there, too.

Now, here I am in Mississippi; working on a literacy program for the Negro sharecroppers in the Delta, getting them registered to vote; grassroots stuff. (Oh yes—somewhere along the way we stopped wearing our Sunday clothes. We wear jeans now.) We've collected thousands of books, trying to fix up centers where they can come and read. There're no real schools for the colored kids down here. Parents can't read or write, most of them. Money? That's funny. You don't sit in restaurants in a place like this. Where would they get money to go to a restaurant? Where would they get clothes to wear? They don't have wants like that. They *need*. *Need everything*. This is zero. You begin here in the mud and dust at nothing and inch up. Got to. No other way. Whites are about as bad off as the Negroes. It is like the Indian villages, a Hindu visitor told us, only maybe worse; more fear, more pressure on the Negroes; hostile police. I didn't know all this existed, had no idea it could exist. In college, we didn't talk about these things, we read *Waiting for Godot*. What you reckon these kids here in the Delta are waiting for; I wish I knew. They're born and then they start waiting, waiting. Sometimes at night, you're riding along one of these bumpy rough roads through the fields, everything stretching away from you, sky tilted, stars spilling out of space, now and then a light way off, a thousand shadows where the shacks are. And you think, They're full of children, real honest-to-God children, and they're all waiting for something to happen here in our country, in the United States; and suddenly the waiting is a ghost choking me and I fight it, I shake it off whispering, Tomorrow I'll teach a kid to read: "This is a book; I want to know what is in it." One inch; one inch up.

✤ 33 ✤

PUBLIC RELATIONS—

THE INVISIBLE SELL

Robert L. Heilbroner

Attempts to make men act collectively (that is, to do the same thing in response to planned stimuli) have commanded the efforts of more and more persons in recent years. One example of this is advertising. Another, examined here, is public relations. The public relations expert often uses data collected under the rigidly controlled conditions specified for scientific research to create—on a mass basis, if possible—predetermined attitudes regarding particular individuals, groups, or products in an attempt to control our behavior with respect to them. The consequences—successful and unsuccessful, intentional and unintentional—are examined in this article.

Mixed up in the affairs of the Atomic Energy Commission, the Institute of Boiler and Radiator Manufacturers, Elvis Presley, and United States Steel; welcomed into the inner sanctum of church, corporation, and cabaret alike; as indispensable to a modern hospital as a surgeon and to a big labor union as an organizer, you will find the representatives of one of the newest, fastest growing, and certainly most significant professions of our times. These are the members of the public relations fraternity—a brotherhood of some 100,000 whose common bond is its profession, and whose common woe is that no two of the practitioners can ever quite agree on what that profession is.

Whatever it is, public relations is the wonder child of our age. Turn back to the Manhattan classified telephone directory for 1935 and look up

SOURCE: *Harper's Magazine*, Vol. 214, No. 1285 (June, 1957), 23–31. Copyright © 1957 by Robert L. Heilbroner. Reprinted by permission of the author. ✧ Robert Heilbroner is a member of the Graduate Faculty of the New School for Social Research. He has written widely on economic subjects. He is the author of *The Worldly Philosophers, The Future as History, The Making of Economic Society, The Great Ascent*, and coauthor of *A Primer of Government Spending*.

the listing for public relations: you will find ten names. Go through the catalogues of the universities twenty years back, and you search for a course on public relations in vain. Investigate the public relations staff of General Motors for 1931, and you will discover one man, Paul Garrett, who had just been hired.

Today the listing in the telephone directory runs on for seven columns and over seven hundred names—in Manhattan alone. Last year 653 colleges taught something called "public relations"; eleven (including such pillars of respectability as Columbia and New York University) offered it as an undergraduate major; and one, Boston University, had a School of Public Relations which gave an M.S. degree. And last December when Paul Garrett retired from General Motors as a full vice president (to set up his own public relations firm), his staff numbered some two hundred people, exclusive of clerical help, and cost well over $1,000,000 a year.

That is, however, only evidence of public relations' meteoric rise. Even more impressive is its present extent. According to *Fortune* magazine, nearly five thousand corporations now support public relations departments or engage public relations counsel. An already outdated report by the Bureau of the Budget lists 5,211 full-time "information officers" for the federal government. Add in the labor unions, the private welfare organizations, the charities, causes, and not least, the celebrities who also buy what public relations men sell, and you arrive at the not unimpressive figure of at least half a billion dollars spent for PR hired help alone. How much is spent not for the hired hands, but on public relations itself, nobody even hazards a guess.

And what is this thing called "public relations" on which all this money is expended? It is not one thing, but many, for the practice in which the brotherhood engages is indeed a motley one. In the name of public relations you will find the boys "institutionalizing" a TV comic, "personalizing" an institution, or just plain peddling a product or an idea. Public relations includes such virtuous aims as making the public "aware" of muscular dystrophy and such dubious ones as putting pressure on a legislature through phony consumer fronts. It runs the gamut from philosophizing on social trends before a board of directors, to advising that same board on how best to pulverize the opposition in a proxy fight. It takes in the planted item in the gossip column and the artfully contrived mention of a client's product in a magazine article ostensibly about something else. It embraces the cozy corporate brochure "About Us Folks," and the hard-breathing advertisements of the "facts" concerning a strike. In a word, public relations covers a lot of acreage—blurring out into advertising, slopping over into selling, dipping down into publicity, and touching—or at least aspiring to—the "making" of public opinion itself.

And what, one may ask, after reading this ill-assorted catalogue, *is* public relations? Perhaps we can sum it up by calling it the business of the Invisible Sell. . . . In the arresting, if chilling, phrase of Edward L. Bernays, a pioneer in the field, public relations is "the engineering of public consent."

And this makes the brotherhood somewhat more interesting than just another bunch of guys out to make a buck. For we are all of us to some extent hooked by the Invisible Sell—enthusiastic about people we have never met, persuaded of the virtues of products and institutions with which we have no direct contact, contented captives of ideas we are scarcely aware of having picked up. If the public relations men are capable of *manufacturing* these enthusiasms, persuasions, and ideas, it would not be too much to claim that they practice the most important occupation of our day. Or perhaps one should say the most portentous. Or perhaps merely the most pretentious. Whatever the final verdict, it would certainly seem worth while to meet the fraternity members themselves.

Up From Broadway

Of the 700-odd public relations firms in New York and the 2,000-odd in the nation, a very considerable number—perhaps as many as two-thirds —represent the ventures of bright young men, who start with a general background in publicity, a client or two, and a few hundred dollars in cash. This is where enterprising youth goes these days, instead of West. A career in point is that of an ex-publicity man named Alan Brandt. Good-looking, voluble, and an absolute garden sprinkler of ideas, Brandt took the plunge sixteen months ago from a well-paid position as publicity director of station WNEW in New York. . . .

"I just got tired of working for someone else," says Brandt, "so I went out and got myself a room with one window, one desk, one phone, one size of stationery, one girl—and one client. I was in business."

The client was the producer of Captain Kangaroo, a TV kiddies' show, and Brandt publicized it as the children's show that *parents* would like. It was a good pitch and made several magazine breaks, and thereupon the phone began to ring. A hair-products firm wanted to know if Brandt could think of some way of publicizing buns and chignons: Brandt got a TV hair styles contest started. A Boston radio station showed up looking for a publicity idea: Brandt printed records which fitted the new Chrysler car-phonograph and which interrupted their music with, "Are you missing the news? Tune in on station WHDH." A TV morning show wanted to be talked about: Brandt put Salvador Dali on to explain that the cauliflower was the basis of all art, and had an art dealer choose between six masterpieces worth over $100,000 and six fake copies worth less than $100, by slashing the fakes—while Brandt quietly perspired behind the camera. A book publisher wondered if something could be done about a novel set in a small New England town. Brandt got an item in the Associated Press about a book that would blow up Gilmanton, New Hampshire, and *Peyton Place* was a best seller before it even reached the bookstores.

❖ ❖ ❖ ❖ ❖

How to Catch a Whale

❖ ❖ ❖ ❖ ❖

Now since there are very few magazines or newspapers which would be interested in running a story about typewriters, wool, or dog food, and still fewer which would give free advertising to Underwood, the Wool Institute, or the Gaines Dog Food company, the public relations man must disguise his hook with fancy feathers. The Underwood people therefore prepare "5 Sprightly Stories" on such themes as *How to Keep Your Boss Happy*, or *The Girl With The Halo* (your secretary); the Wool Institute offers *How's Your AQ?* (Appearance Quotient) and *Wool in History and Legend*—"the fascinating story of the thousands-of-years-old romance of the use of wool"; and the dog food people establish the Gaines Dog Research Center—"a research and educational institution created as a public service." These are offered free to editors.

Needless to say, the mortality rate of such PR productions reaches epidemic proportions, but since the birth rate is high, a certain number of brain-children survive. A considerable number as a matter of fact. No PR firm of any stature cannot boast of having "placed" stories in *Life*, *Look*, *Saturday Evening Post*, or *Reader's Digest*, not to mention the *New York Times*. . . .

One of the most successful product promoters is the firm of Ruder and Finn, which began like Brandt Public Relations, on a shoestring. Not quite ten years ago Bill Ruder, a young publicity man for Sam Goldwyn, and David Finn, a hopeful painter, decided to put their curiously diverse talents together in public relations. They took a room in the Hotel Lombardy—the size of which can be judged by the fact that it is now the hotel linen closet—and landed that essential First Account. It was a promotion job for Perry Como's records, and they performed it so artfully that Como thanked them publicly in an ad in *Billboard*. Then *their* phone began to ring. And they began to think.

"We didn't want to be just publicity boys all our lives," says Finn. "And while we were beating our brains to think of a way not to be, Bill remembered the nation-wide publicity network that Goldwyn used. We decided to try the same deal for product promotion." By writing to independent PRs around the country, Ruder and Finn established a gossamer-thin tie-up with small out-of-town public relations firms, and this they then hawked as the Ruder & Finn Field Network. Into its flimsy meshes promptly swam a whale. A major soap company was about to launch a new soap and it wanted just such point-of-sale promotion. The soap brass descended from its glassy heights to the brownstone basement into which Ruder and Finn had moved their operation (and where they had spent the previous twenty-four hours frantically adding twenty-seven men to their "network"), and—perhaps with suds in its eyes—approved of what it saw.

After that it was easy. Today, with seventy employees, a Field Network of over 190, and a gross take in excess of $1,200,000, Bill Ruder and Dave Finn run one of the six biggest PR firms in the country.

What is public relations at the R & F level? Of course it includes product promotion via the Invisible Sell, as witness a technique used to push Skotch Koolers, a picnic carrier. R & F sent samples of the Koolers to professional photographers and TV studios, merely suggesting that they might be used as studio props. They were. You may have noticed the Kooler alongside the man with the beard in a Schweppes ad, or next to a bathing beauty extolling skin cream. Without spending a nickel on advertising, R & F dangled its product before the eyes of several million people, a pleasing number of whom swallowed the bait.

But the public relations bait does not consist of products only. Indeed, the publics to which R & F professionally relates its clients tend to include fewer and fewer customers, and more and more groups such as stockholders, employees, or even bankers. For these publics Ruder and Finn will design a client's annual report and compose dignified but warm letters to his shareholders, will edit his employee newspaper, or make his name known among the Wall Street community. Or, in the jargon of the trade, they will create and sell his "image."

. . . At the powerhouse of public relations maintained by General Motors, only a fraction of the PR effort is aimed at making people like GM *cars*. . . . Sales Promotion does *that*. What public relations must do is the far more difficult job of selling General Motors itself—as a community asset, a helpful company, a corporation with solid ideas, a big business with its heart in the right place—in a word, as a great institution, and by implication, one which should not be meddled with.

When Paul Garrett arrived in Detroit twenty-five years ago to begin General Motors' public relations program, the first question fired at him was "How do you make a billion dollars look small?" Garrett said damned if he knew, and furthermore damned if he thought that was his job. Public relations, he argued, was not an "act," but a continuing effort on the part of management to win the confidence of the people with whom it came into contact. Hence you will find General Motors engaged in a host of activities in which altruism and self-interest come together in a creamy blend. Plant, City and Field Relations, for example, stimulates local GM participation in the community affairs of the sixty-eight cities where it has factories, thereby helping both the community and itself. Educational Relations works with the schools, providing them with such useful educational material as films on safe driving,. and providing itself with a flow of applicants for jobs. The Speakers Bureau is glad to send a company-sponsored lecturer to your club or association to edify it with an inspirational talk—or to educate it with a "sound" economic one. Institutional Advertising tells the story of GM's role in supporting some twenty thousand suppliers, and leaves you with the pleasant impression that what's good for General Motors is good for small business, too. The billion dollars may not look any smaller as a result of these efforts. But it looks much, much nicer.

The Image-Makers

This same kind of quiet winning of friends and influencing of people is practiced by the biggest public relations firms. At Hill & Knowlton, for instance, which runs neck and neck with Carl Byoir & Associates as the largest PR outfit in the country (H & K's minimum fee $36,000; Byoir's, $50,000, but H & K has more accounts), only 6 or 7 per cent of the firm's effort is spent on publicity. The rest is largely concentrated on showing corporations how to do Good Works and how to present their side of the story—which is always known as The Facts.

Thus for its biggest account, the American Iron and Steel Institute (which is incidentally the biggest PR account in the country), H & K provides a whole panoply of services, none of which is calculated to sell a single ton of steel, but all of which are calculated to sell the steel industry and its point of view. It publishes *Steelways*, a magazine which is sent to 100,000 key people, such as editors and educators, who pass along interesting bits of information to an audience estimated at 12,000,000. It puts out booklets on "timely topics of importance" such as the industry's lagging profit rate. It runs a field service which counsels individual companies on such matters as how to conduct plant tours, or how to work with the local school board, or who should go on the Institute's mailing list.

And it runs such interesting services as the Community Resources Workshop. This is a project to acquaint teachers with industry and its potential helpfulness in providing educational material. It also aims at giving teachers an insight into the problems of steel—not on a "propagandistic" basis, but just the way steel executives honestly see them. Dr. Albert L. Ayars, the educator who heads the Workshop, has stated that he would resign if his project were ever used for the propagation of distorted facts. "I suppose you could say," he admits, "that as a result of these experiences the teachers will be more receptive to some legislation which would be of benefit to industry and the public. But again, not because they have been coerced into it. All that we would have done from the standpoint of our client, American Iron and Steel Industry, is to have exposed them to the facts."

For those who picture public relations at the summit as the cunning manipulation of minds, or the subtle exercise of devious techniques, the actual practice of Big PR must look tame indeed. That it is often transparently self-serving, under the guise of serving the public, is perfectly true; and that the motives which prompt it are not entirely spiritual needs hardly to be pointed out. It is the Invisible Sell on a huge scale, but whereas one may not always particularly like what is being sold, it is hard to get much worked up over the salesmanship.

That goes for nine-tenths of Big PR. Of course there is also the tenth tenth. Witness, for example, the public relations tactics in the Pennsylvania railroad-truckers fight in 1952. The client here was the Eastern Railroads Presidents Conference; the PR firm was that of Carl Byoir & Associates (Hill & Knowlton's big competitor); and the issue at stake was a bill increasing the size and weight limits for trucks on the state roads. It was not by accident that Byoir was chosen for the task of beating the bill. As the company explained in a letter to one of the railroad vice presidents (in charge of public relations), it was good at that sort of thing, modestly mentioning a chain-store bill it had licked in New York State for the A & P, and a tax reduction it had secured in Louisiana for the Freeport Sulphur company. And so, for a fee of $150,000 it got the job.

And brought home the bacon. In due course the bill was vetoed by the Governor.

Not that the Governor acted out of any but the best interest. He had before him, for example, an early report of the Maryland State Roads Commission containing very unfavorable data on road damage. He was faced at every turn by newspaper and magazine articles on the evils of trucking, and across his desk passed a succession of interesting studies by institutions such as the New Jersey Citizens Tax Study Foundation. Certainly not absent from the Governor's mind was the opposition of the State Association of Township Supervisors, which had mailed out thousands of postcards protesting the truck bill, and of the State Grange, a politically powerful organization.

When Governor Fine vetoed the bill, it must have seemed to him that he was only expressing the will of the people; but how much of this will of the people was the result of the activities of the Byoir agency who spent several hundred thousand dollars in their campaign?

All this, however, is aside from the crucial point. It is not the excesses, but the run of the mill of big PR, not its faults but its very virtues which need examination. The basic question is not the power which resides in bad public relations, but that inherent in *good* public relations; not the ability of public relations to subvert, but its capacity to convince. The really important question about the power of public relations is whether it can influence what men *think*.

Where the Doubt Begins

This brings us to an impressive demonstration concerning the making of public opinion that took place in Cincinnati in 1947.

For six months Cincinnati became the focus for an unprecedented crusade—a powerful, well-planned, and well-financed attempt to teach it what to think. Specifically, Cincinnati was the target of an all-out effort to make a typical American city "United Nations conscious."

The crusade was a thorough and intelligent one. It was launched at every level of city life. On blotters, matchbooks, streetcar signs, and billboards. Cincinnatians read "Peace Begins with the United Nations—the United Nations Begins with You." Local radio stations broadcast UN facts and news daily—one of them on 150 spots a week. The newspapers played up the theme. Every schoolchild in the city was given literature about the United Nations to take home; the PTA, the Council of Churches, and the Catholic Church all climbed enthusiastically aboard the bandwagon. Club women rallied round with letters and telegrams pledging their support to the American delegation to the UN. In the last three months as the campaign reached a crescendo, 225 meetings were held, hundreds of documentary films shown, 59,588 pieces of literature distributed.

Then they took a poll of the results.

At the end of six months only *half* as many people considered the United Nations a means of preventing war as thought so at the beginning.

There was almost no change in the number who thought the United States should take an active part in world affairs.

There was a drop in the number of those who were in favor of having the United States join an international police to keep peace.

Fewer people thought there should be some sort of international control of atom bombs.

There was almost no change in the numbers who knew what the main purpose of the United Nations was, or who had heard of the veto power, or who knew how the UN worked.

In a word, the campaign was a gigantic frost.

Why? The answer may be shocking, but it is simplicity itself: people in Cincinnati just didn't give a damn about the United Nations one way or another. For all the matchbooks and the meetings, the UN was something far off, vague, abstract, unconnected with daily life. Hence the propaganda went in one ear and out the other, and save for the pleasant friction stimulated in transit, it left no imprint at all.

And the moral, for public relations, seems to be that most people don't give a damn about most things, unless those things are part and parcel of their concrete lives. They just don't listen. For many years, Hill & Knowlton has sought to put across such simple (and true) messages as that the steel industry is not a dangerous place to work, or that steel's profit margins, by comparison with other industries, have been low. The results: slightly *more* people thought steel was dangerous in 1955 than in 1946 or 1943, and there continues to be "considerable belief" (in Hill & Knowlton's own words) that steel's profits are too high.

Or take the case of General Motors. For nearly twenty years, along with seven other large corporations, GM has tested its popularity by means of a continuing opinion poll called the Link Audit. On the face of it, results were excellent: the proportion of people who "liked" General Motors (and all the other companies) rose from less than 60 per cent in the late 'thirties to over 80 per cent today. The only trouble is, no one quite knows what "like" means. Every time there is a strike in any *one* of the eight companies, the popularity of *all* of them goes down. For some unfathomable reason all the corporations are more popular in fall than spring. And every time there is something to get mad about, the Link Audit "liking" doesn't seem to prevent people from boiling up: when Harlow Curtice, GM's president, testily denied to a Senate Committee last year that there was anything wrong with General Motors' dealer relations, something akin to a whirlwind of angry protests materialized out of the blue. Chastened, Mr. Curtice appeared again in a more conciliatory mood. The whirlwind disappeared. And the Link Audit once again showed that everybody "liked" General Motors.

Hence the public-opinion researchers are, to put it mildly, skeptical about the ability of public relations to engineer the public's consent and dubious about the depth of the affections it arouses. "Give the PR something real and specific—a personality, a product, or even a precise enough idea—and he can usually make an impact," says one professional public-opinion measurer. "But ask him to sell a big fuzzy thing like a 'nice' company or a 'sound' doctrine, and the result is usually an absolutely monumental indifference."

Or worse, skepticism. One opinion researcher, Douglas Williams, measuring the effect of a company's effort to "sell" its employees on Free Private Enterprise, found the net outcome to be an increase in hostility and suspicion. "Those people knew about free enterprise in terms of their own jobs and incomes," he explains. "They didn't like having those realities 'justified' with fancy abstractions. Instead they asked, 'What's really the matter, that they have to sell this thing to me?' "

The wiser public relations men are well aware of these facts. "Make no mistake about it," says Earl Newsom, who counsels, among others, Ford and Standard Oil of New Jersey, "a corporation does not win the confidence of the American people by trying to 'educate' them to its point of view." A case in point is Newsom's client, "Jersey," which has long ago wearily resigned itself to living with the popular opinion that it is still part of the oil trust which broke up some forty years ago. It just doesn't bother to argue any more—because it realizes that it probably wouldn't do any good if it did.

But whereas the public relations men themselves have salutary doubts about the efficacy of their efforts to sell those nice big ideas, their clients share no such hesitations with them. For if there is one part of the public which is really a patsy for the power of public relations, it is that hard-headed pragmatic character, the American big businessman himself. Not content with using public relations to publicize or promote his wares, or to cement his relationships with his employees or stockholders—all of which it can do very well—he is convinced that it can serve to get his "message" across to an eagerly attentive public, and to enshrine his corporation, as well as its products, in their hearts. Nor does he, curiously enough, demand proof of this conviction, for he has swallowed the Invisible Sell hook, line, and sinker.

What Is It Worth?

If the public relations brotherhood is not quite so powerful as its enthusiastic clients think, neither can it be shrugged off as just a collection of publicists, pitchmen, and commercial philosophers. Public relations is more than just an occupation or a bunch of occupations: it is a social force—and as such it has left two indelible marks on our world.

The first mark is its part in the general debasement of communications from which we suffer. It is only a banality to point out the need for effective public communication in today's complex society, but communication has become more of a fetish than a function. Science has a technical term which describes the result of forcing more messages along a carrier than it can accommodate: it calls the result *noise*. We live in a noisy society: one in which everyone talks and few say anything; one in which the spurious, the insincere, the meretricious, and most of all the *empty*, crowd out the meaningful, the useful, the important. People who live in such a society learn not to listen—or worse, when they do listen, they learn to disbelieve what they hear.

In this process of the debasement of communication, public relations must bear its share of the blame. No one can quarrel with the essential function that public relations fills as the purveyor of genuine ideas and information. No one denies that many public relations men, working for corporations as well as for colleges or causes, honestly communicate things which are worth communicating. Nor can anyone absolve public relations for loading the communications channels with noise. We read the news and suspect that behind it lies the "news release." We encounter reputation and ascribe it to publicity. Worst of all, we no longer credit good behavior to good motives, but cheapen it to the level of "good public relations."

It is not *that* bad, of course. But if we step back to view that whole big thing called Public Relations and then attempt to weigh what it has meant to our values and beliefs, it is hard to avoid the conclusion that the net effect of the Invisible Sell has been to further a cynical judgment of the motives behind human behavior.

That is one side of the coin, but there is another, and shinier. If public relations has cheapened the face value of good conduct, at the same time it has enormously increased the prevalence of good conduct. For regardless of its motive or its incessant self-advertisement, good conduct *is* more prevalent on the business scene, and public relations can rightly take much of the credit. The reason is a curious one. It is that something called Good Public Relations has come to be regarded as an indispensable attribute of business—as much a sign that a business is "modern and progressive" as a shiny new glass office building (which is also, of course, a good public relations move). Quite simply, business has sold itself the bill of goods it originally intended to sell the public.

"If you ask me," said one shrewd public relations man, "the aim of a big corporation should be invisibility. But no. It insists on being as visible as possible. Its directors get nervous unless people say what wonderful public relations the company has. So it has to *have* wonderful public relations. It has to *act* lovable. It has to *be* progressive. It has to *become* socially responsible—not because the management necessarily thinks that way, but because that's what Good Public Relations is."

Hence by an unexpected twist, public relations has become a weapon whose recoil is greater than its muzzle blast. Good Public Relations has come to be something very much like the corporate conscience—a commercial conscience, no doubt, but a conscience none the less. If the public relations profession can bolster this role, if it can become the corporate conscience openly, fearlessly, and wisely, speaking not only *for* business but *to* business, then it will have more than redeemed its name.

* 34 *

THE NATURE OF

PERSONAL INFLUENCE

Paul F. Lazarsfeld, Bernard Berelson, and Hazel Gaudet

Collective behavior, like any other form of social behavior, operates within a framework of communication. Even when this framework is an indirect one, involving the use of mass media, it still is heavily dependent upon a system of face-to-face relationships.

SOURCE: Paul F. Lazarsfeld, Bernard Berelson, and Hazel Gaudet, *The People's Choice: How the Voter Makes Up His Mind in a Presidential Campaign* (2d ed., New York: Columbia University Press, 1948), 150–58. Reprinted by permission of the publisher and the senior author. ✧ For biographical data on Paul Lazarsfeld, see selection 3. For biographical data on Bernard Berelson, see selection 2. Hazel Gaudet was associated with the Bureau of Applied Social Research, Columbia University. She assisted Hadley Cantril in writing *The Invasion from Mars*.

Although the principles asserted here have been somewhat modi-
fied and refined by subsequent research, this early study of Lazars-
feld, Berelson, and Gaudet is a classic and still valid analysis of the
role of personal influence in affecting public opinion. The topic
dealt with here is voting behavior, but the generalizations de-
scribed may be applied to many kinds of collective behavior.

The political homogeneity of social groups is promoted by personal
relationships among the same kinds of people. But for a detailed and systematic study of the influence of such relationships—the political role of
personal influence—a systematic inventory would be needed of the various
personal contacts and political discussions that people had over a sample
number of days. . . . Such complete data are not available in the present
study, but enough information has been collected to indicate the importance of personal relationships so far as their direct political influence
is concerned. Our findings and impressions will be summarized without
much formal statistical data. The significance of this area of political behavior was highlighted by the study but further investigation is necessary
to establish it more firmly.

In comparison with the formal media of communication, personal
relationships are potentially more influential for two reasons: their coverage
is greater and they have certain psychological advantages over the formal
media.

Personal Contacts Reach the Undecided

Whenever the respondents were asked to report on their recent exposure to campaign communications of all kinds, political discussions were
mentioned more frequently than exposure to radio or print. On any average
day, at least 10% more people participated in discussions about the
election—either actively or passively—than listened to a major speech
or read about campaign items in a newspaper. And this coverage "bonus"
came from just those people who had not yet made a final decision as to
how they would vote. Political conversations, then, were more likely to
reach those people who were still open to influence.

For example, people who made up their minds later in the campaign
were more likely to mention personal influences in explaining how they
formed their final vote decision. Similarly, we found that the less interested
people relied more on conversations and less on the formal media as
sources of information. Three-fourths of the respondents who at one time
had not expected to vote but were then finally "dragged in" mentioned
personal influence. After the election, the voters were given a check list
of "sources from which they got most of the information or impressions
that caused them to form their judgment on how to vote." Those who had
made some change during the campaign mentioned friends or members

of their family relatively more frequently than did the respondents who kept a constant vote intention all through the campaign.

The Two-Step Flow of Communications

A special role in the network of personal relationships is played by the "opinion leaders." . . . We noted that they engaged in political discussion much more than the rest of the respondents. But they reported that the formal media were more effective as sources of influence than personal relationships. This suggests that ideas often flow *from* radio and print *to* the opinion leaders and *from* them to the less active sections of the population.

Occasionally, the more articulate people even pass on an article or point out the importance of a radio speech. Repeatedly, changes referred to reading or listening done under some personal influence. Take the case of a retired school teacher who decided for the Republicans: "The country is ripe for a change . . . Willkie is a religious man. A *friend read and highly recommended* Dr. Poling's article in the October issue of the *Christian Herald* called 'The Religion of Wendell Willkie.' "

So much for the "coverage of personal contacts." The person-to-person influence reaches the ones who are more susceptible to change, and serves as a bridge over which formal media of communications extend their influence. But in addition, personal relationships have certain psychological advantages which make them especially effective in the exercise of the "molecular pressures" finally leading to the political homogeneity of social groups. We turn now to a discussion of five such characteristics.

Non-Purposiveness of Personal Contacts

The weight of personal contacts upon opinion lies, paradoxically, in their greater casualness and non-purposiveness in political matters. If we read or tune in a speech, we usually do so purposefully, and in doing so we have a definite mental set which tinges our receptiveness. Such purposive behavior is part of the broad area of our political experiences, to which we bring our convictions with a desire to test them and strengthen them by what is said. This mental set is armor against influence. The extent to which people, and particularly those with strong partisan views, listen to speakers and read articles with which they agree in advance is evidence on this point.

On the other hand, people we meet for reasons other than political discussion are more likely to catch us unprepared, so to speak, if they make politics the topic. One can avoid newspaper stories and radio speeches simply by making a slight effort, but as the campaign mounts and discussion intensifies, it is hard to avoid some talk of politics. Personal influence is more pervasive and less self-selective than the formal media. In short, politics gets through, especially to the indifferent, much more easily through personal contacts than in any other way, simply because it comes up un-expectedly as a sideline or marginal topic in a casual conversation. For example, there was the restaurant waitress who decided that Willkie would make a poor president after first thinking he would be good. Said she: "I had done a little newspaper reading against Willkie, but the real reason I changed my mind was from *hearsay*. So many people don't like Willkie. Many customers in the restaurant said Willkie would be no good." Notice that she was in a position to overhear bits of conversation that were not intended for her. There are many such instances. Talk that is "forbidden fruit" is particularly effective because one need not be suspicious as to the persuasive intentions of the speakers; as a result one's defenses are down. Furthermore, one may feel that he is getting the viewpoint of "people gen-erally," that he is learning how "different people" think about the election.

Such passive participation in conversation is paralleled in the case of the formal media by accidental exposure, e.g., when a political speech is heard because it follows a favorite program. In both conversation and the formal media, such chance communication is particularly effective. And the testimony to such influence is much more frequent in the case of per-sonal contacts. The respondents mentioned it time and again: "I've heard fellows talk at the plant . . . I hear men talk at the shop . . . My husband heard that talked about at work. . . ."

Flexibility When Countering Resistance

But suppose we do meet people who want to influence us and suppose they arouse our resistance. Then personal contact still has one great advan-tage compared with other media: the face-to-face contact can counter and dislodge such resistance, for it is much more flexible. The clever campaign worker, professional or amateur, can make use of a large number of cues to achieve his end. He can choose the occasion at which to speak to the other fellow. He can adapt his story to what he presumes to be the other's interest and his ability to understand. If he notices the other is bored, he can change the subject. If he sees that he has aroused resistance, he can retreat, giving the other the satisfaction of a victory, and come back to his point later. If in the course of the discussion he discovers some pet convictions, he can try to tie up his argument with them. He can spot the moments when the other is yielding, and so time his best punches.

Neither radio nor the printed page can do anything of the kind. They must aim their propaganda shots at the whole target instead of just at the center, which represents any particular individual. In propaganda as much as in other things, one man's meat is another man's poison. This may lead to boomerang effects, when arguments aimed at "average" audiences with "average" reactions fail with Mr. X. The formal media produced several boomerangs upon people who resented what they read or heard and moved in the opposite direction from that intended. But among 58 respondents who mentioned personal contacts as concretely influential, there was only one boomerang. The flexibility of the face-to-face situation undoubtedly accounted for their absence.

Rewards of Compliance

When someone yields to a personal influence in making a vote decision, the reward is immediate and personal. This is not the case in yielding to an argument via print or radio. If a pamphlet argues that voting for the opposite party would be un-American or will jeopardize the future, its warning may sound too remote or improbable. But if a neighbor says the same things, he can "punish" one immediately for being unimpressed or unyielding: he can look angry or sad, he can leave the room and make his fellow feel isolated. The pamphlet can only intimate or describe future deprivations; the living person can create them at once.

Of course all this makes personal contacts a powerful influence only for people who do not like to be out of line. There are certainly some people who gain pleasure from being nonconformists, but under normal circumstances they are probably very much in the minority. Whenever propaganda by another person is experienced as an expression of the prevailing group tendencies, it has greater chances of being successful than the formal media because of social rewards. For example, here is a woman who was for Roosevelt until the middle of the campaign: "I have always been a Democrat and I think Roosevelt has been all right. But my family are all for Willkie. They think he would make the best president and they have been putting the pressure on me." She finally voted for Willkie. This aspect of personal contact was especially important for women.

The rewards of compliance to other people are learned in early childhood. The easiest way for most children to avoid discomfort is to do what others tell them to do. Someone who holds no strong opinions on politics and hence makes up his mind late in the campaign may very well be susceptible to personal influences because he has learned as a child to take them as useful guides in unknown territory. The young man who was going to vote for Roosevelt because "my grandfather will skin me if I don't" is a case in point.

Trust in an Intimate Source

More people put reliance upon their personal contacts to help them pick out the arguments which are relevant for their own good in political affairs than they do in the more remote and impersonal newspaper and radio. The doubtful voter may feel that the evaluations he reads or hears in a broadcast are plausible, for the expert writer can probably spell out the consequences of voting more clearly than the average citizen. But the voter still wonders whether these are the issues which are really going to affect *his own* future welfare. Perhaps these sources see the problem from a viewpoint entirely different from his own. But he can trust the judgment and evaluation of the respected people among his associates. Most of them are people with the same status and interests as himself. Their attitudes are more relevant for him than the judgments of an unknown editorial writer. In a formal communication the content can be at its best; but in a face-to-face contact the transference is most readily achieved. For example, here is the case of a young laborer who professed little or no interest in the campaign and who did not even expect to vote until late October: "I've been discussing the election with the *fellows at the shop* and I believe I'll vote, but I haven't decided yet who for." His constant exposure to the views of his fellow workers not only brought him to the ballot booth but also brought out his final Democratic vote in line with his colleagues.

A middle-aged woman who showed great interest in the campaign was undecided until late October and then voted for Willkie: "*I was talking politics just this morning with a friend, a businessman.* He says business will improve if Willkie is elected and that Willkie promises to keep us out of the war. FDR is getting too much power. He shouldn't have a third term." Her friend had apparently run out for her what amounted to a small catalogue of Republican arguments and he was impressive enough to clinch her vote, which had been in the balance throughout the campaign. Her trust in his judgment settled her mind.

Trust in another person's point of view may be due to his prestige as well as to the plausibility of what he has to say or its relevancy to one's interests. It is obvious that in all influences prestige plays a considerable role. The degree of conformity is greater the higher the prestige of the person in our group who seeks to influence us. The plausibility of the consequences he presents will seem greater if he is important. (Of course, the formal media are also important in this respect.) The heightening of trust through the prestige of certain personal contacts was clear in the case of the driver of a bread truck who changed to Willkie because the prominent president of a business firm had done him the honor of persuading him in that direction. Then, too, there is the case of a middle-aged housewife with little education who was for Willkie from May through September, became undecided in October, and finally voted for Roosevelt. She left Willkie because of the statements of people whom she considered authorities: "I talked with *a college student* from Case, in Cleveland, and students are for Roosevelt because he has helped recreation. I talked, too, with a *man from Chicago who is very interested in politics*, and he doesn't seem to think that Willkie is a big enough man to handle international affairs."

Persuasion Without Conviction

Finally, personal contacts can get a voter to the polls without affecting at all his comprehension of the issues of the election—something the formal media can rarely do. The newspaper or magazine or radio must first be effective in changing attitudes related to the action. There were several clear cases of votes cast not on the issues or even the personalities of the candidates. In fact, they were not really cast for the candidates at all. They were cast, so to speak, for the voters' friends.

"I was taken to the polls by a worker who insisted that I go."

"The lady where I work wanted me to vote. She took me to the polls and *they all voted Republican so I did too."*

In short, personal influence, with all its overtones of personal affection and loyalty, can bring to the polls votes that would otherwise not be cast or would be cast for the opposing party just as readily if some other friend had insisted. They differ from the formal media by persuading uninterested people to vote in a certain way without giving them a substantive reason for their vote. Fully 25% of those who mentioned a personal contact in connection with change of mind failed to give a real issue of the campaign as a reason for the change, but only 5% of those who mentioned the formal media omitted such a reason. When personal influence is paramount in this way, the voter is voting mainly for the personal friend, not the candidate.

Practical Implications

In a way the outcome of the election in Erie County is the best evidence for the success of face-to-face contacts. It so happened that for some time the Republican machine in that area worked much more vigorously than its Democratic opponent. When asked whether they knew people who had good ideas about politics, our respondents mentioned considerably more Republican than Democratic local politicians. A few people who did not expect to vote but finally went to the polls mentioned Republican canvassers as the main influence, but we could not trace a similar success for the Democratic machine.

However, one should not identify the personal contacts discussed in this chapter with the efforts of the *professional* political machines. These personal contacts are what one might call *amateur machines* which spring up during elections—individuals who become quite enthusiastic or special groups that try to activate people within their reach. One might almost say that the most successful form of propaganda—especially last-minute propaganda—is to "surround" the people whose vote decision is still dubious so that the only path left to them is the way to the polling booth. We do not know how the budget of the political parties is distributed among different channels of propaganda but we suspect that the largest part of any propaganda budget is spent on pamphlets, radio time, etc. But our findings suggest the task of finding the best ratio between money spent on formal media and money spent on organizing the face-to-face influences, the local "molecular pressures" which vitalize the formal media by more personal interpretation and the full richness of personal relationships into the promotion of the causes which are decided upon in the course of an election.

In the last analysis, more than anything else people can move other people. From an ethical point of view this is a hopeful aspect in the serious social problem of propaganda. The side which has the more enthusiastic supporters and which can mobilize grass-root support in an expert way has great chances of success.

* 35 *

NOTES ON A NATURAL HISTORY OF FADS

Rolf Meyersohn and Elihu Katz

Fads, which are sometimes defined as short-lived or very particularized fashions, are dramatic and often highly visible evidences of the tendency of human beings with similar backgrounds to react similarly to the same stimuli. Fads such as skate boards and Beatle haircuts may sweep across a whole nation, or they may be limited to a single community. In either case, they demonstrate the general phenomenon of human collective behavior. Such collective behavior does not, however, occur simply at random but has what might be termed a "natural history." This is illustrated in the following selection.

The study of fads and fashions may serve the student of social change much as the study of fruit flies has served geneticists; neither the sociologist nor the geneticist has to wait long for a new generation to arrive.

Fads provide an extraordinary opportunity to study processes of influence or contagion, of innovative and cyclical behavior, and of leadership; this has been long recognized by social thinkers, most of whom tended, however, to regard fads and fashions as one form of permanent social change.

SOURCE: Copyright 1957 by The University of Chicago. Reprinted from "Notes on a Natural History of Fads," *American Journal of Sociology*, Vol. 62, No. 6 (May, 1957), 594–601, by Rolf Meyersohn and Elihu Katz, by permission of The University of Chicago Press. ✧ Rolf Meyersohn is assistant professor of sociology at the State University of New York at Stony Brook. He has written in the areas of public opinion and communication. Elihu Katz is associate professor of sociology at The University of Chicago. His major fields of interest include public opinion and communication within small groups. He is a coauthor of *Personal Influence*.

To regard change in fads exclusively as a prototype of social change is to overlook several fundamental distinctions. In the first place, the process by which fads operate is typically confined to particular subgroups in society, and, although fads may change violently and swiftly, the subgroup remains the same; the network of fad communication usually remains stable. On the other hand, patterns of communication that create new social movements—for example, a new religious sect—also create a new social structure; here both the content and the network of communication are new. This distinction is well made by Blumer, who points out that social movement, unlike fads, usually leave stable organizations in their wake:

> Not only is the fashion movement unique in terms of its character, but it differs from other movements in that it does not develop into a society. It does not build up a social organization; it does not develop a division of labor among its participants with each being assigned a given status: it does not construct a new set of symbols, myths, values, philosophy, or set of practices, and in this sense does not form a culture; and finally, it does not develop a set of loyalties or form a we-consciousness.

Popular music illustrates this distinction. Every few months a new "content" in the form of new hits flows through the same "network" of distributors (disk jockeys, etc.) and consumers (primarily teen-agers and other radio audiences). While an occasional song may attract some distributors or consumers who are not regularly a part of the system—for example, the recently popular song "Morität" from Brecht and Weill's *Threepenny Opera* found high-brow listeners outside the regular music audience—these stray elements usually get out as quickly as they came in. The popular-music world as a whole remains unchanged and goes on as before to produce its continuous cycle of discontinuous hits.

Each new fad is a *functional alternative* for its predecessor: this hit for that hit, this parlor game for that one. On the other hand, the processes involved in broader social changes, such as religious conversions, an increase in the birth rate, or a movement toward suburban living, are too complex to permit simple substitution. Following Merton, who, in arguing against the functional indispensability of a social structure, points out that the range of possible variation is more relevant, one may say that in fashion the range of functional alternatives is far greater than in other domains of social change.

Perhaps this is so because fashions are found in relatively superficial areas of human conduct—in the trivial or ornamental. Many more changes have occurred in the styling of automobiles (e.g., in the length of tail lights) than in their engines. In a brilliant essay on fashion Simmel discusses the selective process whereby some cultural items are subject to fashion and others not, and he points out that the former must be "independent of the vital motives of human action."

Fashion occasionally will accept objectively determined subjects such as religious faith, scientific interests, even socialism and individualism; but it does not become operative as fashion until these subjects can be considered independent of the deeper human motives from which they have risen. For this reason the rule of fashion becomes in such fields unendurable. We therefore see that there is good reason why externals—clothing, social conduct, amusements—constitute the specific field of fashion, for here no dependence is placed on really vital motives of human action.

Triviality, of course, does not refer to the amount of emotion, affect, and functional significance surrounding an object but rather to its life-expectancy, its susceptibility to being *outmoded*. Every object has a finite and estimable life-span; a pair of nylon stockings may last a few weeks, a dress a few years, an automobile a decade or two, a house much longer. It is one of the characteristics of fashion that replacement is made before the life-span ends. Such objects are acquired without regard for their durability. This is one definition of "conspicuous consumption."

Hence we arrive at one possible indication whether an item is a carrier of fashion. Simmel has illustrated this point very well:

When we furnish a house these days, intending the articles to last a quarter of a century, we invariably invest in furniture designed according to the vary latest patterns and do not even consider articles in vogue two years before. Yet it is obvious that the attraction of fashion will desert the present article just as it left the earlier one, and satisfaction or dissatisfaction with both forms is determined by other material criteria. A peculiar psychological process seems to be at work here in addition to the mere bias of the moment. Some fashion always exists and fashion per se is indeed immortal, which fact seems to affect in some manner or other each of its manifestations, although the very nature of each individual fashion stamps it as being transitory. The fact that change itself does not change, in this instance endows each of the objects which it affects with a psychological appearance of duration.

Since most fads are of a minority or subculture, they may of course exhibit contradictory or countervailing trends all at once. While the fashion system as a whole may rely on an incompleted life-span for a part of its *élan*, certain subsystems of fashions operate in the opposite way. Thus, the trend today may be to trade in perfectly usable automobiles; yet there are those who drive nothing but antique automobiles. Such people attempt to *exceed* the structural limits of this particular item, and their possessions are as much a part of the fashion system as the latest, newest, the "most unique."

Several approaches to the study of fads can be distinguished. One is concerned with the function of fashion generally for society, groups, and individuals. . . .

Fashions have also been examined in terms of their specific content, and many attempts have been made to relate a particular trend, style, or motif to a *Zeitgeist*, a "climate of opinion," or an ideology. . . .

A third approach to fashion deals not with the content of fashions but with the network of people involved. A fashion "system" may be seen in the interaction among producers, distributors, and consumers, which works as a spiral-like closed circuit. . . .

A fourth approach to the study of fashions, one which differs from the three cited above, though it operates within their orbits, seeks to determine the origin of a given item, the conditions of acceptance by the first participants (the "innovators"), the characteristics of those whom the innovators influence, the shifts from minority to majority acceptance, its waning, and where it goes to die. This is its natural history. The natural history of any phenomenon which is ephemeral and which comprises a specific content (e.g., popular music) with its particular network (e.g., the flow from song writers to publishing companies to record companies to disk jockeys to teen-agers, to juke-box listeners, etc.) can obviously be studied. It is based on the premise that different *stages* of a fad can be isolated and studied. In the past this premise has been used in studies of crowds, race riots, lynching mobs, and even political movements, all of which have been described in terms of discrete evolutionary steps, isolated according to their patterns of person-to-person interaction. Each stage, furthermore, has been described as paving the way for the next stage.

Fads and fashions, too, have been subjected to such analysis. Almost every textbook in social psychology points out how aspirants to social mobility continually try to pre-empt the symbols of higher status, thereby forcing their former holders to search ever for replacements. This is how the story of fashions, and sometimes of all consumer purchasing, is usually told. While it is certainly likely that one function of fashion is in the display of social ascent and that one network for its transmission is from the upper classes downward, the extent to which this traditional view of fashion remains valid cannot be told without refined empirical study— without tracing the diffusion of particular fads and fashions in time and through their relevant social structures.

In the continuing absence of such refined empirical data, this paper presents on the basis of crude observations some notes on the stages in the natural history of any fad; beginning at the point where some change has just begun to occur, it traces very roughly the fad's probable course.

FADS ARE NOT BORN BUT REDISCOVERED   Where do new fads come from? In many instances they have existed all along but not as fads. For example, in the past several years a large number of songs that went under the collective title of "Rhythm and Blues" rose to the top of the "hit parade." Now these songs and this type of music were not new. The music industry had known about them for many years, largely under the title "race records." They had been produced for consumption by a Negro audience, a number of small record companies and publishers devoting themselves almost exclusively to this market. Trade journals carried separate ratings for such music, ranking each new song according to its popularity within this special category.

Then, all of a sudden, "rhythm and blues" songs invaded the general market, and "feedback points" (including the disk jockeys, fan clubs, listings of sheet-music sales, record sales, juke-box sales, etc.) all began to indicate a new trend. This particular new trend had existed for a good long time but in a different audience. It had been a little pocket in the music world as a whole which sustained it not as a fashion but as a "custom." What happened was that minority music was becoming majority music.

These minority social systems seem to feed many kinds of fashions to the majority. This is true not only of racial groups; the word "minority" is here used in the sense of engaging only a small segment of the population. Some "minorities" are more likely to be fashion-feeders, of course; the classic view of fashion assumes that a minority either in the upper classes or tangential to them engages in certain choices, and these are then "discovered" and made fashionable by lower strata.

In areas of life where "new" products are in demand or vital to the continuation of the industry, such "discoveries" are clearly more frequent. Since fashions serve a symbolic function and must be recognized in order to be transmitted, their greatest motility is likely to be found in those areas which are most visible. Thus, changes in dress are likely to be more frequent than in underclothes. Furthermore, the search for something new —what Simmel has called "exceptional, bizarre, or conspicuous"—will be greater there.

In the popular-music industry, where such a search is conducted on a monthly basis, the life-span of a "hit" being approximately that long, new discoveries are essential. Hence, every pocket of the musical world is sooner or later "discovered." "Rhythm and blues" is one of many such pockets, if more successful than some of the others; for a time African songs were hits; South American music has followed this pattern; hillbilly music shows the same trend; even classical music was "discovered" when suddenly the first movement of a Tchaikovsky piano concerto exploded all over America.

Minorities not only provide material to majorities but are also an integral part of the total system. Not only do they offer a pretest—"If it goes well in Tangiers, maybe it has a chance here!"—but they are also a shelf and shelter for dangerous or threatening ideas. Mark Benney suggests that bohemias serve this function. For urban societies their bohemias are a kind of social laboratory. Here something new can be tried out— because it is expected—without threatening either the bohemian minority or the urban population as a whole. The city watches, Benney suggests, and confers respectability on what it likes. Wrought-iron furniture, Japanese scrolls, charcoal-gray flannel suits, not to mention new literary forms and ideological movements, have indeed been bred in these quarters.

THE TASTEMAKERS   While the community, the music industry, or the clothing world as a whole may watch and wait for new ideas in many places, the task of scouting seems to fall to one particular set of people. By the nature of their tasks, they must be intimately acquainted with two worlds, the majority and the minority. . . .

A good example in the popular-music industry is the success of the current artist and repertoire director (the "A&R Man") at Columbia Records, Mitch Miller. A concert oboist himself, he was thoroughly trained as a serious musician. With an established reputation and a semi-bohemian personality which manifests itself in harmless ways, such as the wearing of a beard and keeping odd hours, he has been able to utilize good judgment in the popular-music world not only by being better educated but by having a far broader range of minorities to draw on for inspiration. Thus he is familiar with the attributes of French horns and harpsichords, with echo chambers and goat bells, and has been able to use all to full advantage. One reason for his using esoteric "effects" is that in the music industry any popular hit is immediately copied, but his arrangements have been made so complex by the use of such "gimmicks" —as the music industry calls them—that imitation is very difficult. In addition of course, the gimmicks have given Columbia Records a unique reputation.

In any case, certain individuals in society are equipped to scout for new ideas and products to feed the various fashion systems. What is perhaps more important is to examine the fate of the original producer of the particular minority "custom" once it has been "exported" and translated into a fashion.

THE EXPORTER BECOMES SELF-CONSCIOUS   At some time in the past Parisian clothes were "discovered" and made fashionable throughout "society" in other countries. Before that, undoubtedly, a stable relationship existed between the Paris *couturières* and their customers, and designs were made with a very particular "audience" in mind. In the course of "discovering" these designs, one element which probably attracted the early innovators was precisely the product which emerged from this relationship. But, once discovered, what happened? As Simmel said, "Paris modes are frequently created with the sole intention of setting a' fashion elsewhere." The exporter becomes self-conscious, tries to appeal to his wider circle of customers, and *changes* the product. Another well-known example is found in oriental porcelain. In the nineteenth century, European art collectors "discovered" Chinese and Japanese pottery, and in a very short time the potters began manufacturing "export ware," creating an industry quite separate from the production of domestic "china." Another example is the shift from the 1954 to the 1955 MG car; the most popular British car in this country, the MG had been designed in a some-what old-fashioned way, with a square hood; but recently the British Motor Company decided to build it more along the lines of the latest American styles.

There are, of course, some occasions when the exporter does not be-come self-conscious. This would be most true where there is no return for more: composers who work folk songs into concert music, like Mozart, Beethoven, and Béla Bartók, do not affect the folk "producers."

What happens to the original consumers is not clear. Those who find their own customs—pizza or Yiddish melodies or canasta—becoming widely popular undoubtedly enjoy some sense of pride as well as mixed feelings about the inevitable distortions and perhaps yield to the tempta-tion to make some accommodation from then on in the hope of being "picked up" once again.

STATISTICAL VERSUS REAL FASHIONS: A CASE OF PLURALISTIC IGNORANCE Who can say that something is a fashion? Who knows about it? It may happen that a number of people in various parts of this country, for a variety of reasons, will all buy a certain item. They may all "go in" for "rhythm and blues" music or good musical sound reproduction or raccoon-skin caps, all unaware that others are doing the same thing.

Such situations, in which no one realizes that others are doing the same thing, probably occur all the time. They are similar to what social psychologists have called "pluralistic ignorance," a state in which nobody knows that others maintain an attitude or belief identical with their own. If this coincidence persists long enough, however, the point will be reached at which one cannot help noticing the unself-conscious, "inner-directed" activity of large numbers of people in making identical choices. At this point the phenomenon which had been statistical becomes a real fad; here another important stage is reached—the labeling of a fad.

THE LABEL AND THE COATTAIL The birth of a fad is really accompanied by two labels; the phenomenon is given a name, and it is named as a fad. The fad is defined as real and in consequence becomes so.

Such a definition, however, must be made not only real but public. It must be translated from the specialized professional, business, or trade vocabulary into more popular terms—in short, into a label or a slogan.

While there are certainly plenty of labels which do not represent fads, there are no unlabeled fads or fashions. It is usually through the label that the fashion acquires fame—even beyond its consumer audience. Thus the "New Look," "hi-fi," "motivation research," "automation," and "char-coal gray."

The ground swell immediately after the labeling is caused partly by the activities of indirectly related enterprises. Machines that yesterday were ordinary phonographs and radios are suddenly called "hi-fi"; coon-skin headgear becomes Davy Crockett caps; a lever makes of an industrial machine "automation"; an ordinary open-ended question converts a public opinion survey into "motivation research."

Thus the coattails which dress the fashion. Although the original minorities—whether devotees of recordings of high quality and accurate sound reproduction or Negroes who have been hearing certain kinds of "pop" music for years—may not recognize the $29.95 portable radio as "hi-fi" or the ordinary hit of the week as "rhythm and blues," the respective producers have found something that "works," and every commodity within labeling distance has a chance to be included.

THE FLOW   Where the various fashions find their victims depends on their specific nature. Beginning in the minority, the fad is "discovered," then is labeled, and ultimately reaches the mass audiences. In the case of clothing, there is sometimes a stage, mentioned by Simmel and later by contemporary social psychologists and sociologists, which precedes or accompanies the labeling process, when the fashion is adopted by a group of acknowledged respectability. The fashion is perhaps borrowed from a fringe group within the society, or even outside it, and touted as an "esoteric" discovery. But in a society such as ours very little can be kept private, and providing clues to "better living," tips on the stock market, and advice on clothing, furniture, and virtually every other artifact is the professional job of all the media of communication. Thus, a product associated with a respected group or class is likely to spread, through being publicized, to other groups as well. From here it moves to groups which aspire to be like the advocates. These are not necessarily lower in status, although often so described. It may be that the lower group innovates— as in the "do-it-yourself" fad, a phenomenon which all farmers and lower-income groups have been aware of all their lives—but it is more likely to be a somewhat esoteric group, as the bohemians who flocked to New York's Greenwich Village after World War I, followed by the middle-class New Yorkers after World War II.

Regardless of the direction of the flow, for a time the original possessors of a fashion-to-be will maintain the fashion for themselves and their kind, for people of the same social status are more likely to hear about people of their own level, especially in the upper classes. But after a time the innovation will cross the boundary line of the groups who adopted it and pass into other groups, in the process losing some of its distinguishing characteristics.

THE OLD DRIVES IN THE NEW   The story of fads is, then, one of constant change. And the changes themselves do not change, or at least not so much that they cannot be followed.

The process of change occurs necessarily at every point, leaving, as it were, a vacuum when the fashion departs for its next point. Eventually, the vacuum is filled, even to overflowing, by its successor. When a fad has reached full bloom, its distinguishing features become so blurred that some are totally lost. If everything is called "hi-fi," nothing is high-fidelity.

Furthermore, if more than just certain classes are *aficionados*, the self-conscious among the class-conscious will want something new for themselves.

Thus, at some point before a dress design hits the Sears-Roebuck catalogue, a sports car the secondhand automobile dealer, and a modern chair the suburban rummage sale, once again it is time for a change.

THE FEEDBACK Producers notoriously see an undifferentiated audience before their eyes. They tend so often just to count that they miscalculate demand.

William McPhee and James Coleman have suggested that, while one group may be oversaturated with a fad, another may be very receptive—and only accurate reporting (feedback) about each group can tell the whole story. For example, since teen-agers are the major purchasers of records and sheet music and the major investors in juke boxes, and since these three commodities are the major tests of demand consulted by the producers, teen-agers can make or break a song. Disk jockeys also play a role in feedback, but it is primarily the "top" jockeys with the large teen-age followings who are the key informants. Yet there is another audience for popular music to whom the producers have almost no access—the daytime radio listeners: the housewives, traveling salesmen, commuters. Their tastes are thus inferred—of all places—from teen-agers!

In other words, the skewed feedback of the music industry is responsible in part for the volatility of its fads; exaggerating as it does the tastes of an already erratic group considered as its primary audience, its fads fluctuate beyond all expectation. With perfect information, a normal distribution of tastes can be expected at most times and for most things. In certain industries, and among certain subgroups, the distribution is less likely to be normal, in part due to the pressures for new commodities, to the superficiality of the appeals themselves, to the publicity accompanying every product, and in the case of teen-agers, to their unstable moods. When information comes only or largely from teen-agers, who are at the fringes of the distribution curve, so to speak, then the music industry is rendered excessively phrenetic. Kurt and Gladys Lang, in studying the Chicago MacArthur Day parade of 1951, found that the television reporting of this rather slow-moving and dull event was systematically distorted to give the impression of a vast crowd, a glorious spectacle, and an unremitting enthusiasm. Here, as in the case of the popular-music industry, the requirements to hold an audience from switching to another station or channel or losing interest in popular music or a given song force such emphasis on the manic.

Hence, while the feedback from consumer to producer makes, at first, for a frenzied increase in a fashionable product, it may also make for a more rapid saturation than is warranted or, if the gauge is placed somewhere else in society, for an oversupply.

COMMUNITY IN DISASTER

William H. Form and Sigmund Nosow

Perhaps the most dramatic form of collective behavior is that occasioned by a widespread community disaster. This selection describes the reaction of two groups to a tornado which swept a suburb near Flint, Michigan, in June, 1954. The authors examine the effect of the disaster on the way the members of the two groups—one, a family and the other, a small group of adolescent boys—analyze the problem of determining appropriate roles to play and establish a division of labor among themselves.

After the impact of the tornado, the community was turned into chaos, but rescue behavior was immediately instituted. This postimpact stage (the *emergency stage* of community relations) was marked by three different periods: the first, during which rescue was performed by the victims and persons from the impact and contiguous areas; the second, during which help was supplemented by local organizations; and the third, during which help was supplemented by external agencies. Those periods provide an overall structural view of the disaster process, the relationships among the victims, rescuers, and organizations.

However, from the point of view of the victims and rescuers, the postimpact period was one during which their own patterns of behavior followed given forms, some activities persisting and others changing. It is possible to discern patterns of *personal behavior* and to classify these in terms of different phases. . . .

The *first phase* for an individual was concerned with action immediately after the impact. During this phase dominant activities were checking on the safety of one's family and oneself, appraising the immediate damage, and making decisions as to the appropriate ensuing behavior. This was followed by *phase two*, which reflected a change in

SOURCE: William H. Form and Sigmund Nosow, with Gregory P. Stone and Charles M. Westie, *Community in Disaster* (New York: Harper & Brothers, 1958), 33–46. Copyright © 1958 by William H. Form and Sigmund Nosow. Reprinted by permission of Harper & Brothers. ✧ William H. Form is professor and chairman of the Department of Sociology and research associate in the School of Labor and Industrial Relations, Michigan State University. His chief interests are industrial and occupational sociological research. He is the author of *Industry, Labor and Community* and the coauthor of *Industrial Sociology*. Sigmund Nosow is a professor in the Department of Social Science and in the School of Labor and Industrial Relations, Michigan State University. His major interests are in areas involving both economics and sociology. In addition to *Community in Disaster* he is the coeditor (with William H. Form) of *Man, Work, and Society*.

the patterns of activity, or a change in the site of such activity, or a change in the social orientation of the activities. *Phase three* was also characterized by a shift in activities and social orientations. This was reflected in increased mobility, sporadic activity, and finally, a general withdrawal from the scene of rescue.

The meaningfulness of this classification is best illustrated by . . . contrasting cases of personal behavior in the Flint-Beecher disaster. These case studies are of groups that were more or less enduring, more or less effective, and more or less "spontaneous."

Of the two cases presented, the first dealing with the "Rudenko" family is perhaps the most representative of the types of activities that occurred during the emergency stage. This family is described because most of its members were interviewed and because their case histories contain detailed descriptions of their activities. The second case study of adolescents provides some insights into the types of behavior that might be expected from such a group during an emergency. . . .

I. A Case Study of a Family's Rescue Activities

The family may be considered the basic rescue group within neighborhoods or communities in cases of disaster. Its internal integration is such that the obligations of the members to one another are clearly defined. Its integration into the neighborhood makes it an ideal rescue unit because its members are usually identified with the neighborhood and because they know the physical layout of the homes and the area. This case study of the Rudenko family describes a group consisting of six functioning adult members. The Rudenko house was the only house in its immediate vicinity that survived the tornado.

The active members of the Rudenko family included a 63-year-old grandfather and his 58-year-old wife. Living with them in the same household were their youngest son (25) and his wife (22) and a child. When the tornado struck (8:29 P.M.), the son was at work (did not return until 11 P.M.), but his wife and daughter were at home. Visiting their parents at this time were the oldest son (35), his wife (32), and their three sons (the oldest being 9). The family group, then, was composed of six adults and four children.

The father and son were working in the garden. When it started to rain the father said to his son, "You'd better put that tractor back in the garage—I don't like the looks of that cloud." In the basement of the house, the two daughters were ironing clothes. With them were the two older children, while the grandmother was upstairs with the two babies.

After the rain began, the two men went down to the basement to look at the water pump. The grandmother, upstairs, saw the tornado coming and began to pray. Describing the situation, she said, "I couldn't decide whether to run to the cellar with one baby or go in the dining room for the other baby. People yelled, 'Get the baby and come down here.' I finally went down with one baby."

Fortunately, the house escaped major damage and the second baby was found unharmed upstairs after the tornado had struck.

Not so fortunate was the nearest neighbor, living across the street, whose immediate plight mobilized this rescue group. His account of what happened to him is among the most lucid and complete obtained.

I ran for the house. As I ran, I saw the tornado pick up a car on Clio Road. As I put my foot on the front door steps, it came down the driveway and took me. It didn't seem to come from the west because it carried me north. It threw me into a tree first, then slid me along the grass. . . . I was conscious all the time. It threw me against the basement wall of my house on my head. I just laid there, then looked up and saw the house raising on the foundation. I got up on my hands, raising up; the wind grabbed me again and took me up in the air. While I was going up, something swatted me on top of my head, and I landed right in my basement (the house was gone by then). Incidentally, while I was laying against the basement wall the porch fell on my leg.

Members of the Rudenko family emerged from their house and saw that three of the immediate neighbors' houses were gone or partially destroyed. The father ran to one house and his son to another. The father found his best friend's wife (Mrs. Able) badly injured, but was unable to locate his friend. He ran for aid and located the State Police, who were trying to get into the area. With their aid and that of others, Mrs. Able was placed in a private car and taken to the hospital.

Meanwhile, the son went to Mr. Corn's house, found him and his injured children, and helped them into an automobile, which took them to the hospital. They were careful to withhold from Mr. Corn the information that his wife was dead. Her body had been found by the son 800 feet away from their home. The Rudenko father and son then searched the area and found the body of Mr. Able, who was Rudenko Sr.'s good friend and neighbor. After this, they went to the aid of other victims. Those who were not badly injured were taken to the Rudenko home to be cared for, or given first aid.

The women in the family group remained at home, and for the most part cared for the injured and homeless members of the two families whose other members had been taken to the hospital. In the words of one of the daughters:

"We just tried to calm the Riveras. The Riveras were crying and carrying on. We tried to calm them. . . . We then bandaged them up and took a piece of wood from the Rivera woman's leg."

The above description covers the first phase of activities for most members of this rescue group. This family appears to have followed a rather strict division of labor along sex lines. The women stayed at home, and cared for the children and the injured people whom the men sent to the house. The men remained in the field, performing immediate rescue functions, especially looking for those who they knew were in the area and whose homes were destroyed or damaged.

After the immediate emergency, the father appears to have stayed near the house, while his son worked with others. When the son was asked who helped him, he replied, "I guess I worked with 25 or 30 fellows—Dad, my brother, Mr. Pennel, Fred at the gas station, the man in the white house at the corner of Clio and Coldwater, and Mr. Harris the dairyman. Those are all I knew."

The influx of volunteers from the surrounding area appears to have swelled the membership of rescue groups that started out with a few people in the area working together. Almost no respondent could identify by name more than a half-dozen people with whom he worked during the course of the night.

The Rudenko family rescue group changed its character when most of the rescue work in the immediate neighborhood was finished about 11:00 P.M. After this, the father stayed close to home, while the two sons (one having just returned from work) ranged farther from home. This marked the end of the second phase for most of the Rudenko family.

Later, the eldest son went to inspect his own home some distance away. The parents of the older daughter-in-law arrived about 3:00 A.M. to take their daughter and grandchild to their home.

To summarize, this family rescued, gave first aid to and generally cared for three families of neighbors involving some fifteen to eighteen persons. They located other dead and injured, and looked for and ascertained the welfare and whereabouts of other neighbors who might have been trapped in their homes. They rapidly worked out an effective division of labor according to age and sex role patterns. It was possible for them to devote full energy to the rescue task because all members were aware of the facts that none of the family was injured, that the house was not severely damaged, and that the children were being adequately cared for. Their knowledge of the neighborhood and the family composition of victim groups enabled them to find or account for all potential or actual victims.

When asked whether their group could have done a better job, the oldest son reported: "There wasn't anything else we could do. I did wish I knew how to stop the Rivera kids from crying—you can't stop kids from crying." And the father's reply was, "There wasn't anything else we could do."

Although the Rudenko family constituted perhaps a most highly integrated and most enduring rescue unit, it cannot be conceived of as a team having a high amount of internal cohesion, permanence, and leadership. Rather, these family members set for themselves certain tasks (search, rescue, transportation, calming, first aid, care of children, and checking property). At times they worked with each other, at times with neighbors or friends, and at times with strangers, State Police, ambulance drivers, or others. There was no leadership or authority in the field or in the home. Verbal communication among members apparently was slight, because they were unable to report what functions other members of the family had performed.

The emergent division of labor enabled the Rudenkos to function effectively as individuals because they played appropriate and complementary social roles. Despite the fact that they lived in a marginal area of Beecher that was socially and economically heterogeneous, they had sufficient information about the neighbors to enable an efficient and effective rescue effort to be launched.

II. A Case Study of Adolescent Behavior in Disaster

It is commonly observed that adolescents in contemporary society are denied adult prerogatives that they feel capable of assuming. Some sociologists and anthropologists have challenged the alleged discontinuity between adolescent and adult roles. Disaster conditions, with concomitant relaxation of social controls, initially create a situation that may permit adolescents to assume adult responsibilities. In order to test whether the adolescents in fact can assume adult roles under disaster conditions a sample of 12 boys and girls, ages 15 to 19, were interviewed intensively.

The following case presents materials gathered on the behavior of a group of adolescent boys, ages 14 to 17 years, during the postimpact period. None of the boys resided in the stricken area; all lived in the periphery. However, initially, two of them did not know whether or not their families had been injured. While the activities of five adolescents are described, at no time were there more than three boys in continuous interaction. Two of them very soon dropped out of the group and either went home or worked with adults. The nucleus of this group consisted of Jim Wilson, Lou Olesky, and Ted Braden.

8:25 p.m.

Marty Johnson (age 14) was helping his father and a neighbor (Mr. Blake) repair the door on their house when the siren from the Beecher fire station sounded. Mr. Johnson immediately left for the fire station, since he was a volunteer. As the wind and noise increased in severity, the boy, his mother, and Mr. Blake went into the basement for protection.

Meanwhile Jim Wilson and Ted Braden were driving around Flint just south of Beecher.

Lou Olesky (age 16) was puttering around the drug store where he worked part time. There were no customers in the store. As he looked outside, he saw the trees waving, and thought there was a bad storm brewing.

Hal McNaughton (age 16) was at his next-door neighbor's house when the wind started to blow. He didn't think much about it. About five minutes later, Hal went home. His father, also a volunteer with the Beecher Fire Department, was getting his gear together to join other volunteers at the station. Hal decided to go to the station with his father.

8:32 P.M. (PHASE ONE)

Marty Johnson's father returned from the station to check on his family, and then took Mr. Blake back with him to assist in the rescue activities. Marty remained at home with his mother.

Ted and Jim had driven to an auto parts store and heard over the radio that a tornado had struck the Beecher area. They got into the car and drove toward the stricken area.

Lou was still in the drug store. The lights had gone out, and he saw and heard ambulances going by. He also saw obviously injured people in cars.

8:55 P.M. (PHASE TWO)

Marty was still at home with his mother. Jim and Ted drove their car to where they lived and assured their mothers that they were all right. They then picked up a flashlight at Jim's house and went toward the impact area. On the way they picked up Marty and all three then went toward the fire station.

Lou, who had been joined by his younger brother, was still at the drug store. They saw some injured people being transported in cars toward Flint, and decided to go to the stricken area. They took a flashlight and started off. They wanted to see what had happened and did not particularly anticipate participating in any rescue activity.

9:00 P.M.

While the three boys—Marty, Jim, and Ted—were working their way through the debris toward the fire station Marty became separated from the other two. He was shocked and nearly overcome with nausea at the sight of the dead, the injured, and the damage. He wandered around in this state until he finally went home. He maintained that he went to various parts of the stricken area and its periphery looking for relatives.

Jim and Ted worked their way closer to the fire station. Ted became separated from Jim and never did get to the fire station. He said he worked alone and with different individuals. Meanwhile, Lou Olesky, on his way from the drug store, became separated from his younger brother. When Lou arrived at the fire station he saw Jim and Hal there. From this point on, these three boys—Jim, Hal, and Lou—constituted a group and were together until about 2:00 A.M.

The following is a log of their activities:

The fire station, although partially damaged, was overrun with activity. Not only were there firemen coming and going, but other persons (victims, volunteers, and residents) crowded the station. The boys were asked whether they had or could locate any flashlights and batteries. Since they could not find either in the storeroom of the fire station, they thought they should try to find some at nearby hardware stores.

As they left the fire station they noticed a panel truck belonging to one of the local hardware dealers. Finding the keys in it, Hal decided that they should take the truck and see what they could do to help in the rescue activities. So they loaded some old stretchers, sheets, and blankets in the back of the truck. They then got in and drove off. Later on, the boys revealed that they had had no specific plan in mind, but they had all agreed on the idea of taking the truck anyway. Two of them claimed that they had obtained permission from Mr. Cumberland, the owner, but the other boy denied this.

They drove the truck around the area and into the heart of the damaged sections where a bulldozer had cleared the way. They stopped where they saw a group of firemen digging out bodies, and they let the firemen load the bodies into the truck.

After picking up the first load of victims, they proceeded through the area and stopped at the baseball diamond of the school where some men were working. The workers piled two more victims into the truck. The boys still did not know what to do with the victims. Someone suggested they go to the State Police post. They did, and were told to take the victims to Hurley Hospital.

When they arrived at the hospital, the workers there told them to leave. When the boys informed them that there were victims in the truck, they were let in and the truck was unloaded. The boys then asked if anyone wanted to go back to Beecher with them. They gave one man a ride part of the way back. Then they drove to the area but had to wait in line to get in because the roads were blocked. Since they saw they could not get into the heart of the damaged area, they drove the truck back to the fire department. At the fire station, Jim and Lou got out of the truck.

Hal decided to take the truck to see if he could get water from the dairy back to the fire department. He did not succeed. When he came back he picked up Lou and took him home so that Lou could tell his mother that he was all right. They then went back to the fire station, where Hal dropped Lou off.

At this point, the group of three adolescents had broken up. Jim left the area and could not get back in because the police denied him access. Lou met his father, and went with him to check on some relatives. Hal kept the truck and drove it around performing errands, such as driving a fireman to City Hall to get batteries. He drove the truck around, visited here and there, went back home at 7:00 A.M., and then returned to the area with the truck. He did not return the truck to the owner until noon.

Unlike many of the others involved in rescue the adolescent group did not have injured or threatened family members to hamper their operations. How they would have performed under this kind of stress is, of course, unknown. However, it is clear that they did not behave like adult males. In general, their activity was regulated by others, and they showed only little initiative. At no time did they handle any of the injured, nor did they indicate any desire to do so. The three members of the group did not work out a plan for a division of labor. Any opportunity to utilize their skills was largely dissipated, because they remained together and did essentially what was a one-person job, namely, driving a truck. The fact that they remained together all this time suggests that they needed one another for moral support. Apparently they shunned the opportunities to do different tasks. Thus they neither loaded nor unloaded bodies, searched for victims in any systematic way, nor assumed any systematic liaison function. The implication gained from this case study is that adolescents may perform useful functions in an emergency if they are given task direction by adult members of the community.

The lack of a social definition of useful, responsible roles for adolescents in modern American society is strikingly documented by the behavior of these boys and by the adult attitudes expressed toward them. However, the ability of adolescents to imitate adult activity, assume responsibility, and make decisions was evident in other situations where there was serious doubt about the safety of their own families. At such times they seemed adequate to meet some of the needs of the disaster situation. Without such specific types of social definitions of behavior for *family members* guiding them, the adolescents described in the case study devolved into either errand boys, random wanderers, or emotionally dependent children who could not cope with the terror of the aftermath of the tornado.

This analysis of adolescent behavior underscores the general point that the knowledge, skills, and creativity of any group may just as well not exist if no social definition allows them to be brought into play. . . .

Social Organization:

STRATIFICATION AND MOBILITY

* 37 *

THE NEW MAJORITY

Peter F. Drucker

One of the basic articles of faith in the Marxian creed has been that industrialized societies inevitably produce increasingly large numbers of exploited "blue-collar" workers. Recent research, however, indicates that, in the United States at least, the proportion of manual industrial workers in the total working population is declining sharply. As Peter Drucker here indicates, the largest single American socioeconomic category today is the salaried middle class. He suggests it will soon be realistic, statistically as well as ideologically, to speak of the United States as a middle-class society. The consequences of this development are profound. But one should not conclude from Drucker's analysis that America will become a one-class (or "classless") society. Differences in level and quality of education, and in command of knowledge and skills acquired, will contribute new criteria for status and create new groupings varying in power and prestige. These new groupings will be the social classes of our future American society.

During the past two or three years, professional, technical, and managerial people have become the largest group in the American working population. "Professional, technical, and managerial" is a statistical term. But it is not just a pompous circumlocution for "white-collar employees." "Professional, technical, and managerial" does not include cleri-

S O U R C E : *The Listener* (British Broadcasting Corporation publication), October 23, 30, 1958. Two lectures broadcast on the Third Programme of the BBC. Copyright, 1958, by Peter F. Drucker. Reprinted by permission of BBC and the author. ✧ The author is professor of management at the Graduate School of Business Administration, New York University. Methodology and institutional history are his main interests. Among his books are *Concept of the Corporation*, *The Practice of Management*, and *Landmarks of Tomorrow*.

cal people, or the sales-girl in the shop. It does not even include foremen in the factories. "Professional, technical, and managerial" people, according to our definition in the United States, either determine the work of other people, or apply specialized knowledge in their own work. I know only one short term for these groups: it would be the "salaried middle class."

It is this salaried middle class that has now become our largest working group, larger in fact than the blue collar people, the machine operators. This signals drastic changes in social structure, in the American economy, and in American politics. Thirteen years ago, when we came out of the second world war, the industrial workers were clearly still the largest single group in the American working population—almost one out of every four belonged to it. This was the end of a long historical process that went back to the early years of the 19th century when manufacturing industries were first started on American soil, a process that began to gather momentum in the early years of our century, and that brought about the great changes within the last generation: the change in domestic politics that expressed itself in the New Deal, and the change internationally that led to the emergence of the United States as the greatest industrial and military power in the West. At the end of the war, the professional, technical, and managerial group was already a sizeable group; and it had been growing fast for some time. But it was still one of the smaller groups in the working population, not much more than half the size of the blue-collar workers, that is of industrial labor, and smaller even than office and service employees or farmers. In those thirteen years industrial production in the United States has almost doubled. Both total and working population have been growing fast. But the manual labor needed for this output of goods has remained the same. The number of salaried middle-class people, however, which the economy now requires and which now are employed has almost doubled: it has grown by two-thirds and is growing much faster than either total or working population. By now, one out of every five people at work in the United States works as a professional man, as a technician, or in some managerial capacity—some 13 million of them altogether.

More important than numbers is the direction of the development. All signs point to a further growth of this group, perhaps even a faster growth. By 1975—only seventeen years away—we expect our total production in the United States to be about twice what it is now. Our working population should be one-third larger than it is today. But the only group of employees which will have to grow much faster—a great deal faster than either total population or working population—will again be the salaried middle class. Seventeen years from now, when the boys and girls who are starting their first years in school will have finished their education, in 1975, we should have twice as many people in the salaried middle class as we have today. By then they should be almost two-fifths of the total

working force. While there will be a real and continuing need for more
highly skilled manual workers, we shall not be needing many more of the
"typical" industrial workers, the semi-skilled machine operators, the men
who work on the assembly lines or in the steel mills. Indeed, the three
industries in the American economy where employment is likely to grow
the fastest are education, electronics, and chemistry—and all three employ primarily highly educated middle-class people rather than machine
operators.

Already the machine operators represent the past rather than the
future. Twenty-five years ago they were by and large the youngest group
in our working population. Perhaps the only exception were office personnel where there are so many young unmarried women. Shop stewards
in the plants, for instance, in those days, during the great wave of unionization in the 'thirties, tended to be ten or fifteen years younger on average
than the management people they dealt with. Today the industrial worker
in the United States tends to be older than the population in general.
Union leaders today are almost without exception older by ten years or so
than their negotiating partners in management. The typical industrial
worker, the machine operator, belongs to what is both a stagnant and an
ageing group. Growth and youth are in the professional, technical, and
managerial ranks.

An important question is what this shift in the structure of our work
population might do to the direction in which the economy in the United
States will develop. The large expansion since the end of the war has
been in goods for the consumer—such things as houses, washing machines,
television or furniture. As people's jobs and income improved, they bought
things, that is, material objects. Is this likely to continue as the salaried
middle class becomes the biggest group, and the one that is growing the
most rapidly? Certainly, these salaried, middle-class people will not go
without these consumer goods, without houses or without appliances. But
our manufacturers are finding out that it is the industrial worker who is
more likely to buy a second television set or to trade in an old but still
serviceable washing machine for a new one. The status symbols of the
salaried middle class are much more likely to be different. For instance,
more education both for themselves and for their children. Travel is
another high priority of this group. Also, its members—for whatever reason
—use the telephone much more, especially for toll calls.

Already there are signs of such a shift. The real "growth" industry in
the United States in the last ten years was, for instance, not television,
though it was certainly the most visible one. It was probably the publishing
of paper-back books; and there has been a great shift in their public and
their market and their content: history, foreign affairs, art, and religion are
rapidly becoming paper-back staples. In other words, a paper-back is becom-

ing one of the chief consumer goods of the new middle classes. Schools, travel, paper-backs, or telephone service, require other things. A shift in economic preferences would not necessarily lessen the demand for material production. But in requiring different things, the shift in the structure of our working population raises real questions regarding the direction of American economic growth.

It is not only the American economy which is being transformed; the emergence of the salaried middle class is also affecting our social life— our politics, culture, values, our society as a whole. The new salaried middle class is already the leading group in our society. Take, for instance, the pleasant suburb outside New York City where I live. The people who were the "big men" in the town then, the people who headed the community activities—the hospital board, the vestries of the churches, or the school board, the golf club committee, and the Boy Scouts, and all the thousand-and-one activities for civil and personal improvement which are the real living body of American social life—these people, only thirty years ago, were either respected professional men such as a leading lawyer or owners of businesses. Today, almost all these activities are headed by managerial or professional employees, the chief engineer of this company, the sales manager of another, or the personnel director of a third.

In politics these people are much less likely to form permanent party affiliations than either the industrial worker or the business owner. They tend to be independent in their vote, or, to the pained surprise of the politician, to split their vote. But they also tend increasingly to be impatient with traditional party organization, traditional party slogans, traditional issues.

Both our chief parties, the Republicans and the Democrats, are trying desperately to restore and to maintain their traditional alliances and allegiances, the allegiances of Theodore Roosevelt's or of Franklin Roosevelt's times respectively. Both attempts seem doomed to failure. But the new alignments, which will draw the new salaried middle classes into active politics, are still obscure, the new issues still hidden.

The greatest question, however, may be what the shift in structure of our working population means for our society. There have been many studies of the new salaried middle class of professional, technical, and managerial employees—in England as much as in our country. But we still know little about them. We know even less about a society in which this group predominates and in which it leads. They are "professional people," at least in their own eyes; but they are employed. They are subordinates, as a rule; but they consider themselves part of "management." They are managers or hope to become managers; but they are not "capitalists" any more than they are "proletarians."

The last great theory of society in the Western world was that of Karl Marx: it is now a century old. It was based on the vision—then extremely bold—of the emergence of the industrial worker or the machine operator, as the dynamic, growing class in society. For seventy-five years the machine operators were indeed the most rapidly growing group. Though they never became the majority in any industrial country, they became in every one of these countries the largest single group. This made Marxism such a powerful creed and philosophy despite its many obvious weaknesses. Today —and not only in the United States—an entirely new class is growing and is rapidly becoming the largest single group: the professional, technical, and managerial employees who are neither "capitalists" nor "proletarians," neither "exploiter" nor "exploited." But as yet we have no social theory, no social philosophy, not even adequate facts and knowledge, about the new middle-class society and the new pace-setters within it.

The United States has become, within a short thirty years, an educated society; that is, a society in which almost everybody is expected to have the advanced, long, formal schooling which a generation ago was still confined to a small élite group. It is worth noting that there is only one other country in which something comparable has happened during the same period: the Soviet Union. . . .

Our word "school" and all its synonyms in other European tongues comes from a Greek word meaning "leisure." Thus language still testifies to mankind's old conviction and experience that education unfits man for productive work. Only too obviously the man of education, however limited it may be, will shun the heavy toil, will forsake plough and potter's wheel. Throughout history, therefore, society has never been able to afford more than a small minority of educated people. In fact, ever since systematic education first began, educators themselves have always been haunted by the spectre of the "educated proletariat," by the danger of an unemployable and decaying surplus of educated parasites, too numerous for the few available job-opportunities for educated people, and too highly educated for honest work.

Today, however, we cannot get enough educated people. The job market in the United States last summer [1958] is a good example. With a recession, and with unemployment of six to seven per cent of the total labor force, one would have expected that jobs would be scarce for the newcomers leaving school. So it was indeed for those who had no more education than secondary school—that is no more than twelve years or so of formal schooling. College graduates, who had four more additional years of schooling, usually with some degree of specialization in a major area, all got jobs, though for the first time in five years they had to hunt for them unless they were trained in such highly specialized and still scarce areas as engineering or teaching. But there was no recession for the holders of advanced degrees: indeed, the starting salaries offered them were considerably higher last summer than they had been in 1957 or even in the over-employment of 1956.

Today, in other words, we realize that our economic progress, our defense strength and our political position in the world depend more and more on constantly increasing the supply of highly educated people both in quantity and in quality. This has long been a slogan; Jefferson preached it in the late seventeen-hundreds; Macaulay in the early years of the last century. But now, for the first time, it is fast becoming social reality. Knowledge—rather than "labor" or "capital"—is fast becoming the central and the most productive resource of our society.

In the past the question has always been: How many educated people can a society afford? Today it is increasingly: How many people who are *not* highly schooled can a society afford? For anyone, we are now beginning to realize, who is not educated to the limit of his abilities (and some of us—I belong to them—would greatly prefer to say: who is not educated quite a bit beyond the limit of his abilities) is a social weakness and a productive loss. The knowledge which the educated person brings to work is also a very different resource from either "labor" or "capital." It demands different jobs, different ways of organizing the work, different opportunities, and different rewards. This is true not just for those who hold, or will hold, jobs in management or research or who work in a profession. It is true for the great majority—for they all increasingly have the background and expectations of the highly schooled person.

"Automation" is largely a first impact of this shift in the educational status of the population. Automation is not the replacement of human work by machine. The essence of automation is the replacement of manual labor, whether skilled or unskilled, by knowledge. It is not "saving of labor": automation usually does not mean fewer people at work; often it means more people at work. But it means different people doing different work. It requires such knowledge as is brought to work by the logician, the mathematician, the psychologist, the chemist, the engineer, the economist —a whole host of highly educated people where formerly we employed manual workers.

That we are moving fast to automation in the United States, much faster than anyone thought possible only a few years ago, is precisely because of the changed educational structure of the country. The young people who became available for work today have been sitting on school benches for twelve to sixteen years or more. They may not have learned much—I am not trying to judge the quality of the education they have received, and having four of my own children in school I am sceptical— but they certainly do not look forward to manual work, even to highly skilled manual work, and even to very well paid manual work. They are not looking for jobs, in other words, in the pre-automated factories or the pre-automated office. They expect jobs in which they will put knowledge and theory to work, jobs in which they apply what they have learned rather than jobs in which they apply skill gained through experience. It is no exaggeration to say that the assembly line which only a short time ago was considered really advanced productive technology is, in the United States, already obsolete, socially at least, if not yet technically.

But this raises a big question: just what do these people with their advanced formal schooling expect from work and jobs, from incentives and opportunities, from careers and working conditions? Most of them will stay in modest jobs all their lives. Yet these jobs, too, will be knowledge jobs requiring high-grade theoretical training and considerable judgment. All these people have received an education which, in their fathers' time, was reserved for small, essentially upper and upper-middle class groups.

We have perhaps no idea how one really manages this kind of people. Our personnel management ideas, our personnel management policies, are based largely on experience with rank-and-file manual labor, especially in metal-working industries: essentially this is experience of the first world war. We all know that our ideas were never really effective or successful even for manual workers with a limited degree of formal education and with limited expectations in respect of opportunities. It is unlikely that they have even much relevance to these highly educated people who now come to work in industry and government and the armed forces. It is likely that we face brand-new problems which we do not even understand at all yet.

The greatest impact, however, which the educational revolution in the United States is likely to have is on social values and social structures. It is at one and the same time the fulfilment of the American dream of social equality, and a threat of a new class-structure, of a system of privilege based not on money or birth but on education. As higher education becomes general, access to opportunities becomes increasingly open to all. But at the same time—and the process is going on at high speed—opportunities are increasingly being restricted to the highly educated. It is no longer uncommon for employers to demand a college degree even for sales-girls or secretaries; and without a secondary-school degree even an unskilled factory job may today be hard to get. This is not necessarily absurd. In hiring a sales-girl the employer may hire a future department-head; in hiring a machine operator he may hire a future foreman or works-manager. But the fact remains that the higher degree is rapidly becoming what it never was before in the United States: the passport to opportunities.

I have tried to present two basic changes in American social structure: the emergence of the salaried middle class of professional, technical, and managerial people as the largest and fastest growing group in the United States; and the rapid, almost sudden conversion of the majority of the American people into people of higher, if not of advanced, education. I have tried to report rather than to appraise, and I certainly have not tried to judge.

But, in conclusion, I would like to raise the question whether these two developments have not fundamentally changed the character of American society. For almost 100 years it has been fashionable on both sides of the Atlantic to believe that American social developments follow, with a time-lag, those of Europe; Marx was the first to assert this, and it became almost an article of the faith for people on the left, Americans and Europeans, especially in the 'twenties and 'thirties.

This was always a debatable proposition. But there was some merit to it. It did, in some measure, explain to Europeans what was happening in this complicated, confused, complex country that is America. Thirty years ago, for instance, we in the United States were still much more of an agricultural society than Britain or Germany; and it made sense then to expect that the continuing shift to an industrial economy would produce in the United States such results as the growth of labor unions, of social welfare and state control; in other words, things that paralleled earlier developments in Europe. Thirty years ago we ourselves thought that it was our job to catch up educationally with Europe: the development of the modern American university was one result of this belief.

Today, however, it is the professional, technical, and managerial group that is our leading group; and in education, certainly in respect of quantity and length of schooling, ours is rapidly becoming a society of universal advanced education. These developments may be good or they may be bad. They may be specifically American or they may indicate the roads which Britain and western Europe will travel too. But what is certain is that, for better or worse, we are developing something distinct. What is certain is that to understand this society of ours one will increasingly have to understand these developments. What is certain, finally, is that increasingly the success or failure of this American society of tomorrow will depend on its success or failure as an industrial economy, in which knowledge is the truly scarce and truly productive resource, and as a middle-class society of managerial and professional highly educated people.

WHY WHITE COLLAR WORKERS
CAN'T BE ORGANIZED

Anonymous

Relatively few white-collar workers in this country have belonged to unions. In recent years this situation has changed significantly, particularly among teachers and government employees. The author of this selection discusses the factors associated with the reluctance of teachers and other white-collar workers to organize unions. Despite the fact that they are no better paid than many blue-collar workers, teachers and other white-collar workers tend to follow middle-class values and living patterns. These have traditionally included the belief that if one works hard enough and is virtuous enough, he can rise to the top through his own efforts— without belonging to a union. The recent increase in union membership among white-collar workers may indicate a change in this middle-class attitude as well as in the role of unions in American society. The reader may wish to consider what has caused this increase or produced these changes.

Except for a few highly specialized professions—like musicians, teachers, actors, and newspapermen—white collar workers are largely virgin territory for unionization. Take a look at your own community. Is there a big insurance company? A big department store? A big industrial plant with a substantial office force? Any one of these groups might mean 1,000 or more members in a single local unit—the best kind of target for an organizing campaign.

Workers in small shops are harder to round up than their brothers who share anonymity with hundreds or thousands in a big plant or office. Besides, a large group offers another asset that any businessman understands: the larger the group, the smaller the service cost per member.

"Our job," Industrial Union Department Director Al Whitehouse told the unions' white collar conference, "is to make the white collar worker understand that his interests and ours are one and the same."

If this is true, it seems strange that white collar workers aren't clamoring to be let into unions, as industrial workers did in the 1930s when the Congress of Industrial Organizations first declared that it would "organize the unorganized."

SOURCE: *Harper's Magazine,* Vol. 215, No. 1287 (August, 1957), 44–50. Copyright © 1957, by Harper & Brothers. Reprinted from *Harper's Magazine* by special permission.

A man who was an organizer for several different CIO unions told me how relatively easy his work was in those depression days of despair, hope, cynicism, and optimism.

"An organizer could just walk down the street," he said, "and the workers seemed to come out of the plants to him, begging to be organized. It didn't make any difference what industry you were supposed to be organizing in. Workers from all industries would hear you were around and would come to you. All you had to do was sign them up."

White Collar Workers Are Different

Today, there is no movement among white collar workers that even remotely parallels that surge of the 1930s. The reason, simply, is that white collar workers *are* different.

It might be appropriate to ask, Why *do* people join unions? One reason overshadows all others: the need for dignified treatment. For members of unions, it has found expression in the seniority system rather than promotion based on friendship, and in the grievance procedure which has replaced arbitrary discharges. Wage increases, company-paid insurance plans, pension rights, and all other fringe benefits—including the guaranteed annual wage—are secondary to this goal that the bargaining table itself symbolizes.

When this scale of union values is applied to the white collar worker it goes topsy-turvy. White collar workers are different because they do have a kind of will-o'-the-wisp dignity as part of their occupations. It is manifested in many ways but is most dramatic when contrasted with the plight of industrial workers in the early days of the CIO.

A man who worked in a meat-packing plant in the days before the union once told me what it was like at that time. It was largely seasonal employment and when the "hog rush" was on the hours were unbearably long. Men would stagger to work at four in the morning and work straight through till midnight. My friend told me of men doing the sweaty job of guiding freshly killed hogs through the scalding vat, with steam soaking their clothing so thoroughly that they looked as if they had just climbed out of the vat. A man would ask a foreman to allow him to go to the toilet and would be told to urinate in his clothes since they were all wet anyway.

"In those days," my friend told me, "a man would have joined anything to get help, even if it cost him his job. Things couldn't get any worse for him."

Office workers and department store clerks have suffered indignities too, but they seem to prefer to swallow them in silence.

Even today, when most of the degradation and human misery to which the packing house worker referred have gone out of industrial work, the man or woman who works in a factory has no real attachment to his particular job, unless he is quite highly skilled. To a factory worker, "it's a job," and he shrugs his shoulders when he says it to you. He's interested in what he gets from it in terms of money and other concrete benefits. He can transfer from job to job and feel no emotional loss. Thus, it's not surprising that the names of industrial unions—names like *United Automobile Workers, Amalgamated Clothing Workers*, or *United Steelworkers of America*—contain no reference to the hundreds of specific occupations and trades within the jurisdiction of these unions. Industrial workers invariably refer to their industry rather than their particular job when asked about their occupation.

Listen to a lawyer examining a jury panel:

"Mr. Jones," the lawyer says, "what is your occupation?"

"I work at Minneapolis-Moline," Mr. Jones answers.

"And what is your capacity there, Mr. Jones?"

"I'm a molder in the foundry."

The lawyer turns to a smartly dressed young woman in the second row. "Miss Smith," he says, "what is your occupation?"

"I'm a stenographer," she answers.

"Where are you employed?"

"In the Minnesota Mining and Manufacturing office."

Job-Hopping

The white collar worker thinks in terms of her skill, which she can carry with her from employer to employer. She didn't fall into her job haphazardly as the result of lining up before a personnel supervisor. She has some training, perhaps some talent, invested in it. She is likely to be just as concerned about what she contributes to the job as she is about how well the job pays.

I talked with a time-study man about joining an office union. His first objection was that he was concerned about his own integrity (he sets job standards for production workers). Beyond that, he felt that the union offered him no security that he didn't already have.

"I'm a *good* time-study man," he said. "I can go anywhere in this town and get just as good a salary or better than what I'm getting now."

Moving to another job, incidentally, is the way he and most other white collar workers solve their working problems. Their skill gives them a certain independence and enables them to talk to the boss person to person.

In turn, the clerk or secretary or accountant comes to think that his employer has a right to expect a certain standard of work from him. He asks himself how his demands for better pay or different working conditions will affect that standard. As one sociologist put it, the white collar worker is more *means* conscious while the blue collar worker is more *ends* conscious.

"Sure, I think we need a union in here, but I want to be fair to the company."

Unless he has had some pretty rough treatment from his employer, the average white collar worker with whom I have talked will begin the discussion with words like these: "I think unions have done a good job for some people, but . . ." Or, "I'm not against unions, now, but . . ."

It is these "buts" that loom large when the organizer is trying to get a majority vote for the union in a bargaining election.

There is a tendency among white collar workers to want to look at both sides of the argument about unions—the union's side *and* the company's side. Many of their complaints, moreover, about working conditions are focused against a particular supervisor rather than against a basic company policy. This makes it difficult for an organizer to find a common denominator which he can exploit in an organizing campaign.

Unions which have been successful in the field of white collar organization have encouraged this pride in skill. The *Guild Reporter*, official journal of the American Newspaper Guild, devotes almost as much space to discussion of professional standards and newsy items about members' promotions as it does to bread-and-butter issues. Membership in the Guild, Actors Equity, the musicians' and—in some cities—teachers' unions is considered to be evidence of professional standing.

However, the same "professional" approach cannot be used to appeal to office workers and department store clerks in a town-wide or industry-wide organizing drive. It doesn't work with an office staff which includes stenographers, file clerks, accountants, bookkeepers, dispatchers, receptionists, and a host of other occupational groups, each with its own notion of professional standards.

The American Dream

The Great American Dream still has a firmer hold on white collar workers than on blue collar workers. While a man working in a mine or factory is likely to accept his job as his ultimate lot in life, the white collar worker—except the young woman who thinks of her job as a transition between school and marriage—is likely to aspire to something above and beyond his present occupation. A union may interfere with the promotions of a young man on the make.

I have talked with white collar workers who hesitate to sign membership cards because they have been promised promotions by their employers. In many cases, these turn out to be just promises. However, there are enough examples of ambitious office workers rising to the top to put them in a dilemma about where their future lies. If the labor organizer tries to shatter this dream of upward mobility—as the sociologists call it—he finds himself in the position of apparently blocking a person's advancement, or of talking defeat.

Another problem for the organizer is the average white collar worker's misunderstanding of a union's seniority provisions. Literally dozens of times I have had to explain patiently that such a system does not mean that an incompetent with seniority gets an available promotion. To any honest union, the seniority system means that a *qualified* person with the most seniority gets first chance at an available promotion.

Frankly, however, I doubt if I have changed the feelings of one tenth of the white collar workers I have approached with this argument.

In thinking about personal goals, white collar workers are more inclined to follow the lead of professionals with whom they identify themselves than to respect a union organizer's logic. A teacher, who should have known better explained to me why she decided against joining the teachers' union in her community. "My brother's a chemist and he told me other professionals would look down their noses at me if I joined the union," she said.

White collar workers, in many instances, feel that the status they obtain from their jobs is worth the sacrifice in income. Once, when I explained to a $57-a-week secretary in a factory office that her income was substantially below that of a woman on a common labor rate in the plant, she shot back, "I don't care what they make in the plant. My job is ten times better. I wouldn't work in that plant if they paid me twice what she's making."

Labor leaders feel that white collar workers' attitudes toward union organization have been deliberately shaped by business and industrial leaders. AFL-CIO President George Meany told the union white collar conference:

"The white collar worker has been the victim of propaganda for many years. The boss has always said, 'Well, the union is not for you people. It is all right for the fellow who works in a factory or drives a truck, but a union is not for office workers. You people are above that sort of thing.'"

Actually, Mr. Meany gives management more credit than it deserves. The reasons for a white collar worker's resistance to unions are much deeper than an employer's pep talk. There is a difference in basic attitudes.

Before I went to work for a union I was a newspaper reporter who had covered his share of Rotary lunch speakers and Junior Chamber of Commerce rallies. The first time I went to a local union meeting I was astonished at the candor I found there. It is the same at most local union meetings, I have discovered. If a member thinks another member's motives are questionable, he stands up on the floor of the union hall and says so. There is no beating about the bush, no fear of offense, no hesitation about attacking the other man's integrity. Conflicts are settled right here and now.

The average union member has been largely uncontaminated by the etiquette of "human relations" that has become a way of life for many other groups in our society. Instead, he speaks his mind frankly—with his boss (if he has a strong union), with the officers of his union, with his fellow workers, and probably with the members of his family. There is no good reason why he shouldn't be candid. He earns his living at a job that requires no skill at "getting along" (is there any point to smiling at a lathe or a blast furnace?). Since his contribution to our economy is measured according to his production of things the rest of us can eat, drive, wear, and live in, he can be downright surly if he wants to and fear no reprisal.

Not so with the salesman who lives by the motto, "sell yourself," nor with most of the 26,000,000 persons in our economy who are "meeting the public" through their occupations in wholesale and retail trade, finance, insurance, real estate, government, and service. These are the job-holders who make up the big salesroom that C. Wright Mills wrote about in *White Collar*. David Riesman pointed out in *The Lonely Crowd* that the character of a society depends a good deal on the kind of work it does. So too with the individual. If a production worker were to become a salesman, his personality would change and so would his attitude toward unions and employers.

Thus, it is an oversimplification to say that a white collar worker's resistance to joining a union is a consequence of his being a "victim of propaganda for many years." On the contrary, as one organizer put it, "The white collar worker is just a different breed."

He Wants to Be Loved

Not only does the average office worker look to management for personal models and advancement—he is also often repelled, even frightened, by the idea of getting involved in union activities, chiefly strikes.

"I never saw a group of people so afraid of the idea of a strike," the same organizer said. "They keep asking me if they have to go out on strike if some auto plant across the country walks out. Their ignorance is really something. At first I laughed at some of the things they said, but then I began to realize that this was serious business with them. I leveled with them. I told them it was up to them whether or not they would ever have to strike. I explained how they would have to take a strike vote and all that. Well, finally they understood it, I think, but they sure didn't like the idea."

No one likes strikes. However, a factory worker's life is not so closely tied to a regular weekly income as the white collar worker's. When an Auto Workers representative was trying to explain the guaranteed annual wage to an audience of union members' wives, he asked the question, "How many of you women here can go into a store and buy something and tell the man that you'll be able to make a regular weekly payment for the next fifty-two weeks?" Not a single woman in the audience raised her hand. Certain periods of unemployment—whether through lay-offs or strikes— are an accepted part of a blue collar worker's life. However, to a white collar worker—who mortgages his regular paycheck months in advance and has to meet installments due on his house and refrigerator—a period of unemployment is catastrophic.

Catastrophe, crisis, and militancy are scare words to white collar workers. They want to be dignified, professional, and loved. They want to be promoted; they want to be secure; and they don't want to have to fight. . . .

PORTRAIT OF A STRIVER

John P. Marquand

Here in the colorful fiction of J. P. Marquand is a picture of a young man "trying to get ahead." The interpersonal relations and the private feelings of an upwardly mobile middle-class man are sharply portrayed—the tensions, the insecurities, the necessity to watch every step, and the satisfaction. Vividly illustrated is the importance, if one is to achieve social-financial success in this type of setting, of having many skills other than those required for the mere accurate and rapid performance of one's assigned work.

Shortly before the outbreak of the European war, Charles had begun taking the eight-thirty. This was a privilege that had raised him above the ruck of younger men and of shopworn older ones who had to take the eight-two. It indicated to everyone that his business life had finally permitted him a certain margin of leisure. It meant that he was no longer one of the salaried class who had to be at his desk at nine.

The eight-thirty train was designed for the executive aristocracy, and once Mr. Guthrie Mayhew, not one of the Mayhews who lived on South Street, not George Mayhew, but Guthrie Mayhew, who was president of the Hawthorn Hill Club and also president of Mayhew Brothers at 86 Broadway, had even spoken of getting an eight-thirty crowd together who would agree to occupy one of those club cars with wicker chairs and card tables and a porter, to be attached to the eight-thirty in the morning and again to the five-thirty in the afternoon.

✧   ✧   ✧   ✧   ✧

Charles remembered Mr. Mayhew's idea vividly, if only because it had come up at the same time that Mr. Burton had suggested that Charles call him Tony.

Charles could still recall the glow he had felt on this occasion and the sudden moment of elation. Mr. Burton had been shy about it in a very nice way, as an older man is sometimes shy. Charles remembered that Mr. Burton had fidgeted with his onyx pen stand and that first Mr. Burton had called him "feller." It had all happened one evening when they had stayed

SOURCE: *Point of No Return,* by John P. Marquand, by permission of Little, Brown & Company. Copyright 1947, 1948, 1949, by John P. Marquand. ✧ John P. Marquand (1893–1960) was a well-known American novelist. He also wrote detective stories, short stories and a play. Among his many works are *The Late George Apley* (awarded a Pulitzer prize, 1938), *So Little Time, Stopover Tokyo,* and *Thank You Mr. Moto.*

late talking over the Catlin estate, which was one of the largest accounts in the trust department.

"Now you may remember," Mr. Burton had said, "that Mrs. Burton and I took a little trip in 1933. You hadn't been with us long then, but I don't believe that you or anyone else will forget how tense things were in 1933, and now and then I found I was getting a little taut, so when things eased up I decided to go away somewhere to get a sense of perspective. That was when Mrs. Burton and I went to Bagdad. You ought to go there sometime."

The first morning he and Mrs. Burton had gone to the museum to see the treasure from Ur, parts of which looked like something in a case at Cartier's. You got a lot out of travel if you kept your eyes open. There had been a man in the museum, a queer sort of British archaeologist, who showed him some mud bricks that were actually parts of an account book. When you got used to them, you could see how they balanced their figures; and on one brick, believe it or not, there was even an error in addition, preserved there through the centuries. This had meant a great deal to Mr. Burton.

That clerical error in mud had given him an idea for one of the best speeches he had ever written, his speech before the American Bankers' Association in 1936 at the Waldorf-Astoria. Mr. Burton had opened a drawer and had pulled out a deckle-edged pamphlet.

"Take it home and read it if you have the time," he said, "I dashed it off rather hurriedly but it has a few ideas. It starts with that mistake in addition."

The pamphlet was entitled *The Ancient Art of Banking, by Anthony Burton, President, the Stuyvesant Bank, Delivered before the American Bankers' Association, May 1936.*

"Why, thanks very much, sir," Charles had said, "I certainly will read it." It was not the time to say that he had read the speech already or that for years he had made a point of reading all Mr. Burton's speeches.

"Look here, feller," Mr. Burton said, and he had blushed when he said "feller," "why not cut out this sir business? Why not just call me Tony?"

That was in 1941 but Charles still remembered his great joy and relief, with the relief uppermost, and that he could hardly wait to hear what Nancy would say.

"You know, Charles," Mr. Burton had continued, "Guthrie Mayhew and I have quite an idea. We're going to get hold of Tommy Mapes on the New Haven and see if he can't get us a special car on the eight-thirty. How about getting aboard? My idea is to call it the Crackerbarrel."

"Why, thanks," Charles had said. "I'd like to very much, Tony."

He had worked late that night and he could not remember what train he had taken home, but Nancy had been asleep when he got there.

"Nance," he said, "wake up. I've got something to tell you. Burton's asked me to call him Tony." And Nancy had sat bolt upright in her twin bed.

"Start at the beginning," Nancy had said. "Exactly how did it happen, and don't leave out anything."

They must have talked for a long while, there in the middle of the night. Nancy had known what it meant because she had worked downtown herself.

"Now wait," she had said. "Let's not get too excited. Who else calls him Tony?"

"I don't think anyone else does," Charles had told her, "except the officers, and old Jake when he speaks of him."

"Who's old Jake?" Nancy asked.

It surprised him that Nancy did not know, for she usually kept everything straight, but when he told her that old Jake was a day watchman in the vault who had been there when Mr. Burton had first started at the bank, Nancy had remembered.

"Darling, we ought to have a drink of something, shouldn't we?" she said, but it was pretty late for a drink. "Darling, I knew it would happen sometime. I'm pretty proud of you, Charley."

It was only a week later that they found out that Mr. Burton had also asked Roger Blakesley to call him Tony and they never could find out whom Mr. Burton had asked first.

❖   ❖   ❖   ❖   ❖

Though you seldom talked of salaries at the Stuyvesant, your social status was obvious from the position of your desk. Charles occupied one of the two flat mahogany desks that stood in a sort of no man's land between the roll-top desks of the officers and the smaller flat-tops of lesser executives and secretaries crowding the floor of the bank outside the cages. A green rug extended from the officers' desks, forming a neat and restricted zone that just included Charles's desk and the one beside it which was occupied by Roger Blakesley. Charles could see both their names, Mr. Blakesley and Mr. Gray, in silver letters, and he was pleased to see that he had got there first from the eight-thirty, a minute or two ahead of Roger and Mr. Burton and ahead of everyone else near the windows.

Mr. Burton's desk, which had the best light, was opened already and so was that of Mr. Stephen Merry, the oldest vice-president, and so were all the others except one. This was the desk of Arthur Slade, the youngest vice-president of the Stuyvesant, who had died in a plane accident when returning from the West Coast six months before. The closed desk still gave Charles a curious feeling of incompleteness and a mixed sense of personal gain and loss because he had been more friendly with Arthur Slade than with anyone else in the Stuyvesant—but then you had to die sometime. Once Arthur Slade had sat at Charles's own place but that was before Mr. Walter Harry, who had been president when Charles had first come to the bank, had died of an embolism and everyone had moved like players on bases—Burton to Harry, Merry to Burton, Slade to the vacant roll-top—and so on down to Charles himself. The Stuyvesant was decorously accustomed to accident and death and now it was moving time again and it was so plain where one of two persons might be moving next that it was embarrassing. Any observing depositor and certainly everyone employed in the bank, right up to the third floor, must have known that either Mr. Blakesley or Mr. Gray would move to Arthur Slade's desk by the window. Undoubtedly they were making side bets out in back as Charles used to himself when he had first come there from Boston. Undoubtedly the clerks and the secretaries and the watchmen had started some sort of pool.

✧   ✧   ✧   ✧   ✧

Tony Burton looked very fit, in spite of his white hair and his roll-top desk which both conspired to place him in another generation. For years Charles had accepted him as a model willingly, even though he realized that everyone else above a certain salary rating also used Tony Burton as a perfect sartorial example, and he was pretty sure that Tony himself was conscious of it. Charles never rebelled against this convention because Tony had everything one should expect to find in a president of a first-rate bank. It was amusing but not ridiculous to observe that all the minor executives in the Stuyvesant, as well as the more ambitious clerks, wore conservative double-breasted suits like Tony Burton's at the same time allowing undue rigidity to break out into pin stripes and herringbones, just like Tony Burton's. They all visited the barber once a week. They all had taken up golf, whether they liked it or not, and most of them wore the same square type of wrist watch and the same stainless steel strap. They had adopted Tony Burton's posture and his brisk, quick step and even the gently vibrant inflection of his voice. In fact once at one of those annual dinners for officers and junior executives when everyone said a few words and got off a few local jokes about the bank, Charles had brought the matter up when he had been called upon to speak. Speaking was always an unpleasant ordeal with which he had finally learned to cope successfully largely from imitating Tony. He remembered standing up and waiting for silence, just as Tony waited, with the same faint smile and the same deliberate gaze.

"I should like to drink a toast," he had said, "not to our president but to everyone who tries to look like him. When I walk, I always walk like Tony, because Tony knows just how to walk; and when I talk, I always talk like Tony, because Tony knows just how to talk; and when I dress,

I always dress like Tony, in a double-breasted suit. But no matter how I try, I cannot be like Tony. I can never make myself sufficiently astute."

It was the one time in the year, at that annual dinner, when you could let yourself go, within certain limits, and Tony Burton had loved it. He had stood up and waited for the laughter to die down and then he had spoken easily, with just the right pause and cadence. He had said that there were always little surprises at these dinners. He had never realized, for instance, that there could be a poet in the trust department, but poetry had its place. Poetry could teach lessons that transcended pedestrian prose.

"And I'm not too old to learn," Tony Burton had said, "and I'm humbly glad to learn. Sometimes on a starlit night I've wondered what my function was in the Stuyvesant. I'm very glad to know it is that of a clothing dummy. It's a patriotic duty. It's what they want us to be, in Washington."

That was back in 1941, but Tony Burton still had the same spring to his step, the same unlined, almost youthful face, and the same florid complexion; and he had the same three pictures on his desk, the first of Mrs. Burton in their garden, the second of their three girls standing in profile, like a flight of stairs, and the third of his sixty-foot schooner, the *Wanderlust* (the boat you were invited on once every summer), with Tony Burton in his yachting cap standing at the wheel. Time had marched on. All of the girls had come out and all were married, and the *Wanderlust* had been returned by the navy in deplorable condition, but Tony Burton had no superficial scars.

No matter how well Charles might know him, in that half-intimate, half-formal business relationship, he still had a slight feeling of diffidence and constraint. It was the same feeling that one had toward generals in wartime or perhaps toward anyone with power over one. There was always a vestige of a subservient desire to please and to be careful. You had to know how far to go, how long to laugh, and how to measure every speech.

Sycamore Park had been developed in 1938 on the forty-acre grounds of an old estate and the subdivision had been excellently managed by the local real estate firm of Merton and Pease. As Mr. Merton had said, it was a natural, and he had never understood why someone had not dreamed it up long ago—not too far from the shopping center and the trains, and yet in the neighborhood of other larger places. Every place had its own acre, and no house was to be constructed for a cost of less than thirty thousand dollars. It would have been wiser, perhaps, never to have gone there but to have bought a smaller place.

It would have been wiser, easier, and much safer. He had not at that time been moved up in the trust department and in 1939 all he had was twenty thousand dollars in savings, part of which was in paid-up life insurance. He could never analyze all the urges that made him lay everything on the line in order to live on a scale he could not immediately afford, discounting the possibilities of illness or accident and relying on possibilities of promotion. He only remembered having had an irrational idea that time was of the essence, that he would always stay on a certain business level if he did not take some sort of action, and Nancy too, had shared that feeling.

✧   ✧   ✧   ✧   ✧

Not since he had left Clyde had Charles ever felt as identified with any community as he had since he had been asked to join the Oak Knoll Country Club. They were in a brave new world involving all sorts of things, of which he had scarcely dreamed after they had moved to Sycamore Park. This cleavage between past and present, Charles realized, was a part of a chain reaction that started, of course, with one of those shake-ups in the bank. Charles had known that he had been doing well, He had known for a year or so, from the way Mr. Merry and Mr. Burton and particularly Mr. Slade had been giving him little jobs to do, that something was moving him out of the crowd of nonentities around him. He was aware also that Walter Gibbs in the trust department was growing restless. There had been a premonition of impending change, just like the present tension. One day Walter Gibbs had asked him out to lunch and had told him, confidentially, that he was going to move to the Bankers' Trust and that he was recommending Charles for his place. Charles was not surprised, because he had been a good assistant to Walter Gibbs, and he was glad to remember that he had been loyal to his chief, ever since the old days in the statistical department.

"Charley," Walter Gibbs had said, "a lot of people around here have been out to knife me. You could have and you never did, and I appreciate it, Charley."

He had known, of course, for some time that Walter Gibbs was not infallible, that he was fumbling more and more over his decisions and depending more and more on Charles's support, but Walter had taught him a lot.

"Slade keeps butting in," Walter had said, and then he went on to tell the old story which Charles had often heard of conflicting personalities and suspicions. Walter had felt that frankly he was more eligible for a vice-presidency than Slade, and the truth was he had never been the same after Arthur Slade had been selected. "If they don't like you enough to move you up," Walter had said, "it's time to get out, Charley."

God only knew where Walter Gibbs was now. He was gone like others with whom you worked closely once and from whom you were separated. Walter Gibbs was gone with his little jokes and his bifocal glasses and the stooping shoulders that had given him a deceptively sloppy appearance. He was gone with his personality that would never have permitted him to be a vice-president of anything.

Charles was ready, not surprised, when Tony Burton, though of course he did not call him Tony then, had called him downstairs and had asked him if he knew what was coming, that he had been with them for quite a while and that they had all had an eye on him ever since he had done that analysis on chain stores. Even if you were prepared for such a change there was still an unforgettable afterglow, and an illuminating sense of unrealized potentiality. It was a time to be more careful than ever, to measure the new balance of power, and not to antagonize the crowd that you were leaving. One day, it seemed to Charles, though of course it was not one day, he was living in a two-family house in Larchmont that smelled of cauliflower in the evenings, stumbling over the children's roller-skates and tricycles, taking the eight-three in the morning, keeping the budget on a salary of six thousand a year. Then in a day, though of course it was not a day, they were building at Sycamore Park. The children were going to the Country Day School. They were seeing their old friends, but not so often. Instead they were spending Sundays with Arthur Slade. There was a maid to do the work. He was earning eleven thousand instead of six, and he was an executive with a future. New people were coming to call; all sorts of men he had hardly known were calling him Charley. It was a great crowd in Sycamore Park and he was asked to join the Oak Knoll Country Club. They were a great crowd in Sycamore Park.

It would have made quite a story—if it could have been written down —how all those families had come to Sycamore Park. They had all risen from a ferment of unidentifiable individuals whom you might see in any office. They had all once been clerks or salesmen or assistants, digits of what was known as the white-collar class. They had come from different parts of the country and yet they all had the same intellectual reactions because they had all been through much the same sorts of adventures on their way to Sycamore Park. They all bore the same calluses from the competitive struggle, and it was still too early for most of them to look back on that struggle with complacency. They were all in the position of being insecurely poised in Sycamore Park—high enough above the average to have gained the envy of those below them, and yet not high enough so that those above them might not easily push them down. It was still necessary to balance and sometimes even to push a little in Sycamore Park, and there was always the possibility that something might go wrong—for example, in the recession that everyone was saying was due to crop up in the next six or eight months. It was consoling to think that they were no longer in the group that would catch it first, or they would not have been at Sycamore Park—but then they were not so far above it. They were not quite indispensable. Their own turn might come if the recession were too deep. Then no more Sycamore Park, and no more dreams of leaving it for something bigger—only memories of having been there once. It was something to think about as you went over your checkbook on clear, cold winter nights, but it was nothing ever to discuss. It was never wise or lucky to envisage failure. It was better to turn on the phonograph—and someday you would get one that would change the records automatically. It was better to get out the ice cubes and have some friends in and to talk broad-mindedly about the misfortunes of others. It was better to go to the club on Tuesday evenings and to talk about something else—and that was where Charles Gray was going.

✣ 40 ✣

THE CULTURE OF POVERTY

Oscar Lewis

The preceding selections examine the characteristics of those who are members of the middle and upper-middle strata of society. Because so many of us in the United States come from these strata and because middle class ways of living tend to set the standards for the whole society, it is easy for us to assume that these ways of living permeate all strata from top to bottom. Studies show, however, that even in our "affluent society" there are still countless millions who live meager lives, with no ties to the past, with no present resources, and with no hope for the future. In this selection Oscar Lewis shows that those in these bottom strata—people in poverty—are not simply persons who think and act like everyone else except that they don't happen to have as much money. In actuality, as Lewis demonstrates, their way of life is different, they live in a different culture—a "culture of poverty." Moreover, it is a world-wide phenomenon and, perhaps most significant from a social science point of view, it "has some universal characteristics which transcend regional, rural-urban, and even national differences." That is, among poverty-stricken people in a variety of national settings, in cities as different as "London, Glasgow, Paris, Harlem and Mexico City," there tend to develop remarkably similar traits of this culture of poverty.

SOURCE: Oscar Lewis, *Introduction to the Children of Sanchez.* © Copyright 1961 by Oscar Lewis. Reprinted by permission of Random House, Inc. ❖ The author is professor of anthropology at the University of Illinois. He has been a propaganda analyst for the U.S. Department of Justice and a consulting anthropologist for the Ford Foundation in India. His special interests include comparative analysis of peasant societies, cultural change, and applied anthropology. In addition to *The Children of Sanchez,* Dr. Lewis has written *Life in a Mexican Village: Tepoztlán Restudied,* and *Five Families: Mexican Case Studies in the Culture of Poverty.*

✧   ✧   ✧   ✧   ✧

It is the anthropologists, traditionally the spokesmen for primitive people in the remote corners of the world, who are increasingly turning their energies to the great peasant and urban masses of the less-developed countries. These masses are still desperately poor in spite of the social and economic progress of the world in the past century. Over a billion people in seventy-five nations of Asia, Africa, Latin America, and the Near East have an average per capita income of less than $200 a year as compared with over $2,000 a year for the United States. The anthropologist who studies the way of life in these countries has become, in effect, the student and spokesman of what I call the culture of poverty.

To those who think that the poor have no culture, the concept of a culture of poverty may seem like a contradiction in terms. It would also seem to give to poverty a certain dignity and status. This is not my intention. In anthropological usage the term culture implies, essentially, a design for living which is passed down from generation to generation. In applying this concept of culture to the understanding of poverty, I want to draw attention to the fact that poverty in modern nations is not only a state of economic deprivation, of disorganization, or of the absence of something. It is also something positive in the sense that it has a structure, a rationale, and defense mechanisms without which the poor could hardly carry on. In short, it is a way of life, remarkably stable and persistent, passed down from generation to generation along family lines. The culture of poverty has its own modalities and distinctive social and psychological consequences for its members. It is a dynamic factor which affects participation in the larger national culture and becomes a subculture of its own.

The culture of poverty, as here defined, does not include primitive peoples whose backwardness is the result of their isolation and undeveloped technology and whose society for the most part is not class stratified. Such peoples have a relatively integrated, satisfying, and self-sufficient culture. Nor is the culture of poverty synonymous with the working class, the proletariat, or the peasantry, all three of which vary a good deal in economic status throughout the world. In the United States, for example, the working class lives like an elite compared to the lower class of the less developed countries. The culture of poverty would apply only to those people who are at the very bottom of the socio-economic scale, the poorest workers, the poorest peasants, plantation laborers, and that large heterogeneous mass of small artisans and tradesmen usually referred to as the lumpen proletariat.

The culture or subculture of poverty comes into being in a variety of historical contexts. Most commonly it develops when a stratified social and economic system is breaking down or is being replaced by another, as in the case of the transition from feudalism to capitalism or during the industrial revolution. Sometimes it results from imperial conquest in which the conquered are maintained in a servile status which may continue for many generations. It can also occur in the process of detribalization such as is now going on in Africa where, for example, the tribal migrants to the cities are developing "courtyard cultures" remarkably similar to the Mexico City *vecindades*. We are prone to view such slum conditions as transitional or temporary phases of drastic culture change. But this is not necessarily the case, for the culture of poverty is often a persisting condition even in stable social systems. Certainly in Mexico it has been a more or less permanent phenomenon since the Spanish conquest of 1519, when the process of detribalization and the movement of peasants to the cities began. Only the size, location, and composition of the slums have been in flux. I suspect that similar processes have been going on in many other countries of the world.

It seems to me that the culture of poverty has some universal characteristics which transcend regional, rural-urban, and even national differences. In my book, *Five Families* (Basic Books, 1959), I suggested that there were remarkable similarities in family structure, interpersonal relations, time orientations, value systems, spending patterns, and the sense of community in lower-class settlements in London, Glasgow, Paris, Harlem, and Mexico City. Although this is not the place for an extensive comparative analysis of the culture of poverty, I should like to elaborate upon some of these and other traits in order to present a provisional conceptual model of this culture based mainly upon my Mexican materials.

In Mexico, the culture of poverty includes at least the lower third of the rural and urban population. This population is characterized by a relatively higher death rate, a lower life expectancy, a higher proportion of individuals in the younger age groups, and, because of child labor and working women, a higher proportion of gainfully employed. Some of these indices are higher in the poor *colonias* or sections of Mexico City than in rural Mexico as a whole.

The culture of poverty in Mexico is a provincial and locally oriented culture. Its members are only partially integrated into national institutions and are marginal people even when they live in the heart of a great city. In Mexico City, for example, most of the poor have a very low level of education and literacy, do not belong to labor unions, are not members of a political party, do not participate in the medical care, maternity, and old-age benefits of the national welfare agency known as *Seguro Social*, and make very little use of the city's banks, hospitals, department stores, museums, art galleries and airports.

The economic traits which are most characteristic of the culture of poverty include the constant struggle for survival, unemployment and underemployment, low wages, a miscellany of unskilled occupations, child labor, the absence of savings, a chronic shortage of cash, the absence of food reserves in the home, the pattern of frequent buying of small quantities of food many times a day as the need arises, the pawning of personal goods, borrowing from the local money lenders at usurious rates of interest, spontaneous informal credit devices (*tandas*) organized by neighbors, and the use of second-hand clothing and furniture.

Some of the social and psychological characteristics include living in crowded quarters, a lack of privacy, gregariousness, a high incidence of alcoholism, frequent resort to violence in the settlement of quarrels, frequent use of physical violence in the training of children, wife beating, early initiation into sex, free unions or consensual marriages, a relatively high incidence of the abandonment of mothers and children, a trend toward mother-centered families and a much greater knowledge of maternal relatives, the predominance of the nuclear family, a strong predisposition to authoritarianism, and a great emphasis upon family solidarity—an ideal only rarely achieved. Other traits include a strong present time orientation with relatively little ability to defer gratification and plan for the future, a sense of resignation and fatalism based upon the realities of their difficult life situation, a belief in male superiority which reaches its crystallization in *machismo* or the cult of masculinity, a corresponding martyr complex among women, and finally, a high tolerance for psychological pathology of all sorts.

Some of the above traits are not limited to the culture of poverty in Mexico but are also found in the middle and upper classes. However, it is the peculiar patterning of these traits which defines the culture of poverty. For example, in the middle class, *machismo* is expressed in terms of sexual exploits and the Don Juan complex whereas in the lower class it is expressed in terms of heroism and lack of physical fear. Similarly, drinking in the middle class is a social amenity whereas in the lower class getting drunk has different and multiple functions—to forget one's troubles, to prove one's ability to drink, and to build up sufficient confidence to meet difficult life situations.

Many of the traits of the subculture of poverty can be viewed as attempts at local solutions for problems not met by existing institutions and agencies because the people are not eligible for them, cannot afford them, or are suspicious of them. For example, unable to obtain credit from banks, they are thrown upon their own resources and organize informal credit devices without interest. Unable to afford doctors, who are used only in dire emergencies, and suspicious of hospitals "where one goes only to die," they rely upon herbs or other home remedies and upon local curers and midwives. Critical of priests "who are human and therefore sinners like all of us," they rarely go to confession or Mass and rely upon prayer to the images of saints in their own homes and upon pilgrimages to popular shrines.

A critical attitude toward some of the values and institutions of the dominant classes, hatred of the police, mistrust of government and those in high position, and a cynicism which extends even to the church gives the culture of poverty a counter quality and a potential for being used in political movements aimed against the existing social order. Finally, the sub-culture of poverty also has a residual quality in the sense that its members are attempting to utilize and integrate into a workable way of life the remnants of beliefs and customs of diverse origins.

❖ 41 ❖

THE OTHER AMERICA

Michael Harrington

Although Michael Harrington's book, The Other America, was published only recently, it has already become a classic of social commentary, a well-deserved recognition. For just as we were beginning to think of America as the first truly affluent society, Harrington awakened us to the fact that we have not yet created the economic component of a perfect society. His book has helped to make known to the complacent members of the middle class the plight of the lower one-third of the population, the faceless and voiceless American poor. His vivid descriptions have convinced many that a society can never maintain stability when large segments of that society fail to share in its economic benefits. By bringing these ideas out into the open, Harrington played a significant part in mobilizing public support for the "war on poverty."

❖   ❖   ❖   ❖   ❖

I

The millions who are poor in the United States tend to become increasingly invisible. Here is a great mass of people, yet it takes an effort of the intellect and will even to see them.

I discovered this personally in a curious way. After I wrote my first article on poverty in America, I had all the statistics down on paper. I had proved to my satisfaction that there were around 50,000,000 poor in this country. Yet, I realized I did not believe my own figures. The poor existed

SOURCE: Reprinted with permission of the Macmillan Co. from *The Other America*, by Michael Harrington. Copyright © Michael Harrington 1962. ❖ The author is a free-lance writer. He has been an editor of the *Catholic Worker* and has worked on various projects of the Fund for the Republic. He is a contributing editor to *Dissent* and has written numerous articles for *Commentary*, *Commonweal*, and *Partisan Review*. He is the co-editor of *Labor in a Free Society*.

in the Government reports; they were percentages and numbers in long, close columns, but they were not part of my experience. I could prove that the other America existed, but I had never been there.

My response was not accidental. It was typical of what is happening to an entire society, and it reflects profound social changes in this nation. The other America, the America of poverty, is hidden today in a way that it never was before. Its millions are socially invisible to the rest of us. No wonder that so many misinterpreted Galbraith's title and assumed that "the affluent society" meant that everyone had a decent standard of life. The misinterpretation was true as far as the actual day-to-day lives of two-thirds of the nation were concerned. Thus, one must begin a description of the other America by understanding why we do not see it.

There are perennial reasons that make the other America an invisible land.

Poverty is often off the beaten track. It always has been. The ordinary tourist never left the main highway, and today he rides interstate turnpikes. He does not go into the valleys of Pennsylvania where the towns look like the movie sets of Wales in the thirties. He does not see the company houses in rows, the rutted roads (the poor always have bad roads whether they live in the city, in towns, or on farms), and everything is black and dirty. And even if he were to pass through such a place by accident, the tourist would not meet the unemployed men in the bar or the women coming home from a runaway sweatshop.

❖   ❖   ❖   ❖   ❖

These are normal and obvious causes of the invisibility of the poor. They operated a generation ago; they will be functioning a generation hence. It is more important to understand that the very development of American society is creating a new kind of blindness about poverty. The poor are increasingly slipping out of the very experience and consciousness of the nation.

If the middle class never did like ugliness and poverty, it was at least aware of them. "Across the tracks" was not a very long way to go. There were forays into the slums at Christmas time; there were charitable organizations that brought contact with the poor. Occasionally, almost everyone passed through the Negro ghetto or the blocks of tenements, if only to get downtown to work or to entertainment.

Now the American city has been transformed. The poor still inhabit the miserable housing in the central area, but they are increasingly isolated from contact with, or sight of, anybody else. Middle-class women coming in from Suburbia on a rare trip may catch the merest glimpse of the other America on the way to an evening at the theater, but their children are segregated in suburban schools. The business or professional man may drive along the fringes of slums in a car or bus, but it is not an important experience to him. The failures, the unskilled, the disabled, the aged, and the minorities are right there, across the tracks, where they have always been. But hardly anyone else is.

In short, the very development of the American city has removed poverty from the living, emotional experience of millions upon millions of middle-class Americans. Living out in the suburbs, it is easy to assume that ours is, indeed, an affluent society.

This new segregation of poverty is compounded by a well-meaning ignorance. A good many concerned and sympathetic Americans are aware that there is much discussion of urban renewal. Suddenly, driving through the city, they notice that a familiar slum has been torn down and that there are towering, modern buildings where once there had been tenements or hovels. There is a warm feeling of satisfaction, of pride in the way things are working out: the poor, it is obvious, are being taken care of.

The irony in this is that the truth is nearly the exact opposite to the impression. The total impact of the various housing programs in postwar America has been to squeeze more and more people into existing slums. More often than not, the modern apartment in a towering building rents at $40 a room or more. For, during the past decade and a half, there has been more subsidization of middle- and upper-income housing than there has been of housing for the poor.

Clothes make the poor invisible too: America has the best-dressed poverty the world has ever known. For a variety of reasons, the benefits of mass production have been spread much more evenly in this area than in many others. It is much easier in the United States to be decently dressed than it is to be decently housed, fed, or doctored. Even people with terribly depressed incomes can look prosperous.

This is an extremely important factor in defining our emotional and existential ignorance of poverty. In Detroit the existence of social classes became much more difficult to discern the day the companies put lockers in the plants. From that moment on, one did not see men in work clothes on the way to the factory, but citizens in slacks and white shirts. This process has been magnified with the poor throughout the country. There are tens of thousands of Americans in the big cities who are wearing shoes, perhaps even a stylishly cut suit or dress, and yet are hungry. It is not a matter of planning, though it almost seems as if the affluent society had given out costumes to the poor so that they would not offend the rest of society with the sight of rags.

Then, many of the poor are the wrong age to be seen. A good number of them (over 8,000,000) are sixty-five years of age or better; an even larger number are under eighteen. The aged members of the other America are often sick, and they cannot move. Another group of them live out their lives in loneliness and frustration: they sit in rented rooms, or else they stay close to a house in a neighborhood that has completely changed from the old days. Indeed, one of the worst aspects of poverty among the aged is that these people are out of sight and out of mind, and alone.

❖   ❖   ❖   ❖   ❖

And finally, the poor are politically invisible. It is one of the cruelest ironies of social life in advanced countries that the dispossessed at the bottom of society are unable to speak for themselves. The people of the other America do not, by and large, belong to unions, to fraternal organizations, or to political parties. They are without lobbies of their own; they put forward no legislative program. As a group, they are atomized. They have no face; they have no voice.

Thus, there is not even a cynical political motive for caring about the poor, as in the old days. Because the slums are no longer centers of powerful political organizations, the politicians need not really care about their inhabitants. The slums are no longer visible to the middle class, so much of the idealistic urge to fight for those who need help is gone. Only the social agencies have a really direct involvement with the other America, and they are without any great political power.

❖   ❖   ❖   ❖   ❖

Forty to 50,000,000 people are becoming increasingly invisible. That is a shocking fact. But there is a second basic irony of poverty that is equally important: if one is to make the mistake of being born poor, he should choose a time when the majority of the people are miserable too.

J. K. Galbraith develops this idea in *The Affluent Society*, and in doing so defines the "newness" of the kind of poverty in contemporary America. The old poverty, Galbraith notes, was general. It was the condition of life of an entire society, or at least of that huge majority who were without special skills or the luck of birth. When the entire economy advanced, a good many of these people gained higher standards of living. Unlike the poor today, the majority poor of a generation ago were an immediate (if cynical) concern of political leaders. The old slums of the immigrants had the votes; they provided the basis for labor organizations; their very numbers could be a powerful force in political conflict. At the same time the new technology required higher skills, more education, and stimulated an upward movement for millions.

Perhaps the most dramatic case of the power of the majority poor took place in the 1930's. The Congress of Industrial Organizations literally organized millions in a matter of years. A labor movement that had been declining and confined to a thin stratum of the highly skilled suddenly embraced masses of men and women in basic industry. At the same time this acted as a pressure upon the Government, and the New Deal codified some of the social gains in laws like the Wagner Act. The result was not a basic transformation of the American system, but it did transform the lives of an entire section of the population.

❖   ❖   ❖   ❖   ❖

Out of the thirties came the welfare state. Its creation had been stimulated by mass impoverishment and misery, yet it helped the poor least of all. Laws like unemployment compensation, the Wagner Act, the various farm programs, all these were designed for the middle third in the cities, for the organized workers, and for the upper third in the country, for the big market farmers. If a man works in an extremely low-paying job, he may not even be covered by social security or other welfare programs. If he receives unemployment compensation, the payment is scaled down according to his low earnings.

One of the major laws that was designed to cover everyone, rich and poor, was social security. But even here the other Americans suffered discrimination. Over the years social security payments have not even provided a subsistence level of life. The middle third have been able to supplement the Federal pension through private plans negotiated by unions, through joining medical insurance schemes like Blue Cross, and so on. The poor have not been able to do so. They lead a bitter life, and then have to pay for that fact in old age.

Indeed, the paradox that the welfare state benefits those least who need help most is but a single instance of a persistent irony in the other America. Even when the money finally trickles down, even when a school is built in a poor neighborhood, for instance, the poor are still deprived. Their entire environment, their life, their values, do not prepare them to take advantage of the new opportunity. The parents are anxious for the children to go to work; the pupils are pent up, waiting for the moment when their education has complied with the law.

Today's poor, in short, missed the political and social gains of the thirties. They are, as Galbraith rightly points out, the first minority poor in history, the first poor not to be seen, the first poor whom the politicians could leave alone.

The first step toward the new poverty was taken when millions of people proved immune to progress. When that happened, the failure was not individual and personal, but a social product. But once the historic accident takes place, it begins to become a personal fate.

The new poor of the other America saw the rest of society move ahead. They went on living in depressed areas, and often they tended to become depressed human beings. In some of the West Virginia towns, for instance, an entire community will become shabby and defeated. The young and the adventurous go to the city, leaving behind those who cannot move and those who lack the will to do so. The entire area becomes permeated with failure, and that is one more reason the big corporations shy away.

Indeed, one of the most important things about the new poverty is that it cannot be defined in simple, statistical terms. . . . If a group has internal vitality, a will—if it has aspiration—it may live in dilapidated housing, it may eat an inadequate diet, and it may suffer poverty, but it is not impoverished. So it was in those ethnic slums of the immigrants that played such a dramatic role in the unfolding of the American dream. The people found themselves in slums, but they were not slum dwellers.

But the new poverty is constructed so as to destroy aspiration; it is a system designed to be impervious to hope. The other America does not contain the adventurous seeking a new life and land. It is populated by the failures, by those driven from the land and bewildered by the city, by old people suddenly confronted with the torments of loneliness and poverty, and by minorities facing a wall of prejudice.

In the past, when poverty was general in the unskilled and semi-skilled work force, the poor were all mixed together. The bright and the dull, those who were going to escape into the great society and those who were to stay behind, all of them lived on the same street. When the middle third rose, this community was destroyed. And the entire invisible land of the other Americans became a ghetto, a modern poor farm for the rejects of society and of the economy.

It is a blow to reform and the political hopes of the poor that the middle class no longer understands that poverty exists. But, perhaps more important, the poor are losing their links with the great world. . . . They are no longer participants in an ethnic culture from the old country; they are less and less religious; they do not belong to unions or clubs. They are not seen, and because of that they themselves cannot see. Their horizon has become more and more restricted; they see one another, and that means they see little reason to hope.

❖   ❖   ❖   ❖   ❖

II

There are mighty historical and economic forces that keep the poor down; and there are human beings who help out in this grim business, many of them unwittingly. There are sociological and political reasons why poverty is not seen; and there are misconceptions and prejudices that literally blind the eyes. The latter must be understood if anyone is to make the necessary act of intellect and will so that the poor can be noticed.

Here is the most familiar version of social blindness: "The poor are that way because they are afraid of work. And anyway they all have big cars. If they were like me (or my father or my grandfather), they could pay their own way. But they prefer to live on the dole and cheat the taxpayers."

This theory, usually thought of as a virtuous and moral statement, is one of the means of making it impossible for the poor ever to pay their way. There are, one must assume, citizens of the other America who choose impoverishment out of fear of work (though, writing it down, I really do not believe it). But the real explanation of why the poor are where they are is that they made the mistake of being born to the wrong parents, in the wrong section of the country, in the wrong industry, or in the wrong racial or ethnic group. Once that mistake has been made, they could have been paragons of will and morality, but most of them would never even have had a chance to get out of the other America.

There are two important ways of saying this: The poor are caught in a vicious circle; or, The poor live in a culture of poverty.

In a sense, one might define the contemporary poor in the United States as those who, for reasons beyond their control, cannot help themselves. All the most decisive factors making for opportunity and advance are against them. They are born going downward, and most of them stay down. They are victims whose lives are endlessly blown round and round the other America.

Here is one of the most familiar forms of the vicious circle of poverty. The poor get sick more than anyone else in the society. That is because they live in slums, jammed together under unhygienic conditions; they have inadequate diets, and cannot get decent medical care. When they become sick, they are sick longer than any other group in the society. Because they are sick more often and longer than anyone else, they lose wages and work, and find it difficult to hold a steady job. And because of this, they cannot pay for good housing, for a nutritious diet, for doctors. At any given point in the circle, particularly when there is a major illness, their prospect is to move to an even lower level and to begin the cycle, round and round, toward even more suffering.

This is only one example of the vicious circle. Each group in the other America has its own particular version of the experience . . . . But the pattern, whatever its variations, is basic to the other America.

The individual cannot usually break out of this vicious circle. Neither can the group, for it lacks the social energy and political strength to turn its misery into a cause. Only the larger society, with its help and resources, can really make it possible for these people to help themselves. Yet those who could make the difference too often refuse to act because of their ignorant, smug moralisms. They view the effects of poverty—above all, the warping of the will and spirit that is a consequence of being poor—as choices. Understanding the vicious circle is an important step in breaking down this prejudice.

There is an even richer way of describing this same, general idea: Poverty in the United States is a culture, an institution, a way of life.

There is a famous anecdote about Ernest Hemingway and F. Scott Fitzgerald. Fitzgerald is reported to have remarked to Hemingway, "The rich are different." And Hemingway replied, "Yes, they have money." Fitzgerald had much the better of the exchange. He understood that being rich was not a simple fact, like a large bank account, but a way of looking at reality, a series of attitudes, a special type of life. If this is true of the rich, it is ten times truer of the poor. Everything about them, from the condition of their teeth to the way in which they love, is suffused and permeated by the fact of their poverty. And this is sometimes a hard idea for a Hemingway-like middle-class America to comprehend.

The family structure of the poor, for instance, is different from that of the rest of the society. There are more homes without a father, there is less marriage, more early pregnancy and, if Kinsey's statistical findings can be used, markedly different attitudes toward sex. As a result of this, to take but one consequence of the fact, hundreds of thousands, and perhaps millions, of children in the other America never know stability and "normal" affection.

Or perhaps the policeman is an even better example. For the middle class, the police protect property, give directions, and help old ladies. For the urban poor, the police are those who arrest you. In almost any slum there is a vast conspiracy against the forces of law and order. If someone approaches asking for a person, no one there will have heard of him, even if he lives next door. The outsider is "cop," bill collector, investigator (and, in the Negro ghetto, most dramatically, he is "the Man").

✣ 42 ✣

THE WHITE MAN'S THEORY OF
COLOR CASTE

Gunnar Myrdal

Americans tend to pride themselves on the conviction that this country permits social and economic advancement by able and energetic persons. A society which provides for such mobility is said to have an "open-class" system: one in which persons may move freely up, or down, within the socioeconomic hierarchy. At the other extreme is a "closed-class," or "caste," system. The essence of the caste system is that a person's status is completely determined by biological inheritance, or family identification, and that he is prevented from crossing caste lines through marriage. In his famous study of the Negro in America, Myrdal shows that some aspects of caste are characteristic of our society, despite popular beliefs to the contrary. In this excerpt, based on data collected about 1940,

SOURCE: Gunnar Myrdal, *An American Dilemma*, pp. 57–67. Copyright 1944 by Harper & Brothers. Reprinted by permission of Harper & Row, Publishers. ✧ The author is professor of international economy at the University of Stockholm, Sweden, and a former member of the Swedish senate. He was executive secretary of the United Nations Economic Commission in Europe from 1947 to 1957. Prior to that, from 1938 to 1942, he had studied the American Negro for the Carnegie Corporation of New York, which resulted in *An American Dilemma*. Among his other books are *Population: A Problem for Democracy, Economic Theory and Under-Developed Regions*, and *Challenge to Affluence*.

Myrdal presents the white man's attitudes concerning anti-amalgamation—attitudes which have helped to maintain separate Negro and white social systems in America.

Every widening of the writer's experience of white Americans has only driven home to him more strongly that the opinion that the Negro is unassimilable, or, rather, that his amalgamation into the American nation is undesirable, is held more commonly, absolutely, and intensely than would be assumed from a general knowledge of American thought-ways. Except for a handful of rational intellectual liberals—who also, in many cases, add to their acceptance in principle of amalgamation an admission that they personally feel an irrational emotional inhibition against it— it is a rare case to meet a white American who will confess that, if it were not for public opinion and social sanctions not removable by private choice, he would have no strong objection to intermarriage.

The intensity of the attitude seems to be markedly stronger in the South than in the North. Its strength seems generally to be inversely related to the economic and social status of the informant and his educational level. It is usually strong even in most of the non-colored minority groups, if they are above the lowest plane of indifference. To the poor and socially insecure, but struggling, white individual, a fixed opinion on this point seems an important matter of prestige and distinction.

But even a liberal-minded Northerner of cosmopolitan culture and with a minimum of conventional blinds will, in nine cases out of ten, express a definite feeling against amalgamation. He will not be willing usually to hinder intermarriage by law. Individual liberty is to him a higher principle and, what is more important, he actually invokes it. But he will regret the exceptional cases that occur. He may sometimes hold a philosophical view that in centuries to come amalgamation is bound to happen and might become the solution. But he will be inclined to look on it as an inevitable deterioration.[1]

This attitude of refusing to consider amalgamation—felt and expressed in the entire country—constitutes the center in the complex of attitudes which can be described as the "common denominator" in the

---

[1] The response is likely to be anything but pleasant if one jestingly argues that possibly a small fraction of Negro blood in the American people, if it were blended well with all the other good stuff brought over to the new continent, might create a race of unsurpassed excellence: a people with just a little sunburn without extra trouble and even through the winter; with some curl in the hair without the cost of a permanent wave; with, perhaps, a little more emotional warmth in their souls; and a little more religion, music, laughter, and carefreeness in their lives. Amalgamation is, to the ordinary American, not a proper subject for jokes at all, unless it can be pulled down to the level of dirty stories, where, however, it enjoys a favored place. Referred to society as a whole and viewed as a principle, the anti-amalgamation maxim is held holy; it is a consecrated taboo. The maxim might, indeed, be a remnant of something really in the "mores." It is kept unproblematic, which is certainly not the case with all the rest of etiquette and segregation and discrimination patterns, for which this quality is sometimes erroneously claimed.

problem. It defines the Negro group in contradistinction to all the non-colored minority groups in America and all other lower class groups. The boundary between Negro and white is not simply a class line which can be successfully crossed by education, integration into the national culture, and individual economic advancement. The boundary is fixed. It is not a temporary expediency during an apprenticeship in the national culture. It is a bar erected with the intention of permanency. It is directed against the whole group. Actually, however, "passing" as a white person is possible when a Negro is white enough to conceal his Negro heritage. But the difference between "passing" and ordinary social climbing reveals the distinction between a class line, in the ordinary sense, and a caste line.

This brings us to the point where we shall attempt to sketch, only in an abstract and preliminary form, the social mechanism by which the anti-amalgamation maxim determines race relations. This mechanism is perceived by nearly everybody in America, but most clearly in the South. Almost unanimously white Americans have communicated to the author the following logic of the caste situation which we shall call the "*white man's theory of color caste.*"

1. The concern for "race purity" is basic in the whole issue; the primary and essential command is to prevent amalgamation; the whites are determined to utilize every means to this end.
2. Rejection of "social equality" is to be understood as a precaution to hinder miscegenation and particularly intermarriage.
3. The danger of miscegenation is so tremendous that the segregation and discrimination inherent in the refusal of "social equality" must be extended to nearly all spheres of life. There must be segregation and discrimination in recreation, in religious service, in education, before the law, in politics, in housing, in stores and in breadwinning.

This popular theory of the American caste mechanism is, of course, open to criticism. It can be criticized from a valuational point of view by maintaining that hindering miscegenation is not a worthwhile end, or that as an end it is not sufficiently worthwhile to counterbalance the sufferings inflicted upon the suppressed caste and the general depression of productive efficiency, standards of living and human culture in the American society at large—costs appreciated by all parties concerned. This criticism does not, however, endanger the theory which assumes that white people actually are following another valuation of means and ends and are prepared to pay the costs for attaining the ends. A second criticism would point out that, assuming the desirability of the end, this end could be reached without the complicated and, in all respects, socially expensive caste apparatus now employed. This criticism, however adequate though it be on the practical or political plane of discussion, does not disprove that people believe otherwise, and that the popular theory is a true representation of their beliefs and actions.

To undermine the popular theory of the caste mechanism, as based on the anti-amalgamation maxim, it would, of course, be necessary to prove that people really are influenced by other motives than the ones pronounced. Much material has, as we shall find, been brought together indicating that, among other things, competitive economic interests, which do not figure at all in the popular rationalization referred to, play a decisive role. The announced concern about racial purity is, when this economic motive is taken into account, no longer awarded the exclusive role as the *basic* cause in the psychology of the race problem.

Though the popular theory of color caste turns out to be a rationalization, this does not destroy it. For among the forces in the minds of the white people are certainly not only economic interests (if these were the only ones, the popular theory would be utterly demolished), but also sexual urges, inhibitions, and jealousies, and social fears and cravings for prestige and security. When they come under the scrutiny of scientific research, both the sexual and the social complexes take on unexpected designs. We shall then also get a clue to understanding the remarkable tendency of this presumably biological doctrine, that it refers only to legal marriage and to relations between Negro men and white women, but not to extra-marital sex relations between white men and Negro women.

However these sexual and social complexes might turn out when analyzed, they will reveal the psychological nature of the anti-amalgamation doctrine and show its "meaning." They will also explain the compressed emotion attached to the Negro problem. It is inherent in our type of modern Western civilization that sex and social status are for most individuals the danger points, the directions whence he fears the sinister onslaughts on his personal security. These two factors are more likely than anything else to push a life problem deep down into the subconscious and load it with emotions. There is some probability that in America both complexes are particularly laden with emotions. The American puritan tradition gives everything connected with sex a higher emotional charge. The roads for social climbing have been kept more open in America than perhaps anywhere else in the world, but in this upward struggle the competition for social status has also become more absorbing. In a manner and to a degree most uncomfortable for the Negro people in America, both the sexual and the social complexes have become related to the Negro problem.

These complexes are most of the time kept concealed. In occasional groups of persons and situations they break into the open. Even when not consciously perceived or expressed, they ordinarily determine interracial behavior on the white side.

❖   ❖   ❖   ❖   ❖

It has . . . always been a primary requirement upon every Negro leader—who aspires to get any hearing at all from the white majority group, and who does not want to appear dangerously radical to the Negro group and at the same time hurt the "race pride" it has built up as a defense—that he shall explicitly condone the anti-amalgamation maxim, which is the keystone in the white man's structure of race prejudice, and forbear to express any desire on the part of the Negro people to aspire to intermarriage with the whites. The request for intermarriage is easy for the Negro leader to give up. Intermarriage cannot possibly be a practical object of Negro public policy. Independent of the Negroes' wishes, the opportunity for intermarriage is not favorable as long as the great majority of the white population dislikes the very idea. As a defense reaction a strong attitude against intermarriage has developed in the Negro people itself. And the Negro people have no interest in defending the exploitative illicit relations between white men and Negro women. This race mingling is, on the contrary, commonly felt among Negroes to be disgraceful. And it often arouses the jealousy of Negro men.

The required soothing gesture toward the anti-amalgamation doctrine is, therefore, readily delivered. It is iterated at every convenient opportunity and belongs to the established routine of Negro leadership. For example, Robert R. Moton writes:

> As for amalgamation, very few expect it; still fewer want it; no one advocates it; and only a constantly diminishing minority practise it, and that surreptitiously. It is generally accepted on both sides of the colour line that it is best for the two races to remain ethnologically distinct.

There seems thus to be unanimity among Negro leaders on the point deemed crucial by white Americans. If we attend carefully, we shall, however, detect some important differences in formulation. The Negro spokesman will never, to begin with, accept the common white premise of racial inferiority of the Negro stock. To quote Moton again:

> . . . even in the matter of the mingling of racial strains, however undesirable it might seem to be from a social point of view, he [the Negro] would never admit that his blood carries any taint of physiological, mental, or spiritual inferiority.

A doctrine of equal natural endowments—a doctrine contrary to the white man's assumption of Negro inferiority, which is at the basis of the anti-amalgamation theory—has been consistently upheld. If a Negro leader publicly even hinted at the possibility of inherent racial inferiority, he would immediately lose his following. The entire Negro press watches the Negro leaders on this point.

Even Booker T. Washington, the supreme diplomat of the Negro people through a generation filled with severe trials, who was able by studied unobtrusiveness to wring so many favors from the white majority, never dared to allude to such a possibility, though he sometimes criticized most severely his own people for lack of thrift, skill, perseverance and general culture. In fact, there is no reason to think that he did not firmly believe in the fundamental equality of inherent capacities. Privately, local

Negro leaders might find it advisable to admit Negro inferiority and, particularly earlier, many individual Negroes might have shared the white man's view. But it will not be expressed by national leaders and, in fact, never when they are under public scrutiny. An emphatic assertion of equal endowments is article number one in the growing Negro "race pride."

Another deviation of the Negro faith in the anti-amalgamation doctrine is the stress that they, for natural reasons, lay on condemning exploitative illicit amalgamation. They turn the tables and accuse white men of debasing Negro womanhood, and the entire white culture for not rising up against this practice as their expressed antagonism against miscegenation should demand. Here they have a strong point, and they know how to press it.

A third qualification in the Negro's acceptance of the anti-amalgamation doctrine, expressed not only by the more "radical" and outspoken Negro leaders, is the assertion that intermarriage should not be barred by law. The respect for individual liberty is invoked as an argument. But, in addition, it is pointed out that this barrier, by releasing the white man from the consequences of intimacy with a Negro woman, actually has the effect of inducing such intimacy and thus tends to increase miscegenation. Moton makes this point:

> The Negro woman suffers not only from the handicap of economic and social discriminations imposed upon the race as a whole, but is in addition the victim of unfavourable legislation incorporated in the marriage laws of twenty-nine states, which forbid the intermarriage of black and white. The disadvantage of these statutes lies, not as is generally represented, in the legal obstacle they present to social equality, but rather in the fact that such laws specifically deny to the Negro woman and her offspring that safeguard from abuse and exploitation with which the women of the white race are abundantly surrounded. On the other side, the effect of such legislation leaves the white man, who is so inclined, free of any responsibility attending his amatory excursions across the colour line and leaves the coloured woman without redress for any of the consequences of her defencelessness; whereas white women have every protection, from fine and imprisonment under the law to enforced marriage and lynching outside the law.

But even with all these qualifications, the anti-amalgamation doctrine, the necessity of assenting to which is understood by nearly everybody, obviously encounters some difficulties in the minds of intellectual Negroes. They can hardly be expected to accept it as a just rule of conduct. They tend to accept it merely as a temporary expedient necessitated by human weakness. Kelly Miller thus wrote:

> . . . you would hardly expect the Negro, in derogation of his common human qualities, to proclaim that he is so diverse from God's other human creatures as to make the blending of the races contrary to the law of nature. The Negro refuses to become excited or share in your frenzy on this subject. The amalgamation of the races is an ultimate possibility, though not an immediate probability. But what have you and I to do with ultimate questions, anyway?

And a few years later, he said:

> It must be taken for granted in the final outcome of things that the colour line will be wholly obliterated. While blood may be thicker than water, it does not possess the spissitude or inherency of everlasting principle. The brotherhood of man is more fundamental than the fellowship of race. A physical and spiritual identity of all peoples occupying common territory is a logical necessity of thought. The clear seeing mind refuses to yield or give its assent to any other ultimate conclusion. This consummation, however, is far too removed from the sphere of present probability to have decisive influence upon practical procedure.

This problem is, of course, tied up with the freedom of the individual. "Theoretically Negroes would all subscribe to the right of freedom of choice in marriage even between the two races," wrote Moton. And Du Bois formulates it in stronger terms:

> . . . a woman may say, I do not want to marry this black man, or this red man, or this white man. . . . But the impudent and vicious demand that all colored folk shall write themselves down as brutes by a general assertation of their unfitness to marry other decent folk is a nightmare.

Negroes have always pointed out that the white man must not be very certain of his woman's lack of interest when he rises to such frenzy on behalf of the danger to her and feels compelled to build up such formidable fences to prevent her from marrying a Negro.

With these reservations both Negro leadership and the Negro masses acquiesce in the white anti-amalgamation doctrine. This attitude is noted with satisfaction in the white camp. The writer has observed, however, that the average white man, particularly in the South, does not feel quite convinced of the Negro's acquiescence. In several conversations, the same white person, in the same breath, has assured me, on the one hand, that the Negroes are perfectly satisfied in their position and would not like to be treated as equals, and on the other hand, that the only thing these Negroes long for is to be like white people and to marry their daughters.

Whereas the Negro spokesman finds it possible to assent to the first rank of discrimination, namely, that involving miscegenation, it is more difficult for him to give his approval to the second rank of discrimination, namely, that involving "etiquette" and consisting in the white man's refusal to extend the ordinary courtesies to Negroes in daily life and his expectation of receiving certain symbolic signs of submissiveness from the Negro. The Negro leader could not do so without serious risk of censorship by his own people and rebuke by the Negro press. In all articulate groups of Negroes there is a demand to have white men call them by their titles of Mr., Mrs., and Miss; to have white men take off their hats on entering a Negro's house; to be able to enter a white man's house through the front door rather than the back door, and so on. But on the whole, and in spite of the rule that they stand up for "social equality" in this sense, most Negroes in the South obey the white man's rules.

Booker T. Washington went a long way, it is true, in his Atlanta speech in 1895 where he explained that: "In all things that are purely social we [the two races] can be as separate as the fingers, yet one as the hand in all things essential to mutual progress." He there seemed to condone not only these rules of "etiquette" but also the denial of "social equality" in a broader sense, including some of the further categories in the white man's rank order of discrimination. He himself was always most eager to observe the rules. But Washington was bitterly rebuked for this capitulation, particularly by Negroes in the North. And a long time has passed since then; the whole spirit in the Negro world has changed considerably in three decades.

The modern Negro leader will try to solve this dilemma by iterating that no Negroes want to intrude upon white people's private lives. But this is not what Southern white opinion asks for. It is not satisfied with the natural rules of polite conduct that no individual, of whatever race, shall push his presence on a society where he is not wanted. It asks for a general order according to which *all* Negroes are placed under *all* white people and excluded from not only the white man's society but also from the ordinary symbols of respect. No Negro shall ever aspire to them, and no white shall be allowed to offer them.

Thus, on this second rank of discrimination there is a wide gap between the ideologies of the two groups. As we then continue downward in our rank order and arrive at the ordinary Jim Crow practices, the segregation in schools, the disfranchisement, and the discrimination in employment, we find, on the one hand, that increasingly larger groups of white people are prepared to take a stand against these discriminations. Many a liberal white professor in the South who, for his own welfare, would not dare to entertain a Negro in his home and perhaps not even speak to him in a friendly manner on the street, will be found prepared publicly to condemn disfranchisement, lynching, and the forcing of the Negro out of employment. Also, on the other hand, Negro spokesmen are becoming increasingly firm in their opposition to discrimination on these lower levels. It is principally on these lower levels of the white man's rank order of discrimination that the race struggle goes on. The struggle will widen to embrace all the thousand problems of education, politics, economic standards, and so forth, and the frontier will shift from day to day according to varying events.

Even a superficial view of discrimination in America will reveal to the observer: first, that there are great differences, not only between larger regions, but between neighboring communities; and, second, that even in the same community, changes occur from one time to another. There is also, contrary to the rule that all Negroes are to be treated alike, a certain amount of discretion depending upon the class and social status of the

Negro in question. A white person, especially if he has high status in the community, is, furthermore, supposed to be free, within limits, to overstep the rules. The rules are primarily to govern the Negro's behavior.

Some of these differences and changes can be explained. But the need for their interpretation is perhaps less than has sometimes been assumed. The variations in discrimination between local communities or from one time to another are often not of primary consequence. All of these thousand and one precepts, etiquettes, taboos, and disabilities inflicted upon the Negro have a common purpose: to express the subordinate status of the Negro people and the exalted position of the whites. They have their meaning and chief function as symbols. As symbols they are, however, interchangeable to an extent: one can serve in place of another without causing material difference in the essential social relations in the community.

The differences in patterns of discrimination between the larger regions of the country and the temporal changes of patterns within one region, which reveal a definite trend, have, on the contrary, more material import. These differences and changes imply, in fact, a considerable margin of variation within the very notion of American caste, which is not true of all the other minor differences between the changes in localities within a single region—hence the reason for a clear distinction. For exemplification it may suffice here to refer only to the differentials in space. As one moves from the Deep South through the Upper South and the Border states to the North, the manifestations of discrimination decrease in extent and intensity; at the same time the rules become more uncertain and capricious. The "color line" becomes a broad ribbon of arbitrariness. The old New England states stand, on the whole, as the antipode to the Deep South. This generalization requires important qualifications, and the relations are in process of change.

The decreasing discrimination as we go from South to North in the United States is apparently related to a weaker basic prejudice. In the North the Negroes have fair justice and are not disfranchised; they are not Jim-Crowed in public means of conveyance; educational institutions are less segregated. The interesting thing is that the decrease of discrimination does *not* regularly follow the white man's rank order. Thus intermarriage, placed on the top of the rank order, is legally permitted in all but one of the Northern states east of the Mississippi. The racial etiquette, being the most conspicuous element in the second rank, is, practically speaking, absent from the North. On the other hand, employment discriminations, placed at the bottom of the rank order, at times are equally severe, or more so, in some Northern communities than in the South, even if it is true that Negroes have been able to press themselves into many more new avenues of employment during the last generation in the North than in the South.

There is plenty of discrimination in the North. But it is—or rather its rationalization is—kept hidden. We can, in the North, witness the legislators' obedience to the American Creed when they solemnly pass laws and regulations to condemn and punish such acts of discrimination which, as a matter of routine, are committed daily by the great majority of the white citizens and by the legislators themselves. In the North, as indeed often in the South, public speakers frequently pronounce principles of human and civic equality. We see here revealed in relief the Negro problem as an American Dilemma.

❖ 43 ❖

THE NEGRO'S MIDDLE-CLASS DREAM

C. Eric Lincoln

This selection complements the previous one by describing the middle-class society that has developed among American Negroes as a result of color-caste barriers. Although some "passing" into white society occurs among light skinned Negroes, the author indicates here that "lightness" is no longer a primary status factor in the Negro class system. The same desires for status, respectability, and economic security motivate Negroes as whites, but the symbols and behavior which characterize the Negro middle class are in some respects unique. It is these unique features that are dealt with here.

A famous professor at a large university used to begin one of his lectures in social psychology with a description of the characteristics of a typical American family. After he had described the family's income, address, religion, the kind of car they drove, organizations to which they belonged and the occupation of the father, he would then demand to know what social class the family belonged to. But before the students could answer, the professor would add as an apparent afterthought: "Oh, yes, I forgot to mention that this is a *Negro* family!" Inevitably, the students were stymied. What had begun as a simple problem became insolubly complex by the addition of the word "Negro."

Where do Negroes fit into the prevailing American class structure? Most sociologists say they don't. Negroes have a *parallel* social structure, somewhat—but not entirely—analogous to that of whites. This social

SOURCE: *The New York Times Magazine*, October 25, 1964. © 1965 by The New York Times Company. Reprinted by permission. ❖ C. Eric Lincoln is professor of sociology at Clark College, Atlanta. He is the author of *My Face Is Black*.

parallelism, or two-caste society, is created by the color barrier which, with the rarest exceptions, prevents lateral movement from class to class between Negroes and whites. As a prominent Negro matron said in Detroit, "We Negroes and whites visit each other at times, and frequently we belong to the same civic organizations and attend the same functions, but the lines are there, and no one has to say where they are."

The Negro class structure had its roots in the institution of American slavery, which, in ignoring the African's cultural presumptions, leveled all classes, and force-fused highly disparate individuals and groups into one conglomerate mass—"the Negro slave," or simply, "the Negro," a word which, in America, became synonymous with "slave" or the "descendant of slaves." Prince and servant, Eboe and Mandingo, Moslem and spirit-worshipper were all the same to the slave master, who saw them only as commodities to be bought and sold, or as a labor supply for his vast plantations.

Whatever the basis of past distinctions, the Negro social structure in America had to evolve out of conditions connected with plantation life, and within a context which recognized the absolute superiority of the white slave owner (although not necessarily that of the small, non-slave-holding white farmers, who supplied the "overseer" class, and who were looked upon by house servants and slave owners alike as "poor white trash").

The Negro's "society," then, had four more or less distinct social classes. In ascending order, they were: (1) field hands (who had least contact with the socializing influences of the white environment); (2) mechanics and artisans (bricklayers, carpenters, iron workers, bakers, etc., who were frequently hired by the month or the year to merchants or builders in the cities); (3) valets, butlers, maids, cooks and other household servants (whose frequent personal contact with whites made them the most "acculturated" class); and (4) free Negroes (who had bought their freedom or had become free by manumission—often because of faithfulness or some heroic exploit).

As slaves, the house-servant class had by far the highest proportion of mulattoes. While this did not by any means exempt them from the normal rigors incident to being slaves, including sale, the light-skinned mistresses of the slave masters were often granted petty privileges and their children were more frequently given their freedom than those of any other class.

At the end of the slave period, the mulattoes sought to establish themselves as a distinct occupational and social class within the Negro subculture. For the most part, they continued as servants and retainers to their erstwhile masters—as dressmakers, barbers, coachmen and the like. For more than a generation they clung tenuously to a certain degree of status derived from catering exclusively to the "quality" folk (as they had done in slavery) under the then current slogan of (serving) "mighty few white folks and no niggers a'tall!"

By the turn of the century, however, as the economy of the South began to revive, the mulatto "retainers" were progressively displaced by European immigrants and poor whites who were suddenly willing to do "Negro work." From that date neither occupation nor color has been a reliable index of social standing among Negroes.

Today, a light skin is not an automatic key to social status. In this day of the Negro's increasing race pride and his subtle impulse to nationalism, a light skin *can* be a handicap, especially if it is associated with "recent" miscegenation. Mass education and the discriminate rise of power and money of significant numbers of Negroes irrespective of their grandparents' station in the slave society have all but destroyed the effectiveness of the Negro's private color bar. Leadership in civil rights as well as in the professions has long since passed from the mulatto class. As a matter of fact, the number of mulattoes in the general Negro population seems to be declining steadily, and there is no evidence that legal integration will soon replace clandestine miscegenation in restoring the ratio of light color.

There is no unanimity of opinion as to what proportion of today's Negroes fall into the traditional "lower," "middle" and "upper" classes of the Negro social structure. Prof. Tillman Cothran, head of the graduate department of sociology at Atlanta University, estimates that "not more than 25 per cent of the Negro population can be called middle class by any reasonable standards. And not more than 5 per cent can be called upper class."

Other sociologists have argued that if one applies the full spectrum of criteria by which the white social structure is measured—ranging from income to education, affiliation, residence, etc.—the Negro middle class is reduced to 4 per cent or 5 per cent of the Negro population, and the Negro upper class vanishes altogether.

Such an estimate is, I think, too drastic. If the theory of parallel social structure is valid (and there seems to be no other way to measure "class" in an essentially segregated society), certainly it can be shown that Negroes and whites of similar education and income exhibit many of the same desires, restraints, conformities and general patterns of behavior.

America's self-image is that of an essentially equalitarian society best represented by the middle class. Most Americans concede that there are a few snobs and millionaires at the top, and a few poor people in Appalachia, or somewhere, at the bottom, but America is middle class, and most Americans identify themselves as belonging to the middle class.

Implicit in this identification is a belief in "democracy" and "fair play," and also the expectation of "the good life"—a home, a car, a regular vacation, an education for the children, regular promotions, and maybe even extras like a boat or a summer place. Despite the pessimism of the sociologists, more and more Negroes share this dream, and to an increasing degree they are making it come true for themselves and their children.

The Negro middle class is made up primarily of Negro professionals, with school teachers probably constituting the largest single bloc. Teachers, along with doctors, lawyers, college professors, small businessmen, ministers, and postal workers have traditionally made up the bulk of the Negro middle class.

However, the recent availability of new kinds of jobs not previously held by Negroes has begun to modify the character of this group. Technicians, politicians, clerical and sales personnel, social workers, labor-union officials, minor government bureaucrats, and an increasing managerial class in such agencies as Federal housing and local units of national corporations have helped broaden the occupational range of the Negro middle class.

Under the Kennedy-Johnson Administration a few Negroes have been appointed to the upper echelons of Government officialdom, and within the past two or three years a few Negroes have reached executive status in white corporations. A dinner in New York honored seven Negroes who were vice presidents or held managerial positions in major firms. In Washington, Dr. James Nabrit, president of Howard University, and Dr. Frank Jones have been elected to the board of directors of a major bank. And in that city, several Negroes have been elected to the Board of Trade.

It is difficult to set a salary range for a given social class because social status does not depend upon money alone. Some upper-class whites are impoverished, but their families have once held fortunes and they have traditions of culture and attainment. Since the American Negro's family traditions seldom antedate the Civil War, Negro society puts an undue emphasis on money and material acquisitions. It is often said by Negro critics themselves that "anybody with a dollar, no matter where he stole it, can belong to Negro society."

Most Negroes, like most other Americans, earn their living legitimately, of course, but because of job discrimination and lack of skills, the total income of the typical middle-class Negro family will be substantially lower than that of a typical white family of the middle class. An arbitrary figure of $7,500 a year as the average income of a middle-class family would severely limit the number of Negroes who could be called middle-class.

Some Negro families do exceed a $7,500 income, but the vast majority of those who do are families in which both husband and wife work full time. Very frequently among home-buying Negroes, the head of the family works at two jobs, and occasionally at three. Such supplementary work or "moonlighting"—often driving a taxi, waiting on tables, tending bar or bellhopping—is known as "a hustle," a term quite familiar to the Negro middle class.

In many of the large cities of the North such as New York or Boston where undeveloped land is nonexistent, the middle-class Negro, who has the means and the desire to live elsewhere, is locked in the black ghetto. Only with difficulty can he find a house or apartment outside the ghetto in a white community. As a consequence, many Negroes despair of ever leaving the slums, no matter what their education or income.

Money that would normally go for a new house is spent in the hopeless task of refurbishing antiquated apartments, or in conspicuous consumption which somehow helps them to forget the horror of living in the nation's Harlems. (In the South, the housing problem is not nearly so acute. Space for building can be had in most Southern cities, although it is likely to be in a segregated community.)

The style of living of the Negro middle class does not differ radically from that of its white counterpart. Bridge is a favorite pastime among both men and women. Those who have the leisure belong to innumerable social clubs. An increasing number of Negro men play golf and participate in water sports where facilities are available. In the South, fishing and hunting are favorite pastimes, but only if one has the full regalia of dress, and all the latest equipment shown in the sports magazines.

To a far greater degree than whites, Negroes maintain affiliation in the graduate chapters of their college fraternities and sororities, and these organizations are important indexes of social stratification. Women of a given sorority tend to marry men of its fraternal opposite number. Together, the eight major Negro sororities and fraternities constitute the nucleus of any imaginary "blue book" of Negro society.

The children of the Negro middle class are taught to aspire to middle-class standards. They take lessons in piano and creative dancing on Saturday mornings and attend carefully planned parties on Saturday night. A few are sent East to private schools.

Sometimes the interpretation of middle-class values takes an unusual twist. A Negro matron in a Memphis department store, for example, refused to corral her two children who were busily chasing through the store and littering the aisles with merchandise. She explained: "The white kids do it and the salesclerks think it's cute. I don't want my children inhibited by feeling that they can't do anything any other kids can do."

In Washington, among those aspiring to the middle class, or those who are recently "in," status is measured by the quantity and the cost of whisky served one's guests. The most conspicuous feature in such a home will be the bar appointments, and it is considered equally insulting for a guest to refuse a drink as it is for the host to offer his guests "cheap whisky." One Washingtonian gained prominence in his set by consistently being first to serve rare and expensive imports before they were well known in the Negro community. He learned what was "in" by frequenting an exclusive liquor store patronized by high Government officials.

It used to be said that the difference between a Negro making $50 a week and driving a Cadillac and a white man making $100 a week and driving a Chevrolet was that the Negro, having nowhere to live, needed the bigger car to sleep in! On Atlanta's West Side, where the Cadillac (or Lincoln) frequently comes with a split-level ranch house, it is popular to have the main (or "status") car match the house in color and appointments.

A second car for the Negro professional family is not unusual. Unlike most white middle–class families having two cars, the Negro's second car is likely to be as big and expensive as his first. An expensive automobile to drive to work is often as much a matter of personal prestige for the working Negro woman as for her husband. Hence, it is common to see large numbers of Pontiacs, Oldsmobiles and Mercurys parked near the schools where Negro women are employed as teachers.

A cottage at Oak Bluffs, on Martha's Vineyard, or in Maine or Upper Michigan can be claimed by a few. A very small number of Negroes go to Europe and to the Caribbean or Mexico on vacation. A sort of pilgrimage to Africa has high status value for those seeking to "understand their pre-Western heritage."

Some Negroes are in the middle class because there is nowhere else for them to go. These few might be considered "upper class" but there is a certain incongruity in talking about a Negro "upper class" so long as the color barrier operates to bar Negroes who are otherwise qualified from full participation in American social life. "There may not be an upper class," says Clarence Coleman, southeastern director of the National Urban League, "but there is a 'power élite' which abstracted itself from the rank and file of the middle class and participates to an important extent in the decision-making of the white power structure where Negroes are concerned."

Certainly this power élite does exist. But where it was not created by the white establishment, its power derives from white recognition and respect. Militant civil-rights leaders have discovered this again and again when the white establishment has refused to negotiate with the Negro community except through "recognized channels."

The Negro middle class, like any middle class, is preoccupied with making secure its hard-won social position. This is a characteristic of middle-class aspirations.

Because of this preoccupation the Negro middle class has been criticized frequently for not being more deeply and realistically involved in the struggle for civil rights. The criticism is well placed, for given more manpower, more money and more dedication, it is obvious that more walls could be breached. But this is not the whole story, and the lack of total involvement may not be an accurate index of middle-class feelings and intentions.

Much of the criticism has come from within the ranks of the middle class itself. Clarence Coleman sees the middle class as the buffer between the militants, whose aspirations are frequently unrealistic in terms of present possibilities, and the power élite which seems concerned to protect itself and its privileged positions from too rapid social change.

James A. Tillman Jr., executive director of the Greater Minneapolis Fair Housing Program and a frequent writer on problems of social change, describes the Negro middle class as "that class of Negroes who have bought the inane, invalid and self-defeating notion that the black man can be integrated into a hostile white society without conflict."

Tillman denounces the power élite as "the fixers and go-betweens who cover up rather than expose the violent nature of racism. They are," he declares, "the most dangerous clique in America."

Tillman's sentiments are echoed by Cecil Moore, militant civil-rights attorney and head of the Philadelphia N.A.A.C.P. Moore, who himself came from an accomplished West Virginia family, insists that "the Negro middle class, and all those who consider themselves above the middle class, 'subsist on the blood of the brother down under,' the brother they are supposed to be leading. Who do these Negroes think they're kidding?" he asks, and then answers his own question. "They're kidding nobody but the white folks who are willing to pay 'philanthropy' to keep from having to come to grips with the central problem, which is 'full and complete citizenship for all Americans, *right now!*' "

Despite all such criticism, however, the Negro middle class has borne the brunt of the civil-rights protest. Critics of the so-called "Black Bourgeoisie" have not always given them credit for the maturity and social responsibility upon which the Negro's fight for first-class citizenship has finally depended. The civil-rights fight, at least insofar as it visualizes an integrated society, is a middle-class fight. The N.A.A.C.P., CORE, the Urban League and the followers of Dr. Martin Luther King are all middle-class. (Indeed, the lower-class Negro has yet to be stirred by the promise of integration. He is more concerned with such immediate needs as jobs and housing than with abstract values like integration. He looks neither to Martin Luther King nor to Roy Wilkins; in fact, the leader of the black masses, has yet to appear.)

In Atlanta and other Southern cities during the massive sit-ins of 1962–63, housewives baked pies, made sandwiches and provided transportation for the students. Negro businessmen donated food, gasoline and other supplies. Then doctors, nurses, professors and businessmen walked the picket lines. Similar middle-class support has assisted the activities of CORE in New York, Cleveland and other cities in the North. Voter registration is essentially a middle-class project.

Middle-class leadership and support of the civil-rights movement has not been without ambivalence. Desegregated schools frequently mean that Negro teachers will lose their jobs. Negro businessmen often lose their most competent clerical help to recently desegregated industries. Negro restaurants, drug stores, real-estate firms and the like may be adversely affected by desegregation. Some Negro churches have lost members to white churches. In a fully integrated society, the Negro middle class would lose its identity. Indeed, it would cease to exist.

Some Negroes recognize all this, of course, and fight against it. Nor can it be said that the majority of the middle class is active in the rights struggle. What can be said is that the struggle is for the most part led, financed and supported by the Negro middle class and, of course, its white allies.

Certainly, Negro leadership has become a "profession," and in some cases a lucrative one. Yet most Negroes trying to help improve things are in search of neither fame nor fortune and may be themselves disadvantaged by the race issue. A. Maceo Walker and Jesse Turner of Memphis, for example, both executive officers of a sensitive banking business that has important white as well as Negro depositors, come to mind. These men and others like them have little to gain for themselves personally, yet they have given leadership to the civil-rights movement in their city for years. Other cases could be cited across the country.

In Washington, I talked with the distinguished Negro attorney, Belford Lawson, and his wife, Marjorie McKenzie, who, as associate judge of the Juvenile Court there, is no less distinguished. The Lawsons were undisturbed about the "black backlash" against the Negro middle class, although they felt that the middle class was just beginning to realize its responsibilities to the Negro masses. Nor did they recognize a middle-class backlash against the lower class (which has been roundly criticized by some Negroes for rioting in the streets and undoing the patient and painful accomplishments of middle-class leaders).

"We must press on to the next phase," Lawson said. "And it would be foolish to wait until all of us have reached the place a few of us have reached today. Negroes, like other people, move at different rates of speed. Our circumstances vary. Now we have a handful of civil rights and no money. Our next front is economic. We want to buy stocks in banks and corporations and sit on their boards. Every time a Negro reaches an executive position in a major corporation, he is in a better position to help that Negro in the streets without a job."

Mr. Lawson believes that it is time to stop complaining and to move on into the American mainstream. "Breaking into the white man's economy" he believes to be essential to any further progress on the part of Negroes. "In Washington," he says, "where many social and cultural affairs are integrated, many doors would open if the Negro would only push on them."

Negroes are pushing—for status and respectability and economic security. They are less concerned with integration for integration's sake than they are with being comfortable—middle-class—and unhindered in enjoying all that America has to offer. The riots in the city streets are not the work of sinister Communist agents, except where such agents move in to exploit an already festering social situation. Nor are they the work of hopheads and hoodlums bent on the destruction of the fruits of years of patient interracial effort.

They are the social expressions of pent-up anxiety and frustration which derive from the hopelessness of the conditions under which those people live. *They* cannot hope for "the good life." *They* cannot appropriate the "middle-class image," the American norm for democratic living.

I sat recently in a comfortable middle-class home in northwest Washington talking with Jerry Coward and his wife, both school teachers in the District of Columbia school system. "You know, when we moved into this neighborhood five years ago," Jerry said, "the whites all threatened to move out. A few stayed. And since that time, two brand-new white families have moved in, right down the block. Professional people, too. When white people start moving into, instead of away from, a Negro neighborhood, I guess we've got it made."

I guess they have.

✦ 44 ✦

THE ETA: A MARGINAL
JAPANESE CASTE

Hugh H. Smythe

The two previous selections have described some aspects of a caste-like system in our society. This selection by Hugh Smythe describes a sharply defined caste stratum in Japan and provides an instructive comparison with the American scene. It is well to bear in mind that a pure caste system in which there is no mobility is actually unknown in contemporary society.

Today in Japan there exist some three million persons, ethnically Japanese, who are virtually social outcasts living largely on the margins of Japanese society. These are the Eta. Their racial similarity with other Japanese, coupled with caste status and economic overtones in a society in which Western political patterns have been overlaid on a centuries-old feudalistic foundation, hold out rich promise for those interested in new aspects of the general problem of caste and class.

Foundations of Caste

Historically, the Eta developed out of the feudalistic economy of the Middle Ages, their identity as a special group arising near the close of the fourteenth century. Although work with leather was their major occupation, they performed services as executioners, butchers, handlers of the dead, and disposers of offal and did other jobs avoided by people in general as being unclean. Because of their association with occupations considered degrading they were even refused work as domestics in the homes of

SOURCE: Reprinted from the *American Journal of Sociology*, Vol. 58, No. 2 (September, 1952), 194–96, by permission of The University of Chicago Press. Copyright 1952 by the University of Chicago. ✧ The author is associate professor of sociology at Brooklyn College. He has served on government committees and been a member of various United Nations committees working for UNICEF and UNESCO. His major interests include race and cultural contact, African and Asian affairs, and modern developments and studies in new leadership groups. He is the coauthor of *New Nigerian Elite*.

farmers and merchants. Thus in the feudal social system their status was at the bottom, and they became social outcasts on the basis of occupation. During the long period of internecine warfare in the fifteenth and sixteenth centuries, when the demand for leather goods was great, the Eta occupied a preferred economic position, although their social status remained low. The embattled warlords competed with one another to gain their services and to attract them to their castle towns, and they were given special protection, since their help was indispensable. However, when the long period of isolation and relative peace set in with the inception of the Tokugawa regime at the beginning of the seventeenth century, the demand for leather goods declined, the Eta lost their favored status, and they were segregated in special villages or special sections of towns and villages.

In 1871, soon after the beginning of the modern period in Japanese history in 1868, the identity of the Eta as a special caste was officially abolished by imperial decree, and they were legally absorbed into the category of commoners, being permitted to follow any occupation they wished. But in reality their caste status remained intact, and by 1873 the general population had set them apart as the "new commoners." Socially they were shunned; marriage with them was abhorred, and they were excluded from social functions. They were forced to continue in their traditional occupations and were limited to such others as day laborer, peddler, tenant farmer, and handicraft worker. Their segregated living quarters, although no longer recognized, persist even today: the Eta are referred to as the "special *buraku* people."

The limited and fragmentary work done on the Eta by Japanese scholars has been almost wholly historical; thus there are no substantial sociological or anthropological data available. This limitation of detailed research materials frustrates attempts at even a partial interpretation of their present role and function in Japanese society. Their current situation is, therefore, here empirically discussed for the purpose of pointing the way for detailed and comprehensive study.

General Problem

ECONOMIC ROLE AND MOBILITY   The historical development of the Eta accounts for their concentration today mainly in central and southern Japan, with their population about equally divided between rural and urban areas. There is very little internal migration in Japan, and many Eta, especially those in villages and rural areas, continue to live in localities which they have inhabited for generations. In prewar times the more enterprising sons of Eta sometimes were able to escape their inferior status by emigrating to Japanese-held Dairen, Port Arthur, and Korea. Some attended the Japanese-established imperial universities—Keijo in Korea and Taihoku in Formosa—secured training, returned to Japan, and entered other occupations, losing their identity in new occupations and in the general population of cities. Since their names and physical appearance are in general indistinguishable from those of the general population, their potential mobility is relatively great.

Although the position of the Eta in the post-surrender period was improved somewhat (under the Occupation all forms of social, religious, racial, and political discrimination were made illegal), today the Eta continue to function largely within their traditional occupations as slaughterers of animals; proprietors of butcher shops, shoe stores, and repair shops; leather-workers; basket-weavers; and clog- and sandal-makers. In the villages they usually occupy the bottom rung of the economic ladder and cultivate the smallest farms.

CULTURAL ISOLATION AND COALESCENCE Like the Classic Black Belt, Jewish ghetto, and immigrant slums of American and European cities, the Eta neighborhoods are set apart. But unlike the former, which are customarily large continuous concentrations, the Eta settlements are small and spotty, although there are a few villages populated almost entirely by them. When villages and towns have merged into cities, their settlements have remained as peripheral enclaves and the Eta continue to live in isolation as a marginal neighborhood group.

The period since the surrender has afforded them greater political participation, yet in their villages as well as in the towns and cities they share in political life, as a rule, as Eta. Part of this is due to the fact that in most villages assembly men, in practice, are elected by their own *buraku* rather than by the village-at-large; and because he is segregated in special *burakus* or confined to a certain part of a *buraku* in very small places, an Eta customarily represents his community only when such representation is on a *buraku* basis.

Being Japanese and indistinguishable physically and linguistically from the general population, the Eta are able to participate inside the larger Japanese society. Their problem here appears to be one fundamentally sociopsychological, arising from their occupational caste status and the inhibitions which this promotes. The sociopsychological effect of the term "Eta" is undoubtedly a restraint, since it has a derogatory connotation similar to that of "nigger," "kike," "wop," "greaser," "chink," "monkey chaser," and other terms applied in America to minority groups. Their economic status also isolates them from full cultural participation: generally the poorest group in the population and segregated in special areas, they live a ghetto life, a limited and growth-retarding existence.

INTEGRATION AND ASSIMILATION Considering their physical oneness with the general Japanese population, the constricted status of the Eta makes a vivid impression upon the observer. Superficially they appear to occupy an apparently undifferentiated position, but further examination reveals that they are socially excluded, economically depressed, and politically powerless. The Eta still experiences segregation and discrimination, despite Occupation reforms, and their occupational-caste status continues to be accompanied by social restrictions, particularly in personal relations and in religion.

Even where the Eta have achieved economic success and political acceptance, marriage into the majority group is still rigidly taboo. Since the Japanese place great stress upon the "stock" of a family, non-Eta families never consider the marriage of their son or daughter to an Eta, for they feel that, no matter how much worldly success an Eta might achieve, he can never overcome the taint of his lineage.

The Eta have attempted on a mass scale to escape their proscriptive position. In the early 1920's they formed a nation-wide organization, *Suiheisha* (Levellers Association) to effect their emancipation, and in a national convention in Kyoto on March 3, 1922, they set forth a declaration of equality. In several instances they were forced to resort to force to resist those interested in keeping them in their subordinate status.

The postwar period has helped some of them individually to escape their ethnic enclaves, especially the young women. The Eta women are reputedly among the most attractive in Japan. During the Occupation some of them became *pen-pans* (street prostitutes); others went to the large cities and became taxi dancers in the night clubs, dance halls, and restaurants; still others entered the employment of Occupation dependents. In this way they met Allied soldiers and sometimes married them, while in others they remained in the cities and continued in their newly found pursuits, thus escaping their caste-ridden traditional occupations and conditions.

Summary

In the light of the foregoing and because of their size and dynamic character it is apparent that the Eta merit wide, detailed, and comprehensive study. Research on aspects of the Eta phenomenon can make significant contributions to the study of problems of caste, class, social distance, minority groups, social differentiation, intergroup and race relations, social mobility, and occupation-status relationships. Findings from such research should provide materials useful for comparative treatment with other status and ethnic groups. Among possible research projects are the following: (1) their geographic origin and prior occupational and status characteristics; (2) differences in degrees of social, economic, religious, and political acceptance and nonacceptance, in urban and rural settlements; (3) factors encouraging or mitigating their cultural coalescence and how far they have operated in either direction since the war; (4) studies of their ethnic enclaves, the reduction of their isolation, and possibility of their incorporation into the larger society; (5) the effect of the term "Eta" as a concept of derogation on the stigmatized group and its social function in the larger society; (6) intercaste and intra-caste behavior; (7) majority stereotypes of Eta characteristics; (8) the extent to which caste restrictions operate upon Eta who have obtained a high level of education and wealth; (9) intermarriage between the Eta and other Japanese.

Social Organization:

INSTITUTIONS AND ASSOCIATIONS

* 45 *

PARKINSON'S LAW

C. Northcote Parkinson

Although written with tongue in cheek, Parkinson's "Law" clearly describes one of the most fundamental facts about human society. Human groups, he says, tend to devise increasingly complicated organized ways of doing things (a process that is often termed "institutionalization"), and then frequently keep on doing these things in the established way even when it would appear, from the standpoint of efficiency, not to make sense to do so. Vested interests resist because they might suffer if some change were introduced. The consequences of this tendency are legion: social change is impeded, valuable time and energy are unnecessarily expended, people become more concerned with the procedures and techniques than with goals, more people are assigned to carry out more specialized tasks. Such consequences are specifically illustrated in one aspect or another in the articles by Sanders (46), Boisen (62), and Basch (65).

I. Parkinson's Law or the Rising Pyramid

Work expands so as to fill the time available for its completion. General recognition of this fact is shown in the proverbial phrase "It is the

SOURCE: C. Northcote Parkinson, *Parkinson's Law and Other Studies in Administration*, 2–13, 59–69 passim. Copyright © 1957 by C. Northcote Parkinson. Reprinted by permission of the publisher, Houghton Mifflin Company. ✧ C. Northcote Parkinson is an author, historian, and journalist. He is the President of the Parkinson Institute, a Business Consultants Organization, Amsterdam. He has taught at several universities and was the Raffles Professor of History at the University of Malaya from 1950 to 1958. Among his many published works are *Trade in the Eastern Seas; Parkinson's Law, The Pursuit of Progress; The Evolution of Political Thought;* and *East and West.*

busiest man who has time to spare." Thus, an elderly lady of leisure can spend the entire day in writing and dispatching a postcard to her niece at Bognor Regis. An hour will be spent in finding the postcard, another in hunting for spectacles, half an hour in a search for the address, an hour and a quarter in composition, and twenty minutes in deciding whether or not to take an umbrella when going to the mailbox in the next street. The total effort that would occupy a busy man for three minutes all told may in this fashion leave another person prostrate after a day of doubt, anxiety, and toil.

Granted that work (and especially paperwork) is thus elastic in its demands on time, it is manifest that there need be little or no relationship between the work to be done and the size of the staff to which it may be assigned. A lack of real activity does not, of necessity, result in leisure. A lack of occupation is not necessarily revealed by a manifest idleness. The thing to be done swells in importance and complexity in a direct ratio with the time to be spent. This fact is widely recognized, but less attention has been paid to its wider implications, more especially in the field of public administration. Politicians and taxpayers have assumed (with occasional phases of doubt) that a rising total in the number of civil servants must reflect a growing volume of work to be done. Cynics, in questioning this belief, have imagined that the multiplication of officials must have left some of them idle or all of them able to work for shorter hours. But this is a matter in which faith and doubt seem equally misplaced. The fact is that the number of the officials and the quantity of the work are not related to each other at all. The rise in the total of those employed is governed by Parkinson's Law and would be much the same whether the volume of the work were to increase, diminish, or even disappear. The importance of Parkinson's Law lies in the fact that it is a law of growth based upon an analysis of the factors by which that growth is controlled.

The validity of this recently discovered law must rest mainly on statistical proofs, which will follow. Of more interest to the general reader is the explanation of the factors underlying the general tendency to which this law gives definition. Omitting technicalities (which are numerous) we may distinguish at the outset two motive forces. They can be represented for the present purpose by two almost axiomatic statements, thus: (1) "An official wants to multiply subordinates, not rivals" and (2) "Officials make work for each other."

To comprehend Factor 1, we must picture a civil servant, called A, who finds himself overworked. Whether this overwork is real or imaginary is immaterial, but we should observe, in passing, that A's sensation (or illusion) might easily result from his own decreasing energy: a normal symptom of middle age. For this real or imagined overwork there are, broadly speaking, three possible remedies. He may resign; he may ask to halve the work with a colleague called B; he may demand the assistance of two subordinates, to be called C and D. There is probably no instance in history, however, of A choosing any but the third alternative. By resignation he would lose his pension rights. By having B appointed, on his own level in the hierarchy, he would merely bring in a rival for promotion to W's vacancy when W (at long last) retires. So A would rather have C and D, junior men, below him. They will add to his consequence and, by dividing the work into two categories, as between C and D, he will have the merit of being the only man who comprehends them both. It is essential to realize at this point that C and D are, as it were, inseparable. To appoint C alone would have been impossible. Why? Because C, if by himself, would divide the work with A and so assume almost the equal status that has been refused in the first instance to B; a status the more emphasized if C is A's only possible successor. Subordinates must thus number two or more, each being thus kept in order by fear of the other's promotion. When C complains in turn of being overworked (as he certainly will) A will, with the concurrence of C, advise the appointment of two assistants to help C. But he can then avert internal friction only by advising the appointment of two more assistants to help D, whose position is much the same. With this recruitment of E, F, G, and H the promotion of A is now practically certain.

Seven officials are now doing what one did before. This is where Factor 2 comes into operation. For these seven make so much work for each other that all are fully occupied and A is actually working harder than ever. An incoming document may well come before each of them in turn. Official E decides that it falls within the province of F, who places a draft reply before C, who amends it drastically before consulting D, who asks G to deal with it. But G goes on leave at this point, handing the file over to H, who drafts a minute that is signed by D and returned to C, who revises his draft accordingly and lays the new version before A.

What does A do? He would have every excuse for signing the thing unread, for he has many other matters on his mind. Knowing now that he is to succeed W next year, he has to decide whether C or D should succeed to his own office. He had to agree to G's going on leave even if not yet strictly entitled to it. He is worried whether H should not have gone instead, for reasons of health. He has looked pale recently—partly but not solely because of his domestic troubles. Then there is the business of F's special increment of salary for the period of the conference and E's application for transfer to the Ministry of Pensions. A has heard that D is in love with a married typist and that G and F are no longer on speaking terms—no one seems to know why. So A might be tempted to sign C's draft and have done with it. But A is a conscientious man. Beset as he is with problems created by his colleagues for themselves and for him— created by the mere fact of these officials' existence—he is not the man to shirk his duty. He reads through the draft with care, deletes the fussy paragraphs added by C and H, and restores the thing back to the form preferred in the first instance by the able (if quarrelsome) F. He corrects the

English—none of these young men can write grammatically—and finally produces the same reply he would have written if officials C to H had never been born. Far more people have taken far longer to produce the same result. No one has been idle. All have done their best. And it is late in the evening before A finally quits his office and begins the return journey to Ealing. The last of the office lights are being turned off in the gathering dusk that marks the end of another day's administrative toil. Among the last to leave, A reflects with bowed shoulders and a wry smile that late hours, like gray hairs, are among the penalties of success.

❖   ❖   ❖   ❖   ❖

II. Plans and Plants or the Administrative Block

Every student of human institutions is familiar with the standard test by which the importance of the individual may be assessed. The number of doors to be passed, the number of his personal assistants, the number of his telephone receivers—these three figures, taken with the depth of his carpet in centimeters, have given us a simple formula that is reliable for most parts of the world. It is less widely known that the same sort of measurement is applicable, *but in reverse*, to the institution itself.

Take, for example, a publishing organization. Publishers have a strong tendency, as we know, to live in a state of chaotic squalor. The visitor who applies at the obvious entrance is led outside and around the block, down an alley and up three flights of stairs. A research establishment is similarly housed, as a rule, on the ground floor of what was once a private house, a crazy wooden corridor leading thence to a corrugated iron hut in what was once the garden. Are we not all familiar, moreover, with the layout of an international airport? As we emerge from the aircraft, we see (over to our right or left) a lofty structure wrapped in scaffolding. Then the air hostess leads us into a hut with an asbestos roof. Nor do we suppose for a moment that it will ever be otherwise. By the time the permanent building is complete the airfield will have been moved to another site.

The institutions already mentioned—lively and productive as they may be—flourish in such shabby and makeshift surroundings that we might turn with relief to an institution clothed from the outset with convenience and dignity. The outer door, in bronze and glass, is placed centrally in a symmetrical façade. Polished shoes glide quietly over shining rubber to the glittering and silent elevator. The overpoweringly cultured receptionist will murmur with carmine lips into an ice-blue receiver. She will wave you into a chromium armchair, consoling you with a dazzling smile for any slight but inevitable delay. Looking up from a glossy magazine, you will observe how the wide corridors radiate toward departments A, B, and C. From behind closed doors will come the subdued noise of an ordered activity. A minute later and you are ankle deep in the director's carpet, plodding sturdily toward his distant, tidy desk. Hypnotized by the chief's

unwavering stare, cowed by the Matisse hung upon his wall, you will feel
that you have found real efficiency at last.

In point of fact you will have discovered nothing of the kind. It is
now known that a perfection of planned layout is achieved only by institutions on the point of collapse. This apparently paradoxical conclusion is
based upon a wealth of archaeological and historical research, with the
more esoteric details of which we need not concern ourselves. In general
principle, however, the method pursued has been to select and date the
buildings which appear to have been perfectly designed for their purpose.
A study and comparison of these has tended to prove that perfection of
planning is a symptom of decay. During a period of exciting discovery or
progress there is no time to plan the perfect headquarters. The time for
that comes later, when all the important work has been done. Perfection,
we know, is finality; and finality is death.

❖   ❖   ❖   ❖   ❖

It is natural . . . to ask at this point whether the Palace of Westminster,
where the House of Commons meets, is itself a true expression of parliamentary rule. It represents beyond question a magnificent piece of planning, aptly designed for debate and yet provided with ample space for
everything else—for committee meetings, for quiet study, for refreshment,
and (on its terrace) for tea. It has everything a legislator could possibly
desire, all incorporated in a building of immense dignity and comfort. It
should date—but this we now hardly dare assume—from a period when
parliamentary rule was at its height. But once again the dates refuse to fit
into this pattern. The original House, where Pitt and Fox were matched
in oratory, was accidentally destroyed by fire in 1834. It would appear to
have been as famed for its inconveniences as for its lofty standard of debate.
The present structure was begun in 1840, partly occupied in 1852, but
incomplete when its architect died in 1860. It finally assumed its present
appearance in about 1868. Now, by what we can no longer regard as coincidence, the decline of Parliament can be traced, without much dispute,
to the Reform Act of 1867. It was in the following year that all initiative in
legislation passed from Parliament to be vested in the Cabinet. The prestige attached to the letters "M.P." began sharply to decline and thence-
forward the most that could be said is that "a role, though a humble one,
was left for private members." The great days were over.

❖   ❖   ❖   ❖   ❖

But no other British example can now match in significance the story
of New Delhi. Nowhere else have British architects been given the task
of planning so great a capital city as the seat of government for so vast
a population. The intention to found New Delhi was announced at the
Imperial Durbar of 1911, King George V being at that time the Mogul's
successor on what had been the Peacock Throne. Sir Edwin Lutyens then

proceeded to draw up plans for a British Versailles, splendid in conception, comprehensive in detail, masterly in design, and overpowering in scale. But the stages of its progress toward completion correspond with so many steps in political collapse. The Government of India Act of 1909 had been the prelude to all that followed—the attempt on the Viceroy's life in 1912, the Declaration of 1917, the Montagu-Chelmsford Report of 1918 and its implementation in 1920. Lord Irwin actually moved into his new palace in 1929, the year in which the Indian Congress demanded independence, the year in which the Round Table Conference opened, the year before the Civil Disobedience campaign began. It would be possible, though tedious, to trace the whole story down to the day when the British finally withdrew, showing how each phase of the retreat was exactly paralleled with the completion of another triumph in civic design. What was finally achieved was no more and no less than a mausoleum. . . .

The elaborate layout of the Pentagon at Arlington, Virginia, provides another significant lesson for planners. It was not completed until the later stages of World War II and, of course, the architecture of the great victory was not constructed here, but in the crowded and untidy Munitions Building on Constitution Avenue.

Even today, as the least observant visitor to Washington can see, the most monumental edifices are found to house such derelict organizations as the Departments of Commerce and Labor, while the more active agencies occupy half-completed quarters. Indeed, much of the more urgent business of government goes forward in "temporary" structures erected during World War I, and shrewdly preserved for their stimulating effect on administration. Hard by the Capitol, the visitor will also observe the imposing marble-and-glass headquarters of the Teamsters' Union, completed not a moment too soon before the heavy hand of Congressional investigation descended on its occupants.

It is by no means certain that an influential reader of this chapter could prolong the life of a dying institution merely by depriving it of its streamlined headquarters. What he can do, however, with more confidence, is to prevent any organization strangling itself at birth. Examples abound of new institutions coming into existence with a full establishment of deputy directors, consultants, and executives; all these coming together in a building specially designed for their purpose. And experience proves that such an institution will die. It is choked by its own perfection. It cannot take root for lack of soil. It cannot grow naturally for it is already grown. Fruitless by its very nature, it cannot even flower. When we see an example of such planning—when we are confronted for example by the building designed for the United Nations—the experts among us shake their heads sadly, draw a sheet over the corpse, and tiptoe quietly into the open air.

MUTINY OF THE BOUNTIFUL

Marion K. Sanders

Illustrated here, in a serious vein, is the phenomenon that Parkinson spoofs in his "Law," in the preceding article. Sanders deals with health organizations, but the same behavior she describes can be observed among educational institutions, religious groups, government departments, and business establishments.

A truly appealing picture of a child with a runny nose has yet to be produced. As a result we are denied the privilege of joining in an annual Sniffle Crusade, and the Common Cold Foundation wheezes along on a mere fifty thousand a year, collected mainly from a few industries. This is a puny war chest to fight a public health menace which is said to cost the nation around five billion dollars a year in lost production, wages, and medical bills. But the sniffles, alas, do not tug at the heart strings; and though murderous ills may follow, no one ever died of sneezing. Crusades are built on pity and terror, not statistics.

We contribute, for example, about the same sum in behalf of 150,000 victims of muscular dystrophy as for the nine million who are mentally ill. Arthritis and rheumatism—of which there are said to be more than ten million cases—get less.

No one knows just how many different groups are soliciting funds across the country for how many different diseases. Last spring in a spot check of Chatham County, Georgia, the Savannah *Morning Herald* tallied up nineteen organizations passing the hat for the blind; seven for disabled veterans; six for the crippled; four for mental illness; five for cancer; two each for muscular dystrophy, polio, leprosy, brain injury, and alcoholism; and one apiece for heart disease, retarded children, cerebral palsy, deafness, tuberculosis, multiple sclerosis, arthritis, myasthenia gravis, nephrosis, facial disfigurement, tropical diseases, diabetes, epilepsy, allergic diseases, hemophilia, and paraplegia.

Most American communities of any size are equally lavishly endowed. John A. Lincoln, President of the Stamford, Connecticut, Chamber of Commerce, spoke with the voice of many when he remarked recently,

"We are punch drunk trying to keep up with all these appeals."

SOURCE: *Harper's Magazine*, Vol. 217, No. 1303 (December, 1958), 23–31. © 1958 by Harper's Magazine, Inc. Reprinted by permission of the author. ✧ The author is an editor on the staff of *Harper's Magazine*. She wrote *The Lady and the Vote* as well as numerous articles that have appeared in *Harper's*.

To be sure, not all of these outfits blanket the nation or conduct house-to-house campaigns. Those that do have tried to carve up the calendar into non-overlapping segments. It is not, in fact, considered cricket among fund-raisers to muscle in on someone else's day, week, or month. But with some fifty nationwide campaigns competing with thousands of lesser causes and local appeals it is often impossible to clear the tracks even between major drives. Thus, for instance, a Shellsburg, Iowa, farmer, Glenn McClintock, who was dunning his neighbors for the cancer crusade had the awkward but not unusual experience of being forced to lurk in his car waiting for Mrs. Jim Peacock to finish her pitch for the heart drive. Both of them turned in their campaign kits shortly thereafter.

There are signs of resistance too among the kind-hearted givers. This summer, for instance, I talked with a young matron in Grosse Ile, Michigan, who announced to me firmly that she would no longer part with a dollar for a disease drive even if the solicitor was a personal friend.

"This morning," she said dramatically, "I actually turned down the mother of a retarded child!"

Such protests are, at present, about money and ways of raising it. They are being followed, however, with lively interest by experts in public health and philanthropy who have long held that splintering up the human body into competing sovereignties is a poor way to fight disease or to promote habits of health. For years, no one but other experts paid much attention to them. But of late a number of people have begun to listen and to wonder how such a noble idea as a citizens' war against disease managed to get so far out of hand.

The result is a growing tug of war between local and national interests. Even more sharply in conflict are two opposing philanthropic concepts: the one aims at balancing services with human needs, the other at developing whatever programs the public can be persuaded to support. Both sides have ardent and forceful supporters, who are currently locked in combat. The issues have been obscured by a blinding public-relations barrage from both sides. In essence, however, this is the same struggle which gave birth to the Community Chest movement of the 1920s.

The businessmen in Cleveland, Rochester and other cities who introduced federated fund-raising to the health and welfare scene after World War I did not have clear sailing. There were anguished wails from orphanage boards, scout leaders, hospital superintendents, and other free-wheeling philanthropic types, particularly at the prospect of a budget committee peering over their shoulders. There was trouble too with parochial-minded natives who objected to sharing the local charity pot with national outfits like the Y's and the Salvation Army. These differences were eventually ironed out, and all concerned found it a great relief to devote one strenuous week a year to the Red Feather-Community Chest campaign and the other fifty-one to their own affairs.

Divided They Stand

In the 1930s and 1940s the health appeals began moving into town. As they multiplied, the Red Feather campaign became just another drive, competing with many others for time, newspaper space, and man- and woman-power. When the fund-raisers swarmed not only into homes but into offices and factories their managers began to reckon the cost. The Ford company, for example, calculated that every plant solicitation meant, apart from contributions, a $40,000 loss in executive time and production. Union men, for once, were in hearty agreement with management.

"The results just didn't justify the amount of effort we were putting into all those appeals," said Andy Brown of the United Auto Workers in Detroit. "We had to find a more efficient way to get the job done."

The plan pioneered in Detroit in 1949 was an all-encompassing campaign known as the Torch Drive, which would raise funds for the Community Chest and the national health agencies in a single annual appeal. The auto magnates spearheaded a massive push for substantial gifts from corporations and their executives. The union backed a payroll deduction plan for employee contributions. The Torch Drive was a spectacular financial success and has steadily grown in subsequent years. Variations of the same plan known as United Funds or United Community Chests have since been set up in more than a thousand cities. They have been particularly successful in industrial centers where union members and management, dunned once a year, have become the chief supporters of voluntary philanthropy.

Inside the factories, multiple health drives are vanishing, for industry has shut the door on them. The federal government has also clamped down and now permits (in addition to the Red Cross roll call) just two solicitations a year of its employees on the job—one for community chests, the other for a combined health drive.

Though temporarily routed on these fronts, the health campaigners are regrouping their forces. They assail payroll deductions and plant quotas for charity as "stark unbridled materialism in action." They attribute sinister imperialist aims to the United Funders who are, in truth, all autonomous groups.

"Divided we stand, united we fall!" was the rather odd battle cry sounded last May by Dr. Robert W. Wilkins of the Heart Association. Under such banners the health agencies are currently presenting themselves to the nation as champions of the American Way, freedom of choice, and true charity. In the privacy of their New York offices, however, more practical questions are discussed. Many doubt, with good reason, that people who give a dollar apiece to six drives will kick in six dollars for one campaign however well sold. What will happen to The Organization if it loses its constituents—the door-to-door brigades? For a money-raising outfit without an annual drive is like a political party without an annual election. . . .

From the outset, the TB Association turned thumbs down on joint drives. This caused relatively little fuss since it is generally felt that the Christmas Seals don't compete with anyone but Santa Claus. March of Dimes also declined with great firmness—which surprised no one since its generalissimo, Basil O'Connor, is a celebrated lone wolf who successfully kept the Red Cross out of Community Chests during his tenure as President from 1944 to 1949. In the current controversy, however, the Red Cross has taken a neutral position, leaving the matter up to its local chapters; more than 900 have now joined United Funds.

It has taken the other agencies some time to rally for defense. A number of them were stuck with state and local chapters headed by men who were members of the same bridge games and foursomes as the chiefs of the new United Fund. As a result, it was natural for many local chapters to join up with the united drives despite the dismay of their national offices. Within the past two years resistance has stiffened. The Heart Association will not permit any more chapters to join United Funds. Last June the Cancer Society went a step further by ordering all those now in to get out by 1960.

This edict precipitated a minor civil war. Outraged protests were made in New Orleans and San Francisco. Chapters in Danville, Virginia, Detroit, and Rochester, New York, voted to secede from the parent body. The sounds of this internecine strife reverberated noisily in the local press.

"If the Cancer Society can do it, the Baldheaded League can do it and we'll have a different drive every day of the year," said Msgr. Thomas J. Tobin, one of the founders of the United Fund in Portland, Oregon.

Faced with this prospect, some of the United Funders have resorted to strong counter-measures. In Pittsburgh, for example, when the Heart and Cancer Societies declined to join, the united drive directors none the less included "heart and cancer research, education, and services" in their fund-raising package and in effect incited a boycott of the independent drives. This stratagem was denounced by the Pittsburgh Heart Association as "sheer trickery which shows an amazing lack of integrity by our leading citizens." Even more irate was Dr. John W. Cline, a former AMA President who charged that money raised in this way is "tainted with the spurious claims under which it was raised, the broken promises of professional promoters . . . and the certainty that freedom in research will disappear. . . ."

Despite this dire forecast, the tainted dollars have been happily accepted by local research foundations in more than a dozen cities and states.

In the future, contributions for research may go to a new foundation for the support of basic research set up within the past year by the National Fund for Medical Education, with the blessing of the United Community Funds and Councils of America.

Cuyahoga County Uprising

Meanwhile, the Heart and Cancer Societies along with the March of Dimes have spurned funds collected for their disease rather than their organizations. The million dollars or more that has thus been kept out of their collective treasuries has not, in their view, been too high a price to pay in the defense of autonomy. Most costly in the long run may be the loss in popular esteem, for the fury of a contributor scorned can pack quite a wallop. This was lately demonstrated by some 10,000 Ohio housewives.

Two years ago the women of Gates Mills, a prosperous Cleveland suburb, decided to save time by staging a one-shot combined drive for all the health agencies. Their modest experiment became a *cause célèbre* when the National Foundation ordered its Cleveland chapter to give back $1,322 which the ladies had collected for polio. This was not only a snub to womankind; it was an affront to a native hero, for the local March of Dimes is headed by baseball star Bob Feller. The press was aroused.

"Arrogant blindness," wrote Sidney Andorn in a sizzling column in the Cleveland *News*. "The women who went from house to house collecting gifts are not slaves to the bidding of emperors perched on a national throne in New York. . . . The Health Drives have done and are doing a service for humanity. They couldn't do it at all if it were not for more fortunate humanity at the grass-roots level. On this level they face a strike of the women volunteer workers."

Thus incited, the ladies of Cuyahoga County reacted like an oppressed nation. From the well-nourished grass roots of Gates Mills the revolt spread to humbler back yards and garden apartments. The Gates Mills affair became a prime discussion topic in a dozen towns. Action committees sprang up headed usually by the wives of public officials, officers of women's clubs, and past chairmen of the assorted health drives. Everywhere the motif was the same: the volunteers had stopped volunteering. One weary chairman reported that it had taken 200 phone calls to recruit a captain for her last campaign.

"The situation has deteriorated," said Mrs. Warren North of Middleburg Heights, "to a point where a woman agrees to work only if contacted by a very dear friend. And dear friends are getting fewer by the week."

To all the rebels a combined drive in the Gates Mills style seemed the right solution. Village councils, Rotary Clubs, and Chambers of Commerce seconded the plan enthusiastically. The point was clinched when the ladies circulated a questionnaire and found their neighbors over-whelmingly in favor of having the doorbell ring just once a year in the name of health.

The scattered groups kept in touch with each other by telephone. Sixteen towns to the east of Cleveland set up a joint command post in the home of Mrs. George J. Urban, wife of the Mayor of South Euclid. Here they worked out details, such as a separate listing of the participating agencies on one envelope, allowing the contributor free choice among them. They agreed also to synchronize their drives which were all staged in May.

Last summer, in the course of a cross-country trip, I stopped off in Cleveland to ask Mrs. Urban how they had made out. A forthright, orderly person, she produced neatly-typed tally sheets with the returns tabulated by towns and causes. The total looked impressive—more than $200,000.

"We should have done better than that," Mrs. Urban acknowledged. "The business slump hurt us, I think, and some of the towns got started too late to be well organized."

She was disappointed too because the allocation to cancer was less than the yield of the Society's independent drive the year before.

"I don't say we've found the perfect answer," she said. "We have a lot to learn about how you educate people for this kind of appeal. But I do know we can't handle all those drives. It's always the busiest woman who gets stuck with these jobs—the one who's willing to take on one more task. We can never get help from the ones with time on their hands."

The national health agencies see the matter differently.

"Sure the old pros are tired," I was told by Willis Nichols, an able young Cincinnati businessman who is an ardent Heart Association parti-san. "But there are thousands of women who have never been asked to do anything. All we have to do is find them."

Some of the agencies are doing this by hiring professional solicitors who pick names at random from the reverse (or geographic) telephone directory and keep calling until they recruit enough hands to blanket a neighborhood with campaign literature. This may be a practical way to raise money. But it seems doubtful that the casual labor so assembled can permanently replace the kind of women who are on strike in Cuyahoga County.

Their tribe is the chief treasure of voluntary philanthropy—the dedi-cated few who choose to give their leisure to service. Since they believe in the purposes of the health drives why, one may ask, are they unwilling to make the rounds for them? An evening's stroll through the neighborhood is not an arduous task compared to the labor many of these citizens happily give to the cub scouts, the League of Women Voters, the ambulance corps or, according to their persuasion, to Hadassah or the Society for the Propagation of the Faith.

The trouble may well be that the health agencies are asking not too much but too little of them. The protest is, in large part, against a form of philanthropy which downgrades the volunteer to a mere messenger and coin-collecting machine manipulated by professionals. The health agencies have not, of course, done this deliberately. If they could dream up worthy projects, most of them would like to keep their volunteers happily employed as the Cancer Society proposes to do in its current mammoth statistical research venture. In general, however, since they do not operate community institutions, they are in much the same position as the national committees of political parties which can offer their constituents nothing to do between campaigns.

Resentment against their lowly role in the philanthropic scheme of things appears widespread among women. Although there are few organized resistance movements outside of Cuyahoga County, I have yet to find a housewife who regards door-to-door fund-raising as "a satisfying outlet for creative energy," a claim made by Dr. Lowell T. Coggeshall of the Cancer Society.

"It's like falling into a bottomless well," said an energetic young mother of four who is a pillar of civic and charitable causes in Minneapolis. "Every year there are new drives and all the old ones keep right on going. You would think a couple of them might quit or get together."

Reasonable as this notion sounds, it is like asking Oklahoma to merge with Texas. Causes can multiply like rabbits, but old agencies never die. . . .

❖ 47 ❖

BUREAUCRACY

Max Weber

Contemporary American and other Western societies are characterized by highly bureaucratic organizations. This type of structure is common in business and other private social institutions as well as governmental agencies. Here Max Weber has systematically analyzed the nature of bureaucracies and demonstrated their necessity.

SOURCE: Max Weber, *Essays in Sociology*, edited and translated by H. H. Gerth and C. Wright Mills, 196–244. Copyright 1946 by Oxford University Press, Inc. Reprinted by permission. ❖ The author (1864–1920) was a German sociologist and political economist. He held the Chair of Political Economy at Freiburg. Weber's sociology is based on his extensive knowledge in economic, political, social, legal, military, and religious fields. He is especially well known for his typological studies of charismatic authority, feudalism, and bureaucracy. He was also a pioneer in the sociology of religion. Among his translated works are *General Economic History*, *The Protestant Ethic and the Spirit of Capitalism*, and *The Theory of Economic and Social Organization*.

*Although this analysis was written nearly a half-century ago and is
based largely on observations of German and other European organizations, no more thorough or sociologically significant statement
on the subject has ever appeared.*

Characteristics of Bureaucracy

Modern officialdom functions in the following specific manner:

I. There is the principle of fixed and official jurisdictional areas,
which are generally ordered by rules, that is, by laws or administrative
regulations.

1. The regular activities required for the purposes of the bureaucratically governed structure are distributed in a fixed way as official duties.

2. The authority to give the commands required for the discharge of
these duties is distributed in a stable way and is strictly delimited by
rules concerning the coercive means, physical, sacerdotal, or otherwise,
which may be placed at the disposal of officials.

3. Methodical provision is made for the regular and continuous
fulfilment of these duties and for the execution of the corresponding
rights; only persons who have the generally regulated qualifications to
serve are employed.

In public and lawful government these three elements constitute
"bureaucratic authority." In private economic domination, they constitute bureaucratic "management." Bureaucracy, thus understood, is fully
developed in political and ecclesiastical communities only in the modern
state, and, in the private economy, only in the most advanced institutions
of capitalism. Permanent and public office authority, with fixed jurisdiction,
is not the historical rule but rather the exception. This is so even in large
political structures such as those of the ancient Orient, the Germanic and
Mongolian empires of conquest, or of many feudal structures of state. In
all these cases, the ruler executes the most important measures through
personal trustees, table-companions, or court-servants. Their commissions
and authority are not precisely delimited and are temporarily called into
being for each case.

II. The principles of office hierarchy and of levels of graded authority
mean a firmly ordered system of super- and subordination in which there
is a supervision of the lower offices by the higher ones. Such a system
offers the governed the possibility of appealing the decision of a lower
office to its higher authority, in a definitely regulated manner. With the
full development of the bureaucratic type, the office hierarchy is mono-
cratically organized. The principle of hierarchical office authority is found
in all bureaucratic structures: in state and ecclesiastical structures as well
as in large party organizations and private enterprises. It does not matter
for the character of bureaucracy whether its authority is called "private"
or "public."

When the principle of jurisdictional "competency" is fully carried through, hierarchical subordination—at least in public office—does not mean that the "higher" authority is simply authorized to take over the business of the "lower." Indeed, the opposite is the rule. Once established and having fulfilled its task, an office tends to continue in existence and be held by another incumbent.

III. The management of the modern office is based upon written documents ("the files"), which are preserved in their original or draught form. There is, therefore, a staff of subaltern officials and scribes of all sorts. The body of officials actively engaged in a "public" office, along with the respective apparatus of material implements and the files, make up a "bureau." In private enterprise, "the bureau" is often called "the office."

In principle, the modern organization of the civil service separates the bureau from the private domicile of the official, and, in general, bureaucracy segregates official activity as something distinct from the sphere of private life. Public monies and equipment are divorced from the private property of the official. This condition is everywhere the product of a long development. Nowadays, it is found in public as well as in private enterprises; in the latter, the principle extends even to the leading entrepreneur. In principle, the executive office is separated from the household, business from private correspondence, and business assets from private fortunes. The more consistently the modern type of business management has been carried through the more are these separations the case. The beginnings of this process are to be found as early as the Middle Ages.

It is the peculiarity of the modern entrepreneur that he conducts himself as the "first official" of his enterprise, in the very same way in which the ruler of a specifically modern bureaucratic state spoke of himself as "the first servant" of the state. The idea that the bureau activities of the state are intrinsically different in character from the management of private economic offices is a continental European notion and, by way of contrast, is totally foreign to the American way.

IV. Office management, at least all specialized office management—and such management is distinctly modern—usually presupposes thorough and expert training. This increasingly holds for the modern executive and employee of private enterprises, in the same manner as it holds for the state official.

V. When the office is fully developed, official activity demands the full working capacity of the official, irrespective of the fact that his obligatory time in the bureau may be firmly delimited. In the normal case, this is only the product of a long development, in the public as well as in the private office. Formerly, in all cases, the normal state of affairs was reversed: official business was discharged as a secondary activity.

VI. The management of the office follows general rules, which are more or less stable, more or less exhaustive, and which can be learned.

Knowledge of these rules represents a special technical learning which the officials possess. It involves jurisprudence, or administrative or business management.

The reduction of modern office management to rules is deeply embedded in its very nature. The theory of modern public administration, for instance, assumes that the authority to order certain matters by decree —which has been legally granted to public authorities—does not entitle the bureau to regulate the matter by commands given for each case, but only to regulate the matter abstractly. This stands in extreme contrast to the regulation of all relationships through individual privileges and bestowals of favor, which is absolutely dominant in patrimonialism, at least in so far as such relationships are not fixed by sacred tradition.

The Position of the Official

All this results in the following for the internal and external position of the official:

I. Office holding is a "vocation." This is shown, first, in the requirement of a firmly prescribed course of training, which demands the entire capacity for work for a long period of time, and in the generally prescribed and special examinations which are prerequisites of employment. Furthermore, the position of the official is in the nature of a duty. This determines the internal structure of his relations, in the following manner: Legally and actually, office holding is not considered a source to be exploited for rents or emoluments, as was normally the case during the Middle Ages and frequently up to the threshold of recent times. Nor is office holding considered a usual exchange of services for equivalents, as is the case with free labor contracts. Entrance into an office, including one in the private economy, is considered an acceptance of a specific obligation of faithful management in return for a secure existence. It is decisive for the specific nature of modern loyalty to an office that, in the pure type, it does not establish a relationship to a *person*, like the vassal's or disciple's faith in feudal or in patrimonial relations of authority. Modern loyalty is devoted to impersonal and functional purposes. Behind the functional purposes, of course, "ideas of culture-values" usually stand. These are *ersatz* for the earthly or supra-mundane personal master: ideas such as "state," "church," "community," "party," or "enterprise" are thought of as being realized in a community; they provide an ideological halo for the master.

The political official—at least in the fully developed modern state— is not considered the personal servant of a ruler. Today, the bishop, the priest, and the preacher are in fact no longer, as in early Christian times, holders of purely personal charisma. The supra-mundane and sacred values which they offer are given to everybody who seems to be worthy of them and who asks for them. In former times, such leaders acted upon the personal command of their master; in principle, they were responsible only to him. Nowadays, in spite of the partial survival of the old theory, such religious leaders are officials in the service of a functional purpose, which in the present-day "church" has become routinized and, in turn, ideologically hallowed.

II. The personal position of the official is patterned in the following way:

1. Whether he is in a private office or a public bureau, the modern official always strives and usually enjoys a distinct *social esteem* as compared with the governed. His social position is guaranteed by the prescriptive rules of rank order and, for the political official, by special definitions of the criminal code against "insults of officials" and "contempt" of state and church authorities.

The actual social position of the official is normally highest where, as in old civilized countries, the following conditions prevail: a strong demand for administration by trained experts; a strong and stable social differentiation, where the official predominantly derives from socially and economically privileged strata because of the social distribution of power; or where the costliness of the required training and status conventions are binding upon him. The possession of educational certificates —to be discussed elsewhere—are usually linked with qualification for office. Naturally, such certificates or patents enhance the "status element" in the social position of the official. For the rest this status factor in individual cases is explicitly and impassively acknowledged; for example, in the prescription that the acceptance or rejection of an aspirant to an official career depends upon the consent ("election") of the members of the official body. This is the case in the German army with the officer corps. Similar phenomena, which promote this guild-like closure of officialdom, are typically found in patrimonial and, particularly, in prebendal officialdoms of the past. The desire to resurrect such phenomena in changed forms is by no means infrequent among modern bureaucrats. For instance, they have played a role among the demands of the quite proletarian and expert officials (the *tretyj* element) during the Russian revolution.

Usually the social esteem of the officials as such is especially low where the demand for expert administration and the dominance of status conventions are weak. This is especially the case in the United States; it is often the case in new settlements by virtue of their wide fields for profit-making and the great instability of their social stratification.

2. The pure type of bureaucratic official is *appointed* by a superior authority. An official elected by the governed is not a purely bureaucratic figure. Of course, the formal existence of an election does not by itself mean that no appointment hides behind the election—in the state, especially, appointment by party chiefs. Whether or not this is the case does not depend upon legal statutes but upon the way in which the party

mechanism functions. Once firmly organized, the parties can turn a formally free election into the mere acclamation of a candidate designated by the party chief. As a rule, however, a formally free election is turned into a fight, conducted according to definite rules, for votes in favor of one of two designated candidates.

In all circumstances, the designation of officials by means of an election among the governed modifies the strictness of hierarchical subordination. In principle, an official who is so elected has an autonomous position opposite the superordinate official. The elected official does not derive his position "from above" but "from below," or at least not from a superior authority of the official hierarchy but from powerful party men ("bosses"), who also determine his further career. The career of the elected official is not, or at least not primarily, dependent upon his chief in the administration. The official who is not elected but appointed by a chief normally functions more exactly, from a technical point of view, because, all other circumstances being equal, it is more likely that purely functional points of consideration and qualities will determine his selection and career. As laymen, the governed can become acquainted with the extent to which a candidate is expertly qualified for office only in terms of experience, and hence only after his service. Moreover, in every sort of selection of officials by election, parties quite naturally give decisive weight not to expert considerations but to the services a follower renders to the party boss. This holds for all kinds of procurement of officials by elections, for the designation of formally free, elected officials by party bosses when they determine the slate of candidates, or the free appointment by a chief who has himself been elected. The contrast, however, is relative: substantially similar conditions hold where legitimate monarchs and their subordinates appoint officials, except that the influence of the followings are then less controllable.

When the demand for administration by trained experts is considerable, and the party followings have to recognize an intellectually developed, educated, and freely moving "public opinion," the use of unqualified officials falls back upon the party in power at the next election. Naturally, this is more likely to happen when the officials are appointed by the chief. The demand for a trained administration now exists in the United States, but in the large cities, where immigrant votes are "corraled," there is, of course, no educated public opinion. Therefore, popular elections of the administrative chief and also of his subordinate officials usually endanger the expert qualification of the official as well as the precise functioning of the bureaucratic mechanism. It also weakens the dependence of the officials upon the hierarchy. This holds at least for the large administrative bodies that are difficult to supervise. The superior qualification and integrity of federal judges, appointed by the President, as over against elected judges in the United States is well known, although both types of officials have been selected primarily in terms of party considerations. The great changes in

American metropolitan administrations demanded by reformers have proceeded essentially from elected mayors working with an apparatus of officials who were appointed by them. These reforms have thus come about in a "Caesarist" fashion. Viewed technically, as an organized form of authority, the efficiency of "Caesarism," which often grows out of democracy, rests in general upon the position of the "Caesar" as a free trustee of the masses (of the army or of the citizenry), who is unfettered by tradition. The "Caesar" is thus the unrestrained master of a body of highly qualified military officers and officials whom he selects freely and personally without regard to tradition or to any other considerations. This "rule of the personal genius," however, stands in contradiction to the formally "democratic" principle of a universally elected officialdom.

3. Normally, the position of the official is held for life, at least in public bureaucracies; and this is increasingly the case for all similar structures. As a factual rule, *tenure for life* is presupposed, even where the giving of notice or periodic reappointment occurs. In contrast to the worker in a private enterprise, the official normally holds tenure. Legal or actual life-tenure, however, is not recognized as the official's right to the possession of office, as was the case with many structures of authority in the past. Where legal guarantees against arbitrary dismissal or transfer are developed, they merely serve to guarantee a strictly objective discharge of specific office duties free from all personal considerations. In Germany, this is the case for all juridical and, increasingly, for all administrative officials.

Within the bureaucracy, therefore, the measure of "independence," legally guaranteed by tenure, is not always a source of increased status for the official whose position is thus secured. Indeed, often the reverse holds, especially in old cultures and communities that are highly differentiated. In such communities, the stricter the subordination under the arbitrary rule of the master, the more it guarantees the maintenance of the conventional seigneurial style of living for the official. Because of the very absence of these legal guarantees of tenure, the conventional esteem for the official may rise in the same way as, during the Middle Ages, the esteem of the nobility of office rose at the expense of esteem for the freemen, and as the king's judge surpassed that of the people's judge. In Germany, the military officer or the administrative official can be removed from office at any time, or at least far more readily than the "independent judge," who never pays with loss of his office for even the grossest offense against the "code of honor" or against social conventions of the salon. For this very reason, if other things are equal, in the eyes of the master stratum the judge is considered less qualified for social intercourse than are officers and administrative officials, whose greater dependence on the master is a greater guarantee of their conformity with status conventions. Of course, the average official strives for a civil-service law, which would materially secure his old age and provide increased guarantees against his arbitrary removal from office. This striving, however, has its limits. A very strong development of the "right to the office" naturally makes it more difficult to staff them with regard to technical efficiency, for such a development decreases the career-opportunities of ambitious candidates for office. This makes for the fact that officials, on the whole, do not feel their dependency upon those at the top. This lack of feeling of dependency, however, rests primarily upon the inclination to depend upon one's equals rather than upon the socially inferior and governed strata. The present conservative movement among the Badenia clergy, occasioned by the anxiety of a presumably threatening separation of church and state, has been expressly determined by the desire not to be turned "from a master into a servant of the parish."

4. The official receives the regular *pecuniary* compensation of a normally fixed *salary* and the old age security provided by a pension. The salary is not measured like a wage in terms of work done, but according to "status," that is, according to the kind of function (the "rank") and, in addition, possibly, according to the length of service. The relatively great security of the official's income, as well as the rewards of social esteem, make the office a sought-after position, especially in countries which no longer provide opportunities for colonial profits. In such countries, this situation permits relatively low salaries for officials.

5. The official is set for a *"career"* within the hierarchical order of the public service. He moves from the lower, less important, and lower paid to the higher positions. The average official naturally desires a mechanical fixing of the conditions of promotion: if not of the offices, at least of the salary levels. He wants these conditions fixed in terms of "seniority," or possibly according to grades achieved in a developed system of expert examinations. Here and there, such examinations actually form a character *indelebilis* of the official and have lifelong effects on his career. To this is joined the desire to qualify the right to office and the increasing tendency toward status group closure and economic security. All of this makes for a tendency to consider the offices as "prebends" of those who are qualified by educational certificates. The necessity of taking general personal and intellectual qualifications into consideration, irrespective of the often subaltern character of the educational certificate, has led to a condition in which the highest political offices, especially the positions of "ministers," are principally filled without reference to such certificates.

✧   ✧   ✧   ✧   ✧

Technical Advantages of Bureaucratic Organization

The decisive reason for the advance of bureaucratic organization has always been its purely technical superiority over any other form of organization. The fully developed bureaucratic mechanism compares with other organizations exactly as does the machine with the non-mechanical modes of production.

Precision, speed, unambiguity, knowledge of the files, continuity, discretion, unity, strict subordination, reduction of friction and of material and personal costs—these are raised to the optimum point in the strictly bureaucratic administration, and especially in its monocratic form. As compared with all collegiate, honorific, and avocational forms of administration, trained bureaucracy is superior on all these points. And as far as complicated tasks are concerned, paid bureaucratic work is not only more precise but, in the last analysis, it is often cheaper than even formally unremunerated honorific service.

Honorific arrangements make administrative work an avocation and, for this reason alone, honorific service normally functions more slowly; being less bound to schemata and being more formless. Hence it is less precise and less unified than bureaucratic work because it is less dependent upon superiors and because the establishment and exploitation of the apparatus of subordinate officials and filing services are almost unavoidably less economical. Honorific service is less continuous than bureaucratic and frequently quite expensive. This is especially the case if one thinks not only of the money costs to the public treasury—costs which bureaucratic administration, in comparison with administration by notables, usually substantially increases—but also of the frequent economic losses of the governed caused by delays and lack of precision. The possibility of administration by notables normally and permanently exists only where official management can be satisfactorily discharged as an avocation. With the qualitative increase of tasks the administration has to face, administration by notables reaches its limits—today, even in England. Work organized by collegiate bodies causes friction and delay and requires compromises between colliding interests and views. The administration, therefore, runs less precisely and is more independent of superiors; hence, it is less unified and slower. All advances of the Prussian administrative organization have been and will in the future be advances of the bureaucratic, and especially of the monocratic, principle.

Today, it is primarily the capitalist market economy which demands that the official business of the administration be discharged precisely, unambiguously, continuously, and with as much speed as possible. Normally, the very large, modern capitalist enterprises are themselves unequalled models of strict bureaucratic organization. Business management throughout rests on increasing precision, steadiness, and, above all, the speed of operations. This, in turn, is determined by the peculiar nature of the modern means of communication, including, among other things, the news service of the press. The extraordinary increase in the speed by which public announcements, as well as economic and political facts, are transmitted exerts a steady and sharp pressure in the direction of speeding up the tempo of administrative reaction towards various situations. The optimum of such reaction time is normally attained only by a strictly bureaucratic organization.[1]

Bureaucratization offers above all the optimum possibility for carrying through the principle of specializing administrative functions according to purely objective considerations. Individual performances are allocated to functionaries who have specialized training and who by constant practice learn more and more. The "objective" discharge of business primarily means a discharge of business according to *calculable rules* and "without regard for persons."

"Without regard for persons" is also the watchword of the "market" and, in general, of all pursuits of naked economic interests. A consistent execution of bureaucratic domination means the leveling of status "honor." Hence, if the principle of the free-market is not at the same time restricted, it means the universal domination of the "class situation." That this consequence of bureaucratic domination has not set in everywhere, parallel to the extent of bureaucratization, is due to the differences among possible principles by which polities may meet their demands.

The second element mentioned, "calculable rules," also is of paramount importance for modern bureaucracy. The peculiarity of modern culture, and specifically of its technical and economic basis, demands this very "calculability" of results. When fully developed, bureaucracy also stands, in a specific sense, under the principle of *sine ira ac studio*. Its specific nature, which is welcomed by capitalism, develops the more perfectly the more the bureaucracy is "dehumanized," the more completely it succeeds in eliminating from official business love, hatred, and all purely personal, irrational, and emotional elements which escape calculation. This is the specific nature of bureaucracy and it is appraised as its special virtue.

The more complicated and specialized modern culture becomes, the more its external supporting apparatus demands the personally detached and strictly "objective" *expert*, in lieu of the master of older social structures, who was moved by personal sympathy and favor, by grace and gratitude. Bureaucracy offers the attitudes demanded by the external apparatus of modern culture in the most favorable combination.

---

[1] Here we cannot discuss in detail how the bureaucratic apparatus may, and actually does, produce definite obstacles to the discharge of business in a manner suitable for the single case.

ROLES AND MARITAL ADJUSTMENT

Leonard S. Cottrell, Jr.

Institutions develop to fulfill basic and persistent social needs. Sometimes institutional experience is unsatisfying, however, and the effective operation of the institution is jeopardized, because the roles persons have learned to play and which they bring to the institution are not suited to the institutional situation in which they find themselves. Or, equally disruptive to individual and group, the expectations of persons regarding the behavior of others in the institution are unfulfilled. In this selection L. S. Cottrell, Jr., discusses the importance of an understanding of role-behavior and role-expectation in studying the adjustment of husbands and wives to the institutions of marriage and the family.

There are certain points concerning the concept of the rôle which, though recognized by those who developed and refined the concept, need for our purposes added emphasis.

First, in our use of the concept rôle we are prone to think of certain characteristic responses or tendencies to respond which the person makes or tends to make to persons or situations. Frequently we fail to recognize clearly enough what might be called expectations entertained by the subject as to actions or responses which are to come from other persons. The writer recognizes that it is impossible to separate these two things since in reality they are aspects of the same thing. There is no conception of one's rôle, conscious or unconscious, without reference to what action is expected of the situation of which the rôle is a part. It is well, however, to emphasize the expectancy aspect, particularly in using the notion in the study of marriage situations. A number of our cases of marital difficulty seem capable of analysis in terms of the inability of one mate to fit into the expected response pattern called for by the other.

A second point to be called to mind is that in marriage the partners do not play single rôles with respect to one another, although a single rôle may be most characteristic of a given person in his marriage relations. Cases seem to indicate a multiplicity of rôles. For example, a wife may

SOURCE: Publication of the American Sociological Society, Vol. 27, No. 2, *Papers* (May, 1933), 108–15, University of Chicago Press. Reprinted by permission of the author and the publisher. ✧ Leonard Cottrell, Jr., is Social Psychologist for the Russell Sage Foundation. He is a former president of the American Sociological Association. Among his books are *Delinquency Areas* and *Developments in Social Psychology.* He is the coauthor of *Identity and Interpersonal Competence: New Directions in Family Research* and the co-editor of *Sociology Today.*

play a much depended upon mother-rôle, a hated sister-rôle, and a loved brother-rôle at different times for her husband. The husband may in turn be for his wife her distantly respected father, her hated younger brother, and her loved older sister. The startling ambivalence frequently displayed by married persons for one another may not be true ambivalence in the strict Freudian sense. It may actually be the result of corresponding attitudes for different rôle patterns derived from early family relations. Thus a husband may call out affectionate as well as hostile responses from his wife by playing rôles of members of her family who earlier called out the different responses. Of course it is not at all necessary nor even likely that either husband or wife will be aware that he is playing such rôles.

A third point to be mentioned is that rôles may be stereotyped and unique. The stereotyped rôles, for example, of husband and father, wife and mother, are defined in the folkways and mores of society. But within these definitions by a given culture there are individual patterns or rôles that are determined by the peculiar social experience of the individual. Thus an adult may continue to play an infantile rôle as a result, let us say, of his having been the youngest child in a family that has coddled him a great deal.

A fourth point which needs emphasis is that, frequently, we might say usually, many of the rôles that persons play are unconscious. If all of the rôles a married pair play for one another are not unconscious, the most significant ones are frequently so.

We shall not here attempt an exegesis of the conception of the unconscious. It is sufficient for our purposes to realize that, if we analyze any act or series of actions, we find that there are phases of the act which can be said to be unknown to the actor, and are, moreover, not subject to his unaided conscious scrutiny and reflection. The conscious phase of the act in which the individual has defined for himself or has defined for him his objects and purposes and motives is one phase only. There are preliminary to and concomitant with his acts, goals, motives, etc., of which he is unconscious. Examples might be taken from the cases cited by Mr. H. D. Lasswell in his *Psychopathology and Politics* in which the conscious political activity directed against a present order turns out to be a displacement of drives and hostilities of the child with respect to its parent or sibling. Of these more primary and elementary motives the person is not aware and accepts his own definitions of goals and reasons as the only ones present in the action. Our contention here is that the same kind of unconscious character can be attributed to much of marital activity.

There may be some objection to thinking of rôles as unconscious. We do not hold that all rôles are unconscious. Some seem to be completely unconscious; some only partially so. We are not wedded to a word. If the term "rôle" is to be used only for conscious action patterns and relationships, then we must give another name to these unconscious patterns and relationships that exist in fact.

The narrowed angle of approach represented in this paper, namely, the study of marriage as an adjustment of rôles, may be indicated by laying down certain propositions.

First, marriage adjustment may be regarded as a process in which marriage partners attempt to re-enact certain relational systems or situations which obtained in their own earlier family groups. Or, in other words, marriage partners tend to play the habitual rôles they evolved in their childhood and adolescence.

Second, the kinds of rôles that marriage partners bring to the marriage will determine the nature of their marriage relationship and the degree of adjustment that they will achieve.

Third, that maladjusted marriages may be regarded as results of the failure of the marriage situation to provide the system of relationships called for by the rôles which the marriage partners bring to the marriage.

Now the writer is quite aware that these propositions leave out of account a great many important factors—cultural, economic, etc.—and there is no effort to deny that such factors are of importance. Let it be emphatically affirmed that these propositions are laid down in an effort to make a logical delimitation of the problem. However, there is considerable justification for the opinion that the unique rôle patterns are the chief determinants of the success or failure of marriages in which the persons come from similar cultural backgrounds. And it should not be forgotten that the greater number of marriages are contracted by persons of reasonably similar cultural backgrounds.

Let us consider the case of Mr. and Mrs. A. who have been married about a year.

Mr. A. (aged 24) is the youngest of a family of seven. When asked to tell about his childhood, he launches into a rather enthusiastic account of his happy and satisfactory family life. From his story one gathers that his mother was a powerful and aggressive personality, the chief center, drive, and control factor in the family. She ran the father's affairs, planned the children's vocational and social activities, maneuvered the daughters' marriages, and tried to maneuver the sons' marriages. Mr. A. boasts of her iron will. He is proud of her determined look, and tells how her spirit never sagged. He tells how she faced death with the same unshaken will and determination never to admit defeat.

The father is described as a pleasant, reliable, steady, quiet, and meek person who seemed to figure merely as an unimportant though kindly fixture in the household. He worked steadily, turned his earnings over to his wife, never seriously opposed her, and after her death, agreeably allowed his daughters to place him in an old people's home.

The three sisters are described as being very much like the mother, particularly the two older ones. These two have married husbands to whom they play pretty much the same rôle which their mother played toward her husband. The youngest sister, whom we shall call Martha, is two years older than Mr. A. Although not quite so Amazonian as her sisters, she is fairly aggressive, active, and adequate in meeting situations. She has played a decidedly mothering rôle to Mr. A., especially since the death of their mother when Mr. A. was about fifteen years old. He says of Martha in an interview, "We have always been very close together. She has comforted me and consoled me in my troubles. I have confided in her and she has shielded me. She used to advise me and tell me what to do." He used to sleep with his sister, and he tells of his surprise on discovering recently that people thought such an arrangement strange. He says: "Even after I was 16 or 17 if I was blue or worried about my future she would take me to bed with her and comfort me." This occurred more frequently after the mother's death. Soon after his marriage he felt he *had* to leave his wife, to get away and think things out. He went home for a visit. The first few days he was very worried and upset. He couldn't sleep at night and one night fell to weeping. Martha took him to bed with her and consoled him. He says: "I felt a motherly warmth and felt released from my troubles and went to sleep. After that I slept in her room every night and felt much better." Mr. A. denies ever having sexual impulses or ideas about Martha at any time, although they have discussed sex quite freely.

In speaking of all the sisters he says: "I was always proud to go places with my sisters. They were lively and popular and I was proud of them. I could walk around and enjoy myself and they could take care of themselves." (This was said in comparing his sisters with his wife, who depends too much on him, he says, for pleasant times at social gatherings.)

Mr. A. does not feel that there was much conflict in his home. Things seemed to be secure and to run smoothly under the orderly supervision of the mother. He feels that the home life was happy. He says: "There was always something going on at my home. My mother and sisters were always doing interesting things, having people over and having jolly times that I like to remember. They didn't sit around like she does (alluding to his wife) and wait for something to happen. My father is quiet and never participated much in what was going on, but he enjoyed watching and listening to other people. I am like my father. I liked to watch and listen, and, if I felt like it, put in a word or do something. I hate to feel I *have* to talk or take the initiative." (This remark also was made with reference to his wife's irritating dependence upon him.)

Mr. A.'s two brothers are interesting. The older brother, who is also the oldest child, is called the black sheep. His relations with the mother and with the sister next to him were particularly hostile. He rebelled and left home early. The next brother is the middle child. He was the mother's favorite. He was and still is a dependable, quiet, kindly, non-aggressive person. The children say he is the mainstay of the family. Mr. A. describes him as a kind of parent to the younger children.

Mr. A. says that his parents and siblings were always kind to him.

"They always took care of me, and my brother told me he would send me to school. My sisters like to have me come to their homes, and they enjoy giving me the comforts of a home. They say, 'You need the comforts of a home'; and I believe they are right, because I often wish I could feel that I had a father and mother and a home I could go back to."

He was punished very little. A typical instance is revealing. His mother and brother scolded him and threatened to punish him for not practicing his music. They told him he should be willing to practice for them if they paid for his lessons. Mr. A.'s comment is interesting: "I remember I was very angry that they should expect anything from me just because they paid for the lessons. I hated to feel obligated." (This represents an attitude characteristic of Mr. A.—that of expecting the environment to minister unto him with no obligation or responsibilities on his part.)

One gets the impression from Mr. A.'s conversation that he was an extremely dependent, much indulged, and coddled child; that he resented any responsibility or expectation or demand from him on the part of the environment; and that he felt insecure in situations where he was thrown on his own initiative. He tended to assume a passive rôle, expecting the environment to furnish aggressive support, backing, and leadership. On several occasions he made what he describes as attempts to win his independence by leaving home. He usually went under the tutelage of a decisive and aggressive boy friend who told him he ought to learn to stand on his own feet. On each occasion when he faced a shortage of jobs or money he felt forced to retreat home. After a few attempts he was ashamed to go home and would retreat to the family of the girl he finally married. He said: "I just can't bear feeling all alone in a strange place with no money and no home I can go to."

Mr. A. met his wife shortly before his mother's death. He says: "I was timid and bashful, but she was pleasant and talked to me and I felt comfortable with her." Soon after Mr. A.'s mother died the girl's family moved to another city. A. wept the night before her departure and said: "First I lose my mother; then I lose you." (The girl had the same first name as Mr. A.'s mother.) He told her he loved her at that time, but felt that he had said more than he meant; and the next day he contrived to arrive at the railroad station too late to see her off. Largely through the girl's efforts, a correspondence was kept up between the two. Later, after some of his unsuccessful forays into the world of affairs, he would seek the shelter of the girl's home. She would be very sympathetic about his trials and tribulations and she readily accepted his alibis for failure and excused him to himself. When she consoled him on his retreats from unsuccessful attempts to make good in the world (which, by the way, he expected to do in short order) he would tell her that she was just like his sister. As he was forced to repeat his returns to the girl's family, he became more and more uncomfortable; for he felt himself more and more obligated to assume responsibilities with respect to the girl. He seemed unable to do without a good deal of sympathetic reassurance; but he became increasingly panicky as it grew more evident that marriage was expected of him.

Before we discuss further the relations between Mr. A. and his wife, it is necessary to describe briefly Mrs. A.'s family. The families of both Mr. and Mrs. A. represent the same cultural and economic levels; if there is any difference, it is slight and in favor of Mr. A.'s family.

Mrs. A. (aged 23) describes her father as a successful merchant until a few years ago, when he developed an interest in gambling and taking extended vacations. He had never saved money but his business kept the family in good circumstances. For some time now, however, he had been very improvident and irresponsible. He has obtained good positions, but has given them up for very trivial reasons. Mrs. A. says she used to admire and respect her father, but since he has allowed the family to come upon evil days she has lost respect for him and feels very resentful toward him. The father accuses the mother of being responsible for the condition of the family. He says: "You should have taken the money from me and not allowed me to gamble." And "You should have made me attend to our business." Mrs. A. feels her father has acted as something of a spoiled child toward his wife.

The mother is described as patient, long suffering, submissive. Mrs. A. feels that she is close to her mother because, as she says, "I am very much like my mother and can understand her." She has always taken sides with her mother in family arguments, which seems to align the father and older brother against the mother and Mrs. A. These arguments turn out to be tongue lashings from the father and older brother, with the mother and daughter passively resisting.

The oldest brother is very harsh toward the mother, but she submits to his dominating and overbearing treatment. She appears to resent it somewhat, but she excuses him. When he flies into rages and leaves home to avoid paying room and board, the mother will feel sorry for him and will cook up cakes and other dainties, which she carries to his abode and lays at his feet. She treats the father in much the same way, patiently accepting his occasional beratings. When some of the children complain of their father's incompetence the mother will make excuses for him. She will say, "Your father has worked hard all his life and now just look at him. It isn't fair."

There are three children in the family, an oldest son, Mrs. A., and her younger brother. Mrs. A. speaks bitterly of the intense hatred she bears her older brother, who appears from her description to be a very domineering, overbearing, egocentric person. But she follows her statements of hostility toward him with the admission that she secretly admires his aggressiveness and capabilities and envies his assertiveness. She has wished all her life that he would love her. When on rare occasions he would be kind to her or give her a birthday gift, she would feel much encouraged and hope for better relations. She would experience great disappointment when he would resume his usual tactics.

The son's hostilities toward his mother and sister seem to date from early childhood. Mrs. A. has fought back somewhat, but she usually cries, feels blue, and suffers inwardly. She still dreams of having bitter fights with him, but in these dreams her rôle is one of defending herself against his attacks. Occasionally she will dream of a more aggressive rôle in which she vehemently commands her brother to get out of the house. She says that one reason she liked Mr. A. was that he seemed to be the opposite of her brother in every way.

Mrs. A. is fond of her younger brother and feels that they were quite close as children, though their relationship is not so close now.

Mrs. A.'s conversation gives one the impression of a person with some hostile drives, who, nevertheless, tends to assume a passive rôle in all situations. She tends to wait for something to happen, for others to make suggestions and to take the initiative. Her lack of decisive self-assertion is a characteristic which drives her husband, so he says, to distraction.

With this all too meager account of the backgrounds of our subjects, let us turn again to their relationship with one another.

Mr. A. became more and more frightened and restless as it became clearer to him that the natural and expected result of his relationship to Mrs. A. was marriage. He made some attempts to extricate himself by protesting to her that they were in no position to marry and by leaving her home. Quoting from an interview with him: "I wanted to be away to be free to work out my problems alone, but I felt myself dragged deeper and deeper." Early attempts to leave and get a job resulted in failure and an inevitable return to the girl, who was always ready with her sympathy and mothering solicitude. Her family was hospitable; but what worried Mr. A. was that they assumed his frequent returnings for prolonged visits to mean that he was intent on marriage. The father finally became more urgent and tried to encourage the diffident young man by letting him know that what he needed to settle him down was marriage.

These urgings and expectations on the part of the family plus the pleadings of the girl, plus his own inability to do without some sympathetic reassuring, proved too much for him. Finally, he says, he shut his eyes and jumped. We do not have time to give his description of his mental anguish as he walked the streets for two days trying to make up his mind. "Then," he says, "with super-human effort I forced myself to go to the courthouse and say 'I want a marriage license.'"

After the marriage Mr. A. began to have many fears and forebodings. He was afraid Mrs. A.'s mother or father would die and he would have to help take care of Mrs. A.'s younger brother. He feared that he had wrecked his chances to realize his best self and should get out of the marriage. He began to find Mrs. A. ugly; and this, he said, outraged his aesthetic sensibilities. But the main theme throughout his interviews is: "My wife is a drag on me. She depends too much on me. Instead of feeling myself being pulled forward, I feel like she is pulling me backward. Why can't she be like my sisters? She is weak and casts a gloom over my spirit that I can't shake off. I must go away so I can feel free again and be on my own."

He did break away once to go to his sister for comfort and solace. He said: "While I was there I was happy again unless I thought of my plight. My sister said 'all you need is the comfort of your home' and she was right. While I was with her I felt all right."

The wife complained that she didn't feel secure with her husband. She wished that he could be like other men who seem to know what they want to do and how to go about it, who seem to take charge of things and forge ahead and not appear so helpless. She resented the fact that, although her husband was out of work and she was supporting him, he seemed to take that for granted as his due. Moreover, he showed great irritation toward her if she came home tired and, as he puts it, "sagging and weak looking." He says: "I simply can't stand that sagging, droopy look."

Their sexual adjustment is interesting when seen on this background. Neither knew how to proceed and their first attempts at intercourse were clumsy and unsuccessful. The husband's history shows considerable curiosity during childhood, and avoidance and fear in adolescent encounters. Even after receiving coaching from a physician and becoming somewhat adept in sexual technique, he is still described by his wife as clumsy and diffident in his approaches. He himself reveals a certain resentment and resistance to assuming the rôle of aggressor in relation with his wife. He has to assume a rôle in the sexual situation that runs contrary to his desires.

In both husband and wife there are evidences of strong repressions of sexual drives. These specifically sexual attitudes are undoubtedly a part of the situation, but they may also be thought of as parts of the basic rôle patterns, particularly in the case of the husband.

This represents the barest outline of some of the high spots in the case, but if we could present all of our materials they would hardly do more than amplify the picture which must be evident from even such a scant description.

The central problem in this case is a problem of basic rôles, which are apparently the result of the early family relationships.

The husband is looking for a solicitous, protecting, aggressive, decisive, parent environment which the wife, who expects something of the same sort of environment, cannot supply. She was able to furnish sympathy and to that extent supplied the rôle of mother and sister in the husband's family. But she is not equipped to supply the more positive and aggressive part of the rôles that these people represented in Mr. A.'s personality development.

Neither of them is quite fully aware of what the basis for their trouble is. The husband thinks his marriage is a mistake, that he is not cut out for marriage, that his artistic temperament needs complete freedom to realize itself. The wife thinks the husband is sulky, inconsiderate, selfish, and jealous of her interest in her family. They both think that relief of the financial tension would be a partial solution.

Those who take the psychoanalytic approach would probably classify the man as a homosexual type, and interpret the difficulties on that basis. If we recognize that for the male the category "homosexual" applies to general psycho-sexual traits of passivity rather than to certain specific sexual attitudes merely, then the classification is probably valid. But it should be pointed out that the classification is not fully descriptive of the rôle pattern Mr. A. represents. He is not only passive but has an infantile dependent attitude or rôle which is not necessarily characteristic of the homosexual.

The case might also be interpreted as a result of guilt feelings which arise when Mr. A. engages in sexual activity with a person who stands as a substitute for his sister Martha. Sexual impulses with reference to his sister must have been heavily repressed and, when they are allowed expression on a love object that stands for her, they give rise to strong guilt feelings from which Mr. A. seeks to escape by terminating the marriage. Even here, however, we get into a usage of the notion of rôles. But it is apparent that this specifically sexual explanation leaves out of account too much of Mr. A.'s general pattern of response to all types of situations.

The writer would suggest that, at the present stage of the game, it seems preferable to use concretely descriptive categories of rôle types. It may turn out later that some such set of master categories as those now used in the psychoanalytic field will apply. But their application should be made when empirical evidence justifies such usage.

Turning to a different approach, it should be pointed out that analysis of marital problems in terms of the usual categories of economic, cultural, response, temperamental, health, and other tensions is rather sterile unless such analysis is done with the insight that rôle analysis supplies. Any and all of the usual tensions may and do appear in a given case, but frequently they are meaningless unless seen in reference to the basic problem of rôles.

THE SWEDES DO IT BETTER

Richard F. Tomasson

The family as a social institution is today undergoing change because of scientific and technological developments in the society in general. One feature which has been altered markedly is the opportunity for, and orientation toward, employment of married women. The problems raised by working wives have been handled differently in different cultures. In this selection Tomasson contends that Swedish women, as compared with American women, face fewer role conflicts between work and marriage and between a job and bearing children. Numerous arrangements are designed to make the two roles compatible in their industrialized society. And the result, says Tomasson, is a less child-centered society but one with more stable marriages.

Some rational answers to questions that trouble many American women today—and perhaps some illuminating guidelines for the future—can be found in the experience of Sweden. Our countries, to be sure, are different in many respects: Sweden is a small nation with a homogeneous population. But both nations are attached to a democratic political philosophy, and Sweden comes closer to matching our high standard of living than any other European country. While there are many resemblances between our two societies, the Swedes have come closer to resolving issues which are still being uneasily debated in the United States.

Why, for instance, is the familiar conflict between work and marriage so much less of a problem in Sweden? One reason—though by no means the only one—is the fact that Swedish women devote less time and energy to child bearing.

Sweden has, in fact, one of the lowest birth rates in the world, fourteen per thousand population in 1960 compared with twenty-four per thousand in the United States. This is not due to any great difference in ability to control family size. . . . Nor are economic factors the heart of the matter. In fact the relative cost of rearing a child is greater in America than in Sweden, where an expanding system of welfare legislation has provided

SOURCE: *Harper's Magazine*, Vol. 225, No. 1349 (October, 1962), 178–80. Reprinted by permission of the author and the publisher. ✧ Richard F. Tomasson is assistant professor of sociology at the University of Illinois. His areas of interest include social and cultural aspects of human fertility, differential mortality, social stratification, sociological theory, and Scandinavian societies. He is the author of *Patterns in Negro-White Differential Mortality, 1930–1957* and the coauthor of *Disparities in Visualizing Social Norms* and *Identifiability of Jews.*

increasing financial benefits to mothers and children. This aid began in the 1930s to spur the low birth rate which was below replacement level for several years.

All Swedish mothers, married or not, now receive a grant of $180 when a child is born, as well as free delivery and confinement, grants for post-natal health care for mother and child, and an allowance of $180 a year for each child up to the age of sixteen. (Unmarried mothers receive additional cash compensation in recognition of their greater need when a father does not contribute to the support of the child.) Comprehensive national health insurance makes the child's medical bills negligible and complete dental care is available to all children in the schools. Nor need Swedish parents worry about paying for their children's education. Through the university level, tuition is virtually free and there are generous scholarship and loan programs to help meet students' living costs.

Employers are forbidden by law to discharge a woman employee who gets married or becomes pregnant. She is entitled to a substantial proportion of her pay for a maternity leave of up to six months. With all these inducements one would expect Swedish fertility to exceed ours.

There are, however, important differences in Swedish and American culture which explains the significant disparity in family size. (The Swedish population will probably increase by only 10 per cent between 1960 and 1975 while ours will take a 25 or 30 per cent leap.)

Of prime importance is the simple fact that Swedes marry about four years later than Americans—the median age for Swedish men in the 1950s was twenty-seven; for women, twenty-four. Americans, in fact, marry earlier than the people of any other industrialized nation. This is, of course, one reason for our population explosion. Very young couples have a longer period of fecundity, more energy to deal with the rigors of child-rearing, and a less realistic picture of the burdens of parenthood than those who marry later. It is also true that a girl who goes to marriage directly from her parents' home or the college dormitory adjusts more easily to the confining role of motherhood than one who has had several years of bachelor freedom. And early marriage tends to narrow a woman's horizon to the traditional roles of wife and mother before competing interests have a chance to develop.

Most American wives have worked outside their homes before marriage, a majority do so again some time after marriage, but few—even among college graduates—can be said to have careers. In Sweden, on the other hand, a high proportion of middle-class wives have relatively uninterrupted working lives and there are far more women in the traditionally male occupations than in America.

In Swedish universities, for example, women are now a quarter of the students of medicine, dentistry, and the natural sciences, and 15 per cent of those in law school; a majority of the pharmacy students are women. In all these fields in the United States the proportion of women is small or negligible. Few Swedish wives give up careers when they marry; few American wives have careers to give up.

A Shack in the Country

Family size and behavior are affected too by a difference in attitudes toward city living. Smaller quarters and the distractions and opportunities of the city discourage large families. In all industrial societies urban families have fewer children than those who live in the country. Statistically, Americans are as urbanized as the Swedes but—as William F. Whyte and Jane Jacobs have eloquently charged—we are essentially anti-city; if we can afford it we prefer to live in the suburbs despite the difficulties and deprivations that go with commuting.

The Swedes, on the other hand, do not share our feeling that we are not doing right by our children if we bring them up in the city. Families are generally content to live in apartments in Stockholm or Gothenburg, though many wish they were larger and easier to get. A vacation shack in the country satisfies their bucolic longings.

An even more striking difference is in the permissive single standard of sexual behavior which prevails in Sweden . . . . There are social pressures against promiscuity, but on the whole unmarried young women have about the same latitude as young men. Thus there is little of the guilt and moral ambiguity about sex relations among the unmarried which act as such a powerful inducement to early marriage in the United States.

Interestingly, Sweden has a divorce rate lower by a third than ours. Considering how far Sweden has moved along the road to full equality for women, it is perhaps paradoxical that the roles of husband and wife are more specifically defined than in the United States. This is, in fact, generally true of Europeans who feel that American husbands do much "woman's work." Swedish (or Dutch, French, or Austrian) fathers will seldom be found diapering, feeding, or bathing their children; nor are they dish driers, grocery shoppers, or baby-sitters. (But this is changing among younger Swedes.) Only in America is it not surprising for a university professor to feel that he must be home by five o'clock in order to help his wife with the children. And it may be that the amiable co-operation of their husbands in some of the onerous duties of child care is an extra inducement to American mothers to have more babies.

More probably, however, the decision to have a third or fourth child results from the mother's feeling that she is on full-time duty at home anyhow and has no compelling outside involvements. It takes an exceptionally well organized woman with great vitality to flout convention and play the mother and career roles simultaneously against all the obstacles American middle-class culture puts in her way. Certainly the conventional wisdom makes it clear that home is the only place for the mother of small —and even not so small—children. Family, neighbors, and friends urge her to stay there as do such diverse instructors as Dr. Spock, Ann Landers, and Russell Kirk. Even the government conspires by allowing only slight tax exemption for the child-care expenses of working mothers.

Swedish women too are under some pressure to stay home with their babies, and most of them take more than just a few months out to have them. But a relatively high proportion of middle-class wives with small children work outside their homes. Facilities for the daytime care of small children are more readily available than in the United States and so are competent domestic helpers. But the crucial difference is the fact that it is not generally considered strange, antisocial, or immoral for the Swedish mother of young children to work outside her home.

Recent evidence accumulated in the United States suggests that we too may have reason to reverse our stand on these questions. . . . Three diverse studies all came to the conclusion that maternal employment *per se* does not have the adverse effects on children's lives attributed to it. One study which covered more than a thousand children in the public schools of Cedar Rapids, Iowa, indicated that the academic performance and social adjustment of children—from nursery school through high school—had no perceptible connection with their mothers' employment. Similarly, a study of some six hundred Michigan high-school girls demonstrated that while an employed mother may be under increased physical strain, her dual role does not affect the mother-daughter relationship adversely. The same conclusions were corroborated by interviews conducted in Spokane with 104 nonemployed mothers, 104 who were employed, and 82 mother substitutes. Nothing was found to support the widely held hypothesis that the separation of children from their mothers "has 'bad' psychological, physical, and social effects on children. . . ."

America's Fertility Champs

Findings of this sort have not yet gained much currency. But as the facts become more widely known, they are bound to contribute to a more rational and less child-centered way of life for American women. There are indeed already signs that our birth rate is declining and that families will be smaller in the years ahead. I have asked hundreds of college students over the past couple of years how many children they wanted. As might be expected they overwhelmingly want two, three, or four. But the interesting fact is that more want two than four. Compared to the 1940s and 1950s, this is a significant change. The uninterrupted decline in the American birth rate between 1957 and 1963 from 25.3 to 21.6 births per 1,000 population may well reflect a real decline in average family size.

It may well be, in fact, that American women born in the early 'thirties will turn out to be the fertility champions of the twentieth century. On the other hand, wives of the 1970s and 1980s may find themselves as free as Swedish women are today from the conflict between the traditional woman's role and the opportunities which an affluent industrial society provides.

The distance still to be bridged is epitomized in two sociological studies. Writing about "Student Culture at Vassar," John H. Bushnell observed . . . :

"The Vassar student's future identity is largely encompassed by the projected role of wife-mother. . . . For these young women the 'together-ness' vogue is definitely an integral theme of future family life with any opportunities for independent action attaching to an Ivy League degree being willfully passed over in favor of the anticipated rewards of close-knit companionship within the home that-is-to-be."

In sharp contrast, . . . a Danish sociologist . . . notes:

"But even if she excels in all these respects [being a good housekeeper and hostess, a loving mother, and an attractive spouse], she will reap slight social esteem, because dominant middle-class opinion will insist on the superior value of choosing a career outside the home and of cultivating literary and artistic interests."

✤ 50 ✤

TECHNOLOGY, BIOLOGY, AND
THE CHANGING FAMILY

Meyer F. Nimkoff

Though social institutions tend to be stable, they sometimes change in both form and function. According to this article by Nimkoff, written in 1951, our scientific and technological develop-ments had appeared to have brought us to a point where even the child-bearing function of the family, assumed to be so permanent and fundamental, might become altered beyond recognition. How-ever, persistence of the institutionalized behavior patterns of the family is demonstrated by the fact that relatively little of the change predicted has occurred in the years since this article appeared.

. . . We may experience in the near future a revolution in the biological functions of the family comparable to the revolution which has occurred

SOURCE: Reprinted from "Technology, Biology, and the Changing Fam-ily," by M. F. Nimkoff, *The American Journal of Sociology*, Vol. 57, No. 1 (July, 1951), 20–26, by permission of The University of Chicago Press. Copy-right 1951 by The University of Chicago. ✧ Meyer F. Nimkoff (1904–1965) was chairman of the Department of Sociology, Florida State University. He was the author of *The Child* and *Marriage and the Family*, and the coauthor of *Technology and the Changing Family* and *Sociology*.

in the economic functions during the last two hundred years. This new impact on the family derives from discoveries in the rapidly developing field of the biology of sex and reproduction. . . . As a first example, consider the progress that has been made in determining the sex of the child before conception. This is not to be confused with the prediction of the child's sex before birth, which can now be made in certain cases on the basis of various tests, although with less than 100 per cent accuracy.

For some time we have known that the child's sex is determined by the type of sperm cell contributed by the father. There are two types of sperm cell, the male-producing Y-sperm and the female-producing X-sperm, whereas in the ova there is only one type of sex cell, the X-type. Each parent contributes one sex chromosome to the child; if two X's combine, the child is female; an X and a Y produce a male. So it is the father, or at least his sex chromosomes, that determines the sex of his children, and the mother has nothing to do with it. Yet many a wife in ignorance of this fact has felt guilty because *she* did not present her husband with a son. King Farouk of Egypt divorced his queen, according to press accounts, because she bore him no son.

The X-chromosome is slightly larger than the Y-chromosome, and the female-producing sperm contains slightly more chromosomal material, making it slightly more dense. Harvey has calculated that the Y-sperm should have a density of 1.07132 and the X-sperm a density of 1.1705. By means of a special centrifuge apparatus (the vacuum type turbine centrifuge) and the use of a proper medium for the density gradient (a 20 per cent dextrin in Ringer's solution), Harvey thinks it possible to separate these two kinds of cells. The refinement of technique required for success is comparable, Harvey points out, to that which separated Uranium 235 and 238. For this reason, says Harvey, "we may designate any process of sorting the two kinds of sperm for control of sex as essentially a separation of biological isotopes."

It should be emphasized that the separation of male-producing and female-producing sperm has not yet been accomplished, but one would be bold indeed who would argue that it will not be done in the future. If and when the two cells are separated, use of them for purposes of reproduction would involve artificial insemination. There is, however, at the present time no important objection to this procedure when the donor is the woman's husband.

✧   ✧   ✧   ✧   ✧

Even if scientific research should give us the knowledge of how to control the sex of the child, the question remains: Would we use the knowledge? And, if so, how? Do we have a preference for boys or girls? It may be observed at once that, even if there is no general preference for one sex over the other in a society, individual parents may still prefer one sex to the other, or a certain ordering of their families according to sex, in which case the ability to achieve this end may be deemed to contribute to the happiness of the couple. Margaret Mead in *Male and Female* has stated that there are no social reasons why parents in the United States should prefer boys to girls or vice versa, but there is at least the reason that boys preserve the family name, in which there may be pride. Mead thinks most American parents would like to have a balanced family of boys and girls, but the preference is probably that the firstborn be a boy, which means that a son would be the more common choice of one-child families, if there were control.

This discussion assumes that the mores would be favorable to the new knowledge and that prospective parents would be permitted to utilize it. But we have no assurance that the control, if achieved, would be socially sanctioned, especially if it resulted in an appreciable imbalance in the sex ratio. There seems to be no great demand for control of the sex of the child at the present time. At least such a demand, if it exists, is not evident in any considerable application by scientists to the task of solving the technical problems involved. But if a differential in the size of the male population establishes the superiority of one nation over another in war, then it is conceivable that sex control may be encouraged in the future even as a high birth rate, without reference to the sex of the children, is now encouraged in nearly every Western nation by means of subsidies for babies. Dictatorial governments in particular may find sex control appealing and may derive an advantage from the reluctance of democratic states to adopt the practice and/or to favor male births.

We may consider briefly the implications of an unbalanced sex ratio as it relates to the marriage system. The evidence from primitive peoples indicates that an appreciable surplus of women in a society, resulting mainly from the high mortality of male hunters in late adolescence and early manhood, is a condition disposing to polygyny, whereas a surplus of men, usually resulting from female infanticide and/or religious cloistering, disposes toward polyandry. War in modern times in many Western nations has led to a large surplus of women of marriageable ages, but, barring another war, the imbalance in the sex ratio has been temporary, correcting itself in the next generation. If the sex of the child were controlled by science, and a continuing preference for males were to be expressed by a society, it would seem that the bases would exist for a trend toward polyandry. Considerable changes might be expected in the status of the sexes, their social roles, and their attitudes toward each other.

We may speculate further on what effect, if any, controlling the sex of the child would have on the relations of husbands and wives. If sex control is utilized, then procreation must occur by artificial insemination. During the past century or so, the trend has been to emphasize the psychological rather than the procreative function of coitus, as the reduction in the size of the family bears witness. Sex control would presumably further this trend; indeed, procreation and coitus might be rendered entirely separate functions. The fertile period would be emphasized more, and there would be more birth control. In the latter connection we may note in passing another probable biological development in the near future, namely, a long-term contraceptive. Knowledge of how to inhibit ovulation already exists, but such regulation disturbs the balance of the endocrine system.

A further significant discovery in the biology of sex has to do with the preservation of human germ plasm. Success has been reported in preserving human sperm 125 days in dry ice after vitrification in liquid nitrogen, with no appreciable decline in mortality in this period beyond the decline of the first two hours. As much as 60 per cent of the human sperm survived the treatment so far as motility is concerned. The limit was 125 days, because an assistant failed to resupply the dry ice after that time, and the sperm warmed up. The experiment was not resumed, but the experimenter believes that vitrified sperm will keep indefinitely at the temperature of dry ice. But whether they would be able to fertilize, he, of course, does not know. He reports that he was unable to get an adequate yield of sperm other than human to survive at very low temperatures and was therefore unable to perform fertilization experiments.

The doctors object to using preserved semen in human subjects, since they do not know how it will work. Experience with animal insemination has been limited to using semen that has been kept only a relatively short time, a maximum of about 168 hours. If it could be demonstrated that no harmful effects result from the use of vitrified human sperm, the opposition might disappear. The objection would persist if donor semen were used, but where the male is the woman's husband there probably would be no organized religious objection, to judge by the present position of the churches on artificial insemination. If there is no objection, many new possibilities are opened up. For instance, a woman who is married a short time before a war and who bears no children before being separated from her husband may still bear her husband's child even if the husband is killed in action, if his semen is preserved beforehand. Widowhood under the circumstances may become a somewhat different experience from what it now is. Semen banks are a possibility in such a situation.

✧ ✧ ✧ ✧ ✧

. . . Reference has been made to the use of the sex hormones. This is another brilliant chapter in the book of recent advance in the biochemistry of reproduction, to which we can here refer only briefly. The literature deals mainly with the lower animals, with whom experimentation is permissible. In one experiment a prepubertal castrated chimpanzee was paired with an intact male. The administration of male sex hormones led to the social dominance by the castrated animal, whereas female sex therapy resulted in its subordination. Following injection of a female rat with estrogen and progesterone, mating responses were induced despite the congenital absence of gonadal tissue. Hormone therapy has also succeeded in reversing sex roles. Thus a single-comb Brown Leghorn hen displayed male mating behavior following successive implants of testosterone propionate pellets, in contrast with the earlier negative findings following single daily injections of the hormone. Some experiments on human subjects have also been made. When 101 women under treatment for endocrine disorders were given androgen administered intramuscularly, subcutaneously, or orally, all but 13 reported some increase in libido. In another experiment progesterone depressed excessive libido and androgen decidedly increased both libido and general well-being, with best results obtained by implantations of pellets of testosterone propionate. On the basis of such experiments, it has been conjectured that the amount of androgens greatly affects the vigor of the sex drive and that the absolute or proportionate amount of estrogens affects its direction. It is, of course, not implied that learning and experience are not also important factors affecting the sex drive but only that constitutional factors are important, especially the hormones of the glands of internal secretion.

The foregoing are only a few of the remarkable developments in the biology and chemistry of reproduction, sufficient perhaps to indicate to us what promise for the future this infant science holds. Time does not permit more than the briefest mention of important developments in other areas, notably the biochemistry of nutrition. For instance, aging in rats has been greatly postponed by heavy doses of vitamin A in the early years. If a comparable result were to be achieved in man, this one fact alone could have a significant effect on the relationship between the sexes and on the relations of parents and children.

Confronting these discoveries, sociologists must consider what social implications they may have. An important consideration is the mores: if they are hostile, the new knowledge will not be widely utilized. Hostile mores are also an obstacle to scientific discovery itself. But, as we have seen, many of the changes which would be effected by the new discoveries are possible within the limits of the existing sex mores. There seems to be no objection to new scientific procedures if they are employed exclusively within marriage. For instance, the Roman Catholic church sanctions artificial insemination if the husband is the donor and if insemination by the physician follows normal coitus. Some of the innovations mentioned above can be confined to the marital pair, and presumably on this account there would be no objection. Such would be the case as regards the control of the sex of the child. But this would involve artificial means in separating the two types of sperm, and to this there might be objection from certain groups, though not all, just as there is objection at present to obtaining the husband's semen by methods other than normal marital coitus, for purposes of assisting in the insemination of the wife. So we conclude that certain of the procedures will meet with acceptance and that other procedures may meet with opposition.

We cannot be certain as to what the public practice will be with regard to man of the biological innovations, since they create new situations for which the old definitions are not adequate. Such is the case, for instance, with artificial insemination at the present time. Artificial insemination has been introduced into our culture by the doctors, and thousands of inseminations have been performed. There is as yet no body of law or clearly defined public opinion regarding the practice. Certain church bodies have taken a stand against it when the donor is not the woman's husband, and there are a few contradictory court decisions. In due course public policy may be formulated on the issue, but it may not be the same in all societies, just as public policy on abortion and birth control varies in different cultures at the present time. Moreover, even if at first there is opposition to the practice, the opposition may eventually moderate, for the mores change.

It may also be observed that the systematic opposition of the group to a practice does not necessarily mean that the practice will not exist. There are many thousands of abortions each year despite the taboo against them. Where a need exists, and the knowledge of how to fill it, it is difficult to suppress the practice in a complex, heterogeneous, rapidly changing society. What the doctors and their patients do in our complex society is not generally known: the statement that thousands of persons have been artificially inseminated is probably news to most citizens.

So we conclude that, even if there is opposition to new biological practices and knowledge, there may still be not a little diffusion of the innovations, with considerable effects on family practices. But it is too soon yet to say whether there will be opposition to many of the discoveries that are in process of being made in the field of biology and chemistry of reproduction. It may, furthermore, be noted that not all scientific discoveries are put to use. For one reason and another, the death rate of inventions and discoveries is high. But if the innovation has great human significance and there is a demand for it, there is considerable probability that it will be developed and diffused.

To sum up, the family in the past has been shaped by changes in the social system of which it is a part, and particularly by changes in technology and economic organization, which are among the most dynamic elements of the social system. These changes in technology have during the past century and a half been revolutionary and have forced radical readjustments in the correlated parts of culture, including the family. These technological changes have been exterior to man the animal and have required changes in adaptation without any radical change in the constitution of man. But now the revolution in science has extended to the sciences of man, and the probabilities are great that discoveries in human biology will revolutionize the constitutional bases of human behavior. There are great discoveries also in the psychological realm of which this paper has taken no account; family behavior may be greatly affected in the years ahead by new knowledge regarding the learning process and the way personality is shaped by group and culture. Sociologists seem to be more mindful of the possibilities in the psychological realm, and they have given some attention to the correlations of technology and the rest of the social order. But there does not seem as yet to be much awareness of the social influences that the biological discoveries may exert. . . .

✤ 51 ✤

ILLEGITIMACY
AND VALUE DILEMMAS

Clark E. Vincent

American family norms place great emphasis on limiting sex relations to marriage partners. Illegitimate births are considered a threat to the marriage institution, and though they are few in number, we constantly express concern about them. In this selection Vincent indicates that the problem of illegitimacy arises from our social structure and the values attached to the family social system in the United States. Hence illegitimacy can be eliminated only by altering both structure and values. Vincent explores several factors involved in reducing the frequency of illegitimacy and concludes that any effective measures "will entail changes in some social attitudes and practices which some people prefer not to change." He makes clear that those who would solve such social problems by merely "passing a law" are deluding themselves. This same principle is applicable to other complex problems of society.

If people engaged in efforts to ameliorate the age-old social problem of illegitimacy are to get results, they should begin with an awareness that most if not all social problems persist because of value dilemmas, and that their solution may require changes in social attitudes and practices most of us would prefer not to change.

SOURCE: Copyright 1963 Christian Century Foundation. Reprinted by permission from the June 19, 1963 issue of *The Christian Century*. ✧ The author is professor of sociology at the Bowman Gray School of Medicine and was formerly chief of the Social Science Section, Training Branch, National Institute of Mental Health. His main interests include medical sociology, sociology of child development, marriage counseling, social problems, and social psychology. He has written *Unmarried Mothers* and edited *Readings in Marriage Counseling*.

Illegitimacy could, of course, be eradicated by abolishing marriage. Without marriage as the recognized legitimation of coition and parturition, all births would be licit. But people who espouse the traditional values of our society rate the maintenance of marriage more highly than elimination of illegitimacy. Similarly, legalized abortions and wider dissemination of contraceptive information are solutions rejected by most people. In fact, such means of reducing illegitimacy tend to be discarded so readily that rarely are they considered as alternatives. And our failure to consider alternatives hinders us from realizing that choices are being made that may actually jeopardize the values we profess to cherish.

One area in which an implicit choice has been made is represented by the highly selective and distorted emphases of public information about illegitimacy. The publicity given to illicit births among the nation's very young females might lead one to believe that American young people have completely discarded traditional sex norms. A closer look at the data, however, suggests that the perennial and vociferous censure of youthful misbehavior diverts attention from adult misbehavior and ignores the 90–95 per cent of our young people whose sexual behavior very likely is more exemplary than that of the adults whom they are continually admonished to "grow up and act like." Such censure of course reflects our idealization of youth and our perennial hope of a better world if only young people would follow the teachings—but not necessarily the deeds—of adults.

It is well known that the number of teen-age females in the United States has increased markedly in recent years, but few people are aware that females aged 10–19 accounted for a smaller proportion of illicit births in 1960 (41 per cent) than in 1938 (48 per cent). In fact, the illegitimacy rate, which is the number of illicit births per 1,000 unmarried females, has risen far less among teen-agers than among older females. Why do popular information and prevention programs ignore the fact that rate increases in illegitimacy since 1940 have been far greater among 20–44 year olds than among teen-agers? For one thing, it is the very young unwed mothers who are the most dependent on parents and taxpayers; their illicit sexual behavior offends our sense of morality far more than does similar behavior among older, more independent females. The point, however, is that concentration of attention on very young unwed mothers ill serves preventive efforts when it obscures the fact that about 78 per cent of all unwed mothers are 18 and older. Even this figure is probably an underestimate; very likely the percentage is closer to 80 or 85, since many older, white, middle and upper class unwed mothers-to-be move temporarily to one of the 15 states that do not record illegitimacy on birth certificates.

In the next few years an adequate statistical perspective on illegitimacy will become more and more important. The *number* of 15 to 19-year-old unwed mothers during the 1960s may be almost twice what it was during the 1950s even if there are no rate or percentage increases, since almost twice as many girls were born between 1945 and 1954 than between 1935 and 1944. Continuation of the popular emphasis on young, teen-age illegitimacy may inadvertently influence some young people to accept illicit sexual behavior as normative, and may further postpone the needed scrutiny of illegitimacy among the many unwed mothers who are 18 and older—old enough to know what they are doing, old enough to be emulated by younger girls.

The "Bad Causes Bad" Fallacy

In terms of the intricate network of norms by which we live it is apparent that some unwed mothers are regarded as "more equal" than others. Evoking the strongest censure are those who are young, poor, nonwhite, and dependent on taxpayers' support. The explicit condemnation and frequent exaggeration of illicit births among females possessing these characteristics contrasts sharply with the playing down of such births among older, white, middle and upper class females. This contrast derives in part from the fact that censure of white unwed mothers was tempered in the 1940s and 1950s; at that time they represented the largest single source of adoptable infants and served a useful social function by enabling childless couples to have a family. As physicians, lawyers, and social caseworkers can testify, many of the estimated 1 million involuntarily childless white couples in this country a decade ago would have been highly displeased had this major source of adoptable white infants disappeared. This choice—continued illegitimacy or a reduced supply of adoptable infants—of course was not openly acknowledged. We simply failed to publicize illicit births among white females who had sufficient means and maturity discreetly to leave home during their pregnancy, returning only after they had released their offspring for adoption.

Another area in which alternative means of reducing illegitimacy are obscured is represented by the explanations of what causes illegitimacy. Most explanations of illegitimacy—indeed, of any social problem—are deeply imbedded in the assumption that "bad causes bad." Between the 1920s and the middle 1950s the bourgeois-oriented theories concerning illegitimacy fostered the belief that "bad illegitimacy" is the result of such "bad causes" as poverty, mental deficiency, broken homes, minority group membership and psychological disturbances. This belief was conveniently supported by descriptions of unwed mothers from domestic court files, charity institutions, "wayside homes" and out-patient psychiatric clinics.

To assume that only bad causes bad and selectively to censure some groups of unwed mothers more than others is to obscure the fact that a number of highly valued social practices are relevant to illegitimacy. This relevance can be illustrated by citing certain practices in education, child-rearing and personnel ideology which accompanied the "philosophy of fun morality" of the 1940s and '50s. In education this philosophy found expression in the notion that a child would learn more and faster if he were "having fun" and "enjoying life," if he were "happy" and "popular." The emergence of fun morality in child-rearing was particularly evident during the '40s, when it was assumed that whatever the child enjoyed had to be good for him. Less and less frequently was a distinction made between what the child *needed* and what he *wanted*. As wants came to be regarded as needs, many parents found themselves dominated by their children. This period of permissiveness in child-rearing began to subside with maternal exhaustion and the subsequent reassertion of parental knowledge in the mid-'50s. By then, however, a generation of youngsters had in varying degrees been implanted with a fusion—not to say confusion—of needs and wants.

This implantation, whether occurring through educational procedures at school or child-rearing patterns at home, is currently flowering in adolescents who are predisposed to believing that what is fun is good. And they read, hear and see few denials of the notion that "sex is fun."

The significance of the philosophy of fun morality in the personnel ideology of industry and business has been discussed by C. Wright Mills, William H. Whyte, Jr., Leo Lowenthal and others. The loss of motivation for work in our technological, assembly-line society and the decrease in the inherent rewards of work have necessitated an increasing emphasis on ways to make work "fun" and working conditions enjoyable. Thus employee parties and other instances of "togetherness" help maintain production quotas by keeping workers happy with their on-the-job relationships—if not with their work. Within such a context employees frequently know more about each other's current problems than do members of their own families.

Then there is the expense account, which often permits the young executive to live a kind of life away from home that makes his home life and a vacation with his family seem dull—and expensive—by comparison. Sometimes the lush away-from-home life includes the services of "escort bureaus," provided at out-of-town conventions and sanctioned as promotional means to the "good" goal of future conventions and consequent city revenue. While this promotional spirit gives respectability to the female escorts of visiting businessmen, it also inadvertently lowers the barriers to heterosexual intimacy.

A Web That Ensnares

What does all this have to do with understanding illegitimacy? When viewed separately, such social practices as I have noted may appear to have only enough relevance to illegitimacy to attract the attention of "bluenosed do-gooders." But when viewed collectively, such practices seem to constitute a source of permissive attitudes toward pre- and extramarital sexual relationships—a web that ensnares many an unsuspecting victim as well as many an invited and knowing guest. The fun-morality notion that a person has a *right* to fun and enjoyment makes it easier for the male who is unhappy in marriage to justify, at least to himself, finding his fun outside the home. His selection of a fun partner is simplified, the risk of an initial rebuff minimized, when the emphasis on close-knit relationships in the occupational setting provides a socially sanctioned context for familiarity. A male-female pair of office employees can share coffee breaks and lunch periods much more frequently and with less chance of censure than can a male-female pair of neighbors.

To suggest that illegitimacy can be an inadvertent by-product of a combination of means to conventional goals is to look outside the evil-causes-evil circle. This approach, however, is not popular, nor is it easily brought into focus. Any one social practice reflects a variety of vested interests and conflicting values, and one man's means are sometimes another man's goals. Moreover, strongly to deplore the means used to increase advertising returns, production quotas and box-office successes is to risk being labeled a "busybody," a "do-gooder," an "infringer on freedom of expression." Such labels—particularly the latter—tend to blur the issue; it becomes lost in a polemical discussion on "freedom vs. restriction of expression," in which the questions "freedom for what?" and "freedom for whom?" are never adequately explored.

But the failure to examine the relevance of accepted social practices is not to be attributed solely to the power of vested-interest groups. The bad-causes-bad assumption is frequently welcomed as a protective device against our own fears, struggles and temptations concerning illicit sexual behavior, and is a way of reaffirming our conviction that "it can't happen to me." For to contend that "bad girls" are the result of poverty, ignorance or minority-group membership is to reaffirm that "good girls" are the result of material blessings, a good education and majority-group membership.

Long-Standing Double Standard

The failure to conduct research on unmarried fathers provides another illustration of how value dilemmas impeded our understanding of illegitimacy. Only about one study of unmarried fathers exists for every 30 studies of unmarried mothers. Obviously, illegitimacy cannot be understood, much less remedied, by studying only the female factor. But to observe unwed fathers to the same degree we do their female counterparts requires changes in the conventional double standard by which we judge the sexual behavior of males and females. Semantically, we have no male equivalent of "the fallen woman."

That we generally resist changes in the double standard is evidenced by the following facts: (1) We condemn and stigmatize unmarried mothers far more harshly than unmarried fathers. (2) We tend to express greater indignation over wives involved in extramarital affairs than over husbands. (3) We blame wives more frequently than husbands for unwanted pregnancies occurring within marriage. (4) State legislators frequently consider requiring tubal ligations for recidivist unmarried mothers, but never vasectomies for unmarried fathers.

We inadvertently condone the unmarried father by ignoring him. The unwed mother poses tangible problems, the unmarried father does not. It is she for whom prenatal care, maternity homes and possible child support must be financed; it is her noticeably altering appearance which openly threatens traditional sex mores. The male represents no obvious expense to taxpayers and bears no evidence of unconventional sex behavior. Moreover, the female's need for care during pregnancy and delivery makes her available for study and identifiable for censure; the male's biological role ends at conception, and society's protection of him through disinterest enables him to remain anonymous and unavailable for study.

Comparing Married and Unmarried Mothers

A better understanding of illegitimacy is also hampered by the value dilemma posed by the need to consider similarities in the attitudes of married and unmarried mothers, as well as similarities in the motivations for licit and illicit births. The pregnancies of some married women signify attempts to strengthen a faltering marriage, just as those of some unmarried women signify attempts to obtain a husband. There are those among both married and unmarried females who use pregnancy as a means to resolve emotional problems, just as there are those in both groups who have sexual relations for personal enjoyment with no intent or desire to become pregnant. Moreover, unwanted pregnancies evoke as much indignation, disappointment and emotional upset among some married as among some unmarried women. Conversely, the discovery of pregnancy is welcomed by some women in both groups as the achievement of a much-desired goal and the realization of self-fulfillment.

Open consideration of such similarities could further our understanding of illegitimacy by focusing attention on the more germane problem of unwanted pregnancies. Such pregnancies occurring within marriage may represent a far greater problem, numerically and in terms of abortions and marital strife, than does illegitimacy. However, such a possibility is usually resisted because it poses a dilemma—a choice between either using a more effective approach to understanding illegitimacy or changing some of our cherished assumptions about the relative purity of married mothers' motivations and feelings concerning coition and pregnancy as opposed to those of unmarried mothers.

Toward a More Constructive Approach

In summary, then, there is no simple explanation of illegitimacy, and every effective measure or method for reducing its occurrence will entail changes in some social attitudes and practices which some people prefer not to change. Thus far, those engaged in preventive efforts have generally played it safe by stressing the conventional scapegoats of youth, poverty, ignorance, psychological disturbance; by prescribing tubal ligations for females but not vasectomies for males; by publicizing the number of unwed Negro mothers on Aid to Dependent Children rolls but ignoring the older white females who supply adoptable infants.

Hopefully, an awareness of the contrarieties in attitudes and practices concerning illicit sexual behavior might result in more constructive approaches to illegitimacy. Surely it is inconsistent for a society on the one hand to condone and even to produce and consume in prodigious quantity sex enticements which foster attitudes favorable to permissive sexual behavior, and on the other to become outraged when the protruding anatomy of the unmarried female reveals an out-of-wedlock pregnancy. What would the Martian visitor say about a society that inundates young people with sexual stimuli and then not only castigates them for responding to such stimuli but also denies them the contraceptive means and knowledge whereby they could at least exercise caution?

To interpret what I have just said as an argument in favor of making contraceptives freely available to youth is again to obscure the issue and to deny the dilemma by avoiding the alternative of withdrawing the stimuli. It may be that as a society we prefer to continue piecemeal and largely ineffective approaches to the understanding and diminution of illegitimacy, rather than to deal with basic value dilemmas and seriously to consider making changes in attitudes and practices we prefer not to change. If such is the case, then we might at least stop pretending that we really want to do away with illegitimacy and devote our funds and our research efforts to social problems about which we are less ambivalent.

To continue to support a matrix of social practices which serve to instill permissive attitudes toward illicit sexual behavior and at the same time to intensify efforts to decrease illicit pregnancies is, to say the least, highly illogical.

THE DIVISION OF
LABOR IN SOCIETY

Emile Durkheim

One of the recurring basic criticisms of modern society is that the "whole man"—the personality—has been weakened because of specialization, or "division of labor." Said one philosopher, "It is a sad commentary that we have come to the state where we never do anything more than make the eighteenth part of a pin." Said another, "In so far as the principle of the division of labor receives a more complete application, the art progresses, the artisan retrogresses." Many, comparing the life of the modern workman with the "free, bold life of the 'noble' savage," have found the second much preferable to the first. Adoption of such a philosophy, carried to its logical conclusion, would lead to drastic changes in all of social life. This idea, perhaps most popular in the nineteenth century, still flourishes today. Consequently, in vocational planning, we may be given contradictory advice: Specialize. Do not specialize. The result of specialization, in the thinking of Rousseau and others, is the "splintering" of personalities and societies. Emile Durkheim, however, in this conclusion to his The Division of Labor in Society argues that specialization is the chief source of social solidarity and is becoming the foundation of our present moral order.

I

If there is one rule of conduct which is incontestable, it is that which orders us to realize in ourselves the essential traits of the collective type. Among lower peoples, this reaches its greatest rigor. There, one's first duty is to resemble everybody else, not to have anything personal about one's beliefs or actions. In more advanced societies, required likenesses are less numerous; the absence of some likenesses, however, is still a sign of moral failure. Of course, crime falls into fewer different categories; but today, as heretofore, if a criminal is the object of reprobation, it is because he is unlike us. Likewise, in lesser degree, acts simply immoral

SOURCE: Reprinted from *The Division of Labor in Society*, 396–409, by permission of The Free Press, Glencoe, Illinois. Copyright 1947. ✧ The author (1858–1917) was a French sociologist and philosopher. He taught at the University of Bordeaux and at the Sorbonne, succeeding Auguste Comte. Besides his doctoral dissertation from which this selection is taken, Durkheim's main works are *The Rules of Sociological Method, The Elementary Forms of the Religious Life,* and *Suicide: A Study in Sociology.*

and prohibited ˊas such are those which evince dissemblances less profound but nevertheless considered serious. Is this not the case with the rule which common morality expresses when it orders a man to be a man in every sense of the word, which is to say, to have all the ideas and sentiments which go to make up a human conscience? No doubt, if this formula is taken literally, the man prescribed would be man in general and not one of some particular social species. But, in reality, this human conscience that we must integrally realize is nothing else than the collective conscience of the group of which we are a part. For what can it be composed of, if not the ideas and sentiments to which we are most attached? Where can we find the traits of our model, if not within us and around us? If we believe that this collective ideal is that of all humanity, that is because it has become so abstract and general that it appears fitting for all men indiscriminately. But, really, every people makes for itself some particular conception of this type which pertains to its personal temperament. Each represents it in its own image. Even the moralist who thinks he can, through thought, overcome the influence of transient ideas, cannot do so, for he is impregnated with them, and no matter what he does, he finds these precepts in the body of his deductions. That is why each nation has its own school of moral philosophy conforming to its character.

On the other hand, we have shown that this rule had as its function the prevention of all agitation of the common conscience, and, consequently, of social solidarity, and that it could accomplish this role only by having a moral character. It is impossible for offenses against the most fundamental collective sentiments to be tolerated without the disintegration of society, and it is necessary to combat them with the aid of the particularly energetic reaction which attaches to moral rules.

But the contrary rule, which orders us to specialize, has exactly the same function. It also is necessary for the cohesion of societies, at least at a certain period in their evolution. Of course, its solidarity is different from the preceding, but though it is different, it is no less indispensable. Higher societies can maintain themselves in equilibrium only if labor is divided; the attraction of like for like less and less suffices to produce this result. If, then, the moral character of the first of these rules is necessary to the playing of its role, it is no less necessary to the second. They both correspond to the same social need, but satisfy the need differently, because the conditions of existence in the societies themselves differ. Consequently, without speculating concerning the first principle of ethics, we can induce the moral value of one from the moral value of the other. If, from certain points of view, there is a real antagonism between them, that is not because they serve different ends. On the contrary, it is because they lead to the same end, but through opposed means. Accordingly, there is no necessity for choosing between them once for all nor of condemning one in the name of the other. What is necessary is to give each, at each moment in history, the place that is fitting to it.

Perhaps we can even generalize further in this matter.

The requirements of our subject have obliged us to classify moral rules and to review the principal types. We are thus in a better position than we were in the beginning to see, or at least to conjecture, not only upon the external sign, but also upon the internal character which is common to all of them and which can serve to define them. We have put them into two groups: rules with repressive sanctions, which may be diffuse or organized, and rules with restitutive sanctions. We have seen that the first of these express the conditions of the solidarity, *sui generis*, which comes from resemblances, and to which we have given the name mechanical; the second, the conditions of negative solidarity and organic solidarity. We can thus say that, in general, the characteristic of moral rules is that they enunciate the fundamental conditions of social solidarity. Law and morality are the totality of ties which bind each of us to society, which make a unitary, coherent aggregate of the mass of individuals. Everything which is a source of solidarity is moral, everything which forces man to take account of other men is moral, everything which forces him to regulate his conduct through something other than the striving of his ego is moral, and morality is as solid as these ties are numerous and strong. We can see how inexact it is to define it, as is often done, through liberty. It rather consists in a state of dependence. Far from serving to emancipate the individual, or disengaging him from the environment which surrounds him, it has, on the contrary, the function of making him an integral part of a whole, and, consequently, of depriving him of some liberty of movement. We sometimes, it is true, come across people not without nobility who find the idea of such dependence intolerable. But that is because they do not perceive the source from which their own morality flows, since these sources are very deep. Conscience is a bad judge of what goes on in the depths of a person, because it does not penetrate to them.

Society is not, then, as has often been thought, a stranger to the moral world, or something which has only secondary repercussions upon it. It is, on the contrary, the necessary condition of its existence. It is not a simple juxtaposition of individuals who bring an intrinsic morality with them, but rather man is a moral being only because he lives in society, since morality consists in being solidary with a group and varying with this solidarity. Let all social life disappear, and moral life will disappear with it, since it would no longer have any objective. The state of nature of the philosophers of the eighteenth century, if not immoral, is, at least, *amoral*. Rousseau himself recognized this. Through this, however, we do not come upon the formula which expresses morality as a function of social interest. To be sure, society cannot exist if its parts are not solidary, but solidarity is only one of its conditions of existence. There are many others which are no less necessary and which are not moral. Moreover, it can happen that, in the system of ties which make up morality, there are some which are not useful in themselves or which have power without any relation to their degree of utility. The idea of utility does not enter as an essential element in our definition.

As for what is called individual morality, if we understand by that a totality of duties of which the individual would, at the same time, be subject and object, and which would link him only to himself, and which would, consequently, exist even if he were solitary,—that is an abstract conception which has no relation to reality. Morality, in all its forms, is never met with except in society. It never varies except in relation to social conditions. To ask what it would be if societies did not exist is thus to depart from facts and enter the domain of gratuitous hypotheses and unverifiable flights of the imagination. The duties of the individual towards himself are, in reality, duties towards society. They correspond to certain collective sentiments which he cannot offend, whether the offended and the offender are one and the same person, or whether they are distinct. Today, for example, there is in all healthy consciences a very lively sense of respect for human dignity, to which we are supposed to conform as much in our relations with ourselves as in our relations with others, and this constitutes the essential quality of what is called individual morality. Every act which contravenes this is censured, even when the agent and the sufferer are the same person. That is why, according to the Kantian formula, we ought to respect human personality wherever we find it, which is to say, in ourselves as in those like us. The sentiment of which it is the object is not less offended in one case than in the other.

But not only does the division of labor present the character by which we have defined morality; it more and more tends to become the essential condition of social solidarity. As we advance in the evolutionary scale, the ties which bind the individual to his family, to his native soil, to traditions which the past has given to him, to collective group usages, become loose. More mobile, he changes his environment more easily, leaves his people to go elsewhere to live a more autonomous existence, to a greater extent forms his own ideas and sentiments. Of course, the whole common conscience does not, on this account, pass out of existence. At least there will always remain this cult of personality, of individual dignity of which we have just been speaking, and which, today, is the rallying-point of so many people. But how little a thing it is when one contemplates the ever increasing extent of social life, and, consequently, of individual consciences! For, as they become more voluminous, as intelligence becomes richer, activity more varied, in order for morality to remain constant, that is to say, in order for the individual to remain attached to the group with a force equal to that of yesterday, the ties which bind him to it must become stronger and more numerous. If, then, he formed no others than those which come from resemblances, the effacement of the segmental type would be accompanied by a systematic debasement of morality. Man would no longer be sufficiently obligated; he would no longer feel about and above him this salutary pressure of society which moderates his egoism and makes him a moral being. This is what gives moral value to the division of labor. Through it, the individual becomes cognizant of his dependence upon society; from it come the forces which keep him in check and restrain him. In short, since the division of labor becomes the chief source of social solidarity, it becomes, at the same time, the foundation of the moral order.

We can then say that, in higher societies, our duty is not to spread our activity over a large surface, but to concentrate and specialize it. We must contract our horizon, choose a definite task and immerse ourselves in it completely, instead of trying to make ourselves a sort of creative masterpiece, quite complete, which contains its worth in itself and not in the services that it renders. Finally, this specialization ought to be pushed as far as the elevation of the social type, without assigning any other limit to it. No doubt, we ought so to work as to realize in ourselves the collective type as it exists. There are common sentiments, common ideas, without which, as has been said, one is not a man. The rule which orders us to specialize remains limited by the contrary rule. Our conclusion is not that it is good to press specialization as far as possible, but as far as necessary. As for the part that is to be played by these two opposing necessities, that is determined by experience and cannot be calculated *a priori*. It is enough for us to have shown that the second is not of a different nature from the first, but that it also is moral, and that, moreover, this duty becomes ever more important and pressing, because the general qualities which are in question suffice less and less to socialize the individual.

It is not without reason that public sentiment reproves an ever more pronounced tendency on the part of dilettantes and even others to be taken up with an exclusively general culture and refuse to take any part in occupational organization. That is because they are not sufficiently attached to society, or, if one wishes, society is not sufficiently attached to them, and they escape it. Precisely because they feel its effect neither with vivacity nor with the continuity that is necessary, they have no cognizance of all the obligations their positions as social beings demand of them. The general ideal to which they are attached being, for the reasons we have spoken of, formal and shifting, it cannot take them out of themselves. We do not cling to very much when we have no very determined objective, and, consequently, we cannot very well elevate ourselves beyond a more or less refined egotism. On the contrary, he who gives himself over to a definite task is, at every moment, struck by the sentiment of common solidarity in the thousand duties of occupational morality.

II

But does not the division of labor by making each of us an incomplete being bring on a diminution of individual personality? That is a reproach which has often been levelled at it.

Let us first of all remark that it is difficult to see why it would be

408 · Emile Durkheim

more in keeping with the logic of human nature to develop superficially rather than profoundly. Why would a more extensive activity, but more dispersed, be superior to a more concentrated, but circumscribed, activity? Why would there be more dignity in being complete and mediocre, rather than in living a more specialized, but more intense life, particularly if it is thus possible for us to find what we have lost in this specialization, through our association with other beings who have what we lack and who complete us? We take off from the principle that man ought to realize his nature as man, to accomplish his ὀικεῖον ἔργον as Aristotle said. But this nature does not remain constant throughout history; it is modified with societies. Among lower peoples, the proper duty of man is to resemble his companions, to realize in himself all the traits of the collective type which are then confounded, much more than today, with the human type. But, in more advanced societies, his nature is, in large part, to be an organ of society, and his proper duty, consequently, is to play his role as an organ.

Moreover, far from being trammelled by the progress of specialization, individual personality develops with the division of labor.

To be a person is to be an autonomous source of action. Man acquires this quality only in so far as there is something in him which is his alone and which individualizes him, as he is something more than a simple incarnation of the generic type of his race and his group. It will be said that he is endowed with free will and that is enough to establish his personality. But although there may be some of this liberty in him, an object of so many discussions, it is not this metaphysical, impersonal, invariable attribute which can serve as the unique basis for concrete personality, which is empirical and variable with individuals. That could not be constituted by the wholly abstract power of choice between two opposites, but it is still necessary for this faculty to be exercised towards ends and aims which are proper to the agent. In other words, the very materials of conscience must have a personal character. But we have seen that this result is progressively produced as the division of labor progresses. The effacement of the segmental type, at the same time that it necessitates a very great specialization, partially lifts the individual conscience from the organic environment which supports it, as from the social environment which envelops it, and, accordingly because of this double emancipation, the individual becomes more of an independent factor in his own conduct. The division of labor itself contributes to this enfranchisement, for individual natures, while specializing, become more complex, and by that are in part freed from collective action and hereditary influences which can only enforce themselves upon simple, general things.

It is, accordingly, a real illusion which makes us believe that personality was so much more complete when the division of labor had penetrated less. No doubt, in looking from without at the diversity of occupations which the individual then embraces, it may seem that he is developing in a very free and complete manner. But, in reality, this activity which he manifests is not really his. It is society, it is the race acting in and through him; he is only the intermediary through which they realize themselves. His liberty is only apparent and his personality borrowed. Because the life of these societies is, in certain respects, less regular, we imagine that original talents have more opportunity for free play, that it is easier for each one to pursue his own tastes, that a very large place is left to free fantasy. But this is to forget that personal sentiments are then very rare. If the motives which govern conduct do not appear as periodically as they do today, they do not leave off being collective, and, consequently, impersonal, and it is the same with the actions that they inspire. Moreover, we have shown above how activity becomes richer and more intense as it becomes more specialized.

Thus, the progress of individual personality and that of the division of labor depend upon one and the same cause. It is thus impossible to desire one without desiring the other. But no one today contests the obligatory character of the rule which orders us to be more and more of a person.

One last consideration will make us see to what extent the division of labor is linked with our whole moral life.

Men have long dreamt of finally realizing in fact the ideal of human fraternity. People pray for a state where war will no longer be the law of international relations, where relations between societies will be pacifically regulated, as those between individuals already are, where all men will collaborate in the same work and live the same life. Although these aspirations are in part neutralized by those which have as their object the particular society of which we are a part, they have not left off being active and are even gaining in force. But they can be satisfied only if all men form one society, subject to the same laws. For, just as private conflicts can be regulated only by the action of the society in which the individuals live, so intersocial conflicts can be regulated only by a society which comprises in its scope all others. The only power which can serve to moderate individual egotism is the power of the group; the only power which can serve to moderate the egotism of groups is that of some other group which embraces them.

Truly, when the problem has been posed in these terms, we must recognize that this ideal is not on the verge of being integrally realized, for there are too many intellectual and moral diversities between different social types existing together on the earth to admit of fraternalization in the same society. But what is possible is that societies of the same type may come together, and it is, indeed, in this direction that evolution appears to move. We have already seen that among European peoples there is a tendency to form, by spontaneous movement, a European society which has, at present, some idea of itself and the beginning of organization. If the formation of a single human society is forever impossible, a fact which has not been proved, at least the formation of continually larger societies brings us vaguely near the goal. These facts, moreover, in no wise contradict the definition of morality that we have given, for if we cling to humanity and if we ought to cling to it, it is because it is a society which is in process of realizing itself in this way, and with which we are solidary.

But we know the greater societies cannot be formed except through the development of the division of labor, for not only could they not maintain themselves in equilibrium without a greater specialization of functions, but even the increase in the number of those competing would suffice to produce this result mechanically; and that, so much the more, since the growth of volume is generally accompanied by a growth in density. We can then formulate the following proposition: the ideal of human fraternity can be realized only in proportion to the progress of the division of labor. We must choose: either to renounce our dream, if we refuse further to circumscribe our activity, or else to push forward its accomplishment under the condition we have just set forth.

III

But if the division of labor produces solidarity, it is not only because it makes each individual an *exchangist*, as the economists say; it is because it creates among men an entire system of rights and duties which link them together in a durable way. Just as social similitudes give rise to a law and a morality which protect them, so the division of labor gives rise to rules which assure pacific and regular concourse of divided functions. If economists have believed that it would bring forth an abiding solidarity, in some manner of its own making, and if, accordingly, they have held that human societies could and would resolve themselves into purely economic associations, that is because they believed that it affected only individual, temporary interests. Consequently, to estimate the interests in conflict and the way in which they ought to equilibrate, that is to say, to determine the conditions under which exchange ought to take place, is solely a matter of individual competence; and, since these interests are in a perpetual state of becoming, there is no place for any permanent regulation. But such a conception is, in all ways, inadequate for the facts. The division of labor does not present individuals to one another, but social functions. And society is interested in the play of the latter; in so far as they regularly concur, or do not concur, it will be healthy or ill. Its existence thus depends upon them, and the more they are divided the greater its dependence. That is why it cannot leave them in a state of indetermination. In addition to this, they are determined by themselves. Thus are formed those rules whose number grows as labor is divided, and whose absence makes organic solidarity either impossible or imperfect.

But it is not enough that there be rules; they must be just, and for that it is necessary for the external conditions of competition to be equal.

If, moreover, we remember that the collective conscience is becoming more and more a cult of the individual, we shall see that what characterizes the morality of organized societies, compared to that of segmental societies, is that there is something more human, therefore more rational, about them. It does not direct our activities to ends which do not immediately concern us; it does not make us servants of ideal powers of a nature other than our own, which follow their directions without occupying themselves with the interests of men. It only asks that we be thoughtful of our fellows and that we be just, that we fulfill our duty, that we work at the function we can best execute, and receive the just reward for our services. The rules which constitute it do not have a constraining force which snuffs out free thought; but, because they are rather made for us and, in a certain sense, by us, we are free. We wish to understand them; we do not fear to change them. We must, however, guard against finding such an ideal inadequate on the pretext that it is too earthly and too much to our liking. An ideal is not more elevated because more transcendent, but because it leads us to vaster perspectives. What is important is not that it tower high above us, until it becomes a stranger to our lives, but that it open to our activity a large enough field. This is far from being on the verge of realization. We know only too well what a laborious work it is to erect this society where each individual will have the place he merits, will be rewarded as he deserves, where everybody, accordingly, will spontaneously work for the good of all and of each. Indeed, a moral code is not above another because it commands in a drier and more authoritarian manner, or because it is more sheltered from reflection. Of course, it must attach us to something besides ourselves but it is not necessary for it to chain us to it with impregnable bonds.

It has been said with justice that morality—and by that must be understood, not only moral doctrines, but customs—is going through a real crisis. What precedes can help us to understand the nature and causes of this sick condition. Profound changes have been produced in the structure of our societies in a very short time; they have been freed from the segmental type with a rapidity and in proportions such as have never before been seen in history. Accordingly, the morality which corresponds to this social type has regressed, but without another developing quickly enough to fill the ground that the first left vacant in our consciences. Our faith has been troubled; tradition has lost its sway; individual judgment has been freed from collective judgment. But, on the other hand, the functions which have been disrupted in the course of the upheaval have not had the time to adjust themselves to one another; the new life which has emerged so suddenly has not been able to be completely organized, and above all, it has not been organized in a way to satisfy the need for justice which has grown more ardent in our hearts. If this be so, the remedy for the evil is not to seek to resuscitate traditions and practices which, no longer responding to present conditions of society, can only live an artificial, false existence. What we must do to relieve this anomy is to discover the means for making the organs which are still wasting themselves in discordant movements harmoniously concur by introducing into their relations more justice by more and more extenuating the external inequalities which are the source of the evil. Our illness is not, then, as has often been believed, of an intellectual sort; it has more profound causes. We shall not suffer because we no longer know on what theoretical notion to base the morality we have been practicing, but because, in certain of its parts, this morality is irremediably shattered, and that which is necessary to us is only in process of formation. Our anxiety does not arise because the criticism of scholars has broken down the traditional explanation we used to give to our duties; consequently, it is not a new philosophical system which will relieve the situation. Because certain of our duties are no longer founded in the reality of things, a breakdown has resulted which will be repaired only in so far as a new discipline is established and consolidated. In short, our first duty is to make a moral code for ourselves. Such a work cannot be improvised in the silence of the study; it can arise only through itself, little by little, under the pressure of internal causes which make it necessary. But the service that thought can and must render is in fixing the goal that we must attain. That is what we have tried to do.

✽ 53 ✽

CYBERNATION:
THE SILENT CONQUEST

Donald N. Michael

There are good reasons, according to Donald N. Michael, to challenge the assertion that automation and the use of computers in today's world constitute nothing more than a logical extension of a process that started when man first began to fabricate tools. Michael asserts that we are currently undergoing a work revolution comparable to, and perhaps more far-reaching than, the Industrial

SOURCE: Donald N. Michael, *Cybernation: The Silent Conquest*, Center for the Study of Democratic Institutions. Copyright by the Fund for the Republic, Inc. ✧ The author is Director of Planning and Programs at the Peace Research Institute. His areas of interest include social change in relation to technological change, peace research, disaster behavior, man in space, and mass communication and cybernetics. He has written *Proposed Studies of the Implications of Peaceful Space Activities for Human Affairs, Ritualized Rationality and Arms Control*, and *The Next Generation*.

Revolution, which introduced the factory system to the Western World. The names for the two basic components of this new revolution—automation and computers—have been combined by Michael into a new and widely used word, Cybernation. In this selection, he explores the implications of the expanded use of these "thinking machines" in such matters as employment and unemployment; the availability and use of leisure time; control over governmental and industrial decision making; and the unprece dented potential enhancement of good or evil.

Introduction

Both optimists and pessimists often claim that automation is simply the latest stage in the evolution of technological means for removing the burdens of work. The assertion is misleading. There is a very good possibility that automation is so different in degree as to be a profound difference in kind, and that it will pose unique problems for society, challenging our basic values and the ways in which we express and enforce them.

In order to understand what both the differences and the problems are and, even more, will be, we have to know something of the nature and use of automation and computers. There are two important classes of devices. One class, usually referred to when one speaks of "automation," is made up of devices that automatically perform sensing and motor tasks, replacing or improving on human capacities for performing these functions. The second class, usually referred to when one speaks of "computers," is composed of devices that perform, very rapidly, routine or complex logical and decision-making tasks, replacing or improving on human capacities for performing these functions.

Using these machines does not merely involve replacing men by having machines do tasks that men did before. It is, as John Diebold says, a way of "thinking as much as it is a way of doing. . . . It is no longer necessary to think in terms of individual machines, or even in terms of groups of machines; instead, for the first time, it is practical to look at an entire production or information-handling process as an integrated system and not as a series of individual steps." . . .

The two classes of devices overlap. At one pole are the automatic producers of material objects and, at the other, the sophisticated analyzers and interpreters of complex data. In the middle zone are the mixed systems, in which computers control complicated processes, such as the operations of an oil refinery, on the basis of interpretations that they make of data automatically fed to them about the environment. Also in this middle zone are those routine, automatic, data-processing activities which provide men with the bases for controlling, or at least understanding, what is happening to a particular environment. Processing of social security data and making straightforward tabulations of census information are examples of these activities.*

Cybernated systems perform with a precision and a rapidity unmatched in humans. They also perform in ways that would be impractical or impossible for humans to duplicate. They can be built to detect and correct errors in their own performance and to indicate to men which of their components are producing the error. They can make judgments on the basis of instructions programmed into them. They can remember and search their memories for appropriate data, which either has been programmed into them along with their instructions or has been acquired in the process of manipulating new data. Thus, they can learn on the basis of past experience with their environment. They can receive information in more codes and sensory modes than men can. They are beginning to perceive and to recognize.

As a result of these characteristics, automation is being used to make and roll steel, mine coal, manufacture engine blocks, weave cloth, sort and grade everything from oranges to bank checks. More versatile automatic fabricators are becoming available, too:

U.S. Industries announced . . . that it had developed what was termed the first general-purpose automation machine available to manufacturers as standard "off-the-shelf" hardware. . . . The new machine, called a TransfeRobot, sells for $2,500. . . . The Westclox Company of La Salle, Ill., has been using a TransfeRobot to oil clock assemblies as they pass on a conveyor belt. The machine oils eight precision bearings simultaneously in a second. At the Underwood Corporation typewriter plant in Hartford, the robot picks up, transfers and places a small typewriter component into a close-fitting nest for an automatic machine operation. In an automobile plant, the device feeds partly fabricated parts of a steering assembly to a trimming press and controls the press. The device consists basically of an arm and actuator that can be fitted with many types of fingers and jaws. All are controlled by a self-contained electronic brain.

❖   ❖   ❖   ❖   ❖

The opportunities for man's enhancement through the benefits of cybernation are generally more evident and more expected, especially in view of our proclivity to equate technological advances with progress and happiness. In the words of the National Association of Manufacturers:

* In order to eliminate the awkwardness of repeating the words "automation" and "computers" each time we wish to refer to both at the same time, and in order to avoid the semantic difficulties involved in using one term or the other to mean both ends of the continuum, we invent the term "cybernation" to refer to *both* automation and computers. The word is legitimate at least to the extent that it derives from "cybernetics," a term invented by Norbert Wiener to mean the process of communication and control in man and machines. He derived it from the Greek word for "steersman." The theory and practice of cybernetics underlie all systematic design and application of automation and computers.

For the expanding, dynamic economy of America, the sky is indeed the limit. Now more than ever we must have confidence in America's capacity to grow. Guided by electronics, powered by atomic energy, geared to the smooth, effortless workings of automation, the magic carpet of our free economy heads for distant and undreamed horizons. Just going along for the ride will be the biggest thrill on earth!

But the somber and complex difficulties produced by cybernation, which already are beginning to plague some aspects of our society and economy, are only beginning to be recognized. Thus, although this paper will describe, first, the advantages of cybernation, which make its ever expanding application so compelling, it will, on the whole, emphasize the less obvious, sometimes acutely uncomfortable aspects of this development with which we must successfully contend if we are to enjoy the benefits of both cybernation and democracy.

The Advantages of Cybernation

In recent years deteriorating sales prospects, rising production costs, increased foreign competition, and lower profits have led business management to turn to our national talent for technological invention as the most plausible means of reducing costs and increasing productivity, whether the product is an engine block or tables of sales figures. And the government, faced with the need to process and understand rapidly increasing masses of numerical facts about the state of the nation and the world, is already using 524 computers and is the major customer for more of them.

What are the advantages of cybernated systems that make government and private enterprise turn to them to solve problems?

In the first place, in a competitive society a successfully cybernated organization often has economic advantages over a competitor using people instead of machines. As *U.S. News and World Report* says:

In one line of business after another, the trend is the same. Companies are spending millions of dollars to mechanize their operations, boost output and cut costs. . . . Says an official of a big electrical company: "It is no longer a question of whether or not to automate, but rather it is how far to go and how fast to proceed. If you don't, your competition will."

Not only must many organizations automate to compete, but the same principle probably holds for competing nations. We are by no means the only semi-cybernated society. Europe and Russia are well under way, and their machines and products compete with ours here and in the world market. The U.S.S.R. is making an all-out effort to cybernate as much of its planning-economic-industrial operation as it can.

In the second place, reducing the number of personnel in an organization reduces the magnitude of management's human relations tasks, whether these be coping with over-long coffee breaks, union negotiations, human errors, or indifference.

In the third place, cybernation permits much greater rationalization of managerial activities. The computers can produce information about what is happening now, as well as continuously up-dated information about what will be the probable consequences of specific decisions based on present and extrapolated circumstances. The results are available in a multitude of detailed or simplified displays in the form of words, tables of figures, patterns of light, growth and decay curves, dial readings, etc. In many situations built-in feedback monitors the developing situation and deals with routine changes, errors, and needs with little or no intervention by human beings. This frees management for attention to more basic duties. There is, for example,

. . . an automatic lathe . . . which gauges each part as it is produced and automatically resets the cutting tools to compensate for tool wear. In addition, when the cutting tools have been worn down to a certain predetermined limit, the machine automatically replaces them with sharp tools. The parts are automatically loaded onto the machine and are automatically unloaded as they are finished. These lathes can be operated for 5 to 8 hours without attention, except for an occasional check to make sure that parts are being delivered to the loading mechanism.

Another example, combining built-in feedback with a display capability, adds further illumination:

The Grayson-Robinson apparel chain, which has more than 100 stores throughout the country, receives print-punch tags daily from its stores and converts them to full-size punchcards. The complete merchandise and inventory control function is then handled on a computer. What styles are to be processed first are determined at the computer center. During any given week about 60 per cent of the sales data are received and summarized. On the following Monday morning the remaining 40 per cent of the sales data are received. The computer can then begin running style reports immediately after the tickets have been converted to cards. By this time the company can run up style reports by departments and price lines in order to obtain the necessary merchandising information. The entire reporting job is completed by Wednesday afternoon of each week, including reports on all inactive stockpiles.

Freeing management from petty distractions in these ways permits more precise and better substantiated decisions, whether they have to do with business strategy, government economic policy, equipment system planning, or military strategy and tactics. Thus, management in business or government can have much better control both over the system as it operates and over the introduction of changes into future operations. Indeed, the changes themselves may be planned in conformity with, and guided by, a strategy that is derived from a computer analysis of the future environment.

In the fourth place, cybernation allows government and industry much greater freedom in locating their facilities efficiently in relation to the accessibility of raw products, markets, transportation, and needed (or cheaper) human and material resources. Distance is no longer a barrier to control and coordination. The computers that control automated processes need not be near the factories nor the data-processing computers near their sources of information or users if other considerations are more pressing. Widely dispersed installations can be coordinated and controlled from still another place, and the dispersed units can interact with each other and affect one another's performance as easily, in many cases, as if they were all in the same place.

In the fifth place, some degree of cybernation is necessary to meet the needs of our larger population and to maintain or increase the rate of growth of the Gross National Product. An estimated 80,000,000 persons will be added to our population in the next twenty years. Beyond increases in productivity per man hour to be expected from the projected 20 per cent growth in the labor force during this same period, productive growth will have to be provided by machines.

If the criteria are control, understanding, and profits, there are strong reasons why government and business should want to, and indeed would have to, expand cybernation as rapidly as they can. The versatility of computers and automation is becoming better understood all the time by those who use them, even though, as with the human brain, most present users are far from applying their full potential. Cheap and general purpose computers or modular components applicable to many types of automatic production and decision-making are now being manufactured. In good part, they are cheap because they themselves are produced by automated methods. Techniques for gathering the field data that serve as the "inputs" to the machines are being refined and themselves automated or semi-automated. . . .

These are the advantages for management, for government, and for those parts of the work force whose status has been enhanced because of cybernation. But as cybernation advances, new and profound problems will arise for our society and its values. Cybernation presages changes in the social system so vast and so different from those with which we have traditionally wrestled that it will challenge to their roots our current perceptions about the viability of our way of life. If our democratic system has a chance to survive at all, we shall need far more understanding of the consequences of cybernation. Even the job of simply preserving a *going* society will take a level of planning far exceeding any of our previous experiences with centralized control.

The balance of this paper will point out some of the implications of cybernation that we must recognize in our task of developing a society and institutions in which man may be allowed to reach his full capacities.

The Problems of Cybernation

Unemployment and Employment

BLUE-COLLAR ADULTS

In the highly automated chemical industry, the number of production jobs has fallen 3% since 1956 while output has soared 27%. Though steel capacity has increased 20% since 1955, the number of men needed to operate the industry's plants—even at full capacity—has dropped 17,000. Auto employment slid from a peak of 746,000 in boom 1955 to 614,000 in November. . . . Since the meat industry's 1956 employment peak, 28,000 workers have lost their jobs despite a production increase of 3%. Bakery jobs have been in a steady decline from 174,000 in 1954 to 163,000 last year. On the farm one man can grow enough to feed 24 people; back in 1949 he could feed only 15.

Further insight into the problem of declining employment for the blue-collar worker comes from union statements to the effect that the number of these employees in manufacturing has been reduced by 1,500,000 in the last six years. As one example from the service industries, automatic elevators have already displaced 40,000 operators in New York.

Another disturbing aspect of the blue-collar displacement problem is its impact on employment opportunities for Negroes. There is already an increasingly lopsided Negro-to-white unemployment ratio as the dock, factory, and mine operations where Negroes have hitherto found their steadiest employment are cybernated. This, plus the handicaps of bias in hiring and lack of educational opportunity, leaves Negroes very few chances to gain new skills and new jobs. Continued widespread and disproportionate firings of Negroes, if accompanied by ineffectual reemployment methods, may well produce a situation that will increase disenchantment abroad and encourage discontent and violence here.

SERVICE INDUSTRIES   It is commonly argued that, with the growth of population, there will always be more need for people in the service industries. The assumption is that these industries will be able to absorb the displaced, retrained blue-collar labor force; that automation will not seriously displace people who perform service functions; and that the demand for engineers and scientists will be so great as to provide employment for any number of the young people who graduate with engineering training. (Indeed, some of this demand is expected to arise from the needs of cybernetic systems themselves.)

It is all very well to speak glowingly of the coming growth in the service industries and the vast opportunities for well-paid jobs and job-upgrading that these activities will provide as blue-collar opportunities diminish. But is the future as bright and as simple as this speculation implies? In the first place, service activities will also tend to displace workers by becoming self-service, by becoming cybernated, and by being eliminated. Consider the following data: The U.S. Census Bureau was able to use fifty statisticians in 1960 to do the tabulations that required 4,100 in 1950. Even where people are not being fired, service industries can now carry on a vastly greater amount of business without hiring additional personnel; for example, a 50 per cent increase in the Bell System's volume of calls in the last ten years with only a 10 per cent increase in personnel.

It is possible that as automation and computers are applied more widely an attitude of indifference to personalized service will gradually develop. People will not demand it and organizations will not provide it. The family doctor is disappearing; clerks of all sorts in stores of all sorts are disappearing as well. For example:

The R. H. Macy Co. is trying out its first electronic sales girl. This machine is smart enough to dispense 36 different items in 10 separate styles and sizes. It accepts one- and five-dollar bills in addition to coins and returns the correct change plus rejecting counterfeit currency.

People either get used to this or, as in the case of the self-service supermarket, seem to prefer it.

The greater the indifference to personalized service by both buyers and sellers, the greater the opportunity, of course, to remove human judgments from the system. Cybernation may well encourage acceptance of such depersonalization, and this, in turn, would encourage further reductions in opportunities for service jobs.

MIDDLE MANAGEMENT The blue-collar worker and the relatively menial service worker will not be the only employment victims of cybernation.

. . . Broadly, our prognostications are along the following lines:

1) Information technology should move the boundary between planning and performance upward. Just as planning was taken from the hourly worker and given to the industrial engineer, we now expect it to be taken from a number of middle managers and given to as yet largely nonexistent specialists: "operation researchers," perhaps, or "organizational analysts." Jobs at today's middle-management level will become highly structured. Much more of the work will be programmed, *i.e.*, covered by sets of operating rules governing the day-to-day decisions that are made.

2) Correlatively, we predict that large industrial organizations will recentralize, that top managers will take on an even larger proportion of the innovating, planning, and other "creative" functions than they have now.

3) A radical reorganization of middle-management levels should occur with *certain classes* of middle-management jobs moving downward in status and compensation (because they will require less autonomy and skill), while other classes move upward into the top-management group.

4) We suggest, too, that the line separating the top from the middle of

the organization will be drawn more clearly and impenetrably than ever, much like the line drawn in the last few decades between hourly workers and first-line supervisors.

. . . Information technology promises to allow fewer people to do more work. The more it can reduce the number of middle managers, the more top managers will be willing to try it. . . . One can imagine major psychological problems arising from the depersonalization of relationships within management and the greater distance between people at different levels. . . . In particular, we may have to reappraise our traditional notions about the worth of the individual as opposed to the organization, and about the mobility rights of young men on the make. This kind of inquiry may be painfully difficult, but will be increasingly necessary.

As cybernation moves into the areas now dominated by middle management in government and in business—and this move is already beginning—growing numbers of middle managers will find themselves displaced. Perhaps the bulk of displaced members of the blue-collar and service work force might be trained "up" or "over" to other jobs with, generally speaking, little or no decline in status. But the middle manager presents a special and poignant problem. Where can he go? To firms that are not as yet assigning routine liaison, analysis, and minor executive tasks to machines? This may take care of some of the best of the displaced managers and junior executives, but if these firms are to have a future, the chances are that they will have to computerize eventually in order to compete. To the government? Again, some could join it, but the style and format of governmental operations may require readjustments that many junior executives would be unable to make. And, in any case, government too, as we have seen, is turning to computers, and it is entirely possible that much of *its* middle management will also be absorbed by the computers. Up into top management? A few, of course, but necessarily only a few. Into the service end of the organization, such as sales? Some here, certainly, if they have the talent for such work. If computers and automation lead to an even greater efflorescence of marginally differentiated articles and services, there will be a correspondingly greater emphasis on sales in an effort to compete successfully. But can this be an outlet for a truly significant portion of the displaced? And at what salary? Overseas appointments in nations not yet using cybernation at the management level? Again, for a few, but only for those with the special ability to fit into a different culture at the corresponding level from which they came.

Middle management is the group in the society with the most intensive emotional drive for success and status. Their family and social life is molded by these needs, as the endless literature on life in suburbia and exurbia demonstrate. They stand to be deeply disturbed by the threat and fact of their replacement by machines. One wonders what the threat will do to the ambitions of those who will still be students and who, as followers of one of the pervasive American dreams, will have aspired to the role of middle manager "on the way up."

With the demise or downgrading of this group, changes in consumption levels and patterns can also be expected. These people, although they are not the only consumers of products of the sort advertised in *The New Yorker, Holiday,* and the like, are certainly among the largest of such consumers. They are the style-setters, the innovators, and the experimenters with new, quality products. With their loss of status and the loss of their buying power, one can imagine changes in advertising, or at least changes in the "taste" that this advertising tries to generate. It is possible that the new middle élite, the engineers, operations researchers, and systems analysts, will simply absorb the standards of the group they will have replaced. But they may be different enough in outlook and motives to have different styles in consumption.

OVERWORKED PROFESSIONALS There are service jobs, of course, that require judgments about people by people. (We are not including here the "personalized service" type of salesmanship.) The shortage of people with these talents is evidenced by the 60-hour and more work-weeks of many professionals. But these people are the products of special education, special motives, and special attitudes that are not shared to any great degree by those who turn to blue-collar or routine service tasks. Increasing the proportion of citizens with this sort of professional competence would require systematic changes in attitudes, motives, and levels of education, not to mention more teachers, a professional service already in short supply. Alterations of this magnitude cannot be carried out overnight or by casual advertising campaigns or minor government appropriations. It is doubtful indeed, in our present operating context, that they can be done fast enough to make a significant difference in the employment picture for professional services in the next decade or two. Values become imbedded early in life. They are subject to change, to be sure, but we are not, as a democratic society, adept at or inclined to change them deliberately and systematically.

Even if the teachers and the appropriate attitudes already existed, service needs at the professional level might not be great enough to absorb a large share of the potentially unemployed. Much of the work that now takes up the time of many professionals, such as doctors and lawyers, could be done by computers—just as much of the time of teachers is now taken up by teaching what could be done as well by machines.

The development of procedures for medical diagnosis by machine is proceeding well. A completely automatic analysis of data can produce just as good a diagnosis of brain malfunction as that done by a highly trained doctor.

✧   ✧   ✧   ✧   ✧

UNTRAINED ADOLESCENTS

Altogether the United States will need 13,500,000 more jobs in the Sixties merely to keep abreast of the expected growth in the labor force. This means an average of 25,000 new jobs each week, on top of those required to drain the reservoir of present unemployment and to replace jobs made superfluous by improved technology. In the last year, despite the slackness of employment opportunities, 2,500,000 more people came into the job scramble than left it through death, age, sickness or voluntary withdrawal. This was more than double the 835,000 average annual growth in the working population in the last ten years. By the end of this decade, 3,000,000 youngsters will be starting their quest for jobs each year, as against 2,000,000 now. This almost automatically guarantees trouble in getting the over-all unemployment rate down to 4 per cent because the proportion of idleness among teen-age workers is always far higher than it is among their elders.

The Labor Department estimates that 26,000,000 adolescents will seek work in the Sixties. If present performance is any indicator, in the decade ahead 30 per cent of adolescents will continue to drop out before completing high school and many who could go to college won't. The unemployment rate for such drop-outs is about 30 per cent now. Robert E. Iffert, of the Department of Health, Education, and Welfare, concluded in a 1958 study that approximately one-fourth of the students who enter college leave after their freshman year never to return. Figures compiled since then lead him to conclude that there has been no significant change, in spite of the National Defense Education Act, which was supposed to help reduce this figure.

If some figures recently given by James B. Conant turn out to be typical, at least one situation is much more serious than the average would imply. He found that in one of our largest cities, in an almost exclusively Negro slum of 125,000, 70 per cent of the boys and girls between 16 and 21 were out of school and unemployed. In another city, in an almost exclusively Negro slum, in the same age group, 48 per cent of the high school graduates were unemployed and 63 per cent of the high school drop-outs were unemployed. These adolescents would in the normal course join the untrained or poorly trained work force, a work force that will be more and more the repository of untrainable or untrained people displaced from their jobs by cybernation. These adolescents will have the following choices: they can stay in school, for which they are unsuited either by motivation or by intelligence; they can seek training that will raise them out of the untrained work force; they can compete in the growing manpower pool of those seeking relatively unskilled jobs; or they can loaf.

. . . Persuading drop-outs to stay in school will not be easy. Teachers will not be easy to recruit unless they are well paid. There is already a shortage of teachers. And let no one suggest that an easy source of teachers would be displaced workers. There is no reason to believe that they have the verbal and social facility to teach, and most of them would have nothing to teach but skills that have become obsolete. Some, of course, might be taught to teach, though this would add obvious complications to the whole effort.

Knowing what to teach will depend on knowing what types of jobs are likely to exist when the student finishes his training. This will require knowledge about the trends and plans of local industry, if that is where the youths are to work (and if that is where industry plans to stay!), and of industries in other localities, if the youths are willing to move. Such knowledge often does not exist in a rapidly changing world or, if it exists, may not be forthcoming from businesses more concerned with competition than with the frustrated "delinquents" of their community. As of now, in the words of Dr. Conant, "unemployment of youth is literally nobody's affair."

SOME PROPOSED SOLUTIONS Retraining is often proposed as if it were also the cure-all for coping with adults displaced by cybernation as well as young people. In some circumstances it has worked well for some people, especially with office personnel who have been displaced by data-processing computers and have learned other office jobs, including servicing the computers. But in other cases, especially with poorly educated blue-collar workers, retraining has not always been successful, nor have new jobs based on that retraining been available.

✧ ✧ ✧ ✧ ✧

The problem of retraining blue-collar workers is formidable enough. But, in view of the coming role of cybernation in the service industries, the retraining problem for service personnel seems insuperable. No one has seriously proposed what service tasks this working group could be retrained *for*—to say nothing of training them for jobs that would pay high enough wages to make them good consumers of the cornucopia of products manufactured by automation.

Another proposal for coping with the unemployment-via-cybernation problem is shorter hours for the same pay. This approach is intended to maintain the ability of workers to consume the products of cybernation and, in the case of blue-collar workers, to maintain the strength of unions. This would retain the consumer purchasing capacity for x workers in those situations where the nature of the cybernation process is such that x men would do essentially the same work as x plus y men used to do. But when the task itself is eliminated or new tasks are developed that need different talents, shorter shifts clearly will not solve the problem. The latter conditions are the more likely ones as cybernation becomes more sophisticated.

Proponents of cybernation claim that it should reduce the price of products by removing much of the cost of labor and increasing consumer demand. Whether the price of beef, or milk, or rent will be reduced in phase with the displaced worker's lowered paycheck remains to be seen. So far this has not happened. Whether the price of TV sets, cars, refrigerators, etc. will be reduced substantially depends in part on how much product cost goes into larger advertising budgets aimed at differentiating the product from the essentially same one produced last year or from the practically identical one produced on some other firm's automated production line.

An obvious solution to unemployment is a public works program. If our understanding of the direction of cybernation is correct, the government will probably be faced for the indefinite future with the need to support part of the population through public works. There is no dearth of public work to be done, and it is not impossible that so much would continue to be needed that an appropriately organized public works program could stimulate the economy to the point that a substantial portion of the work force could be re-absorbed into the private sector. That is, although the proportion of workers needed for any particular task will be reduced through the use of cybernation, the total number of tasks that need to be done could equal or exceed the absolute number of people available to do them. It is not known whether this situation would obtain for enough tasks in enough places so that the portion of the population working on public projects would be relatively small. However, if it should turn out that this felicitous state of affairs could be realized in principle, clearly it could only be realized and sustained if there were to be considerable and continuous centralized planning and control over financing, the choice of public projects, and the places where they were to be done. If, for whatever reasons, this situation could not be achieved, the public works payroll would remain very large indeed.

What would be the effects on the attitudes and aspirations of a society, and particularly of its leadership, when a significant part of it is overtly supported by governmental public works programs? ("Overtly" is used because much of the aerospace industry in particular and of the weapons systems industry in general is subsidized by the government right now: they literally live off cost plus fixed fee contracts, and there is no other comparable market for their products.) Whatever else the attitudes might be, they certainly would not be conducive to maintaining the spirit of a capitalistic economy. This shift in perspective may or may not be desirable, but those who think it would be undesirable should realize that encouraging the extension of cybernation, in the interests of free enterprise and better profits, may be self-defeating.

❖   ❖   ❖   ❖   ❖

Whether any of these proposed solutions is adequate to the challenge of unemployment is not known to us or, we gather, to those who have proposed one solution or another. But even if, in principle, some combination of them would be adequate, in order to put them into effect a considerable change would be necessary in the attitudes and voting behavior of Congress and our tax-paying citizens. Preconceptions about the virtues and vices of work, inflation, the national debt, and government control run deep and shift slowly.

Not all of these dire threats would come to pass, of course, if cybernation reduced consumer buying power through unemployment and, thereby, the financial capability of industry and business to introduce or profit from cybernation. In this way we might all be saved from the adverse effects of unemployment from this source. But the economy would still be faced with those threats to its well-being which, as were pointed out earlier, make the need to cybernate so compelling.

Cybernation is by nature the sort of process that will be introduced selectively by organization, industry, and locality. The ill-effects will be felt at first only locally and, as a result, will not be recognized by those who introduce it—and perhaps not even by the government—as a *national* problem with many serious implications for the whole social system. Also, because one of the chief effects of cybernation on employment is not to hire rather than to fire, the economic-social consequences will be delayed and will at any time be exacerbated or ameliorated by other economic and social factors such as the condition of our foreign markets, which also are being changed and challenged by European and Russian cybernation. By the time the adverse effects of cybernation are sufficiently noticeable to be ascribed to cybernation, the equipment will be in and operating.

Once this happens, the costs of backtracking may be too great for private enterprise to sustain. For, in addition to the costs of removing the equipment, there will be the costs of building a pre-cybernation system of operations. But which firms will voluntarily undertake such a job if they are unsure whether their competitors are suffering the same setback—or indeed if their competitors are going to decybernate at all? And, if not voluntarily, how would the government enforce, control, and pay for the change-over?

Additional Leisure

It is generally recognized that sooner or later automation and computers will mean shorter working hours and greater leisure for most if not all of the American people. It is also generally, if vaguely, recognized that there probably are problems connected with the use of leisure that will take time to work out.

Two stages need to be distinguished: the state of leisure over the next decade or two, when our society will still be in transition to a way of life based on the widespread application of cybernation; and the relatively stable state some time in the future when supposedly everybody will have more leisure time than today and enough security to enjoy it. The transitional stage is our chief concern, for the end is far enough off to make more than some general speculations about it footless. At this later time people's behavior and attitudes will be conditioned as much by presently unforeseeable social and technological developments as by the character and impact of cybernation itself.

During the transition there will be four different "leisure" classes: 1) the unemployed, 2) the low-salaried employees working short hours, 3) the adequately paid to high-salaried group working short hours, and 4) those with no more leisure than they now have—which in the case of many professionals means very few hours of leisure indeed.

. . . During the transition period, it is the second group, the low-salaried workers who cannot or will not find another job, that presents the true leisure problem, as distinct from the unemployment problem. Here is where the multiple problems connected with private and public make-play efforts may prove very difficult indeed. We have some knowledge about relatively low-income workers who become voluntarily interested in adult education and adult play sessions, but we have had no real experience with the problems of how to stimulate the interests and change the attitudes of a large population that is forced to work shorter hours but is used to equating work and security, that will be bombarded with an advertising *geist* praising consumption and glamorous leisure, that will be bounded closely on one side by the unemployed and on the other by a relatively well-to-do community to which it cannot hope to aspire. Boredom may drive these people to seek new leisure-time activities if they are provided and do not cost much. But boredom combined with other factors may also make for frustration and aggression and all the social and political problems these qualities imply.

Decisions and Public Opinion

PRIVILEGED INFORMATION   The government must turn to computers to handle many of its major problems simply because the data involved are so massive and the factors so complex that only machines can handle the material fast enough to allow timely action based on understanding of the facts. In the nature of the situation, the decisions made by the government with the help of computers would be based in good part on computers that have been programmed with more or less confidential information—and privileged access to information, at the time it is needed, is a sufficient if not always necessary condition for attaining and maintaining power. There may not be any easy way to insure that decisions based on computers could not become a threat to democratic government.

Thus, even if people may have more leisure time to attend more closely to politics, they may not have the ability to contribute to the formulation of policy. Some observers feel that the middle class does not now take a strong interest in voting and is alienated in its responsibility for the conduct of government. Leisure may not change this trend, especially when government becomes in large part the complex computer operation that it must necessarily become.

Significant public opinion may come from only a relatively small portion of the public: a) those who are able to follow the battles of the computers and to understand the implications of their programs; and b) those who are concerned with government policy but who are outside of or unfamiliar with the computer environment.

✧　✧　✧　✧　✧

PERSONNEL AND PERSONALITIES As for the selection of the men who are to plan or make policy, a computerized government will require different training from that which executive personnel in most governmental agencies has today. Certainly, without such training (and perhaps with it) there is bound to be a deepening of the split between politics and facts. For example, it is evident that the attitudes of many Congressmen toward space activities are motivated more by politics and conventional interpretations of reality than by engineering facts or the realities of international relations.

The same schisms will be compounded as computers are used more and more to plan programs in the Department of Health, Education, and Welfare, urban development, communications, transportation, foreign aid, and the analysis of intelligence data of all sorts.

✧　✧　✧　✧　✧

MASS VS. THE INDIVIDUAL The psychological influence of computers is overwhelming: they symbolize and reenforce the potency of America's belief in the utility of science and technology. There is a sense of security in nicely worked-up curves and complex displays of information which are the products of almost unimaginably intricate and elegant machinery. In general, the influence of computers will continue to be enhanced if those who use them attend chiefly to those components of reality which can be put into a computer and processed by it, and the important values will become those which are compatible with this approach to analyzing and manipulating the world. For example, the influence of computers has already been sufficiently strong to seduce military planners and civil defense planners *away* from those aspects of their problems which are not now subject to data processing. Most of the planning for survival following nuclear attack has to do with those parts of the situation which can be studied by computers. Crucial aspects of psychological and social reorganization have been pushed into the background simply because they cannot be handled statistically with convenience or with the demonstrated "expertness" of the specialist in computers. Thus, the nature of the post-attack situation is argued learnedly but spuriously by those who have the attention of leadership, an attention stimulated by the glamor of computers, the prestige of their scientist-keepers, and the comfort of their "hard facts."

DECISIONS FOR BUSINESS   The implications of the concentration of decision-making within business firms as a result of cybernation are not as clear-cut as the effects for government. In principle, both big and small business will be able to know much more about the nature of their markets and of their organizational operations through cybernation. Whether or not this will help both big and small proportionately is far from clear. Big business will undoubtedly have better facilities for information and decisions, but small business may be able to get what it needs by buying it from service organizations that will come into existence for this purpose. Big organizations will be able to afford high-priced personnel for doing the thinking beyond that done by the machines. If quality of thinking is always related to price, the big organizations will be able to put their small competitors out of business. But the big organizations, precisely because of their size, may have relatively little maneuverability, and some of the best minds may find the little organizations a more exciting game. Whether the little organizations could stay afloat is moot, but one can anticipate some exciting entrepreneurial maneuvers among the small firms while they last.

One thing is clear: among the small organizations, and probably among the big ones too, we can expect disastrous mistakes as a result of poor machine programming or inaccurate interpretations of the directives of the machines. These will be greatest during the early period when it will be faddish to plan via machine and when few organizations will have the brainpower and organization to do so intelligently. Thus, added to the unemployment ranks in the decade or so ahead will be those who have been put out of jobs because their firms have misused computers.

After the Take-Over

In twenty years, other things being equal, most of the routine blue-collar and white-collar tasks that can be done by cybernation will be. Our schools will probably be turning out a larger proportion of the population better educated than they are today, but most of our citizens will be unable to understand the cybernated world in which they live. Perhaps they will understand the rudiments of calculus, biology, nuclear physics, and the humanities. But the research realm of scientists, the problems of government, and the interplay between them will be beyond the ken even of our college graduates. Besides, most people will have had to recognize that, when it comes to logic, the machines by and large can think better than they, for in that time reasonably good thinking computers should be operating on a large scale.

There will be a small, almost separate, society of people in rapport with the advanced computers. These cyberneticians will have established a relationship with their machines that cannot be shared with the average man any more than the average man today can understand the problems of molecular biology, nuclear physics, or neuropsychiatry. Indeed, many scholars will not have the capacity to share their knowledge or feeling about this new man-machine relationship. Those with the talent for the work probably will have to develop it from childhood and will be trained as intensively as the classical ballerina.

Some of the remaining population will be productively engaged in human-to-human or human-to-machine activities requiring judgment and a high level of intelligence and training. But the rest, whose innate intelligence or training is not of the highest, what will they do? We can foresee a nation with a large portion of its people doing, directly or indirectly, the endless public tasks that the welfare state needs and that the government will not allow to be cybernated because of the serious unemployment that would result. These people will work short hours, with much time for the pursuit of leisure activities.

Even with a college education, what will they do all their long lives, day after day, four-day week-end after week-end, vacation after vacation, in a more and more crowded world? (There is a population explosion to face in another ten to thirty years.) What will they believe in and aspire to as they work their shorter hours and, on the outside, pursue their "self-fulfilling" activities, whatever they may be? No one has ever seriously envisioned what characteristics these activities might have in order to be able to engross most men and women most of their adult lives. What will be the relationship of these people to government, to the "upper intellectuals," to the rest of the world, to themselves?

Obviously, attitudes toward work, play, and social responsibility will have changed greatly. Somehow we shall have had to cope emotionally with the vast gap in living standards that will then typify the difference between us and the have-not nations. We shall presumably have found some way to give meaning to the consumption of mass leisure. It would seem that a life oriented to private recreation might carry with it an attitude of relative indifference to public responsibility. This indifference, plus the centralization of authority, would seem to imply a governing élite and a popular acceptance of such an élite.

If this world is to exist as a coherent society, it will have to have its own "logic," so that it will make sense to its inhabitants. Today, for most of our population, our society makes sense, even though some other eyes hardly see us as logical in the formal sense of the word and the eyes of some of our own people look on us as a more or less pointless society. We make and solve our problems chiefly by other than mathematical-logical standards, and so must the cybernated generations. What these standards might be, we do not know. But if they are inadequate, the frustration and pointlessness that they produce may well evoke, in turn, a war of desperation—ostensibly against some external enemy but, in fact, a war to make the world safe for human beings by destroying most of society's sophisticated technological base. One thing is clear: if the new "logic" is to resolve the problems raised here, it will have to generate beliefs, behavior, and goals far different from those which we have held until now and which are driving us more and more inexorably into a contradictory world run by (and for?) ever more intelligent, ever more versatile slaves.

❖ 54 ❖

COMPETITION? YES, BUT . . .

Charles F. Phillips

All major social institutions involve an interacting complex of values, as well as of roles and statuses. One of the values of our economic system has been the idea that competition is "good." Competition has been valued positively because it has been viewed, at least theoretically, as an essential ingredient of free, private enterprise. The phrase "at least theoretically" deserves emphasis because some claim, as Charles F. Phillips contends in the following article, that most American businessmen believe in competition— but not for their business! Whether this is true or not, American businessmen have devised a multitude of ways to minimize serious competition. They believe in competition. But . . .

❖   ❖   ❖   ❖   ❖

To ask an American businessman—whether he be grocer, baker, or candlestick maker—if he believes in competition is almost like asking for a sock on the nose. *Of course*, he believes in competition—and he raises his voice to add emphasis to his answer.

But, after he has cooled off a bit from your question, you may find

s o u r c e :   Charles F. Phillips, "Competition? Yes, but . . ." Address to the 26th Annual Boston Conference on Distribution, October 19, 1954. Reprinted by permission of the author. ❖ The author is President of Bates College, Lewiston, Maine, and a public governor of the American Stock Exchange. He has written *A Tax Program to Encourage the Economic Growth of Puerto Rico*, and has collaborated with Delbert J. Duncan on *Marketing Principles and Methods*.

that he has his own definition of competition. For example, let's walk with him down the street toward the grocery store of which he is the proprietor. Across the way in a window of one of his competitors is a large sign: "Sugar, X cents per pound." You call it to his attention and at once his brow knits. "That's unfair competition," he says. "That so-and-so has cut his price again to attract *my* customers." I remind him that he believes in competition. "Why, yes," he replies, "but not unfair and ruthless competition." And, if you then ask him, "But why is it unfair for a competitor to cut his price?" he will explode, "Why, any darn fool knows that it is unfair to sell sugar for X cents. You can't make any money at that price. There ought to be a law in this state against such practices."

We Are for Freedom, But

I wonder if the reaction of our friend, the grocer, does not illustrate a simple truth which can be expressed in the short but incomplete sentence: "We all like competition, but . . ."

We all like competition since we know it is essential for our type of economy, and we like the freedoms which our economy gives to each of us—the freedom to enter or withdraw from any specific field or career; freedom to set our own prices; yes, even freedom to undersell somebody else and take business away from him.

But . . . all too often when a competitor really acts like a competitor and does something which hurts us—cuts a price, sells harder, improves quality—it becomes "unfair competition" and we run to our trade association, our resources, or the government for protection.

❖   ❖   ❖   ❖   ❖

. . . If we go back to the turn of the present century, we find that small country merchants were going through the mail-order scare. Following the lead of Montgomery Ward Company and Sears, Roebuck & Company, mail-order firms were springing up in many parts of our country. To the small country retailer, this newer form of retailing was unfair. It did not employ salespeople. It did not involve the operation of a retail store. It could purchase in huge quantities. For these and other reasons, the local merchant was undersold and he objected to this result. Obviously, such competition was unfair! In a number of communities, "trade at home" clubs were organized while some local retailers organized mail-order catalogue burning parties.

Unfair, They Say

Along about the same time, the "unfair" competition of the department store was also growing. As a matter of fact, by 1895 the department store had developed to such an extent that a group of retailers meeting in convention, "after an exciting debate," passed a resolution condemning this form of retailing, as it would "result in oppression of the public by suppressing competition (note that word 'suppressing') and causing the consumer in the end to pay higher prices and ultimately create a monopoly . . . and, further, that it (would) close to thousands of energetic young men who lack great capital the avenue of business which they should find open to them." Once again, the bogey of unfair competition had reared its ugly head. Yet, it is probably not being cynical to remark that what these retailers really were opposed to was the fact that the department store was a formidable competitor.

What happened in the late Twenties and early Thirties in the chain store field is known from personal experience to practically all of us . . . . Based on charges that the chains were monopolistic; that they used such unfair practices as loss leaders; that they were a detriment to community life because of their absentee ownership, unfairness to local bankers, failure to pay their fair proportion of taxes; and that they were unfair to their employees through long hours, low wages, and offering little chance of advancement, smaller retailers spent much time, effort, and money in attacking this new method of unfair competition. Customers were urged to curtail their purchases at chains. The Robinson-Patman Act was sponsored, the misnamed Fair Trade laws were encouraged, and in over twenty states special taxes discriminating against the chains were enacted.

We all like competition, but . . .

Of course, this excursion into retail history belongs to the past, and you may ask: Is anything like this going on at the present time? The answer is "yes"—and in practically every area of business. Let's note a few illustrations.

Pick up the trade paper of today, and you will discover that discount houses are a form of unfair competition. All over the country, they are rapidly springing up on the basis of underselling the so-called established retailer, which means, and I now quote the executive secretary of the National Association of Retail Druggists, that they are trying to destroy "every established retailer in the United States . . . by unfair competition. . . ." And he goes on with two sentences which might well have been lifted verbatim from dozens of speeches made against the chain store twenty-five years ago.

Unless the discount house is effectively curbed . . . there will inevitably be anarchy in the market place. The American public must ask itself whether it wishes to sacrifice the legitimate retailers who make outstanding contributions to our economic and community life and who are the backbone of our mass distribution system.

Discount houses are even pointed to as being unfair to the consumer because, after all, they do not offer him all the services of the established retailer. Incidentally, whether the customer wants those services or not is rarely considered when this argument is advanced.

Solution by Elimination

And, what do the established retailers offer as a solution to the discount house? Is it an honest effort on their part to meet this new competitive factor by reducing their own margins and prices—which, if history proves anything, *must* be the way to meet it in the long run? In a few instances, the answer is yes. To illustrate, here is a refreshing statement from the chairman of the board of Sears, Roebuck & Company, Theodore Houser, who says:

I have no patience with people who say that there ought to be some way to stop the discount house. The important thing is to bring down the price to the consumer. If the discount house can do that, good. It's Sears' job to get in there and pitch.

But Houser's statement is really the exception which proves the rule. The majority of established retailers act as if they think the answer is *more* Fair Trade—despite the fact that it is the wide margins set by Fair Trade which are playing an important role in encouraging the growth of the discount house. Consequently, they clamor for the manufacturer to cut off the flow of merchandise to the price cutter and to enforce his Fair Trade contracts. In brief, they say: Let's not meet competition; let's have someone eliminate it for us.

Another form of what some of today's retailers refer to as unfair competition can be discovered by talking with a downtown merchant in any city where one or more major outlying shopping centers have been developed. "Here I am, a well-established retailer," he will tell you. "I have been in this location for thirty years, and I have always given good service to the public. Now, some real estate operator has come along and developed a shopping center five miles outside of this community, and *my* customers are driving out there where they have ample room to park and where they can shop during the evening. In view of all I've done for this community, I don't think it is fair."

Or, again, talk with the president of one of today's drug chains. Twenty-five years ago *his* organization was the culprit. At that time, *he* was the unfair competitor—the price cutter—but, today, he finds that the supermarket has added a drug section and is underselling him. Whereas he opposed resale price maintenance laws twenty-five years ago, today he is one of their strong advocates. His own definition of unfair competition has shifted rapidly, depending upon who is being undersold. Incidentally, this same shift in opinion is becoming evident among the executives of the older and well-established food chains, and the leading trade paper in this area is now an advocate of Fair Trade.

Make Competition Illegal

We see another aspect of the Fair Trade fight in New Jersey. Here—as elsewhere—the supermarkets began to sell packaged medicines at reduced prices. The regular druggists' reaction was not to meet competition in the market place, but to try for a court ruling to prevent sales of packaged medicines in stores not having registered pharmacists. This method of fighting competition is catching: It has also appeared in Minnesota, California, and other states.

We all like competition, but . . .

But, we do not have to limit ourselves to illustrations from what we normally consider the retail field. Did you follow the ten-month strike of Local 15 of the United Hatters and Millinery Workers International Union against the Hat Corporation of America? The strike started in July of 1953, brought on basically by the Union's demand that the company sign a contract containing a clause that would prohibit it from opening new plants outside of the Norwalk area and from transferring work now done in Norwalk to any outside plant.

What the Union wanted was a limit on competition. It did not want its members to compete with workers in some other areas where Hat Corporation might establish a factory. Fortunately, after ten months, the Union lost its fight. It is worth contemplating, however, what would have happened had a similar strike been won when the United States was still located on the East Coast only. Obviously, it would still be located on the East Coast only; and equally obviously, its standard of living today would be far below what it now is.

Then, of course, there is the farmer—the so-called individualist, the man who stands on his own feet, and, as the politician puts it, "is the backbone of the nation." Here, of course, is someone who believes in competition. Yes, he does, but again there comes that but—and the but in his case is a big one, so big that through powerful lobbies he has forced through Congress price support laws which give him protection far in excess of even that provided for the retailer through Fair Trade.

In the foreign trade area, we can find this same attitude. A Randall Commission . . . came up with a program which could be described by the phrase, "more trade, less aid." For a time, it seemed as if practically everyone in the country was in agreement that this slogan would be a good one to put into practice. It looked as if we were going to make progress in minimizing some of our tariff barriers which limit competition and result in lower standards of living both here and abroad. Yet, when a specific program to accomplish these ends was proposed . . . many of those who, at their trade association meetings, are warm advocates of competition, suddenly found that there were certain wage cost differentials which led them to oppose lower tariffs "as posing a grave threat to the domestic economy." As they warmed up to their subject, they pointed out that lower tariffs would throw American workers out of jobs, curtail purchasing power, and send us into a depression. The fact that domestic difficulties in specific areas would be far more than offset by benefits in other areas is something with which they were not concerned.

We all believe in competition, but . . .

. . . Please do not think I am saying there is no such thing as unfair competition. When a competitor resorts to false and misleading advertising, engages in misbranding, and makes false and disparaging statements against competitors or their products he is engaging in practices which all of us would denounce.

What I am saying is this: Much of what we daily refer to as unfair competition is really just keen competition. It is the kind of competition that is essential to our type of economic system. If we want to maintain the freedoms which our system gives us—to enter businesses of our choice, to produce the merchandise we please, to set our own prices—then we must accept the competition which is essential to that kind of an economy. We must not always look to our trade association or our government to protect us from the actions of our competitors.

Do We Want Another System?

Of course, there are other kinds of economic systems. I studied one at first hand . . . when I spent several months in India. There I discovered that if you want to make a substantial capital investment in your plant, you must get the approval of the government licensing committee and this is not easy to do. To illustrate, during 1953, the textile industry in India—as in the United States—was not having a very happy time. A number of companies decided to install automatic looms to reduce their cost and, hence, to compete better both in the domestic and in the world markets. During the year, ten applications for such installations came before the government licensing committee: All ten applications were refused: The committee felt that the automatic looms would create unfair competition for the firms not installing similar equipment. As a result, India's textile industry finds itself increasingly unable to compete in today's market and, what is even more important, Indian customers were continuing to pay the higher prices required by the older, less efficient and, hence, more costly looms. Perhaps it is this kind of reasoning—perhaps it is this limitation on competition—which plays a part in explaining why the average per capita income in today's India is about $39.00 per year.

I would make this positive suggestion. Let us spend more time—in our offices, stores, conferences, and trade association meetings—improving our operations and less time trying to curb our competitors. Not only will individual companies be better off, but so will society. If America wants to continue its long-time development toward a rising standard of living, we need to encourage more, not less, competition.

❖   ❖   ❖   ❖   ❖

✤ 55 ✤

THE FRUITS OF

PRICE INVESTIGATION

Estes Kefauver

The previous selection described the apparent contradiction between, on the one hand, the American ideological commitment to competition, and on the other hand, the widespread practices that nullify competition. In this selection by Senator Kefauver, we see some of the complexities of maintaining a truly competitive economic system under conditions of increasing concentration of economic power and economic control by Federal agencies. Indeed, as brought out before Senator Kefauver's committee, in a market dominated by a few massive firms, it can be argued that "administered prices" are more typical of modern capitalism than prices based on competition. The article also makes clear the value of Congressional committee investigations as a means of informing the public and benefiting consumers through savings which result from such information.

On July 9, 1957, the Subcommittee on Anti-trust and Monopoly of the Senate Committee on the Judiciary began hearings on what Gardiner C. Means in 1935 termed "administered prices." Administered prices are those which, in contrast to competitive prices determined by market supply and demand, are arbitrarily set and held constant, or, on occasion, even increased despite a fall in demand. Now, after four years, twenty-six vol-

SOURCE: *The Progressive*, Vol. 25, No. 7 (July 1961), 12–16. Reprinted by permission of the publisher. ✧ Estes Kefauver (1903–1963) was United States Senator from Tennessee. He was the chairman of the Anti-trust and Monopoly, and the Constitutional Amendments subcommittees of the Senate Judiciary Committee. He was the author of *Crime in America* and *In a Few Hands: Monopoly Power in America*.

umes of hearings numbering 16,505 pages, and four reports, it may be appropriate to inquire what the Subcommittee has accomplished.

The inquiry has rested basically upon a detailed examination of administered prices in four important industries:

The first industry examined, steel, produces one of the nation's most basic materials; it has long been referred to as the bellwether of the economy.

Next came an inquiry into the automobile industry, which is not only the nation's largest but one that exercises a pivotal influence upon the rate of activity in the economy generally.

Bread, the "staff of life," is among the nation's half dozen most important industries. It also presents an interesting example of an industry in which there is no technological basis whatever for the concentration of sales in a few large companies, yet nonetheless is changing from a market-determined to an administered-price status.

Finally, we examined the drug industry. The importance of drugs lies not so much in the overall size of the business (although with annual sales of $2.5 billion this is hardly negligible), but rather in its crucial relationship to health and indeed life itself.

We then turned to the heads of the anti-trust agencies and asked what action could be taken against the simultaneous price increases, identical bids, and similar manifestations of group behavior we had uncovered. In essence, their position was that competition could be restored only if they were fortunate enough to come across "hard-core" evidence of meetings and agreements—overt conspiracy.

These professions of futility dramatize the basic irony underlying the enforcement of the anti-trust laws. Although now and then an exception, such as electrical goods, turns up to prove the rule, the typical "hard-core" case involves enterprises, such as Louisiana strawberry firms or Maine lobster fishermen, so small and so poor that they are unable to afford the legal fees of corporation law firms, and thus go about the business of fixing prices in the direct, old-fashioned way—through meetings and price-fixing agreements. In the process they leave behind all kinds of evidence of "hard-core" violations.

But if the same result is achieved by price leadership, with, say, U.S. Steel raising its price, which is then matched by all of the other steel companies (some of which enjoy even higher profit rates and appear to have lower costs), the anti-trust agencies have insisted that they are powerless to act. This position, expressed before our Subcommittee . . . represents a tragic retrogression in enforcement.

During the late 1940's and early 1950's, the anti-trust agencies had made considerable progress in establishing conspiracy through the economic evidence of its operation and effects. Courts were increasingly holding that such phenomena as identical bids could not possibly be explained as the result of mere chance but must reflect an "implied conspiracy" or "planned common course of action" and that therefore the law had been violated even though no proof of meetings or formal agreements had been uncovered. Unless this doctrine of "conscious parallelism" is revived, the case for new legislation to deal with the problem of administered pricing becomes very strong indeed.

But what kind of legislation? There is the rub. During our hearings outstanding economists who have specialized on this subject described the alternative public policies. On the one hand is the viewpoint, expressed by Dr. Ben Lewis, chairman of the department of economics at Oberlin College, that whether we like it or not the logic of events is working inexorably toward direct controls:

"My own prediction—and I stress that I am predicting, not prescribing —is that the years ahead will see a great increase in conscious, collective, governmental controls and of governmental enterprise; and that bigness will be a major focal point of the development. The development will reflect a growing, intensified concern over the private possession of economic power so vast that even its possessors are frightened by the implications of their holdings. . . . The conviction that great power over the economy must reside only in a government of the people will be acted on relentlessly, bluntly, and with force. Events will count more heavily than fine logic in determining the action, but events will surely occur, and public action to repossess the power to economize will surely follow."

While agreeing on the general nature of the problem, another group of authorities, including Fritz Machlup, Corwin Edwards, and Walter Adams, held that not only is competition preferable to controls but that it is not too late to make competition work; that to this end the government may act in many ways in addition to anti-trust enforcement, such as reducing tariffs; that bigness is not the inevitable result of technology or anything else; and that breaking up the giants would not impair efficiency. In the words of Walter Adams:

"Size, in the sense of market control, is the fact of life, and the essence of the problem, in our concentrated industries. Restrictive practices are merely superficial symptoms of the disease. Given a market structure dominated by a few firms, it seems inevitable that prices be administered. . . . Therefore, if competition is our goal, and I repeat that, if competition *is* our goal, the only real solution, the most effective remedy, is dissolution, divorcement, and divestiture; trustbusting in the literal sense.

"Industrial concentration . . . is not inevitable . . . It is the concomitant of unimaginative, shortsighted, or corrupt exercise of governmental power. It is man-made, not God-made, and since it is made by man, it can be changed by man."

Still, a third group, including Edwin D. Nourse, Gardiner C. Means, and J. Kenneth Galbraith, appeared to express the hope that standards of desirable economic performance and behavior could be evolved and ways and means short of direct governmental intervention in the economic process could be devised to induce the heads of large firms to operate their corporations in accordance with these standards.

Regardless of the differences in their proposed remedies, these authorities seemed to be in general agreement that the time for action is now. But they also recognized that the problem is not going to be solved tomorrow. In this, they were merely manifesting their awareness that an inevitable time lag exists between the advancement of a proposal for legislative action and its final adoption.

But this is not to say that nothing can be done and done now. For one thing, there has come out of our hearings a growing recognition that the consumer is the forgotten man not only when capital and labor sit down to divide up the spoils of technological advance, but when governmental agencies act on matters which impinge directly upon his interests. Together with nineteen other Senators, I have introduced a bill, S. 1688, to establish a Department of Consumers of Cabinet rank which would have the right and duty to call to the attention of the regulatory agencies the effects of their actions on consumers before they are taken. The new department would act as a central clearinghouse for consumer information and complaints, bringing under one roof the varying agencies of the government whose primary responsibility is to the consumer interest. . . .

As another step which need not wait upon any comprehensive solution to the general administered price problem, I recently introduced a bill, S. 1552, designed to stimulate competition and bring about lower prices in the ethical drug industry. From our hearings it has become obvious that by any standard drug prices are excessive and in some cases outrageous, that this is made possible by a tight control of the market by a few big drug companies, and that this tight control in turn stems from three factors: patent monopolies; enormous advertising and promotional campaigns directed to the doctor which the small drug manufacturer cannot possibly match; and the successful efforts of the large drug companies in persuading physicians to prescribe by trade-name rather than by generic name. The bill is directed at each of these sources of market power.

While the drafting of effective legislation on new and complex problems is itself an accomplishment, it is true that neither the consumer bill nor the drug bill has yet become the law of the land. Nor are they likely to become so unless they receive strong public support. Without such support the usual fate of legislation in the public interest, particularly if opposed by powerful groups, is permanent interment in the standing committee to which it is referred.

A particular source of annoyance to me and to other members of Congress is the citizen who consistently deplores the lack of essential legislation but does nothing to communicate his own views to his elected Senators and Representative. The importance of even a small volume of mail from the grass roots is confirmed by the lengths to which large organizations will go to evoke a "spontaneous" flow of mail from "the folks back home."

In addition to these measures which are definitely within the area of the possible, the hearings by the Subcommittee have provided the bases for important additions to the arsenal of anti-trust weapons. Penalties for violation of the statutes have been increased, while orders issued by the Federal Trade Commission under the Clayton Act now become final unless appealed—a significant technical change which the FTC had been urging upon Congress for many years.

In recent years the argument has been made with increasing frequency that the hearings of Congressional committees should be restricted solely to the consideration of legislation. Because of the flagrant abuses of some hearings, such as those of the late Senator Joseph R. McCarthy, this argument has found favor with many individuals of liberal persuasion who formerly would have opposed any restriction on the rights of Congressional committees to get at the facts. Yet, throughout our history most reforms have been preceded by Congressional investigations which were *not* directed toward any specific piece of legislation for the simple reason that no meaningful bill can even be drafted until the facts of the matter are known and understood.

Each of the investigations made by the Subcommittee on Anti-trust and Monopoly *has* been conducted for legislative purposes. Its inquiries have been focused principally on the questions of whether a need for new legislation exists and, if so, what form it should take. But even if they had not been directed to a legislative purpose, these investigations would still have been appropriate as part of what Woodrow Wilson called the "informing function." Indeed, in his celebrated treatise on Congressional government, President Wilson went so far as to say that "The informing function of Congress should be preferred even to its legislative function." With the emergence of big business, big labor, and big government as the central forces in our society, and with the pressures for greater secrecy and non-disclosure coming from everywhere, the need for the "informing function" today is far greater than in the simpler days of Woodrow Wilson.

As a by-product of its legislative work our Subcommittee has carried out this "informing function" which, it appears, has not been without certain beneficial results. A specific example is the failure of the steel companies to raise their prices after the settlement of the steel strike of

1959. Following the strike, conditions were propitious for a price increase. Wage rates had been increased as part of the settlement with the union. Predictions of demand for steel were optimistic. Some of the metal-using companies were looking forward to a price increase as "a good peg on which to hang higher price tags that would recoup even more than the additional steel costs." In each of the previous four years an increase in wage rates had been followed by an increase in price—$4.50 per ton in 1958, $6 in 1957, $8.50 in 1956, and $7.35 in 1955. The 1957 increase, alone, was shown to have cost direct steel buyers $500,000,000 a year, and, because of the pyramiding effect, the cost to the ultimate consumer was several times this amount.

The Subcommittee made it clear that if the price of steel were increased, it would hold public hearings in which steel officials would be asked to compare the price increase with the cost of the wage increase and to explain the need for the price rise in view of their remarkable profit showings. Trade sources suggest that this was a factor in the decision of the steel companies not to raise prices, although there is no way of precisely determining its importance. To assume all of the credit for this new-found rectitude on the part of the steel companies would be presumptuous since other factors were at work, not the least of which was an approaching national election. At the same time, to ignore completely the Subcommittee's role would be to distort reality.

But perhaps an even clearer case in point is provided by the Subcommittee's inquiry into the drug industry, the indirect consequences of which are referred to in the trade press as "fallout effects." For one thing, there has been a number of price reductions which the trade has attributed in considerable part to the Subcommittee's investigation. In actual dollars and cents the savings to consumers have not been inconsiderable. Just one month prior to the Subcommittee's hearings on antibiotics in September, 1960, the price of the largest-selling broad-spectrum antibiotic, tetracycline, was reduced fifteen per cent, the first price reduction since the product was introduced in 1954. Savings to consumers total more than $50,000,000 a year. Immediately prior to the Subcommittee's first drug hearings in December, 1959, the price of the largest-selling oral anti-diabetic drug was reduced ten per cent—an annual saving to consumers of $2,500,000. During the course of the hearings, price reductions were made on still other drug products. (The Subcommittee's total annual appropriation is only $450,000, or less than one per cent of the savings on antibiotics alone.)

Savings have also been effected through the broader use of generic name-prescribing, interest in which has been stimulated by our disclosures that non-patented drugs marketed under their generic names are usually available from smaller drug manufacturers at prices far below those charged by the large companies for their trade-name products. A typical case is the arthritic drug, prednisone, which under the trade-name Meticorten is sold to the consumer for nearly thirty cents a pill. Under its generic name the product can be purchased currently from drug stores in Washington, D.C., for less than four cents a pill.

The growing interest in the subject is evident from the fact that the American Medical Association at its meeting in Washington in November, 1960, recommended the use of generic name prescribing for welfare patients as a means of keeping down drug costs. In August, 1960, the American Hospital Association's House of Delegates strongly urged hospitals to adopt "formularies" which employ generic names as a means of cutting down expenses. . . .

The growing acceptance of generic name-prescribing for welfare patients led Senator Philip Hart of Michigan to raise a logical question. If drugs purchased under generic names are of adequate quality for welfare patients, asked Hart, why should they not be equally acceptable for the general public, and if they are not of adequate quality for the general public, why should they be prescribed for welfare patients?

✧   ✧   ✧   ✧   ✧

Throughout our hearings the Food and Drug Administration was the subject of severe criticisms for its failure to require adequate clinical testing of new drugs prior to clearance for marketing; for its failure to act when new evidence revealed significant undesirable side effects of drugs previously cleared; for inadequate policing of promotional material of drug companies which fell within the agency's power over "labeling"; and for its approval of certain drug combinations which are worthless and in some cases dangerous to public health.

Recently the FDA has taken a number of positive steps to meet these criticisms. It has issued new regulations providing for full disclosure of all information—good and bad—in promotional material. It has inaugurated a plan of action with the American Hospital Association, and others to secure reports of adverse reactions to drugs. It has stiffened its requirements for adequate data in toxicity studies. It has taken a number of drugs with dangerous toxic effects off the market. And on others, such as chloromycetin, it has strengthened the warning language required to appear on labels and in advertisements.

Still another type of indirect result of the Subcommittee's work has been the filing of anti-trust cases. On the basis of material unearthed by the Subcommittee, new actions have been filed in the automobile, bread, and drug industries. But it is in electric machinery that this form of "fallout effect" has been of greatest importance. In September, 1959, the Subcommittee held hearings on identical bids on purchases of electrical equipment by the Tennessee Valley Authority and five municipal distributors of electrical power. Subsequent to the announcement of those hearings the Department of Justice gave notice that it was beginning a grand jury investigation in Philadelphia of identical bidding in the electrical equipment industry. Daily transcripts of the Subcommittee's hearings which showed a consistent pattern of identical bidding on electrical equipment, were made available to the Department of Justice in its investigation. These hearings resulted in a printed record of more than 1,200 pages.

The Justice Department proceedings resulted in the filing of some twenty criminal cases in which twenty-nine corporations and forty-four individuals were charged with conspiracy to fix prices on electrical equipment through identical bids to governmental agencies. Rotation bidding, known as "phases of the moon" in one of the more colorful Department of Justice proceedings, is clearly shown in the documentation of the Subcommittee's hearings.

The results consisted not only of jail sentences and fines for leading company officials but of important savings to buyers as well. In just two categories of products involved in the cases, transformers and switch-gear, manufacturers' shipments in 1958 were valued at $1.6 billion. Press accounts of the cases report that prices for many of the items involved in the conspiracy have been decreased by twenty to thirty per cent since the indictments were returned. If these reductions were to apply to only half the volume of sales in these two industrial groups, the annual savings to industry, public utilities, and governmental agencies would amount to some $200 million. The bid on a single TVA generator was reported by the Knoxville *News Sentinel* in late 1960 to have been reduced by more than five million below a 1959 bid. Recovery by private and governmental purchasers for past overcharges could run well in excess of a year's savings, since the conspiracy ran from 1951 to 1960.

Important as these indirect effects may be, the hard fact remains that the question of what to do about the problem of administered prices remains very much with us. That it is a problem is recognized by members of both parties. Earlier I referred to the inevitable time lag between the instigation of a reform and its final adoption. But recognition of this social phenomenon should not be interpreted as justifying a passive acceptance of things as they are.

LETTER FROM BIRMINGHAM JAIL

Martin Luther King, Jr.

The power necessary to maintain the social control function of government often encourages those in control to perpetuate special privileges to serve their own ends. In these circumstances the disadvantaged may resort to revolution or civil disobedience to overcome the inequities. Through passive resistance, Mahatma Gandhi led a weaponless mass of South Asians in their struggle to end British rule. The contemporary nonviolent action led by Nobel Peace Prize winner Martin Luther King follows the same tradition. In this selection King states his case for nonviolence, the "powerful and just weapon" which he called the Sword That Heals.

April 16, 1963

MY DEAR FELLOW CLERGYMEN:

While confined here in the Birmingham city jail, I came across your recent statement calling my present activities "unwise and untimely." Seldom do I pause to answer criticism of my work and ideas. If I sought to answer all the criticisms that cross my desk, my secretaries would have little time for anything other than such correspondence in the course of the day, and I would have no time for constructive work. But since I feel that you are men of genuine good will and that your criticisms are sincerely set forth, I want to try to answer your statement in what I hope will be patient and reasonable terms.

I think I should indicate why I am here in Birmingham, since you have been influenced by the view which argues against "outsiders coming in." I have the honor of serving as president of the Southern Christian Leadership Conference, an organization operating in every southern state,

SOURCE: "Letter from Birmingham Jail" (April 16, 1963) in *Why We Can't Wait* by Martin Luther King, Jr. Copyright © 1963 by Martin Luther King, Jr. Reprinted by permission of Harper & Row, Publishers. ✧ Martin Luther King is a clergyman and author. He is the president of the Southern Christian Leadership Conference and vice-president of the National Sunday School and Baptist Training Union, Congress of National Baptist Convention. He was awarded the Nobel Peace Prize in 1964 and is the author of *Stride Toward Freedom*. ✧ AUTHOR'S NOTE: This response to a published statement by eight fellow clergymen from Alabama . . . was composed under somewhat constricting circumstances. Begun on the margins of the newspaper in which the statement appeared while I was in jail, the letter was continued on scraps of writing paper supplied by a friendly Negro trusty, and concluded on a pad my attorneys were eventually permitted to leave me. Although the text remains in substance unaltered, I have indulged in the author's prerogative of polishing it for publication.

with headquarters in Atlanta, Georgia. We have some eighty-five affiliated organizations across the South, and one of them is the Alabama Christian Movement for Human Rights. Frequently we share staff, educational and financial resources with our affiliates. Several months ago the affiliate here in Birmingham asked us to be on call to engage in a nonviolent direct-action program if such were deemed necessary. We readily consented, and when the hour came we lived up to our promise. So I, along with several members of my staff, am here because I was invited here. I am here because I have organizational ties here.

But more basically, I am in Birmingham because injustice is here. . . . Moreover, I am cognizant of the interrelatedness of all communities and states. I cannot sit idly by in Atlanta and not be concerned about what happens in Birmingham. Injustice anywhere is a threat to justice every-where. We are caught in an inescapable network of mutuality, tied in a single garment of destiny. Whatever affects one directly, affects all in-directly. Never again can we afford to live with the narrow, provincial "outside agitator" idea. Anyone who lives inside the United States can never be considered an outsider anywhere within its bounds.

You deplore the demonstrations taking place in Birmingham. But your statement, I am sorry to say, fails to express a similar concern for the conditions that brought about the demonstrations. I am sure that none of you would want to rest content with the superficial kind of social analysis that deals merely with effects and does not grapple with underlying causes. It is unfortunate that demonstrations are taking place in Birmingham, but it is even more unfortunate that the city's white power structure left the Negro community with no alternative.

In any nonviolent campaign there are four basic steps: collection of the facts to determine whether injustices exist; negotiation; self-purification; and direct action. We have gone through all these steps in Birmingham. There can be no gainsaying the fact that racial injustice engulfs this com-munity. Birmingham is probably the most thoroughly segregated city in the United States. Its ugly record of brutality is widely known. Negroes have experienced grossly unjust treatment in the courts. There have been more unsolved bombings of Negro homes and churches in Birmingham than in any other city in the nation. These are the hard, brutal facts of the case. On the basis of these conditions, Negro leaders sought to nego-tiate with the city fathers. But the latter consistently refused to engage in good-faith negotiation.

Then, last September, came the opportunity to talk with leaders of Birmingham's economic community. In the course of the negotiations, certain promises were made by the merchants—for example, to remove the stores' humiliating racial signs. On the basis of these promises, the Rev-erend Fred Shuttlesworth and the leaders of the Alabama Christian Move-ment for Human Rights agreed to a moratorium on all demonstrations. As the weeks and months went by, we realized that we were the victims of a broken promise. A few signs, briefly removed, returned; the others remained.

As in so many past experiences, our hopes had been blasted, and the shadow of deep disappointment settled upon us. We had no alternative except to prepare for direct action, whereby we would present our very bodies as a means of laying our case before the conscience of the local and the national community. Mindful of the difficulties involved, we decided to undertake a process of self-purification. We began a series of workshops on nonviolence, and we repeatedly asked ourselves: "Are you able to accept blows without retaliating?" "Are you able to endure the ordeal of jail?" We decided to schedule our direct-action program for the Easter season, realizing that except for Christmas, this is the main shopping period of the year. Knowing that a strong economic-withdrawal program would be the by-product of direct action, we felt that this would be the best time to bring pressure to bear on the merchants for the needed change.

Then it occurred to us that Birmingham's mayoral election was coming up in March, and we speedily decided to postpone action until after election day. When we discovered that the Commissioner of Public Safety, Eugene "Bull" Connor, had piled up enough votes to be in the run-off, we decided again to postpone action until the day after the run-off so that the demonstrations could not be used to cloud the issues. Like many others, we waited to see Mr. Connor defeated, and to this end we endured postponement after postponement. Having aided in this community need, we felt that our direct-action program could be delayed no longer.

You may well ask: "Why direct action? Why sit-ins, marches and so forth? Isn't negotiation a better path?" You are quite right in calling for negotiation. Indeed, this is the very purpose of direct action. Nonviolent direct action seeks to create such a crisis and foster such a tension that a community which has constantly refused to negotiate is forced to confront the issue. It seeks so to dramatize the issue that it can no longer be ignored. My citing the creation of tension as part of the work of the nonviolent-resister may sound rather shocking. But I must confess that I am not afraid of the word "tension." I have earnestly opposed violent tension, but there is a type of constructive, nonviolent tension which is necessary for growth. Just as Socrates felt that it was necessary to create a tension in the mind so that individuals could rise from the bondage of myths and half-truths to the unfettered realm of creative analysis and objective appraisal, so must we see the need for nonviolent gadflies to create the kind of tension in society that will help men rise from the dark depths of prejudice and racism to the majestic heights of understanding and brotherhood.

The purpose of our direct-action program is to create a situation so crisis-packed that it will eventually open the door to negotiation. I therefore concur with you in your call for negotiation. Too long has our beloved Southland been bogged down in a tragic effort to live in monologue rather than dialogue.

One of the basic points in your statement is that the action that I and my associates have taken in Birmingham is untimely. Some have asked: "Why didn't you give the new city administration time to act?" The only answer that I can give to this query is that the new Birmingham administration must be prodded about as much as the outgoing one, before it will act.

. . . My friends, I must say to you that we have not made a single gain in civil rights without determined legal and nonviolent pressure. Lamentably, it is an historical fact that privileged groups seldom give up their privileges voluntarily. Individuals may see the moral light and voluntarily give up their unjust posture; but, as Reinhold Niebuhr has reminded us, groups tend to be more immoral than individuals.

We know through painful experience that freedom is never voluntarily given by the oppressor; it must be demanded by the oppressed. Frankly, I have yet to engage in a direct-action campaign that was "well timed" in the view of those who have not suffered unduly from the disease of segregation. For years now I have heard the word "Wait!" It rings in the ear of every Negro with piercing familiarity. This "Wait" has almost always meant "Never." We must come to see, with one of our distinguished jurists, that "justice too long delayed is justice denied."

We have waited for more than 340 years for our constitutional and God-given rights. The nations of Asia and Africa are moving with jetlike speed toward gaining political independence, but we still creep at horse-and-buggy pace toward gaining a cup of coffee at a lunch counter. Perhaps it is easy for those who have never felt the stinging darts of segregation to say, "Wait." But when you have seen vicious mobs lynch your mothers and fathers at will and drown your sisters and brothers at whim; when you have seen hate-filled policemen curse, kick and even kill your black brothers and sisters; when you see the vast majority of your twenty million Negro brothers smothering in an airtight cage of poverty in the midst of an affluent society; when you suddenly find your tongue twisted and your speech stammering as you seek to explain to your six-year-old daughter why she can't go to the public amusement park that has just been advertised on television, and see tears welling up in her eyes when she is told that Funtown is closed to colored children, and see ominous clouds of inferiority beginning to form in her little mental sky, and see her beginning to distort her personality by developing an unconscious bitterness toward white people; when you have to concoct an answer for a five-year-old son who is asking: "Daddy, why do white people treat colored people so mean?"; when you take a cross-country drive and find it necessary to sleep night after night in the uncomfortable corners of your automobile because no motel will accept you; when you are humiliated day in and day out by nagging signs reading "white" and "colored"; when your first name becomes "nigger," your middle name becomes "boy" (however old you are) and your last name becomes "John," and your wife and mother are never given the respected title "Mrs."; when you are harried by day and haunted by night by the fact that you are a Negro, living constantly at tiptoe stance, never quite knowing what to expect next, and are plagued with inner fears and outer resentments; when you are forever fighting a degenerating sense of "nobodiness"—then you will understand why we find it difficult to wait. There comes a time when the cup of endurance runs over, and men are no longer willing to be plunged into the abyss of despair. I hope, sirs, you can understand our legitimate and unavoidable impatience.

You express a great deal of anxiety over our willingness to break laws. This is certainly a legitimate concern. Since we so diligently urge people to obey the Supreme Court's decision of 1954 outlawing segregation in the public schools, at first glance it may seem rather paradoxical for us consciously to break laws. One may well ask: "How can you advocate breaking some laws and obeying others?" The answer lies in the fact that there are two types of laws: just and unjust. I would be the first to advocate obeying just laws. One has not only a legal but a moral responsibility to obey just laws. Conversely, one has a moral responsibility to disobey unjust laws. I would agree with St. Augustine that "an unjust law is no law at all."

Now, what is the difference between the two? . . . Any law that uplifts human personality is just. Any law that degrades human personality is unjust. All segregation statutes are unjust because segregation distorts the soul and damages the personality. It gives the segregator a false sense of superiority and the segregated a false sense of inferiority. Segregation, to use the terminology of the Jewish philosopher Martin Buber, substitutes an "I–it" relationship for an "I–thou" relationship and ends up relegating persons to the status of things. Hence segregation is not only politically, economically and sociologically unsound, it is morally wrong and sinful. Paul Tillich has said that sin is separation. Is not segregation an existential expression of man's tragic separation, his awful estrangement, his terrible sinfulness? Thus it is that I can urge men to obey the 1954 decision of the Supreme Court, for it is morally right; and I can urge them to disobey segregation ordinances, for they are morally wrong.

Let us consider a more concrete example of just and unjust laws. An unjust law is a code that a numerical or power majority group compels a minority group to obey but does not make binding on itself. This is *difference* made legal. By the same token, a just law is a code that a majority compels a minority to follow and that it is willing to follow itself. This is *sameness* made legal.

Let me give another explanation. A law is unjust if it is inflicted on a minority that, as a result of being denied the right to vote, had no part in enacting or devising the law. Who can say that the legislature of Alabama which set up that state's segregation laws was democratically elected? Throughout Alabama all sorts of devious methods are used to prevent Negroes from becoming registered voters, and there are some counties in which, even though Negroes constitute a majority of the population, not a single Negro is registered. Can any law enacted under such circumstances be considered democratically structured?

Sometimes a law is just on its face and unjust in its application. For instance, I have been arrested on a charge of parading without a permit. Now, there is nothing wrong in having an ordinance which requires a permit for a parade. But such an ordinance becomes unjust when it is used to maintain segregation and to deny citizens the First-Amendment privilege of peaceful assembly and protest.

I hope you are able to see the distinction I am trying to point out. In no sense do I advocate evading or defying the law, as would the rabid segregationist. That would lead to anarchy. One who breaks an unjust law must do so openly, lovingly, and with a willingness to accept the penalty. I submit that an individual who breaks a law that conscience tells him is unjust, and who willingly accepts the penalty of imprisonment in order to arouse the conscience of the community over its injustice, is in reality expressing the highest respect for law.

Of course, there is nothing new about this kind of civil disobedience. It was evidenced sublimely in the refusal of Shadrach, Meshach and Abednego to obey the laws of Nebuchadnezzar, on the ground that a higher moral law was at stake. It was practiced superbly by the early Christians, who were willing to face hungry lions and the excruciating pain of chopping blocks rather than submit to certain unjust laws of the Roman Empire. To a degree, academic freedom is a reality today because Socrates practiced evil disobedience. In our own nation, the Boston Tea Party represented a massive act of civil disobedience.

We should never forget that everything Adolf Hitler did in Germany was "legal" and everything the Hungarian freedom fighters did in Hungary was "illegal." It was "illegal" to aid and comfort a Jew in Hitler's Germany. Even so, I am sure that, had I lived in Germany at the time, I would have aided and comforted my Jewish brothers. If today I lived in a Communist country where certain principles dear to the Christian faith are suppressed, I would openly advocate disobeying that country's antireligious laws.

I must make two honest confessions to you, my Christian and Jewish brothers. First, I must confess that over the past few years I have been gravely disappointed with the white moderate. I have almost reached the regrettable conclusion that the Negro's great stumbling block in his stride toward freedom is not the White Citizen's Counciler or the Ku Klux Klanner, but the white moderate, who is more devoted to "order" than to justice; who prefers a negative peace which is the absence of tension to a positive peace which is the presence of justice; who constantly says: "I agree with you in the goal you seek, but I cannot agree with your methods of direct action"; who paternalistically believes he can set the timetable for another man's freedom; who lives by a mythical concept of time and who constantly advises the Negro to wait for a "more convenient season." Shallow understanding from people of good will is more frustrating than absolute misunderstanding from people of ill will. Lukewarm acceptance is much more bewildering than outright rejection.

I had hoped that the white moderate would understand that law and order exist for the purpose of establishing justice and that when they fail in this purpose they become the dangerously structured dams that block the flow of social progress. I had hoped that the white moderate would understand that the present tension in the South is a necessary phase of the transition from an obnoxious negative peace, in which the Negro passively accepted his unjust plight, to a substantive and positive peace, in which all men will respect the dignity and worth of human personality. Actually, we who engage in nonviolent direct action are not the creators of tension. We merely bring to the surface the hidden tension that is already alive. We bring it out in the open, where it can be seen and dealt with. Like a boil that can never be cured so long as it is covered up but must be opened with all its ugliness to the natural medicines of air and light, injustice must be exposed, with all the tension its exposure creates, to the light of human conscience and the air of national opinion before it can be cured.

In your statement you assert that our actions, even though peaceful, must be condemned because they precipitate violence. But is this a logical assertion? Isn't this like condemning a robbed man because his possession of money precipitated the evil act of robbery? Isn't this like condemning Socrates because his unswerving commitment to truth and his philosophical inquiries precipitated the act by the misguided populace in which they made him drink hemlock? Isn't this like condemning Jesus because his unique God-consciousness and never-ceasing devotion to God's will precipitated the evil act of crucifixion? We must come to see that, as the federal courts have consistently affirmed, it is wrong to urge an individual to cease his efforts to gain his basic constitutional rights because the quest may precipitate violence. Society must protect the robbed and punish the robber.

I had also hoped that the white moderate would reject the myth concerning time in relation to the struggle for freedom. I have just received a letter from a white brother in Texas. He writes: "All Christians know that the colored people will receive equal rights eventually, but it is possible that you are in too great a religious hurry. It has taken Christianity almost two thousand years to accomplish what it has. The teachings of Christ take time to come to earth." Such an attitude stems from a tragic misconception of time, from the strangely irrational notion that there is something in the very flow of time that will inevitably cure all ills. Actually, time itself is neutral; it can be used either destructively or constructively. More and more I feel that the people of ill will have used time much more effectively than have the people of good will. We will have to repent in this generation not merely for the hateful words and actions of the bad people but for the appalling silence of the good people. Human progress never rolls in on wheels of inevitability; it comes through the tireless efforts of men willing to be co-workers with God, and without this hard work, time itself becomes an ally of the forces of social stagnation. We must use time creatively, in the knowledge that the time is always ripe to do right. Now is the time to make real the promise of democracy and transform our pending national elegy into a creative psalm of brotherhood. Now is the time to lift our national policy from the quicksand of racial injustice to the solid rock of human dignity.

You speak of our activity in Birmingham as extreme. At first I was rather disappointed that fellow clergymen would see my nonviolent efforts as those of an extremist. I began thinking about the fact that I stand in the middle of two opposing forces in the Negro community. One is a force of complacency, made up in part of Negroes who, as a result of long years of oppression, are so drained of self-respect and a sense of "somebodiness" that they have adjusted to segregation; and in part of a few middle-class Negroes who, because of a degree of academic and economic security and because in some ways they profit by segregation, have become insensitive to the problems of the masses. The other force is one of bitterness and hatred, and it comes perilously close to advocating violence. It is expressed in the various black nationalist groups that are springing up across the nation, the largest and best-known being Elijah Muhammad's Muslim movement. Nourished by the Negro's frustration over the continued existence of racial discrimination, this movement is made up of people who have lost faith in America, who have absolutely repudiated Christianity, and who have concluded that the white man is an incorrigible "devil."

I have tried to stand between these two forces, saying that we need emulate neither the "do-nothingism" of the complacent nor the hatred and despair of the black nationalist. For there is the more excellent way of love and nonviolent protest. I am grateful to God that, through the influence of the Negro church, the way of nonviolence became an integral part of our struggle.

If this philosophy had not emerged, by now many streets of the South would, I am convinced, be flowing with blood. And I am further convinced that if our white brothers dismiss as "rabble-rousers" and "outside agitators" those of us who employ nonviolent direct action, and if they refuse to support our nonviolent efforts, millions of Negroes will, out of frustration and despair, seek solace and security in black-nationalist ideologies—a development that would inevitably lead to a frightening racial nightmare.

Oppressed people cannot remain oppressed forever. The yearning for freedom eventually manifests itself, and that is what has happened to the American Negro. Something within has reminded him of his birthright of freedom, and something without has reminded him that it can be gained. Consciously or unconsciously, he has been caught up by the *Zeitgeist*, and with his black brothers of Africa and his brown and yellow brothers of

Asia, South America and the Caribbean, the United States Negro is moving with a sense of great urgency toward the promised land of racial justice. If one recognizes this vital urge that has engulfed the Negro community, one should readily understand why public demonstrations are taking place. The Negro has many pent-up resentments and latent frustrations, and he must release them. So let him march; let him make prayer pilgrimages to the city hall; let him go on freedom rides—and try to understand why he must do so. If his repressed emotions are not released in nonviolent ways, they will seek expression through violence; this is not a threat but a fact of history. So I have not said to my people: "Get rid of your discontent." Rather, I have tried to say that this normal and healthy discontent can be channeled into the creative outlet of nonviolent direct action. And now this approach is being termed extremist.

❖   ❖   ❖   ❖   ❖

. . . The question is not whether we will be extremists, but what kind of extremists we will be. Will we be extremists for hate or for love? Will we be extremists for the preservation of injustice or for the extension of justice?

❖   ❖   ❖   ❖   ❖

. . . Perhaps the South, the nation and the world are in dire need of creative extremists.

❖   ❖   ❖   ❖   ❖

Yours for the cause of Peace and Brotherhood,
MARTIN LUTHER KING, JR.

❖ 57 ❖

ONE MAN, ONE VOTE—
YES OR NO?

Andrew Hacker

The shifting of American population from rural to metropolitan areas has affected many social institutions and other aspects of society. One of the most significant effects is the impact on our repre-

SOURCE: *The New York Times Magazine* (November 8, 1964), 30–31, 131–32. © 1964 by The New York Times Company. Reprinted by permission. ❖ The author is associate professor of government at Cornell University. His chief interests are American politics and political sociology. He has written *Politics and the Corporation*.

sentative government. *The legislators from rural areas have resisted reapportionment that would reflect the country-to-city population shift and thereby reduce the political power of their constituents. But the recent Supreme Court opinion holding nonequal representation unconstitutional has resulted and will result in major governmental changes. The arguments for and against the political equality principle on which the court decision was based are analyzed in the following article by Andrew Hacker.*

Since the earliest days of the Republic, the districts of most state legislatures have been so constructed as to give disproportionate representation to rural voters. While this practice was struck down by the Supreme Court in its 1962 Baker *v.* Carr decision, at that time the Justices gave no precise indication of the reform they would require.

Because Baker *v.* Carr was silent on the subject of second chambers, the hope was held out that the upper houses in each state might still be permitted to remain attuned to the interests of the countryside. Then came Reynolds *v.* Sims. In that case the Court held that both legislative chambers had to be based on population alone, that there could be no exceptions to the rule that all districts had to be substantially equal.

The argument for "one man, one vote" is simply an application of the principle of political equality. All votes should carry the same weight, it is said, because no justification can be found for singling out certain citizens for preferred treatment. If minorities are worried about the possibility of majority oppression, the remedy lies not in giving them added electoral weight but rather in settled constitutional procedures.

Moreover, the Fourteenth Amendment stricture that all citizens are entitled to "equal protection of the laws" would seem to require that everyone be permitted to participate in the process whereby those laws are made. Experience has shown that those who are excluded from the polls or who are underrepresented in legislative councils will find themselves having to obey laws that are highly discriminatory. Urban voters, to use the customary example, are taxed to support rural services while city problems are all but ignored. If the majority is not allowed to rule, then power reverts to some accidental or consciously designated minority.

"One man, one vote" may appear to be unexceptionable as a matter of logic. But logic alone is not the only guide in political life. When a national party and a national legislative chamber both propound the argument that some votes ought to be more equal than others, it is time to examine this position with consideration and care:

(1) What is good for the Congress in Washington, it has been suggested, ought also to apply at the state level. The Senate has given equal

representation to each state regardless of size, and by the same token one legislative chamber in each state should be allowed to represent established political units within its own boundaries. As a minimum, the state house might give each county at least a single representative, thus insuring that its interests will have a spokesman.

A Legislature must insure, by one means or another, that small units have an effective voice in its proceedings. This is especially necessary when metropolitan areas elect large blocs of legislators who might easily ignore or drown out rural opinion. The founders agreed that Delaware and Rhode Island should always be able to defend themselves in the Senate. Ought not similar guarantees be given to Schuyler County in New York (population: 15,044) and to Sierra County in California (2,247)?

(2) Rural areas, which benefit most from arrangements as they now stand, actually need additional representation for their well-being—if not their survival. Ours is an urban age, with wealth increasingly concentrated in the cities and surburbs. Small towns and agricultural areas are losing population, which is one reason why they are overrepresented, and industry is by no means reinvigorating rural America to the extent that is necessary. If the logic of equal votes is applied, then back-country legislative seats would in most cases be transferred to the growing suburbs. Yet this would take from the have-nots and give to those who are already doing quite well.

In Illinois, for example, the median family income in Gallatin County (population: 7,638) is $2,711 per year, whereas the Chicago suburbs of Du Page County, which have doubled in numbers in the last decade, have a median annual income of $8,570 per family. Gallatin may be overrepresented in Springfield but it is underequipped with schools, roads, hospitals and other amenities. Were the prosperous and populous to be given their arithmetical due, the odds are great that the flow of public funds to rural sections would come to a halt.

No one will deny that cities and suburbs have problems of their own; but metropolitan areas have the resources to help themselves if only they would set their minds to it. In contrast, the last remaining hope for the countryside lies in its political power at the state capitals.

(3) "Those who labor in the earth are the chosen people of God . . ." Thomas Jefferson once wrote, adding, "the mobs of great cities add just so much strength to the support of pure government as sores do to the strength of the human body." Under this theory—which still prevails in many sections of the country—the America of the provinces is composed of superior stock: independent, self-reliant, and embodying the values which impart integrity to society. The rural and small-town citizen is an individual, uncorrupted by the mass mentality of the city. While such a characterization can verge on caricature, it explains why we hear so much about "bloc voting" in the cities but not about such behavior out where the pavements end. At all events, if rural areas need added representation

because of their economic plight they also deserve such a magnified voice due to their enhanced moral character.

(4) There is no technical difficulty in dividing a state into a series of geometric quadrilaterals, each one having almost precisely the same population as its neighbor. Michigan, in reapportioning its Senate last year, created 38 districts no one of which had less than 205,000 people nor more than 207,000. But to do this is to break up the natural communities of interest and outlook within a state, imposing an artificial political mold on what are really areas having historic identities and social complexions of their own.

Thus, in the cause of arithmetical consistency, a dairying region may be forced into a shotgun marriage with an industrial suburb, resulting in a district that is difficult for one man to represent and lacking a personality of its own. By the same token there is much to be gained in psychic satisfactions, if nothing else, in having "Polish" and "Czech" and "Jewish" districts where voters can be represented by someone of their own ethnic background who understands their particular interests and needs.

(5) There are indications that the voters—and not simply rural voters—are content with arrangements as they now stand; that they see nothing particularly malapropos in malapportionment. In Colorado, for example, a statewide referendum rejected by a 2–1 vote a proposal calling for districting reforms in the direction of greater equality. Moreover, every county in the state, urban as well as rural, registered a majority for retaining the status quo. Thus it would appear, at least in the states that have had such referendums, that the majority is sensitive to minority needs and is willing to dilute its own votes so as to augment those of their fellow citizens who need them more.

Some of these arguments are clearly more persuasive than others. It is hard to prove that while 1,000 city dwellers automatically make up a "mob," 1,000 farmers are all independent yeomen. Even if the innate superiority of rural Americans were demonstrated, it would not necessarily follow that a weightier ballot should be given to those blessed with greater virtue. Among other difficulties there would be the problem of finding virtuous souls, admittedly few and far between, who happen to reside in the cities and suburbs, in order to give them additional votes at election time. For uprightness of character is a condition of spirit and not dependent on where one stakes one's tent.

More to the point is the fact that rural America is indeed poorer, that it needs political leverage more than its metropolitan cousin. The reply here, quite simply, is that if one disadvantaged minority is to have preferential treatment in the chambers where laws are made, then other such minorities should be given similar consideration. Surely Negroes, Mexican-Americans, the indigent aged, mothers supporting fatherless children, and the blind also stand in need of greater-than-average governmental help and protection. If a Downstate Illinois farmer with an annual income of $2,711 deserves to be heard so does a Negro laundress in Chicago who also ends the year with $2,711. The rural areas hardly have a monopoly on those suffering from majority indifference.

The creation of districts of equal population would undoubtedly destroy what are now homogeneous enclaves. Yet one of the troubles with state legislatures is that too many of their members do in fact represent special-interest constituencies, preoccupied with a particular crop or industry or natural resource. Experience has usually shown that the best lawmakers emerge from districts that are diverse in their social characteristics and competitive in their party politics. Such legislators must be able to talk the language of more than a single electoral group and have the skills to win an open fight against more-than-token opposition. Underpopulated districts, whether rural or urban, tend to be one-party domains, with the same seat going to an organization regular. Enlarging these fiefdoms would breathe some fresh air into more than a few musty political corners.

Should each state have a "miniature" Federal system, with one house based on population and the other on some other criterion? There may be good reason for arguing that a bicameral legislature serves some useful purpose (although unicameral Nebraska has not been notable for rushing through hasty or ill-advised statutes). However, the two chambers, as Chief Justice Warren pointed out last June, can both be population-based and still display quite different characteristics.

"One body could be composed of single-member districts while the other could have at least some multi-member districts," he wrote in *Reynolds v. Sims.* "The length of term of the legislators in the separate bodies could differ. The numerical size of the two bodies could be made to differ, even significantly, and the geographical size of districts from which legislators are elected could also be made to differ. And apportionment in one house could be arranged so as to balance off minor inequities in the representation of certain areas in the other House."

What does stand out is the fact that the role of counties, townships and other subdivisions within the states, simply is not constitutionally analogous to the status of the states themselves *vis-à-vis* the Union. Alaska and Utah are "sovereign" entities and hence entitled to as much representation in the Senate as are New York and California. Counties, far from being "sovereign," are convenient governmental agencies which can be created, consolidated, or abolished by the states. The states came together to create a more perfect union; that is why they have "sovereign" status and that is why the Senate exists. Counties and cities are creatures of the states; it is too late to endow them with an immortality they never had.

Most compelling, perhaps, is that the people of a state have on occasion agreed to permitting one of their legislative chambers to give an amplified voice to underpopulated areas. Here the Supreme Court has chosen to stand on slippery political ground, for it has had to justify a judicial veto of arrangements approved by popular referendum. Even if majorities in

Colorado and Michigan and California acted mistakenly, it may be argued that it is part of democracy that the people should be allowed to commit their own errors—and then learn by experience and mend their ways in their own time.

The Court's reply, or at least the reply of six of the nine Justices last June [1964], was that "an individual's constitutionally protected right to cast an equally weighted ballot cannot be denied even by a vote of a majority of a state's electorate."

The issue is the old one of majority rule versus individual rights, but with a new twist. The Court seems to be saying that even if a majority of the citizens are willing to dilute the value of their legislative vote they must be prevented from doing so. For citizens may not trade, barter, or give away their basic political freedoms. These rights are the end-products of an historical evolution, too often imperfectly understood by those who now possess them. And the continuance of democratic government itself requires that such rights be protected and guaranteed. Jean-Jacques Rousseau once said that there are times when citizens must be "forced to be free." Equal votes for equal citizens seems to be just that sort of occasion.

Logic, theory and history can be brought to bear in defense of "one man, one vote." Such a position, moreover, is difficult to compromise. For if a minority can rule in one House of a bicameral legislature, then it could veto the acts of its sister chamber and exact concessions on behalf of the special interests it represents.

The problem, not surprisingly, is one of political power. Those who feel that current arrangements safeguard their interests are understandably disinclined to see changes brought about. While the general public has not become involved in the reapportionment issue, it is plain that many elected officials are deeply concerned. There are more than 7,000 state legislators, more of whom have something to lose than to gain by redistricting, and these local politicians can expect to find fellow feeling among members of Congress and party leaders at all levels.

But it would be idle to mask the fact that state legislatures are not simply rural but conservative citadels. Those who are calling for reapportionment might well ask just how disinterested their own position is. If it were proposed that the U.S. Senate be abolished—after all, it is a far cry from "one man, one vote"—and that all national legislation be left to the House of Representatives the suspicion arises that such a move would arouse little enthusiasm in liberal circles. Much of the rhetoric on both sides tends simply to rationalize a struggle for that oldest of all political commodities: the power of some to make policy for all. . . . Leaders in both chambers have promised to introduce resolutions for amending the Constitution that would permit one House in each state to be based on non-population factors.

Whether such a resolution will be able to muster the required two-thirds vote, especially in the Senate, remains to be seen. Yet if this is accomplished and an amendment is sent to the states, for ratification in 1965, then there will be the curious spectacle of malapportioned state legislatures voting for their own continuation. In the words of Senator Abraham Ribicoff of Connecticut, this will allow "the rotten boroughs to decide whether they should continue to be rotten."

The goal of equal votes for equal citizens, far from being a radical departure in our political tradition, is consistent with this nation's efforts to extend a full franchise to all citizens. Reapportionment, insuring ballots of the same weight for all voters, is not only long overdue but will also lay the groundwork for an updating of our 50 state legislatures.

As matters now stand, those bodies have lost effective contact with all too many of the voters they supposedly represent, and they are unwilling or unable to deal with the most pressing problems within their jurisdictions. One consequence of malapportionment has been public cynicism about state government; the reverse side of the coin is mounting popular approval for the extension of Federal authority to provide services the states have neglected. Representative legislatures, representing people rather than cows or acres or trees, will actually serve to strengthen the states and give new life to the practice as well as the theory of federalism.

✲ 58 ✲

REFLECTIONS ON THE ABILITY
DIMENSION IN HUMAN SOCIETY

Robert E. L. Faris

The processes and organization of American formal educational institutions have generally been based on the assumption that human ability is limited and fixed by genetic forces. But in his 1961 presidential address before the American Sociological Association, Robert Faris challenges such assumptions and marshals evidence to support the contention that societies can and do produce the human abilities they need. His ideas are particularly significant at this time, because the ever-increasing demands for more highly skilled and better educated personnel have made the contemporary processes

SOURCE: *American Sociological Review*, Vol. 26 (December 1961), 835–843. Reprinted by permission of the author and The American Sociological Association. ✧ The author is professor of sociology at the University of Washington. He is a former president of the American Sociological Association. He has written *Social Disorganization* and *Social Psychology* and coauthored *Mental Disorders in Urban Areas*.

of selection and allocation of students to various types and levels of education dysfunctional in our society. The social scientist can play an essential role in designing the types of learning environments that will produce the high levels of educated personnel needed now and in the future.

The survival and welfare of every person on earth rests on organization. In simple organizations, as in prehistoric societies, only small populations can exist. Our immense contemporary civilization survives luxuriously only by virtue of a base of elaborate organization.

More extensive organizations can support more population at high standards of living. As Ogburn has shown, among modern nations differences in living standards are related not so much to inequality of resources as to differences in complexity of organization.

We cannot have intricate systems without a supply of high and conspicuous ability in the population. Scarcity of abilities is palpably a major and conspicuous obstacle to progress in some of the currently developing nations.

It also appears that, in our own economy, the supply of ability is a factor in its potential growth rate. The present concern about automation bears on the point. Assuming that we do not elect to arrest further automation, the solution to technological unemployment must lie in the stimulation of a marked increase in the growth rate of the Gross National Product, and this in turn obviously requires an augmented supply of the various kinds of ability involved in inventing and organizing. There will have to be new products if we are to employ the persons no longer needed on farms and unskilled laboring jobs. These new devices will have to be developed at a greater rate than the already high pace of invention.

The current tempo, which we must outrun, is illustrated by the observation that eighty per cent of the sales of the Radio Corporation of America are of products unknown a little over a decade ago, and by a recent forecast of the Du Pont Company that at least 60 per cent of its 1975 sales revenue will be from products now in their introductory stages or still to be invented. It has also been predicted that within the next three years, in the transportation industry, almost 30 per cent of its sales dollar will come from products either new or so changed as to be considered new. Chemical research, an immensely important component of all inventive activity, measured by published volume, has doubled from 1950 to 1960. While these selected examples may over-represent the present pace of technical innovation, they give a useful impression that the needed acceleration is from an already swift-moving rate of development.

Present population trends do not give a prospect of an early automatic increase in the proportion of productive persons, for the U.S. population is now bulging at the young and old ages. We will have 16 per cent more population in the United States by the end of the present decade, but only a three per cent increase in the most creative ages of 25–44. This fact clearly intensifies the urgency of artificial stimulation of capacities in the part of the population that must bear the mental burdens.

It does not suffice to have a limited stock of geniuses at the top of the productive organization. The need is equally great for a wide distribution, throughout the society, of personal characteristics favorable to the operation of elaborate technology and organization. While mankind has always correctly sought for able leaders, we have chronically over-emphasized the importance of a few great men in the growth of civilization, and have failed to appreciate the importance of distributed ability. Advanced achievements, we now realize, rest not only on the shoulders of generals, statesmen, and inventors, but importantly on the skills, muscles, and morale of the common soldier, the curiosity and optimism of minor technicians, and also the inconspicuous crescive processes of custom and law-building which underlie all governmental structure.

Elaborate technology is not alone capable of upholding a civilization. It fails without a wide distribution of machine skills. The ingenious products of the inventor's mind must be continually maintained, improved, repaired, and properly used. The pre-industrial peasant who has never known gasoline engines may acquire a tractor and learn to drive it, but unless he has also a supply of generalized comprehension of such matters as the effects of overheating, the necessity of lubrication, the function of spark plugs, he will not long till his fields by machinery.

Deficiency of technical ability contributes to the fact that in 1961 the unemployment rate is highest among the unskilled and uneducated workers. Many of these workers, at their present levels of ability, are not qualified for the new jobs created by technical advance. Simple retraining for more skilled tasks will not suffice, for recent studies have revealed a lack of general aptitude in the majority of those with long-term unemployment. Many are in fact on the edge of illiteracy, and their deficiencies are in important part matters of basic schooling.

Our hero-admiring habits have beguiled us into overlooking the significance of the thousands of contributors to the development of every complex machine in favor of the person who made the small step in the middle of the stage that marked the transition from a merely promising device to a functioning but unperfected machine. The jet monster we ride in today is a product of the combined thought of great numbers of uncelebrated innovators, many probably equal in mental capability to the Wright brothers. The point applies also to more commonplace products—a nylon garment, for example, is based on a long series of chemical discoveries, and on an unmeasured amount of anonymous ingenuity involved in the design of the machines that extrude filaments and stretch them into fibers, dye and spin the threads, and fabricate them into serviceable garments. The important brain power responsible for all this is not a possession of a few giants, but is a funded mental wealth which is a characteristic of any civilized population, but is lacking in varying degrees in less developed societies.

The above argument suggests a concept of *collective ability*, denoting the supply and organization within a society of all the relevant abilities which give the society its creativeness and power. This *collective ability* is not only a matter of technical knowledge, but also of general comprehension of social wisdom, as well as of popular aspiration toward excellence in a variety of fields of mental activity. A high level of collective ability produces not only science and machinery, but also efficient organizational behavior; this in turn allows effective complex governmental, economic, and social organization. Responsibility for research in this superorganic form of creative potential must of course be accepted by the science of sociology.

The relative security and power of advanced nations thus lie not in buried gold but mainly in the accumulated capital of collective ability. The statement also applies to the great world society, and to subdivisions within nations. Thus our best defense against discouragement in our flooding tide of troubles would be an acceleration in the development of our collective mental power. This, of course, does not automatically produce a stable Utopia; new problems will erupt forever. To handle them we will need ever further exponential growth of collective ability.

Not long ago the prospect of such a growth seemed hopeless, for ability was generally held to be fixed in biological inheritance, and improvable, if at all, only by a glacially slow and impractical eugenics program. The present argument, however, is that, in a literal sense, and to an important degree, a society generates its level of ability, and further, that the upper limit is unknown and distant, and best of all, that the processes of generation of ability are potentially subject to intentional control.

The foregoing statement is not a new thought. It was familiar to some prominent Nineteenth Century European scholars. But a half-century or so ago a miniature Dark Age descended over the field of human psychology and the doctrines of the mental testers convinced an impressed public with a secular variant of an infant damnation doctrine.

A single illustration is here offered to symbolize the whole movement. The able and distinguished psychologist, Carl E. Seashore, spent much of his research career investigating musical ability, which he analyzed into a few measured elements. Among the most basic of these, he believed, was the ability to discriminate accurately small differences in musical pitch. He held as follows:

[Pitch discrimination is] an immediate impression . . . dependent upon the presence or absence in various degrees of the sensitive mechanism in the inner ear. . . . A good test in the hands of an expert may properly establish the physiological limit of pitch discrimination. . . . The physiological limit for hearing pitch does not improve with training. . . . What a blessing to a girl of the age of eight if the music teacher would examine her, and, if necessary say, "much as I regret it, I must say that you would find music dull and diffi-cult, and I would advise you to take up some other art."

This is, of course, to say that either the ability was there or not, and if not, nothing could be done about it. This view was and still is widely held by educators and the public.

Seashore's conviction was strengthened by the fact that he had made unsuccessful efforts to train persons to improve pitch discrimination. The trouble turned out to be that he apparently did not know how to apply such training—possibly his heart was not in the task. Eventually, however, train-ing did succeed in reversing Seashore's results and the concept of that par-ticular type of fixed innate ability was flatly overthrown.

The same delayed revolution has been, and is now, going on in the field of abilities in general. We no longer heed the doctrinaire testers who pronounce specific individual limits for potentialities in mechanical ability, language ability, artistic ability, and mathematical ability. Their ceilings have all been discovered to be penetrable. Slow readers are being retrained. The linguistic near-imbecility of college students is treated by new teaching methods and motivational stimulation. Barriers in many fields of knowledge are falling before the new optimism, which holds that anybody can learn anything.

In sum, we have turned away from the concept of human ability as something fixed in the physiological structure, to that of a flexible and versatile mechanism subject to great improvement. Upper physiological limits of performance may eventually be shown to exist, but it seems certain that these are seldom if ever reached in any person, and in most of the population the levels of performance actually reached have virtually no relation to innate capacities.

Thus the amount of ability in each person is created in the course of experience, and the supply of ability in any society is at present a conse-quence mainly of impersonal social processes rather than of intentional control.

Any society tends automatically to reproduce its level of achieved ability among its members. The most obvious factor in this continuity is the rich-ness of the social heritage. As we learn in our first course in sociology, a preliterate society can have a culture only as complex as can be carried in the minds of the living generation. With the acquisition of writing this limit is removed, and civilization of unlimited complexity is made possible. The fund of knowledge stored in print and accessible to the population is a major component of the framework of collective ability.

Another variable of obvious importance is the breadth of distribution of advanced knowledge within a population. It makes a difference whether the advanced knowledge is possessed only by a small minority or distributed widely in a population by formal education. Institutionalized schooling, viewed variously as having the purposes of child-tending, job-qualifying, and mate-finding, is above all a potent instrument for raising the ability level of the population. This is done at the lower grades by transmitting important basic aspects of the general heritage, and in the higher levels by developing versatile capacity to face novel problems. Graduate schools in the various fields of science concentrate on this latter capacity by training students for independent and original research, and, to the extent that they succeed in their principal function, constantly and exponentially add to the supply of the most generative type of human ability in the population.

Aware as we all are of the educational boom in the United States, we may still overlook its spectacular implications for the future. What is happening at the present time is that the nation is quietly lifting itself by its bootstraps to an importantly higher level of general ability—an achievement which, though less dramatic than a space voyage to the moon and less measurable than the Gross National Product, may mean more to the national future than either.

A few statistical items may help us to assess the extent and possible consequences of the contemporary educational surge. It was only forty years ago, according to the U.S. Census, that less than 27 per cent of the age group 25–35 completed a high school education or more. The percentage reached 58 in 1950, over 70 in 1960, and is expected to exceed 78 by 1970. College enrollment is of course rising to a similar flood level. A little over 30 years ago the undergraduate enrollment of the United States population ages 18 to 21 was 21 per cent. In 1961, it is over 30 per cent. If intentions could be accepted as reliable for forecasting they would indicate a 1970 percentage at least twice as large.

Graduate school enrollments in the same period have increased from about 200,000 to 330,000, and the prediction for 1970 is 560,000—thus approaching the tripling of the most important source of advanced research ability in only twenty years. Most of this is a net gain in educational achievement, for the majority of the fathers of contemporary graduate students, 62 per cent, never even attended college, and only 13 per cent of the fathers ever had any graduate study. No comparable quantitative expansion in formal education has occurred in all history. Any qualitative improvements, of course, add further to the effects of these trends.

The consequences of such an educational prosperity to the pace of basic research and, therefore, our ability to meet new perils are incalculably great. Our present accomplishments in science arise from the activities of a relatively limited number of trained persons. An estimate by the National Science Foundation indicates that academic research manpower today is not large for a nation of 180 million. In 1953 the full-time equivalent number of faculty members engaged in research was only 16,500. Incidentally, of these only 1,700 were in psychology and the social sciences, which may help to explain why our nation has more success in handling technical problems than human affairs.

It has been estimated that the United States Ph.D. output in all fields of knowledge will nearly double in the decade 1960–70. Any such increase, if maintained, will automatically continue to add to the ability level of the population as the highly trained generation advances through the age levels and replaces the older and less-educated people—thus the force of the present increase alone may not be fully experienced until forty years have passed. Allowing for various uncertainties in all the above statistics, all signs point to a half century of immensely fruitful development in the national supply of formally educated people.

Formal education, for all its importance, is not the only producer of talent in the population. We have abundant reason to recognize the importance of other contributing influences which are less conspicuous and controlled.

Among the most effective of these is the informal influence of the family on the intelligence of children. We have long recognized a relation between abilities of father and son, but here again too much credit has traditionally been given to heredity. Sociologists have had reason to become aware of the fact that mind itself arises in a social process, and this knowledge should suggest a search for intellectual differences resulting from varying qualities of influence from parent to child.

There is now a large and growing body of convincing research which indicates that a factor of central importance in this family transmission of ability is size of vocabulary. Children normally acquire their speech initially within the family, and in harmonious families the degree of richness in parental language becomes a major determiner of the quality and quantity of the child's vocabulary during his growing years. We know that intelligence tests and school success are heavily influenced by verbal facility, and it must follow that the size and precision of the vocabulary used by parents before their children would be a major factor in achieved and measured intelligence.

Size of parental vocabulary is not the whole story, however, and we may be sure that research directed toward subtle influences within the family will yield applicable knowledge. Among the promising objects of such study we may list: the degree of richness and warmth of relation between parents and children, variations in clarity and orderliness of communication, amount of encouragement of the child to take initiative in talking and relating experience, the development of early familiarity and ease with handling quantities and measurements, acquisition of advanced motivation for reading and school learning, the creation of a broad appetite for orientation to the world and a hunger for knowledge of all kinds, a delight in novel thoughts, and the development of a sense of confidence that answers to questions are not hard to find. We may also look within family processes to find how it comes about that some children gain a self concept of a person who expects to be able to do whatever he decides to undertake.

Another research lead of promise is in the field of sources and effects of aspiration. We have much reason to believe that aspiration is a controlling variable of importance within family, peer groups, communities, and other social groupings, and that these groups may affect intelligence upward or downward through supplying or limiting aspiration among its members.

Among the well-known institutionalized obstructions to learning is the informal complex of attitudes long embedded in the special culture of school children. This attitude complex may be the major explanation of the notorious inefficiency of the instructional process in the schools. Experiments of many kinds have abundantly shown that children can learn far more efficiently, and can handle much more complex materials, than they actually do in the schools. There is a minor scandal and mystery in the fact that a child can spend three years in school study of a foreign language and know little of it, while the same child placed in a school abroad may acquire speaking ability within a few months.

A part of the explanation of the disappointing product of the schools thus must lie in the existence among school children of an informal culture that constitutes a destructive influence on aspiration for learning. In general, our schools are burdened by an ancient pupil tradition which defines lessons and study as unpleasant and also as unimportant to the life the children see about them. Probably most children acquire this concept in the first or second grade and never lose it completely even through the college years.

In general, the assurances of teachers that mathematics, languages, history, and science will be of interest and importance in the student's future life is successfully opposed by the child's experience in athletics, activities, and social intercourse. Coleman has recently described the operation of informal prestige systems in a group of public high schools, and has shown how these systems direct energy and aspiration away from scholarship. In each of the schools studied the students who were accepted as members of the "leading crowd" held attitudes involving less emphasis on scholarship than those held by the consensus of all students, and in most schools the leaders differed from the other students in the direction of even greater emphasis on athletics. In each school, athletics appeared to be more influential than scholarship—that is, most students stated that they would generally prefer to be remembered as athletic stars than as brilliant scholars. Of course all this has long been known, and since the days of Woodrow Wilson at Princeton has been a matter of much concern to educators. Our formal educational system, powerful as it is, operates against a heavy braking effect from an informally organized aspect of juvenile society.

The above is only one among various ways in which our society and culture inhibit abilities. Research has shown that one of the most direct of these influences operates through the control of aspiration by the primary groups of school-age children and youth. Abundant evidence supports the principle that primary groups tend to form on the basis of homogeneity in almost every respect observed—age, sex, socio-economic status, activity interests, and intellectual qualities. Furthermore, once established, these primary groups exert pressure on their members to maintain their similarities. This force operates to hold the achievement and aspiration level toward the approved mode for the group.

Such a pull toward mediocrity is of course not limited to school children—it occurs at all ages at which primary groups are spontaneously formed. A potentially superior member comes to realize that he faces the choice between concealing his intellectual interests or finding himself losing his position in the group.

Social life opposes superiority in still another way, through a constant social pressure to communicate intelligibly. Original individual thought develops most readily in privacy, and can be inhibited by a felt need to make sense to others at all times. A rich social life in primary groups allows little opportunity for such mental privacy, and includes an atmosphere of disapproval of the person who at any time expresses a thought difficult for his friends to grasp. This atmosphere may involve implications of conceit and even a touch of mental abnormality.

There is a parallel, though not identical, process which allows for social influences in broader categories of society to limit aspirations. The large family and neighborhood community has been shown to influence attitudes and expectations toward education and mental development. Occupational status of fathers is statistically related to vocational ambitions of sons. Even sons who aspire to a level above that of their fathers usually tend to limit their goals to a moderate ascent above the achievements of their fathers.

At the top limit of performance for some persons there seems to be an additional aspiration barrier, as if a demon were establishing a line beyond which performance could not possibly go. Few persons can summon their maximum effort against what they conceive to be an absolute impossibility, but their powers may be released if they are shown, by the example of achievement by a person they view to be comparable, that the thing can be done. Such an *aspiration boundary* probably accounts for the long delay of track athletes in performing a four-minute mile run. For years great runners had come close but failed to beat the clock across the magic line. Extrapolations from world records over shorter and longer distances indicated that comparable running ability should make the feat possible, but there were athletes and sports experts who questioned that it would ever be done. In 1954, however, Roger Bannister achieved it, breaking not only the record but also the aspiration boundary for many talented athletes. By the end of 1960 the four-minute mile had been performed 66 times.

It appears probable that a similar aspiration boundary effect operates with reference to mental achievements, and that many persons of high ability have to wait for Newtons and Einsteins to show that the looming redoubts are not invulnerable. Persons of lower ability, of course, cannot so readily be inspired by the genius at the top, but the same effect may occur at their level. In the days when all great American writers appeared to be in New England, General Lew Wallace inspired a sequence of worthy Indiana writers by his production of *Ben Hur*. It would seem that we sociologists can learn much, and profitably apply the knowledge, from the study of the effect of successful achievements on lifting the aspiration boundaries of the colleagues of the achiever.

The foregoing discussion is meant only as a sample of some of the ways in which the society, and its subgroups, may regulate in a variety of inconspicuous ways the general level of aspiration and performance among its members. It appears that immense potentialities of human abilities are being smothered by systematic social influences which tend to hold achievement toward the medial level of a group or a community. Only a few escape from such influence—the rest aim and achieve at a level near that of their closest social groups.

The central implication of the present argument is that attractive potentialities of increase in collective ability are possible if we advance our knowledge of the sociological influences that stimulate and limit aspiration and achievement, and find strategic points at which we may establish some control over them. No great difficulties appear to stand in the way. It appears that we only need to apply a massive research effort in the field of the relation of social factors to abilities. Fortunately there exists today a nation-wide enthusiasm for the development of talent resources; a milling crowd is stirring into action even in advance of academic sociological leadership.

All of this school effort is to the good, and vigorous support of it will surely produce rewards. Even greater benefit, however, may in time result from the discovery and application of knowledge in the influence of other aspects of social life on ability. The schools, however improved, will not perform the tasks which belong to the family and the community. It is not enough to know how to offer a subject, say a foreign language, by the most advanced instructional methods if the subject is meaningless to the student. We have not yet faced the question of what the significance of academic study of the Spanish language is to the daughter of a Minneapolis dentist who plans to marry a farm-implement salesman of Norwegian descent. Nor have we learned to bring students to college with an effective appetite for the types of knowledge most useful to themselves and the nation. At present business training, home economics, and physical education outnumber mathematics, physics, sociology, and philosophy in the expressed academic intentions of high school students.

In the present opera on the nature and destiny of man's genius, we have heard only the opening bars of the overture, but the music suggests that the production will some day be a success, and that the amount of effort we put into it will make a difference in the time required. Biology and genetics, while not entirely irrelevant to the cause, promised more than they could deliver in the early years of the century. Individual psychology has taught much, but now we perceive evidence that an important part of the relevant causation of abilities is essentially sociological in nature, and that control is most likely to come through penetration of this aspect of the subject. Research in the sociology of collective ability thus promises to give us an unmatched opportunity to apply advanced techniques of discovery to a matter of critical human importance.

Men of wealth, position, and responsibility wishing to provide security for their children, find that there is actually no way of having absolute assurance that a fortune can survive. Currency can fluctuate in value and deteriorate through war and inflation. Gold and diamonds have arbitrary worth which can vanish with economic disorganization. Land can be taxed away or confiscated by agrarian reformers. No kind of material wealth is more secure than the social organization which stands back of it. The most favorable chance of survival, therefore, eventually goes to persons of highest general ability and wisdom who can deal with problems of complexity in a time of change. Effective intelligence, then, is a richer legacy than acres of diamonds, not only to the heirs of a tycoon, but also to the posterity of a nation. To learn how to expand the heritage of collective intelligence would create the best legacy we could leave to the children of our children.

✦ 59 ✦

REPORT FROM A
SPANISH HARLEM "FORTRESS"

Richard Hammer

In the previous selection and in the one that follows, formally organized educational institutions are the objects of analysis. It is essential for us to recognize that not all education occurs in the classrooms or in the social systems found in schools and colleges. Much education takes place—perhaps more than in the formal school setting—through day-to-day interaction within the family,

SOURCE: *The New York Times Magazine*, January 5, 1964. © 1965 by the New York Times Company. Reprinted by permission. ✦ The author is a member of the staff of the Magazine section of *The New York Times*.

neighborhood, and other social groups. Such informal education may reinforce or complement the behavior taught in school, or it may interfere with the formally organized educational processes. Richard Hammer describes here the informal education that occurs in a minority-group neighborhood in Harlem.

The people will tell you that this block is a fortress. Its walls are invisible; they are inside the mind, built by the people who live on the block and by society outside. But the walls are as real as if they were made of mortar and stone; they keep 3,000 people locked up inside, afraid, and they keep most outsiders away, afraid.

The block is in the middle of Spanish Harlem, a section of New York that runs roughly from 96th Street to 118th Street between Fifth Avenue and Park Avenue. As events constantly make clear, the area is seething. To the outsider, it is a strange and unfamiliar and often frightening world— one he can never know on his own and one he can understand only partially even with the most expert help.

Recently I met a young man, 18 years old, for whom Spanish Harlem is home. He was born on the block on which he lives and has spent his entire life on it, in the same small apartment he now shares with his mother, widowed for 10 years, three brothers, three sisters and three other relatives. From all outward signs, Hiram Gonzales (this is not his name) could be a typical 18-year-old from his block. He has grown up in its poverty and faced discrimination all his life because his skin is dark and he is recognizably of Puerto Rican descent. Twice he has dropped out of high school, once from vocational high school in Brooklyn and later from an academic high school in Manhattan.

But Hiram is articulate beyond his education and background, made so by self-education and by an innate brightness and intelligence, and he has thought long and hard about what it is like to grow up and live in Spanish Harlem. He also has a goal and the talent and determination to realize it: he wants to be a professional photographer . . . and he is driven by a desire to return to school and then go on to college. And he has the sensitivity to see into and beneath the sights and sounds and texture of the life around him.

For several nights, we sat together and talked. At first, he was hesitant and wary, looking for something in the interviews other than interest in him and his problems. "To tell you the truth, man," he said later, "I dislike white men because I feel all the injustice that I, my family, my mother, my friends . . . you know, that all of us have gone through." Later, as respect and trust grew, Hiram led me through his world.

"When you walk through my block," he said, "probably the first thing you realize is that there are a lot of people on the street all the time, from early in the morning to late at night. You'll see that the buildings are old, almost falling apart, but a lot of people have hung curtains in the windows.

"If you are an observing person, you'll notice prostitutes waiting for guys with money, most of them white men from downtown. You'll see drug addicts just moving nowhere; you'll see dope peddlers practically passing the stuff right out in the open. You'll see incidents of theft, you'll just walk along and see them. You'll see a lot of things that are wrong by moral standards and by the moral laws of the rest of society.

"But, man, ever since I was a little kid, this was my block, the block of the fellows who lived in it. It was our property and we govern it and we make our own laws and no outsider or no people who don't live in the block can tell us what to do. There are a lot of people who come up and they try to tell us. But, man, they don't understand, they're living in some kind of dream.

"Their standards and ideas don't belong on this block. Because we've been made to feel like we're different, like we don't fit, like we don't belong any place but on our own crummy little block. And there's nobody up here who's going to listen until the white man lets us become a part of his society outside, and I don't mean just a couple of guys who are really exceptional, who've got a lot of brains, but I mean everybody who can make it."

One of the things the rest of society has to understand, Hiram thought, was that the people on his block are not different or strange. "To live on my block," he said, "is to live anywhere where there are a lot of people who are poor and who don't have any place else to go. There's a lot of pain and a lot of sorrow, but underneath there's also a lot of glory and happiness and love. Sure, there are a lot of problems on my block, and maybe more problems than a lot of other places. And everybody on the block knows that you think we brought all the problems with us. Well, man, we didn't. The problems were all here before the people came, or anyway, the things that made the problems. For every unjust act done by the people in my neighborhood, there was an unjust act, directly or indirectly done to these people by society."

By indirect, Hiram meant the often unthinking attitudes of whites. "There was this white woman from downtown," he said, "who sometimes came into the neighborhood to help my mother when she was sick. One day this woman said to me, 'Now, I don't have anything against the Irish or the Italians, but I just don't like most Negroes and I don't like most Puerto Ricans.'

"Now, man, even though she was helping us when we needed help, I got damn mad. 'Now just a minute,' I said to her, 'how many Puerto Ricans or Negroes do you know? How many do you associate with? Where do you come off saying something like that?'

" 'Well,' she told me, 'I see lots of Negro and Puerto Rican boys hanging on the street corners who look tough, and I'm afraid of them.'

" 'You go out to Bedford-Stuyvesant and you'll see plenty of white boys hanging on the street corners who are just as tough; you go anywhere

where people have to live in this kind of filth and you'll see the same damn thing. When you and your kind first came here, you weren't any better.' "

Later, Hiram said, "You know, I'd like to move all the people from Scarsdale, N.Y., right into my block, into the same apartments where some of them have to pay maybe $70 for a couple of crummy little rooms for 10 or 11 people and have to share a bathroom in the hall with the door falling off. Let them live in a place where somebody throws a tire in the furnace and stinks out the place and then the cops come along and tell you that it's nothing and laugh when they're telling you.

"I'll tell you, I think they'd make just as much of a mess as we do, maybe more, because we're used to it, we're used to dodging those weak spots in the floors and not leaning on the wall because it will fall in.

"I don't think those people from Scarsdale could take it. In Scarsdale, the first things the kids learn are how to read and write; that's taken for granted. In my neighborhood, the first things the kids learn are how to fight and steal and not take any crap from anyone. We grow up knowing about narcotics, I mean we don't even remember when we didn't know about them, and everybody just takes that for granted.

"In my block, there are five places where you can buy marijuana cigarettes and I know, even though he's never said anything, that my little brother who's 14 knows where most of them are, that he's known for a long time."

I suggested that nobody forces the kids to use narcotics. "Of course nobody comes up to us and says, 'Man, here's some pot, you *got* to take a drag; man, here's some horse, you *got* to shoot.' But, man, these little kids look at the teen-agers who are using, and they *look* bigger, and, man, they can laugh and forget everything that's around. So, the little kids think, 'That's a tough man; he's great.' And then they see the pushers and racketeers in their $50 shoes and $100 suits, driving a big car, and they think, 'Man, he's tough; he's into some money, and he's doing good.' So, when the pusher talks, they listen."

Hiram told me that by the time the boys on the block get to be 20 probably 95 per cent of them have tried some kinds of drugs and about 40 per cent of them are hooked.

"We aren't fooling ourselves," he said, "when we try drugs. We know what can happen. When I was 13, I saw somebody die of heroin. I went up to the roof of the house next door . . . I think it was to fly my kite . . . anyway, when I came out the door I nearly fell over these addicts who were sort of sitting around in the hallway next to the door. They saw I was only a kid, so they kept right on shooting.

"All of a sudden, I heard a lot of rumbling and this one guy leaped out through the door and started running and turning and jumping all over the roof. Man, he still had the needle sticking in his arm. His friends, and they were still half asleep, sort of staggered out and grabbed him and held him down until he was quiet; then they started walking him back and forth to keep him awake. After a while, they sent me downstairs to get some milk, and more people began coming up to try to help. But nobody could do nothing, and by the time the ambulance got there, he was dead."

Most of the young people in Spanish Harlem are bitter and disillusioned. They sit on the stoops because there isn't anything else most of them can do, and they play cards and they joke. "Our goal is to have a good time, to keep having fun so we don't have to think," said Hiram. "You know what we're doing? We think we're sending the world on its own way while we go on ours. But we know, and, man, that's the trouble, we know that we can't send the world away, that we're part of the world and the world is looking down at us and snarling and laughing at us."

Isn't there, I asked, a desire to get out of the block and into that world to stop that sneering?

"Man, when I was a kid, I used to have dreams that maybe I'd be a scientist and discover all kinds of things. But they were only dreams; when I woke up, there wasn't anything real about them, there couldn't be anything real about them. I've never seen a scientist; I don't understand anything about them; there aren't any scientists, or anybody else who has a big job on my block, so I haven't got the least idea of what they're like. It's hard to even picture them mentally. These things are so far above us they aren't real. They're like a cloud that looks solid until you grab it and find it falls apart in your hands."

The boys on the block feel that even with an education they have no hope of realizing any dreams. "I know guys with a diploma who start looking for jobs. You know what they can get? A stockboy or a delivery boy or something like that, but not something where they feel they can move ahead.

"I've got a friend who wants to be a mathematician and he's a real smart guy. But when he graduated from high school, an academic one, too, not a lousy vocational one like most of us dropped out of, he went looking for a job so he could make the money to go to college. Nobody had nothing for him. Finally, he answered an ad for a lousy busboy's job at a crummy cafeteria.

"You know what they told him? They told him that he had too much education, that they were afraid he would quit. Now this kid would have worked like hell because he needed the money; but he couldn't even get that crummy job, a job any fink who didn't even know how to read could handle."

So most of the boys just sit. They are convinced that if they went back to school, it would not assure them of a decent job; besides, they are disenchanted with the schools themselves. "When I reached sixth grade, I couldn't read," said Hiram. "The teachers, most of them, didn't give a damn."

The school, instead of revealing the world, merely mirrored the world the young people from the block already knew. "But when I was in seventh grade, I went to a Catholic school for a year. They put a kind of wrench in my mind and opened it a crack and I began to see that there was a world outside my block. Man, that school cared about me and about everybody, and they wanted to teach and they wanted me to learn.

"Then I went back to public school because, man, the work just got too hard and I wasn't ready for it. In public school, the only thing the teachers wanted was quiet. If they thought we didn't want to learn, they'd sit there smoking and reading and if you got out of line, sometimes they'd curse at you: 'You little spic, sit down.' "

But in that school Hiram's horizons were broadened by one teacher of a subject he hated, English. "One day, the teacher came in and played us 'The Three Penny Opera,' and there was something about this 'Mack the Knife' character that really hit us. We asked him to play it over and over, and the next day he brought in 'West Side Story,' and every day he played us records for a while. Then he began to read to us. He read 'The Old Man and the Sea,' 'The Most Dangerous Game,' and a lot of others.

"Now, man, we weren't angels after that; we still carried on, maybe even more because we were getting some freedom, but when that man asked for silence, he got it, and when he began to suggest things, they began to move."

While there were some who managed to get an education, Hiram explained that they paid a terrible price for it. They had to be the teacher's pet, and this put them at the mercy of their fellows, who were not slow to deal out fitting punishment. For most, however, "this was the white man's education, taught the way the white man wanted it taught, without giving it any meaning for us. It was routine, do this and do that, and today we try to escape routine all the time. And it was using things from the white man's world which didn't mean anything to us or things that were so completely against everything we knew that we laughed at them. They even had books telling us what great guys the cops are.

"Now look, man, I know that most cops are just doing their jobs and trying to protect people most of the time. But I've grown up admiring people, I mean *admiring*, who would fight back at cops; to some extent, I still admire them. Why, I think that if right now, right this minute, a cop walked into this room and told me to do something, I don't think I'd do it, just because he was a cop."

This is the way Hiram and his friends see the law. "In my neighborhood, the cops feel that they're superior to the people, and, man, they let us know they think they're better than us. They walk into our homes and look around and tell us to open up, and we're afraid, and I mean afraid, to do anything or say anything. We just do what the cops say.

"And they'll come walking down the street and see us sitting on the stoop, and you know what they do? They come up to us, asking us who we're going to rape next and what job we're planning to pull, and then they tell us to get moving. Man, it can be our stoop, right in front of our house, with our mothers watching out the windows, and the cops are cursing and, man, even demanding that we show them identification."

Another group of "outsiders," youth board and social workers, also rank low in the opinion of the block, Hiram said. "They're all around the neighborhood and most of them are rat fink types. They act like they think that we're not human. They think they've got all there is and all they've got to do is convert us to think and do what they think and do. Then, everything will be just great. But, man, these jerks pop up in the morning with their little briefcases and they cut out for their homes a hell of a way away around 5 or 6 at night, and that's it. If you ever are nuts enough to go to one of them, they hand you the old crap, 'Now, son, you shouldn't feel that way.'

"Now, look, I don't think these guys mean any harm. I think the least thing they want is to do any harm. But harm comes in many forms."

So Hiram and the people on the block have come to distrust those who arrive with good words and offers of help. They feel that they have only themselves to depend on, that only within their group is there reliability.

"As bad as things are here," Hiram said, "in my lifetime I have seen more good things on this block than I have seen bad. On my block, people help each other and most of them do the right things, for themselves and for everybody. Man, I have seen thieves help thieves; I have seen thieves help other guys; I have seen guys who have to rob for a living, and I mean really rob because they don't have any other way, I have seen them give their money to make another guy a little happier.

"I have seen an addict—and this guy was nearly crying for a fix and practically running across the street to get one—stop and shove his last $3 in the shirt pocket of another guy who was married and had a lot of kids but who couldn't find a job and didn't have any money. And this junkie went walking away, kicking himself and cursing, 'Now, why the hell did I do that?'

"Now, man, this may not sound like much, but that one incident, for me, could equal 50 unjust things, because it shows that these people do have concern about each other, even though it may be hard for them to show it or express it or maybe even to understand it."

The people on the block are not unconscious of the horror and the filth and destitution around them. They know that it is bad and, at times, they talk of leaving it, though few ever do. But now, today, most of them are afraid. They are afraid because their block is going; all around, new housing projects have risen and this is almost the last block to remain unchanged. It will not remain so for long, and the people know it. Hiram said that most of them would not be able to get into the new projects; some because they wouldn't be able to afford the rents, some because they have an addict or a criminal in the family and the rules of projects forbid such tenants.

"The people are going to have to move, like up to the Bronx, and the landlords know that these people are going to need houses, so instead of $50 they'll make it $70 or $100 an apartment; they're already doing it.

"Man, this is the end of my block," said Hiram. "This is something that we all evade; like, this has been going on for five years. All the other blocks have been going, and this has been in my mind, in everybody's mind, but I haven't really given it any thought, but it scares me. I fear it. But wherever, any place, there is poverty and minorities like us, you will find another block like this one, with all the same problems and the same horrors that we have. Maybe that's where we will have to go. Forget it, man, let me live in this rathole that I have now, that I know, instead of some other new rathole that I don't know."

* 60 *

WHAT DO THEY REALLY LEARN
AT COLLEGE?

Howard S. Becker

Most people think of a college education as something which takes place in the formally organized activities of the classroom, the laboratory, and the library. As the institution of higher education has evolved, however, most colleges also provide an opportunity for students to learn many of the other skills they will need as adults. In this article Becker examines some of these (usually) less-planned-for educational experiences occurring in college. Perhaps the reader should ask himself, as he studies this selection, whether it is time, as Becker says, that students know that these skills will be important and so "act accordingly." So also, perhaps, should the reader ask himself what the consequences might be if more systematic and self-conscious attention were given to make certain that these aspects of "socialization" were imparted to students rather than leaving them to the kind of informal machinery described here.

When we talk of education, we ordinarily refer to the conventional institutions in which it is carried on: elementary schools, secondary schools, colleges and universities, graduate and professional schools. When we talk

SOURCE: Reprinted from *Trans-Action*, Vol. 1, No. 4 (May, 1964), 14–17, a publication of the Community Leadership Project, Washington University, St. Louis, Mo. ✧ The author is a Senior Associate of the Institute for the Study of Human Problems at Stanford University and the editor of *Social Problems*. His special interests include sociology of work, deviant behavior, and social psychology. He has written *Outsiders: Studies in the Sociology of Deviance*, has coauthored *Boys in White*, and has edited *The Other Side*.

of what students learn at school, we usually refer to the things adults want them to learn there. What do people learn as they grow up in our society? Where do they learn it? It may be that the important things that happen to students in college do not happen in the library, the laboratory, or in the classroom.

Most middle-class boys and girls graduate from high school and go on to college. Many, perhaps most, college-goers learn in college precisely what they need to know to get along as adults in a middle-class world. The middle-class worlds of business and the professions demand a number of specific skills and abilities and the experience of college is such as to provide college students with training in precisely those skills and abilities. I shall discuss a number of the demands made by the adult middle-class world, indicating in each case how the world of the college is organized to provide relevant training. Most of what I will talk about is not conventionally regarded as an important part of the college curriculum; nevertheless, these are matters which are important for college students while they are in school and afterward. They know it and they act accordingly.

Independence from Home

Ours is one of the most mobile societies ever known. People move frequently and they move great distances. Unlike nomadic groups, they do not move together, taking their families and communities with them. They move because opportunity beckons elsewhere and it beckons to individuals, not groups. Moving for the sake of opportunity is very common in the middle class. As more and more people enter itinerant professions or go to work for one of the national organizations which ships its men around from city to city, more and more members of the middle class find themselves, as young adults, leaving their homes, neighborhoods, and families behind and setting out for new territory. Friends, instead of being furnished almost automatically by family connections and neighborhood contiguity, must be made without that help. To make the break from family and community requires an independence of spirit that does not come naturally.

Going away to college provides a rehearsal for the real thing, an opportunity to be away from home and friends, to make a new life among strangers, while still retaining the possibilities of affiliation with the old. In the dormitory, and even more so in the fraternity and sorority, one finds himself on his own but at the same time surrounded by strangers who may become friends. One has the experience of learning to shift for oneself and making friends among strangers.

Further, all the little chores that one's family did for you now have to be taken care of in some other way. You get your own meals, take care of your own room, make your own bed, clean your own clothes. These are small things but difficult until one has learned to do them. They are a kind of training for the passage from home, whether it is geographical or simply the making of a new home upon marriage. Going away to college provides an opportunity to play at moving away from home for good and it prepares the youngster for the world in which he will have to live.

Dating, Marriage, and Poise

We normally expect young people to achieve some kind of workable relationship with members of the opposite sex, to learn how to get along with them and eventually to choose or be chosen for marriage. For middle-class youth, the problem is complicated by the requirement of the adult work world that he choose a wife who will be "culturally adequate" for the circles his business or profession will require him to move in. He must acquire the ability to attract and marry the kind of woman who can run a proper house for him and entertain for him. And for women, this means that they must learn how to perform these functions in an adequate middle-class way. It means for both men and women that they must learn the kind of manners, poise, and cultural skills necessary to move in such a world and to attract such a mate.

Again, the college (and particularly the large state university) provides the proper kind of training. Although it is not part of the curriculum, training in manners, poise, and cultural skills is given in a wide variety of places on the campus. Fraternities and sororities specialize in it. Pledges are taught in formal classes how to introduce themselves to strangers, how to ask for a date or accept one, how to behave on a date, how to handle silverware at a formal dinner, and so on. The need for this training is obvious if one watches incoming freshmen during orientation week. The people who prepare dinners for these students know that, in order to avoid embarrassments, they had better not serve any strange dishes which require more than rudimentary skill with silver. The formal training is reinforced by constant practice. A stranger who walks into a fraternity house finds himself assaulted by a stream of young men rushing up to introduce themselves, fearing that if they do not one of the active members will punish them.

The Marriage-Hunting Ground

The dating system and the round of formal and informal social functions provided by both the Greek system and the university proper provide a fine training ground for meeting the opposite sex and finding a proper mate. Some pledges are required to have a certain minimum number of dates per month; most students feel some vague pressure to date, even though they find it anxiety-provoking. By participating in a round of parties and social functions, students learn the kind of manners and poise necessary for the social life of the country club or civic organization, skills that will stand them in good stead in their later middle-class lives.

In addition, many, though by no means all, students receive training in dealing socially with "important people." Fraternities, dormitories, and other kinds of student groups make a practice of inviting important people, both campus personages and visitors, to meet with them. Students may have experience socializing with the governor of the state, the chancellor of the university, national political figures, or important visitors from overseas.

Work Skills

The middle-class occupational world demands a number of generalized work skills from its recruits. They must, first of all, acquire some skills needed for their prospective occupations which the university is set up to teach. It may be that they need to learn the analytic techniques of chemistry or engineering; they may need to learn the skills of reading, writing, and the use of a library. Whatever it is, the university has courses which teach them some of the knowledge and technique necessary to hold a job.

We must not overstate this. Many businesses, industries and professional and graduate schools feel that an undergraduate college cannot, or at least does not, teach the required skills in the proper way. They prefer to train their recruits from scratch. To this end, many firms have in-service training programs which provide the specific knowledge recruits need.

More important than the specific knowledge and techniques necessary for entrance into an occupation is a more generalized kind of work skill, one that in older days was referred to as "stick-to-it-iveness." The entrant into the middle-class occupational world must have the ability to see a job through from beginning to end, to start a project and keep his attention and energy focused on it until it is completed.

The ability to get things done does not come naturally to young people; it is a hard-won skill. In acquiring it, the middle-class youth must learn to defer immediate gratifications for those that are longer in coming; he must learn to give up the pleasures of the moment for the larger rewards that await a big job well done. Most students have not had to learn this in high school, where the parade of daily requirements and assignments places the emphasis on receiving the immediate gratification of having done this day's job well.

College . . .

For many students, it is only when one reaches college that one is required to plan ahead in units of four or five months, keeping attention focused on the long-range goal of passing the course without the constant prodding of the daily assignment. In learning to organize himself well enough to get a good grade in a college course, in learning to keep his mind on one job that long, the college student learns the middle-class skill of getting things done, so important in business and industry.

Finally, the middle-class world demands of those who enter it that they be able to juggle several things at once, that they be able to handle more than one job at a time and to keep them straight. He must learn to manage his time successfully and not fritter it away in actions that produce no reward. At least some college students get magnificent training in how to budget time and energy. The kind of student, of whom there are many, who does well in his courses and at the same time is, let us say, a high-ranking officer in several campus-wide organizations and an officer of his fraternity or dormitory, learns that he cannot waste his time if he is to achieve anything. He learns to set aside particular times for study and not to allow anything to intervene; he learns to handle organizational matters with dispatch; he learns to give up or strictly ration the joys of watching television and drinking beer with the boys. He learns, in short, how to have a time for everything and to do everything in its time.

Organizational Skills

The typical middle-class career now takes place in a bureaucratic organization. Even the professions, which used to be the stronghold of the individual practitioner, now tend increasingly to find the locus of their activities in a complex organization rather than a professional office; the doctor spends more of his time in the hospital and is responsive to the social control of the bureaucratically organized hospital, rather than practicing independently in his own office. The recruit to the middle-class occupational world requires, if he is to operate successfully in it, the ability to get along in a mass of organization and bureaucracy. If the rules and constraints of large organizations frighten or anger him, he will not be able to achieve what he wants nor will he be an effective member of the organization.

Among the specific things an effective member of a large organization must know and be able to do we can include the following: He must be willing and able to take the consequences for his own actions, to see ahead far enough to realize how what he does will affect others and the organization. He must have some skill in manipulating other people, in getting them to do what he wants without the use of force or coercion; he must learn to be persuasive. He must have the ability to compromise, to give up some of what he wants in order to gain the rest; he must not be a narrow-minded fanatic, who either has his way or not at all. And he must, finally, be knowledgeable and skillful in manipulating the rules and impersonal procedures of bureaucratic organizations to his own advantage, rather than being stymied and buffaloed by them.

Rehearsal for Management

The network of extracurricular organizations characteristic of the large state university provides a perfect context in which to learn these skills.

The student can participate in student politics, either as an active candidate or as a behind-the-scenes organizer. He can become an officer of one of the organizations that helps run campus activities. He can work on the student newspaper. He may be an officer of his fraternity or dormitory. A large number of students have experiences in one or more such organizations during their four years in college.

Melville Dalton, in tracing the antecedents of successful industrial managerial careers, argues that experience in this realm of campus life is a perfect background for success in industry.

Our observations at the University of Kansas corroborate Dalton's findings. Let me point out some sources of experience, important for the recruit to the middle-class occupational world. Many officers of campus organizations find themselves exercising responsibility for large amounts of money; they may administer budgets running as high as $50,000 a year. Some of them administer programs of activity in which it is necessary to coordinate the efforts of several hundred or more of their fellow students. You have only to think, for an example, of the effort and organization necessary for the traditional Homecoming Weekend at any big university.

Some students even have the experience of discovering that the important people with whom they come in contact have feet of clay. As they deal with officers of the university in the course of their organizational work, they discover that these officers may ask them to do things they regard as improper. A typical case, which occurs in many universities, arises when some university officer requests or attempts to coerce the student newspaper into not publishing matter he believes harmful to the university. The student reporters and editors discover, in such a situation, that university officials are, after all, only human too; it is a shocking and educational discovery for a nineteen-year-old to make.

Motivation

The recruit to the middle-class world must, finally, learn to attach his own desires to the requirements of the organizations he becomes involved in. He must learn to have what we might call *institutional motivation*. He must learn to want things simply and only because the institution in which he participates says these are the things to want.

College provides practice at this linking of personal and institutional desires. The student learns that he requires, at the least, a degree and that he must do whatever it is the college asks of him in order to get that degree. This attachment to the long-range goal furnishes him with the motivation to continue in classes that bore or confound him, to meet requirements that seem to him foolish or childish. The college student learns to want to surmount the obstacles posed for him by the college, simply because they are there. He learns to regard these external obstacles as marks of his own ability and maturity, and because he interprets the obstacles that way, sees his success in college as a sign of his own personal worth. The ability to link institutional and personal desires is an important prerequisite for occupational success in adult life.

Through participation in the college community, the student comes to define himself as the kind of person who ought to have the skills of the middle-class occupational world. He pins his self-respect, his sense of personal worth, on acquiring them. He feels that he will have properly become an adult only when he has all these qualities and skills. He directs his effort and organizes his life in such a way as to achieve them and thus to prove to himself and others that he has grown up. It may be that these are the really important things he learns at college.

It is too bad that convention requires the college studiously to ignore what it really teaches students.

✤ 61 ✤

SCIENCE AND THE
HUMAN COMMUNITY

J. Robert Oppenheimer

It should be quite obvious even to the casual observer that formal processes of education, which usually end at twenty-two to twenty-five years of age, are not enough to carry a person through his lifetime. The object of higher education should, therefore, be not only to impart what we think is now known but also to help students to "learn how to learn." In later life, then, both on their own and through the increasing number of institutions set up to help adults continue to learn, many people will need to constantly upgrade their understanding and skills. This need for continued education is growing at an accelerated pace. In this selection, the eminent scientist Oppenheimer reviews the startling growth and complexity of science and describes the demands that this growth places upon man and upon the "institution of education."

✧   ✧   ✧   ✧   ✧

. . . In the seventeenth century the sense of a new world began to spread, and the feeling that the old order had been shot out from under

SOURCE: *Issues in University Education*, 52–61, edited by Charles Frankel. Copyright © 1959 by Harper & Brothers. Reprinted by permission of Harper & Row, Publishers. ✧ The author was Director of the Institute for Advanced Study, Princeton, New Jersey, from 1947 to 1966. He is now Professor of Theoretical Physics. From 1943 to 1945 Oppenheimer was the Director of the Los Alamos Scientific Laboratory, New Mexico. He received the Enrico Fermi award in 1963.

was sharply articulated. Some of the finest poetry of our history was written as a result. And people also began to talk about a possibility which, in the eighteenth century, especially in France and England, was referred to with awe and apprehension. A time might not be far off, it was suggested, when the sum of human knowledge would double every half century. It is arguable whether the doubling time of knowledge today is eight years or eleven years; but it is something like that. And this extraordinary acceleration has been achieved by the development in the full, broad, noble sense of the word *science*. It is most strikingly true in the natural sciences and can even be measured by volume of publication. And this increase in quantity does not signify by any means that quality has declined. A society will protect itself from really trivial things: a group of physicists or a group of biochemists will manage their journals in such a way that what is in those journals is worth reading to the specialist. The quality, I would say, in all branches of science in which I have either knowledge or competence or interest has gone up with the fantastic increase in quantity.

Now this knowledge is, of course, not without its order. In fact, it is all about order. Its whole purpose is to relate experiences to each other and to show that not everything in human experience is arbitrary. But it is not orderly in the sense that there are a few general premises from which you can deduce everything else. And it never will be. The conviction which the physicist may have that the facts of chemistry could be deduced from physics if someone tried doesn't mean that chemistry is a part of physics. And it should not be at all. The interesting parts of chemistry are those which no physicist would ever have thought of deducing. Similarly, we may be confident about the great insights into the origin of life, and the nature of genetic material, and the coding techniques which all living organisms have and which dominate such primitive things as perception. We may be confident that there will be a total lack of gap between the biological and psychological descriptions of man. Still, this will never reduce the parts of psychology to biology.

This enormous house of science has its inner relatedness, which is very subtle and beautiful, but it is not the sort of edifice that was imagined in the enlightenment of a century ago. What we have is entirely different from the early nineteenth-century nightmare of Laplace, who thought that one had only in a static moment to be temporarily omniscient and all history could be predicted out of this moment of insight. What we have today corresponds to an entirely different ideal of human knowledge, in which from the very beginning it is understood that if you pursue one means of sorting out our experience, you exclude many or all others. From the very beginning, starting with the most elementary, common-sense things, scientific activity today marches off in different technical and specialized directions and adopts and cultivates a view of knowledge as something which, in its nature, cannot be total, but is always partial and self-limited.

Now all this means that the problem of acculturation, and the problem of community, and the problem of education—they are all related problems—have a character for us which is quite different from any they have had in the past. I have often been led to recall with interest a metaphor which William James used fifty years ago to describe the nature of the interrelations in our cognitive world. He saw this world not as global, not as made up of the kind of description which one would give of a finite, closed object, like a temple, which was there for all time and which one might survey and describe and come back to again and again until no further detail needed to be added. He saw it rather as an affair of networks or interconnections of relevance, some explicit, some remote: an affair in part of analogies, some recognized and some not recognized, perhaps formal analogies of the kind that mathematics uses so much, perhaps logical analogies, perhaps often analogies that are verbal and rather thin, and sometimes even the affective analogies which play so enormous a part in the arts. It is a set of interconnections, not themselves exhaustible, between rapidly growing, highly specialized, and enormously fruitful ways of knowing about the world. And the problem of domesticating this intricate and novel system of beliefs and procedures in the more general culture around us has, therefore, certain distinctive and troublesome features.

Before proceeding, there are two points I should like to add which may make matters a little sharper. The first has to do with our knowledge of man. I believe there is a good chance that what have been the protosciences of man are now rather close to becoming the many, many different sciences of man. I do not think that in the world fifty years from now there will be a subject called *psychology*, any more than there is now a subject called *natural philosophy*. I think that different ways of studying man will lead to disciplines which for convenience will have different names, be in different buildings, and will have different professors. But I believe that we are on the threshold of an enormous enrichment in what we know about man. I do not mean that we will ever know more, in a certain sense, than we can find from the greatest art. But that is something very different. It is something that we rightly cherish, and it must be evident that I am not trying to exclude it from the sum of human life. But it is not the kind of knowledge I am talking about. I have in mind rather the same sort of homely, and in the end sometimes forbiddingly dull, knowledge that we get to have about such magic things as the stars and about life itself. In fact, we never answer the questions which people thought would be answered when they asked, "Will we ever understand life?" or "Will we ever understand what makes the stars move in their courses?" We understand other things and we answer other questions. And so it will be with the sciences of man. But I do have the impression that all the way from history to biology a great arc of science is about to catch fire. We have to be prepared to deal with this and to see that it does not throw us off balance and does not even further corrupt and corrode the vitality of our society.

The second point about the growth of modern knowledge, which I should like to stress before proceeding to the broader cultural and educational problem, has to do with the nature of scientific communities. The receptacle of all the knowledge we have, the agencies to whom this knowledge is entrusted and who create it, are not individual men. They are communities of men. They are the specialized professions, often increasingly specialized. The world of knowledge is a world held together by little bands of people who know a great deal about some particular field but whose relations with neighboring fields, while warm, are often not very intense. As far as the world of learning goes, we live in a way in a kind of generalization of the old medieval guilds, a kind of syndicalism which is a cognitive syndicalism, a syndicalism in which the true community, the true intimate collaboration of men, is best exemplified by groups of specialists who understand each other and help each other. Every scholar is in some sense or other a member of such a group. To use the image of a network again, these communities offer a picture of internal intimacy, cognitive intimacy, an intimacy of understanding and clarity, and usually also of good will and cordiality; and these communities stretch through all parts of the world. One notices this fact with hope, but one notices it also with melancholy. For one thinks of these communities as networks holding the world together, and one cannot believe that these bonds are strong enough for the times we live in.

But now we must come to the relation of this knowledge and these communities to the larger world in which they have emerged and which they affect. There are two traits of this world that I would stress, two things which seem to me to mark it off from past times—certainly from the Athens that we love, certainly from the high times in Elizabethan England, or the Enlightenment, or the great days of the Renaissance: all of them times of change, of great discovery, of unmooring. The first thing I would single out about the present scene is the overwhelming predominance of things that are new over things that are old. This is, of course, a consequence of the fact that knowledge doubles every ten years. It expresses itself in the fact that no professional man can really be any good if he does not, either by formal schooling or by reading and his own efforts, really keep at school constantly. No engineer can leave school today and hope to be a competent engineer in relation to the problems of twenty years from now if he has not gone back to school or done the equivalent. And this phenomenon shows itself, of course, not only in matters of sheer knowledge. The application of knowledge changes the face of the earth. It is brilliantly illustrated in towns like São Paulo in Brazil, which simply grew as you watched. It has been very much illustrated on the face of Europe, and it is of course illustrated in the United States. People do not live as they did even ten, twenty, or thirty years ago. The kinds of practices their parents engaged in, the kind of sensibility their parents had, live on in a new and rather alien soil. This has come about partly from mechanical changes, partly from the changes brought about by communication, partly from the actual change in what people know. And this imbalance between the new and the old, although it is not beyond endurance for man, is something to which man is unaccustomed and for which his tradition has not fully prepared him.

The second trait of the present scene which I would stress is another kind of imbalance. If we look at what is known, the proportion that is known by specialized groups is very large, and the proportion that gets back into the common knowledge of man is very small. I have a prejudice—perhaps some Englishman will correct me—that England has done best in putting special knowledge into the common pool of knowledge of educated men. It is not put in very deeply; it is not put in with terribly much reverence. But that is the price you pay for putting it in at all. And this is almost not done at all in the United States. As a result, there is a deep attrition of the common culture. The common culture does not receive the kind of resources which it should be getting from the special expeditionary forces that are going off in all directions and learning so many new things. These expeditions do not enrich the common culture because almost no solid report comes back from them. The transmittal back is entrusted too much to woefully superficial and often meretricious popularizations, which do not get the meaning, or the beauty, or the weight of the experience communicated, and which do not, in a certain sense, engage or involve the general public. Even within a large part of science itself, I know that one specialist does not get a feeling for what goes on in a contiguous specialty. As I have been forced to note with amazement, there is today practically no understanding among physicists, for example, of what modern mathematicians are doing. There is a good deal of, perhaps not boredom, but suspicion that mathematicians are engaged in a game that will never be a part of the physicists' world. And I am afraid the mathematicians hold the same attitude in reverse and think the physicists are bothering about rather foolish things, which, if only they could really be cleared up, the mathematician would understand very clearly. But the mathematician is not going to turn his mind to such problems for a long, long time.

We have, then, a predominance of novelty on the present scene, and also an absence of common knowledge, or at least a thinning of common knowledge, together with an enormous growth of specialized and available knowledge, but not vital, living knowledge. And both these tendencies give one the sense that what in the past people have called *values* are bound to suffer. For whatever values may be, they rest in areas of life which are familiar and deeply intimate. Though one can think of exceptions, they have for the most part a dual character. On the one hand, they are commitments, commitments as to where one stands, and where one acts, and what one will be, and what one cares for. On the other hand, they always involve memories. Thus, in values, commitment and memory unite the past and the future. And so, with the enormously rapid change in our lives, partly cognitive, partly technical and practical, it is not unnatural that we should have a sense of evaporation and emasculation and vagueness in this area. Our past is not so manifestly meaningful for our future. The problems that we meet in our future are not like those which we suffered and from which we learned in our youth, even though there are some analogies. And the danger is that if people today articulate what they think about the good and the beautiful, their words will have a kind of awesome vagueness, an awesome lack of the specific and the robust and the intimate. The business of human life, after all, has to be the business of using what we were to become what we shall be. And this means that just the things that you have been close to, that you have felt as well as learned, that you have learned to do and learned about, that you have learned as arts, things that you have been with for a while and have not changed too rapidly—these must still be present, and they must be relevant to you, to your colleagues, your associates, your community, your society, and your future.

But if human values are so much a matter of familiarity and intimacy, one might reply, "Why can't all this rapid change be stopped?" But it is obvious that such a change can be stopped only by two kinds of things. There was a great Moslem renaissance, for example, which lasted over three centuries, but which stopped about the year 1100. And what stopped it can take place again. It was military conquest and religious orthodoxy. But without some horrible combination of these two devices, it is clear that men's curiosity, their adventuresomeness, even their cupidity, will all conspire to favor the conditions for the wonderful growth of knowledge with which we live. There are countries where the pace of change is something which people would have liked to resist, countries where many people would prefer not to let things like mechanization and large-scale industrialization go very fast. But in our world this course is not open; it is not a real possibility, short of a total calamity or a total tyranny. I think that it is our mission—if we have any influence—to avoid such an apocalypse and to avert the kind of fanatic ordering of belief and knowledge and activity which could put some fixity back into our cultural and practical lives. I think that we have to accept the situation that I have outlined.

But if we do, then, above all, we have to recognize that the notions of education and the notions of culture which we have inherited, and which were natural a century ago and still more natural several centuries ago, are today misleading and quite sure to lead us to do the wrong things. And while we recognize this, it must bring us to cherish the thing which is so in danger in the world. This is just the touch of intimacy, of craftsmanship, of skill, of true, deep understanding, ranging all the way from simple things in human life to the most recondite things that one can learn in mathematics or biology or history: love of the expert, love of style, love of technical competence. We have to do this at the same time that we know that whatever little we happen to have that is familiar and intimate is only one of an incredible number of things, most of which are rather remote from us. We learn about them through friends, through reading, by luck. We shall not learn them unless we are very fortunate—and very talented. There is a balance we must strike: on one side there must be a kind of openness and skepticism, a welcoming of the new and the unfamiliar; on the other side, there must be a passionate devotion and appreciation of intellectual excellence among all excellencies, of intimacy among all intimacies.

This view has implications for higher education. I shall not labor all of them. But one basic implication is that no man should escape our universities without knowing how little he knows. He must have some sense of the fact that not through his fault, not through his sloth (though he may be lazy and not very bright) but inherently in the nature of things, he is going to be an ignorant man and so is everyone else. It would be nice, however, if this great achievement could be complemented by another great achievement, which is to make a man, although he may be ignorant of almost everything, not quite ignorant of everything. My own feeling is that for education it is indeed necessary that it accomplish these two purposes. If I had to advise a young man, to give him some rule to live by, I know that the rule would be wrong most of the time and that my advice would only be safe if it were ignored. But if I did have to give such advice, I would be inclined to say, "Try to learn something very well indeed. And do not just learn what it is in general terms. Learn it as a practitioner; learn how to do it. And stop while you are doing it long enough to see the beauty of it." But I would not quite stop with that. I would add, "But learn something else as well that is quite different. Get some sense of the span of things human, the span of things that the intelligent man can cope with."

* 62 *

DIVIDED PROTESTANTISM
IN A MIDWEST COUNTY:
A STUDY IN THE NATURAL HISTORY
OF ORGANIZED RELIGION

Anton T. Boisen

Sociologists study religion—its structure and function—as another of the institutions basic to the lives of people everywhere. As an institution, Protestant religion (in America, at least) exhibits some

SOURCE: "Divided Protestantism in a Midwest County: A Study in the Natural History of Organized Religion," by Anton T. Boisen. From *The Journal of Religion*, Vol. 20, No. 4 (October, 1940), 359–81. Reprinted by permission of the University of Chicago Press. ✧ The author was formerly Chaplain of Elgin State Hospital. He has written *Lift Up Your Heart: A Service Book for Use in Hospitals, Explorations of the Inner World, Problems in Religion and Life* as well as numerous papers for professional sociological, religious, and psychiatric journals.

interesting phenomena. Protestant churches, when they grow in size and power, tend to become more complex and formal. When segments within a church disagree with the main body of belief, they often break away and form a separate denomination, resulting in a proliferation of competing sects. The larger and more powerful a church becomes, the more likely it is to be concerned with maintenance of its organization and the less likely it is to be concerned with its particular theological reason for being. These generalizations are illustrated by Anton T. Boisen, who writes from the standpoint of a participant observer.

Sociology and history are commonly distinguished one from the other on the basis that history is the record of temporal sequences which are not likely to be repeated, whereas sociology is the attempt to discover relationships which are recurrent and universal. It follows that sociology must in many cases turn to history for its data and that history may find in sociology a valuable ally in the interpretation of its findings. This paper is an attempt to study the history of a particular middle western county with special reference to a pattern which appears to be recurrent in the development of organized religion and the forces which are operative in determining this pattern.

I

The county in question [Monroe] was selected from among a number of sample areas which I have studied because it is the one I know best. More than that, the data are unusually full and the situation revealed presents some unusually interesting features. This county is located in southern Indiana about fifty miles southwest of Indianapolis and about ninety miles northwest of Louisville. It was first opened for settlement in 1818. In 1820 it was designated as the seat of the state university— Indiana Seminary, as it was called originally.

❖   ❖   ❖   ❖   ❖

We have . . . in this early period in Monroe County three groups of churches: (1) There was, in the first place, a more or less liberal group consisting of the two Presbyterian churches and the Episcopal church. These were composed chiefly of college people and of those who wished to be identified with college people. (2) There was a very conservative group consisting of the four psalm-singing Presbyterian churches. These were characterized by great loyalty to family and clan, by their emphasis upon Old Testament morality, and by their requirement of an educated ministry. Their services were long, their sermons doctrinal and dry, and church attendance was compulsory on the part of all members of the family. Family "worship" was held every day, often morning and evening. There was among them no appeal to the emotions and no attempt to win converts. Their growth came through birth and immigration. (3) There were the churches which represented the new revivalistic movement which was sweeping the Ohio Valley. Of these the Methodists, the Disciples, the Baptists, and the Cumberland Presbyterians were represented in Monroe County. From the standpoint of our inquiry it is important to recognize that in contrast to the liberal and conservative groups this group sprang out of the spontaneous religious fervor of the common people. Instead of appealing to the desire for culture or status, instead of clinging tenaciously to the symbols of an inherited culture, these groups were attempting to meet pioneer conditions and to grapple with the moral problems of pioneer men. They brought people together in great numbers at their camp meetings, and there under the spell of vigorous singing, of stirring testimony, of exhortations by able, but often poorly educated, preachers strong emotions were often aroused. Many individuals felt themselves released from a burdening sense of sin and received the "baptism of the Spirit." Such individuals often became zealous missionaries, serving as lay leaders or being ordained as ministers to serve a group of struggling churches under the circuit-rider plan. It was through such men that Methodist, Disciples, and Baptist churches were planted throughout Monroe County, while the Presbyterians remained under the shelter of the county seat.

II

For many years the situation remained essentially unchanged. The six Presbyterian churches were, however, in time reduced to three. In 1858 the Associate and the Associate Reformed bodies merged to form the "United Presbyterian Church." The national union was marked by the characteristic "come-outer" reaction on the part of minority groups, so that the union resulted in three churches where only two had been before. Locally, however, there was agreement, as Professor Woodburn puts it, that the only differences between them were that one sang the Psalms of David and the other David's Psalms. Late in the sixties the New School and the Old School bodies succeeded in resolving their differences. In 1868 the New Side Covenanters disbanded, most of their families joining the United Presbyterian, the rest the Presbyterian Church. Here again the local action was the result of national developments, which are not without significance from the standpoint of this inquiry.

From the beginning of its existence in this country the Covenanter church had been strongly opposed to slave-holding. When in 1800 Alexander McLeod received a call from the First Reformed Presbyterian Church in New York City, he made it a condition of his acceptance that the church must be free from all slave-holding. In 1802 he and Samuel Brown

Wylie were commissioned to visit the Carolinas and take counsel with their brethren there regarding the sin of slave-holding. In 1806 the church formally declared itself against slave-holding. Apparently, therefore, the opposition to slavery, which had had not a little to do with the migration from the Carolinas, was not motivated entirely by economic considerations. In any case, the Bloomington Covenanters were active in the Underground Railroad before the Civil War, and they even received Negroes into their fellowship. When war was declared, they gave vigorous support to the Union side. Among the Covenanters who took a prominent part was George H. Stuart, the leading layman of the First Church in Philadelphia. He served as national president of the Christian Commission, an organization which corresponded somewhat to the Y.M.C.A. of the World War. It thus became his duty to visit other churches. This was all right so long as the war lasted, but after it was over he was admonished by the Synod regarding the sin of "occasional hearing" and especially regarding the practice of singing hymns of non-Davidic origin. When he refused to heed the Synod's admonitions, he was excluded from membership. The First Church thereupon severed its connection with the General Synod, and the Bloomington Church, in accordance with my grandfather's advice, did likewise.

In my own early years in Bloomington at a time when the population was about five thousand and the university enrolment about five hundred we had, therefore, three different brands of Presbyterian churches. As David Starr Jordan used to put it, we had the United Presbyterians, the Reformed Presbyterians, and the Presbyterians who were neither united nor reformed. There was also a strong Methodist church, a strong Disciples church, a Baptist church, a Church of Christ (known locally as the "Sassafras Church"), a weak Episcopal and a small Catholic church. The general grouping was much the same as in the 1840's. The Presbyterian church had become mildly evangelistic in its emphasis, but this church and the Episcopal church were still made up chiefly of college people, and of those who associated with college people. The United and the Reformed Presbyterians were still very conservative in their practices, even though the former was under very able and enlightened leadership. Both of them still made exclusive use of the Psalms of David in their services of worship, while the Reformed Presbyterians still refused to allow instrumental music, and they still forbade their members to vote. The Methodists, the Disciples, and the Baptists were still dominant among the rank and file of the population, while in the county at large their sway was undisputed except for two Cumberland Presbyterian churches, a few Churches of Christ and an occasional Separate, Regular, and Primitive Baptist organization. These churches were still evangelistic in their emphasis. They were concerned with the task of "saving souls," and they held that a man must be "converted" in order to be saved. They had their annual revival meetings, and they still encouraged or tolerated emotional expression on the part of their people. Young people from the more sedate communions would frequently attend these revivals to see the fun.

Going back after many years, I find some striking changes. The town has now eighteen thousand inhabitants, and the university six thousand students. The churches also have grown. More than that, there have been some changes of type. The Methodists today worship in a large and costly building. The older people with their "Amens" have long since passed away. There is now a stately service which appeals to college people. And the old efforts to induce the conversion experience have been discontinued. What is true of the First Methodist Church is true also of the Disciples of Christ, of the First Baptist Church, and also of the fine new Methodist church on the other side of the tracks. Among all these, conversion experiences of the old type are now very rare.

But I find also a number of churches of which I had never heard in the 1890's. Among the thirty-two churches within Bloomington's city limits are three Pentecostal Assemblies of Jesus Christ, two Nazarene churches, an Assembly of God, a Wesleyan Methodist, a Free Methodist, and a Church of God. In these new churches I find somewhat the same type of service and somewhat the same message which I used to hear in the Methodist church years ago. They are interested in saving souls, and they believe that men need to be converted in order to be saved. They emphasize the reality of sin and guilt, and they proclaim deliverance through the wonder-working power of the Blood of the Lamb. Like the Methodists and Baptists of the days gone by, they have sprung from the spontaneous religious fervor of the common people, and they are propagated through the missionary zeal of those who feel that they have found the greatest of all blessings. Their membership is made up of working-class people, who have been drawn in from the surrounding countryside to man the mills and the quarries and who, since the beginning of the depression, have had tough going.

In the county at large, outside of Bloomington, there are now sixty-two churches, some of which, however, are rather feeble. Of this number fourteen are Methodist (three of these having been Methodist Protestant); ten, Baptist; two, Separate Baptist; one, Regular Baptist; one, Primitive Baptist; nine, Disciples of Christ; eight, Church of Christ; while four are union chapels. The newer churches include one Nazarene, one Assembly of God, seven Pentecostal Assemblies of Jesus Christ, and four Trinity Pentecostal. Of the latter at least two are off-shoots of the Assembly of God in Bloomington.

Therefore, we still have today the same three groups of churches— the conservative churches, which persist by reason of their great resistance to change; the churches composed of college people and of those who accept the standards of college people; and the churches which spring out of the common soil of human nature. The alignment is, however, different today. The Methodists, the Disciples, and the Baptists have taken their place alongside of the Presbyterians and Episcopalians as respectable, middle-class churches, and a new group of churches has sprung up to meet the needs which formerly they had met.

III

The situation in Monroe County is by no means an average one. Its significance is rather to be found precisely in the unusually clear relief with which certain factors, which are, I think, operative in all organized religion, stand out. Let me call attention to the following considerations: (1) the coexistence throughout the one hundred and twenty years of Monroe County's history of the beginning, of the middle, and of the terminal stages of institutional religion, the types thus represented being constant as regards their general characteristics but shifting as regards the identity of the constituent bodies; (2) the presence throughout this period of a group of churches characterized by a strong clan loyalty and by a marked tendency toward splitting over relatively trivial issues; (3) the existence, especially during the early and the later years, of a considerable body of economically distressed folk, nearly all Protestants of English and Scotch-Irish descent, among whom the emotional cults have found their greatest following; and (4) the presence of an important university, which, especially in recent years, has accentuated the cultural differences and has speeded up the processes of liberalization and secularization within the larger churches.

Notice first of all that we have in this country a fine exemplification of Professor H. Richard Niebuhr's thesis regarding the life-history of organized religion. According to that thesis, the religious denomination begins usually among the underprivileged with a group of believers banded together on the basis of some vivid religious experience and the new vision which accompanies it. As time goes on, these believers' groups develop in accordance with a fairly definite pattern. They become more prosperous, and the original believers are replaced by their children. The process of institutionalization then sets in. The children accept the faith of their parents without sharing their experience. Short-cuts and protective devices are introduced. The sacraments become means of grace rather than symbols of belief. The creeds become standards of doctrine rather than confessions of faith. Even religious experience itself tends to become standardized in the form of patterns of behavior, which have to be induced by artificial devices. In general, the process is one of leveling. The prophetic forward movements are leveled down and conventionalized. The eccentric and regressive manifestations are leveled up and become respectable. This process is exemplified most strikingly in the Methodists, the Disciples, and the Baptists of Bloomington. They began under the impulse of a vital religious movement. They were believers' groups, characterized by strong emotion, insisting upon first-hand religious experience, and propagated spontaneously through the missionary zeal of their converts. They have now taken their place among the respectable. The newer cults represent the period of spontaneity and creativity. In the course of time they, likewise, will become respectable middle-class churches. And the Presbyterians? Their period of spontaneity and creativity lay in the time of John Knox three hundred years ago. They are merely a little further along in the process which characterizes any vital religious movement. In their psalm-singing offshoots we already see the terminal stages of institutional religion.

These Scotch-Irish psalm-singers, who are so unusually well represented in Bloomington, are worthy of careful consideration. In any attempt to understand them and the tragedies of loyalty presented by their much subdividing, we may begin by recognizing that a church is first of all a fellowship. It is a group banded together on the basis of a loyalty which is accepted as supreme. Doctrine and ritual are of secondary importance. These are taken over from those who represent authority and are thus functions of the social relationships, particularly to the parents and early guides. The persistence of these groups is due to that principle. If a great and beloved president of the university throughout his long period of service has remained a leader in the United Presbyterian Church in Bloomington, it is not due to any conviction on his part regarding the unique claims of the Psalms of David. So also the dean of the school of education in the university, who is equally active in the Old Side Covenanter Church, has no determining views regarding instrumental music in the church. Neither is he opposed to voting. Both these men are guided rather by considerations of loyalty. They have felt it a point of honor to be true to the church of their fathers. They have stayed with it, not because of doctrine but in spite of it.

Loyalty to family and clan is, in fact, so important in these churches that they may be said to represent tribal religion. The maintenance of group integrity in the face of changing conditions and against the onslaughts of an alien culture is with them a primary concern, and for this reason obedience and conformity to established patterns are required. The past rather than the future is the focus of attention. The German and the Scandinavian Lutherans in this country are examples. They are struggling to maintain their group identity and integrity, and in so doing they have become more conservative than their kindred in the old country. Religion of this type is especially likely to appear where the group has been subjected to pressure or to persecution. The ecclesiastical zeal of the Irish Catholics as compared with the Italians may thus be accounted for; so also the rigid attitudes of the various religious groups in Asia Minor and the legalism of the ancient Pharisees. The Scotch-Irish psalm-singers were just such a group. They had been solidified by persecution in the old country. In this country they were facing the disintegrating forces of impoverishment and disheartenment, which changed so many of their fellow-country-men into the "poor-white" or "hill-billy" type. They therefore stuck together throughout their wanderings. They clung to a faith in education. They retained a pride of race and clan.

The divisive tendencies which we find among them may be explained by the removal of external pressure and persecution and by the attempt to maintain loyalty, not through reason and love but through force and fear and arbitrary authority. The children who grow up under such conditions are likely to feel strong resentment, which sometimes takes the form of open rebellion and the disowning of the loyalty. More frequently, however, love is mingled with fear, loyalty with resentment. The individual may then accept the faith of his father, but the repressed hostility may be ready to seize upon some trivial doctrinal or ritualistic pretext in order to express itself. Divisions in the church then result, not from real issues of belief and practice but from unrecognized antagonistic social attitudes.

No consideration of these psalm-singing Presbyterians should fail to do justice to their sturdy character. They are a fine lot—strong, honest, neighborly, thrifty. Nonetheless, it must be recognized that their loyalty to race and clan is too often divorced from clear objectives. There is, in consequence, confusion as to what is important and what is unimportant in the principles emphasized and in the means employed. Therefore, their religion becomes static. There is fear of deviating even in the slightest from what is already established, and the confusion is accentuated by lurking antagonisms which are ready to find expression in church quarrels.

IV

The astonishingly rapid growth of new cults of the Holiness and Pentecostal types cannot be explained in terms of any one factor. The fact that this growth has taken place among the economically distressed factory and quarry workers and has been especially rapid since the depression is, however, significant. This is true not merely in Bloomington but in the country at large. It has also been true of other periods of economic distress. It brings to our attention the fact that the mystical experiences out of which such movements arise are most likely to occur in periods of stress and crisis. Under normal conditions the individual is busy with his customary pursuits, and his reflections upon matters philosophical and religious are generally in terms of an accepted currency of ideas. His personality may, in fact, be regarded as a reflection of the social organization and as the subjective aspect of his particular culture. His attitudes, his beliefs, his standards of value are taken over from his environment without much thought on his part. They are functions of his social relationships, particularly to those whom he admires and whose authority he accepts. In time of crisis, however, the individual finds himself face to face with the ultimate issues of life, and as his mind is stirred through strong emotion ideas come flooding in as from an outside source. These ideas he is likely to attribute to a divine or to a demonic origin. In so far as he does come to feel himself in contact with a superhuman world there will be for him a new social frame of reference. The accepted bases of judgment and reasoning no longer apply. There is a transvaluation of values—a break with the culture pattern of his particular time and race. Face to face with what he regards as ultimate reality, philosophy and theology become for such an individual no mere matters of academic concern but matters of life and death. Under such conditions meaning and emotion outstrip symbol. Instead of beginning with words and concepts according to the common practice, he is forced to seek new words to express the new ideas which come thronging in upon him. Such experiences may open the eyes to a larger universe and give insights which are new and creative. Again they may give new life and meaning to traditions and concepts which before had been stale and profitless. Frequently, they leave the individual cut loose from his moorings—perplexed, bewildered, sure only that things are not what they seem. They may thus be either constructive or destructive. They may be associated with mental disorder of the type, however, which should be recognized as an expression of nature's power to heal. They are likewise looked upon as wellsprings of religion. Even the unlettered laborer who passes triumphantly through such an experience may, like John Bunyan, emerge a poet and theologian of no mean order.

The danger of mental unbalance is at a minimum where the strain is shared by a group; it is at a maximum where the experience is a solitary one. Studies which have been made of the effect of the economic depression upon the mental health of our people thus show that there has been no demonstrable increase in the incidence of mental disorder. The explanation is to be found in the fact that economic distress tends to increase the sense of fellowship and forces people to think together about the things that matter most. It thus tends to lessen the sense of isolation and guilt which is the primary evil in the functional types of mental illness.

The revivalism of the early nineteenth century would thus be related to the impoverishment and disheartenment of those who had been forced to seek new homes in the wilderness. Its reappearance today in this college town is to be explained in large part by the suffering and privation to which working-class families have been subjected by reason of the hard times in the stone industry. It is religion of the type which tends to appear spontaneously wherever men are grappling desperately with the issues of spiritual life and death. Such religion is rooted in the creative forces latent in struggling humanity. It is a manifestation of nature's power to heal in the face of overwhelming difficulties. Its primary concern is release from the sense of sin and guilt. It finds the solution in the acceptance of personal responsibility and emotional identification with a fellowship conceived as universal and abiding. The individual who has that experience is thereby given a role in a great world-drama. He finds a new purpose in life and goes forth with a contagious enthusiasm which communicates itself to other individuals. The group is thus formed on the basis of a shared experience, and it grows of itself through the zeal of its converts.

It is characteristic of this type of religion that it tends to break down old culture patterns and to create new social alignments. In a recent study of the Holy Roller cults I have reported the case of an intelligent, well-educated, economically well-to-do white man who received the "baptism of the Spirit" and identified himself with a Negro Holy Roller group. This is not an isolated case. Whites are not infrequently found in Negro Holy Roller meetings, and sometimes Negroes are welcomed in white groups of the Pentecostal variety. Apparently, the mystical experience means a new social identification, which tends to create new values and to break across the lines of class and caste, even lines so fixed as those which separate the Negroes from the whites. We may therefore say that the revivalism of the early part of the nineteenth century served as a solvent to many old social formations and that it was instrumental in creating a new culture suited to the pioneer conditions of the Middle West. . . .

❖ 63 ❖

TIME ON OUR HANDS

Russell Lynes

The shorter work week and the extensive development of mechanical devices to ease the burden of our daily tasks have made possible much more opportunity for leisure-time activities. Man's adjustment to this change is only now beginning to be studied by sociologists. It is a subject deserving serious attention, and this article by Russell Lynes describes some of the consequences of poorly conceived use of this newfound resource of "time." He then moves to a special plea for intellectually challenging activities as the best means to make leisure most rewarding.

Recently I discovered among some papers that my mother had stowed away in a deserted file a clipping from a magazine of the 1920s. It was headed "Schedule for a One-Maid House." The house, it said, "has seven

SOURCE: Russell Lynes, "Time on Our Hands," *Harper's Magazine*, Vol. 217, No. 1298 (July, 1958), 34–39. Copyright © 1958, by Harper's Magazine, Inc. Reprinted by permission of the author. ❖ The author is Managing Editor of *Harper's Magazine*. An astute literary interpreter of sociological phenomena, he has written *Highbrow, Lowbrow, Middlebrow; Snobs; Tastemakers;* and *A Surfeit of Honey*.

rooms; a living-room, dining-room, porch, kitchen, maid's room and bath, three bedrooms, and two baths." The schedule starts with:

6:45 A.M. *Wash and Dress*

and ends with:

8:00 P.M. *Plans for the evening will be adapted to the household convenience.*

Bridget, if that was her name, was busy in the intervening hours with cleaning, cooking, bed-making, baking, and polishing silver and brass. Her respite came sometime between 1:30 and 3:00 P.M. when, according to the schedule, she was to "clear table, wash dishes, go to own room to rest, bathe, and change dress." At 3:00 she was back in the kitchen, "ready to answer door, etc."

Leisure was not much of a problem for Bridget at work in a one-maid house. Her schedule covers six days (on Saturday it says: "Bake cake for Sunday") and like everyone else she had Sunday as her only day off. (She doesn't seem to have had "maid's night out" on the customary Thursday.)

The familiar picture of the maid on her day off was of a girl dressed "fit to kill" on her way to meet her friends at church. The equally familiar picture of the man of the house was father asleep in a hammock buried under the Sunday paper. Leisure in those days was merely a restorative for work. Now leisure has become work in its own right . . . and a worry to lots of earnest Americans.

Last year at the commencement exercises at New York University a clergyman said to the graduating class: "America can be undone by her misuse of leisure. Life is getting easier physically, and this makes life harder morally."

There are, of course, a great many professional and business men who wonder what all this talk about leisure is: somehow it is no problem to them—or so they think. There are also a good many women, especially young married women, who would give their heirlooms for a few minutes to themselves. They have only to wait.

But leisure is making some thoughtful people uneasy. In January the American Council of Churches met in Columbus to discuss the spare time of our increasingly urbanized populace. The Twentieth Century Fund is deep in an investigation of leisure and the University of Chicago is (with the help of Ford Foundation funds) making a study of the nature of leisure and how people use it. Corporations not only worry about the leisure of their employees; they do something about it. Schoolteachers and social workers and local politicians worry about it, about footloose youngsters, about long summer vacations for teen-agers, and about juvenile delinquency. City planners, safety experts, highway engineers watch the growing number of hours when families are not at work and feel they have to go somewhere. Where? To what extent is the boredom of leisure responsible for young drug addicts, for the common cold, for muggings on city streets?

Every new scientific development, whether it is aimed at saving our skins or washing our dishes, leads in one way or another to reducing still further the sweat of the public brow. The four-day week which looms on the immediate horizon (and which causes such consternation in the corporate breast) is, of course, less the product of labor's demands than of manufacturing genius. Machines not men have created the three-day weekend.

✧   ✧   ✧   ✧   ✧

How to Keep the Idle Rich from Committing Suicide

But these efforts to sponge up the ocean of the so-called leisure time which has engulfed us can only put a few drops in the bucket. The truth is that while the new leisure has come on us fairly gradually, it has found us not at all prepared. If we are to cope agreeably with it, we are going to have to change our minds about some shibboleths and even some rather basic beliefs. To do this, we need to understand what has happened to the pattern of our leisure and where it is likely to lead.

Leisure is not a new problem born of automation, but it is a new problem for a great many kinds of people who were never much concerned with it when Bridget was working her seventy- or eighty-hour week in the one-maid house. America has had a leisure class since the industrialization of our country began, and in the 1850s the art critic James Jackson Jarves complained in shocked tones of the number of scions of wealthy families who threw themselves into rivers because they were so bored that life seemed not worth living. (Mr. Jarves wanted to interest such young men in the arts as a suitable outlet for their energies and money.) These young men, whom we would call the idle rich, had on a large scale the same problem that nearly everybody in America has today on a small scale. In its simplest terms, the primary problem of leisure is how to avoid boredom.

We used to be more accomplished at being bored than we are today, or at least we seem to have taken boredom with better grace in the days of party calls and decorous parlor games. We assumed a high moral tone toward leisure, and in some respects this tone persists. "The devil finds work for idle hands," our parents said and shook their heads; and when they said, "All work and no play makes Jack a dull boy," they meant, of course, that Jack should work most of the time but not quite all of it. Primarily leisure was thought of as a way to get a man back on his feet so that after Sunday he could put in sixty or so productive hours from Monday through Saturday. Leisure for women (few women in those days had jobs) was something quite else—it was the custody of culture and good works. Women in their spare time were expected to cultivate the arts, foster the education of their children, and play the role of Lady Bountiful in the community.

It was a neat division of family functions and a tidy way of life. Father's leisure was restorative; mother's was extremely productive. But more has changed than just the roles of men and women; the whole complex machinery of leisure has changed.

Briefly the changes are these:

In the last few decades what had started about a century ago as a trickle of people from the country and small towns to the cities became a torrent. Cities filled like cisterns and overflowed into suburbs, and as we shifted from a predominantly agricultural economy to a predominantly industrial one, we changed the nature of much of our leisure from what might be called a natural one to an artificial one, from pleasures provided by nature to pleasures concocted by man. Ways of using leisure began to come in packages—in cars, in movies, in radios, and most recently in television sets, and what was once the sauce only for the city goose became the sauce for the country gander as well. City culture is now within easy reach of everyone everywhere and everyone has the same access to talent that only a few decades ago used to be reserved for the rich and the urbane.

During the time when we were changing from a rural to an urban culture, the length of the work-week fell from sixty hours or more to forty or thirty-five. Gradually the five-day week became an almost universal reality, and the four-day week is on the immediate horizon. With more leisure time, men have, quite naturally, taken on some of the household chores that only a short while ago they wouldn't have been caught dead at, and have assumed some of the cultural responsibilities which were once the domain of their wives. They have also, with time on their hands and cars at their disposal, turned again to many kinds of rural recreation . . . to fishing and hunting especially, but also to sailing and skiing. The most solitary of all sports, fishing, is also the most popular of all sports with American men.

The Cash Value of the Devil's Work

But the greatest assault on old patterns of leisure and on the shibboleths about devil's work for idle hands, has been industry's discovery that it needs the consuming time of workers as much as it needs their producing time. In an economy geared as ours is to making life comfortable for everyone, it is essential to business that people have time to enjoy their comfort and to use up the things that make life comfortable.

A tremendous part of our production plant is committed to promoting leisure—to automobiles, to television sets, to time-saving gadgets, to sports equipment, and to hundreds of services which are unnecessary to life but which contribute to relaxed living. Our economy, in other words, is more and more involved with Time Off. Think of the industries, the purveyors of pleasure, that would collapse if we were to go back to the sixty-hour week. It looks as though we were far more likely (and not because of pressures from labor but the demands of technology and automation) to go to a twenty-eight hour week.

Urbanization, the shorter working day and week, and the changing roles of the sexes have, heaven knows, produced tremendous changes in the ways Americans live. But the premium put on the consuming time of the worker by our economic system presents us with a tidily packaged moral dilemma. When idleness is a public virtue, what becomes of the moral value of work? What are we going to substitute for the old adages on which we were brought up? What are we going to tell our children? What will happen to the economy if we go on saying that virtue is its own reward, that work is good for the soul, and that leisure is only a reward for toil? What happens to the Calvinist ethic?

This is a problem I would rather refer to a dilettante than to an economist or a clergyman or certainly to an engineer. The economist would consider it from the point of view of wealth, the clergyman of the after life, and the engineer of production. The dilettante can be counted on to look at it from the point of view of life, liberty, and especially the pursuit of happiness.

A Special Kind of Lover

I would like to contend in all seriousness, at this moment when there is such a cry for engineers and when our theological seminaries are bursting at the doors, that what we need is more dilettantes. Compared with good dilettantes, good engineers and good clergymen are a dime a dozen. Every newspaper account of the engineering shortage is contradicted by another story of how big corporations are hoarding engineers the way people hoarded butter during the last war. Recently, Dr. Robert J. Havighurst of the University of Chicago made it quite clear that the number of engineers and technologists being trained in our technical schools is more than adequate to our needs; the shortage, he said, is in good teachers. In the long run our civilization will be measured more accurately by our know-why than by our know-how.

It is probably because in the triumvirate of our ideals—life, liberty, and the pursuit of happiness—the last of these has always seemed to our Calvinist society rather naughty, that we have come to look down our noses at the dilettante. We have dismissed him as a trifler: we have despised him as a parasite on other people's work, the fritterer, the gadfly. But there was a time when the word dilettante was by no means the term of opprobrium it has become.

Originally *dilettante* meant a lover of the fine arts (it comes from the Latin word for delight) and it was used to distinguish the consumer from the producer. Its application spread beyond the arts in England, and in the eighteenth century the Society of the Dilettanti was a club of influential men interested not only in the arts but in the sciences and in archaeology. It meant the man of intellectual curiosity who devoted part of his time to the intelligent cultivation of the arts and sciences, to the resources of leisure and the satisfactions of the mind.

If you transplant the idea of the eighteenth-century dilettante from England to America, you discover that he was Thomas Jefferson and Benjamin Franklin—one a farmer who dabbled in architecture and introduced a new style to America, the other a printer who dabbled in natural science and flew a kite into a thunderstorm. You discover several others who got together and started a talkfest and became the Philosophical Society of Philadelphia, and others who, dabbling in the arts, somehow founded a string of distinguished museums across the nation and filled them with masterpieces, and, of course, a good many bad guesses. These men were dilettantes. There is no other word that fits them.

❖   ❖   ❖   ❖   ❖

. . . What we need in our society, I contend again, is more real dilettantes, and we need to extend the meaning of the word to many delights besides the arts and sciences.

The dilettante is just a consumer. He is a man who takes the pursuit of happiness seriously, not frivolously, and he works at it. He is part sensualist, part intellectual, and part enthusiast. He is also likely to be a proselytizer for those causes in which his interests are involved, and to be rather scornful of those people who do not take their pleasures seriously and who are passive instead of active in the cultivation of them. But whatever else he may be he is not lazy. He may or may not have a job that he finds interesting, but he does not use his leisure in a miscellaneous and undirected fashion. He knows what he wants out of life and will go to a lot of trouble to get it. Primarily, in Voltaire's sense, he wants to cultivate his own garden.

The Crank on Quality

You will find dilettantes everywhere and in every aspect of our culture. I found one a few weeks ago driving a taxi in New York. He was a man in his early sixties.

"I only drive this hack three days a week," he said. "The other four days I go fishing. I like to fish and I'm pretty good at it."

By the time he had delivered me home I knew what he fished for at what times of year, what bait he used and where and in what weather, and which were the best fishing boats and captains going out of New York harbor. I asked him what he did with all the fish he caught.

"I got a son-in-law runs a saloon," he said. "I give them to his customers."

Probably the most common and in some ways the most accomplished of American dilettantes is the baseball fan, though the national pastime is being crowded out of its position as top banana of entertainment these days by serious music. The baseball fan knows his subject with something very close to genuine scholarship. He is an expert in the minutiae of its history and understands the nuances and subtleties of its performance. He takes as much pleasure from the refinements of its details as from the outcome of any single game, and he enjoys the company of others with whom he can argue the relative virtues of performance and make comparisons with other similar situations. He demands skill on the field of a truly professional caliber, and he lets his displeasure with anything less be known in the most direct and uncompromising manner. He is, by and large, a less tolerant dilettante than the one whose interest is devoted to art, for his expert eye is less subject to changes in fashion. Unquestionably without him the standards of baseball would long since have gone to pot.

The simple fact is that the dilettante is the ideal consumer, not ideal, perhaps, from the point of view of those producers who would like their customers to accept their products with blind confidence, but ideal from the point of view of maintaining standards of quality . . . whether material or cultural. He takes his functions as a consumer seriously. He takes the trouble to know what he likes and to sort out the shoddy and the meretricious from the sound and reasonable. If he is a dilettante of music, for example, he demands the best performance from his record-player. He is unimpressed by an imitation mahogany cabinet in the Chippendale manner, but he knows that the components of his hi-fi equipment are the very best that he can afford. (He can, in fact, be credited with the very great improvement in mass-produced sound equipment; it was his interest in high-fidelity that spread the word to the general public and raised the level of public acceptance.)

We are likely to associate the dilettante only with the arts, which is one reason why he has such a bad name in America. In the rambunctious and expansive days of the nineteenth century when America was growing and fighting its way across the continent, toil was man's business; culture was left to women. So were most other refinements of life, and the arts were thought of as sissy and men who showed any interest in them as something less than virile. A man who didn't sleep through a concert or an opera was regarded with suspicion. It was only when a man retired from business that it was considered suitable for him to spend his money on art—not necessarily because he liked it or knew anything about it but because it gave him social prestige. Except in a few Eastern Seaboard cities, the arts were women's work, and there was no time and place for the dilettante.

The Ascent of Babbitt

The nature of our new-found leisure is rapidly changing the old stereo-types. The businessman who doesn't make some pretense at an interest in culture, who doesn't support the local symphony and museum, who isn't on the library board or out raising money for his college is looked upon as not doing his duty, much less serving his own interests. Babbitt isn't Babbitt any more. Babbitt is by way of becoming a dilettante. A lot worse things could happen to him. In no time at all being a dilettante will not be considered un-American.

The point at which the dilettante becomes an "expert" but not a "pro-fessional" is an indistinct one. Two successful businessmen who have, in their leisure time, become naturalists of considerable reputation are an officer of J. P. Morgan & Co., R. Gordon Wasson, who has recently pro-duced an important book of original research on mushrooms, and Boughton Cobb, a textile manufacturer who is one of the world's leading authorities on ferns. A few years ago an ancient language known to scholars as "Minoan Linear B" that had had scholars completely at sea for years was "broken" by an English architect, Michael Ventris, for whom cryptanalysis was a leisure activity. These three men became experts, not professionals, dilet-tantes in the best sense, not amateurs.

Obviously not many men in any generation are going to be able to extend their leisure activities to such levels of distinction. But leisure with-out direction, without the satisfaction of accomplishment of some sort is debilitating to anyone brought up in an atmosphere, like ours, in which the virtues of work have been so long extolled and are so deeply imbedded in our mythology. The greatest satisfaction of the dilettante is not in doing but in discovering, in discriminating, and in enjoying the fruits of his knowledge and his taste.

There will, of course, always be those who can only find satisfaction in making something, the eternal do-it-yourselfers, the cabinetmakers, and needlepointers, and gardeners, and model builders, and rug hookers. These are the amateur craftsmen who often achieve professional competence. There are also those who will find their only satisfactions apart from work in sensuous pleasures, in sports, and food and drink, and love. The dilet-tante finds his satisfactions primarily in the mind. He is the ideal traveler, the perfect audience, the coveted reader, and the perceptive collector.

Is He a Highbrow?

But he is not by any means necessarily a highbrow. Indeed the ideal dilettante is not. He may be a professional intellectual or he may not, but he does not pose as what he isn't. His tastes and his knowledge may well run to abstruse and esoteric things, to the dances of Tibet or the jewelry of pre-Columbian Mexico, but they may just as well run to the square dance and baseball cards. The dilettante of jazz, the man who knows the names of the instrumentalists in all of the great bands of the last thirty years, is as important a dilettante as the man who knows his Mozart by Koechel numbers. It is genuine, not simulated, enthusiasm that counts. The function of the dilettante is to encourage a high degree of performance in whatever field of interest happens to be his, to be an informed, but by no means conventional, critic, and to be a watchdog. He must be both an enthusiast and irritant who will praise what measures up to his standards and needle producers into doing as well as they know how, and better. He is an incorrigible asker of hard questions. He keeps controversy in our culture alive, and if he is sometimes proved to be dead wrong, he is at least never dead on his feet. He is the want-to-know-why man and the traditional anathema of the know-how man.

Several months ago I found myself in an argument, or the beginnings of one, in a radio interview with a well-known broadcaster. "Our colleges need to produce more and better trained men," he said, and I countered with the suggestion that they needed to produce better educated men. "We need experts," he said.

"We need dilettantes," I replied, and the word so surprised him that he gingerly changed the subject to safer ground.

I would like to change my position, but only slightly. What we need are trained men with the capacity for being dilettantes. There can be no argument with the fact that an industrialized society must have a great many highly trained men and women with specialized knowledge and skills. But in this country the consumers and the producers are the same people; all of us work both sides of the economic street. We are, the great majority of us, the part-time idle rich, and no nation, so far as I know, has ever found itself in such a position before. Ours is a society in which no man's nose need be permanently to the grindstone, and where every man is a potential dilettante.

We have thought of our know-how as our most exportable commodity, and when somebody else demonstrated, moon-fashion, a superior know-how, we took it as a blow to our "national prestige." In fact our most exportable commodity has been a cultural one, a way of life that balances work and leisure for almost everyone and distributes the fruits of labor with astonishing, if not complete, evenness. Our most effective know-how has been in the production of leisure, a commodity filled with promise and booby traps. It is the engineer with his slide rule who knows how to produce leisure, but it is the dilettante who knows how to use it and make it productive.

It will be as dilettantes and consumers that we will, in the long run, determine the quality of our culture. We will determine not only the gadgets of our civilization but the fate of its arts as well. We will determine whether the pursuit of happiness has, after all, been worth it.

THE FUNCTION OF THE ORCHESTRA
IN COMMUNITY AND NATION

John H. Mueller

Leisure takes a variety of institutionalized forms in any society. One of these is the symphony orchestra. In this selection J. H. Mueller shows the particular way in which certain musical arts are institutionalized in American society. His analysis demonstrates how the functional approach to social phenomena (described and used by Merton in selection 4) can often lead to insights which would be denied to those ignoring the sociocultural setting within which an activity takes place.

The symphony concert is not exclusively, nor in one sense primarily, a musical event. For, so complex and inseparable are human interests, that every social occurrence is a blended experience of varied and simultaneous motives. A concert is comparable, perhaps, to a dinner party, where the interest in food may be subordinated to business contacts, social prestige, ceremonial display, or mere convivial association. No hostess would be flattered to be assured merely that the food was nutritious, nor even that it was tastily served; for such an affair has well-accepted ramifications into many other avenues of social intercourse. A symphony concert is similarly a pluralistic event, which may supply an outlet for fashion, prestige, civic pride, heightened national consciousness, as well as musical delight. It is therefore no disparagement, but a psychological and sociological truth, that music is often secondary to nonmusical considerations.

Since music, too, is laden with these derivative functions, which vary considerably in character and proportion from person to person, the quality and meaning of "enjoyment" of a concert displays a wide range of variation in different epochs. When, for example, we reflect on the strenuous content of our recent and contemporary symphony programs, the awe in which the masterpieces are held, the reluctance with which the audience pits its taste and judgment against that of the critic and conductor, and the frankly tentative and reserved judgments of the critics themselves, it is difficult for the modern patron to realize that in the classic period, often

SOURCE: From *The American Symphony Orchestra* by John H. Mueller, published by Indiana University Press. Reprinted by permission. ✦ John H. Mueller (1895–1965) was chairman of the Department of Sociology, Indiana University, from 1953 to 1960. He is the author of *The American Symphony Orchestra: A Social History of Musical Taste*, and the coauthor of *Music and Education: A Sociological Approach* and *Statistical Reasoning in Sociology*.

called the "golden age," music was generally considered a matter of sheer pleasure, a forthright delectation of the senses, without any pretense of satisfactions of a more edifying nature. It is quite evident from Mozart's letters that he contemplated very little beyond the pleasure of the moment and harbored no conceit about the sacredness of his scores.

Although much of Mozart's music is still played and enjoyed today, his guileless conception of its function has suffered eclipse, for the typical aesthetician of the romantic nineteenth century (descended, however, from eighteenth century antecedents) held in scorn the theory that music is made merely for pleasure. In fact, it need not even be beautiful. In reviewing Sibelius' Second Symphony, the late Richard Aldrich, then of the *New York Times*, expressed that notion as follows:

There is absolutely nothing in this symphony that is written to please the ear as many wish to be pleased. There is much that sounds chaotic and disordered; but it is evident to the listener who can take a larger measure of it, that it is all very definitely related, the coherent expression of a consistent idea. It is not too much to say that this Second Symphony of Sibelius is one of the strongest compositions in the symphonic form that have been heard in a considerable period.

Such a sanction for what was then cerebral cacophony would have been inconceivable to Haydn, Mozart, Beethoven, and their contemporaries. Mozart, Handel, and Bach had great difficulty in producing music in sufficient volume and at a rate to satisfy the honest appetite for novelty on the part of their audiences, while today a novelty is something the modern audience is expected to endure for the sake of possible habituation and future delight. To explain this complete reversal in the conception of the psychological function of the repertoire, in the criterion of aesthetic judgment, and in the relation between the artist and his public, one must examine the intervening period: the nineteenth century and its Romantic revolt.

The shift is largely attributable to the complete sociological metamorphosis of the audience and of the social status of the musician. During the previous century, the pre-Napoleonic era, the musician had been an employee, who performed a skilled service according to contractual obligations—analogous to the twentieth-century staff musicians in a radio or motion picture studio, allowing, of course, for the divergent requirements of the period and the much greater sense of social stratification than now prevails. His secular audience consisted primarily of the nobility, many of whom were themselves adequate performers, and who sometimes arrogated to themselves the privilege of joining the orchestra. Some even utilized their leisure moments for composing. In fact, as late as 1905 Breitkopf and Haertel published a catalogue of compositions by German royalty, including Kaiser Wilhelm—which serves to recall the piquant warning attributed to Brahms that "one should never criticize the compositions of royalty, for you never know who may have written them."

Composers were craftsmen who composed to order and who, like the architect, the portrait painter and the cook, expected their work to be appreciated forthwith. It would not have occurred to Bach, Mozart, Haydn, and the other *Kapellmeistern* of the day to ignore the interest of the current generation by writing *Zukunftsmusik*, nor could they have had the temerity to expect their socially superior patrons to sit through repeated hearings of a suite or symphony on the chance that they or their descendants might possibly enjoy it at some future time. The liveried Haydn admitted that he experimented, but such experimentation was mild and inoffensive, and therefore tolerated and even enjoyed by the prince whom he was paid to serve.

By the turn of the eighteenth century, a social and political transformation had occurred with rather dramatic suddenness, as historical events go. In the history of music this consisted in the catastrophic bankruptcy, and consequent decline in power, of the musician's two richest employers: the church and the court. To gratify those who feel that they must pinpoint evolving historical events, one may suggest that it was the bombardment of Vienna in 1809, sheltering at once the aged Haydn, the middle-aged Beethoven, and the twelve-year-old Schubert, which actually and symbolically gave the *coup de grâce* to the feudal era and marked the transition from the old order to the new. The musician lost his job and became a free-lance composer and an itinerant performer, with all the risks appertaining thereto.

His audience was no longer the closed group of cultivated nobles and their leisurely satellites, before whom the composer was honored to display his accomplishments. Instead, the nineteenth century performer now served the emerging middle-class audience, the third estate, in a commercialized concert to which anyone had access who was able and willing to pay the price of admission. In this new pecuniary social order, the bourgeois audience was not sophisticated, nor well-schooled; but it was ready to be impressed by the virtuosity and the eccentricities of a Paganini, a Liszt, and a host of other virtuosi who mushroomed from that soil. Instead, therefore, of an attitude of reverence and awe on the part of the musician toward his noble audience, it was now the audience which sat in bewilderment before the musician. The artist, in fact, held his audience—his new patrons—in disdain for its crude and undeveloped aesthetic tastes. In art the customer was never right. The mass of anonymous urbanites, newly hatched under the wings of the industrial revolution, issued from office and shop, from banks and colleges, from the professions and public services. Occupied, as they were, full time in gaining a livelihood from the new competitive world, they were by no means a leisure class, they felt keenly their inadequacies in the arts, and acquired a veritable inferiority complex in their presence. They suffer from this debilitating affliction to this very day. They eagerly emulated the standards of the decaying, but still glamorous, aristocracy by cultivating and supporting the arts, and stood ready to be instructed.

Now, if the audience generated by the bourgeois social revolution thus drew away from the artist, the artist on his part also drew away from the audience. Being no longer in the immediate employ of a master whom he was being paid to serve, he developed a sense of autonomy and self-expression in standards of composition as well as in interpretation and execution. The artist even erected an ivory tower where he could commune with his aesthetic conscience and protect himself from any insinuation of being responsible to the audience.

The evolutionary development of the musical arts abetted the artist in his new independence. Orchestral instruments were being improved, orchestras were being enlarged, and composition was becoming more difficult and esoteric. Beethoven's orchestral scores looked "so black" that they literally sounded the death-knell of the amateur player-cooks who had infested the mixed ensembles during the courtly era. Music was now becoming a learned profession which a lifetime was too short to master. Art was really long, and time fleeting. Liszt and Mendelssohn contributed enormously to the enhancement of the prestige of the once lowly profession. As a consequence of these social and technical revolutions, the artistic gap between audience and musician, which had been negligible a generation or two before, was now widening; and the evident explanation was to be sought not only in musical terms, but still more significantly in terms of the social, economic, political, and technological changes unfolding during that period. It is only against such a social background that the problems of the contemporary "heavy" repertoire can be comprehended.

Synchronized with these social changes, philosophers, as is their wont and function, were drafting a system of thought designed to rationalize and buttress these overt historical trends, which were rendering music incomprehensible even to an intelligent audience. By an evolution too complex to rehearse at this point, music was elevated to the most exalted position among the arts; and in its unfettered creativeness, it approximated "pure spirit," universal and absolute Truth. Because of its mystical and supernatural characteristic, it possessed the power to exert a spiritual and ethical influence upon its auditors superior to that of any other medium. Such neo-Platonic doctrines of Hegel and Schopenhauer inevitably placed the great musician in a position of ethical leadership, conferred a certain sacrosanct validity on his "inspiration," and elevated him into the realms of near-infallibility. Music, the most exalted art, was not only a reflection of ultimate ideas and sentiments, but was actually a form of thinking in tones—an abstract, subtle, and direct communication superior to crude verbal symbols, independent of the physical actualities of the world, and therefore a "universal" language. The inspiration of the artist was thus of higher validity than the uninstructed taste of otherwise intelligent people. This was the ideology propagated by such philosophers as Schopenhauer, whose concepts dominated his disciple, Richard Wagner.

This dogma of artistic supremacy was imported to the United States from Germany in the baggage of musicians and conductors, and has set the standards for the musical repertoire to this very day. Indeed, in this country, where vertical mobility was much more rapid than in Europe, where class relations were elastic, where wealth was easier to come by, and the middle class musically unsophisticated, the musical gap was probably still wider than in the old country. Precisely because of this, the conductors assumed, and were given, greater latitude and freedom in America than in Europe. The programs in Boston and Chicago were much more radical—or "progressive"—than they ever were in London, Vienna, Leipzig, and Berlin, both in relation to the maturity of the audience and in absolute terms, as far as the latter can be measured.

It is not at all obvious, nor even probable, that the industrial philanthropists, who liquidated the deficits incurred by Theodore Thomas, Gericke, Mahler, and Stokowski, necessarily shared these mystical convictions with the crusading conductors whom they sponsored. Some were indeed musical and philosophical dilettantes, while many of them were downright metaphysical illiterates and calculating businessmen to whom the ethical import of the Beethoven Third probably did not make much sense. However, in the meantime, the orchestra, with its conductor and esoteric programs, had achieved a certain prestige and glamour. Like fine churches, public buildings, and parks, it soon became an element in the complete apparatus of civic life which focused not unwelcome attention upon the community, and consequently deserved support. Such "tycoon" pride was characteristically expressed by the orator of the occasion at the dedication of Orchestra Hall, December 14, 1904:

Chicago has been the most public spirited city in the world. We are proud of our rapid growth in wealth and population, but we are not satisfied with the merely industrial growth of our city—we demand something more and something better. We look through the dust and smoke of Chicago as she is, to see the fair and noble form of our city as she will be, a center of influence, intellectual and artistic as well as industrial, a school for the nation, as Pericles declared Athens was the school for Greece.

Intercity rivalry was a constant factor that stimulated audience, management, and conductors. Even the idealistic Thomas used this motif on his rebellious constituents in defense of his uncompromising stand on program construction:

The announcement of a symphony on the program was enough to keep many people from the concert. . . . When fault was found with the severity of the programs I would say: Do you wish our program to be inferior in standard to those of the Boston Orchestra? "No" was the answer . . .

That an orchestra had merit as an investment that would redound to the economic benefit of a city was a frequent theme. It was agreed, however, that a city's musical life serves as an enticement to visitors and settlers, and the tours of the orchestra are considered favorable publicity. In one instance, the orchestra was declared to be a force in "helping to sell shoes" for the greatest shoe center in the country.

There are many who are neither sensitive to the supposed ethical overtones of a symphony, nor concerned with the commercial potentialities of a fine civic orchestra, but whose private social ambitions are gratified by indulgence in such an honorific enterprise. These impulses manifest themselves in diverse ways: maintenance of boxes or other preferred locations in the auditorium; program listing as patron; socially exclusive erudition on matters artistic; all the subtle satisfactions accruing from the wide range of contact and intimacy with a fashionable concern, from the occasional ticket purchaser to the confidential relation with conductor and steering members of the board, with all its invidious prestige. The concert-hall box has now all but disappeared in the relentless democratization of audience and patrons. But it once reflected the highly prized perquisite of the social elite. The private corridor and the anteroom, which conferred a sense of aloof distinction, translated the symphony and opera into a social ritual more highly regarded than the aesthetic relaxation derived from the actual music, which, in fact, was often sacrificed.

Musical politics may run deep, and orchestras have at times been a "football of society." With motives something less than sublime, various groups have often rallied around rival conductors, thus literally splitting the resources of the community to the detriment of higher values. On occasion, however, such competition has had its salutary moments. Witness the case of the prolonged feud between the followers of Damrosch and Thomas in New York, during which two orchestras challenged each other for supremacy. But in other less inspiring circumstances, two orchestras have been supported when nourishment was insufficient for one. That pioneer period has, in general, passed. Though factions will always exist, funds are not nowadays so plentiful as to permit the luxury of such wasteful competition.

Since 1893, when Walter Damrosch first organized them, many of the responsibilities for carrying on orchestral affairs have fallen to the ladies, whose efforts have proven indispensable to the solvency of the harassed orchestral institution. Largely for the benefit of the fashionable world, the matinee concerts (usually Friday afternoon) are maintained. Originally instituted by the New York Philharmonic as a public rehearsal which would offer bargain rates to students, musicians, or others who might wish to hear repeated performances, these matinee programs have long since graduated into more or less exclusive afternoon affairs, constituting an integral part of the winter social season. In Boston and Philadelphia, where this "Friday Spell" exerts its full potency, this particular division of the audience into two segments has been profitable, for the house is sold out. However, in other cities, for various reasons, the Friday patronage, though involving a similar principle, has for some time been hardly sufficient in volume to persuade the management that the retention of the traditional weekday matinee was practicable. History may be repeating itself, for the economic aristocracy today, analogously to the feudal aristocracy of 150 years ago, is declining in power and is relaxing its control over our artistic institutions. Musically this may mean a popularization of the repertoire and a significant alteration in the role played by the orchestra in its community relations. . . .

* 65 *

THE PAINS OF A NEW IDEA

Shirley Basch

Although social institutions have great stability, sometimes amounting to the rigidity that the pioneer sociologist Edward A. Ross called "ossification," this does not mean that they never change. They do change, but not easily, nor without pain. A dramatic recent example was the enactment in late 1965 of federal legislation providing national health insurance benefits, popularly known as "Medicare," to older Americans. This law was passed despite decades of well financed, sophisticated, organized, nationwide opposition by the American Medical Association. But the basic point of the following selection remains valid and significant even though, with the passage of Medicare, the situation is drastically different now. The same arguments and impassioned language were used a century ago to oppose tax-supported education by those who feared institutional changes as are now being used to oppose tax-supported medical care.

Americans a century ago were fiercely divided on the question of tax supported education for all children. No punches were pulled. The opponents had ten main arguments and in flowing oratory they presented them.

History seems to be running the film over again today. Americans once more have two different opinions, this time on national health insurance. The fight is on, no punches are pulled, and once more the oratory is loud and passionate.

SOURCE: *Survey Graphic*, Vol. 84 (February, 1948), 78–79. Reprinted by permission of the author and the publisher. ✦ At the time this selection was written, the author's husband was a physician in the United States Public Health Service.

The strange thing is that the current arguments are exactly the same as those of a hundred years ago. And they are presented in almost exactly the same words! Then it was the public's education, today it is the public's health. That seems to be the only difference. The record speaks for itself. The quotations in the column to the left, with one exception, are from the *Philadelphia National Gazette*, 1830, those at the right from recent writings and speeches.

| UNIVERSAL EDUCATION | NATIONAL HEALTH INSURANCE |

1. Only Those Who Can Pay Have a Right to It

"Literature cannot be acquired without leisure, and wealth gives leisure. . . . The 'peasant' must labor during those hours of the day, which his wealthy neighbor can give to the abstract culture of his mind; otherwise the earth would not yield enough for the subsistence of all. Languor, decay, poverty, discontent would soon be visible among all classes."

"This attitude arose, in part from the false premise that it is a function of government or philanthropy to '*give* health to the people' whereas in truth, health, like freedom and wealth, cannot be given, but must be earned. . . . The assumption that people have a 'right' to health is as false as the notion that everyone is entitled to freedom from want. Nothing could be more viciously destructive of initiative, effort and progress. Health is a privilege, not a right. . . ."—*Edward J. Stieglitz, M.D. in "A Future for Preventive Medicine." 1945*

2. The Idea Is Foreign to Our Country

"Some of the writers about universal public instruction and discipline seem to forget the constitution of modern society and declaim as if our communities could receive institutions . . . like those of Sparta. . . . No government, no statesman, no philanthropist can furnish what is incompatible with the very . . . being of civil society."

"In my view we need look no further for evidence that this legislation embodies proposals which find no roots in the soil of free America. . . . The system here proposed is alien to the deepest instincts of the American people."—*National Physicians Committee in "Compulsion the Key to Collectivism." 1946*

3. It Should Be Left to Private Enterprise

"Education generally, to be effective, must be left to the enterprise and competition of individuals, to the sagacity and liberality of parents, and to the efforts of enlightened associations."

"I believe that the whole business of teaching school should be thrown

"All these activities demonstrate that an effort is being made to change radically the free system of caring for the sick as we have always known it. The broad purpose is nothing less than the shifting of responsibility from its threefold traditional base—the individual, the medical profession, and the

open to private enterprise and free competition, just like . . . running a shoe factory." *From Zachery Montgomery in "The School Question." 1866*

local community—to the federal government and the states."—*From* The Nation's Business. *1940*

4. Government Must Not Concern Itself with It

"It is an old and sound remark that government cannot provide for the necessities of the people; that it is they who maintain the government, and not the latter the people. Education may be among their necessities; but it is one of that description which the State or National councils cannot supply except partially and in a limited degree."

"That the protection of the health of the citizen is a natural function of government is debatable. The best government is that which governs least, and all history persuades us that freedom is smothered by increasing government paternalism."—*L. S. Goin, M.D., California Medical Society, in the Twentieth Annual Debate Manual. 1946*

5. If Public Funds Support It, Political Bureaucracy Will Be Rampant

"In this country, nothing could prevent [public education] from becoming a political job, if a government concern."

"Shall patients and doctors retain their freedom of judgment in this matter of medical care or shall this freedom be surrendered to a federal bureaucracy?"—*H. H. Shoulders, M.D. in his 1946 presidential address to the American Medical Association*

6. Requiring People to Pay for Its Support Is Dangerous

"Authority—that is, the State—is to force the more eligibly situated citizens to contribute a part . . . of their means for the accommodation of the rest, and this is equivalent to the idea of an actual, compulsory partition of their substance. . . . We have no confidence in any compulsory equalizations."

"Compulsion is the key to Collectivism. If the Wagner-Murray-Dingell proposals were enacted into law they would introduce a compulsory tax to pay for a compulsory service—medical, dental, and nursing care—directly affecting the most vital and most sacred functions of each individual citizen of the United States."—*National Physicians Committee. 1946*

7. It Is "Agrarianism"—or "Socialism"

"The Scheme of Universal Equal Education at the expense of the State is virtually Agrarianism. It would be a compulsory application of the means of the richer for the direct use of the poorer classes."

"Such frauds like compulsory health insurance . . . anticipate the establishment of universal state medical service for everybody. That is socialism as unadulterated as if it came from the sanctified pen of Karl Marx himself."—*From* The Nation's Business. *1940*

8. It Will Destroy Initiative and Ambition

"One of the chief excitements to industry among the working classes is the hope of earning the means of educating their children respectably and liberally; that incentive would be removed, and the scheme of State and equal. education be thus a premium for comparative idleness, to be taken out of the pockets of the laborious and conscientious."

"Ambition is destroyed in a large percentage of the population when all the provisions of socialized medicine are put into effect. . . . The proposed bill . . . makes it possible for the government to take directly . . . earnings . . . of conscientious moral workmen . . . and give them to the lazy, shiftless, immoral individuals for sickness which they may have largely brought on themselves by riotous, immoral living."—*Edward H. Ochsner, M.D., Chicago Medical Society in 1946 Senate Committee hearings on a National Health Program*

9. It Will Lower Standards

"Universal Equal Education is impossible . . . unless the standard of education be greatly lowered and narrowed."

". . . any attempt to introduce compulsory health insurance in the United States . . . would inevitably result in a serious—even criminal—deterioration in the quality of medical care."—*National Physicians Committee. 1946*

10. It Is Best to Insure It Only for the Needy

"[State and National Governments] may endow public schools only for the indigent. . . . But to create or sustain seminaries for the tuition of all classes . . . is beyond their province and power."

"It is our recommendation that the Federal government consider some plan for aid to the states in taking care of those persons who cannot pay for it."—*Peter D. Ward, M.D., American Hospital Assn. in the Twentieth Annual Debate Manual. 1946*

And after all the smoke of the century-ago battle cleared away, we had the start of a public school system unsurpassed in the world. The dire predictions of its calamitous effect are now a shadowy memory.

CHAPTER VIII

Social Organization:

ECOLOGICAL

❖ 66 ❖

COMMUNITY AND ASSOCIATION

Robert M. MacIver

The nature of the modern state has been treated by Robert Mac-
Iver in three of his works. The groundwork for his approach to the
subject is suggested in the following article. When MacIver wrote
this, the modern totalitarian state with its dreadful tyrannies had
not yet appeared. Yet this sociological analysis of the nature of
community as distinguished from the state is so powerful a refuta-
tion of the governmental theories upon which totalitarianism is
based that one has difficulty believing it was not written after the
fact. The confusion of thought that identifies community as such
with its instrument, the state, is here exposed; and the results of
such identification are foreseen.

The General Relation of Community and Association

One of the greatest of the difficulties which at the present day beset
the social analyst is the confused nature of his vocabulary. Unlike the students of most other sciences he must accept the terms of everyday life.
These terms are lacking in all precision, and if the sociologist is to avoid
disaster he must not hesitate to refine them to his own purposes. This is
the case with the essential terms of our subject-matter, the terms society,
community, association, and State. The looseness with which these terms
are often used even by professed authorities is remarkable, and the results

SOURCE: *Community: A Sociology Study*, 22–28, Copyright 1924, 1928
by the Macmillan Company and used with their permission. ❖ Robert Mac-
Iver is Lieber Professor Emeritus of Political Philosophy and Sociology, Columbia University. He is a former president of the American Sociological
Association and the author of several books, among which are *Society: Its
Structure and Changes*, *The Web of Government*, and *Life: Its Dimensions
and Its Bounds*.

most unhappy. That must be our excuse if at the outset we insist, in spite of popular usage, on limiting each of these terms to a single and definite meaning.

Society, the most general term of all, I intend to use in a universal or generic sense to include every willed relationship of man to man. If, then, we distinguish community, association, and State from society, it must be by delimiting the former as special kinds or aspects of social fact. The essential distinction here involved, one of the utmost importance, is that between community and association.

By a community I mean any area of common life, village, or town, or district, or country, or even wider area. To deserve the name community, the area must be somehow distinguished from further areas, the common life may have some characteristic of its own such that the frontiers of the area have some meaning. All the laws of the cosmos, physical, biological, and psychological, conspire to bring it about that beings who live together shall resemble one another. Wherever men live together they develop in some kind and degree distinctive common characteristics—manners, traditions, modes of speech, and so on. These are the signs and consequences of an effective common life. It will be seen that a community may be part of a wider community, and that all community is a question of degree. For instance, the English residents in a foreign capital often live in an intimate community of their own, as well as in the wider community of the capital. It is a question of the degree and intensity of the common life. The one extreme is the whole world of men, one great but vague and incoherent common life. The other extreme is the small intense community within which the life of an ordinary individual is lived, a tiny nucleus of common life with a sometimes larger, sometimes smaller, and always varying fringe. Yet even the poorest in social relationships is a member in a chain of social contacts which stretches to the world's end. In the infinite series of social relationships which thus arise, we distinguish the nuclei of intenser common life, cities and nations and tribes, and think of them as *par excellence* communities.

An association is an organisation of social beings (or a body of social beings as *organised*) for the pursuit of some common interest or interests. It is a determinate social unity built upon common purpose. Every end which men seek is more easily attained for all when all whom it concerns unite to seek it, when all co-operate in seeking it. Thus you may have an association corresponding to every possible interest of social beings. Community bubbles into associations permanent and transient, and no student of the actual social life of the present can help being struck by the enormous number of associations of every kind, political, economic, religious, educational, scientific, artistic, literary, recreative, philanthropic, professional, which to-day more than ever before enrich communal life.

A community is a focus of social life, the common living of social beings; an association is an organisation of social life, definitely established for the pursuit of one or more common interests. An association is partial, a community is integral. The members of one association may be members of many other and distinct associations. Within a community there may exist not only numerous associations but also antagonistic associations. Men may associate for the least significant or for the most significant of purposes; the association may mean very much or very little to them, it may mean merely the excuse for a monthly dinner-party, or it may be the guardian of their dearest or highest interests—but community is something wider and freer than even the greatest associations; it is the greater common life out of which associations rise, into which associations bring order, but which associations never completely fulfil. If we reflect, we perceive at once that there is a vast difference between the living together of men which makes a village or city or country on the one hand, and the association of men in a church or trade-union—or even, as we shall see, in a State—on the other. Often state-areas do not even coincide with the areas of effective community, as, for instance, when a subject-people, incorporated in an alien State, continues to lead its own manner of life. A distinction of name is essential.

It may be well to show how infinitely associations vary in degree of permanence and significance, and the main reason of these variations, before we consider the relation to community of the most permanent and most comprehensive of all—the State.

Men may *mass* together without becoming organised. A mere aggregation is not an association. Take the case of a crowd casually collected to watch a fire. The aggregation serves no end, each individual of the crowd could watch the fire quite as well—better in fact—if the others went away. A common interest keeps them together, but it does not bind them to one another; it need bring no individual into social contact with any other. It is a physical and not a social contiguity. No association is dissolved when the fire burns out—or when the policeman moves the crowd away. But suppose the crowd had resolved to fight the fire and had organised themselves to that end. At once the aggregation would have been transformed into an association, its individuals would have fallen into social relations with one another, and the order which is attendant on social purpose would have permeated the whole. As soon as men see that any interest they share is furthered by organisation, they are preparing an association. So here an association would have come into being for an hour—and in an hour would have passed away.

Take next the case of men gathered to celebrate some occasion, say the centenary of some historical event. Here there is a purpose depending on and realised through association. The meeting-together is an essential element of the celebration. Time and place and procedure are predetermined; it is an organised association, not a casual aggregation. But the purpose may be only a trivial thing in the life of each member of the assemblage. It brings him into social contact, but a very transient and partial contact, with the rest. There is a consciousness of common interest realised in association, but it finds only a momentary expression. When the parade is over or the procession has passed, or the bonfire turned to ashes, or the dinner and the speeches are ended, the association dissolves. Because the purpose was transient, the association it created could not endure.

Consider next an association created for the achievement of some specific reform, political or religious, say for the passing of a bill or the formulation of a creed. Here a more permanent purpose animates the association, and works a deeper organisation. Each member of the association has a definite point of contact with every other. It is because each member has a certain individuality that he is a member. If he were different in a certain important way, he would not be a member. And in the association each holds a definite place, determined in part at least by his individuality. (For it is a general law of association that the deeper the purpose at work, the more complex becomes the organisation.) Yet since the purpose is specific and temporary, the association which pursues it pursues its own dissolution. When the bill is enacted or the creed formulated, in the fulfilment of its sustaining purpose the association itself dissolves. When slavery was abolished, the associations for the abolition of slavery were abolished also. Every such association dies of its success. Sometimes an association lives on when its primary purpose belongs to the past, becoming either a venerable relic, like, say, the Honourable Society of Fishmongers, or a social obstruction, like the Grand Army of the Republic.

Let us turn next to an association of a very different type, the association of marriage. The purpose on which this association rests is the deep foundation of all life, and that purpose is fulfilled not in the mere procreation of offspring and their tutelage until they attain the autonomy of manhood or womanhood. The profound purpose of the marriage-association includes the present as well as the future generations, and fulfils the lives of those who enter into it no less than it creates and develops the lives of those who issue from it. It is, therefore, a continuous and—unless perverted —permanent purpose of human life, and the association it creates is likewise continuous and permanent, strongly rooted in the heart of life.

Thus to a permanent purpose there always answers, in the nature of things, a permanent association. This appears still more clearly when we turn to such associations as Church and State. These rest on purposes more lasting than any individuals, and are thus maintained through periods of time infinitely larger than the life-periods of individuals. In so far as they are purposes necessary to the fulfilment of life, they create associations as immortal as life. And as the most enduring purposes are also those which grow and change the most, there is a continuous evolution of the greater associations.

Lastly, associations vary as much in extent as in permanence, and for the same reason. Wherever there is a character common to social beings, a common interest is implicit, an interest, that is, which can be furthered by organisation, by association. The extent of a common interest *should* measure the extent of its correspondent association. The most intimate interest is that which most directly unites just two human beings, as in the association of marriage; but at the other extreme are interests universal as mankind—the interest we call justice, for example—and the history of society is in part a history of the widening of associations (and therefore of community) as men more and more recognise how much they have in common with other men, and more and more understand that every common value is protected and furthered by association. So out of the small circles of primitive society have grown the great and ever-widening associations of the modern world.

We have been speaking of the State as simply one among other associations, but the State has obviously a very peculiar and distinctive place. Other associations are limited to the pursuit of one or at most a few interests, the State seems to have some care for nearly every interest. Other associations cannot on their own initiative enforce their decisions on recalcitrant members, the State can and does. Other associations have their members scattered over a city or district or country, the State includes within its membership, or at least within its control, all the dwellers within determined communal frontiers. It is, therefore, highly important to determine the relation of the State, first to community itself, and next to the other associations within community.

Community and State

Because the State, like community, has territorial frontiers and because it exercises control over all, or nearly all, other associations, many writers speak as if community and State were one. This seems to have been the view of Hegel and is certainly the doctrine of the neo-Hegelian writers on the State, as well as of many others to whom that epithet scarcely applies. Here is a representative statement of this doctrine from the late M. Fouillée: "Imagine," he wrote, "a great circle within which are lesser circles combining in a thousand ways to form the most varied figures without overstepping the limits that enclose them; this is an image of the great association of the State and of the particular associations that it embraces." (*La Science Sociale Contemporaine*, p. 13.)

We shall see later that this doctrine, which makes the State the limit of community and makes all other associations but elements of the State, is contradicted by the whole evolution of the modern State. For the present it will suffice to show that the doctrine, so strangely maintained in the face of history, is contrary to the present fact. Here we are not concerned with what the State ought to be and to include, but with what the State actually is and does include. So regarded, it is quite obvious that the State is neither conterminous nor synonymous with community. Every State has rigid territorial limits, but the modern world, marked off into separate States, is not partitioned into a number of isolated communities. We have already seen that community is a matter of degree, that it is a network of social inter-relations, here denser, here thinner, whose ever new-woven filaments join men to men across countries and continents. The State, unlike community, is exclusive and determinate. Where one State ends, another begins; where one begins, another ends. No man can without contradiction owe allegiance to two States, any more than he can serve two masters, but he can enter into the life of as many communities as his sympathies and opportunities will allow.

Quite obviously the metaphor of Fouillée is false. Let us draw our exclusive circles and call them England, France, Germany, and so on. By hypothesis, all associations fall within these circles, and do not intersect them. Well, in which circle shall we place the international economic associations without which none of the great States could to-day exist at all? In which shall we place the numerous international unions, industrial, scientific, religious, and artistic? "Without overstepping the limits that enclose them"—that is the foundation of the neo-Hegelian doctrine of the State, and it is a foundation which is false in fact.

But, it will be answered, every association, international or intrana-tional, is controlled by the State. Intranational associations are controlled by the separate States, international associations by agreement between States. No members of any State can enter into any association whatever unless that State permits it. Thus every other association is subordinate to the State.

We may grant the contention. At a later stage we shall see more clearly whence and why the will of the State has this pre-eminence. At that stage we shall understand more fully the distinction between community and State. Meantime we must insist that there is a false inference if we say that because the State has control over every other association, therefore all other associations are absorbed into the State, are simply parts of the State, or are completely circumscribed by its frontiers. If we hold this view, the process of conflict through which modern States have attained their present democratic forms, and in especial the long agony of strife due to the opposing claims of churches and of States, is without meaning for us.

There is an easy and direct way by which we can discover the limits of the State. The essential feature of the State is political order, the *primary* instrument of the State is political law. There has been community where no State yet existed, and even to-day we may discover, among certain Eskimo peoples, for instance, primitive forms of communal life still un-coordinated within a State. Where there is no political law, there is no State. Political law is thus the criterion of the State, and in learning the nature and limits of political law we are learning the nature and limits of the State.

Political law is in its proper nature unconditioned, formulated, and mainly negative. These characters reveal the limits of the State.

It is unconditioned. The laws of other associations bind their members, but if you don't like the laws you can leave the association—unless the *State* forbids. If you disapprove of the laws of your club or business-association or trade-union or church, you can resign. If any such association tries of its own accord to enforce its laws on you, it comes into collision with the powers of the State. It can properly do no more than deny you its special benefits and privileges. So with communal or customary law, properly so-called. If you break the customs, traditions, fashions prevalent in your community, you may expect its disapprobation. It will boycott you, refuse to enter into social relations with you, but unless you break also the law of the State, it cannot otherwise visit upon you its displeasure. But if you break a political law, you do not merely lose privileges. The State will do more than deny its benefits, it will punish. It has behind it the united force of the community, the final sanction attached to no other kind of social law. Nor can you simply resign your membership of the State to escape its law. Even if you go beyond its frontiers its claims may follow you, and within the State, even if you shut yourself up within your walls, you are subject to the laws of the State, to all the conditions it may impose either directly or by delegation of authority.

Why does the State hold this unique position? Why has it behind it the united force of the community? The force of the law is not an ultimate thing, it is always and essentially dependent upon will. The State has this power of compulsion because its members *will* that power, because they subject themselves to its law and unite their force to maintain it. To what end?

No man can wholly cut himself off from social relations while he remains in the world of men. We are forced, from all sides, by every instinct and every need, into society, into relations with our fellows. Such relations must be *ordered*, or life is impossible. Mutual good demands mutual service, mutual forbearance and restraint. Thus wherever society exists there exists a system of obligations and rights. Society incessantly creates these reciprocal relations between every man and all other men. Sometimes they remain unformulated and traditional, as in a primitive community ruled by "unwritten law," but nearly always the most essential of these relationships of right and obligation are set out in clear formulæ, as political laws, and protected by a central authority endowed with communal power. Any body of men so organised that a central institution or government takes over the maintenance and development of the essential system of rights and obligations accepted among them is properly called a State. A State is thus the fundamental association for the maintenance and development of social order, and to this end its central institution is endowed with the united power of the community. It is not meant that the members of a State consciously realise why they give or permit it this final authority—if they did they would never have suffered the endless perversions of government—but only that as their political consciousness emerges, as they ask themselves why they should contribute this might to the State, the answer appears in this form. As the State develops, as its members grow in social wisdom, in the consciousness of their own needs and the possibilities of satisfying them through political order, the power of the State comes to rest more and more on its service of that end—or else there is distraction, weakness, cleavage, finally perhaps revolution.

Subjection to law is political obligation, which is only the reverse side of political right. Beyond law, beyond government, and beyond force lie the common ends, the common will of community. The end is here as always the revelation of meaning and the justification of existence. If the citizen owes obedience to government it must be in virtue of some social good which in turn determines the respect the government shall show to him. Political right and political obligation, as all right and obligation, are derived from the same source and are meaningless if separated. Already we see that the State and its government are not ultimate social phenomena but rest on what is yet deeper, communal life and will.

The special limits of the State are revealed when we consider the further characteristics of political law.

In the second place, political law is expressed in definite formulæ. A political law defines certain categories of persons as coming within its scope, and prescribes for them as precisely as possible certain forms of conduct. It is obvious, therefore, that it can apply only to general situations and can enforce only *external* fulfilments. Thus the State is at once outside large spheres of human activity. It cannot control motives save indirectly. It can enjoin actions, or rather activities, but not the spirit of their fulfilment. But large classes of action are wholly dependent on the spirit in which they are fulfilled, and many associations exist simply to foster types of ideal or spiritual values. The State *cannot* determine these associations, and it *should not* prescribe any of those actions which derive their only value from the spirit of their performance. The State can compel people to attend church, but it cannot compel them to worship, and therefore the former compulsion is folly. The State cannot create by its *fiat* a church or an artistic or literary association. It can protect and maintain and even organise such associations—to do so may be part of its function—but it cannot, if it is true to its own nature, determine and control them. Further, in its generality and externality it cannot touch (save by way of repression) that spontaneity and initiative of individual life which is the beginning of all social process and the root of all social value. There are times, pre-eminently the time of war, when cumulative force matters for the time being more than spontaneity, and the State inevitably becomes repressive. But this, like nearly all the special phenomena of war, is a throwback to the barbaric order. Certainly this repressiveness, when continued into the time of peace by the momentum of the war-habit, of necessity breeds grave social disturbance and dissension. The State must, therefore, be clearly distinguished from the community which creates it. Community is the common life of beings who are guided essentially from within, actively, spontaneously, and freely (under the conditions prescribed by the laws they make) relating themselves to one another, weaving for themselves the complex web of social unity. But the State works with an instrument which is necessarily formal, prescribing the general external conditions of social life, upholding the main system of those social obligations which may be externally fulfilled. Its instrument resembles, in Aristotle's phrase, no "leaden rule" which can adapt itself to the actual mouldings of the social structure, but an unbending rod which can measure only its general outlines.

Because it can determine only the external forms of conduct, the law of the State must be mainly (though by no means wholly) negative. It must for the most part be content (as the neo-Hegelians themselves are forced to admit, though they do not see the significance of the admission) to "hinder hindrances" to social welfare. It can prevent or punish wrong-doing rather than endorse right-doing. It can create for men the external social conditions necessary for the well-living of their lives. It can enforce these outer obligations without the fulfilment of which the inner obligations cannot be fulfilled. For this reason the sanction of political law is punishment and not reward. We reward and honour only what the theologian called "works of supererogation," not the minimal fulfilment of external law.

It is needless to say that in thus stating the limits of political activity we are not belittling the immeasurable value of that activity. The point is that the State is not equivalent to community, that the political association does not include and cannot control the whole life of men. The State is seen to be not community but a peculiarly authoritative association within it. The State is determinate, a closed organisation of social life; community is indeterminate, an ever-evolving system spreading beyond and only partially controlled within the definite framework of any State. That framework gives to the portion of community which it encloses a certain unity and definition, but neither cuts it off from a wider community of which it is essentially part nor within that portion substitutes its own external mode of action, its necessity, for the spontaneity that is the mark of all life, social and other. Social life can no longer in practice and should no longer in theory be summed up in political life. The individual should not be summed up in his citizenship, otherwise the claim of citizenship will itself become a tyranny and its essential moral value be lost. "The modern wilderness of interests" is not to be straightened out into the simple road of citizenship. For the main road of citizenship, which we must make straight as possible, though it intersects a thousand paths of social interest, cannot and should not absorb them.

These paths of social interest do not stop at the frontiers of States. The political interest is determinate and has limits, the social has none. Hence for the proper understanding of international relations it is most necessary to distinguish community and State. On the assumption of identity we can have no social unity among the nations until they are absorbed within some world-state. For each State by its very definition is a determinate and self-contained unit. In this respect of the sphere of its sovereignty every State is demarcated absolutely from every other. Consequently, if political relationship were identical with social relationship, the members of one State would remain totally alien from the members of every other State. Communities would stand to one another as Spinoza and Hobbes imagined them to stand, isolated as the pre-civil individuals of their imaginations, totally irresponsible until some contract is agreed upon, even then totally irresponsible because there is no possible higher will to make agreement binding. But, of course, it is in international relations that the distinction of State and community is most clearly revealed and that the common interests of universal society most manifestly weave new unities in spite of political separation. A man may perhaps "denationalise" himself (though that is hardly the proper word) by leaving his country, but he cannot "desocialise" himself without leaving the world of men, or at least of civilised men.

Community, therefore, and not the State, is the "world the spirit has made for itself." "The spirit" does not isolate itself in States, as Hegel's argument assumes. On the contrary, the growth of civilisation means the growth of ever-widening community, the "realisation" of social interest beyond the limits of politically independent groups. Society widens and the sense of community grows. In particular, the privileged classes of the different peoples, the authors of most past wars, become more and more allied by social intercourse, by common commercial and intellectual interests. M. Tarde has pointed out how classes of men whose occupation, even if in a competitive way, brings them into constant association with one another, develop a friendlier spirit towards one another than classes not subject to this socialising influence. The same holds of peoples. It is not civilisation but intercivilisation that develops mutual sympathy between States. The highly socialised Greek cities, because each held to an ideal of autonomy and self-sufficiency, the ideal of "completely independent totality," were not intersocialised, and, accordingly, displayed the intensest hostility to one another. But the aloofness of Greek states is impossible in the modern world, which is pervaded by intersocialising influences of literature and commerce. Common ideas and common trade have formed everywhere social bonds which cut across the line of States, and have made western Europe, looked on as a whole, an effective community. Thus an educated Englishman comes to have more in common with an educated Frenchman than he has, say, with an English agricultural labourer. The alien, shut out from his State, may yet have a closer, social affinity to him than his fellow citizen. And yet the prevalent political philosophy blindly declares that "the State" is "the world the spirit has made for itself," and that "between State and State there can be no consciousness of common good." Because certain dangerously antiquated modern governments retained that philosophy, they have overwhelmed our common civilisation in the consciousness of common evil.

If we turn for a moment from fact to ideal—two things which the neo-Hegelians constantly confuse—we may admit the desirability of a wider political co-ordination of community than at present exists. This is to be achieved not by our going backwards and cutting off the bonds of relationship which make community wider in area than any single State, but by our going forward on the road of federation and making a union of States great enough to comprehend the existing intercommunity. The recognition of likeness of interests, purposes, and needs is increasing and not diminishing in the people of different nations. It is the State that is inadequate, not community that is overstepping its due bounds. The State must always, as we have seen, remain inadequate to comprehend and regulate *all* community. But it is more inadequate than need be, so long as the political relations of States are capricious and uncoordinated. At present civilised States are like masters who maintain splendid order and discipline within their workshops, and thus feel free to go out and racket in the streets.

✦ 6 7 ✦

LITTLETOWN: THE STORY OF
AN AMERICAN VILLAGE

William G. Mather, Jr.

Some elements of human ecology may be seen more clearly when they are examined in a relatively simple setting. Such a view is provided in this selection, in which the author takes a single rural community in upstate New York, and after briefly reviewing its history, he describes the way of life in the village. The picture he paints is a dismal one, but not an uncommon one for many rural communities at the time this article was written (1935). The concluding paragraphs suggest, however, that many communities have a way of persisting, even though their character may distinctly change because of shifts in the organization of American society.

The other day a farmer called on Jonas Handman to deliver a basket of apples. He knocked on the kitchen door, waited for a while, then went

SOURCE: *Harper's Magazine*, Vol. 170 (January, 1935), 200–208. Reprinted by permission of the author. ✦ The author is professor of sociology at Pennsylvania State University. His interests center in rural sociology, the church, and health, in each of which fields he has published.

round to the front door and knocked there. Nobody came. Handman had said that he wanted those apples, so the farmer put the basket down on the porch and went back of the house to the barn. There he found Jonas hanging by his neck, dead.

Jonas had never been known to do any real work about Littletown; while his father was living he never had to. And when his father died he left him the store blocks downtown. Jonas seemed to get along very well on the rents up to a few years ago, and was in the pool room most of the time. There were two stores, one with a hall over it that hasn't been used for years except for a few months some time ago by the Girl Scout troop. Last year Bill and Ed Brown started a garage in the store part of that block, when the grocery which Jed Simmons had run was closed out after his funeral. The other block had been vacant for a few years, except for a rummage sale or bake-sale in it now and then. The garage did not pay much rent, and you can't charge a women's society for sales, so it seemed that things had turned out badly for Jonas. We hadn't realized they were that bad though.

The truth is, we don't miss Jonas Handman very much. He was never, so to speak, a contributing member of our community. But his suicide is the third within the past year.

Littletown is small, as its name implies, with only some fourteen hundred people. And three suicides in one year are altogether too many for that population.

Some of us are beginning to worry about what is going to happen to our town. The past thirty years have seen many changes in the world, and from the point of view of the small-town man they have not all been good in their effect. There seems to be a sinister force at work, threatening the very existence of many small towns.

Take the little hamlet a few miles from us called The Flats. Thirty years or so ago The Flats was a busy little crossroads with two cheese factories, two stores (one with a hall over it), a blacksmith shop, a shingle mill that took its power from the creek, a school, and a church. They had great times with family reunions, square dances, warm-sugar parties, and the like, and it was known as one of the best communities in our neighborhood.

To-day not a single one of those signs of business life remains. There is only the old church, empty and unused, and the school with only a handful of pupils. One out of three of the houses within two miles of the crossroads in every direction is unoccupied and falling to pieces.

No wonder that we in Littletown are becoming nervous. As the advertising posters begin to be pasted on the inside of the show windows of store after store of ours that closes, the ghost of The Flats comes over the hill and haunts us. Twenty years, forty years—and shall we also belong to the Past?

II

Littletown is a cozy village in a hollow of the beautiful, surprisingly abrupt hills of southwestern New York. The Baptist church, a few rods down Spring Street from the main corner, is at an elevation of 1400 feet above sea level, while the tops of the hills round about are 1800 and 1900 feet. The only flat land is found in the valleys, and in only small patches there; in one summer alone three men, tilling the rolling slopes, were hurt by the overturning of tractors. The land has been farmed for a century and a third but is untamed yet!

An ancient glacial lake lay to the north of Littletown long before even the foot of a Seneca Indian had disturbed the deep grass of the pastures of the deer, and the lake left behind, with its shoreline and outlet banks, a level but tortuous passage through the hills to the more gently rolling valley of the Genesee. Along this path wound the old cart road to the cities of the north in the early days of settlement in the 1790's; and when Clinton's Ditch traversed the State from east to west a canal was dug over the same gentle path to connect Rochester, with her port on Lake Ontario, to the Allegheny River. It was possible in those days to move slowly up the canal, through Littletown and across to Oleander, where one turned down the Allegheny to the Ohio, thence to the Mississippi and the Gulf. The canal is gone now, but the locks still stand, with now and then a crumbling skeleton of a gate between them; and there are men in Littletown who will tell you of unloading salt at the Port of Littletown in those days, and women who remember the Sunday School outings when heavily loaded, bunting-draped barges moved off for a day in some grove along the canal.

The Pennsylvania Railroad bought the canal and used the tow path as a base for its rails; part of the Erie main line follows the same route, and is well traveled; but the Pennsylvania is a branch line, built to serve the little towns along the old artery of travel. Such is the way of Time that it is running fewer trains each year, the rails are beginning to gather rust, and a concrete highway makes the tires whine as cars speed over the old route of the post road, the canal, and the iron horse.

It was nearly a century and a half ago that a group of men discovered the valley in which Littletown lies. It seemed a good place for a town, this little flat patch with passes through the hills to all four points of the compass, so they took up land rights. One faction wanted the village at the north end of the hollow; the other, at the south, against the hills. Each set up a store and a tavern on its chosen spot; but the liquor must have been better at the latter place, for North Littletown is now just a filling station, a house for tourists and a school.

The village grew slowly but was regarded as a coming town. A new post road from Buffalo to Pennsylvania was surveyed about 1870, and

Littletown was on one of the two possible routes. The village was astir; two post roads, a canal—what more could one ask to insure prosperity? And then the road went through Oleander, a village of the same size, almost a day's journey (in reality, only sixteen miles) up the swampy valley to the west. Old timers shake their heads and date that city's rise from the changing of the road. "When I was a boy Oleander wasn't as big as we are now," they say, and sigh the sigh of men who have guessed wrong.

But the long grass was still there, and the cows were there, going about the business of the cud unmindful of the fate of village empires down below them. Within ten years after the incident of the road, the milk from more than two thousand cows was being handled in the many cheese factories tucked away in the folds of the hills, and more than three-quarters of a million pounds of rich, mild-flavored cheese were marketed through the Littletown exchange each year. Almost all of the land, even in the remotest hills, was in pasture or grain.

The little cheese factories are just about all closed now, for cheese can be made at lower cost in Wisconsin and Minnesota; but there are a few left, and a chain store and a national meat packer still maintain cheese warehouses in Littletown. The War helped to change the nature of the dairy industry, as it boosted the sale of condensed milk, and several large condensaries were established in and near our village. One of them is still operating, the milk being hauled in by trucks that rumble through when the sleepy storekeepers are sweeping out in the morning.

Milk prices are low now, and the dairymen who have to pay for long hauls of milk are finding it hard to keep going. The old days of milk-prosperity—if they could be called that—do not seem likely to come again; dairying is a serious, corner-cutting, belt-tightening business, and a good many hill pastures are growing up to brush and scrubby timber.

There was another time when Fortune gave her Mona Lisa smile to Littletown, and now and again we get a little publicity in some newspaper because of it.

It seems that away back in the early days a bowlegged man called Seneca Pete used to drive an old gray mule down from Buffalo with two empty kegs strapped on her back. A mile or so from the village is a scummy spring in a swampy hollow, that used to form a thin film of oily substance over its surface. When flint and steel were struck close to its edge, it would burn for a time. The Senecas guarded it as a treasure, dipping their blankets into it and straining out the precious oil that had oozed up from the rock below. It was thought to be good for a snakebite, good for wounds, good for general principles; and Seneca Pete would load up his mule and plod back to Buffalo, there to sell the famous "Seneca Oil" to the doctors. It was the first petroleum discovered in America.

When Drake proved the worth of drilling a shaft for oil Littletown heard the news with joy. When oil ran out of its own accord, without need of a drilled hole, how much more must there not be below the surface, waiting for the bit to free it and send it spouting up into the sun?

A well was drilled close to the edge of the old spring. The top of the casing still stands in the weeds, ragged, rusty, ashamed. But over the hills, only eight miles away, begins the rich oil field from which the world's best crude is pumped. Fortune missed us by that slight a margin.

A few years ago the men whom oil had made rich came to our town and built a monument in tribute to the spring that had led the way. We are proud of that bowlder with its bronze slab and generally motor our visitors out to see it. But we would rather have a derrick.

In the first decade of the present century, Littletown made its bid as a manufacturing center. A knife factory, a pulley works, a cheese-box factory, and a novelty concern erected buildings and began operations. Perhaps a hundred men were employed, with two dozen others in the two older mills that had been long established for the grinding of feed and flour and the sawing of lumber. An enterprising citizen with little taste put up a whole street of somber houses, all alternately alike, on the edge of town. We had our factories and our slums. We were on the way to becoming a big town.

The knife factory died first and one of the banks took it over. The novelty firm moved on. The pulley works went under two years ago. The box factory merged with the sawmill.

The buildings still stand there, sagging, empty, and the Chamber of Commerce is busy dangling bait before the eyes of small city businesses, hoping to entice them here. A year or so ago some of the younger business men became impatient and from somewhere managed to raise two thousand dollars, which they gave, together with an old barnlike structure, to a man with an idea for an airplane. The plane almost flew, at that.

Commerce, oil, manufacturing—they have all paid us but fleeting visits. They roused our hopes, they made us dream. Yet on the hillsides the sleek cows still graze, the milk trucks roll through town in the early morning, and the only mills that stood the test of time are the feed and flour mills, grinding out food for the cows. Even the sawmill is owned by the same men that own the feed mill. And it makes cheese-boxes. We have not wanted to be rural, but it seems that we cannot help it.

III

Although Littletown is small, it does not lack facilities for trade. There are three chain groceries in town, hated like poison by the proprietors of the locally owned groceries, of which there are also three. The local stores are forever urging us to keep our dollars at home, to support home industries, to remember old friends; but so far only one of them has cleaned up his place of business, painted the front an attractive color, enamelled the shelves, and removed the cat from the warm show window. He gets some of the business that the bright, neat chains get, but the other two have their troubles.

We did have two bakeries, one of them half a grocery also. The bakery has gone bankrupt; the combination hangs on. Bread trucks come in daily from Oleander with fresh rolls and bread and pastry, attractively done up in boxes or transparent paper with no flies inside, and most of our housewives prefer to buy their baked goods that way.

If you wish to buy a pair of shoes in our town, you have many opportunities. When the last census was taken, there were only two thousand eight hundred and forty-four feet in the village, but there are six places in which to buy shoes. There are two men's clothing stores, one pool room, one men's and women's clothing store, and two drygoods stores—all selling shoes. Of course, no one of them has a large assortment of either sizes or styles, but you may find what you want if you are lucky.

There are two meat markets, one run by the man who also manages the moving picture theater. But two of the chain groceries also carry meat, and so one of the markets has put in a line of bread and rolls, cakes, and canned goods. He is new to town and swears that if the competition extends to other stores he will put in dresses and cameras and a soda fountain.

There is the ever-present ice cream parlor, whose owner, in partnership with his brother, also runs an ice cream factory. They make very good ice cream, putting real cream from the local dairies into it; thus it costs more to make than do the frozen puddings turned out by the Buffalo factories, and so their business remains small. The drugstore on the opposite corner from the ice cream parlor carries the Buffalo brand.

There are two drugstores and they both sell drugs in addition to watches, alarm clocks, cameras, radios, candles, wall paper, candy, mirrors, pictures, greeting cards, toys, and what not. And there are two pool rooms, two hardware stores, two electric stores, the proprietor of one of which doubles as funeral director, three restaurants, two gift shops with jewelers' counters, two hotels, four garages.

Yes, we have the facilities for doing business. Two of everything at least, including two banks to handle the inevitable bankruptcies that come more frequently in recent years. If Prosperity ever dared walk down our main street it would be plucked raw before it had gone half a block.

We used to have business too. The farmers' teams crowded the streets, and their children the stores, and everyone was happy. They used to give you a bag of candy when you paid your bill. But business is drifting to Oleander now, with its ten-cent stores and its larger stocks of suits and dresses and furniture, only twenty-five minutes away over a good paved road that we were mighty pleased with when it was first laid down.

Sometimes we look back on the paving of that road and grin crookedly. We were proud as Punch when the job was finished. There were editorials in the paper, photographs of leading citizens, and all that. We came within an inch of having one of these celebrations with a symbolic wedding too. If our storekeepers could have seen how much of their business was going to roll over that road to Oleander, they would have worked for a symbolic funeral instead.

But they didn't see it and went right on doing business as they had done it for years before, when we had to buy from them or go without. But now, if we don't like what they have or the price that they set upon it we can try in Oleander without much trouble. A lot of small-town business men are making that same mistake; they do not seem to realize that the swamps and hills that cut their customers off from the rest of the world are being filled and levelled now, and that their business is in competition with every other store of the same line within forty miles. Even Oleander, now with nearly twenty thousand people, complains that some of its trade is going to Buffalo, seventy miles to the northeast; and Oleander has some large stores.

Of course, it is true that a man in a small town like ours cannot expect to have a large store; but sometimes I wonder if it is necessary to break up what little business we do have among so many men and make it still smaller.

One of the things that keeps business poor is the fact that there just aren't as many people to buy goods as there used to be. Our village declined 11.7 per cent in population between the last two federal censuses. As for the countryside round us, a drive over the dirt roads in any direction will show what is happening there, as house after house stands empty with its shutters banging in the wind. It does no good to call those dirt roads "side" roads; they were main roads when our village was growing and our present number of stores were founded, and the people who traded with us came over them to market.

Modern methods of agriculture have made it possible for one farmer to handle more stock and more land than several farmers could in the former days, and the surplus farmers have moved away. The poorer land is going out of cultivation, as not worth a man's time, and the better land is being tilled more cheaply and better. The population of the old canal and post road days is not needed any more. Men do not go down the meadows four and six abreast, swinging their scythes, at harvest time; one man rides round on a mower. One man sitting on a tractor turns two or three furrows at once. One man milks two cows at once while leaning against a post and watching the machine suck and blow. Farming is a business now, and the sheriff sells out the man who cannot run his farm in a business way.

I cannot sigh over the departure of the old days of hand agriculture. I was raised on a farm. I have had a double-shovel give my ribs a Dutch rub when plowing corn in the old stump field, and I am glad that men can farm now more safely for their bones and their religion. The women in farm homes too do not long for the days when the dining room was full of harvesters and the kitchen full of the fumes of hell. The new ways are better. But that does not alter the fact that they mean fewer feet to be shod, fewer legs to be overalled, fewer freckled, sun-browned misses to wear the new, soft dresses.

IV

The people that live in Littletown are nice. The Legion and the Ku Klux would accept them all. We have very few foreign families— you could count them on one hand—and still fewer colored. There are the usual number of faithful elderly spinsters waiting to join Ma and Dad, who died and left them without the job that had been husband and children to them; the usual number of widows and widowers living alone with their memories in rambling, solitary houses; the usual number of retired farmers sniffing the wind wistfully in the morning; the usual number of children playing in the yards of the smaller houses on the side streets. There are not many young people though; the population takes a running jump over the twenties, and the few that are left keep asking, "What's doing in the city? Are jobs opening up there yet?"

It makes it rather hard on the young folks in high school. They are determined not to be like Mother and Dad, but there are few in between to copy after. So they read the magazines and go to the movies and get their styles of dressing and acting from there. A little too much lipstick, talk rather coarse and loud, clothes just a bit extreme, and a faraway look of cities over the horizon when the school bell has rung for the last time, tell their story.

A year or two ago one of the men from the college of agriculture gave the young folks in our high school a questionnaire about their choice of a vocation. Only 16.5 per cent of them said they were planning to do work similar to their father's, and only 13.8 per cent were intending to stay in town. Their dreams will change of course, and disappointment will also come; but that does not change the present situation much. Our young folks do not like us and see no future for themselves with us.

On Sunday morning the bells in five steeples ring the call to worship, and the doors of five churches open for the crowds of worshippers who will not come. All of our churches have a seating capacity far in excess of their resident membership. Yet we are a fairly religious town; for a census that the churches took one year showed that over half of our population belonged to some church, and the average for the United States is less than that. The proportion is considerably smaller, however, among the country people; relatively few of them come to our churches, and they have none of their own. They say that their clothes are inferior to ours, and that we are not friendly with them. I think that their clothes are on the whole as good as ours, but they are probably right about the lack of cordiality; we have had our eyes fixed on the dream of being a big city for so long that we have forgotten the people who tend the cows that fill the milk trucks that rumble through town.

Our churches are costly affairs. In 1930 we spent, one of the ministers estimated, $17,507 for the four Protestant churches alone. Thirty years before that the records show that the cost of those same churches, with more members, was only $7,089. I do not attribute this rise to extravagance but to the upward tendency of our necessities; thirty years ago we did not feel that a college education was necessary for our ministers; but we do now, for so many of us are college-educated that we abhor scientific blunders in the pulpit. And college men cost us more than illiterate, or semi-so, ministers. The same is true of our pipe organs, our redecorated buildings, our robed choirs. Those things are part of our modern culture.

Our extravagance comes, however, in our insistence that each small church group must have those things for itself. The Methodists, with only ninety-four members, must have those things just as do the Baptists, with two and one-half times as many people over whom to spread the cost. Some people I know have actually declined to join one of our churches, not because they did not feel spiritually ready, but because they knew that they could not stand the financial pressure that is put upon its members. The gospel is far from free in our town.

Some efforts have been made toward inter-church co-operation. Union services are held on summer evenings, and even the smallest building is adequate to hold the combined audiences. The young people of three of the churches began a joint society, but the older folks of one church withdrew their young people after a few weeks, saying that they were having too good a time with the others and feared they might be "weaned away" from their own church. Two of the churches have had a joint men's class for a few years, and the men got along with one another there as well as they did in the lodges or the business men's clubs; but when talk began of union of the two churches at a time when one of them was without a minister some of the women said things that put a stop to it.

It may be after we have had a few more burials in our beautiful green cemetery on the hill that church union will come nearer, and we shall become fellow-Christians as well as fellow-Littletownians—but there are those who will term my hope sinful.

Although we are losing population, our school is becoming more crowded every year. The classrooms are full of seats. It seems that out in the country districts, as the little schools lose students until only a few are left and the cost per pupil becomes high, the schools are closed and those few children are taken in to our school by buses. Also, more young people above the age at which they are legally required to go to school are wanting to continue on through the high school; they feel the need of higher education in this day. We shall have to build a new building for them eventually, and yet we hesitate at the cost and keep putting it off. A large part of our taxpaying townsmen are retired farmers whose income is small and limited, whose children are already educated and gone, but whose influence is great.

We have a beautiful little library, built by funds which a good woman left for the purpose, and the young folks use it very well. Their parents, except for women who do a deal of novel-reading, do not use it much. We are not enthusiastic in the cultivation of our minds but are fairly satisfied to let them be as they are. One of the doctors was fuming the other day that there were eight card clubs in town but not one mother's club.

When evening settles down upon us there are several things that we can do. Generally we sit at home and listen to the radio, which is pleasant in the summer when it can be heard through an open window on the porch. If the night is fair we visit friends; and if there is something extra on at one of the lodges those of us who are not officers, who would go anyway, attend.

We have two lodges, the Odd Fellows and the Masons, the former with a large proportion of farmers in its membership. The leaders of both complain that meetings are poorly attended, not like the good old days. But the rooms are open in the afternoons, and the older men drop in to play checkers and cards and talk. The women have their Rebekahs and Eastern Star and put on bake-sales now and then.

There are, besides the Legion—which is getting a bit fat—and the Grange, a number of other organizations in town. A D.A.R. chapter that was recently formed by some lady who belonged to no other club, I think, and who wanted to join one; a chapter of Daughters of Union Veterans; a Current Topic club that should properly be called Current Gossip; the Shakespeare Club that discusses astronomy and art; any number of card clubs that are the breath of life to the two little gift shops; and in each section of town a "sunshine" club that sends flowers and gifts to the sick. The women spend a great deal of time at these various clubs; for they are, like most small-town women, forever lonesome and inquisitive about one another's affairs.

We have two business men's clubs, whose main occupation is talking about bringing "new business" to town, but none of them includes in its membership farmers, whose milk trucks bring in all the new business that ever does come.

For sport, the younger men have organized a soft-ball league that fights noisy battles in the park at twilight. The barbers have a team, the railroad men, the feed-mill men, and so on; "Lucky Tigers," "Keystones," "Barney Googles" they call them, and get real sport out of the games. Baseball loosens up the muscles that have been fighting rust on the rails or waiting behind the counters for business to come home and be forgiven, and also takes their minds off the complaining women who wait for their men folk to return at sundown and listen respectfully while they retail the gossip of the day.

V

Last year the farmers took a step that disgusted the business men. They organized a co-operative feed store in one of the empty buildings, to handle feed and flour and the like, buy seeds and fertilizer, and ship some produce as well. The business men regard it as very ungrateful of them, especially in the midst of this business depression. If they had only taken some stock in the knife factory or the airplane industry now, the farmers would have been showing real co-operation. But this event proves to them that the farmers do not understand civic needs.

One would think that the young people, even more than the women, would be very busy; for they have any number of organizations for them in the school and the churches and the Scouts and the Hi-Y. Some organization is putting on a sale of some kind, raising money for some purpose, almost all the time. But the truth is, as I have observed, that a few of them belong to nearly everything, with no time even to study, while a great many belong to nothing and do nothing except stand on the street corners and giggle.

There really is not much else for those who are not dashing off to some meeting or other to do. They can go to the movies, which cost money, or they can shoot pool, which also costs money and is not too well thought of, or they can go home. They rarely do that except to work at their lessons. What they fall back upon is the promenade. From the library they drift down one side of the street to the filling station, then cross over and back up the other side, and so on around again. Now and then they pair off and slip away down a side street where the lights are more dim.

One winter a new minister suggested opening up some of the rooms of a church and installing ping-pong tables, checkers, a piano, and the like on Friday and Saturday nights. He didn't get far with that idea. "What for?" was the attitude of his board. "We spend a lot of money on our young folks now, and then when they get through school they go off to the city and we never get it back. And besides it isn't right to use the church property that way."

So the card-tables gossip about the goings-on among the younger generation of this awful day; one of the older ministers fulminates weekly about the drinking and necking proclivities of youth, and the business men complain that the young people do not remain to marry and settle down and breed a trading population for the town. And all the while the more ambitious and worthy of the young folks are whispering impatiently among themselves, "Let's get out of here to where something's doing!"

And that probably is the very spirit that led their ancestors to come to Littletown in the first place.

We used to have, not so long ago, considerable doing in our town. Every fall we had a fair, of which we were justly proud. We had halls for exhibits, a race track, a grandstand. I can remember when I used to swallow a whole bag of popcorn without tasting it, as La Paloma won by a nose from Gelter's Pride or while I watched Zanzibar the snake eater for one dime, ten cents, the decimal part of a dollar. But the fair stopped some years ago for lack of entries, and enthusiasm, and patrons, and money; and last year we arranged to sell the old buildings that remained in order to pay off a debt we owed the printer.

The grove just south of town, a clean place of hard maples lifting round bare trunks above the grass, used to be the scene of camp meetings, chautauquas, and political rallies. Tents were pitched amid the trees, water brought from the spring, horses staked out, and the whole family settled down to enjoy religion or whatever there was, while one of the boys ran the farm between hayings. Jolly, informal, full of fist fights and love-making, of prayer and mud-slinging, summer camp meetings were the balm of sultry days. Brush grows up in the old grove now, and the cows scratch their lean necks against well-nigh obliterated hearts with arrows stuck through and letters, "H. C. and V. T." O Time, how could you?

Here it lies, the little village in the lap of the hills, about it the marks of its former happiness and hope, and before it the shadows seen only by itself and the old men who sit on the bench before the pool room on calm afternoons. They too have lived and dreamed.

And the storekeepers agitate home trade, dangle decaying buildings before decaying industries as an attraction to come to Littletown and die, and at the last do as Jonas Handman did. Just between the main highways of travel, just on the edge of the oil field, not big enough to be a city, not small enough to be a hamlet—wanting things, almost getting things, too alive to die and too dead to grow, what shall become of us?

We have the poor comfort of knowing that our lot is not solitary. There are many villages like ours to-day, facing what we face. We hear talk of the decentralization of industry, of the putting of great factories into small units scattered over many towns, but we know that salvation for us does not lie in the scheme. It may be done, but we know that it will be the villages nearer the great cities than we are that will profit. And the extent of their profit is doubtful; industry began in small towns once and left them; we had factories once, and they are gone; nor have the prodigals shed many tears of penitence as yet. Many villages like us are waiting for either factories or farmers to come back; for over one hundred thousand acres of farm land have been abandoned in our county alone, many times that in the State, and millions in the whole country.

Everywhere that this has occurred there are villages with Jonas Handmans.

Of this, I think we are certain: that the process of shrinking will go on until there are just enough farmers left outside our village to supply the milk that the market demands. And when that point is reached there will also be just enough stores left in Littletown to supply the needs of these farmers. The churches will either die or merge the one with the other until there are just enough churches to accommodate us all, villagers and farmers, in our worship. The little district schools will probably draw together in consolidation until our youth can find in the minimum number of good schools the maximum preparation for life.

These things will not happen easily. They will be accompanied by struggle and pain. But if we can see where we are going, and help one another on the way, we may be able to reduce the Jonas Handmans.

Littletown is not going to die. Littletown is going to start over again, this time with its eyes open, its goal more real. We shall gain a spiritual dividend from the re-organization of our village life, I think; for whatever we do we shall have to do together—and that is good for the soul. One with the countryside, with the old false barrier between village and farm forgotten, with the common interest of storekeeper and dairyman at last known and understood, the renascent Littletown may be a better place than before.

For life still goes on about us. Lovers marry and are given in marriage; children play in the front yards; men sweat in the fields; women peel vegetables in the kitchens; and the cows come home at evening in long patient lines, trailing down from the hill pastures.

And wherever there is life there are the needs of life, that cannot be met by any one man alone.

* 68 *

VILLAGERS IN METROPOLIS

Svend Riemer

Are city planners following a mistaken lead when they attempt to revive villagelike structures in the metropolis? Do we need to shift our thinking about the neighborhood so as to emphasize less its characteristic as an "area clearly delineated in space" and empha- size more the fact that it is a "phenomenon anchored in the mind"? These are some of the questions to which the author ad- dresses himself and in so doing shows some of the consequences of increasing urbanization to a society.

SOURCE: *British Journal of Sociology*, Vol. 2, No. 1 (March, 1951), 30– 43. London: Routledge & Kegan Paul Ltd. Reprinted by permission of the author and the publisher. ✧ Svend Riemer is professor of sociology, University of California, Los Angeles. His main interests are family, housing and family living, and urban planning. He has written articles for many professional jour- nals and is the author of *The Modern City*.

I. *Rural and Urban Social Control*

While village structures vanish more and more from the urban environment, the professional city planner endeavours to keep alive or to
revive in the city a social climate characterized by close internal cohesion
among neighbours. The paradox ventured in the title of this article presents
a goal, a desideratum rather than a fact.

Village structures are determined by a way of life (1) deeply embedded in tradition and (2) controlled by a close-knit welter of informal
social relationships among the members of the group. Geographically,
the village is characterized by close residential propinquity of those members of the community who—at work and play—are bound to each other
by frequent social contacts.

In the large modern city of the United States, all these criteria were
realized only in the flourishing immigrant neighbourhoods of the nineteenth century. Here, indeed, the village pattern of the old world was
frequently transferred to urban residential sections in the new world. These
immigrant neighbourhoods, however, were never successful in retaining
their populations.

Successive waves of European and other nationality groups moved
through the quasi-village environment of the American immigrant neighbourhood. In the process of urbanization, immigrant populations gradually lost themselves in the anonymous environment of other residential
sections where they established themselves individually as members of
the urban community at large without intermediate in-group loyalties.
Since the cessation of large-scale immigration to the United States in
1924, these village-like immigrant communities have gradually evanesced.
Some nationality groups moved to secondary settlements of higher status
in a more Americanized, i.e., urbanized, environment; others lost control
over their members in the younger generation who spread wide and far
over the entire city.

Suburban real estate developments have attempted, at times, to provide
their customers with an arrangement of construction that promised village
comforts lost in the large city. With a village green and possibly a swim-
ming-pool, a community centre or a country club in the middle of the
settlement, and a protecting wall surrounding the entire area, these "guaranteed neighbourhoods" found their greatest advantage in the exclusion of
others than the residential population from expensive recreational facilities.
They promised protection against invasion by lower status groups. They
guaranteed permanence of the family residence unendangered by the
degrading influence of undesirable association.

Such village construction in the parkland of the dormitory suburb
serves only the purpose of segregation without necessarily creating that
overlapping and intertwining of economic and social interests in the
resident group characteristic for true village structures. As a matter of

fact, residential anonymity reaches its highest degree in the suburban settlement of advanced status groups. Neighbouring, in this environment, tends to be limited to the children as the only constant users of joint recreational facilities.

Rapid urban growth, of course, ensnares actual village communities in the orbit of urban extension, either at the periphery of the growing metropolis or in the midst of vast connurbations. Again, true village structures are lost as peasants and farmers turn into commuting city workers, as close economic interdependence fails to coincide with residential propinquity, and as the common interests of the residents are reduced to the private or consumption aspects of their lives.

Thus, while actual village structures are gradually being lost in the urban environment, the efforts of the planners point in the opposite direction. The planner endeavours to revive village structures in the city. He promotes a type of neighbourhood planning which by the arrangement of construction, by landscaping and by the provision of a full scope of services for purposes of everyday living, by visual separation of the area from adjacent territories and its orientation inwards towards the playground—and other recreational facilities offer the physical setting for the development of social relations typical for the village rather than the city. The reason for this anachronism lies in the attempt to stem the tide of social disorganization which—like delinquency, divorce, crime, suicide and vice—is attributed to the anonymity of urban living.

The planned neighbourhood in the city is considered a substitute for those informal means of social control assumed to keep the villager and the small town dweller in line, forcing him—through gossip, ridicule, contempt and ostracism—into the wholesome strait-jacket of provincial conformity. Two questions arise at this juncture:

1. Whether it is indeed these informal means of social control that keep the small town clean from undesirable symptoms of social disorganization, and
2. Whether the typical city dweller is susceptible to a transfer of these means of social control to the urban environment.

To both questions, our considered answer is "No."

Small town and village people are made to conform to socially approved behaviour by the inescapability of economic pressures. The overlapping of numerous economic as well as social relationships within a limited geographical area gives to even the most superficial of social contacts economic significance. Any displeasure aroused within the sphere of leisure-time activities might have economic repercussions. The people with whom financial negotiations are entertained are the same with whom the villager rubs elbows in his private life. If the minister's son steals apples, he might find that he did so in the orchard of that member of the congregation who decides about his father's reappointment. If the local grocer becomes negligent in his church attendance, a malicious whispering campaign may cost him a lot of patronage. Informal means of social control—such as gossip and spying upon each other—are certainly at work. But they could remain powerless were it not for the fact that they are backed up by economic pressures in an environment where confinement in space forces all residents either to buy from or sell to each other.

The low level of social disorganization in the non-urban environment does not necessarily reflect upon social controls in the village, the small town and the farm. Delinquents bent upon a criminal career sooner or later vanish from the small town environment and move to the city. They move because of economic pressures exerted upon them and their families. All non-conformists tend to withdraw from an environment in which their deviant behaviour is easily discovered. They move to the city where employment is not dependent upon the private conduct of the individual.

What are the chances for the transfer of these controls to the urban environment? Without proof to the contrary, we must be sceptical about their efficacy in the city. Even in the best-planned urban neighbourhood, economic pressures upon the private conduct of the individual are lacking. Whether informal social contacts by themselves will turn the trick of reducing deviant behaviour has yet to be shown. In the small town, the combination of economic with social contacts keeps the individual in line. This combination is absent from the urban neighbourhood planned for the private spheres of daily living only.

Even in leisure-time activities, the typical city dweller is not at all prone to limit himself to contacts with neighbours dwelling in close propinquity to his own home. Apart from very special situations such as recent arrival to the city with few pre-established personal or institutional contacts, or apart from special local conditions with numerous small children in families thus restricted in their movements, apart from such special situations the city dweller tends to take advantage of his unique privilege to roam far and wide in search of a select group of friends and select recreational facilities to serve his very special needs for entertainment and self-expression.

The "freedom of the city" is the freedom to choose from innumerable potential social contacts. Social contacts are not forced upon the city dweller on the basis of residential propinquity. It is doubtful that the city dweller will ever forgo the privilege of association by choice. Under the circumstances, many planned neighbourhoods will never function as cohesive social units. The generous provision of park- and play-space within the confines of the planned neighbourhood may well be enjoyed as an unusual asset of the individual dwelling unit. Still, the neighbourhood and its facilities may fail to promote that experience of belonging which the planner—following the example of the village and the small town—tries to reproduce in the large city.

II. Neighbouring Patterns

To assess the city dweller's readiness to avail himself of the facilities provided in the conventional neighbourhood unit plan, we have to know about his propensity to "neighbour" under conditions of planned or unplanned urban environment. Such information is sorely lacking. Most neighbourhood planning has proceeded on the basis of foregone conclusions.

Experimental research about actual neighbourhood experiences has provided the author with two types of pertinent documentation. Family contact patterns were ascertained by way of interview in both Milwaukee and Madison, Wisconsin. In addition, students of the University of Wisconsin were induced to write about their individual neighbourhood experiences with the help of a Problem Guide. The materials so collected cover a wide range of actual neighbourhood experiences in communities of different size and families of different composition. No attempts were made to apply sampling methods that would have provided reliable conclusions. The intent of this research was truly "experimental." It was devised to produce that familiarity with a new field of investigation without which the formulation of pertinent hypotheses is impossible. The resultant conceptualization of the field of neighbourhood study appears on the following pages.

The empirical approach to our problem may concern itself with either

1. Neighbourhood consciousness, or
2. Neighbouring behaviour.

At closer scrutiny, neighbourhood consciousness reveals itself as an elusive phenomenon. Residents in a limited residential area of Milwaukee were asked what they considered "their" neighbourhood. Fifty-three out of 197 interviewees responded by pointing to an area of not more than a city block. Another 78 of the interviewees referred to an area of more than seven blocks. Obviously, these two groups did not have the same thing in mind when talking about their neighbourhood. Nearly all answers to this question were introduced with expressions of doubt such as "I don't know," "never thought about it," etc. These people were not only vague about the subject of discussion, but felt actually forced to make a choice between different types of experiences to which the term "neighbourhood" could be applied.

The neighbourhood may be considered as either a geographical or a social unit. As a geographical unit, the neighbourhood is considered a contiguous territory in which close neighbourly relations exist. As a social unit, the neighbourhood refers to social relations which may or may not pre-empt a contiguous city area. Neighbourhood consciousness as a social experience is subject to different interpretations.

WHAT DO YOU CONSIDER "YOUR" NEIGHBOURHOOD?

*(Responses from a residential environment
in the city of Milwaukee)*

One block or under	53
Two to three blocks	12
One square block	14
Three to six blocks	11
Two square blocks	13
Seven to ten blocks	20
Eleven to twenty blocks	21
Over twenty blocks	37
Whole city	2
Area outside neighbourhood	4
No neighbourhood	10

To consider the neighbourhood as a phenomenon anchored in the mind, rather than a phenomenon located in an area clearly delineated in space, a phenomenon resting in prevailing attitudes, customs and preferences, rather than a certain number of square miles of real estate, such shift in our thinking about the neighbourhood presents a departure from the customary approach. Uncritically, the neighbourhood has been discussed as a unit that combines both spatial and social characteristics. For purposes of analysis, we have to separate from each other the social and the spatial aspect of the phenomenon under observation. Only in this manner can we do justice to the practical problem that consists of placing these two aspects in best possible relationship to each other.

From the same urban environment, we receive most contradictory statements about neighbourhood experiences and neighbourhood activities prevailing in the area. The same residential area will be assessed very differently by people living at close distance from each other. More than that: neighbourhood experience is under the influence of individual dynamics. It does not change only from individual to individual but undergoes continuous changes in the individual life history. Neighbouring means something different at elementary-school age, at high-school age, at the age of family formation and in old age.

Furthermore, neighbourhood experiences may be associated by the same individual with different dimensions of social participation. Education and occupation, informal and organized leisure-time activities may lead to different clusters of social contacts which—rightly or wrongly— are referred to by the term "neighbourhood relations." These distinctions will stand out more clearly in our discussion of neighbouring behaviour.

If the existence of neighbourhood relations is to be based on overt behaviour, we must focus on behaviour that establishes social contact. We ask ourselves to what extent these social contacts remain confined to a contiguous city area. To make a "true" neighbourhood, one further condition would have to be satisfied. The neighbour—according to the history of the word—means literally near-dweller. Residential propinquity, therefore, is a necessary prerequisite to neighbourhood formation.

In the early cities of Western Civilization, residential propinquity led unavoidably to social interrelationship. In the farming environment, near-dwellers depended upon each other for help in emergency situations. City living diminished the exchange of mutual help among those living close to each other. In the city, distances were not such as to prohibit help from others than those living nearby in the large population settlement. Near-dwellers in the city were held together in the city by co-operative municipal function. Neighbourhood groups developed social cohesion by assuming collectively the responsibility for urban defence, water supply, fire protection, etc. In the course of the centuries since medieval city foundation, such responsibilities were gradually centralized and placed upon the shoulders of the urban community at large. Deprived of definite service functions, the urban neighbourhood retained only the loose bonds of informal social contacts which previously had flourished as adjuncts to decentralized urban self-government.

Even the informal social relations between neighbours in the city are withering away to-day. Many informal social relations take the city dweller far away from his family residence. The same is certainly true for formal social relations which carry the city dweller to the residential, commercial and industrial sections of town.

It is not necessary to demonstrate that the dormitory suburb is far removed from urban places of employment. It is more interesting to show that even such important functions as shopping and worship have been far removed from the range of what might properly be called a contiguous residential neighbourhood.

The extension of shopping relations beyond the confines of the residential neighbourhood is dependent upon new developments in urban food distribution. It is dependent upon improved storage facilities in the individual family home in the form of sizeable refrigerators or freeze lockers. It is dependent upon the availability of private motor-transportation. It is dependent, finally, upon the concentration of commercial food distribution in the hands of large chain-stores able to offer lower prices than the local grocery store. Weekly rather than daily shopping needs are carried beyond the confines of the individual neighbourhood. We venture to guess, however, that the volume of weekly shopping is continuously being enlarged at the cost of daily shopping. The long-term destiny of the local grocery store is easy to predict.

Worship is not necessarily confined within the residential neighbourhood. Due to prevailing heterogeneities, it takes more people than those living in easy walking distance from each other, to provide sufficient numbers for the operation of a church. Urban residential settlement is not based on denominational segregation. Consequently, church membership must reach out beyond spatial proximity to the individual church building. Those affiliated to a certain religious denomination are too sparsely settled in the urban fabric to draw desired facilities for worship close to all individual family homes.

Similar conditions prevail in other urban activities. If we consider all city contacts of the individual family, the limited importance of "neighbouring" becomes immediately apparent. The activity radius of the individual family extends over the entire city. The family picks and chooses from what the city has in store for it. In the process of choice, proximity to the family residence is obviously not the only principle of selection.

Still, family contacts are not spread at random over the entire urban fabric. They tend to cluster in characteristic patterns. . . .

❖   ❖   ❖   ❖   ❖

Seen within this broader framework of family contact patterns, the urban "neighbourhood" appears as a special case within the pattern of selective contact clusters. It forms a selective contact cluster, with the added criterion of being contained in close proximity to the family residence. It becomes an empirical question, then, what contact terminals are—and under what conditions—contained close to the urban residence.

Our observations, then, reveal a phenomenon closely related to neighbouring although not identical with it: namely, the phenomenon of contact clusters established either close to the family home or close to any of the more important contact points in the city area. They are not neighbourhoods proper because this term cannot be divorced from the circumstance of "near-dwelling" or from "proximity to residential location." Different walking distance areas, not necessarily close to the family home, gain social significance for the city dweller.

Walking distance areas tend to be of either of the five following types:

1. Residential.   4. Commercial.
2. Occupational.   5. Associational.
3. Educational.

They shall be so designated according to the most frequent activity around which other contact points are clustered. In practice, an overlapping of several important activities within one and the same walking distance area will be the rule rather than the exception. The reason for the formation of such contact clusters is found in the ease of communication between one contact point and the others. It is invited also by the initiation of contacts due to chance of physical presence. The dentist close to the place of work and the ice-cream parlour close to the high school are most likely preferred to others in less accessible location. Different recreational facilities in close proximity to each other appeal to the same patronage.

In the course of the individual life cycle, the total contact pattern of the individual city dweller is subject to continuous change. Before the contact pattern reaches out to city areas far remote from the individual residence, and when they shrink again in old age, or as long as they are limited due to new arrival in the city, the "neighbourhood," i.e., the residential walking distance area, gains overwhelming importance by default. The pre-school child may be limited to contacts within the city block. The schoolchild branches out, and at high-school age, friendship and recreation and education pull the young city dweller out over a considerable section of the city. Occupational activities establish new clusters of contacts close to place of work. Shopping activities extend farther for adults and with the availability of private motor-transportation. Friendship established at work will open new contact areas for the individual city dweller in other residential areas than his own. Marriage and movements of friends and relatives and the city dweller himself furthermore extend and complicate the picture. In old age, the pattern is apt to shrink due to decreasing mobility and diminishing interests.

If the primary group is to be discovered as a socializing factor in the city environment, it will not necessarily have to be tied to the residential neighbourhood. Close and intimate contacts are established in those contact areas of the city which gain significance for the individual not only due to number of repetitive contacts and waking hours spent in this environment, but in addition due to the importance of different overlapping social contacts.

III. From Neighbourhood to City Planning

Unfortunately, the endeavour to reactivate primary group relations in the large modern city has been tied to the assumption that such primary group relations are worth promoting only in the vicinity of the family home. Our thinking about social relations in the city has been dominated by the spatial dimension. A small town culture trait has thus been superimposed upon the urban environment. In the small town, the coincidence of intense social relations with proximity to the individual residence can be taken for granted. This need not be so in the city. In the city, man has gained the freedom of making social contacts with little regard to geographical distance.

The city offers opportunities to select social contacts from a large number of people and facilities gathered in the urban environment and connected by convenient and rapid means of transportation. These conditions permit the city dweller to pick and choose the social relations he wants to bother with. He does not find, like the small town dweller, the opportunities for personal and institutional contacts limited to the walking-distance area surrounding his living quarters. Social relations are not thrust upon him. He enjoys the freedom of choice.

City planning is needed in view of limitations in the urban transportation system. Transportation may be inconvenient or unduly time-consuming. For these reasons, the arrangement in space of different urban construction has to be carefully planned. Exclusive concentration upon neighbourhood planning, i.e., the planning of the walking-distance area around the individual family home, neglects those manifold opportunities which alone justify the urban way of life, which have led to city formation and which draw the farmer and the small town dweller into cityward migrations. One-sided attention to residential neighbourhood planning runs the danger of ignoring fundamental advantages that led to large population settlements in the first place. It clashes with the attitude of the typical city dweller who wants to roam within the entire urban fabric in search for occupational, educational, recreational and associational opportunities, assisted by an efficient system of transportation that releases him from the fetters of spatial confinement.

We have not yet freed ourselves, however, in thought and action, in scientific observation and planning, from domination by the spatial dimension. Preparatory to planning, urban sociology starts with the observation of "natural areas" in the urban environment and promotes the correction of minor inadequacies. The full scope of city planning invites the analysis not of urban environment as it has grown at random. It challenges the social scientist and the planner to deal with more elementary data. These data may be found in individual and family contact needs.

Such contact needs may reach out for either informal or formal personal relations. By and large, informal personal relations call for the proximity of certain residential units to each other. Formal personal relations, on the other hand, are tied to and carried out within commercial and public urban construction. For planning purposes, we have therefore to ascertain

1. The spread of family contact patterns in the city.
2. The service radius of commercial and public facilities in the city.

The purpose of functional city planning can be no other than to relate to each other family contact needs and the service areas of commercial and public facilities. They have to be related to each other in such a manner as to minimize inconvenient and time-consuming transportation.

In a well-structured urban environment services and people must be related to each other in an economical manner. Optimal conditions can be obtained by the promotion of walking-distance areas which tend to grow out of individual adjustments to the urban environment anyway. In terms of urban construction, such walking-distance areas require the clustering of commercial and public construction. Such groupings of urban construction cannot be called "neighbourhoods" because most of them will be located at longer than walking distance from the majority of family residences which they serve. These walking-distance areas have one thing in common, however, with our concern for urban neighbourhoods. They establish walking-distance areas at some maximum distance from the city residence. Here they are contained in walking distance from each other, albeit not in walking distance from the residences of most city dwellers.

The city planner must concern himself with the relative desirability of different possible clusterings of commercial and public facilities in the urban environment.

The service radius of urban facilities is not entirely a matter of choice and desired convenience. If it were so, every city dweller would want to have *all* services located either next door or—if they entail nuisances—at close distance hidden by a pleasant group of trees. To provide for the satisfaction of such needs is economically impossible. To operate economically, with a profit or at reasonable cost, all urban services demand recruitment areas of different size from which to draw their clientele. The more specialized the type of service, the fewer the people who avail themselves of the service at all, and the less frequently they will make use of the service, the larger the service area will have to be.

To establish walking-distance areas in the city environment, the city planner is charged with the task of combining into a cluster of construction commercial and public facilities dependent upon service areas of equal size. A number of concentric service areas will thus be made to overlap. With increasing specialization of service, ever larger areas will be required to provide sufficient patronage. The deciding factor for the combination of some and not other services is the service radius of these facilities, which also determines the distance at which these service clusters will have to be located from each other to operate efficiently.

While a well-structured urban environment may thus be planned for, an environment that does not leave any service loopholes in the urban fabric and meets the demand for "walking-distance areas" at varying distances from the city residence, the need for informal personal relations is thereby not considered. Informal social relations call for proximity to each other of those residences the occupants of which want to associate frequently, at a minimum of inconvenience and time spent.

The scope of neighbourhood planning becomes apparent if it is realized that either of two conditions must be fulfilled to encourage the city dweller to limit his informal associations to near-dwellers. The city dweller must be either:

1. Willing to limit the majority of his leisure-time activities to association with those people who live by chance next door or in easy walking distance, i.e., he must be void of personal or activity interests that will draw him to some other location, leaving the planned neighbourhood without social function; or he must be

2. Willing to congregate within the residential neighbourhood with like-minded and like-interested people, i.e., he and his friends must stand ready to move to put life into well-planned neighbourhood construction.

Such conditions are the exception in the modern city. It is doubtful, therefore, that even a semblance of village life will find acceptance in the modern metropolis.

THE STRANGEST PLACE IN CHICAGO

John Bartlow Martin

Sometimes a purely descriptive piece of writing brings to life with startling impact ideas that otherwise seem dull and mechanical, commonplace, or meaningless. In this article John Bartlow Martin performs such a feat. He never uses the social science terms "invasion," "succession," or "segregation." He does not discuss rentals, slum areas as such, city planning, or race discrimination in its varied aspects. He simply describes a building in its physical aspects, its locale, the life that goes on there, and the differences between that place as it was years ago and at the time when he was writing (the building has subsequently been torn down). He makes it live for us. Invasion and succession—that's what happened here!

From the Chicago loop, where sunlight off the lakefront strikes the shining towers, State Street runs straight south, wide, busy with streetcars and heavy trucks. Quickly the buildings get shabby—little stores selling auto parts, a junkyard crammed with rusting wreckage. The city is harsh: concrete streets, brick building walls, black steel viaducts. Beyond 22nd Street the faces of the people are black. This is the South Side Negro section. Here the street is quieter, the sun is hazy and dirty and pale, the sky is a network of trolley wires. Across an expanse of new-turned earth stretches a new public housing project, with a play-yard for the children, and at 32nd Street begins the new campus of the Illinois Institute of Technology, sleek brick-and-glass buildings surrounded by new trees and new grass. And just beyond the Institute rises a great gray hulk of brick, four stories high, topped by an ungainly smoke-stack, ancient and enormous, filling half the block north of 34th Street between State and Dearborn. It is the Mecca Building.

Let us note its setting. Across State Street are a cleaning shop, a barber shop, a grocery, the Railroad Men's Social Club, McClain's Hair Goods, a Bar-B-Q, the office of H. Young the Icer, the Church of God & Saints of Christ in an old storefront. An old man pulls a handcart filled with junk across an empty lot. From a deep hole tunneled under the sidewalk emerges

SOURCE: *Harper's Magazine*, December, 1950. Copyright © 1950 by Harper & Brothers. Reprinted by permission of Harold Ober Associates Incorporated. ❖ John Bartlow Martin is a former Ambassador to the Dominican Republic and a member of the Board of Directors, Chicago Institute for Psychoanalysis. He has written many books, among which are *Call It North Country: The Story of Upper Michigan, Indiana: An Interpretation, Break Down the Walls, The South Says Never, My Life in Crime,* and *Jimmy Hoffa's Hot.*

the head of a little Negro boy, playing. The sidewalk is cracked and broken. Nearby are rickety wooden tenements.

The Mecca Building is U-shaped. The dirt courtyard is littered with newspapers and tin cans, milk cartons and broken glass. Pigeons roost on a car on blocks. A skinny white dog huddles in a doorway. Iron fire escapes run up the building's face and ladders reach from them to the roof. There are four main entrances, two on Dearborn and two on State Street. At each is a gray stone threshold and over each is carved "The Mecca." The Mecca was constructed as an apartment building in 1891, a splendid palace, a showplace of Chicago. Today it is still an apartment building and a show-place but of a very different sort. It has become one of the most remarkable Negro slum exhibits in the world. Let us pass through the arched doorway of the Mecca; let us see what the Mecca looks like inside, see who the people in it are and how they live, whence they came and why they stay.

Inside, a powerful odor assails the visitor at once, musty, heavy, a smell compounded of urine and stale cooking and of age, not necessarily an un-pleasant odor but a close powerful one, which, like that of marijuana, once smelled is never forgotten. The stone slab step is hollowed. The lower part of the walls of the vestibule once was covered with marble but now the marble has been stripped away in ragged patches, revealing naked brick and mortar. It is dark here. Ahead stretches a corridor; it is like a tunnel, it seems endless and it is indeed a block long, running all the way to the Dearborn Street entrance; down its whole length hang only five light bulbs, glowing feebly in the gloom. Tan paint is peeling from the wall, the doors of apartments open into the corridor. This is the base of the U in the U-shaped building.

The arms of the U are identical. They are great halls, each lit by a skylight four stories overhead which, because of the dirt that has accumu-lated on the glass through years of neglect, admits the kind of unreal light found underseas. This light slants down in great long angling shafts filled with floating dust, shifting as the sun moves across the sky, falling in fitful patches on the floor. Around the walls run three balconies guarded by ornate wrought-iron grillwork, and off these balconies open the doors to the apartments, like tiers of cells in a prison cellblock. The floor in the center of the well is of hardwood, splintered now, and beneath the bal-conies it is of tile, broken in many places. A janitor with a wheelbarrow is slowly patching the tile with concrete; his shovel makes a rasping, scraping sound. From somewhere in the building comes always the sound of distant human voices—women talking, a baby squalling, children screaming, men muttering, no words distinguishable. Spittle splats flatly on the tile floor, falling from a great height, spat by a man or a woman standing on an upper balcony. All day long people stand at the balconies, leaning on the wrought-iron railings with hands clasped out over them, gazing out at the other people facing them across the well in silence, gazing down at the floor far below, spitting, small human figures in a vast place, two or three on each of the four floors, occasionally calling back and forth to one another but most of the time just standing silent. The building is never entirely quiet, not even very late at night, since so many people live here; but it is so vast that it seems quiet, even amid uproar.

In the center on the ground floor is a long narrow bank of mailboxes, tarnished brass, 176 of them. One has thirteen names on it, including seven different family names, indicating that thirteen adults expecting mail occupy that particular apartment. Late in the morning the postman comes, a man in blue. Three tenants wait respectfully at the side while he distributes the mail. On the balcony above, two men leaning on the railing watch him critically. "He'll never get it all done doing it one at a time," and, "He's a new man." At last he finishes, and tenants emerge from their apartments to get their mail. From a high balcony a toddler throws a chunk of broken tile; it bounces on the floor by the mailboxes. A stooped old woman wearing a black sweater and black shawl, only her hair and her eyeballs white, moves slowly and painfully in the shadows beneath the balcony, keeping close to the wall as long as possible, touching it with bony fingers, and only leaving it when she must to venture across the open floor to the mailboxes; gets her mail, then retreats along the wall to the stairs, where a man steps aside, saying kindly, "You come down to see what you got, didn't you?" and she says, in a gasping voice, "I'm going take my good time," then begins to ascend, pulling herself up by the railing, first her right foot up one step, then the left slowly after it, her body bent so low that her face almost touches the next step, stopping at the landing to rest and stare at the peeling walls with watery, half-blind eyes. Near the mailboxes three children are jumping rope, using a double rope, two boys swinging the two long strands in sweeping arcs while a girl rocks to and fro at one side to get into the rhythm before jumping in. Children ride battered tricycles across the floor, safe here from the traffic of the streets. On a balcony children are playing store, using a cardboard box. One of them throws a fistful of paper over the railing and it flutters down: policy slips, there must be a policy station here.

The wind blows in off Dearborn Street and a young woman neat in black enters, walking a leashed dog and humming a hymn. Somewhere a child is crying over and over, "Mummy, Mummy." In the long dark corridor a dog is nosing at garbage from an upset garbage can. From somewhere comes a clatter, perhaps of a falling garbage-can lid, and the high mad cackling laughter of an old man. A very young child standing on the third floor balcony urinates through the ornate iron grillwork and the urine falls to the ground floor far below and a woman calls to him, "Don't you do that, you got no right to do that, I'm going to tell your mother." The ice man comes wearing a leather protector on his shoulder and back, carrying a cake of ice that gleams whitely against his black face and hat. A woman calls from the third floor, "Bring fifty pounds to 304½," and he plods to the stairs.

In the shadow against a pillar marked with match-strikes leans a man, his shirt-collar buttoned but without a necktie, his hat-brim slanting low over his scarred face, a cigarette slanting from his mouth; he is just standing there watching. How many people live here? He laughs. "I don't know." Two thousand? "Oh, more than that. There's 176 apartments and some of 'em's got seven rooms and they're all full." A heavy round-faced man in a long white apron holding a ball-peen hammer approaches: "You are visiting some of the historic sites of the city? You found one all right. If it don't fall in on you while you're lookin'." How many people live here? "That," he says, "is a mystery. You'll find them sleeping in bathtubs, sleeping in the kitchen under the sink, anywhere they can sleep." Nobody, in truth, knows how many people inhabit the Mecca Building. The janitor, Jimmy Sanders, estimates 2,300; the Democratic precinct captain, William Patrick Fitzgerald, who has lived here eighteen years, estimates 1,400; the owner doesn't know. All the inhabitants except one woman are Negroes. The Mecca Building contains more people than most Chicago precincts; indeed, it constitutes a precinct in itself, the 27th Precinct of the 2nd Ward.

On the third floor an old woman stands by the railing, a towel wound round her head, a big gold ring on her finger. Watching dispassionately as children run in from school for lunch, their screams ringing piercingly through the building, she says judiciously, "That size runs to roller skates," and then, "When I first came here they used to control the children. White people hadn't been gone so long, 1917 it was. They used to have a policeman here nights, you could hear a needle drop. Now they's shooting here five times a night. Them young men and the young girls is the worst. I'd move out tonight if they'd find me a house. I moved out for a while once but I came back to have company, my daughter lives here and my granddaughter was born here," and she turns and shuffles into her flat.

In the flat, wallpaper hangs from the walls in great sheets. Clean newspapers are spread on the floor. Over the dresser are some artificial flowers, and a transparent plastic wrapper covers the bed. The sideboard, radio, and table are cluttered with family photographs. Mottoes and pictures hang on the walls, a picture of Jesus Christ and a crucifix put out by a liquor store, a plaque, "My Help cometh from the Lord," and also secular shrines: a large frame holding the pictures of Abraham Lincoln and Frederick Douglass flanked by Booker T. Washington, Paul Laurence Dunbar, W. E. B. DuBois, and other race leaders. And a framed faded campaign picture of Franklin D. Roosevelt. She calls Lincoln "Abraham." She was born in Alabama. She is bent and stooped, aged. She says, "I live here all by myself, me and my Lord," and then, as her visitor departs, she touches his arm and says gently, "Do you know anything about that man we call Jesus, do you know him personally, you ought to get in touch with him." Outside her door a teen-age boy is standing at the balcony railing, trying to spit clear across to the other side.

In the long first-floor corridor the janitor passes, Jimmy, a short squat man in a leather cap and jacket, ambling along with a Yankee drill in his hand. "I'm the maintenance man," he says. "I do a little of everything— work a little, fight a little, sleep a little, play a little." Right now he is accompanying the rent collector, a white man, a wiry Scot named John. "I go around with him," Jimmy says, shifting the stub of his dead cigar to the other corner of his mouth, "because the young fellas in the building think he's got money with him." About a year ago the young fellows robbed an insurance collector of $17. The rent collector, John, says, "I lost all my hair fighting with these people," and laughs. Actually, he has little trouble collecting rents, which are cheap. His troubles are of a different sort: he and Jimmy fight a hopeless rearguard action against decay and vandalism. "Last night they shot out the light bulbs," says Jimmy. "And the windows —in the last year I bet I put in over two hundred windows. They break 'em fast as you put 'em in." Who does it? "Outsiders, most of it. And the kids here. The kids get to playin' and throwin' at one another and first thing you know they break the glass. There's nothin' you can do about it. You can't kill one 'cause he broke the glass."

As the rent collector walks along, a woman calls from the third-floor balcony, "Hold your head up, John, John, hold your head up, I want to talk to you," but John plods on, grinning secretly. A sign by the basement stairs reads, "Put All Complaints in Mail Box." Near the State Street entrance another janitor has temporarily left his job of cementing a broken place in the floor and is stooping over at an apartment door, digging with a knife at something in the door. He gets it out: a bullet. "That's a thirty-eight," he says, turning it over in his hand, shiny and twisted. Then, to a woman who has come to the door, "They try to shoot you out last night?" She laughs. "Yeh, try to kill me. Like shootin' rabbits in a swamp down yonder." He says, "They was really shootin' here last night. Some of 'em shootin' for fun, some of 'em fightin'. That's every night around here. Couple of 'em got shot the other night." Any ever killed? "Oh, yes, one got killed summer before last up there in that corner," pointing upward. Why? "I don't know."

Down the stairs comes a man on crutches, his left leg off above the knee, his pants leg pinned up, coming down the steps, the crutch and his good leg visible first, then the man, thin, wearing white pants and a brown coat and hat; he walks diagonally past the mailboxes to the grocery, pausing to adjust his pipe.

High on the fourth west gallery, close up under the skylight, the balcony seems narrow. Two boys wrestle on it, and one falls heavily against the iron railing, which trembles but holds firm. It is four stories down to the ground floor; nobody ever heard of a child falling. An old woman is sweeping the floor. High up here at the north end a dozen young men and women are congregated, well-dressed, two of the men off to one side leaning idle on the railing and peering sullenly down, the others close together, laughing, fooling around with each other, the girls in tight white sweaters, the young men in snapbrim hats and suitcoats over sweaters.

❖   ❖   ❖   ❖   ❖

When the Mecca Building was constructed it was considered one of the largest and finest apartment buildings in Chicago if not in America. It catered (almost needless to say) to a white clientele. But after 1900 the Negro migration to Chicago forced the black belt to expand, and by 1912 the Mecca Building was the home of the Negro elite—doctors, lawyers, business men.

A woman who lives there still, Mrs. Florence Clayton, arrived in 1916, and she remembers, "There were carpets on the stairs and halls. There were goldfish in the fountain. On the first floor there were lounge chairs and outdoors we had a flower garden and beautiful trees and green grass, you could go out there, oh, it was lovely. The courtyard was all fenced in and there was a lovely walk through the flowers."

The building started to deteriorate during the 1917–18 war. So did the whole neighbourhood. Booming war industries pulled thousands of Negroes to Chicago. The luckier ones abandoned the region of 35th and State to the poor and the wicked. The black-and-tans where Chicago jazz flowered were right here. Jimmy, the janitor, recalls, "There were lots of fights and cuttings. Building was full of prostitutes. I saw a man throw a prostitute over the third floor railing—from the third floor to the first floor. Didn't hurt her much. She only weighed ninety pounds, kind of light. Finally one of the pimps killed the building watchman. Did it over a woman. And she wasn't even living with him." Jimmy pushes his leather cap back off his forehead. "That about ended it, though. They got a new watchman and he was a killer. He was just a little man but he had great big eyes and he'd shoot you with either hand. He had a cemetery of his own before he died. He only killed nine people—between the basement here and that wire fence. The building got kind of decent after that— families, working people."

And then the Depression came along, and the wicked left, and almost none but the poor remained. The Depression was awful in the black belt. About 1932 the bottom fell out. One woman who lived here then recalls, "The building was partly empty. One lady told me she was sitting down on the curb and the police passed and it was cold and they asked her what was the matter and she said she'd been set out and they told her to come on in here and the first flat she'd find, sit down. They carried her to court later but they didn't make her get out, they couldn't, people had no work to do then. It was always warm and nice in here during the Depression."

The Depression accounts for the presence today of the building's only white tenant, a heavy, soft-faced, white-haired woman of sixty-six. "I'd been a housekeeper at a hotel and one of my maids, a colored girl, she was married to a white doctor and they lived here in the Mecca Building. I couldn't find a job, I just got stuck, I couldn't make it, and they took me in." Some of the Mecca inhabitants who moved in while they were on relief are now earning good money in the steel mills or on Pullman cars and one or two earn upward of $5,000 a year, but they are imprisoned here by the scarcity of dwellings for Negroes. A few of the longtime tenants remain by choice, oddly proud of the building. A few earn money by living there—they sublet rooms in their apartments for as much as $12 a week. The janitor Jimmy says, "Every day people come in, many as ten or twelve a day, lookin' for a place, they been walkin' the street, lookin' for some place to go, say, 'Janitor, if you can get me an apartment in here I'll give you $100,' but there ain't none."

There are several women's clubs in the building, such as the Old-Age Pensioners Club and the Twelve Tribes. Fitzgerald, the Democratic precinct captain, has been elected sweetheart of these. Fitzgerald, a neat, well-dressed, youngish man, has said, "If there's a weddin' I'm there, if there's a death I'm there, if there's a birth I'm there. I had a baby born in my car a while back, trying to get the mother to the hospital." Fitzgerald is a court bailiff by day. The Mecca precinct has voted Democratic since 1932. Like the other tenants, Fitzgerald worries about the children. "In summertime the police chase them off the street. One day I come home and the police had backed up a wagon ready to take a whole load to the station for standing in front of the building. I had to put a stop to it. I had three ball clubs last summer and got uniforms for 'em all."

In a vacant store on the ground floor is the Mecca Center, for children. Nobody knows how many children are being raised in the Mecca Building but most people guess five hundred, and now at 4:30 P.M. on a Thursday fifteen of the five hundred are in the Mecca Center. The Center is a big square bare room, a dais at one side, a great clutter of dusty newspapers behind a desk, a piano and a windup Victrola against one wall, a tom-tom and Indian heads in the display window. Two older boys are playing Ping-pong and at a small table two younger ones are playing checkers but the rest of the younger ones, probably from nine to twelve years old, are chasing each other around the room, snapping cap-guns at each other, and soon the checker game stops and all thirteen of the younger ones are chasing each other, climbing over tables and chairs, leaping through the air onto each others' backs, screaming wildly; the Ping-pong players, older, proceed with their game, each with an arm outstretched to fend off the littler kids, occasionally pausing to take a cut at a near one's head; a dozen chairs stacked against a wall collapse as a boy's body crashes into them. A man in a hat is standing in a corner watching, saying vaguely, "She was supposed to come and be a musical program but I ain't seen her come in."

On the wall is a program schedule allotting various hours of the week to such activities as "Teen-Age Club," "Children's Story-Telling Hour," "Parents' Club Meeting." Right now, it is "Children's Game Period." The man watching says sharply, "You—let that Victrola alone," to a boy climbing onto it in order to leap onto another boy's back. A woman arrives bustling in. "I teach music and dramatics and folk dancing. I have about sixty enrolled. From six to eight we have singing and at nine physical culture and clubs." She is taking off her gloves, as unmindful of the children as they are of her; the children are growing more serious in their play, the temper has changed, ugliness has crept in, they battle silently, not laughing or screaming, only panting hard. The man is making plans to take some of them to the circus.

In one apartment in the building a woman and her husband are raising nine children, raising them in one room. This summer afternoon she is sitting in a chair by the door of the one room, her baby on the bed, evidently asleep but looking dead it is so thin and still, and the mother is saying, "It is hot at night, at night you burn up. My husband and I sleep in the bed. The kids sleep on the cot." The nine kids. They are from nine months to fifteen years in age. The room is eight feet by eleven. In it are one bed, one davenport, one radio, one light bulb, one picture, two straight wood chairs, one wicker table (on which stand a seashell, a jar of deodorant, and a can of face powder), one calendar. Back of the bed is a closet curtained with a rag. One necktie hangs on a nail in the wall. The plaster is broken. Her husband earns $45 a week as a machine operator. They pay $6 a week for this room. They have lived in this room four years.

The mother is twenty-nine years old. When she and her husband first came to Chicago they lived in one room on Wentworth Avenue, then in three rooms on Prairie Avenue until "the lady sold the building," then in five rooms elsewhere on Prairie Avenue again "till the lady sold the building," then in four rooms elsewhere on Prairie "till the man sold the building," then here. They came here on August 6, 1946. "My husband knew the man that had this apartment so he let us have a place in it that same evening. We were out on the street." They can find no other place to live. "I looked so much that I'm just disgusted about it. They say you're a citizen of Chicago and on votin' day they're right up to your door to vote. My husband, he wrote to the Mayor of Chicago and everyone else and I don't see no results," and she rises and fumbles behind a curtain on the window ledge and finds two letters. She is young, quick-moving, pretty; her teeth flash and she wears big gold earrings and she appears about the age of her oldest daughter, fifteen, who now comes in and stands in the doorway looking reproachful. One letter is a long form letter from the Chicago Housing Authority:

"Dear Friend,

". . . The housing projects now in operation have such lengthy waiting lists that no additional applications are being taken at this time. . . ." The other is a personal letter from a Housing Authority official: "Mayor Kennelly has referred to us for reply your letter of March 2, concerning your need for adequate housing. We are very sorry."

"All this stuff's just a racket," says the mother of nine. "They ain't doing nothing about it. Makes me sick." She hitches her chair around to face the wall. "After all, my husband works and makes an honest livin' and he do support his family the best that a workin' man can. His children do get clothes, the onliest kick that they can have is that they don't have no place to live. And that's not his fault." The baby on the bed stirs a little, then lies still again.

Until 1941 the Mecca Building was owned by a New York estate. The janitor Jimmy only once saw a representative of the estate. In 1941 the estate sold the Mecca to its next-door neighbor, the Illinois Institute of Technology. The Institute bought the building for only one purpose: to tear it down. The Institute was expanding its campus in accordance with a neat plan integrated with the neat plans of numerous other agencies for clearing the South Side slums. It wanted to replace the Mecca Building with a laboratory. But its plans ran head-on into an important need of the people who dwelt in the Mecca Building, the need for a place to live.

For nine years it has tried to evict them, taking them to court and warning them the Mecca is a firetrap. Thus far the tenants have managed to generate enough political pressure to stay. Recently, when the Institute again started eviction proceedings, State Senator C. C. Wimbish, a lawyer who has represented the tenants in court, said, "If they try to put these people out, they'll have a race riot down there on State Street and I intend to make it as tense as possible. Any roof is better than no roof."

It is quiet in the building on a summer morning, quiet as a tomb. Spit falls flatly on the ground floor, spat by a silent watcher high on the balcony, and in a dark corner recess on the topmost floor a young girl, pretty, wearing a tight white sweater, strains against a young man leaning on the wall. An old man in blue pajamas, his eyes wild and staring, his body very thin, totters along, clutching at the railing, saying in a high, cracked voice, to a visitor, "Call me a telephone number please, mister, will you call me a telephone number," but a large woman steps from a doorway and shakes her head at the visitor, making circling motions beside her temple, and moves to take the old man's arm, and seeing her he starts, as though to run, then weeps, and she leads him away. A puff of blue smoke hangs in the dead air on the second balcony where a man is leaning on the railing, smoking. A janitor collects garbage in a cart that rumbles on the broken tile like a tumbril. Everything echoes in the halls, voices are hard to comprehend, are confused with distant sounds.

A visitor twists the bell on Mrs. Griffin's apartment and she calls, "Who is it?" then unfastens the chain. Her mother is sitting by the window in the sun, as always. Mrs. Griffin says that when she got the most recent notice to vacate, she went house-hunting: "I found a place to buy at a real estate office way up on the North Side but no other colored people live right there, and I don't want to get bombed on," as indeed many Chicago Negroes have been when they tried to leave the black belt. She goes over beside her mother, who is rocking. "I think this housing situation is terrible, it's all politics, that's all. I'm not mad at the school. It's their property, we know that. I'm mad 'cause all this politics. Put 'em in office and they didn't did nothin'. They build streets and superhighways and recreation—not houses. They should turn that money loose and stop it—people has got to have some place to live. They gonna do *anything* if they don't."

She laughs, but does not sound amused: "They say they gonna place us somewhere. *Place* us! I don't wanta be placed anywhere myself. They might place me in some mudhole somewhere and I never did live in that," and she laughs again. Her mother mutters something. "I don't know what they going to do with us. After all, there's no use in pushing us around from one place to another, that's no way to live." And then, after a pause, "It's all so mean."

Her mother, rocking, has started muttering steadily; she is looking out the window, her head in its white lace cap bobbing gently up and down. What is Mrs. Griffin going to do?

"I don't know. I'll have to have a place for my mother. I couldn't tell you what I'm going to do, to save my neck." Her mother, rocking, begins to mutter louder, but her words are not intelligible, it is just a human voice, muttering, and it is impossible to tell whether in anger or in joy, it is only sound.

* 70 *

EFFECTS OF THE MOVE

TO THE SUBURBS

Herbert J. Gans

One aspect of the urbanization process in America, especially since World War II, has been an extensive migration from the central city to the suburbs. For some time now this suburban life has been subjected to scathing criticism, especially by essayists and journalists who claim the move to the suburbs creates many social and social-psychological problems. Most of this writing, however, is impressionistic and based on little careful, empirical study of those who have moved from city to suburbs. In this selection Gans analyzes data from several systematic studies and concludes that suburban pathology is more myth than fact.

SOURCE: "Effects of the Move from City to Suburb," from *The Urban Condition*, chap. 14, edited by Leonard J. Duhl with the assistance of John Powell, © 1963 by Basic Books, Inc., Publishers. ✧ Herbert J. Gans is Research Associate, Institute of Urban Studies, and associate professor of sociology, Teachers College, Columbia University. His interests include community studies, stratification, mass media of communication, popular culture, and city planning. He has written *Urban Villagers: Group and Class in the Life of Italian-Americans* and was a contributing author to *Human Behavior and Social Processes*.

Of the many changes that have taken place in America since World War II, one of the most important, and certainly the most visible, has been the migration of the white middle class from the city to the suburbs. Every American city, large and small, is now ringed by suburban subdivisions of varying sizes and price levels, and where once farmers raised fruits and vegetables for city tables, young families are now raising children.

Much has been written about the suburban exodus, and much of that has been critical. Journalists, essayists, social workers, psychologists, and psychiatrists have argued that the departure from the city, and suburban life itself, have had undesirable effects on the people involved and on the larger society. The critics have suggested that suburbia is one of the slayers of traditional American individualism, that it has made people more conforming and other-directed. They have argued that there is too much socializing, useless hyperactivity in voluntary associations, competition, and conspicuous consumption. Many of these evils are thought to be the result of boredom produced by the demographic homogeneity of suburban life, and by the loss of the stimulation associated with city life. The critics have also described a matriarchy and child-dominated society, resulting from the lack of job opportunities within the average suburb and the husband's consequent absence from the home during the children's waking hours. More recently, a psychiatrist has argued that the suburban way of life is a product of excessive social mobility and is so full of stress that it increases psychosomatic illness, divorce, alcoholism, suicide attempts, and mental illness generally. In short, suburbia is thought to be a source of negative effects in American life.

Although the concept of suburban pathology has entered our folklore, empirical studies of people who have moved from city to suburb suggest that the concept is false, that it is a myth rather than a fact. This paper attempts to describe the actual effects of the move, and to consider the implications these create for city planners, social planners, and the professions which Erich Lindemann has aptly described as caretakers.

Effects of the Move from City to Suburb

The effects of suburban life can best be determined through an investigation of behavior changes which people undergo after the move. A number of sociological studies have now been made of this topic. My own analysis will be based primarily on preliminary conclusions from my own research among people who moved from Philadelphia and other nearby cities to a new suburban community of low-priced single-family homes. My findings are similar to those of Berger's study of factory workers who moved from Richmond, California, to a suburban tract in Milpitas; and to Willmott's study of London slum dwellers who moved to Dagenham, a quasi-suburban municipal housing estate. These studies suggest the following conclusions:

1. For the vast majority of city dwellers, the move to the suburb results in relatively few, and for the most part, minor changes in the way of life. As one respondent explained: "I don't know how a new house changes your life. You have a pattern you go by, and that stays the same no matter where you live."

2. The most frequently reported changes that do take place are not caused by the move to the suburb, but are reasons for moving there in the first place. These reasons are based on aspirations for ownership of a single-family house that are today satisfied only in suburbia. These aspirations have not been created by the suburbs, however, and are therefore not effects of the move.

3. A few changes in behavior can be traced to life in the suburb itself, independent from aspirations people held before they moved. Some of these can therefore be designated as effects of the move. Most of the changes are positive in nature, but a few result in problems that require solutions.

4. Most of the effects described by the myth of suburbia either can be traced to factors other than the move to suburbia, or do not take place at all.

Each of these conclusions will now be discussed in further detail. The studies I have cited are in agreement that people's lives are not changed drastically by the move to the suburb. Berger found, for example, that factory workers continued to maintain their working-class styles when they became homeowners, and showed no interest in adopting the patterns of social life, religious activity, voting behavior, status-striving, or class mobility predicted by the suburban myth. My own study reached the same conclusions about a more middle-class population. These two studies are based on interviews with people about two years after the move to the suburbs. The same results have been obtained by Willmott's study, however, which indicated that after twenty to forty years of life in Dagenham the residents maintained most of the working-class ways of life that they had pursued in the slums from which they came.

My own research asked people specifically what changes they had experienced as a result of the move. Although the analysis of these interviews is still in process, a preliminary review of the data suggests the following changes as most important: the satisfactions of a new home and of home ownership, the availability of more living space, increased social life, somewhat greater organizational participation, and the development of family and community financial problems. Adolescents and culturally deviant people experience some social isolation, and adaptation problems.

Most of these changes fall into the second category mentioned above: they are the results of pre-occupancy aspirations, rather than the effects of the suburb. Thus, the changes reported most often derive from owning a home, and having more space inside and outside the house. Home ownership gives people the feeling of having an equity—or sharing it with the bank—more privacy from neighbors than they had either in apartments or Philadelphia row-houses, and an opportunity to improve the house and yard in their own, individual way. This not only satisfies desires for self-expression and creativity, but for joint family activity around the house that brings the family closer together. The house is also a locale for the relaxation that many working- and lower middle-class Americans derive from "puttering" and "tinkering." The increased living space which people have obtained as a result of their move permits adults and children to get out of each other's way more easily than before, and this in turn reduces family conflict.

The crucial change here is that of house type, rather than community: from the rented apartment or row-house to the single-family house. Since the opportunity for home ownership is by and large available only in the suburb, at least for new houses in the low and medium price ranges, this is primarily why young families move from the city to the suburb. Even so, I suspect similar changes would be reported by people who move from an apartment to a house within the city limits, or within the suburbs.

Other frequently mentioned changes are an increase in social life and in organizational activity. These have been reported in many new suburbs, and can be traced to the newness of the communities, rather than to the fact that they are suburban. Moving into a new community creates an initial feeling of cohesion and universal friendliness, especially if there are shared problems. These feelings may disappear as people settle down, the novelty of the community wears off, and class and other cultural differences make themselves felt. Even so, there is probably more social life among suburbanites than among city dwellers of equal age and socio-economic level. There are several reasons for this difference. First, many people move to the suburbs with the hope of making new friends, and those that come with this purpose are able to do so. For example, the interviews I conducted six to nine months after the move show that 23 out of 55 couples wanted to do more visiting with other couples and 83 per cent achieved their wish. (These interviews were conducted among a random sample of *all* residents, not just ex-city dwellers, but among the 13 ex-city dwellers in this sample, the 5 who wanted to do more visiting in their new home all achieved their aim.) Also, there are many people of similar age and with similar interests, and many opportunities to meet them. And finally, a new house encourages entertaining, while the absence of movies and restaurants in a new community discourages other forms of diversion.

The increase in community activity can also be attributed to the newness of the community. A new suburb usually lacks the basic church and voluntary organizations which residents need. Consequently, even people who have never been active before and had no intention of becoming so find themselves helping to start organizations in their new community. Once the organization is safely under way, they drop out, and eventually the typical pattern develops, in which a small number of people are active in many organizations and the large majority are inactive.

The remaining changes listed earlier can be attributed to the move itself, and are thus an effect of suburban life. Probably the most important one—at least in a low price suburb—is the development of family and community financial problems. Since a house is more expensive to keep up than the apartments from which most people come, suburban life adds new expenditures to the family budget. Many of them are unavoidable ones. If they coincide with the increasing expenditures of a growing family, as they usually do, the household budget is often under considerable strain. Since the preponderance of young families also creates new needs for classrooms and teachers, the tax rate is likely to rise at the same time, thus increasing the financial burden even further.

This in turn has a number of other effects, most of them undesirable. Financial problems are a prime cause of marital conflicts, or a new source of discord for couples already saddled with marital difficulties. Moreover, these problems have consequences for the entire community. In American society, private expenditures have traditionally had higher priority than public ones. As the former rise, people try to reduce their financial problems by demanding reductions in public expenditures. This hampers the provision of needed community services, and especially so in a new community. Moreover, political conflicts develop between those who want additional services, and can pay the taxes, and those who want services cut to the bone because they are unwilling or unable to pay for them. Since school expenditures constitute about three-fourths of the local public expenditures, this conflict often focuses around the school and may extend to curriculum questions as well. This problem is typically found in the low and medium price suburbs, especially those which lack industrial taxpayers.

The move to the suburbs also creates behavior changes of a largely negative type for the adolescents and for those who deviate culturally from the majority of their neighbors. Adolescents are perhaps the most enthusiastic city dwellers in our society, since they are frequent users of urban entertainment facilities. Many of them suffer in the move to the low density suburb. Unless they have cars, they cannot easily get to the nearby shopping centers; and if they do go there, the proprietors object because high shopping center rents make adolescent trade unprofitable. As a result, the teen-agers become bored, and may turn to vandalism and miscellaneous mischief to get even with the adults who have inflicted suburbia—or what some teen-agers have called "endsville"—on them. Nevertheless, the actual delinquency rate remains low, mainly because the large majority of adolescents are middle-class ones whose life is taken up with school work and friends.

In the community I studied, the cultural minorities were not ethnic or religious groups, but cosmopolite middle- and upper middle-class families, and working-class people. The cosmopolites may move to suburbia because it is easier to raise their children there, but they miss the city's cultural facilities, as well as people with interests similar to their own. Although they become unhappy, their discontent has positive functions for the community. Quite often, they take more part in community activities than they would have in the city or in a more cosmopolite suburb because, like other minorities, they stream to organizations to find friends. Also, they set up civic groups which try to persuade the community to accept their ideas and high standards for education and municipal government. While the cosmopolites generally lack the votes to implement their standards, they are more influential than their numbers, and contribute organizational skill and knowledge to the community. Moreover, their ability to express themselves in the larger community adds to the total set of alternative policies under public discussion, thus improving the quality of the policy-making process.

A second group of cultural deviants is the working-class population from the city. Not only do they feel the economic pinch most severely, but some report that the distance from the city, and the lack of public transportation have cut them off from relatives and old friends. The ones who suffer most are the people who have come directly from neighborhoods in which they grew up, and especially those who cannot make friends in the new community. Since they may lack the social skills and the geographical mobility of the cosmopolites, they cannot defend themselves as easily against social isolation.

It should be noted that the problems of both the cosmopolites and the working-class people result from being in a numerical minority, rather than from suburban residence. They do not suffer from pressures to conform, but from a shortage of like-minded people in their surroundings. Were they to live in communities with more compatible people, many of their problems would disappear.

Most of the changes attributed to suburban life by the myth of suburbia are either insignificant, or not supported by the available evidence. For example, the increase in commuting time seemed, in my study, to be lower than is often thought. Fifty per cent of 400 people responding to a mail questionnaire indicated their journey to work was longer; 37 per cent, that it was now shorter. For the entire sample, the median journey was only thirty-three minutes each way. Among those interviewed, only about 10 per cent reported spending less time with their family, but about 40 per cent reported spending more time than they did in their previous residence. Moreover, 39 per cent of the respondents reported that the family did more things together than in their previous residence. Fifty-nine per cent reported no change, and only one person reported fewer joint activities.

As I noted earlier, most of the joint family activity is stimulated by the new house, and is likely to decrease as its novelty wears off. Nevertheless, two years of observation revealed no evidence that suburban life had any unilaterally harmful effect on either the quality or quantity of family life. The myth-makers' claim that suburbia is creating a new matriarchy in America is not justified either. Women may have greater equality and more influence in the home than their mothers and grandmothers, but this is a universal trend in American society, especially among working-class and lower middle-class people.

Maladies such as status-striving, competition, and conformity, which are prominent in the suburban myth, are less so in the actual suburb. My observations suggested that much of what is called competition or status-seeking is really an expression of normal class differences, as seen by those of lower status. Thus, lower income respondents described the way of life of their more affluent neighbors as "showing off," or "trying to keep up with the Joneses," an interpretation that minimized their resentment over income inequalities. Higher income people had similarly deprecating comments about those behavior patterns of lower income people which differed from their own. At the same time, they ascribed similarities in the ways of life of lower income neighbors to a desire for conformity.

Enforced conformity has often been described as the scourge of suburban life; yet in the community I studied, instances of this were rare. Most people are willing to tolerate differences of behavior that do not affect them personally. The vast majority of suburbanites are therefore free to live as they please, and their frequent reports of having more privacy in the suburbs than they had in the city is one illustration of this freedom. People do conform in such matters as lawn care—and demand it from their neighbors—largely because they share personally in the appearance of the entire street front. Suburbanites also conform by copying each other's ideas in home improvements, but only those which they consider desirable or useful. People who deliberately strive to maximize their prestige, show off status symbols, or resort to conspicuous consumption are usually socially marginal types who have difficulty in relating to other people. Their neighbors feel sorry for them even while they criticize them. Such strivers are few in number.

Finally, there is no reason to believe that the move from the city to suburb, or suburban life itself, has any effect on mental health, other than a positive one. Most interview respondents report improvements in health and disposition. The number of crimes, suicide attempts, serious delinquent acts, and cases of mental illness, as noticed by doctors and ministers, are comparatively few in the community I studied; and if translated into rates, far below those reported for city inhabitants. Since the suburbs lack the lower class populations which account for the majority of such pathologies, this is not surprising. I was able to get information about many of the people whose behavior suggested serious mental illness; and in almost every case, they had histories of similar disturbance in previous residences. Some of them moved to the suburb I studied in the false hope that the newness of the community and the change of environment would solve their problems.

Nor does the move to the suburbs lead to increased boredom and loneliness. Most people find that the house, the yard, and the increased social life leave them less time to be bored—in fact, less spare time generally —than life in a city apartment. For example, 40 per cent of fifty-five ex-Philadelphians interviewed on this question said they had never been bored, either in the city or in the suburb. Of the twenty-three who said they were sometimes bored, 9 reported no change, 8 were less bored in the suburb, and 6, more. These were mainly women, but the reasons for their boredom have little to do with the community. It was the result of the children growing up and needing them less, of husbands whose work kept them away from home too much, or of anxieties brought on by economic and marital problems.

This analysis may be summarized as follows. The move from city to suburb creates relatively few changes in behavior. Most of these, representing the achievement of aspirations held prior to the move, can be described as *intended* changes. They are effects not of suburban life, but of the larger cultural milieu in which people form their aspirations. This milieu has traditionally stressed the desirability of home ownership, and life in a single-family house. Since most of the intended changes stem from the change in house type, rather than the change in settlement type, the move to the suburb may be considered as the most recent form of a traditional aspiration.

A number of behavior changes which took place after people moved to the suburbs had nothing to do with pre-occupancy aspirations or contradicted them. They may be described as *unintended* changes. Some of them result from the newness of the community, but others can be traced to one or another aspect of suburban life. Economic problems, and the difficulties of the adolescents, are two examples. These, then, can be considered as effects of suburban life, although even they are not entirely caused by suburbia. But most of the effects which have been attributed to the suburb by the myth of suburbia are not supported by empirical evidence.

Why then, does the myth exist? By far the most important reason for its existence is the fact that, since World War II, many people have been able to raise their standards of living, and adopt styles of consumption previously available to the upper middle class only. One part of this change has been the move to the suburbs. Since the post-war subdivisions are a new phenomenon and a highly visible one, the ways of life which have been observed there have been attributed to the community, rather than to the age and class position of the people involved.

Most of the people who have written about suburbia come—like other writers—from the cosmopolite upper middle class. Their criticism of suburban life is actually directed at working- and lower middle-class, non-cosmopolite ways, which can be found in most city neighborhoods as well, but are not as visible there as they are in suburbia. For example, the suburbanites are criticized for turning their back on the city's cultural facilities, but what little evidence exists on the use of such facilities suggested that they are avoided by working- and lower middle-class people who live in the city as well. In short, the myth of suburbia is an implicit criticism of the non-cosmopolite nature of the working class and lower middle class, and is only a contemporary variation of a theme that has been prominent in American critical writing for many decades. The major innovation—and one that must be considered undesirable—is for the critic to invoke concepts of mental health and illness, and thus to identify as pathological what is in reality mainly a difference of class cultures between him and those he criticizes.

Implications for Physical and Social Planning

My analysis of the alleged and real effects of suburbia has a number of implications for social theory, for city or physical planning, for social planning, and for the caretaking professions.

With respect to social theory, the fact that people's lives are not changed drastically by the move from city to suburb suggests that the differences between these settlement types are either fewer, or, more likely, less relevant to the way people live than has been traditionally believed. In short, the community itself does not shape people's ways of life as significantly as has been proposed by ecological and planning theory. The major behavior patterns are determined, rather, by the period of the life-cycle, and the opportunities and aspirations associated with class position.

At one time in American history, the local community did shape the processes that determine ways of life. When the country was rural, income, education, and occupational opportunity were determined within a small area. Today, however, many patterns of life are determined by national economic and social structures, and given the ease of geographical mobility, the community has become less important.

Physical planners, especially those with architectural training, believe that the physical characteristics of the community have important influences on people's ways of living, and that changes in housing and site design, density of structures and amount of open space can change their behavior. The findings I have reported here, and other studies of the impact of physical features on behavior, suggest that this belief is open to serious question. It fails to recognize some of the more important, but non-physical, causes of human behavior. For example, the planners who aim to eliminate urban sprawl—the discontinuous spreading of suburban subdivisions over the rural landscape—and who also wish people to make greater use of the city's downtown districts, have usually proposed that suburbanites move into urban elevator apartments, or into row-house neighborhoods closer to the edge of the city. It is not at all certain that this will solve the problem. Most of the suburbanites I interviewed have little interest in using downtown facilities, and would not move into the city or closer to it for the sake of shortening the journey to work and the wife's monthly or semi-monthly trip to the department store. Urban sprawl and the decline of the downtown can be halted only if more people want to make greater use of the city. These goals cannot be achieved solely by physical design, or even by mass transportation schemes; they require the development of cosmopolite interests among people. This in turn requires—among other things— changes in the education offered in public high schools and most colleges.

Ways of life are determined principally by economic and social conditions, not by architectural schemes. This means that future suburban planning must place greater emphasis on the problems of the suburban population, and this in turn requires the use of social planning methods that involve changes in the social, economic and political structure of our society, and in the programming of public services and caretaking functions.

Despite the generally positive effect of the suburban move, suburban residents have their share of problems. These problems are neither as sensational nor as distinctive to suburbia as the myth-makers have suggested, however. They are old and familiar ones that exist in the city as well, and have not yet been solved there—or wherever people may live.

Perhaps the most important problems are located in the family, both in the marital relationship and among the children. As I have already suggested, ex-city residents find family life improved after the move to the suburbs, but couples who had marital problems in the city have them in the suburbs too. These are familiar difficulties, brought about by sexual or cultural incompatibility, personality clashes, and emotional disturbances in one or both of the spouses. The children's problems are also familiar ones; for example, learning difficulties, serious emotional disturbances, conflicts over discipline with parents and teachers, as well as organic impairment and retardation.

One of the major causes of marital problems, in the suburbs as elsewhere, is economic. In many cases, it is not the lack of money per se which causes problems, since there is usually enough for the basic needs. The conflicts result from disagreement about the allocation of money for items other than food and shelter, and often reflect cultural differences and blocked communication between the spouses. Even so, there are also people for whom the problem is first and foremost financial; who could not really afford to move to the suburbs but have done so nevertheless. It would be arrogant—and useless—to recommend that they go back to the aging apartment buildings or crowded city neighborhoods from which they came. The only real solution is an economic one. Our society may be wealthy compared to others, but families who try to raise three children on $6000 a year are hardly affluent. In the short run, housing subsidies will help, but in the long run, further increases in real income are necessary. These—as well as changes in the tax structure—will subsequently reduce the financial difficulties of suburban municipalities.

My study supports previous findings that unhappy suburbanites are more likely to be women than men. For the latter, the suburb is a peaceful retreat from the city and the job. Most of the women are also content there. The wives of traveling salesmen, airplane pilots, and of other men whose work takes them out of the house for days or weeks on end are probably most unhappy. Many of the marital problems in the community I studied were found among such families. Their problem is not a suburban one, and indeed, the women seem to feel less isolated in the suburb than they did in their previous residence.

A less serious but numerically more important problem is that of the women who want to be more than housekeepers and mothers, especially among those who have gone to college. Some have solved this problem by taking part-time jobs, or by finding satisfying unpaid work in voluntary organizations and community service, meanwhile sending their children to nursery schools or day-care centers. Their problem is not unique to suburbia, and it is likely to become more widespread as larger numbers of women obtain college educations.

Adolescents, as I have already noted, face problems in suburbia, because they lack the after-school facilities that are available to them in the city. If these cannot be supplied commercially, they will have to be made available from public resources, with care being taken that they are pro grammed on the basis of adolescent needs, rather than by adult desires. This is more easily said than done. Adults have reacted quite negatively to the development of the adolescent youth culture that has developed in America, as elsewhere, over the past two decades. Many adults, especially in the working and lower middle classes, stereotype all teen-agers as delinquents. As a result, community leaders are hesitant about providing them with recreational facilities for fear that gang fights, sexual episodes, and other forms of misbehavior will upset the voters and cause them to blame the public officials.

The problems of bored middle-class adolescents are much less serious than those of working-class and lower-class ones. As Paul Goodman and others have noted, our society provides no function for the teen-ager who does not want to remain in school. This problem, which has nothing to do with the suburbs, is exacerbated in middle-class suburbs by the fact that such teen-agers are a hostile and unhappy minority in a predominantly middle-class environment.

Finally, another group who suffer in the suburbs—as they do everywhere—are people who differ too greatly from their neighbors and other residents, and are therefore socially isolated. As I noted earlier, in the community I studied, this affected primarily the cosmopolite minority, and working-class women. The former can fend for themselves, and eventually move to a community of more compatible people. In this process, however, the original community loses their participation in civic problem-solving activities. I am frankly uncertain whether or not this is a serious loss in a working-class or lower middle-class community. While upper middle-class people have the intellectual and administrative skills I described earlier, they also tend to see community problems—and their solutions—from an upper middle-class perspective, and they are often blind to the problems faced by the other classes. This question urgently requires empirical research.

Working-class women—as well as their families—who are in a minority in the neighborhood cannot solve their isolation problem as easily as others, especially those who have difficulty in entering into new roles. They might be better off if they remained in their old neighborhoods in the city, or if they moved into the modern dwellings being made available there by urban renewal projects in their price range.

I have tried to describe what appear to be the major problems of suburban residents, especially in low and medium priced communities. Few are distinctive to suburbia, and they bear little resemblance to those described in the myth of suburbia. The problems aired by the myth-makers are principally those of their suburban cosmopolite friends, and of the upper middle class generally.

Needless to say, most suburbanites are not cosmopolites; they are people who lived in the city more from necessity than from choice. Thanks to the FHA, the suburbs have made it possible for them to achieve much of what they want out of life, although the suburban exodus has in turn raised yet unsolved problems in metropolitan government, such as the financing of public services, which I have not discussed here.

Because suburbanites are above average in education, income, and many other characteristics—even in a lower middle-class suburb—their life is comparatively problem-free, and the problems I have listed are much less serious than those of less fortunate Americans. Indeed, the most critical problems in American society are to be found among the people who cannot move to the suburbs, who are doomed to a deprived existence in urban and rural slums because of low income, lack of occupational skill, and racial discrimination. Their needs take precedence over all of the problems I have described here.

THE SQUEEZE:
CITIES WITHOUT SPACE

Edward Higbee

The combination of burgeoning population growth and increasing urbanization places more and more pressure upon land that can be converted from farms to residential, business, and industrial uses. Yet institutional arrangements for controlling this conversion —in order to protect the interests of farmers on the one hand and to provide a maximum degree of rational and aesthetic urban space development on the other—have yet to be devised. In this selection, Higbee explores the nature of this ecological phenomenon and describes some of the attempts that have been made to cope with it justly and efficiently.

New Space for the City

The disappearance of farms on the edges of growing cities is a matter to which few urbanites have given thought; yet it is more important to their welfare than to that of the agriculturists who are displaced. Land to the farmer is basically a business medium. While he may have a personal preference for one place rather than another, and it may be an inconvenience to give up a homestead so that a city may grow, the affected husbandman is not damaged irreparably. He may keep his business alive by shifting to a rural district. For the moment at least the total farm economy is not hurt by urban raids on agricultural lands. In fact the net result is to reduce surpluses slightly, stiffen prices, and enrich the individual farmer. However, land is a substance of more intrinsic significance to the growing city. It is the basic raw material of its existence. It is not soil but rather space—for which there is no substitute anywhere else. The city, unlike the farmer, cannot move. It is committed forever to its location. As it consumes space to expand, it makes commitments which, while they may be modified, may never be undone completely. Only a Carthaginian annihilation could remove a city and restore the land to a pastoral condition.

SOURCE: *The Squeeze: Cities Without Space* by Edward Higbee. Copyright © 1960 by Edward Higbee. Reprinted by permission of William Morrow and Company, Inc. ❖ The author is professor of geography at the University of Rhode Island. His publications include *American Oasis—The Land and Its Uses; American Agriculture—Geography, Resources, Conservation;* and *Farms and Farmers in an Urban Age.*

In his use of land the farmer harvests a crop, plows under the useless aftermath, and starts afresh with each new seeding. He repeats this cycle over and over, year after year. If he is an intelligent man he learns from this experience and his techniques improve as time goes by. To the agriculturist land is a renewable resource, capable of restored fertility and ever better crops. He does not plant for permanence but for the season, and he expects that each new effort will eventually be superseded by another even better. The farm is an enormous blackboard upon which the operator continuously draws and erases patterns of use. Its function is to be neutral—constantly subject to change and improvement under increasingly better management.

The city uses land differently. What it plants it cannot plow under except at a sacrifice. Buildings and streets are not crops to be harvested but useful facilities to be preserved with care, and utilized where they stand decade after decade. Though a city may learn from experience how to make better use of land, only in the most exceptional circumstances can it afford to apply this knowledge by tearing down and starting over. If it learns anything that is widely applicable, it is how to plan the future consumption of virgin space so as to avoid the mistakes of the past. A growing city which cannot learn from its own experience how to utilize newly acquired farm lands more appropriately than in the past is destined to consume this irreplaceable resource to the ever-increasing expense and dissatisfaction of its citizens. It is difficult for the American city to adopt such an attitude of self-criticism toward its own growth because throughout our history the conquest of space has been glorified. Almost invariably it has been considered an obstacle to be overcome rather than a limited asset to be handled with thrift.

In a country of continental size it is too easy to look upon space as an obstacle to efficient organization. It means long routes of transportation, sometimes across deserts and wastelands, to connect the really productive and inhabited centers. The American urbanite has not been conditioned to look upon space as a limited commodity because the occasion for this point of view is recent, and a rural heritage still dominates our thinking. The very flight to suburbs reflects an unwillingness to face the basic problems of city planning. The sprawl of suburbs over the landscape without a coordinated design for their expansion suggests a complacent belief that space for expansion and linkage is inexhaustible. If there were a consciousness of the actual limited supply of space where populations are concentrated, it would have provoked by now more positive civic action. As it is, the waste and misuse of space by both government and private investors is creating a situation which could destroy the fiscal solvency of communities as well as their usefulness as habitats for the human organism.

From the standpoint of the greatest good for the greatest number of American citizens at this particular moment in the nation's development, the most important function of the farm on the urban fringe is as a reservoir of space which eventually will be urbanized. Unless a growing community regards the farms on its periphery as the most important raw material out of which its future will be molded and treats them accordingly, there can be no sensible policy for the eventual allocation of their space to urban uses. If a community must first misuse land, create congestion, license inefficiency, and promote dissatisfaction before it is shocked into seeing the importance of rational space allocation, there can be no hope. We shall have to live with folly if we are not wise enough to prevent it, and this will become a permanent drag on our economy and a constant irritation to our daily living. That we have muddled through in the past will not comfort us in the future. Effective urban renewal is already far beyond the financial means of our economy; yet the speed-up in population growth and metropolitan expansion has only begun. The deluge is yet to come and we have only a sieve to bale out the boat.

It is a function of the human mind to anticipate danger and to keep the human organism out of trouble. In no matter related to the domestic environment is there more urgent need for intelligent foresight than in directing the final disposition of farm space as it is incorporated into the city and suburb. Yet, at present, this vital community matter is generally ignored and left to contending speculators as though it were an old bone to scrap over. Those who look upon the consumption of farm space by the spreading city as progress, regardless of the ultimate use and arrangement of that space, are a type of Chamber of Commerce enthusiast with little understanding of man's basic biological and psychological needs. It may be good business and good politics to think of the farm on the edge of the city as an anachronism that should be prematurely taxed into submission and sold into the hands of land jockeys who are out to snare the developer with the deepest pockets and strongest nerve. To be sure, this is growth. This is action. A city with friends of this conviction needs no enemies to create a troubled future.

It is not surprising that the average metropolitan citizen has given no thought as to how open farm space should be converted into cities and suburbs. Even professional planners must be content with the piecemeal niceties of street patterns for new plats and the pretty colored lines that separate single-family districts from multifamily districts on zoning maps. Very few are permitted to think about master designs for the detailed uses that should be made of all the fields and pastures on metropolitan outskirts that are positively destined to eventual urbanization. The civic architect is buried under the minutiae of spot planning without the benefit of guiding concepts of how the whole community should grow. No responsible person would invest in a projected office building for which there were no blueprints, yet every property holder in practically every city is an investor in a community which has no detailed blueprint for what lies ahead. A building contractor would lose his mind if he had no master plan and at every stage of construction a different architect showed up to insist upon structural innovations that had occurred to him the night before. Yet this is the way additions are made to cities.

While usually there is no basic concept of community organization to guide the growth of a metropolis in a rational manner, there is a plethora of ideas about the design of disjointed parts. There are superb plans for each new subdivision, and each new shopping center, and each new school. But these are only pieces to the total puzzle. The fact that they are ultimately destined to fit badly, with no reasonable suggestion of over-all design, seems to be no one's concern. The fact that the whole should be an entity superior to the sum of its parts is universally ignored by cities. Planners could do this job easily and well. That is their profession, but they are not given the green light. While hack work is turned over to these professionals, the basic decisions which really determine a city's future are made by speculators and politicians. The growing metropolis is in the curious position of allowing its future to be determined by amateurs and promoters, while specialists stand on the sidelines to give the game some semblance of respect. Yet this is the home of the American people. It is the environment in which they live out their lives. It is the backdrop which colors each day's existence. It is the setting for the private dwelling, and the stage upon which every social function is performed. This is the environment which arouses our emotions and influences our thoughts. There is no function without form and if the form is cockeyed the function is bound to be screwy. We could do better but we refuse to give the professionals a chance.

In areas where large cities lie close together there is no co-ordinated effort whatever between these neighbors to plan together so that they do not bump into one another. In fact when two cities such as Philadelphia and Trenton are only a few miles apart, there seems to be a fatal impulse to close the gap. Such "urbitraction" may be temporarily forestalled by active farming in the space between, but there is a limit to the farmer's ability to hold out until communities come to their senses and realize that space is an exhaustible resource that should be allocated with the most cautious respect rather than with a promoter's eagerness "to get things going" so as "to close a deal." The disappearance of farms on the urban fringe is not the "farmer's problem," but it is a matter of health or disease to the city. It is like the passage of years to an aging organism. Something irretrievable is gone, and the span of what remains depends almost entirely upon whether the past was spent in health or dissipation. Let the young city with big ideas look at Boston and its suburbs to study the frightful consequences of metropolitan growth without order or discipline. Let the young city on-the-make study Boston's tax rate and take heed lest it too travel the same road to bankruptcy.

Use According to Capability

The ways cities and suburbs consume farm space in their ever-spreading growth should be guided by the physical capabilities of the land and by the human needs of the community. Without a grasp of these principles and an adherence to them in planning, the eventual cityscape is certain to be sheer potluck or deliberate abuse. People need space in which to reside, work, shop, move around, play, pray, study, exercise, relax, love, entertain, and carry on government. The more people there are, the more space is needed for all these activities. A metropolis will be off-balance just as a diet may be off-balance if any necessary ingredient is omitted as the organism grows. Any landscape which is brought into metropolitan development through suburbanization must plan for all human needs by an allocation of space for their purposes. Just a casual acquaintance with the way suburbia is growing in most places will reveal neglect of fundamental human activities and civic needs. Only at the risk of drying up the diversity and vitality of American life may we neglect to provide space for every human exercise.

Attention to the bare subsistence details of housing and shopping are not enough. No community could get along without water, yet how many suburban communities have set aside space for reservoirs that will assure an adequate water supply when present populations have quadrupled? Where would they expect to find the space for reservoirs when the time comes when there will be four times as many houses, shopping centers, factories, schools, streets, and service stations scattered around? In December, 1957, soil conservationist Edwin F. Owens made a reconnaissance study of land use on 41,000 acres of the Wissahickon-Sandy Run Valley, which is on the outskirts of Philadelphia in Montgomery County. Among the suburban towns in the area are Roslyn, Willow Grove, Ambler, and Flourtown. The purpose of Mr. Owens' study was to locate, if possible, open areas where several water impoundments could be made without condemnation of houses or the relocation of power lines and roads. As suburbanization has progressed in the valley the rate of storm water run-off has increased. Roofs and pavements of new suburban areas, by shedding water more rapidly than farm land, have hastened flood discharge that has damaged urbanized areas farther down the valley. Land use at the time of the survey was found to be: agricultural, 25–30 per cent; forested, 10 per cent; urbanized, 35–40 per cent; idle, 25 per cent.

The idle land consisted chiefly of abandoned farms and pieces of farms which had been sold to investors and were awaiting urbanization. Many years may pass before all this idle land is utilized, but because it is scattered among built-up zones it has already lost much of its value as far as regional planning is concerned. Of seventeen possible sites for the construction of impoundment areas, only three were "open." That is, these were the only places with enough acres grouped together to make a catchment basin where there were no houses to condemn or roads and power lines to relocate. Urban-suburban construction on thirty-five to forty per cent of the land is so sprinkled through the old farm country that the opportunity to acquire undeveloped space for flood control and water-storage reservoirs has almost disappeared. There is no point in training professionals in the principles of urban planning if their brains are used only to write expert post-mortems.

In 1958 the suburban town of North Providence, Rhode Island, had about fifty per cent of its land developed and fifty per cent awaiting some-one to build on it. However, the two types of land were so intermingled that the town, in looking for a school site, could not find five acres of open land in one piece in a suitable location. The same community wants light industry to improve the tax base and provide employment. Yet with all its parcels of open land it does not have sufficient in any appropriate location for commercial construction. The best sites for industry, which are fairly level areas near railroad tracks and above the natural flood plain, are sprinkled with an assortment of residences, stores, and small factories. Only the latter are where they logically belong.

This kind of conglomerate development is happening in hundreds of communities at the present time. Clutter and scatteration distinguish their landscapes whereas there should be orderly separation of incompatible types of development. When space is abused and wasted in this way, a com-munity is likely to be functionally obsolete before it is half finished. It will resemble a bargain basement stocked for a remnant sale. The customers it attracts will certainly not be the most affluent or discriminating. The city that wants to attract the best will have to practice snob appeal in its use of space or, like an inept swain, it will be rejected by the most desirable damsels.

Not only must there be a place for everything that communities should provide, but the place for each activity should enhance the value and function of all other places for all other activities. This calls for intelligent arrangement and a subtle consciousness of what goes into the physical construction of a community so that human lives will not be underprivileged. It enhances the value of a residential area to be within reasonable commuting distance to work, but certainly the place where people live should not look like a factory district nor should it be so close to one as to smell like it or sound like it. But there are new housing sub-divisions around Gary and Hammond, Indiana, where people will never know what it means to live in a residential neighborhood. Schools do not belong in commercial districts, but practically every large city and some new suburbs have built them there. On the other hand a school may enhance the function of a park and a park may protect the function of a school. Certainly a church would be a more delightful place for contempla-tion and worship if it were set apart on a green landscaped square rather than at a highway intersection or next to a supermarket. This is a horse-sense concept as old as the colonial New England village, the physical charm of which is eternal in the annals of church location, but now seldom copied.

   ✧   ✧   ✧   ✧   ✧

The Control of Metropolitan Space

The dream boat of state is wrecked upon the shoals of reality. The abstract idea, that the development of space in metropolitan areas should be guided, sounds nice, but a community can do very little without controls. There are strict limits to a community's authority over landowners and what they should do with their real estate. This is as it should be for, otherwise, the very ownership of property would be a delusion. It would be clearly unethical and illegal for a public authority to permit one farmer to sell his land for great profit to real-estate developers and to deny this right to his neighbors on the assumption that their acres should be conserved as open space until the community approved conversion to other uses. This would be an arbitrary and a discriminatory exercise of police power out of keeping with constitutional guarantees.

Certainly it is unrealistic to expect that the average farmer or land investor would forgo voluntarily the speculative advantages of possession. Population increase is the best guarantee that land values will increase substantially in metropolitan areas, and the average owner naturally wants to cash in on a good thing if the spread of suburbia comes his way. This is certain to happen in approximately two hundred metropolitan areas in the United States which comprise about seven per cent of the nation's surface and where sixty per cent of the population lives. Within these areas about half the land is still in farms but their life expectancy is limited for the rate of population growth is running seven times faster in the suburbs than in the central cities. If these communities wish to protect their futures, they must buy that protection from the landowner or buy the land itself just as they would buy any other commodity or service. If a city or county is too stingy to pay space insurance, it will have to suffer the consequences. It is not the duty of farmers or land speculators to save the health of the community. Theirs are legitimate businesses and they have as much right as anyone else to try for as much profit as they can possibly make. The community that seeks salvation must save itself.

While no large landowner in a metropolitan county has lived through the past decade without being intoxicated by the real-estate boom, the voting public remains pretty much in the dark about the kick in that potent brew. Most citizens have no acquaintance with real estate beyond their F.H.A. and G.I. insured mortgages. Under the circumstances they do not realize how fantastically open land increases in market price as it passes from farm to suburban development. Given time, which is another way of saying, "Let population pressure develop," an acre that is worth no more than $400 as cropland may sell for $4000 as house lots or $40,000 if it is in a choice commercial location. This can and does happen very frequently in a matter of ten or twenty years.

✧   ✧   ✧   ✧   ✧

If communities want to get in on the ground floor of their own future they, too, will have to "play with land" and they will have to get at least a twenty-year head start. If communities want to plan their growth and dictate the way space should be used when it passes from farm to city, then they will have to do more than pass ordinances. They will have to gain control of the land. To get control they will have to buy it just as any individual would. Cities do not normally engage heavily in the real-estate business but they will have to if the pattern of their future growth is to be rational. Planning without control is idle dreaming. There are several ways by which a community could purchase control. It could buy land on the open market when it is in farms and hold it until it is ripe for development. It could then sell its holdings with restrictions in the deeds so that developers would have to build whatever the community would have planned for that particular space. This approach would be impossible for most cities or counties. They are already in debt for current needs and could scarcely find funds to invest in properties they could not use or sell for twenty years.

William H. Whyte, Jr., one of the authors of *The Exploding Metropolis*, has proposed that communities purchase "development easements" from farmers on the urban fringe. By the sale of such easements farmers would surrender the right to use their land for anything but agriculture. Space would then lose its speculative value because developers would scarcely care to collect cornfields and pastures if that were all the land could be used for. Possibly only farmers, who want to continue farming on their present properties, would be interested in forfeiting development privileges. Many estate owners who are harried by mounting taxation might sell such easements if their preference were to live on their properties indefinitely rather than to sell them for a profit. Local real-estate taxes would certainly be lower on farms and estates stripped of their speculative prospects because their market values would be comparatively low.

The "development easement" idea is a good one and a farmer who would sell such rights need not necessarily be a financial dimwit. Either he could charge a high price for parting with the speculative value of his land or he could afford practically to give away development rights if he were to reserve an option to repurchase them for a nominal fee at any future time the community should decide that his farm space were needed for urban development. By these devices a community could be protected against premature and disorganized expansion. It would gain control of its own future growth pattern because it could specify the uses to which the land might be put when it eventually released the rights which it had held in trust. The farmer would not be chased away until his land was urgently needed and meanwhile he would enjoy low taxes. Also the farm community could not be infiltrated and split up by other types of land uses if all farmers in the vicinity were to make similar sales of development rights simultaneously. Obviously the time for a community to buy development rights is not when the land is almost ripe for urbanization but when that day is twenty, fifty, or a hundred years away. The more remote the prospect, the easier and cheaper it should be to acquire them.

There are other ways to skin the cat. A community could establish a revolving fund with which it would purchase farms on the urban fringe. Once they were in legal possession, then restrictions could be written into deeds that any change of use would have to conform to the development plans of the community. With these restrictions recorded the land could then be resold immediately into private hands for farming or speculation. Such a program would be senseless unless the community had a comprehensive plan for its future expansion. Another device would be for private citizens to establish a corporation either for profit or as a nonprofit foundation which would acquire farms and sell them with restrictions in their deeds that would conform to uses designated in a community's master plan. By processing properties in such ways as these relatively little capital would need to be tied up at any particular moment. Also, the chances are that while farms are in the temporary possession of the processing agency they could be rented so as to return a reasonable interest on the invested capital.

The basic reason for any approach to rational space design is that expanding metropolitan areas are so large that controls must be of a similar magnitude. Such space design on a large scale and fortified with legal teeth could go far beyond the capacities of zoning ordinances and actually blueprint specific patterns of future land use that would stick. No speculator could cry "foul" because he would buy land with its future clearly specified on the label.

The capital-gains tax on real estate is the logical source of the funds with which communities either might buy space for future public needs or acquire land temporarily in order to write development restrictions into deeds. These capital-gains taxes, which can amount to as much as twenty-five per cent of profits made on real-estate transactions, are now collected by the Federal Government as though they were ordinary revenue. Capital gains on real estate are actually the product of local community growth and should properly be collected by the community which created them rather than by the Federal Government. Either that or the Federal Government should return revenues to the communities which produced them with the proviso that they be used only for planning and for the acquisition of land. They should be spent to buy space for future roads, parks, reservoir areas, school sites, airports, disposal areas, and other public facilities. These funds should also be available to buy development right from landowners.

Revolving funds built up out of capital-gains taxes on real estate could be used to buy and sell land in order to amend deeds so that they would conform to master plans for future growth. The capital-gains tax on real estate should be regarded not as revenue but as a vital instrument with which to obtain control over the way a community grows. It is no mystery why the Federal Government has preempted the capital-gains tax, which

should have been a local privilege. Most local communities do not take
planning seriously enough to realize that the way they grow either makes
or breaks the real-estate market and that if they grow in a rational way
then they, and not the Federal Government, should get the credit. Planning the ultimate use of space is one of the most important, if presently
neglected, functions of local governments. Usually they have not progressed
beyond the kindergarten stage of zoning. It is therefore no wonder that they
have not reached the sophisticated level where they feel competent to
control their own growth or realize what is the origin of capital gains in
land.

* 72 *

THE AMERICAN WAY OF LIFE:
REGIONAL VARIATIONS

Anonymous

*This selection is an antidote to the belief that mass production and
mass communication have reduced all Americans to identical ro-
bots; that the exciting variations which gave our nation strength
through the stimulation of contrasts and differing modes of life
have disappeared. Though brief, the presentation is clear and effective in showing that diversities still exist in this country. The reader
is invited to look for himself, using the insightful ideas and approaches presented here, for differences between regions, and even
between cities, as he may have visited them.*

. . . It will be found . . . that there is not just one American way of life
There are American *ways* of life, almost without number. For example,
there are the great regional differentiations, where nature herself has conspired with American institutions to create ways of life as different from
each other as those of two nations might be. It is true that these American
"sub-nations" are bound together by many common ties, including the
important tie of language; yet their temperamental characteristics, their
customs, their values and views, their personal objectives differ so greatly
that a man who is happy and effective in one might be miserable and frustrated in another.

Take the Far West. This vast area, which begins, roughly speaking,
just east of Colorado, has of course many important things in common with

SOURCE: Reprinted from "The American Way of Life" in the February,
1951, issue of *Fortune Magazine* by special permission; © 1951 Time Inc.

the rest of the U.S. Yet the ways of those people are very different from the ways of the Easterner. Nature herself has made sure of that, for the Far West is a region of majestic drama, of mountains and buttes and deserts, beside which the woods and streams of the east coast look puny. The western people, generally speaking, are more outspoken than the Easterners, more cordial, more generous of their time and money; they speak slower, and they have a way of cutting through a lot of argument to reach a quick conclusion on which they are willing to stand or fall. The Easterner is endlessly fascinated by them; but he considers them naive, unsophisticated, lacking in perspective in the ways of the world. In fact, the West is to the East as the East is to Europe.

And yet, as anyone knows who has lived out there, these generalizations misrepresent the realities. The Far West itself includes many ways of life. Take, for example, the differences between the Pacific Northwest and California. In the Pacific Northwest the great rivers rise in snow-capped mountains and wind down through gorges to the sea. The cities are incredibly young—Seattle has not yet celebrated its centenary. It is trade-union country and the standard of living is high. But happiness is pursued in the Northwest with a certain calm simplicity that is rare in America. For all the youth of his region, the Northwesterner is something of a philosopher; he expects a lot out of life, but he doesn't aim to get very rich. He attends to his business all right, but he is more interested in his mountains and his waters; he would rather pack up with his wife and kids, with about $200 worth of camping gear in the back of his car, and push off for a ten-day tour of his magnificent state parks; or go cruising in a small boat, or salmon fishing in the foaming streams of the Columbia River watershed, or skiing on the mighty slopes of Mount Rainier.

In the eyes of the Northwesterner, the Californian, therefore, is a noisy fellow. The Californian goes about in bright informal clothing of many colors and lolls on bright beaches along the shores of the bright-blue Pacific and grows oranges that shine brightly from the dark-green foliage of the orange trees. That is to say, the southern Californian does; the northern Californian is altogether different. Northern California merges with the Pacific Northwest and has its roots firmly planted in San Francisco, the westernmost metropolis of Western civilization. San Francisco has become a place where a man can find anything he wants to find, which is perhaps the best definition of metropolitanism.

But Los Angeles, which is the headquarters of the southern Californian, is not like that. Los Angeles is big and boastful and overrun with Easterners and movie actors and cultists of infinite variety. It is also the mecca of the retired couple who took the life-insurance ads seriously and have come out here to enjoy "beauty" and "leisure" and watch the sun set westwardly over the Pacific. But the Northwesterner has the feeling, as he passes the innumerable little "bungalows" that sprawl out into what was only a few decades ago a near desert, that the beauty is wasted here, that it is not appreciated as in the Northwest, that it has not been absorbed. Somehow, like the movie industry that it houses, southern California seems to be removed one step from the real, to live in a world that nature never made—or, for that matter, man. That is the big difference between southern California and the Northwest.

Then there is that other vast region of the U.S., lying between the Rocky Mountains and the Appalachians, where a river may be a thousand miles long, and where everything drains into the Mississippi. Here all lines are horizontal, life is intensely practical and "real," and the quarter sections and the fields and the towns duplicate themselves, league after league, in seemingly endless repetition. It is here in this great "valley" that the itinerant lecturer has his worst time and reaches his most pessimistic conclusions; for unless these people are studied community by community, they appear to vanish into sociological generalizations.

But actually when you come to know Kansas you find it very different from Minnesota, for example, with its high percentage of Swedes and Germans and a better-balanced economy than Kansas has ever had. Kansas, Nebraska, and the Dakotas are heavy agricultural exporters; their way of life is based upon the soil, and even their towns exist for the farmers, not the townspeople. This makes town life quite different from that of an eastern town, or even a town in a manufacturing area of the Midwest (such as Chicago or St. Louis, for example), where the town exists, so to speak, for itself, and lives on its own exports. The Midwest farmer is fat with the world's riches—and safe from its depredations. But he is not in the least soft. On the contrary, he has time after time challenged the power of the East, which he regards with a congenital suspicion that is much more marked in the Midwest than in the Far West.

The Midwest merges into the South, and as it does the standard of living declines. The South is problem country. It grew up differently from the rest of the nation, with an economy based on big landholdings and slave labor. It still has with it the problem of the Negro; in many towns of Mississippi and Alabama the Negroes outnumber the whites, who cling to their political power by any means, fair or foul. The southern way of life differs radically from other American ways of life. The pace is slower. The extremes of poverty and riches are greater. The traditions are better preserved. The storied southern "aristocracy" is becoming something of a myth; but it has left behind it the tradition of southern cooking, which is supposed to be the best in the U.S. (though no vestige of it is to be found in the hotels and public eating places); of hospitality, which makes the New Yorker look like a boor; of flirtatious women; and of peaceful ways whose like is to be found nowhere else in the U.S.

And then there is Texas, the independent nation that became a state in 1845. Geographically Texas belongs to both the Midwest and the South, but in terms of its way of life it belongs to neither. Maybe California has outstripped Texas in population growth, but Texas has got rich faster than any comparable region of the U.S. ever has. Oil derricks, skyscrapers, flamboyant hotels, oil and gas pipelines, canals, piers, and great industrial shapes have sprung like mushrooms from a landscape that the Northwesterner would consider quite drab. It is the land of the big rich; the making of wealth dominates the way of life. And yet wealth is really only a symbol for the Texan; he likes to spend it just as wildly as he makes it; he loves the "feel" of struggle, the exhilaration of victory, of "getting ahead." Everything here is on a big scale, as if the gods had lifted the curtain for a drama on Valhalla. The young folks associate in droves—one of their barbecues will be attended by a hundred or more. As an Easterner once complained, he wished that Texans could be friendly on a neighborhood basis instead of on a state basis. The ordinary Texan thinks nothing of driving two or three hundred miles just to see a "local" football game.

The Texan way of life, indeed, represents an extension into the twentieth century of certain ideas that animated all Americans up to the first world war. Here is the land of opportunity, where anybody can rise to the "top," where tomorrow is unpredictable and yesterday unnecessary. Here the intrepid individual, the risk, the adventure, the fabulous reward, have somehow come to fruition in a world largely occupied with the less romantic problems of social "security" and social "science." It is possible for the modern American to feel somewhat nostalgic about Texas, however he may smile   or cringe—at its excesses.

But in the East the way of life is crowded. In the winter the Easterner takes to the trains and planes if he wants to go anywhere; in the summer he chugs despondently along obsolete highways, breathing carbon monoxide from the car ahead, snarled in the traffic of his innumerable cities. He lives in an industrial jungle. His most awe-inspiring sights are not the works of nature but the works of man. He is caught in a maze of brick walls and steel shapes, communications lines and enormous switchboards, six-lane clover-leaf highways and railroad switchyards of such complexity that the eye cannot predict the path that a train will follow through them. The island of Manhattan consists of only twenty-two square miles of rocky land; but two million people live on it, tier above tier, with the subways and three trunkline railroads underneath them, and tunnels under the subways, and tunnels under the rivers, and eighteen bridges gripping Long Island and the mainland. And all around them are clustered miles on miles of houses, and highways extending outward to the "dormitory towns." The Westerner could not endure it.

Yet the East is exciting, too. It generates ideas—big, continental ideas that have had enormous influence in the development of America. The ideas radiate outward and merge with native ideas in the different regions, to bring forth new ventures and new shapes. Thus from the Manhattan apex there extends westward an enormous triangle, one side 900 miles to Chicago, the other 1,000 miles to St. Louis. This is the "industrial triangle," the jugular vein of Western civilization. If an enemy could knock it out, or any substantial part of it, the U.S. would be unable to fight. For it contains more than half of all the capital investment of American industry and employs more than half of the industrial workers. Yet even within the triangle the ways of life differ. The people of Pittsburgh, who live among the ruddy fires of the steel mills, are "Westerners" to the New Yorker, who works òr lives several hundred feet above the earth, has two martinis for lunch, and charges the rest of the country exorbitant sums for the use of his fertile imagination. And the people of Chicago really belong to the Midwest.

Nor is the way of life in New York City the same as the way of life in Boston, the hub of another industrial complex, composed chiefly of textiles, machine tools, high skills, and industrial specialties. Perhaps New England contains more incongruities than any region. The "elite"—for here, at any rate, there are such—still cling to a great cultural tradition that reached its climax with Ralph Waldo Emerson and shed a mellow light into the twentieth century through the pen of Henry Adams. Boston still has in the Athenaeum the nation's most notable private library, whose shelves are accessible only to "proprietors"; and it also has in the Widener at Harvard the biggest university library in the world. Yet the casual visitor to New England, including the American tourist who goes there for his summer vacation, has increasing difficulty in finding vestiges of the cultural tradition; for a large part of New England is encased like one of its famous clams in a shell of modern industrialization, in all of its ugliest aspects, including a plethora of billboards and hot-dog stands, together with an ex-Governor recently released from jail.

Up in Vermont and New Hampshire you will find a stubborn folk who have never yielded to the most "advanced" versions of the industrialized life—on a number of instances they have even refused to accept federal aid. And it is commonly said that this ruggedness, for which New England was once famed, is on the wane. Yet this is not really the case, as anyone who tries to live there will soon discover. Within its industrialized shell the New England clam still flourishes—sober, hard-working, inventive, prudent, much more reserved than the Westerner, and downright unsympathetic to the flashy airs of the California goldfish.

Which one of these ways of life does the American mean by "the American way of life"? The answer is none of them. New England is no more "American" than the Northwest, nor Denver more so than Atlanta. This diversity itself is the way of life—nations within nations.

Nor can the way of life be defined by the life of any one particular community—the late Sinclair Lewis notwithstanding. For it is at the community level that America really begins to get diverse, because American life is not regional but local. The life of one town is influenced by a newspaper editor who wrote a history of his county and is a specialist on Indian warfare; the life of another, by a doctor interested in psychology. Here is a town addicted to schottisches, another whose social life centers around a Norwegian Harmony Club, another that features Czech gymnastic festivals. Here is a town with a Chinese restaurant, over there a town with German *verein*; over there a town, redolent of frijoles, that speaks mostly Spanish. All cultures are cherished—interwoven—modified. Here there are no memories and the town is flat and everyone eats out of cans. But there the memories of the old country are strong; the housewives treasure old Finnish recipes handed down from grandmothers who never saw America; or creole dishes, or Irish remedies for the gout.

And all this is accented by the extremists, the individualists, the eccentrics: the man with a thousand canaries; the man who keeps five buffalo in Connecticut; the electrician with odd working hours who spends his mornings in the town library in blue jeans reading Shakespeare; the nudists, the vegetarians, the Indian fortunetellers, the perpetual-motion inventors; the Amish who won't wear buttons; the old lady who writes poetry in the manner of Sara Teasdale. And then there are the hobbyists—the carpenters and gardeners—the man in the Great Plains who builds model ships—the amateur painters—the man who plays the flute in the morning, and the expert on Japanese prints, and the collector of chess sets. The way of life is none of these ways of life. And as for "standardization," it is lost in a forest of human foibles.

And yet, also, the way of life is *all* of these. For there is an extraordinary unity in this diversity, a coherence that resists all eccentricities, all power concentrations even. And this unity, which is not merely national in the ordinary sense of the word, pertains to quite another level of existence, another level of values from that which manifests itself with such diversity. It has to do with ideals, with a complex of principles and beliefs, to which all American life has reference. The truth, which has thus far been difficult for the rest of the world to grasp, is that Americans live on two planes at once—the practical and the ideal. The conflicts created by this ambivalent existence, which worry other people so much that they often feel constrained to reject one plan or the other, bother the American scarcely at all. . . .

THE DOMINANT VALUE PROFILE
OF AMERICAN CULTURE

Cora Du Bois

The preceding selection described regional variations in "The American Way of Life." Here Cora Du Bois, an anthropologist trained to view a sociocultural system as a single entity, presents us with a picture of the basic values of middle-class Americans considered as a total and distinctive configuration. It should be noted that opinions differ on how valid it is to describe a large and complex society in the same way that one describes the small and relatively simple groupings traditionally studied by anthropologists. However one may feel about this issue, Du Bois has here presented a number of penetrating insights and provocative ideas about American culture.

This paper is an attempt to synthesize and systematize the relevant insights on American values advanced by a diverse group of writers from De Tocqueville through Myrdal to the authors of the polemic or conversational pieces that have been so numerous in the last decade. It will be addressed to the dominant value system of middle-class Americans. This system is rooted in the Protestant ethic and eighteenth-century rationalism. Many of its specific values are shared with other societies, but its configuration has come to be considered peculiarly American.

✧   ✧   ✧   ✧   ✧

Four Basic Premises

For our purposes the value premises of any culture can be considered to rest upon the assumptions made concerning man's cognitive view of the universe, man's relation to it, and man's relation to other men. For the American middle class it is postulated that: (1) the universe is mechanistically conceived, (2) man is its master, (3) men are equal, and (4) men are perfectible. From these four basic premises alone many of the focal

SOURCE: *American Anthropologist*, Vol. 57, No. 6, Part 1 (December, 1955), 1232–39. Reprinted by permission. ✧ Cora Du Bois is Zemurray-Stone Professor of Anthropology at Harvard and Radcliffe. She has received the Order of the Crown of Thailand and Santimola Peace Medal and the Exceptional Civilian Service Award, United States Department of the Army. Her chief interests are personality and culture. She is the author of *People of Alor, Social Forces in Southeast Asia,* and *Foreign Students of Higher Education in the United States.*

and specific values, as well as the directives, of the American value system can be derived. In the context of the last three hundred years of American history these assumptions have proved valid both experimentally and integratively (i.e., in a self-reinforcing sense) for the United States as a whole, and, more specifically, for the American middle class. Despite changed situations and therefore the potential loss of experiential and integrative validation, we may nevertheless expect these assumptions to persist for a considerable period of time. There may be lags in a value system as there are in other aspects of culture.

Focal Values and Their Directives

The four premises given above yield at least three major focal values: material well-being that derives from the premise that man is master of a mechanistic universe; conformity that derives from the premise of man's equality; effort-optimism that derives from the premise of man's perfectibility. . . .

The nexus of specific values and directives clustering around each of these focal values can now be considered. Simultaneously the mutual reinforcement that occurs between the basic premises and their focal values, as well as the constant effort to resolve spurious oppositions through change, can be underlined. The inner consistency of the value system here presented accounts for much of the traditional vigor of "the American way of life" in the past. However, such vigor could not have existed without the reinforcement provided by the geographic setting of the American nation and the historic forces operative in the broader setting of Western European commercial, industrial, technical, and scientific growth in which the American nation shared.

1. Effort-Optimism

Work is a specific value in American society. It is not so much a necessary condition of existence as a positive good. It is a specific instrumental value through which man strives to reach not only the goal of his own perfectibility but also the goal of mastering a mechanistically conceived universe. But in values Vaihinger's "law of the preponderance of the means over the ends" is frequently operative. Thus work becomes a goal in itself and in the process may acquire the quality of activity for its own sake. Thus recreation, although theoretically the antithesis of work, nevertheless in its activism shows many of the aspects of work. "Fun" is something that most Americans work hard for and at, so that they must be warned at forty to give up tennis for golf, or hunting trips for painting. Touring, whether at home or abroad, acquires the quality of a marathon. And this in turn is closely associated with another specific value linked with the effort-optimism syndrome, the importance placed on education. However, as we shall see later, the educational effort acquires a particularly American cast when taken in conjunction with the other two focal values, material well-being and conformity. In sum, as many foreigners have observed, American life gives the impression of activism. The directives, as well as the virtues and vices, associated with this optimistic activism are numerous: "If at first you don't succeed, try, try again"; or, in the more contemporary idiom, "Let's get this show on the road." The optimistic quality that pervades the American mood is clearly conveyed by the "bigger ergo better" mentality; the "never say die"; the "up and at 'em."

Vigor, at least as motility, connotes biologic youth. The cult of youthfulness in this society is again a specific value frequently commented upon by foreign observers. This observation is borne out by the popularity of the heroes manufactured in Hollywood and in the world of sports, by the advertisements of styles and cosmetics. As the average age of the population increases, this value is already showing signs of being given new interpretations in terms of geriatrics, etc. This will be alluded to again in following paragraphs.

2. Material Well-being

If indeed effort is optimistically viewed in a material universe that man can master, then material well-being is a consistent concomitant value. Not only is it consistent within the value system, but it has been amply demonstrated in our national experience. It has been manifest in the American standard of living. The nation's geographic frontier and its natural resources, combined with an era of invention, have convinced most Americans of the validity of such a proposition. In the American scene progress and prosperity have come to have almost identical meaning. So deeply convinced are most Americans of what is generally called "prosperity" that material well-being is close to being considered a "right" due to those who have conscientiously practiced the specific value of work. The congruence of this view with the new science of geriatrics, social insurance, and the growth of investment trusts is obvious. It represents a consistent adjustment of specific values to a changing situation. However, as the situational context changes it may weaken the present linkage between effort and optimism with the resulting devaluation of both and thereby set up a new strain for consistency that may alter the present configuration of the American value system.

One of the most common stereotypes about the United States is its materialism. Viewed in the context of the value system presented here, materialism is less a value *per se* than an optimistic assertion of two value premises (mastery over material nature and the perfectibility of man) that have operated in a favorable environment. What foreign observers may call materialism, with derogatory or envious innuendos, is to the American a success that carries the moral connotation of "rightness"—of a system that proves itself or, as Americans would say with complete consistency, that "works." Within the frame of American value premises, success phrased as material well-being resolves the material-spiritual opposition and becomes a proof of right-mindedness. "Hard work pays off." The old and widely known proverb that "Virtue is its own reward" has a particularly American slant, meaning not that virtue is in itself a reward but rather that virtue is rewarded.

If hard work is a "good thing" in a material universe and since it has been rewarded by material well-being, consistency requires that manual labor should be accorded dignity or, at least, should not be considered undignified. Furthermore, manual labor is an unambiguous manifestation of that activism alluded to earlier.

The salience of material well-being as a focal value in American life leads into many by-ways, some of which confuse and confound members of societies founded on a different value configuration. In military terms, for example, Americans are so profoundly convinced of the correctness of the material well-being formula that logistics forms our basic strategy. Personal heroism, though it may amply exist, is not assumed to be the fundamental requisite for victory, as it is in France. In American terms, victory is won by the sheet of material laid down in front of advancing infantry and by the lines of supply that must be built up to provide such a barrier between hand-to-hand combat.

In the same vein, there is little room in the American middle-class value system for the realities of physical pain, brutality, and death. Since they are nonetheless natural and undeniable, they are given a highly stylized treatment in detective fiction, newspapers, and movies that provide an acceptable discharge of tension created by the discrepancy between values and reality. Many Americans are alienated and morally repelled when they encounter the poverty and misery prevalent in certain lands. They manage to go through life untouched experientially even by those in our own population who have not succeeded—those who exist hopelessly in rural or urban slums or those who are victims of physical or psychic disasters. We have provided for the latter so effectively that they are whisked away into institutions that our national surpluses permit us to provide comparatively lavishly. Death itself has been surrounded with appurtenances of asepsis. Evelyn Waugh's *The Loved Ones* could never have been written with India as a setting. The compelling quality of this value emerges when we consider world statistics on human welfare facilities. In this respect, the United States is consistently in the lead. Yet, if we compare these statistics with the outbursts of compassion that a newspaper account of a "blue baby" will elicit, we become aware not only of the power of this focal value but also the resultant constellation that might be summarized as compulsive compassionate activism.

3. Conformity

Viewed historically it seems probable that conformity is a more recent focal value in American culture than effort-optimism and material well-being. It may represent one of the valuational changes induced by the strain for consistency assumed earlier in the paper to be one of the forces that alter value systems. Over a century ago De Tocqueville saw with singular clarity the potential threat to national solidarity inherent in the values of individual liberty, on the one hand, and of the sovereignty of enfranchised masses, on the other hand. In the contemporary American value system, conformity represents an attempt to resolve this dilemma. The France of today, with a comparable dilemma, has still to find a resolution.

If the premises of perfectibility and equality are linked with the focal value labeled effort-optimism, then each middle-class American may legitimately aspire to maximal self-realization. But, if man is to master through his efforts a mechanistic universe, he must co-operate with his fellow-men, since no single man can master the universal machine. In other words, people are individuated and prized, but if they are to co-operate with their fellow-men for mastery of the universe or, in more modest terms, of the immediate physical and sociopolitical environment, too great a degree of individualization would be an impediment. Also since the American value premises—in contradistinction to much of the rest of the world—include equality, the realization of the self in such a context would not necessarily imply the development of highly personalized and idiosyncratic but rather of egalitarian traits. Self-cultivation in America has as its goal less the achievement of uniqueness and more the achievement of similarity. This is a proposition many Frenchmen, for example, find difficult to grasp. The Japanese, with their stress upon self-cultivation in order more perfectly to discharge the obligations they owe their family and society, might come closer to understanding this American formulation. . . .

The assimilation of diverse immigrant groups to middle-class American values has been one of the remarkable sociopolitical achievements of the nation and testifies to the compelling vigor of its value systems. As resources and space were more fully manned, the very lack of tolerance for differences that facilitated assimilation was finally to curtail the admission to this country of those who presented such differences.

Earlier in our history self-reliance and initiative were specific values attached to the focal value of liberty. Today these specific values have a new focus. Individual self-reliance and initiative are attached to the promotion of the commonweal and to the progress of society. Conformity has replaced liberty as a focal value to which these specific traits are attached. Co-operation has been added as a specific value that has facilitated the shift-over. The present American value system manifests a highly effective integration of the individual to society.

The ramification of this nexus into the sphere of education has been alluded to already. Education is envisaged as a means by which all men through effort can realize themselves. But since co-operativeness is a specific value also inserted into this equation, education comes to be envisaged as a means to make more men more effective workers and better citizens. The land-grant colleges, the vast network of public schools, and the system of free and compulsory education with its stress on education for citizenship and on technical skills have set the American educational system apart from that of many other countries. In the American context the linkage between conformity, effort-optimism, and material well-being leads inevitably to mass education with the emphasis on the common man rather than the uncommon man, to its technical and practical cast, to what seems to many observers its low standards. Simultaneously, to many Americans schooling has acquired the weight of a goal rather than a means. A college degree is a "good thing" in itself, whether or not the education entailed is prized. This concatenation does not lead one to expect perfection as a directive for performance in American life.

In a society where co-operation and good citizenship are valued and where the commonweal is served by having each man develop himself through his own efforts, a generous friendliness, openness, and relaxation of interpersonal relations are not only possible but desirable so long as the associated expanding economy furnishes the situational possibilities. Rigid class structures and protective privacies are inconsistent with the values here enumerated. Doors need not be closed to rooms; fences need not be built around properties. The tall hedges of England and the enclosing walls of France are not appropriate to the American scene, where life faces outward rather than inward. If every individual is as "good as" the next and all are good citizens—what is there to hide? The open front yards, the porches, or more recently the picture windows that leave the home open to everyone's view, the figurative and literal klieg lights under which our public figures live are all evidence of the value placed in American life on likeness and the pressure exerted for conformity. This is very different from saying that American middle-class individuals are in fact all alike. It means merely that likeness is valued.

The American hostility to figures in authority has been frequently noted, and in this connection the almost placatory informality and familiarity of American manners that serve to play down status differences have been pointed out. The apparent contradiction between the striving for upward mobility and the distrust of those who achieve pre-eminent positions can now be seen in more balanced terms. If the argument advanced here is correct, upward mobility is valued as successful activity, but when it reaches a point where it outstrips the premise of equality and the focal value of conformity it borders on *hubris*.

In this connection then the relaxed, friendly manner of American life so frequently commented upon by foreign observers can be gauged in the broader context of an adjustment to incompatible values. The search for popularity, the desire to be liked, the wish to be considered a "good fellow," are searches for reassurance that, in striving to achieve all the ends implied by the focal value of effort-optimism, one has not exceeded the bounds set by the other focal value of conformity. That this process can operate at any level of actual achievement, from the presidency of the United States to chairmanship of an Elks Club committee, need not be stressed. It is the boss, the politician, the teacher, the "big shots" who are disvalued figures to the extent that their superordinate position implies authority. It is the movie star and the baseball hero who are valued figures since their pre-eminence connotes no authority but at the same time dramatizes the meteoric rise to fame and popularity through hard work and youthful striving.

Another aspect of American social life is thrown into relief in the effort to balance effort-optimism, material well-being, and conformity and their linked specific values. In the business and financial world, despite conservative tendencies, there has been a steady trend toward consolidation and standardization. Although the familiar and now perhaps inappropriate hue and cry is still raised about monopoly and big business, the latter, at least, serves the greater material well-being of the American mass consumer, whose values are geared to conformity. "Big business" is consonant with the American value system here portrayed so long as the owners of such enterprises are pictured as the American middle class, so long as savings are invested in the stocks and bonds of these enterprises so that the middle class shares "equally" in its successes, and so long as the authorities in such enterprises are presented as servants of the people. In these terms the American value system is served. The dangers of a too extreme individualistic power-centered authority are thus allayed, and competitive rivalry is brought under control. . . .

THE LOSS OF PEASANT HERITAGE
IN JAPAN

Iwao Ishino and John D. Donoghue

Each culture and subculture has basic values and patterns of behavior that distinguish it from others. We commonly associate such
values and behavior with types of communities or regional areas.
The range of regions and community types for which we hold
images has expanded greatly but has not kept pace with change
brought about by technological advances and other factors. Thus
the images held of a given community type sometimes persist long
after extensive changes have occurred. Just as many Americans talk
of rural and urban communities in terms that are no longer valid,
so the anthropologists who wrote this selection held preconceptions
about the Japanese village and villager based on their study of the
research literature. Here they describe contemporary Japanese villages and villagers as they observed them. There were significant
differences between preconceptions and observed reality.

. . . Since October [we] . . . have visited nine of the thirteen villages surveyed a decade ago by a team of Japanese and American social scientists;
and examined three of these nine more intensively with the aid of 15 students from the University of Tokyo. These three villages . . . exemplify
respectively an isolated mountain village, a marginal coastal community,
and a lowland plains village.

The authors arrived in the field with certain preconceptions and beliefs
about the nature of Japanese peasantry. Some of these beliefs were implicit,
but most were explicit because they have been a familiar feature of the
literature of both American and Japanese scholars. The writers wish to take

SOURCE: Prepared for the Annual Meetings of the Central States Anthropological Society, Madison, Wisconsin, May, 1959 ❖ Iwao Ishino is
professor of anthropology and a member of the staff of the Institute for
Community Development at Michigan State University. He has done extensive
field work in Japan, was formerly a Fulbright Lecturer at the University of
Tokyo, and was Chief of Party, Michigan State University, Ryukyus Project,
Okinawa. He is the author of *Paternalism in Japanese Economy* and a coauthor of *Social Problems: Dissenters and Deviation in an Industrial Society.* ❖
John D. Donoghue is associate professor of anthropology and a member of
the staff of the Institute for Community Development at Michigan State University. He was formerly a Fulbright Research Scholar, Tohoku University, and
spent five years doing field work in rural Japan and Viet Nam. He is the
author of *My Thuan: A Mekong Delta Village in South Viet Nam* and *Cam
An: A Fishing Village in Central Viet Nam.*

this opportunity to examine these preconceptions in the light of new evidence. The purpose of this paper, then, is to review these early assumptions and to summarize the authors' present views.

Our Preconceptions

We knew that Japan was an over-populated country and poorly endowed with natural resources. The amount of arable land—only 16 per cent of the total area—had reached its upper limits long ago. Further reclamation and conversion of the hillsides into arable land was deemed impossible. We also knew that a land reform program had been carried out several years before in which tenancy was drastically reduced. We had figures which told us that the average farm household operated a strip of land of only two-and-a-half acres or, more accurately, 5.9 separate strips of land totalling only 2.5 acres. We read that this rural population of 36 million represented 40 per cent of the nation's population, and that it was able to produce up to 80 per cent of the nation's food requirements.

Yet this 40 per cent earned only 17 per cent of the total national income. These figures were sufficient to suggest that the farmers of Japan were living at a standard considerably below that of the city workers and that they indeed were "peasants." What else could they do but to live frugally and to cherish the classic peasant values that hard work is a virtue in itself and that farming is not a money-making business but a way of life? How else could they maintain their self-respect if they did not maintain a closely integrated natural community which insulated itself from the impersonal, competitive, and frivolous life of the urbanite?

Such were our thoughts and impressions about Japanese peasantry before we began our studies. But this picture did not hold its shape for long. As we visited one village after another the image began to fade. The "peasant" image gave way to an image of a hard-headed commercial "farmer." The reasons for the change in image ran somewhat as follows:

Are Japanese Agriculturalists "Peasants"?

While we did not quite expect the Japanese "peasant" to be following the same cultivation methods his great grandfather used, we thought the technical advances would be limited. We were surprised, however, at the refinements that had developed. We came to the conclusion that the Japanese farms may be small, but that it was not merely "gardening" activity.

The successful farmer must not only work with his hands, but also with his head in order to make his 2.5 acre farm produce as efficiently as it does. He works on a small margin and so he must be careful that each decision he makes is the best one. But in these days, the Japanese peasant is confronted with many kinds of decisions his grandfather never had to make. Dozens of basic innovations about farming have been placed before him in recent years. The information about them comes to him from many directions: from the farmer in the next hamlet, the local agricultural agent, the technical advisor for the cooperative, the salesman of fertilizers and farm equipment, the canning company looking for raw materials, the popular farm journal issued by the cooperatives, and his wife who might have learned about the new idea at the local Women's Club lecture meeting.

The officers in agricultural cooperatives have told us that farm families most resistant to new ideas are "holiday" farmers who work in a nearby factory or office while their women folk and children operate the farm. Perhaps these represent the small, but significant, number of farmers who are leaving the farms, after they get their sons educated and placed in a town occupation. On the other hand there are the eager farmers who actively seek technological improvements. These progressive farmers, by their example, encourage other less imaginative farmers to follow suit. They are the ones who are first to use farm machinery. Those whose role is to promote the new farm technology—like the farm extension agent and the technical advisors of the cooperatives—introduce the innovations through these action-oriented farmers.

The kinds of changes taken over by the peasants can be readily observed in the villages. The use of plastic covering to hasten the maturation of rice seedlings and to protect other kinds of crops has become a familiar part of the landscape. The characteristic odor from "night soil" fertilizers is absent even though they are still used in large quantities. The rhythmic coughing sounds of small cultivators can be heard. Technical progress can also be indicated by statistics. For instance, in five years from 1948 to 1952, the rice yields per hectare increased 64 per cent.

The Japanese peasant must use his head not only for increasing his yields but also in other ways, for example in marketing. Like farmers elsewhere he is concerned with locating the best market for his crops. Except for rice, which is usually handled through the agricultural cooperatives, other commodities require personal attention and sometimes long term planning. In one of our sample villages, for example, the farmers lobbied for the construction of a highway that would lead into the city of Hiroshima. If such a road were built, this would enable them to double their income from the vegetables which they already raise, and also to raise such quality items as late season tomatoes. Where the locality has many producers of a single crop—such as silk, mandarin oranges, milk, and tea—marketing cooperatives are available. Peasants located near large cities often transport their products by their own three-wheeled trucks or contract someone to do it.

Financial problems are also matters of great concern to the Japanese peasant, particularly for obtaining farm credit. Interest rates are high and so are taxes. It is interesting to note that some farm families have incorporated themselves as a business and thereby claim tax deductions not given to farmers. Court decision on this is pending. The government has put in a crop insurance system which provides a kind of protection the farmer never had before. Farm credit, interest rates, taxes, and crop insurance are financial problems that rarely concerned the grandfather of today's peasant.

As we said before, then, the management of a two-and-a-half acre farm is a complicated business. The Japanese "peasant" is learning to adapt himself to the modern world and, incidentally, to the Great Traditions. We conclude, therefore, that the Japanese peasant is being rapidly transformed into something else: a hard-headed and hard-working commercial farmer.

But this peasant-turned-farmer is still caught in the inexorable vise between too many people on the one hand and not enough land on the other. Seen in the large perspective, however, he is not retreating to the security of his traditional ways nor escaping into the world of supernaturalism. Neither is he a revolutionist wishing to upset the existing political order. We think some of the reasons for this lie in the nature of his local community.

The Hamlet

The face-to-face, natural community of the Japanese rural population is the hamlet. Other than the family or household there is probably no other social grouping that exerts so much influence upon the peasant's daily activities and his social outlook. Its members operate farm plots in adjoining areas, manage the communally owned pastureland and forest reserves, share the water from the same irrigation system, repair and maintain their common roads; pay their respects at the common tutelary shrine; and celebrate their annual festivals.

In this kind of tightly knit community of several dozen families, then, the Japanese farmer can and does find a certain degree of security, in spite of whatever inequities there might be between him and the city dweller. Interestingly enough, certain events have taken place in the postwar period to increase the solidarity of the hamlet. The prime motive for this was the land reform program which removed the economic dependence of the tenants upon the landlords. Social distance between the top families and those lower has decreased; overt deference patterns are diminishing; and some cases of inter-marriage between classes have been noted. Numerous members of the former tenant class have been elected to the village assembly and hold other positions of influence in the hamlet. Most of these positions were not formerly open to the tenant class. We can also say that in general the prestige of the individual has come to be based less on his family background and more on his personality and accomplishments. In this sense the hamlet has become more democratic.

Another reason for the generally healthy outlook of the Japanese farmer is that the gap in the living standards between him and his city cousin is being closed. This is not only reflected in the national statistics on income and nutrition, but can be directly observed in the villages. The range and quality of merchandise carried in the village stores are good and cannot easily be distinguished from that found in suburban shops in Tokyo. New roads have been constructed, telephone lines put in, temples renovated, and thatched roofs replaced with tile. In every village we visited, we saw hundreds of bicycles, and dozens of motorcycles, trucks, and busses. We have noted five to ten television sets in eight of the nine villages visited. The ninth village was not within the existing television telecast zone. Washing machines were becoming popular and the farmers' wives were buying ready-made work clothes at the cooperative store. They said it was cheaper to buy them than to sew them at home.

Some Differences Between Villages

The foregoing, we hope, is sufficient to suggest how the Japanese peasant is adjusting to the situation of too many people and not enough land. Scientific and technological advances have come into the peasant's way of life and as a result he is becoming less a peasant and more a commercial farmer. We see the hamlet and the favorable conditions in it, playing a vital role in helping him make this transition.

But to look more closely at the facts, we see a basic difference among the communities in which the Japanese peasant lives—a difference which is important for understanding his adjustment to modern conditions.

Japanese rural communities have to be classified in many ways—by size, by kinship structure, by crops raised, etc. But for our purposes the most significant classification is in terms of degree of isolation from major urban centers. For convenience, let us call those which are located near the large cities or close to the major railroad lines as "hinterland" villages; while those located in remote regions such as those in the mountain areas are "isolated" communities.

With regard to these two types of villages, we note a very interesting difference. Paradoxically, the isolated villages seem to be further advanced and more progressive than hinterland communities in taking over innovations in agricultural techniques, in home improvements, in family relations (e.g., mother-in-law and daughter-in-law adjustments) and in birth control measures. The "backwardness" of these isolated villages is no longer so apparent as it was before. The reason for this, we think, is that the social solidarity is greater in the isolated communities and local pride in making it a shining example gains wider appeal. Furthermore, the capable persons and potential leaders do not leave these villages to the same extent as they do in other types. The temptations to be drawn away into the town and city are not as strong nor as real. This is to say, then, that compensating factors are operating here. The isolated villages help the Japanese peasant make a better adjustment to life by providing him with a comparatively active and progressive social environment. In the case of the peasant in the hinterland communities, his opportunities to move into the urban centers are greater and his dependence upon fellow villagers for recreation, part-time employment, and friendship is less.

These differences between village types, however, can be overstressed. We reiterate the original statement that the opportunities of the Japanese peasant to participate in the Great Tradition have increased immeasurably. His stake in the economy is larger and his status in the society is higher. The confining pressure of too many people and not enough land is still there, but what has been accomplished within this framework is remarkable. . . .

❊ 75 ❊

THE COMMUNITY OF MAN: A STUDY IN THE THIRD CULTURE

John Useem

There has been a drastic increase in contact between cultures in the past quarter century, which has meant intimate and prolonged contact between members of different societies. In the process of interaction new cross-cultural patterns of behavior, roles and expectations, values and norms, have tended to develop. John Useem here shows the nature and importance of such groups of foreigners and nationals who develop mutually acceptable patterns of living and working together and gradually create a distinctive new international "third culture." The specific group chosen to illustrate this important concept—the third culture that emerges among such "middle-men between societies"—is the community of Americans and Indians who live and work together in India.

It has become commonplace within American society during recent years to depict the need for mutual understanding between the peoples of different societies, to propose that a more authentic image of American life and values be projected in foreign countries and, in the process of anxious evaluation, to speculate about the effectiveness of Americans overseas in fulfilling these related goals. Beneath the surface of these manifest national

SOURCE: *Centennial Review*, Vol. 7, No. 4 (Fall 1963), 481–98. Reprinted by permission of the author and the publisher. ❖ John Useem is professor of sociology at Michigan State University and a member of the advisory committee of the Edward W. Hazen Foundation. He is coauthor with Dr. Ruth Hill Useem of *The Western-Educated Man in India* and is a contributing author to *Human Problems in Technological Change, Cultural Patterns and Technical Change,* and *The Underdeveloped Areas.*

concerns can be traced deeper preoccupations: we have witnessed in our times a new vision for mankind—one world, and experienced a haunting fear of there being no world for man.

For the social scientist, the evolving patterns of cross-cultural relationships in an interdependent world, including changes on an unprecedented scale in the relationships among western and non-western societies, pose a complex series of new variables for study. They call for more sophisticated theorizing and more empirical research over a wide range of relatively new phenomena. Thus the ever-widening scope of interpersonal contacts between members of disparate cultures and the burgeoning social systems which govern their behavior require detailed study. We must learn a great deal more than we presently know about how people act in their roles as middlemen between societies, what actually occurs within each society as a consequence of the flow of persons across its national boundary lines, and how members of intersecting societies relate themselves to one another.

This discussion selects from the larger set of variables a limited group for two purposes: first, to reformulate the concepts of community and culture for the study of social groups in cross-cultural relations; and second, to present some relevant findings derived from a field survey of Americans who live and work in India.

I. The Community and the Third Culture

To serve as a guideline to the new social arrangements in cross-cultural relations, we shall use the international community to refer to any group formed of people who stem from disparate societies, who regularly interact through interpersonal contacts and communications networks, and who share mutual interests and a common ethos. This usage detaches the sociological meaning of the community from its conventional geographical reference points. Throughout much of man's past, we described the community primarily in terms of people who resided together within a delimited area of land and who participated during their lifetime in the social institutions sustained by local groups.

Put on the widest social scale, one can refer to world-encompassing types of international communities. A prominent case in point is the diplomatic community which includes men from over a hundred countries. The members associate together in various national capitals, have interlocking roles, conform to well-established codes of personal behavior, are stratified in a formal hierarchy of ranks, and have a "consciousness of kind." More recent developments consist of scientific communities grouped around specialized disciplines which are in the process of extending into most societies around the globe. The International Geophysical Year dramatically symbolizes one community of scientists working across national boundaries. In the same fashion, we can note the collectivity of leaders on the European continent who currently are designing an economic community through the common market, or the Christian ecumenical movement aspiring to build a world-wide community encompassing diverse religious groups, or the more informal association of leaders of newly-independent countries which prefer non-alignment in a polarized political world.

On a more delimited scale in social space, and of direct interest for the case study which follows, are the groupings composed of foreigners and nationals located in any particular society. The foreigners normally have a representational function with respect to one or more aspects of their homeland and, typically, are regarded as temporary residents irrespective of their actual length of stay. Accordingly, excluded from this classification are refugees, immigrants, and those who by marriage or other reasons identify with or are identified by the host society as permanent members.

Every society in Asia and Africa contains a foreign group; however, the aftermath of independence combined with the modernizing of traditional cultures has profoundly altered the symbiotic basis of the foreigners' association with local people. Alien governors are supplanted by envoys and technical assistants; the authority and status of the foreign administrators —in business firms, mission enterprises, educational institutions—are diminished with the "nationalizing" of managerial positions. Changes in the myths, customs, and social rules occur as superordinate-subordinate divisions give way to new kinds of coordinate, foreign-national communities.

Just as we enlarged the concept of the community to delineate the newer groupings of people across societies, we expand the term culture to fit modern-day, cross-cultural relations. Out of early anthropological study of preliterate societies, two major generalizations emerged: (1) that each culture is firmly anchored in an ageless heritage which is transmitted from generation to generation in a relatively unchanged form; (2) that each culture in fundamentals is homogeneous, integrated, and coherent. These coefficients of culture when tested in subsequent research proved true for comparatively stable, isolated, small populations. The ongoing process of decision making in a primitive society is over-shadowed by its powerful traditions which endow succeeding generations with ready-made solutions to life's problems. The search for consensus among factions is not permeated by vigorous dialogues in which people question the priority of their goals or ask what they are trying to accomplish by new plans.

Later studies of primitive societies undergoing acculturation as a consequence of the enveloping impact of western cultures on them, and studies of modern societies with their pervasive inner differentiation and high rates of culture change, revealed additional dimensions of culture. These dimensions are even more apparent as one begins to explore the milieu of cross-cultural relations, a milieu which we shall term the third culture.

The third culture signifies the patterns generic to a community of men which spans two or more societies. It consists of more than the mere accommodation or fusion of two separate, juxtaposed cultures, for as groups of men belonging to different societies associate together and interact with each other, they incorporate into their common social life a mutually acknowledged set of shared expectations. A third culture cannot be understood fully without reference to its mediating functions between societies nor apart from the cultures of the several societies in which its participants learned how to behave as human beings. Nonetheless, each third culture generates a composite of values, role-related norms, and social structures which distinguish its patterns from any of the societies it spans. Perhaps the most conspicuous feature of third cultures is the self-conscious effort on the part of its carriers to create the common grounds for living and working together.

A newcomer to an established third culture, whatever the character of the society in which his personal life and occupation have been embedded, is socialized through learning and adjusting to the group's mores, institutions, and world view. The new man, for example, who seeks to identify himself with an international community of scientists, assimilates its methods for the discovery of knowledge, the profession's heritage of information, and its specialized language. As he becomes familiar with the present work of his colleagues, he, in turn, further contributes to the shared behavior by building a "name" for himself.

It would be generously optimistic to assume that men drawn from different societies can easily formulate a uniform set of expectations or transcend the misunderstandings and tensions between societies; it would be excessively pessimistic to underestimate the creativity of a generation insistently challenged by the problems of a nascent interdependent world. There is universal concern over the existing shortcomings in cross-cultural relations and how they might be lessened. It is evidenced by western administrators of foreign public and private endeavors in their constant search for better formulae for the selection of persons to represent their programs in an alien country. It is apparent in the stress on pre-departure orientation schemes to help first-time-outers adjust. It is visible in the intermittent reorganizations intended to strengthen programs and upgrade the level of intercultural performance.

The concern to improve cross-cultural relations is also found among those communities of men who are carrying out programs in other lands. In the "foreign communities," their designations by the host country, one hears anxious talk about how well the policymakers back home really comprehend the critical issues, how communications can be improved between the host society and the "home office," and how best to relate to "local" people. Infra-groups of a foreign community, united by some common role of men in the middle of two societies, often disagree as to how men should act. The short-term residents shake their heads over the social enclaves of the long-term residents and the manner in which they live, voice doubts as to whether a "golden ghetto" comprises a suitable environment for fostering personal contacts across cultures. Old foreign hands often look askance when the newcomer on a once-in-a-lifetime stay "goes native" and reaches out indiscriminately for social contacts. And each person, according to his own private experience, projects an ideal model of cultural middlemen. Comparable sorts of apprehensions, cleavages, and hopes can be discerned within most groups of non-western people who are directly involved in a third culture.

An international community with its third culture is like a bridge between societies. A bridge, however, is worthless unless pathways and roads connect the bridge into segments of each society. Some groups traverse national boundary lines without actually bridging societies—the leisure-attuned elite who freely move around the world, the peasants and laborers who migrate from one country to another, and the mutant ethnic minorities such as the Anglo-Indian and Eurasian communities of South Asia. Some groups are demolishing the old bridges of colonialism; others have become the victims of bridges suddenly demolished, as in Indonesia, Rhodesia and Burma. The pathways and roads have been' more completely laid out among the cosmopolitan than among the provincial segments of both western and non-western societies. Notwithstanding, new bridges are going up all over the world—frail ones between Russia and America, rebuilt ones between Japan and America, new ones between the western world and the newly independent nations of Asia and Africa, rebuttressed ones between the societies of the western world. Meanwhile, the provincial-minded in every society are discovering new social routes from the outside world leading into their midst.

Important sociological questions, therefore, must be raised as to who uses these bridges, where do the outlets actually lead in the connected societies, what happens to the pathways when they reach their destinations, how are the bridges maintained? The account which follows endeavors to find some answers about a particular bridge between the United States and India.

❖   ❖   ❖   ❖   ❖

III. Who Participates in the Indo-American Community

The Indo-American community, for the purpose of this analysis, is defined as being composed of the representatives of India and of the United States who are relating their societies to each other through their interpersonal relationships within the setting of India. There are, of course, many more who are indirectly members of the community—Americans once resident in India and Indians once resident in the United States who continue their membership through indirect contacts and through their concerns about cross-cultural relations between the two countries.

Our survey confirms an often-sketched image of the cohesiveness of Americans in a foreign land and disputes an equally common inference as to its significance. An abundance of collected facts shows the extent of group cohesion. Two-thirds of the Americans reside near other Americans or within easy commuting distance; seventy-five per cent of those with a dwelling in close proximity to other Americans participate in the social life of American groups. Under a tenth of the residents associate with no Americans except on special occasions.

Less attention has been paid to the conditions which motivate Americans to stay together than to the fact of their close association. The average newcomer reports that although he had given little thought before his arrival as to what his interaction with Americans in India might be, it loomed forth as a major factor during his initial decisions and adjustments. Americans live near other Americans largely because of lack of choice in accommodations. Only certain more westernized areas of the big cities offer the facilities and amenities American families want and landlords in these neighborhoods specialize in leasing homes to foreigners. Additionally, some American organizations have found it essential to have adequate quarters ready for the newcomer's family so that he might start on his job instead of spending months establishing a place to live. And these, too, are usually near other Americans.

Most Americans soon find themselves caught up in a series of informal relationships with their fellow countrymen. For some, such contacts provide a feeling of identity with their native culture at a time when everything else is strange; for old foreign hands, they assure a continuity in their private lives as they move over the world; for all, and especially dependents, they offer patterns of mutual aid in getting settled in a strange environment. Newcomers find American groupings an important learning resource. As one put it: "Talking and listening to Americans in touch with reality helps you to clarify your own impressions. Indians don't always understand what you don't understand; you can get closer to what you are trying to figure out with another American." They also serve as secure media for catharsis, allowing the individuals to admit to frustrations which might be thought of as insulting if said to another Indian. "When I found other Americans who also felt Calcutta was a difficult place to live in, it helped me to keep confidence in myself." Whatever the specific factors which make for American groups, we cannot discount the importance they have in the year-round life of the typical American resident.

Contrary to popular folklore, American groups normally open channels into Indian society rather than cutting their members off from social life with Indians. We shall cite a few observations from a large body of supporting evidence. Among those integrated into an American group, two-thirds also regularly join in mixed Indian-American gatherings—receptions, dinners, teas, cocktail parties, home visits, and so forth. Only a fifth of them have no recurrent personalized social contacts with Indians. Factors other than belonging or not belonging to an American group are more decisive in accounting for lower interaction with Indians—as examples, having a work role which does not stress the need for mingling socially with Indians;

individual preference for no social life beyond the family circle whether in the United States or India; inarticulateness in any language including English, a characteristic which Indians equate with low intelligence.

Instead of creating social walls, most American groups function as the foremost means by which newcomers are introduced into the segment of Indian society where they find many of the Indians with whom they continue to associate during their stay. Around each of the well-established American groups is located a particular constellation of Indians; whereas Americans come and go, these Indians preserve their social ties with the current members of the American group.

The American community as a whole tends to move on social pathways and roads into a small yet influential sector of the host society. The social identity of the Indians can be summarized as being primarily upper middle class Hindus and Parsis who are English speaking and westernized in style of life and whose life histories are characterized by high mobility. They have reputations in their Indian circles as the prominent in various fields of endeavor; they are the local elites, the figures of power, or they have attachments to the newer power structures of post-independence India. Of course, not all the people in this sector of a massive society have direct contacts with Americans but most who interact with Americans exhibit these attributes.

Few persons and no groups in the American community have a social life which regularly includes the backbone of the country, the cultivators in some five hundred thousand villages. There is also little social interaction with the lower and lower middle classes of the city for there is little in common to foster close personal ties with the laborer, small shopkeeper, or clerk. Missionaries have contacts with some of these groups in their "service" relationships but seldom in their social relationships. Orthodox Hindus of higher socio-economic background usually neither savor contact with foreigners nor welcome invitations to mingle with them.

The structure of binational groups affects the scope and content of interpersonal behavior. There are two discernible, although sometimes overlapping, types of groups—functional and locality-bound. Functional types are composed of Indians and Americans with complementary interests converging around work roles, professional affiliations, organizational loyalties, or other salient values. Some of the members of functional groups may be found locally but functional groups also extend widely over the country. A grouping of persons sharing a unique interest (e.g., those who prize the fine arts, big game hunters, Quakers, intellectuals concerned with East-West understanding) sustains an intricate series of large and small networks.

Interpersonal relations in these varied functional groups develop at a faster pace and more smoothly than most other types of social contacts. From their initial meeting as strangers, the Indian and American geologists can talk the language of their profession, cultivate a feeling of intimacy as they gossip about mutual acquaintances in the profession, and exchange views on aspects of India and America. Their shared third culture gives them a common frame of reference. Functional affiliations tend to minimize the obstacles to rapport in three ways. First, Indians and Americans are somewhat alike in cross-cultural communications in that both are more skilled at telling than at listening; that is, both sides seem more adept in expressing their ideas than in discerning what has been conveyed in the thoughts of people from another society. We noticed that in a functional type of gathering, the conversations were less beclouded by misunderstandings as to what was meant than in other forms of Indian-American communications. Second, they impose less demands on the host-guest pattern which commonly engenders subtle personal stresses between Indians and Americans. The former may feel impelled to offer amenities they can little afford; the latter may feel uneasy to be the recipient of so much hospitable treatment. In addition, the customs of acting as host and guest differ in the two cultures. In functional associations less of the social interaction focuses on this phase of the relationship. Third, they seldom involve the complete self or the wife of the involved. This alleviates the likelihood of interpersonal clashes because much of each self seems irrelevant, and whether or not the wives have something in common is not germane. In addition, functionally-linked associations have a higher rate of survival for they continue as social ties even when the American departs for his homeland.

In contrast, locality-bound groups of Indians and Americans occur among residents in a population center, usually a city. They are characterized by a common style of life and interpersonal congeniality patterns. The newcomer geologist from America who lacks a professional counterpart in the place he lives, finds social company in a circle of kindred spirits. With them he can play golf, meet at the club, celebrate holidays, attend an Indian wedding, entertain the "visiting firemen" from the United States. The larger the American population in an Indian city, the more likely is it to subdivide the local American community into tight social circles with each American crowd having a specific set of Indian participants. The Americans are sufficiently numerous in the main urban centers of Bombay, Calcutta, and New Delhi that they often have several different social crowds, each one linking members into functional and local ties.

These concentrations offer a full life to those who are integrated; the newcomer is not expected to possess great social talents or an exceptional personality, the only demands being that he adopt the folkways of the group—if golf is the recreation, then he learns to play golf; and if politics is not an appropriate topic at parties, then he learns to avoid the subject.

The smaller and more heterogeneous the American population, the greater the self and superimposed pressures to find a common basis for doing things together. Under these conditions, interpersonal conflicts sometimes flare into rather intense factionalism and intra-group feuds. Scattered Americans in outlying towns and cities sometimes travel for miles to secure meaningful companionship or join mixed groups of Europeans and Indians in the locality of residence. Whatever the social arrangement, locality groups generally are comprehensive associations of Americans and Indians in that they encompass a large portion of the social self plus the wife of the man. The social interaction is geared to the social seasons, the reciprocities of giving parties and paying back social debts, and the routine built into the yearly cycle of events.

IV. The Inter-Societal Functions of a Third Culture

Beyond the social arrangements and interpersonal behavior of group life, how does the Indo-American community mediate between societies?

We must briefly review the limiting factors of this bi-national group before we can appraise the net influence of its third culture on a cross-cultural relationship. (1) A group of this character may not be viewed realistically as a superordinate community that wields power over the societies its members represent, nor can the bi-national community be construed as a subordinate instrumentality of nation-states. To be sure, the foreign policies of the two governments affect directly or indirectly all groups of the Indo-American community, but most do not act merely as means to political ends and some explicitly detach themselves from the political sub-community. Business and missionary groups, in addition to their primary purposes for being in India, do regard themselves as cultural ambassadors of American society but not on behalf of the State Department. Both governments can restrict the Americans who enter India but neither has the authority to govern the community of Americans in their associations with Indians.

(2) Although the people in the Indo-American community over recent years stem from wider segments of both societies, the populations involved do not comprise a cross-section of either one. Therefore they cannot be expected to represent fully the total societies in their person-to-person contacts. Furthermore, the current participants move within a narrow range of Indian life. The Indians who participate are identified more with the westernized and society-wide culture; their high mobility allows them to say about the place in which they now live: "I am a stranger here myself." Cosmopolitan in outlook and style of life, few have significant roles in provincial and orthodox groups. Another group also exposed to the western world, the American-educated Indians, have relatively little contact with the Americans in India but they do have significance for cross-cultural relations because of their distribution within sectors of Indian society relatively untouched by Americans abroad.

(3) The first generation in a third culture encounters the dual tasks of learning how to act as cultural middlemen and developing the social patterns appropriate for the roles. The biographies of the Indians and Americans who associate together show the average man as being born in

1916 and growing up in a period which offered few adult models of success-ful cross-cultural behavior between co-equals; only a handful had personally experienced in their prior adult life the anxieties, stresses, ambiguities, and bright hopes of men in the middle of two cultures.

The third culture, despite these conditions, has a manifold and signifi-cant impact. It functions at the lowest common denominator as the social basis for people from different societies "getting along" together. The most universally specified norms (originating out of rejection of the colonial heritage) are social acceptance of persons as equals and freedom from racial bias and attitudes of superiority and inferiority. In the words of a leading American figure: "If Indians think you are condescending, patron-izing, acting like a *burra sahib*, you are through." The glaring social mistakes which evoke sensitivities and create hostilities are held in check by these social ground rules of mixed Indian-American groups. Contrasting with more casual social contacts in which Indians and Americans may become entrapped in dissonance, the third culture infuses each ongoing social group with a pattern of mutual expectations.

At a higher level, it improves the prospects for understanding between societies under circumstances which enhance the chances of new informa-tion being absorbed. All Americans have questions put to them about America: family life (with special emphasis on divorce and sex-related cus-toms), racial discrimination, juvenile delinquency and crime, military aid to Pakistan, atomic weapons, and the cold war. The mass media as sources of information on America, notably moving pictures and the press, are par-tially counteracted by the interpretation of these events by Americans known to Indians. American domestic customs and foreign policies do not come up for searching questions in most of the mixed Indian-American congeniality groups of long standing—the Indians are past the stage of asking elementary questions or they do not feel the need to "tell off" an American or they are so deeply committed to a western style of life that they do not challenge its shortcomings. However, when a dramatic episode pertaining to America galvanizes public attention in India, then the Ameri-can contribution to understanding is evidenced in the explanations, "inside facts," and background which the Americans offer about the disturbing event. In turn, Indians offer Americans knowledge and insights into aspects of Indian society which enter their threshold of awareness. The underlying circumstance is the readiness of both Indians and Americans to accept as reasonable and understandable what they hear from members of another society they personally know and trust. The newer social groups do reveal a broader flow of factual information.

The cross currents of Indian-American misunderstandings seem evanes-cent to people caught up in the great social and economic tides set in motion by a changing world. They feel the challenge to build on the solid bedrock of the common faith in democratic values, of the shared commit-ment to advance underdeveloped countries, and of the ideal of a peaceful world. The individual American is not prone to voice these lofty sentiments in person-to-person contacts, nor for that matter are Indians, yet as they find in their common life together a larger vision for mankind, they contribute to their fulfillment.

The process of living together does more than hold forth the promise of greater unity among people from different societies; it gives fresh perspective to each society and to the larger world. A midwest county agent said: "I have thought more about America, its customs, family life, standard of living and foreign policies since I have been here than in my entire life. I have never realized so clearly our good points and our bad points. You see things more vividly here and you want to know the whys of our own country. You start thinking about things you took for granted all your life." Seven out of ten newcomers learn about their own country as they learn about India.

In general, two changes in outlook occur. First, there is a deeper sense of self-identification with the homeland. "Here you realize how lucky you are to be an American." Second, there is an awareness of belonging to a community of man. "We have learned that the differences between the East and the West grow out of their conditions and not out of the nature of mankind." "You find the same fundamental characteristics with them as with us." "It's plain to see that human emotions are the same everywhere. Regardless of national boundary lines, all people are very human." Those who make the long journey across cultures see the great panorama of human life; those who make a short journey see much less. The Indian members of the third culture in India do not have as clear a perspective on, nor as great an appreciation of, their own civilization as do the Indians who go to the west for their education. Nonetheless, India is enriched by the presence of its third culture as symbolic of a new age.

Rabindranath Tagore, one of the first of the first generation in the third culture, wrote: ". . . from the sunset-created end of my road, I feel proud that I have been born in this great Age. I know that it must take time before we can adjust our minds to a condition which is not only new, but almost exactly the opposite of the old. Let us announce to the world that the light of the morning has come, not for entrenching ourselves behind barriers, but for meeting in mutual understanding and trust on the common field of cooperation; never for nourishing a spirit of rejection, but for that glad acceptance which constantly carries in itself the giving out of the best we have."

CHANGE IN RED CHINA TODAY:
THE CASE OF HIGHER EDUCATION

Edgar Snow

Where once even neighboring tribes or communities were "cultural islands" having relatively little contact with each other, today entire nations and continents are involved in constant interchange. Whole cultures are modified by these interchanges even though the traits acquired are often altered in special ways to harmonize with the new setting. A striking exception to the world-wide trend toward increasing inter-societal contacts, as described in the preceding selection, is the absence of normal communications between The People's Republic of China and the United States. Edgar Snow, perhaps more than any other American, has tried to bridge this communications gap. This selection gives an idea of the unique form higher education is taking in mainland China today, in part because of its isolation from other cultures.

The evening before I visited the Iron and Steel Institute I saw in a Peking theater a contemporary drama about two girls, two boys and a commune against a swamp. The swamp lost; one of the boys was a party veteran and naturally he won the confidence of the peasants and with their faith and his courage they drained the swamp just before the winter frost set in. Humor was provided by the Intellectual, a malingerer afraid to soil his hands by labor; nobody was surprised when it turned out that his father had been an oppressive landlord. A Student Agronomist who knew her books but not life was now learning the hard way, from the Wise Old Peasant. The W.O.P.'s daughter was ambitious; she wanted to drive a truck, a tractor, or anything at all as long as it gave her equal status with a man.

All these were stock caricatures, but the next day I met a girl at the Iron and Steel Institute who was exactly like the peasant's daughter. Her name was Chiang Chu-hsing and I nicknamed her Hsiao-shan or Small Lightning. Her story literally corresponded to that of the character in the play, but in this case life was larger than "art" and more interesting.

SOURCE: © Copyright 1962 by Edgar Snow. Reprinted from *The Other Side of the River*, Chaps. 32, 33, by Edgar Snow, by permission of Random House, Inc. ✧ The author is a journalist specializing in the Far East. In 1960, he became the only American writer accredited by the United States State Department and The People's Republic of China to travel throughout Communist China. His publications include *Far Eastern Front, Red Star over China, The Pattern of Soviet Power*, and his autobiographical *Journey to the Beginning*.

I spent the morning talking to the director, Hu Ying, and inspecting the institute. It was one of twenty wholly new universities and colleges, built north and west of Peking, with a combined enrollment which exceeded the total number of students on that level in all prerevolutionary China.

Every province has its own higher educational system, but Peking is still regarded as the Athens of China and attracts more than 100,000 college students, or about 15 per cent of the current national enrollment. They still tend to think of themselves as China's intellectual *crème de la crème*. Old Peking had eleven colleges and about 10,000 students, and foremost of the colleges was the Pei-ta, Peking National University. Pei-ta is still the goal of ambitious arts and sciences students and graduate research workers. Enrollment was now about 11,000. Outside the city, near the Summer Palace, was the "rich man's university" of Yenching, founded by missionaries; nearby was Tsing Hua, which also had a foreign background. Yenching had now been absorbed by Tsing Hua, a greatly enlarged university with an enrollment exceeding 7,000. I revisited both of them, and went on to the new institutes north of the city walls.

The focus of this recently developed university city is the Chinese Academy of Sciences, which embraces institutes of meteorology, economics, geophysics and physics, linguistics, philology and others. Around it are the spacious new campuses of universities, institutes and colleges which specialize in medicine, normal training, petroleum technology, aeronautics, agriculture, mining and metallurgy, music and art. As an illustration of their impact, the new geological institute now had more students than the total number of graduate geologists produced in all the years before 1949.

At the Iron and Steel Institute, Hu Ying was both chief administrator and party leader, a combination I had learned to welcome. One could accomplish one's business much more smoothly and rapidly wherever a party man was in titular as well as factual control rather than operating under some euphemism such as secretary. The party man may or may not answer all one's questions, but he is in a better position to make the decisions. Hu Ying proved so cooperative that I returned to the school a second time to get a picture story of student daily life.

Director Hu was a Manchurian, born in Fushun, the coal town, and educated at Shenyang Normal College. As a young teacher during the war he had joined the anti-Japanese underground, at first simply as a national patriot, so he said. Later he escaped to the hills and the partisans and there became a Communist and fought with the guerrillas until victory. Assigned to help establish the Iron and Steel Institute in 1953, he had been there ever since. The chancellor and vice-chancellors were professional engineers, but Hu Ying was boss. Wearing blue slacks and a blue cotton shirt, Hu received me in a spacious reception room furnished with semimodern Chinese furniture, the walls decorated with Sung and Ming paintings, the windows draped in silk with golden bees embroidered on it. He offered me innumerable cups of scalding tea served by a student assistant.

The institute's well-landscaped campus covered thirty acres and its plant included forty-one completed buildings, with eleven more under construction. It had 6,000 students, of whom 916 were women. The largest institute of its kind in the country, it had a staff of 700 professors, assistants and instructors. It operated fifty-seven laboratories, more than ten experimental factories, and a small modern steel plant with an electric blast furnace where men and women students were trained. The plant had a 1962 target of 100,000 tons. In the middle of the campus were adequate athletic fields and a large swimming pool built by spare-time student labor—as was common now at many universities.

"Our curriculum includes twenty-three subjects," said Hu, "and all varieties of steel processing. We train research specialists and teachers. The full course is five years and we offer one and two years of post-graduate work. There are more than thirty different student activity organizations such as photography, radio, dancing, opera, dramatics, orchestra, chorus, Chinese and Western music appreciation—"

"How about cooking—or is it going to become a lost art in an age of communal eating?"

"There is a cooking club; also a sewing club."

Hu went on to say that tuition and rent were paid by the state, and that 80 per cent of the students drew a stipend which covered the cost of food—twelve and a half yuan a month—and provided pocket money of three yuan for undergraduates and five yuan for graduate students. The other 20 per cent of the students, who came from families with an income of more than sixty yuan per month (that excludes most peasants), were obliged to pay for their food in whole or in part, "depending on circumstances." Institute students included forty-three Mongols and "about fifty" assorted Moslems, Uighurs from Turkestan, Chuangs from Kwangsi, and Thais from Yunnan.

"There must be stiff competition to get into a school like this. How are students selected?"

"That's right. The demand is greater than the supply. High schools annually yield from two to three hundred thousand graduates who are qualified to apply, but our own institute can't admit more than about fifteen hundred a year. Applicants are judged by scholarship, character and health status."

"Children from ex-landlord families, too?"

"Yes, we have some. But most of our students come from peasant and working-class families. We also admit a limited number of students who are substandard in scholarship—most of the minority nationalities students, for example. They get special tutoring or spend an extra year or two with us. An especially promising peasant from a revolutionary family, or the son of a veteran, naturally has a good chance to be recommended."

"By the party?"

"By the party—and the school authorities, too."

"Your teachers must average out pretty young?"

"Most of them are under forty. Quite a few were educated in Russia. We have about sixty 'old boys'—over forty—trained before the war."

"Would you say your teaching methods follow Soviet lines or develop independently?"

"In some basic respects they are the same; we use a lot of translated Russian texts. But the teaching revolution going on here now is our own development. We call it a three-in-one technique. It combines, in all grades, teaching, practical research work, and actual production. All students spend some time in our factories where we make some of the materials used in the buildings you see being constructed here. We designed and helped build our steel plant. You'll see it, if you wish. We are working on more than a hundred research projects—real, exciting, practical problems passed on to us by various industries. We also send students to outside factories to study and work."

"How many months a year?"

"It depends on the kind of work—whether it's a special project, a whole class under the guidance of a professor, or a student's combined research-and-work project—what his year in school is—and so on. Some students spend most of their four weeks' vacation time working. In 1958 practically all of them did."

"Why 1958?"

"We sent two thousand students to build small blast furnaces during the first Great Leap Forward drive."

"Do you count that a waste of time, materials and money? Critics said the people fell behind in their regular work, the back-yard furnace product was useless, the whole thing had to be abandoned. What about that?"

"You have to remember two things. First, our steel output in 1957 was less than a fourth of this year's target. The movement was launched in a countryside where the level of understanding of industry was very low. Many peasants looked upon steel-making as a mystery; they were afraid of it. When the campaign ended, millions of people had learned the principles. Do you know how to smelt iron or steel, Mr. Snow?"

"Never touch the stuff."

"Well, lots of our peasants are ahead of you. You may not need to know, that's true, but in a socialist country just beginning to industrialize, it's important for the people to know what's going on, and what they're working for."

"But your government admitted that 3,000,000 tons of the pig iron smelted was unfit for industrial purposes."

"Yes, there was waste, but not all waste. Don't forget, China can always use scrap iron. We have a big shortage. The educational result of the campaign was not the only thing. Our two thousand students helped build 25,000 furnaces—"

"Out of 600,000 all told, as I remember the claim?"

"Most of those were tiny brick hearths intended only for demonstration purposes. With the furnaces our students built we trained 67,000 skilled workers. The best furnaces were then combined and modernized. Last year China's small blast furnaces made 5,000,000 tons of usable iron and steel. That's more than our whole national production a few years ago.

"Another permanent result of the Great Leap Forward was that we discovered new sources of ore. A few of our students went as far west as Sikang and Chinghai and came back with rich ore from deposits we didn't know existed. Thousands of peasants helped us."

Hu took me through some classrooms and labs. They were less impressive within than outside; interiors were cheaply finished and furnished and classroom equipment seemed mediocre, if adequate. The labs had good instruments; China now makes most of her scientific equipment, including microscopes and some fine lenses. The library held 300,000 books, with journals in foreign languages.

Men's dormitories were two-story brick buildings where students lived in cramped quarters: four to six in a room, with double tiers of bunks, and not much working space. (Not much more, in fact, than I later saw in the Peking jail.) The showers and washrooms, dining rooms and kitchens were clean, Spartan and as dreary as army barracks.

This was the school routine:

5.30 A.M.	Ablutions, dress.
6:00— 7:00	Physical exercise, en masse.
7:30— 8:00	Breakfast.
8:00—11:30	Classrooms, lab, or workshops.
11:30—13:30	Lunch, rest and study hours.
13:30—16:30	Classroom study or workshop.
16:30—17:30	Play or study.
17:30—18:00	Supper.
18:30—22:30	Study, club meetings, political lectures.
22:30	Curfew.

Saturdays and Sundays are free days used for study, club activities, sports, theater or special group projects. There was a college dance every Saturday.

"Would you like to see the girls' dormitories?" asked Mr. Hu as I was about to leave.

I hadn't talked to a girl engineer since I left Russia. I had never talked to a Chinese girl engineer. I said, "Of course." That's how I happened to meet Small Lightning and her roommates.

Hu Ying led me down a willow-lined path to a girls' dormitory, a long brick building with a simulated tile roof and numerous casement windows. Two girls in maroon slacks and white cotton pullovers, their hair braided, were hanging laundered underwear on the unpainted wooden stairway banisters. They looked up and laughed confusedly. The student house chairman appeared and led us to the second floor, where some girls skipped past, their long hair damp from a shower.

"Is it all right to just walk in like this—?"

"They're expecting us," said Mr. Hu. The house chairman cried out our arrival and mobilized girls in half a dozen rooms that were in order; she invited me to inspect any of them. I looked into two or three, and their occupants bowed invitingly. Then a girl with an engaging smile above two pigtails called out, "*Wo-men ch'ing nin tao li-pien lai*," welcoming me to visit them, and three roommates behind her nodded affirmation.

Inside were two sets of double-tiered bunks in a room ten feet by twelve. Under the French windows and between the bunks was a work table covered with a white cloth and on it stood a small lamp and the usual teapot and statuette of Mao Tse-tung. Under the bunks was just enough space to store the regulation small canvas or wooden traveling boxes which contained the girls' personal belongings. There were two cheap chairs and another small table. From the white walls in rough plaster hung a few dresses, slacks and coats. Overhead there was one unshaded light bulb.

The girl who had beckoned to me was slightly pockmarked and not very pretty, but she radiated personality. She had bright, merry, bold eyes —not so much bold as direct. Women of her province, Honan, are not shy or cringing but are noted for their independence. Most Honanese women are also large and deliberate in their movements, but this girl was diminutive and quick; she was **Chiang Chu**-hsing.

I asked the same questions of six girls who crowded into the room and here quote their answers, from my notes.

First (Chiang): Born near Chengchow (northern Honan, central China). Age twenty-two. Daughter of poor tenant peasants. Neither could read or write; mother now just able to read Small Lightning's letters. Two brothers, one sister. During childhood Chiang Chu-hsing worked as a scullery maid in local landlord's house. One year's schooling before "liberation" (1949), when she was eleven. "Liberation" obviously had literal meaning for her. She had worn only rags till then. She remembered a famine year of a diet of tree bark. Never owned a dress. (Now owns three.) Her parents got some land and security; she was sent to school; life completely changed, "like crossing a bridge to heaven." Worked hard, with party support. Now a sophomore, three years older than average in her class. Will graduate at twenty-six. She belongs to the Communist Youth League.

Second (Ho): Born Hopei province (where Peking is situated). Age nineteen. Parents small landlords; left home and went to Tangshan, mining town on the Hopei coast, during war. Land confiscated; they stayed in Tangshan. Now both parents work in factory there. "They like it."

Third (Lin): Born Hunan (South China). Age nineteen. Pretty girl. Daughter of small landlords. Land redistributed—taken by village cooperative. Parents went through six months of "re-education" and then rejoined community. No discrimination against her? (She would have been a small child at the time.) Not at all, she says. Went through regular schools, won place at institute on high scholarship after close examination. Now in her third year.

Fourth (Sung): Born Kiangsu (where Shanghai is located). Age twenty. Father an "intellectual." Meaning, middle school teacher. Non-party but helped revolution. He now teaches in Yangchow. Three younger brothers. She is sophomore—and a Young Communist.

Fifth (Wang): Born Shantung (east coast). Age twenty. Third year. Father a railway worker. Two brothers, also railway workers, both party men.

Sixth (Hsu): Hopei girl, age eighteen. Father was scavenger—peddler of coal balls (made of coal scrap) in Tientsin. After liberation he became skilled worker. Mother and father both work in factories, have good three-room apartment, new building, living "better than ever dreamed."

"Why did you choose to become engineers?" Some answers:

"We want to build socialism." "Heavy industry is the foundation of socialism." "We want to build China into a strong, modern nation and help the world get rid of imperialist oppression." "Engineers are the spine of a modern nation."

"Those answers are out of a book," I said. "Before you ever heard of heavy industry, socialism or imperialism, you must have formed an ambition. I met a nurse at a hospital recently who told me she had begun to long to be a nurse from the moment when, as a small child, she first saw a woman wearing a cool, crisp, clean white uniform, 'looking like one of the immortals.' Don't any of you remember wanting to be an engineer before you knew the country needed them?"

Small Lightning spoke up, the most articulate of the group.

"When I was a very small girl I saw a truck for the first time in my life. I said, 'I'd like to drive that truck.' My older brother laughed at me. For a long time I was determined to be a truck driver. After liberation, going to and from school, I saw many trucks, tractors and bulldozers working on a dam but I saw that it was the engineers who told them what to do, and where to put their loads. I knew that I couldn't compete with those strong men driving bulldozers, but by using my brains I could become an engineer."

Freudians may recognize some familiar patterns in that frank statement.

"Many men would say that women shouldn't be engineers," I said provocatively, "especially iron and steel specialists. The work is too tough. Research, draftsmanship, building design, maybe, but can women really do the heavy jobs?"

They all heatedly asserted that they did everything men students did. There was a tendency to give them light work but they all did their time at the furnaces, the same carrying work, the same risks; they wanted complete equality in work assignments. Did I know who was the first volunteer to carry a cable across the Yellow River rapids at San Men Hsia at the start of the big dam there? A woman engineer!

They were beginning to boil when I apologized by saying that I had already heard from factory chiefs and engineers that women make better operators of heavy-duty cranes than men and are more reliable at tasks where a precise sense of timing may mean the difference between life and death. I quickly put myself on record as being in favor of women engineers.

"I hope you will admit," I said, shifting to safer ground, "that two sexes are better than one. Better a two-sex institute than a one-sex institute, for example? There must be advantages in being a girl student in an institute with nine males for every female?"

Nobody denied that coeducation was a good thing. "Much better than an all-girls' school." "Very nice!" "Sex doesn't come into our work here. We are all engineers!" "There is no sex discrimination here."

"Do many girls get married while they are students?"

"Very few. Usually we get married right after graduation." The others laughed at the pretty Hunanese girl, Miss Lin, who said that. "You mean *you're* going to get married," they said. Student marriages were distinctly discouraged now. Although the legal age for marriage is twenty for men and eighteen for women, these young ladies considered the "correct" age to be at least twenty-two or twenty-three for a man and twenty or twenty-one for a woman.

They said they usually dated for Saturday night dances, for Sunday walks, for games or sports like swimming. They often paired up on "teams" for field-work assignments. "We have most of our fun in collective living rather than dating."

Mr. Hu had gone off somewhere, so I asked my interpreter's advice about whether anyone would be offended if I asked their views on birth control. He thought I might try.

"Do any of you object to family planning?"

"Certainly not," said Miss Chiang. The rest looked blank.

"Let me put it this way. How many children do you intend to have when you get married?"

"That won't be my decision alone but my husband's—and the needs of socialism," said the Shantung girl. "Personally, I think two are enough."

"Two!" "Three!" "Two!" The small family was definitely preferred.

"What if you have two or three and they're all daughters? Won't you need at least one boy?"

"That's feudal thinking! We don't make such distinctions any more," said the little Honanese spokesman. They all joined in pouncing on the old attitude that males have superior value.

A few more questions elicited the information that birth control techniques were understood by all, from group discussions on social hygiene. It was also pointed out that the "facts of life" were discussed on daily radio programs which explained contraceptive methods, for listeners of any age, in most precise detail. I was tempted to solicit their views on premarital relations, but this was not a clinic. I had already learned that such questions were often regarded as too prying and rather shocking even to some fully matured adults. I deferred them for another occasion.

"This is too one-sided," I said. "You're doing all the answering. Would you like to ask me any questions for a change?"

They shouted in a chorus and held up their hands.

"You said you lived in Peking before, and taught at Yenching University. How do things in New China impress you?"

"Infinitely more opportunity for the poor, that's obvious. Certainly a poor peasant woman in college was almost unheard of. College was mainly for the upper class."

"How is it in America? Can women study engineering in your schools?"

"They can, and do, but I'd say the cards are stacked—I mean there's a lot of prejudice against that. On my plane to Moscow last June I met an American woman engineer from San Francisco—a Mrs. Henry Taylor, whose husband was a doctor. She was the only American woman engineer I ever heard of. They exist, but they're as scarce as hens' teeth."*

They all smiled. It was what they had expected to hear.

I asked, "Do you think you are happier than American students?"

Howls of derision greeted this, laughter and exclamations of surprise. "What an odd question!" "How could American students possibly be happy—slaves of American capitalism!" "We feel sorry for them; they have yet to win their freedom." "How different it is with us, who are free and have a glorious and victorious future ahead of us!"

"I must tell you that most American women students would say they feel sorry for you. Some might also tell you that the proportion of women to men college graduates in America is still higher than it is in China. There it is about one to two while here it is still one to four, is it not?"

"But here we are changing that very rapidly," said Small Lightning. "We will soon make it fifty-fifty. Besides, in your country only daughters of the rich get to college. Would any peasant have a chance?"

This was going to be a hard one. How explain that the average American farmer never thought of himself as a peasant? That it takes only about 5,000,000 farmers to produce more than enough to feed America? That on the same percentage basis only 20,000,000 farm workers should be needed to feed China instead of the 200,000,000 to 250,000,000 now required? Well . . .

"Yes, farmers go to college—yes, they do. Probably in a higher proportion than urban people. I'm not sure."

* Not quite: in 1958–59 6,755 master's degrees in engineering were granted, 24 to women; 121 women and 38,013 men received bachelor's degrees as engineering majors. One woman and 713 men received doctor's degrees in engineering. (U.S. Office of Education, *World Almanac*, 1961.)

This was news a little beyond their information and was received skeptically.

"*Poor* peasants can go to college?"

"Not so many poor peasants—I mean poor *farmers*. Of course it takes money to go to college—"

"That's the difference. Here education is free, it's for the working class. In America colleges are run for the rich—and to make money."

"No, it's more accurate to say they are run to teach *students* how to make money. But let's not forget that America had a free educational system long before any other country. We have free primary and high school education—compulsory, in most places. Even in higher education there are some tuition-free local colleges. But good colleges and universities charge heavy tuition—too heavy for most families to bear. Students have to pay for their room, board, everything. That's where discrimination in favor of the rich comes in."

"Naturally," said Small Lightning. "Marx said that bourgeois education means bourgeois class domination. Bourgeois education seeks to perpetuate the enslavement of the working class. That's the kind of system we used to have in China."

"A high percentage of Americans from working-class families get through college with the help of scholarships and part-time jobs. It's quite possible. You believe in struggle, don't you?"

"Struggle is important but it has meaning only if it's conscious class struggle. Individualistic struggle in bourgeois society only means that the one who succeeds joins the exploiters."

"Not always. Sometimes it produces a Lenin or a Mao Tse-tung, does it not? The real weakness of education run by private enterprise, like the real weakness of an unplanned economy, is the amount of sheer waste involved. Someone here in China quoted to me a statement he had read, by an American admiral, Rickover, complaining about the fact that half of the top-ranking students in American high schools never get to college or are forced to drop out. It was an anomaly that America, the richest country in the world, able to spend billions on bombs and nuclear weapons that could be used only in mutual suicide, could yet not afford to provide a proper education for its best brains."

"The people can afford it but monopoly capitalism does not want to educate the poor. That is inevitable under an imperialist system," Small Lightning recited.

Curiously, and to my relief, they had spared me questions about segregation in the South. My last remark had put them back on terra cognita and it would have been an appropriate moment to leave. The normal suppertime had come and gone and I had been pressed to eat with them. Each time I was invited I had declined, because I had a late dinner engagement, but whenever I rose to leave they insisted that I stay. They were genuinely curious, perhaps even more curious about me than I was about them; three of them had never seen an American. I could not leave without finding out a little more about how well they had learned their Mao Tse-tung.

"It may surprise you," I said, "to hear that few American youths believe they live under a system of imperialism. The average American believes imperialism means owning colonies, and Americans think they own no colonies. Students of history might ask you why, if America is an aggressive imperialist country, it supported Russia during the war against Hitler. After victory America had half the wealth of the world, fresh armies of fifteen million men, the best navy, the strongest air force, and men in occupation of a dozen countries and colonies. Why didn't America hold them and build a colonial empire?"

"The imperialists were afraid of Russia."

"Russia was bleeding then, and truly very weak. And she had no defense against the atom bomb."

Hu Ying had returned, but he was taking no part in the students' responses. I got the impression that such a question had never been raised for them in just that way.

They were silent for a moment. Then one of the younger girls, who had said little, remarked thoughtfully, "The American people would not have supported such a thing." To me that was a heartening statement.

Small Lightning would not leave it at that. "Of course imperialism is not just owning colonies in the old way," she said. "It means monopoly capital ownership of the means of production in countries economically colonial to it. It means keeping economic control and enslavement of peoples in order to make great profits. The people's revolutions were becoming powerful in some countries and American imperialism's role was to prevent revolution and to support counter-revolution, in that way maintaining its control.

"America did not really leave any of those countries. She tried to defeat revolution in China and she failed—except in Taiwan, for the moment. She tried to defeat it in Korea and failed. She is trying the same kind of aggression in Vietnam and Laos and she will fail there, too. There are American advisers and bosses in Pakistan and others in India, giving Nehru money to fight socialism. America has two hundred military bases, all the way from Germany to Japan, combining its forces with the native reactionaries to protect U.S. investments and profits and to hold down the people. What we don't understand is why American students tolerate all that—and the great risk of war that goes with it."

"Why? Some of them would agree with some of what you say, but most would say that these bases are necessary defenses against the danger of Communist aggression—"

"Communist aggression! Is China's fleet occupying Hawaii, or is China flying planes over America? Are Chinese troops in Canada or Mexico? No! We haven't a soldier on foreign territory. Are Americans in Taiwan, Japan, Laos, Vietnam? Yes!"

What about Korea? Yes, what about it? That could have meant another six hours and it was really late. I had heard enough to know that these young people, the generation being prepared for leadership, were well indoctrinated in the politics of the land. They had answers to all the questions—or thought they had.

I promised to continue the discussion when I returned on Saturday, but that day was full of activity. Small Lightning was the star in a picture story I did of a day in the life of a student. She was a good actress: getting up, eating breakfast, working in the lab, walking in the park with a boy friend. She wore a light summer frock and black pumps and had her hair put up. In the afternoon we went to the steel mill, where she donned white overalls, helmet and glasses and pulled out half a dozen testings of flaming metal before it was poured. I went with her to the swimming pool, which was crowded with students. Finally she took me for some shots of her, with another partner—she was not sticking to one—dancing decorous fox trots and waltzes.

All this, I had persuaded her and the college authorities, would greatly interest youth in America, and help to correct some distorted impressions there about the slave lives of Chinese students. The pictures were not bad, but American magazine editors did not consider them worth using. Like the Chinese students, they already had the right answers—though not the same ones.

CHAPTER IX

Social Processes

HOW PEOPLE INTERACT IN
CONFERENCES

Robert F. Bales

*Ordinarily sociologists direct their energies to a consideration of
the structure and functioning of human groups and leave to social
psychologists the study of the behavior of individuals within small
groups. Nevertheless, it is useful to those interested in sociology to
observe in a simple setting the operation of the social processes, for
they have their parallel in the activity that may be observed
within and between larger and more complex groups and organizations. In this selection, Bales describes some significant findings
from the study of small problem-solving groups.*

Social interaction is made up largely of the talking that people do when
they get together. Talk is an elusive object of study, in spite of the fact that
a good deal of it exists. It is also a rather sensitive subject. Even a friend
might find it hard to put up with a dissection of the following kind: "I
was just noticing how much you talk. In the last 10 minutes I noticed
that you made a total of 114 remarks, while I made a total of 86. According
to my count you have about twice as many opinions as facts. Although I
agreed with you 15 times and didn't disagree at all, I noticed that you
stammered once and blushed twice."

I first began to develop a systematic procedure for analyzing social

SOURCE: *Scientific American*, Vol. 192, No. 3 (March, 1955), 31–35. By
permission of the author and the publisher. ❖ Robert F. Bales is Director of
the Laboratory of Social Relations, Harvard University, and a consultant to
the Rand Corporation. His special areas of interest include small groups and
small-group interaction. He is the author of *Interaction Process Analysis: A
Method for the Study of Small Groups*, the coauthor of *Working Papers in
a Theory of Action*, and the coeditor of *Small Groups*.

interaction when I became interested in trying to account for the success of Alcoholics Anonymous in helping apparently hopeless drinkers to stop drinking. Although I attended meetings and talked with many members, I did not feel free to ask all the questions I wished. Consequently I fell back on observation and began to develop crude methods for recording who did what, who spoke to whom, and how. Eventually even this quiet occupation began to appear sinister and the effort was abandoned. But by this time my fascination with the process of social interaction had developed to the point of no return. I decided that I must pursue my studies in the more favorable conditions of a laboratory.

A number of laboratories for the study of social interaction within small groups and organizations have been started in the last 10 years—in hospitals, clinics, special research centers and military installations. The studies and experiments I shall describe were conducted in one of the earliest of these laboratories, established in 1947 at Harvard University.

The laboratory consists of a large, well-lighted room for the group under study and an adjoining room for observers, who listen and watch from behind windows with one-way vision. The subjects are told at the beginning that the room has been constructed for the special purpose of studying group discussion, that a complete sound recording will be made and that there are observers behind the one-way mirrors. The purpose of the separation is not to deceive the subjects but to minimize interaction between them and the observing team.

After much research we developed a standardized task from which significant generalizations could be drawn. A group of persons (ranging from two to seven in number) is asked to discuss a complex human relations problem of the sort typically faced by an administrator. Each member of the group first reads a five-page presentation of facts about the case to be discussed, but each is left uncertain as to whether he has been given exactly the same range of facts as the others in the group. The members are not introduced to one another or coached in any way; they must develop their own organization and procedure. They are to consider the facts and report to an administrator, as if they were his staff, their joint conclusions concerning the problem and what should be done about it. They are allowed 40 minutes for the discussion. The group is observed for four such sessions.

On the other side of the one-way screen the observers systematically record every step of the interaction, not omitting such items as nods and frowns. Each observer has a small machine with a moving paper tape on which he writes in code a description of every act—an act being defined essentially as a single statement, question or gesture. Acts ordinarily occur at the rate of 15 to 20 per minute. The recorded information on each includes identification of the person speaking and the person spoken to and classification of the act according to predetermined categories. There are

12 categories, covering positive and negative reactions, questions and attempts to solve the problem by the offering of information, opinion or suggestions.

... On the average about half (56 per cent) of the acts during a group session fall into the categories of problem-solving attempts; the remaining 44 per cent are distributed among positive reactions, negative reactions and questions. In other words, the process tends to be two-sided, with the reactions acting as a more or less constant feed-back on the acceptability of the problem-solving attempts. The following is a typical example of the pattern of interchange:

Member 1: "I wonder if we have the same facts about the problem? [Asks for opinion.] Perhaps we should take some time in the beginning to find out." [Gives suggestion.]

Member 2: "Yes. [Agrees.] We may be able to fill in some gaps in our information. [Gives opinion.] Let's go around the table and each tell what the report said in his case." [Gives suggestion.]

This example illustrates that a speaker's first remark is likely to be a reaction, and if he continues speaking, the probability is very high that his second act will be a problem-solving attempt. ... About 50 per cent of the time a member's first remark in a series is a reaction; if he continues, about 80 per cent of the succeeding comments are opinions or other offerings classed as attempts to solve the problem.

When we examine the reactions, we find that positive reactions commonly outnumber negative ones about two to one during a session. It is as if after every negative reaction, the members of the group feel they must make another problem-solving attempt which meets with a positive reaction "just to catch up," and net forward progress is felt to be sufficiently secure only when a repetition of the problem-solving attempt meets unopposed acceptance. It may be that members employ repetition, or near repetition, as an error-checking device to determine whether the others "really agree." Social interaction, in common with many other goal-seeking control mechanisms, seems to depend upon error and correction of error for guidance.

The process of attempting to arrive at a group decision through discussion is in many ways very like the operation of a large-scale communication and control system such as an air-defense network. I recently compared the two processes in collaboration with John Kennedy of the Systems Research Laboratory at the Rand Corporation.

In the military case there are three functions to be performed: surveillance of the air by radar, identification of planes as friendly or unknown and direction of fighters sent out to intercept unknown planes. These are something like the three problems confronting our groups in the standard interaction task: assembling the given information on the case, evaluating it and proceeding toward a solution as the goal. Now the stepwise operations involved in the air defense system may be tolerably well described as an interlocking series of seven types of information-processing operations (see chart). Here x stands for the path of a plane tracked by radar, and O represents the class of objects unknown. If no known flight plan of a friendly plane coincides with x—a fact represented by the symbol y—then x must belong to the class O. Since there is a general rule, W, that all unknown planes are to be intercepted, the conclusion is that a specific order, w, should be given to intercept x. Such a decision, involving many groups and interlocking processes, is obviously a very complicated affair, socially as well as technically. The job of the decision-making organization is essentially to build and maintain through means of communication and evaluation a sufficiently complex and commonly accepted symbolic structure to guide or control the stages of behavior of all the operating units. Effective decision making is basically a continuous process of building and maintaining a structure of cultural objects which in their totality constitute the common culture of the organization affected.

The seven types of acts, or stages, just described are very general: they apply quite as well to the interaction of five experimental subjects in the laboratory group, trying to decide in 40 minutes what the administrator in their case should do about his problem, as to the large-scale operations of an air-defense network. Not all of the elements in the process are primarily logical in character. They involve elements of perception, memory, association and perhaps inductive insight. All sorts of motivational and evaluative pressures affect the process. The steps make sense not as a formally perfect chain of logic, but rather as a set of symbol transformations which help to guide, although in an imperfect way, a process of decision-making behavior. Error checking is an integral part of this fallible process.

The reason for calling attention to the seven-step structure of the process is that it may help to explain the unequal ratios of suggestions, opinions, and information offered in the problem-solving attempts of the groups in our tests. . . . Of every seven problem-solving attempts, on the average four are opinions, two are offers of information and one is a suggestion. It seems significant that in the idealized seven-step outline of the air-defense operation two steps have the interaction form of giving information, four intermediate steps have the interaction form of giving opinion and only one step, the final one, has the form of giving a suggestion.

From the transcription of a group discussion it is often possible to reconstruct complete seven-step chains leading to agreement on specific points and the final conclusion. In a general way there is even a tendency for the steps to proceed in a regular order in time. During a session the rates of giving information tend to be highest in the first third of the meeting and to decline in the next two thirds. Rates of giving opinion are usually highest in the middle portion of the meeting. Rates of giving suggestion are generally low in the early period and reach their high point

1 STATES PRIMARY OBSERVATION:
I Observe a Particular Event, x

2 MAKES TENTATIVE INDUCTION:
This Particular Event, x, May Belong to the General Class of Objects, O

3 DEDUCES CONDITIONAL PREDICTION:
If This Particular Event, x, Does Belong to the General Class, O, Then It Should Be Found Associated with Another Particular Event, y

4 STATES OBSERVATION OF CHECK FACT:
I Observe the Predicted Particular Event, y

5 IDENTIFIES OBJECT AS MEMBER OF A CLASS:
I Therefore Identify x-y as an Object Which Is a Member of the Predicted General Class of Objects, O

6 STATES MAJOR PREMISE RELATING CLASSES OF OBJECTS:
All Members of the General Class of Objects, O, Should Be Treated by Ways of the General Class, W

7 PROPOSES SPECIFIC ACTION:
This Particular Object, x-y, Should Therefore Be Treated in a Particular Way, w

PROCESS IN REACHING A GROUP DECISION *is analogous to the operation of a large-scale communication and control system such as the air-defense network. The steps consist of observing an object or event, comparing it with several possible identifications, considering the associated facts and, once its nature is understood, taking the appropriate action.*

in the last third. These increases may be connected mainly with social and emotional problems of the group process itself. The ratio of negative to positive reactions tends to be higher in response to suggestions than in response to factual statements. The decision point is a critical bottleneck in the process. Once the decision point has been passed, however, the rates of negative reaction usually fall off and the rates of positive reaction rise sharply. Joking and laughter, indicating solidarity and tension release, become more frequent. With the problems of the task and common values stabilized for the time being by the decision, the interaction process apparently turns to restabilizing the emotional states of the individuals and their social relations to one another.

There is a good deal of evidence that the process of social interaction, like other processes involving feedback tends to fall into oscillation as it "hunts" around a hypothetical steady state. Over a small time span the action tends to alternate every few acts between the problem-solving attempts of one person and the social-emotional reaction of some other. But this rapid oscillation is not quite rapid enough to keep all elements of the process in perfect balance. There is a drift toward inequality of participation, which in time has cumulative effects on the social relationships of the members. The reason for this drift may be seen fairly easily. When a person has completed one act, the chances are a little better than even that he will continue for another act. After each succeeding act his probability of continuing drops, but never so far as if he simply flipped a coin at each point to determine whether to continue or to yield the floor. In fact, relatively speaking, he exceeds this chance probability by a larger and larger fraction with each succeeding act.

We have already noted that when a person continues several acts in succession the probability is very high that he is giving information, opinion or suggestion—in other words, specializing in problem-solving attempts. We may also infer from the seven-step theory of problem-solving attempts that the tendency to continue for several acts in succession is probably due in part to a felt need on the part of the speaker to provide inferences and check facts which will result in the acceptance of a more advanced step in the series, with an accepted suggestion as the goal.

This tendency toward inequality of participation over the short run has cumulative side effects on the social organization of the group. The man who gets his speech in first begins to build a reputation. Success in obtaining acceptance of problem-solving attempts seems to lead the successful person to do more of the same, with the result that eventually the members come to assume a rank order by task ability. In some groups the members reach a high degree of consensus on their ranking of "who had the best ideas." (The members are interviewed by questionnaire after each meeting.) Usually the persons so ranked also did the most talking and had higher than average rates of giving suggestions and opinion.

While one person becomes a specialist in advancing ideas, another is apt to be developing a specialization on the reactive side. The men most commonly rated "best liked" typically have higher than average rates of showing tension release (mainly smiling and laughing) and showing agreement. It is not impossible for the man ranked at the top in ideas also to be best liked, but apparently it is difficult. In one set of experiments the top idea man had about an even chance of also being best liked at the end of the first meeting, but by the end of the fourth meeting his chances were only about one in 10. The best-liked man is usually second or third in the participation hierarchy.

The task specialist seems to "lock onto" the person who is most responsive to what he is saying and address more remarks to him than to the others. In turn, the best-liked man talks more and agrees more with the top-ranking idea specialist than with any other member. The idea specialist and the best-liked man often form a mutually supporting pair. However, the best-liked man may attract the idea specialist even though they are not always in agreement. Indeed, in order for a person to become established in the minds of other members as a social-emotional specialist, it is probably more important that he be representative of their reactions, both positive and negative, than that he should ardently support everything the task specialist says. Apparently, reactions that are emotionally gratifying to other members tend to be generalized by them into liking for the person who expresses the reactions.

Giving suggestions, necessary as it may be for accomplishment of the task, is more likely to arouse negative reactions than is giving information or opinion. This tends to put the task specialist in a vulnerable position. The group commonly develops a certain amount of negative feeling toward him. Not only is he likely to lose the status of being best liked, but he may lose his position as task leader unless he is sensitive to the problem and is well supported by other members. Even in a group which ends its first meeting with a high consensus on who has the best ideas, the second meeting is apt to see a challenge to his leadership, with a rise in rates of disagreement and antagonism and a precipitous drop in his popularity. But then, in a group where the original consensus was high, a peculiar thing seems to happen. Apparently as progress toward accomplishment of the task slows down, some members rally around the leader again and his popularity tends to rise. By the third meeting the rates of disagreement and antagonism go down. The task leader may not retain all the liking that was transferred to him in his time of need, but the net effect of the hunting kind of oscillation that takes place is a tendency to maintain the original rank order of task ability.

In a group that starts with a low degree of consensus on who has the best ideas, the developments usually are more dismal. There tends to be a high turnover in the top ranks throughout the four meetings, with one would-be leader replacing another. In such a group the man ranked as having the best ideas is less apt to be best liked. Furthermore an additional specialist is likely to appear—a man who talks more than anybody else but is neither best liked nor most highly respected for his task ability.

It appears probable that whether the members will agree on who has the best ideas depends to a large degree on how well they agree on basic premises or norms—what we may call the "common culture." If such consensus is not present, at least implicitly, at the beginning, it may take a long time to build. While consensus on major values does not solve all the problems of arriving at a stable social organization, probably no stable organization is possible without this control factor. If it is lacking, the interaction process becomes primarily a means for the expression of individual emotional states.

Our studies have made clear that social stability is an extremely complex achievement: it takes time and patience to arrive at a common culture extensive enough and sensitive enough to regulate strong counter motives, to promote task accomplishment, to harmonize social relationships and to rejuvenate itself whenever the conditions demand. A clear recognition of the complexity of cultural control of behavior should encourage us to believe that interminable series of meetings around the conference table, international and otherwise, are perhaps worth while after all.

✢ 78 ✢

EXPERIMENTS IN GROUP CONFLICT

Muzafer Sherif

This selection by Sherif not only explores the concept of "conflict" but also illustrates one of the methods used by social scientists in their research. By providing a relatively natural setting in which interaction can take place, while at the same time introducing inconspicuous but effective controls over certain crucial elements or variables, Sherif has been able to obtain new evidence about the behavior of individuals and groups in conflict situations. The reader should be cautioned, of course, not to assume that the conclusions drawn from such an experimental setting are applicable without further testing to all kinds of groups under all circumstances.

SOURCE: *Scientific American*, Vol. 195, No. 5 (November, 1956), 54–58. By permission of the author and the publisher. ✧ Muzafer Sherif is professor of sociology at Pennsylvania State University. Born in Turkey, he was educated in his native country and in the United States. He is the author of *The Psychology of Social Norms* and the coauthor of *An Outline of Social Psychology* and *Groups in Harmony and Tension*.

Conflict between groups—whether between boys' gangs, social classes, "races" or nations—has no simple cause, nor is mankind yet in sight of a cure. It is often rooted deep in personal, social, economic, religious and historical forces. Nevertheless it is possible to identify certain general factors which have a crucial influence on the attitude of any group toward others. Social scientists have long sought to bring these factors to light by studying what might be called the "natural history" of groups and group relations. Intergroup conflict and harmony is not a subject that lends itself easily to laboratory experiments. But in recent years there has been a beginning of attempts to investigate the problem under controlled yet lifelike conditions, and I shall report here the results of a program of experimental studies of groups which I started in 1948. Among the persons working with me were Marvin B. Sussman, Robert Huntington, O. J. Harvey, B. Jack White, William R. Hood and Carolyn W. Sherif. The experiments were conducted in 1949, 1953 and 1954; this article gives a composite of the findings.

We wanted to conduct our study with groups of the informal type, where group organization and attitudes would evolve naturally and spontaneously, without formal direction or external pressures. For this purpose we conceived that an isolated summer camp would make a good experimental setting, and that decision led us to choose as subjects boys about 11 or 12 years old, who would find camping natural and fascinating. Since our aim was to study the development of group relations among these boys under carefully controlled conditions, with as little interference as possible from personal neuroses, background influences or prior experiences, we selected normal boys of homogeneous background who did not know one another before they came to the camp.

They were picked by a long and thorough procedure. We interviewed each boy's family, teachers and school officials, studied his school and medical records, obtained his scores on personality tests and observed him in his classes and at play with his schoolmates. With all this information we were able to assure ourselves that the boys chosen were of like kind and background: all were healthy, socially well-adjusted, somewhat above average in intelligence, and from stable, white, Protestant, middle-class homes.

None of the boys was aware that he was part of an experiment on group relations. The investigators appeared as a regular camp staff—camp director, counselors and so on. The boys met one another for the first time in buses that took them to the camp, and so far as they knew it was a normal summer of camping. To keep the situation as lifelike as possible, we conducted all our experiments within the framework of regular camp activities and games. We set up projects which were so interesting and attractive that the boys plunged into them enthusiastically without suspecting that they might be test situations. Unobtrusively we made records of their behavior, even using "candid" cameras and microphones when feasible.

We began by observing how the boys became a coherent group. The first of our camps was conducted in the hills of northern Connecticut in the summer of 1949. When the boys arrived, they were all housed at first in one large bunkhouse. As was to be expected, they quickly formed particular friendships and chose buddies. We had deliberately put all the boys together in this expectation because we wanted to see what would happen later after the boys were separated into different groups. Our object was to reduce the factor of personal attraction in the formation of groups. In a few days we divided the boys into two groups and put them in different cabins. Before doing so, we asked each boy informally who his best friends were, and then took pains to place the "best friends" in different groups so far as possible. (The pain of separation was assuaged by allowing each group to go at once on a hike and camp-out.)

As everyone knows, a group of strangers brought together in some common activity soon acquires an informal and spontaneous kind of organization. It comes to look upon some members as leaders, divides up duties, adopts unwritten norms of behavior, develops an *esprit de corps*. Our boys followed this pattern as they shared a series of experiences. In each group the boys pooled their efforts, organized duties and divided up tasks in work and play. Different individuals assumed different responsibilities. One boy excelled in cooking. Another led in athletics. Others, though not outstanding in any one skill, could be counted on to pitch in and do their level best in anything the group attempted. One or two seemed to disrupt activities, to start teasing at the wrong moment or offer useless suggestions. A few boys consistently had good suggestions and showed ability to coordinate the efforts of others in carrying them through. Within a few days one person had proved himself more resourceful and skillful than the rest. Thus, rather quickly, a leader and lieutenants emerged. Some boys sifted toward the bottom of the heap, while others jockeyed for higher positions.

We watched these developments closely and rated the boys' relative positions in the group, not only on the basis of our own observations but also by informal sounding of the boys' opinions as to who got things started, who got things done, who could be counted on to support group activities.

As the group became an organization, the boys coined nicknames. The big, blond, hardy leader of one group was dubbed "Baby Face" by his admiring followers. A boy with a rather long head became "Lemon Head." Each group developed its own jargon, special jokes, secrets and special ways of performing tasks. One group, after killing a snake near a place where it had gone to swim, named the place "Moccasin Creek" and thereafter preferred this swimming hole to any other, though there were better ones nearby.

Wayward members who failed to do things "right" or who did not contribute their bit to the common effort found themselves receiving the "silent treatment," ridicule or even threats. Each group selected symbols and a name, and they had these put on their caps and T-shirts. The 1954 camp was conducted in Oklahoma, near a famous hideaway of Jesse James called Robber's Cave. The two groups of boys at this camp named themselves the Rattlers and the Eagles.

Our conclusions on every phase of the study were based on a variety of observations, rather than on any single method. For example, we devised a game to test the boys' evaluations of one another. Before an important baseball game, we set up a target board for the boys to throw at, on the pretense of making practice for the game more interesting. There were no marks on the front of the board for the boys to judge objectively how close the ball came to a bull's-eye, but, unknown to them, the board was wired to flashing lights behind so that an observer could see exactly where the ball hit. We found that the boys consistently overestimated the performances by the most highly regarded members of their group and underestimated the scores of those of low social standing.

The attitudes of group members were even more dramatically illustrated during a cook-out in the woods. The staff supplied the boys with unprepared food and let them cook it themselves. One boy promptly started to build a fire, asking for help in getting wood. Another attacked the raw hamburger to make patties. Others prepare a place to put buns, relishes and the like. Two mixed soft drinks from flavoring and sugar. One boy who stood around without helping was told by the others to "get to it." Shortly the fire was blazing and the cook had hamburgers sizzling. Two boys distributed them as rapidly as they became edible. Soon it was time for the watermelon. A low-ranking member of the group took a knife and started toward the melon. Some of the boys protested. The most highly regarded boy in the group took over the knife, saying, "You guys who yell the loudest get yours last."

When the two groups in the camp had developed group organization and spirit, we proceeded to the experimental studies of intergroup relations. The groups had had no previous encounters; indeed, in the 1954 camp at Robber's Cave the two groups came in separate buses and were kept apart while each acquired a group feeling.

Our working hypothesis was that when two groups have conflicting aims—i.e., when one can achieve its ends only at the expense of the other —their members will become hostile to each other even though the groups are composed of normal well-adjusted individuals. There is a corollary to this assumption which we shall consider later. To produce friction between the groups of boys we arranged a tournament of games: baseball, touch football, a tug-of-war, a treasure hunt and so on. The tournament started in a spirit of good sportsmanship. But as it progressed good feeling soon evaporated. The members of each group began to call their rivals "stinkers," "sneaks" and "cheaters." They refused to have anything more to do with individuals in the opposing group. The boys in the 1949 camp turned against buddies whom they had chosen as "best friends" when they first arrived at the camp. A large proportion of the boys in each group gave negative ratings to all the boys in the other. The rival groups made threatening posters and planned raids, collecting secret hoards of green apples for ammunition. In the Robber's Cave camp the Eagles, after a defeat in a tournament game, burned a banner left behind by the Rattlers; the next morning the Rattlers seized the Eagles' flag when they arrived on the athletic field. From that time on name-calling, scuffles and raids were the rule of the day.

Within each group, of course, solidarity increased. There were changes: one group deposed its leader because he could not "take it" in the contests with the adversary; another group overnight made something of a hero of a big boy who had previously been regarded as a bully. But morale and cooperativeness within the group became stronger. It is noteworthy that this heightening of cooperativeness and generally democratic behavior did not carry over to the group's relations with other groups.

We now turned to the other side of the problem: How can two groups in conflict be brought into harmony? We first undertook to test the theory that pleasant social contacts between members of conflicting groups will reduce friction between them. In the 1954 camp we brought the hostile Rattlers and Eagles together for social events: going to the movies, eating in the same dining room and so on. But far from reducing conflict, these situations only served as opportunities for the rival groups to berate and attack each other. In the dining-hall line they shoved each other aside, and the group that lost the contest for the head of the line shouted "Ladies first!" at the winner. They threw paper, food and vile names at each other at the tables. An Eagle bumped by a Rattler was admonished by his fellow Eagles to brush "the dirt" off his clothes.

We then returned to the corollary of our assumption about the creation of conflict. Just as competition generates friction, working in a common endeavor should promote harmony. It seemed to us, considering group relations in the everyday world, that where harmony between groups is established, the most decisive factor is the existence of "superordinate" goals which have a compelling appeal for both but which neither could achieve without the other. To test this hypothesis experimentally, we created a series of urgent, and natural, situations which challenged our boys.

One was a breakdown in the water supply. Water came to our camp in pipes from a tank about a mile away. We arranged to interrupt it and then called the boys together to inform them of the crisis. Both groups promptly volunteered to search the water line for the trouble. They worked together harmoniously, and before the end of the afternoon they had located and corrected the difficulty.

A similar opportunity offered itself when the boys requested a movie. We told them that the camp could not afford to rent one. The two groups then got together, figured out how much each group would have to contribute, chose the film by a vote and enjoyed the showing together.

One day the two groups went on an outing at a lake some distance away. A large truck was to go to town for food. But when everyone was hungry and ready to eat, it developed that the truck would not start (we had taken care of that). The boys got a rope—the same rope they had used in their acrimonious tug-of-war—and all pulled together to start the truck.

These joint efforts did not immediately dispel hostility. At first the groups returned to the old bickering and name-calling as soon as the job in hand was finished. But gradually the series of cooperative acts reduced friction and conflict. The members of the two groups began to feel more friendly to each other. For example, a Rattler whom the Eagles disliked for his sharp tongue and skill in defeating them became a "good egg." The boys stopped shoving in the meal line. They no longer called each other names, and sat together at the table. New friendships developed between individuals in the two groups.

In the end the groups were actively seeking opportunities to mingle, to entertain and "treat" each other. They decided to hold a joint camp-fire. They took turns presenting skits and songs. Members of both groups requested that they go home together on the same bus, rather than on the separate buses in which they had come. On the way the bus stopped for refreshments. One group still had five dollars which they had won as a prize in a contest. They decided to spend this sum on refreshments. On their own initiative they invited their former rivals to be their guests for malted milks.

Our interviews with the boys confirmed this change. From choosing their "best friends" almost exclusively in their own group, many of them shifted to listing boys in the other group as best friends. They were glad to have a second chance to rate boys in the other group, some of them remarking that they had changed their minds since the first rating made after the tournament. Indeed they had. The new ratings were largely favorable.

Efforts to reduce friction and prejudice between groups in our society have usually followed rather different methods. Much attention has been given to bringing members of hostile groups together socially, to communicating accurate and favorable information about one group to the other, and to bringing the leaders of groups together to enlist their influence. But as everyone knows, such measures sometimes reduce intergroup tensions and sometimes do not. Social contacts, as our experiments demonstrated, may only serve as occasions for intensifying conflict. Favorable information about a disliked group may be ignored or reinterpreted to fit stereotyped notions about the group. Leaders cannot act without regard for the prevailing temper in their own groups.

What our limited experiments have shown is that the possibilities for achieving harmony are greatly enhanced when groups are brought together to work toward common ends. Then favorable information about a disliked group is seen in a new light, and leaders are in a position to take bolder steps toward cooperation. In short, hostility gives way when groups pull together to achieve overriding goals which are real and compelling to all concerned.

CONFLICT IN A
NEW ENGLAND COLLEGE TOWN

Victor A. Rapport

Many American colleges and universities with fairly large staffs are located in relatively small communities. These staff members often have characteristics and values that differ from those of the towns-people. In such situations the townspeople tend to regard the staff of the institution of higher learning as an out-group, and vice versa. It is often but a small step further till hostile feelings develop. From his own experiences V. A. Rapport describes one such "town-gown" conflict. Though it has certain unique characteristics, it illustrates university-community conflicts that may take other forms in other places. The cultural difference between the two groups often tends to make conflict a relatively permanent, insti-tutionalized relationship.

A conflict situation which exists between college and town groups is neither new nor unusual, yet the conflict manifesting itself around Storrs, the seat of Connecticut State College, seems sufficiently individual in certain particulars, typical in others, to warrant description. Deep-seated hates, the products of years, do not prevail since the college itself is young. Antagonisms which have festered with time are absent. Instead, however, is the intensity accompanying new suspicions and dislikes, the force of pioneers who inherit no traditions of struggle but, rather, live the struggle themselves. And the conflict, although new, expresses ancient motivations to conflict, rallying cries of past centuries and foreign places.

An investigation made by the author over a period of two years pro-vides illustrations of certain characteristics of conflict and demonstrates conflict patterns. Some doubt is cast by the facts on the accepted outcomes of conflict, although there is a partial manifestation of several of these effects. The research was by personal interview with a large number of the residents of the Town of Mansfield (in which Storrs is located), and with members of the college faculty. The results do not adapt themselves to statistical interpretation; they are exclusively opinions expressed in con-versation of a purposely casual nature.

SOURCE: *Social Forces*, Vol. 17 (May, 1939), 527–532. Reprinted by permission of the author and the publisher. ✧ The author is professor of so-ciology and anthropology and Dean for International Studies, Wayne State University. His interests include manpower planning in the field of education, criminology, and social implications of selective service. He is the coauthor of *The Recreational Uses of Land in Connecticut*.

Out of the statements, the following characteristics and patterns of conflict became evident: (1) the groups are highly self-conscious with respect to status and welfare; (2) organization both with and without recognized leaders is frequent, although the organizations are transitory; (3) propaganda and false reports are constant; (4) there is distinct confusion between the accepted and assigned reasons for the conflict and what appear to be the real reasons; (5) the unifying and (6) the disorganizing effects of conflict are both apparent. Finally, (7) whether the conflict will be resolved by the operation of accommodation, assimilation, or amalgamation is open to question despite indications of the existence of these processes in the present situation.

Before entering upon a description of the conflict, it would be best to clarify the peculiarities of the New England setting. Connecticut State College is located in Storrs, a village in the Town of Mansfield.

It should be remembered that the New England town is a relatively autonomous political division of the state, somewhat corresponding to the western township. Since county organization and function are relatively insignificant in New England, the town becomes a highly important grouping. Within the town are districts or villages—sometimes cities—which may or may not be separately incorporated, but which still owe a responsibility to the town. Thus, any resident of the Town of Mansfield, be he in Eagleville, Merrow or Gurleyville, is concerned with Storrs and the doings of its people, the college group.

This demarcation of the college group from the remainder of the town is indicative of the self-consciousness with respect to status and welfare. One frequently hears the former referred to as "the college" rather than as a group of individuals. Many of the townspeople make a clear distinction between themselves, who are residents of the town, and the college people who are in the same category as summer residents in a resort town. This is true despite the fact that many of the faculty have been taxpayers and property owners in the town for a score of years. Within the town group, one is "new people," according to one informant, for at least thirty years; the acceptance after that length of time does not appear to hold for those at the college. The college group, on the other hand, generally restricts its social life to colleagues and, in general, is quite ignorant of the town affairs. The self-consciousness with respect to welfare will be discussed later under organization.

Certain individuals, it should be indicated, are excluded from the conflict because of either or both of two reasons: (1) non-participation and (2) exemption. The *non-participants* are in both groups; these people do not feel antagonistic toward the other group, mix freely, and tend to merge with the *exempts*, those college people who are stamped as "regular" by the town group, and vice versa. The reasons for inclusion in the exempted group vary considerably with no characteristic pattern. In many instances, the older professors are included, though not all the older professors are exempted nor are all the exempts of the older group at the college. The exempted townspeople are frequently retired or professional men who reside in Mansfield, though not all the exempts are of this category nor is this whole group exempt. Young professors, recently arrived in Connecticut, and old farmers are accepted by the opposite groups—just why, nobody seems to know.

An illustration of the operation of the self-consciousness with respect to status is seen in Mansfield Center, another village of the Town of Mansfield, located about four miles from the college. Many residents of this community have long felt strongly about the college group. Some years ago a lone professor and his family took up residence in the village. They were not a part of it for several years and were constantly made to feel that they did not "belong." Cracks finally began to appear in the icy reception they met, and in time they found themselves accepted as satisfactory citizens. What they had done to effect this change, they were unaware. They had merely continued about their own business, greeted people pleasantly but without trying to make friends, cultivated their garden, trimmed their lawn, and lived. It is probable that the combination of all these factors was the successful formula to break down the conflict attitudes. More and more of the college families moved into Mansfield Center as Storrs became overcrowded. The village soon heard mutterings about "The college people are taking over all the fine old houses," and "A farmer can't get a place any more with the rents that these college people pay" and "The Center ain't the same with all these new people coming in." As time went by, some of the new people became exempts, others did not.

The organization of the conflicting groups is primarily for political purposes. When the townspeople believe that "the college" is coming to the town meeting (a good old New England custom) for the purpose of promulgating legislation designed to further the ends of the college group, word goes out to the back country that all are needed to fight the measure. On the other hand, the college faction is constantly cautious about being absent lest "the town" force an ordinance prejudicial to the interests of the college. That each is motivated by selfish interests which are not conducive to the greatest welfare of the town is the firm belief of the opposing groups. Leaders are self-constituted or chosen from time to time in these political controversies, but frequently the groups follow concerted action without individuals at their head. A particularly serious issue arose about ten years ago when it was proposed to replace the antiquated grammar school at Storrs with a modern building. The opposition from the town centered around the argument that the existing school had been satisfactory for a great many years and ought to be good enough now, and, further, that "the college" felt that it needed something better for its children than was provided for the remainder of the town. That the children of faculty members represented only about one-third of the school population was overlooked. The building was approved at a town meeting and erected, but the wounds of the conflict have not yet healed. It is chiefly in these political disagreements that the propaganda and false reports are most current. The latter also are frequent in personal gossip principally concerning faculty members.

The confusion between assigned reasons and real reasons is particularly interesting. Among those persons who were interrogated, few had any real justification for disliking the other group, they "just felt that way." In most instances, when pressed for a reason, the informant was forced to pause for reflection before the "reason" was forthcoming.

The "reasons" on both sides are fundamentally the same. The objections of the people of the town to the college group fall under five general headings. The college group (1) takes no interest in the town; (2) is trying to run the town for its own selfish interests; (3) is "too snooty"; (4) represents impractical and incompetent theorists; (5) is composed of non-Connecticut newcomers. The college group felt that the townspeople (1) are trying to run the town for their own selfish interests; (2) are old-fashioned, stubborn Yankee farmers; (3) lack intellectual stimulation; (4) lack broad vision.

An analysis of the assigned reasons for the antagonisms reveals that some are justified while others are merely rationalizations. The political situation, which has been discussed in part previously, has counted heavily in arousing opposition attitudes. The charge has frequently been levelled at the college group that it lived in houses rented from the college (thus not contributing to taxation), traded outside the town, and in general represented no financial gain to town funds. These facts are generally untrue. A large number of the faculty live in non-college houses, almost all have automobiles which are taxable, and even those who live in college houses contribute indirectly to the town in that Mansfield receives a special grant from the State to compensate for the tax-exempt property which the State of Connecticut holds in the town. Regardless of the general untruth of the claim, it still carries great weight in the minds of the townspeople. They resent the "non-contributing" college people coming to town meeting and voting how the town's money shall be spent. A feeling common to many of the townsfolk is that the faculty receives instructions from the administration of the college—or some unnamed group in power—and must vote accordingly.

Some years ago, "the college" was accused of taking no interest in town affairs. When a few members of the faculty interested themselves to the extent of running for office as members of the school board or for other minor offices, the tune changed to one charging an attempt to dominate town affairs. One professor who served for ten years on the school board was complimented implicitly by having a candidate placed in the field for the express purpose of opposing the professor's policies on the board. It was felt that Professor X could not be defeated for office—"the college" would elect him—but the town's leading merchant was elected to fight every proposal which the learned gentleman might make. It is interesting to note that the merchant, who was an "exempt" as far as the college was concerned, found himself agreeing with Professor X, much to the displeasure of the former's constituents.

That the college group is "snooty" is both a justified and a false accusation. While certain of the faculty hold themselves aloof from the non-college group, others are anxious to be felt a part of the town. Their isolation is often more a result of exclusion by the townspeople than a product of their own desire. Herein is manifested a situation common to groups considered "clannish"; they are frequently so because they are not *allowed* to participate. In Mansfield, a number of the residents say that they want nothing to do with the college group, and then charge them with feeling themselves "too good to associate with plain people." An illustration of this occurred when a faculty member went into the village store one day attired in the old clothes in which he had been working in his garden. There he met one of the townspeople who was noted for his dislike of "the college." The two fell into a long conversation about a variety of things, and then the faculty member left. After his departure, the townsman asked, "Who is that fellow? He seems mighty pleasant." When told that it was Professor Y, the man felt that he had been imposed on, and continued in his opinion that the college group was "snooty."

The charge that the people at the college are theoretical and impractical is largely derived from the origin of the college as a land-grant and primarily agricultural institution. The proposals of the agricultural faculty for improvement of farming techniques are frequently met with the statement that if those men had to farm like other farmers, they couldn't get along. "As long as they've got the State to pay for all their nonsense, they can try out those damn fool notions." Or, as a variant of that theme, "Anybody could be a successful farmer if he had all the money in the world to buy equipment in the first place." With the introduction and increase of non-agricultural subjects, the attitude of the townspeople was strengthened by the strange fields and the more citified men who were brought in to teach. Now, more than ever, the rift widened.

Not only were the new faculty members urban products, in the large, but they were often from places far distant from Connecticut or even New England. Here the political conflict arose again when it was felt that persons not familiar or sympathetic with local problems were dictating (or attempting to dictate) how town affairs were to be conducted. This is not particularly strange when it is realized that many of the families have been in Mansfield for many generations, and at least five of these families antedate the Revolution by almost a hundred years. One of the local families is directly descended from a Mayflower pioneer who left the Massachusetts Colony and settled in Mansfield. That "Westerners" (people from Ohio, Illinois, Indiana, Kansas, and Iowa) should tell them how to run *their* town was something to resent. One local resident feels that the cause of the confusion in the United States today is the adoption of all these new-fangled devices, and that all the country needs to restore equilibrium is a return to the old ways of doing things. Automobiles and telephones are foolishness, the local store should resume business on a barter basis with the farmers, and we should drive oxcarts to Norwich, twenty miles away, to do our "trading." Why we have to import strangers to teach weird subjects when there are a lot of Connecticut boys and girls available is a mystery.

The college group, on the other hand, cannot sympathize with the Connecticut tradition of proceeding slowly. Its belief that the towns-people are trying to run the town for their own selfish interests and that they are old-fashioned and stubborn arises from the reluctance of the town to accept in their entirety the proposals for radical change in school and fiscal matters. With all the experts in education and finance it is not surprising that there should exist a desire to operate a sort of laboratory here in Mansfield. The people of the town are not ready to enter whole-heartedly into such proposals. Impatient with this attitude, the college group becomes rapidly critical.

The charges that the local people lack intellectual stimulation and broad vision impress the writer as coming frequently from the fact that the townspeople "don't talk our language." This conflict situation is not limited to gown versus town; it is frequent within the college itself. We of the faculty often become so engrossed in our own fields that we are unwilling or unable to talk with someone else about his work, and his unwillingness becomes to us a sign of his narrowness. The definition of a bore as "a person who always wants to talk when I want to talk" is applicable with slight transformation in this situation.

The real reasons for the conflict are common to all conflict situations. There is a clash of mores, a conflict of interests, which cannot be resolved. The jealousy of success by either group cannot be overcome by rational argument. That there is some justification on both sides is without question, but that much of the dispute is rooted in lack of understanding, in untruths, and an unwillingness to see the opposite side is equally evident.

The unifying effect of conflict is seen in the coming together of disputing groups of the townspeople to oppose the faculty, which, in turn, disagrees about many matters of college policy but which is quite homogeneous in opinions as to town affairs. The disorganization which conflict brings is retarding the normal progress which the town would make were these two factions not present.

Accommodation and assimilation are not totally absent, although whether either process will ever be complete is doubtful. Each side accepts the presence of the other, occasional joint efforts are carried out with the usual pattern being that of the college group joining the town group; rarely does the reverse occur. Such groups as the local Red Cross, the Parent-Teachers Association, and a choral society are effecting certain joint association, but it should be noted that these are primarily groups of women. Less association of the men takes place. As has already been mentioned, exempts of both groups are universally welcome and represent well assimilated individuals. A negligible amount of intermarriage between the groups has occurred.

Discussion of this type of conflict is usually designated as "town versus gown"; the implication is that the town is the aggressor, the college the defender. Long before Simmel, Gumplowicz or Marx, men knew that "it takes two to make a fight." It is the writer's opinion that the gown versus town phase of the conflict has been neglected. The college group, it would appear, is equally responsible for the existence and preservation of the conflict situation.

Finally, the question arises as to whether, as is frequently stated regarding conflict, this situation is true only during a period of change. It may be said that the conflict is occurring while the college is growing, but the writer believes that such divergent groups will not, as has been said, complete the processes of accommodation, assimilation and amalgamation with the eventual eradication of the conflict. Each group is protected from being absorbed by the culture of the other, and, as a result, each will continue with its own culture. Evidence in support of this is seen in towns where colleges have existed for several hundred years and where the town versus gown and the gown versus town conflicts still prevail.

❖ 80 ❖

THE TOOTHPASTE TOURNAMENT

Walter Goodman

The social process of competition—the individual or intergroup struggle for a mutually desired goal—can be illustrated in many different settings. This goal may be material, like goods, money, or property; or nonmaterial, like prestige or popularity. Of all the examples that might be chosen, the techniques used by many manufacturers to attract and hold customers illustrate the competitive process particularly well. Walter Goodman contributes an amusing case study of the extremes to which some industries go in the competition for markets. This selection not only demonstrates "competition" but also exhibits one form of collective behavior by showing

SOURCE: *New Republic*, Vol. 135, No. 5 (July 30, 1956), 15–17. Reprinted by permission. ❖ Walter Goodman is senior editor at *Redbook Magazine* and head of a restaurant chain in Chicago. He is the author of *All Honorable Men* and *The Clowns of Commerce*.

that clever advertising campaigns can sometimes convince a great many people by appealing primarily to their emotions rather than by convincing them with logical and scientific evidence.

In 1859 a wholesale druggist from New York named William Henry Hall presented America with a product called Sozodont, a red liquid containing 37 per cent alcohol. The nation was informed that it had been blessed with "the most convenient, efficacious and beneficial article for the teeth the world has ever seen." We've come a long way since.

While scientists in other fields have been inching their way modestly toward such attainments as hydrogen bombs and deep freezes, the dentifrice people have advanced with seven-league boots, conquering new terrain four times in the past decade. Since all toothpastes and powders are made of substantially the same three simple ingredients—soap that foams, an abrasive that scrapes and a flavorer that makes the stuff tolerable—this is no small trick. The credit for it belongs less to the men in the laboratories than to the men in the advertising agencies.

A late 19th Century ad circulated by Dr. I. W. Lyons, innovator of tooth powder in a can, stated flatly:

It is useless to say that any dentifrice will whiten the teeth or change their color one particle—anything which professes to do it is an acid.

Fortunately for the industry, more imaginative copywriters were to take over from Dr. Lyons, as promotion-minded soap firms ("soapers" to the trade) ousted the drug companies from their positions of dentifrice leadership. The family-sized tube of soap, abrasive and flavorer which costs about 10 cents to produce (including tube), ordinarily receives about a dime's worth of advertising. Americans had been made tooth-conscious enough by 1954 to spend more than $150 million for pastes and powders, and the figure is going up all the time.

How, exactly, have the admen aroused all this enthusiasm for so grubby a chore as brushing one's teeth? Well, in the early days they could alert people to the fact that tooth-brushing was good for them (although certain African tribes are said to keep their teeth strong and shining with a vigorous tongue motion after meals, and some people in the West are still devoted to dental floss). Then there was the novelty of nationally advertised brands that tasted better than baking soda, not to mention the convenient packaging. "Comes out like a ribbon, lies flat on the brush," sang a turn-of-the-century ad for Colgate's. Between wars, the toothpaste makers discovered a great number of foul ailments which had heretofore gone neglected by the nation's medical men. Acid-mouth; pink toothbrush; germ mask; smoker's teeth; gingivitis; pyorrhea; halitosis.

As a matter of fact, pink toothbrush is a rather common phenomenon; bad breath generally starts in the stomach; and nobody's teeth are precisely white—the shades range from a pale ivory to a positive yellow. But you'd never know *that* from the ads—"You'll wonder where the yellow went when you brush your teeth with Pepsodent."

By the end of World War II, the persuasive powers of Colgate's ("It cleans your breath while it cleans your teeth") had won 40 per cent of the national market. Tied for second place, with 15 per cent apiece, were Lever Bros.' Pepsodent (which had coined the phrase "clinging film," destined to endure through generations of dentifrice ads) and Ipana, put out by Bristol-Myers, a drug firm.

Pepsodent is generally credited with pioneering the way into the postwar phase of toothpaste wonders with its discovery of Irium. The American Dental Association found this "special ingredient" to be sodium alkyl sulfate, a simple foaming compound. Said the ADA: "The firm has attempted to endow the word 'irium' which is applied to the soap substitute used in its products with extraordinary virtues which it does not possess." Irium did, however, possess one extraordinary virtue: it rhymed with Miriam in the jingle about that poor girl's failings chorused twice each week for several seasons on the Bob Hope radio show.

Early in 1949, a new brand of tooth powder appeared on the neighborhood drug and supermarket counters in everybody's neighborhood, and almost immediately became one of the industry's leaders. By April, Amm-i-dent, a powder manufactured by the Block Drug Co., had garnered almost 20 per cent of the market. A $2 million advertising campaign that year helped retain much of this. "Genuine Amm-i-dent Ammoniated Toothpaste Is Here to Reduce Tooth Decay!" the ladies' magazines announced that autumn. It did this, explained Block, by virtue of the carbamide (synthetic urea) and dibasic ammonium phosphate sparkling in every tube. In 1934, it seemed a pair of Minnesota dentists had found a higher percentage of ammonia nitrogen in the saliva of people naturally immune to decay than of those subject to caries. This, they decided, was nature's way of fighting the microorganism Lactobacillus acidophilus, colonies of which swarm around every cavity. Amm-i-dent claimed that its "exclusive formula" released ammonium ions, which thereupon engaged those villainous Lactobacilli, etc., in mortal combat.

Amm-i-dent's formidable discovery presented the major firms with a dilemma. A rash of obscure ammoniated brands appeared almost at once, and the sales of the top pastes were being hurt. But to alter the chemistry of the long-established favorites was fraught with hazard. Still, who could hold out? Ipana surrendered, and soon even the front runner had added a new product to its line—Colgate's Ammoniated Tooth Powder, containing those "wonder ingredients" compounded by University of Illinois scientists —dibasic ammonium phosphate and carbamide. (The very names were enough to scare a young Lactobacillus out of a year's growth.) "Yes, Colgate's Great Dentifrice Gives *Extra Protection!*" affirmed the ads for the new ammoniated powder, while a page or two away it was reported that Colgate's good old unammoniated toothpaste "has been proven to contain all the necessary ingredients, including an effective *patented* ingredient, for effective daily dental care."

Amm-i-dent retorted peevishly that it had "more anti-decay ingredients than any other toothpaste." Un-ammoniated Listerine stood above the battle: "What about tooth decay?" It asked—and answered: "It's mainly up to *you!* If you will always brush your teeth right after eating, you will almost certainly help reduce decay in your teeth." (What an opening for the product directed at "the man who can't brush after every meal.")

Nineteen-fifty was a relatively quiet year. The Andrew Jergens Co. came up with Dentocillin, a powder containing penicillin which, in one test, reportedly reduced cavities by 55 per cent. But the item somehow failed to capture the popular imagination and the latest revolution was stillborn.

Another event in 1950, however, was destined to launch one of those recurrent crazes in tooth care. The Rystan Co., a drug firm headed by a former adman named O'Neill Ryan Jr. obtained a patent on the therapeutic use of chlorophyll, the substance that makes alfalfa green. Rystan had been channeling the alfalfa extract to dentists for a decade; now it was looking toward the world at large. In the fall of 1951, Lever Bros. obtained a license from Ryan to use a water-soluble chlorophyll derivative in a commercial toothpaste. Thus was born Chlorodent, which guaranteed America a "Fresh Mouth . . . ALL DAY LONG!" The arrangement made a million dollars for Ryan and moved Lever Bros. into a second-place position where it breathed its sweet, minty breath onto Colgate's neck. . . .

After some legal preliminaries, other dentifrice manufacturers jumped onto the alfalfa wagon. In April, 1952, Amm-i-dent became Amm-i-dent Ammoniated Chlorophyll and upped its share of the national market from 10 to 14 per cent. Ipana became Ipana A/C; Colgate, Kolynos and Iodent also turned green.

Commenting on the newest achievement of dental science, Dr. J. Roy Doty, secretary of the ADA's council of dental therapeutics, said:

. . . evidence presently available does not warrant claims that dental products containing chlorophyll derivatives are useful or beneficial in preventing or curing dental decay. . . . Concerning claims for breath deodorization, the evidence as to the usefulness of products containing chlorophyll derivatives is inconclusive.

After slightly less than a year's run—about par for this course—chlorophyll was winded and the front position was taken by still another sensational additive. Experiments—at Northwestern University this time—had resulted in the discovery of two chemicals that were reputed to neutralize cavity-producing enzymes in the mouth. The Lambert Pharmaceutical Co., makers of Listerine, quickly announced that hereafter it wanted to be known as the maker of Listerine Anti-Enzyme. The trade-name developers for Colgate's burst forth joyfully: "What's new in Colgate Dental Cream that's MISSING-MISSING-MISSING in every other leading toothpaste? It's Gardol!" Lever Bros., for its part, quietly began to test-market Shield, a new paste that contained a marvelous anti-biotic.

Barely a handful of enzymes had been destroyed, however, before Procter & Gamble, the only one of the three big soapers which had heretofore refrained from attacking man's teeth, entered the lists with Gleem. "Just *one* brushing destroys decay- and odor-causing bacteria. After one Gleem brushing, up to 90 per cent of bacteria are destroyed. Only GLEEM has GL-70 to fight decay."

"*Any* toothpaste can destroy decay- and odor-causing bacteria," sneered Colgate's. "But new bacteria come back in minutes, to form acids that cause decay. Colgate's, unlike any other leading toothpaste, *keeps on* fighting tooth decay 12 hours or more."

GL-70, in case anybody is interested at this point, is a "surface-active" detergent of the variety used to brighten clothes and dishes. Procter & Gamble has devoted an estimated $15 million to spreading the news of its contribution to America's bicuspids. Ipana, lately possessed of dibasic ammonium phosphate, carbamide and chlorophyll, now shot itself full of WD-9. "Ipana destroys decay bacteria best of all leading toothpastes." Pepsodent, for its part, added IMP (insoluble Meta-Phosphate, you know) to good old Irium.

But the latest and greatest toothpaste additive is something related to fluoride, the ingredient found in drinking water in certain areas of the country, which is thought to harden tooth enamel and thereby frustrate bacteria.

1796: Triumph Over Contagious Diseases. First inoculation by Dr. Jenner.
1848: Triumph Over Pain. Dr. Morton's discovery of ether.
1929: Triumph Over Bacterial Infections. Fleming discovers penicillin.
    Now—1956—Procter & Gamble proudly announces . . .
            TRIUMPH OVER TOOTH DECAY.
Crest Toothpaste with Fluoristan strengthens tooth enamel to lock out decay from within. Crest with Fluoristan is the only toothpaste ever developed that makes possible a major reduction in tooth decay, for people of all ages. Thereby, Crest marks the turning point in man's age-old struggle against this almost universal disease.

About the time that several million households had used up their sample tubes of CREST, they received sample tubes of BRISK. The Colgate Company, late again, had bounced back with its customary verve. "Only BRISK has FLUORIDE/85 . . . HARDENS TOOTH ENAMEL, MAKES TEETH STRONGER, starts working instantly TO DEFEAT DECAY." Good old unfluorided Colgate's thereupon advertised, snidely, that kiddies under six could eat its merchandise with complete safety. Fluoride yellow seems about to join halitosis among America's major oral ailments.

(Amm-i-dent, by the way, is at present the world's first and only toothpaste containing all three of the best decay fighting ingredients known to dental science: Fluoride, Ammoniated and Anti-Enzyme SLS.2.)

Is Colgate's Fluoride/85 better than Procter & Gamble's Fluoristan? Dr. Harold Hellenbrand, secretary of ADA, takes an impartial view:

The American Dental Association is not aware of evidence adequate to demonstrate the claimed dental caries prophylactic value of Crest. . . . Published evidence to support the usefulness of adding a fluoride in other dentifrices is even less convincing. The Association therefore believes that all fluoride dentifrices are being marketed prematurely.

In a full-page newspaper advertisement on its 150th birthday in April, the Colgate-Palmolive Co., the world's largest manufacturer of toilet goods, revealed its "infallible rules for a long happy life for a business or organization. The first is to make products that are genuinely useful to people." Continued Colgate's:

We intend to go right on trying, for another 150 years, to outdo our competitors in devising new ways to serve the desire of people everywhere to be clean, attractive, healthy. The gainer from all this will be the public—that ever-youthful, open-minded, hard-to-please, impossible-to-fool public. . . .

Happy birthday, Colgate's. You Ammoniated, Chlorophylled, Gardolled, Fluoridated Colgate's.

* 81 *

COOPERATIVES IN EAST PAKISTAN: A SUCCESSFUL EXPERIMENT

Akhter Hameed Khan,
Henry W. Fairchild, and M. Zakir Hussain

Among the social processes that characterize American economic behavior, competition may seem most typical; cooperation, however, is also very important. During the past century many systems of cooperative societies of various types have been organized throughout the world. Usually the purpose has been to help poor people improve their general welfare through working together. The following selection, in two parts, describes one such undertaking in a developing new nation, and then shows dramatically what successful cooperation can mean to the individual member of a cooperative society.

Mr. Khan

The government of Pakistan has various kinds of training institutions, one of which is this Academy for the training of officers who are connected with rural work. It was started in 1959 and is supported by the Ford Foundation, with advisory services being supplied by Michigan State University. The faculty is from the social sciences. Let me make it clear that the instructors are not experts in agriculture itself but are social scientists from the fields of public administration, agricultural economics, statistics, education, community development, and so on. The original idea of the Academy was to bring into contact the instructors and the officers who were engaged in field work and to give the officers some idea of the social and economic problems of the villagers, to introduce some kind of insight and depth into their work, and to apply social science to public administration, especially rural administration. . . .

I asked the Government to allocate the adjoining area to us as a kind of laboratory where we could demonstrate our ideas, and the Government was pleased to allocate the Comilla Thana to us. I think I should explain to you the term, "thana." A thana is an administrative unit of the Government, and there are about 400 of them in East Pakistan. Six or seven thanas form a subdivision; three or four subdivisions form a district; and there are 17 districts in East Pakistan.

The area in which the Academy is located is the Comilla Thana. It is about 107 square miles and has a population of a little more than 200,000, of which the city contains about 57,000. The rural population is just about 150,000, and there are about 300 villages in this Thana. This is our "laboratory area." I think we were so dominated by the scientific approach from the very beginning that we used that term. The officers found the term very funny, but we kept using it until it was finally accepted. . . .

The area itself is used as a demonstration model. For instance, take cooperatives. "Well," the officers say, "we have had fifty years of experience with cooperatives in Pakistan, and cooperatives have not succeeded. It is impossible. It has been tried." Now we can tell them, "No, this idea is all wrong. Theoretically, cooperatives can be organized, and practically too. Come and have a look. Sit down with these villagers. Here are some cooperative groups. See how they have been organized. Talk with them. Look at the figures. Go and visit the villages."

. . . Our worst problem is the feeling of skepticism among the officers,

SOURCE: *Rural Development in East Pakistan, Speeches of Akhter Hameed Khan* (East Lansing, Mich.: Asian Studies Center, Michigan State University, 1965), 21–37. Reprinted by permission. ✧ Akhter Hameed Khan is Director of the Pakistan Academy for Rural Development, Comilla, East Pakistan. He received the Ramon Magsaysay Award Foundation award for government service in 1963. He was formerly a member of the Indian Civil Service and has held several positions of leadership in Pakistan government and education.

a kind of hopelessness and despair that nothing can be done. A result of that is a pretension that they are doing something, but really their hearts are not in it. They are not convinced that something can be done. That is the first problem we have to tackle: how to remove the skepticism from the officers and to convince them that something can really be done. That is how we are using the pilot project. . . .

I'll begin the analysis of the cooperative project by first outlining the old cooperative structure that already existed because Comilla Thana was not, you know, a blank slate when we arrived. We found everything there —the cooperatives, the agricultural extension, the local government—they were all there. And our policy, from the very beginning, was not to destroy things, but to reform them. We do not set up new institutions or new departments unless it is absolutely necessary, till we are convinced that the old departments and the old institutions cannot be vitalized. The old structure, which was not working, which unfortunately was completely dormant, was based on a Union Multipurpose Society. Now, as I will be using these words, I think I should explain them to you.

In East Pakistan, we have a federal system of government. The first unit is a district. The second is the subdivision. The third is the thana. And the fourth is the union. We have 4,000 unions in East Pakistan. A union will generally have about 10 or 15 villages and a population of ten or fifteen thousand people. Here was a Union Multipurpose Cooperative Society based on the assumption that small village units are not economically viable. Therefore, a bigger unit was needed, the Union Multipurpose Society.

The Union Multipurpose Society was supposed to get loans from the District Cooperative Bank. There was no bank at the thana nor, generally, at the subdivision levels, but at the district headquarters, the Cooperative Department had a Bank. From there the loans were to come to the union. The District Bank, in its turn, was to get its loan from an apex bank because the cooperative banks did not have any funds of their own. Their savings deposits were nominal, and they had no reserves. So the district bank was to have its loan from the apex bank and the apex bank, in its turn, was to take a loan from the State Bank.

You can very well imagine how efficiently a system like this would work. It generally took six months for the money to move from the State Bank to the apex bank to the district bank to the union cooperative. But a six months' delay can make complete nonsense of a crop loan, especially if it is followed, allowing two or three weeks for distribution, with a demand to repay it as the time for repayment has arrived. Now, in this system there were very few savings. The Union Multipurpose Societies had no deposits. Although large sums of money were being distributed every year, the collection, the realization of loans, often was less than 50 per cent. If the price of jute fell down too much, then the realization might be only 30 per cent. This made the State Bank very angry. It said, "The Cooperative System is no good. Perhaps we should discard it and have something better. Let's have an agricultural bank because the cooperatives don't work. The agricultural bank possibly can serve everybody more effectively."

There were other weaknesses of the Societies such as the lack of relationship between the cooperatives and their credit policy and agricultural extension and marketing. There was also little relationship among the membership itself; it was too scattered. There was no social cohesion, no solidarity. Our problem, as we saw it, was to work with existing situations, existing institutions and to revise them whenever possible so that they would work.

First we studied more thoroughly the village as it exists in East Pakistan. The villages are very small, about 50 to 100 families living in the middle of their land which surrounds the village. The village might have 100 to 200 acres of land. The population of East Pakistan is now 50,000,000 in an area of 55,000 square miles. . . .

When we studied the farmers living in the villages, we found that they fell into three categories: there was a very small minority of what I call "surplus farmers" who had 10 or 15 acres of land each. They produce a surplus; they can save money. Second, there is the big majority of small farmers who have only one or two acres, at the most three or four. At the bottom, are the landless laborers. It might be added here that there are no landlords, no class of big money-lenders, in East Pakistan. They were completely eliminated by our Debt Settlement Acts. That problem, at least, has been solved; but the small farmers still have problems. Some of them are trying to come up but in the process of disintegration many of them are falling down.

Of course, there is a natural fragmentation due to the increase in population. But more important than that is the squeeze put on the small farmers because they are in great need of credit. They cannot carry on their monsoon operations without credit. And as the need, the demand, for credit rises the rates also rise. In East Pakistan, in most places, if a man borrows 100 rupees he has to repay two maunds of rice every year. The two maunds of rice mean about 60 or 70 rupees. Now, if any one of these people can save 100 rupees, there are ten of his neighbors who are willing to take it from him and pay him back two maunds of rice. Naturally, everybody being an economic man, that's what he does. He invests all his surplus savings either in loans to his neighbors or in buying rice from them and stocking it for a short time after harvest when prices will rise. And that is the second squeeze which is causing the disintegration of the small farmer class. First is the need for credit and the second is the selling by the small farmers of their paddy or their jute immediately after the harvest. Therefore, in Pakistan you find that the prices of jute or paddy fluctuate enormously. After the harvest, let's say the price of paddy is 10 rupees. Four months later it's 18 rupees, an 80 per cent rise.

What it means in human terms is that the small farmers are being disinvested in a double sense. First they are paying very high rates of interest, and so losing part of their capital, and then they are getting very low prices for their produce. And it is their neighbors who are profiting by this, not some vicious person from outside, not an absentee landlord, not city people, but their own neighbors. So, the natural tendency is for the number of landless laborers to grow. If the economic forces were allowed free play, this is what would happen in East Pakistan: we would have a lot of landless people, consolidation would take place as the clever and the intelligent people would buy up the land, and the others would be pushed down.

That might happen, but it cannot be permitted because it may create violence; and, once violence starts, then all hope of a reasonable solution to the problem will disappear. We will see in East Pakistan the beginning of a true revolution if violence breaks out. And violence is sure to break out if the base widens, and we have a lot of landless people staying in the village. If we could take them out of the village and provide them with non-agricultural employment then things might be all right.

Another fact which adds to the process of disintegration is that the people are not investing their money back in the village. What they are doing is disinvesting their neighbors and investing this money in the education of their children, or in trade and business. Most of their money is going out of the village. That is what makes it so very difficult to set the village up on its own feet. Education also is really another way of taking people out of the village so we are having a dual migration from the village: first, the rich people are going out, acquiring education; and secondly, the poor people are going out as destitute beggars, or as laborers, and filling up the slums.

That was the situation we discovered in the village. What do we do? The village level workers were mostly going to the rich people and not to the small landowners. Even if they had gone to the small farmers, as almost everybody knows, such farmers did not have the capacity to adopt improved methods without a good system of credit. So what we decided was to try to see if the small farmers would form a group in order to protect themselves. Here we followed, not the advice of the Community Development people, but the advice of a man dead long ago, that is, Raiffeisen. We took the Raiffeisen cooperative as the model; here are the small farmers; they are completely helpless individually, so let them come together. Their cooperative group would be based on the three old principles: Raiffeisen's principle of thrift, that they would all save money and try to create some capital, however absurd that might appear; that they would support each other; and, in another way, that they would also restrain each other, that is, they would engage in a lot of joint planning.

That is how we began with our idea of the small village group consisting mostly of the small farmers. The rich people were out. They hated the cooperative. They loved the Union Multipurpose Cooperative, but a cooperative which would eliminate money-lending and trading they hated because they were the money-lenders and the traders. So, if the small farmers could form a group, then there was some hope that the process of disintegration or disinvestment would stop. But for the landless laborers the cooperative is no solution at all. It has nothing to offer them. It was for them that we devised the rural public works program, which would provide them employment during the four idle months of the year when there is no agricultural work. Their problem would be partly solved if we could have year-round agriculture, that is, instead of depending on the monsoon, have perennial irrigation. Then they would find more employment. We could also educate them and send them into the towns.

We decided on the village cooperatives to help solve some of our many problems, but let me not give you the impression that it all came as a kind of inspiration. It was all very slow work, evolved step by step, working with the people. We spent many evenings, sometimes talking up to one o'clock, late in the night. Not I—I did it sometimes, but most of the time it was my associates who did it. All these ideas were evolved slowly and painfully.

When it was decided to have a village cooperative, then we were face to face with that old controversy which had led to the establishment of the Union Multipurpose Cooperative and which is bothering the whole subcontinent—what is the viable economic unit? If you form a group of 40 or 50 families, how do they manage their affairs? Can they do banking? Can they have machines? Can they do marketing? Of course not. Therefore, it's argued that we should have a bigger unit. Now if you have a bigger unit, if you lump 10 or 15 villages together, you find that social cohesion does not exist. All your hopes for the bigger unit to be more economically viable are mere hopes. It is an illusion. When you make a big unit it's no cooperative at all. It becomes a paper organization.

After a lot of trial and effort and thought and discussion with the local people, we discovered a kind of solution. For the sake of social unity—because only that can be the foundation of the cooperative—their knowing and trusting each other, we decided to have small, village cooperatives. But for the real economic operations, we combined the cooperatives into a federation. Thus we evolved the pattern of the village unit and a thana association—the Thana Cooperative Federation or Association—where they can have any number of village cooperatives federated into a central association set up at the thana headquarters. These thana headquarters, by the way, are not really in a village but are now the nucleus of a small urban community. It is set up there and connected, mostly by some kind of road or a railway, with the main markets. At its headquarters, this federation is going to set up its own bank. It's going to set up its marketing section. It's going to have a tractor station. It's going to have an agricultural extension program. And in this way it becomes the supporting institution for the village reorganization.

Above all, we found that for sustaining morale the central association occupies the key position because in the village conditions are so frustrating —people are so full of factions and despair and hopelessness—that if we start something and then leave, the whole thing falls to pieces again. What is the remedy for that?

For that we devised two things: first there was the training center, to which the village representative—the manager of the group or, as we first called him, the organizer—would come every week. This was a weekly conference of all the village organizers at the training center. We argued in this way—and this we learned, of course, from the Danish folk-school model—that if there is frustration generally, then the best remedy for that is to bring together the most active, the most hopeful people again and again from different places. In this way is formed a kind of brotherhood of active and hopeful people. Then they go back and rejuvenate the village. They are not submerged by the general atmosphere of hopelessness and despair. But for that it is necessary that they should be drawn, again and again, back to the center, first to be trained, but second, and more important, to come in contact with many of their peers placed in situations similar to their own and to be mutually reinforced by their constant association.

The central federation at the thana headquarters was to have its own resources and its own authority to make decisions. The former pattern was completely nonsensical, that the village should go for a loan to the district. It didn't make any sense. It's just not possible. The power to make decisions must come down to the thana. And in the course of time, the central federation may also be completely owned and operated by the village cooperatives.

So we got some funds which were placed with the thana association, and it set up its banking functions, a tractor station, brought in machines and so on. Here we were enormously helped by the Ford Foundation. They gave us a large grant for the central association which gave us the necessary flexibility. We were often asked by visitors, "Now, who decides this?" So we said, "God, and nobody else!" . . . .

Now, in the village cooperative the first principle was that each group of small farmers should select one of themselves as their organizer or manager, and he would come to the training center every week. He must be a man who could afford much time and energy. At the same time we were saying that—in the beginning we were insisting very strongly—"He must be a man whom you trust. We don't care whether he can read or write; that is immaterial because, in any case, we are going to talk Bengali, not English. So if he can understand Bengali it's all right. If he cannot read it, well, we'll run a literacy class for him. But you send somebody whom you trust." Why? Because the second important thing was that every week the group would assemble and every one of them put in a small deposit, however small it might be. It would be a ritual, which would have to be performed, because it's only through this that the habit of thrift will come.

Our next task was to get credit for the villagers. I had read in the books of economics that capital formation is very, very important, so I explained to the villagers that capital formation was very, very important. "You must make deposits; otherwise how can there be a credit system?" And they said, "Sir, what are you saying? How can we poor people save? We are so poor that we cannot save." And everybody said that in Pakistan the poor villagers could not save. So I argued with them, "Well, it's the poor who have got to save. The rich people are already rich. You have *got* to save." Finally they acquired the habit of saving. I can give you the latest figures. We now have 160 cooperative groups. At the end of May, 1964, there were 5,980 families as members of the cooperatives. Up till now 486,978 rupees have come in small deposits from these people, and some of these cooperatives may be only six months old, or even less. Nearly half a million rupees have come from these poor villagers. They have purchased 61,000 rupees worth of shares, and they hold 23,000 rupees of reserve in the central association. So much for the weekly deposits.

The third principle was that they must make joint production plans. We made no effort to pool their land, and they have no intention whatsoever of doing so. The land was to be left completely alone. They have individual ownership. They do individual work. They have individual proprietorship of the produce. But some of the operations have to be done jointly. So some members of a cooperative wanted a loan; the entire group sat down in a meeting and, after prolonged discussion, made a list of the persons who wanted the loan and their assets, including the land, deposits, and shares of all members of the family. Then they itemized what the loan was for: how much for fertilizers, how much for seed, how much for labor, and how much for hiring of tractors. All of these were totaled, and the total was brought to the central association by the organizer or manager. In this way the central association would examine one loan request from 40 or 50 members who owned together about a hundred acres of land, or more sometimes.

In the beginning we gave small loans. They might be only about 6,000 rupees. We followed the principle of the ceiling, which is quite opposed to the principle of giving the small farmer everything he needs. That is wrong. In our opinion that should not be done in the beginning. In the beginning he should be given a little help, taught strongly to increase his income and in this way to repay his old loans. Gradually the amount of the ceiling can be increased.

The production plan was linked with improved methods. They must adopt improved methods which were being taught to the organizer and another farmer selected by the group, the model farmer, who was coming to the center where, as I will tell you, we had put all the officers, the experts, together as a team of teachers. If they did not adopt any improved methods they would not get a loan.

Then credit was linked with marketing. Immediately after the harvest they were given the choice either to pay their loan in cash or put their crop in deposit, and the central association accepted that as payment. When there was a good price for the produce they could sell it, adjust their loan, and take back the surplus. In this way, in the village, the organization was built, slowly. But what had been missing in the former cooperative setup was this habit of meeting together and discussing and establishing what we call a bond of trust.

It would be interesting to observe the failure of the managing committee system in the underdeveloped countries. I offer you this explanation: when the British administrators sent out some of their best men, at the end of the 19th century, to study the cooperatives in Denmark and Germany, they came back full of enthusiasm. They said, "We have found the solution which would remove the indebtedness of the Indian peasant." And they brought the whole cooperative system back to India. It was a beautiful system, no doubt, and they thought it *could* solve their problem. But unfortunately they also brought back the idea of the managing committee—that the cooperative would select a number of persons who could discharge all the work during the year; and then, at the end of the year, there would be a general meeting of the cooperative. Of course, there are many reasons for the failure of the cooperatives. I won't be so foolish as to say that there were no other reasons. There were economic reasons, there was the failure of crops, there were low prices, and all that. But one of the reasons why cooperatives in our country had not been working was that the managing committee was never trusted. The managing committee generally consisted of the well-to-do people, and the small farmers did not trust them. They were not worthy of trust. They were misusing their authority most of the time.

Here again, instead of suggesting that there should be no managing committee, which seems logical, we said, "All right, keep the managing committee. The letter of the law will be followed completely, but we are going to have a general meeting every week." It was this which made our cooperatives, the small village groups, suddenly alive. Every week, all the members assembled. They discussed everything. The accounts were shown to them. They deposited money and it was entered right in the presence of the members. The passbook was handed out. We were very meticulous about these small "insignificant" details for they were crucial; everything should be done in the farmers' presence, should be explained to them all the time. They should have full opportunity to discuss, and this is going on all the time. The weekly general meeting has put life into the cooperatives. It has enabled the villagers to start to understand the elements of planning. . . .

The model farmer also helps in these discussions. He is the best farmer, selected by the village cooperative group. He comes and learns directly from the experts whom we had placed at the training center, from the team of Japanese agricultural experts, and from our own animal husbandry and plant protection experts. All the instruction is written on a sheet of paper, and each of the model farmers takes back the sheet and reads it out in the village meeting. It is a continuous educational program for the model farmer, to make him more and more expert, and for the organizer, to teach him the managerial skills and to pass on all the information to the village group.

And they send other persons too. There is the teacher selected by the group, the Imam of the village, the religious—it is difficult to call him a leader—the religious functionary from the village whom we made the teacher. There are a driver, a mechanic, and an accountant. All of them are selected by the group and are trained continuously by the central association.

We found that the role of machines is crucial. Now this, I know, is very controversial, but we approached it experimentally. We said, "Let's find out whether tractors are economical, whether they really displace labor, whether they cause dislocation, instead of condemning or promoting them without trial. Let's test them and see the results." Two of the most important machines we have experimented with are the pump and the tractor.

The pump is important for irrigation in our monsoon agriculture. Most farmers grow only two crops, two of rice or one of rice and one of jute, and these crops depend upon the monsoon rains. For the farmer to improve his condition it would be necessary to grow a third crop. In some cases we found that the farmers were already growing a third crop, but only in very small patches where water was available and could be pumped by hand. So we had only to extend this process, so that instead of lifting water by hand, they could do it by pumps. The pump was crucial. If we want to introduce a big change in the East Pakistan village, the irrigation pump has to be set up and the water supply has to be ensured. But if we want that, it's necessary that the whole group should be reorganized to handle the pump. They are organized now for monsoon agriculture, they are not organized for irrigation. The cooperative helped us in setting up this new organization, and the organization itself was strengthened by the introduction of the pump.

Then the tractors. It's often said that in such countries, where the holdings are so small and the farmers are so poor, the tractor may not be a good thing to bring in. What we found was that 20 per cent of the small farmers had lost their bullocks and had to hire bullocks from their neighbors. This was another squeeze put upon them. We found that the cost of hiring bullocks was quite high. Not only was the cost high, but they had to wait. First, their neighbors, the owners of the bullocks, did their own plowing. Then if there was spare time, they could hire the bullocks. And in the case of rice cultivation a delay can be quite harmful. The farmer can lose a substantial part of the crop in monsoon agriculture by flooding if it is sown late. So the demand for the tractor from the poorest farmer was the highest. Just as the "surplus" farmers were not interested in cooperatives, they were also not interested in agricultural investment because already they were making a much more profitable investment, from their point of view—that is, in the education of their children and in loans—and they did not want to put their investment in agriculture. As a matter of fact, if a man had 10 acres of land he found it more profitable to lease it out to his neighbors than to cultivate it himself. The rental was 250 rupees per acre for one year, without any risk at all. Such a man was not at all interested in agricultural improvement. He was also not interested in tractors. But we found that the small farmers wanted tractors. We now have a lot of data on this. Our tractor station has been going on for three years. We have suffered a lot of losses because the drivers also have to be trained. And at first there were no roads. But we have gained enormous experience which would be of much use to the economists for analysis. . . .

But I must say this: just as the horse carriage had completely disappeared from the East Pakistan town (you won't see many horse carriages now in Dacca) because we have got motor buses and trucks, which have expanded the town economy, I think the tractor will do the same for the village economy. The tractor will do for the village economy what the bus and the truck have done for the town economy. They have expanded it greatly, and it seems to me to be inevitable.

Finally, we are experimenting with introducing electric power. We are very lucky that a hydroelectric project, from the Karnafuly river, has just been completed and that the lines are passing right through our thana. So there is a program now to electrify all the villages, to take power there, and to sink deep six-inch tubewells—four are being sunk now every month —and then to introduce more pumps and more tractors, and see what happens. The results already are quite visible. When along with the cooperative, with the production plan, and with supervised credit, we also introduce the tubewell and the pump, the whole village becomes transformed within one or two years. The farmers begin to grow three crops. They change the pattern of cropping. They do a lot of marketing to distant places. The impact is massive and almost immediate. Ten years of extension work without the tubewell may mean nothing, but the tubewell and the cooperative make all the difference.

Mr. Fairchild and Mr. Hussain

Abdul Wahab Mia—height five feet one inch, weight one hundred five pounds, leathery black bony face, black wavy hair, thin, slight build, age

SOURCE: Henry W. Fairchild and M. Zakir Hussain, "Abdul Wahab Mia," *Second Annual Report on the Rural Co-operative Pilot Experiment* (Comilla, Pakistan: Pakistan Academy for Rural Development, July, 1962), Case No. 2, pp. 69–73. ✧ Henry W. Fairchild is on the professional staff of the United Nations Food and Agriculture Organization at its headquarters in Rome, Italy. A specialist in rural resource development planning, he was a Michigan State University advisor of the Pakistan Academy for Rural Development, Comilla, East Pakistan, from 1960 to 1963. ✧ M. Zakir Hussain is Project Director, The Comilla Kotwali Thana Central Co-operative Association, Ltd., Abhoy Asram, Comilla, East Pakistan. He has worked in the East Pakistan Civil Service and was a pioneering Development Officer of the Village Agricultural and Industrial Development Administration.

thirty-five, profession, rickshaw puller—rested easily on the crumpled seat of his cycle rickshaw, idly turning the pedals backwards. He threw the butt of a bidi cigarette away and sat fingering the handle bars. His soiled T-shirt was rolled up to his armpits exposing his flat muscular stomach. His *lungi* of worse-for-wear gingham was hoisted above his knees for easier pedalling. His head was uncovered. His feet were bare.

It was a Bengal twilight. The clouds always low and threatening rain this time of year, were now fringed with gold from the setting sun. It was hot. At the faucet the men were washing their feet readying themselves for prayer.

It was six-fifty-six. The "Green Arrow" led by its big green diesel loco-motive pulled into the tin-roofed, red-brick station at Comilla. It tooted twice, slowly ground to a halt, then stood impatiently while passengers tumbled down from the compartments all along its shiny green sides.

There was a great din and confusion. Hawkers cried their wares: Cigarettes! Mangoes! Pineapple! Pan! Porters rushed pell mell with great loads on their heads. Veiled women in black *burkas* tugged at sweaty painted-eyed children. Men in white, in black, in almost nothing pressed for the exit.

Suddenly the tall sahib was outside. The evening monsoon breeze cooled his face. A hundred male voices cried "Rickshaw! Rickshaw sahib! A little beggar urchin pulled at the tall man's leg. He cried *"baksheesh sahib sa-a-a-hib Baksheesh?"*

The tall stranger looked about him. It was his first visit to this place. He motioned for the coolie with his suitcase to follow him. He paused momentarily to look at a sign on the back of a rickshaw: "Dider Rickshaw Pullers' Co-operative Society," it said. He crawled into this rickshaw, tipped the coolie and said, "Academy for Village Development, please."

Swiftly the station slid behind. It was pleasant with only the click of the cycle chain after the noise of the station. The tall sahib watched the rippling shoulder muscles and the pistoning legs of the rickshawman. "What is your name?" asked the tall stranger suddenly.

"My name? You want to know my name?" asked the rickshaw man, surprised, turning his head to look at the tall man. "My name is Abdul Wahab Mia. But what does my name matter? A rickshaw puller has a name only to other rickshaw pullers. Am I not a part of my rickshaw, like a bullock, to a bullock cart driver?"

The tall sahib laughed "Ahcha! You are a philosopher I see. How long have you been pulling this rickshaw?" "This rickshaw, only two years but before that I pulled many rickshaws, for eighteen years I pulled rick-shaw."

"How old are you?" asked the stranger. "You don't look like you have pulled a rickshaw for eighteen years. You don't look old enough."

"But I am," said Abdul, turning again to look with a toothless grin at the stranger. "I am thirty-five years old. I have been pulling a rickshaw since I was a boy."

"Do you like your work?" asked the stranger. "Do you like being a rickshaw puller?" "No one likes to be a rickshaw man" said Abdul, "But it is better now that I own my own rickshaw."

"Own your own rickshaw?" asked the stranger, surprised. He knew that none of the rickshawmen ever owned their own rickshaws. "What do you mean, own your own rickshaw?"

"It *is* my rickshaw," said Abdul proudly, "I bought it. The society helped me buy it." "The society," thought the stranger, "Oh you mean this rickshaw belongs to a Co-operative?" "No! It belongs to me. The co-operative only helped me get it."

"I saw your sign on your rickshaw—'Dider Co-operative' or something like that."

"Pardon me, Sahib, but it is a wonderful blessing. It is a miracle that Allah has made."

"You speak in riddles, Abdul Wahab Mia. Explain yourself."

"It is no riddle, Sahib. It is the truth. It is a miracle. I shall explain to you."

"Since I was seventeen I have pulled a rickshaw. Ballarampur, my village, is three miles west of Comilla on the Kotbari road. In my village there are only two kinds of people. There are people like me who are without land. We are poor. Then there are the *mahajans*, the money-lenders. There are only a few of them, but they are rich.

"For sixteen years I rented a rickshaw from a *mahajan* in my village. I paid him two rupees a day for his rickshaw. I had to pay all the repairs on his rickshaw. Sometimes if I sulked because I didn't like this or didn't pay the proper respect to the *mahajan*, he wouldn't rent me the rickshaw. There were always more rickshaw pullers than rickshaws.

"I used to earn about fifty rupees a month of my own. But some months I earned nothing. My family has eighteen members. I am the eldest son, so I am the family head. My next younger brother is a mason. He works about half the year. Last year however after the great storm he worked all year. He earns four rupees a day. My next younger brother is also a rickshaw puller. My youngest brother works in Comilla. He owns a little stall in the bazar. He earns about one hundred rupees per month. We barely scrape along. We are always in debt, but it is better than it used to be.

"Every year since I can remember we have lived this hand-to-mouth way. My father was a day laborer. He had no land. We never had any money. We are only an ignorant poor family.

"Then three years ago a great thing happened. There was in my village a worker, a Village-AID worker, you know. Gulam Mustafa Faruqui was his name. He was a young man and a good man. He used to come almost every day to the tea stall of Mohammad Yasin. This was where we rickshaw men used to gather in my village. We would sit there using up our money drinking tea and gambling. There between rides we would gossip. We would smoke *bidis* and drink many glasses of tea. We would grumble about being helpless and poor. This V-AID worker Faruqui used to ask us, 'Why do you smoke so much? Why do you gamble all your money away? Why don't you save your money? Why don't you try to pay your debts and get away from the grasp of the *mahajan?*' Then we would say to Mr. Faruqui, 'That would be nice. It is a nice dream. But we are poor men.'

"But one day Yasin the tea stall owner asked us, 'Why do you always grumble? Why do you always dream? Why don't you combine together to do something?' 'Do what?' we asked. 'What can we do?'

"There is here in Comilla," the rickshaw puller said, "an Academy. The very Academy we are riding to now. This Academy is run by a strange tall man like yourself. He is called Khan Sahib. He does not dress as other officers. He dresses only in village clothing. I have seen him in my village several times. . . . He speaks my language with a foreign accent. Do you know him?" the rickshaw man suddenly asked. "Yes," the stranger nodded, "I know him well! I know Khan Sahib."

"Well, Khan Sahib was going about the villages trying to get people to organize co-operatives. And somehow Yasin the tea stall owner and Faruqui met him. Together they planned our Dider Rickshaw Pullers' Co-operative."

"Tell me about it," said the stranger.

"It was two and one-half years ago" said Abdul. "One evening Yasin asked us to attend a meeting. He said at that meeting that he had talked with some officers at the Academy and they had told him how to start a co-operative. He told us that we should save some money. After we had saved some money we should buy ourselves a rickshaw.

"This is the way we started. There were nine of us. We started to save a few annas* a day. Yasin made us stop smoking so many *bidis*. He told us to stop drinking so much tea. We had to stop gambling.

"This is the way we went for a few months, saving a little but without a plan of what to do. Then one day Khan Sahib sent Mr. Nurul Huq of the Academy to us to help us. Later Khan Sahib came himself. They helped us plan what to do.

"They said we should make a co-operative and save money each week. Mr. Yasin would be our Organizer. Another man, Mr. Shamsul Haq, another officer of the Academy, helped us too.

"To make a long story short, we began to save money every day and deposit it. The Academy showed us how to purchase rickshaws with these savings. When we had Rs. 600 we decided to buy two old rickshaws. Every member wanted one of these rickshaws but we couldn't decide who of the members should be given them. There were two ideas. One member thought we should flip a coin. Yasin thought that there should be a savings contest. He said that the two rickshaw men who saved the most money should be awarded the rickshaws. Yasin's proposal was accepted."

---

* An anna is a coin that represents 1/16 of a rupee, or slightly more than 1 cent.

"In that way I got this rickshaw. Each week we saved. When we had three hundred rupees—there were by that time about thirty members saving—we would buy another rickshaw and give it to the member who had saved the most and who didn't yet have a rickshaw.

"After I got this rickshaw I had to pay one rupee eight annas a day until it was paid for. I paid three hundred rupees for this rickshaw plus twenty-five rupees interest. I remember it took me just over seven months to pay for it. Now I earn just about five rupees a day. All I have to spend on my rickshaw is a little for repairs. I don't have to pay the two rupees rent any more. I save these two rupees in my savings account. Each member has a pass book.

"My co-operative has more than one hundred members. In the beginning we were only nine. Now my co-operative has forty-five rickshaws. Twenty-four of them have been paid for like mine. We have a building in Ballarampur also. You should come and see it, Sahib."

"That I should," said the tall stranger. "Are you happier than you were, Abdul Wahab Mia?" "Yes, certainly I am happier. I *said* it was a miracle. It *is* a miracle. In sixteen years I saved nothing. I had nothing. But now both my brother and I have our own rickshaws. I have more than one hundred rupees in savings now. I take only two cups of tea a day. I don't gamble any more. I used to go to the cinema three times a week. I don't do that any more. I say my prayers five times a day and keep fast during Ramazan. Before I always had worries. In our house there was hunger every year. Now we still don't have much, but we have food to eat all the time. Sahib, it is a miracle for a poor man."

The tall man looked at the little rickshaw puller before him, "Abdul Wahab Mia, you are a lucky man to be able to be happy."

Swiftly the paddy fields went by. The yellow flat roof of the Academy office came into view. The rickshaw decorated with its red and blue plastic hood swung to the right, into the Academy entrance, and stopped. "How much is the ride?" asked the stranger. "As you like," said Abdul. "Here is a rupee for the ride and a rupee for the savings account," said the stranger. "Salaam-aleikum," said the stranger. "O-aleikum-salaam," said Abdul as he wheeled off.

GOSSIP IN THE SMALL TOWN

Albert Blumenthal

Social control—the process by which society induces conformity to group norms—is actually one of the social processes, although it is not ordinarily included with them in introductory texts. Social control can be of the informal type (for example, praise or blame) or the formal type, as by laws and codes. This selection by Albert Blumenthal well illustrates informal social control by gossip, a method that is especially effective in small towns. Says E. W. Burgess of the book from which this selection is taken, "The main characteristics of small town life stand out in clear perspective: close acquaintanceship of everyone with everyone else, the dominance of personal relations, and the subjection of the individual to continuous observation and control by the community."

One of the favorite themes of novels, stage plays, and jokes has long been the petty gossiping in small towns. Even the small-town residents themselves poke some fun at the inevitable and perennial gossiping in their midst, and are continually crying out against it and grumbling about it. For all that is so traditional about the small and isolated community is woven about the far-reaching power of gossip—of communication by word of mouth.

In Mineville, "gossip" is a term much used, especially by women and in description of them. It has two general meanings. Sometimes it includes all local news which is transmitted by word of mouth; and at other times it means only that information involving a fellow-resident which any particular resident would not want told of himself, or which people feel they must whisper stealthily lest they incur the displeasure of someone. Whether or not the resident wishes the word to carry a derogatory stigma is told by the intonation of his voice or by other gestures. In the following discussion it will be used in both senses under the assumption that the context will indicate to what extent a distinction is meant to be made between mere talk, and that sort of talk which anyone thinks should be whispered or not told.

SOURCE: *Small-Town Stuff* (Chicago: The University of Chicago Press, 1932), 128–43. Reprinted by permission of the author and the publisher. ◇ The author is associate professor of sociology, Wisconsin State College, Eau Claire. *Small-Town Stuff* was his Ph.D. dissertation, University of Chicago, under the title "A Sociological Study of a Small Town." His interests include criminology, juvenile delinquency, the family, and sociological theory.

Who Are the Gossipers?

Over the telephone a Mineville woman may quite frankly say, "I thought I would call up and see if you have heard the latest gossip." But while she is herself in the midst of spreading a scandal she is not unlikely to cast discredit upon another woman by calling her a "terrible old gossip." This illustrates the tendency of the people to make light of their own gossiping and that of their friends and to condemn it in others. For whether or not a person is rated as a gossip in the discrediting sense of the term depends not upon what he actually says but upon the attitude toward him held by the person making the rating.

Violent outbursts of anger and disgust at the "damned gossipers" are characteristic of most Minevillers when some of their own private affairs are aired in public. The part they themselves play in airing the affairs of others they seem to overlook. While it is true that most of them pretend to refrain from circulating information which will be harmful to the other fellow, all townsfolk (excepting infants and very small children) are dispensers of gossip, be it harmful or not. Those persons who might locally be known as non-gossipers are merely persons who are comparatively little interested in collecting whispered information and who, when they secure it, impart it more tactfully and considerately than the people as a whole. But even they have a few strong dislikes which cause them to show little consideration for some people.

In classifying the gossiping proclivities of the people the first criterion to suggest itself is that of sex, because from time immemorial men have jested about woman's tendency toward personal gossip. The explanation is clear. She merely talks of that about which her life is centered. She spends comparatively little time discussing the stock market, sports, politics, and impersonal problems of workaday life such as do the men. Her preoccupation is with local events—particularly those local events which have a strong tinge of the personal such as bridge parties and moral scandals. She frankly admits that when she goes calling she "talks about everybody in town." She touches at great length upon the care of babies, children, and husbands; illnesses, childbirth, cooking, clothing, and other subjects closely related to the home—always illustrating her theory in terms of Mineville personalities. Unlike her husband, she never tires of talking shop, and when she talks shop, persons are generally involved. Also, she can gossip for an hour over the telephone at will while he works with a lone partner in a dark recess far below the surface of the earth. In this way she may act as a gossip collector for him during the day and detail her findings to him when he returns from work. He may tell her what he has heard "at the mine," but this usually is much less than she has to tell him, and less personal.

A usual remark about those in the community who are known as "gossips" is: "Tell Mrs. So-and-So anything as a secret if you want it advertised all over town in a hurry." But Mineville has so many proficient gossipers that to select only those who are reputed to be gossips and to ignore the rest would be to produce an erroneous picture. A few typical examples will serve to bring out this point.

First we may note some factors which cause Mrs. Dunwell to be rated as the community's leading female "gossip." Mrs. Dunwell occupies a position of social prominence which normally places her somewhat in the public eye aside from publicity which she might derive from her gossiping. She is frank and quick to "jump to conclusions"; she spares no one, not even herself, when she decides to give her opinion. This impulsive frankness causes her to reveal passing flurries of envy and jealousy which would remain undisclosed in the case of the ordinary woman. Consequently, she is readily accused of having a tendency to exaggerate and distort, and is feared and disliked by many. But there is no doubt that were she less prominent and less frank to all persons anywhere, she might gossip equally as much without being renowned as a community gossip, in the derogatory sense of the term.

The leading gossips tend to be persons with unusual ability to remember "everything about everybody." One of these is Ed Slade, who is known more as a "talker" than as a "gossip" because he is not a woman. Another was Mrs. Drake, who was not known as a gossip mainly because she was a recluse. Both Mr. Slade and Mrs. Drake were recognized as vocal social historians of the community, as can be seen from the following advice given when certain inside information was sought:

Miss X: You should see Ed Slade. He can tell you anything you want to know.

Mr. X [*her father—interrupting*]: Yes, see Ed Slade. He knows all about everything in town. I came in 1889 and he was tending bar before he worked for me at that time. He can tell you lots and more too.

Mrs. X: And he will be glad to tell you things. It's odd how some people can remember things. There was Mrs. Drake. Whenever I wanted to know anything I used to go over to her. She seemed to know everything about everybody and everything in town. It's too bad she died. She could have helped you.

She was not a gossip. She never told unless you asked but when you asked she sure knew.

Mr. X: Sid Marshall is quite a talker. He came here after I did but he sure could tell you about everything since he came.

It is interesting that the men are especially prone to speak of the talkative members of their sex as "talkers" while females with the same propensities are classified as "gossips." In reply, the women contend, and perhaps not without justification, that the men are the "worst gossipers." Whatever the truth may be, Mineville has some very talkative males who are much better situated to secure and spread the news than are the women. Among these is Sid Marshall.

"Sid" is the proprietor of a tailor shop in which an almost perpetual talk-fest is in progress throughout the day and often until late at night. Man after man "drops into Sid's place" for a sociable chat and leaves such news as he has in return for a large supply from Sid and others who may have been present. Everything is discussed: from the habitual debtors of Mineville to the debtor nations of the World War; from the scandal of a Mineviller who just passed by the window to that involving presidents and kings. Religion, politics, psychology, economics, milady's styles, fishing trips, smutty stories, the weather, and the merits of one another's chewing tobacco—nothing is barred. But it would be a mistake to conceive of this visiting center as those of small towns are so often caricatured, that is, as made up of men of naïve intelligence who presume great wisdom. Their ideas and attitudes on problems of larger import are not provincialisms, but rather are the same as those had by city people, because of being derived from the same immediate sources: editors of leading periodicals, the radio, and the movies. On the other hand, on local matters the individuals force one another to keep close to facts by the ruthlessness by which they pounce upon him who errs.

There is no better place in Mineville to sense shifts in public opinion than Sid's tailor shop. For news generally is not "out" long before someone brings it to Sid's, whose position is much like that of the editor of a paper in that he tends to hear all sides of questions more rapidly than people in general. From these diverse points of view he tries to arrive at the true statement of a situation. He becomes one of the best-informed men in town on local affairs, and his shop is one of Mineville's best substitutes for a daily newspaper and scandal sheet—a function pleasant to him and in no sense to his discredit, even though he is subjected to criticism by women who imagine that they are the particular objects under discussion in his shop.

❖   ❖   ❖   ❖   ❖

There are, of course, other outstanding agents of gossip and other gossiping centers on Main Street. Not only are there several business men who are very proficient gossips, but most of the business establishments have particular persons who "hang around and talk." In fact, wherever the people assemble informally a gossiping center tends to arise.

Those traditional gossip-dispensing bureaus, the barber shops, where the barber tries to talk about as many interesting things as possible to his customers, have changed somewhat since the war. One of the barbers observes:

Do you remember how there always used to be a gang of men hanging around the barber shops? I try to discourage them from hanging around my place nowadays since women and girls are an important part of my trade. Boy, how the guys used to talk in the old days! I'll bet there were more dirty jokes and more dirty remarks passed in the barber shops than anywhere in town. And how they gossiped! But things have changed. If the fellows do hang around now they have to be careful what they say in the presence of women and girls and so there isn't much to encourage them to loiter in a shop. Besides, women don't like to come into a shop if a lot of men are sitting around. There is plenty of talk now, but the subjects are different—as long as women are in the shop, at least.

Away from Main Street and from home the men do most of their gossiping in the mines and mills. Each group of workers tends to have certain members who stand out for their general talking abilities. Of forty-six men on one shift at the Salmon Mine two of these entertainers are in the limelight. To quote a fellow-workman:

Talk about gossip! On our shift we have Fred Hare and Charlie Ratner in the center of the bunch before we go down the mine and at eating time, and I'll bet there ain't a woman in town who can equal those fellows. They never run out of gossip. You ought to see how they monopolize the conversation. It seems almost impossible that they can possibly know so much. Month after month their supply of gossip holds out.

Even among children there are prominent agents of gossip. They function much as do their elders, and when they are indiscreet they are subjected to the same disrepute. Breta Gaynor (age eleven) is a good example in the grade school. She talks incessantly and keeps widely informed upon the affairs of the school children, and upon those of adults as well. At a tender age Mineville children commence to take a naïve interest in the events of community gossip because they are likely to have had some acquaintance with a large share of persons and things of which they hear adults talk. The more intelligent five-year-old kindergarten children, for instance, have already reached a stage at which they are able to impart surprising bits of information to their teacher.

Influenced by small-town conditions, as are mature residents, Mineville children have leisure time, frankness, curiosity, and close contacts with large numbers at school to facilitate their gossiping. Through the grade school and through the high school waves of gossip of all sorts surge. Indeed, the schools are the largest gossiping centers in town although townsfolk, as a rule, are not aware of the fact.

Gossip and the Formation of Public Opinion

Talking of things in general appears to be the favorite indoor and outdoor sport in Mineville. This is due in part to the neighborliness and community of interest among the people, and in part to the deficiency of other leisure-time activities in which there is an element of sociability. An interesting sidelight upon the effect of a community of interest was observed by a candidate for a county office:

I'll tell you something that surprised me. Because I was never much of a mixer, I thought I would have a hard time when I ran for office. I thought I wouldn't be able to find anything to talk about to people I didn't know. It sure surprised me how easy it is to find something to talk about. We have so much in common with one another in this town, and even in the county, that we know a lot about people we've never talked to. For that reason I found that I could predict pretty well what would be an interesting topic of conversation to nearly everyone. I always knew some of their friends, where they worked, something about their children, and so forth. In a jiffy I could bridge the gap between not knowing people and becoming intimate with them. The trouble was not in finding something to talk about but rather that I had to be careful not to talk too much about intimate things for fear someone would start talk going around that the people shouldn't vote for me because I'm just an old gossiper anyhow. And then, I was pretty sure that some of the people were trying to get me to feel intimate with them so that I would confide things in them which they could use against me politically.

With such community of interest, and a general desire to tell the other fellow the latest news, it is not surprising that an exceptionally live bit of news, such as the death of a prominent citizen, attains almost complete circulation in the community in about two hours. Most of the people are likely to have the news in an hour. In a few minutes it reaches all of the business establishments on Main Street. "Too bad about Mr. So-and-So," the merchant characteristically says to his customers one by one. And wherever a group is congregated along the street the death becomes a topic of conversation. Meanwhile, with half of the people in town having telephones and by the age-old practice of "running in" to tell a neighbor, the news soon reaches those who perchance have not visited Main Street or otherwise encountered someone who might tell them. Community expectation of rapidity of circulation is attested by the fact that should such a death occur at nine o'clock in the morning and the information not reach a resident until late in the afternoon, his usual expression is, "I can't understand why I didn't hear that sooner," and others say to him, "Where have you been? Everybody knew that by noon."

For several days such a topic is likely to be focal in the community. The man, his last illness, his family, etc., are discussed and rediscussed. A multitude of diverse bits of information and points of view have been brought into play before the subject drops out of the limelight.

Because as a social unit it is small and isolated, Mineville offers a most interesting laboratory for the study of public opinion. The participant-observer can witness the crystallizing of opinion in detail from its initial gropings to the final product in which more or less uniform attitudes and ideas in respect to a matter are characteristic over the whole community or in large factions. He will be struck with the rapid and varied shifts of opinion from one side of a question to another. He will see occasional cases when opinion becomes so fixed that there is a community-wide tendency for the people to become emotional if they are asked to consider the merits of the minority side of a matter. But he will find that such cases of callousness are usually temporary periods of high resistance, and that in the long run the "truth" is acknowledged by the people as a whole, if an item of gossip is sufficiently alive to keep it before them long enough. The people are so persistently confronted with untruths or partial truths in local rumor that they have a wholesome skepticism regarding it which naturally results in a rigorous, although often unconscious, piecing-together of evidence before a final conclusion is reached.

When news "gets out," one of the first steps of a resident is to trace it, and, as a rule, he is quite keen in tracing the origins and course of gossip because of his insight into the relations of Minevillers to one another. Resolutely he sets about to build his theory as to the channels through which an item of gossip has passed, through certain outstanding gossipers, and through a network of relatives, friends, and others who have frequent and intimate contact with one another. He knows much of the probable motives of these people and of the reliability of what they might say. In questioning the truth of a bit of news, for instance, he will say, "She got it from Mrs. Jacobs and it's a cinch Mrs. Jacobs got it from Mrs. Black and you know what a liar Mrs. Black is."

How Gossip Destroys Privacy

We have already indicated how gossip brings together odds and ends of one's private life which he reveals about himself to numerous persons over a long period of time. We have not yet discussed the factor which accounts for the feeding of most of the very intimate personal information into the streams of gossip, that is, betrayed confidences.

Everyone trusts that certain persons in possession of intimate facts of his personal life will not betray him. He would feel most wretched if he actually believed that no one is to be trusted to hold such knowledge in due respect. His father, mother, wife, brother, and several good friends he assumes will shield parts of his life from the public gaze. And while we have no evidence upon which to assert that his faith is not justified for the most part, bit by bit details of his private affairs sift out by way of betrayed confidences. This happens everywhere, but the consequences are especially serious in a small town such as Mineville where people seize with alacrity upon such information and shortly insure its perpetuation by making it a public acquisition. Husbands, for instance, little know what information of their private affairs their wives may have told "in confidence" to women friends who in turn have broadcast it to the community "in confidence." It is by means of just such a network of interlocking confidences that the "whole town" secures the most whispered of information almost as readily as it does ordinary news, despite the strong inhibitions the people have regarding "talking about" others because of being afraid that their words will "get back" to the person "talked about." Fortunately, however, most Minevillers do not seem to realize how well others know them, and so the human longing for someone in whom to confide, to whom to unburden the weight of troubles, still finds extensive expression in the town.

By way of illustration, the following phenomena attending broken confidences may be noted as commonplace in Mineville, as elsewhere:

a) There are irresponsible information purveyors—persons who must tell.
b) While people are on intimate terms they normally confide in and otherwise learn a great deal about one another. When their relations are temporarily or permanently broken, the situation is ripe for the wholesale breaking of confidences.
c) The desire to appear interesting to others often causes indiscretion to the point of violation of confidences.
d) Persons are led into disclosing confidential information in order to prove points in arguments.
e) There are "accidental slips" which are not realized as broken confidences until after they have occurred.
f) Many confidences are broken because as time passes people are likely to forget that they received the information concerned in confidence.
g) Some people care less about privacy than others and so they easily disregard what are to them the excessive requests of others for secrecy. The leading female gossip of the town, as has been indicated, secures her disrepute largely because of telling about others that which she does not care if others tell about her.

Scandals

Novelists have painted vivid pictures of small-town life which have captured the popular imagination and have made small-town people appear to be a peculiar species of scandal-hungry creatures. Somehow the lurid exposés featured by city daily papers have been considered to be more worthy of sophisticated people than rural gossip, and there has been a tendency to minimize the fact that city folks do a great deal of gossiping among their more intimate associates.

If Minevillers have a greater interest in scandal than urbanites, it is because of a difference in situation, not in people. It so happens that besides sensational news derived from city dailies, the residents of the town are living under conditions conducive to the ferreting-out, spreading, and perpetuation of an extensive fund of local scandal. And this news is the more interesting because it affects the status of persons with whom they are obliged to have close social relationships. Certainly it would be more interesting if one were to know that the only iceman in town has tendencies to be a paramour than it is to read in a city paper of the same proclivities on the part of some strange iceman one has never seen.

There is a fund of whispered gossip about every resident of a small town. Actually but an infinitesimal part of this is communicated directly to the person concerned, although the people say, "Everything gets back sooner or later in this town." Such news characteristically travels in channels which avoid him. It frequently buzzes among his closest friends and yet escapes him. This is particularly true of scandal. . . .

Fear of Gossip

In Mineville, individual variation in respect to fear of gossip is very wide. There is to be found the whole gamut of degrees from persons who are excessively fearsome lest their affairs become matter of gossip to those who defy, ignore, or are not well cognizant of the relentlessness with which news travels and the thorough circulation which it attains.

In the main, however, Minevillers wittingly and unwittingly are affected by a strong fear of gossip. Long experience has shown them that information tends to become distorted in passing from person to person, and so, even though the public in question is small enough that the truth is likely to become generally known in time if it is known to a few persons, the people do not wish to have their affairs thrown into the gristmill of conversation and argument through which so much news must pass before it is accurately consumed. This reluctance to be "talked about" does much to inhibit the circulation not only of reprehensible gossip but of permissible news. A warning voice is ever ready to whisper into the resident's ear, "Be careful! It will get all over town," or "What will people say?" And even in formal meetings someone may arise to say, "We'd better watch our step or the whole town will be on our necks before we adjourn."

No resident of Mineville supposes that he is not "talked about." Even obscure townsfolk complain that they live under the spotlight of the public eye and hence must become hardened to the inevitable gossip, if they are to have peace of mind. But withal, there is so much open defiance to gossip as to suggest that many residents do not realize the harm which their acts may bring upon their reputations at present, and even twenty years in the future.

SOCIAL CONTROL
AND NON-CONFORMITY
IN A SOUTHERN TOWN

Edgar A. Schuler and Robert L. Green

In the previous selection we have seen how gossip functions as a means of social control in a small community. In this selection Schuler and Green have edited an extended interview that the senior author had with a prominent educator in a southern town. In the interview Dean Gordon Moss relates how shunning and other processes of social control operated in efforts to force his compliance with the local norms regarding segregated schools. This case study also illustrates how belief in educational opportunity for all, and other values acquired in the larger society, produced the non-conformity of a respected community leader. The analysis of the conflicting social forces with his resolution of them and the stages of non-conformity and ostracism in the community is an insightful documentation of these social processes.

Prince Edward County, located in south-central Virginia, is a predominantly rural area containing approximately 8,000 whites and 5,000 Negroes. Both the County and the town of Farmville, its County seat, manifest the cultural, social, economic, and interracial situations typical of many southern counties and towns. The children of both Negro and white families come primarily from lower and lower-middle class socio-economic backgrounds, and the same social and racial barriers exist as are normally found in comparable southern communities.

For the past thirteen years Prince Edward County has exhibited a

SOURCE: Interview with Dean Gordon Moss, Dean of Longwood College, Farmville, Va. (May 23, 1963). Conducted and recorded by Edgar A. Schuler in connection with a study directed by Professor Green, which was financed by the U.S. Office of Education, Grant 2321. ❖ Edgar A. Schuler is professor of education and sociology, and a staff member of the Social Science Teaching Institute, Michigan State University. From 1959 to 1962 he was senior advisor of the Pakistan Academy for Village Development at Comilla. One of the editors of this book, he is also the coauthor of *Medical Public Relations* and *Public Opinion and Constitution Making in Pakistan, 1958–1962.* ❖ Robert L. Green is associate professor of educational psychology, Michigan State University. He was the administrator of the Citizenship Education Program for the Southern Christian Leadership Conference during 1965–66. He wrote *The Educational Status of Children in a District Without Public Schools,* in which he reported the study of Negro children in Prince Edward County, Virginia.

*pattern of growing interracial conflict, emerging openly in 1951 in a strike
engineered by Negro high school students to obtain more adequate educational facilities.*

*During this period the Negro citizens of Prince Edward County began
to perceive the issue of equal school facilities and education as being
integrally related to the more basic problem of school desegregation. After
a number of lawsuits had been initiated by local Negro citizens, the County
Board of Supervisors in 1959 closed both the white and Negro public
schools rather than comply with court-ordered desegregation. Shortly
thereafter certain members of the white community established privately
financed segregated schools for their children. Since 1959 approximately
1,300 of the 1,700 Negro children of school age who live in Prince Edward
County have had almost no formal, and very little informal, education.
In the summer of 1963 and continuing through September of 1965 a team
of social scientists under the direction of Robert L. Green of Michigan
State University has been involved in a research project in Prince Edward
County, Virginia, supported by the U.S. Office of Education. The major
objective of the project is to assess what effect four years of non-schooling
has had upon the achievement and aptitude levels of the Negro school-age
children in this county. Furthermore, an analysis is being made of the
social impact of the schools' closing upon the community.*

*As the school issue developed and gained in momentum a number of
prominent Prince Edward County residents became involved in the school
controversy. Outstanding among these individuals has been C. G. Gordon
Moss, Dean of Longwood College, a State-supported institution of higher
education located in Farmville, which enrolled only white students up to
the time of the interview. In connection with initiation of the field activities of the research team the senior author of this paper, a faculty member
in the Colleges of Education and Social Science at Michigan State University and sociological consultant to the research project, interviewed
Dean Moss at Farmville, Virginia, in May of 1963 in an attempt to gather
information pertinent to the research project. Except for the italicized
paragraphs and the topical subheadings, the following is an edited version
of the transcribed recording of what Dean Moss had to say.*

Personal Background

We are getting to a sort of impasse here in Farmville, insofar as our
local situation is concerned. We have been in such an impasse for some
months now, since we are really awaiting court decisions and neither side
can do anything one way or the other until the legal situation is clarified.

With regard to my own background, I should begin with the fact that
I am just fifty miles away from my birthplace. I was born in Lynchburg,
Virginia, at the end of the 19th century, and I have lived in Virginia all
my life except some three years of residence in New Haven when I did

my graduate work at Yale and the one year that I taught in North Carolina. Other than those four years, I have spent my entire life in Virginia: in Lynchburg, in Fredericksburg to the north, in Alexandria for three years back at the beginning of my teaching career, and here in Farmville. I certainly grew up in the normal, the average, and the traditional southern atmosphere. I can remember, as a child, having several Negro friends— one, in particular, was a close friend. But, of course, as I grew up, I was unconsciously subjected to the normal 19th century southern attitudes regarding the Negro. I can remember having jumped right over a seat in a streetcar in Washington when a Negro sat down beside me. That must have been around 1912 or 1913—when I was just a very young boy.

I can remember avoiding eating with Negroes at various public meetings and conferences into my adult life. But I can also remember that in my home there was never any hatred or fear of Negroes, and that we maintained an attitude that was normal in the era—the kindliest possible relationship with the Negro servants. I did not become aware, and certainly not intensely aware, of any major issue in regard to Negroes until this situation developed here in Prince Edward County.

I have no recollection of even being aware of the difficulties Negroes were having with regard to education until at least the 1940's. The only thing I do remember was my relief when my mother-in-law sold some Negro residential property that she had inherited down in the slum areas of the town. I felt relieved because it was perfectly obvious that the property was being used for economic exploitation. By "economic exploitation" I mean that it was the cheapest, slummiest, scummiest type of property on which she had spent nothing in the way of improvement and consequently all of the rent was pure profit to her. She spent nothing on physical improvements, neither as an investment nor in improving her inheritance, and I couldn't have been a normal rational human being if I hadn't realized that such disinterest was not the best way to behave.

Paternalism as a Salve for the Troubled White Conscience

If I may attempt to summarize as briefly as possible, first the developments in Prince Edward County, but more particularly, my reaction and relationship to the developments, it would have to begin with the fact that as a normally sensitive person, I have been aware at least subconsciously for as long as I have known anything about Farmville in Prince Edward County—and that would go back to 1926—of the most paternalistic attitude maintained by the ruling white majority toward the Negro in this community. This was and is an attitude of love for the Negro, if the Negro will accept everything from the white rulers—if he will, to use common southern language, "stay in his place." But I would say that this paternalistic attitude toward the Negro is probably stronger in this particular locality than generally throughout Virginia.

I believe this attitude represents an unconscious salving of the conscience of the white man in this community. The white men have known that the Negroes who made up almost 50 per cent of the population were uneducated, patient, and willing to remain in its low situation. They wanted that Negro population for the dirty work of raising tobacco on farms or laboring in the local tobacco processing plants. The housewives of the County wanted that Negro population for household servant work. And, whether they were able to consciously admit it to themselves or not, I believe that they have known that by keeping the Negro uneducated, poor, available for what they wanted from him was unjust to the Negro, and as a result they had to in some manner protect their own consciences against what they were doing. Consequently, they have developed the feeling that they were the benefactors of the Negro. They treated Negroes personally and individually in a friendly and kindly way, and were helpful to them in their personal problems—give or lend the Negro who is becoming a drunkard money when he needs to buy another bottle of cheap wine, pay his fine so he can get out of jail in order that he can work your garden for you again. This protective position or attitude was both beneficial to the Negro and to the white man in easing the latter's conscience with regard to what he was doing to the Negro. This preserves the kind of image that we like to hold of ourselves . . . that we are kindly masters concerned with the personal life of our servants (no longer our slaves but now our servants) and that we want to make them as happy as possible, always assuming that they can be entirely happy in this totally subservient status.

Inferior Education for Negroes

The paternalistic attitude as a salve for the white man's conscience had its most specific social reaction and implication in terms of the educational system maintained by the County for the Negroes. All through the 1930's and into the 1940's an admittedly inferior school system for the Negroes was manifested in the buildings, in the teachers, and in the school administration, and as a result, in inferior educational content. But the white man eased his conscience by thinking and by assuming that this very modicum of education was all that the Negro wanted, and that he was entirely satisfied with it. When, in the 1930's, and on into the 1940's, the schools for the Negroes—particularly in the town of Farmville in contrast to the surrounding County community—became severely overcrowded, the white people were not willing to spend the necessary money to relieve the crowded condition in any reasonable and effective manner. They were only willing to do this inch by inch, as they were forced to do so, and to do it in the cheapest way possible, such as putting up temporary buildings—tar paper shacks.

I recall now that around 1945 a friend of mine from Longwood College was asked to give a science lecture at the Negro high school. When he came back, he told me how impossibly crowded the high school building was, that he could barely get to the platform to deliver the lecture because every square inch of space was taken up by the students. I believe that this was my first concrete, specific realization of the crowded conditions.

Negro Efforts to Improve Negro Education

I am aware that throughout the 1940's the Negroes through their Parent-Teachers Association were persistently and continuously urging the School Board to build adequate structures for the education of their children. There was no effort then to build for integration. It was merely an effort to increase the physical facilities for the admittedly "Negro" schools. The whites resisted any such obligations to provide such needed facilities. As a result, if I recall correctly, the Negro children by 1951 had become utterly disillusioned and thought that there would never be any schools.

So in the spring of 1951, the Negro children initiated on their own, without any adult help or even knowledge, a strike in the Negro high school. They went out on strike and declared that they were going to stay out on strike until the School Board agreed to build a structure. The strike brought in the N.A.A.C.P. led by Reverend L. Francis Griffin who is the local Baptist Negro minister and now President of the local and state N.A.A.C.P. This group sought to help the Negro children in their endeavors and led to the initiation of a legal suit originally designed, I believe, to promote more adequate physical facilities for the Negro children, but eventually demanding that segregation in the school system be abandoned. I am quite certain that suit was in the Federal Courts in 1952, and it was the beginning of the combination of suits which reached the Supreme Court in 1954.

With the above threat hanging over the heads of the ruling whites of the County they *did* go ahead and find the money which they had previously said they were unable to find. They found the money, and borrowed to build an entirely adequate high school for the Negro children of the town and the County. This new school, the Moton High School located on the southern outskirts of the town, is far and away the best school building in the entire County, white or Negro. The white people were trying to "buy the Negroes off" by giving them more than they had asked for in the way of physical facilities and thus hoped to stop the desegregation suit. The new school was in use when the Supreme Court decision of May 1954 was handed down.

Popular Reactions to the Supreme Court Decision

The next milestone to be considered is the reaction of the people of the County to the Supreme Court decision of 1954. I believe the white community's reaction was originally one of utter confusion and dismay, and then, very rapidly, of anger and determination to resist to the utmost the decision and all of its implications. This feeling resulted in the formation of the so-called Defenders of State Sovereignty—a southside Virginia organization, not merely a Prince Edward County organization—an organization that was determined to resist by all possible legal means, as they said, any end of segregation whatsoever.

My reaction to the decision was one that I did not have to make publicly for a while. However, when the occasion arose, I did make it known whenever possible—that the County should open the white schools immediately to the Negro children and abandon segregation at once. The schools would be crowded with Negroes for the first week or two or for a brief interval of time, and then it would become difficult to find even a· single Negro—certainly not more than a bare sprinkling—who would be able to persist in the white schools with the latter's higher standards and the difficult social situation for the Negro children. No consideration was given to my proposal by anybody in authority whatsoever.

Then, after the second Supreme Court decision of 1955, with its implementation of the 1954 decision, there was the immediate local reaction—a public county-wide meeting to consider action. Undoubtedly careful preparation was made for that meeting in terms of speakers and proposals. The attendance was just about as large as one could expect—it overflowed the 1,200 seat auditorium of Longwood College. There was essentially no opposition voice raised in the meeting at all, and it was at that meeting that they organized their Prince Edward Educational Foundation Corporation to conduct private schools for the white children if and when that became necessary. That was in the spring of 1955. I had no opportunity to participate at that time since I was in the hospital with a coronary thrombosis and under doctor's orders not to become involved in the local controversy until well into 1956.

I believe that my first public statement was at a meeting of the high school Parent-Teachers Association when I was the only person who voted "No" on a resolution that the P.T.A. would resist integration of schools by all possible means. I had to ask specifically for the opportunity to cast my negative vote—the chairman did not think it was necessary even to ask for the negative vote. From that time, which was probably somewhere in the spring of 1956, until 1959, there has been really no opportunity for public protest whatsoever. I became known throughout the community as a proponent for public schools and for whatever integration was necessary to maintain the public schools. I doubt that I had developed my own thinking to any appreciable point bcyond merely believing that the Negroes should be allowed to continue to have the right to education, and for those Negroes who wanted it, integrated education.

Refusal to Compromise Leads to Private Schools for Whites, 1959

Finally in May 1959 the Board of Supervisors refused to adopt a budget providing for the continuance of public schools because the Federal District Court decision had been rendered, demanding that such schools would have to be integrated in the fall of 1959. In June of 1959 the Board of Supervisors decided to hold a public hearing on that action of May 1959. The public hearing was the occasion of my first real public expression of opinion. At that time I protested against the closing of schools and insisted that there was no necessity for such closing even to preserve segregation (if they wanted to preserve segregation) because not a single Negro had applied for admission to the white schools in June of 1959 for the subsequent September opening of the schools. There were several white citizens that did make such protests in that public meeting, but it was an entirely futile action because the Board of Supervisors merely went through the motions but not the reality of listening to us. I recall definitely that Henry Bittenger, a colleague of mine on the Longwood College faculty, also spoke. Possibly, he and I were the only two white people at the first to protest.

After the public hearing, upon realizing that there was no possible local way of preventing the closure of the schools, Bittenger and I, wondering if there was anything else we could do, began to meet from time to time. By September 1959 we succeeded in finding two Negro leaders who were willing to meet with us to explore the possibilities of maintaining free public education. We proposed that they, speaking for the Negroes, accept voluntary segregation for three years with the possibility of continued voluntary segregation beyond that point as the only possible way to having schools in the County in the year 1959–1960. They agreed to this proposal, but admitted that their agreement did not necessarily mean that all of the Negroes of the County would go along with them. We carried that agreement to the State Government, as well as to . . . , the outstanding spokesman of the white supremacists in the County. [He] . . . refused to consider it at all. He said that he would not discuss anything with the two Negro leaders and that he would only discuss private education with Negroes of his own choice, but that he would not discuss resumption of public education with anyone.

I consider it highly significant to call attention to this situation in the fall of 1959—that the white supremacists were determined to have no public schools at all, segregated or integrated. They rejected the opportunity to have segregated schools, as I have indicated. It was only after their Prince Edward Foundation had begun to operate the white private schools that they organized a separate group, claiming that this would assist the Negroes in establishing a private school for the Negro children in the County. They attempted to get an academic friend of mine, a sort of "academic son" of mine of the Longwood College faculty, to head the organization for private schools for Negroes—a move, I assume, to undercut any opposition on my part. I did succeed in persuading that young man not to accept the position. Late in the fall of 1959—it was possibly as late as December 1, I am not certain—they issued what in a sense was an ultimatum to the Negroes: they would give them until the first of January to accept the idea of these private schools, and if the Negroes did nothing about it, the project would be dropped. This ultimatum was delivered, and if I recall correctly, in the form of a circular letter to every parent requesting their replies as to whether or not they would send their children to the private school system if established. January 1, 1960, arrived with only one Negro family having indicated that it would place its children in such a school—and within two weeks time the white Foundation had made an official request to the School Board to rent the white public school buildings for the private school system. I do not think there is a mere coincidence involved in those dates. It is definitely known that during the fall of 1959 they had found the lack of adequate buildings to be the greatest difficulty in running the white private school system. They realized their desperate need for the public white schools, and saw that if they could get the Negroes to accept the token of a private school system and the use of Negro public schools, then they would have no difficulty whatsoever in obtaining the use of the white schools for the white private school system.

I am stressing the above point at considerable length because ever since the winter of 1959–1960, recurrently until it has become virtually a monotonous sing-song, they keep on repeating that they offered the Negroes a private school system, that they offered it honestly, that the Negroes refused it, and therefore the whites were absolved from any guilt caused by the Negro children not having an education. The offer was a mere paper offer and nothing was done in any sense to actually organize the private schools such as obtaining school teachers or determining the location of the buildings or of acquiring money to operate them. It was a paper offer made by and for the white people in an effort to be able to use the white schools.

I personally did not sense any real criticism, or hatred by the white people of the County, until I spoke in strong opposition at a public meeting of the School Board in late January or early February of 1960 held to consider whether or not to grant the request for the use of the white school buildings by the private school system. The School Board members turned down the request. I believe they had decided to do so before they even held the public meeting. They simply wanted to show at least some support from the public for such an action.

Emergence of the New View: Negroes Are Fellow Human Beings

My next personal crisis in the conflict came in January and February of 1961 when I attended the national annual meeting at Williamsburg of the Episcopal Society for Cultural and Racial Unity. The incidents and details of the matter are not of any public concern, but the local people used them in an attempt to pin on me the label of a total integrationist—even to the extent of believing in intermarriage of the two races. This resulted in a turmoil in my own church and in strained relations for me there ever since.

I have talked every time, every year—1959, 1960, 1961, 1962—when the Board of Supervisors held their annual public meeting with regard to a budget to include schools. I have, I think, gone through a very definite progression in my own thinking. I believe I have already referred to the fact that in 1959, at that first Board of Supervisors meeting at which I spoke, I was initially simply a proponent for public education for Negroes and whites regardless of whether it involved integration or not. But during the four years of the non-school system, as a result of my continuous private biracial conferences that had begun in 1959 between the two Negro leaders and Bittenger and myself, my thinking regarding the issue has changed. The conferences have become more frequent, with meetings approximately once a month from 1959 to the present, the spring of 1963. As a result, I have had to reexamine my own thoughts on the racial situation, and I think I have grown.

To me, the question of integrated schools is a very minor part of the problem in even so peaceful a county as Prince Edward. The real issue has grown beyond the mere question of integration to nothing more nor less than whether or not the white people are going to accept the Negroes as fellow human beings. And I doubt very much if even 10 per cent of the white population of the County would consider looking at the issue in so fundamental a form as that. And among that 10 per cent, one would be more likely to find the better educated (for example, members of the faculties of the two colleges in the County).

I do not believe that religion, however, would be a factor in determining whether one would look at Negroes as fellow human beings. Essentially all of the white churches and the white ministers of the County have refused to look at what has happened as a moral issue. One Presbyterian preacher was driven away at the beginning of the controversy in 1956 or 1957 because he insisted upon recognizing the problem as a moral issue. There is one Presbyterian minister out in the County now—has been there since 1962—who accepts it as such. But with the exception of those two men, I do not know of any white minister anywhere in the town or County who, in the last ten or twelve years, has ever been brave enough to accept it as such.

We have also had one physician who from the first has been very sympathetic to the Negroes, but who has not been willing to take a public and open stand, although he has allowed his wife to do so with moderation. Another physician was originally sympathetic and started out admitting that the Negroes had been grossly mistreated. However, he has now succeeded in rationalizing his withdrawal from the issue and his acceptance of the status quo. A third physician did accept the chairmanship of the County School Board in 1961, at the time the previous chairman and most of the School Board resigned. He was a very beloved physician who unfortunately has since died, and I never had the opportunity to discuss the matter with him. I believe he accepted the position with the hope that he could do something constructive by working from within with those who controlled the situation. He certainly never made any public statement advocating integration or advocating that we ought to do something for the Negroes in the County.

As to those who controlled the situation, I have already mentioned one person.

The open, entirely known, active leaders of the movement are, however, few in number but without them I don't believe the situation would have developed, and I doubt very much if, without them, there would have been any controversy and concrete issue here at all.

Whether or not it is true that one man, or several men, are behind these recognized leaders has always been a question in my own mind. I have very strong reasons to believe that there is one person, but I have no proof of it and so I will not even name that person. But it is altogether likely that in the final analysis the County's actions have resulted from one person's beliefs and ideas.

The local bar has not supported the cause of the Negroes. One member of that bar was legal counsel for the School Board at the beginning of the case. That was W. Cabell Fitzpatrick. He was gravely mistreated at the time when the lease or sale of the school buildings was an active issue. But he has never taken any open stand. Only one other person, who was trained for the law (but did not actively practice it) for a time took an active stand in favor of the Negro.

Social Mechanisms to Maintain Conformity

Though Dean Moss has not himself referred to this, Reverend L. Francis Griffin, the local Negro minister, has described the kind of ostracism to which Dean Moss has been exposed. This is a kind of punishment the community has imposed on him because he spoke out and purportedly advocated not only integrated education but also intermarriage.

The senior author notes, in passing, that this kind of social control, i.e., ostracism, operates in much the same manner in the East Pakistani villages he had occasion to visit. There the mechanism was called "outcasting." The ruling group of old men led by the headman would investigate a case and tell the individual what he must do if he would accept their control. If the individual refused to conform to the traditional ideals of this local leader and the others comprising the village power group, there was a formal outcasting procedure after the completion of which he was cut off from any communication and all social contacts within the village. This process of social action is known as "Ek ghore," i.e., "keeping the person in solitary confinement."* In rural East Pakistan, where everyone depends on others for almost all types of daily services, this is the most severe type of punish-

---

* Personal communication from Dr. Sheikh M. A. Noor of Dacca, East Pakistan, a graduate of the College of Education, Michigan State University.

ment which the village community can impose. No one will speak to him. The grocer will not sell his merchandise to him. The banker will not offer his services. Teachers will not instruct his children. The religious leader will not give his blessings. The rickshaw puller will not transport him. In other words, all types of specialized skills and services available in the villages are denied to him. At the same time, no one will buy his services, thus imposing on him an economic boycott. In addition, a type of social stigma is attached to his personality. If any villager sees him in the morning before breakfast that villager will refrain from taking breakfast himself as evidence of protest at his non-conformity. According to Dean Moss, in general terms, his experience and that of certain other people in the Farmville community could be used as illustrations of the mechanism presented above.

Here I am, a native of Virginia, born in Lynchburg, only 50 miles to the west of Prince Edward County. My ancestors on both sides of my family have been in Virginia since the 17th century. I came to Farmville, Virginia, in 1926 to begin my college teaching. I married a native of Farmville in 1929. I returned to Farmville to teach in 1929 and 1930 and left only because the substitute position I took in 1929 and 1930 did not develop into the permanent position I had hoped it would. I was continuously visiting in the town from 1930 until my return to the faculty of Longwood College in 1944. I have been associated with various civic organizations, such as the Rotary Club and so forth.

However, because I do not accept the Farmville interpretation of the racial issue, I am a foreigner, as much of a foreigner as if I had come from Iowa or even East Pakistan I expect. On the contrary, one of the principal spokesmen for the white supremacists is a native of Pennsylvania and is the mouthpiece of the publisher of the *Farmville Herald* and is a member of the Board of Supervisors. He married, not a native of Prince Edward County, but the widow of a native of Prince Edward County. But because he goes along with the ruling clique, he is a native and not a foreigner.

My sin, really, is that I am a scalawag: a native but a non-conformist. The Foundation people have continuously argued that this matter should be settled by natives of Farmville, but look at this situation: When they needed legal counsel, they took a lawyer from Blackstone, Virginia, as their principal legal counsel. Blackstone is 35 miles to the east, which is almost as far as Lynchburg, 50 miles to the west; however, I suppose the eastward direction is all-important! And furthermore, when they needed additional legal counsel, they took another outsider, a lawyer from Richmond, Virginia, and became very much incensed when, in the public hearing on school leases, I insisted upon establishing the fact that their principal counsel was not a native. I was accused of being most impolite to a person who had been invited into the County. It is not who you are or where you are from; it is whether or not you go along with the rules that determines your nativity.

I do not think that I have particularly suffered, personally, because of my criticism of the local situation. I have been snubbed on Main Street by virtually lifetime friends. I sit in a pew by myself in church every Sunday. I am not allowed to serve on the vestry although they are quite willing to accept my work as treasurer of the church.

On the positive side, let me add this. When the schools were closed in 1959, I had one remaining child in public school. He was ready for the eighth grade and I publically refused to allow him to go to the Prince Edward County school even though it was going to have the same faculty it had had for years as a public school, for the County school was, according to my views, based upon evil principles. So I refused to allow my son to go to that school and sent him away at the age of 13 to a boarding school much against his personal wishes, and he has been away from the local schools throughout the four years. Nevertheless, that boy has retained all of his friends in the Prince Edward Academy and his principal desire throughout these four years has been to get home as frequently as possible in order to be with his friends. So far as I know, he has never been snubbed in any way by any of his age peers.

I would therefore like to think that the attitudes of the adolescents differ from their parents and thus make the future look more hopeful, and that is what I thought for a good while—possibly for the first two years of the private school system.

It would be a bit difficult to prove, but I have increasingly gotten the impression for the past two years that the white children in the private school system are beginning to inherit and adopt their elders' ideas and that they are beginning to develop in themselves positive attitudes of hatred toward the Negroes. That is difficult to prove, and I would not attempt to do so now.

Foundations of a Philosophy of Total Integration

Actually, I have prevented any too strong personal attack being launched upon myself since I have always insisted that my opposition was based upon, first, my belief that public education was an absolutely necessary foundation stone for America if America was going to be a leading world nation.

Second, I have insisted that my opposition was based upon my belief in democracy, and that in a democracy you cannot have second-class citizens.

And, finally, I based my opposition, and insisted that it be so recognized, on Christianity—on the principle that Christianity forbade the mistreatment of any subordinate group in the society.

Accordingly, I have virtually defied people and insisted that if they wanted to criticize me, they would have to admit that they did not believe in public education, that they did not believe in democracy, and that they did not believe in Christian principles. Even so, it has threatened my life professionally and economically. Within a matter of days after my first public speech for public schools, a delegation was in the office of the president of Longwood College demanding that I be fired.

In the winter of 1961, an attempt was made to circulate a petition to the State Board of Education to fire me. They could not get enough signatures on the petition to make it of any weight, but they did carry it privately to the State Board of Education. An effort was made at that time to shut me up with the threat that if I did not stay quiet, I might lose my job. I guess what rankles the leaders of the opposition most is that in 1956–1959, when I began my opposition, I was merely Chairman of the History Department of Longwood College, but since then I have been promoted to Associate Dean and finally to the position of Academic Dean of the College, which is a rather bitter pill for most people in the community to take.

Present Status of Public Schools

A *private foundation known as the Prince Edward Free School Association was organized in September 1963. It made available elementary and secondary education to all Prince Edward County children on a desegregated basis. The Free School Association was financed by grants and contributions from foundations and private citizens. Although approximately 1,500 Negro youngsters attended the Free Schools, only four out of approximately 2,000 white school-age children were enrolled. Among the four white children was a 17-year-old senior named Richard Moss, the son of Dean Gordon Moss.*

A court order which directed the reopening of public schools in the county on an integrated basis in the Fall of 1964 rendered unnecessary continuation of the Free School Association's educational operation. Most white children of school age in Prince Edward County, however, are still attending—in 1965—the segregated private academy.

PICTURES IN OUR HEADS

Otto Klineberg

*Several years ago Walter Lippmann made a classic analysis of what
he referred to as the stereotypes that people hold of other persons
and groups. He termed those stereotypes "pictures in our heads"
and indicated how these images, often based on inadequate knowledge and overgeneralized ideas, provide the basis for our behavior
in relation to others. Here Otto Klineberg examines some of the
stereotypes commonly held of several national groups and discusses
the consequences of spuriously based images.*

About a year ago I was in London at the invitation of British psychologists and sociologists in order to lecture on "National Stereotypes."
Throughout the preceding day, during which I was undoubtedly made
more sensitive by my preoccupation with this topic, I kept running into
examples of such stereotyped thinking.

In my hotel, I heard someone say, "Oh, she has that Scottish stubborn-
ness, you know." A book review in a newspaper used the phrase, "With true
Gallic wit." At the theatre that evening, during the interval, I caught part
of a conversation in which a pretty girl said to her escort, "I know that all
Americans have a 'line' "; and in a mystery story that I read before retiring,
there was a reference to "typical German thoroughness."

These are all instances of those "pictures in our heads" to which
Walter Lippmann gave the name of stereotypes. They are typical of the
ease with which most of us generalize about national or ethnic groups,
usually without even stopping to think where such "information" comes
from, and whether it represents the truth, the whole truth, or anything
like the truth.

There are certainly very few, if any, among us who have not succumbed
to the temptation to stereotype nations. One might almost describe the
tendency as inevitable, or at least very nearly so. We *know* that Englishmen
are reserved, and Irishmen pugnacious; we have heard it all our lives;
besides most people agree with us. If we are asked, however, *how* we know,
we would not easily find a suitable answer.

SOURCE: UNESCO *Courier*, Vol. 8, No. 4 (September, 1955), 5–9.
Reprinted by permission. ✧ The author is professor of psychology, Columbia
University. He was formerly Director of Research for the "Tensions Project,"
UNESCO. His chief interests are race differences, national differences, and
attitudes. He has written *Race Differences, Social Psychology,* and *Tensions
Affecting International Understanding.*

One of the earliest careful studies of this tendency was made by Katz and Braly, in 1932, in connexion with the stereotypes held by Princeton University students. The technique was simple.

Each student was given a list of traits, and a list of nationalities; from the first list he chose the five traits which he regarded as characteristic of each national or racial group.

The results showed a fair degree of unanimity, e.g. out of 100 students, 78 described the Germans as "scientifically minded," and 65 described them as "industrious"; 53 students used the adjective "artistic" for the Italians; the same percentage described the English as "sportsmanlike"; 79 agreed that the Jews were "shrewd" and 54 stated that the Turks were "cruel"; 84 regarded Negroes as "superstitious," and 75 described them as "lazy."

We may summarize the results in a slightly different manner by indicating the three or four characteristics most commonly ascribed to each nationality. These included, for the Germans: scientifically-minded, industrious, stolid; the Italians, impulsive, artistic, passionate; Negroes, superstitious, lazy, happy-go-lucky, ignorant; the Irish, pugnacious, quick-tempered, witty; the English, sportsmanlike, intelligent, conventional; the Jews, shrewd, mercenary, industrious; the Americans, industrious, intelligent, materialistic, ambitious; the Chinese, superstitious, sly, conservative; the Japanese, intelligent, industrious, progressive; the Turks, cruel, religious, treacherous.

A recent study of the stereotypes of German students at the Free University of Berlin by Sodhi and Bergius showed a similar willingness to stereotype nations and, on the whole, comparable results. Americans, for example, were described as sportsmanlike, democratic, materialistic; the Italians as warmblooded, musical, light-hearted; the Chinese as poor, inscrutable, modest; the German as conscious of duty, loving their homeland, intelligent; the English as proud of their nation, bound by traditions, sportsmanlike. There were some variations between the German and the American stereotypes, but on the whole the overlapping is considerable.

On a more extensive scale, a study conducted in 9 countries under the auspices of UNESCO in 1948 and 1949, showed that such stereotyped thinking could easily be elicited almost anywhere. In each country approximately 1,000 respondents, representing a cross-section of the population, were given a list of 12 traits, and asked to choose those which they thought were most applicable to themselves, to Americans, to Russians, and in some cases, to two or three other national groups as well. They could choose as many of the traits as they wished.

The British, for example, thought of Americans as primarily progressive, conceited, generous, peace-loving, intelligent, practical. The Americans regarded the British as intelligent, hard-working, brave, peace-loving, conceited and self-controlled. The Norwegians described the Russians as hard-working, domineering, backward, brave, cruel and practical. The full results can be found in the volume by Buchanan and Cantril, "How Nations See Each Other."

The "self-image" is also revealing. The British saw themselves as peace-loving, brave, hard-working, intelligent; the French saw themselves as intelligent, peace-loving, generous, and brave; the Americans saw themselves as peace-loving, generous, intelligent and progressive. All the groups agreed on one item: their own nation was the most peace-loving of all!

Few people realize how much the existence of stereotypes may colour our relations with other people, even to the extent of seeing them differently as a result. Psychologists have long known that our perceptions of the external world, and particularly of human beings, are determined not only by what is *out there*, but also by what is *in ourselves*. What we see is determined in part by what we expect to see. If we believe, for example, that Italians are noisy, we will have a tendency to notice those Italians who are indeed noisy; if we are in the presence of some who do not fit the stereotype, we may not even realize that they, too, are Italian. If someone points that fact out to us and says: "Look, those people are Italians, and they are not noisy," we can always dismiss them as exceptions.

Since there is no limit to the number of cases that can be so dismissed, we may continue to cling to the pictures in our heads, in spite of all the facts to the contrary. This does not always happen. Stereotypes do sometimes change in the light of new experiences, and evidence for this is presented later. If we have had them for a long time, however, we surrender them with great reluctance.

A number of significant investigations have shown in a very dramatic manner how our stereotypes may determine our perceptions. Some years ago Allport and Postman, psychologists at Harvard University (Cambridge, U.S.A.) studied some of the phenomena associated with the spread of rumours, making use of a technique known as "serial reproduction," a very simple device which anyone can use with a group of friends in his own home. They showed a picture to one student, and he described to a second student what he saw in the picture. The second then told a third what the first had told him; the third told the fourth, and so on, through a series of 8 to 10 reproductions. Then a comparison was made between the final result and the original presentation.

One of the pictures used in this investigation showed a scene in a subway in which, in addition to a number of people seated, there were two men standing, one a white man, the other a Negro. The white man was dressed in working clothes, with an open razor stuck in his belt. It so happens that the stereotype of the Negro held by some people in the USA includes the notion that Negroes carry with them an open razor, of which they make ready use in an argument.

The psychologists were able to demonstrate that in half of the groups who served as subjects in these experiments, before the end of the series of reproductions had been reached, the razor had "moved" from the white man to the Negro. In some instances, the Negro was even represented as brandishing the razor violently in the face of the white man. This does not mean that half of the subjects in the experiment saw the Negro with the razor, since if only one person in the chain made this error, it would be repeated by those that followed. Interestingly enough, this did not occur when the subjects were Negroes (who rejected the stereotype), or young children (who had not yet "learned" it).

Another study conducted by Razran in New York points in the same direction. A group of college students in the USA were shown photographs of 30 girls, and asked to judge each photograph on a 5-point scale, indicating their general liking of the girl, her beauty, her intelligence, her character, her ambition, and her "entertainingness." Two months later, the same students were again shown the same photographs, but with surnames added. For some of the photographs Jewish surnames were given, such as Rabinowitz, Finkelstein, etc.; a second group received Italian names, such as Scarano, Grisolia, etc.; a third group Irish surnames, such as McGilli-cuddy, O'Shaughnessy, etc.; a fourth, "old American" names like Adams and Clark.

The investigator was able to demonstrate that the mere labeling of these photographs with such surnames definitely affected the manner in which the girls were perceived. The addition of Jewish and Italian names, for example, resulted in a substantial drop in general liking, and a similar drop for judgments of beauty and character. The addition of the same names resulted in a rise in the ratings for ambition, particularly marked in the case of the Jewish surnames. It seems clear that the same photographs *looked different* just because they could now be associated with the stereotype held by these students.

If a great many people agree that a particular trait is associated with a particular nation, does that make it true? There is a fairly widespread theory to the effect that "where there's smoke there's fire"; or, in other words, that the very existence of a stereotype is, to some extent at least, an argument in favour of its truth. Otherwise, the argument runs, where does the stereotype come from? How would it come into existence?

There is, however, a good deal of evidence as to the possibility that stereotypes may develop without any kernel of truth whatsoever. We all know how widespread is the notion that intelligent people have high foreheads, yet scientific investigation in this field has failed to reveal any such relationship. The stereotype of the criminal as bearing in his features the mark of his criminality is widely accepted, but it is equally without foundation; the famous British criminologist, Sir Charles Goring, was able to demonstrate that a composite photograph, representing criminals in British gaols, bore no resemblance to the accepted stereotype of the criminal.

Stereotypes frequently change. In some cases it may be argued that this corresponds to a real change in the characteristics of the people; in others, however, it seems much more likely to be due to external circumstances which have little or nothing to do with the group concerned. The Dutch sociologist, Shrieke, has, for example, made a collection of some of the descriptive phrases applied to the Chinese during the course of their residence in the state of California, U.S.A.

When the Chinese were needed in California, in order to carry on certain types of occupation, they were welcome there; during that period, newspapers and journals referred to them as among "the most worthy of our newly adopted citizens"; "the best immigrants in California"; they were spoken of as thrifty, sober, tractable, inoffensive, law-abiding. This flattering picture prevailed over a considerable period of time, but around 1860, presumably because economic competition had grown much more severe, there was a marked change in the stereotype of the Chinese. The phrases now applied to them included: "a distinct people," "unassimilable," "their presence lowered the plane of living," etc. They were spoken of as clannish, criminal, debased, servile, deceitful, and vicious.

This startling change can hardly be accounted for by any real modification of the characteristics of the Chinese population of California. The most acceptable explanation is that when it became advantageous to reduce the competition from the Chinese, the stereotype was altered in a direction which would help to justify such action. In this historical case it seems reasonable to conclude that the change in the characteristics ascribed to the Chinese throws doubt on the notion that stereotypes must necessarily contain some truth.

Another Dutch sociologist, Den Hollander, has studied the historical changes in the stereotype of the Hungarians in Europe. He points out that for centuries after the migration of Hungarians to Central Europe, they had a bad reputation, and were regarded as culturally different, and therefore inferior, to Europeans generally. During the 15th and 16th centuries, however, when they joined in the war against the Turks, they were pictured as a brave, devout, and chivalrous people.

By the second half of the 18th century their popularity had again declined, and they were described as savage, lazy, egotistical, unreliable, and tyrannous. This picture changed again a little later, when the Hungarians became romanticized and idealized. Den Hollander believes that the image followed the pattern of political interrelationships; it seems unlikely that there was sufficient transformation in the character of the people to justify the change in the national image.

One of the most amusing examples of a stereotype which has apparently developed without any kernel of truth emerges from an investigation by Schoenfeld on stereotypes associated with proper names. Here again the technique used was a simple one. The American students who served as subjects in this study were given a list of eight proper names and a list of eight adjectives; their task was to "match" or pair each name with the adjective regarded as most appropriate.

Since there were 120 students, and eight names, the results to be expected by chance alone, that is to say, if no stereotype existed, would be 120 divided by eight, or 15 for each name. The actual results showed that 63 out of the 120 judges matched Richard with "good looking"; 58 judged Herman to be "stupid"; 59 judged Rex as "athletic"; 71 associated Adrian with "artistic"; and 104 agreed that Cuthbert was "a sissy." In a similar experiment with American girls judging feminine names, 54 regarded Minnie as stupid; 60 saw Linda as sophisticated; 69 said that Mary was religious; 58 that Maisie was talkative; and 73 that Agatha was middle-aged.

Although this study was done with American students, it seems quite certain that comparable stereotypes would be found in languages other than English.

In any case, it can hardly be argued that Richard is really better looking than John, or Herman more stupid than Cuthbert. To return to ethnic stereotypes, one significant study may be cited which demonstrates the manner in which stereotypes may develop without any basis in truth. The American sociologist, La Piere, studied the attitudes of residents of California towards first and second generation Armenian immigrants in Fresno County in that State. There was almost complete agreement that these Armenians had more than their share of faults, and the general attitude toward them was relatively unfriendly.

La Piere proceeded to question non-Armenians as to the reasons for their antipathies, and he was able to classify the answers into three stereotypes. In the first place, it was stated that Armenians were treacherous, lying, deceitful. In actual fact, when measured by the criterion of business integrity, the Armenian merchants turned out to be equal and frequently superior to others. In the second place, they were alleged to be parasites, making excessive demands upon charitable organizations, free clinics, etc. Actually, such demands by them were less than half of what would be expected in terms of their proportion of the population.

Finally, it was said that they had an inferior code of morality, and they were always getting into trouble with the law. In fact, police records showed that they appeared in only 1.5% of Police Court cases, although they constituted approximately 6% of the population. La Piere concludes that all of these stereotypes have one factor in common, viz. that they are definitely false. This does not mean that stereotypes *never* contain any truth. It does mean that they *can* develop without any truth whatsoever.

There is, however, the possibility that a little truth may enter into a stereotype through the back door, so to speak. A Frenchman, with considerable experience of international meetings, once said that when he had occasion to address such a meeting he usually did so in a rather oratorical, flowery, "Latin" style. He said that otherwise his Anglo-Saxon colleagues would be disappointed! When he was with other Frenchmen, he reverted to a quieter, more matter-of-fact, "un-Latin" manner, which really suited him personally much better.

In this case, the stereotype itself determined his behavior under certain circumstances, and undoubtedly reinforced the conviction of the Anglo-Saxons that they really knew what Frenchmen were like. More rarely, the stereotype may operate in reverse. A member of a group with the reputation for frugality, may go out of his way to spend freely, and tip lavishly; if the stereotype calls for lack of punctuality, he may make it a point to arrive at his destination well before the hour specified. Since, in that case, as was indicated above, he will probably be regarded as an exception, the stereotype will still prevail.

Stereotyped thinking may be *almost* inevitable, but there is good evidence that it can at least be reduced, if not eliminated. Eighteen years after the Katz and Braly study, another psychologist (Gilbert) applied the same technique to a new generation of Princeton students. He found that there was some persistence of stereotypes, but also a very important change which he describes as "a fading effect."

There is much less agreement among the students in 1950 than in 1932; any specific trait is usually checked by a much smaller proportion of students in the later study. In 1932, for example, 84% of the students described the Negroes as lazy; in 1950 the percentage had dropped to 31. The description of Italians as artistic drops from 83 to 28.

In London, a UNESCO study conducted by H. E. O. James and Cora Tenen, showed how specific personal experiences might affect the nature and content of stereotypes. What they did was to obtain from school-children their opinions of other ethnic groups, particularly of African Negroes, and then bring them into contact with two able African women teachers who spent a few weeks in the schools.

The "before and after" picture is very striking. As an example, a child before the experience stated that "I do not like black people; it's the colour; it makes me nervous; they might be savage . . . they are different in nature to us, more savage and cruel sometimes, so you don't trust them ever." The same child after the experience said: "Miss V. and Miss W. were nice people . . . there does not seem any difference between them and us except the colour. I think that Negroes are like that—just like us, except for the colour. I like them. They are nice people."

The authors give many examples of similar changes that occurred. Stereotypes cannot always be modified so strikingly nor so fast, but the fact that they can be changed at all as a result of experience is itself encouraging.

Sometimes just growing older helps. In a study sponsored by UNESCO, Plaget and Weil report the results of a series of interviews with Swiss children of different ages. One interview with a little girl aged eight years ran as follows:

"Have you heard of foreigners?—Yes, there are Germans and French.—Are there any differences between these foreigners?—Yes, the Germans are bad, they are always making war. The French are poor and everything is dirty there.

Then I have heard of Russians, but they are not at all nice.—Do you have any personal knowledge of the French, Germans, or Russians, or have you read something about them?—No.—Then how do you know?—Everyone says so."

On the other hand, a boy aged thirteen years, after having mentioned a large number of foreign countries of which he had heard, was asked, "Are there any differences between all those countries?", and his answer was, in part, *you find all types of people everywhere.*" We are not all as "mature" as this 13-year-old boy, but perhaps we can move in that direction. Or is it possible that the Swiss are . . . ? Oh no! No stereotypes!

The understanding of national characteristics represents an important task for all of us. . . . The difficulties in the way are great: nations are made up of many different kinds of individuals, and generalizations are dangerous if they do not give adequate consideration to the range of individual variations.

An important first step will be taken if we treat "the pictures in our heads" with a strong dose of scepticism, and if we keep our minds closed to stereotypes and open only to facts. No one is denying the existence of national characteristics.

A knowledge of them can aid our understanding of people, as well as our enjoyment of the varieties of behaviour and personality that are found in different parts of the world. We need to make sure, however, that the "pictures in our heads" correspond as closely as possible to reality.

✦ 85 ✦

RACE RELATIONS AND
THE SOCIOLOGICAL IMAGINATION

Everett C. Hughes

In the current era of racial demonstrations and conflict, character-ized by strongly held beliefs, the sociologist may miss his oppor-tunity to analyze the social processes and problems in which he is involved as a member of society. Hughes, on the other hand, has capitalized on this and shows here, through a comparative exam-

SOURCE: *American Sociological Review*, Vol. 28, No. 6, (December, 1963), 879–90. Reprinted by permission of the author and the publisher.
✧ The author is professor of sociology at Brandeis University. He was formerly president of the American Sociological Association, and this selection is from his presidential address. He is coauthor of *Where Peoples Meet: Racial and Ethnic Frontiers, Twenty Thousand Nurses Tell Their Story,* and *Boys in White: Student Culture in Medical School.* He is also the coeditor of *Race: Individual and Collective Behavior.*

ination of race relations in the United States and Canada, that such relations can provide a laboratory for sociological study. The struggle of the Negroes and of the French Canadians for equal rights has given rise to strong social movements—the aims of which are to improve the status of the members. But the direction of change desired by these groups varies greatly. The French Canadians wish to become more distinct as a group, while the Negroes seek to become less distinct. Gaining an understanding of such movements and predicting their outcome require imaginative and rigorous social research.

What is there new to say about race relations? A colleague with great knowledge and deep experience of American race relations—he is a Negro —asked me that. I could have answered that new things are happening in race relations here and all over the world; things from which we can still learn.

A younger colleague who builds models and tries them out in the laboratory wanted to know to what general theoretical problem I would direct this discussion. I could have answered that race relations are so much a feature of most societies, and that they are in such flux that one could find in them a living laboratory for almost any problem of social interaction, social identity and social structure which one could imagine.

While these points are indeed part of my discussion, a deeper question concerning sociology and social life lurks in the background: Why did social scientists—and sociologists in particular—not foresee the explosion of collective action of Negro Americans toward immediate full integration into American society? It is but a special instance of the more general question concerning sociological foresight of and involvement in drastic and massive social changes and extreme forms of social action.

Robert E. Park defined race relations thus:

. . . the term . . . includes all the relations which exist between members of different ethnic and genetic groups which are capable of provoking race conflict and race consciousness, or of determining the relative status of the racial groups of which a community is composed. . . .

Park's definition makes study of race relations a part of the study of society itself, not a peculiar problem requiring special concepts for its analysis.

In the same paper Park—it was in 1939—spoke of a great movement among "national minorities to control and direct their own destinies;" a movement "which began in Europe in the early part of the last century, and has now spread, as if it were contagious, to every part of the world; every part of the world at any rate, which has felt or still feels itself oppressed in its provincial, autonomous life, or for any other reason, inferior in its international status."

The relations among races are now even more disturbed than when Park wrote. They offer a richer and more varied living laboratory than ever for any of us sociologists who would consider going abroad other than to attend conferences. But it is not precisely a laboratory which they offer, for we have but one chance to observe, to understand and to act.

Of course, we need not go abroad. Racial turmoil is here at home. In North America, two elderly nation-states—as those things go—contain two of the oldest established minorities of the world, Negro Americans and French Canadians. When I call them old, I refer to the duration of their position in the nation-states of which they are a part. Negro Americans, aided by some others, are engaged in their most massive, determined, urgent and detailed struggle for equality. French Canadians are vigorously demanding an overhaul of the century-old bargain sealed by the Confederation of the provinces into a single dominion.

Although there have always been agitators in both minorities, there have been long periods of quiet in which there was an entente between the leading classes of each minority and the dominant groups and implicit acceptance of it by the masses of the people. During these periods the dominant group apparently thought that an equilibrium had been established for an indefinite period, with changes going on so slowly as not to upset it. One might have said of both American and Canadian society what Park says of all:

Every society represents an organization of elements more or less antagonistic to each other but united for the moment, at least, by an arrangement which defines the reciprocal relations and respective sphere of action of each. This accommodation, this *modus vivendi*, may be relatively permanent as in a society constituted by castes, or quite transitory as in societies made up of open classes. In either case, the accommodation, while it is maintained, secures for the individual or for the group a recognized status. . . .

In the accommodation, then, antagonism of the hostile elements is, for the time being, regulated, and conflict disappears as overt action, although it remains latent as a potential force. With a change in the situation, the adjustments that had hitherto held in control the antagonistic forces fail. There is confusion and unrest which may result in open conflict. Conflict . . . invariably issues in a new accommodation or social order, which in general involves a changed status in the relations among the participants.

Park's view of society is that status arrangements are always tentative and likely to be questioned. In our two minorities, many of the younger people are questioning the bargain—the status arrangement—made by their forebears and consented to by their elders (for failure to act is considered consent). But what is the time perspective of parties to a bargain? The group with the greatest interest in the status quo may be expected to think of the arrangement as permanent, and to justify it by various devices —such as the doctrine of racial superiority and inferiority. The group disadvantaged in status may use some principle of permanency, which has been violated by the status-bargain forced upon them. Thus a national minority, such as the French Canadian, will prove that it was there first; that it is an older nation than the oppressor. The function of folklore is to establish antiquity and the rights based upon it. . . .

In both our minorities, the Negro-American and the French-Canadian, the time perspectives of past bargains are being called into question; in both cases, the dominant group asks either that the bargain be permanent or that it be changed but slowly.

Why the great outbreak of unrest and demand for change in these two minorities at just this moment? Certainly there have been great changes in the situation of both. At the last census, French Canadians had become more urban than other Canadians; Negroes, more urban than other Americans. With the precipitous drop in the agricultural labor force of both countries, these minorities have undergone changes of occupational structure probably greater than those of the rest of the population. Both minorities, in the industrial and urban order in which their fate now lies, are concentrated at lower points of the socio-economic scale than are the dominant groups.

These similarities may appear strained. They cover great differences. French Canadians do not, and never have, suffered civil or personal disabilities; they have not had to give deference to others. No social rank inheres in being French Canadian; the only aristocracy Canada ever had was French. French institutions in Canada are more venerable than English. French Canadians have headed the national government and always control the governments of their province and of most cities within it.

The two minorities are alike in that they have gone from a rural condition to an urban and see themselves as thereby put into a position of increased disadvantage; and at precisely that time in history when such disadvantage is no longer a purely domestic matter. But they seek opposite remedies. The Negro Americans want to disappear as a defined group; they want to become invisible as a group, while each of them becomes fully visible as a human being. Only so will they, in the myriad relations of American life, be judged by the characteristics pertinent to each. They want to be seen, neither as Negroes nor as if they were not; but as if it did not matter. The French Canadians, on the other hand, struggle not for survival as individuals—in which their problems are those of other Canadians—but for survival as a group with full social, economic and political standing.

These two apparently opposite goals represent one of the dialectics of human beings and the groups with which they identify themselves and are identified. How like others, how different from them shall I, shall we, can I, can we, be? And in what respects? Jews in the western world are generally thought to find these questions difficult, and the solutions unstable. Such a group as Negro Americans is at one pole—where all is to be gained from reduction of the social perception of differences. Their end will have been gained when Negroid characteristics and African descent matter no more and no less than other physical traits and quirks of ancestry. At that point, there would be no racial bargain. Whether all persons known as Negroes—and their descendants of that future day—would be content to wipe out their collective past and all features of Negro-American culture is another matter.

Some Negro Americans have given up hope that white Americans will ever live up to the bargain of the American ideology of equal rights for all. They reject everything American—the country, the Christian religion, their Anglo-Saxon names; as so-called Black Muslims they claim complete and eternal difference from white Americans and seek to develop such solidarity among Negroes as will enable them to fight and bargain for a separate realm. To support their claim, they have imagined themselves a glorious past as the Muslims who were the scourge of Europe and Christianity throughout the centuries. They project themselves into an apocalyptic future when . . . their ship will come in and the evil white race will be destroyed. This, mind you, is not in the South Seas, in Black Africa or among dispossessed American Indians, but among urban Americans. The question one must ask is this: at what point do people so far lose confidence in the "others" with whom they are destined to live as to reject all the collective symbols of the common society, and to erase from their talk all phrases which imply common humanity. Such symbolic Apartheid has not been the prevailing mind of Negro Americans, but it lurks ready to be called into the open with every alienating rebuff. The balance is still with the movement for complete integration.

Indeed it is so much so that some Negroes are claiming special treatment in order to make the integration more rapid, on the ground that past discrimination has loaded them with a competitive disadvantage which it will take a long time to overcome. Thus, for the moment, they appear to be asking that their Negro-ness be not forgotten, in order that, in the long run, it may be. It is the vigor and urgency of the Negro demand that is new, not its direction or the supporting ideas. It was the vigor and urgency that sociologists, and other people, did not foresee, even though they knew that Negroes would not be content forever with their situation, and should have sensed that the contradiction between "speed" and "deliberate" would become the object of both wit and anger.

In Canada, the tension between French and English has always existed, and has always turned upon the question of the survival and status of the French as a linguistic, cultural and political entity. French Canadians believe that a large proportion of English Canadians assume that French Canada will and ought to cease to exist, just as English Canadians believe that many Americans assume that Canada itself will and ought to cease to exist. From time to time, the tension becomes great and various French nationalist movements arise. In time of war, English Canadians accuse French Canadians of less than full devotion to the cause, while French Canadians resent the attempt of the others to tell them their duty. In the great depression there was tension over jobs and the burden of unemployment centering about the fact that management and ownership of industry were English, while labor was French.

The present movement is the first major one in time of peace and prosperity, when critics can say, and do, "They never had it so good. What do they want anyway?" To be sure it is a *drôle de paix* in which some other Canadians wish the French might join more heartily in the campaign against Castro—as they ought, it is said, being Catholics and therefore presumably leaders in the battle against Communism. Not only are the circumstances different from the times of earlier national upsurgings, but the very rhetoric is contrary, and some of the most ardent of earlier leaders are dubbed compromisers, or even traitors.

Most earlier French nationalist leaders called upon their fellow Canadians to respect the bargain of Confederation everywhere in Canada; bilingualism and public support of Catholic schools should prevail, or at least be tolerated, everywhere, not only in Quebec. The French were to have parity, their just proportion of all positions in government, and eventually in business and industry. But to merit their survival French Canadians should retain their rural virtues, including a high birth rate which would win for them, in due time, a victory of the cradle. To retain those virtues, their unemployed and the extra sons of farmers should go north to clear and settle new lands. Only so would they save themselves from the vices of the city, which were alleged to be English, American—and Jewish. To document their charter-membership of Canada, they cultivated folklore and song; their novelists wrote of the clearing of the land, of the drive of logs down the rivers after the spring thaw, of the land passing from father to son. They emphasized their place as the true Canadians—*Canadiens* without qualifying adjective—while English Canadians were *Anglais*, or perhaps *Canadiens anglais*.

Thus equal rights with English in a common country was the theme of most of the earlier leaders, and was the sentiment of most French Canadians, whether active in any movement or not. But the new movement talks of separation of the State, not Province, of Quebec from Canada; if not separation, then a new constitution giving Quebec a special status. It calls the French people of Quebec by the name *Québecois*. English Canadians are called Canadians, with English spelling, and the French word Canadien, is avoided. The government in Ottawa is spoken of as an alien power maintaining unjust colonial rule; the *Québecois* are chid for allowing themselves to remain the only white colonized people in the world and, indeed, one of the few colonized peoples, white or colored. Instead of seeking bilingualism everywhere in Canada, the more extreme wing—and even some quite conservative groups—ask for a Quebec with one language, French, and complete fiscal independence from Canada. The movement takes the doctrine of the nation-state in its extreme form as defining the goal to be attained.

Instead of praising rural life, they speak of an urban and industrial Quebec, which will solve its problems by becoming master in its own house. They dismiss return to the land and the victory of the cradle as dreams that divert French Canadians from attaining realistic goals. Those goals of well-being for an urban and industrial people are to be gained by socialistic means, and by breaking the power of Yankee capitalism.

The new rhetoric may not be used in extreme form by many, but it has permeated a great deal of French-Canadian writing and political talk. It has spread much more rapidly than any one expected. There are indeed some extreme groups who have turned to the bombing of symbols of British hegemony—a statue of Queen Victoria, an army recruiting station, and mailboxes in what is considered a well-to-do English quarter. The members of this small terrorist sect are not the leaders of the separatist movement, but their existence and temper indicate the intensity of the general feeling of malaise. Those arrested and accused of the bombings are alienated young men of the city, not intellectuals, but part of the white-collar Lumpen-proletariat, semi-employed. It has been said that the whole separatist movement is one of the little bureaucrats of business and government. In its more moderate form, the movement has certainly been joined by many people of various classes, whose rhetoric also turns in the direction of a special status for the State of Quebec, of a renegotiation of the terms of Confederation.

To return to this country, the new things about the Negro movement are not its ultimate goals and its rhetoric, but its immediate goals, its mass and its structure. It got under way and took on mass as a struggle for the equal right to consume goods and services—food, transportation, education, housing and entertainment. This is a goal of people with at least some money to spend and with the aspiration to spend as others do. The Negro Americans who led those first sit-ins were indeed so American that they seem more humiliated by not being able to spend the dollar than they would be at not having a dollar to spend. "My money is as good as the other fellow's," is probably the ultimate expression of American democracy. Here we meet the great paradox in American social structure. While our race line is, next to South Africa's, the world's tightest, we have the times-over largest Negro middle class in the world, and the largest group of Negroes approaching middle-class western tastes and with the money to satisfy them in some measure. This may be due to the fact that we are that country in which industry first depended upon its own workers to be its best customers, and in which movement has gone farthest in that direction. Handicapped though Negro Americans are in employment and income, they are well-enough off to resent the barriers which prevent them from keeping up with the white Joneses. This reflects a great change in the Negro social structure itself; goal and social structure are doubtless functions of each other. In the struggle for consumption it appears generally to have been true that the Negro participants were of higher social class than the whites who have set upon them, or perhaps it is that racial struggles bring out the low-class side of white people.

The older Negro middle class—in the clergy, teaching, law, medicine, insurance and undertaking—had its being in segregated institutions. They got support from white people and organizations with an implicit bargain that there was to be no Negro middle class except what could be supported by giving services to Negro clients and customers; as Park said, the accommodation gave certain Negroes a defined place and field of activity. Now that these institutions are undergoing changes . . . the very basis of the older Negro elite would be shaky even without changes in the race line itself.

But that line is changing. With every increase of access of Negroes to consumption and service institutions, the security of the older Negro middle class, which depended upon segregated delivery of services takes another blow; and another front is opened in the battle for equality in the production and distribution of goods and services. Like so many battles in time of great change, it is in part a battle of the generations. In the larger, more itinerant and cosmopolitan system of distributing professional services in which younger men must make their careers, sponsorship of specialized colleagues and the good opinion of their peers about the country counts more than favor with a local clientele or local white leader. While the standards of judgment among professional peers are in some respects objective and universal, yet the specialized colleagueships of the academic, scientific and professional world are small and relations are quite personal. People are loath to hire a stranger. . . .

Another new feature of the present movement is that some white people have joined not merely in financial support but in direct action itself. A few white Protestant, Catholic and Jewish religious dignitaries have lent not merely their voices, but also their bodies to the demonstrations. Larger numbers of young white persons, mainly students, have joined, perhaps at somewhat greater risk, in marches, demonstrations and sit-ins in both South and North.

Obstinate and irrational resistance is certainly in evidence, and apparently more on the consumption front than on the job front. Perhaps the American ego is more centered on symbolic consumption of housing among the right neighbors than on having the right job and colleagues. But what about those white people who join in the lively action on behalf of Negro equality? Are they really nothing more than sympathetic spectators? This raises questions concerning the part of people without status disadvantage in the struggles of those who have a disadvantage. The clergy and many white people are, for the first time, going into overt action on behalf of an external principle which they presumably believed and preached all the time. In this case, conscience seems to have been aroused only after the movement, initiated and led by the injured party, got momentum and showed some signs of success. This somewhat cynical suggestion is no answer to this problem: What circumstances so re-define a social situation that some espoused eternal moral principle is considered not merely to apply to it, but to require immediate drastic action of kinds the keepers of the principle ordinarily would not consider proper? Some years ago Samuel Stouffer discovered that the leaders of American communities are more liberal on many issues than are people of less influence. What his study did not throw light on is this: When do those tolerant leaders initiate action to implement their views? The answer on many issues is that they do not initiate action. In some Southern cities those leaders of the business community who would answer to Stouffer's description, enter to support the Negroes when the movement is under way and when stubborn opposition from another kind of community leader endangers prosperity and peace.

Whether white people will remain sympathetic is one question; whether they will remain spectators is another. The alternative to being a spectator is entering the action. The more insistent Negroes become on equality now, the more other people will be forced to act one way or another.

❖   ❖   ❖   ❖   ❖

I should not like to predict what equilibrium, what compromises, supported by what bargains, will be reached in American race relations. But it looks as if no long-term bargain short of fully equal status is likely to be accepted by Negroes. Compromises in some groups and structures will last longer than in others, depending in part upon how rapidly participants turn over. Customers can turn over quickly; where kinship, seniority and long tenure prevail, as in some occupations and organizations, new kinds of people can come in only very slowly. Institutional time is not the time of social movements. Whether Negroes will be content to let old bargains stand where turn-over is slow, and whether they will be able to break slow-moving institutional processes are both questions which cannot be answered now. We must ask: What will be the rate of breakdown of the race line in various segments of society?

Even if we cannot answer these questions about the future state of things, we might at least speculate on them and even on that state in which it could be said that there is no longer a race problem. We might imagine a state of things in which Negroes and whites, as both are defined in our society, would be distributed in their chance proportions among all the occupational, income, educational, residential, or other cells in a great table of the population. That unlikely ultimate state could not be the immediate result of any bargain; it could come about only after a very, very long time in which Negroes could have penetrated, like some slow-moving dye, into the many small capillaries of our complex social system. Indeed, by the time it occurred, Negro and white, as discernible racial types, might long since have disappeared. That would take a long time, even if race as a barrier to inter-marriage were to disappear.

Last year I asked some students this question: "Suppose that tomorrow morning Americans were to wake up blind to all the distinguishing marks of race; what would be the long- and the short-term results?" One student, a mathematician, figured how many people of white, Negro, and mixed ancestry there would be in the country after certain numbers of generations. There were, in her formula, certain assumptions which do not correspond to the present reality, but we must allow that license to mathematicians. Another student thought that we are so in need of someone to subordinate, that we would immediately visit upon the Jews or some other minority all we now visit upon Negroes; that might be called the "sick" answer. Others based their answers to this science-fiction question on other assumptions and worked out other possibilities. One student, of his own initiative, imagined that all the inhabitants of Samoa, whom we affect to love and admire, landed one morning, miraculously multiplied but penniless, in Los Angeles—to stay. Whether things would have worked out as he described them, I do not know. The only sociologist of note who ever did anything of the sort in print, was Gabriel Tarde. He imagined a society in which men were all assured of plenty of food and other comforts with but a few minutes of labor each day; the economic friction was taken out of human interaction. He then gave his notions of what would happen to sex, music, the mind, and many other things. He even gave a gently satirical account, by members of that society, of a group called sociologists who had existed in some ancient time—Tarde's own time.

I do not claim that either Tarde or those students to whom I gave that absurd assignment produced probable predictions. At least, they exercised their sociological imaginations in ways that are unaccustomed. Some of them may, in the future, attack problems not by making predictions based on projecting slow trends of opinion a few years into the future, but by imagining a wide range of possibilities, and following out the fantastic and improbable ones as well as those which seem most likely and immediate.

❖   ❖   ❖   ❖   ❖

Some have asked why we did not foresee the great mass movement of Negroes; it may be that our conception of social science is so empirical, so limited to little bundles of fact applied to little hypotheses, that we are incapable of entertaining a broad range of possibilities, of following out the madly unlikely combinations of social circumstances.

It is sometimes said that sociology deals with only those processes of social behavior which are repeated again and again. That statement, useful in its way, may have been taken too seriously. A process may be repeatable, but it may occur in some set of circumstances which has never happened before or yet. Whenever before was there a race-caste of 20,000,000 people, literate, with the aspirations and basic skills of a modern industrial society, with money to spend and the tastes which make them want to spend it on the same things as do other people of highly industrial societies, yet limited by others in their full realization of all these things; living in a society which has preached that all men are created free and equal, and has practiced it not fully, but enough so that with every increase of education, standard of living and of middle-class achievement of the race-caste, the discrepancy between partial and full practice of equality becomes a deeper, more soul-searing wound. Why should we have thought, apart from the comfort of it, that the relations of the future could be predicted in terms of moderate trends, rather than by the model of the slow burn reaching the heat of massive explosion?

Another possible impediment to claiming our full license to consider every possible human arrangement is that we internalize limits on our sociological imagination. Most of us apparently go about tacitly accepting the cliché that whites and Negroes don't want to marry each other, and that white women are never attracted sexually by Negro men, without considering the circumstances in which it would no longer be true (if it is indeed true now). One of the accomplishments of Freud was to break the bonds of repression so that a person could make his memory match his outrageous impulses. One function of the sociologist is to be that sort of analyst *cum* model-building mathematician for human society, who will break the bonds of ordinary thought and moral inhibition so as to conceive a great variety of human situations, even the most outrageous. Perhaps we failed to foresee present racial movements because our whole inward frame is adapted to study of the middle range of behavior, with occasional conducted tours toward, but not dangerously near, the extremes.

The kind of freeing of the imagination that I am speaking of requires a great and deep detachment, a pursuit of sociological thought and research in a playful mood. But it is a detachment of deep concern and intense curiosity that turns away from no human activity. Such curiosity is not likely to develop in minds which are not deeply involved in human affairs, and not concerned with our impossible human race. Detachment and indifference are not the same. I believe those sociologists who will contribute most of the fundamental, comparative and theoretical understanding of human society and of any of its problems are those so deeply concerned with it as to need a desperate, almost fanatical detachment from which to see it in full perspective.

Our problem is not that we are too deeply involved in human goings-on but that our involvement is so episodic and so bound to the wheel of particular projects with limited goals; in short, that we are too professional. While professionalizing an activity may raise the competence of some who pursue it by standardizing methods and giving license only to those who meet the standard, it also may limit creative activity, by denying license to some who let their imagination and their observations run far afield, and by putting candidates for the license (Ph.D.) so long in a straitjacket that they never move freely again. Our problem, as sociologists, in the next few years will be to resist the drive for professionalizing, and to maintain broad tolerance for all who would study societies, no matter what their methods.

❖   ❖   ❖   ❖   ❖

. . . Finally there are among us some who look about the world for laboratory cases in which to study the problems of human society; and those who, deeply and passionately involved in some problem of real life, describe reality both with the intimacy and detail which comes from close participation and observation and with that utopian imagination which can conceive of all sorts of alternatives to the way things are now. If we encourage each other, and our students, to work in a variety of ways, and if we all make our projections into the future, the greater the chance that once in a while some of us will hit upon a prediction that will be right.

❖ 86 ❖

THE FIRE NEXT TIME

James Baldwin

This selection is presented in the chapter on social process to illustrate the failure and distortion of communication between dominant and subordinate strata of society. Such communication blockage may generate conflict. With blunt honesty, as essential to inter-racial understanding as it has been infrequent, Baldwin tells what his life was like as a black boy growing up in a Harlem dominated by inescapable and terrifying white authority. His revealing account can help the non-Negro reader grasp the deeper

SOURCE: James Baldwin, *The Fire Next Time* (New York: Dial Press, 1963), 29–41, 61–72, 80–96. Reprinted by permission of the author and the publisher. ❖ James Baldwin is a well-known American writer and is also active in the civil rights movement. Some of his works include the novels *Go Tell It on the Mountain, Giovanni's Room,* and *Another Country;* the book of essays *Notes of a Native Son;* and the plays *The Amen Corner* and *Blues for Mr. Charlie.*

meaning and more painful implications of the Black Muslim
movement and violent local racial explosions for modern America.

I underwent, during the summer that I became fourteen, a prolonged
religious crisis. I use the word "religious" in the common, and arbitrary,
sense, meaning that I then discovered God, His saints and angels, and His
blazing Hell. And since I had been born in a Christian nation, I accepted
this Deity as the only one. I supposed Him to exist only within the walls
of a church—in fact, of *our* church—and I also supposed that God and
safety were synonymous. The word "safety" brings us to the real meaning
of the word "religious" as we use it. Therefore, to state it in another, more
accurate way, I became, during my fourteenth year, for the first time in my
life, afraid—afraid of the evil within me and afraid of the evil without.
What I saw around me that summer in Harlem was what I had always
seen; nothing had changed. But now, without any warning, the whores and
pimps and racketeers on the Avenue had become a personal menace. It had
not before occurred to me that I could become one of them, but now I
realized that we had been produced by the same circumstances. Many of
my comrades were clearly headed for the Avenue, and my father said that
I was headed that way, too. My friends began to drink and smoke, and
embarked—at first avid, then groaning—on their sexual careers. Girls,
only slightly older than I was, who sang in the choir or taught Sunday
school, the children of holy parents, underwent, before my eyes, their
incredible metamorphosis, of which the most bewildering aspect was not
their budding breasts or their rounding behinds but something deeper and
more subtle, in their eyes, their heat, their odor, and the inflection of their
voices. Like the strangers on the Avenue, they became, in the twinkling
of an eye, unutterably different and fantastically *present.*

❖   ❖   ❖   ❖   ❖

. . . And I began to feel in the boys a curious, wary, bewildered despair,
as though they were now settling in for the long, hard winter of life. I
did not know then what it was that I was reacting to; I put it to myself
that they were letting themselves go. In the same way that the girls were
destined to gain as much weight as their mothers, the boys, it was clear,
would rise no higher than their fathers. School began to reveal itself, therefore, as a child's game that one could not win, and boys dropped out of
school and went to work. My father wanted me to do the same. I refused,
even though I no longer had any illusions about what an education could
do for me; I had already encountered too many college-graduate handymen.
My friends were now "downtown," busy, as they put it, "fighting the man."
They began to care less about the way they looked, the way they dressed,
the things they did; presently, one found them in twos and threes and
fours, in a hallway, sharing a jug of wine or a bottle of whiskey, talking,
cursing, fighting, sometimes weeping: lost, and unable to say what it was

that oppressed them, except that they knew it was "the man"—the white man. And there seemed to be no way whatever to remove this cloud that stood between them and the sun, between them and love and life and power, between them and whatever it was that they wanted. One did not have to be very bright to realize how little one could do to change one's situation; one did not have to be abnormally sensitive to be worn down to a cutting edge by the incessant and gratuitous humiliation and danger one encountered every working day, all day long. The humiliation did not apply merely to working days, or workers; I was thirteen and was crossing Fifth Avenue on my way to the Forty-second Street library, and the cop in the middle of the street muttered as I passed him, "Why don't you niggers stay uptown where you belong?" When I was ten, and didn't look, certainly, any older, two policemen amused themselves with me by frisking me, making comic (and terrifying) speculations concerning my ancestry and probable sexual prowess, and for good measure, leaving me flat on my back in one of Harlem's empty lots. Just before and then during the Second World War, many of my friends fled into the service, all to be changed there, and rarely for the better, many to be ruined, and many to die. Others fled to other states and cities—that is, to other ghettos. Some went on wine or whiskey or the needle, and are still on it. And others, like me, fled into the church.

For the wages of sin were visible everywhere, in every wine-stained and urine-splashed hallway, in every clanging ambulance bell, in every scar on the faces of the pimps and their whores, in every helpless, newborn baby being brought into this danger, in every knife and pistol fight on the Avenue, and in every disastrous bulletin: a cousin, mother of six, suddenly gone mad, the children parcelled out here and there; an indestructible aunt rewarded for years of hard labor by a slow, agonizing death in a terrible small room; someone's bright son blown into eternity by his own hand; another turned robber and carried off to jail. It was a summer of dreadful speculations and discoveries, of which these were not the worst. Crime became real, for example—for the first time—not as *a* possibility but as *the* possibility. One would never defeat one's circumstances by working and saving one's pennies; one would never, by working, acquire that many pennies, and, besides, the social treatment accorded even the most successful Negroes proved that one needed, in order to be free, something more than a bank account. One needed a handle, a lever, a means of inspiring fear. It was absolutely clear that the police would whip you and take you in as long as they could get away with it, and that everyone else—housewives, taxi-drivers, elevator boys, dishwashers, bartenders, lawyers, judges, doctors, and grocers—would never, by the operation of any generous human feeling, cease to use you as an outlet for his frustrations and hostilities. Neither civilized reason nor Christian love would cause any of those people to treat you as they presumably wanted to be treated; only the fear of your power to retaliate would cause them to do that, or to seem to do it, which was (and is) good enough. There appears to be a vast amount of confusion on this point, but I do not know many Negroes who are eager to be "accepted" by white people, still less to be loved by them; they, the blacks, simply don't wish to be beaten over the head by the whites every instant of our brief passage on this planet. White people in this country will have quite enough to do in learning how to accept and love themselves and each other, and when they have achieved this—which will not be tomorrow and may very well be never—the Negro problem will no longer exist, for it will no longer be needed.

People more advantageously placed than we in Harlem were, and are, will no doubt find the psychology and the view of human nature sketched above dismal and shocking in the extreme. But the Negro's experience of the white world cannot possibly create in him any respect for the standards by which the white world claims to live. His own condition is overwhelming proof that white people do not live by these standards. Negro servants have been smuggling odds and ends out of white homes for generations, and white people have been delighted to have them do it, because it has assuaged a dim guilt and testified to the intrinsic superiority of white people. Even the most doltish and servile Negro could scarcely fail to be impressed by the disparity between his situation and that of the people for whom he worked; Negroes who were neither doltish nor servile did not feel that they were doing anything wrong when they robbed white people. In spite of the Puritan-Yankee equation of virtue with well-being, Negroes had excellent reasons for doubting that money was made or kept by any very striking adherence to the Christian virtues; it certainly did not work that way for black Christians. In any case, white people, who had robbed black people of their liberty and who profited by this theft every hour that they lived, had no moral ground on which to stand. They had the judges, the juries, the shotguns, the law—in a word, power. But it was a criminal power, to be feared but not respected, and to be outwitted in any way whatever. And those virtues preached but not practiced by the white world were merely another means of holding Negroes in subjection.

It turned out, then, that summer, that the moral barriers that I had supposed to exist between me and the dangers of a criminal career were so tenuous as to be nearly nonexistent. I certainly could not discover any principled reason for not becoming a criminal, and it is not my poor, God-fearing parents who are to be indicted for the lack but this society. I was icily determined—more determined, really, than I then knew—never to make my peace with the ghetto but to die and go to Hell before I would let any white man spit on me, before I would accept my "place" in this republic. I did not intend to allow the white people of this country to tell me who I was, and limit me that way, and polish me off that way. And yet, of course, at the same time, I *was* being spat on and defined and described and limited, and could have been polished off with no effort whatever. Every Negro boy—in my situation during those years, at least—

who reaches this point realizes, at once, profoundly, because he wants to live, that he stands in great peril and must find, with speed, a "thing," a gimmick, to lift him out, to start him on his way. *And it does not matter what the gimmick is.* It was this last realization that terrified me and—since it revealed that the door opened on so many dangers—helped to hurl me into the church. And, by an unforeseeable paradox, it was my career in the church that turned out, precisely, to be my gimmick.

For when I tried to assess my capabilities, I realized that I had almost none. In order to achieve the life I wanted, I had been dealt, it seemed to me, the worst possible hand. I could not become a prizefighter—many of us tried but very few succeeded. I could not sing. I could not dance. I had been well conditioned by the world in which I grew up, so I did not yet dare take the idea of becoming a writer seriously. The only other possibility seemed to involve my becoming one of the sordid people on the Avenue, who were not really as sordid as I then imagined but who frightened me terribly, both because I did not want to live that life and because of what they made me feel. Everything inflamed me, and that was bad enough, but I myself had also become a source of fire and temptation. I had been far too well raised, alas, to suppose that any of the extremely explicit overtures made to me that summer, sometimes by boys and girls but also, more alarmingly, by older men and women, had anything to do with my attractiveness. On the contrary, since the Harlem idea of seduction is, to put it mildly, blunt, whatever these people saw in me merely confirmed my sense of my depravity.

It is certainly sad that the awakening of one's senses should lead to such a merciless judgment of oneself—to say nothing of the time and anguish one spends in the effort to arrive at any other—but it is also inevitable that a literal attempt to mortify the flesh should be made among black people like those with whom I grew up. Negroes in this country—and Negroes do not, strictly or legally speaking, exist in any other—are taught really to despise themselves from the moment their eyes open on the world. This world is white and they are black. White people hold the power, which means that they are superior to blacks (intrinsically, that is: God decreed it so), and the world has innumerable ways of making this difference known and felt and feared. Long before the Negro child perceives this difference, and even longer before he understands it, he has begun to react to it, he has begun to be controlled by it. Every effort made by the child's elders to prepare him for a fate from which they cannot protect him causes him secretly, in terror, to begin to await, without knowing that he is doing so, his mysterious and inexorable punishment. He must be "good" not only in order to please his parents and not only to avoid being punished by them; behind their authority stands another, nameless and impersonal, infinitely harder to please, and bottomlessly cruel. And this filters into the child's consciousness through his parents' tone of voice as he is being exhorted, punished, or loved; in the sudden, uncontrollable note of fear heard in his mother's or his father's voice when he has strayed beyond some particular boundary. He does not know what the boundary is, and he can get no explanation of it, which is frightening enough, but the fear he hears in the voices of his elders is more frightening still. The fear that I heard in my father's voice, for example, when he realized that I really *believed* I could do anything a white boy could do, and had every intention of proving it, was not at all like the fear I heard when one of us was ill or had fallen down the stairs or strayed too far from the house. It was another fear, a fear that the child, in challenging the white world's assumptions, was putting himself in the path of destruction. A child cannot, thank Heaven, know how vast and how merciless is the nature of power, with what unbelievable cruelty people treat each other. He reacts to the fear in his parents' voices because his parents hold up the world for him and he has no protection without them. I defended myself, as I imagined, against the fear my father made me feel by remembering that he was very old-fashioned. Also, I prided myself on the fact that I already knew how to outwit him. To defend oneself against a fear is simply to insure that one will, one day, be conquered by it; fears must be faced. As for one's wits, it is just not true that one can live by them—not, that is, if one wishes really to live. That summer, in any case, all the fears with which I had grown up, and which were now a part of me and controlled my vision of the world, rose up like a wall between the world and me, and drove me into the church.

✧   ✧   ✧   ✧   ✧

I had heard a great deal, long before I finally met him, of the Honorable Elijah Muhammad, and of the Nation of Islam movement, of which he is the leader. I paid very little attention to what I heard, because the burden of his message did not strike me as being very original; I had been hearing variations of it all my life. I sometimes found myself in Harlem on Saturday nights, and I stood in the crowds, at 125th Street and Seventh Avenue, and listened to the Muslim speakers. But I had heard hundreds of such speeches—or so it seemed to me at first. Anyway, I have long had a very definite tendency to tune out the moment I come anywhere near either a pulpit or a soapbox. What these men were saying about white people I had often heard before. And I dismissed the Nation of Islam's demand for a separate black economy in America, which I had also heard before, as willful, and even mischievous, nonsense. Then two things caused me to begin to listen to the speeches, and one was the behavior of the police. After all, I had seen men dragged from their platforms on this very corner for saying less virulent things, and I had seen many crowds dispersed by policemen, with clubs or on horseback. But the policemen were doing nothing now. Obviously, this was not because they had become more human but because they were under orders and because they were afraid. And indeed they were, and I was delighted to see it. There they stood, in twos and threes and fours, in their Cub Scout uniforms and with their Cub Scout faces, totally unprepared, as is the way with American he-men, for anything that could not be settled with a club or a fist or a gun. I might have pitied them if I had not found myself in their hands so often and discovered, through ugly experience, what they were like when *they* held the power and what they were like when *you* held the power. The behavior of the crowd, its silent intensity, was the other thing that forced me to reassess the speakers and their message. I sometimes think, with despair, that Americans will swallow whole any political speech whatever—we've been doing very little else, these last, bad years—so it may not mean anything to say that this sense of integrity, after what Harlem, especially, has been through in the way of demagogues, was a very startling change. Still, the speakers had an air of utter dedication, and the people looked toward them with a kind of intelligence of hope on their faces—not as though they were being consoled or drugged but as though they were being jolted.

Power was the subject of the speeches I heard. We were offered, as Nation of Islam doctrine, historical and divine proof that all white people are cursed, and are devils, and are about to be brought down. This has been revealed by Allah Himself to His prophet, the Honorable Elijah Muhammad. The white man's rule will be ended forever in ten or fifteen years (and it must be conceded that all present signs would seem to bear witness to the accuracy of the prophet's statement). The crowd seemed to swallow this theology with no effort—all crowds do swallow theology this way, I gather, in both sides of Jerusalem, in Istanbul, and in Rome—and, as theology goes, it was no more indigestible than the more familiar brand asserting that there is a curse on the sons of Ham. No more, and no less, and it had been designed for the same purpose; namely, the sanctification of power. But very little time was spent on theology, for one did not need to prove to a Harlem audience that all white men were devils. They were merely glad to have, at last, divine corroboration of their experience, to hear—and it was a tremendous thing to hear—that they had been lied to for all these years and generations, and that their captivity was ending, for God was black. Why were they *hearing* it now, since this was not the first time it had been said? I had heard it many times, from various prophets, during all the years that I was growing up. Elijah Muhammad himself has now been carrying the same message for more than thirty years; he is not an overnight sensation, and we owe his ministry, I am told, to the fact that when he was a child of six or so, his father was lynched before his eyes. (So much for states' rights.) And now, suddenly, people who have never before been able to hear this message hear it, and believe it, and are changed. Elijah Muhammad has been able to do what generations of welfare workers and committees and resolutions and reports and housing projects and playgrounds have failed to do: to heal and redeem drunkards and junkies, to convert people who have come out of prison and to keep them out, to make men chaste and women virtuous, and to invest both the male and the female with a pride and a serenity that hang about them like an unfailing light. He has done all these things, which our Christian church has spectacularly failed to do. How has Elijah managed it?

Well, in a way—and I have no wish to minimize his peculiar role and his peculiar achievement—it is not he who has done it but time. Time catches up with kingdoms and crushes them, gets its teeth into doctrines and rends them; time reveals the foundations on which any kingdom rests, and eats at those foundations, and it destroys doctrines by proving them to be untrue. In those days, not so very long ago, when the priests of that church which stands in Rome gave God's blessing to Italian boys being sent out to ravage a defenseless black country—which until that event, incidentally, had not considered itself to be black—it was not possible to believe in a black God. To entertain such a belief would have been to entertain madness. But time has passed, and in that time the Christian world has revealed itself as morally bankrupt and politically unstable. The Tunisians were quite right in 1956—and it was a very significant moment in Western (and African) history—when they countered the French justification for remaining in North Africa with the question "Are the *French* ready for self-government?" Again, the terms "civilized" and "Christian" begin to have a very strange ring, particularly in the ears of those who have been judged to be neither civilized nor Christian, when a Christian nation surrenders to a foul and violent orgy, as Germany did during the Third Reich.

❖   ❖   ❖   ❖   ❖

The treatment accorded the Negro during the Second World War marks, for me, a turning point in the Negro's relation to America. To put it briefly, and somewhat too simply, a certain hope died, a certain respect for white Americans faded. One began to pity them, or to hate them. You must put yourself in the skin of a man who is wearing the uniform of his country, is a candidate for death in its defense, and who is called a "nigger" by his comrades-in-arms and his officers; who is almost always given the hardest, ugliest, most menial work to do; who knows that the white G.I. has informed the Europeans that he is subhuman (so much for the American male's sexual security); who does not dance at the U.S.O. the night white soldiers dance there, and does not drink in the same bars white soldiers drink in; and who watches German prisoners of war being treated by Americans with more human dignity than he has ever received at their hands. And who, at the same time, as a human being, is far freer in a strange land than he has ever been at home. *Home!* The very word begins to have a despairing and diabolical ring. You must consider what happens to this citizen, after all he has endured, when he returns—home: search, in his shoes, for a job, for a place to live; ride, in his skin, on segregated buses; see, with his eyes, the signs saying "White" and "Colored," and especially the signs that say "White Ladies" and "Colored Women"; look into the eyes of his wife; look into the eyes of his son; listen, with his ears, to political speeches, North and South; imagine yourself being told to "wait." And all this is happening in the richest and freest country in the world, and in the middle of the twentieth century. The subtle and deadly change of heart that might occur in you would be involved with the realization that a civilization is not destroyed by wicked people; it is not necessary that people be wicked but only that they be spineless. I and two Negro acquaintances, all of us well past thirty, and looking it, were in the bar of Chicago's O'Hare Airport several months ago, and the bartender refused to serve us, because, he said, we looked too young. It took a vast amount of patience not to strangle him, and great insistence and some luck to get the manager, who defended his bartender on the ground that he was "new" and had not yet, presumably, learned how to distinguish between a Negro boy of twenty and a Negro "boy" of thirty-seven. Well, we were served, finally, of course, but by this time no amount of Scotch would have helped us. The bar was very crowded, and our altercation had been extremely noisy; not one customer in the bar had done anything to help us. When it was over, and the three of us stood at the bar trembling with rage and frustration, and drinking—and trapped, now, in the airport, for we had deliberately come early in order to have a few drinks and to eat—a young white man standing near us asked if we were students. I suppose he thought that this was the only possible explanation for our putting up a fight. I told him that he hadn't wanted to talk to us earlier and we didn't want to talk to him now. The reply visibly hurt his feelings, and this, in turn, caused me to despise him. But when one of us, a Korean War veteran, told this young man that the fight we had been having in the bar had been his fight, too, the young man said, "I lost my conscience a long time ago," and turned and walked out. I know that one would rather not think so, but this young man is typical. So, on the basis of the evidence, had everyone else in the bar lost *his* conscience. A few years ago, I would have hated these people with all my heart. Now I pitied them, pitied them in order not to despise them. And this is not the happiest way to feel toward one's countrymen.

While I was in Chicago last summer, the Honorable Elijah Muhammad invited me to have dinner at his home. This is a stately mansion on Chicago's South Side, and it is the headquarters of the Nation of Islam movement. I had not gone to Chicago to meet Elijah Muhammad—he was not in my thoughts at all—but the moment I received the invitation, it occurred to me that I ought to have expected it. In a way, I owe the invitation to the incredible, abysmal, and really cowardly obtuseness of white liberals. Whether in private debate or in public, any attempt I made to explain how the Black Muslim movement came about, and how it has achieved such force, was met with a blankness that revealed the little connection that the liberals' attitudes have with their perceptions or their lives, or even their knowledge—revealed, in fact, that they could deal with the Negro as a symbol or a victim but had no sense of him as a man. . . .

I began to see that Elijah's power came from his single-mindedness. There is nothing calculated about him; he means every word he says. The real reason, according to Elijah, that I failed to realize that the white man was a devil was that I had been too long exposed to white teaching and had never received true instruction. "The so-called American Negro" is the only reason Allah has permitted the United States to endure so long; the white man's time was up in 1913, but it is the will of Allah that this lost black nation, the black men of this country, be redeemed from their white masters and returned to the true faith, which is Islam. Until this is done— and it will be accomplished very soon—the total destruction of the white man is being delayed. Elijah's mission is to return "the so-called Negro" to Islam, to separate the chosen of Allah from this doomed nation. Furthermore, the white man knows his history, knows himself to be a devil, and knows that his time is running out, and all his technology, psychology, science, and "tricknology" are being expended in the effort to prevent black men from hearing the truth. This truth is that at the very beginning of time there was not one white face to be found in all the universe. Black men ruled the earth and the black man was perfect. This is the truth concerning the era that white men now refer to as prehistoric. They want black men to believe that they, like white men, once lived in caves and swung from trees and ate their meat raw and did not have the power of speech. But this is not true. Black men were never in such a condition. Allah allowed the Devil, through his scientists, to carry on infernal experiments, which resulted, finally, in the creation of the devil known as the white man, and later, even more disastrously, in the creation of the white woman. And it was decreed that these monstrous creatures should rule the earth for a certain number of years—I forget how many thousand, but, in any case, their rule now is ending, and Allah, who had never approved of the creation of the white man in the first place (who knows him, in fact, to be not a man at all but a devil), is anxious to restore the rule of peace that the rise of the white man totally destroyed. There is thus, by definition, no virtue in white people, and since they are another creation entirely and can no more, by breeding, become black than a cat, by breeding, can become a horse, there is no hope for them.

There is nothing new in this merciless formulation except the explicitness of its symbols and the candor of its hatred. Its emotional tone is as familiar to me as my own skin; it is but another way of saying that *sinners shall be bound in Hell a thousand years.* That sinners have always, for American Negroes, been white is a truth we needn't labor, and every American Negro, therefore, risks having the gates of paranoia close on him.

In a society that is entirely hostile, and, by its nature, seems determined to cut you down—that has cut down so many in the past and cuts down so many every day—it begins to be almost impossible to distinguish a real from a fancied injury. One can very quickly cease to attempt this distinction, and, what is worse, one usually ceases to attempt it without realizing that one has done so. All doormen, for example, and all policemen have by now, for me, become exactly the same, and my style with them is designed simply to intimidate them before they can intimidate me. No doubt I am guilty of some injustice here, but it is irreducible, since I cannot risk assuming that the humanity of these people is more real to them than their uniforms. Most Negroes cannot risk assuming that the humanity of white people is more real to them than their color. And this leads, imperceptibly but inevitably, to a state of mind in which, having long ago learned to expect the worst, one finds it very easy to believe the worst. The brutality with which Negroes are treated in this country simply cannot be overstated, however unwilling white men may be to hear it. In the beginning— and neither can this be overstated—a Negro just cannot *believe* that white people are treating him as they do; he does not know what he has done to merit it. And when he realizes that the treatment accorded him has nothing to do with anything he has done, that the attempt of white people to destroy him—for that is what it is—is utterly gratuitous, it is not hard for him to think of white people as devils. For the horrors of the American Negro's life there has been almost no language. The privacy of his experience, which is only beginning to be recognized in language, and which is denied or ignored in official and popular speech—hence the Negro idiom —lends credibility to any system that pretends to clarify it. And, in fact, the truth about the black man, as a historical entity and as a human being, *has* been hidden from him, deliberately and cruelly; the power of the white world is threatened whenever a black man refuses to accept the white world's definitions. So every attempt is made to cut that black man down —not only was made yesterday but is made today. Who, then, is to say with authority where the root of so much anguish and evil lies? Why, then, is it not possible that all things began with the black man and that he was perfect—especially since this is precisely the claim that white people have put forward for themselves all these years? Furthermore, it is now absolutely clear that white people are a minority in the world—so severe a minority that they now look rather more like an invention—and that they cannot possibly hope to rule it any longer. If this is so, why is it not also possible that they achieved their original dominance by stealth and cunning and bloodshed and in opposition to the will of Heaven, and not, as they claim, by Heaven's will? And if *this* is so, then the sword they have used so long against others can now, without mercy, be used against them. Heavenly witnesses are a tricky lot, to be used by whoever is closest to Heaven at the time. And legend and theology, which are designed to sanctify our fears, crimes, and aspirations, also reveal them for what they are.

I said, at last, in answer to some other ricocheted questions, "I left the church twenty years ago and I haven't joined anything since." It was my way of saying that I did not intend to join their movement, either.

"And what are you now?" Elijah asked.

I was in something of a bind, for I really could not say—could not allow myself to be stampeded into saying—that I was a Christian. "I? Now? Nothing." This was not enough. "I'm a writer. I like doing things alone." I heard myself saying this. Elijah smiled at me. "I don't, anyway," I said, finally, "think about it a great deal."

Elijah said, to his right, "I think he ought to think about it *all* the deal," and with this the table agreed. But there was nothing malicious or condemnatory in it. I had the stifling feeling that *they* knew I belonged to them but knew that I did not know it yet, that I remained unready, and that they were simply waiting, patiently, and with assurance, for me to discover the truth for myself. For where else, after all, could I go? I was black, and therefore a part of Islam, and would be saved from the holocaust awaiting the white world whether I would or no. My weak, deluded scruples could avail nothing against the iron word of the prophet.

I felt that I was back in my father's house—as, indeed, in a way, I was—and I told Elijah that I did not care if white and black people married, and that I had many white friends. I would have no choice, if it came to it, but to perish with them, for (I said to myself, but not to Elijah), "I love a few people and they love me and some of them are white, and isn't love more important than color?"

Elijah looked at me with great kindness and affection, great pity, as though he were reading my heart, and indicated, skeptically, that I *might* have white friends, or think I did, and they *might* be trying to be decent—now—but their time was up. It was almost as though he were saying, "They had their chance, man, and they goofed!"

❖ ❖ ❖ ❖ ❖

Elijah's intensity and the bitter isolation and disaffection of these young men and the despair of the streets outside had caused me to glimpse dimly what may now seem to be a fantasy, although, in an age so fantastical, I would hesitate to say precisely what a fantasy is. Let us say that the Muslims were to achieve the possession of the six or seven states that they claim are owed to Negroes by the United States as "back payment" for slave labor. Clearly, the United States would never surrender this territory, on any terms whatever, unless it found it impossible, for whatever reason, to hold it—unless, that is, the United States were to be reduced as a world power, exactly the way, and at the same degree of speed, that England has been forced to relinquish her Empire. (It is simply not true—and the state of her ex-colonies proves this—that England "always meant to go.") If the states were Southern states—and the Muslims seem to favor this—then the borders of a hostile Latin America would be raised, in effect, to, say, Maryland. Of the American borders on the sea, one would face toward a powerless Europe and the other toward an untrustworthy and non-white East, and on the North, after Canada, there would be only Alaska, which is a Russian border. The effect of this would be that the white people of the United States and Canada would find themselves marooned on a hostile continent, with the rest of the white world probably unwilling and certainly unable to come to their aid. All this is not, to my mind, the most imminent of possibilities, but if I were a Muslim, this is the possibility that I would find myself holding in the center of my mind, and driving toward. And if I were a Muslim, I would not hesitate to utilize—or, indeed, to exacerbate—the social and spiritual discontent that reigns here, for, at the very worst, I would merely have contributed to the destruction of a house I hated, and it would not matter if I perished, too. One has been perishing here so long!

And what were they thinking around the table? "I've come," said Elijah, "to give you something which can never be taken away from you." How solemn the table became then, and how great a light rose in the dark faces! This is the message that has spread through streets and tenements and prisons, through the narcotics wards, and past the filth and sadism of mental hospitals to a people from whom everything has been taken away, including, most crucially, their sense of their own worth. People cannot live without this sense; they will do anything whatever to regain it. This is why the most dangerous creation of any society is that man who has nothing to lose. You do not need ten such men—one will do. And Elijah, I should imagine, has had nothing to lose since the day he saw his father's blood rush out—rush down, and splash, so the legend has it, down through the leaves of a tree, on him. But neither did the other men around the table have anything to lose. "Return to your true religion," Elijah has written. "Throw off the chains of the slavemaster, the devil, and return to the fold. Stop drinking his alcohol, using his dope—protect your women—and forsake the filthy swine." I remembered my buddies of years ago, in the hallways, with their wine and their whiskey and their tears; in hallways still, frozen on the needle; and my brother saying to me once, "If Harlem didn't have so many churches and junkies, there'd be blood flowing in the streets." *Protect your women:* a difficult thing to do in a civilization sexually so pathetic that the white man's masculinity depends on a denial of the masculinity of the blacks. *Protect your women:* in a civilization that emasculates the male and abuses the female, and in which, moreover, the male is forced to depend on the female's bread-winning power. *Protect your women:* in the teeth of the white man's boast "We figure we're doing you folks a favor by pumping some white blood into your kids," and while facing the Southern shotgun and the Northern billy. Years ago, we used to say, "*Yes,* I'm black, goddammit, and I'm beautiful!"—in defiance, into the void. But now—now—African kings and heroes have come into the world, out of the past, the past that can now be put to the uses of power.

And black has *become* a beautiful color—not because it is loved but because it is feared. And this urgency on the part of American Negroes is *not to be forgotten!* As they watch black men elsewhere rise, the promise held out, at last, that they may walk the earth with the authority with which white men walk, protected by the power that white men shall have no longer, is enough, and more than enough, to empty prisons and pull God down from Heaven. It has happened before, many times, before color was invented, and the hope of Heaven has always been a metaphor for the achievement of this particular state of grace. The song says, "I know my robe's going to fit me well. I tried it on at the gates of Hell."

It was time to leave, and we stood in the large living room, saying good night, with everything curiously and heavily unresolved. I could not help feeling that I had failed a test, in their eyes and in my own, or that I had failed to heed a warning. Elijah and I shook hands, and he asked me where I was going. Wherever it was, I would be driven there—"because, when we invite someone here," he said, "we take the responsibility of protecting him from the white devils until he gets wherever it is he's going." I was, in fact, going to have a drink with several white devils on the other side of town. I confess that for a fraction of a second I hesitated to give the address—the kind of address that in Chicago, as in all American cities, identified itself as a white address by virtue of its location. But I did give it, and Elijah and I walked out onto the steps, and one of the young men vanished to get the car. It was very strange to stand with Elijah for those few moments, facing those vivid, violent, so problematical streets. I felt very close to him, and really wished to be able to love and honor him as a witness, an ally, and a father. I felt that I knew something of his pain and his fury, and, yes, even his beauty. Yet precisely because of the reality and the nature of those streets—because of what he conceived as his responsibility and what I took to be mine—we would always be strangers, and possibly, one day, enemies. The car arrived—a gleaming, metallic, grossly American blue—and Elijah and I shook hands and said good night once more. He walked into his mansion and shut the door.

The driver and I started on our way through dark, murmuring—and, at this hour, strangely beautiful—Chicago, along the lake. We returned to the discussion of the land. How were we—Negroes—to get this land? I asked this of the dark boy who had said earlier, at the table, that the white man's actions proved him to be a devil. He spoke to me first of the Muslim temples that were being built, or were about to be built, in various parts of the United States, of the strength of the Muslim following, and of the amount of money that is annually at the disposal of Negroes—something like twenty billion dollars. "That alone shows you how strong we are," he said. But, I persisted, cautiously, and in somewhat different terms, this twenty billion dollars, or whatever it is, depends on the total economy of the United States. What happens when the Negro is no longer a part of this economy? Leaving aside the fact that in order for this to happen the economy of the United States will itself have had to undergo radical and certainly disastrous changes, the American Negro's spending power will obviously no longer be the same. On what, then, will the economy of this separate nation be based? The boy gave me a rather strange look. I said hurriedly, "I'm not saying it *can't* be done—I just want to know *how* it's to be done." I was thinking, In order for this to happen, your entire frame of reference will have to change, and you will be forced to surrender many things that you now scarcely know you have. I didn't feel that the things I had in mind, such as the pseudo-elegant heap of tin in which we were riding, had any very great value. But life would be very different without them, and I wondered if he had thought of this.

How can one, however, dream of power in any other terms than in the symbols of power? The boy could see that freedom depended on the possession of land; he was persuaded that, in one way or another, Negroes must achieve this possession. In the meantime, he could walk the streets and fear nothing, because there were millions like him, coming soon, now, to power. He was held together, in short, by a dream—though it is just as well to remember that some dreams come true—and was united with his "brothers" on the basis of their color. Perhaps one cannot ask for more. People always seem to band together in accordance to a principle that has nothing to do with love, a principle that releases them from personal responsibility.

Yet I could have hoped that the Muslim movement had been able to inculcate in the demoralized Negro population a truer and more individual sense of its own worth, so that Negroes in the Northern ghettos could begin, in concrete terms, and at whatever price, to change their situation. But in order to change a situation one has first to see it for what it is: in the present case, to accept the fact, whatever one does with it thereafter, that the Negro has been formed by this nation, for better or for worse, and does not belong to any other—not to Africa, and certainly not to Islam. The paradox—and a fearful paradox it is—is that the American Negro can have no future anywhere, on any continent, as long as he is unwilling to accept his past. To accept one's past—one's history—is not the same thing as drowning in it; it is learning how to use it. An invented past can never be used; it cracks and crumbles under the pressures of life like clay in a season of drought. How can the American Negro's past be used? The unprecedented price demanded—and at this embattled hour of the world's history—is the transcendence of the realities of color, of nations, and of altars.

"Anyway," the boy said suddenly, after a very long silence, "things won't ever again be the way they used to be. I know *that*."

❖   ❖   ❖   ❖   ❖

CHAPTER X

Social and Cultural Change:

DISORGANIZATION, PLANNING, AND VALUES

❦ 87 ❦

THE PROCESS OF ADJUSTMENT
TO NEW INVENTIONS

William Fielding Ogburn

We accept many miracles of modern scientific technology as commonplace: spacecraft that circle the globe in ninety minutes;
navigational aids that permit safe airplane travel regardless of local
visibility; on-the-spot and up-to-the-minute reports and interpretations of significant recent events in foreign capitals around the
globe by means of communication satellites; the atom-splitting
technology of nuclear physics that overnight makes necessary a
re-examination of the geography of crucial natural resources. The
list could be extended almost indefinitely. In this selection, William F. Ogburn's primary concern is "with how invention and
science affect international relations," a subject of overwhelming
importance. Incidental to this discussion, the principle of multiple
causation—almost always operative in social and cultural phenomena—is also clearly illustrated.

The subject of international relations is often presented in terms of
policies. These policies are generally seen in terms of choice, will, and action
by leaders. Bismarck's policy was one of moderation as compared to that

SOURCE: William Fielding Ogburn, Ed., *Technology and International
Relations* (Chicago: The University of Chicago Press, 1949), 16–27. Reprinted
by permission of the publisher. ✧ William Fielding Ogburn (1866–1959) was
professor of sociology, University of Chicago. His major interests were in sociology, social statistics, and statistical research. He was credited with the coinage
of the phrase "cultural lag." He is the author of *Social Change, American
Marriage and Family Relationships, You and Machines,* and *The Social Effects
of Aviation.*

of Kaiser Wilhelm. Or Bismarck chose to wage war. Stories of alliances, of national commitments, and of diplomatic strategy are dramatic accounts of human behavior. Then, too, the explanations of international action are frequently in terms of principles. The enemy wants to enslave the world; or we wish to make it safe for democracy.

Into such an atmosphere technology appears as a strange intrusion. Against the mighty force of morals it seems incidental rather than a determining force to be reckoned with seriously. For is not an invention an instrument to do man's bidding for such ends as he chooses?

Yet few would doubt that the early acquisition of steam power by the British before other states acquired it helped them to become the leading world power of the nineteenth century and thereby made the task of British diplomacy much easier. Britain's steel mills, with their products for peace and for war, enabled her to spread much more effectively the ways of European civilization into Africa and southern and southeastern Asia. Yet we are disposed to give credit to Gladstone, or even to Queen Victoria. Another illustration is the praise we extend to Columbus for the discovery of America. Yet without the new large boats and their equipment, this continent would not have been discovered from Europe; and with such boats, if Columbus had not lived, some other adventurous navigator would have made the discovery. No one thinks of attributing the discovery of America to a boat, though.

We may say, then, that technology makes possible certain human achievements, and we may also admit that without such material aids these achievements would not be possible. But there are other ways in which invention affects human action. The purpose of this chapter is to inquire into these processes.

Some Basic Conceptions

We begin by pointing out a restriction of the subject. We are concerned here only with how invention and science affect international relations and not with how international relations affects science and invention. Though we recognize that international relations, to wit, war, was a factor in developing the submarine, for instance, a more proper concern under this limitation would be with how the submarine affected international relations, to wit, Germany's relations with Britain, whose ships could, without the submarine, blockade the Baltic Sea.

Furthermore, when it is found that technology affects international relations, it is not to be implied that no other factor is of any influence. Several causes often exist, of which only one is a new invention. Thus the development of heavy industry, driven with mechanical power, in the Soviet Union will increase her might as a state. But so will the growth of her population of military age, which will occur at the same time that her factory production will be increased. The problem here, however, is to trace out the processes of one factor, technology, and not to appraise the relative strength of each of the many factors involved.

Quite a problem in analysis is what to do with the factor that does not change. For instance, shall we credit Britain's increase as a power in the nineteenth century to her coal mines? But the island had coal when it was not a power, as when the Romans or the Normans occupied it. Coal only becomes useful when there are steam engines in which to burn it. The coming of the steam engine, not coal, is the variable which explains the increase of Britain as a power in the nineteenth century.

The phenomenon we seek to explain is a variable, namely, a change in Britain's position as a power. A change must be explained in terms of a change. Thus the reader is reading this page not because there is oxygen in the air but for some other reason. The necessity of the oxygen in reading is apparent, but it is useless as an explanation of why a reader is reading this page instead of attending a theater, say, or reading something else.

Returning to the illustration of coal, while it has been a constant over time in Britain and hence could not explain a change in her position, coal is not a constant between two nations. Thus, France has little coal and Germany has much; hence coal is a factor in explaining why Germany is a greater power than France. In these illustrations coal is a variable over space but not over time.

An interesting question is whether human nature should be considered a constant. Sometimes it is and sometimes it is not. Between individuals there is great variation in some traits—desire for power, for instance. But between large populations, perhaps, the percentage of the population that desires power may be about the same.

If a new invention calls forth the same response from human beings in the societies being compared which use it, we think of the new invention, a variable, as a causative factor and not human behavior, which is in this situation a constant. Thus, in all cities, automobiles have developed suburbs. Human beings in all cities want more space in which to live. The desire for more space is a constant, then, from one large city to another. Hence we do not say that the desire for space caused the suburbs. The desire for space is a variable, though, between the open country and the city. Ranchers do not desire more space in which to live and do not use the automobile for that purpose.

Inventions are made relatively suddenly and are dropped, so to speak, into a social situation. Often this social situation is the same as to basic human attitudes before the invention occurs and after the invention is adopted. So we do not say that the attitude is a factor in explaining a change following the invention, because the attitude is a constant. These social situations may vary, though, from one country to another. Thus, the appearance of contraceptives in China may not lead to the same results as did their appearance in Protestant western Europe, for attitudes on the Chinese desire for children is different, with their ancestor worship and their familial institutions. So also the effect of the airplane on international relations would be quite different in a world situation which is not warlike from what it is in a world in which a power struggle is going on.

In international relations the variables often stressed are leaders, personalities, social movements, and organizations. These are important variables in explaining particular actions and specific achievements. But because of their significance the variations of the technological factors should not be obscured. . . .

One reason technological factors are obscured is that causes appear in a sequence like the links of a chain, and the link signifying the factor of technology is often somewhat removed and not so close to the change being explained as is the leader of a movement or the head of an organization. Thus, we observed the prime minister of the United Kingdom, as World War II came to a close, repeatedly advancing the interests of France in international conferences. But back of this British policy we note the invention of the rocket carrying an explosive and the airplane, both of which have rendered water barriers to Britain less effective and have increased the value of defense in depth. Britain becomes increasingly eager for a strong and a friendly France. Thus, the inclusion of France in many postwar actions is caused first by the political leaders, but also a cause back of that is the changed nature of war occasioned by new transportation inventions. This is not to say that there were not other factors or that Britain has not wanted the support of France long before these inventions of the airplane. It is rather that the increased need of Britain for France is caused by a change in technology.

One final observation should be made on the idea of inevitability, often implied in speaking of the influence of an invention. It is as though men had no choice in the matter. Thus, we think of the invention of gunpowder as inevitably changing the course of feudalism. But, it may be argued, men had the "choice" of using the explosive to propel missiles. The Chinese did not so use it. In the past, where the effect of invention in history has already occurred, we more readily admit inevitability than we do in looking to the future, where we seem to have choice, for instance, as to what we shall do about using the atomic bomb. We are using the word "choice" as it is popularly used and shall here not go beyond this conception. It may be preferable in referring to the future to speak of "adjustment to technology" rather than to the "effect of technology."

Inevitability and choice are a dichotomy of extremes. A more realistic approach is to think in terms of degrees of a continuum rather than of two extreme categories. Hence, it is preferable to think of the influences of invention in terms of probabilities. A good way of visualizing probabilities of a relationship of two variables is in terms of a correlation table, in which the coefficient may vary from zero to one, and, when it does, there are other factors involved which if unknown may carry the idea of chance or choice. It does not appear necessary that ideas of free will complicate the analysis in the paragraphs which follow.

The First Effects of an Invention

Let us start our inquiry with the fact of an invention. A new invention is made. It is here. In what ways will civilization be different because of it?

The first stage of inventional influence is in its use. It should be observed, however, that not every invention is used. Probably more than 90 per cent of them are not used. There appears to be a "choice" as to whether we shall make use of a scientific discovery or not. We did not choose to use poison gas in World War II. In other cases, where the demand is strong, continuous, and widely spread, the use is assured, as in the case of the discovery of anesthetics. All of us, except a few eccentrics, want to avoid pain.

Once a significant invention is widely used, there follow changes in the habits of the users. Steamships change the habits of sailors. So an early stage in the social effects of an invention is changes in the habits of users.

For an invention to be used, it must be produced. So, parallel with these changes due to use, there occur changes due to production. If we decide to use the atom bomb, new types of factors are set up. Using an invention makes changes due to its production inevitable, though there are some choices, as in the location of factories or in the materials to be used. The impact of an invention upon consumers and producers is generally recognized.

Derivative Influences

That the impact of inventions upon society extends beyond their influence upon consumers and producers is not generally appreciated. The influence of the long-range air bomber does not cease with its changes in the usages of warfare. It extends beyond and affects the foreign policies of states during peacetime. This influence on foreign policies is derived from its use and is therefore called a "derivative influence."

Derivative influences of science flow not only from users but also from producers. For instance, the changes in the production of explosives due to atomic fission have a derivative influence upon the relation of small states or outlying areas, with possible or actual uranium deposits, to great powers making atomic bombs. The competition for atomic bombs thus leads through the first stage of production to rivalries in the search for raw materials—a derivative effect from the production of the invention.

Why There Are Derivative Effects

The reason derivative influences spread from users and producers to social institutions is the existence of interconnections between the parts of civilization. Our modern culture is put together more like a clock, with its interrelationships of parts, than it is, let us say, like a chain, where some links may be changed without greatly affecting the whole. In a total war today almost every institution, every organization, is affected, so closely interconnected are the different parts of modern civilization.

Hence, if an invention through its use changes one part of our social organization, its influence does not stop there but extends toward the other parts of our social order which are connected with it. For instance, in societies, travel is interconnected with a system of lodgings. When one travels a long distance, one must have a place to spend the night away from home. If the method of travel which depends upon time schedules and a few fixed tracks is changed by the addition of the private automobile, independent of schedules and for which there are many different highways, a change in the system of lodging is inevitable, whether it be tourist camps, motels, or guest homes. Once we decide to use private automobiles for traveling long distances, the derivative change in the hotel system follows.

Sometimes the linkages between the parts of the social order are not so strong as that between travel and inns, in which case the derivative effect is not so certain. A rather weak linkage exists, for instance, between the transportation system and resettlement—not so strong as between transportation and temporary lodgings. The addition to overseas transportation of fast and large steamships with regular schedules was accompanied by an increase in emigration from Europe to America; but such a derivative effect as migration does not appear to follow inevitably solely because of the new invention of the steamboat. For, later, this immigration was stopped while the steamboats continued to run; nor did immigration occur in transportation across the Pacific Ocean. Thus it is not at all certain that resettlement will be a derivative influence of transportation changes.

The reason resettlement is not always a derivative effect of a new transportation invention is that transportation is only one of many factors in peoples' determining to change their home. Other factors are economic opportunity, population pressure, the fluctuations of the business cycle, and political barriers. Most social phenomena, like immigration, are the products of many different variables.

Convergence

Often several of these variables which operate to produce a social change are influences from several different inventions. The influences of these inventions are said to converge to bring about a result. A good illustration is the widening differential between the small powers and the large ones since the second World War. This is one of the effects of the air bomber. Small countries with few heavy industries cannot well provide the necessary defenses in fighter planes and antiaircraft guns to stop a great power's large destructive fleet of bombers. Furthermore, the development of the airplane is achieved much better in states with a great expanse of territory, which a small state does not have. With the ability of the air bomber to hit military objectives anywhere, the resistance of a small state is greatly weakened.[1]

The invention of the armored tank has the same general effect on widening the comparative military strengths of small and large states. So also do rockets and guided projectiles, especially if there are many cities in the small state. A great power can have more scientific laboratories and greater use of mass production. There then is the convergence of the influence of many different inventions to make the great power stronger and the little power weaker. In this case the influence of these different converging inventions is additive. In convergence the contribution of any invention to a social change is a fraction.

Successive Derivatives

We have shown that the effect of an invention does not stop with its uses. Nor does it stop with its first derivative influence. It proceeds to still other linked institutions. The process of successive derivative influences is much like the game of billiards when the cue ball strikes another, which in turn hits still another, and so on.

The invention of the cotton gin, for example, by removing a bottleneck to cotton utilization, led to increased production of cotton in the southern states by an expansion of slave labor, since the world demand for cotton cloth from the mills of England was very great. There followed a struggle for new slave territory in the western states about ready to be admitted to the Union as states. This struggle for political power between the northern and southern states accentuated the issue of a high tariff versus free trade, since the South could export more cotton with free trade and since the industries of the North could grow faster under the protection of a tariff. This struggle reached a climax in the War between the States. There were, then, a succession of derivative influences following the invention of the cotton gin.

It seems absurd to imply that the invention of the cotton gin caused the war of 1860–64. But such is not the implication. The cotton gin was only one factor, large or small, in a series of successive convergences of derivative influences, such as the expanding market for textiles from British factories, the opening of new lands for settlement, the development of new factories in northern states, etc.

The proportional influence of the cotton gin becomes smaller as new influences are added in successive convergences. If an inventional influence is one in three other influences on convergence No. 1, and the influence of convergence No. 1 is one in four other influences on convergence No. 2, then the invention's influence is only one in seven on the second con-

---

[1] Editors' Note: This selection was published in 1949. In 1966 the author would no doubt have discussed "missiles" instead of "bombers."

vergence. So the proportional influence of an invention diminishes through a succession of derivatives.

It is not customary to think of an invention like the cotton gin of the 1800's as having an influence on the tariff of the 1850's, for the invention of the gin is far removed not only in time but in successive convergences. Nevertheless, we may ask the pertinent question: "If the cotton gin had never been invented, would the tensions between the northern and southern states have reached an intensity great enough to start a conflagration of war?" The removal of an invention from society, if no substitute is provided, would show how far-reaching are its derivative influences.

Resistances to Technological Influences

Convergence is a phenomenon of social change. In a stationary society its analogue would be a pattern of linked parts of society. The family as an institution is linked to education, to production, to protection, etc. The appearance of a new invention in a system of linked material objects, institutions, and habits may modify the system, that is, the system adjusts to the invention.

These adjustments do not take place easily. Sometimes the pattern of a culture cannot assimilate a new invention. An area without coal and iron cannot assimilate the blast furnace, though it could buy the products of the Industrial Revolution. Japan could incorporate into its system the steam and steel complex, but the Australian aborigine could not. In other cases assimilation may be readily accomplished. To adopt the jet fighter plane by a country engaged in the war production of planes was not difficult.

An invention is, then, like a seed which may fall on different kinds of soil. The soils that are too sandy, too wet, too dry, or too rocky may be said to offer resistances to the growth from the seed. So there are obstacles to the adoption of inventions. A law was passed in Hungary in 1523 to prevent the use of four-wheeled coaches, since there was fear that the training of cavalry would be less effective. It should be observed that eventually the people of Hungary did use coaches.

There are also resistances to the derivative influences, as in the case of inventions of local transportation which have spread the economic city beyond the boundaries of the political city. There is great resistance to extending outward the political boundaries of an expanding city.

Similarly, the influence of various transportation, communication, and military inventions is to spread the influence of a state, which is a great center of dispersal, outward to the small border states, sometimes called a "zone of influence." But the influence of large states over the small neighboring political units is resisted. Any loss of sovereignty or change of boundary lines particularly is expected to be resisted. There are many linkages of different parts of a state with its political structure.

Lags

This resistance, which inventions and their influences meet, means delays in time in the spread of technological effects on society. One such delay is that of straightening highways and rail tracks to permit the speeds which new engines yield. The linkage is close, but the adjustment to the new speeds lags.

Some of these lags are very long indeed. The uniting of the European states economically or politically has lagged a long time after the inventions of production and transportation have made it possible and desirable and long after the disadvantage of this lack of union is evident in comparison with large united areas like the United States and the U.S.S.R.

The long lag in yielding to the influence of technological developments has made the correlation between technological change and social change more difficult to see. An illustration is the counties in the United States. The political units were laid out in the days of horse-drawn transportation and when the technology of production was on farms fairly equably distributed. Now the administration of counties would probably be better and cheaper per capita if a state had five or ten counties instead of a hundred. If the county lines are not changed, they will become less and less functional, and the adjustments to the new technological developments will be made by grants-in-aid, new taxation procedures, and the shifting of functions to states and cities. The long delays in adjustments obscure the correlation.

The Weight of the Technological Factor

We have now traced the main steps in the process of social changes flowing from inventions and scientific discoveries. But an analysis of the process is not an assessment of the importance of technology as compared with other factors. An analysis of ideational innovations would probably have shown somewhat similar processes. Regarding the relative importance of technological forces, a few remarks in the nature of theory will be made.

The Variability of Modern Technology

One reason we think technology is important in international relations is its great variability. There are many new and important inventions occurring every decade; facsimile transmission, radio telephone, jet propulsion, rockets, helicopters, radar, television, photography, litho-printing, plant hormones, alloys, atomic fission, and many others. Indeed, the number of inventions tends to grow exponentially.

The significance of the variability of invention lies in the fact that we do not consider a constant as a causal factor in change. It must be a variable that explains a variation. Thus a variation from sailing ships to steamships led to changes in British foreign policy. National interest is, of course, a factor in British foreign policy, but that is a constant which was present both before and after the appearance of the steamship, and does not explain the changes.

Another constant in international relations, at least for a time, is the desire for national security. The new inventions of war give emphasis to the policy of the Soviet Union to obtain a zone of security around it. The ideological constant is the desire for security. The new inventions lead to policies regarding particular countries.

The Variation in Ideologies

Ideologies vary, too; and, in so far as they do, they must be given weight. We have no conclusive answer as to whether in modern times as many important ideological factors vary as do important technological factors. We have recently seen the rise of fascism and communism, important ideological developments. It should not be assumed, however, that fascism and communism originated independently of technological changes. In some cases the technological factor in the origin of ideologies or their variation is clear. The safety-first movement, incorporating the social invention of workmen's compensation, was occasioned by the invention of fast-moving metal machines and vehicles. It may also be argued that the idea of the federation of the Western nations arises in part because of the variation in the transportation and military inventions. The ideology of "isolationism," so prominent in the United States, is being eliminated, by the airplane.

On the other side, ideologies cause changes in technology. The atom bomb, jet propulsion, and radar were creations of the war ideas. The influence of war on creating inventions is more the influence of demand arising from a social condition than the force of an ideology.

War is an illustration of a nontechnological factor that is not always a constant, not so much so as national interest and national security. The prospects of war vary from decade to decade and from one continent to another. Indeed, one foreign policy in which the people of the United States are deeply interested is to produce a more marked variation in this factor of war, that is, to eliminate it.

The foregoing discussion does not settle the question of the relative importance of technology but is rather an exploration of some aspects of the problem. In any case, the purpose of this paper is rather to describe the processes whereby technological change influences society.

Summary

We may now summarize the processes of change instituted by the appearance of an invention in our culture. Society is different, first, because of the new habits of users and producers of the invention, assuming the invention meets a demand and is not rejected. This first step in the impact of technology upon civilization is common knowledge. But the effect of an invention is not restricted solely to its direct influence on its users and its producers. Institutions and ideologies may also make adjustments to the new habits of users and consumers. Thus an invention has a derivative influence upon social institutions indirectly through its users or producers. This derivative influence is often not recognized by casual observers because it is once removed from the invention. This observation is most commonly left unmade in the case of a chain of successive derivative influences. The phenomenon of derivative influences arises because of the inter-correlation of the parts of culture.

The derivative influence of any particular invention is often not appreciated because it is only one of many converging influences, many of which flow from other inventions, mechanical or social. In the case of successive derivative convergences of inventions, the influence of one early invention may be comparatively small.

Because of the intercorrelation of the parts of culture and the fact that many social phenomena exist because of the presence of many factors, the effects of inventions are resisted or delayed until a favorable situation develops. Sometimes the derivative influence of an invention requires for an adjustment an ideational or social invention.

All these processes may be observed in the influence of the inventions of steam and steel, aviation, and other means of transportation, the atom bomb and the mass-communications inventions, upon the ranking of powers, the federation of nations, spheres of influence, and diplomatic procedure.

DEATH BY DIESELIZATION:
A CASE STUDY IN THE REACTION
TO TECHNOLOGICAL CHANGE

W. Fred Cottrell

The preceding selection discussed the "derivative effects" of new inventions or ways of doing things. These derivative effects occur because the parts of a society are interconnected. If a new development is generally considered "good," the public commonly takes the position that any derivative effects in the way of "costs" to small segments of the population are more than offset by the benefits to "society as a whole." We may even consider it unpatriotic or immoral for groups unfavorably affected by technological changes to call for reparations for the losses they suffer. This selection by W. Fred Cottrell dramatizes the widespread derivative effects of an invention and helps us to understand something of the position of those on whom the social costs of that invention fell most directly.

In the following instance it is proposed that we examine a community confronted with radical change in its basic economic institution and to trace the effects of this change throughout the social structure. From these facts it may be possible in some degree to anticipate the resultant changing attitudes and values of the people in the community, particularly as they reveal whether or not there is a demand for modification of the social structure or a shift in function from one institution to another. Some of the implications of the facts discovered may be valuable in anticipating future social change.

The community chosen for examination has been disrupted by the dieselization of the railroads. Since the railroad is among the oldest of those industries organized around steam, and since therefore the social structure of railroad communities is a product of long-continued processes of adaptation to the technology of steam, the sharp contrast between the technological requirements of the steam engine and those of the diesel

SOURCE: *American Sociological Review*, Vol. 16, No. 3 (June, 1951), 358–65. Reprinted by permission of the author and The American Sociological Association. ❖ The author is professor of sociology and political science at Miami University, Oxford, Ohio. He is interested in the effects of technology upon society and has written *The Railroader*, *Men Cry Peace*, and *Energy and Society*.

should clearly reveal the changes in social structure required. Any one of a great many railroad towns might have been chosen for examination. However, many railroad towns are only partly dependent upon the railroad for their existence. In·them many of the effects which take place are blurred and not easily distinguishable by the observer. Thus, the "normal" railroad town may not be the best place to see the consequences of dieselization. For this reason a one-industry town was chosen for examination.

In a sense it·is an "ideal type" railroad town, and hence not complicated by other extraneous economic factors. It lies in the desert and is here given the name "Caliente" which is the Spanish adjective for "hot." Caliente was built in a break in an eighty-mile canyon traversing the desert. Its reason for existence was to service the steam locomotive. There are few resources in the area to support it on any other basis, and such as they are they would contribute more to the growth and· maintenance of other little settlements in the vicinity than to that of Caliente. So long as the steam locomotive was in use, Caliente was a necessity. With the adoption of the diesel it became obsolescent.

This stark fact was not, however, part of the expectations of the residents of Caliente. Based upon the "certainty" of the railroad's need for Caliente, men built their homes there, frequently of concrete and brick, at the cost, in many cases, of their life savings. The water system was laid in cast iron which will last for centuries. Business men erected substantial buildings which could be paid for only by profits gained through many years of business. Four churches evidence the faith of Caliente people in the future of their community. A twenty-seven bed hospital serves the town. Those who built it thought that their investment was as well warranted as the fact of birth, sickness, accident and death. They believed in education. Their school buildings represent the investment of savings guaranteed by bonds and future taxes. There is a combined park and play field which, together with a recently modernized theatre, has been serving recreational needs. All these physical structures are material evidence of the expectations, morally and legally sanctioned and financially funded, of the people of Caliente. This is a normal and rational aspect of the culture of all "solid" and "sound" communities.

Similarly normal are the social organizations. These include Rotary, Chamber of Commerce, Masons, Odd Fellows, American Legion and the Veterans of Foreign Wars. There are the usual unions, churches, and myriad little clubs to which the women belong. In short, here is the average American community with normal social life, subscribing to normal American codes. Nothing its members had been taught would indicate that the whole pattern of this normal existence depended completely upon a few elements of technology which were themselves in flux. For them the continued use of the steam engine was as "natural" a phenomenon as any other element in their physical environment. Yet suddenly their life pattern was destroyed by the announcement that the railroad was moving its division point, and with it destroying the economic basis of Caliente's existence.

Turning from this specific community for a moment, let us examine the technical changes which took place and the reasons for the change. Division points on a railroad are established by the frequency with which the rolling stock must be serviced and the operating crews changed. At the turn of the century when this particular road was built, the engines produced wet steam at low temperatures. The steel in the boilers was of comparatively low tensile strength and could not withstand the high temperatures and pressures required for the efficient use of coal and water. At intervals of roughly a hundred miles the engine had to be disconnected from the train for service. At these points the cars also were inspected and if they were found to be defective they were either removed from the train or repaired while it was standing and the new engine being coupled on. Thus the location of Caliente, as far as the railroad was concerned, was a function of boiler temperature and pressure and the resultant service requirements of the locomotive.

Following World War II, the high tensile steels developed to create superior artillery and armor were used for locomotives. As a consequence it was possible to utilize steam at higher temperatures and pressure. Speed, power, and efficiency were increased and the distance between service intervals was increased.

The "ideal distance" between freight divisions became approximately 150 to 200 miles whereas it had formerly been 100 to 150. Wherever possible, freight divisions were increased in length to that formerly used by passenger trains, and passenger divisions were lengthened from two old freight divisions to three. Thus towns located at 100 miles from a terminal became obsolescent, those at 200 became freight points only, and those at three hundred miles became passenger division points.

The increase in speed permitted the train crews to make the greater distance in the time previously required for the lesser trip, and roughly a third of the train and engine crews, car inspectors, boilermakers and machinists and other service men were dropped. The towns thus abandoned were crossed off the social record of the nation in the adjustment to these technological changes in the use of the steam locomotive. Caliente, located midway between terminals about six hundred miles apart, survived. In fact it gained, since the less frequent stops caused an increase in the service required of the maintenance crews at those points where it took place. However, the introduction of the change to diesel engines projected a very different future.

In its demands for service the diesel engine differs almost completely from a steam locomotive. It requires infrequent, highly skilled service, carried on within very close limits, in contrast to the frequent, crude adjustments required by the steam locomotive. Diesels operate at about 35 per cent efficiency, in contrast to the approximately 4 per cent efficiency of the steam locomotives in use after World War II in the United States. Hence diesels require much less frequent stops for fuel and water. These facts reduce their operating cost sufficiently to compensate for their much higher initial cost.

In spite of these reductions in operating costs the introduction of diesels ordinarily would have taken a good deal of time. The change-over would have been slowed by the high capital costs of retooling the locomotive works, the long period required to recapture the costs of existing steam locomotives, and the effective resistance of the workers. World War II altered each of these factors. The locomotive works were required to make the change in order to provide marine engines, and the costs of the change were assumed by the government. Steam engines were used up by the tremendous demand placed upon the railroads by war traffic. The costs were recaptured by shipping charges. Labor shortages were such that labor resistance was less formidable and much less acceptable to the public than it would have been in peace time. Hence the shift to diesels was greatly facilitated by the war. In consequence, every third and sometimes every second division point suddenly became technologically obsolescent.

Caliente, like all other towns in similar plight, is supposed to accept its fate in the name of "progress." The general public, as shippers and consumers of shipped goods, reaps the harvest in better, faster service and eventually perhaps in lower charges. A few of the workers in Caliente will also share the gains, as they move to other division points, through higher wages. They will share in the higher pay, though whether this will be adequate to compensate for the costs of moving no one can say. Certain it is that their pay will not be adjusted to compensate for their specific losses. They will gain only as their seniority gives them the opportunity to work. These are those who gain. What are the losses, and who bears them?

The railroad company can figure its losses at Caliente fairly accurately. It owns 39 private dwellings, a modern clubhouse with 116 single rooms, and a twelve-room hotel with dining-room and lunch-counter facilities. These now become useless, as does much of the fixed physical equipment used for servicing trains. Some of the machinery can be used elsewhere. Some part of the round-house can be used to store unused locomotives and standby equipment. The rest will be torn down to save taxes. All of these costs can be entered as capital losses on the statement which the company draws up for its stockholders and for the government. Presumably they will be recovered by the use of the more efficient engines.

What are the losses that may not be entered on the company books? The total tax assessment in Caliente was $9,946.80 for the year 1948, of which $6,103.39 represented taxes assessed on the railroad. Thus the railroad valuation was about three-fifths that of the town. This does not take into account tax-free property belonging to the churches, the schools, the hospital, or the municipality itself which included all the public utilities. Some ideas of the losses sustained by the railroad in comparison with the losses of others can be surmised by reflecting on these figures for real estate alone. The story is an old one and often repeated in the economic history of America. It represents the "loss" side of a profit and loss system of adjusting to technological change. Perhaps for sociological purposes we need an answer to the question "just who pays?"

Probably the greatest losses are suffered by the older "non-operating" employees. Seniority among these men extends only within the local shop and craft. A man with twenty-five years' seniority at Caliente has no claim on the job of a similar craftsman at another point who has only twenty-five days' seniority. Moreover, some of the skills formerly valuable are no longer needed. The boilermaker, for example, knows that jobs for his kind are disappearing and he must enter the ranks of the unskilled. The protection and status offered by the union while he was employed have become meaningless now that he is no longer needed. The cost of this is high both in loss of income and in personal demoralization.

Operating employees also pay. Their seniority extends over a division, which in this case includes three division points. The older members can move from Caliente and claim another job at another point, but in many cases they move leaving a good portion of their life savings behind. The younger men must abandon their stake in railroad employment. The loss may mean a new apprenticeship in another occupation, at a time in life when apprenticeship wages are not adequate to meet the obligations of mature men with families. A steam engine hauled 2,000 tons up the hill out of Caliente with the aid of two helpers. The four-unit diesel in command of one crew handles a train of 5,000 tons alone. Thus, to handle the same amount of tonnage required only about a fourth the man-power it formerly took. Three out of four men must start out anew at something else.

The local merchants pay. The boarded windows, half-empty shelves, and abandoned store buildings bear mute evidence of these costs. The older merchants stay, and pay; the younger ones, and those with no stake in the community will move; but the value of their property will in both cases largely be gone.

The bondholders will pay. They can't foreclose on a dead town. If the town were wiped out altogether, that which would remain for salvage would be too little to satisfy their claims. Should the town continue there is little hope that taxes adequate to carry the overhead of bonds and day-to-day expenses could be secured by taxing the diminished number of property owners or employed persons.

The church will pay. The smaller congregations cannot support services as in the past. As the church men leave, the buildings will be abandoned.

Homeowners will pay. A hundred and thirty-five men owned homes in Caliente. They must accept the available means of support or rent to those who do. In either case the income available will be far less than that on which the houses were built. The least desirable homes will stand unoccupied, their value completely lost. The others must be revalued at a figure far below that at which they were formerly held.

In a word, those pay who are, by traditional American standards, *most moral*. Those who have raised children see friendships broken and neighborhoods disintegrated. The childless more freely shake the dust of Caliente from their feet. Those who built their personalities into the structure of the community watch their work destroyed. Those too wise or too selfish to have entangled themselves in community affairs suffer no such qualms. The chain store can pull down its sign, move its equipment and charge the costs off against more profitable and better located units, and against taxes. The local owner has no such alternatives. In short, "good citizens" who assumed family and community responsibility are the greatest losers. Nomads suffer least.

The people of Caliente are asked to accept as "normal" this strange inversion of their expectations. It is assumed that they will, without protest or change in sentiment, accept the dictum of the "law of supply and demand." Certainly they must comply in part with this dictum. While their behavior in part reflects this compliance, there are also other changes perhaps equally important in their attitudes and values.

The first reaction took the form of an effort at community self-preservation. Caliente became visible to its inhabitants as a real entity, as meaningful as the individual personalities which they had hitherto been taught to see as atomistic or nomadic elements. Community survival was seen as prerequisite to many of the individual values that had been given precedence in the past. The organized community made a search for new industry, citing elements of community organization themselves as reasons why industry should move to Caliente. But the conditions that led the railroad to abandon the point made the place even less attractive to new industry than it had hitherto been. Yet the effort to keep the community a going concern persisted.

There was also a change in sentiment. In the past the glib assertion that progress spelled sacrifice could be offered when some distant group was a victim of technological change. There was no such reaction when the event struck home. The change can probably be as well revealed as in any other way by quoting from the Caliente *Herald*:

. . . [over the] years . . . [this] . . . railroad and its affiliates . . . became to this writer his ideal of a railroad empire. The [company] . . . appeared to take much more than the ordinary interest of big railroads in the development of areas adjacent to its lines, all the while doing a great deal for the communities large and small through which the lines passed.

Those were the days creative of [its] enviable reputation as one of the finest, most progressive—and most human—of American railroads, enjoying the confidence and respect of employees, investors, and communities alike!

One of the factors bringing about this confidence and respect was the consideration shown communities which otherwise would have suffered serious blows when division and other changes were effected. A notable example was . . . [a town] . . . where the shock of division change was made almost unnoticed by installation of a rolling stock reclamation point, which gave [that town] an opportunity to hold its community intact until tourist traffic and other industries could get better established—with the result that . . . [it] . . . is now on a firm foundation. And through this display of consideration for a community, the railroad gained friends—not only among the people of . . . [that town] . . . who were perhaps more vocal than others, but also among thousands of others throughout the country on whom this action made an indelible impression.

But things seem to have changed materially during the last few years, the . . . [company] . . . seems to this writer to have gone all out for glamor and the dollars which glamorous people have to spend, sadly neglecting one of the principal factors which helped to make . . . [it] . . . great: that fine consideration of communities and individuals, as well as employees, who have been happy in cooperating steadfastly with the railroad in times of stress as well as prosperity. The loyalty of these people and communities seems to count for little with the . . . [company] . . . of this day, though other "Big Business" corporations do not hesitate to expend huge sums to encourage the loyalty of community and people which old friends of . . . [the company] . . . have been happy to give voluntarily.

Ever since the . . . railroad was constructed . . . Caliente has been a key town on the railroad. It is true, the town owed its inception to the railroad, but it has paid this back in becoming one of the most attractive communities on the system. With nice homes, streets and parks, good school . . . good city government . . . Caliente offers advantages that most big corporations would be gratified to have for their employees—a homey spot where they could live their lives of contentment, happiness and security.

Caliente's strategic location, midway of some of the toughest road on the entire system has been a lifesaver for the road several times when floods have wreaked havoc on the roadbed in the canyon above and below Caliente. This has been possible through storage in Caliente of large stocks of repair material and equipment—and not overlooking manpower—which has thus become available on short notice.

. . . But [the railroad] or at least one of its big officials appearing to be almost completely divorced from policies which made this railroad great, has ordered changes which are about as inconsiderate as anything of which "Big Business" has ever been accused! Employees who have given the best years of their lives to this railroad are cut off without anything to which they can turn, many of them with homes in which they have taken much pride; while others, similarly with nice homes, are told to move elsewhere and are given runs that only a few will be able to endure from a physical standpoint, according to common opinion.

Smart big corporations the country over encourage their employees to own their own homes—and loud are their boasts when the percentage of such employees is favorable! But in contrast, a high [company] official is reported to have said only recently that "a railroad man has no business owning a home!" Quite a departure from what has appeared to be [company] tradition.

It is difficult for the *Herald* to believe that this official however "big" he is, speaks for the . . . [company] . . . when he enunciates a policy that, carried to the letter, would make tramps of [company] employees and their families!

No thinking person wants to stand in the way of progress, but true progress is not made when it is overshadowed by cold-blooded disregard for the loyalty of employees, their families, and the communities which have developed in the good American way through the decades of loyal service and good citizenship.

This editorial, written by a member of all the service clubs, approved by Caliente business men, and quoted with approbation by the most conservative members of the community, is significant of changing sentiment.

The people of Caliente continually profess their belief in "The American Way," but like the editor of the *Herald* they criticize decisions made solely in pursuit of profit, even though these decisions grow out of a clear-cut case of technological "progress." They feel that the company should have based its decision upon consideration for loyalty, citizenship, and community morale. They assume that the company should regard the seniority rights of workers as important considerations, and that it should consider significant the effect of permanent unemployment upon old and faithful employees. They look upon community integrity as an important community asset. Caught between the support of a "rational" system of "economic" forces and laws, and sentiments which they accept as significant values, they seek a solution to their dilemma which will at once permit them to retain their expected rewards for continued adherence to past norms and to defend the social system which they have been taught to revere but which now offers them a stone instead of bread.

Implications

We have shown that those in Caliente whose behavior most nearly approached the ideal taught are hardest hit by change. On the other hand, those seemingly farthest removed in conduct from that ideal are either rewarded or pay less of the costs of change than do those who follow the ideal more closely. Absentee owners, completely anonymous, and consumers who are not expected to co-operate to make the gains possible are rewarded most highly, while the local people who must cooperate to raise productivity pay dearly for having contributed.

In a society run through sacred mysteries whose rationale it is not man's privilege to criticize, such incongruities may be explained away. Such a society may even provide some "explanation" which makes them seem rational. In a secular society, supposedly defended rationally upon scientific facts, in which the pragmatic test "Does it work?" is continually applied, such discrepancy between expectation and realization is difficult to reconcile.

Defense of our traditional system of assessing the cost of technological change is made on the theory that the costs of such change are more than offset by the benefits to "society as a whole." However, it is difficult to show the people of Caliente just why *they* should pay for advances made to benefit others whom they have never known and who, in their judgment, have done nothing to justify such rewards. Any action that will permit the people of Caliente to levy the costs of change upon those who will benefit from them will be morally justifiable to the people of Caliente. Appeals to the general welfare leave them cold and the compulsions of the price system are not felt to be self-justifying "natural laws" but are regarded as being the specific consequence of specific bookkeeping decisions as to what should be included in the costs of change. They seek to change these decisions through social action. They do not consider that the "American Way" consists primarily of acceptance of the market as the final arbiter of their destiny. Rather they conceive that the system as a whole exists to render "justice," and if the consequences of the price system are such as to produce what they consider to be "injustice" they proceed to use some other institution as a means to reverse or offset the effects of the price system. Like other groups faced with the same situation, those in Caliente seize upon the means available to them. The operating employees had in their unions a device to secure what they consider to be their rights. Union practices developed over the years make it possible for the organized workers to avoid some of the costs of change which they would otherwise have had to bear. Feather-bed rules, make-work practices, restricted work weeks, train length legislation and other similar devices were designed to permit union members to continue work even when "efficiency" dictated that they be disemployed. Members of the "Big Four" in Caliente joined with their fellows in demanding not only the retention of previously existing rules, but the imposition of new ones such as that requiring the presence of a third man in the diesel cab. For other groups there was available only the appeal to the company that it establish some other facility at Caliente, or alternatively a demand that "government" do something. One such demand took the form of a request to the Interstate Commerce Commission that it require inspection of rolling stock at Caliente. This request was denied.

It rapidly became apparent to the people of Caliente that they could not gain their objectives by organized community action nor individual endeavor but there was hope that by adding their voices to those of others similarly injured there might be hope of solution. They began to look to the activities of the whole labor movement for succor. Union strategy which forced the transfer of control from the market to government mediation or to legislation and operation was widely approved on all sides. This was not confined to those only who were currently seeking rule changes but was equally approved by the great bulk of those in the community who had been hit by the change. Cries of public outrage at their demands for make-work rules were looked upon as coming from those at best ignorant, ill-informed or stupid, and at worst as being the hypocritical efforts of others to gain at the workers' expense. When the union threat of a national strike for rule changes was met by government seizure, Caliente workers like most of their compatriots across the country welcomed this shift in control, secure in their belief that if "justice" were done they could only be gainers by government intervention. These attitudes are not "class" phenomena purely nor are they merely occupational sentiments. They result from the fact that modern life, with the interdependence that it creates, particularly in one-industry communities, imposes penalties far beyond the membership of the groups presumably involved in industry. When make-work rules contributed to the livelihood of the community, the support of the churches, and the taxes which maintain the schools; when feather-bed practices determine the standard of living, the profits of the business man and the circulation of the press; when they contribute to the salary of the teacher and the preacher; they can no longer be treated as accidental, immoral, deviant or temporary. Rather they are elevated into the position of emergent morality and law. Such practices generate a morality which serves them just as the practices in turn nourish those who participate in and preserve them. They are as firmly a part of what one "has a right to expect" from industry as are parity payments to the farmer, bonuses and pensions to the veterans, assistance to the aged, tariffs to the industrialist, or the sanctity of property to those who inherit. On the other hand, all these practices conceivably help create a structure that is particularly vulnerable to changes such as that described here.

Practices which force the company to spend in Caliente part of what has been saved through technological change, or failing that, to reward those who are forced to move by increased income for the same service, are not, by the people of Caliente, considered to be unjustifiable. Confronted by a choice between the old means and resultant "injustice" which their use entails, and the acceptance of new means which they believe will secure them the "justice" they hold to be their right, they are willing to abandon (in so far as this particular area is concerned) the liberal state and the omnicompetent market in favor of something that works to provide "justice."

The study of the politics of pressure groups will show how widely the reactions of Caliente people are paralleled by those of other groups. Amongst them it is in politics that the decisions as to who will pay and who will profit are made. Through organized political force railroaders maintain the continuance of rules which operate to their benefit rather than for "the public good" or "the general welfare." Their defense of these practices is found in the argument that only so can their rights be protected against the power of other groups who hope to gain at their expense by functioning through the corporation and the market.

We should expect that where there are other groups similarly affected

by technological change, there will be similar efforts to change the operation of our institutions. The case cited is not unique. Not only is it dupli-
cated in hundreds of railroad division points but also in other towns
abandoned by management for similar reasons. Changes in the location of
markets or in the method of calculating transportation costs, changes in
technology making necessary the use of new materials, changes due to the
exhaustion of old sources of materials, changes to avoid labor costs such
as the shift of the textile industry from New England to the South, changes
to expedite decentralization to avoid the consequences of bombing, or
those of congested living, all give rise to the question, "Who benefits, and
at whose expense?"

The accounting practices of the corporation permit the entry only
of those costs which have become "legitimate" claims upon the company.
But the tremendous risks borne by the workers and frequently all the
members of the community in an era of technological change are real
phenomena. Rapid shifts in technology which destroy the "legitimate"
expectations derived from past experience force the recognition of new
obligations. Such recognition may be made voluntarily as management
foresees the necessity, or it may be thrust upon it by political or other
action. Rigidity of property concepts, the legal structure controlling directors in what they may admit to be costs, and the stereotyped nature of
the "economics" used by management make rapid change within the
corporation itself difficult even in a "free democratic society." Hence while
management is likely to be permitted or required to initiate technological
change in the interest of profits, it may and probably will be barred from
compensating for the social consequences certain to arise from those
changes. Management thus shuts out the rising flood of demands in its
cost-accounting only to have them reappear in its tax accounts, in legal
regulations or in new insistent union demands. If economics fails to
provide an answer to social demands then politics will be tried.

It is clear that while traditional morality provides a means of protecting
some groups from the consequences of technological change, or some
method of meliorating the effects of change upon them, other large segments of the population are left unprotected. It should be equally clear
that rather than a quiet acquiescence in the finality and justice of such
arrangements, there is an active effort to force new devices into being which
will extend protection to those hitherto expected to bear the brunt of these
costs. A good proportion of these inventions increasingly call for the
intervention of the state. To call such arrangements immoral, unpatriotic,
socialistic or to hurl other epithets at them is not to deal effectively with
them. They are as "natural" as are the "normal" reactions for which we
have "rational" explanations based upon some pre-scientific generalization
about human nature such as "the law of supply and demand" or "the
inevitability of progress." To be dealt with effectively they will have to be
understood and treated as such.

EXTINCTION BY THRUWAY:
THE FIGHT TO SAVE A TOWN

Polly Praeger

The preceding selection describes an as yet unsuccessful attempt to avoid, or at least reduce, the unfavorable derivative effects of a new invention on a minority. This selection, by Polly Praeger, illustrates the successful modification of a new development so that its harmful derivative effect on a minority is reduced. It also demonstrates the difficulties which may arise, even in a representative democracy, when citizens in a local area attempt to question decisions made by centralized bureaus and commissions at the state level.

It began inconspicuously—just a brief legal notice in the newspaper announcing a public hearing to be held in the County Courthouse on January 9, 1957, in regard to the route of a federal super-highway through Broome County. But for us in Hillcrest, where surveyors had already been sighting along the quiet streets, the announcement had a note of doom.

You will probably not find Hillcrest (population approximately 3,000) on your map of upper New York State. It is an unincorporated suburb of Binghamton—and, although it is small, there is an unusually strong community spirit among its middle-class home owners. We have a progressive Board of Education and two new schools of which we are very proud—as we are of most things about Hillcrest.

Most people were too busy with Christmas to see the legal notice, but a few of us were among the hundred or so who turned out for the hearing. I had no idea what to expect and listened with great interest to the District Engineer's technical description of the beautiful expressway that was to cost at least a million dollars a mile. Of even greater interest was the map of Broome County he displayed. Hillcrest was not even marked on it. All I could see clearly was a wide black line cutting a swath through the county.

The Engineer called for statements from organizations first. Understandably, representatives from the Chambers of Commerce, banks, unions, and auto clubs were enthusiastic about the economic advantages of a new highway that the area badly needs. But in spite of my naïveté, I felt there was a kind of "pre-sold" quality to their glowing endorsements.

SOURCE: *Harper's Magazine*, Vol. 217, No. 1303 (December, 1958), 61–64, 69–71. © 1958, by Harper's Magazine, Inc. Reprinted by permission of the author. ✧ The author studied at Radcliffe and taught English in Hawaii. She is now living in Binghamton, New York, and is active in A.A.U.W. and civic affairs.

There was no such quality in the statements from the Town of Fenton (in which Hillcrest is located). Robert Ford, our politically shrewd supervisor, and cautious but worried Raymond H. Moody, the town attorney, declared they could say nothing unless they knew where the route was to go in relation to Hillcrest.

Clayton Axtell, Jr., the school-board attorney—single-purposed in his causes, caustic in cross-examination—forcefully pressed the point: "This hearing is inadequate by law. Even today the route does not deal with specific localities."

But the District Engineer remained adamant: "Details cannot be given now. The route could go one way or the other."

Since Hillcrest lies between the Chenango River and the hills and is only approximately a mile long and a half mile wide, a mile could mean the difference between bisecting and by-passing.

When the District Engineer asked for individual comments, three or four men tried, without success, to get specific information on the route. . . .

Hillcresters left the hearing feeling frustrated and helpless. Every time someone asked, "What can we do?" the answer was, almost universally, "Nothing. What chance do we have against the State Department of Public Works and the U.S. Bureau of Public Roads?"

A lot of people all over America are going to feel this same bewilderment and frustration during the next few years, as the $50 billion-plus federal highway program gets under way. I don't for a minute suggest that everyone who will have his home destroyed by a super-highway should promptly object. But I do believe that citizens have the right to expect good planning from an over-all community point of view.

"The new highway program furnishes a great, if fleeting, opportunity; its new rights-of-way and interchanges will set the basic structure of the metropolitan areas of the future, and whether those areas will be livable will depend on the foresight of the communities involved as much as it will depend on the engineers," says William H. Whyte, Jr. in "Urban Sprawl" in the January 1958 *Fortune*.

"Not to act now," he continues, "is to make a decision. . . . Planners can help, so can more studies. But the citizens must not merely acquiesce; it is they who must seize the initiative. Their boldness and vision will determine the issue."

My own home, according to rumor, would not have been taken, but I felt the community would be ruined. Beyond that, I was concerned with the whole problem of sensible planning. And, for that reason, perhaps my experience—local though it is—may prove useful to others who will soon find themselves in a similar fix.

A Letter of Protest

If Clayton Axtell had not questioned the legality of the hearing, I might never have thought of taking action. Since he had, I called him up and asked if anything could be done. He said he was looking into the legal angles and was in touch with our then representative in Congress, the Honorable W. Sterling Cole.

But I was still not satisfied. I asked if he didn't think the citizens should do something—say, pass a resolution at the meeting of the Hillcrest Community Association which was about to take place.

"Sure thing. Go to it," he said.

The Hillcrest Community Association is primarily devoted to sponsoring youth programs. But my belief—from many years of working in the League of Women Voters—that citizens' efforts *can* count gave me the courage to make my suggestion: "I think the Hillcrest Community Association should write a letter of protest to John W. Johnson, Superintendent of Public Works for New York State, over the conduct of the hearing and request permission to have a statement from Hillcrest made part of the record."

That's how the fight began.

✧   ✧   ✧   ✧   ✧

A lively meeting produced what we felt was a very restrained letter. . . .

The wait for the reply seemed much longer than it actually was, but the answer made us jubilant. Johnson said in part, "The official newspaper notice failed to disclose the general location of the route as is prescribed in our Department regulations. . . . The purpose of these public hearings is to permit presentation of all known factors and we would request that you file your statement as soon as possible. . . ."

Then the sentence which we read and reread: "The Department of Public Works will attempt to consider such changes in alignment as may be possible, in order to minimize destruction of property and still maintain an economical route for the project."

The State's willingness to restudy the route made us feel that it would be worth our while to do a thorough job of presenting facts in our behalf. But facts are hard to come by—especially from the Department of Public Works. Repeated visits to the District Office failed to give us the specific route.

Actually, I was the first person to see a detailed map. I happened to be in Albany for a meeting, and I could not bear to be so close to the Department of Public Works without trying to get the information we were so desperate to have. My State Senator, Warren M. Anderson, made an appointment for me. I was not able to see anyone in command, but I did see an assistant deputy engineer who was wonderfully helpful and spread a large-scale map of Hillcrest before my startled eyes. Either the point of view in Albany was different, or else I just happened to hit a psychological moment when there was a general change of heart.

For the first time, we were sure of what we were up against. The worst rumors were, in reality, the truth. You cannot superimpose a six-lane highway with four access roads and four traffic circles on an already developed community the size of ours without making mincemeat of it. A more thorough job could hardly have been done, in terms of destroying the water wells, taking a third of the new elementary-school property, some of the buildings of the Wyoming Conference Children's Home, and knocking out over a hundred new houses, the loss of which would take at least a half a million in assessed valuation from the town tax rolls. There was also an estimated loss of a million dollars in assessed valuation to the Board of Education because the area affected across the river is in our Chenango Valley Central School District.

Worst of all, the community as a community would be destroyed. All available land is already developed, and displaced people would not be able to move from one section to another. Their hardship would be great, and so would that of the people who remained—separated into little "islands" by the limited access expressway and faced with a much heavier tax burden.

We went to work to get as many facts as we could. Our committee had a session in the State's District Office in Binghamton. By now, maps were available for our inspection, and we spotted a line called "Alternate A" which obviously went outside Hillcrest, and, as we later discovered, outside the village of Port Crane as well.

"Why can't Alternate A be used?" asked Bill Morgan.

"The State never really considered that because it is too far from Binghamton," the District Engineer explained to him. "No one would use it."

"But it is only seven miles to the Courthouse at the center of the downtown area," objected Joe Norris. "That's by a four-lane divided highway most of the way. If I could go to Syracuse by a seventy-mile-an-hour expressway, I'd drive farther than that to get on it."

"No one would use it," insisted the District Engineer.

We ourselves studied the two possibilities. We had interviews with civil-defense authorities on locations of defense highways (preferably twelve miles outside of critical target areas like Binghamton). We had interviews with bankers on increased interest rates and the difficulty of getting mortgages; with realtors on the existing housing shortage; and we held a conference with the director of the Broome County Planning Board and all manner of officials. We studied highway law, all earlier arterial plans for the area, the Planning Board's recommended land-use studies near Port Crane, construction magazines, and articles on metropolitan planning. And ceaselessly we kept Albany and the Washington Bureau of Public Roads and our legislators at all levels apprised of what we were doing. . . .

I admit engineers have their problems with our hills and narrow river valleys, and I think if they had ever told us categorically that Hillcrest was the only possible way that the road could be constructed from the engineering point of view, we would, as public-spirited citizens, have given up the fight. But the two major reasons given for the choice of the Hillcrest route were: (1) Hillcrest was closer to Binghamton by three miles, and (2) the Port Crane route had one sharper curve and hill. For these arguments, we could not see having our community ruined.

The battlefront widened. Our committee felt it would be fairer to have the entire community represented, even though most families already belonged to the Community Association. Every possible group joined with us in a large committee that included Rotary and Kiwanis, churches, the American Legion, PTA, Town Board, Board of Education, Children's Home, and garden clubs. So the Community Association Committee resigned. But the large committee promptly re-elected it to serve as a small executive committee, and we more or less officially became the Hillcrest Committee on the Penn-Can Highway.

In the meantime, we had organized a subcommittee of prominent engineers who live in Hillcrest and work for such companies as General Electric, Ansco, and Link Aviation. What had begun in self-interest as a local protest over the conduct of the hearing had become a plea for more imaginative planning. Incidentally, there was no opposition by citizens to the Port Crane route.

To bring our fellow citizens up-to-date on what we committee members were doing we held a New England style town meeting. Over five hundred residents turned out. Normally, only basketball games can produce this kind of attendance! . . .

By this time, both daily newspapers—the Binghamton *Press* and the Binghamton *Sun*—were covering the controversy in detail and publishing many letters to the editor. I received all kinds of mail. There was one anonymous clipping:

"Good Morning! Being as smart as a steel trap means knowing when to shut up."

But there was also a letter from a prominent Binghamton attorney with "congratulations to a gallant and fearless fighter" and quotations from "Gentleman Jim Corbett" which urged "Fight one more round." Most letters contained suggestions on where to place the route.

The Battle Is Joined

✧   ✧   ✧   ✧   ✧

The State had agreed to restudy the route and hold an "informational" meeting (not another public hearing) at which their decision would be announced to the people of Hillcrest. There was scarcely another topic of conversation until that day arrived, and eight hundred citizens gathered to hear the outcome.

We on the committee already knew the answer. We had requested an advance meeting, and on the afternoon before, we heard the results from the consulting engineers and the Department of Public Works. That was the night we worked until 2:00 A.M. preparing a rebuttal, for we could see no evidence of a real review of alternate possibilities. No ground survey had been made of the Port Crane route, but we had all seen the surveyors busy again on the streets of Hillcrest.

The informational meeting was charged with excitement. Maps and reports were the first order of the day. Then came the climax: Hillcrest was still the recommended route—because it would be cheaper than the Port Crane route by $9,500,000!

Inevitably, most of the taxpaying audience was amazed and speechless. The consultants admitted that acquisition costs would be higher for the closely populated Hillcrest route than for the undeveloped Port Crane route. But they argued that if the expressway were built near Port Crane (with the necessary inclusion of a bridge) another $5 million six-lane bridge would still be needed at Hillcrest. They further claimed that if the highway were built three miles farther out on the Port Crane route, there would be additional costs to the road users which would amount to $4,500,000 over a twenty-year period.

Then came the people's turn. The District Engineer announced that each person might speak once and only at the time he was offered the microphone by an engineer who went up and down the aisle. No committee member would be allowed to ask questions.

I asked if, in that case, I might read a prepared statement from the committee before the questioning began. Permission was granted. I stood at the dais with my back to the State officials or I could never have done it. Our rebuttal was couched in strong words.

We denied the need of an additional bridge until the Penn-Can bridge could be tested under the resulting new traffic pattern, for the Hillcrest bridge had originally been part of a ten-year-old arterial plan. And we claimed that road users' costs were not properly costs to the taxpayers as such. We thought it only fair, if the State were going to include social costs, that it should also admit all other social and economic costs which would have to be paid by the people of Hillcrest, residents of the town, and the school district. We estimated them in dollars over the twenty-year period and found they greatly outweighed users' costs.

For the State's District Engineers the matter was ended; they were forwarding their recommendation to Albany. But what was to be our course of action? At the end of my statement I turned to the audience and said, "It is the recommendation of our committee that we continue to seek a genuine consideration of all factors. We will appreciate an expression of your opinion."

Nearly everyone in that huge group spontaneously applauded and stood up. We had our answer.

Carrying the Fight to the Top

Shortly thereafter, I received an answer of another sort from the Director of Public Relations of the State Department of Public Works in Albany, in which he said: ". . . while we are in complete agreement with your right to be heard on this matter we are somewhat concerned with the lack of factual data to support statements which infer that the department does not have the knowledge, judgment, or know-how to design a highway."

(We had never questioned the design of the highway—only the location of it in terms of good planning.)

He went on, "We would be most interested to know whose judgment is used to substantiate your 'challenge the validity of the District Engineer's analysis' . . . or 'so-called users' costs are based on questionable premises.' This unsupported verbal gymnastics smacks of plain rabble rousing. . . .

"In spite of this type of abuse let us assure you that we are giving this matter a truly impartial study. Our final determination will be based on sound engineering and economical judgment taking into account those legitimate local objections which are offered in a spirit of good will and without malice."

Swallowing our resentment at the charge of rabble rousing, the committee wrote a reply in which our sources were given for every point. But on second thought we never sent it! We decided instead to secure the services of an impartial expert to assess the validity of our position.

Since the issue was not the engineering feasibility of one route over the other but the social and economic costs to the area, we felt that we needed not an engineer but a community planning expert. One of the professors at Harpur, the State's liberal-arts college in nearby Endicott, was Dr. Seymour Z. Mann, who had been active in community and county planning in our general area. We approached him, but he refused to accept unless he was free to draw his own conclusions. To this we agreed.

On Dr. Mann's visit to the District Engineer, he was asked, "How can you deal with these emotional people who run to their elected representatives in Albany and Washington?"

"If people feel strongly about a problem that requires political action, then citizens should use all legitimate means at their disposal," Dr. Mann replied. "It is part of the representative process. This is what I teach my students in political science."

Aside from Dr. Mann, elected representatives now seemed our only hope. Congressman W. Sterling Cole, who had earlier blasted the public hearing as a "Star Chamber procedure," assured us that the position of the community would be given thoughtful consideration by the federal Bureau of Public Roads. Senators Javits and Ives looked into the matter. A petition with over a thousand signatures, telegrams, and letters appealed to Governor Harriman. His office wrote that the Governor was concerned and had been in touch with the State Department of Public Works.

State Senator Warren M. Anderson, after attending a meeting of the Hillcrest Committee on the Penn-Can Highway, decided that our objections were valid and promised to arrange a meeting between some of the committee and Superintendent Johnson in Albany. After considerable pressure from the Senator, Mr. Johnson agreed but only on condition that the Senator be present, that there be no more than three committee members—and that under no circumstances Mrs. Praeger be one of them.

Dr. Mann's excellent analysis—which upheld our position—was first presented at this meeting. One of the many interesting points he made was that "citizens who participate in the activities that lead up to the public decisions which affect their individual persons or communities will have less reason and less desire to obstruct improvements for the public good even against their own short-run interests."

After the Albany conference in May, Superintendent Johnson ordered the full review we wanted, and the citizens' committee rested its case.

Citizens vs. Super-Highways

From January 9 to October 20 is a long time when you are waiting to know the fate of your home or community. But on that day came the eventful words, "Hillcrest 'By-passed,'" and the headlines announcing a totally new concept for two major routes. We read for the first time of a proposed common route for several miles through Binghamton and Johnson City for both the Penn-Can and Route 17 (the East-West state highway). This confluence was to make the area a transportation crossroads and bring great economic prosperity.

The Binghamton *Press* did an outstanding job and devoted many pages to delineating every aspect of the proposed routes. Quite a change from the original legal notice!

Whether the new route is the best possible one is another story—one which I have not studied. At least this time, many community leaders have been consulted. Mayor Burns of Binghamton has given his approval. The Broome County Planning Board, which played no part in the location of the first route, has worked with the engineers and endorsed the new routes as the best possible use of city land. Highly publicized hearings have been held, both Albany and Washington have approved the new routes, and the design contracts have been let.

We Hillcresters will never know how much our stand had to do with the new plan. Our recommended alternate was not chosen, but it is impossible to contrast the new plan with ours because it is concerned with two highways, not one. It seems evident, however, that the original plan failed to consider the relationship of Route 17 to the Penn-Can, although they have been concurrent problems. In fairness, I must say that the District Engineer was new here and it has been said that he inherited the former plan. Perhaps the more thorough study called for by the citizens of Hillcrest gave him an opportunity to develop his own more comprehensive plan. In any case there is evidence that the State is realizing, belatedly, the need for improved road-building public relations.

Governor Harriman at the eighteenth annual convention of the New York State Association of Highway Engineers called for a better job of public relations on the part of engineers: "We ought to recognize that in government the public is always right." The State Department of Public Works has itself recognized that there is more to the new super-highway program than merely designing good highways.

Better public relations is a step in the right direction, it seems to me. If we expect to build 41,000 miles of interstate highways within the next fifteen years, it is obvious that there will be a tremendous number of persons affected. If the officials responsible for the program do a constant educational job, citizens and super-highways need not be incompatible.

Unfortunately, many bureaucrats are not yet convinced that the home-owning citizen has an important stake in this vast new program. They apparently feel that public hearings and consultation with citizens' groups merely delay "progress," and that we must keep moving at all costs—even if costs include citizens' rights and vital community considerations.

Our experience has convinced me that Congress was wise in providing citizens with the opportunity to be heard on a program that deeply affects so many lives.

It is understandable that many a highway official, beset by a multitude of problems and harassment on all sides, will regard the old approach to highway building with nostalgia. But if the new program is to do its job for community as well as for the transcontinental road user, citizen and highway engineer must work together.

This new program, as John T. Howard, associate professor of city planning at MIT, has pointed out, forces highway engineers to make decisions that have repercussions far outside their field—the highways to be built during the next twenty years "will have more effect upon all form and pattern of growth, and therefore upon the character and structure of our metropolitan areas, than all the metropolitan planning done by city planners between 1945 and now." And he added, "Just as wars are too important to be left to generals, so the building of the new super-highways is too important to leave just to engineers."

A network of super-highways across the face of America will be an empty achievement if it kills democratic processes and ignores long-range community planning. There is good evidence that the best in American life has always been achieved through co-operation between citizens and government.

THE "NEW BREED" OF AMERICAN CATHOLICS

Joseph L. Walsh, C.S.P.

Nearly a century ago Walter Bagehot used the term "cake of custom" to describe institutional resistance to change. Until recently such resistance has been well exemplified by the stable patterns of the Roman Catholic Church. But today's American Roman Catholics, says Father Walsh, are no longer content to do things as they have always been done, no longer willing to accept traditional authority, no longer interested in being anonymous members of a large and depersonalized organization. Modern American Catholics, he says, call for a change. The "New Breed" of Catholic is suspicious of bigness and of authority in general, and is openly expressing this suspicion in numerous, sometimes spectacular, ways. The fact that this sympathetic description of the modern American Catholic was written by a priest rather than a layman makes it all the more significant.

Something different is happening in American Catholicism today. One can point to a number of incidents. The picketing of the Archdiocesan chancery building in Los Angeles with its stated criticism of the handling of the race issue. Mumblings of conflicts in seminaries over authority and integrity. Catholic University students in Washington passing out to Cardinals and Archbishops in solemn procession a prayer asking forgiveness for the hierarchy and laity for the sin of silence on race. Books like Mary Perkins Ryan's *Are Parochial Schools the Answer?* attacking the great sacred cow of American Catholic life. Boston College students censuring their university for violating the academic freedom of a professor. Notre Dame students exercising new freedom to severely criticize the university administration. Sociologist Gordon Zahn's documented indictment of the German bishops on the Nazi issue.

All these give evidence of a new spirit at work, almost revolutionary in its ignoring of past custom and tradition, and startling in its passion for an honest confrontation with failure.

SOURCE: *Newman Review*, Vol. 16, No. 2 (Fall, 1964), pp. 2–9. Reprinted by permission of the author. ✧ Reverend Joseph L. Walsh is Catholic Chaplain and Director of the Newman Apostolate at Wayne State University, and is currently working on his doctorate in Modern Intellectual History. He has written articles for *Cross Currents* and *Commonweal*.

Father Andrew Greeley has perceptively described the new spirit as well as some of the achievements of this "new breed" of American Catholics. According to Greeley, they are concerned most "about things like honesty, integrity and authenticity." The new breed "is not flexible, it is not gradualist. It wants a Church that is relevant to its own needs and the needs it sees in the world, and it wants it now, not next week." Though severely critical, they are not "going to leave the Church, either by apostasy or alienation. It is their Church and it would be difficult even to drive them out of it." Unlike Catholic reformers of recent decades, they are not content to be a tiny minority working for a far-off, distant reform. "They have tasted enough change in the last few years to want much more," Greeley says. The new breed is trying to tell us "that you cannot have a half-souled *aggiornamento*, that if you open the window you are not going to be able to close it again and that the wind that blows in is likely to bring all sorts of strange things with it."

Though it is true, as Greeley says, that the "new breed" are proportionately few, they are everywhere, and for every two or three who can articulate their views there are many others who are sympathetic and thinking generally in the same direction. Though it is also true that the pure "new breed" are still or were recently students, their heroes and leaders are a significant band of professors, priests and writers who are articulating the unspoken beliefs of the new generation of American Catholics who want a different sort of Church from the one their fathers built.

America's Impact

Perhaps the most significant aspect of the new spirit in American Catholicism is its consonance with the spirit of the society at large. The very fact of the self-criticism itself reveals a security about Catholics' place in the society as a whole. American Catholics apparently now feel sufficiently secure enough that they no longer fear to air their dirty laundry in public and do not feel compelled to present a "united front" against "the others."

Another interesting aspect of the contemporary American Catholic ferment is the increasing role of opinion. Catholics have long been conditioned to look to their publications and platforms as well as the pulpit for generally accepted views of belief and action. When the secular news media and opinion magazines like *Time* and *The New Yorker* decided to treat the Second Vatican Council with the same techniques used on public political and cultural life, they caused a revolution. Catholic publications were forced to compete for readers and attention. The result was an honesty about disagreement and opinions that had never before been present. Catholic readers find themselves for the first time confronted with a wide variety of opinions on what is right and wrong in the Church. This pro-liferation of often opposing and contradictory opinions has in turn given rise to a further freedom of speech and choice that is totally new and exhilarating to many American Catholics.

It is also difficult not to see parallels between the search for integrity and authenticity in the Catholic new breed and the student volunteers in Mississippi and in our big cities. In each is a need to face problems their elders had ignored or covered over. In each is a dissatisfaction with large-scale bureaucratic techniques and a need for person to person contact to change things now. In each group there is a passionate desire to eliminate present evils and little appreciation for the real but limited successes of their fathers. Politically this gives rise to an increasing dissatisfaction with representative democracy as a means of bringing about social reform and an increasing attention to direct action and demonstration to bring about change. In the Church, this dissatisfaction questions the honesty and integrity of officialdom. This is of great significance in a Church which, particularly since the Protestant Reformation, has stressed divine guidance and direction of the official hierarchy.

Bigness Taboo

The new breed is suspicious of authority . . . [and] bigness in whatever form as being unresponsive to personal needs, whether it be Big Govern-ment, Big Business, Big Labor or even the Big Church. There is no strong sense of emotional loyalty to institutions in the new generation. This is the generation which considers patriotism phony. One's government and its symbols are part of the establishment, things taken for granted, and not the sort of thing to arouse emotion.

The same attitude affects religion. There is little emotional pride in the Roman Catholic Church as a far-flung institution having weathered the storms of history. Much less is there any sort of institutional loyalty to one's parish church, or school (or Newman Center) in the new breed. All these are part of the structured, given (soon to be automated?) aspects of life. The new breed looks elsewhere for spirit and life. In Catholic circles one looks for small, almost intimate groups gathered around a personalist liturgy where the spirit of community—the true Christian gift—can be experienced in a way not possible in a huge suburban parish. For the new breed, the experience of community—a shared experience of unity, respect and mutual acceptance in and through the presence of Christ—has become the purpose and value of Christian living. In an age of anxiety, alienation and organization, the young turn to the Church to offer an antidote to the problems of the age.

The Father Dubay incident of June [1964] is in many ways a perfect case-study of the new attitudes at work. A young priest of the Archdiocese of Los Angeles, Father Dubay wrote a letter to Pope Paul VI asking for the removal of Cardinal McIntyre of Los Angeles on the grounds that he had not given sufficient leadership to his people on the matter of racial injustice. Dubay called a press conference to make his views public and his case became a national incident immediately.

Dubay Significance

It would be easy to miss the real significance of the Dubay incident. One could interpret it as the action of a naive and impetuous young man who didn't understand the uses of power and the mechanics of bureaucracy. Or one could see it as the inevitable emergence in the Catholic structure of the kind of independence and courage too often missing since Luther. Or one could interpret the affair as essentially local: in which an isolated minority of liberal Catholics found an issue and a willing spokesman to vent their long pent-up frustration at the political and religious conservatism of the majority around them and the authority over them.

Whatever truth there may be in any or all of these interpretations, they reflect only a partial and lesser side of the story. Dorothy Day and other old-line Catholic liberals have criticized Dubay and his followers for seeking hierarchical approval and leadership in their offbeat and far-out endeavors for social reform. "Why not," they ask, "go ahead and operate independently, and be content to operate in the shadow of a dark cloud from the Chancery office, attracting to the cause only those with enough courage to be daring?" This is to judge the new breed, however, by 1933 standards. Dorothy Day and her generation were concerned over social injustice, at hunger and bread lines and skid rows. The new breed, in Los Angeles and everywhere, weren't nearly as upset about racial injustice as they were angry against the Church. I would suggest that they are much more worried about the Church as a bureaucratic, impersonal, unfeeling corporation than they were about the remains of segregation in exclusive Los Angeles suburbs.

For the new breed, the supreme evil of our time is depersonalization. It is not precisely that a man is starving or being deprived of his rights that bothers them, but that others can be insensitive to this deprivation. The *New York Times* interviews of the students training in Oxford, Ohio, to go to Mississippi this past summer were most enlightening. Time and time again the same pattern emerged: the students were going to Mississippi not precisely to register voters and certainly not to help give an education. They were going to express their solidarity with the Mississippi Negro and as a sign of protest with so much that they considered wrong and rotten in our society. This twentieth century Children's Crusade was not a reform movement; it was human beings trying to express deep, personal human feelings. If some other good like registration and education came out of it, that, too, was fine. But being *there* (and not just *here*)—that was the big thing.

Seeking Community

If depersonalization is the new breed's evil, personalism is its good. Father Greeley says of the new breed: "They feel that they can help others only if they can relate as persons . . ." and "they are not attracted by a task that seems to rule out the possibility of an 'I-Thou' deed." The new breed is the product of the mass-produced, ticky-tacky civilization that moves them from home to home, school to school, neighborhood to neighborhood every few years. In the 1930's young radicals found solidarity while seeking justice for the oppressed. Today's young discontents are seeking that solidarity itself.

I would suggest that it is this same revulsion against depersonalization and a search for solidarity that gives the key to the whole recent rash of impudent outbreaks against authority in American Catholicism.

Past generations of Catholic leaders and its present top echelon wondered whether the Church could survive in American life. Whether American society would find Catholicism acceptable and whether Catholics could keep the faith here. Thus they built the Catholic school system, perhaps the greatest instrument ever devised for educing continued allegiance in an alien culture. The middle generation of leaders (now in their forties), while keeping a watchful eye on survival, began to worry about quality: making Catholics as informed, articulate and knowledgable as "the others." They wanted to be sure that American Catholics possessed the good fruits of American culture and that they were not only better than non-Catholic Americans by possessing the true religion, but at least as good in other things as well.

Too Much Alike

The new breed understands none of this. They take survival for granted. How could anyone ever question the survival of an institution that in their experience builds bigger schools (and football teams) than the city government? As for being as good as the others: don't Catholic schools win all the science fairs and debating tournaments? They have never experienced the feeling of alienation from American culture which led the preceding, middle generation of leaders to call for the end of the Catholic ghetto. The new breed isn't afraid of being too different from American culture; they are afraid of being too much like it.

When Father Dubay, whether as leader or spokesman is still unclear, asked Cardinal McIntyre for leadership on civil rights and wrote a letter to the Pope asking for removal, he was making an act of faith in the Church as a community not a bureaucracy. He was saying that its leaders must feel what its people feel and that in this electric age they must be as near as the nearest telephone or airmailed envelope.

Conflict between the new breed and their elders in the Church is obviously inevitable, and is already widespread. Part of it is just the perennial conflict between the old and the young, heightened in an era in which the old live longer and the young are more self-consciously "a threshold generation" bred through the long years of adolescence, college and now graduate school. As such, one could see the conflict merely as one of many stages, with the present new breed destined to pass on and become essentially like their elders, having added only their own special bit of flavor to the mixture.

It is my belief, however, that much more is involved in the present situation. We have no guarantee that the present new breed will not capitulate and almost completely adopt the standards and attitudes of the preceding generation. Some such mellowing and softening is indeed inevitable as the new breed confronts the hard realities of life. But with the new breed, the mellowing and compromise that usually marks the move into middle age will not be enough to completely dilute an attitude toward the Church and its place in the world that is revolutionary when compared with that of their elders.

New Standards

The new generation of Catholics views success for the Church in almost totally different terms from the older and middle generation of leaders. For the older and middle leaders the obligations of the Church to the social order are definitely secondary. Few of them would agree with the Southern bishop who in 1963 defended the Church's long toleration and acceptance of racial segregation on the grounds that the Church's duty was to save souls and preach the gospel while leaving the problems of society to the political power. Nevertheless, for most Catholic clerics and laymen, social problems (labor, race, poverty, etc.) were things to be looked after only when the essential business of preaching the gospel and administering the sacraments (and of course building the structures for these activities) was accomplished.

The new breed thinks differently. It is not that they have sat down and logically thought out the matter of priorities. But instinctively they have felt a great sickness in our society, a lack of personal concern, a preoccupation with techniques and procedures as a substitute for personal involvement, a loneliness among men whose echo is captured in a folk song and whose antidote is a small group of friends, who really care, gathered around a Man who cared the most. They do not have to read Father Congar to know that the Church best manifests its divinity by being a servant to needing, bleeding humanity. The new breed have felt the new deep sickness in humanity and have instinctively turned to their Church to heal it. They can't understand the workings of power, why bishops must be aloof in order to save face, why one must work through proper channels in order to get things done. To the new breed this is the way everything else works (the way the whole *world* is) and they have, naively perhaps, come to expect something else from the Church.

✧　✧　✧　✧　✧

The problems of the future are upon us and are different. We are entering the era of vast populations, of total urbanization, of complete automation and bureaucratization, or as Pope John's *Mater et Magistra* described it, socialization. Ours is the era in which technology will make possible and necessary the minute regulation and control of our lives. As *Mater et Magistra* repeatedly says, in this era the essential problem for mankind is the preservation of human dignity and individuality. It is time now for the Church to turn its attention to this human and social problem in the same way its bishops and monks once built bridges and roads to lead men out of chaos into medieval civilization. It can begin well by listening to the voices of its own new breed, the first products of the new age of material abundance and spiritual starvation.

✤ 91 ✤

STEEL AXES FOR
STONE AGE AUSTRALIANS

Lauriston Sharp

Perhaps oversimplifying somewhat to make his point, Lauriston Sharp illustrates in this selection how the introduction of a single new culture trait into a closely integrated society can undermine it. These unwanted results—demoralization of the individual, disintegration of the culture, and perhaps even dissolution of the society as a viable distinct entity—were nonetheless unavoidable once the trait was widely adopted. One writer has referred to this particular article as the story of "The Steel Axe That Destroyed a Tribe." It is important to note that a similar story could hardly be written about a complex and less integrated society such as ours. But problems that are only quantitatively (not qualitatively) different from those faced by the Yir Yoront appear in every society that undergoes change.

SOURCE: Edward H. Spicer, ed., *Human Problems in Technological Change* (New York: Russell Sage Foundation, 1952), Case 5, pp. 69–90. ✧ The author is professor of anthropology and Director of Cornell University Studies in Culture and Applied Science. His chief interests are in the study of Oceania and Southeast Asia. He has written *Siamese Rice Village, Bibliography of Thailand,* and has edited *Handbook on Thailand.*

The Problem

Like other Australian aboriginals, the Yir Yoront group at the mouth of the Coleman River on the west coast of tropical Cape York Peninsula originally had no knowledge of metals. Technologically their culture was of the old stone age or paleolithic type; they supported themselves by hunting and fishing, obtaining vegetable foods and needed materials from the bush by simple gathering techniques. Their only domesticated animal was the dog, and they had no domesticated plants of any kind. Unlike some other aboriginal groups, however, the Yir Yoront did have polished stone axes hafted in short handles, and these implements were most important in their economy.

Toward the end of the nineteenth century metal tools and other European artifacts began to filter into the Yir Yoront territory. The flow increased with the gradual expansion of the white frontier outward from southern and eastern Queensland. Of all the items of western technology thus made available, none was more acceptable, none more highly valued by aboriginals of all conditions than the hatchet or short-handled steel axe. . . .

Relevant Factors

If we concentrate our attention on Yir Yoront behavior centering about the original stone axe, rather than on the axe—the thing—we should get some conception of the role this implement played in aboriginal culture. This conception, in turn, should permit us to foresee with considerable accuracy some of the results of the displacement of stone axes by steel axes acquired directly or indirectly from Europeans by the Yir Yoront.

The production of a stone axe required a number of simple skills. With the idea of the axe in its various details well in mind, the adult men—and only the adult men—could set about producing it, a task not considered appropriate for women or children. . . .

The use of the stone axe as a piece of capital equipment for the production of other goods indicates its very great importance in the subsistence economy of the aboriginal. Anyone—man, woman, or child—could use the axe; indeed, it was used more by women, for theirs was the onerous, daily task of obtaining sufficient wood to keep the campfire of each family burning all day for cooking or other purposes and all night against mosquitoes and cold (in July, winter temperature might drop below forty degrees). In a normal lifetime any woman would use the axe to cut or knock down literally tons of firewood. Men and women, and sometimes children, needed the axe to make other tools, or weapons, or a variety of material equipment required by the aboriginal in his daily life. . . .

While the stone axe helped relate men and women and often children to nature in technological behavior, in the transformation of natural into cultural equipment, it also was prominent in that aspect of behavior which may be called conduct, primarily directed toward persons. Yir Yoront men were dependent upon interpersonal relations for their stone axe heads, since the flat, geologically recent alluvial country over which they range, provides no stone from which axe heads can be made. The stone they used comes from known quarries four hundred miles to the south. It reached the Yir Yoront through long lines of male trading partners, some of these chains terminating with the Yir Yoront men, while others extended on farther north to other groups, having utilized Yir Yoront men as links. Almost every older adult man had one or more regular trading partners, some to the north and some to the south. His partner or partners in the south he provided with surplus spears, and particularly fighting spears tipped with the barbed spines of sting ray which snap into vicious fragments when they penetrate human flesh. For a dozen spears, some of which he may have obtained from a partner to the north, he would receive from a southern partner one stone axe head. . . . Thus trading relations, which may extend the individual's personal relationships out beyond the boundaries of his own group, are associated with two of the most important items in a man's equipment, spears and axes, whether the latter are of stone or steel. Finally, most of the exchanges between partners take place during the dry season at times when the great aboriginal fiestas occur, which center about initiation rites or other totemic ceremonials that attract hundreds and are the occasion for much exciting activity besides trading.

Returning to the Yir Yoront, we find that not only was it adult men alone who obtained axe heads and produced finished axes, but it was adult males who retained the axes, keeping them with other parts of their equipment in camp, or carrying them at the back slipped through a human hair belt when traveling. Thus, every woman or child who wanted to use an axe—and this might be frequently during the day—must get one from some man, use it promptly, and return it to the man in good condition. While a man might speak of "my axe," a woman or child could not; for them it was always "your axe," addressing a male, or "his axe."

This necessary and constant borrowing of axes from older men by women and children was done according to regular patterns of kinship behavior. A woman on good terms with her husband would expect to use his axe unless he were using it; a husband on good terms with his wives would let any one of them use his axe without question. If a woman was unmarried or her husband was absent, she would go first to her older brother or to her father for an axe. Only in extraordinary circumstances would she seek a stone axe from a mother's brother or certain other male kin with whom she had to be most circumspect. A girl, a boy, or a young man would look to a father or an older brother to provide an axe for her or his use, but would never approach a mother's brother, who would be at the same time a potential father-in-law, with such a request. Older men, too, would follow similar rules if they had to borrow an axe.

It will be noted that these social relationships in which the stone axe had a place are all pair relationships and that the use of the axe helped define and maintain the character of the relationships and the roles of the two individual participants. Every active relationship among the Yir Yoront involved a definite and accepted status of superordination or subordination. A person could have no dealings with any other on exactly equal terms. Women and children were dependent on, or subordinate to, older males in every action in which the axe entered. Among the men, the younger was dependent on the older or on certain kinds of kin. The nearest approach to equality was between brothers, although the older was always superordinate to the younger. Since the exchange of goods in a trading relationship involved a mutual reciprocity, trading partners were usually a kind of brother to each other or stood in a brotherly type of relationship, although one was always classified as older than the other and would have some advantage in case of dispute. It can be seen that repeated and widespread conduct centering on the axe helped to generalize and standardize throughout the society these sex, age, and kinship roles, both in their normal benevolent and in exceptional malevolent aspects, and helped to build up expectancies regarding the conduct of others defined as having a particular status.

The status of any individual Yir Yoront was determined not only by sex, age, and extended kin relationships, but also by membership in one of two dozen patrilineal totemic clans into which the entire community was divided. A person's names, rights in particular areas of land, and, in the case of a man, his roles in the totemic ceremonies (from which women are excluded) were all a function of belonging to one clan rather than another. Each clan had literally hundreds of totems, one or two of which gave the clan its name, and from any of which the personal names of clan members were derived. These totems included not only natural species or phenomena like the sun, stars, and daybreak, but also cultural "species": imagined ghosts, rainbow serpents, heroic ancestors; such eternal cultural verities as fires, spears, huts; and such human activities, conditions, or attributes as eating, vomiting, swimming, fighting, babies and corpses, milk and blood, lips and loins. While individual members of such totemic classes or species might disappear or be destroyed, the class itself was obviously ever present and indestructible. The totems therefore lent permanence and stability to the clans, to the groupings of human individuals who generation after generation were each associated with one set of totems that distinguished one clan from another.

Among the many totems of the Sunlit Cloud Iguana clan, and important among them, was the stone axe. The names of many members of this clan referred to the axe itself, or to activities like trading or wild honey gathering in which the axe played a vital part, or to the clan's mythical ancestors with whom the axe was prominently associated. When it was necessary to represent the stone axe in totemic ceremonies, it was only men of this clan who exhibited it or pantomimed its use. In secular life the axe could be made by any man and used by all; but in the sacred realm of the totems it belonged exclusively to the Sunlit Cloud Iguana people.

Supporting those aspects of cultural behavior which we have called technology and conduct is a third area of culture, including ideas, sentiments, and values. These are most difficult to deal with, for they are latent and covert or even unconscious and must be deduced from overt actions and language or other communicating behavior. In this aspect of the culture lies the "meaning" of the stone axe, its significance to the Yir Yoront and to their cultural way of life. The ideal conception of the axe, the knowledge of how to produce it (apart from the purely muscular habits used in its production) are part of the Yir Yoront adult masculine role, just as ideas regarding its technical use are included in the feminine role. These technical ideas constitute a kind of "science" regarding the axe which may be more important in relation to behavioral change than are the neurophysiological patterns drilled into the body by years of practice. Similarly there are normative ideas regarding the part played by the axe in conduct which constitute a kind of "morality" of the axe, and which again may be more important than the overt habits of social interaction in determining the role of the axe in social relationships. More than ideas regarding technology, ideas regarding conduct are likely to be closely associated, or "charged," with sentiment or value. Ideas and sentiments help guide and inform overt behavior; in turn, overt behavior helps support and validate ideas and sentiments. . . .

Important for an understanding of the Yir Yoront culture is a system of ideas, which may be called their totemic ideology. A fundamental belief of the aboriginal divided time into two great epochs, a distant and sacred period at the beginning of the world, when the earth was peopled by mildly marvelous ancestral beings or culture heroes who in a special sense are the forebears of the clans; and a second period, when the old was succeeded by a new order that includes the present. Originally there was no anticipation of another era supplanting the present; the future would simply be an eternal continuation and reproduction of the present, which itself had remained unchanged since the epochal revolution of ancestral times.

The mythical sacred world of the ancestors with which time began turns out on investigation to be a detailed reproduction of the present aboriginal world of nature, man, and culture altered by phantasy. In short, the idea system expressed in the mythology regarding the ancestral epoch was directly derived from Yir Yoront behavior patterns—normal and abnormal, actual and ideal, conscious and unconscious. The important thing to note, however, is that the native believed it was just the other way around, that the present world, as a natural and cultural environment, was and should be simply a detailed reproduction of the world of the ancestors. He believed that the entire universe "is now as it was in the beginning" when it was established and left by the ancestors. The ordinary cultural life of the ancestors became the daily life of the Yir Yoront camps, and the extraordinary life of the ancestors remained extant in the recurring symbolic pantomimes and paraphernalia found only in the most sacred atmosphere of the totemic rites.

❖ ❖ ❖ ❖ ❖

Analysis

The introduction of the steel axe indiscriminately and in large numbers into the Yir Yoront technology was only one of many changes occurring at the same time. It is therefore impossible to factor out all the results of this single innovation alone. Nevertheless, a number of specific effects of the change from stone axes to steel axes may be noted; and the steel axe may be used as an epitome of the European goods and implements received by the aboriginals in increasing quantity and of their general influence on the native culture. The use of the steel axe to illustrate such influences would seem to be justified, for it was one of the first European artifacts to be adopted for regular use by the Yir Yoront; and the axe, whether of stone or steel, was clearly one of the most important items of cultural equipment they possessed.

The shift from stone to steel axes provided no major technological difficulties. While the aboriginals themselves could not manufacture steel axe heads, a steady supply from outside continued; and broken wooden axe handles could easily be replaced from bush timbers with aboriginal tools. Among the Yir Yoront the new axe never acquired all the uses it had on mission or cattle stations (carpentry work, pounding tent pegs, use as a hammer, and so on); and indeed, it was used for little more than the stone axe had been, so that it had no practical effect in improving the native standard of living. It did some jobs better, and could be used longer without breakage; and these factors were sufficient to make it of value to the native. But the assumption of the white man (based in part on a realization that a shift from steel to stone axe in his case would be a definite regression) that his axe was much more efficient, that its use would save time, and that it therefore represented technical "progress" toward goals which he had set for the native was hardly borne out in aboriginal practice. Any leisure time the Yir Yoront might gain by using steel axes or other western tools was invested, not in "improving the conditions of life," and certainly not in developing aesthetic activities, but in sleep, an art they had thoroughly mastered.

Having acquired an axe head through regular trading partners of whom he knew what to expect, a man wanting a stone axe was then dependent solely upon a known and an adequate nature and upon his own skills or easily acquired techniques. A man wanting a steel axe, however, was in no such self-reliant position. While he might acquire one through trade, he now had the new alternative of dispensing with technological behavior

in relation with a predictable nature and conduct in relation with a predictable trading partner and of turning instead to conduct alone in relation
with a highly erratic missionary. If he attended one of the mission festivals
when steel axes were handed out as gifts, he might receive one simply by
chance or if he had happened somehow to impress the mission staff that
he was one of the "better" bush aboriginals (their definition of "better"
being quite different from that of his bush fellows). Or he might—but
again almost by pure chance—be given some brief job in connection with
the mission which would enable him to earn a steel axe. In either case, for
older men a preference for the steel axe helped create a situation of
dependence in place of a situation of self-reliance and a behavior shift
from situations in technology or conduct which were well structured or
defined to situations in conduct alone which were ill defined. It was
particularly the older ones among the men, whose earlier experience or
knowledge of the white man's harshness in any event made them suspicious,
who would avoid having any relations with the mission at all, and who thus
excluded themselves from acquiring steel axes directly from that source.

The steel axe was the root of psychological stress among the Yir
Yoront even more significantly in other aspects of social relations. This was
the result of new factors which the missionary considered all to the good:
the simple numerical increase in axes per capita as a result of mission
distribution; and distribution from the mission directly to younger men,
women, and even children. By winning the favor of the mission staff, a
woman might be given a steel axe. This was clearly intended to be hers.
The situation was quite different from that involved in borrowing an axe
from a male relative, with the result that a woman called such an axe "my"
steel axe, a possessive form she never used for a stone axe. (Lexically, the
steel axe was differentiated from the stone by an adjectival suffix signifying
"metal" the element "axe" remaining identical.) Furthermore, young men
or even boys might also obtain steel axes directly from the mission. A result
was that older men no longer had a complete monopoly of all the axes
in the bush community. Indeed, an old man might have only a stone axe,
while his wives and sons had steel axes which they considered their own
and which he might even desire to borrow. All this led to a revolutionary
confusion of sex, age, and kinship roles, with a major gain in independence
and loss of subordination on the part of those able now to acquire steel
axes when they had been unable to possess stone axes before.

The trading partner relationship was also affected by the new situation.
A Yir Yoront might have a trading partner, in a tribe to the south whom
he defined as a younger brother, and on whom as an older brother he would
therefore have an edge. But if the partner were in contact with the mission
or had other easier access to steel axes, his subordination to his bush colleague was obviously decreased. Indeed, under the new dispensation he
might prefer to give his axe to a bush "sweetheart" in return for favors or
otherwise dispose of it outside regular trade channels, since many steel

axes were so distributed between natives in new ways. Among other things, this took some of the excitement away from the fiesta-like tribal gatherings centering around initiations during the dry season. These had traditionally been the climactic annual occasions for exchanges between trading partners, when a man might seek to acquire a whole year's supply of stone axe heads. Now he might find himself prostituting his wife to almost total strangers in return for steel axes or other white men's goods. With trading partnerships weakened, there was less reason to attend the fiestas, and less fun for those who did. A decline in one of the important social activities which had symbolized these great gatherings created a lessening of interest in the other social aspects of these events.

Not only did an increase in steel axes and their distribution to women change the character of the relations between individual and individual, the paired relationships that have been noted, but a new type of relationship, hitherto practically unknown among the Yir Yoront, was created in their axe-acquiring conduct with whites. In the aboriginal society there were almost no occasions outside the immediate family when one individual would initiate action to several other people at once. For in any average group, while a person in accordance with the kinship system might be superordinate to several people to whom he could suggest or command action, at the same time he was also subordinate to several others, in relation with whom such behavior would be tabu. There was thus no over-all chieftainship or authoritarian leadership of any kind. Such complicated operations as grass-burning, animal drives, or totemic ceremonies could be carried out smoothly because each person knew his roles both in technology and conduct.

On both mission and cattle stations, however, the whites imposed upon the aboriginals their conception of leadership roles, with one person in a controlling relationship with a subordinate group. Aboriginals called together to receive gifts, including axes, at a mission Christmas party found themselves facing one or two whites who sought to control their behavior for the occasion, who disregarded the age, sex, and kinship variables among them of which they were so conscious, and who considered them all at one subordinate level. Or the white might impose similar patterns on a working party. (But if he placed an aboriginal in charge of a mixed group of post hole diggers, for example, half of the group, those subordinate to the "boss," would work while the other half, who were superordinate to him, would sleep.) The steel axe, together, of course, with other European goods, came to symbolize for the aboriginal this new and uncomfortable form of social organization, the leader-group relationship.

The most disturbing effects of the steel axe, operating in conjunction with other elements also being introduced from the white man's several subcultures, developed in the realm of traditional ideas, sentiments, and values. These were undermined at a rapidly mounting rate, without new conceptions being defined to replace them. The result was a mental and moral void which foreshadowed the collapse and destruction of all Yir Yoront culture, if not, indeed, the extinction of the biological group itself.

From what has been said it should be clear how changes in overt behavior, in technology and conduct, weakened the values inherent in a reliance on nature, in androcentrism or the prestige of masculinity, in age prestige, and in the various kinship relations. A scene was set in which a wife or young son, his initiation perhaps not even yet completed, need no longer bow to the husband or father, who was left confused and insecure as he asked to borrow a steel axe from them. For the woman and boy the steel axe helped establish a new degree of freedom which was accepted readily as an escape from the unconscious stress of the old patterns, but which left them also confused and insecure. Ownership became less well defined, so that stealing and trespass were introduced into technology and conduct. Some of the excitement surrounding the great ceremonies evaporated, so that the only fiestas the people had became less festive, less interesting. Indeed, life itself became less interesting, although this did not lead the Yir Yoront to invent suicide, a concept foreign to them.

The whole process may be most specifically illustrated in terms of the totemic system, and this will also illustrate the significant role which a system of ideas, in this case a totemic ideology, may play in the breakdown of a culture.

In the first place, under pre-European aboriginal conditions in which the native culture has become adjusted to a relatively stable environment in which there can occur few, if any, unheard of or catastrophic crises, it is clear that the totemic system must serve very effectively to inhibit radical cultural changes. The closed system of totemic ideas, explaining and categorizing a well-known universe as it was fixed at the beginning of time, presents a considerable obstacle to the adoption of new or the dropping of old culture traits. The obstacle is not insurmountable and the system allows for the minor variations which occur about the norms of daily life, but the inception of major changes cannot easily take place.

Among the bush Yir Yoront the only means of water transport is a light wood log, to which they cling in their constant swimming of rivers, salt creeks, and tidal inlets. These natives know that forty-five miles north of them are tribes who have a bark canoe. They know these northern tribes can thus fish from midstream or out at sea, instead of clinging to the river banks and beaches, and can cross coastal waters infested with crocodiles, sharks, sting rays, and Portuguese-men-of-war without the recurring mortality, pain, or anxiety to which they themselves are constantly subjected. They know they lack any magic to do for them what the canoe could do. They know the materials of which the canoe is made are present in their own environment. But they also know, as they say, that their own mythical ancestors lacked the canoe, and therefore they lack it, while they assume that the canoe was part of the ancestral universe of the northern tribes. For them, then, the adoption of the canoe would not be simply a matter of learning a number of new behavioral skills for its manufacture and use. The adoption would require at the same time a much more difficult procedure, the acceptance by the entire society of a myth, either locally developed or borrowed, which would explain the presence of the canoe, associate it with some one or more of the several hundred mythical ancestors (and how decide which?), and thus establish it as an accepted totem of one of the clans ready to be used by the whole community. The Yir Yoront have not made this adjustment, and in this case we can only say that ideas have for the time being at least won out over very real pressures for technological change. In the elaborateness and explicitness of the totemic ideologies we seem to have one explanation for the notorious stability of Australian cultures under aboriginal conditions, an explanation which gives due weight to the importance of ideas in determining human behavior.

At a later stage of the contact situation, as has been indicated, phenomena unaccounted for by the totemic ideological system begin to appear with regularity and frequency and remain within the range of native experience. Accordingly, they cannot be ignored (as the "Battle of the Mitchell River" was apparently ignored), and an attempt is made to assimilate them and account for them along the lines of principles inherent in the ideology. The bush Yir Yoront of the mid-1930's represent this stage of the acculturation process. Still trying to maintain their aboriginal definition of the situation, they accept European artifacts and behavior patterns, but fit them into their totemic system, assigning them as totems to various clans on a par with original totems. There is an attempt to have the myth-making process keep up with these cultural changes so that the idea system can continue to support the rest of the culture. But analysis of overt behavior, of dreams, and of some of the new myths indicates that this arrangement is not entirely satisfactory; that the native clings to his totemic system with intellectual loyalty, lacking any substitute ideology; but that associated sentiments and values are weakened. His attitudes toward his own and toward European culture are found to be highly ambivalent.

All ghosts are totems of the Head-to-the-East Corpse clan. They are thought of as white, and are, of course, closely associated with death. The white man, too, is white and was closely associated with death, so that he and all things pertaining to him are naturally assigned to the Corpse clan as totems. The steel axe, as a totem, was thus associated with the Corpse clan. But it is an "axe," and is clearly linked with the stone axe, which is a totem of the Sunlit Cloud Iguana clan. Moreover, the steel axe, like most European goods, has no distinctive origin myth, nor are mythical ancestors associated with it. Can anyone, sitting of an afternoon in the shade of a ti tree, create a myth to resolve this confusion? No one has, and the horrid suspicion arises that perhaps the origin myths are wrong, which took into account so little of this vast new universe of the white man. The steel axe, shifting hopelessly between one clan and the other, is not only replacing the stone axe physically, but is hacking at the supports of the entire cultural system.

The aboriginals to the south of the Yir Yoront have clearly passed beyond this stage. They are engulfed by European culture, in this area by either the mission or cattle station subcultures, or for some natives a baffling, paradoxical combination of both incongruent varieties. The totemic ideology can no longer support the inrushing mass of foreign culture traits and the myth-making process in its native form breaks down completely. Both intellectually and emotionally a saturation point is reached, so that the myriad new traits which can neither be ignored nor any longer assimilated simply force the aboriginal to abandon his totemic system. With the collapse of this system of ideas, which is so closely related with so many other aspects of the native culture, there follows an appallingly sudden and complete cultural disintegration and a demoralization of the individual such as has seldom been recorded for areas other than Australia. Without the support of a system of ideas well devised to provide cultural stability in a stable environment but admittedly too rigid for the new realities pressing in from outside, native behavior and native sentiments and values are simply dead. Apathy reigns. The aboriginal has passed beyond the reach of any outsider who might wish to do him well or ill. . . .

* 92 *

IMAGINATION AND HALLUCINATION
IN AFRICAN EDUCATION

John W. Hanson

During the 1960's, called the Decade of Development by the United Nations, attempts at rationally planned change have greatly expanded in the underdeveloped countries of the world. The creation of viable "knowledge centers" to promote social change has received increasing emphasis as a crucial element in the total devel-

SOURCE: John W. Hanson, *Imagination and Hallucination in African Education* (East Lansing: Institute for International Studies, College of Education in Cooperation with African Studies Center, Michigan State University, 1965). Reprinted by permission. ✧ John W. Hanson is professor of education at Michigan State University, and a member of the University's African Studies Center and of the Institute for International Studies in Education. He is a contributing author to *Language and Concepts in Education* and *African Education* and coauthor of *School and Society* and *Education and the Development of Nations*.

opment process. *This selection by Hanson illustrates both the problems and the potentials of modern nation-building through the formation of educational institutions. The article is based on his participation in the Michigan State University program at the University of Nigeria and on extensive field research and travels in a score of African countries.*

High in the hills above Bujumbura, in the very heart of Central Africa, situated so that all who come into the city cannot but be struck by its presence, stands the Collège du Saint Esprit. On sunny days its white walls and inspiring tower shine like polished ivory, clearly visible to any air visitors; on more cloudy days it stands high enough above the city and lake that the gray clouds move in upon it, burying it in their soft folds. If a person takes the trouble to ascend by foot or car the road which climbs up the twelve hundred feet above the city, he finds himself standing in the court of as magnificent a secondary school as he is apt to find anywhere in the world. Airy classrooms, fully equipped laboratories, a luxurious and well-supplied audio-visual room, and a line of student dormitories surround the expanse of paved playing fields. An inspiring chapel raises the eyes of each student to still higher things, while his more mundane needs are provided for by dormitories equipped with individual rooms and private showers. "Indeed," confided one of its professors to me, "I know of only one secondary school in all of Europe which is its equal in magnificence. But sometimes I wonder . . ."

There was much to wonder about. Founded in 1952 as an interracial collège of international standing through the munificence of the Belgian government, the Collège has offered the customary Belgian metropolitan curriculum, modified only in detail to make use of the existing environment in its science courses and to give, nowadays, some increased place to African geography and history. After six years of study, the recruits, once raw from the hills, are ready to leave the college as graduates, having in hand the diploma in humanities which assures them they have met the metropolitan standards and that they are, insofar as any school can assure it, the carbon-copies of their white counterparts in Liège, Antwerp, or Brussels. Below the edifice as they leave it, and in the hills behind it to which they hope to return as rarely as possible, and then only for short visits, are the huts and hovels of the people of Burundi who number over two hundred persons to a square mile and who produce each year less than forty dollars in products per person. No one doubts that this school was designed as a monument to the beneficence of the former "tutorial" power; but to a greater or lesser extent it is a monument to the recent past in most types of African education, a symbol of those hallucinations that confuse *schooling* with *education* and still bid fair to blind the muse to the problems of the times. The blindness lies not in the opulence of the school (though opulence can be blinding), but in its basic irrelevance. The true cost of such conceptions of education is not to be counted in the Belgian francs of their construction, or in any of the hard currencies of the world, but in the unnumbered graves still being filled by tribal strife, in the frustration and tensions of lives dwarfed by every form of impoverishment, in elites that vaunt their education rather than serve their people, in minds that imitate rather than create—in short, education that frustrates rather than liberates.

In a significant sense the problem of the Collège du Saint Esprit is the root problem of African education in general. African education is plagued neither by lack of faith in schooling nor by low priority in government or private budgets. If anything, the African faith and investment in schooling promises to be greater than the return. Unfortunately, the hardest problems of African education cannot be solved solely by budgets. They are not problems of educational expansion, but of educational re-thinking. Education has become equated with schooling; and the entrenched educational establishment—ministries, universities, and foreign assistance experts—much too often appears circumscribed in its vision and its thinking by the blank walls of schools as we have known them.

I am reminded of the multitude of schools I visited a few years ago in the back country of one of the new African nations. Instruction had reached that point in the syllabus where the root systems of trees were to be learned. Although the compounds of the schools I was visiting were literally cut from the surrounding forest, which provided a green wall to each of their playing fields, in school after school I watched youngsters parade to the inevitable chalkboard and dutifully retrace from their copybooks diagrams carefully copied from those previously drawn on the same chalkboard by their teachers—the "four basic types of roots." Live roots were all about them, but the chalk-pale imitation of the classroom held sway. Similar ghosts haunt most of African education today; and although it may be easy to "retrain" teachers to take an occasional excursion into the real and living forest, there is little sign that we have learned much about helping educational leaders search out the significant, living roots of education in the startling new environments which now surround them.

Educational expansion is difficult in countries with limited economic resources and qualified personnel; educational re-thinking is difficult everywhere. The tragedy in African education in our time is not, as is so often stated, that there is too little schooling; the tragedy is that what there is of it is inappropriate, partakes too much of the superficial attributes of schooling everywhere and too little of the qualities of education which make a difference. Equally tragic, and of course even less often mentioned, is the fact that the schoolmen, both Africans and foreigners, have thus far, by and large, failed significantly to demonstrate the imaginative vision which alone will permit education to fulfill its promise in a continent which places all its faith in this magic elixir.

The great hurdle for African education may prove to be those of us in the educational establishment itself—an establishment, both in Africa and in those nations overseas which would help Africa, that has not yet broken the bounds of conventional and imitative thinking. Conventional minds, as Mill reminded us a century ago, are good equipment for conventional times; but these are anything but conventional times in Africa. What Africa needs today is unconventional minds capable of finding unconventional answers to problems certain to stagger any but the most imaginative. If education would serve to treat the ills, present and potential, of the new African states, it is true that it must treat its own ills—but the most important of these are not to be found in the minutiae of pedagogy (minutiae which we educators are happy to explore endlessly), but in the root orientation of education to the wider problems and forces which are becoming all too clear on the African scene. Such an orientation must get quickly beyond happy educational sloganeering about "meeting needs" and must amount to a genuine educational revolution. If schoolmen are incapable of meeting this challenge, governments will (as they have already tentatively begun to do in some African countries) turn away from the schoolmen and the schools, and provide education by new agencies and other means, often losing the benefits of our knowledge in attempting to escape the limitations of our biases. A far happier solution would be for schoolmen to take part in the adventure of reshaping education; but any such partaking will come about only if we frankly prove ourselves capable of recognizing the nature of the problems we are confronting and the inadequacies of our past conventional answers in meeting them. Most of these problems and many of these inadequacies are by now becoming clear.

❖　❖　❖　❖　❖

It is not unusual when confronting difficult problems to search for panaceas. Today, vocational schools appear to be viewed by many as the panacea for the educational and social ills of Africa. There is a growing belief—especially encouraged by Americans—that Western vocational education will somehow solve developmental problems which Western academic education is unfortunately not solving. In a country such as Nigeria, for example, the faith in vocational education is to be seen in the secondary modern school program in Western Nigeria, in a policy statement that would transform grammar schools into comprehensive high schools in Eastern Nigeria, and in the attempt to build the University of Nigeria in the practical "land-grant" tradition of American university education. The same vocational emphasis is to be noted in greater or lesser degrees throughout Africa, from the *ferme écoles* and new rural education programs in numerous French-speaking countries to the American-sponsored Polytechnic School in Malawi, an expensive new school going into operation in an economy where even existing vocational schools have been unable to place their graduates. Vocational education would, of course, appear to have face-value validity in nations which hope for rapid economic development. Yet it has in the past seldom fared well in Africa, and there is reason to question how well it may fare in the future—or *under what conditions,* it may fare well. One scholar with long experience in Africa has, in fact, pointedly referred to this panacea as the "vocational education fallacy."

Whether vocational education succeeds appears to be related to at least five factors: the perception of the students and potential students that vocational courses will actually "pay off"; the development of work habits and attitudes which subsequently enable students to make a success of manual vocations; the relevance of courses of study to African conditions; the existence of bridges over the chasms that separate school from successful earning power; and the reinforcement which comes from continuing help, follow-up, or cooperation. Educators and the school must demonstrate leadership and ingenuity which take these factors into account before vocational education has much chance of succeeding. In order to illustrate what such ingenuity and imagination might mean in practical terms, we will consider several promising current practices—although most of them are so new that one cannot be certain that time will bear out the promise they now seem to hold.

An illustration of what can be accomplished through the agency of the vocational school can be drawn from Uganda. In a report that was strongly critical of past agricultural education, the Uganda Education Commission singled out the Wairaka Farm School as a bright light in this otherwise dark plain. Founded in 1958, Wairaka appears to be in the process of overcoming the usual barriers to effective farm education in East Africa and well on the way toward building self-respect among agricultural students, leading them to view agriculture as an attractive life alternative, and helping them over the gap to initial employment. The success of the Wairaka school in breaking through the anti-agricultural bias in those seeking education is shown by the fact that in 1964 over a thousand applicants had to be turned away, and Wairaka's present student body includes sons of legislators, judges, and other "prestige" individuals.

What is the magic which leads to success, when all the same problems potentially exist here as elsewhere? What makes the difference? The answer seems to lie in the practical implementation of a school philosophy of education which is realistically addressed to preparing students to face the hard facts of life in African agriculture. The school does not aim at producing farm laborers but at producing young men who can start their own farms and run them profitably. Graduates who lack sufficient holdings of their own to support profitable modern farming are encouraged to go to the new farm settlement areas. But encouragement means more than verbal encouragement—it means sound preparation and practical enabling or supporting action from the school itself.

The success of the school seems to be compounded out of what the school does for the student *while he is in* school and what it does for him *after he leaves* school. What is it about the *in*-school program which is unique? First of all, the school curriculum is specifically designed to produce a farmer who can make a reasonable living for himself. The school course of study places emphasis on the *principles* of science and agriculture and their application to various situations, rather than upon rules-of-thumb for farming; mathematics has been geared to farm planning and yield and marketing accounts; social studies are pointed toward helping students understand and cope with market conditions; field work provides experience in improvising with free and inexpensive local materials (for example, chicken houses are built with a cost for purchased parts of one penny per chicken).

But the conception of education which is exemplified here is concerned not only with factual knowledge and principles—it attempts to get at a value or attitude dimension—especially through the monumental task of building a respect for self, a respect for labor, and a respect for farming as a way of life. The school is run as a profitable farm operation—but the students are also brought to see that it would not be a profitable operation if the farmer limited himself to an 8-hour shift. (The school program runs all hours of daylight, and night hours are frequently thrown in.) Students can build up capital savings from their own individual crops or fields, but they soon recognize the hard work involved if these individual fields are actually to pay off. Everybody at the school does the hard work and the dirty work—including a principal who takes his occasional turn cleaning up in the kitchen, but apparently something about the real meaning of the dignity of labor rubs off on the student.

Students are given much more freedom and far fewer directions than at most African schools—and as a result they make mistakes, but they are helped to learn from their mistakes. Experiments are encouraged and often fail—but the love of "trying out" has apparently been fostered. Wairaka may be a farm school but, as the Principal commented to me, "The fact that it is a farm school doesn't mean that we expect students to behave like cabbages, just sitting in rows and growing bigger and bigger. We expect our students to be lively, mistake-making, learning human beings." Finally, in order to stress that its graduates will find a good life in rural areas only if they help make it a good life, the school attempts to incorporate in its own life those programs which will produce noteworthy community members—programs in self-government, debating, music, and dramatics. "Unless rural life is worth living," the Principal observed, "agricultural education can never succeed." This is social philosophy of education at its best.

This brings the student to the key "point of departure"—and the problem of the school and the society in helping him bridge the chasm between school attendance and productive life in the rural area. The student has already begun this bridging while in school. Each student leaves school with his own tool kit for farming, which he has built himself in school shops or bought through farm profits; each has a small amount of capital which he has earned through sales of crops on his own individual plots at the school; each has earned a "credit" which will enable him to receive from the school help in kind—seeds, poles, and the like—as these are needed on his own farm. But this is not all that is done to bridge the gap; the school follows him to his own farm—or to the farm settlement area, if he lacks sufficient farm land for modern farming back home. This school extension includes advice and help in dealing with specific problems he encounters, whenever and as often as needed. Equally important, it involves a claim by the recent graduates on the use of the very scanty and overworked equipment which the school does possess—as for example, when the school's *one* tractor is made available to a graduate to help remove those last intractable stumps in the first field he is clearing. Effective farm education, or preparation for effective farm living in Africa, cannot abruptly terminate with the award of a diploma or certificate.

As agriculture is, and must for some time remain, the vocation of an overwhelming proportion of Africans, occasional farm schools at the post-primary level cannot alone meet the educational need. If agricultural education is to play its legitimate role in the solution of social problems it must become far more extensive than this. Here the more extended experience of the United Arab Republic in attempting to introduce genuine rural education into its regular primary schools in non-urban areas is relevant, for in the U.A.R. the social drives and forces are not entirely unlike those further south in Africa. The initial Egyptian experiment in rural education began in the late 1930's and included some sixty schools. Each of these traditional "Western-type" primary schools was provided with equipment deemed necessary to adapt it to the rural environment—namely land, cattle, beehives, poultry—and an agriculture teacher. Apart from the additional classes, equipment and teachers, Western-style primary education remained intact—the same curriculum, the same academic teachers, the same principals. The result was emphatic: cows and agricultural teachers proved about equally alien to the school, and the experiment had to be abandoned as a failure after some ten years. The addition of agricultural courses and teachers to traditional schools left the schools and the communities which they served unchanged, and the drift to the cities unchanged.

The second phase of the Egyptian experiment was built on the basis of this initial failure. It was decided that the answer to rural regeneration lay not in Western-type primary schools with agricultural appendages, but in the creation of genuine rural schools. The creation of such schools was to be achieved largely through rural training colleges for primary teachers. In colleges such as Minshat-el-Kannater, teachers lived, worked, and studied in a rural environment for five years—practicing rural industries themselves, engaged in agricultural work as well as studies, and carrying out social services in the surrounding villages. At the same time the primary school syllabus was made flexible, permitting the teachers to put into practice upon leaving that which they had learned and practiced while in the rural teacher training college—not only what they had learned about agriculture, but what they had learned about improving rural life in general. In essence, this was the *penetration* principle rather than the *addition* principle in attempting to change schools. Here the result seemed to be successful as far as meaningful schooling was concerned, but it was found that this was still not enough.

Problems of rural backwardness and rural attrition through migration of potential leadership to the cities are not easily solved. The third step in the U.A.R. has been not only to make education—and the training of teachers for rural schools—part of the total rural environment, but to make the school a central part of a rural "social unit." This has come about through the creation in some three hundred rural areas of combined social units—consisting of hospitals, agricultural extension centers, social welfare centers, and rural schools—in an attempt to create a new composite-type social institution really designed to deal with the full range of rural needs. It is these principles of rural education—first making rural life the center of the total curricula; second, training all teachers for rural schools in and through the rural environment; and third, using the school as one of a complex of social agencies designed to make living in the rural community a reasonably attractive alternative—which appear to give greatest promise of providing sound programs in rural education. It is unfortunate that in times of potential social catastrophe so many African nations seem intent upon retracing the whole series of painful steps themselves, all the way from that first step of attempting to integrate school gardens into school programs to which they are in every way alien.

Although the problem of rural education varies from one African nation to another, depending upon the attractiveness of the perceived urban environment, the availability of land unencumbered by highly resistant tenure systems, and factors such as soil fertility and produce marketability, the principle still stands that no system of rural or agricultural education is going to make much sense, or achieve any measure of success, if it is not built into larger plans which give promise that agricultural life can afford the individual a decent living. "We must repeat that no plans for agricultural education will meet with success unless provision is made for settling young farmers on the land," the Uganda Education Commission concluded. "Young people must be convinced that plans exist to carry them forward in the difficult pioneer period. They need land, capital and tools; and also oversight, advice and encouragement. These they cannot provide for themselves."

Fortunately a number of experiments which apply this principle in very different ways are currently being tried in Africa south of the Sahara. It is worthwhile noting some of these experiments, not because their success is assured but because wide-ranging experimentation will be necessary if solutions are to be found. One experimental program underway is that of the *Centres des Jeunes* (Youth Centers), organized in Congo/Brazzaville as a joint project of the Ministry of Agriculture and the High Commission for Youth. This program consists of a number of *chantiers*—communal farms which have been constructed for youth. In the initial phase of the project, one *chantier* has been located in each of the agricultural regions of the country, but it is hoped that as a more extended rural renovation movement gets underway with Food and Agriculture Organization help it will be possible to expand this pilot scheme into a mass social-educational movement. Each *chantier* has a common foyer, common dining and sports facilities, and individual rooms in addition to agricultural holdings. The initial centers were opened in the south and consisted of approximately thirty youths each, ranging between 17 and 21 years of age. These youths were largely recruited from those leaving the *service civique*, and apart from very rudimentary vocational and civic training which they had acquired in that program, they possess no specific advanced training for life at the centers. Although government of each center is democratic, being conducted by an elected committee and president, instruction is given by an agricultural teacher provided by the Ministry of Agriculture and by a basic education teacher provided by the High Commission for Youth. Members, during the initial period, receive a small monthly stipend in addition to their share of the *chantier's* profits. It remains to be seen whether or not such communal living, which will ultimately be expanded to provide for family life, will be sufficient to counteract the attractions of Brazzaville (which I recall a young traveling companion on a Congo train referring to excitedly as "the Paris of Africa!"). Obviously it can succeed only if its members come to see it as assuring them both a reasonable standard of living and some of the excitement and advantages which they view as being part of "modernity."

A second essentially non-school approach to education, and one which has received considerable attention, is that of *animation rurale*, especially as this has been developed under the effective leadership of Cissé Ben Mady in Senegal. In many respects rural animation is about as far from school education as one can get. Most schoolmen would even question if it should be classified as "education." Rural animation is an attempt to revolutionize both a tradition and a society by working from within that tradition and that society. In this program young men, usually between the ages of 25 and 40, are selected by their fellow villagers to receive brief training aimed at helping them carry out projects which their villagers see as important. The basic principle in "teacher" selection is thus that of *paysans parmi les paysans*—those who are to receive the instruction which they will subsequently pass on to their fellows are chosen by villagers from among their own number. These animators are given a brief training session of about twenty days' duration at a Center of Animation. During this period they learn much about Senegal and its development plans, about applying new techniques in improving rural life, and about the principles and practices of cooperation. Returning to the communities which had selected them for the training, they decide with their fellow villagers upon actions to be undertaken in the village—actions which promise rather immediate observable returns, such as the improvement of cultivation methods, building a school, or improving a local cooperative. With the training they have received, plus periodic additional training periods of even shorter duration and aimed at specific problems of a region, they provide leadership ("education," if you will) for their fellow villagers. The essential instructional principle involved is "that the peasant must not be alienated from his traditional society and his society must not consider him an outsider." The expectation is that the enthusiasm generated—as individual improvements are agreed upon and effectuated—can begin a genuine reconstruction of rural life and, through rural life, of the entire nation.

A third experimental approach to rural education has been the attempt to link formal agricultural schools directly to land resettlement schemes, as has been tried with Israeli technical assistance in both Togo and Western Nigeria. In Togo the first two agricultural schools, at Glidji and Tsevie, were opened in 1962. Tied in with government plans to develop two relatively unsettled river valleys in southern Togo, these schools prepare the youngster to participate in a cooperative village; and upon completion of his agricultural school training program, each student receives some twenty acres of land in such a pilot village. In Western Nigeria, under the leadership of Chief Deko, a similar program was instituted and five Farm Institutes were established. Here, in an atmosphere that attempts to develop both understanding of and practice in cooperative organization, students are likewise prepared for farming in land resettlement areas. Upon completion of the Institute portion of their training, students move to the settlement sites, and for the succeeding two years receive additional training, even as they are allocated their own land holdings. Once again, as in most sound agricultural education schemes, a serious attempt is made to assure that no insurmountable barrier separates the instruction received from the chance actually to put that instruction into use.

Perhaps the most encouraging of the agricultural schemes, however, are those which are parts of broader attempts at educational reconstruction— reconstruction such as seems to be the current educational environment in countries such as Mali on the economic and political Left, and the Central African Republic, more centrally situated in the French "cultural sphere." It is not only educational planning which is needed in Africa, but educational planning which can somehow or other be freed from the firm grip of traditional educational thinking.

✧   ✧   ✧   ✧   ✧

. . . It is difficult to predict where fully satisfactory answers will be found, but in the light of experience currently available it would seem we might do better if we were to think more in terms of *education* and the social and institutional arrangements which make productive education probable, and less in terms of *schools per se*. We might do better if we begin thinking in terms of broad educational-social matrices which would give promise of bridging the chasms between formal education and nation-building. Educational thinking concerned only with schools does not necessarily do this.

What would it mean to consider *educational matrices* rather than merely *schools* as variables in developing an educational plan or altering an educational system? Essentially it would require considering as variables institutions or social arrangements which cut across our traditional distinctions between preparation and contribution, training and employment, school and life. It would be difficult to find a case where this is actually the dominant educational approach in any African nation today; yet if imagination and imaginative ways of overcoming almost insurmountable obstacles are to replace persistent hallucinations about the magic of schooling, this is precisely what is needed.

In order to illustrate how educational thinking can simultaneously use both traditional and non-traditional educational variables in tackling an enormous educational problem, we shall use the generally unheralded example of the Central African Republic. The example is of value, not for what has been accomplished, but for what seems to be in the process of being accomplished. I have had the good fortune to visit the country twice within the span of its first four years of independence. As a new nation it possesses most of the problems of the other new African states. Located in the heart of Africa far from the sea coast, it must rely for transportation on the Chari River flowing north to equally land-locked Lake Chad and, more importantly, the Oubangi flowing to the Congo and the sea. Its population consists of numerous tribal groups, sometimes referred to as the frightened people, as this was an area into which slave raiders made incursions even as late as this century. Many of the groups were originally refugees from such incursions. The population is divided between Islam, Christianity, and the indigenous tribal religions. The people suffer the usual deficiencies in nourishment; and traditional social structures, rural and family restraints, are showing signs of decomposition. Although in the past the nation was overwhelmingly rural, the general problems of the uprooting of peoples and the rural exodus are now in evidence. Large numbers of unemployed and unemployable youth are already congregating in such centers as Bangui. Rural and remote areas are becoming increasingly depopulated as people move either to roadsides or into the few cities and towns.

When I first visited its capital, Bangui, several years ago, I left with mixed impressions of soft nights scented by the perfume of tropical plants, of myriads of glorious tropical butterflies frolicking along the roads that wind into the hills above the city—and of a moribund educational system, built around that unadulterated French metropolitan education which had been equal partner in the team of French colonialism, French cultural hegemony, and French economic monopoly. When I returned to Bangui several months ago my impressions were sharply changed. I was treated early to a symbol of the change which had taken place. As one of the rather infrequent American visitors to this off-route African nation, I was invited to a dinner given by the American Ambassador for the visiting ambassador of another nation. The prescribed dress was shirtsleeves and no tie, the dress which President Dacko has initiated as the down-to-work symbol for himself and his government, and which he has requested the foreign embassies to accept as well. Symbols of a working approach to problems mean little if they stop at symbolism, but as I had subsequent occasion to explore what was going on in education, I became convinced that this was more than an empty sign—that here was a government working at its problems in ways that for Africa were fully as unconventional as ambassadorial dinners *sans cravate*.

But what are the educational problems in this nation *sans cravate?* The customary types of educational statistics begin to give a clue: The Central African Republic is a land in which only 10 per cent of those who enter the primary school at grade one receive their certificate (only 30 per cent even reach grade five); of those who enter general secondary school, only 1 per cent receive their *baccalauréat*; only half as many teachers, trained with the minimum qualifications, are being produced as new classrooms are being opened each year; with independence the only technical school closed, because it had been deemed to be too expensive; the number of African university graduates scarcely reaches a two-digit figure; uneducated, semi-educated, and minimally educated youth are flocking into the few urban areas which exist and once there, find little or nothing to do. Against this kind of background, in a country possessing an annual government budget in the neighborhood of approximately twenty million dollars, what can be done?

Although scarcely underway, the Central African Republic's approach to education for development does suggest both that education for developmental purposes need not discard what is relevant in the Western tradition of formal schools, but also that it need not stop there: in short, it stresses the applicability of old and new concepts, conventional and unconventional approaches, in facing the broad problems of education. At this point the most important thing about education in the Central African Republic is not that the answers to its educational problems have been found, much less that the answers to the overwhelming economic and social problems of the nation have been found through education, but that there is a spirit of innovation and experimentation in seeking out the answers.

This spirit is to be seen at all levels of education. It is to be seen both in the creation and program of its new regional higher education institution, the *Institut d'Études Agronomique d'Afrique Centrale* (one part of a four-nation foundation), which has devised an instructional program in which formal course work is supplemented by extended work training stages in research institutes,. rural cooperatives, government extension agencies, plantations and agricultural processing enterprises. This Institute has further discarded the traditional curriculum of the French agricultural university in order to provide one which places emphasis on adaptation, regional planning, administration, general education, and field experience. The spirit of innovation is also to be seen in thinking about the academic *lycée*. Plans are being considered whereby its program can be accelerated by at least one year—both through elimination of cultural content relevant to France but irrelevant to Africa, and through the reduction of wasteful school vacations and holidays. The same innovative spirit reveals itself in the teacher training and improvement program. The Pedagogical Bureau has, for example, developed a new reading program now being instituted through materials produced by cheap local reproduction processes (which must substitute for non-existent printing presses), through weekly radio programs built around these materials and their use, through short courses given in the field, and through a *Revue Pedagogique* which reaches all teachers with help on their teaching problems. (This review is also being used to help even the most remote teacher feel he has a unique stake in cultural renaissance through collecting and publishing accounts or works of local culture which might otherwise be lost!) Finally, this same spirit of innovation is to be seen in the primary school program, where an attempt is underway to supplement traditional schools with forty diversified upper primary schools, staffed to teach four trade subjects each, designed to familiarize their students with the principles of cooperative work and to provide them with practical experience in using local materials and maintaining farm machinery. Whether these new schools will in fact prove effective in educating and holding youth in the country remains to be seen; that they represent an experimental step toward creating an elementary program better adapted to the needs of a large number of rural youth seems clear.

Although these programs in their totality reflect a recognition of the need for broad educational change if harmonious development is to occur, they do not represent sharp departures from traditional approaches to education, approaches which essentially isolate education in school buildings and treat it as preparation for later productive life. As such they represent not the radical but the conservative part of the educational advance in the Central African Republic. More radical, both in the sense of manipulating social-educational matrices rather than just formal school units, and in the sense of challenging the assumption that education should be pre-service preparation sharply delineated from later productive life, is the complementary program in agricultural development through the National

Pioneer Youth. This program, carried on with Israeli expert assistance and with some American and French aid, indicates somewhat more clearly what is meant by taking broader social-educational matrices as variables which can be changed, rather than just concentrating on units in the formal school system.

The fundamental orientation of the project has been described as follows:

The aim of the project is to transform young Africans from tribal backgrounds into modern agriculturalists and to establish new cooperative farm villages, as one of the means toward rapid, practical agricultural development in the Central African Republic . . . Agricultural development in its initial stage is primarily a problem of attitudes, of a willingness on the part of villagers to change work habits, of a receptivity for new ideas, of a certain discipline in their daily work—in short, of a reorientation of their frame of mind. The greatest obstacle to agricultural growth in the Central African Republic is the present backward state of the rural African. The traditions and customs of the tribal society are incompatible with the requirements of modern agriculture. The National Pioneer Youth project has been conceived on the premise that a completely fresh start with the youth of the nation holds the most promise for success and rapid results.

The scheme involves progressive movement by a youngster—socially and educationally—from being a non-productive and unwanted youth wandering in town to the point where he is not only a self-sustaining, productive member of society but has accepted the responsibility of providing leadership in improving rural life through example and extension. There is no sharp division between education and productive contribution: the one grows systematically and smoothly into the other.

A youngster starts out by joining a youth club, of which there are now about ten with a total enrollment of some three thousand youth. (Original membership has been drawn largely from *abandonés*, youngsters wandering in the towns and having no place in the modernizing society, albeit they may have had a few years of formal schooling.) The club program is designed to have high appeal for youth and includes a wide variety of activities, including patriotic observances, athletics, classroom talks and instruction, and even physical labor at the club location. The instructional part of the program includes both general education and an introduction to modern agriculture. Club members are expected to put this instruction to use in their club program by cultivating garden plots, caring for poultry, and tending oxen. Some common meals are provided from their own produce. It is hoped that in the near future it will be possible to add to these activities the care and use of farm machinery, as American technical assistance makes such machinery available. The youth-oriented activities of the club are designed to build up enthusiasm and *esprit-de-corps*, restore self-confidence lost in idling, and develop the skills and values required for cooperation.

Those who acquire these qualities and demonstrate their dedication and sincerity by regular club attendance (not over three absences a year) are rewarded with a two-month session at an agricultural education "camp," located adjacent to a cooperative village. Here members continue with their club program part of each day, but are able to spend the remainder of the time in the cooperative village, working jointly with members of that village and perfecting their own skills in working together cooperatively. Even this experience serves as a trial period, however. Those who "measure up" to the challenge of this group living and service go on to a further agricultural training center where they receive a final brief period of training pointed specifically at preparing them to serve as the nucleus for a cooperative village of their own. Leaving this final training, the youngsters form such a cooperative village which, in a short period of time, serves as a center of rural regeneration, a pool of sound agricultural knowledge and mechanized farm equipment for extension work in the surrounding area. Education in the form of help and guidance continues to be provided in the village by Israeli technical assistants who are able to reinforce the formal and informal learnings which have been acquired during the club and camp programs. While no attempt is being made to convert all rural areas into cooperative villages, each village is seen as a pilot station which can in its own turn "multiply" education by demonstrating and spreading modern agricultural practices to those farmers within a forty kilometer radius who are willing to try out improved agricultural techniques.

The reasons for the initial success of this project are not hard to find. It promises the rewards which are necessary if young Africans are going to look at agricultural education as a desirable choice. The project does not rely heavily upon formal schools, where many youngsters may already have experienced humiliating defeat, but upon the activities and exciting cooperative programs characteristic of all good youth clubs or organizations. It does not separate schooling from the successful use of what has been learned: learning is put to use immediately—at the club site, in the cooperative village adjacent to the agricultural camp, in their own new cooperative. The program leads quickly and systematically from town clubs to actual memberships in a cooperative village. The steps are clear-cut and—to the student who applies himself diligently—certain. The village at the end of the road is characterized not by rural life as they might have previously known it, but by a better life and a more exciting life, a life which can be made to pay off financially in a village where they have both equipment to farm profitably and a social and cultural program—occasional motion pictures, a small library, dances and sports—capable of making rural living attractive. Finally, they have a chance to show leadership and to share in promoting the economic development of their country by serving as demonstrators, extension helpers, and leaders for others less fortunate than themselves.

The momentum gained appears to be paying off, if enthusiasm, high demand, and a rapidly expanding program are to be used as criteria. The program, operated outside of the Ministry of Education and under the direct auspices of the President's office, has a degree of freedom, flexibility, and imagination which seldom characterizes programs in education. It is certainly a far cry from our usual conceptions of schooling, but it does represent an imaginative adaptation of education to the needs of an African nation beset by all the usual problems of agricultural backwardness and unemployable youth. The ultimate test of educational development in the Central African Republic will be the nation's ability to capitalize on changes both within and outside the formal educational system; to provide for the cross-fertilization of ideas from each to the other, and thus to shape a comprehensive program that will provide a basis not only for national economic development but for satisfying, productive lives for all its people.

❖   ❖   ❖   ❖   ❖

Education for the reconstruction of societies is unlikely to take place without thorough-going reconstruction of education itself. This is the fundamental problem of African education: it must change rapidly enough, and fundamentally enough, to make the contribution to the solution of these problems of nation-building which it is potentially capable of making. One cannot determine with certitude the exact form this educational reconstruction should take; but it does seem clear that it will have the greatest promise of success if it is closely and directly tied in with the process of nation-building—a potentially tremendous educative process itself! This means education must do more than produce certain "quotas" of primary, secondary or technical school graduates, as is called for by too much current educational "planning." It means active programs and new educational strategies which will capture the energy of youth and turn it to worthwhile needs, which will prepare their minds to deal with the complicated forces that are already shaping their destinies, and which will assure that the skills they are acquiring lead directly into productive employment and nation-building. Traditional Western models of school-ing, and particularly their African imitations, rarely do this; but with suffi-cient modification and imaginative adaptation they might become func-tionally related parts of a broader educational system truly adapted to African needs.

To what extent our own educational experience, and that of the other Western nations, will be relevant in making these adaptations is uncertain. Had we the Poverty Program under our belts, our experiences might better qualify us to make a contribution. (Ironically, had we more often encour-aged such imaginative planning or experimentation in African develop-mental situations, we might now be in a better position to deal with our own Poverty Program!) In any event, if we are seriously concerned about

African development we must seek out fundamentally altered programs and bold strategies where these appear and render them every assistance we can. Merely using our aid to reinforce inherited educational systems, or furthering their routine expansion, will no longer be enough. In some cases we must face the likelihood that such reinforcement is already threatening to prove counterdevelopmental. Encouraging the African equivalent of our own tradition of educational experimentation and innovation might be our greatest potential contribution today.

✤ 93 ✤

THE CHANGING VALUES AND INSTITUTIONS OF VICOS IN THE CONTEXT OF NATIONAL DEVELOPMENT

Allan R. Holmberg

One of the most successful cases of planned modernization of a problem-ridden peasant community in an underdeveloped country is the Cornell Peru Project at Hacienda Vicos. This summary of an experiment in applied social science was written by the anthropologist who, in cooperation with Peruvian leaders and with very modest American assistance, conceived and led the effort.

More than fifty per cent of the world's population is peasantry, the large majority of whom are living in the so-called underdeveloped countries or newly emerging nations under natural conditions and social structures that have denied them effective participation in the modernization process. In the context of a modern state, this peasantry plays little or no role in the decision-making process; its members enjoy little access to wealth; they live under conditions of social disrespect; a large majority of them are illiterate, unenlightened, and lacking in modern skills; many are victims of ill health and disease. Characteristic of this sector of the world's population is a deep devotion to magico-religious practice as a means of miti-

SOURCE: *The American Behavioral Scientist*, Vol. 8, No. 7 (March, 1965), 3–8. Reprinted by permission of the author and the publisher. ✧ The author is professor of anthropology at Cornell University. From 1946 to 1948 he served as a cultural anthropologist in the Institute of Social Anthropology of the Smithsonian Institution, and he is a past president of the American Ethnological Society. His areas of interest include ethnology of the tropical forest and Andean regions of South America, culture and personality, applied anthropology, economic development and culture change.

gating the castigations of a harsh and cruel world over which it has little or no control. Such, in fact, were the conditions of life on the *Hacienda Vicos*, . . .

Operating on the assumption that these conditions of human indignity are not only anachronistic in the modern world but are also a great threat to public and civic order everywhere, Cornell University in 1952—in collaboration with the Peruvian Indianist Institute—embarked on an experimental program of induced technical and social change which was focused on the problem of transforming one of Peru's most unproductive, highly dependent manor systems into a productive, independent, self-governing community adapted to the reality of the modern Peruvian state.

Up until January, 1952, Vicos was a manor or large estate, situated in a relatively small intermontane valley of Peru, about 250 miles north of the capital city of Lima. Ranging in altitude from about 9,000 to 20,000 feet, Vicos embraced an area of about 40,000 acres and had an enumerated population of 1,703 monolingual Quechua-speaking Indians who had been bound to the land as serfs or peons since early colonial times.

Vicos was a public manor, a type not uncommon in Peru. Title to such properties is frequently held by Public Benefit or Charity Societies which rent them out to the highest bidder at public auction for periods ranging from 5 to 10 years. Each such manor has particular lands, usually the most fertile bottom lands, reserved for commercial exploitation by the successful renter who utilizes, virtually free of charge for several days of each week, the serf-bound labor force, usually one adult member of every family, to cultivate his crops. The rent from the property paid to the Public Benefit Society is supposed to be used for charitable purposes, such as the support of hospitals and other welfare activities, although this is not always the case. Under the contractual arrangements between the renter and the Public Benefit Society (and sometimes the indigenous population) the former is legally but not always functionally bound to supply, in return for the labor tax paid by his serfs, plots of land (usually upland) of sufficient size to support the family of each inscribed peon.

Manors like Vicos are socially organized along similar lines. At the head of the hierarchy stands the renter or *patron*, frequently absentee, who is always an outsider and non-Indian or Mestizo. He is the maximum authority within the system and all power to indulge or deprive is concentrated in his hands. Under his direction, if absentee, is an administrator, also an outsider and Mestizo, who is responsible to the renter for conducting and managing the day-to-day agricultural or grazing operations of the property. Depending on the size of the manor, the administrator may employ from one to several Mestizo foremen who are responsible for the supervision of the labor force. They report directly to the administrator on such matters as the number of absentee members of the labor force, and the condition of the crops regarding such factors as irrigation, fertilization, and harvest.

Below and apart from this small non-Indian power elite stands the Indian society of peons, the members of which are bound to a soil they do not own and on which they have little security of tenure. The direct link between the labor force and the administration is generally through a number of Indian straw bosses, appointed by the *patron* and responsible for the direct supervision of the labor force in the fields. Each straw boss or *Mayoral*, as he was known at Vicos, had under his direction a certain number of *peones* from a particular geographic area of the manor. In 1952 there were eight straw bosses at Vicos, with a total labor force of about 380 men. In addition to the labor tax paid by the Indian community, its members were obligated to supply other free services to the manor such as those of cooks, grooms, swineherds, watchmen, and servants. The whole system is maintained by the application of sanctions ranging from brute force to the impounding of peon property.

In the matters not associated directly with manor operations, the Indian community of Vicos was organized along separate and traditional lines. The principal indigenous decision-making body consisted of a politico-religious hierarchy of some seventeen officials known as *Varas* or *Varayoc*, so named from the custom of carrying a wooden staff as a badge of office. The major functions of this body included the settling of disputes over land and animals in the Indian community, the supervision of public works such as the repair of bridges and the community church, the regulation of marriage patterns, and the celebration of religious festivals. The leading official in this hierarchy was the *Alcalde* or mayor who assumed office, after many years of service to the community, by a kind of elective system and who occupied it for only one year. The *Varayoc* were the principal representatives of the Indian community to the outside world.

In 1952 all Vicosinos were virtual subsistence farmers, occupying plots of land ranging in size from less than one-half to about five acres. The principal crops raised were maize, potatoes and other Andean root crops, wheat, barley, rye, broad beans, and quinoa. In addition, most families grazed some livestock (cattle, sheep, goats, and swine) and all families raised small animals like guinea pigs and chickens as a way of supplementing their diets and their incomes. After thousands of years of use and inadequate care, however, the land had lost its fertility, seeds had degenerated, and the principal crops and animals were stunted and diseased. Per capita output was thus at a very low level, although the exact figure is not known.

In addition, many Vicosinos suffered from malnutrition; most were victims of a host of endemic diseases. Studies in parasitology demonstrated that 80 per cent of the population was infected with harmful parasites, and epidemics of such diseases as measles and whooping cough had been frequent over the years. There were, to be sure, native curers employing magico-religious practices and ineffectual herbal remedies to cope with these well-being problems but it can be said that the community had little or no access to modern medicine. The goal of the traditional Vicosino was simply to survive as long as he possibly could, knowing full well that he might be a victim of fate at any moment.

The principal avenue for gaining respect in traditional Vicos society was to grow old and to participate in the politico-religious hierarchy, the top positions of which could be occupied only after many years of faithful service to the community. Wealth was also a source of gaining prestige and recognition but it could not be amassed in any quantity, by native standards, until one's elders had died or until an individual himself had lived frugally and worked very hard for many years. In other words, the principal role to which high rank was attached was that of a hard working, muscle-bound, virtual subsistence farmer who placed little or no value on other occupations or skills. Consequently there was just no place for a rebellious or symbolically creative individual in traditional Vicos society. The manor system was, of course, in large part responsible for this. It needed few skills beyond brawn, and enlightenment could not be tolerated, because the more informed the population, the more it might become a threat to the traditional manor system. Records show that all protest movements at Vicos had been pretty much squelched by a coalition of the landlords, the clergy, and the police. As a result, over a period of several hundred years the community had remained in static equilibrium and was completely out of step with anything that was occurring in the modern world. The rule at Vicos was conformity to the status quo. It pervaded all institutions and dominated the social process. The peon was subservient to the overlord; the child, to the parents; and both were beaten into submission. Even the supernatural forces were punishing, and the burdens one bore were suffered as naturally ordained by powers beyond one's control.

Intervention From Without

The Cornell Peru Project intervened in this context in 1952 in the role of *patron*. Through a partly fortuitous circumstance—the industrial firm which was renting Vicos on a ten year lease that still had five years to run went bankrupt—we were able to sublease the property and its serfs for a five year period. For a couple of years prior to this time, however, the Peruvian anthropologist, Dr. Mario Vazquez, had conducted a very detailed study of this manor as a social system, as part of a larger comparative study of modernization of peasant societies that the Department of Anthropology at Cornell was conducting in several areas of the world. Thus when the opportunity to rent the *hacienda* arose, we seized upon it to conduct our own experiment in modernization. In its negotiations prior to renting the *hacienda*, Cornell received full support of the Peruvian Government through its Institute of Indigenous Affairs, a semi-autonomous agency of the Ministry of Labor and Indigenous Affairs. In December, 1951, a formal Memorandum of Agreement was drawn up between Cornell and the Institute of Indigenous Affairs, and the Cornell Peru Project became a reality at Vicos on January 1, 1952.

Several months prior to assuming the responsibilities of the power role at Vicos, a plan of operations was drawn up which was focused on the promotion of human dignity rather than indignity and the formation of institutions at Vicos which would allow for a wide rather than a narrow shaping and sharing of values for all the participants in the social process. The principal goals of this plan thus became the devolution of power to the community, the production and broad sharing of greater wealth, the introduction and diffusion of new and modern skills, the promotion of health and well being, the enlargement of the status and role structure, and the formation of a modern system of enlightenment through schools and other media. It was hoped that by focusing on institutions specialized to these values as independent variables this would also have some modernizing effect on the more dependent variables, namely, the institutions specialized to affection (family and kinship) and rectitude (religion and ethics), which are sensitive areas of culture in which it is generally more hazardous to intervene directly.

In designing our program and a method of strategic intervention, we were very much aware of two, among many, guiding principles stemming from anthropological research: First, innovations are most likely to be accepted in those aspects of culture in which people themselves feel the greatest deprivations; and second, an integrated or contextual approach to value-institutional development is usually more lasting and less conflict-producing than a piecemeal one. Consequently, we established our operational priorities on the basis of the first principle but tried to optimize change in all areas at the same time, realizing, of course, that with scarce resources, all values could not be maximized concurrently. Perhaps a few examples will best illustrate our use of the method of strategic intervention.

Our first entry into more than a research role at Vicos coincided with a failure of the potato harvest of both the *patron* and the serf community due to a blight which had attacked the crop. The poor of the community were literally starving, and even the rich were feeling the pinch. Complaints about the theft of animals and food were rife. At the same time, previous study of the manor had enlightened us about the major gripes of the serfs against the traditional system. These turned out not to be such things as the major commitment of each head of household to contribute one peon to the labor force for three days of each week, but the obligation of the Indian households to supply the extra, free services to the manor previously mentioned. Since we were in a position of power, it was relatively easy to abolish these services. A decision was made to do so, and volunteers were hired to perform these jobs for pay. Thus an immediate positive reinforcement was supplied to the community in our power relationship with it.

An added incentive to collaborate with the new administration resulted from the fact that we as *patrones* reimbursed the serfs for labor which they had performed under the previous administration but for which they had not been paid for approximately three years. Under the traditional system, each peon was entitled to about three cents per week for the work performed under the labor tax. In some Peruvian manors this is paid in the form of coca leaves, which most adult males chew, but at Vicos it was supposed to have been paid in cash. By deducting the back pay from the cost of the transfer of the manor to our control, we fulfilled earlier commitments, with the money of the previous administration, and received the credit for it. Through such small but immediately reinforcing interventions, a solid base for positive relations with members of the community was first established. In this regard, of course, we were greatly aided by Dr. Vazquez, who had previously spent almost two years in the community, living with an Indian family, and who personally knew, and was trusted by almost every one of its members.

Increasing Agricultural Productivity

As mentioned above, one of the most immediate and urgent tasks at Vicos was to do something about its failing economy which, in reality, meant increasing its agricultural productivity. Manors like Vicos are never productive because the renter during his period of tenure puts as little as possible into the operation and exploits the property for as much as he possibly can. The serfs, on the other hand, make no improvements on their lands, or other capital investments, because they, too, have no security of tenure. As a consequence, most such manors are in a very bad state of repair.

Since the Cornell Peru Project possessed funds only for research and not for capital development, the wealth base had to be enlarged by other capital means. It was decided, in consultation with Indian leaders, who were early informed about the goals of the Project, that no major changes would be initiated immediately in the day-to-day operations of the manor. We even retained the former Mestizo administrator, a close friend of the Project Director and Field Director, who agreed to reorient his goals to those of the Project.

The principal resources available to the Project were the labor of the Indian community and the lands which had been formerly farmed by the overlord. By employing this labor to farm these lands by modern methods (the introduction of fertilizer, good seed, pesticides, proper row spacing, etc.), and by growing marketable food crops, capital was accumulated for enlarging the wealth base. Returns from these lands, instead of being removed from the community, as was the case under the traditional system, were plowed back into the experiment to foment further progress towards our goals. Profits from the Project's share of the land were not only employed further to improve agricultural productivity but also to construct health and educational facilities, to develop a wider range of skills among the Indian population, and to reconstruct what had been a completely abandoned administrative center of operations. At the same time, new techniques of potato production and other food crops, first demonstrated on Project lands, were introduced to the Indian households which, within a couple of years, gave a sharp boost to the Indian economy. In short, by 1957 when Cornell's lease on the land expired, a fairly solid economic underpinning for the whole operation had been established, and the goal of considerably enlarging the wealth base had been accomplished.

Devolution of Power

From the very first day of operations, we initiated the process of power devolution. It was decided that it would be impossible to work with the traditional V*aras* as a leadership group, because they were so occupied during their terms of office with religious matters that they would have no time to spend on secular affairs. On the other hand, the former straw bosses, all old and respected men, had had a great deal of direct experience in conducting the affairs of the manor for the *patron*. It was decided not to bypass this group even though we knew that its members had enjoyed the greatest indulgences under the traditional system and, being old, would be less likely to be innovative than younger men. Under prevailing conditions, however, this seemed to be the best alternative to pursue. As it turned out, it proved to be an effective transitional expedient. Gradually, as success was achieved in the economic field, it became possible to replace (by appointment) the retiring members of this body with younger men more committed to the goals of modernization. For instance, men finishing their military service, an obligation we encouraged them to fulfill, returned home with at least an exposure to other values and institutions in Peruvian society. In pre-Cornell days such returning veterans were forced back in the traditional mold within a few days time, with no opportunity to give expression to any newly found values they may have acquired. Insofar as possible, we tried to incorporate people of this kind into decision-making bodies and tried to provide them opportunities to practice whatever new skills they had acquired. In the first five years of the Project, not only did age composition of the governing body completely change, but decision-making and other skills had developed to a point where responsibility for running the affairs of the community was largely in indigenous hands. A complete transfer of power took place in 1957, when a council of 10 delegates, and an equal number of sub-delegates, was elected to assume responsibility for community affairs. This council, elected annually, has performed this function ever since.

In the area of well-being it was much more difficult to devise a strategy of intervention that would show immediate and dramatic pay-off. This is a value area, to be sure, in which great deprivation was felt at Vicos, but it is also one in which the cooperation of all participants in the community was necessary in order to make any appreciable impact on it. The major well-being problems at Vicos, even today, stem from public health conditions. All individuals are deeply concerned about their personal well-being but are unwilling to forgo other value indulgences to make this a reality for the community as a whole. Nor were the resources available to do so at the time the Project began.

A variety of attempts was made to tackle the most urgent health problems. In collaboration with the Peruvian Ministry of Health and Social Welfare, a mobile clinic was started at Vicos, which made at least one visit to the community each week. Support for this effort came from the community itself in the form of the construction of a small sanitary post at which the sick could be treated. It was hoped to staff this clinic through the Public Health services of Peru, but all attempts to do so were frustrated by lack of budget and responsibly trained personnel. In Peru, such services seldom extend into rural areas because the preferred values of the medical profession are, as almost everywhere, associated with city life. Consequently, no major public health effort was launched and the community's state of well-being has shown little net gain. What gains have been made stem principally from improved nutrition, but as enlightenment about the germ theory of disease diffuses and the results of modern medicine are clearly demonstrated, through the application of public health measures that take negative beliefs into account, we expect a sharp rise in the well-being status of the community to follow.

Optimizing Goals

Strategies for optimizing Project goals for the respect, affection, and rectitude values, first rested heavily on the examples set by Project personnel. From the very beginning, for example, an equality of salutation was introduced in all dealings with the Vicosinos; they were invited to sit down at the tables with us; there was no segregation allowed at public affairs; Project personnel lived in Indian houses. At the same time, we attempted to protect the constitutional rights of Vicosinos, which had been previously flagrantly violated by the Mestizo world. Abuses by Mestizo authorities and army recruiters were no longer tolerated. The draft status of all Vicosinos was regularized; they were encouraged to fulfill their legal obligations to the nation. While not directly intervening in the family, or tampering with religious practice, the indirect effect of optimizing other values on the respect position of the community soon became evident. As Vicosinos mastered modern techniques of potato production, for example, they were approached by their Mestizo compatriots in the surrounding area, seeking advice as to how to improve their crops.

Even the rectitude patterns at Vicos began to change. When we first took control of the manor, rates of theft were extremely high. Every peon farmer, as his crops were maturing, had to keep watchmen in his fields at night. As the Indian economy rose and starvation was eliminated, this practice disappeared completely. Even the parish priest became an enthusiastic supporter of the Project. His services were more in demand, to say nothing of their being much better paid.

A strategy of promoting enlightenment at Vicos was initiated through the adaptation of a traditional manor institution to goals and values of the Project. In most Andean manors run along the lines of Vicos, the peons, after completing their three days labor, must report to the manor house where they receive their work orders for the following week. This session of all peons, straw bosses, and the *patron* is known as the *mando*. We devised a strategy of meeting the day before the *mando* with the *mayorales* or decision-making body and utilizing the *mando* to communicate and discuss the decisions taken. Since heads of all households were present, the *mando* provided an excellent forum for the communication of news, the discussion of plans, progress towards goals, etc.

A long-run strategy of enlightenment rested on the founding of an educational institution at Vicos that could provide continuity for Project goals, training of leadership dedicated to the process of modernization, and the formation of a wide range of skills. Through collaboration with the Peruvian Ministry of Education and the Vicos community itself, this became a possibility. Within the period of Cornell's tenure, levels of enlightenment and skill rose sharply and their effects have been substantial throughout the society.

Transfer of Title

In 1957, at the time Cornell's lease in Vicos expired, the Project made a recommendation to the Peruvian Government, through its Institute of Indigenous Affairs, to expropriate the property from the holders of the title, the Public Benefit Society of Huaraz, in favor of its indigenous inhabitants. By this time we felt that a fairly solid value institutional base, with the goals of modernization that we had originally formulated, had been established in the community. The Peruvian Government acted upon the recommendation and issued a decree of expropriation.

It was at this point that the experiment became especially significant, both in the local area and throughout the nation, for national development. Prior to this time, although considerable favorable national publicity had been given to the Project, little attention had been paid to it by the local power elite, except in terms of thinking that the benefits of the developments that had taken place would eventually revert to the title holders. It was inconceivable in the local area that such a property might be sold back to its indigenous inhabitants. Consequently, local power elites immediately threw every possible legal block in the way of the title reverting to the Indian community. They set a price on the property that would have been impossible for the Indian community ever to pay; members of the Project were charged with being agents of the communist world; the Vicosinos were accused of being pawns of American capitalism; Peruvian workers in the field were regarded as spies of the American government. Even such a "progressive" organization as the Rotary Club of Huaraz roundly denounced the Project, accusing its field director of being an agent of communism.

Fortunately, the Project had strong support in the intellectual community of the capital and among many of Peru's agencies of government. The co-director of the Project and President of the Indigenous Institute of Peru (also an internationally recognized scholar in high altitude biology), Dr. Carlos Monge M., was tireless in his effort to see justice done to the Vicosinos. But even his efforts did not bear fruit until almost five years had passed. The reason for this was that not only were the legal blocks of the resistance formidable, but the central government of Peru at this time was an elite government, which, while giving great lip service to the cause of the Vicosinos, was reluctant to take action in their favor. It is a matter of record that many high officials of government were themselves *hacendados*, hesitant to alter the status quo. Consequently, they were able to delay final settlement.

Meanwhile the Vicosinos, now renting the manor directly, were reluctant to develop Vicos because of the danger of their not being able to enjoy the fruits of their labor. While agricultural production rose through the stimulation of a loan from the Agricultural Bank of Peru, other capital investments were not made because of the fear that the price of the property would rise with every investment made. Finally, through pressure exerted by the President of the Institute of Indigenous Affairs and U.S. government officials in Peru, an agreement was reached between the Public Benefit Society and the Vicos community for the direct sale of the property to the Vicosinos at a price and on terms that they could realistically pay. Thus, after a five year wait following the devolution of power, the community actually became independent in July, 1962. Since that time Cornell has played largely a research, advisory, and consultant role, although the Peruvian National Plan of Integration of the Indigenous Populations has had an official government program of development at Vicos since Cornell relinquished control in 1957.

Results

What can be said in a general way about results of the Vicos experience so far? In the first place, if one criterion of a modern democratic society is a parity of power and other values among individuals, then vast gains have been made at Vicos during the past decade. Starting from the base of a highly restrictive social system in which almost all power and other value positions were ascribed and very narrowly shared, the Vicosinos have gradually changed that social system for a much more open one in which all value positions can be more widely shared and they can be attained through achievement. This in itself is no mean accomplishment, particularly since it was done by peaceful and persuasive means.

In the second place, the position of the Vicos community itself, vis-à-vis the immediately surrounding area and the nation as a whole, has undergone a profound change. Starting at the bottom of the heap, and employing a strategy of wealth production for the market place and enlightenment for its people, the community of Vicos has climbed to a position of power and respect that can no longer be ignored by the Mestizo world. This is clearly indexed by the large number of equality relationships which now exist at Vicos (and in intercommunity relationships between Vicos and the world outside), where none existed before.

Finally, of what significance is Vicos in the context of national development? Peru is a country with a high degree of unevenness in its development. The highly productive agricultural coast, with off-shore fishing grounds that are among the richest in the world, is moving ahead at a modern and rapid pace. In contrast, the overpopulated sierra, containing major concentrations of indigenous populations, many of whom live under a medieval type agricultural organization, such as exists at Vicos, is lagging far behind. The major lesson of Vicos, for Peru as a whole, is that its serf and suppressed peasant populations, once freed and given encouragement, technical assistance and learning, can pull themselves up by their own bootstraps and become productive citizens of the nation. It is encouraging to see that the present Peruvian Government is taking steps in the right direction. Its programs of land reform and Cooperation Popular may go a long way towards a more peaceful and rapid development of the country as a whole.

✤ 94 ✤

DESCENT TO ANOMY

Robert M. MacIver

Our social ties, the values by which we live, and our sense of "belonging" are so much a part of most of our lives that we have little conception of their deep significance to us and to our society. Hence, we are inclined to take social cohesion for granted. But this social cohesion through which the unity of our personalities is secured and maintained always rests in delicate balance. In a complex society, even under the most favorable conditions,

SOURCE: *The Ramparts We Guard,* chap. 10 (New York: Macmillan Co., 1950), 84–92. Reprinted by permission. ✤ For biographical data on Robert M. MacIver, see selection 66.

there are individuals who fall into anomy (now usually spelled anomie)—a condition where the sense of "belonging" to the group is lost and the norms or values of society are ignored or rejected. In times of crisis such as these, "whole groups are exposed to the malady." In this selection, MacIver describes the anomic person, and shows how the presence of anomy is evidenced in a modern society.

Let us look next at *anomy*, the other malady of democratic man that becomes most virulent in times of crisis and turbulent change, the breakdown of the individual's sense of attachment to society, to all society. Anomy is not simply lawlessness. A gangster or a pirate or a mere law-evading rogue is not as such, indeed is not likely to be, anomic. He has his own code of law against law and is under strong sanctions to obey it. He need not be the victim of that inner detachment, of that cleavage between the real self and the projected self, of that total rejection of in-doctrinated values that characterizes the anomic person. Anomy signifies the state of mind of one who has been pulled up from his moral roots, who has no longer any standards but only disconnected urges, who has no longer any sense of continuity, of folk, of obligation. The anomic man has become spiritually sterile, responsive only to himself, responsible to no one. He derides the values of other men. His only faith is the philosophy of denial. He lives on the thin line of sensation between no future and no past.

In any times particular individuals may fall into anomy. It happens when sensitive temperaments suffer without respite a succession of shocks that disrupt their faith. And not a few men have temporary moods that resemble anomy, periods when the spirit of denial rules them, after they have experienced some grave bafflement. But there are times of profound disturbance when whole groups are exposed to the malady. The soldiers in Mailer's novel, *The Naked and the Dead*, talk the language of anomy. They have been torn in youth from their environments, their careers, their dreams, their hopes, to face laborious tedium and the ugliest forms of death. They have been bereft of the sustaining ways of their culture. They are thrust back on the immediate needs and demands of each perilous hour. The present offers nothing but sensations; there are periods of boredom and drudgery, and then they are alone with nature and sudden death. So they use the language of sensation—there is nothing else to express. It means little but there is nothing else to mean. The livid, gory, sexy words they utter soon convey precisely nothing, nothing but the denudation they feel. For them, however, for those who survive, there is a return to nearly all the things they have lost. For most of them anomy wears away in their restoration to their society. But there are others, the hopelessly displaced, the totally uprooted, the permanently insecure, those who need the support of authority and have lost it without hope of recovery, the over-sophisticated who find that the challenges of life cannot be met by sophistication—among such people anomy takes full command.

Anomy is a state of mind in which the individual's sense of social cohesion—the mainspring of his morale—is broken or fatally weakened. In this detachment of the anomic person from social obligation his whole personality is injured. He has lost the *dynamic unity* of personality. The anomic fall into various types, though we do not have so far the psychological researches necessary for the adequate classification of these types. We can, however, broadly distinguish the following.

First, there are those who, having lost altogether, or in great measure, any system of values that might give purpose or direction to their lives, having lost the compass that points their course into the future, abandon themselves to the present, but a present emptied of significance. They resort, in other words, to a sophisticated cynicism, by aid of which they rationalize their loss. They live by the hour, seeking immediate gratification on whatever level it is available. They tend to be sensationalists and materialists. It is their defense against the ghosts of perished values.

Second, there are those who, having lost their ethical goals, having no longer any intrinsic and socialized values to which they can harness their drive to action, transfer this drive to extrinsic values instead, to the pursuit of means instead of to the pursuit of ends beyond them, and particularly to the pursuit of power, so far as that lies within their reach. It has been claimed that there is a "strain toward anomy" in modern capitalistic society, with its emphasis on competitive success measured by the purely extrinsic standard of money-making. There can be little doubt that engrossment in the competitive struggle, especially when it is carried on under the aegis of the "soul-less body-less" corporation, diverts men from the search for intrinsic satisfactions and erodes their recognition of the common interests of their society, the inclusive more abiding interests that bind men in the responsible fellowship of their community. At the same time, the experience of the past two generations suggests that it requires the violence of change, the deeper perturbations that disorient and displace men from their former ways, their former goals, their former faiths, to bring anomy to its full being, and in particular this second type of anomy. Those who exhibit it tend to be domineering, sadistic, ruthless, irascible, vain, inherently destructive. Unlike the first type, they live for a future, they have objectives that bind today to the further tomorrow, but these objectives are self-centered, ego-glorifying, bereft of social obligation. Often they profess adherence to some intrinsic faith or value, but primarily because that profession enhances their private designs. They are then like Machiavelli's prince, who must appear to be religious and high-minded if he is to retain his prestige and power. Moreover, they make the creeds of other men the instruments of their own aggrandisement, the utilitarian myths of their authority. On another level they are racketeers, buccaneers of industry or finance, unprincipled exploiters of whatever position, privilege, or power they acquire. All men or nearly all men cherish their private interest and frequently enough they allow it to overcome their public obligation. But they are restrained within certain limits set by loyalties of one kind or another, and when they transgress they are conscious of dereliction. But the truly anomic man has no limit short of necessity and no conscience that is more than expediency.

Third, we may distinguish a type of anomy that is characterized above all by a fundamental and tragic insecurity, something that cuts deeper than the anxieties and dreads that beset other men. It is the insecurity of the hopelessly disoriented. They have lost the ground on which they stood, the ground of their former values. Usually it happens when they have lost also their former environment, their former connections, their social place, their economic support. In the profoundest sense they are "displaced persons." The displacement, however, may not be physical. There is, for example, the social alienation of those who feel themselves rejected and become the victims of a persecution complex. This is perhaps the bitterest of all forms of anomy. There is a crushing sense of indignity, of exclusion, of injustice, of defeat, arousing feelings of intense hate, counter-aggressiveness, total revulsion from things as they are, sometimes accompanied by unquiet introspection and self-torture.

This cursory review is intended to suggest types, not to classify them. In any event there is a considerable overlapping of attributes between our types. We should also remember that many people approach the full bent of anomy in various degrees. As we have already suggested, the conditions of our civilization create some predisposition to it and when our kind of civilization is racked by abrupt and violent change anomy grows rampant. Anomy is a disease of the civilized, not of the simpler peoples. As Durkheim pointed out, one index of anomy is the number of suicides, and suicide is much more frequent among the civilized.

It is noteworthy that modern doctrines of violent social change are initiated by those who have at least a tendency to anomy. Let us take for example the case of Karl Marx. He was from his early youth subjected to some of the conditions that breed anomy. His family belonged to the rabbinical elite in Germany. While he was still an infant his father, to the general surprise, announced his conversion to the Protestant Evangelical Church. This was the cause of a bitter dispute between his father and his mother. In the end, when Karl was six years old, his father had his way, and Karl, along with the six other children of the family, was baptized into the new faith. We know from modern studies how deeply disturbing it is to the mind of a child to have his first indoctrinations shattered by a "culture clash" on the hearth. The secret churning of the young boy's mind was the first preparation of the revolutionist-to-be, greatly heightening that sense of aloofness and disorientation that is the lot of many a Jewish boy in a society that stupidly clings to its hoary prejudices. The first obvious effect on Karl Marx was his loathing of all religions.

He grew into an impetuous, irascible, opinionated, and still idealistic youth. Then his ambitions suffered a series of reverses and frustrations. At this stage he fell in with the "communist rabbi," Moses Hess. He was ripe for the new gospel. He embraced it avidly, inclining at first toward the French socialists but soon repudiating and scorning them to assert his own truly scientific brand. It was the culmination of a process that began in the disorientation of childhood. Marx had become completely alienated from the society in which he lived, not its economic order particularly but its whole being and all the culture it nourished. In the background of his mind there flickered visions of an ideal society. But his love of the ideal was pale and distant compared with his hatred of the actual. He turned early to dreams of power, of lonely mastery. He was at enmity with the world. He denounced with incredible bitterness his own best friends the moment they ventured to question in any way his authority.

A man may condemn the society in which he lives without being himself anomic. But only if he is sustained by the engrossing vision of a better society, only if he is working to hasten the coming of some "new Jerusalem," only if he lives in fellowship with some brotherhood of the faithful who share his vision, only, in the last resort, if he is already, prophetically, a member of the society for which he yearns. There are those who believe the main inspiration of Marx was just some such redemption of mankind, that he was filled with the vision of a world in which men would be liberated from exploitation and injustice, from the gross oppression of every form of power. To the present writer that seems a mistaken interpretation. In the voluminous writings of Marx there are only one or two most fleeting references to "the good society." There is no evidence that he really cared for his fellowmen. He never uses kindly language except for those who looked upon him as their infallible leader. He hated those of his own party who showed any independence of thought. He was venomous toward all whom he could not dominate.

Marx focused his sharp intelligence on the worst sore of the society he hated. A new industrial system had been growing up. It was being exploited with callous disregard for the welfare of the workers. In the "dark Satanic mills," as the poet Blake called them, men, women, and young children labored endlessly long days, under the worst conditions, for subsistence wages or less. There were riots and threats of revolution. The French Revolution had shown how a class system could be overthrown. Here Marx found his opportunity. With immense vigor and remarkable propagandistic skill he proclaimed the inevitable victory of the proletariat. Marx had never mixed with any proletarians. He was himself a bourgeois. He never showed any interest in proletarians as human beings—only as a class. As he himself said, he found in the proletariat the "material weapon of philosophy," of his philosophy, of his revenge on society, of his triumph. He was the wrathful divider. The "bourgeoisie" became the fixed objective of his hate, the source of all evil. He identified it with the society that had rejected him. It was anathema. He devoted his being to its destruction.

The presence of anomy in modern society is evidenced by the spread of violently divisive doctrines, doctrines of all-or-nothing, doctrines that loudly preach a reactionary or a revolutionary authoritarianism, doctrines that appeal to men not as human beings but as de-individualized masses in motion. The anomic and near-anomic persons of the second and third types are particularly prone to such doctrines. For they offer a congenial release from anomy, a drastic remedy for its bitterness and frustration, a refuge from its insecurity, a means of reconciling its destructive tendencies with its secret need for social reintegration.

All these doctrines are enemies of democracy. They reject its tolerance, its acceptance of difference, its respect for the individual, its faith in the healing processes of free opinion. The anomic man has lost the balance of social health, mostly through no fault of his own. In his alienation he seeks a quick and false prescription. The anomic who cannot be masters are often ready to be slaves. They cry out for the superman to save them, for some equivalent of a Providence, a God, the ineluctable authority who will end their alienation by saying, "I command you to follow," making his command ring with the magic of a lost obligation.

What then can democracy do to meet these two perils that threaten it in this age of violent change—group anarchy and individual anomy? We remarked in passing that we should not blame the anomic for their plight; they are suffering from a disease incident to our civilization. The remark may seem at best a truism—of what other social ailment might not the same be said? But it was said to call attention to the proper ways in which democracy can safeguard itself against these dangers. When we seek to heal a social ailment—or a physical one—we should always treat it as a disease and not as a sin. Unfortunately we often proceed on the latter assumption, as we have been doing, for example, in our "denazification" policies, with mostly unhappy consequences. To protect democracy against anomy or against group anarchy we must endeavor to get at and to remove their causes.

In the first place we should realise that all our efforts to protect democracy against these and other dangers are wholly futile unless we can protect it first against the catastrophe of war. For war has now become so immeasurably ruinous that the shaken and impoverished survivors would be driven to desperate measures that might be fatal to the very existence of democracy. Therefore while we still possess the inestimable spiritual heritage of democracy we must assure it against the very possibility of war, showing an alertness and a forethought that in the past two generations the democratic world most deplorably failed to show.

To achieve this end democracy must be strong in its quality as democracy, not only in its arms. The spiritual weakness of democracy is the strength of its enemies. In some respects we still make only a pretence at democracy. Ask the Mexican-Americans within our borders, whom we do not permit to sit at the same table with our noble Nordics. Ask the Negroes, whom we segregate as pariahs, so that we may not be contaminated by the social presence of a lower caste. Ask the Jewish people, who cannot live in the same hotels, sometimes cannot even be treated in the same hospitals as their democracy-loving fellow-Americans. Ask the Eastern Europeans, who are still frequently treated as second-class citizens, especially if their names have a Slavic sound. Ask the Chinese among us, the Japanese, the Filipinos, the Hindus—and remember that by our treatment of these people we are betraying our democracy before the greater part of the human race; remember also that the Orient is now stirring to new political life and that its decision between democracy and dictatorship will profoundly affect our future and the future of all mankind. Ask these questions, remember these things, and you must see that *our* failure to be true to *our* democracy is in the last resort the main reason why democracy is in danger.

The diseases of group anarchy and of personal anomy are peculiarly incident to modern democracies. The unfree systems are authoritarian; by authority and by sheer compulsion they suppress such manifestations. Democracy places responsibility in the individual and in the group—it asks their free allegiance, their free cooperation. But it must on that account assure its citizens the conditions in which they can exercise their freedom. It must guard them from haunting economic insecurity or their civic freedom becomes a mockery. It must guard them against the rank prejudice that cuts them off from the equal partnership of democratic society. Otherwise democracy will breed the seeds of its own destruction.

Lastly, it must make its own meaning, its own philosophy, its own spirit, positive and vital. It cannot rest in the outworn liberalism that never rose above the negative of non-intervention. No vague negative faith can meet men's needs in this age where dogmatic authoritarian creeds deride the democratic ideal, and promise men, however falsely, a greater security and a greater reward. Democracy must become self-conscious of its own worth. Here we reach a theme that needs our most earnest attention.

WHY AMERICANS FEEL INSECURE

Arnold W. Green

We Americans frequently pride ourselves on the flexibility and social change that characterize our society. But we pay a price for this fluid setting and rapid change in our patterns of living, for we need at least a few consistent and dependable social and physical anchorages to which we can attach ourselves. If we are constantly faced with new or ambiguous situations, we may become uncertain as to how to act and thus develop feelings of insecurity. It is because it is often but a short step from feelings of insecurity to neurosis to complete mental breakdown that social scientists need to study seriously the nature and origins of insecurity. In this selection, by A. W. Green, are portrayed some of the factors that produce insecurity in Americans. To counterbalance the rather strong charges implied here against our way of life, it should be pointed out that societies that are extremely rigid, inflexible, and stratified may err in the direction of defining appropriate behavior so completely as to produce their own special form of frustration.

Historically, from the ancient Hebrews, Greeks, and Romans, through the Middle Ages, and down to recent decades, a basic family tradition has been preserved in the West: the patriarchal, rural-familistic system. Within that system, the person lived out his life, rooted to the land and to a way of life that encompassed all his activities. Unquestioned duties and obligations were enforced, but there was financial and emotional security, intimate emotional ties, and close identification with one's fellows.

The division of labor was familial, all working together toward a common goal of family maintenance and perpetuation. The family circle and the local community comprised a complete and virtually isolated social world. Economic life, recreation, education, religious observances, were all a matter of intimate association among a small group of life-long relatives and friends. While the pressures to conformity were overwhelming, the individual nevertheless controlled his fate in ways denied to modern man.

He, in his family, owned or had equity in his own land and tools of production. He was not swept hither and thither by the vagaries of a

SOURCE: *Commentary*, Vol. 6, No. 1 (July, 1948), 18–28. Reprinted by permission of the author and the publisher. ✧ The author is a writer of monographs, articles, and textbooks in sociology. He was formerly professor of sociology at Pennsylvania State University. He has written *Henry Charles Carey: Nineteenth-Century Sociologist; Sociology, An Analysis of Life in Modern Society;* and *Recreation, Leisure, and Politics.*

market economy. Many of the important economic and political issues were local ones, and he could directly affect their development. In this isolated world, social action did not ramify out in unanticipated ways to produce incalculable results. There was an obvious and close relationship between social cause and effect, reward and punishment. As one moved from childhood into adolescence, courtship, and marriage, and the assumption of adult responsibilities, the blueprint for behavior was stable, consistent, unquestioned. Finally, the individual possessed a single status in all of the intimate groups of which he was an important part.

Over against this description—made extreme for the sake of contrast— of the traditional family, another can be placed: the modern, secular, individualized conjugal unit, composed of a restricted unit of husband, wife, and one or two offspring, living in an urban apartment. It finds itself in an impersonal world, in which personal relationships are scattered, partial, specialized. The old familial functions are no longer home-centered: the husband works away from home, among strangers; the children are educated outside the home by hired specialists; religious observances have waned; and each member of the family goes his own way in seeking recreation, which is today highly specialized for each age group.

Rights and duties are no longer rigidly defined. The demands of shifting and specialized groups with which the individual is associated in home, office, social and professional contacts, require specialized conformities, and not the total personality, but different parts of it, are involved. Emotional security has diminished. The roles assigned the person at different stages in his life history within the family are inconsistent and contradictory; similarly, one's status ebbs and flows as one moves rapidly from one association to another, one career situation to another. Under the impact of the competing needs and value of the various individuals in the unit, the family's solidarity is destroyed, leaving in its wake dissatisfaction, frustration, and intra-familial conflict.

✧   ✧   ✧   ✧   ✧

What does this mean psychologically? Since the family is no longer empowered to make plans and decisions and direct its own operations to anywhere near the extent that once was possible the *individuals* who make it up are pushed and pulled by forces of which they are only dimly aware, and which they can neither control nor stop. A new technological development, a bank failure in Austria, an unidentifiable bureaucrat's decision, the rise to power of a fanatic across the Atlantic, any and all of these may blast and ruin. And all the individual citizen can do is read about it. The concrete world of reality in which he, his family, his associates operated becomes less real than the "paper world" which informs him what "they" are doing, what "they" are planning, what decisions "they" have made, what new scientific discoveries "they" have blessed him with.

Can the laborer find out whether his union leaders are taking him out on strike only to secure a higher wage for him, as they may claim, instead of political advantage for themselves? Can the citizen actually find out what is going on in one of the federal agencies, or the stockholder how the affairs of "his" corporations are being administered? How much control does the voter have over either of the two political machines he has the political right to help into office? As bureaucracy extends, power and responsibility become more and more hidden, with greater possibilities of setting off forces that will ramify out to change, disrupt, control, and manipulate individual lives. The average American scorns the average German's plea that he had no responsibility for the concentration camps, but the average American knows that *he* had nothing to do with the development of the atomic bomb. And, indeed, he did not.

The individual finds himself in a world in which personal and business ethics increasingly go by the board as personal long-range planning becomes more difficult, and life-long residence in one location is no longer the pattern. It is a world of insecurity and uncertainty, blaring headlines and sudden shocks, in which the accumulation of experience is insufficient preparation for the next, unforeseen stimulus. And meanwhile a tremendous discharge of nervous energy runs into a hundred deviant channels. Bitterness, despondency, dependency spread like a pall, along with the belief that all is chance. We are still oriented, in terms of thought pattern and emotional pattern, to the slow, stable rhythms of family life on the farm. But the structure that created this basic ideology of living is gone.

We have already spoken of the confusion of statuses in the new way of life. At one time, status, taken over from the family, was relatively fixed and definitive. Today, the person interacts within a plethora of groups, and will be accorded a *different* status as he steps from one to another: the moral religious adolescent may be praised at home and vilified in school; the liberal may be appreciated by his college professor and scoffed at later by his business associates. Under the dispensation of modern success-striving, social approbation and a sense of security must be constantly reaffirmed, and this pressure is aggravated by the fact that one is really not in control of one's economic fortunes, the chief determinant of status. Thus it happens that anxiety and conviction of personal failure are endemic in our society.

The psychological pressures thus created impinge directly upon the life of the family, since they divert energy, time, and talent away from the home. And the new economic order, with its demands for rationality, its dividing-up of the personality, its schooling of impulses, combined with the constant threat of sheer job-insecurity as well as ultimate failure, places a tremendous emotional overload on the modern family. Within it love-relationships must compensate for all the shocks, frustrations, and damming up of impulse that success-striving demands.

The function of "love" in modern society is peculiarly complex. With the partial disintegration of the rural-familistic system, the actual day-by-day involvement of personal relations—both in work and play—disappeared, and the improvisation and demonstration of a total *emotional* involvement became doubly important as an ideal. The emphasis on such emotional involvement was stepped up as codes of proper conduct with various kinds of persons became increasingly vague. When the behavior of husband and wife, for example, became more and more a matter to be settled in each marriage, rather than by reference to convention, the answer of the culture was to jazz up the tempo of romantic love.

The concept of romantic love rests on a myth. Two young persons arrive at an indeterminate age, meet, and a mysterious cosmic process informs each that this is the "one." They marry, and live happily ever after, constantly fulfilling in every act their *unique* relationship. Marriage becomes, then, not so much an institutional arrangement as a device by which each can secure his or her *individual* desire for personal happiness. Sadly enough, the very fact of basing marriage on romance operates to create a well-nigh universal frustration of the prized sentiment.

In the first place, romantic love is a highly stylized drama that demands some modicum of natural physical endowment and fitting surroundings. But the majority of men are not handsome, the majority of women are not beautiful, and the majority of both are poor. Frustration is inevitable.

Second, success and love, particularly for that segment of the population known as the "middle class," work at cross-purposes. Marriage is still the woman's chief career. The middle-class girl hopes to marry not only a man but a bank balance, so that she may combine the two major goals of her career in a single activity—courtship. But when a man is striving toward success, early marriage seriously interferes with his career. In the rural-familistic system a man's wife was a necessary adjunct to his economic activity; today, a wife is an unproductive luxury that an ambitious young man cannot afford. He needs time, energy, and his available funds for education and to get started in his individual career, a career that is no longer integrated with family life. Thus, at the very time when the culture demands the intensive idealization of courtship, the stage is set for a battle of the sexes, often involving sexual exploitation, in a context of what Dr. Willard Waller has called "pluralistic ignorance of each other's motives," where pre-marital relations are no longer supervised closely by family and community.

Third, the romantic concept of love in marriage must carry a tremendous overload of emotion engendered through success-striving. With marriage less "practical," there tends to arise a constant questioning of the extent to which one is receiving the expected emotional service: a ceaseless seeking-out of the other's motivations, with the feeling of betrayal if the other does not conform to expectations. . . .

Fourth, while romantic love appears to be needed in modern society in order to get people married, serving as an emotional drive that smashes past individualistic considerations of success, it cannot be depended upon to keep a marriage together through the years. The family remains, in however truncated a form, an *institution* with a certain minimum of obligations that must be met in a certain way regardless of the present emotional tone of relations between husband and wife. The tragedy of love, as Somerset Maugham has so honestly observed, is that it does not last. Marriage, as sexual-emotional interaction, in time inevitably seeks a lower level of habitual expression, and the aging mate no longer fulfills the romantic ideal. Sociologists in the field of marriage and the family have been somewhat dishonest in this regard, writing confidently of "another kind of love" which replaces the erotic euphoria of the honeymoon. Perhaps there is such a love, but it most certainly is not the kind of love that moderns have been specifically conditioned to expect in their marriage —an effortless, timeless ecstasy. And so we have the phenomenon of "romantic divorce"—if this other person no longer fits the romantic ideal, I will retain my ideal intact, and seek another love-object. That the same failure will only be repeated with another partner is not considered, and so, in 1946, there was one divorce for every three marriages.

It is questionable whether the new freedom in marriage has appreciably raised the general level of happiness. In most cultures, and in our own historical perspective, people have not married for individual happiness or the development of their personalities, but to form a necessary basic economic unit, and the necessity of maintaining it was as unquestioned as it was unquestionable.

Interestingly enough, various schools of psychotherapy have recently been soft-pedalling the neo-Freudian injunction to allow children to develop their egos without restriction, in favor of pointing out the valuable psychological security that can derive from a child's knowledge of absolute limits to "freedom." A similar formulation has yet to be devised for the child's parents. Paradoxically, "freedom" for the individual has value, or even meaning, only in terms of some indeterminate authoritarian framework. The divorce rate does not begin to measure the amount of dissatisfaction, the wistful longing for escape, that is generated by the mere knowledge that the back door of divorce is swinging wider. (No advocacy of restricting divorce legislation is implied here. To do so would be to mistake effect for cause.) It may be that the Victorian, with all his "repressions," had the better of the argument. His marriage and family were buttressed by a no-nonsense set of community, family, and religious exactions. He was not at the same time forced to uphold an institution and impelled to "develop his own personality," i.e., fulfill individualistic cravings at the expense of that institutional structure.

Mental health or emotional stability (the term used is not a critical matter, being imprecise in any case) in a sociological framework, depends upon a continuity of conditioning and group-expectation: either personal roles, goals, and self-conceptions remain fairly uniform throughout the life-history, or undergo a series of easy transpositions. The typical modern family, which contains the majority of the population and embodies the dominant social trends, rips that continuity to shreds.

Let us consider what happens in such a family—let us say, a family of the Protestant, urban, college-educated, lower-middle income group. (The training of children born to parents who can thus be characterized is so consistent as to permit prediction, in a certain range.)

The father's primary goal is success; yet he cannot use his *child* to this end. The child, far from being an economic asset as he was under rural-familistic conditions, has become a serious liability: the sheer dollar-outlay for medical care, diets, lengthening schooling, etc., represents a diversion of energy as well as funds at the very time when the father's career is in its early, and crucial, stages. This is made more painful by the feeling that the child will in all probability never contribute to his father's support.

The child also interferes with pleasures. Modern recreation is no longer designed for family-wide participation: rather, whether in the form of movies, sports events, plays, golf, bridge, tennis, dinner parties, it is designed for individual or couple participation.

And what is the role of so-called scientific child care in this complex? The child must not be spanked, parents must be patient, the child's ego development must not be curbed. The assumption of much of the literature on child rearing seems to be that the parents have a combined culinary, nursing, and psychiatric function, and nothing more. But note that in a commercial, industrial, specialized job-world, cooks, nurses, and psychiatrists are paid for what they do.

In other words, the father's duties and obligations constantly increase, while his rights diminish. An ambivalence toward his child emerges, which is more or less widespread, though very rarely admitted, even to confidants.

The child's mother also feels somewhat ambivalent toward him. Nurtured on the romantic concept of love, possessing a success-drive only slightly less intensive than her husband's, having embarked upon a career of her own prior to marriage, or at least dallied in fantasy with the idea of a career, she is left ill-fitted for the drudgery of house-cleaning, child care, and the preparation of meals. The freedom that modern household conveniences have brought her has been commonly misinterpreted as well as exaggerated. While the housewife in the past had more work to do, that work was part of a well-integrated system of household and community activities. The modern housewife, with more leisure time, still must work at a number of household tasks for which she has not been trained, for which she has no respect, and which are isolated from her social activities.

Having little to do, in or out of the home, she is her child's constant companion. So-called scientific child care enforces a ubiquitous supervision and diffused worrying over the child's health, diet, and ego development; this is complicated by the expenditure of much energy aimed at forcing early walking, toilet-training, talking, because in an intensively competitive milieu the parents are constantly comparing their own child's development with that of the neighbor's children.

Under constant supervision, with limited play area in a house touching other homes on all sides, or in an apartment, and lacking companions, the child's physiological expansiveness, fed by his boredom, persists in getting him into trouble. Similar behavior was not so likely to occur in the rural-familistic household, and even when it did, it did not constitute so much of a crisis.

Already the parents have made "love" of supreme importance in their relation to their child, theirs for him and his for them, partly because of the love complex of our time, and partly as a compensation for the many sacrifices they have made for the child, long debated before and after its arrival. The child, in turn, comes to need love desperately, precisely because he has been conditioned to need it. Now, the more ambivalent the parents are towards the child, the more seriously is the "trouble" he causes them interpreted. He should not act in such a way because of the sacrifices they have made on his behalf, and the least he can do is show his gratitude by "loving" them in turn, i.e., keeping out of "trouble." When the trouble inevitably occurs, the most effective punishment imaginable is the threat to withdraw love from him. To the extent that the child's personality has been absorbed and blanketed by lack of companionship other than with his parents, he will be thrown into a panic, and will develop guilt feelings to help keep him from getting into further trouble.

But obedience and propitiation are not enough. The modern child, particularly the boy, having tried to escape from anxiety and guilt by blind obedience and "love" for his parents, finds he cannot stabilize his relationships with others on that basis. His play group, which may be denied him until he has reached school age, makes him feel a certain shame and inadequacy in approaching its members with his accustomed techniques. He also discovers that he is involved in competition with others—as an individual with his contemporaries, and as a representative of his family unit with other families. Before he has developed a real self-awareness he becomes part of a process of invidious comparison with other families.

But effective competition demands a certain degree of independence, firmness of purpose, perhaps aggressiveness. His earliest conditioning was toward obedience, dependence, and love, and he is still expected to exhibit these virtues within the home, but he must "do things" outside the home. In the case of the boy, the father, as the representative of the outside male world, makes this demand uncompromisingly—this, incidentally, may be one of the unsuspected sources of the so-called Oedipus complex. In any event, contradictory demands are made on the child, and an integration of the conflicting roles is virtually impossible. Thus is laid the basis for so many self-blocking drives in modern society, and the widespread feeling of frustration and inadequacy.

In the earlier years, the girl's training tends to be not so traumatic as the boy's. Girls are still for the most part being prepared for marriage as an ultimate goal. Girls are not subjected to so much familial pressure to assume early roles of independent, aggressive action. For both sexes, however, but perhaps especially in the case of the boy, adolescence is a period of "storm and stress," not so much because of the biological changes taking place at that period, but rather because the parents received their basic life-orientation as children in a milieu that was radically different from the one the modern adolescent encounters outside the home. Thus the parents attempt to impose on the child a life-organization that is out of gear with the adolescent's outside experience. Also, the period of dependence upon parents is steadily lengthening.

The adolescent of either sex must defer sexual satisfaction and the assumption of responsible adult activities until long after the period when he is biologically and intellectually (if not emotionally) mature. This is complicated by the fact that the culture has not worked out guides for the gradual relinquishment of parental authority over children, so that a conflict tends to arise: the parents attempting to lengthen the period of parental authority, the adolescent attempting to cut it short. Since the job world has no place for the adolescent, the age at marriage is on the average increasing,[1] he must fight out the battle on minor personal issues, such as when he must get home from the dance, the use of the family automobile, the right to "express" himself. Postponement of adult roles slows the process of emotional maturity, and represents malpreparation for marriage.

The girl's childhood may not be beset by so many contradictory familial demands as the boy's, but as she grows older, the inchoate values of "female emancipation" involve her. Perhaps she won't get married. There is always the possibility of a career. In any event, she also has been caught up in the new values of individualism and success and is no longer willing to accept the subordinate role in marriage that once was unchallenged. If marriage can be used to secure a high standard of living, she

---

[1] Editors' Note: The author's statement concerning the average age at marriage is in error, but this does not deny the major theme.

"succeeds," otherwise she may be assailed by doubts. The writer has traced, in case records taken over a period of years in a university psychological clinic, the educated woman's reluctance to accept *any* marriage as a way out.

A new role is emerging for the woman in marriage, the role of equal partner, which is more acceptable to her than the traditional housewife-and-mother role. Yet, despite the growing tendency to regard marriage not as an institutional complex but as an opportunity to get something for herself, to fulfill the romantic ideal, to develop her own personality, there remains a widespread reluctance to renounce the protection and security of the older role. At the same time the bearing of children, and the domestic service performed for the husband, are unacceptable. And her husband hardly simplifies her problem. He was raised in a home which had its chronological setting two decades ago, but centuries ago in terms of social change. His recollection of his own father's role is strikingly patriarchal compared to his wife's expectations of him. He is not ready to forgo the rights accruing to the patriarch though he may be perfectly willing that his wife work, assume equal responsibility in making decisions, manage family finances. And so the stage is set for a conflict of expectations.

It is questionable that moral exhortation will change this whole picture. Family stability in the modern world (as Lewis M. Terman thoroughly demonstrated in his *Psychological Factors in Marital Happiness*, 1939), as well as individual adjustment within it, are dependent upon the preservation of older patterns, since no new bases for the family have taken their place. At the same time, the socio-economic structure which was the underpinning of the older values has been too greatly modified to support an effective demand that a generation of vipers cease chasing its strange new gods. We may well have to reconcile ourselves to the fact that we will have to live, for some time to come, in a society increasingly made up of persons subjected to the process we have described. . . .

NAGASAKI'S MAGIC MOUNTAIN

Norman Cousins

The development of a plan to prevent forever the outbreak of nuclear war is without doubt the most urgent human problem of our time. War has always been a desperate, destructive, and costly way of resolving disagreements between nation states; but today we are capable of total annihilation anywhere in the world within minutes of the irrevocable decision. And such an action could be the logical consequence of the Soviet-American race to achieve world superiority in destructive capacity. This "deterrent approach" to world peace has developed on a scale totally inconceivable to the isolationist and peace-loving Americans of only a short generation ago. Dispute about which nation is superior in destructive power seems pointless since facts are hard to come by, and an empirical test, unthinkable. A decade has now passed since Norman Cousins first aroused the conscience of Americans by quoting the disturbing questions raised by the young Nagasaki college instructor. These questions are still unanswered. They remain the inescapable concern of all citizens of the world.

Fumiko Narahara is a seamstress in Nagasaki. When the bomb fell eight years ago she had just turned fifteen. She is alive today because of Nagasaki's magic mountain. And so are at least seventy-five thousand of her fellow citizens who happened to be on the right side of the mountain on August 9, 1945.

It isn't much of a mountain. More precisely, it is a ridge, a high and uneven lump of land jutting into the heart of the city. The ridge falls away quickly where it approaches the sea. A road skirts the shore and connects a network of streets on both sides of the mountain. The far or Urakami side of the mountain is where most of the heavy industry used to be located. It is also a densely populated area. For the people of Nagasaki today all life is reckoned according to the side of the mountain you were on when the bomb fell. The bomb fell low enough for the mountain to contain the radioactive ball of fire to the Urakami valley. If you were on the right side of the mountain you felt the shock—but you lived.

On the morning of August 9, 1945, Fumiko Narahara was at the home of her aunt on the right side of the mountain. The aunt had been ill and Fumiko's mother had sent the girl to care for her. Fumiko's mother was

SOURCE: *Saturday Review*, Vol. 36, No. 2 (January 9, 1954), 22–24. Reprinted by permission. ❖ For biographical data on Norman Cousins, see selection 31.

unable to come because she was employed. Fumiko's father worked at the iron smelting plant on the wrong side of the mountain, where the Narahara home was also located.

At two minutes past eleven the explosion occurred. The aunt's home shook at the impact and the windows were smashed. But the house itself remained erect; it was not touched by the ball of fire that mushroomed through the Urakami valley, consuming seventy thousand lives and severely burning fifty thousand others. When Fumiko rushed outside her aunt's home she saw that the houses nearby were all right; but beyond the mountain the city was a vast furnace. The Narahara home was inside the furnace. So was the weaver's shop where her mother worked. So was the foundry where her father worked.

Fumiko was one of many thousands of survivors who experienced the agonizing wait of endless days on the fringe of the furnace until the fires died down. When, finally, she was able to go around the mountain she took the road skirting the shore and passed the foundry, now a charred skeleton. But the road ended at about that point. Beyond that were no streets, no landmarks, no homes. There was not even a city. There were only acres of smoking black rubble. Except for a vague idea where her home had been Fumiko had no way of identifying the site. The bodies of her mother, father, and two smaller brothers were not recovered from any of the ruins

For the first few years after the bomb Fumiko lived with a deep sense of guilt for having survived. She says now that whenever she took the shore road to Urakami in the early days she hated herself for not having been in Urakami with the others. This feeling was not hers alone. There were many who had homes on the far side of the mountain but who were outside the valley on the day of the bomb, leaving their wives or husbands or children behind. Like Fumiko, they felt cut off from their real selves, unable to understand why they should have been spared. But with the passing of the years the guilt feeling has tended to lose its heaviness, returning only now and then when something special happens, like a medical examination by doctors assigned to study the effects of the bombing, or a propaganda movie put out by people who are trying to stir up passions against America.

Fumiko says she no longer hates the mountain for having spared her. She no longer cringes when she hears people refer to the mountain as a blessing. For she knows the good the magic mountain has done for Nagasaki. Unlike Hiroshima, which suffered almost total devastation within one mile of the center of the bomb and severe fire damage beyond that, Nagasaki's death toll and damage was largely confined to one section of the city. Consequently, in the emergency period after the bomb the city could mobilize some of its own medical and hospital facilities from the undamaged part that remained. And, though the bomb was a more powerful type than the one that fell on Hiroshima, there were fewer casualties, thanks not only to the magic mountain but to the early care of many of the victims.

Today the Urakami valley of Nagasaki has been almost completely rebuilt. Some of the scars remain. The old iron and steel works is still in its charred skeletal state. And on the beginning of the ridge, only a few hundred yards from the center of the explosion, is the empty shell of the Church of Urakami, once the largest Catholic cathedral in the Orient, with a capacity of almost 9,000. A temporary church has been built alongside the old one; there is the hope that someday soon the means may be forthcoming to put up a new cathedral every bit as magnificent as the old.

At what is believed to be the center of the explosion a memorial park has been laid out, with a high tower in the center and appropriate exhibits at various spots, such as a crumpled steel girder or slate that had melted and fused again. A small museum facing the tower contains some notable mementoes of the bombing, such as a grandfather's clock that was stopped by the bomb at exactly two minutes past eleven. The clock was in a home at the end of the valley some six miles from the center of the explosion. The city plans to erect a large cultural center around a mammoth statue dedicated to the peace, on the present site of the memorial. This, too, awaits necessary funds.

✧   ✧   ✧   ✧   ✧

There are still some inner scars. As more and more is known about the period immediately preceding the end of the war the feeling has grown that the bomb may not have been as essential to ending the war as at first was widely believed. The memoirs of Secretary Stimson, Secretary Forrestal, and General Eisenhower have thrown a new light on the decision to drop the bomb. On August 9, three days after the Hiroshima bomb, there was no doubt about the fact that Japan would surrender. The only doubt concerned the circumstances of the surrender. America wanted no discussion about terms or anything else. We wanted absolute surrender and we wanted it within a matter of hours, and the bomb of Nagasaki was designed to achieve just that, which it did.

But today, as we prod Japan to become a mighty military nation again, there are people in Nagasaki who cannot convince themselves that seventy thousand of their number died because there was a good reason for it, or because there was no other way. At a college not very far from the new memorial park a young instructor put it to me succinctly during a small open forum following my talk.

"History now knows," he said, "that Japan asked for peace terms even before Hiroshima was bombed. And history knows that Japan was certainly ready to surrender after Hiroshima. But the Americans were afraid perhaps that Japan would not want to give up as much as you wanted her to give up in defeat. So you used the atomic bomb for the second time on Nagasaki and you got what you wanted. You said that what you wanted was a Japan which would completely destroy its military machine and the spirit of militarism and nationalism which built it. We agreed. You tore down our armaments plants, and you dumped all our munitions and weapons into the sea, and you put our military leaders in jail, and you wrote new textbooks for us in which you denounced militarism and war, and you helped us to write a new Constitution in which we said we would never arm or fight again.

"But now you are telling us that it was all a big mistake. You tell us that it was a mistake to get rid of the military machine, a mistake to say all those terrible things about our militarists and nationalists, a mistake to have written that clause in our Constitution against war and the means of war.

"Very well. If we are to believe you now what are we to think of the bombing of Nagasaki and the seventy thousand who died here? If the reason for your bombing of Nagasaki was to get Japan to agree to do the very things you now say was a mistake, then you can only mean that you acknowledge that the bombing of Nagasaki was a mistake, too. And a mistake such as this is not something that passes easily. We are talking now about an atomic explosion over a living city and about what happened to the people who are inside it. Some people say that one way to die is as bad as another, and that death by atomic bomb is no worse than death by any other means. But what about the people who were not quite killed? We had many thousands of them, people with atomic disease who died very slowly over a long period of time. We had thousands of children with new kinds of scars and burns that have not yet been treated adequately—even now, eight years after the bomb. Should I say to them that your policy about Japan has now changed, that the bomb wasn't really necessary after all, and that therefore there is no real reason for their burns?

"I am no Communist, although there are many Communists who hate America and are doing everything possible to make you look ridiculous because you don't seem to know what you want in the world or where you're going. I don't side with the Communists, because where they say they are going is all wrong, and it will be a bad thing for Japan if we become a totalitarian nation again, whether Communist or militarist. But it is true that you can't expect people to follow America when you make so many big mistakes. How do we know that what you are telling us now will not turn out to be another mistake that you will admit a few years from now after even more damage is done?

"When you go back to America I wish you would tell the American people that it's not what the Communists are saying about you that is what is really hurting you. The main thing that is hurting you is that you never sit still long enough to think deeply before you do something. You change from day to day, and no one on the outside ever really knows who speaks for your country. We know that at heart you are all right but we aren't sure you know enough about the people outside America whom you expect to follow you. You have so much power and so little purpose. We'd like to follow you but it's not easy when you make so many strange turns and when you seem to be more afraid of yourself than of the power you identify as your enemy.

"You have probably visited the office of the Atomic Bomb Casualty Commission in Nagasaki, where American doctors examine Japanese who survived the explosion. They are wonderful men, these doctors, and they have made many friends among the Japanese people, for they have done things as individuals which their official jobs try to discourage them from doing. I am talking about the fact that these doctors are not officially able to do anything but examine the people here. They are not allowed to treat the Japanese they examine, by American law. But as individuals they have done a great deal to help us and we are grateful to the United States for sending them.

"But what puzzles many Japanese every time we pass the ABCC is this: now that America knows all the terrible things that happen to people during an atomic explosion, what new ideas do you have to do away with atomic explosions altogether—on us, on you, or on anyone else?"

❖ 97 ❖

ENCOUNTERS BETWEEN
CIVILIZATIONS

Arnold J. Toynbee

One professor of sociology used to take his classes on an airplane ride over the city so they could see the general ecological pattern of the total area. From such a vantage point one gets a special perspective. Details become smaller and often obscured, but relationships between elements stand out. In this article, historian Arnold Toynbee takes us up above the confining horizon of our own immediate time and culture and reveals to us the broader panorama of interaction among societies. We see civilizations growing, blending, and dying. We see our own culture as it relates to this larger pattern. Some aspects of our civilization take on greater significance, while others shrink in proportion. We see that some of

SOURCE: *Harper's Magazine*, Vol. 194 (April, 1947), 289–94. Reprinted by permission of the author. ❖ Arnold J. Toynbee is a British historian and economist, and professor emeritus of history, University of London. Among his many publications are A *Journey to China*, *Study of History* (12 vols.), *Civilization on Trial*, A *Survey of International Affairs*, and *East to West: A Journey Round the World*.

*our assumptions and interpretations may be time-bound and pro-
vincial. Cultural variability and diffusion become more meaningful
concepts.*

What will be singled out as the salient event of our time by future
historians, centuries hence, looking back on the first half of the twentieth
century and trying to see its activities and experiences in that just proportion which the time-perspective sometimes reveals? Not, I fancy, any of
those sensational or tragic or catastrophic political and economic events
which occupy the headlines of our newspapers and the foregrounds of our
minds; not wars, revolutions, massacres, deportations, famines, gluts,
slumps, or booms, but something of which we are only half-conscious, and
out of which it would be difficult to make a headline. The things that
make good headlines attract our attention because they are on the surface
of the stream of life, and they distract our attention from the slower,
impalpable, imponderable movements that work below the surface and
penetrate to the depths. But of course it is really these deeper, slower movements that, in the end, make history, and it is they that stand out huge in
retrospect, when the sensational passing events have dwindled, in perspective, to their true proportions.

Mental perspective, like optical perspective, comes into focus only
when the observer has put a certain distance between himself and his
object. When, for example, you are traveling by air from Salt Lake City
to Denver, the nearest view of the Rockies is not the best one. While you
are actually over the mountains, you see nothing but a maze of peaks,
ridges, gullies, and crags. It is not until you have left the mountains
behind you and are looking back at them as you fly over the plains that
they rise up before you in their magnificent order, range behind range. It
is only then that you have a vision of the Rockies themselves.

With this vision in my mind, I believe that future historians will be
able to see our age in better proportion than we can. What are they
likely to say about it?

Future historians will say, I think, that the great event of the twentieth
century was the impact of the Western Civilization upon all the other
living societies of the world of that day. They will say of this impact that
it was so powerful and so pervasive that it turned the lives of all its victims
upside down and inside out—affecting the behavior, outlook, feelings, and
beliefs of individual men, women, and children in an intimate way, touching chords in human souls that are not touched by mere external material
forces—however ponderous and terrifying. This will be said, I feel sure, by
historians looking back on our times even from as short a time hence as
A.D. 2047.

What will the historians of A.D. 3047 say? If we had been living a
century ago, I should have had to apologize for the fantastic conceit of
pretending to speculate about anything that might be said or done at so

immensely remote a date. Eleven hundred years was a very long time for
people who believed that the world had been created in 4004 B.C. But I
need not apologize today; for, since our great-grandfathers' time, there has
been so great a revolution in our time scale that, if I were to try to plot
out to scale, on one of these pages, a chart of the history of this planet since
its birth, I should not be able to make so short a period as eleven hundred
years visible to the naked eye.

The historians of A.D. 3047, then, may have something far more interesting than those of A.D. 2047 to say, because they, by their time, may
know much more of the story of which we, today, are perhaps in a rather
early chapter. The historians of A.D. 3047 will, I believe, be chiefly interested
in the tremendous countereffects which, by that time, the victims will
have produced in the life of the aggressor. By A.D. 3047, our Western
Civilization, as we and our Western predecessors have known it, say, for
the last twelve or thirteen hundred years, since its emergence out of the
Dark Ages, may have been transformed, almost out of all recognition, by
a counterradiation of influences from the foreign worlds which we, in our
day, are in the act of engulfing in ours—influences from Orthodox Christendom, from Islam, from Hinduism, from the Far East.

By A.D. 4047 the distinction—which looms large today—between the
Western Civilization, as an aggressor, and the other civilizations, as its
victims, will probably seem unimportant. When radiation has been
followed by counterradiation of influences, what will stand out will be
a single great experience, common to the whole of mankind: the experience
of having one's parochial social heritage battered to bits by collision with
the parochial heritages of other civilizations, and then finding a new life—
a new common life—springing up out of the wreckage. The historians of
A.D. 4047 will say that the impact of the Western Civilization on its contemporaries, in the second half of the second millennium of the Christian
Era, was the epoch-making event of that age because it was the first step
toward the unification of mankind into one single society. By their time,
the unity of mankind will perhaps have come to seem one of the fundamental conditions of human life—just part of the order of nature—and it
may need quite an effort of imagination on their part to recall the parochial
outlook of the pioneers of civilization during the first six thousand years or
so of its existence. Those Athenians, whose capital city was no more than
a day's walk from the farthest frontiers of their country, and those American contemporaries—or virtual contemporaries—of theirs, whose country
you could fly across from sea to sea in sixteen hours—how could they behave (as we know they did behave) as if their own little country were the
universe?

And the historians of A.D. 5047? The historians of A.D. 5047 will say,
I fancy, that the importance of this social unification of mankind was
not to be found in the field of technics and economics, and not in the field
of war and politics, but in the field of religion.

II

Why do I venture on these prophecies about how the history of our own time will appear to people looking back at it several thousand years hence? Because we have about six thousand years of past history to judge by, since the first emergence of human societies of the species we call "civilizations."

Six thousand years is an almost infinitesimally short time compared to the age of the human race, of mammals, of life on earth, of the planetary system round our sun, of the sun itself, and of the star-cluster of which our sun is a not particularly conspicuous member. Still, for our present purpose, these last six thousand years—brief though they are—do provide us with other examples of the phenomenon we are studying—examples of encounters between different civilizations. In relation to some of these cases, we ourselves, in our day, are already enjoying the advantage—which the historians living in A.D. 3047 or 4047 are going to have in looking back at us—of knowing the whole story. It is with some of these past encounters in mind that I have been speculating on how our own encounter with our own contemporaries is likely to turn out.

Take the history of one of our predecessors, the Græco-Roman civilization, and consider how this looks to us in the fairly distant perspective in which we are now able to see it:

As a result of the conquests of Alexander the Great and of the Romans, the Græco-Roman civilization radiated over most of the old world—into India, into the British Isles, and even as far as China and Scandinavia. The only civilizations of that day which remained untouched by its influence were those of Mexico and Peru, so that its expansion was not incomparable to our own in extent and vigor. When we look back on the history of the Græco-Roman World during the last four centuries B.C., it is this great movement of expansion and penetration that stands out now. The wars, revolutions, and economic crises that ruffled the surface of Græco-Roman history during those centuries, and occupied so much of the attention of the men and women who were struggling to live through them, do not mean much to us now compared with that great tide of Greek cultural influence invading Asia Minor, Syria, Egypt, Babylonia, Persia, India, China.

But why does the Græco-Roman impact on these other civilizations matter to us now? Because of the counterattack of these other civilizations on the Græco-Roman World.

This counterattack was partly delivered in the same style as the original Græco-Roman attack: that is, by force of arms. But we are not much interested today in the forlorn hope of Jewish armed resistance to Greek and Roman imperialism in Palestine; or in the successful counterattack of the Parthians and their Persian successors under the Sassanian Dynasty east of the Euphrates; or in the sensational victories of the early

Muslim Arabs, who in the seventh century of the Christian era liberated the Middle East from Græco-Roman rule in as short a number of years as it had taken Alexander the Great to conquer it a thousand years earlier.

But there was another counterattack, a non-violent one, a spiritual one, which attacked and conquered, not fortresses and provinces, but hearts and minds. This attack was delivered by the missionaries of new religions which had arisen in the worlds which the Græco-Roman civilization had attacked by force and submerged. The prince of these missionaries was Saint Paul, who, starting from Antioch, made the audacious march on Macedonia, Greece, and Rome which King Antiochus the Great had once attempted unsuccessfully. These religions were different in kind from the native religion of the Græco-Roman World. The gods of Græco-Roman paganism had been rooted in the soil of particular communities; they had been parochial and political: Athene Polias, Fortuna Praenestina, Dea Roma. The gods of the new religions that were making this non-violent counterattack on Greek and Roman hearts and minds had risen above their original local origins. They had become universal gods, with a message of salvation for all mankind, Jew and Gentile, Scythian and Greek. Or, to put this great historical event in religious terms, one might say that the One True God had taken this opportunity of the opening of men's minds through the collision and collapse of their old local traditions; He had taken advantage of this excruciating experience in order to illuminate these momentarily open minds with a fuller and truer vision of His nature and purpose than they had been capable of receiving before.

Take the two words "Jesus Christ," which are so very important for us, and which, we may venture to prophesy, will still be important for mankind two or three thousands years hence. These very words are witnesses to the encounter between a Græco-Roman civilization and a Syrian civilization out of which Christianity came to birth. "Jesus" is the third person singular of a Semitic verb; "Christ" is the passive participle of a Greek verb. The double name testifies that Christianity was born into this world from a marriage between those two cultures.

Consider the four higher religions, with a world-wide mission, which exist in the world today: Christianity, Islam, Hinduism, and the Mahayana form of Buddhism which prevails in the Far East. All four are, historically, products of the encounter between the Græco-Roman civilization and its contemporaries. Christianity and Islam arose as alternative responses of the Syrian World to Græco-Roman penetration: Christianity a non-violent response, Islam a violent one. Mahayanian Buddhism and Hinduism are the gentle and the violent responses of the Hindu World to the same Græco-Roman challenge.

Looking back on Græco-Roman history today, about thirteen hundred years after the date when the Græco-Roman civilization became extinct, we can see that, in this perspective, the most important thing in the history of the Græco-Roman World is its meeting with other civilizations; and these encounters are important, not for their immediate political and economic consequences, but for their long-term religious consequences. This Græco-Roman illustration, of which we know the whole story, also gives us some idea of the time-span of encounters between civilizations. The Græco-Roman World's impact upon other contemporary civilizations, which corresponds to the modern Western World's impact on its own contemporaries since the turn of the fifteenth and sixteenth centuries, started with the conquests of Alexander the Great in the fourth century B.C.; and the Middle Eastern World was still translating the classical works of Greek philosophy and science some five or six centuries after the liberation of the Middle East from Græco-Roman rule by the early Muslim Arabs in the seventh century of the Christian era. From the fourth century B.C. to the thirteenth century of the Christian era, it took the best part of sixteen hundred years for the encounter between the Græco-Roman civilization and its contemporaries to work itself out.

Now measure against that span of sixteen hundred years the duration, to date, of the encounter between our modern Western Civilization and its contemporaries. One may say that this encounter began with the Ottoman attack on the homelands of the Western Civilization and with the great Western voyages of discovery at the turn of the fifteenth and sixteenth centuries of our era. That makes only four-and-a-half centuries to the present.

Let us assume, if you like, that people's hearts and minds move rather faster nowadays (though I know of no evidence that the unconscious part of the human psyche ever greatly varies its pace)—even so, it looks as if we were still only in an early chapter of the story of our encounter with the civilizations of Mexico and Peru and Orthodox Christendom and Islam and the Hindu World and the Far East. We are just beginning to see some of the effects of our action on them, but we have hardly begun to see the effects—which will certainly be tremendous—of their coming counteraction upon us.

It is only in our generation that we have seen one of the first moves in this counteroffensive, and we have found it very disturbing; whether we have liked it or not, we have felt it to be momentous. I mean, of course, the move made by the offshoot of Orthodox Christendom in Russia. It is momentous and disturbing not because of the material power behind it. The Russians . . . have already shown (and this is the point) the power to convert Western souls to a non-Western "ideology."

The Russians have taken up a Western secular social philosophy, Marxism; you might equally well call Marxism a Christian heresy, a leaf torn out of the book of Christianity and treated as if it were the whole gospel. The Russians have taken up this Western heretical religion, transformed it into something of their own, and are now shooting it back at us. This is the first shot in the anti-Western counteroffensive; but this Russian counterdischarge in the form of Communism may come to seem a small affair when the probably far more potent civilizations of India and China respond in their turn to our Western challenge. In the long run India and China seem likely to produce much deeper effects on our Western life than Russia can ever hope to produce with her Communism. But even the comparatively feeble native civilization of Mexico is beginning to react. The revolution through which Mexico has been passing since A.D. 1910 may be interpreted as a first move to shake off the top-dressing of Western Civilization which we imposed on Mexico in the sixteenth century; and what is happening today in Mexico may happen tomorrow in the seats of the native civilization of South America: in Peru, Bolivia, Ecuador, and Colombia.

III

Before leaving off, I must say a word about one question which I have begged up to this point, and that is: what do we mean by a "civilization"? Clearly, we do mean something, for even before we have tried to define what our meaning is, this classification of human societies—the Western Civilization, the Islamic, the Far Eastern, the Hindu, and so on—does seem to make sense. These names do call up distinct pictures in our minds in terms of religion, architecture, painting, manners, and customs. Still, it is better to try to get closer to what we mean by a term which we have already been working so hard. I believe I do know what I mean by a civilization; at least, I am sure I know how I have arrived at my own idea of it.

I mean, by a civilization, the smallest unit of historical study at which one arrives when one tries to understand the history of one's own country: the United States, say, or the United Kingdom. If you were to try to understand the history of the United States by itself, it would be unintelligible: you could not understand the part played in American life by federal government, representative government, democracy, industrialism, monogamy, Christianity, unless you looked beyond the bounds of the United States— out beyond her frontiers to Western Europe and the other overseas countries founded by West Europeans, and back beyond her local origins to the history of Western Europe in centuries before Columbus or Cabot had crossed the Atlantic. But, to make American history and institutions intelligible for practical purposes, you need not look beyond Western Europe into Eastern Europe or the Islamic World, nor behind the origins of our Western European civilization to the decline and fall of the Græco-Roman civilization. These limits of time and space give us the intelligible unit of social life of which the United States or Great Britain or France or Holland is a part: call it Western Christendom, Western Civilization, Western Society, the Western World. Similarly, if you start from Greece or Serbia or Russia, and try to understand their histories, you arrive at an Orthodox Christendom or Byzantine World. If you start from Morocco or Afghanistan, and try to understand their histories, you arrive at an Islamic World. Start from Bengal or Mysore or Rajputana and you find a Hindu World. Start from China or Japan and you find a Far Eastern World.

While the state of which we happen to be citizens makes more concrete and more imperious claims on our allegiance, especially in the present
age, the civilization of which we are members really counts for more in our
lives. And this civilization of which we are members includes—at most
stages in its history—the citizens of other states besides our own. It is older
than our own state: the Western Civilization is about thirteen hundred
years old, whereas the Kingdom of England is only one thousand years old,
the United Kingdom of England and Scotland less than two hundred and
fifty, the United States not more than one hundred and fifty. States are
apt to have short lives and sudden deaths: the Western Civilization of
which you and I are members may be alive centuries after the United
Kingdom and the United States have disappeared from the political map
of the world like their late contemporaries, the Republic of Venice and the
Dual Monarchy of Austria-Hungary. This is one of the reasons why I have
been asking you to look at history in terms of civilizations, and not in terms
of states, and to think of states as rather subordinate and ephemeral political phenomena in the lives of the civilizations in whose bosoms they appear
and disappear.

❖ 98 ❖

ILYA EHRENBURG'S AMERICA:

TRANSLATIONS OF SIX ARTICLES

PUBLISHED IN IZVESTIA

Ilya Ehrenburg

*Many scholars, journalists, and photographers seek as much infor-
mation as they can about life in Soviet Russia today. In the
restrictive context of the continuing Cold War, however, the end
products of this long and involved international communications
process often leave much to be desired on both sides of the Iron
Curtain. The following selection by Ilya Ehrenburg, then known
to the West as "the foremost Soviet journalist," dates from the
early post-war period when mutual esteem largely characterized relations between nationals of the victorious and cooperative military
allies. It is enlightening to see ourselves and our institutions*

SOURCE: *Harper's Magazine*, Vol. 193 (December, 1946), 562–76. ❖
The author is a Russian novelist, poet, and short-story writer. He has also
been a war correspondent and a broadcaster on Moscow Radio. Ehrenburg
has written some eighty books, including *Out of Chaos; Moscow Does Not Believe in Tears; The Love of Jeanne Ney;* and *The Fall of Paris,* which won
him a Stalin Prize.

*through the eyes of someone from a different social milieu, espe-
cially from a social, political, and economic system so much at
variance with ours that its proponents show hostility to much that
we cherish. We may wince at the ridicule and resent the misleading distortions. Though the picture seems out of focus, we cannot
but acknowledge the validity of some of Ehrenburg's criticisms.*

In my time I have traveled a good deal and have been all over Europe.
I sometimes thought I had lost the ability to be amazed. Upon arriving
in America I realized that there was much of which I had no conception.
Everything here is different—the cities, the trees, and the customs. The
summer here is very hot, but the heat is not European; the air is damp,
as in a hothouse. The olives here are larger than plums and devoid of taste.
People gesticulate more often with their legs than with their arms, and
in the theaters spectators who wish to show approval whistle deafeningly.

Modernity cannot be understood without understanding America.
Hundreds of odes and pamphlets have been dedicated to her; she can be
exalted or ridiculed with ease. But this is not merely a peculiar country,
but also a diverse one, difficult to understand. It is hard to set forth vivid,
often contradictory, impressions in brief notes. Behind the complexity of
technology there is sometimes concealed spiritual simplicity, and behind
this simplicity—unexpected complexity.

I rate American literature very highly. It is not easy now to find writers
in Western Europe equal to Hemingway, Faulkner, Steinbeck, or Cald-
well. I might venture to add two or three more names. Right behind them
is a vacuum—stories in illustrated weeklies which are so cheap and stupid
that even the most unexacting readers in Europe would recoil from them.
There is no intermediate literature here, just as there are no four- or five-
story houses. The skyscrapers of New York are justified by geography: this
is a huge city built on small islands. But in any provincial city one may see
several skyscrapers surrounded by thousands of single-story houses.

At the railway station in Atlanta I was amazed by the automatic
checking booths which have replaced the cloakroom. You insert a coin,
receive a key, and can lock up your baggage yourself. I was about to say
to my American companion, "You know how to make human existence
easier," but before I could speak I noticed a dark, noisome room marked
"For non-Whites" in which Negroes and mulattoes were dozing. In the
state of Mississippi I saw the home of a plantation owner. It had a refrigerator, a washing machine, a marvelous radio, and wonderful ventilators. The
planter calmly explained to me that black-skinned people aren't people at
all. Neither the radio nor the ventilators had any reflection on the mental
development of this slave-owner.

I stayed in several university towns. In America a great deal is done
to elevate knowledge to its proper height. I saw superb libraries and laboratories: I saw scientists surrounded with attention. But in Tennessee pro-

fessors told me they were not allowed the right to expound the theory of evolution in the schools: the law forbids any departure from the biblical myth of Adam and Eve.

In all American cities are are "lions'" clubs: I was fortunate enough to attend a luncheon at such a club in one town. Respectable business men assembled there, each one wearing a tag indicating the place and nature of his business; luncheons are closely associated with business. Before those present at the luncheon began to eat their compotes and mayonnaise and ham with raisins, the chairman banged the table with a wooden hammer and exclaimed: "Greetings, lions!" The middle-aged business men at once rose and chorused: "Woo-woo-woo-woo." I quailed, but they explained that they were imitating the lion's roar.

Naturally, the sound-imitations of dealers in suspenders are an innocent affair. There are worse ideas. A parade of the Ku Klux Klan recently took place in Georgia. The members of this supposedly secret society donned fools' hoods and took an oath of loyalty to the local fascist *führer*, whom they called the "Grand Dragon." Then they swore to hang several Negroes and kill several freethinkers.

Everyone knows that in America money is surrounded with respect. Apart from many hundreds of registered churches and sects there is still another cult—the dollar. An art critic, after introducing a young artist to me, reeled off his surname and then, enunciating precisely, said, "Three thousand dollars." A master of ceremonies at a cabaret announced that eminent visitors were present: an actress, a senator, and a business man "who has tripled his capital turnover since the war." I attended many dinner meetings with a program much like this one: first, everybody quickly chews the chicken, then orators give lengthy speeches; then a female singer renders a sentimental ballad; and finally a pastor takes a collection for charity. He recites the names of the liberal donors: "Mr. Smith gave five hundred dollars." Everyone applauds and Mr. Smith rises and bows.

It is not well known that, along with brisk business men, there are also many naïve day-dreamers and noble idealists in America. I met a prominent inventor who renounced a fortune, fearing that the machine he invented would deprive hundreds of thousands of workers of their bread. I spoke to provincial Utopians who go without food and sleep, devoting their money and energy to the fantastic project of creating a "world government." In one town I found a circle of eccentrics who were convinced that they could render the atomic bomb harmless with the aid of Esperanto. Everywhere there are societies to protect the rights of Negroes. Every year innocent Negroes are condemned and put to death in the electric chair, and every year the best people in America protest against racial barbarism. Yes, the cult of the dollar does exist in America, but in America there are also people who deny themselves a pair of shoes and tickets to the cinema in order to send gifts to Yugoslav children.

There is much that is childish in Americans. They are not artificial; they are frank, curious, and noisy. The oldest part of America is called New England. Everything in America is new; everything is young. In New Orleans, however, houses built in the seventeenth and eighteenth centuries have been preserved in the French Quarter. Such houses are legion in Europe and are ignored by even the most painstaking tourists. But the "Old Quarter" of New Orleans is like Pompeii—a real center of pilgrimage. There is either an antique shop or a stylized tavern in almost every house. I was in New Orleans on a very sultry day (the tropics are not far off), and a fire was burning in the grate of one house—to re-create the atmosphere of a bygone epoch. Perspiring Americans were sitting by the fire drinking iced water; they wanted to spend several minutes in an *old* house. One must remember the age of the country to understand Americans.

People here like to wander about. If they are sitting in a room, they jump up from time to time and change seats; they move readily from city to city and from state to state. They regard a person who lives in the place where he was born as a rarity.

There is nothing more the reverse of the British character and customs than the character and customs of the average American. The Englishman is polite and phlegmatic; he loves to live out his life in the home of his grandfather; he orders his suit of first-quality material, expecting to wear it, if not until he dies, at least until the next elections. The American likes only new clothes. Hardly has he furnished his apartment than he is looking for another. He never has a suit made to order; why should he? In any shop he can find a cheap, well-made suit; can wear it a little and then throw it out. He will buy a shirt that is not worth washing. He respects old stones, but loves flashy new ties—and noise.

The history of the United States is indeed a new history. I might say, incidentally, that history studied by school children appears to vary in different states: in the North the Southerners are called "defenders of slavery," and in the South the Northerners are called "oppressors." Vexed issues here frequently hide the feeling of history. For the average American nearly a whole epoch passes between the morning and evening papers; he doesn't always remember in the evening exactly what disturbed him in the morning. One lady told me: "Don't read this novel. It's not a new one; it came out two years ago."

Anti-Soviet ideologists like to depict our country as a sort of barracks in which everyone is deprived of individuality. The Soviet reader will be amused by the surprise of some American editors who, on seeing us three visitors, said in amazement: "Why, they don't look much like one another."

As a matter of fact, I don't know of any country which has achieved such perfection in standardization as the United States. I was in dozens of American cities—which were impossible to distinguish from each other.

Every city has its Main Street—the principal street—with fashion shops, a cinema, and lighted signs advertising cigarettes or Coca-Cola. Not a single American can distinguish Main Street in one town from Main Street in one of a hundred others from a photograph. . . .

Trousers, percolators, and armchairs are standardized, too. I do not say this reproachfully, for Americans have succeeded in raising the material level of life, thanks to mass production. I think we can learn something from the Americans: how to turn out shoes or saucepans quickly and well. However, almost all luxury articles in America are imported and a salesman who wishes to explain why this or that is expensive says, "But this is *imported*."

There is a certain depression in such uniformity: the same houses, the same furniture, the same crockery; men in identical suits, women in identical dresses. But still I do not agree with the European aesthetes who have ridiculed the standardization in America. Perhaps all the suits are alike; on the other hand, they are accessible to all.

Much more deplorable is a certain spiritual standardization. Americans are fond of speaking about their liberty; but their views, tastes, emotions, and consequent behavior are regulated from outside. The cinema, for instance, lays down the standard for beauty, and the papers supply all the details of the "ideally shaped" woman. This is the standard of desire. All American women are guided by these references in their efforts to resemble some film star, while men fall in love according to the same references without noticing it. There are no books with average circulation. Even the most remarkable book will not be circulated in more than several thousand copies unless it has been pronounced worth reading by some "book club," in which case it will be published in hundreds of thousands of copies. Since the average American does not like to choose, he entrusts the right to choose to his "club." The press and cinema de-personalize the ideas of people who stroll along thousands of Main Streets in the evening. This forms the key to the sense of depression which is linked with leisure in America.

Americans know very well how to earn money, but they have not yet learned to spend it. I do not mean that they are mean; they spend money swiftly and energetically—but without originality. They work with much greater talent than they amuse themselves. I would say that the gayest times in America are when townspeople meet nature; on the seashore, for instance, youth is full of *joie-de-vivre*. But in the cinema one is struck by their drowsiness and torpor, the rare laughter in response to the most humorous, or apparently humorous, situations.

There are many drunks, despite the fact that the sale of strong drink is restricted in one way or another in the majority of states. There are "dry" states, those in which whiskey is rationed, those in which liquor sales cannot be made on Sunday, and those in which one may drink sitting but not standing.

Automobiles in America are wonderful and numerous, and the average American loves a car. . . . I understand the love of Americans for cars. But I do not understand why some of them turn their car into a home. There are restaurants which one is not allowed to enter; dinner is brought out on a tray and people eat in their cars. There are cinemas outside towns where people can draw up in their cars in the yard in front of the screen and watch the films without getting out. Finally, it is sufficient to take a walk through Central Park, New York, in the evening to see yet another purpose of the automobile: it replaces the nuptial bed for lovers. Such habits make life somewhat mournful, not because people wear fashionable jackets, but because underneath these fashionable jackets there are at times fashionable feelings. . . .

In a relatively short time the Americans have created an astonishing technology. I saw how swiftly they build skyscrapers, how well and with what precision they produce automobiles in Detroit, and how many inventions they possess which ease the daily life of man. How can one not praise American roads, with their cheap and comfortable roadhouses for motorists who decide to spend a night on the road? Some Americans, glancing at the factories, the excellent bridges of New York, the automatic restaurants, and the electric razors, are prepared to believe that the whole of human culture is concentrated in America. One journalist in Jackson said to me: "Rome is a dirty and ugly city; there is nothing to look at in it—not a single skyscraper or a good drug store. After Rome, Jackson seemed to me more like a capital." How is one to explain to such a man that the ancient basilicas and palaces of the Renaissance are worth the skyscrapers of Jackson, or that, besides drug stores where cigars, fountain pens, chewing gum, and even sausages may be bought, there also exist the mosaics of Byzantium and the frescoes of Raphael?

The Americans are inadequately acquainted with the rest of the world. They do not know the history and geography of the Old World. One group of school children was not able to name to me a single city in the Soviet Union. Their political level is just as low. People know the intimate side of the lives of different senators, but in many states the word "Socialist" (let alone "Communist") is considered offensive. American papers frequently write that the existence of two parties is a guarantee of genuine democracy. One might note that no one is capable of explaining where the ideological demarcation line runs between the two parties, and in what way the Northern Republicans differ from the Southern Democrats.

Some Europeans have ridiculed America for her cult of technology. Now the same Europeans look to their ridiculed cousins with servility in the hope of obtaining from them an old car or an out-dated suit. There is nothing to laugh at here and nothing to flatter. American development has proceeded along a different path from the ways of old Europe. France started almost from the Gothic cathedral and the troubadours. America started with automobiles, drug store feeding houses, and gold fever. She swiftly reached a high level of material culture, but her spiritual culture is only awakening. Knowing the intelligence, liveliness, and energy of the Americans, we have the right to say that the spiritual culture of this great people will be great and independent.

Certain changes have taken place in the political consciousness of the average American; he is gradually moving away from the abyss. Roosevelt was surrounded by people who were honest thinkers, capable of realizing the trend of history. Even if these people have now been removed (or have removed themselves), there is still a trace of the late President's activity. I observed a beginning of independent thought, genuine solidarity, and a consciousness of their national mission among many workers. The era in which they were led only by demagogues and adventurers is coming to an end. We see the contributions made to the world by American scientists. The American writers are not renegades or salon aesthetes; they are people connected with the nation, even though the reading masses don't read them. In contrast to French writers, American writers seem to me organic, like huge trees with tenacious roots. The American cinema has already created genuine, universal humor; apart from the genius Chaplin, I will name the Brothers Marx. The cinema has also created the multiplicity of Disney, real poetry capable of stirring a man devoid of all lyricism. Finally, there is beauty—uneasy, but indisputable—in the architecture of New York.

The American intelligentsia has been born. It is still weak and lacks self-confidence; it hides from the illuminated advertisements, from the deafening juke-boxes in the bars, from ecclesiastical sermons with references to business firms, and advertisements with quotations from the Bible. It hides itself in a melancholy which I call Chekhovian, sometimes in cynicism and sometimes in Utopianism. But among the intelligentsia more and more bold people are appearing. They understand that salvation does not lie in flight or repulsion or solitude. The spiritual world of the average American must be raised to the level of the technology which surrounds him from the maternity home to the crematorium.

✧   ✧   ✧   ✧   ✧

It would seem that in this country of diverse races united by patriotism, national equality would prevail. However, America, which never knew feudalism, has established a *racial* hierarchy. The aristocracy are the English, Scotch, and Irish. After them come the Scandinavians and Germans, then the French and Slavs; much lower are the Italians, even lower still the Jews and Chinese; lower still the Puerto Ricans, and finally, at the bottom of the scale, the Negroes.

In the war against Hitlerism America played a prominent part; yet racialism here has a legal standing. When I entered America I had to fill out a questionnaire which contained the question: "Race—White or Colored?" If a person has a "colored" great-grandfather he is designated as "colored" and is subject to various restrictions. We were the guests of the government, and I was often amused by the thought of the reaction the representatives of the State Department might have had if Pushkin had come to America. I met a lawyer in Nashville who spent a long time trying to persuade me that there are "inferior and superior races." He reiterated the theories of Rosenberg and other ideologists of the Third Reich. Then he showed me the portrait of his brother who was killed on the Rhine; he was proud of his brother, who had perished in the struggle against racialists.

Anti-Semitism is an ordinary phenomenon to most Americans; it seems quite natural to them that some institutions accept only Aryans and that certain hotels do not admit Jews. On the West Coast the Chinese are the pariahs. There are organizations in which Italians are not accepted as members. The fate of the Negroes is especially tragic. There are twelve million of them in the United States, and it may be said that one out of every ten Americans is deprived of all human rights.

Natives of New York like to emphasize the liberalism of the North—"Our grandfathers fought against slavery." In any Southern town, on the other hand, you may see a monument to the soldiers of the Southern Army. This is a monument to the vanquished, because in the war which shook America the Southerners were defeated. However, it seemed to me more than once that these were monuments, not to the vanquished, but to the victors; since the South not only preserved the principles of slavery but was able, in some degree, to inject them into the North. Certainly equal rights among the races exist *theoretically* in New York. A Negro may not be ejected from a restaurant because he is a Negro, but not a single well-ordered American restaurant will admit a Negro. If it occurs to him to persist, he is told that the empty tables are reserved. A Negro cannot rent a room anywhere except in a Negro "ghetto." He may work in the most different sort of quarters, but he is obliged to live in Harlem, a Negro city within a city—dirty and impoverished, unhappy but still gay. New Yorkers amuse themselves in the cabarets in Harlem. The Negroes are the best dancers and musicians in America; they are gifted with a high sense of rhythm and are not as inherently mechanical as other Americans. In the center of New York there are theaters where Negro troupes perform excellently and are willingly applauded by the whites. But if a Negro wants to have a snack in a restaurant near the theater in which he is playing, he is calmly evicted.

Real estate speculators have a favorite trick; they buy a house in a good residential district and settle a Negro in it. The quarter then becomes taboo immediately, and all the whites depart. The speculator then buys the neighboring houses for a song, moves out the single Negro, and the section again becomes respectable—and the houses rise in price.

Still, in order to understand the place of the Negro in America, it is essential to see the South. When we were asked which part of America we wanted to see, my fellow-travelers chose California and Chicago. I wanted to see the Southern states. Remembering stories I had read—the novels of Steinbeck and Faulkner—I wanted to find out if reality resembled literature. Thus, after the skyscrapers of New York I saw Uncle Tom's Cabin, and I can say that this cabin has changed little.

In all the Southern states there is a "segregation of the races" law. Negroes are not forbidden to use railroads, but they must travel in special cars (always over-crowded). In streetcars, seats are set aside for Negroes in the rear. A car frequently leaves almost empty while Negroes stand and wait for the next one, as the seats for them are occupied. Negroes may not attend meetings of whites, they dare not enter a church where white people are praying, and of course they must not even dream of entering theaters or cinemas for whites.

The Constitution of the United States guarantees that all citizens, male and female, have the right to take part in elections. However, the Negroes in the Southern states do not possess the right to vote. In the state of Alabama there are three million inhabitants, of whom 1,100,000 are Negroes. Among the voters of the state are 496,000 whites and 4,000 Negroes. In Birmingham, Alabama, there are 130,000 Negroes who have reached the age of twenty-one, but the total number of Negro voters is only 1,400. How do the Southern states get around the federal Constitution? There are several ways: one, the poll tax; another, examinations. The qualified voter must know and "be able to interpret" the Constitution. Clearly the examiners can cut out many Negroes. Finally, if the Negroes pay their poll tax, pass the examination, and go to the voting places, the guardians of slavery frighten away the unwanted voters with sturdy clubs. Obviously they do indeed know how to "interpret" the Constitution in the Southern states! In the state of Mississippi, Negroes form half of the population; half the inhabitants of the state are deprived of the right to vote. All this is done cynically and is well-known to all Americans both in the North and the South.

✧   ✧   ✧   ✧   ✧

Not a few Negroes have been in Europe; many fought for America against racialist Germany. They saw that in Paris or Rome no one looked at them as though they were plagued, and they returned home with even greater bitterness. The South is on the eve of a decisive event: either the owners will yield, or the Negroes—yesterday's men of the front line—will open the struggle for equality.

I am convinced that in the end racialism will be overthrown in America; but it must be understood that this disease has penetrated deeply into the mind of the average American. I did not meet a single white in the South who was not contaminated with racialism. One of the most fervent opponents of the slaveowners admitted to me in a frank and intimate conversation: "Yes, I defend the Negroes, but just the same, for me these are not people. I was playing yesterday with our Negro maid's child and found myself thinking that I was playing, not with a child, but with a nice puppy." Racialism has infected even the persecuted; I met Negro anti-Semites and Jews convinced of the superiority of whites over blacks. . . .

The famous journalist, Walter Lippmann, said that in my article on America I was criticizing what was easy to criticize—racial intolerance; Americans themselves know about this vice and are happy to be able to criticize their own vices. Lippmann says that when we Soviet people are capable of appreciating the merits of America and criticizing our own faults, then he, Lippmann, will agree to accept us as "real people." Yes, I know that the best people are ashamed of their attitude toward the Negro. But in my opinion doctors are good, not because they treat, but because they heal. It is no easier for Negroes because Lippmann recognizes Senator Bilbo as an evil and writes articles in New York, while Bilbo and others like him are oppressing Negroes in Mississippi. As for ourselves, we have never denied the merits of America, nor have ever hidden from ourselves or others our own faults. In America, for instance, there are wonderful tele-phones; from New York it is easier to speak by telephone to San Francisco than from Moscow to Tula. In America there are good passenger planes which fly from city to city every hour day and night. Perhaps Lippmann will say that I am limiting myself to praising technology. No, I have already written that I like American literature. I think we can learn much from American writers, American architects, and even (despite the shattering cheapness of the average production) from American cinema producers. We know our own faults—we criticize our own bureaucracy, our rudeness, and at times our technical backwardness—but we do not criticize just to criticize, but to improve. We have no slaveowners, and it is not a question of whether Lippmann recognizes us as a people, but of whether we recog-nize racialists and slaveowners as people. I believe in the great future of America, and I am convinced that the American nation will soon be healed of its most bitter and shameful ailment.

When American friends asked me what should be done to improve our mutual relations, I replied: "Set up a single standard." The reader must not think that I am proposing that the Americans introduce the metric system; I have no wish to interfere in their affairs. If they like having water freeze at 32 degrees Fahrenheit, that is their business. But a single standard should be set up in evaluating behavior. Too frequently I saw two standards here: one for the virtuous Anglo-Saxons and another for the dishonorable "Reds." If the Americans consider Iceland their base, it is called a "guaran-tee of security for the entire world"; but if the Soviet Union does not wish to have states which neighbor upon it become bases for an attack upon Russia, this is "Red imperialism." When the Americans are engaged in manufacturing atom bombs, this is an innocent game like football; but when Red Army men play football in the suburbs of Moscow, this is "preparation for conquering the world."

The American people are kind-hearted and industrious; they do not want war. At present the country is rich, particularly as compared with a Europe ravaged by war. In Detroit the automobile plants are working at top speed and still cannot satisfy all the would-be customers. People "sign up" for refrigerators, vacuum cleaners, and radios. America did not feel the iron boot of war; inconveniences which are trifling to a European seem to be great deprivations here. You will hear amusing complaints here: "There is little butter . . . poultry or mutton instead of beefsteak . . . the line for nylon stockings . . . it is hard to get white shirts, only colored ones." Here and there strikes are breaking out; the workers are seeking an increase in wages to match the rising cost of living. Demobilized servicemen have returned. The country reminds one of a housewarming or of the beginning of the school year. The people are thinking with pleasure about tomorrow, which will certainly be better than today. They have long since forgotten yesterday, and they are little concerned with the day after tomorrow. If occasionally someone stops to think that suddenly a depression and unemployment may be upon him, he at once drives away these gloomy thoughts. These are people who do not want to look into the future. Many of them have more than once lived through the transitions from wealth to poverty and from poverty to wealth. They have adopted a peculiar fatalism and take things in their stride. They do not want a depression and they do not want war. Newspaper articles about a "Third World War" make them justly indignant. But such articles, talks, and sermons repeated too often are designed to accustom the average American to the idea that a Third World War is inevitable.

I left many sincere friends in America—not only personal friends, but friends of the Soviet people, friends of thought and conscience. Americans are fond of directness. I stated frankly what I liked and did not like in America. Only the sick and impotent should have their feelings spared. Americans have a super-abundance of youth and health. Besides, they now have many European flatterers, eager for loans, trousers, and canned goods. And the Americans themselves love to judge—to judge and condemn. I know that they will receive my words as the words of a friend. This great people has great strength and great will. Its history must be worthy of it.

IGNORANCE IS STRENGTH

George Orwell

Lightened in part though it is by a boy-meets-girl theme, the novel 1984 from which this selection is taken is a deadly serious, satirical exposition of life as it might become in a totalitarian society. Its author, George Orwell, develops to their logical limits the characteristics of the institutions in modern authoritarian cultures. By the device of a book-within-a-book he presents, in this selection, the core of the theory of his 1984 society. The central feature of the theory seems to be this: Modern science, mass production, and technology offer the possibility of practically eliminating the great class differences in material and mental well-being that, up to now, have always characterized the major societies of the world. Under these conditions, how can a hierarchical society, with all the tangible and intangible differential benefits this implies, be indefinitely maintained by the "ruling class"?

Throughout recorded time, and probably since the end of the Neolithic Age, there have been three kinds of people in the world, the High, the Middle, and the Low. They have been subdivided in many ways, they have borne countless different names, and their relative numbers, as well as their attitude toward one another, have varied from age to age; but the essential structure of society has never altered. Even after enormous upheavals and seemingly irrevocable changes, the same pattern has always reasserted itself, just as a gyroscope will always return to equilibrium, however far it is pushed one way or the other. . . .

The aims of these groups are entirely irreconcilable. The aim of the High is to remain where they are. The aim of the Middle is to change places with the High. The aim of the Low, when they have an aim—for it is an abiding characteristic of the Low that they are too much crushed by drudgery to be more than intermittently conscious of anything outside their daily lives—is to abolish all distinctions and create a society in which all men shall be equal. Thus throughout history a struggle which is the same in its main outlines recurs over and over again. For long periods the

SOURCE: *1984* by George Orwell. Copyright, 1949, by Harcourt, Brace and World, Inc. Reprinted by permission of Brandt & Brandt. ✧ George Orwell (1903–1950), a nom de plume for Eric Arthur Blair, was a British novelist and essayist. He was born in Motihari, India, of Anglo-Indian parents. He served on the Republican side in the Spanish Civil War, and one result of his time as a soldier was his book *Homage to Catalonia*. He wrote many other books as well, among which are *Down and Out in Paris and London, Burmese Days,* and *Animal Farm.*

High seem to be securely in power, but sooner or later there always comes a moment when they lose either their belief in themselves, or their capacity to govern efficiently, or both. They are then overthrown by the Middle, who enlist the Low on their side by pretending to them that they are fighting for liberty and justice. As soon as they have reached their objective, the Middle thrust the Low back into their old position of servitude, and themselves become the High. Presently a new Middle group splits off from one of the other groups, or from both of them, and the struggle begins over again. Of the three groups, only the Low are never even temporarily successful in achieving their aims. It would be an exaggeration to say that throughout history there had been no progress of a material kind. Even today, in a period of decline, the average human being is physically better off than he was a few centuries ago. But no advance in wealth, no softening of manners, no reform or revolution has ever brought human equality a millimeter nearer. From the point of view of the Low, no historic change has ever meant much more than a change in the name of their masters.

By the late nineteenth century the recurrences of this pattern had become obvious to many observers. There then arose schools of thinkers who interpreted history as a cyclical process and claimed to show that inequality was the unalterable law of human life. This doctrine, of course, had always had its adherents, but in the manner in which it was now put forward there was a significant change. In the past the need for a hierarchical form of society had been the doctrine specifically of the High. It had been preached by kings and aristocrats and by the priests, lawyers, and the like who were parasitical upon them, and it had generally been softened by promises of compensation in an imaginary world beyond the grave. The Middle, so long as it was struggling for power, had always made use of such terms as freedom, justice, and fraternity. Now, however, the concept of human brotherhood began to be assailed by people who were not yet in positions of command, but merely hoped to be so before long. In the past the Middle had made revolutions under the banner of equality, and then had established a fresh tyranny as soon as the old one was overthrown. The new Middle groups in effect proclaimed their tyranny beforehand. Socialism, a theory which appeared in the early nineteenth century and was the last link in a chain of thought stretching back to the slave rebellions of antiquity, was still deeply infected by the Utopianism of past ages. But in each variant of Socialism that appeared from about 1900 onwards the aim of establishing liberty and equality was more and more openly abandoned. The new movements which appeared in the middle years of the century, Ingsoc in Oceania, Neo-Bolshevism in Eurasia, Death-worship, as it is commonly called, in Eastasia, had the conscious aim of perpetuating unfreedom and inequality. These new movements, of course, grew out of the old ones and tended to keep their names and pay lip-service to their ideology. But the purpose of all of them was to arrest progress and freeze history at a chosen moment. The familiar pendulum swing was to happen once more, and then stop. As usual, the High were to be turned out by the Middle, who would then become the High; but this time, by conscious strategy, the High would be able to maintain their position permanently.

The new doctrines arose partly because of the accumulation of historical knowledge, and the growth of the historical sense, which had hardly existed before the nineteenth century. The cyclical movement of history was now intelligible, or appeared to be so; and if it was intelligible, then it was alterable. But the principal, underlying cause was that, as early as the beginning of the twentieth century, human equality had become technically possible. It was still true that men were not equal in their native talents and that functions had to be specialized in ways that favored some individuals against others; but there was no longer any real need for class distinctions or for large differences of wealth. In earlier ages, class distinctions had been not only inevitable but desirable. Inequality was the price of civilization. With the development of machine production, however, the case was altered. Even if it was still necessary for human beings to do different kinds of work, it was no longer necessary for them to live at different social or economic levels. Therefore, from the point of view of the new groups who were on the point of seizing power, human equality was no longer an ideal to be striven after, but a danger to be averted. In more primitive ages, when a just and peaceful society was in fact not possible, it had been fairly easy to believe in it. The idea of an earthly paradise in which men should live together in a state of brotherhood, without laws and without brute labor, had haunted the human imagination for thousands of years. And this vision had had a certain hold even on the groups who actually profited by each historic change. The heirs of the French, English, and American revolutions had partly believed in their own phrases about the rights of man, freedom of speech, equality before the law, and the like, and had even allowed their conduct to be influenced by them to some extent. But by the fourth decade of the twentieth century all the main currents of political thought were authoritarian. The earthly paradise had been discredited at exactly the moment when it became realizable. Every new political theory, by whatever name it called itself, led back to hierarchy and regimentation. And in the general hardening of outlook that set in round about 1930, practices which had been long abandoned, in some cases for hundreds of years—imprisonment without trial, the use of war prisoners as slaves, public executions, torture to extract confessions, the use of hostages and the deportation of whole populations—not only became common again, but were tolerated and even defended by people who considered themselves enlightened and progressive.

It was only after a decade of national wars, civil wars, revolutions and counterrevolutions in all parts of the world that Ingsoc and its rivals emerged as fully worked-out political theories. But they had been foreshadowed by the various systems, generally called totalitarian, which had appeared earlier in the century, and the main outlines of the world which would emerge from the prevailing chaos had long been obvious. What kind of people would control this world had been equally obvious. The new aristocracy was made up for the most part of bureaucrats, scientists, technicians, trade-union organizers, publicity experts, sociologists, teachers, journalists, and professional politicians. These people, whose origins lay in the salaried middle class and the upper grades of the working class, had been shaped and brought together by the barren world of monopoly industry and centralized government. As compared with their opposite numbers in past ages, they were less avaricious, less tempted by luxury, hungrier for pure power, and, above all, more conscious of what they were doing and more intent on crushing opposition. This last difference was cardinal. By comparison with that existing today, all the tyrannies of the past were half-hearted and inefficient. The ruling groups were always infected to some extent by liberal ideas, and were content to leave loose ends everywhere, to regard only the overt act, and to be uninterested in what their subjects were thinking. Even the Catholic Church of the Middle Ages was tolerant by modern standards. Part of the reason for this was that in the past no government had the power to keep its citizens under constant surveillance. The invention of print, however, made it easier to manipulate public opinion, and the film and the radio carried the process further. With the development of television, and the technical advance which made it possible to receive and transmit simultaneously on the same instrument, private life came to an end. Every citizen, or at least every citizen important enough to be worth watching, could be kept for twenty-four hours a day under the eyes of the police and in the sound of official propaganda, with all other channels of communication closed. The possibility of enforcing not only complete obedience to the will of the State, but complete uniformity of opinion on all subjects, now existed for the first time.

After the revolutionary period of the Fifties and Sixties, society regrouped itself, as always, into High, Middle, and Low. But the new High group, unlike all its forerunners, did not act upon instinct but knew what was needed to safeguard its position. It had long been realized that the only secure basis for oligarchy is collectivism. Wealth and privilege are most easily defended when they are possessed jointly. The so-called "abolition of private property" which took place in the middle years of the century meant, in effect, the concentration of property in far fewer hands than before; but with this difference, that the new owners were a group instead of a mass of individuals. Individually, no member of the Party owns anything, except petty personal belongings. Collectively, the Party owns everything in Oceania, because it controls everything and disposes of the products as it thinks fit. In the years following the Revolution it was able to step into this commanding position almost unopposed, because the whole process was represented as an act of collectivization. It had always been assumed that if the capitalist class were expropriated, Socialism must follow; and unquestionably the capitalists had been expropriated.

Factories, mines, land, houses, transport—everything had been taken away from them; and since these things were no longer private property, it followed that they must be public property. Ingsoc, which grew out of the earlier Socialist movement and inherited its phraseology, has in fact carried out the main item in the Socialist program, with the result, foreseen and intended beforehand, that economic inequality has been made permanent.

But the problems of perpetuating a hierarchical society go deeper than this. There are only four ways in which a ruling group can fall from power. Either it is conquered from without, or it governs so inefficiently that the masses are stirred to revolt, or it allows a strong and discontented Middle Group to come into being, or it loses its own self-confidence and willingness to govern. These causes do not operate singly, and as a rule all four of them are present in some degree. A ruling class which could guard against all of them would remain in power permanently. Ultimately the determining factor is the mental attitude of the ruling class itself.

After the middle of the present century, the first danger had in reality disappeared. Each of the three powers which now divide the world is in fact unconquerable, and could only become conquerable through slow demographic changes which a government with wide powers can easily avert. The second danger, also, is only a theoretical one. The masses never revolt of their own accord, and they never revolt merely because they are oppressed. Indeed, so long as they are not permitted to have standards of comparison they never even become aware that they are oppressed. The recurrent economic crises of past times were totally unnecessary and are not now permitted to happen, but other and equally large dislocations can and do happen without having political results, because there is no way in which discontent can become articulate. As for the problem of overproduction, which has been latent in our society since the development of machine technique, it is solved by the device of continuous warfare, which is also useful in keying up public morale to the necessary pitch. From the point of view of our present rulers, therefore, the only genuine dangers are the splitting-off of a new group of able, underemployed, power-hungry people, and the growth of liberalism and skepticism in their own ranks. The problem, that is to say, is educational. It is a problem of continuously molding the consciousness both of the directing group and of the larger executive group that lies immediately below it. The consciousness of the masses needs only to be influenced in a negative way.

Given this background, one could infer, if one did not know it already, the general structure of Oceanic society. At the apex of the pyramid comes Big Brother. Big Brother is infallible and all-powerful. Every success, every achievement, every victory, every scientific discovery, all knowledge, all wisdom, all happiness, all virtue, are held to issue directly from his leadership and inspiration. Nobody has ever seen Big Brother. He is a face on the hoardings, a voice on the telescreen. We may be reasonably sure that he will never die, and there is already considerable uncertainty as to when he was born. Big Brother is the guise in which the Party chooses to exhibit itself to the world. His function is to act as a focusing point for love, fear, and reverence, emotions which are more easily felt toward an individual than toward an organization. Below Big Brother comes the Inner Party, its numbers limited to six million, or something less than two per cent of the population of Oceania. Below the Inner Party comes the Outer Party, which, if the Inner Party is described as the brain of the State, may be justly likened to the hands. Below that come the dumb masses whom we habitually refer to as "the proles," numbering perhaps eighty-five per cent of the population. In the terms of our earlier classification, the proles are the Low, for the slave populations of the equatorial lands, who pass constantly from conqueror to conqueror, are not a permanent or necessary part of the structure.

In principle, membership in these three groups is not hereditary. The child of Inner Party parents is in theory not born into the Inner Party. Admission to either branch of the Party is by examination, taken at the age of sixteen. Nor is there any racial discrimination, or any marked domination of one province by another. Jews, Negroes, South Americans of pure Indian blood are to be found in the highest ranks of the Party, and the administrators of any area are always drawn from the inhabitants of that area. In no part of Oceania do the inhabitants have the feeling that they are a colonial population ruled from a distant capital. Oceania has no capital, and its titular head is a person whose whereabouts nobody knows. Except that English is its chief lingua franca and Newspeak its official language, it is not centralized in any way. Its rulers are not held together by blood ties but by adherence to a common doctrine. It is true that our society is stratified, and very rigidly stratified, on what at first sight appear to be hereditary lines. There is far less to-and-fro movement between the different groups than happened under capitalism or even in the pre-industrial ages. Between the two branches of the Party there is a certain amount of interchange, but only so much as will ensure that weaklings are excluded from the Inner Party and that ambitious members of the Outer Party are made harmless by allowing them to rise. Proletarians, in practice, are not allowed to graduate into the Party. The most gifted among them, who might possibly become nuclei of discontent, are simply marked down by the Thought Police and eliminated. But this state of affairs is not necessarily permanent, nor is it a matter of principle. The Party is not a class in the old sense of the word. It does not aim at transmitting power to its own children, as such; and if there were no other way of keeping the ablest people at the top, it would be perfectly prepared to recruit an entire new generation from the ranks of the proletariat. In the crucial years, the fact that the Party was not a hereditary body did a great deal to neutralize opposition. The older kind of Socialist, who had been trained to fight against something called "class privilege," assumed that what is not hereditary cannot be permanent. He did not see that the continuity of an oligarchy need not be physical, nor did he pause to reflect that hereditary aristocracies have always been shortlived, whereas adoptive organizations such as the Catholic Church have sometimes lasted for hundreds or thousands of years. The essence of oligarchical rule is not father-to-son inheritance, but the persistence of a certain world-view and a certain way of life, imposed by the dead upon the living. A ruling group is a ruling group so long as it can nominate its successors. The Party is not concerned with perpetuating its blood but with perpetuating itself. *Who* wields power is not important, provided that the hierarchical structure remains always the same.

All the beliefs, habits, tastes, emotions, mental attitudes that characterize our time are really designed to sustain the mystique of the Party and prevent the true nature of present-day society from being perceived. Physical rebellion, or any preliminary move toward rebellion, is at present not possible. From the proletarians nothing is to be feared. Left to themselves, they will continue from generation to generation and from century to century, working, breeding, and dying, not only without any impulse to rebel, but without the power of grasping that the world could be other than it is. They could only become dangerous if the advance of industrial technique made it necessary to educate them more highly; but, since military and commercial rivalry are no longer important, the level of popular education is actually declining. What opinions the masses hold, or do not hold, is looked on as a matter of indifference. They can be granted intellectual liberty because they have no intellect. In a Party member, on the other hand, not even the smallest deviation of opinion on the most unimportant subject can be tolerated.

A Party member lives from birth to death under the eye of the Thought Police. Even when he is alone he can never be sure that he is alone. Wherever he may be, asleep or awake, working or resting, in his bath or in bed, he can be inspected without warning and without knowing that he is being inspected. Nothing that he does is indifferent. His friendships, his relaxations, his behavior toward his wife and children, the expression of his face when he is alone, the words he mutters in sleep, even the characteristic movements of his body, are all jealously scrutinized. Not only any actual misdemeanor, but any eccentricity, however small, any change of habits, any nervous mannerism that could possibly be the symptom of an inner struggle, is certain to be detected. He has no freedom of choice in any direction whatever. On the other hand, his actions are not regulated by law or by any clearly formulated code of behavior. In Oceania there is no law. Thoughts and actions which, when detected, mean certain death are not formally forbidden, and the endless purges, arrests, tortures, imprisonments, and vaporizations are not inflicted as punishment for crimes which have actually been committed, but are merely the wiping-out of persons who might perhaps commit a crime at some time in the future. A Party member is required to have not only the right opinions, but the right instincts. Many of the beliefs and attitudes demanded of him are never plainly stated, and could not be stated without laying bare the contradictions inherent in Ingsoc. If he is a person naturally orthodox (in Newspeak, a *goodthinker*), he will in all circumstances know, without taking thought, what is the true belief or the desirable emotion. But in any case an elaborate mental training, undergone in childhood and grouping itself round the Newspeak words *crimestop*, *blackwhite*, and *doublethink*, makes him unwilling and unable to think too deeply on any subject whatever.

A Party member is expected to have no private emotions and no respites from enthusiasm. He is supposed to live in a continuous frenzy of hatred of foreign enemies and internal traitors, triumph over victories, and self-abasement before the power and wisdom of the Party. The discontents produced by his bare, unsatisfying life are deliberately turned outwards and dissipated by such devices as the Two Minutes Hate, and the speculations which might possibly induce a skeptical or rebellious attitude are killed in advance by his early acquired inner discipline. The first and simplest stage in the discipline, which can be taught even to young children, is called, in Newspeak, *crimestop*. *Crimestop* means the faculty of stopping short, as though by instinct, at the threshold of any dangerous thought. It includes the power of not grasping analogies, of failing to perceive logical errors, of misunderstanding the simplest arguments if they are inimical to Ingsoc, and of being bored or repelled by any train of thought which is capable of leading in a heretical direction. *Crimestop*, in short, means protective stupidity. But stupidity is not enough. On the contrary, orthodoxy in the full sense demands a control over one's own mental processes as complete as that of a contortionist over his body. Oceanic society rests ultimately on the belief that Big Brother is omnipotent and that the Party is infallible. But since in reality Big Brother is not omnipotent and the Party is not infallible, there is need for an unwearying, moment-to-moment flexibility in the treatment of facts. The key word here is *blackwhite*. Like so many Newspeak words, this word has two mutually contradictory meanings. Applied to an opponent, it means the habit of impudently claiming that black is white, in contradiction of the plain facts. Applied to a Party member, it means a loyal willingness to say that black is white when Party discipline demands this. But it means also the ability to *believe* that black is white and more, to *know* that black is white, and to forget that one has ever believed the contrary. This demands a continuous alteration of the past, made possible by the system of thought which really embraces all the rest, and which is known in Newspeak as *doublethink*.

The alteration of the past is necessary for two reasons, one of which is subsidiary and, so to speak, precautionary. The subsidiary reason is that the Party member, like the proletarian, tolerates present-day conditions partly because he has no standards of comparison. He must be cut off from the past, just as he must be cut off from foreign countries, because it is necessary for him to believe that he is better off than his ancestors and that the average level of material comfort is constantly rising. But by far the more important reason for the readjustment of the past is the need to safeguard the infallibility of the Party. It is not merely that speeches, statistics, and records of every kind must be constantly brought up to date in order to show that the predictions of the Party were in all cases right. It is also that no change of doctrine or in political alignment can ever be admitted. For to change one's mind, or even one's policy, is a confession of weakness. If, for example, Eurasia or Eastasia (whichever it may be) is the enemy today, then that country must always have been the enemy. And if the facts say otherwise, then the facts must be altered. Thus history is continuously rewritten. This day-to-day falsification of the past, carried out by the Ministry of Truth, is as necessary to the stability of the regime as the work of repression and espionage carried out by the Ministry of Love.

The mutability of the past is the central tenet of Ingsoc. Past events, it is argued, have no objective existence, but survive only in written records and in human memories. The past is whatever the records and the memories agree upon. And since the Party is in full control of all records, and in equally full control of the minds of its members, it follows that the past is whatever the Party chooses to make it. It also follows that though the past is alterable, it never has been altered in any specific instance. For when it has been recreated in whatever shape is needed at the moment, then this new version *is* the past, and no different past can ever have existed. This holds good even when, as often happens, the same event has to be altered out of recognition several times in the course of a year. At all times the Party is in possession of absolute truth, and clearly the absolute can never have been different from what it is now. It will be seen that the control of the past depends above all on the training of memory. To make sure that all written records agree with the orthodoxy of the moment is merely a mechanical act. But it is also necessary to *remember* that events happened in the desired manner. And if it is necessary to rearrange one's memories or to tamper with written records, then it is necessary to *forget* that one has done so. The trick of doing this can be learned like any other mental technique. It *is* learned by the majority of Party members, and certainly by all who are intelligent as well as orthodox. In Oldspeak it is called, quite frankly, "reality control." In Newspeak it is called *doublethink*, although *doublethink* comprises much else as well.

Doublethink means the power of holding two contradictory beliefs in one's mind simultaneously, and accepting both of them. The Party intellectual knows in which direction his memories must be altered; he therefore knows that he is playing tricks with reality; but by the exercise of *doublethink* he also satisfies himself that reality is not violated. The process has to be conscious, or it would not be carried out with sufficient precision, but it also has to be unconscious, or it would bring with it a feeling of falsity and hence of guilt. *Doublethink* lies at the very heart of Ingsoc, since the essential act of the Party is to use conscious deception while retaining the firmness of purpose that goes with complete honesty. To tell deliberate lies while genuinely believing in them, to forget any fact that has become inconvenient, and then, when it becomes necessary again, to draw it back from oblivion for just so long as it is needed, to deny the existence of objective reality and all the while to take account of the reality which one denies— all this is indispensably necessary. Even in using the word *doublethink* it is necessary to exercise *doublethink*. For by using the word one admits that one is tampering with reality; by a fresh act of *doublethink* one erases this knowledge; and so on indefinitely, with the lie always one leap ahead of the truth. Ultimately it is by means of *doublethink* that the Party has been able—and may, for all we know, continue to be able for thousands of years —to arrest the course of history.

All past oligarchies have fallen from power either because they ossified or because they grew soft. Either they became stupid and arrogant, failed to adjust themselves to changing circumstances, and were overthrown, or they became liberal and cowardly, made concessions when they should have used force, and once again were overthrown. They fell, that is to say, either through consciousness or through unconsciousness. It is the achievement of the Party to have produced a system of thought in which both conditions can exist simultaneously. And upon no other intellectual basis could the dominion of the Party be made permanent. If one is to rule, and to continue ruling, one must be able to dislocate the sense of reality. For the secret of rulership is to combine a belief in one's own infallibility with the power to learn from past mistakes.

It need hardly be said that the subtlest practitioners of *doublethink* are those who invented *doublethink* and know that it is a vast system of mental cheating. In our society, those who have the best knowledge of what is happening are also those who are furthest from seeing the world as it is. In general, the greater the understanding, the greater the delusion: the more intelligent, the less sane. One clear illustration of this is the fact that war hysteria increases in intensity as one rises in the social scale. Those whose attitude toward the war is most nearly rational are the subject peoples of the disputed territories. To these people the war is simply a continuous calamity which sweeps to and fro over their bodies like a tidal wave. Which side is winning is a matter of complete indifference to them. They are aware that a change of overlordship means simply that they will be doing the same work as before for new masters who treat them in the same manner as the old ones. The slightly more favored workers whom we call "the proles" are only intermittently conscious of the war. When it is necessary they can be prodded into frenzies of fear and hatred, but when left to themselves they are capable of forgetting for long periods that the war is happening. It is in the ranks of the Party, and above all of the Inner Party, that the true war enthusiasm is found. World-conquest is believed in most firmly by those who know it to be impossible. This peculiar linking-together of opposites—knowledge with ignorance, cynicism with fanaticism

—is one of the chief distinguishing marks of Oceanic society. The official ideology abounds with contradictions even where there is no practical reason for them. Thus, the Party rejects and vilifies every principle for which the Socialist movement originally stood, and it chooses to do this in the name of Socialism. It preaches a contempt for the working class un-exampled for centuries past, and it dresses its members in a uniform which was at one time peculiar to manual workers and was adopted for that reason. It systematically undermines the solidarity of the family, and it calls its leader by a name which is a direct appeal to the sentiments of family loyalty. Even the names of the four Ministries by which we are governed exhibit a sort of impudence in their deliberate reversal of the facts. The Ministry of Peace concerns itself with war, the Ministry of Truth with lies, the Ministry of Love with torture, and the Ministry of Plenty with starvation. These contradictions are not accidental, nor do they result from ordinary hypocrisy: they are deliberate exercises in *double-think*. For it is only by reconciling contradictions that power can be retained indefinitely. In no other way could the ancient cycle be broken. If human equality is be forever averted—if the High, as we have called them, are to keep their places permanently—then the prevailing mental condition must be controlled insanity.

But there is one question which until this moment we have almost ignored: It is: *why* should human equality be averted? Supposing that the mechanics of the process have been rightly described, what is the motive for this huge, accurately planned effort to freeze history at a particular moment of time?

Here we reach the central secret. As we have seen, the mystique of the Party, and above all of the Inner Party, depends upon *doublethink*. But deeper than this lies the original motive, the never-questioned instinct that first led to the seizure of power and brought *doublethink*, the Thought Police, continuous warfare, and all the other necessary paraphernalia into existence afterwards. This motive really consists. . . .

INAUGURAL ADDRESS,
JANUARY 20, 1961

John Fitzgerald Kennedy

The Inaugural Address of John F. Kennedy will long be remembered as one of the most eloquent and inspiring statements of modern American values. It was delivered at a time when there was doubt, uncertainty, confusion, and skepticism concerning the values in which Americans really believe. Within this forbidding context President Kennedy won a world-wide following of enthusiastic admirers, among both young and old, for his courage, his integrity, and his articulate idealism.

We observe today not a victory of party, but a celebration of freedom—symbolizing an end, as well as a beginning—signifying renewal, as well as change. For I have sworn before you and Almighty God the same solemn oath our forebears prescribed nearly a century and three quarters ago.

The world is very different now. For man holds in his mortal hands the power to abolish all forms of human poverty and all forms of human life. And yet the same revolutionary beliefs for which our forebears fought are still at issue around the globe—the belief that the rights of man come not from the generosity of the state, but from the hand of God.

We dare not forget today that we are the heirs of that first revolution. Let the word go forth from this time and place, to friend and foe alike, that the torch has been passed to a new generation of Americans—born in this century, tempered by war, disciplined by a hard and bitter peace, proud of our ancient heritage—and unwilling to witness or permit the slow undoing of those human rights to which this Nation has always been committed, and to which we are committed today at home and around the world.

Let every nation know, whether it wishes us well or ill, that we shall pay any price, bear any burden, meet any hardship, support any friend, oppose any foe, in order to assure the survival and the success of liberty.

This much we pledge—and more.

To those old allies whose cultural and spiritual origins we share, we pledge the loyalty of faithful friends. United, there is little we cannot do

SOURCE: *Inaugural Address of President John Fitzgerald Kennedy, January 20, 1961*, Doc. No. 9, 87th Cong., 1st Sess. ❖ John Fitzgerald Kennedy (1917–1963) was President of the United States from 1961 to 1963. He had served in both houses of Congress from 1947 to 1961. He was the author of *Why England Slept*; *Strategy of Peace*; *To Turn the Tide*; and *Profiles in Courage*, which was awarded the Pulitzer prize for biography in 1957.

in a host of cooperative ventures. Divided, there is little we can do—for we dare not meet a powerful challenge at odds and split asunder.

To those new States whom we welcome to the ranks of the free, we pledge our words that one form of colonial control shall not have passed away merely to be replaced by a far greater iron tyranny. We shall not always expect to find them supporting our view. But we shall always hope to find them strongly supporting their own freedom—and to remember that, in the past, those who foolishly sought power by riding the back of the tiger ended up inside.

To those peoples in the huts and villages across the globe struggling to break the bonds of mass misery, we pledge our best efforts to help them help themselves, for whatever period is required—not because the Communists may be doing it, not because we seek their votes, but because it is right. If a free society cannot help the many who are poor, it cannot save the few who are rich.

To our sister republics south of our border, we offer a special pledge—to convert our good words into good deeds, in a new alliance for progress, to assist free men and free governments in casting off the chains of poverty. But this peaceful revolution of hope cannot become the prey of hostile powers. Let all our neighbors know that we shall join with them to oppose aggression or subversion anywhere in the Americas. And let every other power know that this hemisphere intends to remain the master of its own house.

To that world assembly of sovereign states, the United Nations, our last best hope in an age where the instruments of war have far outpaced the instruments of peace, we renew our pledge of support—to prevent it from becoming merely a forum for invective—to strengthen its shield of the new and the weak—and to enlarge the area in which its writ may run.

Finally, to those nations who would make themselves our adversary, we offer not a pledge but a request: that both sides begin anew the quest for peace, before the dark powers of destruction unleashed by science engulf all humanity in planned or accidental self-destruction.

We dare not tempt them with weakness. For only when our arms are sufficient beyond doubt can we be certain beyond doubt that they will never be employed.

But neither can two great and powerful groups of nations take comfort from our present course—both sides overburdened by the cost of modern weapons, both rightly alarmed by the steady spread of the deadly atom, yet both racing to alter that uncertain balance of terror that stays the hand of mankind's final war.

So let us begin anew—remembering on both sides that civility is not a sign of weakness, and sincerity is always subject to proof. *Let us never negotiate out of fear. But let us never fear to negotiate.*

Let both sides explore what problems unite us instead of laboring those problems which divide us.

Let both sides, for the first time, formulate serious and precise proposals for the inspection and control of arms—and bring the absolute power to destroy other nations under the absolute control of all nations.

Let both sides seek to invoke the wonders of science instead of its terrors. Together let us explore the stars, conquer the deserts, eradicate disease, tap the ocean depths, and encourage the arts and commerce.

Let both sides unite to heed in all corners of the earth the command of Isaiah—to "undo the heavy burdens and to let the oppressed go free."

And if a beachhead of cooperation may push back the jungle of suspicion, let both sides join in creating a new endeavor, not a new balance of power, but a new world of law, where the strong are just and the weak secure and the peace preserved.

All this will not be finished in the first 100 days. Nor will it be finished in the first 1,000 days, nor in the life of this administration, nor even perhaps in our lifetime on this planet. But let us begin.

In your hands, my fellow citizens, more than in mine, will rest the final success or failure of our course. Since this country was founded, each generation of Americans has been summoned to give testimony to its national loyalty. The graves of young Americans who answered the call to service are found around the globe.

Now the trumpet summons us again—not as a call to bear arms, though arms we need; not as a call to battle, though embattled we are; but a call to bear the burden of a long twilight struggle, year in, and year out, "rejoicing in hope, patient in tribulation"—a struggle against the common enemies of man: tyranny, poverty, disease, and war itself.

Can we forge against these enemies a grand and global alliance, North and South, East and West, that can assure a more fruitful life for all mankind? Will you join in that historic effort?

In the long history of the world, only a few generations have been granted the role of defending freedom in its hour of maximum danger. I do not shrink from this responsibility—I welcome it. I do not believe that any of us would exchange places with any other people or any other generation. The energy, the faith, the devotion which we bring to this endeavor will light our country and all who serve it—and the glow from that fire can truly light the world.

And so, my fellow Americans, ask not what your country can do for you: Ask what you can do for your country.

My fellow citizens of the world: Ask not what America will do for you, but what together we can do for the freedom of man.

Finally, whether you are citizens of America or citizens of the world, ask of us the same high standards of strength and sacrifice which we ask of you. With a good conscience our only sure reward, with history the final judge of our deeds, let us go forth to lead the land we love, asking His blessing and His help, but knowing that here on earth God's work must truly be our own.

APPENDICES

Sociologists at Work

APPENDIX A.

CAREERS IN SOCIOLOGY

Department of Sociology, University of Kentucky

In the preparation of this volume the editors have been primarily concerned with providing an understanding of sociology for students in general. This and other experiences may lead some to pursue further work in the field and consider careers as sociologists. Sociologists at the University of Kentucky have prepared the following statement on careers in sociology for undergraduates who wish to know what opportunities are available to them at various levels of preparation. Students in other colleges and universities should also find it helpful in making decisions about work in sociology.

Young men and women starting careers as sociologists face almost unlimited opportunity in the sense that a vast, almost totally unexplored, field of endeavor is before them. Of course, leading thinkers in all ages have been concerned about society, human conduct, and the creation of a social order that would bring forth the best that man is capable of. But, the study of these problems with the techniques and approaches of science is only a little more than a century old.

It was only about 125 years ago that Auguste Comte published his *Cours de philosophie positive* which first included sociology as one of the scientific disciplines. No course in sociology was available in an American University until 1876 at Yale, and not until after 1890 at the University of Chicago could students in the United States obtain an undergraduate major in social science. Before 1900 all the men who identified themselves as professional sociologists were trained originally in other fields such as

SOURCE: *Should You Be a Sociologist?* Prepared by the Department of Sociology, University of Kentucky, Lexington, Ky. Reprinted by permission.

history, politics, economics, law, and religion. Today, undergraduate students can obtain training in sociology in almost all American four-year liberal arts colleges and in many agricultural colleges and specialized schools; more than 70 schools offer a doctoral program in sociology and many additional schools offer Masters' degree programs. Opportunities and rewards to those trained in the field have expanded with equal, almost explosive rapidity.

Before World War I the opportunities for employment of men and women with professional training in sociology were largely limited to college teaching and research. Besides teaching and research, sociologists today are engaged in more than 25 different kinds of work in professional schools, in local, state, federal, and private agencies, and in business. They work in the fields of education, medicine, law, theology, corrections, agricultural extension, welfare, population study, community development, health, technological change, and the like. In short, sociologists are working on almost all the problems that concern man in relation to his fellow man and the consequences of this relationship for himself and others.

What Does a Sociologist Do?

You are familiar with what a teacher of sociology in a college or university does, but let's see what some other persons who are professional sociologists or who have had training in sociology are doing.

Here is a *research sociologist* in a social research institute interviewing a cross-section of people in a community which has been struck by a hurricane. His purpose is the systematic collection of information on the different responses people make in potential and actual disaster situations. Why are some people more successful than others in their attempts to protect themselves and their property? From his careful study and those of other researchers he develops a theory of human behavior in disaster situations. His insights and the facts he has collected enable public and private agencies to develop more effective programs in preparation for such emergencies—to plan ways of minimizing damage and speeding recovery.

In another locale a *community development specialist* is meeting with the Industrial Development Committee of a local Chamber of Commerce. He is advising the Committee on needed information and educational programs, techniques of community organization, and ways of gaining local support for the development program. A year or so later the same community development man may be found in India, Pakistan, or some other underdeveloped country, working with local officials there in planning self-help development programs.

In a firm designing and producing electrical equipment, gradual changes in the company organization over a period of time have reduced the status of the design engineers and affected their enthusiasm, spontaneity, and cooperativeness, with consequent effects on production. The *personnel director*, whose college training included courses in sociology, recognizes the importance of job-status to satisfaction with work and persuades the company to modify its organization, thereby alleviating their dissatisfaction.

An *urban planning specialist*, employed by a local planning and zoning commission, is assembling information on the probable social consequences of a proposed zoning change for the schools, churches, and families in the affected area and for the larger community. On the basis of this information and that from other sources the Commission must decide whether or not the proposed change is likely to result in net benefits to most of the people in the community.

Here is a *minister* who finds that people in the community in which his new church is located are troubled because their teen-age young people patronize undesirable establishments outside the community for their recreation. Owing to his earlier studies in sociology he recognizes the need to provide more opportunity locally for recreation appealing to today's youth. Under his leadership youth programs in the church and community are being expanded, thereby enriching the lives of the young people, the church, and the community.

Here is an *inter-group relations specialist* meeting with a local Board of Education. They are trying to work out a plan for compliance with the 1954 Supreme Court decision on school desegregation in a way that is most satisfactory to Negroes and white persons in the community. He is helping the School Board understand how the feelings of all people can be considered and what must be done to minimize misunderstanding and to guard against groups of people thinking that they must take matters into their own hands. On the wisdom and carefulness of their planning hinges the possibility of peaceful integration with a minimum of dissatisfaction— or the possibility of mutual distrust and possible violence.

In an industrialized community an *industrial relations specialist* is preparing a written report to the Board of Directors of a manufacturing company. They are concerned with worker absenteeism and low morale. His report includes findings as to the basis of this problem and his recommendations on how the management might work more closely with the workers to reduce worker dissatisfaction, to increase production, and to improve the firm's competitive position.

Here is a sociologist who is a member of a therapeutic team in a mental hospital. Should the relationships of aides and nurses to patients be close and informal or reserved and authoritarian? Should patients be given responsibilities and freedom of movement or should they be carefully watched and guarded? Progress in therapy hinges on making correct assessments of the impact of the hospital environment on the patient at each stage in his treatment, and of what changes must be made at each stage in order to insure continued progress.

A young *housewife*, who majored in sociology in college, recognizes that the future consequences of failure to establish a full-time planning commission in the local government will be real estate deterioration, increasing crime rates, loss of community pride, and the like. Being concerned with the growth and development of the community in which she lives she is working energetically with civic groups helping to organize a planning committee and develop citizen support for its activities.

An *extension rural sociologist*, employed in the Cooperative Extension Service in Agriculture and Home Economics, is conducting a leadership training course for 4-H Club workers in X County. He is demonstrating how the skilled leader can help young people to analyze a social situation and make intelligent choices. Tomorrow he may be working with an Extension Committee in another county, helping to set up a study to evaluate the effectiveness of a new health program.

A *research sociologist* in a university is studying the characteristics of the manpower available for industrial employment in a region. Other sociologists are studying the decision-making processes of doctors, of farmers, of industrial plant managers, and of community groups. Still others are studying factors in the development of a delinquent career, a medical career, the decision to go to college, and many more problems having theoretical and practical significance.

From this list, you can see that the sociologist may teach, he may do research in the advancement of scientific knowledge or in the solution of a practical problem, he may serve as a consultant to agencies and organizations which have international, national, state, and local community programs, or he may possibly combine several of these activities . . . all providing opportunities to find satisfaction in a lifetime of activity. In almost any field the person who has had college work in sociology finds daily uses for his knowledge in his work, civic, familial, and leisure activities.

How Does a Young Man or Woman Become a Sociologist?

The kinds of jobs and activities that are open to you as a sociologically trained person greatly depend on your interests and the kind and the extent of your training. The more professional training you get the more qualified you become to work as a professional sociologist. In some respects the training requirements and job opportunities can be represented by a tree at different stages of its growth.

By fulfilling the requirements for an undergraduate major in sociology or rural sociology, your career tree has gained the proportions, perhaps, of a sapling. If you terminate your academic education at this point a variety of job opportunities await you. Actually the number of different jobs which may be attractive to you is probably greater than it will be if you continue your education. The reason is that, while having majored in sociology, your primary qualification is your liberal arts training which enables you to enter a broad range of nontechnical occupations. Your professional identification in this case is primarily with the job that you get (e.g., recreation worker, agency representative, personnel assistant, or salesman) rather than with the sociological training that you have had and will use in the performance of your duties.

To be sure, however, there are a number of jobs for which an undergraduate major in sociology is especially appropriate. Personnel officers considering applicants for jobs in health programs, social and welfare work, community planning and zoning, farm organization work, and the like, give special consideration to graduates who have had a major in sociology.

The value of an undergraduate major in sociology is not limited to persons who plan to take a job on graduating or to continue on to graduate work in sociology. An undergraduate major or minor in sociology will provide an especially valuable background if you plan eventually to become a clergyman, attorney, economist, psychologist, political scientist, or historian, or to enter many other professional fields.

It is with graduate training in sociology that you begin especially to be identified by the particular type of professional training that you have had and this tendency increases the further you go in your training. By the end of the first or second year of your graduate study you should obtain your Master's degree. At this time you qualify as a sub-professional specialist for jobs in planning and zoning, extension education, social services, community development, research, small college teaching, and the like. Since you are to some extent identified as a sociologist, your opportunity is greater to obtain a job in which a degree of competence in sociology is expected and desired.

If you plan for a career as a full-fledged professional sociologist your academic goal is the Doctor of Philosophy degree in sociology. The occupational fruit of this tree is usually harvested in the third to fifth year of graduate work. Depending on your interests you may accept a job as a teacher or researcher, or join agencies concerned with a variety of human problems in public affairs that require sociological knowledge for their solutions.

If you plan to end your education with an A.B. or B.S. degree, you may want to develop the trunk of your career tree somewhat differently than if you plan to continue academic work beyond that point. If you do not plan to continue your academic training you may emphasize "practical" courses in sociology; but courses in philosophy, mathematics, scientific methods, and in the principles of different scientific disciplines should be your fare if you are looking forward to graduate work. Your major advisor can help you make wise selections from among approved courses.

The academic "trees" of persons who pursue graduate studies in sociology differ in other respects from those who stop with the bachelor's degree. If your undergraduate studies have included a broad range of basic science, philosophy, history, mathematics, and English, a major in sociology will enable you to move directly into professional sociology courses in graduate school. But many graft a sociological career tree on other roots; you may decide to begin graduate studies in sociology after having majored as an undergraduate in history, psychology, political science, engineering, animal husbandry, mathematics, and the like. While in the beginning you may have to take some of the basic courses that a sociology major already will have had, your background in another field is likely to be an asset as you continue your professional training and later work.

Graduate education is not as expensive as it seems at first. Most students are able to obtain financial support while they are in graduate school. This may come from a fellowship or scholarship which does not have a work commitment, or an assistantship which is usually for half-time work in a Department of Sociology. Increasingly, there are opportunities for able students to engage in part-time semi-professional work outside the university while pursuing their advanced studies.

What Are the Rewards and Drawbacks?

One of the most tempting aspects of professional work in sociology is its broad and expanding horizon. It is exciting to be a part of something with ever enlarging opportunities and rewards.

Thirty years ago few people made their living as professional sociologists. Today, there are more than 4,300 Fellows, Active members and Associate members of the American Sociological Association. In ten years the number of student members—about 2,000 in 1960—has increased by 60 per cent, indicating that young men and women increasingly recognize the opportunities to have satisfying careers as sociologists. The many occupations that professional sociologists have now mean that ambitious young men and women can move readily from one interesting job to another in search of variety of experience and opportunities for promotion.

The starting salaries for sociology majors with a bachelor's degree compare favorably with those of other liberal arts and agriculture graduates. Because of the demand for trained people, advancement within a company or agency can be quite rapid. In college teaching and research, starting salaries for young men and women with a Ph.D. degree in sociology range between $7,500 and $10,000 . . . . (For those who go into the civil service or private industry, as more and more are doing, starting salaries average somewhat higher.) Nationally, these figures are increasing at the rate of 2 to 3 per cent a year. The annual salaries of a few top sociologists are now in excess of $20,000. Such salaries are exceptional today, but so were salaries of $12,000 a few years ago, and the record amply indicates that becoming a professional sociologist does not demand a vow of poverty as many people mistakenly believe.

However, a high order of social, emotional, and intellectual maturity is required to earn a Master's and a Doctor's degree. To take these as your academic goals you must find satisfaction in working *toward* answers to human problems rather than in *having* the "right" answer beforehand. You must be willing to view people and their behavior objectively—to suspend judgment of whether their behavior is "good" or "bad" in terms of conventional morality. You must be willing to develop competence in mathematics and written and oral communications, and to pursue intellectual interests in the broad range of the humanities and sciences. It isn't easy to understand the significance of so intangible a thing as society to the attainment of individual and group purposes. But, if you are intellectually curious, and especially if you are interested in people—in understanding and helping them, in discovering why they behave as they do, and how human needs are satisfied in society—you will find a career as a sociologist exciting, rewarding, and satisfying.

"More important than any amount of money or medals to me," writes one research sociologist, "is the thrill in suddenly discovering that in deciding between alternative courses of action for which the precise consequences are unknown a person needs the emotional support of a friend and confidant. On the basis of this insight a number of puzzling and apparently inconsistent facts about the process of human decision-making are given coherence and meaning." An extension sociologist felt forever rewarded, even though he obtained no tangible benefit, on being told that what he had said and done in a crisis faced by a local community recreation committee had led not merely to saving the recreation program and the Recreation Director's job but to the expansion of the program to embrace all groups in the entire community.

We would be less than candid, however, if we left the impression that the job of the sociologist is all fun and satisfaction. First, the task of gaining a graduate degree requires hard, unremitting labor. It requires personal dedication and intellectual endeavor of the highest order; but only in this manner can one gain the confidence and competence necessary to perform one's professional responsibilities with credit to oneself, one's profession, and one's society.

As a sociologist you frequently will find that the people and groups whom you are able to help are unaware of what you can do or sometimes even disparage your abilities. Often it is necessary to sell yourself and your field before you can begin work on the problem needing your attention. But this difficulty confronts the pathmaker in all new fields of endeavor, and herein lies much of the challenge and opportunity awaiting professional sociologists.

Hard to take, sometimes, is the feeling that your job is never done, no matter how much you do; and your failures as a human relations specialist or as a researcher can keep you awake nights wondering, "What should I have said to that committee to enable them to see the significance of approaching the problem in this way?" "What have I failed to take into account in attempting to explain the behavior of that organization paralyzed by conflict and poor morale?"

The fact that the rewards far outweigh the drawbacks, however, is indicated each year by the increasing number of young people like yourself who become professional sociologists. In 1940 only 155 men and women were awarded Master's degrees in sociology in the United States and only 50 were awarded the Doctor of Philosophy degree in sociology. In 1963, however, 684 received a Master's degree and 208 the Doctor's degree.

If you think you might be interested in becoming a sociology or rural sociology major, or in taking several courses in sociology, you will want to find out more about the opportunities, rewards and requirements than is provided here. The undergraduate and graduate advisors in Sociology can supply additional helpful information and help you plan an interesting and rewarding program of study. They will welcome the opportunity to meet you and to discuss with you what courses would be most helpful to you in preparing for your career. You can arrange a meeting with an advisor through an instructor in one of your sociology courses. . . .

APPENDIX B.
SOCIOLOGY AS A PROFESSION
Alex Inkeles

In Appendix A we are given an overview of the various types of work for which sociological training might prepare an individual. In this selection Alex Inkeles analyzes sociology as a profession. Students with only undergraduate education in the field are not likely to become identified as professional sociologists, but those who choose to prepare themselves for professional roles through advanced study will find this article useful. A brief historical analysis is followed by an examination of the professional sociologist's role in contemporary society.

Sociology is not only an intellectual discipline; it is also a profession. When we consider any branch of learning as an intellectual discipline, we have in mind the premises on which the men in the field rest their work,

SOURCE: Alex Inkeles, *What Is Sociology?* © 1964. Reprinted by permission of Prentice-Hall, Inc., Englewood Cliffs, N.J. ✧ The author is professor of sociology at Harvard University; Director, Studies in Social Relations, Russian Research Center; and Director, Studies of Non-Economic Aspects of Development, Center of International Affairs. His main interests include comparative social structures, modal personality patterns, and social stratification. He is the coauthor of *How the Soviet System Works, Public Opinion in Soviet Russia: A Study in Mass Persuasion,* and "National Character" in *The Handbook of Social Psychology.*

the ideas and currents of thought which unite or separate them, the characteristic styles of reasoning or argument which they use, the types of data
considered, the way in which they are collected, and the manner in which
they are treated. When we speak of a profession, we refer mainly to such
themes as the uses or applications of a body of knowledge—for example,
whether to teach or to heal; to the context in which the discipline is used,
whether in public or privately, with large groups or face to face with one
individual; to the way in which those concerned with a given realm make
their living; how they are related to their "client," to one another, and to
the larger society; how much freedom and autonomy they enjoy; how well
or poorly organized they are, and the like. The nature and practice of a
discipline determine the kind of intellectual enterprise and profession it
may become.

Sociology as a Teaching Profession

Teaching absorbs by far the largest part of the nation's sociological
energies. Approximately three fourths of those holding the Ph.D. in sociology teach in university or college programs. Professional schools, especially
of education and social work, but increasingly those of business, law, and
medicine as well, also employ sociologists as teachers. Of those sociologists
with an academic connection, 1 in 7 is affiliated with a professional school,
a research institute within a university, or an other-than-sociology teaching
department.

The development of sociology in American universities is distinguished
by the following facts: it came very late to the academic scene; its bearers
could neither point to a well-established and venerable intellectual tradition, nor claim for themselves superior and distinguished personal social
origins; and it nevertheless grew at a phenomenal rate. These facts played
an important role both in shaping the reception sociology received in the
American academic community and the reaction of sociologists to that
reception.

Growth of Sociology in America

All of the social studies had to struggle to win a place for themselves
in the traditional or classical program of the American college and university. The task was probably easiest for history, which could trace its origins
to Herodotus and readily pass for a humane branch of learning. Economics
was less readily accepted, but the distinction of Adam Smith and the
importance of the subject to English and American societies undergoing
rapid economic development greatly smoothed the way. Sociology came
along at the end of this chain of development. The first department of
sociology was not established until 1893 at Chicago. The American Sociological Association was formed by a rump group which broke away from the

parent Economic Association in 1905. Although Spencer's evolutionary theory had had some vogue in the United States, very few people had at the time heard of sociology and fewer still knew the meaning of this strange new term only recently coined.

The newer Midwestern colleges and universities, state supported and generally more democratic, welcomed the new discipline and it grew up along with them. Yet sociology was by no means excluded in the East. Brown, Columbia, Dartmouth, Pennsylvania, and Yale introduced sociology courses prior to the founding of the Sociological Society, and Yale was host to William Graham Sumner, one of the first of the great American sociologists. There were, however, major pockets of resistance to this new and strange discipline among the more conservative, private and elite eastern schools. Harvard did not establish a department of sociology until Sorokin came to the University in 1930. It is striking that as late as 1960, 5 of the nation's 20 "leading" liberal arts colleges still did not offer any instruction in sociology.

Sociology's late arrival on the academic scene was compensated for neither by the social standing of its partisans nor the inherent status of its subject matter. Very few representatives of the older and wealthier families of the eastern seaboard took up sociology as they did the classics, literature, or history. The early American sociologists were distinctively products of the rural rather than the urban segment of the country. Almost without exception the first two dozen presidents of the American Sociological Association were of rural origin. So pervasive was this characteristic that C. W. Mills detects in the work of American students of social pathology a typical rural prejudice against the city, a tendency to see it as the source and natural home of vice, crime, broken families and the like. The rural origins of the early sociological leaders frequently combined with a connection with the ministry. A surprisingly high proportion of the early sociologists were descended from ministers or were themselves trained in the ministry. The list includes such outstanding figures as Lester Ward, early disciple of Comte and often regarded as the father of American sociology, Franklin Giddings, founder and longtime head of the Department of Sociology at Columbia, Albion Small, founder and chairman of the great department at Chicago, and many others.

The early sociologists in Europe dealt mainly with theories of history or drew on the lives of primitives to illustrate their ideas about evolution, religion, and society. Although similar themes and sources figured prominently in the work of Ward and Sumner, early American sociology gave a much greater share of its attention to the pressing social problems which seemed to spring up everywhere in the rapidly changing American society. This was especially true at the University of Chicago, which for more than two decades (1915–1940) was virtually unchallenged as the leading center of sociological training in America. Chicago sociologists in the living laboratory provided by the city studied the slum and ghetto, the prostitute and juvenile delinquent, the professional criminal, jazz, and drug addiction.

Despite the plain origins of its practitioners and the often raw quality of its subject matter, or perhaps because of them, sociology grew rapidly, indeed phenomenally. The hundred-odd members who had founded the American Sociological Society in 1905 had increased almost sevenfold by the time the United States entered World War I. After the war it experienced another spurt of growth, more than doubling in size in the next 10 years. Although the number of members decreased during the depression years, the period after the Second World War saw the resumption of growth. Indeed, the membership of the Sociological Association has been growing in the postwar period at the exceptional rate of some 10 per cent a year, and in 1960 included more than 6,000.

There is hardly a college or university where sociology is not taught today. One study of a sample of 263 colleges revealed that they offered an average of about 14 courses in sociology at each school. In 1958–1959 the U.S. Office of Education reported that 641 universities and colleges (exclusive of schools of social work) awarded bachelors degrees in sociology to almost 7,000 students graduating that year. The number of graduates majoring in sociology is slightly larger than in political science and slightly smaller than in psychology and economics. In the face of such growing interest and increasing acceptance, sociologists have come to feel about their discipline much as Lavoisier did about chemistry when he said in 1805: "I do not expect my ideas to be adopted all at once. . . . Those who have envisaged nature according to a certain point of view during much of their career, rise only with difficulty to new ideas. It is the passage of time, therefore, which must confirm or destroy the opinions I have presented. Meanwhile, I observe with great satisfaction that the young people . . . are beginning to study the science without prejudice. . . ."

❖   ❖   ❖   ❖   ❖

Sociology as a Research Enterprise

With few exceptions sociologists make their living by teaching or research, or some combination of the two. Even those in administration usually work in the context of a university, a government agency, or a business corporation. The 1959 census of members of the American Sociological Association showed 70 per cent affiliated with universities and colleges, 5 per cent working for the federal government, 6 per cent employed by business and industry, and the remainder mainly in state and local organizations such as schools, hospitals, prisons, and the like. Among those professions which it is reasonable to compare with sociology, this pattern is probably most like that for economists. Historians, by contrast, are found almost exclusively in teaching posts, whereas psychologists are found in large numbers in private practice, which is rare among sociologists.

Unfortunately, we cannot trace this pattern very far back to discover its stability or variability. A census comparable to that for 1959 is available only for 1950. Even over this short span, however, several trends emerge which are probably of long-term significance.

Between 1950 and 1959 the proportion of sociologists with a university or college affiliation decreased from 75 to 70 per cent of the total, while those with a government or other types of affiliation increased from 22 to 26 per cent. While a shift of this magnitude hardly suggests a radical transformation of the profession, it points to the increasing representation of those engaged either in full-time research or in applications of sociology. This trend is strengthened by the fact that of those in colleges and universities, an increasing proportion are affiliated with professional schools. Such schools increased their share of sociological employment from 8 to 11 per cent. The available facts may be used to argue that sociology is becoming less exclusively an academic discipline or a pure science, and is more and more developing a major component of applied work.

❖   ❖   ❖   ❖ ʹ ❖

The Bureaucratic Milieu and the Individual Scholar

The sociological profession is growing very rapidly. In 1960 there were about 2,100 living holders of the Ph.D. in sociology. Over half had received their degrees in the preceding 10-year period. Since new Ph.D.'s are graduating at a rate close to 200 per year, in another decade the number will again have doubled. Some critics, for example, C. Wright Mills, would have us believe that this growing corps of highly trained social scientists is being marched, rank on rank, into the insatiable maw of vast research bureaucracies in the government, especially the military establishment, and in advertising offices of business and industry. There these poor young sociologists presumably toil as routinized and bureaucratized intellectual slaves, doing the bidding of masters who have no real interest in social science or its future development. This outcome is a real possibility in the modern world. But the available data fail to support those who claim that the once free intellectual discipline of sociology has been subverted and reduced to a condition of servitude and impotence.

Among the youngest holders of the Ph.D., those under 35, as among the older groups over 55 years of age, approximately three fourths are employed not by large formal research organizations but by colleges and universities. A 1960 survey located only 170 sociologists in the federal government, and of these by far the largest group, numbering 63, was employed in the health, education, and welfare services. There were only 16 in the Department of Defense. Even in the academic world, only 2 per cent of those in regular sociology departments are exclusively in research.

Among those not in regular departments, only about 1 in 5 are full-time researchers.

These facts make it difficult to accept C. W. Mills' description of social science as having become bureaucratized, ready "to serve whatever ends its bureaucratic clients have in view." Nor can we quite accept his assertion that: "The idea of a university as a circle of professorial peers, each with apprentices and each practicing a craft, tends to be replaced by the idea of a university as a set of research bureaucracies, each containing an elaborate division of labor, and hence of intellectual technicians."

While acknowledging the growth of large bureaucratic research organizations, we should realize that their activities do not basically change the situation of the individual scholars who still make up the overwhelming majority of the profession. Because some work on "projects" arising out of "programs" of research, rely on professional interviewers and paid research assistants, run their data through IBM machines, and juggle their figures on computers, it does not follow that others must do the same.

In any event, the critical fact is that most sociologists are and continue to remain outside of the research bureaucracies. The libraries relied on by the classical sociologists who worked as individual craftsmen are as open and free now as they were when Durkheim and Weber wrote their books. It is weak indeed to excuse the failure of one's research to yield results by charging that the other fellow uses bad methods. And many a sociologist who works as an individual craftsman relies heavily on materials assembled by research bureaucracies. There is no other way to collect statistics about a large national population or a complicated economic or political system save by developing such an organization. The critical issue is not whether we have research bureaucracies, but what we do with their products. The young sociologist today has the same freedom to do good work, and runs the same risk of doing poor work, as did his predecessor before the era of large-scale research bureaucracies.

Sociology and Social Criticism

Gunnar Myrdal, in a brilliant essay on "The Relation Between Social Theory and Social Policy," argued that the social sciences are important to a democracy because they encourage the open discussion of important issues by appealing to the people's rationality rather than to superstition and narrowness. The sociologist can make this contribution, however, only if his situation affords him reasonable freedom and security.

No doubt some societies and bureaucracies will be more tolerant than others of those who "step out of line." And there are, of course, ways in which the social scientist can work for his ideas within any bureaucracy. Nevertheless, most of those employed in public and private agencies which are organized as bureaucracies and enforce discipline and loyalty to superiors, will understandably be constrained from playing an independent role either in opening up important issues or in leading people toward their resolution through free public discussion.

Since the overwhelming majority of sociologists are not employed by such special-interest bureaucracies but rather serve as free scholars in the universities and colleges, we might conclude that the situational pressures which might induce them to neglect their obligations to democracy are not great. Ideally the university professor is, in Myrdal's words, "free to pursue the truth without anxiously seeking public acclaim or avoiding public anathema." In practice, as Myrdal, Mills, and others have been quick to point out, the conditions which underlie the professor's independent status may be either very imperfectly assured or lacking altogether.

❖   ❖   ❖   ❖   ❖

Sociology and the Free Society

Late in life, Durkheim prepared a contribution on sociology for the volume *La Science Française,* assembled in connection with the San Francisco Exposition of 1915, in which he wrote that sociology could be conceived and develop only in a society which met two conditions:

First, traditionalism had to have lost its domain. Among a people who consider their institutions everything they ought to be, nothing can incite thought to apply itself to social matters. Second, a veritable faith in the power of reason to dare to undertake the translation of the most complex and unstable of un-realities into definite terms was necessary.

France, said Durkheim, satisfied this double condition. I think we can say that the United States also distinctively fulfilled these conditions. By contrast, the Soviet regime was not long in power in Russia before most of her sociologists were either driven out of the country or purged. Sociology is defined in the Soviet Union as a bourgeois social science, engaged in only by "lackeys" and "wage slaves" of capitalism who use it to counter the "true" Marxist-Leninist social science. Sociology suffered a similar fate in Communist China. Before the Communist takeover, there were more than 1,000 students studying sociology under some 140 teachers in Chinese colleges and universities. The new regime stamped out these activities completely, to replace them by new courses on Marxism. Those sociologists who survive live under a cloud because of their former profession. Dr. Sun Pen-wen, author of what was the leading treatise on sociology before the new regime took over, sent the following chilling response to an American sociologist who wrote requesting a set of his works: "I have come to understand that all my books are only good for burning and hence I have none to send you. I have also learned that I formerly neglected to study the works of Karl Marx which I am now doing many hours a day. Please don't write again."

American society has characteristically subjected itself to a constant process of self-examination and critical reappraisal which has produced a steady stream of proposals for change. Moreover, a surprisingly large number of these has been adopted. As a result, the United States is viewed by most peoples of the world as dynamic and progressive to a degree which they hardly can imagine, and certainly do not expect to realize, for their own countries. This readiness to change has provided an environment conducive to the development of sociology. Americans may justly be proud of the United States' standing as the undisputed world leader in contemporary sociology. This may be considered one of the important confirmations of its outstanding tradition of freedom of thought and inquiry. But that which confirms can also disconfirm. We must acknowledge the recurrent tendencies in American life to subject to political attack those whose scientific investigations are thought too dangerous or whose ideas are too disturbing.

To fulfill the function Myrdal assigns them as searchers for truth and as leaders of the public discussion of basic social issues, sociologists must have security of tenure and some reasonable immunity against political persecution. In England, and probably France, both the tradition and the institutional arrangements guaranteeing independence to the university professor are stronger than in the United States. Where institutional supports are weak, the climate of opinion is all the more important. Dr. Myrdal has said that the "most unfortunate and potentially enormously dangerous effect of the cold war is that even academic discussion tends to be hampered by anxious fore-thoughts and clamped in opportunist stereotypes." The United States has not escaped these effects. The consequences of the atmosphere of suspicion, of thought control, and of punitiveness which prevailed during "the McCarthy era" cannot be realistically assessed by pointing to the small number of professors actually dismissed, nor even by proving that they were really subversives. Much more important is the effect on the free expression of those who were not subversive and who were not dismissed.

Those effects are well-documented in Lazarsfeld and Thielen's study, completed in 1955, of almost 2,500 social-science teachers, including historians, carefully chosen to represent all the colleges and universities in the United States. Of those teaching in larger schools rated as of high quality, 70 per cent reported that they were familiar with at least one "incident" involving an attack on a fellow faculty member for his views or associations. In the smaller and less outstanding schools, 28 per cent of the teachers knew of such incidents. It should not be surprising, therefore, that 40 per cent of college teachers in the social sciences reported that they worried lest some student inadvertently pass on a warped version of what they said, and 22 per cent admitted direct self-censorship of one kind or another. Under such circumstances it is, of course, not only the professor who suffers but equally the students and the community, which are denied the chance to hear a frank expression of the views of men especially well-qualified to analyze our society and its problems.

Sociology can thrive only under freedom. Indeed, the extent to which sociologists may pursue their interests, fully publish their results, and freely state their conclusions is one important index of the degree to which a nation qualifies as a free and open society. A nation cannot have quality in sociology by fiat. It can, if it chooses, write a kind of "contract" for that kind of sociology which guarantees, in advance, to produce results which affirm the established order and confirm received doctrine. It may then get what it orders, as it does in the Soviet Union, but it will not get good sociology. Only a nation which provides the conditions for free inquiry may with reason hope for the development of social-science knowledge which permits ever deeper understandings of man in society.

APPENDIX C.
THE RELEVANCE OF HISTORY
TO THE SOCIOLOGICAL ETHOS

Hans Gerth and Saul Landau

The range of the phenomena treated in sociological research and writings during the past 150 years has been very broad: from microscopic examinations of small groups for short periods to sweeping analyses of whole societies over the centuries. But the overwhelming majority of American sociologists today have generally focused on phases of social reality which were rather sharply limited in both space and time. This tendency has resulted from a general preference for empirical methods and has caused a strengthening of such methods. As a result, the larger scale social phenomena— and unfortunately often the most relevant for policy decisions—

SOURCE: *Studies on the Left*, Vol. 1, No. 1 (Fall, 1959), 6–14. Reprinted by permission. ❖ Hans Gerth is professor of sociology at the University of Wisconsin. His special interests include social psychology, sociological theory, and political sociology. He is the coauthor of *Character and Social Structure* and the coeditor of *Freedom, Power and Democratic Planning.* He has also translated Max Weber's *The Religion of China* and was the co-translator of Weber's *The Religion of India.* ❖ Saul Landau has written for many magazines including *Studies on the Left* and *Ramparts.* He is the author of *The Minstrel Show or Civil Rights in a Cracker Barrell,* a play, and co-authored *The New Radicals.*

have been regarded as beyond the scope of available and feasible sociological methods or not properly the concern of the discipline. This selection emphasizes anew the early concern for increasing sociological knowledge in order to achieve rational control of human destiny. The authors call for the restoration of historical perspective as essential to an understanding of the dynamics of the major social structures.

Sociological thought emerged in response to the crisis of a newly dynamic European society, fresh from industrial and political revolution. The aim of this new thought process was to forge intellectual tools which would make the complex web of social relations more transparent. Sociology was born and grew in a rapidly changing world, a world that seemed to be drifting, and in which man was again and again surprised and frightened by experiencing the unforeseen and unintended consequences of his actions. From the Enlightenment, the wars for revolution and independence on the European and American continents, the Napoleonic conquests and defeats, the czarist and Metternichean reaction, and the explosion of British industrial and commercial energies, emerged sociology—the intellectual quest pursued by a new type of scholar.

In 1816, Friedrich Buchholz, in Germany, saw this quest as "the advent of a science of which former centuries could not dream; namely the science of society in its necessary and fortuitous relations." Buchholz did not have a name for these new scholars, but he described them as special minds whose "entire endeavor aims at bringing science nearer the state of society, as it actually is, and adjusting science to it." Later, Auguste Comte, the disciple of Saint Simon, named the new intellectual approach "sociology," and sloganized its ethos as *"Savoir pour prévoir, prévoir pour pouvoir."* This new science of society, as its originators thought of it, was designed to overcome blind drift, fate, or the unforeseen and unintended consequences of man's action. The end of knowledge was to be prediction, the end of prediction, control.

The great founders of sociology were not traditional academicians in any sense. Men like Buchholz, Comte and Spencer were academic outsiders; Ferdinand Tönnies and, later, Max Weber were at least relative outsiders. Those that were in the academy did not behave like the average college professor, for they would not, and could not, be confined to one academic discipline. Buchholz, a pastor's son from Brandenburg, was a free lance writer and critic. Karl Marx, the "non Jewish Jew," was an economist, philosopher, sociologist, historian, and social revolutionary. And not only was he obviously outside traditional academic life, but, as an exile who did not assimilate, he was a cultural outsider as well. Certainly for Tönnies and Simmel, Spencer, Weber, and Durkheim (a Jew in Paris in the days of Dreyfus and Zola), the narrow confines of the traditional professor were intolerable.

This fact is related to the nature of the contribution which these men made; for to probe deeper into the analysis of society, to see society in its transition toward a world market, supported by world wide industrialization, required a sense of time and reality, and a breadth of vision, that could only be possessed by men outside, or at least partially outside academic walls. Most of the older academicians were involved in a process of division of labor which increasingly tended to confine their scholarship to expertness (the expert has rightly been defined as a man who knows more and more about less and less), and the court historian of old, the biographer of kings and captains, was giving way, in an age of high pitched nationalism, to the national historian concerned with the heroes and martyrs of his nation. But at the same time, and in opposition to this tendency to contraction, the great minds were developing a sense of world history. Men like Adam Smith, Hegel and Marx, Burckhardt, Ranke and Mommsen, all tried to see the world as a whole.

To the sociologists, seeing the world in totality involved the concrete comprehension of historical causality, not to be explained by reference to "the spirit of the times." For to them, "spirit of the times" seemed a handy phrase that begged the real issues, a slogan substituted for real knowledge. Interestingly, Goethe, who coined the term "world literature," spoke through Faust on the same subject:

> The spirit of the times,
> At bottom merely the spirit of the gentry
> In whom each time reflects itself,
> And at that it often makes one weep
> And at the first glance run away,
> A lumber room and a rubbish heap,
> At best an heroic puppet play
> With excellent pragmatical Buts and Yets
> Such as are suitable to marionettes.

From the inception of sociology as a way of thinking, its practitioners conceived of decision making as a property of all men and women. History was made by all men, albeit some contributed minutely and some grandly. But each individual in his society meant something, and, since he was a maker of history, all parts of his life had to be studied and analyzed. His vocational life and his political life were inseparable; and so, for the sociologist, history and biography merged in the analysis of society.

The case study was born as a stepping stone to the construction or documentation of *types*. It was the use of these types that helped the sociologist to conceptualize society as a whole. Each individual was important, but for the purposes of analysis he had to be seen with reference to a type construct, whether it was "intellectual" or "yeoman farmer," Marx's "bourgeois" or "lumpen proletariat," or Max Weber's heroic Puritan. The heroic individual and unique individual of historical biography was now replaced on the analytical pedestal by the type. The individual could be measured as an approximation of, or deviation from what was typical. Type man enabled the sociologist to broaden the intellectual horizon by making comparative studies of societies and groups of men. Thus, the study of "Caesarism" replaced the study of Caesar, so that Alexander the Great and Napoleon could now be studied comparatively as "Caesarists." The type approach did not deny the importance of great historical personages, but rather, it made for analysis of the great man in a different way, concretely and comparatively. Men like Jay Gould and John D. Rockefeller might be used to study economic supermen, or "robber barons" as they were called by the muckrakers. These Promethean bourgeois, in turn, could be compared with the English merchant capitalists from Sir Walter Raleigh to Smythe and his cohorts on the Muscovy, East India and Virginia companies.

Thus, whatever the limitations of the great social analysts, it is apparent that they attempted to see things in their interconnections, and on a world scale. They all consciously worked within a dynamic social structure, and each saw his own age as one of crisis and transition. For Marx it was an age of transition from Capitalism to Socialism; for Spencer it was an age of conflict between peaceful industrial society running according to natural law, and despotic military society which threatened chaos. For Max Weber, the revival of imperialism spelled disaster for Germany, which he feared would be divided, along with the rest of Europe, between the "rule of the Russian official's ukase and Anglo-Saxon conventionality with a dash of Latin *raison* thrown in."

II

The coming of the twentieth century saw America's emergence as a world power. The nineteenth century sociologist's schematization of the past, whether in terms of evolutionism, or progress toward national efficiency and/or "virtuous perfection," seemed to have been outgrown. By 1919, the Kaiser and his armies were no more. The world should now have been safe for democracy, and The War had supposedly ended all wars. The obstacles to the Wilsonian mission—the guilty Germans and the stubborn Bolsheviks—were placed in the diplomatic dog house where they belonged for not cooperating. The prophet of the western world, President Wilson, sailed to Paris with a proposal for a League that would usher in a new age of mankind. The United States sat on top of the world. Its age in world history had been reached.

Just as United States leaders began to realize their dream of a world economic empire headed by American corporate power, the American sociologist dispensed with world concepts. He dismissed, as metaphysics, all thought and theory that dealt with world or total structures. The world simply was taken for granted. To be sure, there was still work to be done, but it was no more than a scattering of problems that remained to be solved, involving industrial efficiency and the rational adjustment of certain immigrant-alien milieux to the American system. The integration of the world was left to the businessmen and politicians. The sociologist wanted to routinize the functioning of the good society at home, focusing on industrial problems, the family, and the behavior of groups in their natural setting.

To do this, statistical and survey techniques, and small precision group work had to be perfected. Robert Park, in Chicago in the 1920's, contributed more than any other man to the origination of milieu sociology. Park was fascinated by the cultural hybrid, the bilingual immigrant, the marginal man. As a journalist, he offered rich descriptive techniques, in the tradition of Balzac's realism, to help conceptualize the changing milieux in the post World War I United States. Sociologists became intrigued by this kind of study. Following the old maxim that "nothing human is alien to me," but without the "let's go slumming" attitude of the debutante, sociologists descended upon the slums and studied the sex codes of slum dwellers. They also associated with Cafe Society to study the behavior patterns of the night life set. Humanity was studied in the raw, and in its environment— Chinese peasants in their villages, bandits of the Robin Hood type in forests, gunmen in the old west, and Al Capone and Anastasia types in American gangland. Salesladies at Macy's, school teachers, Chicago and New York street gangs, POW's—all were studied in their respective roles in their respective settings.

This analysis of society into segments for separate study, necessarily led to specialization. Comte and Spencer, the nineteenth century mainstays of United States sociology, gave place to the empirical scholars, who proceeded to tackle problems, small and smaller, of milieu, families, and small groups in general, until a sociologist was no longer just a sociologist, but a specialist in family sociology, public opinion, criminology, statistics, small groups, methodology and methods, race relations, and so on, *ad infinitum*. The "experts" and "specialists" emerged and conquered. Fame went to the innovating specialist, the more so if his new specialty fed material into IBM statistical machines. The kind of material fed into the machines came to matter less and less. The synthesizing minds, both past and present, that possessed what C. Wright Mills calls the "sociological imagination," began to be berated as impractical and unscientific. Karl Mannheim and Pitirim Sorokin were dismissed by many of the new "expert specialists" as out of date. The questions that Marx, Comte, Spencer, Ross and Weber had wrestled with, and the great theoretical legacy they had bequeathed were cast into limbo. Their works were largely unread: in some academic circles they were unknown; in others they were sanctified as classics, and so did not have to be read. And one result of this intense division of labor was that sociologists failed to predict anything. Meanwhile, the war that had ended all wars generated steam for a second war to end war, while bolshevism, fascism and nazism made a mockery of the Wilsonian dream.

Certainly, society had to be broken down and studied in its units. Certainly, too, milieu sociology refined and broadened the tools of the trade, developing advanced techniques of inquiry and scientific methods of analysis. The closeup-microcosmic lens was utilized with admirable pictorial results, and observations were made with millimetric exactitude. But all this was achieved at the expense of total structure; that is, by disjoining history and sociology. And such exactitude, even when applied to a society as a whole, cannot be a substitute for the examination of social movements in terms of their roots and far reaching consequences.

The impact of the Bolshevik revolution on the structure of the western world, to say nothing of the Asian world, cannot be revealed through milieux studies, no matter how thorough. The history of czarist Russia, in the context of world history, must be analyzed in order that the sociologist may see the roots of the upheaval and its future direction. A study of Russian workers or peasants, while valuable, could not reveal much more than some aspects of worker and peasant attitudes. Even if several milieu studies were put together, they would only form an incomplete compilation of some of the clues. Without a view of the total structure, from a historical bridge, only narrow currents can be analyzed, and much more of their content will necessarily remain unknown. Similarly, to take a less revolutionary example, the far reaching results of the long Slavonic migration to Prussian Junker labor barracks, or of immigrants arriving in boat loads from Poland, and heading to the mines, mills and factories of the new world in Pennsylvania, Chicago and Milwaukee, cannot be grasped through the close up camera, or attitude studies of changes in old world patriarchalism. While such studies by Thomas and Znaniecki, and other milieu sociologists greatly enriched the tool kit of the profession, the more basic issues were neglected: the analysis of *structures*, which *cause* milieu changes, was forsaken for more "empirical" investigation.

Thus, compartmentalization and the confinement of precision work to milieu and industrial sociology have threatened to smother the original sociologists' ethos. Interest in sterile verbal systems and faddist professional jargon have often replaced the concern with the substance of society. The fact that "all the facts are not in" has been used as an excuse for the failure to examine important problems, and the failure to examine important problems has, of course, resulted in the failure to predict. It was not until 1940, after the hot war was underway, that the *American Journal of Sociology* decided to publish an article on the Nazi Party. In all, from 1933 to 1947, only two articles on National Socialism appeared in the *Journal*. A fifty year index of the *Journal* shows exactly three listings under Marx or Marxism, and under Lenin (or Leninism) there are no citations. By and large, the sociologists of today have shut the world crisis out of their vision, focusing their intellectual energy on the crisis of the family, while the Chinese revolution, involving 600,000,000 people—perhaps the greatest mass movement of mankind—is totally neglected.

III

Hot and cold wars have tortured the earth since the beginning of this century. No one has escaped the horrors of the age of imperialism and its wars, or the effects of the rapid bureaucratization of industrial societies and their empires, and of the movement toward centralized control in almost all areas of the world. The effects of all this on the social sciences are hard to measure. Bureaucracy of all sorts has built high walls of "necessary secrecy" (official secrecy classified from confidential to top secret), and has befogged the human mind with the "necessary" vapors of publicity and rival propagandas. Mass media, themselves products of the age of total warfare and bureaucratization, have transformed the journalist of old into an adjunct of a state and/or business bureaucracy (who sees him anymore as a crusader and fighter for truth, except in grade B movies?). Likewise, the academician, although one step removed from the market place and the political arena, does not escape, and does not want to escape, his obligation to state and corporate power. "Science in uniform" is the order of the day, and the sociologist, along with his colleagues, has become an auxiliary of the bureaucracies, in an age in which bureaucracies have become almost universal.

But there are hopeful signs.

❖   ❖   ❖   ❖   ❖

Concern . . . with the drift of social structures and the concatenation of institutional orders and social strata accounts, in part, for the recently greater receptivity on the part of sociologists to the work of Max Weber, who epitomizes the former sociological concern with the totality of man's social life and future. Weber, who practiced what Comte preached as a motto for sociology, wrote comparatively little on the methodology of prediction, but he predicted much, fusing history with sociology. The death of czarism in Russia and the subsequent rise of Bolshevism did not surprise Weber, who had devoted 200 pages to the study of Russia since Admiral Togo sank the Czar's Baltic navy in the Tsushima straits and General Nogi's troops killed 90,000 Russian soldiers and took 40,000 prisoners of war in 1906, in the battle of Mukden. And in his study of Confucian China, its village and agrarian problems, he expressed his awareness of what lay ahead by apprehending the attraction that agrarian Bolshevism might have for the Chinese peasantry. On the basis of his study of Chinese society, Weber was able to predict the future of China. The same professor, who accompanied the German peace delegation to Versailles, had no Wilsonian illusions. He warned his students about the "polar night of icy darkness" that lay ahead for Germany after World War I.

The revolutionary transitions of large parts of the world since World War I make it urgent for sociologists to study the historical backgrounds of value systems and social structures other than those of the United States, and it is in this direction—with the aid of Fulbright grants—that we hope to see a reorientation of American sociology in the post war generation, in an age in which the maintenance of peace is a more urgent necessity than ever before. Historiography offers a great storehouse of facts and ideas to the sociologist in quest of insight into total social structures, their phases of growth, decline and destruction. Only in this way, with one eye on history and one on the future, can the sociologist broaden his scope to meet the obligations of the contemporary world.

Index